Inventions of NASA: Patents from the Space Program

For Educational Purposes Only

Not To Be Used To Recreate Active Patents

Table of Contents

WITHDRAWN FROM COLLECTION

US007375826B1

(12) **United States Patent**   (10) **Patent No.:**   **US 7,375,826 B1**

Lavelle et al.   (45) **Date of Patent:**   **May 20, 2008**

(54) **HIGH SPEED THREE-DIMENSIONAL LASER SCANNER WITH REAL TIME PROCESSING**

(75) Inventors: **Joseph P. Lavelle**, Los Altos, CA (US); **Stefan R. Schuet**, Sunnyvale, CA (US)

(73) Assignee: **The United States of America as represented by the Administrator of the National Aeronautics and Space Administration (NASA)**, Washington, DC (US)

(*) Notice: Subject to any disclaimer, the term of this patent is extended or adjusted under 35 U.S.C. 154(b) by 548 days.

(21) Appl. No.: **10/956,517**

(22) Filed: **Sep. 23, 2004**

(51) **Int. Cl.**
G01B 11/24   (2006.01)
G01B 11/30   (2006.01)

(52) **U.S. Cl.** **356/607**; 356/606

(58) **Field of Classification Search** .... None
See application file for complete search history.

(56) **References Cited**

U.S. PATENT DOCUMENTS

4,158,507 A *	6/1979	Himmel	....	356/608
5,118,192 A *	6/1992	Chen et al.	....	356/602
5,198,877 A *	3/1993	Schulz	....	356/614
5,495,337 A *	2/1996	Goshorn et al.	....	356/601
5,654,800 A	8/1997	Svetkoff et al.		
5,818,061 A *	10/1998	Stern et al.	....	250/559.29
5,969,822 A *	10/1999	Fright et al.	....	356/608
6,031,225 A *	2/2000	Stern et al.	....	250/235
6,064,759 A *	5/2000	Buckley et al.	....	382/154
6,181,472 B1	1/2001	Liu		
6,205,243 B1 *	3/2001	Migdal et al.	....	382/154
6,577,405 B2 *	6/2003	Kranz et al.	....	356/601
6,603,103 B1 *	8/2003	Ulrich et al.	....	250/205
2002/0140949 A1 *	10/2002	Sasaki et al.	....	356/606
2004/0100639 A1 *	5/2004	Sung et al.	....	356/605

OTHER PUBLICATIONS

Lavelle, et al., High Speed 3D Scanner with Real-Time 3D Processing, SIcon/04—Sensors for Industry Conference, Jan. 27-29, 2004, New Orleans, Louisana.

(Continued)

Primary Examiner—Michael P. Stafira
(74) *Attorney, Agent, or Firm*—John F. Schipper; Robert M. Padilla

(57) **ABSTRACT**

A laser scanner computes a range from a laser line to an imaging sensor. The laser line illuminates a detail within an area covered by the imaging sensor, the area having a first dimension and a second dimension. The detail has a dimension perpendicular to the area. A traverse moves a laser emitter coupled to the imaging sensor, at a height above the area. The laser emitter is positioned at an offset along the scan direction with respect to the imaging sensor, and is oriented at a depression angle with respect to the area. The laser emitter projects the laser line along the second dimension of the area at a position where a image frame is acquired. The imaging sensor is sensitive to laser reflections from the detail produced by the laser line. The imaging sensor images the laser reflections from the detail to generate the image frame. A computer having a pipeline structure is connected to the imaging sensor for reception of the image frame, and for computing the range to the detail using height, depression angle and/or offset. The computer displays the range to the area and detail thereon covered by the image frame.

26 Claims, 6 Drawing Sheets

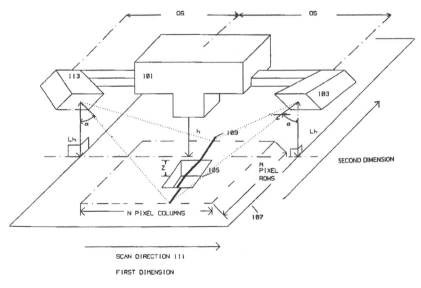

OTHER PUBLICATIONS

Lavelle, et al., High Speed 3D Scanner with Real-Time 3D Processing, IMTC 2004—Instrumentation and Measurement Technology Conference, May 18-20, 2004, Como, Italy.

Lavelle, et al., High speed 3D scanner with real-time 3D processing, ODIMAP IV Optoelectronic Distance/Displacement Measurements and Applications, Jun. 16-18, 2004Oulu, Finland.

Lavelle, et al., High-speed 3D scanner with real-time 3D processing, SPIE Photonics East 2003, Oct. 27-30, 2003.

* cited by examiner

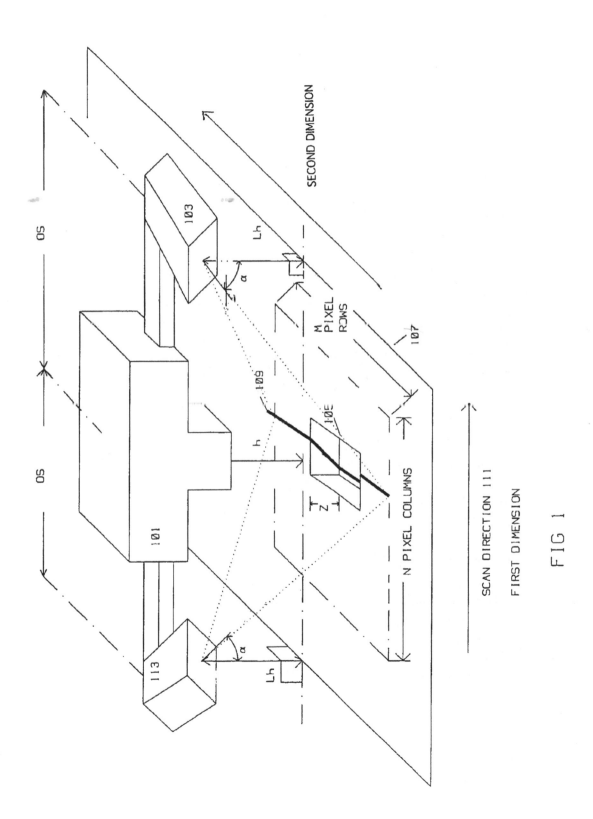

FIG 1

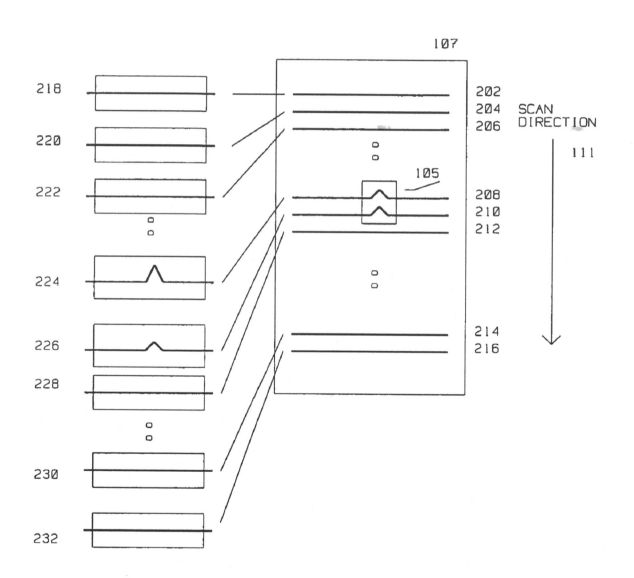

FIG 2

4

SCAN DIRECTION 111

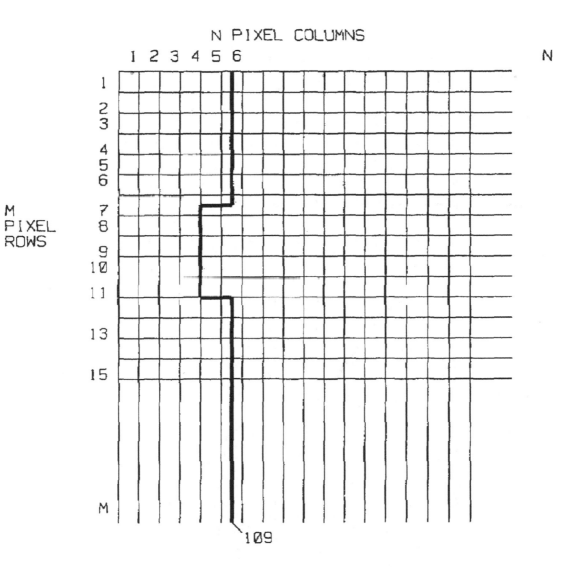

N PIXEL COLUMNS

FRAME STRUCTURE

FIG 3

5

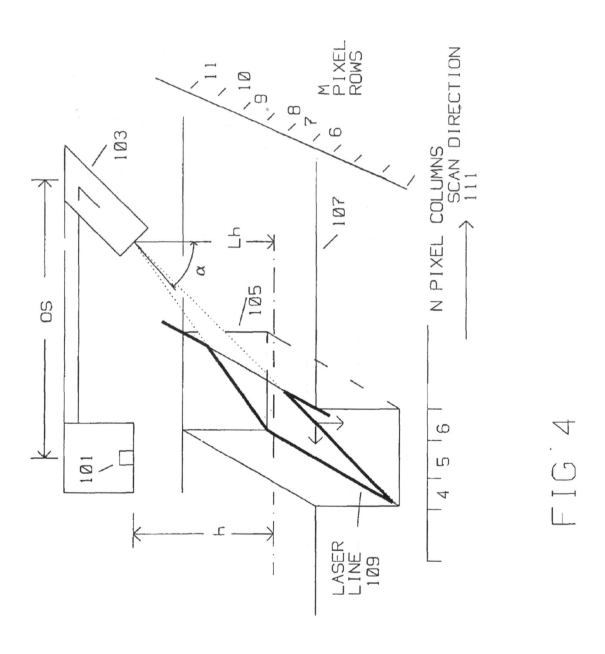

FIG. 4

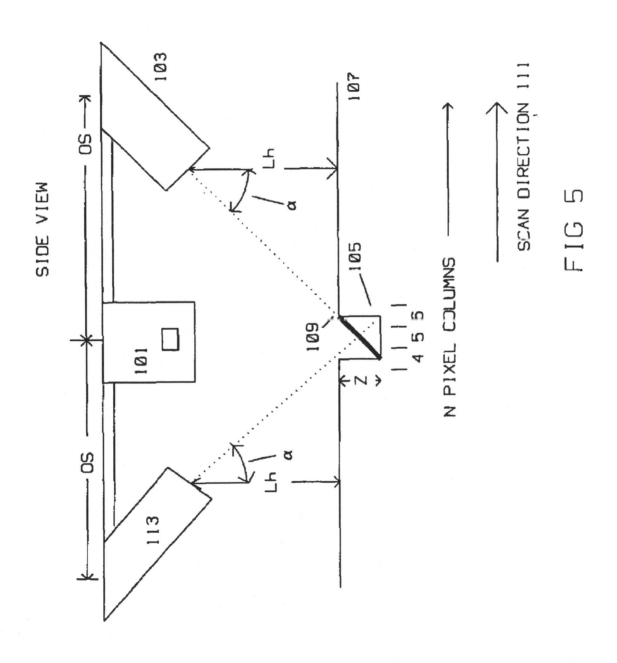

FIG 5

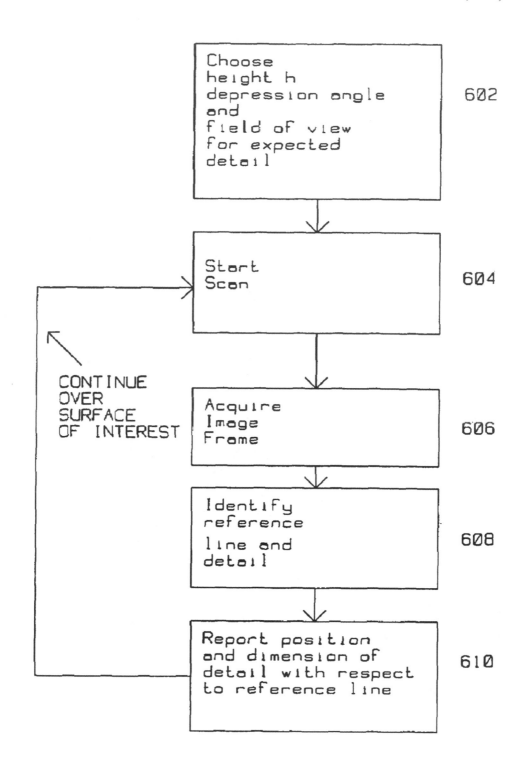

FIG 6

HIGH SPEED THREE-DIMENSIONAL LASER SCANNER WITH REAL TIME PROCESSING

BACKGROUND OF THE INVENTION

1. Field of Invention

This invention is in the field of laser scanners used for detection and measurement of three dimensional details on a target area.

2. Description of the Related Art

One challenge of scanning technology is that of translating the dimensions of an object into a computer compatible format. The idea is to acquire the object's image and digitize it for further digital manipulation. In this context, area scanners have been described to acquire the contours of an object by scanning the object and converting the image into a digital representation. For example, U.S. Pat. No. 5,969, 822 to Fright et al. titled Arbitrary Geometry Laser Area Scanner describes an optical non-contact area scanning apparatus and method. The three dimensional coordinates of an illuminated profile or spot on the object are recorded and the area is reconstructed using spatial location and orientation information from a spatial location system associated with the object, illumination means and image recording means. The digitized output from Fright contains information about the image scanned by the apparatus.

Similarly, another example, U.S. Pat. No. 5,198,877 to Shulz titled Method and Apparatus for Three Dimensional Non-Contact Shape Sensing also describes sensing of numerous points on the area of an object utilizing two stages to sense a shape.

While both above systems and others in the prior art digitize an image into a computer file, at least two critical factors are only tangentially addressed, and need to be considered with respect to the present invention:

a) the time necessary to acquire the image inclusive of the time to process the acquired image information to detect small details in the image;

b) the degree of resolution to which the image has to be digitized to detect relatively small details within the image.

Typically, in the prior art, the object to be analyzed is presented to the image sensor, for example a Charge Coupled Device (CCD). The image of interest is contained in the output generated by the CCD, a large two dimensional array of individual pixel amplitudes. The output of the CCD is representative of the object presented to the camera and is processed to extract the image contained therein to create a usable computer file. The output from such a scanner is typically a large amount of data. For example, a digital image having 1024 by 1024 pixels, each pixel represented by 16 bits of amplitude to resolve small details, translates to approximately 16 million bits per image. The 16 million bits represent a substantial computational load, especially if thousands of images have to analyzed in minutes.

An approach towards reducing the time to process images of objects is to use an increased scan rate, that is, acquire more information per unit time. Such an approach is discussed in U.S. Pat. No. 6,031,225 to Stern et al, titled System and Method of Selective Scanning of an Object or Pattern Including Scan Correction. Here, an optical system quickly sweeps a light beam over the image to be acquired. A scan correction is applied to compensate for motion related errors.

However, even with the faster scan rate of the '225 patent, the rate of creating and analyzing images may be insufficient when a large number of images have to be captured and analyzed to detect small details in a short time. For example,

where thousands of tiles each 3 in by 3 in have to be analyzed to detect relatively small details, such as area flaws in the order of 0.1 in by 0.1 in at a depth of 0.008 in, the prior art may not be satisfactory because of the delay involved to image the overall area of each tile and extract all features to the level where a small (0.1 by 0.1 by 0.008 in) detail is reliably detected. The prior art may require relatively large memories to store the output of high resolution analog to digital (A/D) converters. The high A/D resolution is needed to detect the small change corresponding to a small flaw in the object being examined, in the order of one part in 10000 (approximately 3 in/0.01 in). This means the computing load is quite large, and the analyzed results probably delayed, not available in real time. This is because a large amount of detailed (possibly 16 bit resolution) CCD data has to be stored, then processed to extract and detect the existence of small flaws on a large object. The large object is represented by a relatively vast digital output from the image(video) A/Ds, while the flaws are a small part ($\frac{1}{10000}$) thereof. Hence, the large computing load in detecting small flaws in a large digital image would delay output and the utility of a prior art system.

SUMMARY OF THE INVENTION

A laser scanner computes a range from a laser line to an imaging sensor. The laser line is emitted from a laser emitter, said laser line illuminating a detail within an area covered by said imaging sensor, said area having a first dimension and a second dimension, said detail having a dimension perpendicular to said area. The scanner comprises a traverse for moving said laser emitter coupled to said imaging sensor. Said traverse moves parallel to said first dimension of said area in a scan direction for a scan. The scan may be circular or rectilinear. The imaging sensor and said laser emitter are at a height above the area. The laser emitter is positioned at an offset along said scan direction with respect to said imaging sensor. Said laser emitter is oriented at a depression angle with respect to said area, said depression angle invariant during said scan. For a rectilinear scan, said laser emitter is projecting said laser line along said second dimension of said area at a frame first dimension position, said second dimension perpendicular to said scan direction over said area. The imaging sensor is sensitive to laser reflections from said detail produced by said laser line, said imaging sensor imaging said laser reflections from said detail within said area to generate a image frame, said image frame second dimension aligned along said second dimension and inclusive of said frame first dimension position. A computer, having a pipeline portion and auxiliary portion is connected to said imaging sensor for reception of said image frame. Said pipeline portion examines said image frame for the presence of reflections from said laser line illuminating said detail. The auxiliary portion of said computer computes the range to said laser line and said detail using said height, said depression angle and/or said offset.

The computer displays said range to said detail as indicative of said dimension of said detail on a display at a coordinate within said second dimension and said first dimension over said area covered by said image frame (the scan). It is envisioned that the pipeline portion of said computer and the auxiliary portion are combined into one, fully integrated computer where both the pipeline architecture is implemented as well as that of the auxiliary portion.

BRIEF DESCRIPTION OF THE DRAWINGS

In the drawings:

FIG. **1** describes an angle view of the scanner of the present invention where two laser emitters illuminate an area

FIG. **2** describes a plurality of regions covering the area to be imaged;

FIG. **3** describes a image frame of the present invention where a detail is reflecting laser energy from the area being scanned;

FIG. **4** describes the effect of a detail having a vertical dimension extending below the imaged area and the associated shift in the imaged position of a straight laser line;

FIG. **5** describes a side view of the scanner of this invention; and

FIG. **6** describes the method steps of this invention.

DETAILED DESCRIPTION

The present invention describes an apparatus and method for an improved laser scanner for ranging a laser line illuminating a three dimensional detail on a target area such as, for example, a flaw in a tile, facial features for human physiognomy, parts on a printed circuit board, or machined features on mechanical components. The target area is NOT stored in memory, but rather incorporated into the operation of the scanner by virtue of the structure and method of this invention. A fast range measurement is thus obtained from a composite image of the target area and details thereon derived from the laser reflections sensed by an imaging sensor.

The operation of the scanner is further accelerated by the use of a pipeline processor matched in performance to the output of an imaging sensor **101** acquiring the image. Because the image pixels are delivered in compatible increments and rate to the pipeline processor, and there is no need to store large intermediate results, the overall operation of generating range measurements is accelerated to obtain real time results.

As shown in FIG. **1**, in one embodiment, a rectilinear laser scanner detects a three dimensional detail **105** on a (typically) flat area **107**. Area **107** has a first dimension along a scan direction **111** and a second dimension perpendicular to said first dimension. Detail **105** has a dimension z perpendicular to area **107**. While z is shown to have a dimension below area **107**, it can also extend above area **107**. The scanner comprises a traverse for moving a first laser emitter **103** coupled to an imaging sensor **101**. In an embodiment where the traverse moves rectilinearly, the traverse moves parallel to the first dimension of said area **107** in scan direction **111**. The imaging sensor **101** and a first laser emitter **103** are at a height h above area **107**. Laser emitter **103** is positioned behind imaging sensor **101** by a fixed offset OS. The effect of offset OS is to orient laser emitter **103** at a depression angle α with respect to area **107** so that the emitted laser beam from laser **103** meets area **107** within the bounds of the image scan second dimension and image scan first dimension of imaging sensor **101**. Depression angle α is in a plane oriented along the first dimension of area **107**, and scan direction **111**. The plane of angle α is perpendicular to area **107**. Offset OS is further detailed in FIG. **5**.

In another embodiment, the traverse can also move circularly along a circumference having a radius around a point. The scan direction is now circular, following the circumference. The imaging sensor is displaced with respect to the laser emitter by a fixed number of degrees. The laser emitter is radially located to generate a radial laser line. The imaging sensor is displaced along the radius with every rotation. The same range measurement concepts apply, but using a cylindrical coordinate system.

Returning to the embodiment of FIG. **1**, when used in conjunction with first laser emitter **103**, second laser emitter **113** is located at a spacing OS from imaging sensor **101** along the first dimension of area **107**. The first laser emitter **103** projects a first laser line **109** along the second dimension of said area **107** at a frame first dimension position. Typically, the Z dimension of detail **105** is much less than the image frame first dimension or second dimension.

Second laser emitter **113** is located a spacing OS from imaging sensor **101** and also pointed at a depression angle α to the scan direction. Thus second laser emitter **113** and first laser emitter **103** straddle imaging sensor **101**. Second laser emitter **113** projects a second laser line, for example, superimposed over, and aligned with the same location on area **107** as that covered by laser line **109**, at the same frame first dimension position, across the second dimension of said image frame. In one embodiment, second laser emitter **113** is activated at alternate times with first laser emitter **103** to perform alternate measurements, thereby reduce shadow related errors. It is envisioned that first laser emitter **103** and second laser emitter **113** may also be activated concurrently.

Imaging sensor **101** is sensitive to laser reflections from laser line **109** illuminating area **107** and detail **105**. The reflections are produced by laser line **109** illuminating both area **107** and detail **105**. Imaging sensor **101** images a region of area **107**, including the laser reflections from area **107** and from detail **105** to generate a image frame. The image frame has a image frame first dimension and a image frame second dimension. The image frame second dimension is aligned along the second dimension of area **107**. The image frame covers reflections from detail **105** induced by laser line **109** as well as area **107**.

A computer, having a pipeline portion and an auxiliary portion, preferably internal to imaging sensor **101**, is connected to imaging sensor **101** for reception of the image frame. The pipeline portion examines the image frame for the presence of reflections from area **107** as well as reflections from detail **105** within particular pixels acquired by imaging sensor **101**. Reflections from area **107** induced by laser line **109** are imaged as a (straight) line within the image frame. Conversely, reflections from detail **105** produced from laser line **109** are imaged at a distance from the line imaged from area **107** as present within the image frame.

In a preferred embodiment, a pipeline portion of the computer calculates the location of the laser line on the examined surface. The output from the pipeline portion is reduced substantially as compared to the raw image input. This reduces the amount of data to be used for further calculations in the auxiliary portion of the computer. The auxiliary portion computes depth, the Z dimension, of detail **105** using the geometry shown in the figures, using data generated by the pipeline portion. The Z dimension is computed from the reflections generated by detail **105** using depression angle α, offset OS and known height h of imaging sensor **101** and laser emitter above area **107**.

The auxiliary portion reports the range of the z dimension of the detail at a coordinate within the second dimension and first dimension of area **107** covered by the scan. A constant may be subtracted from the range measured to laser line **109** for each pixel to improve image rendition.

It is envisioned that the auxiliary and pipeline portions are combined in a single computer, reducing costs and increasing speed of the interface(s) linking the two portions.

The computer also synchronizes the movement of the traverse connecting first laser **103**, second laser **113** and image sensor **101**, and reception of the image frame in a plurality of regions, the regions aligned along scan direction **111**. The regions are imaged parts of area **107** and any details that may be thereon. The multiple regions are detailed in FIG. **2**. Regions **218**, **220**, and **222** correspond to an image frame around laser line **202**, **204** and **206** respectively. Thus, when shown over area **107**, regions **218**, **220** and **222** overlap in the direction of scan direction **111**. Since the laser line is detected by imaging sensor **101** as a straight line, no details are found in either frame **218**, **220** or **222**.

Similarly, region **224**, **226** and **228** correspond to laser lines **208**, **210** and **212** over area **107**. Laser lines **208**, **210**, and **212** have encountered detail **105** on area **107**. Hence, laser lines **208**, **210**, and **212** have straight portions, corresponding to reflections from flat area **107** as well as reflections imaged at a distance from the straight portions corresponding with the presence of detail **105**, detail **105** having a dimension perpendicular to area **107**. The image of the dimension of detail **105** is manifested by portions of laser lines **208**, **210** and **212** being located at a distance from the laser line reflected by area **107** along the image frame first dimension. The reflection of the laser line from flat area **107** corresponds to the straight portion of each of the laser lines.

Regions **230** and **232** correspond to imaged laser lines **214** and **216**. Regions **230** and **232** overlap, and are the last regions to be examined on area **107**. No details are present, thus imaged laser lines **214** and **216** are straight lines.

The size of a region such as **224**, **226** or **228** is chosen as a tradeoff between scan speed and expected maximum z depth. If the details to be found are relatively large, then the imaging sensor **101** is positioned further away from area **107** (h large). Now each pixel of sensor **101** covers a larger area, and fewer regions are required to cover the whole of area **107**.

The spacing of regions along scan direction **111** is determined by the expected size of the detail to be analyzed on area **107**. For example, if detail **105** is expected to occupy one pixel dimension over area **107**, then a typical separation between adjacent projected laser lines, as determined by the scan rate, is ½ pixel along area **107**, or less.

FIG. **3** shows a typical image frame of this invention. The image frame is generated from imaging sensor **101** imaging a region, such as **208**, containing detail **105**. The image frame is formed from a plurality of pixels. The pixels are organized in an orthogonal coordinate system of M pixel rows and N pixel columns. The N pixel columns are aligned with scan direction **111**, covering a image frame first dimension. The M pixel rows are aligned with the second dimension of area **107**, and covers an image frame having a second dimension. The frame second dimension and frame first dimension are dependent on the optical characteristics of imaging sensor **101**, that is, its field of view as well as the height h optical sensor **101** is above area **107**. Thus, h is known, as well as the solid angle covered by optical sensor **101**, thus the image frame second dimension and first dimension can be computed a priori, before the start of scan. Choosing h in advance determines the position of a frame as imaged by imaging sensor **101**.

Each pixel is digitized in optical sensor **101** and has an intensity described by A bits, for example A=8. The A bits are representative of the amplitude of laser emissions reflected from either a first laser line, a second laser line, or both laser lines simultaneously, interacting with detail **105**

and area **107**. This intensity corresponds to the image formed onto a pixel by the imaging sensor **101** generating the image frame.

Further defining terms:

1, 2, . . . K is the number of rows in the subset of pixels read off the image sensor per clock cycle at a selected rate;

1, 2, . . . L is the number of columns in the subset of pixels read off the sensor per clock cycle at said rate;

1, 2 . . . M is the total number of rows generated by the image sensor (array);

1, 2, . . . N is the total number of columns generated by the image sensor (array);

A is the number of bits used to resolve the light intensity at each pixel location, i.e. the amplitude of light intensity is digitized, and represented with A number of bits.

The laser line **109** is oriented such as shown in FIG. **3**, along the M pixel rows, perpendicular to the scan direction.

Using these variables, the computer computes the central location of laser line **109** from reflections induced by laser line **109** on area **107** as well as detail **105**, and imaged within the image frame by performing a calculation characteristic of a center of mass calculation, (described elsewhere herein).

The image frame from the imaging sensor includes imaging one of the regions formed from a plurality of pixels. The pixels from the region are delivered at a rate compatible, or matching with the processing speed of pipeline(s) within the computer. The pixels forming the image frame are organized in an orthogonal coordinate system of M pixel rows and N pixel columns. The N pixel columns are aligned with said scan direction covering the image frame first dimension. M pixel rows are aligned with the second dimension covering the second dimension. Each pixel has an intensity described by A bits, said A bits representative of the amplitude of laser emissions reflected from said laser line interacting with said detail and said area, and imaged onto said pixel by said imaging sensor. The processing step uses a pipeline portion of the computer. The computer has a first pipeline and a second pipeline. The first pipeline and the second pipeline processing speed is matched to the pixel delivery rate from the imaging sensor for computing a central location of the laser line as imaged within the image frame by performing the following steps.

First, comparing within said first pipeline said intensity described by A bits of a subset of K pixel rows by L pixel columns starting at a N1 pixel column position within said M pixel rows by N pixel columns within said image frame against a threshold, retaining said intensity for said subset of K pixel rows by L pixel columns above said threshold while setting the rest to zero, thereby generating a K by L thresholded subset. This results in a K by L thresholded subset starting at N1 Pixel column position.

Next, multiplying in said first pipeline said K by L thresholded subset intensity of A bits of said K pixel rows by L pixel columns by their respective L column position within said image frame and summing across each of said K rows to obtain K partial numerators. This results in K partial numerators for a particular K by L block. In one embodiment, K=1, L=8, (e.g. 8 by 1) at pixel column N1 in the first pipeline.

Next, summing across said K pixel rows of said thresholded subset for each L pixel column to obtain K partial denominators in said second pipeline. This results in K partial denominators for a particular K by L block at pixel column N1.

The K partial denominators are delayed from the second pipeline until the K partial numerators are available from the first pipeline.

The comparing, multiplying, summing and delaying steps are repeated at said rate starting at column locations N1, N1+L, N1+2L . . . N/L times to cover the N pixel columns. The K partial numerators and K partial denominators are concurrently accumulated (summed) over each of the K pixel rows. After N/L iterations this result in one total numerator and one total denominator for each of the K pixel rows.

Where K is greater than one, i.e. two or more rows are processed concurrently, the steps are exactly the same, but duplicated because of the higher computing capacity. That is, above steps are performed at the same rate, starting at row locations K1, K1+K, K1+2K . . . M/K times to cover all M rows.

Next, divide the total numerator by its respective K total denominator for each of said K rows thereby identifying the location of a maximum value present within the image frame. This maximum value is indicative of the column where the laser line has been imaged said image frame. That is, the result is indicative of the location of the imaged (straight) laser line on area 107, in one of the N pixel columns for each of M pixel rows.

In a best mode implementation A is 8 bits, K rows is one pixel and L columns is 8 pixels. _is typically 20 degrees. These quantities optimize the use of a readily available pipeline processor to perform above steps efficiently without the need to store large amounts of image data.

In yet another best mode implementation, A is 10 bits, K rows is one pixel, and L columns is 16 pixels.

FIG. 3 further details operation of the algorithm. For example, identifying the location of the laser line proceeds down M=1 pixel row and identifies the presence of laser line 109 in column N=6. The algorithm examines all N pixel columns, typically 1024, at row 1. Then row M=2 is examined for all N pixel columns. The process is repeated for all M pixel rows. This row by row examination outputs the position of the laser line across the field of view, image frame first dimension and image frame second dimension, for imaging sensor 101.

As shown in FIG. 3, the laser line reflected from area 107 is continuous up to M pixel row 7 the laser line present in N pixel column 6. At M pixel row 7, the laser line is reflected from detail 105 in rows 4 and 5. The shift of the laser line from N pixel column 6, to columns 4 and 5, in this image frame, shows that the laser line has "advanced" about 1.5 rows, indicative of laser line 109 illuminating a detail at a range above or below area 107. The reflections at a distance from N pixel column 6, shown in column 4 and 5, come from the bottom area of detail 105, an amount z below area 107, reflecting laser line 109. Thus the dimension Z, the depth of detail 105 below area 107 (shown in FIG. 5) is computed from the angle α (function of OS, h and the extent of a pixel, for example, frame first dimension/1024 by frame second dimension/1024. More simply, if high accuracy of depth is not required, and only a depression in area 107 need be identified, a fixed number is subtracted from the computed range (e.g., the difference of 1.5). The resulting difference is directly displayed on the display at the column/row position it is found. For example, the factor 1.5 is obtained from subtracting the position of the reflections from the area 107 (column 6) from those generated by detail 105 (col 4, 5). For example, a gray scale on the display is calibrated to display shade 1 to be equivalent to a difference of 1, shade 2 for a difference of 2, shade 3 for a difference of 3 etc. The display

will now show a map of gray scales of differences from the area at the proper second dimension/first dimension location.

A color display, instead of the gray scale, enhances the visibility of the differences by assigning contrasting colors to each difference value, such as red for 1, blue for 2, yellow for 3 etc.

Shadow Processing

The geometry for computing the dimension z of detail 105 in the presence of shadows is shown in FIG. 5. When illuminating area 107, reflection from laser line 109 (generated by laser emitter 103) off area 107 are imaged in N pixel column 6 for M pixel rows 1 to 7. Once detail 105 is encountered, a few N pixel columns (e.g. 5, 6) will not be illuminated by reflections from the laser line 109, as they are in the shadow cast by the edge formed by the intersection of area 107 and the vertical extent of detail 105. The shadow is computed from depression angle α, location L_n of laser emitter 103, spacing OS, with respect to detail 105. In addition, depth z of detail 105 along with the other variables will determine how many pixels along laser line 109 will be shadowed when laser emitter 103 is illuminating. Depression angle α is measured perpendicular to the plane of area 107, along the scan direction.

As shown in FIG. 5, the laser line from laser 103 on area 107 is presented to imaging sensor 101 at frame first dimension, N pixel col N=6. When encountering depth Z, the laser line is presented to imaging sensor 101 at frame first dimension N=4. Thus the position of the laser line has shifted because of detail 105 from N=6 to N=4, indicating the presence of detail 105 on area 107. The computation of Z from the known variables, as shown in FIG. 4, are performed within the computer, part of imaging sensor 101. z is displayed on a monitor as a departure from area 107 or printed out for each pixel within the image frame.

To avoid the shadow cast by laser emitter 103, laser emitter 113 having the same geometric location vertically as laser emitter 103, the same offset OS, but behind imaging sensor 101, is activated. Now, with laser illumination from behind, a laser line emitted from laser 113 will illuminate the originally dark pixels N=5, 6 avoiding the original shadow from laser emitter 103.

Therefore, to reduce or avoid shadows, laser emitter 103 is coupled to a second laser emitter 113, both oriented at the same depression angle α. Laser emitter 103 is aimed at a first depression angle α The second laser emitter 113 is oriented at a second depression angle $-\alpha$. The first depression angle and the second depression angle are measured in a plane perpendicular to area 107, with respect to scan direction 111, and are typically equal.

The laser emitter 103 and laser emitter 113 straddle image sensor 101 along said scan direction at a spacing OS. Laser emitters 103 and 113 are offset with respect to imaging sensor 101 by an offset +/−OS along scan direction 111. It is this offset OS that allows viewing area 107 with illumination from an angle α with respect to area 107. The image collected by imaging sensor 101 is along the axis of imaging sensor 101. Imaging sensor 101 is displaced by offset OS in front of the source of laser emitters 103 and 113 along scan direction 111.

FIG. 5 presents a side view for the case where either one or two laser emitters are used to illuminate narrow laser line 109 upon area 107. Laser emitter 103 is directly superimposed on laser emitter 113, or can operate singly, depending on the need for shadow corrections. Depression angle α of laser emitter 103, is determined by laser emitter 103 height over area **107**, L_h, and offset OS. Because of α, the bottom area of detail **105**, located Z below area **107**, is mapped in image frame pixel rows M=4–5 instead of row M=6 where area **107** is expected, as detailed in FIG. **3**. Imaging sensor **101** captures the image frame inclusive of the position of laser line **109** on area **107** and detail **105**.

Two Parallel Pipelines

The Center of Mass Calculation for identifying the position of laser line **109** within the image frame is performed in a pipeline processor. This special purpose processor can be used because no significant amount of storage is required to complete the location and computation of dimensions of detail **105** within the image frame. Because the need for large amounts of storage are avoided, the high performance of the pipeline processor can be fully exploited yielding a scanner that can scan large areas for small details in a relatively short time, presenting real time results.

The application of the Center of Mass calculation on each column of an image frame will convert the image frame into one line of values (equal to the number of columns) identifying of the row position at each column of the laser line reflected from the area **107** and detail **105** therein. This calculation can be summarized by:

$$\Sigma(Row\text{–}Position \times Intensity)/(\Sigma Intensity)$$

Two pipelines are used to calculate the central location of the laser line **109** from the input pixel intensity data, for example, in 64 bit parallel increments, 8 pixels, 8 bits each. The calculation is repeated for each column making up the image frame.

First Pipeline

The stage 1 operation is a threshold function. Here, each of the 8 input pixel intensities are output only if the intensities are above a certain specified threshold. When any pixel intensity is below or equals the threshold, a zero intensity is presented at the output in its place. This operation occurs over one stage or clock cycle.

Next, the numerator is computed. The numerator is part of the center of mass formula and as such multiplies the 8 input intensities by their respective sensor array positions and adds them together. The multiplication process is implemented, for example, using core module multipliers and occurs over a four-stage pipeline. The accumulation of the multiplication results occurs over an additional four-stage pipeline. The pipeline stages and their functions are:

Stage 2 Function: The sensor position for each input pixel intensity is generated based on an input counter.

Stages 3-6 Function: Each of the 8 parallel input intensities are simultaneously multiplied by their respective array positions, resulting in 8 separate multiplication results.

Stage 7 Function: The first of the 8 multiplication results is added to the second, the third result is added to the fourth etc. producing the first set of four partial sums.

Stage 8 Function: The second set of partial sums is calculated by adding the first of the four results from above to the second and the third result to the fourth. Two partial sums remain at this point.

Stage 9 Function: The final partial sum is calculated by adding the 2 partial sums from the above step. This sum represents the total all parallel intensities multiplied by their respective positions.

Stage 10 Function: The running total is updated by adding the result from step 7 into the current total.

Second Pipeline

The denominator is also part in the center of mass formula and as such accumulates the input intensities in an eight-stage pipeline. The denominator calculation works in parallel with the numerator using the second pipeline within the processor.

Stage 2 Function: The first set of partial sums is calculated by adding the first of the eight inputs to the second, the third to the fourth, etc. Each addition results in one partial sum for a total of four.

Stage 3 Function: The second set of partial sums is calculated by adding the first of the four results from above to the second and the third result to the fourth. Two partial sums remain at this point.

Stage 4 Function: The final partial sum is calculated by adding the 2 partial sums from the above step. This sum represents the total all parallel intensities input to the module from step one.

Stage 5 Function: The running total is updated by adding the total from stage 3 into the current total.

Stage 6-10 Function: The result from this second pipeline is delayed by 4 stages (clock cycles) so the total delay in this module is equal to the delay in the computation of the numerator.

Hardware Divider performs the division operation in the center of mass calculation. It is implemented with an available FPGA module. While FPGA is a convenient implementation, other options can be used, such as a DSP unit. The 16-bit output from the divider module represents the laser position corresponding to a particular sensor row. This laser position is then used to triangulate the distance z from known geometric information. The same function could also be performed by a Digital Signal Processor (DSP) core programmed for the particular function.

Method

FIG. **6** details the major steps in operating the scanner of the present invention. Selection step **602** is the first part of the method of using the scanner described herein. The user selects the height h and area of coverage (in a manner similar to selecting a focal first dimension of the imaging lens) for imaging sensor **101** in accordance with expected dimensions z of a detail on area **107**. This optimizes the scanner to detect details in a certain range of dimensions, and also assumes some a priori knowledge of the detail dimension to be detected.

Having made that selection, the method for detecting a three dimensional detail **105** on flat area **107** where flat area **107** has a first dimension and a second dimension, and detail **105** has a dimension perpendicular to said area (e.g. depth), comprises the steps of:

a) Step **604**—Start scan by moving a laser emitter **103** mechanically coupled to imaging sensor **101** parallel to the first dimension of area **107** in scan direction **111**, where imaging sensor **101** and laser emitter **103** are at the pre-selected height h above flat area **107**, and laser emitter **103** is oriented at pre-selected depression angle α with respect to area **107**, depression angle α in a plane along the first dimension of flat area **107**, and perpendicular to area **107**. The scan direction can be along a straight line (rectilinear) or circular, along the circumference of a circle.

b) Step **606**—for the rectilinear case, acquire an image frame by projecting laser line **109** using laser emitter **103** along the second dimension of area **107**, the second dimension perpendicular to the scan direction **111** over area **107**. Imaging sensor **101** is sensitive to laser reflections from area **107** and from detail **105** produced by the interaction with laser line **109**. Generate an image frame using imaging sensor **101**, the image frame including the laser reflections from area **107** and from detail **105**, the image frame second dimension aligned along the second dimension of area **107**.

c) Step **608**—Identify laser line and detail **105** on area **107**, if any, by processing the image frame in the pipeline portion of the computer connected to imaging sensor **101** for reception of the image frame. The pipeline portion examines the image frame pixel by pixel for the presence of reflections from area **107** and reflections from detail **105**, where reflections from area **107** produced from interactions with said laser line **109** are imaged as a line within the image frame. Conversely, laser reflections from detail **105** produced from interactions with the same laser line **109** are imaged at a distance from laser line **109** within the image frame. The laser line reflection is straight for an exemplary flat area **107**.

For example, steps **604** and **608** are performed up to 500 times per second while the traverse is moving along the scan direction.

d) Step **610**—Report range of detail **105** as illuminated by laser line **109** to a display by computing the dimension of detail **105** in a direction perpendicular to area **107** using the distance of said reflections derived from detail **105**, with respect to the laser line **109**, depression angle α, and height h. The actual depth of detail **105** is computed in the auxiliary part of the computer by triangulation. The reporting of the dimension of detail **105** is done for every column within the image at the end of the computation for that column, at a coordinate within the second dimension and first dimension over area **107** covered by the image frame. Thus for each of N pixel columns, a value indicative of the M row position of the laser line will be retained for each scan. This value, subtracting the value associated with the area, is shown on a display. The display becomes the "memory" of N pixel column by column results for this scanner, precluding the need for digital storage of intermediate results within the scanner itself. If the display is to show actual depth Z, the values can be further refined for accurate depth rendition.

All references cited in this document are incorporated herein in their entirety.

Although presented in exemplary fashion employing specific embodiments, the disclosed structures are not intended to be so limited. For example, although a straight laser line is used as a best mode embodiment, a curved laser line can be used instead. The curved laser line is made to conform to specific contours of interest of the area to be inspected. The laser line, when encountering a spherical area, can be tailored in shape to produce a straight line in two-dimensional space seen by the imaging sensor. Ranging to this laser line are now interpreted in accordance with this invention to identify dimensions of details illuminated by the line. Using concepts described herein, a curved laser line increases the scanners sensitivity to details having specific contours, thus increasing its utility.

Similarly, while a plurality of lasers can be used for multiple laser lines from different heights above the area to be inspected and positioned at different depression angles. Multiple laser positions can be customized for specific dimensions of details on the area, again increasing the utility and accuracy of the laser scanner while preserving its high scan rate.

Those skilled in the art will also appreciate that numerous changes and modifications could be made to the embodiment described herein without departing in any way from the invention.

What is claimed is:

1. A laser scanner for computing a range from a first laser line illuminating a detail to an imaging sensor, said first laser line emitted from a first laser emitter, said first laser line illuminating said detail within an area covered by said imaging sensor, said area having a first dimension and a second dimension, said detail having a dimension perpendicular to said area, said scanner comprising:

a traverse for moving said first laser emitter coupled to said imaging sensor, said traverse moving parallel to said first dimension of said area in a scan direction for a scan, said imaging sensor and said first laser emitter at a height above said area, said first laser emitter positioned at an offset along said scan direction with respect to said imaging sensor, said first laser emitter oriented at a depression angle with respect to said area, said depression angle in a plane along said first dimension, said plane perpendicular to said area, said depression angle invariant during said scan, said first laser emitter projecting said first laser line along said second dimension of said area at a frame first dimension position, said second dimension perpendicular to said scan direction over said area;

said imaging sensor sensitive to laser reflections from said detail produced by said first laser line, said imaging sensor imaging said laser reflections from said detail within said area to generate a image frame, said image frame second dimension aligned along said second dimension and inclusive of said frame first dimension position;

a computer connected to said imaging sensor for reception of said image frame, said computer examining said image frame for the presence of reflections from said detail;

said computer computing said range to said detail from said imaging sensor using said height, said depression angle and said offset; and

said computer displaying said range to said detail as indicative of said dimension of said detail on a display at a coordinate within said second dimension and said first dimension over said area covered by said image frame.

2. The laser scanner as in claim **1**, wherein said computer displays said dimension of said detail within said image frame from said range of said reflections from said detail by subtracting a fixed distance from said range.

3. The laser scanner as in claim **2**, wherein said computer synchronizes the movement of said traverse and reception of said image frame in a plurality of regions, said regions part of said area, said regions aligned along said scan direction, said regions overlapping over said first dimension so that one or more of said details are detected over said first dimension and said second dimension of said area.

4. The laser scanner as in claim **3**, wherein said image frame from said imaging sensor imaging one of said regions is formed from a plurality of pixels, said pixels delivered at a rate, said pixels organized in an orthogonal coordinate system of M pixel rows and N pixel columns, said N pixel columns aligned with said scan direction covering an image frame first dimension and said M pixel rows aligned with said second dimension covering an image frame second dimension, each pixel having an intensity described by A bits, said A bits representative of the amplitude of laser emissions reflected from said laser line interacting with said detail and said area, and imaged onto said pixel by said imaging sensor;

wherein said computer uses a first pipeline and a second pipeline, said first pipeline and said second pipeline operating at said rate to compute a central location of said first laser line as imaged within said image frame by performing the steps of:

comparing within said first pipeline said intensity described by A bits of a subset of K pixel rows by L pixel columns starting at a N1 pixel column position within said M pixel rows by N pixel columns within said image frame against a threshold, retaining said intensity for said subset of K pixel rows by L pixel columns above said threshold while setting the rest to zero, thereby generating a K by L thresholded subset; first multiplying in said first pipeline said K by L thresholded subset intensity of A bits of said K pixel rows by L pixel columns by their respective L column position within said image frame and summing across each of said K rows to obtain K partial numerators;

first summing across said K pixel rows of said thresholded subset for each L pixel column to obtain K partial denominators in said second pipeline; delaying said K total denominators from said second pipeline until said K partial numerators are available from said first pipeline; repeating said comparing, said first multiplying, said first summing and said delaying step at said rate starting at column locations N1, N1+L, N1+2L . . . N/L times to cover said N pixel columns, and concurrently summing said K partial numerators and K partial denominators for each of K pixel rows in said second pipeline N/L times obtaining one total numerator and one total denominator for each K pixel row;

repeating said comparing, said first multiplying, said first summing and said delaying step at said rate starting at row locations K1, K1+K, K1+2K . . . M/K times to cover said M rows; and

dividing each of said K total numerator for each K row by its respective K total denominator for each K row thereby identifying a maximum value, said maximum value indicative of said row where said laser line has been imaged within said image frame.

5. The laser scanner as in claim 4, wherein said first laser emitter is coupled to a second laser emitter, said first laser emitter and said second laser emitter oriented at said depression angle along said area with respect to said first dimension;

said first laser emitter and said second laser emitter straddling said image sensor along said first dimension at a spacing; and

said depression angle orienting said first laser emitter to illuminate said first laser line at said frame first dimension position, said depression angle orienting said second laser emitter to illuminate a second laser line at said frame first dimension position, said first laser line and said second laser line superimposed to cover at said frame first dimension position across said image frame second dimension within said region imaged by said image frame.

6. The laser scanner as in claim 5 wherein said computer activates said first laser emitter to obtain a first laser line and computes a first measurement of said dimension of said detail from reflections from said first laser line; and wherein

said computer de-activates said first laser emitter and activates said second laser emitter to obtain said second laser line, and computes a second measurement of said dimension of said detail from reflections from said second laser line; said

computer extracting a combined measurement of said detail from said first measurement and said second measurement, said combined measurement compensated for the presence of shadow e_ffects from the interaction of said first laser line and said second laser with said detail using said depression angle, said height and said spacing.

7. The laser scanner as in claim 6, wherein said computer activates said first laser emitter and said laser emitter concurrently to generate said first laser line and said second laser line, said computer computing said dimension of said detail from said image frame created from reflections from said first laser line superimposed on reflections from said second laser line.

8. The laser scanner as in claim 7, wherein A is 8 bits, K is 1 pixel and L is 8 pixels.

9. The laser scanner as in claim 7, wherein A is 10 bits, K is one pixel, and L is 16 pixels.

10. The laser scanner as in claim 3, wherein said scan direction is a circular path, said second dimension is a radius defining said circular path, said imaging sensor positioned along said radius by said traverse for every revolution along said circular path.

11. A method for computing a range from a first laser line illuminating a detail to an imaging sensor using a laser scanner, said first laser line emitted from a first laser emitter, said first laser line illuminating said detail within an area covered by said imaging sensor, said area having a first dimension and a second dimension, said detail having a dimension perpendicular to said area, said method comprising the steps of:

moving a traverse coupling said first laser emitter to said imaging sensor, said traverse moving parallel to said first dimension of said area in a scan direction for a scan, said imaging sensor and said first laser emitter at a height above said area, said first laser emitter positioned at an offset along said scan direction with respect to said imaging sensor, said first laser emitter oriented at a depression angle with respect to said area, said depression angle in a plane along said first dimension, said plane perpendicular to said area, said depression angle invariant during said scan, said first laser emitter projecting said first laser line along said second dimension of said area at a frame first dimension position, said second dimension perpendicular to said scan direction over said area;

generating a image frame from said imaging sensor, said imaging sensor sensitive to laser reflections from said detail produced by said first laser line, said imaging sensor imaging said laser reflections from said detail within said area to generate said image frame, said image frame second dimension aligned along said second dimension and inclusive of said frame first dimension position;

processing said image frame in a computer connected to said imaging sensor for reception of said image frame, said computer examining said image frame for the presence of reflections from said detail; computing said range to said detail from said imaging sensor using said height, and said depression angle; and

displaying said range to said detail as indicative of said dimension of said detail on a display at a coordinate within said second dimension and said first dimension over said area covered by said image frame.

12. A method as described in claim 11, further including displaying said dimension of said detail by subtracting a fixed number from said range, said dimension of said detail at a coordinate within said second dimension and first dimension over said area covered by said image frame.

13. A method as in claim 12, further including the step of synchronizing the movement of said traverse and reception of said image frame in a plurality of regions, said regions

15

16

aligned along said scan direction, said regions overlapping over said first dimension so that one or more of said details are detected over said first dimension and said second dimension of said area.

14. A method as in claim 13, wherein said processing step of said image frame from said imaging sensor includes imaging one of said regions formed from a plurality of pixels, said pixels delivered at a rate, said pixels organized in an orthogonal coordinate system of M pixel rows and N pixel columns, said N pixel columns aligned with said scan direction covering an image frame first dimension and said M pixel rows aligned with said second dimension covering an image frame second dimension, each pixel having an intensity described by A bits, said A bits representative of the amplitude of laser emissions reflected from said laser line interacting with said detail and said area, and imaged onto said pixel by said imaging sensor,

wherein said processing step uses a pipeline processor, said pipeline processor having a first pipeline and a second pipeline, said first pipeline and said second pipeline matched to said rate for computing a central location of said first laser line as imaged within said image frame by performing the steps of:

comparing within said first pipeline said intensity described by A bits of a subset of K pixel rows by L pixel columns starting at a N1 pixel column position within said M pixel rows by N pixel columns within said image frame against a threshold, retaining said intensity for said subset of K pixel rows by L pixel columns above said threshold while setting the rest to zero, thereby generating a K by L thresholded subset;

first multiplying in said first pipeline said K by L thresholded subset intensity of A bits of said K pixel rows by L pixel columns by their respective L column position within said image frame and summing across each of said K rows to obtain K partial numerators;

first summing across said K pixel rows of said thresholded subset for each L pixel column to obtain K partial denominators in said second pipeline;

delaying said K total denominators from said second pipeline until said K partial numerators are available from said first pipeline; repeating said comparing, said first multiplying, said first summing and said delaying step at said rate starting at column locations N1, N1+L, N1+2L . . . N/L times to cover said N pixel columns, and concurrently summing said K partial numerators and K partial denominators for each of K pixel rows in said second pipeline N/L times obtaining one total numerator and one total denominator for each K pixel row;

repeating said comparing, said first multiplying, said first summing and said delaying step at said rate starting at row locations K1, K1+K, K1+2K . . . M/K times to cover said M rows; and

dividing each of said K total numerator for each K row by its respective K total denominator for each K row thereby identifying a maximum value, said maximum value indicative of said row where said laser line has been imaged within said image frame.

15. A method as in claim 14, wherein:
said first laser emitter is coupled to a second laser emitter, said first laser emitter and said second laser emitter oriented at said depression angle, said depression angle measured perpendicular to said area with respect to said first dimension, said first laser emitter and said second laser emitter straddling said image sensor along said first dimension at a spacing; and

said depression angle orienting said first laser emitter to illuminate said first laser line at said frame first dimension position, said depression angle orienting said second laser emitter to illuminate a second laser line at said frame first dimension position, said first laser line and said second laser line superimposed to cover same frame first dimension position across said image frame second dimension within said region imaged by said image frame.

16. A method as in claim 15, wherein said computer activates said first laser emitter to obtain a first laser line and computes a first measurement of said dimension of said detail from reflections from said first laser line; and wherein said computer de-activates said first laser emitter and activates said second laser emitter to obtain said second laser line, and computes a second measurement of said dimension of said detail from reflections from said second laser line;

said computer extracting a combined measurement of said detail from said first measurement and said second measurement, said combined measurement compensated for the presence of shadow effects from the interaction of said first laser line and said second laser with said detail using said depression angle, said height and said spacing.

17. A method as in claim 16, wherein said computer activates said first laser emitter and said laser emitter concurrently to generate said first laser line and said second laser line, said computer computing said dimension of said detail from said image frame created from reflections from said first laser line superimposed on reflections from said second laser line.

18. A method as in claim 17, wherein A is 8 bits, K is 1 pixel and L is 8 pixels.

19. A method as in claim 17, wherein A is 10 bits, K is one pixel, and L is 16 pixels.

20. A system for illuminating non-planar detail in a substantially planar sheet, divided into a rectangular array of rows (numbered m=1, . . . , M) and columns (numbered n=1, . . . , N) of pixels and containing information, the system comprising:

a light source, spaced apart from a substantially planar sheet and oriented at a selected depression angle $\alpha 1$ relative to a normal direction, substantially perpendicular to a plane parallel to the sheet, that provides a narrow, substantially linear first segment of light that is received and reflected by the sheet, where a selected pixel with (row, column) location (m,n) in the pixel array has first measured light intensity value i1 (m,n) when a portion of the linear segment of light lies in the selected pixel, and has a second, distinct light intensity value when no portion of the first linear segment of light lies in the selected pixel;

a light scanner, spaced apart from the planar sheet and oriented to receive light from the light source that has been reflected from the sheet in approximately the normal direction, to form an image of a first scanner-illuminated portion of the planar sheet;

a computer that is programmed to perform at least the following procedures:

for each row, number m, in the pixel array, to compute a center of mass location or position CM1(m) in the row using a relation

16

$$CM1(m) = \left\{ \sum_{n1=1}^{N} n \cdot i1(m, n1) \right\} \Big/ \left\{ \sum_{n2=1}^{N} i1(m, n2) \right\}$$

to compare the center of mass locations, CM1(m1) and CM1(m1+1) for at least two consecutive rows number m1 and m1+1 (m1=1, . . . , M–1);

when the center of mass locations, CM1(m1) and CM(m1+1), are substantially the same, to interpret this condition as indicating that the sheet is planar in a neighborhood of the rows m=m1 and m=m1+1;

when a center of mass location difference satisfies |CM1(m1=1)–CM1(m1) |≧ΔCM(thr), where ΔCM (thr) is a selected positive value, to interpret this condition as indicating that the sheet is not planar in a neighborhood of at least one of the rows, number m=m1 and m=m1+1.

21. The system of claim 20, further comprising

a second light source, spaced apart from said substantially planar sheet and oriented at a selected depression angle α2 relative to said normal direction, that provides a narrow, substantially linear second segment of light that is received and reflected by the sheet, where a second selected pixel with (row, column) location (M', n') in said pixel array has a third measured light intensity value i2(m', n') when a portion of the second linear segment of light lies in the second selected pixel, and has a fourth, distinct light intensity value when no portion of the second linear segment of light lies in the second selected pixel;

wherein said light scanner is oriented to receive light from the second light source that has been reflected from said sheet in approximately said normal direction, to form an image of a second scanner-illuminated portion of said planar sheet;

wherein said computer is programmed to perform at least the following procedures;

for each row, number m', in said pixel array, to compute a center of mass location or position CM2(m') in the row using a relation

$$CM2(m') = \left\{ \sum_{n1'=1}^{N} n \cdot i2(m', n1') \right\} \Big/ \left\{ \sum_{n2'=1}^{N} i(m', n2') \right\}$$

to compare the center of mass locations, CM2(m1') and CM2(m1'+1) for at least two consecutive rows number m1' and m1'+1 (m1'–1, . . . , M–1);

when the center of mass locations, CM2(m1') and CM2(m1'+1), are substantially the same, to interpret this condition as indicating that said substantially planar sheet is planar in a neighborhood of the rows m=m1' and m=m1'+1;

when a center of mass locating difference satisfies |CM2(m1'+1) –CN(m1') |≧ΔCM(thr), to interpret this condition as indicating that said substantially planar sheet is not planar in a neighborhood of at least one of the rows, number m=m1' and m=m1'+1.

22. The system of claim 21, wherein each of said first light segment and said second light segment has a longitudinal axis, and the first and second longitudinal axes are substantially parallel to each other.

23. The system of claim 20, wherein said computer is further programmed so that:

when said location difference |CM1(m1+1)–CM1(m1)| is equal to a distance value h1, to interpret this difference condition as indicating that at least a first portion of said first scanner-illuminated portion of said sheet is displaced from a second portion of said first scanner-illuminated portion of said sheet, by a positive distance that is proportional to h1, in a direction substantially parallel to said normal direction.

24. The system of claim 20, wherein:

said illuminated portion of said planar sheet is chosen to be a narrow quadrilateral of said sheet that has a width less than a width of one of said pixels.

25. The system of claim 20, wherein said computer is further programmed to replace said measured first light intensity i1(m,n) associated with a pixel at said (row,column) location (m,n) by a processed light intensity pi1(m,n) that is 0 if said first measured light intensity is less than a selected positive threshold value i1(thr) and is equal to said measured light intensity if i1(m,n) is at least equal to i1(thr).

26. The system of claim 20, wherein said computer is further programmed to perform computation of said center of mass location CM1(m) in real time, without storage of any of said measured light intensity values i1(m,n).

* * * * *

(12) **United States Patent**
Landis

(10) **Patent No.:** **US 6,967,462 B1**
(45) **Date of Patent:** **Nov. 22, 2005**

(54) **CHARGING OF DEVICES BY MICROWAVE POWER BEAMING**

(75) Inventor: **Geoffrey A. Landis**, Berea, OH (US)

(73) Assignee: **NASA Glenn Research Center**, Cleveland, OH (US)

(*) Notice: Subject to any disclaimer, the term of this patent is extended or adjusted under 35 U.S.C. 154(b) by 149 days.

(21) Appl. No.: **10/455,139**

(22) Filed: **Jun. 5, 2003**

(51) Int. Cl.^{7} **H01M 10/46**
(52) U.S. Cl. .... **320/101**; 320/109; 322/2 R
(58) Field of Search .... 320/101, 106, 320/110, 108, 109; 322/2 R

(56) **References Cited**

U.S. PATENT DOCUMENTS

3,971,454 A	7/1976	Waterbury
3,989,994 A	11/1976	Brown
4,685,047 A	8/1987	Phillips, Sr.
5,210,804 A	5/1993	Schmid
5,260,639 A	11/1993	De Young et al.
5,396,538 A	3/1995	Hong
5,503,350 A	4/1996	Foote
5,733,313 A	3/1998	Barreras, Sr. et al.
5,982,139 A	11/1999	Parise
6,114,834 A	9/2000	Parise
6,127,799 A	10/2000	Krishnan
6,239,879 B1	5/2001	Hay
6,310,960 B1	10/2001	Saaski et al.
6,474,341 B1	11/2002	Hunter et al.
6,489,745 B1	12/2002	Koreis
6,498,455 B2	12/2002	Zink et al.
2002/0027390 A1	3/2002	Ichiki et al.

OTHER PUBLICATIONS

Prado, Mark "Environmental Effects—The PowerSat Beam and the Environment" 1983 P.E.R.M.A.N.E.N.T.

Primary Examiner—Edward H. Tso

(57) **ABSTRACT**

A system for providing wireless, charging power and/or primary power to electronic/electrical devices is described whereby microwave energy is employed. Microwave energy is focused by a power transmitter comprising one or more adaptively-phased microwave array emitters onto a device to be charged. Rectennas within the device to be charged receive and rectify the microwave energy and use it for battery charging and/or for primary power. A locator signal generated by the device to be charged is analyzed by the system to determine the location of the device to be charged relative to the microwave array emitters, permitting the microwave energy to be directly specifically towards the device to be charged. Backscatter detectors respond to backscatter energy reflected off of any obstacle between the device to be charged and the microwave array emitters. Power to any obstructed microwave array emitter is reduced until the obstruction is removed. Optionally, data can be modulated onto microwave energy beams produced by the array emitters and demodulated by the device, thereby providing means of data communication from the power transmitter to the device. Similarly, data can be modulated onto the locator signal and demodulated in the power transmitter, thereby providing means of data communication from the device to the power transmitter.

20 Claims, 4 Drawing Sheets

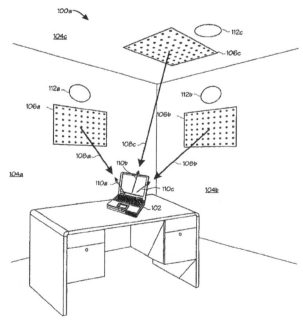

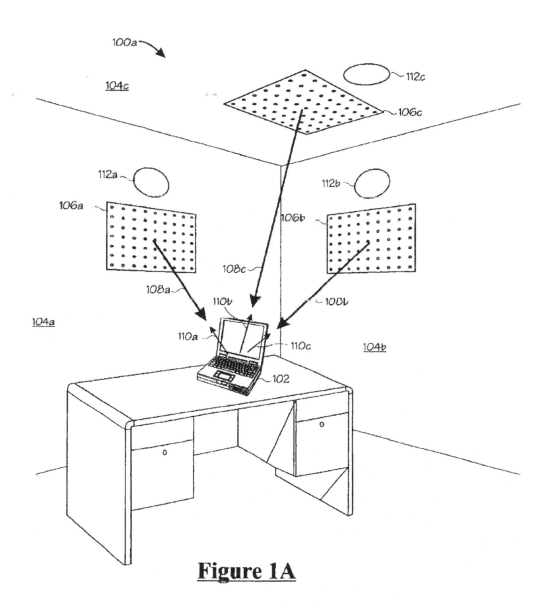

Figure 1A

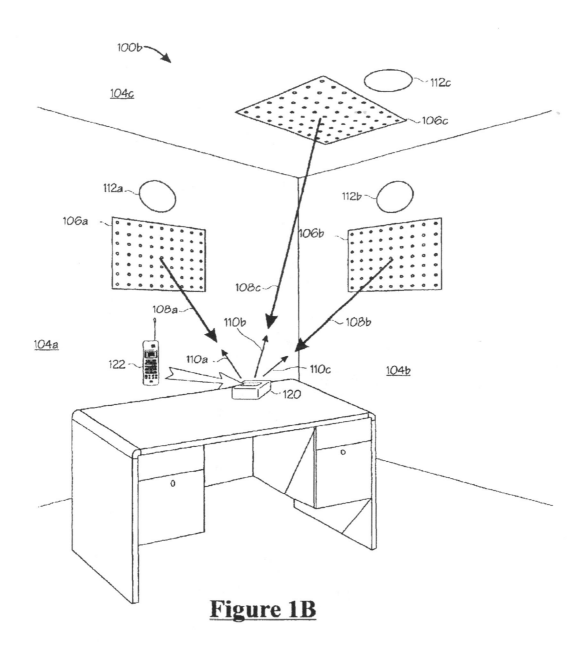

Figure 1B

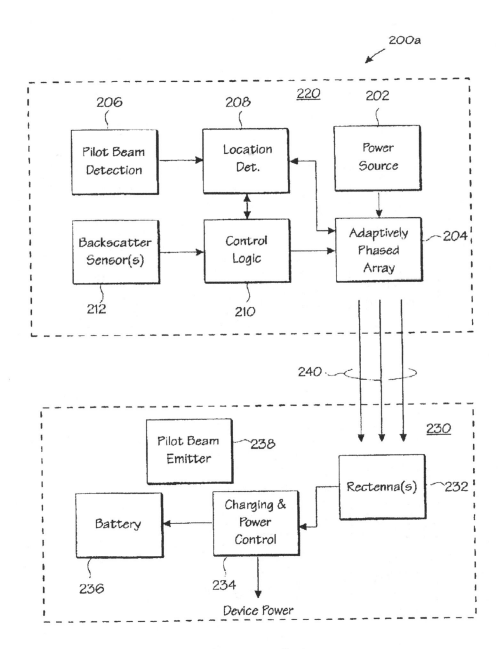

Figure 2A

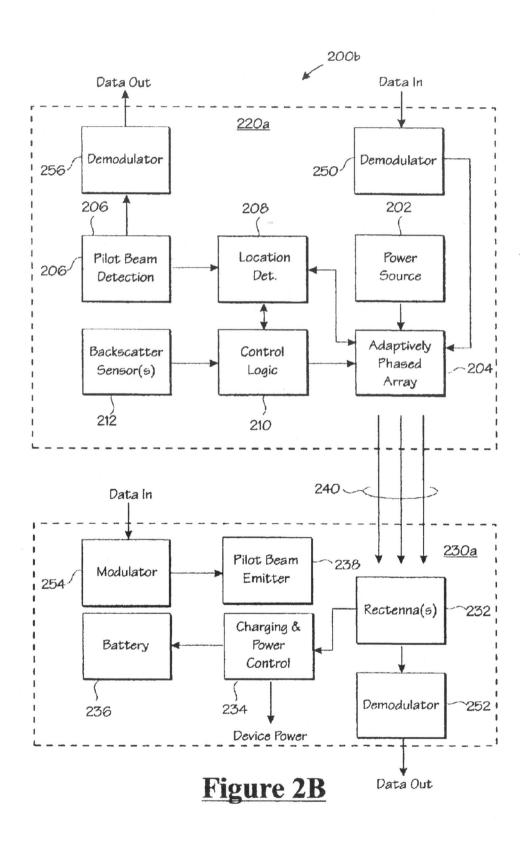

Figure 2B

1

CHARGING OF DEVICES BY MICROWAVE POWER BEAMING

ORIGIN OF THE INVENTION

The invention described herein was made by an employee of the United States Government and may be manufactured and used by or for the Government for Government purposes without the payment of any royalties thereon or therefore.

TECHNICAL FIELD

The present invention relates generally to wireless charging and powering of battery-powered electrical/electronic devices, including consumer devices.

BACKGROUND ART

A recent trend in consumer electronic devices is small, battery operated devices with on-board rechargeable batteries that are recharged by using a small, external charging adapter. These consumer devices can be, e.g., cell phones, personal digital assistants (PDAs), personal stereo devices (e.g., "Walkman", or MP3 Player), laptop computers, calculators, pagers, etc. Typically, the charging adapters for these devices are wall-plug AC adapters that provide bulk, low-voltage AC or DC charging power to the consumer device for operating the device and/or charging the device's on-board battery. Often, cigarette lighter adapters and similar charging adapters are provided for charging the consumer devices from a car's electrical system.

A typical consumer device charging system comprises a source of charging power, a charging circuit and a rechargeable battery. The charging circuit typically controls the amount of charging current delivered to the consumer device's battery, sensing and adjusting the current according to the battery's state of charge. Often, such charging circuits provide additional power for operating the consumer device while it is connected to charging adapter, dividing available power between battery charging and device operation as required.

Sometimes the charging circuit resides within the consumer device; other times the charging circuit is built into the charging adapter. The practice of putting the charging circuit into the charging adapter can be particularly advantageous for very small consumer devices, as it eliminates circuitry from the consumer device itself. Although such charging circuits are typically very small themselves, they can be large in comparison to other circuitry in consumer devices and the space saved by eliminating them can have a significant effect on the size, complexity and cost of the consumer device.

Usually, the charging adapter plugs into the consumer device by means of a wired connection. Sometimes, a connector or a set of contacts on the exterior of the consumer device is arranged so that the act of placing it into a charging "cradle" establishes a physical/electrical connection for charging the device. In this case, the "cradle" is a part of the charging adapter. Most charging systems for consumer devices require a direct electrical connection of this type between the device to be charged and the charging adapter. Over time, these contacts can become worn, loose or dirty, compromising their physical and/or electrical integrity and making them unreliable.

One scheme for powering and/or charging electrical/ electronic devices involves electromagnetically coupled coils. A first coil (or antenna) is disposed within a charging

2

apparatus. A second coil (or antenna) is disposed within the device to be charged. A "transmitting" circuit drives the first coil with an AC waveform. The device to be charged is placed in close proximity to the charging apparatus such that an electro-magnetic field produced by the first coil induces a corresponding AC electrical signal in the second coil. By rectifying the electrical signal in the second coil, a source of charging energy for the device to be charged is realized. In effect, the two coils (or antennae) form a transformer by which electrical power and/or signals can be communicated between the charging apparatus and the device to be charged. Such non-contacting charging systems have also been adapted to provided data communication over the same electro-magnetic coupling that provides the charging energy by modulating the charging signal and/or load impedance.

SUMMARY OF THE INVENTION

The present inventive technique provides for wireless, charging power and/or primary power to electronic/ electrical devices whereby microwave energy is employed. The microwave energy is focused by one or more adaptively-phased microwave array emitters in a power transmitter portion of the system onto a device to be charged. Rectennas within the device to be charged receive and rectify the microwave energy and use it for battery charging and/or for primary power. A locator signal generated by the device to be charged is analyzed by the system to determine the location of the device to be charged relative to the microwave array emitters, permitting the microwave energy to be directed specifically towards the device to be charged. Backscatter detectors respond to backscatter energy reflected off of any obstacle between the device to be charged and the microwave array emitters. Power to any obstructed microwave array emitter is reduced until the obstruction is removed. Optionally, data can be modulated onto microwave energy beams produced by the array emitters and demodulated by the device, thereby providing means of data communication from the power transmitter to the device. Similarly, data can be modulated onto the locator signal and demodulated in the power transmitter, thereby providing means of data communication from the device to the power transmitter.

The power transmitter portion of the system includes one or more (preferably planar) adaptively-phased microwave array emitters, and location detection means responsive to the location signal generated by the device to be charged. Typically, the array emitters would be mounted to walls and or floors of a room in which the device to be charged resides. The phase of microwave energy produced by the array emitters is continuously varied across the face(s) of the array emitter(s) to produce the effect of a focused beam of microwave energy, converging at the device. One or more rectennas within the device receive the transmitted microwave energy, converting and rectifying it into DC electrical energy useful for battery charging and/or device power.

According to an aspect of the invention, device location is determined by producing "pilot beams" (locator signal) at the location of the device to be charged to be received by the power transmitter. By analyzing timing characteristics of the received signal (e.g., by triangulation) the power transmitter determines the exact location of the device to be charged relative to its array emitters and adjusts phase of the microwave energy across the surface of the array emitters to focus the energy on the device.

According to another aspect of the invention, the array emitters produce continuous-wave microwave energy in the

3

frequency range between 2 GHz and 10 GHz inclusive. Frequencies higher than 10 GHz can be employed (e.g., millimeter wave), but using current rectenna technology, there would be a loss of efficiency.

According to another aspect of the invention, each individual microwave array emitter produces energy at a frequency close to, but different from that produced by any other microwave array emitter in the system. This reduces loss of energy in sidelobes, and minimizes interference issues.

According to another aspect of the invention, the power transmitter includes backscatter detectors for detecting backscatter energy reflected off of any obstruction between the microwave array emitters and the device to be charged. When an obstruction is detected, the obstructed, the power output of the obstructed microwave array emitter is reduced to a low level until the obstruction is removed, thereby reducing lost power and preventing injury to humans or damage to objects that obstruct the power transmission path between the arrays and the device.

According to another aspect of the invention, conventional electrical/electronic devices (i.e., those not specifically adapted to microwave charging) can be accommodated by means of a microwave charging adapter/cradle that embodies the inventive technique for receiving and converting microwave energy. In this case, the charging cradle/adapter would generate the locator signal and receive the microwave energy.

According to another aspect of the invention, data can be modulated onto the microwave energy produced by the adaptively phased microwave array emitters by means of a modulator function, thereby producing microwave energy beams having a (DC) power component and a (AC) data component. A demodulator function in the device (or charging adapter/cradle) demodulates the data component of the microwave energy beam as received by the rectennas. This provides means of communicating data from the power transmitter to the device.

According to another aspect of the invention, data can be modulated onto the locator signal produced by the device to be charged (or by the charging cradle/adapter) by means of a modulator function. A corresponding demodulator function in the power transmitter demodulates the data modulated onto the locator signal, thereby providing means of communicating data from the device to the power transmitter.

BRIEF DESCRIPTION OF THE DRAWINGS

These and further features of the present invention will be apparent with reference to the following description and drawing, wherein:

FIG. 1A is a view of a system for direct microwave charging of an electrical/electronic device, in accordance with the invention.

FIG. 1B is a view of a system for microwave charging of an electrical/electronic device in a charging cradle, in accordance with the invention.

FIG. 2A is a block diagram of a system for microwave charging, in accordance with the invention.

FIG. 2B is a block diagram of a system for microwave charging, including means for data exchange, in accordance with the invention.

DETAILED DESCRIPTION OF THE INVENTION

The present inventive technique provides for charging and/or powering of an electrical/electronic device using

4

microwave energy. One or more adaptive-phased arrays are used to focus one or more "rectennas" (rectifying antennas) disposed within the consumer device. Microwave energy reaching the rectenna(s) is converted into DC electrical energy that is used to charge a battery or other energy storage device within the consumer device. The DC electrical energy can also be used to provide primary power for the consumer device while the battery or storage device is being charged.

FIG. 1A is a view of a system **100a** for direct microwave charging of an electrical/electronic device **102**, wherein a plurality of adaptive-phased array microwave emitters **106a**, **106b** and **106c** are disposed on walls **104a**, **104b** and ceiling **104c**, respectively of a room in which the electrical/electronic device **102** resides. Pilot beams **100a**, **100b**, **110c** from the electrical/electronic device **102** permit the system **100** to determine the exact location of the electrical/electronic device **102** within the room. Each of the adaptive-phased arrays **106a**, **106b** and **106c** is then driven to emit continuous-wave microwave energy with varying phase across the array surface in order to effectively focus a respective beam **108a**, **108b**, **108c** of microwave energy directly at the electrical/electronic device **102**. One or more rectennas (described in greater detail hereinbelow) within the electrical/electronic device **102** receive the microwave energy focused thereupon and convert it into a source of charging and/or operating power therefor. Backscatter detectors **112a**, **112b** and **112c**, mounted in close proximity to adaptive-phased arrays **106a**, **106b** and **106c**, respectively, detect "backscatter", i.e., microwave energy reflected off of any obstacle (e.g., a human) that might enter the beam path. When significant backscatter is detected by one of the backscatter detectors **112a**, **112b** or **112c**, its respective adaptive-phased array **112a** is either turned off completely or reduced to a low level of power emission until the beam is clear of the obstruction. This prevents transmission of wasted microwave power that will not reach the electrical/electronic device **102**, and also guards against injury or damage to a human (or other obstacle) that enters a beam path. If any beam is obstructed (**108a**, **108b** or **108c**), the remaining beams can still power the electrical/electronic device **102**.

Preferably, the adaptive-phased arrays operate in the range of 2 to 10 GHz (2×10^9 Hz to 10×10^9 Hz). Higher frequencies, e.g., "millimeter wave" frequencies can be employed, but current millimeter wave rectenna technology is lower in efficiency than rectenna technology designed for the 2 to 10 GHz range. It is also preferable that the adaptive phase arrays (**106a**, **106b** and **106c**) operate at slightly different frequencies, i.e., it is preferable that the adaptive-phased arrays **106a**, **106b**, **106c** transmit mutually incoherent microwave signals. While having all of the adaptive-phased arrays operate on the same frequency would result in a smaller beam "spot" (focal point) on the electrical/electronic device to be charged/powered, it would also result in more of the beam power being scattered into sidelobes, yielding lower efficiency (wasted power in the sidelobes) and greater interference between arrays.

The "pilot beams" **110a**, **110b** and **110c** are essentially a locator signal, and can be provided by any suitable means of identifying the location of the electrical/electronic device **102** relative to the adaptive-phased arrays **106a**, **106b** and **106c**. This can be an RF signal, a microwave signal, or any other suitable locator signal from which the location of the electrical/electronic device **102** can be determined by the system **100a**.

Data transfer between the charging system **100a** and the electrical/electronic device **102** is readily accomplished by modulating data onto one or more of the charging beams **108a**, **108b**, **108c**, and demodulating the modulated component in the electrical/electronic device. Similarly, the electrical/electronic device **102** can modulate either one or more of its pilot beams **110a**, **110b** or **110c** (or whatever "locator" signal it employs) with data to be transferred to the system **100a**. This data transfer mechanism is described in greater detail hereinbelow with respect to FIG. 2B.

FIG. 1B is a view of a similar system **100b** for microwave charging of an electrical/electronic device **122** in a charging cradle/adpater **120**. This embodiment is essentially identical to that of FIG. 1A, except that the electrical/electronic device **102** of FIG. 1A had the beam-receiving rectennas and pilot beam generation built-in, while the implementation of FIG. 1B separates the beam-receiving rectennas and pilot beam generation into a separate charging cradle/adapter **120**. In effect, the combination of electrical/electronic device **122** and charging cradle/adapter **120** in FIG. 1B is comparable to the electrical/electronic device **102** of FIG. 1A. Pilot beams **110a**, **110b**, and **110c** can be "gated" such that they are only generated when the electrical/electronic device **122** is "docked" in its charging cradle/adapter **120**, thereby signaling to the system **100b** that the adaptive-phased arrays can be powered down, since there is no need for powering/charging otherwise.

One advantage of the system **100a** of FIG. 1A over the system **100b** of FIG. 1B is that the fully-integrated electrical/electronic device **102** required no charging adapter, and can be charged or powered simply by being placed in the vicinity of a suitable charging system. The system **100b** of FIG. 1B has the advantage that it readily adapted to accept existing electrical/electronic devices such as cell phones and PDAs without modification.

FIG. 2A is a block diagram of a system **200a** for microwave charging an electrical/electronic device **230** by means of focused, microwave beams **240**. A power transmitter portion **220** of the system comprises a power source **202** that powers one or more adaptively-phased arrays **204** to produce one or more directed ("focused") beams **240** of microwave energy aimed at the electrical/electronic device **230**. Pilot beam detection **206**, detects a locator signal emitted by a pilot beam emitter **238** in the electrical/electronic device. A location detection function **208** analyzes the timing of the locator signal to determine the location of the electrical/electronic device **230** relative to the one or more adaptively-phased arrays **204**. The phase of transmitted microwave energy is varied continuously across the face of the adaptively-phased arrays **204** to produce beam(s) **240** that converge on one or more rectenna elements **232** in the electrical/electronic device. Microwave energy received by the rectennas **232** is rectified and converted thereby into DC electrical energy which is in turn presented to a charging and power control function block **234** for charging a battery **236** and/or for providing primary power to the electrical/electronic device **230**.

Backscatter sensors **212** in the power transmitter portion **220** detect reflected microwave energy indicative of an obstacle in the microwave beams. Control logic responds to signal from the backscatter detector and reduces (or cuts off) the power transmitted by any adaptively-phased array **204** whose beam path is obstructed. Preferably, the power of the obstructed beam is lowered to a "safe" level and the backscatter detectors are continually monitored to determine when the beam is clear, at which time full power to the affected beam can once again be restored. Additionally, the location detection function **208** can provide an indication of presence or absence of an electrical/electronic device **230** to

be charged, enabling power transmission by the adaptively-phased arrays **204** only when an appropriately adapted electrical/electronic device **230** is present.

FIG. 2B is a block diagram of a similar system **200b** for microwave charging of an electrical/electronic device **230a** (compare **230**) by a power transmitter portion **220a** (compare **220**) of the system, but adding means for data exchange between the electrical/electronic device **230a** and the power transmitter portion **220a** As in the system **200** of FIG. 2A, the power transmitter portion **220a** of the system comprises a power source **202** that powers one or more adaptively-phased arrays **204** to produce one or more directed ("focused") beams **240** of microwave energy aimed at the electrical/electronic device **230a**. In addition, however, a Modulator function **250** modulates the microwave energy generated by the adaptively phased arrays **204** such that the focused power beams **240** carry both power (a "DC" or continuous beam component) and data (an "AC" or varying beam component). A demodulator function **252** in the electrical/electronic device **230a** demodulates or "decodes" the varying beam component as received by the rectennas **232**, and reproduces the data used to produce the modulation.

Pilot beam detection **206**, detects a locator signal emitted by a pilot beam emitter **238** in the electrical/electronic device **230a** In this case, however, a modulator function **254** modulates data onto the locator signal produced by the pilot beam emitter. A demodulator function **256** in the power transmitter portion **220a** decodes (demodulates) the data modulated onto the locator signal. A location detection function **208** analyzes the overall timing of the locator signal to determine the location of the electrical/electronic device **230a** relative to the one or more adaptively-phased arrays **204** The phase of transmitted microwave energy is varied continuously across the face of the adaptively-phased arrays **204** to produce beam(s) **240** that converge on one or more rectenna elements **232** in the electrical/electronic device. Microwave energy received by the rectennas **232** is rectified and converted thereby into DC electrical energy which is in turn presented to a charging and power control function block **234** for charging a battery **236** and/or for providing primary power to the electrical/electronic device **230a**.

As in the system **200** of FIG. 2A, backscatter sensors **212** in the power transmitter portion **220a** detect reflected microwave energy indicative of an obstacle in the microwave beams. Control logic responds to signal from the backscatter detector and reduces (or cuts off) the power transmitted by any adaptively-phased array **204** whose beam path is obstructed. Preferably, the power of the obstructed beam is lowered to a "safe" level and the backscatter detectors are continually monitored to determine when the beam is clear, at which time full power to the affected beam can once again be restored. Additionally, the location detection function **208** can provide an indication of presence or absence of an electrical/electronic device **230a** to be charged, enabling power transmission by the adaptively-phased arrays **204** only when an appropriately adapted electrical/electronic device **230a** is present.

Those of ordinary skill in the art will immediately understand that the electronic/electronic device **230** of FIG. 2A could be charged by the power transmitter portion **220a** of FIG. 2B, but that there would be no data exchange capability due to the lack of compatible data exchange circuitry in the electrical/electronic device **230**. Similarly, the electrical/electronic device **230a** of FIG. 2B could be charged by the power transmitter **220** of FIG. 2A, but there would be no data exchange capability due to the lack of compatible data exchange circuitry in the power transmitter **220**.

7
8

Those of ordinary skill in the art will immediately understand that the systems **200** and **200***a* of FIGS. 2A and 2B, respectively, can be applied either to fully-integrated, microwave-chargeable electrical/electronics devices (e.g., **102**, FIG. 1A) or to microwave charging stations for conventional electrical/electronic devices (e.g., **122**, **120**, FIG. 1B) by making the appropriate functional divisions. Specifically, only the battery (e.g., **236**, FIG. 2B) need reside within a conventional electrical/electronic device (e.g., **122**, FIG. 1B). All other components of the microwave-chargeable electrical electronic device (see **230**, **230***a*, FIGS. 2A, 2B) can be integrated into a charging station (e.g., **120** FIG. 1B).

Although the invention has been shown and described with respect to a certain preferred embodiment or embodiments, certain equivalent alterations and modifications will occur to others skilled in the art upon the reading and understanding of this specification and the annexed drawings. In particular regard to the various functions performed by the above described components (assemblies, devices, circuits, etc.) the terms (including a reference to a "means") used to describe such components are intended to correspond, unless otherwise indicated, to any component which performs the specified function of the described component (i.e., that is functionally equivalent), even though not structurally equivalent to the disclosed structure which performs the function in the herein illustrated exemplary embodiments of the invention. In addition, while a particular feature of the invention may have been disclosed with respect to only one of several embodiments, such feature may be combined with one or more features of the other embodiments as may be desired and advantageous for any given or particular application.

What is claimed is:

1. A system for charging of devices, comprising:
a power transmitter having a plurality of adaptively-phased microwave array emitters;
a device to be charged having one or more rectennas associated therewith; and
location determining means for determining a location of the device to be charged relative to the adaptively-phased array emitters;
wherein each individual microwave array emitter produces energy at a frequency close to, but different from that produced by any other microwave array emitter in the system.

2. A system according to claim 1, further comprising:
means for exchanging data between the power transmitter and the device to be charged.

3. A system according to claim 2, further comprising:
modulating means for modulating a data signal onto a locator signal produced by the device to be charged; and
demodulating means within the power transmitter for demodulating the data modulated onto the locator signal.

4. A system for charging of devices, comprising:
a power transmitter having one or more adaptively-phased microwave array emitters;
a device to be charged having one or more rectennas associated therewith;
location determining means for determining a location of the device to be charged relative to the adaptively-phased array emitters; and
one or more backscatter detectors associated with the adaptively-phased microwave array emitters for detecting microwave backscatter energy reflected off of any obstruction between the adaptively-phased microwave array emitters and the device to be charged.

5. A system according to claim 4, wherein:
the location determining means are employed to focus energy produced by the adaptively-phased microwave array emitters onto the device to be charged.

6. A system according to claim 4, wherein:
the location determining means further comprise:
a pilot beam emitter in the device to be charged for producing a locator signal;
a pilot beam detector in the power transmitter for detecting the locator signal; and
location detection means for analyzing the locator signal to determine the location of the device to be charged.

7. A system according to claim 4, wherein:
the adaptively-phased microwave array emitters produce continuous-wave microwave energy in the frequency range between 2 GHz and 10 GHz inclusive.

8. A system according to claim 4, wherein:
each separate adaptively-phased microwave array emitter produces microwave energy at a unique frequency close to but different from the frequency produced by any other adaptively-phased microwave array emitter in the system.

9. A system according to claim 4, further comprising:
means for reducing power transmitted by any adaptively-phased microwave array emitter for which an obstruction exists between it and the device to be charged.

10. A system according to claim 9, further comprising:
means for restoring full power to the obstructed adaptively-phased microwave array emitter upon removal of the obstruction.

11. A system according to claim 4, wherein:
the device to be charged is connected to a charging cradle/adapter within which the rectennas are disposed that receives microwave energy transmitted by the one or more adaptively-phased microwave array emitters and transfers it to the device to be charged.

12. A system according to claim 4, further comprising:
means for exchanging data between the power transmitter and the device to be charged.

13. A system according to claim 12, wherein:
the location determining means are employed to focus energy produced by the adaptively-phased microwave array emitters onto the device to be charged.

14. A system according to claim 12, wherein:
the location determining means further comprise:
a pilot beam emitter in the device to be charged for producing a locator signal;
a pilot beam detector in the power transmitter for detecting the locator signal; and
location detection means for analyzing the locator signal to determine the location of the device to be charged.

15. A system according to claim 12, further comprising:
means for reducing power transmitted by any adaptively-phased microwave array emitter for which an obstruction exists between it and the device to be charged.

16. A system according to claim 15, further comprising:
means for restoring full power to the obstructed adaptively-phased microwave array emitter upon removal of the obstruction.

17. A system according to claim 12, further comprising:
modulating means for modulating data onto microwave energy beams produced by the one or more adaptively-phased microwave array emitters; and

9

demodulating means for demodulating the data modulated onto the microwave energy beams.

18. A system according to claim **17**, wherein:

the rectennas and demodulating means reside within the device to be charged.

19. A system according to claim **17**, wherein:

the rectennas and demodulating means reside within a charger adapter/cradle to which the device to be charged is connected,

the device to be charged is situated in a charging cradle/ adapter that receives microwave energy transmitted by the one or more adaptively-phased microwave array emitters and transfers it to the device to be charged.

20. A system for device charging, comprising:

a power transmitter portion further comprising:

a power source;

one or more adaptively-phased microwave array emitters;

means for receiving a location signal indicative of the location of a device to be charged;

10

location detection means for determining the location of the device to be charged from the locator signal;

means for focusing energy produced by the one or more adaptive-phase microwave array emitters onto the devices to be charged; and

control logic means for reducing the amount of energy produced by any obstructed adaptively phased microwave array emitter until the obstruction is removed; and

a device to be charged comprising:

a battery;

one or more rectennas for receiving and rectifying energy produced by the adaptively-phased microwave array emitters; and

charging and power control means for charging the battery from rectified energy received by the rectennas.

* * * * *

UNITED STATES PATENT AND TRADEMARK OFFICE
CERTIFICATE OF CORRECTION

PATENT NO.   : 6,967,462 B1
DATED   : November 22, 2005
INVENTOR(S) : Landis

Page 1 of 1

It is certified that error appears in the above-identified patent and that said Letters Patent is hereby corrected as shown below:

<u>Column 10,</u>
Line 3, after "means for focusing energy produced by the one or more adaptively-phased microwave array emitters onto the device to be charged;" insert the following paragraph: -- backscatter detection means for detecting microwave energy reflected off of any obstruction between the one or more adaptively-phased microwave array emitters and the device to be charged; and --.

Signed and Sealed this

Twenty-eighth Day of February, 2006

JON W. DUDAS
Director of the United States Patent and Trademark Office

28

US007655145B1

(12) **United States Patent**
Gormly et al.

(10) **Patent No.:** **US 7,655,145 B1**
(45) **Date of Patent:** **Feb. 2, 2010**

(54) **CONTAMINATED WATER TREATMENT**

(75) Inventors: **Sherwin J. Gormly**, Carson City, NV (US); **Michael T. Flynn**, Corte Madera, CA (US)

(73) Assignee: **United States Government as represented by the Administrator of the National Aeronautics and Space Administration (NASA)**, Washington, DC (US)

(*) Notice: Subject to any disclaimer, the term of this patent is extended or adjusted under 35 U.S.C. 154(b) by 276 days.

(21) Appl. No.: **11/543,275**

(22) Filed: **Sep. 28, 2006**

(51) **Int. Cl.**
C02F 1/44 (2006.01)
B01D 15/00 (2006.01)
B01D 61/00 (2006.01)

(52) **U.S. Cl.** **210/649**; 210/652; 210/694; 210/724

(58) **Field of Classification Search** .... None
See application file for complete search history.

(56) **References Cited**

U.S. PATENT DOCUMENTS

5,281,430	A	1/1994	Herron et al.	
6,436,282	B1 *	8/2002	Gundrum et al.	210/117
6,656,361	B1	12/2003	Herron et al.	
6,849,184	B1	2/2005	Lampi et al.	
2004/0004037	A1 *	1/2004	Herron	210/321.83
2005/0155939	A1 *	7/2005	Stadelmann	210/764
2007/0181497	A1 *	8/2007	Liberman	210/636

OTHER PUBLICATIONS

Beaudry, et al., Direct Osmotic Concentration of Waste Water, Final report, Osmotek, Inc. NASA contract No. NAS2-14069, 1999.
Cath, et al., New Concepts and Performance of the Direct Osmotic . . . , Proceedings of 36th International Conference on Environmental Systems, Jul. 17-20, 2006, Norfolk, VA, USA.
Exploration Systems Architechture Study (ESAS), NASA-TM-2005-214062, Nov. 2005, 234.
Gormly, et al., Direct Osmotic Concentration: A Primary Water . . . , Proceedings of the 33rd International Conference on Environmental Systems, Jul. 2003, Vancouver BC, Canada.
Horan, et al., Application of Granular Activated Carbon-Biological Fluidized Bed for the Treatment of Landfill Leachat . . . , Wat. Sci. Tech., 1997, 369-375, 36-No. 2-3, IWAQ.
Kliss, Water Regeneration Technologies for Human Space . . . , Proceedings of Conference on Innovative Technologies in the Water Sector, May 15-17, 2006, Rotterdam, Netherlands.

* cited by examiner

Primary Examiner—Krishnan S Menon
(74) *Attorney, Agent, or Firm*—John F. Schipper; Robert M. Padilla

(57) **ABSTRACT**

Method and system for processing of a liquid ("contaminant liquid") containing water and containing urine and/or other contaminants in a two step process. Urine, or a contaminated liquid similar to and/or containing urine and thus having a relatively high salt and urea content is passed through an activated carbon filter to provide a resulting liquid, to remove most of the organic molecules. The resulting liquid is passed through a semipermeable membrane from a membrane first side to a membrane second side, where a fortified drink having a lower water concentration (higher osmotic potential) than the resulting liquid is positioned. Osmotic pressure differential causes the water, but not most of the remaining inorganic (salts) contaminant(s) to pass through the membrane to the fortified drink. Optionally, the resulting liquid is allowed to precipitate additional organic molecules before passage through the membrane.

8 Claims, 4 Drawing Sheets

(21)

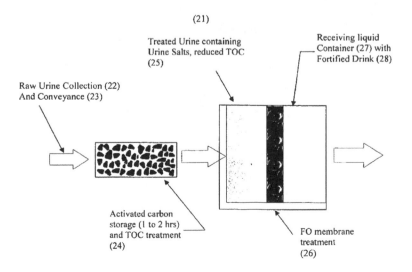

Raw Urine Collection (22) And Conveyance (23)

Treated Urine containing Urine Salts, reduced TOC (25)

Receiving liquid Container (27) with Fortified Drink (28)

Activated carbon storage (1 to 2 hrs) and TOC treatment (24)

FO membrane treatment (26)

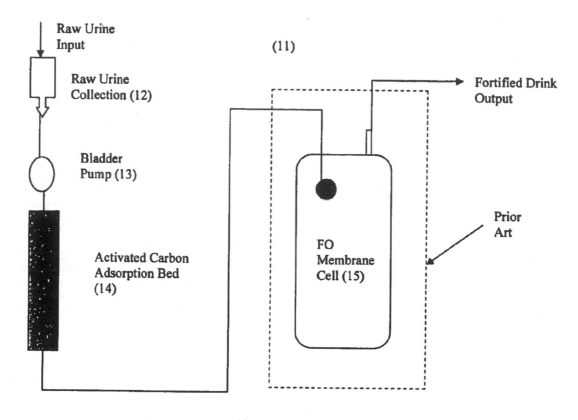

Figure 1

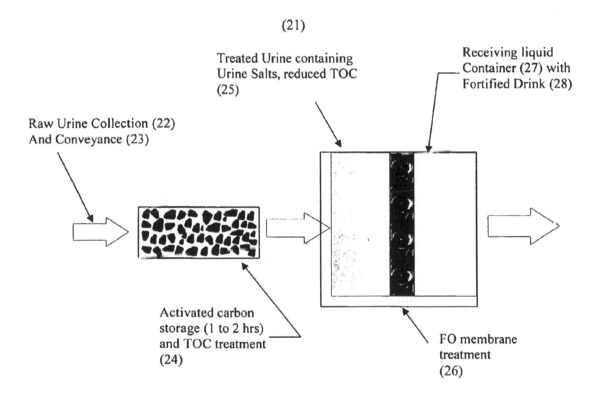

Figure 2

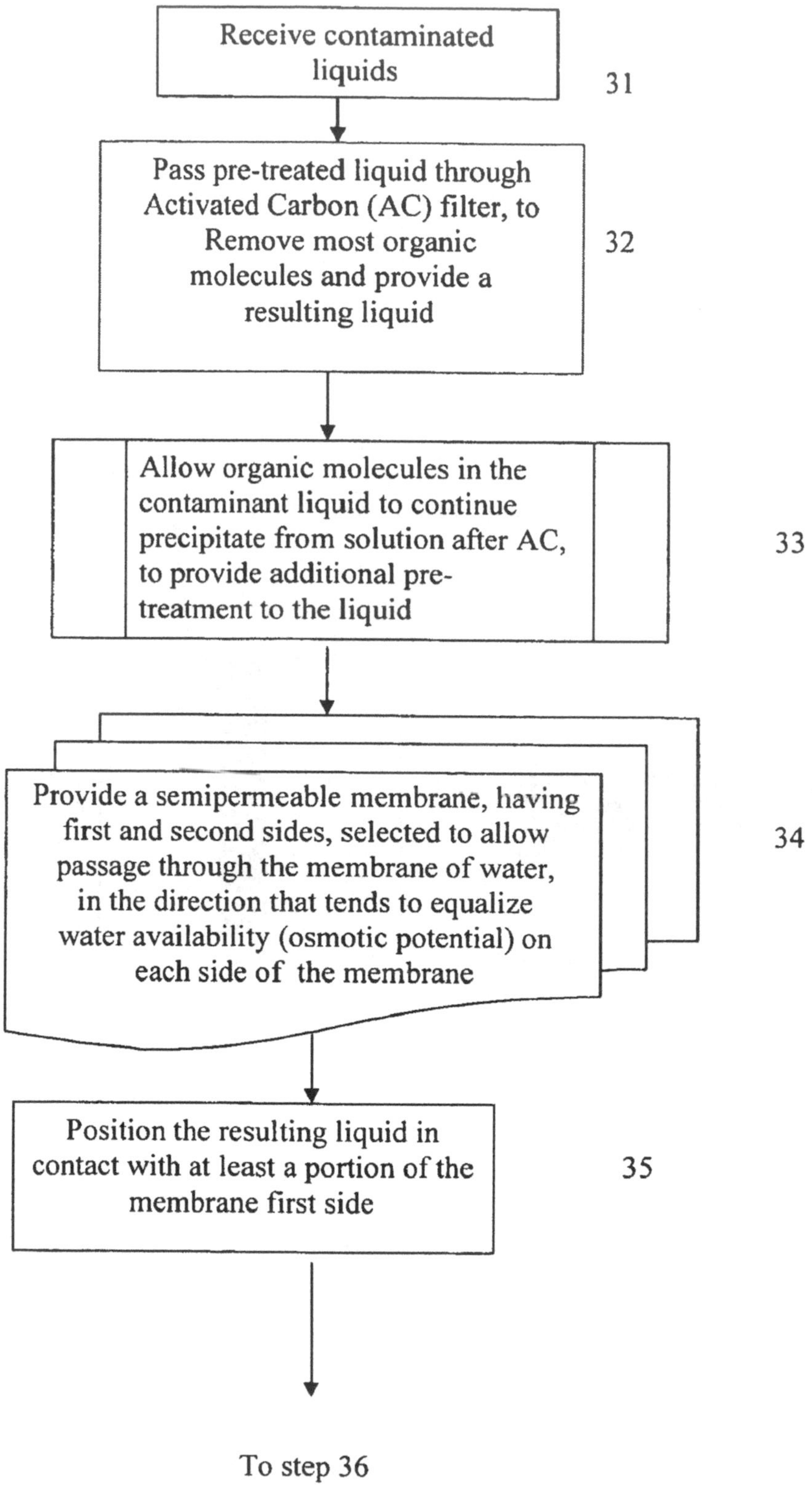

Receive contaminated liquids   31

Pass pre-treated liquid through Activated Carbon (AC) filter, to Remove most organic molecules and provide a resulting liquid   32

Allow organic molecules in the contaminant liquid to continue precipitate from solution after AC, to provide additional pre-treatment to the liquid   33

Provide a semipermeable membrane, having first and second sides, selected to allow passage through the membrane of water, in the direction that tends to equalize water availability (osmotic potential) on each side of the membrane   34

Position the resulting liquid in contact with at least a portion of the membrane first side   35

To step 36

Figure 3A

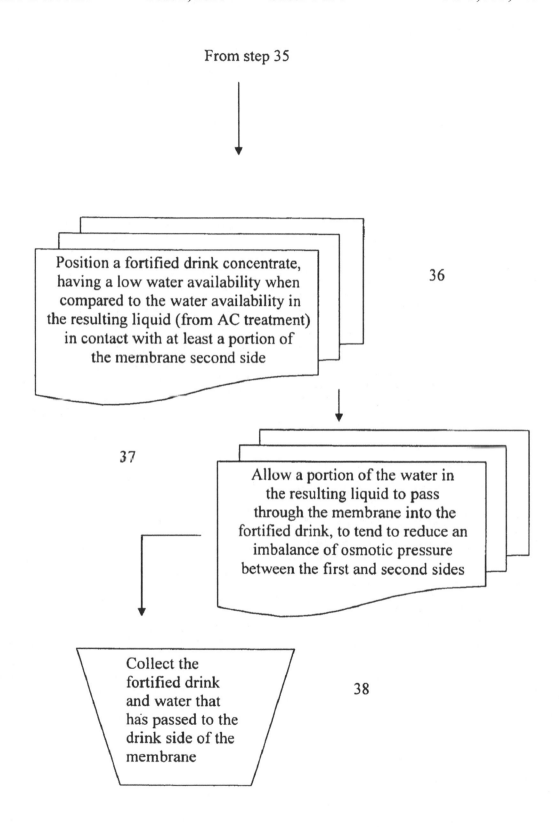

From step 35

Position a fortified drink concentrate, having a low water availability when compared to the water availability in the resulting liquid (from AC treatment) in contact with at least a portion of the membrane second side

36

37

Allow a portion of the water in the resulting liquid to pass through the membrane into the fortified drink, to tend to reduce an imbalance of osmotic pressure between the first and second sides

Collect the fortified drink and water that has passed to the drink side of the membrane

38

Figure 3B

33

1

CONTAMINATED WATER TREATMENT

FIELD OF THE INVENTION

This invention relates to processing and recycling of liquid, including urine, to remove contaminants in the liquid.

BACKGROUND OF THE INVENTION

The Crew Exploration Vehicle ("CEV") and the Lunar Surface Access Module ("LSAM"), to be used for space exploration, will require new life support systems to support the crew on journeys lasting from a few days to several weeks, or longer. These life support systems should also be designed to reduce the mass required to keep humans alive in space. Water accounts for about 80 percent of the daily mass intake required to keep a person alive. As a result, recycling water offers a high return on investment for space life support. Water recycling can also increase mission safety by providing an emergency supply of drinking water, where another supply is exhausted or contaminated. For a three-day CEV mission to the International Space Station (ISS), water recycling can reduce the mass required to be transported to provide drinking water by 65 percent, when compared to stored water. For an 18-day Lunar mission, a mass savings of about 70 percent is possible. These technologies also increase safety by providing a lightweight back-up to stored supplies, and they allow astronauts to meet daily drinking water requirements by recycling the water contained in their own urine. During a three-day CEV emergency return to Earth, this capability could be critical to the crews' survival. These technologies also convert urine into a concentrated brine that is biologically stable and non-threatening and can be safely stored onboard. This approach eliminates the need to have a dedicated vent to dump urine overboard. This would result in one less through hull fitting on the CEV spacecraft (a significant safety advantage).

What is needed is a system for recycling urine (1) to provide a renewable source of drinking water, (2) to reduce the mass of water initially stored aboard a spacecraft, (3) to provide a temporary source of additional nutrients for use by a spacecraft occupant, (4) to reduce the volume of, and provide a biologically safe form of, urine residuals (i.e. waste or non-water residues from urine) temporarily stored aboard a spacecraft and (5) reduce or eliminate the need for urine dumping during a space voyage.

SUMMARY OF THE INVENTION

These needs are met by a system and associated method that provides a contaminant treatment pouch, referred to as a "urine cell" or "contaminant cell," that converts urine or another liquid containing contaminants into a fortified drink, engineered to meet human hydration, electrolyte and caloric requirements, using a variant of forward osmosis ("FO") to draw water from a urine container into the concentrated fortified drink as part of a recycling stage. An activated carbon pre-treatment removes most organic molecules. Salinity of the initial liquid mix (urine plus other) is synergistically used to enhance the precipitation organic molecules so that activated carbon can remove most of the organics. A functional osmotic bag is then used to remove inorganic contaminants. If a contaminant is processed for which the saline content is different than optimal for precipitating organic molecules, the saline content of the liquid should be adjusted toward the optimal value for that contaminant.

2

The development of a water recycling systems to support CEV and LSAM missions can significantly reduce the mass of life support mechanisms. Current plans for the CEV assume that water is "tanked" and that urine is vented overboard. This open loop approach does not attempt to minimize launch mass, and it requires provisions of at least one additional through-wall penetrations. The CEV is, by definition a pressure vessel upon which the crew's life depends and thus any through wall fitting represents a potentially fatal (to the crew) failure point in vehicle design. The CEV, Block 1 mission, which is to transfer crew and limited cargo to ISS, and Block 2, a Lunar mission, are both relatively short flight duration vehicles, at most a few weeks. Short duration missions can be addressed by the use of consumable water treatment products. These products offer reduced mass and produce recycled water for only a fraction of the weight of the water itself. For example, a disposable water purification system, such as the urine cell, could produce 1 Kg of drinking water from urine with only 300 gm of water purification equipment, a 70 percent reduction in mass below what is required with stored water.

BRIEF DESCRIPTION OF THE DRAWINGS

FIG. 1 schematically illustrates the location of the basic X-Pack configuration (prior Art).

FIG. 2 illustrates an embodiment of the invention.

FIGS. 3A and 3B show a flow chart of a procedure for practicing the invention.

DESCRIPTION OF BEST MODE OF THE INVENTION

An FO based urine cell 11 utilizing both activated carbon (AC) and the X-Pack™ technology, disclosed by Hydeation Technologies, Inc., is illustrated in FIG. 1. See, for example U.S. Pat. No. 6,849,184, issued to Lampi et al for previous disclosure of FO membrane cell 15. In the invention a bladder pump 13 is fed by a urine collector 12 and moves the liquid through an activated carbon (AC) filter 14 into a membrane container in a pouch 15. The membrane promotes separation of water from urine, and the product, having a lowered urea content, is drawn off as product.

The invention 21, illustrated in FIG. 2, is an improvement of technologies similar to the X-Pack™ device. The liquid to be treated is passed through an activated carbon filter 24 (granules or porous block or another suitable filter mechanism), which absorbs a majority of the remaining organic molecules to provide a resulting liquid. The resulting liquid is received by a container 25 that is positioned adjacent to a first side of a semipermeable, preferably hydrophilic, membrane 26 (e.g., cellulous triacetate) that allows water diffuse through it, but blocks most contaminants (urea, brine, etc.) due to a micro-porous construction of the filter. A container 27 of a concentrated fortified drink 28 is positioned adjacent to a second side of the membrane 26. Some precipitation of the remaining organic molecules occurs within the container 25.

Water is drawn through the membrane 26, from the first side to the second side, by an osmotic potential differential ΔOP, generated by the feed (urine or another contaminated liquid) and by sugars and electrolytes contained in the fortified drink 28 that is concentrated (strength range 2-20 times normal strength, or more if desired). Water diffuses across the membrane 26 from the urine (water-rich) first side to the concentrated fortified drink (water-poor) second side in order to (partly) equalize the osmotic potential. During this diffusion process, the concentrated fortified drink 28 will become

3

diluted through uptake of water, and the urine will become more concentrated by loss of water. The fortified drink concentrate has the sugars, electrolytes and calories needed by a human and is formulated so that the final product is diluted to a level appropriate for human consumption. Because the process uses osmotic potential OP rather than hydraulic pressure, the process is referred to as forward osmosis ("FO"), which can be thought of as running reverse osmosis ("RO") in reverse. Because the process uses osmotic potential instead of hydraulic pressure, it has been shown to have fewer membrane fouling problems that are inherent to RO and microfiltration.

Table 1 presents data on the treatment of organic compounds using the membranes and AC filter selected for use in the urine cell (more generally, contaminant cell). Table 2 provides the results of bacteriological and viral rejection tests of the X-Pack™ membranes.

TABLE 1

Projected Performance of the Urine Cell	
Stage of Treatment	Typical Values (in mg/L TOC)
Raw Urine	2,500 to 5,500 mg/L
After GAC Treatment	50 to 100 mg/L
After CTA (stock) Forward Osmosis Membrane	20 to 30 mg/L
Theoretical System Performance Limit with Optimal Membranes	1 to 2 mg/L

TABLE 2

Bacterial and Viral Testing		
Test Description	1 hr sample	24 hr sample
Anthrax Permeation		
1.200,000/ml Pigment Ink Dilution	—	0
0.4-1.0 micron E. Coli Permeation	0	0
colony counts 1,000,000/ml	0	0
colony counts 100,000,000/ml M 13 phage Permeation	0	0
phage counts 10,000,000/ml	0	0
phage counts 1,000,000,000/ml MS2 phage Permeation	0	0
phage counts 1,000,000/ml	0	0
phage counts 100,000,000/ml M13 phageDNA Permeation	0	0
2 mg in 4 liters	0	0

Although a technology, such as the basic X-Pack™ device, is capable of removing most inorganic compounds, this device will not reliably remove small non-polar organics or ammonia; up to 50 percent of these compounds will pass through the membrane. Urine contains many of these types of contaminates. Activated carbon, as granules or in a porous block, is used to pre-treat the urine and to remove many, but not all, organic molecules, including most non-polar organics. Activated carbon also has a weak affinity for ammonia. The relatively high concentration of salts in urine in FIG. 2 works synergistically to improve the performance of the activated carbon. Commercially available AC is used.

4

Preferably, the system 21 provides for the collection 22 (12 in FIG. 1) and movement 23 (13 in FIG. 1) of the urine, preceding to an activated carbon ("AC") porous filter 24. The relatively high salinity of the urine enhances the performance of the AC filter 24 by decreasing the solubility of organic molecules in the input liquid, significantly increasing the affinity of these molecules for AC, resulting in a product with approximately 50 mg/liter total organic carbon (TOC) remaining, as compared to about 200 mg/liter TOC (as urea), after AC treatment of fresh water, with no urine salts present. Preferably, the urine temperature and the fortified drink temperature are in a range between room temperature and about 20 to 30° C.; and/or the pH of the fortified drink is adjusted to be no higher than about 8.

FIG. 3 is a flow chart of a procedure for practicing the invention. In step 31, a liquid containing at least one contaminant ("contaminant liquid"), usually urine or a substantially similarly contaminated liquid, is received. In step 32, the contaminant liquid is passed through an activated carbon filter to produce a resulting liquid in which a majority of organic molecules have been removed. In step 33 (optional), a remainder of organic molecules in the resulting liquid are allowed to precipitate from solution, before passage through a membrane (step 34). In step 34, a semipermeable membrane is provided, having a first side and a second side, and being selected to allow passage therethrough of water in a direction that tends to equalize concentration of water on the first and second sides of the membrane. In step 35, the resulting liquid is positioned in contact with at least a portion of the membrane first side.

In step 36, a concentrated fortified drink, having a low concentration of water compared to a concentration of water in the resulting (from AC treatment) liquid, is positioned in contact with at least a portion of the membrane second side. In step 37, a portion of the resulting liquid is allowed to pass through the membrane, from the first side to the second side into the fortified drink, to reduce an imbalance of concentration of water on the first and second sides of the membrane. In step 38, the fortified drink and the water that has passed through the membrane are collected.

Tests performed on the urine cell indicate that: (1) raw urine has a total organic content ("TOC") of 2,500-5,000 mg/liter, before treatment; (2) after treatment, TOC lies in a range of 25-50 mg/liter; and (3) an optimal treatment according to the invention can theoretically lower TOC to 1-2 mg/liter. Urea is the source of the majority of TOC present in urine, and testing indicates that as much as 95-97 percent of urea can be removed using the invention.

The membranes used in the urine cell should be an effective barrier to inorganic compounds. Cellulose tri-acetate (CTA) membranes, similar to those used in the urine cell, are widely used in reverse osmosis (RO) applications and inorganic rejection data are available from suppliers and from published technical articles. Ammonia is present in low or modest percentages in fresh urine. The normal range of urine ammonia for healthy adults is 200-500 ppm. This is a product of urea hydrolysis, a relatively slow process, and treatment within 1 hour of urine generation should help to keep concentrations of ammonia low in the feed and in the product. Most ammonia and nitrogen that is present will be removed from the feed by an AC filter.

In future urine cell designs it may be desirable to enhance the ammonia removal beyond the capabilities of the current (above claimed) design. This would be accomplished through the addition of a 3rd treatment step located between the AC and the FO membrane steps of the urine cell, and would simply require a chemical addition during step 33 (FIG. 3:

5

Step **33**). Ammonia that is not removed by the AC filter can be further reduced by pH adjustment and/or by supplemental absorption using diatomaceous Earth or an amine chemical addition following AC treatment but prior to FO treatment. Low pH (highly acidic) values ensure that ammonia in solution exists predominantly as the ammonium ion. Ammonium ions can be removed by micro-porous membranes. Ammonia can also be removed by diatomaceous Earth or amines. In ether case the additional pH adjustment and/or chemical addition would be provided between to AC and FO treatments (at step **33**) and is claimed as a process improvement option to be freely exercised (without farther patenting applications to the primary invention) should it become desirable or necessary.

The urine cell may be usable more than once, until the osmotic strength of salt in the bag approach the osmotic strength of the sugar in the fortified drink. The urine cell is relatively small and can be incorporated into a flight suit or a space suit and thus become an integral part of a spaceworker's apparel. If the urine cell is made part of a pressure suit the cell may be useful during a specified 120-hour un-pressurized emergency return to Earth capability in a CEV. During an emergency, the urine cell can provide emergency urine collection and drinking water supplies, as a redundant backup. The urine cell uses no electrical power, has no complicated mechanical parts to break or to require maintenance, is silent, and has a shelf life in excess of one year. The cell includes a flexible plastic pouch, surgical tubing, an AC filter, and a water collection device.

The membrane may be hydrophilic, where the membrane pore diameters are as large as, or slightly larger than the minimum diameter required allow liquid phase water to flow, but are smaller than required to pass most organic molecules. Some relatively small organic, non-polar compounds will pass through these pores. The preferred design utilizes hydrophilic membranes, but hydrophobic membranes, in which pore diameters are much smaller, can also be used when desirable. Hydrophilic membranes are preferable for the current design because they achieve reasonable flux or throughput (water production rates), but future application may chose to reduce flux rate for better rejection of urea, in which case hydrophobic membranes would be used without further modification to the concept design. Water transfer rates are about 14 liters/hour/(meter)^2 and 0.04 liters/hour/(meter)^2 for the hydrophilic and hydrophobic membranes, respectively. The membrane surface area can be increased by using a pleated membrane sheet or by using a plurality of helices to increase the effective surface area of the membrane.

6

What is claimed is:

1. A method for treatment of a liquid containing urea, the method comprising:

receiving a liquid containing urea (urea containing liquid or "UCL"), having a salt content of at least 5 gm/liter and having a total organic content ("TOC") of at least 2500 mg/liter;

passing the UCL through an activated carbon filter to produce an intermediate liquid, in which at least 90 percent of organic molecules have been removed, within about one hour after the UCL was generated;

providing a semipermeable membrane, having a first side and a second side, and being selected to allow passage therethrough of water in the intermediate liquid in a direction that tends to equalize osmotic potential of water on the first and second sides of the membrane;

positioning the intermediate liquid in contact with at least a portion of the membrane first side;

positioning a concentrated fortified drink, having a higher liquid osmotic potential for water than a UCL osmotic potential for water on the membrane first side, in contact with at least a portion of the membrane second side; and

allowing a portion of the intermediate liquid to pass through the membrane from the first side to the second side to tend to reduce an imbalance of osmotic potential of the liquids on the first and second sides of the membrane, and to produce a processed liquid having a TOC of no more than 25-50 mg/liter.

2. The method of claim **1**, further comprising collecting at least a portion of a mixture of said fortified drink and said water that has passed through said membrane, on said membrane second side.

3. The method of claim **1**, further comprising maintaining or increasing salinity of said UCL before passing said UCL through said activated carbon filter, to promote additional removal of organic molecules by said activated carbon filter.

4. The method of claim **1**, further comprising providing a hydrophilic membrane as said semipermeable membrane.

5. The method of claim **1**, further comprising providing a hydrophobic membrane as said semipermeable membrane.

6. The method of claim **1**, further comprising adjusting pH of said UCL after passing said UCL through said activated carbon filter, to promote separation of a selected contaminant from said by said membrane.

7. The method of claim **1**, further comprising removing at least 95 percent of urea from said UCL.

8. The method of claim **5**, further comprising removing at least 99 percent of said urea from said UCL.

* * * * *

UNITED STATES PATENT AND TRADEMARK OFFICE
CERTIFICATE OF CORRECTION

PATENT NO.   : 7,655,145 B1   Page 1 of 1
APPLICATION NO. : 11/543275
DATED   : February 2, 2010
INVENTOR(S)   : Gormly et al.

It is certified that error appears in the above-identified patent and that said Letters Patent is hereby corrected as shown below:

On the Title Page:

The first or sole Notice should read --

Subject to any disclaimer, the term of this patent is extended or adjusted under 35 U.S.C. 154(b) by 403 days.

Signed and Sealed this

Twenty-third Day of November, 2010

David J. Kappos
Director of the United States Patent and Trademark Office

US007261783B1

(12) **United States Patent**
MacKay et al.

(10) Patent No.: **US 7,261,783 B1**
(45) Date of Patent: **Aug. 28, 2007**

(54) **LOW DENSITY, HIGH CREEP RESISTANT SINGLE CRYSTAL SUPERALLOY FOR TURBINE AIRFOILS**

(75) Inventors: **Rebecca A. MacKay**, Strongsville, OH (US); **Timothy P. Gabb**, Independence, OH (US); **James L Smialek**, Strongsville, OH (US); **Michael V. Nathal**, Strongsville, OH (US)

(73) Assignee: **The United States of America as Represented by the Administrator of NASA**, Washington, DC (US)

(*) Notice: Subject to any disclaimer, the term of this patent is extended or adjusted under 35 U.S.C. 154(b) by 203 days.

(21) Appl. No.: **10/946,286**

(22) Filed: **Sep. 22, 2004**

(51) Int. Cl.
C22C 10/05 (2006.01)

(52) U.S. Cl. **148/428**; 420/443; 420/445; 420/448

(58) **Field of Classification Search** .... None
See application file for complete search history.

(56) **References Cited**

U.S. PATENT DOCUMENTS

RE29,920 E	*	2/1979	Baldwin	
4,284,430 A	*	8/1981	Henry	148/404
4,388,124 A	*	6/1983	Henry	148/404
4,683,119 A	*	7/1987	Selman et al.	420/444
5,077,141 A	*	12/1991	Naik et al.	428/680
5,395,584 A	*	3/1995	Berger et al.	420/443
5,916,382 A	*	6/1999	Sato et al.	148/404
6,096,141 A	*	8/2000	King et al.	148/429
6,177,046 B1	*	1/2001	Simkovich et al.	420/444

* cited by examiner

Primary Examiner—John P. Sheehan
(74) *Attorney, Agent, or Firm*—Arlene P. Neal; Kent N. Stone

(57) **ABSTRACT**

A nickel-base superalloy article for use in turbines has increased creep resistance and lower density. The superalloy article includes, as measured in % by weight, 6.0-12.0% Mo, 5.5-6.5% Al, 3.0-7.0% Ta, 0-15% Co, 2.0-6.0% Cr, 1.0-4.0% Re, 0-1.5% W, 0-1.5% Ru, 0-2.0%-Ti, 0-3.0% Nb, 0-0.2% Hf, 0-0.02% Y, 0.001-0.005% B, 0.01-0.04% C, and a remainder including nickel plus impurities.

10 Claims, 4 Drawing Sheets

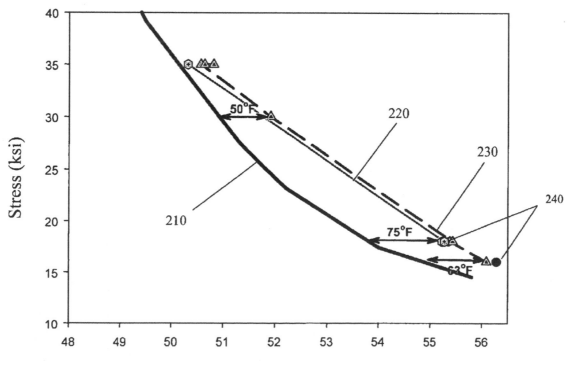

Larson Miller Parameter
$$[(^{\circ}F + 460)*(20 + \log t_f)/1000]$$

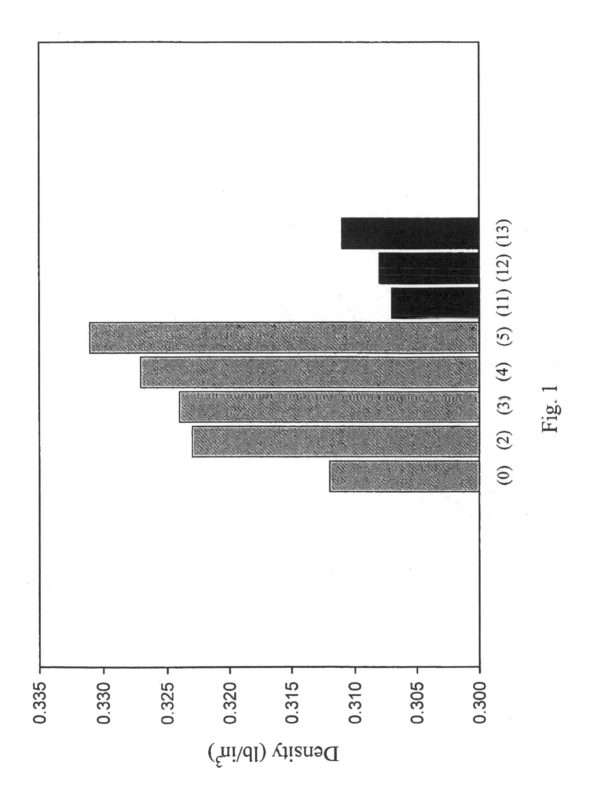

Fig. 1

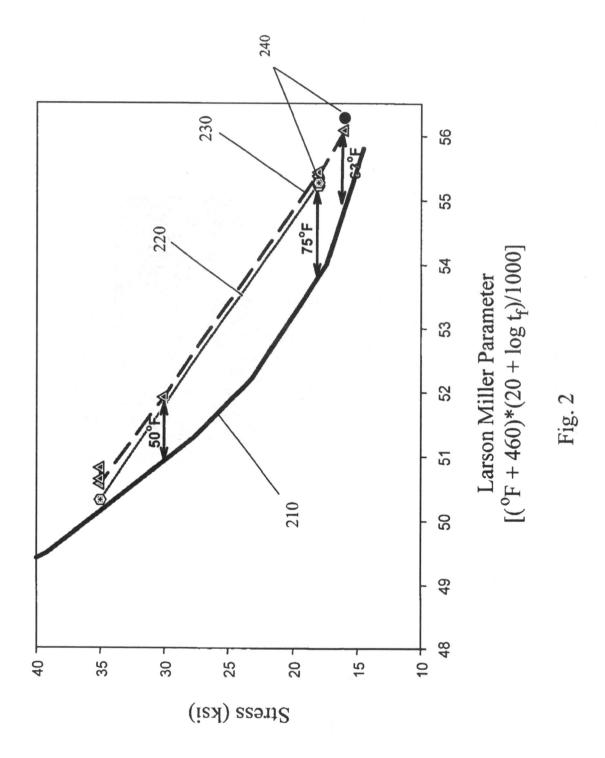

Larson Miller Parameter
$[(^{\circ}F + 460)*(20 + \log t_f)/1000]$

Fig. 2

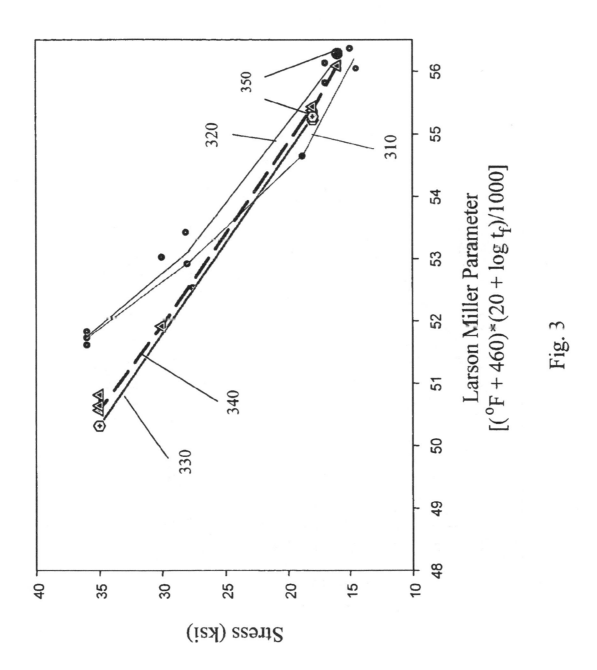

Fig. 3

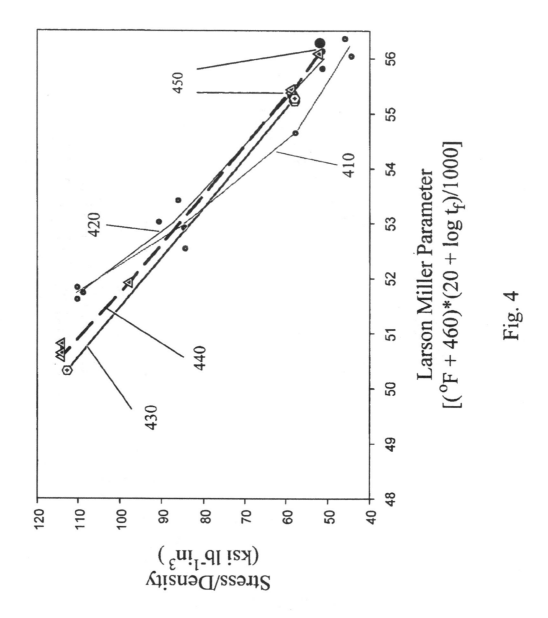

Larson Miller Parameter
$[(^\circ F + 460)*(20 + \log t_f)/1000]$

Fig. 4

1

LOW DENSITY, HIGH CREEP RESISTANT SINGLE CRYSTAL SUPERALLOY FOR TURBINE AIRFOILS

ORIGIN OF THE INVENTION

The invention described herein was made by employees of the United States Government and may be manufactured and used by or for the Government for Government purposes without payment of any royalties thereon or therefore.

BACKGROUND OF THE INVENTION

1. Field of the Invention

The present invention relates to production and use of materials that can be used with turbine airfoils. In particular, the present invention is directed to low density nickel-base superalloys with improved specific creep resistance and strength properties.

2. Description of Related Art

Nickel-base superalloys are used in the construction of some of the components of gas turbine engines that are exposed to severe temperatures and environmental conditions in the engines. For example, the turbine blades and vanes, seals, and shrouds are typically formed of such nickel-base superalloys. During service, these components are exposed to temperatures of 2000° F. or more. To perform at this high temperature for many engine cycles, the materials used in the components must have good rupture strength, a sufficiently high melting point, good thermal shock resistance, and good oxidation resistance at such high temperatures.

Turbine blades have been made from nickel-base superalloy single crystals for over twenty years. The first generation of single crystal superalloys contained no rhenium (Re). Second generation alloys typically contained 3 w/o Re and have attained successful application in commercial and military aircraft engines. Examples of these alloys include Rene N5, CMSX-4, and PWA 1484.

Third generation alloys were designed to increase the temperature capability and creep resistance further by raising the refractory metal content and lowering the chromium (Cr) level. These alloys had Re levels of ~5.5 weight percent (w/o) and Cr levels in the 2-4 w/o range. Examples of these alloys include Rene N6 and CMSX-10. A fourth generation alloy (EPM 102) was developed in the 1990's with NASA sponsorship; it is a very strong alloy due to the increased levels of rhenium and other refractory metals. EPM 102 is considered to be the state-of-the-art.

Second generation alloys are not exceptionally strong, although they have stable microstructures and good oxidation resistance. Oxidation resistance has been achieved in second generation alloys with either yttrium additions or low sulfur (<1 ppmw or 0.0001 w/o) contents. Low sulfur contents can be commercially produced in castings by using melt desulfurization or by using effective hydrogen annealing after the casting has been directionally solidified.

Third and fourth generation alloys have considerably stronger creep resistance due to the use of high levels of refractory metals in the alloy. In particular, high levels of tungsten, rhenium, and sometimes ruthenium are used for strengthening in these alloys, and these refractory metals have densities much higher than that of the nickel base.

The impact of these refractory additions is that the overall alloy density is significantly increased, such that the fourth generation alloy is about 6% heavier than second generation alloys. This weight increase may seem small, but any weight

2

increase to the blade also cascades to the disk, shaft, etc., and increases the overall vehicle system weight by a factor of 8 to 10x. High alloy densities limit the use of the superalloy, and third and fourth generation alloys are used only in specialized applications.

The use of third and fourth generation alloys is also limited by microstructural instabilities which can debit long-term mechanical properties. The alloys are sometimes more difficult to manufacture due to additional processing steps that are needed to mitigate these microstructural instabilities. Additional processing steps add cost to the manufacturing of these alloys, and unfortunately these steps are not always successful in eliminating these instabilities. Thus, there is a need in the prior art for a unique alloying approach in order to achieve microstructural stability, high creep resistance and strength in a turbine blade alloy with low density.

SUMMARY OF THE INVENTION

According to one embodiment of the invention, a nickel-base superalloy article is disclosed. The superalloy article includes, as measured in % by weight, 6.0-12.0% Mo, 5.5-6.5% Al, 3.0-7.0% Ta, 0-15% Co, 2.0-6.0% Cr, 1.0-4.0% Re, 0-2.0% W, 0-2.0% Ru, 0-2.0% Ti, 0-3.0% Nb, 0-0.2% Hf, 0-0.02% Y, 0.001-0.04% C, and a remainder including nickel plus impurities.

Additionally, the nickel-base superalloy article can include 7.0-9.5% Mo, 5.75-6.25% Al, 6.0-6.25% Ta, 0-10% Co, 2.25-5.0% Cr, 1.5-3.25% Re, 0.00% W, 0.00% Ru, 0.00% Ti, 0.00% Nb, 0-0.1% Hf, 0.0015-0.005% Y, 0.001-0.004% B, 0.01-0.02% C, and a remainder including nickel plus impurities. Also, the nickel-base superalloy article may include 7.10% Mo, 6.00% Al, 6.25% Ta, 9.85% Co, 4.70% Cr, 2.95% Re, 0.00% W, 0.00% Ru, 0.00% Ti, 0.00% Nb, 0.00% Hf, 0.0050% Y, 0.004% B, 0.010% C, and a remainder including nickel plus impurities. Alternatively, the nickel-base superalloy article may include 9.45% Mo, 6.00% Al, 6.15% Ta, 4.90% Co, 2.40% Cr, 1.45% Re, 0.00% W, 0.00% Ru, 0.00% Ti, 0.00% Nb, 0.00% Hf, 0.0045% Y, 0.003% B, 0.015% C, and a remainder including nickel plus impurities. Alternatively, the nickel-base superalloy article may include 9.00% Mo, 6.00% Al, 6.05% Ta, 0.00% Co, 2.35% Cr, 2.95% Re, 0.00% W, 0.00% Ru, 0.00% Ti, 0.00% Nb, 0.00% Hf, 0.0095% Y, 0.004% B, 0.015% C, and a remainder including nickel plus impurities.

Additionally, the superalloy article can include the alloy described above, but without yttrium and with extra low sulfur (i.e., less than 0.0001% sulfur). The composition range would be, as measured in % by weight, 6.0-12.0% Mo, 5.5-6.5% Al, 3.0-7.0% Ta, 0-15% Co, 2.0-6.0% Cr, 1.0-4.0% Re, 0-2.0% W, 0-2.0% Ru, 0-2.0% Ti, 0-3.0% Nb, 0-0.2% Hf, <0.0001% S, 0.001-0.005% B, 0.01-0.04% C, and a remainder including nickel plus impurities. Within those ranges, the article may include 7.0-9.5% Mo, 5.75-6.25% Al, 6.0-6.25% Ta, 0-10% Co, 2.25-5.0% Cr, 1.5-3.25% Re, 0.00% W, 0.00% Ru, 0.00% Ti, 0.00% Nb, 0-0.1% Hf, <0.0001% S, 0.001-0.004% B, 0.01-0.02% C, and a remainder including nickel plus impurities. Also, the nickel-base superalloy article may include 7.10% Mo, 6.00% Al, 6.25% Ta, 9.85% Co, 4.70% Cr, 2.95% Re, 0.00% W, 0.00% Ru, 0.00% Ti, 0.00% Nb, 0.00% Hf, <0.0001% S, 0.004% B, 0.010% C, and a remainder including nickel plus impurities. Alternatively, the nickel-base superalloy article may include 9.45% Mo, 6.00% Al, 6.15% Ta, 4.90% Co, 2.40% Cr, 1.45% Re, 0.00% W, 0.00% Ru, 0.00% Ti, 0.00% Nb, 0.00% Hf, <0.0001% S, 0.003% B, 0.015% C, and a remainder

3

including nickel plus impurities. Alternatively, the nickel-base superalloy article may include 9.00% Mo, 6.00% Al, 6.05% Ta, 0.00% Co, 2.35% Cr, 2.95% Re, 0.00% W, 0.00% Ru, 0.00% Ti, 0.00% Nb, 0.00% Hf, <0.0001% S, 0.004% B, 0.015% C, and a remainder including nickel plus impurities.

Alternatively, the article may be a single-crystal component of a gas turbine, or may be a blade of the gas turbine. The article may have a density of less than about 0.311 pounds per cubic inch. Also, the sum of tungsten, ruthenium, titanium and niobium may be less than 0.1 percent or may be essentially zero.

According to another embodiment, a composition of matter is disclosed. The composition consists essentially of, in weight percent, from about 6 to about 12 percent molybdenum, from about 5.5 to about 6.5 percent aluminum, from about 3 to 7 percent tantalum, from 0 to about 15 percent cobalt, from about 2 to about 6 percent chromium, from about 1 to about 4 percent rhenium, from 0 to about 2.0 percent tungsten, from 0 to about 2.0% ruthenium, from 0 to about 2 percent titanium, from 0 to about 3 percent niobium, from 0 to about 0.2 percent hafnium, from 0 to about 0.02 percent yttrium, from about 0.001 to about 0.005 percent boron, from about 0.01 to about 0.04 percent carbon, balance nickel and minor elements.

According to another embodiment, a composition of matter is disclosed that includes the above compositional ranges but without yttrium and with extra low sulfur. The composition consists essentially of, in weight percent, from about 6 to about 12 percent molybdenum, from about 5.5 to about 6.5 percent aluminum, from about 3 to 7 percent tantalum, from 0 to about 15 percent cobalt, from about 2 to about 6 percent chromium, from about 1 to about 4 percent rhenium, from 0 to about 2.0 percent tungsten, from 0 to about 2.0% ruthenium, from 0 to about 2 percent titanium, from 0 to about 3 percent niobium, from 0 to about 0.2 percent hafnium, less than 0.0001 percent sulfur, from about 0.001 to about 0.005 percent boron, from about 0.01 to about 0.04 percent carbon, balance nickel and minor elements.

These and other variations of the present invention will be described in or be apparent from the following description of the preferred embodiments.

BRIEF DESCRIPTION OF THE DRAWINGS

For the present invention to be easily understood and readily practiced, the present invention will now be described, for purposes of illustration and not limitation, in conjunction with the following figures:

FIG. 1 provides a comparison of the densities of superalloy materials according to the prior art and the densities of superalloy materials according to several embodiments of the present invention;

FIG. 2 provides graph illustrating the temperature advantages of superalloy materials according to several embodiments of the present invention when compared with the prior art material Rene N5;

FIG. 3 provides a graph illustrating the comparable strengths of superalloy materials according to several embodiments of the present invention when compared with the prior art third and fourth generation alloys in a high temperature and low stress regime; and

4

FIG. 4 provides a graph illustrating the strength advantages of superalloy materials according to several embodiments of the present invention when compared with the prior art materials when alloy density is taken into account.

DETAILED DESCRIPTION OF PREFERRED EMBODIMENTS

A new low density nickel-base superalloy with improved specific creep resistance and strength properties has been developed for use in, for example, turbine blades of aircraft engines. The levels of alloying elements and the combination of alloying elements used in embodiments of the present invention are unique and allow for the attainment of these improved properties. The alloys developed have significantly lower densities than state-of-the-art alloys and have elevated temperature creep resistance that meet or exceed those of alloys currently in production, as well as state-of-the-art alloys.

The present invention, according to various embodiments, is directed to a single crystal superalloy composition that incorporates lower density refractory metals which provide creep strengthening without the high density. Specifically, molybdenum is the refractory metal employed to provide the bulk of the strengthening, and this element has a density that is close to that of the nickel base. High density alloy elements, such as tungsten and ruthenium, were largely not incorporated in the alloy composition, and low levels of rhenium were used. Cobalt was added to the alloy because it stabilizes the microstructure of the alloy, in a manner similar to ruthenium. Yttrium was added for improved oxide scale adhesion; alternatively, reducing the sulfur impurity level to less than 0.0001% by techniques known to those in the art can have the same effect as an yttrium addition.

Chromium was added to the alloys of the present invention to improve the oxidation resistance. However, adding too much chromium can also cause instabilities thereby reducing the alloy strength. Thus, the chromium levels were kept at modest levels in an effort to achieve a sufficient balance of properties between oxidation resistance, stability, and strength. One feature of this invention is that it provides a novel, highly advantageous combination of the low density of some second generation blade alloys with the high creep strength of the fourth generation superalloy.

TABLE 1 lists some examples of compositions and densities of the alloys according to the present invention. For comparison purposes, the chemistries and densities of the second, third, and fourth generation alloys are also listed in the table. Comparison of the individual alloying elements and their corresponding levels reveals that the alloys in this invention are unique. The high level of molybdenum, the absence of tungsten and ruthenium, the useful range of cobalt, and the lower tantalum contents in particular distinguish the present invention from the prior art materials. The use of these alloying elements in the present invention results in markedly lower alloy densities than second, third, and fourth generation alloys.

TABLE 1

	(11) LDS-1101	(12) LDS-5555	(13) LDS-5051	(0) Rene N5	(1) CMSX-4	(2) PWA 1484	(3) Rene N6	(4) CMSX-10 Ri	(5) EPM 102
Ni	bal	bal	bal	bal	bal	bal	bal	bal	bal
Mo	7.10	9.45	9.00	2.00	0.60	2.00	1.40	0.60	2.00
Al	6.00	6.00	6.00	6.20	5.60	5.60	5.75	5.80	5.55
Ta	6.25	6.15	6.05	7.00	6.50	8.70	7.20	7.50	8.25
Co	9.85	4.90	0.00	8.00	9.00	10.00	12.50	7.00	16.50
Cr	4.70	2.40	2.35	7.00	6.50	5.00	4.20	2.65	2.00
Re	2.95	1.45	2.95	3.00	3.00	3.00	5.40	5.50	5.95
W	0.0	0.0	0.0	5.00	6.00	6.00	6.00	6.40	6.00
Ru	0.0	0.0	0.0	0.0	0.0	0.0	0.0	0.00	3.00
Ti	0.0	0.0	0.0	0.0	1.00	0.0	0.0	0.80	0.00
Nb	0.0	0.0	0.0	0.0	0.0	0.0	0.0	0.40	0.00
Hf	0.0	0.0	0.0	0.20	0.10	0.10	0.15	0.06	0.15
Y	0.005	0.004	0.010				0.010		0.01
B	0.004	0.003	0.004				0.004		0.004
C	0.010	0.015	0.015				0.050		0.03
Density (lb/in^3)	0.311	0.308	0.307	0.312	0.314	0.323	0.324	0.327	0.331

In TABLE 1, (11) is LDS-1101, (12) is LDS-5555 and (13) is LDS-5051. These represent different examples of the present invention. The comparison materials are: (0) as Rene N5, (1) as CMSX-4, (2) as PWA 1484, (3) as Rene N6, (4) as CMSX-10 R1 and (5) as EPM102. The above discussed properties of present invention in comparison with the prior art are also presented graphically in FIG. 1. The exemplary alloys of the present invention, (11), (12) and (13), have densities lower than second, third, and fourth generation alloys (0) and (2)-(5). The numbers used in FIG. 1 for the alloys are the same as those discussed above for TABLE 1.

The creep resistances of different alloys are often compared using a Larson Miller Parameter plot, which enables alloys to be compared over a range of applied stresses and creep testing temperatures. A series of Larson Miller Parameter plots in FIGS. 2 through 4 demonstrate several advantages of the alloys of the present invention. It is noted that while CMSX-4 was discussed above, it is not represented in FIGS. 2-4, although other prior generation alloys are represented for comparison. A first advantage demonstrated is that the creep rupture strength of the present invention materials exceeds that of second generation production alloy Rene N5. This second generation production alloy is disclosed in W. S. Walston et al., "René N6: Third Generation Single Crystal Superalloys," in *Superalloys* 1996, R. D. Kissinger et al., eds., Minerals, Metals & Materials Society, (1996), pp. 27-34. FIG. 2 illustrates that a very significant 50 to 75° F. temperature advantage is provided by the present invention over a wide range of stresses. The curve indicated by 210 is that for Rene N5 and curves 220 and 230 correspond to LDS-5051 and LDS-1101, as discussed above. Data at 16 and 18 ksi indicated by the closed circle are labeled 240 and correspond to LDS-5555. The alloys of the present invention also have slightly lower densities than Rene N5, and thus the temperature advantage of those alloys would be increased slightly if the stress was corrected for density.

FIG. 3 provides the creep test data for the alloys of the present invention, third generation CMSX-10, and fourth generation EPM 102. The curve indicated by 310 is that for CMSX-10, the curve indicated by 320 is that for EPM 102 and curves 330 and 340 correspond to LDS-5051 and LDS-1101, respectively, as discussed above. Data at 16 and 18 ksi indicated by the closed circle are labeled 350 and correspond to LDS-5555. CMSX-10 is discussed in G. L.

Erickson, "The Development and Application of CMSX®-10," in *Superalloys* 1996, R. D. Kissinger et al., eds., Minerals, Metals & Materials Society, (1996), pp. 35-44. EPM 102 is discussed in *Enabling Propulsion Materials Program: Final Technical Report*, Volume 4, Task J—Long-Life Turbine Airfoil Materials System, 1 Oct. 1998 to 31 Oct. 1999, NASA Contract NAS 3-26385, May 2000. Duplicate test results were obtained from the above references and are included in the figure.

FIG. 3 shows that the third and fourth generation alloys have significantly greater creep resistances than the present invention at high stress levels. However, for the lower stress regime, the creep data for the third and fourth generation alloys converge with those of the present invention. In the 14 to 22 ksi stress range, EPM 102 has only slightly improved creep strengths than the alloys of the present invention, and in turn, the alloys of the present invention have slightly improved creep strengths over CMSX-10. However, the alloys of the present invention provide these creep strengths at significantly reduced densities relative to EPM 102 and CMSX-10, and FIG. 3 does not take into account these substantial density differences. The densities of the alloys of the present invention are 6 to 7% lower than EPM 102 and 5 to 6% lower than CMSX-10.

When the creep strengths are normalized for alloy density, the alloys of the present invention have creep strengths very similar to fourth generation EPM 102 over a wide range of stresses. This is illustrated in FIG. 4. The curve indicated by 410 is that for CMSX-10, the curve indicated by 420 is that for EPM 102 and curves 430 and 440 correspond to LDS-5051 and LDS-1101, respectively, as discussed above. Data in the low applied stress regime indicated by the closed circle are labeled 450 and correspond to LDS-5555. Furthermore, it may be seen that the alloys of the present invention provide up to a 40° F. temperature advantage over third generation CMSX-10. Thus, alloy density plays a significant role and the strength capability of the low density alloys of the present invention provides potential benefits for turbine blade applications. The low applied stress regime represents high temperature turbine blade applications, and it is under these conditions that the present invention can be used to great benefit.

Thus, a new low density nickel-base superalloy with improved specific creep resistance and strength properties has been developed for use in turbine blades of aircraft

7

engines. The levels of alloying elements and the combination of alloying elements used in the embodiments of the present invention are unique and result in improved properties. The alloys developed have significantly lower densities than state-of-the-art alloys and have elevated temperature creep resistance that meet or exceed those of alloys currently in production, as well as state-of-the-art alloys. Alloy density has a significant impact because overall vehicle system weight can be reduced, and a reduction in the density of rotating parts results in a 8 to 10× multiplier in total engine weight savings, which translates into reduced fuel consumption and reduced emissions.

Although the invention has been described based upon these preferred embodiments, it would be apparent to those skilled in the art that certain modifications, variations, and alternative constructions would be apparent, while remaining within the spirit and scope of the invention. In order to determine the metes and bounds of the invention, reference should be made to the appended claims.

The invention claimed is:

1. A nickel-base superalloy article, comprising (measured in % by weight):
6.0-12.0% Mo;
5.5-6.5% Al;
3.0-7.0% Ta;
0-15% Co;
2.0-6.0% Cr;
1.0-4.0% Re;
0-2.0% W;
0-2.0% Ru;
0-2.0% Ti;
0-3.0% Nb;
0-0.2% Hf;
0-0.02% Y;
0.001-0.005% B;
0.01-0.04% C;
and a remainder including nickel plus impurities wherein the article is a single crystal component of a gas turbine.

2. A nickel-base superalloy article as claimed in claim 1, comprising (measured in % by weight):
7.0-9.5% Mo;
5.75-6.25% Al;
6.0-6.25% Ta;
0-10% Co;
2.25-5.0% Cr;
1.5-3.25% Re;
0.00% W;
0.00% Ru;
0.00% Ti;
0.00% Nb;
0-0.1% Hf;
0.0015-0.005% Y;
0.001-0.004% B;
0.01-0.02% C;
and a remainder including nickel plus impurities.

3. The nickel-base superalloy article as claimed in claim 2, comprising (measured in % by weight):
7.10% Mo;
6.00% Al;
6.25% Ta;
9.85% Co;

8

4.70% Cr;
2.95% Re;
0.00% W;
0.00% Ru;
0.00% Ti;
0.00% Nb;
0.00% Hf;
0.0050% Y;
0.004% B;
0.010% C;
and a remainder including nickel plus impurities.

4. The nickel-base superalloy article as claimed in claim 2, comprising (measured in % by weight):
9.45% Mo;
6.00% Al;
6.15% Ta;
4.90% Co;
2.40% Cr;
1.45% Re;
0.00% W;
0.00% Ru;
0.00% Ti;
0.00% Nb;
0.00% Hf;
0.0045% Y;
0.003% B;
0.015% C;
and a remainder including nickel plus impurities.

5. The nickel-base superalloy article as claimed in claim 2, comprising (measured in % by weight):
9.00% Mo;
6.00% Al;
6.05% Ta;
0.00% Co;
2.35% Cr;
2.95% Re;
0.00% W;
0.00% Ru;
0.00% Ti;
0.00% Nb;
0.00% Hf;
0.010% Y;
0.004% B;
0.015% C;
and a remainder including nickel plus impurities.

6. The nickel-base superalloy article as claimed in one of claims 1-5, wherein the yttrium is 0.0015% by weight and sulfur content is less than 0.0001% by weight.

7. The nickel-base superalloy article as claimed in claim 1, wherein the single-crystal component comprises a blade of the gas turbine.

8. The nickel-base superalloy article as claimed in claim 1, wherein the article has a density of less than about 0.311 pounds per cubic inch.

9. The nickel-base superalloy article as claimed in claim 1, wherein the sum of tungsten, ruthenium, titanium and niobium is less than 0.1 percent.

10. The nickel-base superalloy article as claimed in claim 9, wherein the sum of tungsten, ruthenium, titanium and niobium is essentially zero.

* * * * *

US008375675B1

(12) **United States Patent**

Fernandez

(10) **Patent No.:** **US 8,375,675 B1**

(45) **Date of Patent:** **Feb. 19, 2013**

(54) **TRUSS BEAM HAVING CONVEX-CURVED RODS, SHEAR WEB PANELS, AND SELF-ALIGNING ADAPTERS**

(75) Inventor: **Ian M. Fernandez**, Boulder Creek, CA (US)

(73) Assignee: **The United States of America as Represented by the Administrator of the National Aeronautics & Space Administration (NASA)**, Washington, DC (US)

(*) Notice: Subject to any disclaimer, the term of this patent is extended or adjusted under 35 U.S.C. 154(b) by 714 days.

(21) Appl. No.: **12/574,493**

(22) Filed: **Oct. 6, 2009**

(51) **Int. Cl.**
E04H 12/10 (2006.01)

(52) **U.S. Cl.** **52/650.1**; 52/843

(58) **Field of Classification Search** 52/80.1, 52/80.2, 639, 644, 650.1, 656.9, 691, 843; 403/263, 267

See application file for complete search history.

(56) **References Cited**

U.S. PATENT DOCUMENTS

1,298,927	A	*	4/1919	Goiffon 52/691
1,656,810	A	*	1/1928	Arnstein 52/634
2,415,240	A	*	2/1947	Fouhy 52/745.08
2,612,854	A	*	10/1952	Fuge 52/86
2,704,522	A	*	3/1955	Frieder et al. 52/641
3,283,464	A	*	11/1966	Litzka 52/636
3,330,201	A	*	7/1967	Mouton, Jr. 52/81.2
4,003,168	A	*	1/1977	Brady 52/118
4,400,927	A	*	8/1983	Wolde-Tinase 52/745.08
4,557,097	A	*	12/1985	Mikulas et al. 52/646

4,729,605	A		3/1988	Imao et al.
4,829,739	A	*	5/1989	Coppa 52/745.2
4,924,638	A	*	5/1990	Peter 52/86
4,932,807	A		6/1990	Rhodes
5,052,848	A	*	10/1991	Nakamura 403/268
5,350,221	A		9/1994	Pearce et al.
5,560,174	A	*	10/1996	Goto 52/655.1
5,575,129	A	*	11/1996	Goto 52/655.1
5,655,347	A		8/1997	Mahieu
5,704,169	A	*	1/1998	Richter 52/81.2
6,374,445	B1		4/2002	Fuessinger et al.
6,446,292	B1		9/2002	Fuessinger et al.
7,347,030	B2	*	3/2008	Lewison 52/693
8,186,124	B2	*	5/2012	Bathon 52/701
2003/0177735	A1	*	9/2003	Seeba et al. 52/726.2
2009/0142130	A1	*	6/2009	Frisch et al. 403/267

* cited by examiner

Primary Examiner — Christine T Cajilig

(74) *Attorney, Agent, or Firm* — John F. Schipper; Robert M. Padilla

(57) **ABSTRACT**

A truss beam comprised of a plurality of joined convex-curved rods with self-aligning adapters (SAA) adhesively attached at each end of the truss beam is disclosed. Shear web panels are attached to adjacent pairs of rods, providing buckling resistance for the truss beam. The rods are disposed adjacent to each other, centered around a common longitudinal axis, and oriented so that adjacent rod ends converge to at least one virtual convergence point on the common longitudinal axis, with the rods' curvature designed to increase prevent buckling for the truss beam. Each SAA has longitudinal bores that provide self-aligning of the rods in the SAA, the self-aligning feature enabling creation of strong adhesive bonds between each SAA and the rods. In certain embodiments of the present invention, pultruded unidirectional carbon fiber rods are coupled with carbon fiber shear web panels and metal SAA(s), resulting in a lightweight, low-cost but strong truss beam that is highly resistant to buckling.

20 Claims, 10 Drawing Sheets

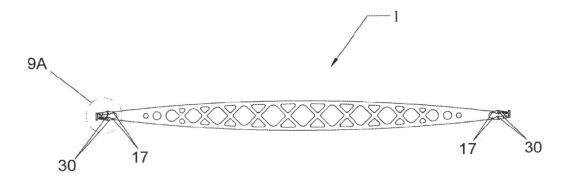

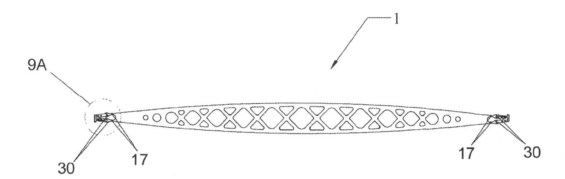

FIG. 1A

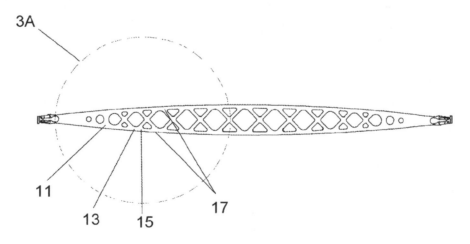

FIG. 1B

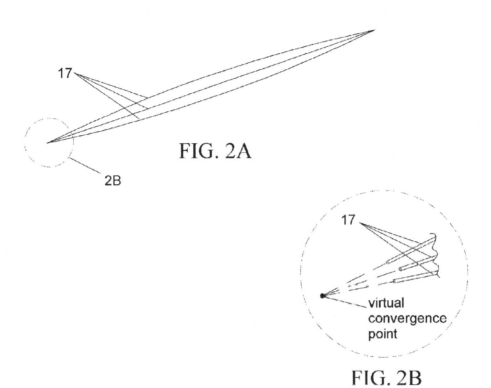

FIG. 2A

FIG. 2B

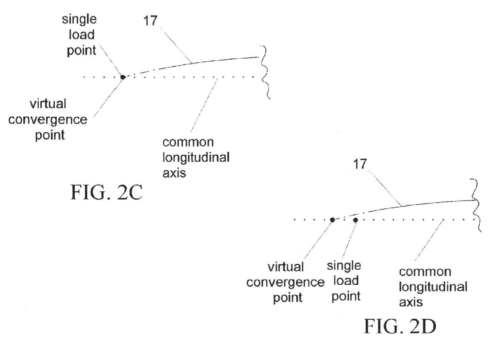

FIG. 2C

FIG. 2D

49

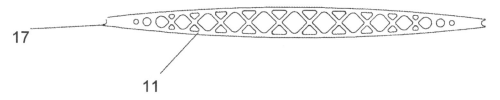

17

11

FIG. 3A

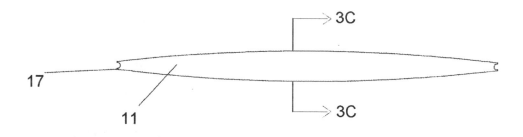

3C

17

11

3C

FIG. 3B

FIG. 3C

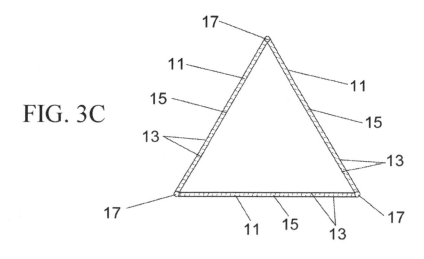

17

11

11

15

15

13

13

17

11

15

13

17

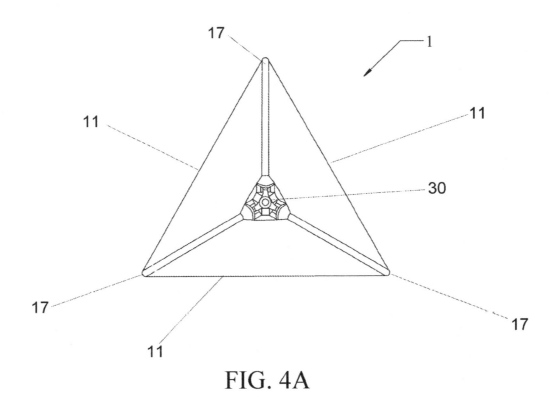

FIG. 4A

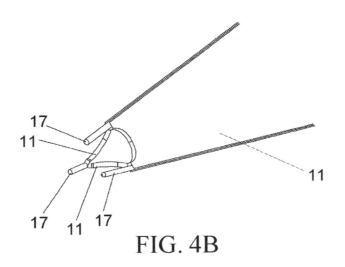

FIG. 4B

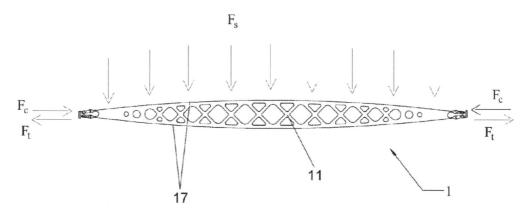

FIG. 5

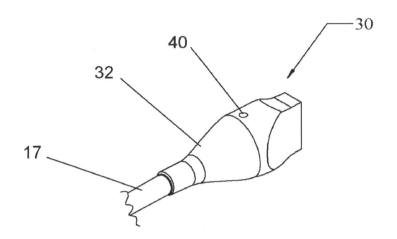

FIG. 6A

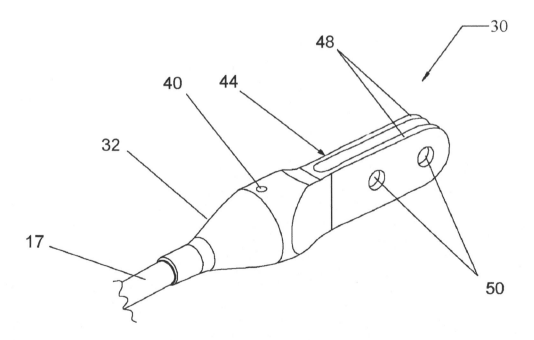

FIG. 6B

FIG. 7A

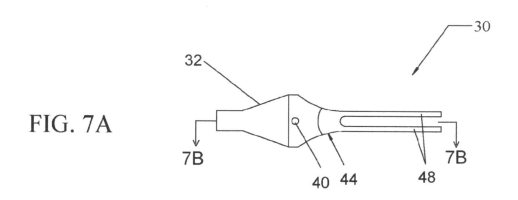

FIG. 7B

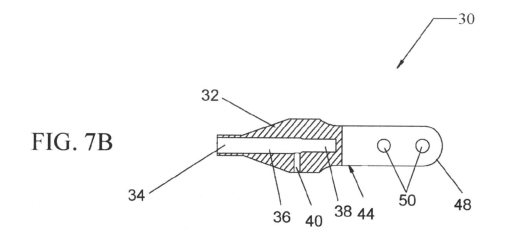

FIG. 7C

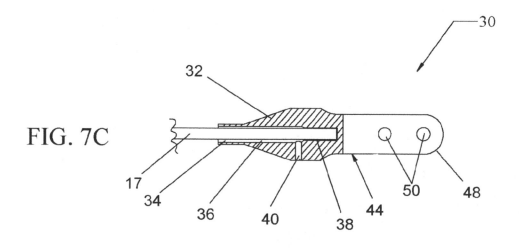

FIG. 8A

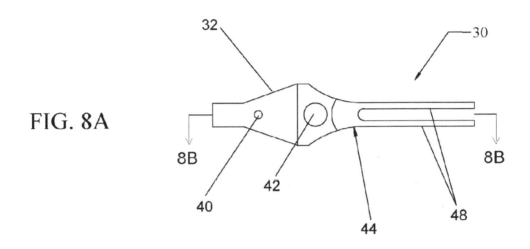

FIG. 8B

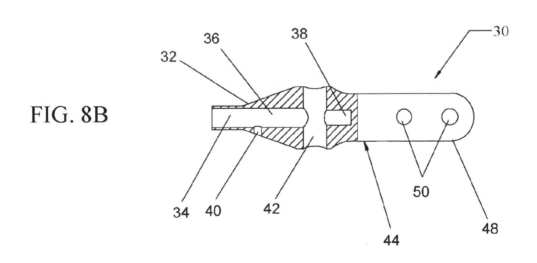

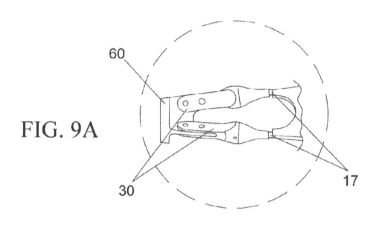

FIG. 9A

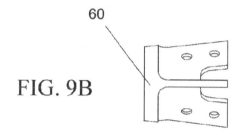

FIG. 9B

FIG. 9C

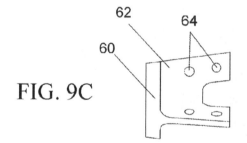

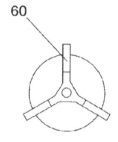

FIG. 9D

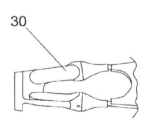

FIG. 9E

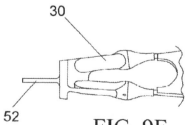

FIG. 9F

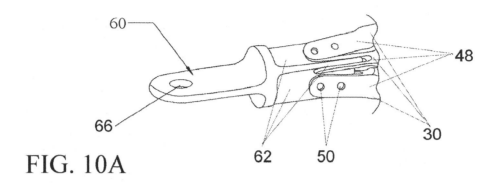

FIG. 10A

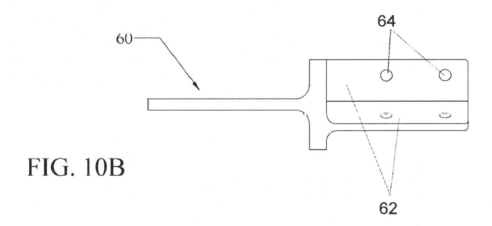

FIG. 10B

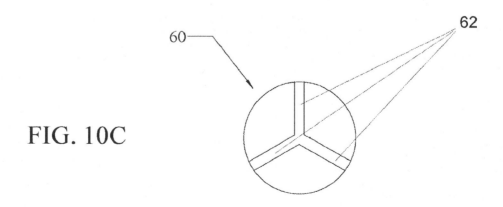

FIG. 10C

1

TRUSS BEAM HAVING CONVEX-CURVED RODS, SHEAR WEB PANELS, AND SELF-ALIGNING ADAPTERS

CROSS-REFERENCE TO RELATED APPLICATIONS

Not Applicable

ORIGIN OF INVENTION

The invention described herein was made by (an) employee(s) of the United States Government and may be manufactured and used by or for the Government of the United States of America for governmental purposes without the payment of any royalties thereon or therefor.

BACKGROUND OF THE INVENTION

1) Field of the Invention

The present invention relates generally to a truss beam, and particularly to a truss beam comprised of rods, shear web panels, and self-aligning adapters.

Unidirectional fiber composite rods present an attractive option for structural members for use in applications requiring high strength and minimum weight, including but not limited to: spacecraft, aircraft (especially rigid airships), high performance ground vehicles, sports equipment (e.g. hang gliders), and tall architectural structures. To fully exploit the bending and compressive strengths of such assemblies composed of unidirectional fiber composite rods, one must provide for buckling stability.

The enormous strength of unidirectional fiber composite rods is difficult to fully exploit because of the difficulty in joining the rod ends to metal components. Bolting does not work with unidirectional composites, and bonding is difficult due to stiffness mismatches between the composite and metal components and the general lack of surface area per volume. Ideally, a thick bond is desired so that the relatively softer adhesive can shear and distribute shear stresses more uniformly instead of peaking at the ends of the bond. Thick bonds are difficult to obtain and repeatably control with conventional methods of beads, bonding wire, shim, or tooling. Most of these methods control the minimum thickness of the bond, but do not control the maximum thickness. In addition, traditional joint types such as lap, strap, scarf, etc. are not ideal for this purpose due to the non-planar nature of rods, fabrication costs, and strength issues.

2) Description of the Prior Art

U.S. Pat. No. 4,729,605 by Imao et al discloses a bicycle wheel spoke comprising a fiber reinforced plastic rod having metal parts adhesively bonded to the ends of the plastic rod, the plastic rod ends having been inserted into bores in the metal parts. U.S. Pat. No. 5,350,221 by Pearce et al discloses a wheel spoke comprising a fiber reinforced plastic shaft having metal end pieces adhesively bonded to the ends of the plastic shaft. U.S. Pat. No. 6,374,445 by Fuessinger et al discloses a tension rod for a chord for a bridge comprising a middle part made of a fiber composite material, the ends of which are glued to metallic end parts. U.S. Pat. No. 5,655,347 by Mahieu discloses a biarch framing member wherein at least one of the arches is made from a fiber reinforced polymer. U.S. Pat. No. 6,446,292 by Fuessinger et al discloses a mobile bridge utilizing composite fiber belts (for tensile forces) to which are attached shear ribs (for shear forces).

2

U.S. Pat. No. 4,932,807 to Rhodes discloses an example of a clevis joint for use in a truss structure.

SUMMARY OF THE INVENTION

A truss beam comprised of a plurality of joined convex-curved rods ("rods"), shear web panels ("panels"), and one or more self-aligning adapters (SAA) disposed at each end of the truss beam, with each rod end being adhesively bonded to an SAA, is disclosed. Shear web panels are attached to adjacent pairs of rods, providing local buckling resistance for the rods, torsional buckling resistance, shear strength, and global stability of the truss beam. In various embodiments, shear web panels comprise face sheets, with a spacer layer disposed between and bonded to the face sheets to provide local buckling resistance. In various embodiments, the shear web panels have perforations to provide weight savings. The rods are disposed adjacent to each other and centered around a common longitudinal axis and oriented so that adjacent rod ends converge to virtual convergence points on the common longitudinal axis, with the rods' convex curvature designed to increase buckling resistance for the truss beam. The SAA(s) have longitudinal bores that provide self-aligning of the rods in the SAA(s), the self-aligning feature enabling creation of strong adhesive bonds between the SAA(s) and the rods. In various embodiments, the rods are fiber composite rods (filament wound or unidirectional), preferably pultruded carbon fiber rods. In various embodiments, the cross-sections of rods may be tubular, annular, solid, or combination of the foregoing. The cross-sectional shapes of the rods may be polygonal, elliptical (including circular, ellipsoid, and ovate), or combination of the foregoing. In various embodiments, an SAA comprises: an adhesive section and an adhesive injection bore. The adhesive section has a longitudinal bore to receive a rod. The longitudinal bore comprises an adhesive region and an alignment region. The adhesive region has a diameter sized relative to the diameter of the rod to provide an optimal radial spacing (between the inner surface of the adhesive region and the rod outer surface) for adhesive bonding. The adhesive injection bore enables adhesive to be inserted into the adhesive region. The diameter and depth of the alignment region is sized relative to the diameter of rod to provide a snug fit when the rod is passed through the adhesive region and seated in the alignment region. The snug fit maintains the rod in concentric alignment within the adhesive region. In some embodiments, the outer diameter of the SAA increases, preferably near the midpoint of the adhesive region, and continuing to increase as one proceeds along the longitudinal bore towards the alignment region. In various embodiments, the SAA(s) are comprised of materials having properties selected according to the following criteria: a) strength to weight ratio appropriate for the intended truss beam application; b) suitability for adhesive bonding to the rods.

BRIEF DESCRIPTION OF THE DRAWINGS

FIGS. 1A and 1B illustrate an embodiment of the truss beam of the present invention. In the figures, like or similar elements (such as truss beam 1) utilize the same reference characters throughout the various views.

FIGS. 2A to 2D illustrate various aspects of embodiments of the present invention with respect to the convex curvature of the rods, and convergence of the rod ends to common points on the common longitudinal axis.

FIGS. 3A to 3C illustrate various aspects of an embodiment of the present invention, with respect to exemplary shear web panels connecting adjacent pairs of rods.

FIGS. 4A and 4B provide end views of a truss beam embodiment of the present invention.

FIG. 5 illustrates various forces exerted on a truss beam embodiment of the present invention.

FIGS. 6A and 6B provide perspective views to illustrate various aspects of embodiments of a self-aligning adapter (SAA) of the present invention.

FIGS. 7A to 7C provide side and cutaway views to illustrate various aspects of an embodiment of a self-aligning adapter of the present invention.

FIGS. 8A and 8B provide side and cutaway views to illustrate various aspects of an embodiment of a self-aligning adapter of the present invention.

FIGS. 9A to 9F provide views to illustrate various aspects of embodiments of the present invention with respect to combining of loads from rods to single load points.

FIGS. 10A to 10C provide views to illustrate various aspects of embodiments of the present invention with respect to combining of loads from rods to single load points.

DETAILED DESCRIPTION OF THE INVENTION

FIGS. 1A and 1B illustrate a truss beam embodiment of the present invention, comprising: a) at least three (three rods shown in the figure) convex-curved rods ("rods") 17 disposed adjacent to each other and centered around a common longitudinal axis; b) shear web panels ("panels") 11 bonded to adjacent pairs of rods 17, and c) at least one self-aligning adapter (SAA) 30 disposed at each end of the truss beam, with each rod end being adhesively bonded to an SAA to handle transfer of loads at the rod ends. In various embodiments, shear web panels comprise face sheets 13, with spacer layer 15 disposed between and bonded to the face sheets 13 to resist local buckling of the panel. In various embodiments, the rods 17 are fiber composite rods (filament wound or unidirectional), preferably pultruded carbon fiber rods. In various embodiments, the cross-sections of rods 17 may be tubular, annular, solid, or combination of the foregoing. The cross-sectional shapes of rods 17 may be polygonal, elliptical (including circular, ellipsoid, and ovate), or combination of the foregoing. In various embodiments, the SAA(s) are comprised of materials having properties selected according to the following criteria: a) strength to weight ratio appropriate for the intended truss beam application; b) suitability for adhesive bonding to the rods. In preferred embodiments, the rods are fiber composite, and the SAA(s) are metal.

FIGS. 2A to 2D illustrate various aspects of embodiments of the present invention with respect to the convex curvature of the rods 17, and the convergence of the ends of the rods 17 to virtual convergence points on the common longitudinal axis. Convex-curved rods 17 transfer loads directly from node point to node point, with the rods' convex curvature designed to increase mid span section properties of the truss beam thereby providing resistance to overall buckling of the truss beam 1. The amount of convex curvature may be selected by means well known in the art (e.g. Euler's buckling theory for columns), taking into consideration the desired span, expected loads, the truss beam cross-section, and material properties of the components being used. As shown in FIG. 2A, the rods 17 are disposed adjacent to each other and centered around a common longitudinal axis, with the fibers in the rods 17 being disposed in the same local direction as the rods. As illustrated in FIG. 2B, the rods 17 are oriented so that the adjacent ends of the rods 17 converge to a virtual convergence point on the common longitudinal axis. In various embodiments of the present invention, at each end of the truss beam 1 the loads from each of the rods 17 are combined to a

single load point (point from which the combined load may be transferred to component(s) separate from the truss beam 1). In various embodiments, as shown in FIG. 2C, the virtual convergence points coincide with the single load points. In various embodiments, as shown in FIG. 2D, the virtual convergence points are spaced a distance outward from the single load points, providing increased torsional buckling resistance. In further embodiments, the virtual convergence points are spaced a distance equal to 10 percent of the length of the truss beam 1. In embodiments of the present invention, the number of rods 17 is equal to or greater than three. A single fiber composite rod has little resistance to buckling. Two fiber composite rods, even if joined by a shear web panel would still be susceptible to side buckling. For numbers of rods 17 greater than three, without additional bracing, the cross-sectional stability of the rods 17 and shear web panels 11 combination may be difficult to maintain (in manufacture and/or in use). For example, it may be difficult to prevent four rods 17 in a square configuration from buckling to non-orthogonal parallelogram shapes.

FIGS. 3A to 3C illustrate various aspects of an embodiment of the present invention, with respect to exemplary shear web panels 11 connecting adjacent pairs of rods 17. In various embodiments, the shear web panels have perforations to enable savings in weight of the truss beam. FIG. 3A provides a side view of a shear web panel 11 with exemplary perforations, the perforations having a common X pattern (typical for the majority of the shear web panel) that transitions to a series of circles as one approaches each end of the truss beam. In various embodiments, the shear web panels do not have perforations (e.g. FIG. 3B), since such panels would cost less (elimination of manufacturing costs associated with the perforations). FIG. 3C illustrates a cross-sectional view of an exemplary shear web panel 11. In various embodiments, the shear web panels comprise two face sheets 13 FIG. 1B, of material having high strength to weight ratio and high strength in several directions for overall buckling resistance and a spacer layer 15, disposed between and bonded to the face sheets 13 to provide local buckling resistance. Face sheets 13 and spacer layer 15 may be bonded to each other by means well known in the art. In various embodiments, face sheets 13 are fiber composite sheets, preferably carbon fiber sheets, more preferably ±45 carbon fiber (±45 being the orientation of the fibers relative to the longitudinal beam axis). In various embodiments, spacer layer 15 is a honeycomb material (for weight savings), preferably an aromatic polyamide honeycomb, more preferably a meta-aramid honeycomb. The shear web panels 11 may be bonded to rods 17 by means well known in the art.

FIGS. 4A and 4B provide end views of a truss beam embodiment of the present invention. FIG. 4A provides an end view of a truss beam 1 embodiment having: three rods 17, shear web panels 11 (no perforations) bonded to adjacent pairs of rods 17, and self-aligning adapter 30 adhesively bonded to the ends of rods 17. FIG. 4B provides a perspective view of one end of the same truss beam 1 embodiment, with the self-aligning adapter 30 removed to show the ends of rods 17.

FIG. 5 illustrates an embodiment of the present invention with respect to various forces exerted on the truss beam 1. The truss beam 1 can be expected to experience tensile, compressive, and side forces. The tensile and compressive forces would be primarily borne by the rods 17, while the side forces would be further borne by the shear web panels 11.

FIGS. 6A and 6B provide perspective views to illustrate various aspects of embodiments of a self-aligning adapter (SAA) 30 of the present invention. As shown in FIG. 6A, the

5

6

end of rod **17** is received in the adhesive section **32** of SAA **30**. Adhesive section **32** has an adhesive injection bore **40** enabling adhesive (not shown) to be injected into adhesive section **32** to adhesively bond rod **17** to SAA **30**. In various embodiments, an SAA would have a section enabling mechanical engagement with (by means well known in the art) other components. As shown in FIG. **6B**, SAA **30** further comprises a clevis joint section **44**. The clevis joint section comprises a U-shaped shackle with two protruding lugs **48**. Each lug has at least two transverse bores **50** (two bores shown in the figure) for bolting to a typical mechanical interface (such as would be well known in the art) of another component.

FIGS. **7A** to **7C** provide side and cutaway views to illustrate various aspects of an embodiment of a self-aligning adapter (SAA) **30** of the present invention. As shown in FIG. **7A**, SAA **30** comprises: adhesive section **32**, adhesive injection bore **40**, and clevis joint section **44**. Clevis joint section comprises a U-shaped shackle with two protruding lugs **48**. As can be seen in cutaway views FIGS. **7B** and **7C**, adhesive section **32** has a longitudinal bore **34** to receive rod **17**. Longitudinal bore **34** comprises adhesive region **36** and alignment region **38**. Adhesive region **36** has a diameter sized relative to the diameter of rod **17** to provide an optimal radial spacing (between the inner surface of the adhesive region and the rod outer surface) for adhesive bonding. Adhesive injection bore **40** provides fluid communication between adhesive region **36** and the exterior of SAA **30**, enabling adhesive (not shown) to be inserted into adhesive region **36**. The diameter and depth of alignment region **38** is sized relative to the diameter of rod **17** to provide a snug fit when rod **17** is passed through adhesive region **36** and seated in alignment region **38**. The snug fit maintains rod **17** in concentric alignment within adhesive region **36**. Thus, adhesive region **36** and alignment region **38** of longitudinal bore **34** provide a capability for self-alignment of rod **17** with SAA **30**. In preferred embodiments, adhesive injection bore **40** is located near the transition between adhesive region **36** and alignment region **38**. The adhesive to be used may be selected from among those well known in the art that are appropriate for the particular application.

FIGS. **8A** and **8B** provide side and cutaway views to illustrate various aspects of an embodiment of a self-aligning adapter (SAA) **30** of the present invention. As shown in FIGS. **8A** and **8B**, SAA **30** comprises: adhesive section **32**, adhesive injection bore **40**, inspection bore **42**, and clevis joint section **44**. Clevis joint section comprises a U-shaped shackle with two protruding lugs **48**. Protruding lugs **48** have transverse bores **50** (two shown in the figure). Adhesive section **32** has a longitudinal bore **34** to receive rod **17** (not shown). Longitudinal bore **34** comprises adhesive region **36** and alignment region **38**. Adhesive region **36** has a diameter sized relative to the diameter of rod **17** to provide an optimal radial spacing (between the inner surface of the adhesive region and the rod outer surface) for adhesive bonding. Adhesive injection bore **40** provides fluid communication between adhesive region **36** and the exterior of SAA **30**, enabling adhesive (not shown) to be inserted into adhesive region **36**. The diameter and depth of alignment region **38** is sized relative to the diameter of rod **17** to provide a snug fit when rod **17** is passed through adhesive region **36** and seated in alignment region **38**. The snug fit maintains rod **17** in concentric alignment within adhesive region **36**. Thus, adhesive region **36** and alignment region **38** of longitudinal bore **34** provide a capability for self-alignment of rod **17** with SAA **30**. Maintenance of rod **17** in concentric alignment obviates the need for conventional bond line control methods (e.g. beads, wire, or mesh) which are typically used (albeit imperfectly) to maintain the proper minimum gap spacing between pieces being bonded. In addition, these conventional bond line control methods do not provide a means to control the maximum gap spacing (a parameter which is also important for optimum bond strength), and are not ideal for cylindrical bonding. Inspection bore **42** (connecting to longitudinal bore **34** and preferably disposed between the adhesive region **36** and the alignment region **36**), provides the capability to: a) verify that rod **17** is properly seated in the alignment region **38**; b) verify that sufficient adhesive has been inserted into adhesive region **36**; and c) any combination of the foregoing. In some embodiments, the outer diameter of SAA **30** increases, preferably near the midpoint of adhesive region **36**, and continues to increase as one proceeds along longitudinal bore **34** towards alignment region **38**. In a typical adhesive bond, peak stresses are focused more towards each end of the bond, less so at the middle of the bond. By increasing the diameter of the SAA **30**, more of the load is distributed to the middle of the bond, not just at the bond ends. The point at which the SAA diameter begins to increase creates a stress concentration; the resulting increased stress causes metal SAA(s) to yield (with eventual strain hardening) before the adhesive fails. Thus, more effective matching of the SAA **30** material's stiffness to the rod **17** material's stiffness is achieved.

FIGS. **9A** to **9F** provide views to illustrate various aspects of embodiments of the present invention with respect to combining loads from rods **17** to single load points. As mentioned with respect to FIGS. **2A** to **2D**, at each end of truss beam **1** loads from rods **17** are combined to a single load point (point from which the combined load from the rods **17** may be transferred to a component separate from the truss beam **1**). Referring to FIG. **9A**, an SAA **30** is attached to each rod **17**. Load bearing fitting (LBF) **60** is adapted to mechanically couple with multiple SAA(s) **30** (in FIGS. **9A** to **9D** LBF **60** is configured to couple to three SAA(s) **30**), providing a single load point for the loads from the coupled SAA(s) **30**. In FIGS. **9A** (perspective), **9B** (top view), **9C** (side view), and **9D** (end view), mechanical coupling is exemplified via a clevis joint arrangement, wherein LBF **60** has three protruding tangs **62** (with transverse bores **64**) to engage with SAA(s) **30** (as exemplified by SAA **30** shown in FIG. **6B**). Each tang **62** has the corresponding number of transverse bores **64** to match the bores **50** in the SAA lugs **48** that the LBF **60** couples with. Secure engagement of LBF **60** to SAA(s) **30** occurs via clevis joint securing members (bolts or pins) (not shown in the figures) disposed within the LBF tang bores **64** and SAA lug bores **50**. In FIG. **9E**, SAA **30** has multiple adhesive sections (each receiving a rod **17**), the SAA **30** itself providing a single load point for the rods **17** it is bonded to. In FIG. **9F**, SAA **30** has a protruding lug **52** enabling mechanical coupling to a component external to the truss beam.

FIGS. **10A** (perspective), **10B** (side view) and **10C** (end view) provide views to illustrate various aspects of another embodiment of an LBF **60**. Analogous to LBF **60** described in FIGS. **9A** to **9D**, LBF **60** has protruding tangs **62** (with transverse bore **64**), and mechanically couples to SAA(s) **30** in a clevis joint arrangement. LBF **60** provides a single load point for the loads from the coupled SAA(s). LBF **60** further has a protruding tang **66** enabling mechanical coupling a component external to the truss beam.

EXAMPLE

Shear web panels were constructed using: face sheets of two ply ±45 carbon fiber, with a ³⁄₁₆" thick 1.5 lbs/ft3 Nomex honeycomb spacer layer disposed between and adhesively (syntactic epoxy) bonded to the face sheets. The shear web panels were fabricated flat and curved to match three twelve foot, ¼" diameter pultruded carbon fiber rods, each having convex curvature of 172 degrees of arc. The rods were adhesively bonded (epoxy) to the shear web panels (a pair of rods for each panel). Self-aligning adapters (SAA) were fabricated from aluminum alloy 1" round, 0.1 lbs per SAA and adhesively bonded (Hysol EA 9360 epoxy injection) to each rod end.

Obviously numerous modifications and variations of the present invention are possible in the light of the above teachings. It is therefore to be understood that within the scope of the appended claims the invention may be practiced otherwise than as specifically described therein.

What is claimed is:

1. A truss beam comprising:

at least three convex-curved fiber composite rods disposed adjacent to each other and centered around a common longitudinal axis, the rods' convex curvature being selected to increase buckling resistance of the truss beam, said rods being oriented so that adjacent rod ends on each side of said truss beam converge to virtual convergence points on said common longitudinal axis;

a shear web panel bonded to each adjacent pair of said rods, each said panel acting to stabilize said rods and carry side loads, each said panel comprising: two face sheets of high strength to weight ratio material with a layer of spacer material disposed between and bonded to said face sheets to resist local buckling of said panel;

one or more self-aligning adapters disposed at each end of the truss beam, with each rod end being adhesively bonded to a self-aligning adapter, said self-aligning adapters each having:

a longitudinal bore to receive said rod end, said longitudinal bore having an adhesive region and an alignment region, the diameter of said adhesive region sized relative to the received rod diameter to provide an optimal radial spacing between the inner surface of the adhesive region and the rod outer surface for adhesive bonding, the diameter and depth of said alignment bore sized to provide a snug fit when the received rod passes through the adhesive region and is seated in the alignment region, thereby maintaining said received rod in concentric alignment within said adhesive region, and an

adhesive injection bore providing fluid communication between said adhesive region and the exterior of the self-aligning adapter enabling adhesive to be injected into said adhesive region.

2. The truss beam of claim 1 wherein:

the number of said rods is three.

3. The truss beam of claim 1 wherein:

said rods are selected from the list of rods consisting of unidirectional, filament wound, and any combination of the foregoing; and

the cross-sections of said rods are selected from the list consisting of tubular, annular, solid, and any combination of the foregoing.

4. The truss beam of claim 3 wherein:

said rods are pultruded unidirectional circular solid cross-section carbon fiber rods.

5. The truss beam of claim 1 wherein:

the outer diameter of said self-aligning adapter is tapered along the longitudinal axis.

6. The truss beam of claim 1 wherein:

said shear web face sheets are comprised of fiber composite material, and said spacer layer is comprised of a honeycomb material.

7. The truss beam of claim 6 wherein:

said fiber composite material is a carbon fiber material, and said honeycomb material is a aromatic polyamide honeycomb material.

8. The truss beam of claim 1 wherein:

said self-aligning adapter further comprises:

an inspection bore connecting to said longitudinal bore and disposed between said adhesive region and alignment region, providing the capability to:

a) verify that the received rod is properly seated in the alignment region,

b) verify that sufficient adhesive has been inserted into the adhesive region, and

c) any combination of the foregoing.

9. The truss beam of claim 1 wherein:

said shear web panels have transverse perforations.

10. The truss beam of claim 9 wherein:

said shear web panels do not have perforations in the last 10 percent of the panel length region adjacent to the rod ends on each end of the truss beam.

11. The truss beam of claim 1 further comprising:

a single load point at each end of said truss beam, said single load points comprising points from which the combined load from the rods may be transferred to component(s) separate from the truss beam.

12. The truss beam of claim 11 wherein:

said single load points are coincident with said virtual convergence points.

13. The truss beam of claim 11 wherein:

said virtual convergence points are a distance outward along said common longitudinal axis from said single load points.

14. The truss beam of claim 13 wherein:

said distance outward is 10 percent of the length of the truss beam.

15. The truss beam of claim 11 wherein:

said single load points are represented by components selected from the list consisting of:

a) a load bearing fitting being mechanically coupled to multiple self-aligning adapters, each self-aligning adapter having a single adhesive section with which to receive a rod;

b) a self-aligning adapter having an adhesive section configured for receiving a rod; and

c) any combination of the foregoing.

16. The truss beam of claim 15 wherein:

said single adhesive section self-aligning adapters each have a clevis joint section comprised of a U-shaped shackle section of two protruding lugs having transverse bores;

said load bearing fitting has protruding tangs;

and said mechanical coupling comprising said load bearing fitting tangs engaging with the single adhesive section self-aligning adapters' U-shaped shackle sections in a clevis joint arrangement.

17. The truss beam of claim 1 wherein:

said self-aligning adapters are comprised of materials having properties selected according to the following criteria:

a) strength to weight ratio appropriate for the intended truss beam application;

b) suitability for adhesive bonding to the rods.

61

18. The truss beam of claim **17** wherein:

said self-aligning adapters are comprised of metal.

19. A truss beam comprising:

three convex-curved circular cross-section pultruded uni-directional carbon fiber rods disposed adjacent to each other and centered around a common longitudinal axis, the rods' convex curvature being selected to increase buckling stability of the truss beam, said rods being oriented so that adjacent rod ends on each side of said truss beam converge to virtual convergence points near single load points on said common longitudinal axis, said single load points comprising points from which the combined load from the rods may be transferred to component(s) separate from the truss beam;

a shear web panel attached to each adjacent pair of said rods, each said panel acting to stabilize said rods and carry side loads, each said panel comprising: two face sheets of carbon fiber material with a layer of aromatic polyamide honeycomb spacer material disposed between and bonded to said face sheets to resist local buckling of said panel;

one or more metal self-aligning adapters disposed at each end of the truss beam, with each rod end being adhesively bonded to a self-aligning adapter, said self-aligning adapters each having:

a longitudinal bore to receive said rod end, said longitudinal bore having an adhesive region and an alignment region, the diameter of said adhesive region sized relative to the received rod diameter to provide an optimal radial spacing between the inner surface of the adhesive region and the rod outer surface for adhesive bonding, the diameter and depth of said alignment bore sized relative to the received rod diameter to provide a snug fit when the received rod passes through the adhesive region and is seated in the alignment region, thereby maintaining said received rod in concentric alignment within said longitudinal bore;

an adhesive injection bore providing fluid communication between said adhesive region and the exterior of the self-aligning adapter enabling adhesive to be injected into said adhesive region; and

an inspection bore connecting to said longitudinal bore and disposed between said adhesive region and alignment region.

20. The truss beam of claim **19** wherein:

the outer diameter of said self-aligning adapter is tapered along the longitudinal axis.

* * * * *

US 20080011904A1

(19) **United States**

(12) **Patent Application Publication** (10) Pub. No.: **US 2008/0011904 A1**

Cepollina et al. (43) Pub. Date: **Jan. 17, 2008**

(54) **METHOD AND ASSOCIATED APPARATUS FOR CAPTURING, SERVICING, AND DE-ORBITING EARTH SATELLITES USING ROBOTICS**

(75) Inventors: **Frank J. Cepollina**, Annandale, MD (US); **Richard D. Burns**, Annapolis, MD (US); **Jill M. Holz**, Laurel, MD (US); **James E. Corbo**, Columbia, MD (US); **Nicholas M. Jedhrich**, Annapolis, MD (US)

Correspondence Address:
NASA GODDARD SPACE FLIGHT CENTER 8800 GREENBELT ROAD, MAIL CODE 140.1 GREENBELT, MD 20771 (US)

(73) Assignee: **United States of America as represented by the Administrator of the NASA**, Washington, DC

(21) Appl. No.: **11/671,062**

(22) Filed: **Feb. 5, 2007**

Related U.S. Application Data

(62) Division of application No. 11/124,592, filed on May 6, 2005, now Pat. No. 7,240,879.

Publication Classification

(51) **Int. Cl.**
B64G 4/00 (2006.01)

(52) **U.S. Cl.** **244/172.6**; 901/2; 901/30

(57) **ABSTRACT**

This invention is a method and supporting apparatus for autonomously capturing, servicing and de-orbiting a free-flying spacecraft, such as a satellite, using robotics. The capture of the spacecraft includes the steps of optically seeking and ranging the satellite using LIDAR; and matching tumble rates, rendezvousing and berthing with the satellite. Servicing of the spacecraft may be done using supervised autonomy, which is allowing a robot to execute a sequence of instructions without intervention from a remote human-occupied location. These instructions may be packaged at the remote station in a script and uplinked to the robot for execution upon remote command giving authority to proceed. Alternately, the instructions may be generated by Artificial Intelligence (AI) logic onboard the robot. In either case, the remote operator maintains the ability to abort an instruction or script at any time, as well as the ability to intervene using manual override to teleoperate the robot. In one embodiment, a vehicle used for carrying out the method of this invention comprises an ejection module, which includes the robot, and a de-orbit module. Once servicing is completed by the robot, the ejection module separates from the de-orbit module, leaving the de-orbit module attached to the satellite for de-orbiting the same at a future time. Upon separation, the ejection module can either de-orbit itself or rendezvous with another satellite for servicing. The ability to de-orbit a spacecraft further allows the opportunity to direct the landing of the spent satellite in a safe location away from population centers, such as the ocean.

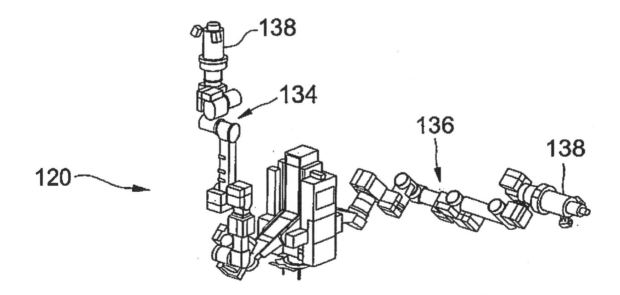

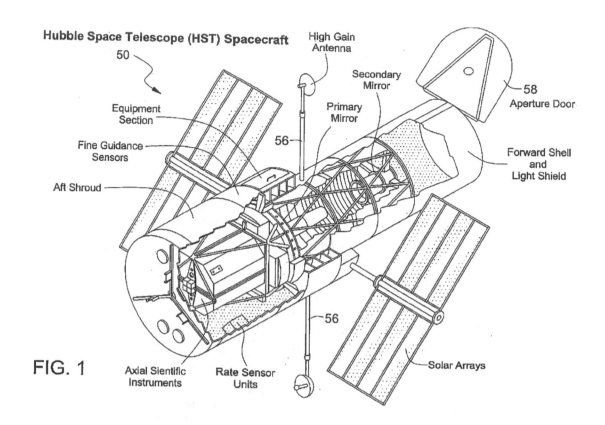

Hubble Space Telescope (HST) Spacecraft

50

Equipment Section

Fine Guidance Sensors

Aft Shroud

High Gain Antenna

Secondary Mirror

Primary Mirror

56

58
Aperture Door

Forward Shell and Light Shield

56

FIG. 1

Axial Sientific Instruments

Rate Sensor Units

Solar Arrays

Optical Telescope Assembly (OTA) Components

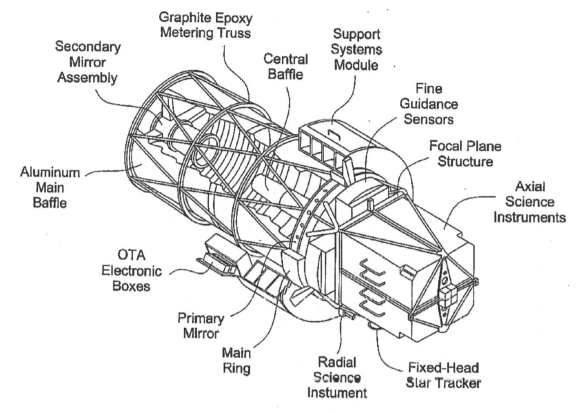

FIG. 2

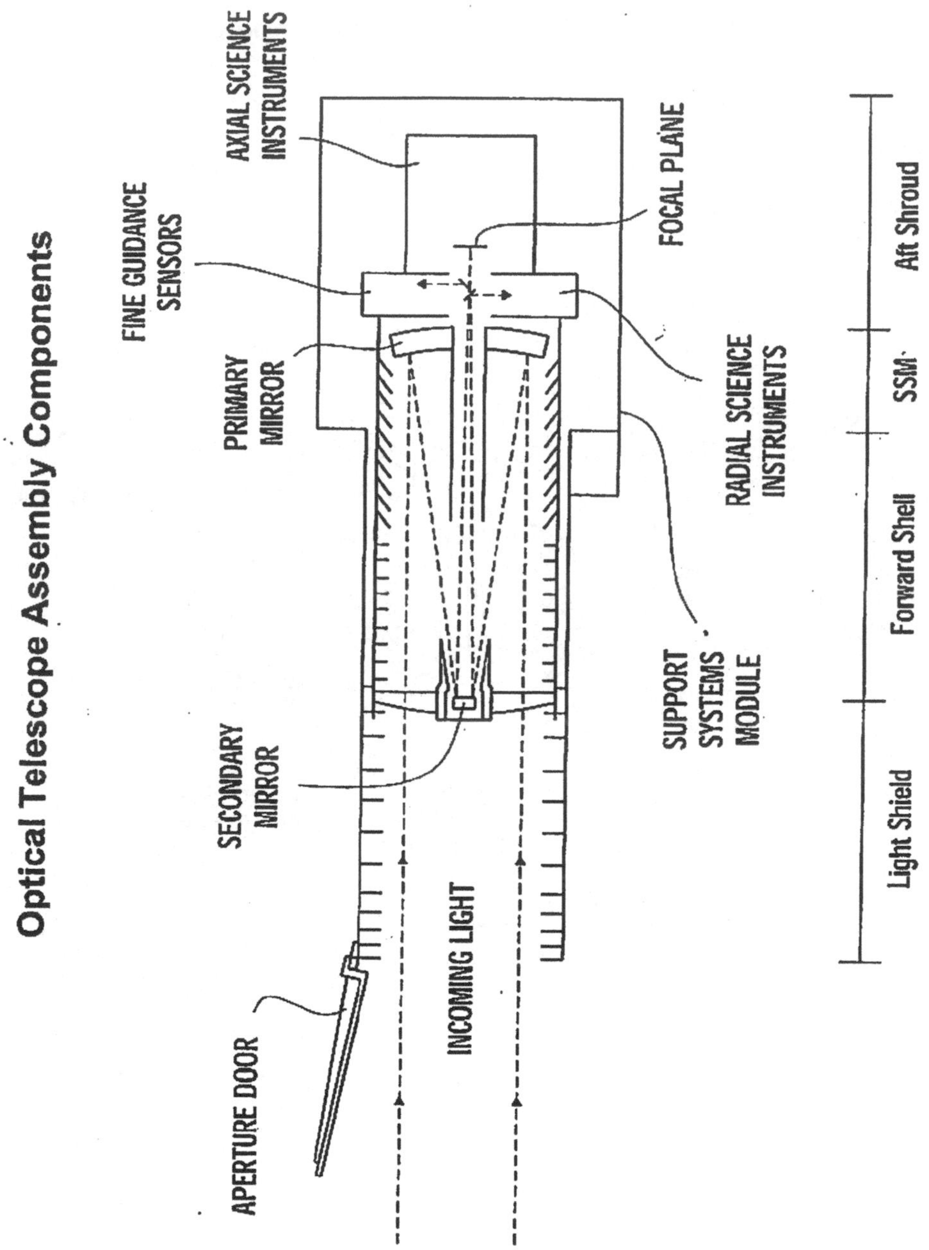

Optical Telescope Assembly Components

APERTURE DOOR

SECONDARY MIRROR

INCOMING LIGHT

PRIMARY MIRROR

FINE GUIDANCE SENSORS

AXIAL SCIENCE INSTRUMENTS

FOCAL PLANE

RADIAL SCIENCE INSTRUMENTS

SUPPORT SYSTEMS MODULE

Light Shield | Forward Shell | SSM | Aft Shroud

FIG. 3

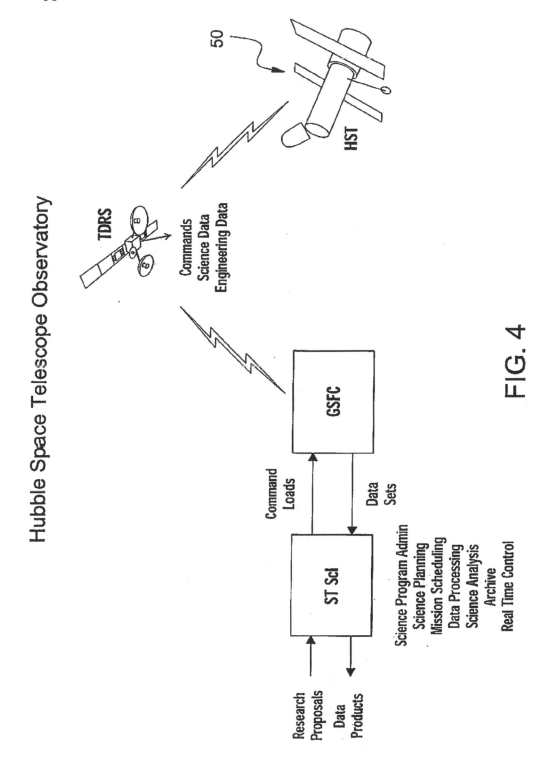

FIG. 4

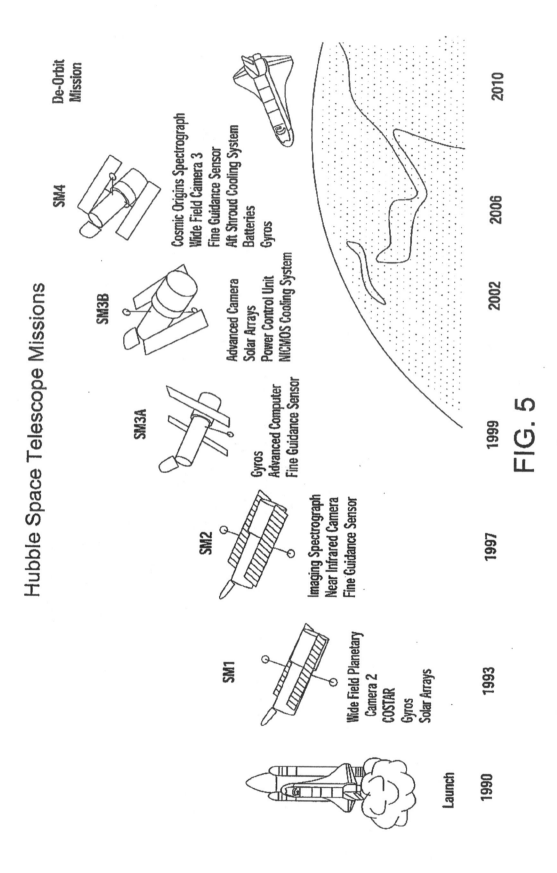

FIG. 5

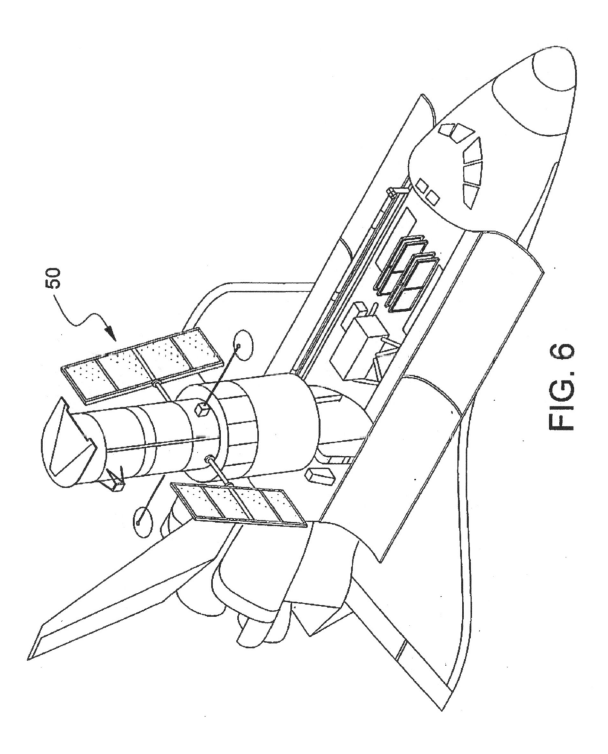

50

FIG. 6

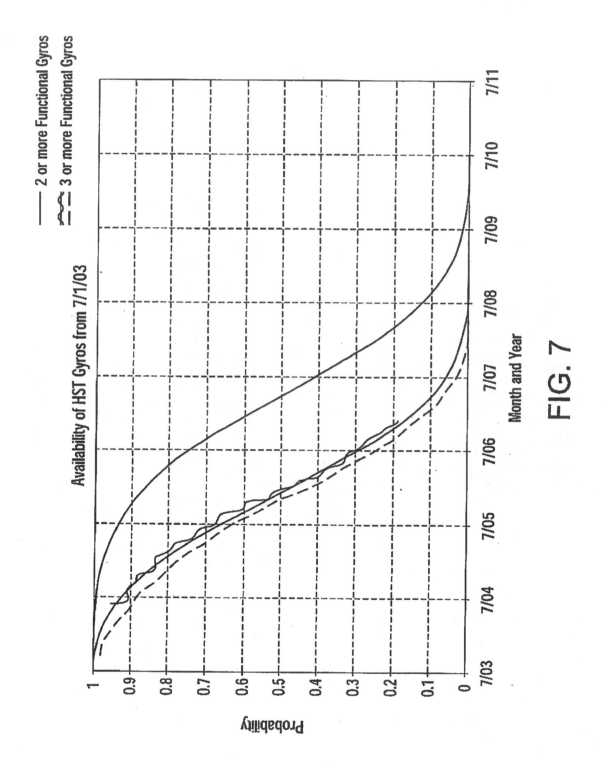

Availability of HST Gyros from 7/1/03

—— 2 or more Functional Gyros
~~~ 3 or more Functional Gyros

FIG. 7

Month and Year

Probability

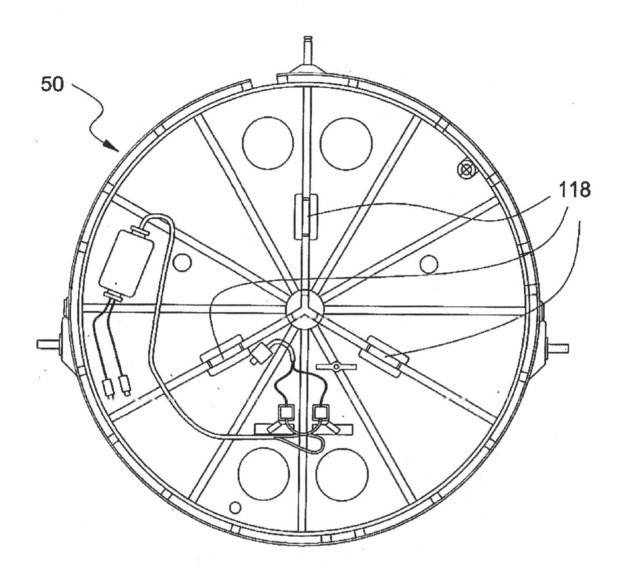

FIG. 8

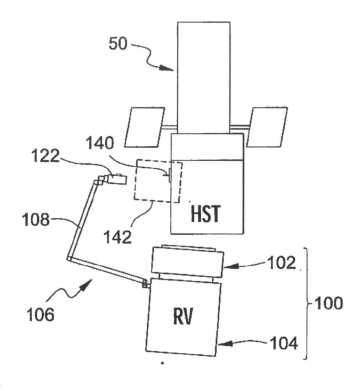

FIG. 9

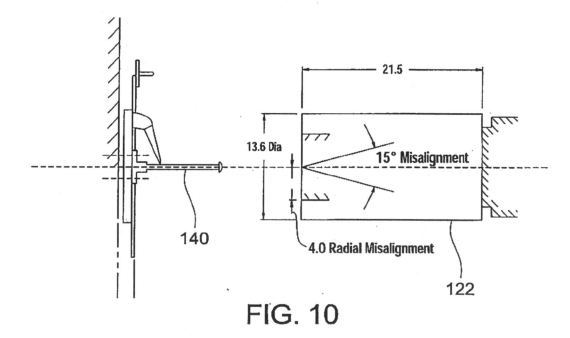

FIG. 10

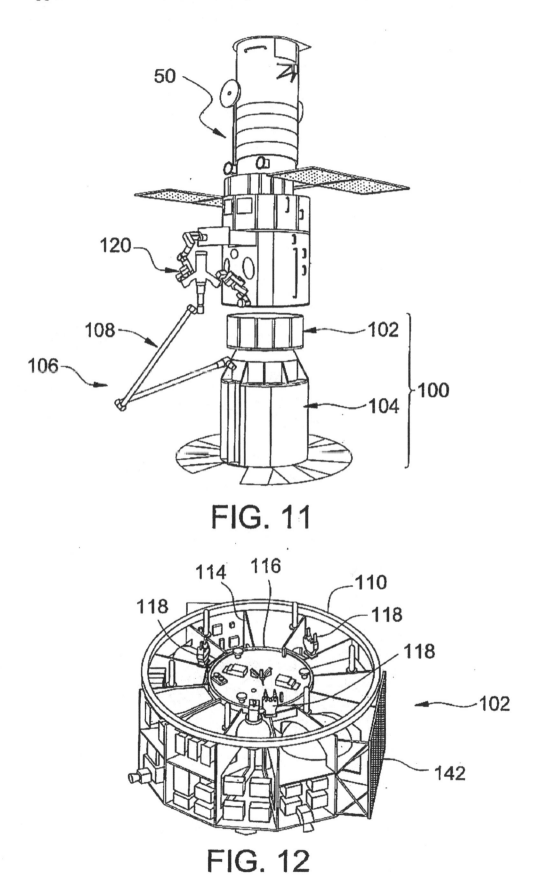

FIG. 11

FIG. 12

FIG. 13

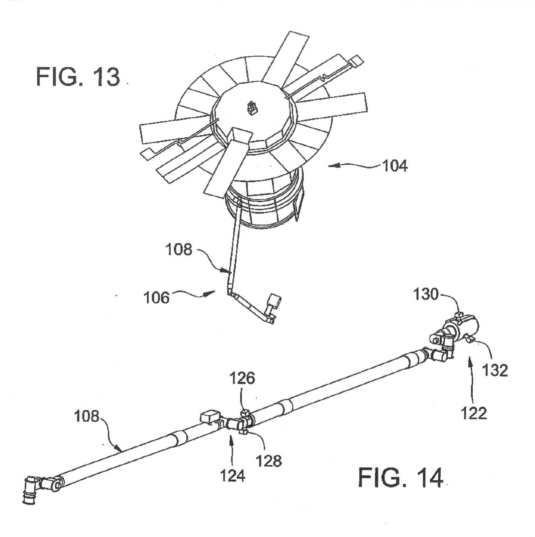

104

108

106

130

132

122

126

108

128

124

FIG. 14

FIG. 15

138

134

136

138

120

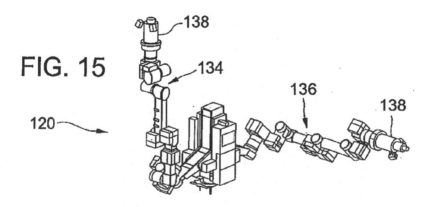

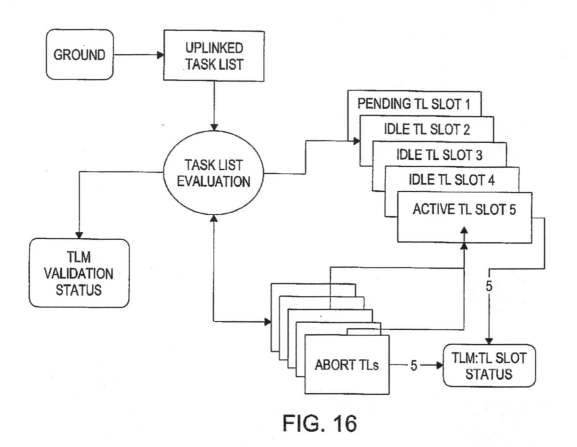

FIG. 16

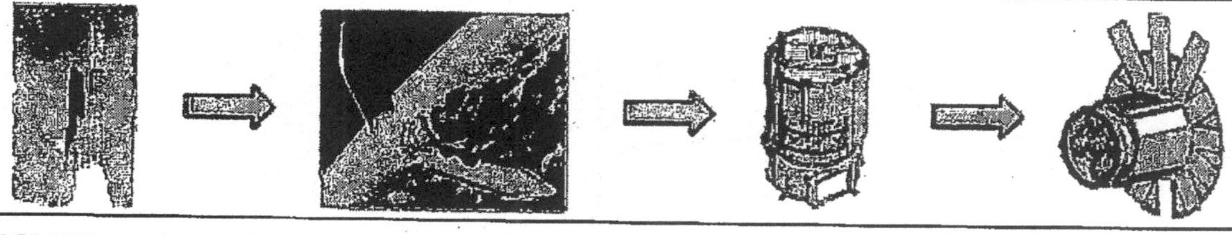

HIGHLIGHTS: Launch/LV Separation/Rate Null/Sun Acquisition/EM SA Deploy

PHASE BEGINS: T-0   **Duration:** 2-3 Hours

PHASE ENDS: HRV-H1 Sun-pointing and Power Positive

INSERTION ALTITUDE: ~540 km+/- 10 km (20 km below HST at time of mission)

ATTITUDE: Launch Vehicle Controlled -> Rate Null -> -H1 Sun Point

EPS: EM Array Retracted -> EM Array Deployed (excluding GA Panel)/DM Array Retracted
Battery Power- Only (up to 180 minutes) -> - H1 Sun Point

DM OPS MODE: Idle (breakwire-based) -> Safe -> Normal -> Standby
EM OPS MODE: Safe -> Free Flight -> Idle

GN & C: Rate Damp -> Sun Search/Tracker-Based Attitude Determination -> -H1 Sun Point

COMMUNICATIONS: HST S-Band (Pri) - NA
Shared { DM S-Band (Pri) - Rx 2 kpbs SSAF, Tx 2-8 kbps SSAR
EM S-Band (Pri) - Rx 2kbps SSAF, Tx 2-8 kbps SSAR
EM Ku-Band (Pri) - NA

FIG. 17A

76

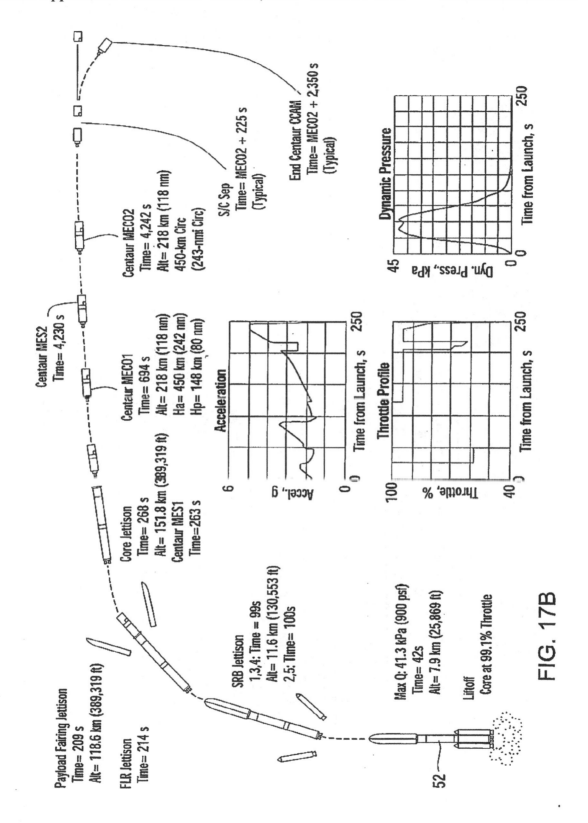

FIG. 17B

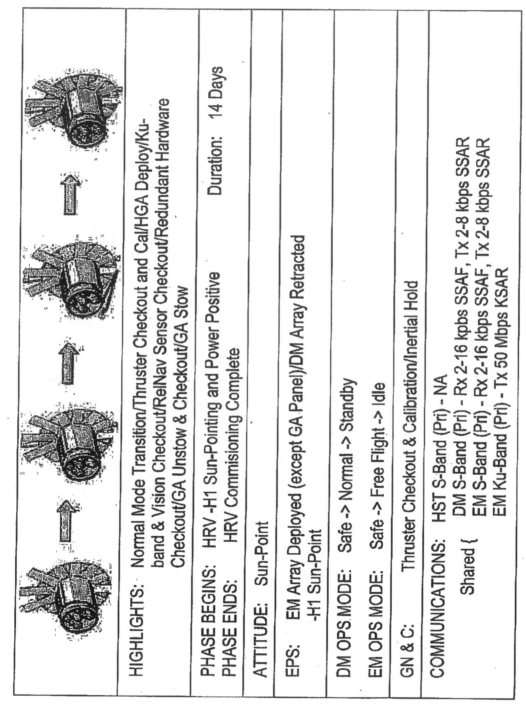

HIGHLIGHTS: Normal Mode Transition/Thruster Checkout and Cal/HGA Deploy/Ku-band & Vision Checkout/RelNav Sensor Checkout/Redundant Hardware Checkout/GA Unstow & Checkout/GA Stow

PHASE BEGINS: HRV -H1 Sun-Pointing and Power Positive   Duration: 14 Days
PHASE ENDS: HRV Commisioning Complete

ATTITUDE: Sun-Point

EPS: EM Array Deployed (except GA Panel)/DM Array Retracted
       -H1 Sun-Point

DM OPS MODE: Safe -> Normal -> Standby

EM OPS MODE: Safe -> Free Flight -> Idle

GN & C: Thruster Checkout & Calibration/Inertial Hold

COMMUNICATIONS: HST S-Band (Pri) - NA
                  DM S-Band (Pri) - Rx 2-16 kpbs SSAF, Tx 2-8 kbps SSAR
         Shared { EM S-Band (Pri) - Rx 2-16 kbps SSAF, Tx 2-8 kbps SSAR
                  EM Ku-Band (Pri) - Tx 50 Mbps KSAR

FIG. 18

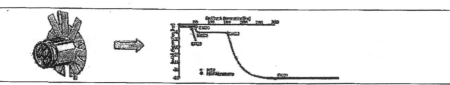

HIGHLIGHTS:	Orbit Adjust Burns: Remove launch residuals/Raise HRV to Coelliptic Orbit 5km below HST Planar Correction/Raise HRV to Coelliptic Orbit 1 km below HST
PHASE BEGINS: PHASE ENDS:	HRV Commissioning Complete Duration: 1-3 Days HRV in Coelliptic Orbit just prior to the maneuver to the safety ellipse
ATTITUDE:	-H1 Sun-Point -> Burn (~15 minutes in altitude) -> -H1 Sun-Point (multiple times)
EPS:	EM Array Deployed (except GA Panel)/DM Array Retracted -H1 Sun-Point -> Battery Power Only (~30 minutes) -> -H1 Sun-Point
DM OPS MODE: EM OPS MODE:	Safe -> Normal -> Standby Safe -> Free Flight -> Idle
GN&C:	Inertial Nav/Inertial Hold -> Slew -> Inertial Hold (burn ~31 sec max) -> Slew -> Inertial Hold (multiple X)
COMMUNICATIONS: Shared {	HST S-Band (Pri) - Rx 1 kbps SSAF, Tx 4 kbps SSAR DM S-Band (Pri) - Rx 2-16 kpbs SSAF, Tx 2-8 kbps SSAR EM S-Band (Pri) - Rx 2 kbps SSAF, Tx 2-8 kbps SSAR EM Ku-Band (Pri) - Tx 50 Mbps KSAR

FIG. 19

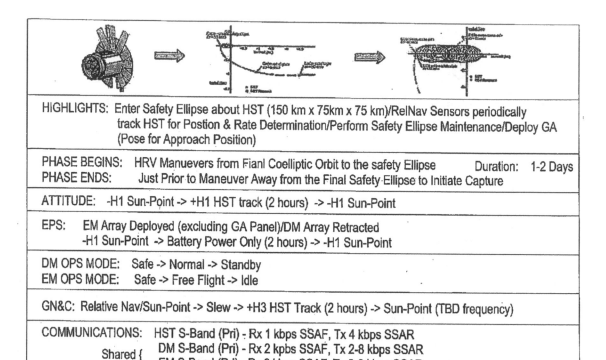

HIGHLIGHTS: Enter Safety Ellipse about HST (150 km x 75km x 75 km)/RelNav Sensors periodically
track HST for Postion & Rate Determination/Perform Safety Ellipse Maintenance/Deploy GA
(Pose for Approach Position)

PHASE BEGINS: HRV Manuevers from Fianl Coelliptic Orbit to the safety Ellipse   Duration: 1-2 Days
PHASE ENDS: Just Prior to Maneuver Away from the Final Safety Ellipse to Initiate Capture

ATTITUDE: -H1 Sun-Point -> +H1 HST track (2 hours) -> -H1 Sun-Point

EPS: EM Array Deployed (excluding GA Panel)/DM Array Retracted
-H1 Sun-Point -> Battery Power Only (2 hours) -> -H1 Sun-Point

DM OPS MODE: Safe -> Normal -> Standby
EM OPS MODE: Safe -> Free Flight -> Idle

GN&C: Relative Nav/Sun-Point -> Slew -> +H3 HST Track (2 hours) -> Sun-Point (TBD frequency)

COMMUNICATIONS: HST S-Band (Pri) - Rx 1 kbps SSAF, Tx 4 kbps SSAR
Shared {   DM S-Band (Pri) - Rx 2 kpbs SSAF, Tx 2-8 kbps SSAR
EM S-Band (Pri) - Rx 2 kbps SSAF, Tx 2-8 kbps SSAR
EM Ku-Band (Pri) - Tx 50 Mbps KSAR

FIG. 20

HIGHLIGHTS:	Deploy GA/Intercept HST-V1 Axis/Match Rated & Hold @ 30 m/Approach to 10 m and Hold/Move GA EE inside Capture Box/Grapple HST Grapple Fixture (in ellipse) GA Null Rates/HRV Maneuver Stack to -H1 Sun-Point/GA Maneuver to Berth & Soft-Dock/Near Close Berthing Latches/Thermally Equilibrate (TBD hours)/Clamp Berthing Latches/Engage J101/Deploy Outriggers	
PHASE BEGINS: HRV Leaves Safety Ellipse PHASE ENDS: HRV Berthed to HST		Duration: 1-2 Days
ATTITUDE: -H1 Sun-Point -> +H1 HST track (3 hours) -> -H1 Sun-Point		
EPS: EM Array Deployed (excluding GA Panel)/DM Array Retracted -H1 Sun-Point -> Battery Power Only (up to 3 hours) -> -H1 Sun-Point		
DM OPS MODE: Safe -> Normal -> Standby EM OPS MODE: Safe -> Free Flight -> Idle		
GN&C: Relative Nav/Sun-Point -> Slew -> +H1 HST Track (2 hours) -> Stabilize/Slew Sun-Point (TBD frequency) -> -H1 Sun-Point Relative Nav/-H1 Sun-Point (free-drift during GA maneuver and berthing)		
COMMUNICATIONS: HST S-Band (Pri) - Rx 1 kbps SSAF, Tx 4 kbps SSAR Shared { DM S-Band (Pri) - Rx 2 kpbs SSAF, Tx 2-8 kbps SSAR EM S-Band (Pri) - Rx 2-16 kbps SSAF, Tx 2-8 kbps SSAR EM Ku-Band (Pri) - Tx 50 Mbps K3AR		

FIG. 21

81

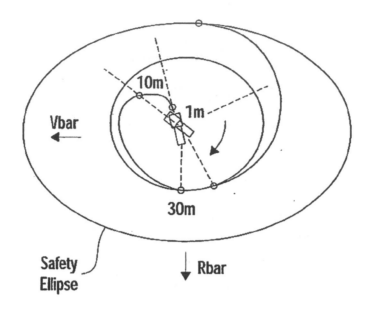

FIG. 22A

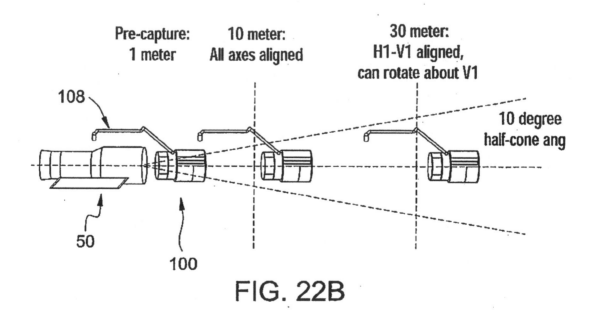

FIG. 22B

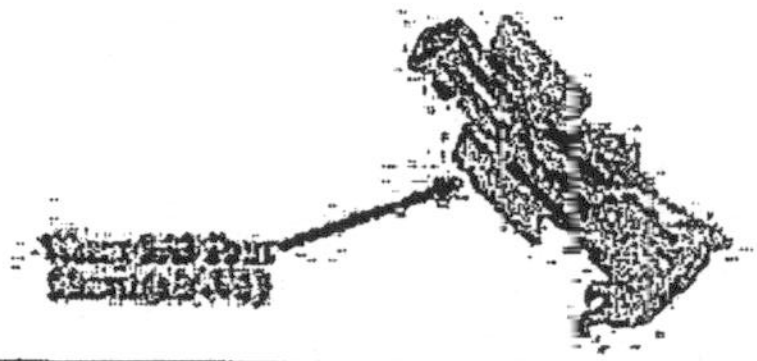

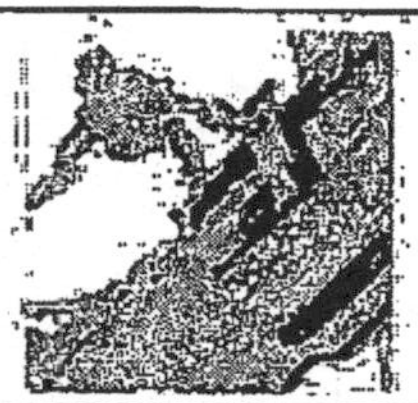

HIGHLIGHTS: Deploy EM GA Solar Panel/DR/Unstow and Commissioning Telerobotically Install:
+ and -SA3 Power Taps (Battery Augmentation), 1553 Harness/NCS Power Harness
WFC3 with New Gyros & GyroPower Harness, Cos,
FGS/Dr Stow

PHASE Begins   HRV Berthed to HST   Duration: 30+ Days
PHASE ENDS: Prior to EM Given Control Authority Prior to Ejection

ATTITUDE: -H1 Sun-Point; Periodic Sun Avoidance (bias off -H1, task specific)

EPS: EM Arrays Deployed/DM Arrays Stowed/SA3 Taps Mated (early task)/
HST Power Augmentation Checkout

DM OPS MODE: Safe -> Normal -> Standby
EM OPS MODE: Safe -> Free Flight -> Idle

GN&C: DM Inertial Nav

COMMUNICATIONS: HST S-Band (Pri) - Rx 1 kpbs SSAF, Tx 4 kbps SSAR
DM S-Band (Pri) - Rx 2-16 kpbs SSAF
Shared {   EM S-Band (Pri) - Rx 2-16 kbps SSAF
EM Ku-Band (Pri) - Tx 50 Mbps KSAR

FIG. 23

83

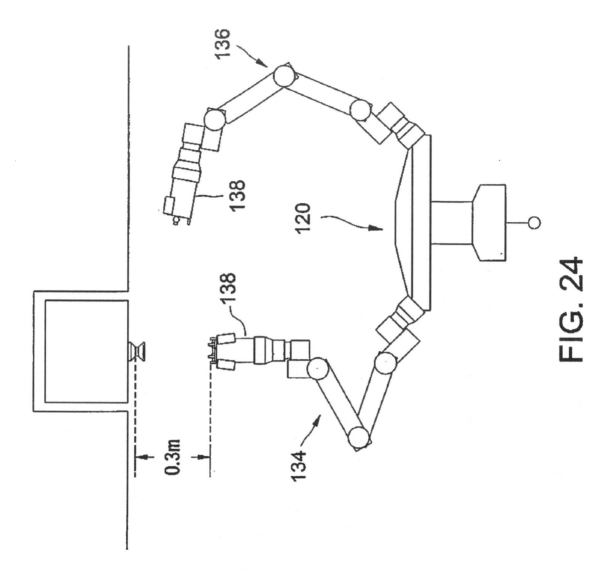

136

138

138

134

120

0.3m

FIG. 24

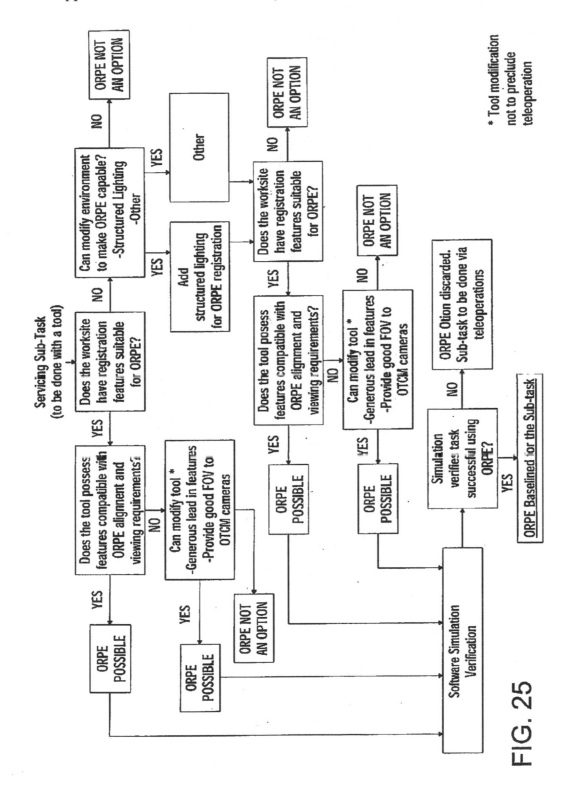

FIG. 25

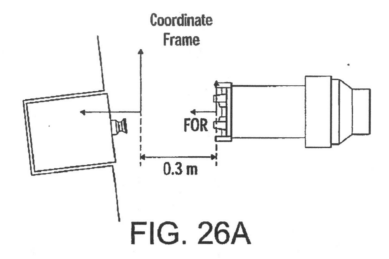

FIG. 26A

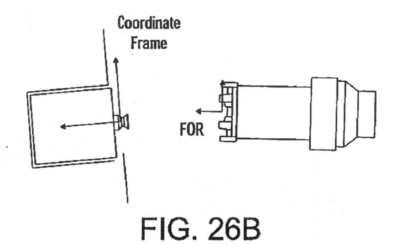

FIG. 26B

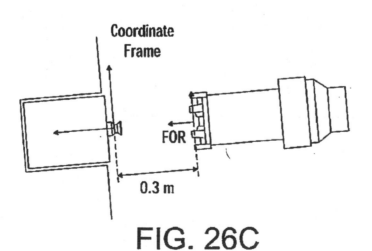

FIG. 26C

HIGHLIGHTS: Control Authority Reverts to EM/Retrograde, spring Assisted EM Ejection from HST-DM/
Stack Control Reverts to HST (Sun-Point)/EM NullRates & Perform 2-3 Sep Burns/Mass
Property Calibration Burns/Retrograde De-Orbit Burns to Lower Perigee to 250 km
Then to 50 km/Impact in Pacific

PHASE Begins   EM Receives Control Authority of the Stack   Duration: 4 Days
PHASE ENDS: Impact in Pacific

ATTITUDE: -H1 Sun-Point -> +H1 VV -> Sep -> Sun-Point -> +H1 VV -> -H1 Sun-Point (2x)

EPS: EM Array Deployed/DM Array Deployed/SA3 Taps Mated/HST Power System Augmented by DM

DM OPS MODE: Safe -> Normal -> Standby
EM OPS MODE: Safe -> Free Flight -> Idle

GN&C: EM Inertial Nav/Perform EM Mass Properties Calibration/De-orbit Burns

COMMUNICATIONS: HST S-Band (Pri) - Rx 1 kbps SSAF, Tx 4 kbps SSAR
Shared {   DM S-Band (Pri) - Rx 2-16 kpbs SSAF, Tx 2-8 kbps SSAR
EM S-Band (Pri) - Rx 2-16 kbps SSAF, Tx 2-8 kbps SSAR
EM Ku-Band (Pri) - TBD

FIG. 27

87

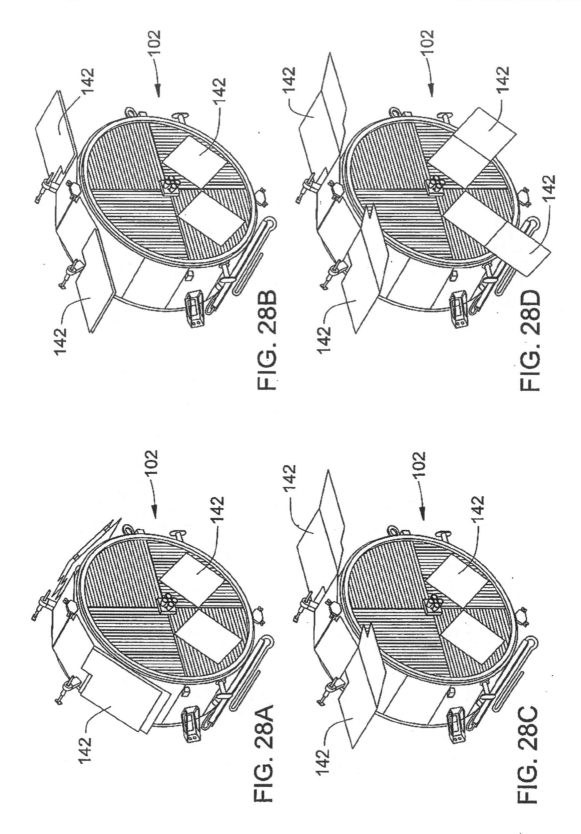

FIG. 28A

FIG. 28B

FIG. 28C

FIG. 28D

HIGHLIGHTS: Normal HST Science Operations/DM Quiescent Monitor Mode

PHASE BEGINS: Ejection Complete   Duration: 4 Days
PHASE ENDS: End of Science Operations and End of Life Testing

ATTITUDE: Normal HST Science Attitudes

EPS: DM Array Deployed- SA3 Taps Mated- HST Power System Augmented by DM

DM OPS MODE: Safe -> Normal -> Standby
EM OPS MODE: N/A

GN&C: HST Standard Operations/DM Monitor Mode

COMMUNICATIONS: HST S-Band (Pri) - Rx 1 kbps SSAF, Tx 32 kbps SSAR/MAR, Tx (SSR) 1 Mbps SSAR
                   DM S-Band (Pri) - Rx 2 kpbs SSAF, Tx 2-8 kbps SSAR
     Shared {   EM S-Band (Pri) - N/A
                   EM Ku-Band (Pri) - N/A

FIG. 29

89

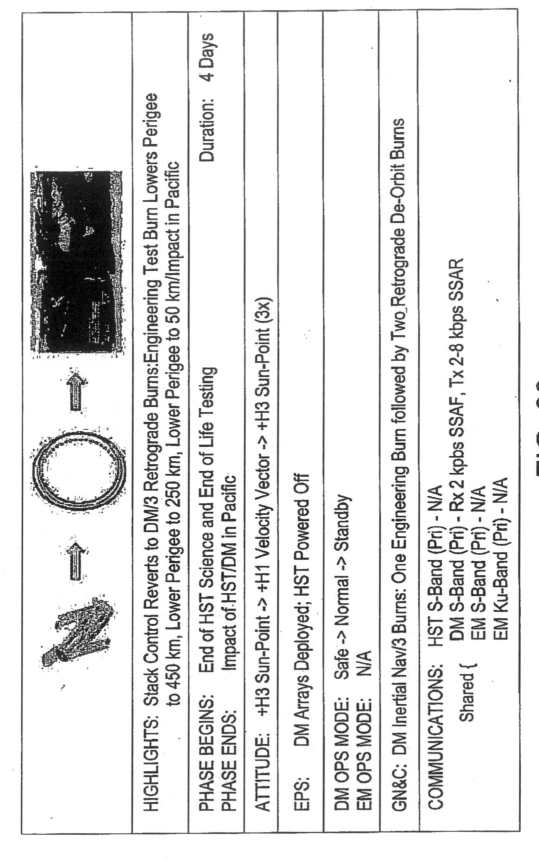

HIGHLIGHTS: Stack Control Reverts to DM/3 Retrograde Burns:Engineering Test Burn Lowers Perigee
to 450 km, Lower Perigee to 250 km, Lower Perigee to 50 km/Impact in Pacific

PHASE BEGINS: End of HST Science and End of Life Testing   Duration: 4 Days
PHASE ENDS: Impact of HST/DM in Pacific

ATTITUDE: +H3 Sun-Point -> +H1 Velocity Vector -> +H3 Sun-Point (3x)

EPS: DM Arrays Deployed; HST Powered Off

DM OPS MODE: Safe -> Normal -> Standby
EM OPS MODE: N/A

GN&C: DM Inertial Nav/3 Burns: One Engineering Burn followed by Two Retrograde De-Orbit Burns

COMMUNICATIONS: HST S-Band (Pri) - N/A
                  DM S-Band (Pri) - Rx 2 kpbs SSAF, Tx 2-8 kbps SSAR
         Shared { EM S-Band (Pri) - N/A
                   EM Ku-Band (Pri) - N/A

FIG. 30

METHOD AND ASSOCIATED APPARATUS FOR CAPTURING, SERVICING, AND DE-ORBITING EARTH SATELLITES USING ROBOTICS

RELATED APPLICATION

[0001] This application is a divisional application and claims the benefit of U.S. Non-provisional application Ser. No. 11/124,592, filed May 6, 2005 under 35 U.S.C. 121.

INCORPORATION BY REFERENCE

[0002] This application incorporates by reference U.S. Non-provisional application Ser. No. 11/124,592 filed May 6, 2005.

ORIGIN OF THE INVENTION

[0003] This invention was made by employees of the United States Government and contractors operating under a contract with the United States Government, and thus may be used by or for the Government for governmental purposes without the payment of any royalties thereon or therefor.

BACKGROUND OF THE INVENTION

[0004] 1. Field of Invention

[0005] This invention relates generally to the field of man-made earth satellites and more specifically to a novel method and associated apparatus for capturing, servicing and de-orbiting such satellites.

[0006] 2. Background of the Invention

[0007] The last half-century has been a watershed for the development and implementation of earth-orbit satellites for various purposes. Different types of earth satellites include those designed for communications, earth remote sensing, weather, global positioning, and scientific research. A typical example of a communications satellite might be EchoStar 3, which is used to send television signals to homes throughout North America. Communication satellites act as relay stations in space. They are used to "bounce" digital messages, such as telephone calls, television pictures and internet connections, from one part of the world to another. EchoStar 3 and many other communications satellites are in geosynchronous orbit. There are more than 100 such communication satellites currently orbiting earth.

[0008] Earth remote sensing satellites, such as the LandSat series (LandSat 1 through LandSat 7), study the earth's surface. From 300 miles above the earth's surface, and more, these satellites use powerful cameras to scan the planet. Their instruments study earth's plant cover, chemical composition, surface temperature, ice cap thicknesses, and many other earth systems and features. Such data is useful in vital industries such as farming, fishing, mining, and forestry. Moreover, remote sensing satellites are used to study changes in global environments caused by man. Examples of this include areas that are turning into desert (desertification), and the destruction of rain forests (deforestation).

[0009] TIROS (Television Infrared Observational Satellite), operated by NOAA (National Oceanic and Atmospheric Administration), is a representative weather satellite. TIROS is one of several weather satellites making up a system operated by NOAA, which produces data used to forecast weather, track storms, and otherwise engage in meteorological research. There are two TIROS satellites circling earth over the poles while satellites from another part of the system, the Geostationary Operational Environmental Satellites (GOES), operate in geosynchronous orbit. Using this system of satellites, meteorologists study the weather and climate patterns around the world, such as temperature, moisture, and solar radiation in the atmosphere. Also, many weather satellites are equipped with sensors that aid search and rescue operations.

[0010] The Global Positioning System (GPS) satellites are in geosynchronous orbit and are able to identify latitude, longitude and altitude with great precision. Originally developed by the military, GPS satellites are now used by a wide variety of people everywhere to find their exact position. Airplanes, boats, cars and virtually any transportation apparatus are equipped with GPS receivers. Even hand-held GPS devices have become a norm with pedestrians and other travelers.

[0011] While there are many examples of satellites engaged in scientific research, Hubble Space Telescope (HST) is perhaps the best known. Since 1990, when HST was launched, the world has had access to remarkable visual images that have significantly advanced our understanding of the cosmos. HST's optics, science instruments and spacecraft systems work together to capture light from far reaches of the universe, convert it into digital data, and transmit it back to earth. Because application of the current invention to HST represents an exemplary mode contemplated of carrying out the invention at the time of filing for a United States patent, an overview of HST's systems is appropriate. However, one skilled in the art will recognize that the method of this invention can be applied and adapted to virtually any man made earth satellite.

[0012] HST optics are collectively called the Optical Telescope Assembly (OTA), which includes two mirrors, support trusses and the apertures of the accompanying instruments. OTA's configuration is that of a well-known, straightforward design known as Ritchie-Chretien Cassegrain, in which the two specialized mirrors form focused images over the largest possible field of view. Referring now to FIGS. 1 through 5, HST and OTA are graphically illustrated. While FIG. 1 shows a three dimensional cutaway view of HST, FIGS. 2 and 3 specifically illustrate OTA and the principles of its operation. As best seen in FIG. 3, light enters through the main aperture and travels down a tube fitted with baffles that keep out stray light. The light is collected by the concave primary mirror and reflected toward the smaller, convex secondary mirror. The secondary mirror bounces the light back toward the primary mirror and through a smaller aperture in its center. The light is then focused on a small area called the focal plane, where it is detected by the various science instruments.

[0013] OTA's mirrors are necessarily very smooth and have precisely shaped reflecting surfaces. They were ground so that their surfaces do not deviate from a mathematically perfect curve by more than 1/800,000 of an inch. According to this precision, if the primary mirror were scaled up to the diameter of the earth, the biggest bump would be only six inches tall. Shortly after HST was deployed, it was discovered that the curve to which primary mirror was ground was incorrect, causing a spherical aberration. Fortunately, corrective optics, much like a contact lens, were able to solve this problem.

[0014] The mirrors are made of ultra-low expansion glass and kept at a nearly constant room temperature (about 70 degrees Fahrenheit) to avoid warping. The reflecting surfaces are coated with a 3/1,000,000-inch layer of pure aluminum and protected by a 1/1,000,000-inch layer of magnesium fluoride, which makes the mirrors more reflective of ultraviolet light.

[0015] HST contains five science instruments, namely the Advanced Camera for Surveys (ACS), the Wide Field and Planetary Camera (WFPC2), the Near Infrared Camera and Multi-Object Spectrometer (NICMOS), the Space Telescope Imaging Spectrograph (STIS), and the Fine Guidance Sensors (FGS). These instruments work either together or individually to observe the universe in a unique way.

[0016] Installed in the latest space shuttle servicing mission in March of 2002, the ACS represents the third generation of science instruments flown aboard HST. It occupies the space vacated by the Faint Object Camera, HST's "zoom lens" for nearly twelve years. Among other tasks, ACS is used to map distribution of dark matter, detect the most distant objects in the universe, search for massive planets in other solar systems, observe weather on other planets in our solar system, and study the nature and distribution of galaxies. With its wider field of view, sharper image quality, and enhanced sensitivity, ACS expands HST's capabilities significantly; its cutting edge technology makes HST ten times more effective and prolongs its useful life. Designed to study some of the earliest activity in the universe, ACS detects electromagnetic waves in wavelengths ranging from far ultraviolet to infrared.

[0017] On the inside, ACS is actually a team of three different cameras, specifically the wide field camera, the high-resolution camera, and the solar blind camera. The wide field camera conducts broad surveys of the universe, which reveal clues about how our universe evolved. In contrast, the high-resolution camera takes detailed pictures of the inner regions of galaxies. The solar blind camera, which blocks visible light to enhance ultraviolet sensitivity, focuses on hot stars radiating in ultraviolet wavelengths.

[0018] HST's "workhorse" instrument, WFPC2, is behind most of the famous images it produces. This main camera includes 48 filters mounted on four filter wheels, which allow scientists to study precise wavelengths of light and to sense a range of wavelengths from ultraviolet to near-infrared light. Four postage stamp-sized pieces of circuitry called Charge-Coupled Devices (CCDs) collect and record information from stars and galaxies to make photographs. These detectors are very sensitive to the extremely faint light of distant galaxies. In fact, CCDs can see objects that are one billion times fainter than the human eye can see. Less sensitive CCDs are now found in some videocassette recorders and virtually all new digital cameras. Each of the four CCDs on HST contains 640,000 pixels. The light collected by each pixel is translated into a number. These numbers are then transmitted to ground-based computers, which convert them into an image.

[0019] NICMOS is HST's "heat sensor" and can see objects in deepest space—objects whose light takes billions of years to reach earth. The instrument's three cameras, each with different fields of view, are designed to detect near-infrared wavelengths, which are slightly longer than the wavelengths of visible light. Much information about the birth of stars, solar systems, and galaxies are revealed in infrared light, which can penetrate the interstellar dust and gas that often block visible light. In addition, light from the most distant objects in the universe "shifts" into the infrared wavelengths, and so by studying objects and phenomena in this spectral region, astronomers can probe the past, learning how galaxies, stars and planetary systems form.

[0020] Just as a camera for recording visible light must be dark inside to avoid exposure to unwanted light, so must a camera for recording infrared light be cold inside to avoid unwanted exposure to unwanted light in the form of heat. To ensure that NICMOS is recording infrared light from space rather than heat created by its own electronics, its sensitive infrared sensors must operate at very cold temperatures—below 77 degrees Kelvin (–321 degrees Fahrenheit). The instrument's detectors were initially cooled inside a cryogenic dewar (a thermally insulated container much like a thermos bottle), which contained a 230 pound block of nitrogen ice. While successful for about two years, the nitrogen ice cube melted prematurely. NICMOS was rechilled during the last HST servicing mission of March 2002 with a "cryocooler," an apparatus that operates much like a household refrigerator.

[0021] STIS in essence acts like a prism to separate detected light into its component colors. This spectrograph instrument thus provides a "fingerprint" of the object being observed, which reveals information about its temperature, chemical composition, density and motion. Spectrographic observations also show changes in celestial objects as the universe evolves. STIS spans ultraviolet, visible and near-infrared wavelengths. Among other tasks, STIS is used to search for black holes. The light emitted by stars and gas orbiting the center of a galaxy appears redder when moving away from earth (redshift) and bluer when coming toward earth (blueshift). Thus, STIS looks for redshifted material on one side of the suspected black hole and blueshifted material on the other, indicating that this material is orbiting at a very high rate of speed, as would be expected when a black hole is present. STIS can sample 500 points along a celestial object simultaneously, meaning that many regions in planet's atmosphere or many stars within a galaxy can be recorded in one exposure. STIS was installed on HST during the 1997 shuttle servicing mission.

[0022] HST's Fine Guidance Sensors, its targeting cameras, provide feedback used to maneuver the telescope and perform celestial measurements. While two of the sensors point the telescope at a desired astronomical target, and then hold that target in an instrument's field of view, the third sensor is able to perform scientific observations. The FGS aim HST by locking onto "guide stars" and continuously measuring the position of the telescope relative to the object being viewed. Adjustments based on these constant, minute measurements keep HST pointed in the desired direction with an accuracy of 0.01 arcsec. The FGS detect when HST drifts even the smallest amount and return it to its target. This gives HST the ability to remain pointed at that target with no more than 0.007 arcsec of deviation over long periods of time. This level of stability and precision is the equivalent of being able to hold a laser beam focused on a dime 200 miles away for 24 hours.

[0023] Additionally, FGS provide precise astrometrical measurements of stars and celestial objects, which are advancing the knowledge of stars' distances, masses and motions. FGS provide star positions that are about ten times more accurate than those observed from ground-based telescopes. When used as science instruments, the sensors allow HST to search for a "wobble" in the motion of nearby stars, which may indicate that they have planets orbiting around them; determine if certain stars are actually double stars; measure the angular diameter of stars and other celestial objects; refine the positions and the absolute magnitude (brightness) scale for stars; and help determine the true distance scale for the universe.

[0024] All telescopes have optical systems, and some even have specialized instruments, but HST is almost unique in that it operates in space; the telescope is actually "flown" as a spacecraft. Therefore, several space craft systems are required to keep HST functioning smoothly. The essential systems are communications antennae, solar arrays for power, computers and automation, and housing.

[0025] HST performs only in response to detailed instructions from a ground-based control center, and thus communications antennae are necessary to transmit and receive such instructions between the telescope and the Flight Operations Team at the Space Telescope Science Institute. The four antennae on HST transmit and receive data via one of the constellation of Tracking and Data Relay Satellites (TDRS) operated by NASA. In order for this system to be operational, at least one TDRS satellite must be visible within HST's line of sight. Direct interaction can occur between HST and the control center only when this line of sight exists. When none of the TDRS satellites are visible from HST, a recorder stores the accumulated data until visibility is resumed. A flow diagram of the communications process is provided as FIG. 4.

[0026] Flanking HST's tube are two thin, blue solar panel arrays. Each wing-like array has a solar cell "blanket" that converts the sun's energy directly into electricity to power HST's various systems. Some of the energy generated by the arrays is stored in onboard batteries so that HST can operate while traveling through earth's shadow (about 36 minutes out of each 97 minute orbit). Fully charged, each battery contains enough energy to sustain HST in normal science operations mode for 7.5 hours, or five orbits. The solar arrays are designed for replacement by visiting astronauts aboard a space shuttle.

[0027] In order to run all the many subsystems onboard HST, several computers and microprocessors reside in the body of HST, as well as in each science instrument. Two main computers, which girdle HST's "waist," direct all operations. One communicates with the instruments, receives their data and telemetry, sends the data to interface units for transmission to the ground, and sends commands and timing information to the instruments. The other main computer handles the gyroscopes, the pointing control subsystem, and other HST-wide functions. Each instrument itself also houses small computers and microprocessors that direct their activities. These computers direct the rotation of the filter wheels, open and close exposure shutters, maintain the temperature of the instruments, collect data, and communicate with the main computers.

[0028] In space, HST is subject to the harsh environment of zero gravity and temperature extremes—more than 100 degrees Fahrenheit difference in temperature during each trip around earth. To accommodate this operating environment, HST has a "skin," or blanket, of multilayered insulation, which protects the telescope during temperature shifts. Beneath this insulation is a lightweight aluminum shell, which provides an external structure for the spacecraft and houses the OTA and science instruments. The OTA is held together by a cylindrical truss made of graphite epoxy, the same material used to make many golf clubs, tennis racquets and bicycles. Graphite is a stiff, strong and lightweight material that resists expanding and contracting in extreme temperatures.

[0029] The following table summarizes some of the relevant facts about HST:

TABLE 1

Weight	24,500 Lbs.
Length	43.5 Ft.
Diameter	14 Ft. (Aft Shroud)
Optical System	Ritchey-Chretien Design Cassegrain Telescope
Primary Mirror	94.5 Inch Dia.
Pointing Accuracy	0.007 Arcsec for 24 Hours
Magnitude Range	5 Meters to 30 Meters (Visual Magnitude)
Wavelength Range	1,100 Angstroms to 24,000 Angstroms
Angular Resolution	0.1 Arcsec at 6328 Angstroms
Orbit	320 Nautical Miles Inclined at 28.5 Degrees
Orbit Time	97 Minutes per Orbit

[0030] As indicated by the foregoing narrative, HST was designed to be serviced and upgraded periodically throughout its lifetime. Specifically, as illustrated in FIGS. 5 and 6, the space shuttle program had planned missions dedicated to servicing and upgrading HST scheduled until 2010, at which time HST would be retired and de-orbited in favor of the new James Webb Space Telescope (JWST). However, in January of 2004, NASA Administrator Sean O'Keefe announced that he was canceling shuttle Service Mission 4 (SM4) because of safety issues identified by the Columbia Accident Investigation Board (CAIB) Report. The CAIB Report was issued as a result of the Space Shuttle Columbia disaster of Feb. 1, 2003, when all seven astronauts aboard Columbia were tragically killed on reentry into the atmosphere.

[0031] Administrator O'Keefe's announcement presented the scientific community with at least two problems. First, without SM4, regularly scheduled upgrades to HST's scientific instruments could not be made, thereby confining scientific use of HST to out-dated technology. Second, and of graver concern, without SM4, wearable parts on HST could not be replaced. More specifically, gyroscopes necessary for HST's Pointing Control System (PCS) are degrading and will probably cease to operate within the next three to five years, as indicated by the chart of FIG. 7. The current PCS requires sensing from three gyros, and already only four of the six gyros aboard HST are operational. Best estimates show that a less than 50 percent probability exists that three gyros will be operational by the late 2005 or early 2006. Although scientists are developing a two-gyro pointing system, that solution may add only 12 to 18 months of additional life.

[0032] Moreover, batteries that power HST's computers, instruments and virtually all vital systems are at risk. Based on recent tests, each of HST's six batteries is losing its charging capacity at a rate of 5.9 amp hours per year. This is far higher than previous tested loss rates of about two amp hours per year, and points out a tendency for capacity loss rate to accelerate nonlinearly over time. Without intervention, as scheduled by SM4, it is projected that by the end of 2005 science operations will likely require block scheduling and a lowering of the safemode trigger. By 2006, it is probable that the state-of-charge at the end of orbit night will be near the hardware sunpoint safemode trigger, which is the lowest level of safemode that protects the vehicle.

[0033] Accordingly, there is a need for a method and attendant apparatus for autonomously servicing HST and other free-flying satellites during flight using robotics.

BRIEF DESCRIPTION OF THE INVENTION

[0034] The problems and shortcomings experienced in the prior art, as detailed above and otherwise, are substantially alleviated by this invention, as will become apparent in the following recitation of the objects and brief description thereof.

[0035] One object of this invention is to provide servicing of satellites and other spacecraft without human presence on or near the spacecraft being serviced.

[0036] Another object is use the principle of supervised autonomy to control one or more aspects of a spacecraft servicing mission.

[0037] Still another object is to provide a method of de-orbiting a spacecraft that was not originally designed for de-orbit.

[0038] Accordingly, one method of the present invention comprises the nominal steps of autonomously establishing a link between a spacecraft needing servicing and a servicing vehicle, and sending commands to a robot system aboard the servicing vehicle, such commands addressing the servicing needs of the spacecraft. The commands may be pre-scripted or generated on board the servicing vehicle by using embedded Artificial Intelligence (AI) logic or other on board processing in response to sensed conditions. The robot system preferably comprises a grappling arm and a dexterous robot, which, in combination, provide for most servicing needs, such as replacing degraded batteries and upgrading the scientific capabilities of the spacecraft by replacing scientific instruments. The servicing vehicle may aid in other ways as well, such as by providing stowage area for replacement parts, by shielding the spacecraft from the harmful effects of the sun during servicing, and by boosting the altitude of the spacecraft's orbit by firing its thrusters.

[0039] Of course, one skilled in the art will appreciate that executing the commands effectuates the servicing procedure. Preferably, other such commands are also used and may include capturing the spacecraft to be serviced while still in free-flight by the robot system and providing the spacecraft with an ability to de-orbit.

[0040] Under the principle of supervised autonomy, the commands sent to the robot system can be overridden by a ground-based operator, who is in telecommunication with the servicing vehicle. In one embodiment, the remote operator may be ground based. In another embodiment, the remote operator may be space based, i.e. resident on the

Space Shuttle, International Space Station, or other human occupied spacecraft. In yet another embodiment, the operator may be based on a seaborne platform or airborne platform. Thus, any command that may need to be changed can be done with little or no interruption of the servicing procedure, or, alternatively, the operator can manually carry out the servicing procedure without using the autonomous commands. It is also preferred that one or more of the pre-scripted commands require validation by the ground-based operator prior to it being carried out, thereby providing a stop-check against accident or error.

[0041] The preferred apparatus to provide a de-orbiting capability to the spacecraft includes a de-orbit module, which has thrusters and a guidance, navigation and control system for directing the flight path of the spacecraft as it de-orbits. Moreover, the apparatus also may include an ejection module, which contains the robot system, as well as parts for servicing the spacecraft. One skilled in the art will understand that the de-orbit module and the ejection module may separate after servicing is complete, with the de-orbit module staying with the serviced spacecraft until it is ready for de-orbit at a future time. Meanwhile, the ejection module, after separation from the de-orbit module, may de-orbit itself immediately, or, alternately, may proceed to capture another spacecraft in need of servicing. The ejection module optionally may be placed in a parking orbit for some period of time to await instructions to rendezvous with and service and/or deorbit another spacecraft, either at a predetermined time or in response to some unforeseen contingency or component failure on the other spacecraft in orbit.

[0042] Tools and space parts for a plurality of spacecraft may be transported on the ejection module to facilitate servicing and/or de-orbit of a plurality of satellites. Such a generic or multi-satellite serving vehicle may be of particular interest to manufacturers of families of satellites using multiple substantially similar satellites with common components. Such a vehicle could potentially reduce or eliminate the need for costly on-orbit or ground based spare satellites. Rather than placing one or more on orbit spares in orbit in anticipation of potential failures, the present invention provides an alternative means to provide a flexible servicing capability that may enable rapid return to service of a variety of satellites without requirement for entire dedicated spares for each type of satellite. Use of modular design and construction of satellites and commonality among satellite designs can be used to maximize the potential repairability of future satellites. Constellations of substantially identical satellites, such as Iridium, GlobalStar and other communications satellites, stand to gain the greatest potential benefit of the repair capabilities of the present invention due to the use of common parts and their relative accessibility to repair vehicles due to their relatively low earth orbit.

[0043] Even for satellites in higher orbits, such as geostationary orbits, it may be more cost effective to conduct a robotic repair/servicing mission to extend the useful life of valuable communications and other satellite payloads presently on orbit, rather than to construct and launch entire replacement satellites. The use of the present invention also has the potential to reduce the amount of orbital debris in orbit by removing inoperative satellites from orbit.

[0044] In the geostationary band, it is generally considered cost-prohibitive to deorbit spent satellites, and satellites are generally boosted to a higher orbit that will not affect satellites in the geostationary band. Use of a repair mission in accordance with the present invention potentially could reduce the problem of clutter from spent satellites above geostationary orbit by extending the useful life of satellites and delaying their eventual boost to higher orbit. Even if it is necessary to boost the ejection module into higher-than-geostationary orbit, one such module may be used to service multiple geostationary satellites, resulting in a lower net contribution to the clutter in the higher-than-geostationary band.

[0045] One cause of end-of-life, particularly in geostationary satellites, is exhaustion of fuel used for stationkeeping and other maneuvers. Attaching a deorbit module to a geostationary satellite to provide for end-of-life boost above geostationary orbit can permit the use of fuel onboard the geostationary satellite for revenue producing purposes that was previously reserved (as required by international law and conventions) for the end-of-life boost maneuver. Exhaustion of fuel for attitude control thrusters may also cause a satellite to lose attitude control capability and thus reach the end of its useful life. In accordance with the present invention, it is possible for the servicing vehicle to transfer additional fuel to the target satellite for stationkeeping in the geostationary band or continued use of attitude control thrusters to allow it to extend its useful life.

[0046] The invention preferably also includes a method for capturing a free-flying spacecraft with a second free-flying spacecraft, the second spacecraft including the autonomous operation abilities already described. This method includes the steps of autonomously identifying and pursuing the second spacecraft and then securing the two spacecraft together. Preferably, the second spacecraft has a grappling arm or other device that aids in attaching the two spacecraft together, while the first spacecraft may have affixed berthing pins that facilitate attachment. One of skill in the art will recognize that a variety of docking mechanisms can be employed without departing from the scope of the present invention.

[0047] One skilled in the art may realize that the steps of autonomous identification and pursuit might be carried out by comparing file images of the first spacecraft with real time images taken continuously by the second spacecraft. Of course, in this situation the second spacecraft includes appropriate equipment to create images.

[0048] One method for capturing the spacecraft further includes the steps of launching the second spacecraft into space and establishing a link between the second spacecraft and a remote operator. Alternately, a second spacecraft previously launched and optionally used to conduct a prior servicing/de-orbit mission can be directed to initiate pursuit, capture, and repair/deorbit of a target satellite, either from a parking orbit or directly from a first servicing rendezvous. In either case, the operator can use a communication link to the second spacecraft to override the autonomous identification and manual pursuit, and manually control the entire procedure or any part thereof as desired. Similarly, the step of securing the two spacecraft together can be done either autonomously or manually. If AI logic onboard the second spacecraft is used to conduct the autonomous pursuit, capture, and repair/de-orbit of the target satellite, the ground operator preferably may take manual control at any time

either at his discretion or based on predetermined criteria. In addition, the second spacecraft may propose a particular action and await approval from the ground operator to execute that action depending on the inputs received by the AI logic or Authority to Proceed conditions either preset in the AI logic or directed by the ground operator.

[0049] Another method of this invention includes the steps of securing a de-orbit module to the spacecraft to be serviced and commanding the de-orbit module to de-orbit the spacecraft. For the purposes of the present invention, de-orbit includes both the removal of a spacecraft from orbit through reentry or transfer of a satellite to a disposal orbit, i.e. transferring a geostationary satellite to higher than geostationary orbit for disposal at end of life. One skilled in the art will appreciate that the de-orbit module allows for the flight path of the spacecraft to be controlled so that population centers can be avoided and impact can be targeted for an ocean or other desired location. If it is desired to de-orbit multiple satellites, a plurality of de-orbit modules can be transported by a single ejection module. Through sequential rendezvous and attachment of a de-orbit module followed by detachment of the ejection module, a plurality of satellites not originally designed for de-orbit can be provided with a de-orbit capability. Alternately, a satellite that has suffered a kick motor failure that prevented it from reaching its desired orbit similarly can have the faulty kick motor replaced with an operational replacement to permit the affected satellite to reach its design orbit.

DESCRIPTION OF THE DRAWINGS

[0050] In order that the claimed invention may be better made and used by those skilled in the art, and that the best mode of carrying out the invention may be more fully appreciated, the following drawings are provided, in which:

[0051] FIG. 1 is a cutaway three-dimensional perspective view of the Hubble Space Telescope (HST), illustrating major components and systems.

[0052] FIG. 2 is a cutaway three-dimensional perspective view of the Optical Telescope Assembly (OTA) of the HST.

[0053] FIG. 3 is a side view of the OTA illustrating major components and the operation of the Ritchie-Chretien Cassegrain telescope design.

[0054] FIG. 4 is a schematic diagram showing the flow of data between HST and remote control centers.

[0055] FIG. 5 is time chart showing the scheduled HST servicing missions by the space shuttle.

[0056] FIG. 6 is a three-dimensional perspective representation of the space shuttle servicing HST.

[0057] FIG. 7 is graph illustrating the projected deterioration of HST's gyroscopes.

[0058] FIG. 8 is a bottom end view of the aft bulkhead of HST illustrating the berthing pins to which the Hubble Robotic Vehicle (RV) attaches at berthing.

[0059] FIG. 9 is a schematic of HST in alignment with the RV immediately prior to berthing, illustrating a preferred capture box and grapple fixture for initial connection of the RV to HST.

[0060] FIG. 10 is a close-up view of the grapple fixture of FIG. 9.

[0061] FIG. 11 is a three-dimensional perspective view of the RV connected to HST, and shows the robotic servicing concept using a preferred grapple arm.

[0062] FIG. 12 is an isolated three-dimensional view of the De-orbiting Module (DM).

[0063] FIG. 13 is a three-dimensional perspective view of the Ejection Module (EM), illustrating the solar array panels in their open position.

[0064] FIG. 14 is a three-dimensional perspective view of the Grapple Arm (GA) shown in the extended position.

[0065] FIG. 15 is a three-dimensional perspective view of the Dexterous Robot (DR) shown with one arm in the extended position.

[0066] FIG. 16 is a schematic representation of the "Mission Manager" concept.

[0067] FIG. 17A is a chart summarizing the launch phase of a preferred method according to the present invention.

[0068] FIG. 17B is a graphic representation showing a typical ascent for an Atlas V rocket, which could be used in conjunction with this invention, embarking on a Low Earth Orbit (LEO) mission.

[0069] FIG. 18 is a chart summarizing the commissioning phase of an embodiment according to the present invention.

[0070] FIG. 19 is a chart summarizing the pursuit phase of an embodiment according to the present invention.

[0071] FIG. 20 is a chart summarizing the proximity operations phase of an embodiment according to the present invention.

[0072] FIG. 21 is a chart summarizing the approach and capture phase of an embodiment according to the present invention.

[0073] FIG. 22A is a diagram representing the safety ellipse of the approach and capture maneuver profile of an embodiment according to the present invention.

[0074] FIG. 22B is a diagram representing the approach range of the approach and capture profile of an embodiment according to the present invention.

[0075] FIG. 23 is a chart summarizing the servicing phase of an embodiment according to the present invention.

[0076] FIG. 24 is a top view of the DR shown after coarse positioning is complete.

[0077] FIG. 25 is a schematic representation of a decision tree for determining whether a task is "robot-friendly."

[0078] FIG. 26A is a side view of one end of a DR arm and a proposed target, illustrating the coordinate frames before calibration.

[0079] FIG. 26B is a side view of one end of a DR arm and a proposed target, illustrating the coordinate frames after calibration.

[0080] FIG. 26C is a side view of one end of a DR arm and a proposed target, illustrating the end of the arm in a hover position after correction.

[0081] FIG. 27 is a chart summarizing the ejection and disposal phase of an embodiment according to the present invention.

[0082] FIGS. 28A through 28D are three-dimensional perspective views of the DM illustrating sequential deployment of its solar arrays after separation of the EM.

[0083] FIG. 29 is a chart summarizing the science operations phase of an embodiment according to the present invention.

[0084] FIG. 30 is a chart summarizing the HST/DM disposal or de-orbiting phase of an embodiment according to the present invention.

DETAILED DESCRIPTION

[0085] Reference is now made to the drawings, in which like numbers are used to designate like features throughout. Some of the preferred objectives of this invention are to robotically service a target satellite, such as the Hubble Space Telescope (HST) 50, and then provide HST 50 with a de-orbit capability, which will be used upon the completion of the HST mission life. While this specification is describing the invention as it relates to HST 50 as an example, one skilled in the art will recognize that the methods and apparatus disclosed herein are given only as exemplary embodiments. Other embodiments exist that fit within the scope of the invention as defined by the appended claims. Thus, for example, one skilled in the art will readily see that this invention has application to any number of existing free-flying satellites needing servicing and/or de-orbiting, and not just to HST 50.

[0086] One embodiment of this invention comprises the Robotic Vehicle (RV) 100, which preferably is launched on an Expendable Launch Vehicle (ELV) 52. The RV 100 preferably includes three basic components: a De-orbit Module (DM) 102, an Ejection Module (EM) 104, and a Robot System (RS) 106 contained within the EM 104. Whereas previous HST servicing missions employed astronauts, the method of this invention is conducted using robotics. After the completion of the servicing mission, the EM 104 and RS 106 preferably are released from HST 50 and optionally de-orbited for a targeted impact into the Pacific Ocean. Alternatively, the released EM 104 and RS 106 may be placed in a parking orbit until needed for servicing another satellite. In contrast, the DM 102 preferably stays attached to HST 50 and eventually provides the de-orbit capability at the end of the HST science mission.

[0087] As indicated, the RV 100 preferably includes the DM 102 and EM 104 spacecraft, together with the RS 106. Preferably, a two-fault tolerant separation clamp band (not shown) releasably joins the DM 102 and EM 104 segments mechanically, while electrical harnesses support various Command & Data Handling (C&DH), Guidance, Navigation & Control (GN&C), and Electrical Power System (EPS) functions across the interface. The RV 100 is preferably launched in this combined state and remains combined until the completion of the servicing phase of the mission, at which time the EM 104 separates from the DM 102, while the DM 102 remains attached to HST 50 through end-of-mission. One of skill in the art will recognize that a variety of mechanism for separating DM 102 and EM 104 may be employed without deviating from the scope of the present invention. In addition, the combination of DM 102 and EM 104 into a single spacecraft is also within the scope of the present invention.

[0088] In one embodiment of the combined vehicle configuration, the DM **102** provides the "brains" and the EM **104** provides the "muscle," with respect to overall vehicle control. The relative navigation sensors and the algorithms to determine absolute RV **100** attitude and relative attitude (RV **100** to HST **50**) reside in DM **102**. The GN&C system actuators, thrusters and momentum management devices reside in the EM **104** and respond to the DM **102** commands to obtain the required RV **100** vehicle state. The respective locations of the sensors, actuators, and momentum management devices can be redistributed between the two vehicles in a plurality of combinations without deviating from the scope of the present invention.

[0089] In one embodiment, the primary functions of the DM **102** are to provide GN&C attitude determination and control functions for the RV **100**, mechanical and electrical interfaces to HST **50**, mechanical and electrical interfaces to the EM **104**, and controlled reentry of the DM **102**HST **50** combined vehicle at end-of-mission

[0090] The DM **102** GN&C subsystem preferably includes relative and absolute attitude sensors and their associated algorithms, and actuation hardware to provide three-axis stabilized attitude control. The preferred sensor suite comprises sensors that are both independent and over lap in coverage (range to target) capability, and provides data used by the control algorithms to determine the HST **50** relative state (or orientation) during the automated rendezvous and capture tasks, as described hereafter. Other sensors provide absolute attitude information to maintain desired vehicle pointing during all mission phases This system, when combined with the actuators in the EM **104**, brings the RV **100** into a position that facilitates either a first embodiment wherein the capture of HST **50** is accomplished using the RS **106** Grapple Arm (GA) **108** to capture one of the HST **50** grapple fixtures (see FIGS. **9** and **10**) or a second embodiment wherein direct docking to the HST **50** berthing pins located on the aft bulkhead (see FIG. **8**) is used. The system allows for capture even in the case where HST **50** is unable to maintain a controlled attitude due to degradation of its pointing and control system, which occurs as a result of failing gyroscopes. The GN&C subsystem also supports the controlled HST reentry task at end-of-mission.

[0091] The relative navigation sensor selection is based on requirements for redundancy, range capabilities, and Technology Readiness Level (TRL). Two different types of sensors are required for redundancy. The following exemplary sensors may be used under this criteria, although one skilled in the art will understand that other sensors and combinations of sensors fall within the scope of this invention:

Longer Range Sensors (Beginning at 5-3 km):

[0092] Primary: Optech Light Detection and Ranging (LIDAR)—Manufactured by MDR

[0093] Secondary: Laser Camera System (LCS)—Manufactured by NEPTEC Close Range Sensors (10 m and closer):

[0094] Primary: Enhanced Advanced Video Guidance Sensor (EAVGS)

[0095] Secondary: Natural Feature Imaging Recognition (NFIR)—System of Eight Digital Video Cameras with Various Focal Lengths Specifically Positioned to Align with Various HST Features/Targets

[0096] The following table summarizes the sensor effective ranges for the exemplary sensors relative to HST **50**. The dark grey shading shows the effective range of the selected sensor. The light grey shading for the LCS shows the extended range for secondary preferred sensors.

TABLE 2

Sensor	Field of View (FOV)	Target	Unit	Pursuit (>150 m)	Prox Ops <150 m	<50 m	<30 m	Capture (~0.3 m)
NFIR	8 degree	Hubble	Camera 9					
	(Long Range)	Hubble	Camera 8					
	12 degree	Aft Bulkhead	Camera 7					
	(Mid Range)	Aft Bulkhead	Camera 6					
	70 degree	Latch/Berthing Pin	Camera 5					
	(Berthing)	Latch/Berthing Pin	Camera 4					
		Latch/Berthing Pin	Camera 3					
EACVS	22 degree	Berthing Target	Camera 2					
	(Close Range)	Berthing Target	Camera 1					
LCS	TBD	Hubble	Primary					
			Secondary					
LIDAR	N/A	Hubble	Primary					
			Secondary					

[0097] The DM **102** preferably includes a propulsion subsystem, which comprises a number of Small Reaction Control System (RCS) thrusters coupled to four large primary thrusters, a plurality of propellant tanks, and associated valves, filters, and lines. Monopropellant (high purity) propellant is preferably used to fuel the thrusters in order to minimize plume contamination. The DM **102** propulsion subsystem preferably is only used for the DM **102**/HST **50** controlled reentry mission phase (described hereafter) in order to minimize propellant slosh during attached science operations. Thus, the DM **102** propulsion subsystem preferably remains pressurized and sealed until actual use in de-orbiting HST **50**. At that time, the RCS thrusters are used to point the combined vehicle to the correct attitude in response to the GN&C commands and the primary thrusters will perform the large delta-v burns required for controlled reentry. One of skill in the art will recognize that the foregoing propulsion system is merely exemplary and that a variety of propulsion designs and components alternatively, including, but not limited to, cold gas thrusters and bipropellant liquid rocket thrusters, may be used without deviating from the scope of the present invention.

[0098] The C&DH provides the functions required for acquiring, processing, storing, and transferring commands and telemetry. More specifically, the DM **102** C&DH also performs integrated operations with the EM **104** and a safe hold computer. The next table provides a breakdown of an embodiment of a C&DH control and operation for one procedure or method of this invention. All functions, with the exception of input/output to some specialized equipment, preferably utilize a MIL-STD-1553 for exchange of data and commands. The preferred processor is a RAD750 on a Compact Peripheral Component Interface (CPCI) Bus based on a heritage processor design used on the Mars Reconnaissance Orbiter program. Also, a VIRTEX II based imaging processing platform is preferably used for simultaneous processing of multiple (at least five) video sensors. Hot redundant operation of the system preferably provides for concurrent processing.

system. High-rate DM **102** data, e.g. video, required during pursuit, capture, proximity operations, and servicing phases is passed through the EM **104** communications system (described hereafter) Ku-band transmitters and high-gain antennas for downlink through the TDRS.

[0100] The preferred DM **102** S-band system through the TDRS is capable of command reception at 2 Kbps and 16 Kbps, and transmits telemetry at between 2 and 16 Kbps. Similarly, the preferred DM **102** S-band system routed through EM**104** will be capable of command reception at 2 Kbps and transmit between 4 and 16 Kbps.

[0101] As one skilled in the art will see, the DM **102** mechanical subsystem design is driven by requirements of the launch and science operations mission phases. During the launch phase, the DM **102** structure preferably is connected to and interfaces with the Expendable Launch Vehicle (ELV) **52** Payload Adapter Fitting (PAF) **54** on one side and to the DM **102**/EM **104** separation ring **110** on the other. In this configuration, the DM **102** has to support the EM **104** mass during the launch phase and meet primary mode requirements levied by the ELV **52** provider. Requirements for the science operations phase push the design to be as light and stiff as possible (preferably moments of inertia below 166,000 kg m2 and an approximately 20 Hz first mode).

[0102] One embodiment of a structural design that meets these requirements is aluminum honeycomb forward and aft panels **112** with a segmented center bulkhead **114** attached to a central tube **116** for internal frame attachment. FIG. **12** presents an embodiment of a structural design with a typical component layout.

[0103] The DM **102** electrical power system (EPS) provides power for the DM **102** during all flight phases and power augmentation to HST post-servicing. One embodiment includes about 90 ft^2 of effective solar array area using triple-junction GaAs cells, ten 55 amp hour Li-ion batteries, and associated power conditioning and distribution hardware known to one skilled in the art.

TABLE 3

Mission Phase	RV Control	DM C&DH Mode	EM C&DH Mode	DM RIU	EM ACE
Launch	ELV/DM	Idle to Safe (Breakwire-based)	Idle	Disabled	Enabled
Commissioning	DM	Normal	Idle	Disabled	Enabled
Pursuit	DM	Normal	Idle	Disabled	Enabled
Prox Ops	DM	Normal	Idle	Disabled	Enabled
Approach & Capture	DM	Normal (Warm-Backup)	Idle	Disabled	Disabled (Extended Time-out)
Servicing	DM	Normal	Idle	Disabled	Enabled
EM Jettison & Deorbit	EM	Standby	Free-Flight	Enabled	Enabled
Science	HST/ DM (Safemode)	Standby	NA	Disabled	NA
DM/HST Deorbit	DM	Normal	NA	Enabled	NA

[0099] The DM **102** communications subsystem is preferably made up of an S-band system using two multi-mode transceivers routed to a pair of low-gain antennas (LGA) for command uplink and telemetry transmission at low data rates through the Tracking and Data Relay Satellite (TDRS)

[0104] In one embodiment, the DM **102** thermal control subsystem must control temperatures within hardware limits and insure that there is no greater than about 5 W of thermal conductivity from the DM **102** and HST **50** during attached science operations. One embodiment, based on prior known and proven methodology, utilizes heat pipes and software controlled heater circuits to provide the required hardware component thermal environments for all mission phases. Thermal isolation of the berthing latches or pins **118** minimizes heat conducted to HST during science operations.

[0105] Turning attention now to the EM **104**, best seen in FIG. **13**, in one embodiment, EM **104** preferably functions to provide and/or perform:

[0106] GN&C actuation for the RV **100**.

[0107] Provide all propulsion during pursuit, rendezvous, capture and servicing of HST **50**.

[0108] Equipment stowage for items that will be replaced on HST **50** as well as for the removed equipment.

[0109] Mechanical and electrical interfaces to the RS **106**.

[0110] Mechanical and electrical interfaces to the DM **102**.

[0111] Controlled reentry of itself and/or rendezvous with another satellite.

[0112] Provide high-rate Ku-band high-gain-antenna communication system.

[0113] Provide shadowing for instruments during servicing.

[0114] Provide solar array (SA) for electrical power when charging HST **50** during servicing.

[0115] Provide reaction wheel assembly (RWA) control.

[0116] The EM **104** GN&C subsystem preferably comprises primarily actuators, such as momentum and/or reaction wheels, magnetic torquers, and thrusters, to enable RV **100** pointing, and sensors, such as coarse sun sensors, a plurality (preferably three or more) of axis magnetometers, IMUs and GPS, to enable three-axis stabilized attitude control during EM **104** controlled reentry. The relative navigation sensors and the algorithms to determine absolute RV **100** attitude and relative attitude (RV **100** to HST **50**) reside in the DM **102**, as explained above. During the majority of the mission, the EM **104** GN&C system actuators, thrusters and momentum management devices preferably respond to the DM **102** commands to obtain the required RV **100** vehicle attitude, i.e. the DM **102** controls the EM **104**/DM **102** stack. However, the EM **104** Actuator Control Electronics (ACE) preferably controls its own propulsion system and the EM **104** provides thruster and momentum/reaction wheel actuation throughout all of its primary mission phases. RV **100** attitude control may be provided by the DM **102** during pursuit, proximity operations, capture, docking and servicing. The DM **102** preferably also controls the attitude of both RV **100** and HST **50** throughout the servicing phase of the mission, except when the EM **104** enters into a contingency safehold status. This safehold status preferably is entered if communication is lost between the DM **102** and the EM **104**, but may also be entered if another unsafe condition is detected or if commanded by the ground operator. Further, the EM **104** ACE software can provide nominal attitude control during EM **104** separation and de-orbit. In order to establish positive

control, the EM **104** computer will assume attitude control of the RV **100**/HST **50** stack just prior to separation.

[0117] An embodiment of the EM **104** propulsion subsystem includes a number of RCS thrusters coupled to four large primary thrusters. In one embodiment of the invention, the EM **104** propulsion system is only used during mission phases involving the RV **100** as a whole, and, after separation, is used for EM **104** controlled reentry and/or rendezvous with another satellite. One skilled in the art will appreciate that the RCS thrusters and momentum management hardware can point the RV **100** to the correct attitude in response to the GN&C commands received from the DM **102** and the primary thrusters will perform the large delta-v burns required for rendezvous operations with HST **50**. The RCS and momentum management hardware will be used during proximity operations to bring the RV **100** into position for HST **50** capture.

[0118] Post-capture, this propulsion system preferably is used to maintain the attitude of the RV **100**/HST **50** combined vehicle. Upon completion of servicing, the EM **104** may separate from the DM **102** and perform a controlled reentry and/or second rendezvous using these RCS thrusters for pointing and the primary thrusters for any large delta-v burns. The current preference is that EM **104** will carry 4800 lbs of hydrazine fuel distributed among five tanks. Thruster impingement will be controlled to reduce contamination and attitude disturbances to reasonable levels established in the art. In another embodiment, the EM **104** propulsion system is made up of four 100 lb, four 20 lb and 36 7 lb thrusters. One of skill in the art will recognize that a wide variety of thruster sizes and combinations can alternately be used without deviating from the scope of the present invention.

[0119] Preferably, the EM **104** C&DH functions to collect and downlink telemetry, collect and downlink video, receive and process spacecraft and robot commands and perform EM **104** separation and de-orbit tasks. The C&DH communication board (not shown) provides a preferred S-band uplink with a nominal 16 Kbps command rate and a 2 Kbps command rate contingency mode. The EM **104** C&DH in one embodiment can service up to 16 hardware discrete commands. The S-band downlink rates are preferably 2, 4, 8 and 16 Kbps, where 8 Kbps is the nominal rate. Ku-band downlink rate preferably is approximately 50 Mbps. The Ku-band downlink may be Reed-Solomon encoded, although one skilled in the art will recognize that other types of encoding may also be used without changing the scope of this invention. Furthermore, all data preferably is delivered to the Ku-band receiver within 200 ms of generation. This C&DH embodiment preferably also provides a continuous command stream at a rate of 10 Hz to the RS **106**. In one embodiment, the C&DH main components are a RAD750 processor board, RS interface card, S-band communication card, Ku-band card and a low voltage power supply card.

[0120] The EM **104** communications system preferably contains an S-band system using two multi-mode transceivers routed to a pair of Low Gain Antennas (LGA) for command uplink and telemetry transmission at low data rates through the TDRS system. In addition, the preferred system also contains a pair of Ku-band transmitters and steerable High Gain Antennas (HGA) to transmit real-time video and high-rate engineering telemetry through TDRS.

[0121] The EM **104** S-band system through the TDRS system is preferably capable of command reception at 2

Kbps and 16 Kbps, and will transmit telemetry at between 2 and 16 Kbps, while the EM **104** Ku-band system preferably transmits channeled video and telemetry at 50 Mbps and 128 Kbps, respectively. The EM **104** S-band system through the Ground Network/Deep Space Network will be capable of command reception at 2 Kbps and transmit telemetry at between 4 and 16 Kbps.

[0122] The mechanical subsystem of the EM **104** preferably includes four main sections, namely structure, mechanisms, solar array, and high gain antenna systems. Preferably, structures include propulsion, avionics, and robotic and instrument modules. One skilled in the art will understand that the propulsion module houses propulsion tanks, valves, plumbing, and fill and drain valves, while the avionics module houses batteries and electronics boxes, except for placement of critical GN&C sensors and actuators. Also, the majority of the harnesses preferably are housed in this section. In one embodiment, the robot and instrument module houses replacement instruments for HST **50**, such as the Wide Field Camera 3 (WFC**3**), Cosmic Origins Spectrograph (COS), and Fine Guidance Sensors (FGS), as well as the Dexterous Robot **120**, the GA **108**, conduits, tools, and tool caddies. Each of these components will be better described hereafter.

[0123] The mechanisms subsystem preferably includes the compartment door mechanisms and orbit replacement instrument (ORI) stowage bays. In one embodiment, the WFC**3**, COS and FGS stowage bays are designed to provide adequate mechanical isolation during all phases of the RV **100** mission. The EM **104** solar array subsystem preferably provides solar shadowing protection to the ORIs and exposed HST **50** cavities during transport and servicing activities. This is done while minimizing the shadowing impingement onto the HST **50** solar arrays. One embodiment of the solar array for the EM **104** is a 14-string daisy-style solar array providing shadowing across the servicing workspace and recharging batteries for the EM **104** during servicing activities. Ten Li-ion batteries are preferred that provide EM **104** power of approximately 3700 W (payload is about 3000 W) during servicing.

[0124] An embodiment of the HGA subsystem has an azimuth motor with 360 degree rotational freedom coupled with a ±90 degree elevation motor which allows the EM **104** HGAs complete hemispheric visibility.

[0125] In another embodiment, the EM's electrical power subsystem switches the primary DC power to the EM **104** actuators, mechanisms, sensors, antennas, DR **120**, Grapple Arm **108**, and electronics boxes. One skilled in the art will understand that the EM **104** electrical power system measures and reports voltages, currents and status of components connected to the EM power bus. In one embodiment, electrical power may be provided for operation of about 200 temperature sensors and approximately 22 heaters.

[0126] Referring more specifically to FIGS. **14** and **15**, the RS **106** is now discussed. Preferably, RS **106** is housed in the EM **104** and comprises generally the GA **108** and the DR **120**, along with appropriate control electronics, such as a vision system (VS), tools and tool caddies for servicing HST **50**.

[0127] Preferably, the GA **108** is a multi-axis manipulator with a Grapple Arm End Effector (GAEE) **122** on one end

providing a power/data/video interface. One embodiment calls for the GA **108** to be responsible for capturing HST **50** via either of the two grapple fixtures (in conjunction with GN&C system), as shown in FIGS. **9** and **10**, and for positioning the DR **120** for servicing as required. This preferred GA **108** provides six degrees of freedom and a 39 ft. total reach (one 20 ft and one 19 ft link). There are preferably two cameras **126** and **128** on the elbow **124** and two cameras **130** and **132** on the GAEE **122**. The GA **108** of this embodiment weighs about 1500 lb and will operationally require approximately 210 W. peak, 100 W. average, power. One of skill in the art will recognize that the foregoing robot system is merely exemplary and a variety of robotic mechanisms and techniques known in the art could be substituted without departing the scope of the present invention.

[0128] One embodiment of DR **120**, illustrated in FIG. **15**, is responsible for servicing HST **50**, in conjunction with the GA **108** and attendant tools. It is comprised of dual manipulator arms **134** and **136** (about 11 ft total length each) with 7 degrees of freedom each, multiple camera units with lights, and an Orbital Replacement Unit (ORU) Tool Change-out Mechanism (OTCM) **138** or end-effector (not shown) on the end. The DR **120** of one embodiment weighs approximately 2950 lb. and will operationally require 2000 W. peak, 1700 W. average, power. The size, weight, and power requirements for the DR and its robotic mechanisms may be varied to accommodate servicing missions on satellites of various sizes and complexities

[0129] Preferably, the VS is responsible for and displays situational awareness during RV **100** mission phases. The VS provides an integrated camera and video delivery system comprising a series of cameras, lights, and electronic boxes that reside at various locations on the RS **106** and the RV **100**. The VS provides visual verification and active vision, using still and streaming video from its complement of cameras, feed back for automated sequencing, manual and scripted servicing, visual inputs to AI logic, and error model correction, and HST **100** inspection and survey activities.

[0130] One embodiment of a VS complement of cameras includes eight on the robot torso, eight on the OTCM **138**, two LIDAR cameras, two on the GA **108** elbow **124**, two on the GAEE **122**, two on the bay and about fourteen situational awareness cameras for a total of 38 cameras. Those skilled in the art will realize that each of these cameras is connected to a Video Control Unit (VCU). The VCU collects the video data from the active cameras connected to it and converts the raw image data, preferably to JPEG2000. The JPEG2000 format includes any compression, if selected.

[0131] Moreover, one embodiment of the VS contains a command and telemetry interface to the EM **104** C&DH that enables VS control, configuration, state of health and video distribution. Remote commands may be used to control power, frame rates, and compression ratios of each camera. Two additional stereoscopic cameras may be used to provide detailed worksite views and support machine vision function for worksite localization that allow the remote operators to monitor robot configuration, servicing task operations, and other activities

[0132] Looking now at the method of carrying out the invention, one skilled in the art will readily observe that the preferred objectives of the methods for the exemplary HST servicing mission are threefold:

[0133] To enable the safe disposal of the HST **50** when it reaches the end of its useful life.

[0134] To implement life extension measures that will assure HST **50** mission life for at least five years beyond the completion of the servicing mission.

[0135] To enhance the scientific capability by installing the scientific instruments planned for SM-4.

[0136] One embodiment of the invention meets these objectives as follows. Towards meeting the first objective, the DM **102** may to be attached to the HST **50** for later use as a de-orbit vehicle. To meet the second, a new set of gyroscopes, batteries, and a replacement FGS may be installed. And, to meet the third objective, the WFC3 and COS instruments may be installed. Each of these procedures, as well as a preferred over-all mission procedure, will be described in greater detail.

[0137] One embodiment of a Robotic Servicing and De-Orbiting Mission (RSDM) mission may be defined by the following phases or steps: launch, RV commissioning, pursuit, proximity operations, approach and capture, servicing, EM ejection and disposal, science operations, and HST/DM disposal. The description that follows will specifically discuss a servicing mission to HST **50**. However, one of skill in the art will recognize that the principles disclosed herein can be applied to servicing and/or de-orbiting of a variety of spacecraft in orbit around the earth or elsewhere in space. It will also be clear to one of skill in the art that the robotic servicing and de-orbit phases may be implemented independently; servicing without de-orbit or de-orbit without servicing may be implemented for a particular spacecraft if desired. If the target satellite is in an orbit, such as geostationary, where de-orbit may not be practical or cost effective, a de-orbit module can be used to place the target satellite into a disposal orbit, for example above the geostationary band. The following table summarizes each phase of the exemplary mission.

TABLE 4

Phase	Duration	Phase Begins	Phase Ends	Highlights
Launch	2-3 hours	Launch	RV in a power positive configuration	Launch, stage 1 ignition/separation, stage 2 ignition/separation, RV separation, EM establishes power positive attitude with solar panels deployed.
RV Commissioning	14 days	RV has established power positive configuration.	Checkout activities complete.	Checkout RV systems and GA.
Pursuit	2-12 days	RV commissioning completed.	Ends just prior to maneuver to the safety ellipse.	Includes orbital maneuvers to bring the RV to the final co-elliptic orbit within relative navigation sensor range of the HST.
Proximity Operations	1-2 days	Begins with the maneuver from the final co-elliptic orbit to the Safety Ellipse.	Ends just prior to leaving the final safety ellipse.	Enter safety ellipse, survey HST, HST and RV preparations for capture.
Approach and Capture	2 hours	RV maneuvers away from the safety ellipse to the capture axis.	Ends with the completion of the mechanical berthing/docking of the RV to HST with the mated spacecraft (RV/HST) in a preferred sun-pointing attitude.	Deploy GA, grapple HST, position HST in berthing latches and partially close latches, maneuver stack to sunpoint attitude, complete latch closure.
Servicing	30+ days	Mechanical docking complete.	Ends when the EM receives authority to take control of the HST/RV stack prior to separation.	Battery augmentation, WFC3/RGA II, COS, FGS, reboost (optional).
EM Ejection & Disposal	4 days	EM takes control of HST/RV stack from the DM.	Completion of controlled disposal of the EM.	Separate EM from DM, perform evasive maneuvers, perform de-orbit

TABLE 4-continued

Phase	Duration	Phase Begins	Phase Ends	Highlights
				burns, impact in Pacific. EM continues this phase while HST/DM enters science operations.
Science Operations	5+ years	EM ejection from HST/DM stack.	End of science observations and end of life testing.	Verification, nominal science operations.
HST/DM disposal	4 days	End of science operations.	Safe disposal of HST/DM.	De-orbit burns, impact.

[0138] In one embodiment, RV **100** and HST **50** each have their own safing systems. Accordingly, prior to initiation of the capture phase, the HST safing system is disabled to prevent any unintended change in attitude or solar array motion. The system will remain disabled until after the EM **104** has separated from the DM **102**, although some HST **50** tests may be enabled during the mission to protect against inadvertent solar array motion. The following table shows which vehicle has primary safing authority for each mission phase in one embodiment.

TABLE 5

Vehicle Configuration	Mission Phase	Software Safing Strategy	Hardware Safehold
RV	Launch, Pursuit and Proximity Operations	DM Software Safe Hold, Mission Manager Abort	EM
RV	Capture	DM (Use Redundancy), Mission Manager Abort	EM
RV + HST	Servicing	DM Software Safe Hold	EM
EM	Ejection	EM	EM
EM	EM De-orbit	EM	EM
DM + HST	Science	HST with DM backup	HST PSEA DM SHM Disabled
DM + HST	HST De-orbit	DM Software Safe Hold, Mission Manager Abort	DM

[0139] Preferably, the DM **102** will utilize previously known Mission Manager (MM) software for most Guidance, Navigation and Control (GN&C) commanding requirements, although one skilled in the art will observe that other software can used to accomplish this function without departing from the scope of this invention. MM allows the RV **100** to implement the GN&C sequences autonomously with optional remote intervention programmed in at key points. FIG. **16** graphically depicts the MM concept. As indicated, this software utilizes task lists that are tied to the mission phases as discussed in the following sections. MM may hold up to five nominal and five abort task lists that are uploaded one at a time from the remote operator, each containing up to 100 tasks per list, although only one task list will be active at any given time. When received by MM, a remote-specified task list preferably is validated, and then

moved to the specified task list slot. Each task in a nominal task list preferably has a corresponding abort task list slot. If an abort occurs during a task, the associated abort task list will be initiated for the abort sequence. A task list preferably is not allowed to span mission phases, and a separate GN&C remote command is required in order to change a mission phase. Each task within a task list may contain an Authority To Proceed (ATP) flag that, if set, will allow that task to proceed to the subsequent task in the list upon nominal completion. If the ATP is not set (i.e. ATP flag=0), the task will suspend upon nominal completion and await explicit authorization to proceed from the remote operator. If desired, a second task list may be set to "pending," such that it will automatically execute pending nominal completion of the active task list. Preferably, only one task list can be defined to be active, and only one task list can be defined to be pending at any given time.

[0140] Referring now to FIGS. **17**A and **17**B, the preferred launch phase starts at T-0 and terminates when the RV **100** achieves a power positive configuration after separation from the second stage. FIG. **17**A is a summary of the launch phase and FIG. **17**B shows a typical ascent for an Atlas V expendable launch vehicle **52** engaged in a low earth orbit (LEO) mission. Based on the size of the RV **100**, an Evolved Expendable Launch Vehicle (EELV) **52**, i.e. an Atlas V or a Delta IV rocket with a five meter fairing could be used.

[0141] The major systems of the RV **100** preferably are configured for launch as follows:

[0142] DM **102** C&DH prime on

[0143] EM **104** C&DH prime and redundant on

[0144] All receivers on

[0145] ACE box off

[0146] Reaction wheels off

[0147] The launch dispersions for the ELV **52** currently provide the following preferred accuracies: altitude ±10 km and inclination ±0.04°. In order to further protect HST **50** from the RV **100** and to provide time for vehicle checkout after separation from the ELV **52** upper stage, the following conditions are preferred in one embodiment:

[0148] Circular orbit 20 km below the altitude of HST **50** at the time of launch.

[0149] Initial in-plane separation (phase angle) of 0-360 degrees, which varies with launch epoch.

[0150] Right ascension difference to target HST **50** plane at end of pursuit phase:

[0151] Allows relative drift of ascending node due to differential gravitation (J_2).

[0152] A function of initial phase angle, semi-major axis difference and time to rendezvous.

[0153] This drift constrains maximum time before first pursuit phase maneuver.

[0154] The difference in semi-major axes will drive a differential rate of regression of the Right Ascension of the Ascending Node (RAAN). Consequently, the target orbit may include a RAAN offset such that the orbit planes align at the nominal end of the pursuit phase. This differential RAAN constrains the allowable time before the first maneuver is executed; the first burn is nominally at launch +14 days.

[0155] Preferably, all activities in the launch phase are nominally to be performed autonomously, meaning that each task is carried out without direct human intervention. In one embodiment, each task may be pre-scripted. In another embodiment, at least some of the tasks may be initiated by Artificial Intelligence (AI) logic resident in RV **100**. As in the case of pre-scripted commands, a capability for the remote operator to override any AI-generated commands may be provided. Alternately, the AI logic may propose a course of action that must be concurred in by the remote operator before being executed. In yet another embodiment, the remote operator pre-loads the GN&C launch task list into the DM **102**, and after separation from the ELV **52**, a breakwire—based DM **102** transition from idle mode to safe mode occurs. This also initiates the execution of the launch task list. The following events then may occur within the EM **102**:

[0156] Turn on S-band transmitter

[0157] Turn on ACE

[0158] Power on the reaction wheels

[0159] Turn on the catalyst-bed heaters

[0160] Delay ten minutes

[0161] Open propulsion system valves

[0162] Activate thruster power bus

[0163] Start solar array deployment sequence (except the sections that cover the stowed GA **108**)

[0164] Next, the RV **100** preferably uses the reaction wheels to damp any tip off rates and then maneuvers to a −H1 sunpoint attitude. Torquer bars preferably are used to dump momentum. If the wheels saturate, the DM **102** preferably activates momentum damping using thrusters, after allowing sufficient time for heaters to warm up the catalyst-beds. In another embodiment, a momentum wheel or wheels may be used to manage the tip off rates and to control the pointing attitude of RV **100**.

[0165] RV commissioning preferably begins with the RV **100** in a power positive attitude with the EM **104** daisy solar array deployed, and ends when checkout of the RV **100** is complete and the maneuvers to initiate pursuit of the HST **50** are about to occur. FIG. **18** is a summary of the RV commissioning phase.

[0166] Once on orbit, RV systems preferably are activated and verified for proper performance. Commanding comes from a combination of real-time and stored commands. In one embodiment, this process takes approximately 14 days and is summarized as follows:

[0167] RV **100** orbit determination.

[0168] RV **100** GN&C checkout.

[0169] Activate Ku-band downlink.

[0170] Check out DM **102** sensors.

[0171] Activate LIDAR.

[0172] Activate and checkout GA **108**.

[0173] The objective of these tests is to verify proper operation of the GA **108** and measure performance that could not be verified directly on the remote station before it is used near HST **50**. Each test includes aliveness, functional and zero-gravity performance tests. Preferably, the pursuit phase begins after the RV commissioning is completed and terminates just prior to the maneuver to place the RV **100** on the safety ellipse. All the GN&C activities preferably are contained in the pursuit phase task list and are performed autonomously with appropriate Authority to Proceed (ATP) points for any actions that require a remote command to authorize continuation of the task list. FIG. **19** is a summary of the pursuit phase.

[0174] The pursuit phase preferably includes a number of burns, detailed in the table below. Preferably, the EM **104** provides the propulsion during this phase using its RCS with the DM **102** providing the vehicle navigation control. In one embodiment, the first two burns are executed to raise the co-elliptic orbit to 5 km below HST **50** and are executed after the 14 day commissioning phase. This slows the relative in-plane drift between the RV **100** and HST **50**. Initial sensor acquisition preferably happens at this point. As RV **100** closes on HST **50** from below and behind, two more maneuvers preferably are made to raise the orbit to about 1 km below HST **50**. Again the relative in-plane drift is slowed. A maneuver may then be made to correct for any out of plane error that may be due to launch dispersion or timing errors of the first two orbit boosts of the RV **100**. The acquisition of HST **50** with relative navigation sensors such as LIDAR may now happen as RV **100** approaches within 5 km of HST **50**, still from below and behind. After HST **50** acquisition, the RV **100** can now get nearly continuous range measurements to HST **50**.

TABLE 6

Maneuver	MET	Action	Delta V m/s	ft/s	Fuel Mass Consumed kg	lbm	Contingency?
1	Launch plus 14 days	Remove inclination error (max 0.04 deg)	5.3	17.4	37.9	83.6	Launch dispersion
		Remove RAAN error from 2 weeks inclination error	2.2	7.2	15.7	34.6	Launch dispersion
		Remove RAAN error from HST state error	0.8	2.6	5.7	12.6	Launch dispersion
2-3	Launch plus 14 days	Remove altitude error from launch	5.5	18.0	39.2	86.4	Launch dispersion
4-5	Launch plus 14-30 days	Achieve coelliptic 5 km below HST	8.2	26.9	58.5	128.9	
6	Launch plus 16-31 days	Remove remaining out of plane error	0.5	1.6	3.5	7.8	
7-8	Launch plus 17-33	Achieve coelliptic 1 km below HST	2.2	7.2	15.6	34.3	
9-10	As required	Achieve coelliptic 1 km above HST	1.1	3.6	7.8	17.2	Launch dispersion or failure to acquire rel-nav
Total (no margin included)			25.8	84.6	184	405	

[0175] The proximity operations phase preferably begins with the maneuver from the final co-elliptic orbit to the safety ellipse. And the proximity operation phase ends just prior to the maneuver to leave the final safety ellipse to initiate the capture phase. Commanding of the RV **100** in this phase is autonomous with ATP points. FIG. **20** is a summary of the proximity operations phase.

[0176] In one embodiment, as RV **100** passes below HST **50**, the LIDAR acquires HST **50** and a sequence of small

intersect coincide with maximum RV **100**/HST **50** radial separation. The relative along-track RV **100**/HST **50** separation can be controlled by periodic small maneuvers (low delta-v). Another advantage of the WSE is that it allows a thorough inspection of HST **50** as RV **100** circumnavigates it, thereby increasing the ability to observe HST **50**. If the LIDAR does not acquire the HST **50**, then the RV **100** passes safely under HST **50** and the maneuver plan will be revised. Burns for this phase are detailed in the following table:

TABLE 7

Maneuver	Duration	Action	Delta V m/s	ft/s	Fuel Mass Consumed kg	lbm	Contingency?
1-3	45 min	Target safety ellipse 1 km ahead of HST	0.59	1.94	4.12	9.09	
		Midcourse correction	0.10	0.33	0.70	1.54	
		Achieve safety ellipse 1 km ahead of HST	0.39	1.28	2.72	6.01	
	as required	Recover to 1 km above or below HST, approach HSt and repeat 1-3	2.77	9.09	19.33	42.62	Failure to achieve safety ellipse
4-11	18 hrs	Maintain SE 1 km ahead for 18 hrs (TBR)	0.03	0.11	0.23	0.51	
12-17	18 hrs	Walking safety ellipse to center HST	0.05	0.17	0.36	0.80	
as required	10 days	Remove relative drift and maintain HST-centered safety ellipse (every 3 orbits for 10 days)	0.44	1.44	3.07	6.77	Provides 10 days on SE to determine HST relative attitude state
Total (no margin included)			3.30	10.81	30.54	50.70	

maneuvers is performed in order to put RV **100** on a 100 m×50 m×50 m Fehse-Naasz Walking Safety Ellipse (WSE) about HST **50**. The WSE is a natural relative motion, best described as a path along the surface of a cylinder with an axis along the HST **50** velocity vector. Consequently, the WSE is preferably strictly non-interfering with HST **50** as the points where the RV **100** and HST **50** orbital planes

[0177] In one embodiment, the approach and capture phase begins when RV **100** leaves the WSE and terminates with the completion of the mechanical berthing/docking of the RV **100** to HST **50** with the mated spacecraft in a preferred sun-pointing attitude. FIG. **21** is a summary of the approach and capture phase. Commanding of the RV **100** during this phase will be primarily autonomous with ATP points programmed in.

[0178] In another embodiment, the approach and capture phase begins with a sequence of maneuvers that puts the RV 100 on the capture axis of HST 50. The capture axis is currently preferred to be the –V1, or in other words the negative end of HST's main longitudinal axis. In another embodiment, the –V3, or in other words negative lateral axis might be used since it has certain advantages in some situations (notably GS 108 reach). The RV 100 preferably maintains its position on the capture axis at a fixed range (nominally 30 meters, but certainly outside the geometry of HST 50) by matching rates with HST 50. Once the RV 100/HST 50 relative rates are stabilized, and authority to proceed is granted, the RV 100 will descend down the capture axis to a stand-off distance ~1.7 m (for –V1 approach) from the capture target.

[0179] The preferred plan for the capture phase is dependent on the state of HST 50 at the time of capture. If HST 50 is not functioning, or non-cooperative, the nominal capture strategy will be as described above, with RV 100 approaching HST 50 along a potentially tumbling capture axis. If HST 50 is functioning and cooperative, the nominal capture strategy will be a traditional approach approximately along the R Bar (from the center of the earth outwards) to HST 50 in an inertial attitude configuration, with HST 50 pointing along the radial direction at the time of capture. This approach is accomplished by performing a sequence of predominantly velocity direction maneuvers to allow RV 100 to approach HST 50 from the nadir direction while minimizing thruster plume contamination of HST 50. FIGS. 22A and 22B show a typical capture maneuver profile. The two tables immediately below show the maneuver plans for a controlled and uncontrolled HST50, respectively.

TABLE 8

| Maneuver | Duration | Action | Delta V | | Fuel Mass Consumed | |
			m/s	ft/s	kg	lbm
R-Bar approach	30 min	Transfer along R-Bar to 30 m-V1 hold from SE below HST	0.56	1.84	3.88	8.55
LVLH Stationkeep	20 min	20 minute hold at 30 m-V1 separation	0.14	0.46	0.98	2.16
HST Stationkeep	10 min	Approach to 10 m hold point	0.10	0.33	0.67	1.48
HST Stationkeep	10 min	10 minute hold at 10 m hold point	0.05	0.16	0.52	1.15
HST Stationkeep	10 min	Approach to 1 m hold point	0.04	0.13	0.37	0.82
HST Stationkeep	10 min	10 minute hold at 1 m hold point	0.02	0.07	0.19	0.42
HST Stationkeep	10 min	retreat to 10 meter hold point	0.08	0.26	0.78	1.72
HST Stationkeep	10 min	hold at 10 meter hold point for 10 minutes	0.16	0.52	1.56	3.44
2 burn	45 min	Safe return to safety ellipse	1.12	3.67	7.81	17.22
Total per capture attempt (no margin included)			2.27	7.45	16.76	36.95
Total for 4 capture attempts (no margin included)			9.08	29.79	67.04	147.80

[0180]

TABLE 9

| Maneuver | Duration | Action | Delta V | | Fuel Mass Consumed | | Contingency? |
			m/s	ft/s	kg	lbm	
2 burn	45 min	Maneuver to predicted docking axis from SE	1.50	4.92	10.47	23.08	
HST Stationkeep	20 min	20 minute hold at 30 m-V1 separation	4.00	13.12	39.02	86.04	
HST Stationkeep	10 min	Approach to 10 m hold point	1.90	6.23	18.55	40.90	
HST Stationkeep	10 min	10 minute hold at 10 m hold point	0.90	2.95	8.79	19.38	
HST Stationkeep	10 min	Approach to 1 m hold point	0.40	1.31	3.90	8.60	
HST Stationkeep	10 min	10 minute hold at 1 m hold point	0.20	0.66	1.95	4.30	

TABLE 9-continued

Maneuver	Duration	Action	Delta V		Fuel Mass Consumed		Contingency?
			m/s	ft/s	kg	lbm	
HST Stationkeep	10 min	retreat to 10 meter hold point	0.40	1.31	3.90	8.60	Failed capture
HST Stationkeep	10 min	hold at 10 meter hold point for 10 minutes	0.90	2.95	8.78	19.36	Failed capture
2 burn	45 min	Safe return to safety ellipse	1.50	4.92	10.44	23.03	Failed capture
Total per capture attempt (no margin included)			11.70	38.39	105.82	233.29	
Total for 4 capture attempts (no margin included)			46.80	153.54	423.28	933.17	

[0181] At the hold point, the RV **100** preferably deploys the GA **108**, as shown in FIG. **9**, and captures either of the two grapple fixtures **140** located on the –V3 side of HST **50**, as shown in FIG. **10**. The preferred candidate vehicle control configurations would have HST **50** in an inertial hold (if the PCS system is active) or tumbling, and the RV **100** going to free drift once the GAEE **122** is inside a predefined capture box **142**. The capture box **142** defines a set of conditions (position, orientation) within which the GA **108** can capture a grapple target. The GA **108** preferably will be positioned so that a GAEE **122** camera **130** or **132** is centered on the capture box **142**. Capture is preferably planned so as to occur during orbit night so the GA **108** lights can be used to control the lighting. Once the command to initiate the final capture sequence has been given, the sequence preferably requires no operator intervention. However, manual override by ground control can always be done if necessary at any point.

[0182] In one embodiment, the RV **100** will notify the GA **108** when the grapple fixture **140** enters the specified capture box **142** with the required rates. The on-board vision software can then acquire the target and communicate its status to the RV **100**. At that point the attitude control may be turned off to avoid inducing disturbance on the GA **108**, and the GA **108** then moves to put the GAEE **122** on the grapple fixture **140**, snare the grapple or berthing pin **108**, and rigidize. The GA **108** will absorb residual relative vehicle rates. Subsequently, the GA **108** will apply its brakes and the RV **100** will null the combined vehicles rates to achieve a power positive, thermally stable, attitude profile. It may be necessary to maneuver the stack to a –V1 sunpointing attitude to charge the RV **50** batteries prior to berthing.

[0183] Once the rates have been nulled, the GA **108** will maneuver the HST **50** to a pre-defined pre-berth position relative to the RV **100**. The operator can validate the script to maneuver to the berthing position at the robotics console using script rehearsal software, or can manually maneuver to the berthing position. Preferably, the operator then will bring the HST **50** berthing pins **118** into the capture mechanism on the DM **102** using a combination of scripts and hand controller operations. The operator will then limp the GA **108** joints and allow the capture mechanism to complete the berthing sequence. Initially, the berthing latches preferably are not completely closed. But after a predetermined time to allow the mechanism to equilibrate thermally, the latches may be closed completely. In another embodiment, AI logic

on RV **100** can execute the capture/berthing process with or without oversight and/or intervention from a remote operator.

[0184] An alternate preferred method of capture is to dock directly to the HST **50** aft bulkhead at the berthing pins using a mechanism(s) on the RV **100**. The candidate vehicle control configurations could have HST **50** in an inertial hold (if the PCS system is active) or tumbling at a rate of up to 0.22 deg/sec per axis and the RV **100** remaining in an active control state through capture.

[0185] The HST **50** could be in one of several attitude control modes for the RSDM, with the status of the Rate Gyro Assemblies (RGA) being the primary determining factor. If three good RGAs remain, the HST **50** may be conducting normal science operations and the normal attitude control law can be used. In this scenario, science operations will be terminated at the beginning of proximity operations so the HST **50** can be prepared for capture and berthing. The science plan may include breakpoints at one day intervals so that science observations can be extended if proximity operations are delayed. In this case, the HGA booms will be retracted and the aperture door closed.

[0186] Given the history of the RGAs, it is quite possible that fewer than three healthy gyros will be available by the RSDM time frame. The HST Project is developing alternate attitude control modes for science that will allow control on two or one gyro(s). Therefore, if one of these modes is in use at the time, the HST could terminate science observations and remain in that control mode, either Magnetometer 2 Gyro (M2G) or Magnetometer 1 Gyro (M1G) mode. If no gyros remain, the HST **50** preferably will be in safemode. However, if inadequate hardware remains on HST **50** to perform an attitude control function, the RV **100** can still perform a capture either with the GA **108** or by direct docking. One of skill in the art will recognize that the above procedure can be modified to accommodate capture and service of three-axis stabilized, spin stabilized, or even satellites with non-functioning or partially disabled attitude control systems.

[0187] Preferably, the servicing phase begins once the RV **100** is completely berthed to the HST **50**, or other satellite to be serviced, and terminates when the EM **104** is given the control authority prior to EM **104** ejection. The hardware systems augmentation and science instrument change-outs may occur during this phase. During the servicing phase there preferably are no HST **50** maneuvers required, and thus, in a preferred embodiment, the RV **100** controls the combined vehicle attitude to maintain a power positive, thermally stable profile while accommodating any constraints that are imposed by the replacement instruments or apparatus, called Orbit Replacement Units (ORU). FIG. **23** summarizes the servicing phase.

[0188] The preferred servicing tasks are planned to extend the life of HST **50**, or other satellite to be serviced, and may provide enhanced science or other operational capabilities. To achieve these objectives the RS **106** carries out a series of tasks, as described hereafter. Preferably, any new hardware to be installed on HST **50** by the RS **106** is equipped with robot-friendly interfaces that allow the ORU Tool Change-out Mechanism (OTCM) **138** end effecter to directly grasp and handle the ORU, including the new science instruments to be installed and interfaces on the RV **100** to be actuated by the DR **120**. However, the HST **50** or other satellite to be serviced may not be equipped with the necessary handling interfaces for the DR **120** to manipulate it directly. To address this problem, a preferred suite of specialized tools (not shown) has been developed to create the environment necessary for the RS **120** to carry out the servicing tasks on HST. One skilled in the art will recognize that other specialized tools could be used in conjunction with the servicing of other satellites that would still fall within the purview of this invention. In one embodiment, the tools for use with the HST **50** include devices to open the aft shroud, the radial bay, and bay doors; tools to actuate the latches to release the science instruments and remove these instruments from HST **50**; and tools to mate and de-mate connectors, actuate bolts, and the like.

[0189] In addition to appropriate tools for the DR **120**, successful completion of the preferred servicing objectives may require that the remote operators receive visual confirmation of the tasks being performed. Therefore, a vision system comprising multiple cameras with various functions and specifications may be used to provide views of on board activities. In one embodiment, the preferred vision system, already described above, is integrated with the DR **120**, GA **108**, EM **104** and servicing tools.

[0190] One skilled in the art will understand that due to the potential for damage to detectors and thermal degradation of adhesives, the science instruments, and the open cavities in which they are mounted, preferably are protected from direct sun exposure. In one embodiment, the combination of shading from the EM **104** solar arrays, vehicle attitude, and robot positioning, meets the sun protection requirements. In addition, the translation paths taken by the RS **106** when moving instruments preferably will be bounded based on both sun protection and thermal constraints.

[0191] According to one embodiment, prior to using the DR **120** for servicing, the GA **108** retrieves the DR **120** from the EM **104**. The remote team then initiates a series of procedures to verify the performance of the DR **120** and the total RS **106** system. Preferably, the GA **108**, and the DR **120** arms, **134** and **136**, are moved sequentially. In one embodiment, the RS **106** control system does not allow simultaneous motion of any arms **108**, **134** or **136**. However, one skilled in the art will see that such simultaneous motion, and other types of synchronized motion, are contemplated by this invention and fall within its scope. Thus, according to one preferred embodiment, in order to move one of the arms GA **108**, **134** or **136**, motor power is disabled for the other

two. In this embodiment, removing motor power engages the brakes for that motor. Also, the command for putting on the brakes can be part of a script, or can be a single command issued from the remote operator, or can be part of an electrical or electromechanical interlock that automatically engages to prevent simultaneous motion of two or more of the arms GA **108**, **134** or **136**.

[0192] As indicated below, two tests preferably are carried out on the DR **120** to verify readiness, include the following steps.

DR Aliveness Test

[0193] Once the GA **108** and the DR **120** are mated, heater power is applied to the DR **120** until it reaches operating temperature. This can be verified via EM **104** bay temperature telemetry.

[0194] The DR **120** VCUs are powered and the flight software is loaded into the DR **120** flight computers.

[0195] Communication between the DR **120** computers and the VCUs is verified.

[0196] All DR **120** joints are verified by issuing commands for small, benign movements to each joint against the DR **120** launch locks.

[0197] The DR **120** down-locks are released and the DR **120** is retracted by the GA **108** from the EM **104** and moved to a hover position away from the structure.

DR Functional Test

[0198] A VCU test verifies the use of each DR **120** camera in still and streaming mode, as applicable. All DR **120** cameras **130** and **132** are tested in both still and streaming mode. In addition, all DR **120** light sources are tested, which ensure proper video and still photo capabilities for both teleoperation and supervised autonomy.

[0199] The joint range of motion is verified by commanding each joint through the widest practical range and polarity.

[0200] The dexterous motion of the DR **120** is verified by moving to several preplanned locations that are away from any hardware to test the inverse kinematics and singularity avoidance software. Verification is accomplished via joint angle telemetry and streaming video feeds.

[0201] Two performance tests are executed to verify the transient response of the DR **120** arms **134** and **136** in several poses and modes. Various disturbances are introduced and arm performance is verified via camera views and joint angle sensors. The first test, summarized in Table 10 below, is the DR transient response test. Each test category is repeated with the opposite DR **120** arm stabilized and free. The second performance test, summarized in Table 11 below, verifies GA **108** transient response while mated to the DR **120**.

[0202] The OTCM **138** cameras are calibrated using a calibration fixture on the task board. The DR **120** arms **134** and **136** then translate to the high hover position directly over the calibration fixture. Still images are downlinked and compared to expected image fidelity.

TABLE 10

Test Category	Arm Pose	DR Arm Mode	Disturbance Input	Objective
1	Various elbow joint	Position Hold	Fire Thruster	Damping,
2	angles	Brakes Engaged	Fire Thruster	natural
3	(outstretched, right angle, folded up)	Position hold	Arm slew (in free drift)	frequency, link flexibility, joint flexibility.
4	Stretched Out	Brakes Engaged	Fast arm slew (in free drift)	Stopping Distance
5	Various approaches to Task Board.	Tele-operated.	Small arm slew (in free drift)	Positioning resolution, ergonomics

[0203]

TABLE 11

Test Category	GA Arm Pose	GA Arm Mode	Disturbance Input	Objective
1	Two nominal	Position Hold	Fire Thruster	Damping,
2	servicing	Brakes Engaged	Fire Thruster	natural
3	configurations: One at EM, other at HST	Position hold	Arm slew (in free drift)	frequency, link flexibility, joint flexibility.
4	Stretched Out	Brakes Engaged	Fast arm slew (in free drift)	Stopping Distance
5	Various approaches to HST Bay.	Tele-operated.	Small arm slew (in free drift)	Positioning resolution, ergonomics

[0204] Once the OTCM **138** cameras are calibrated, a test of the Object Recognition and Pose Estimation (ORPE) system can be done. Preferably, a DR **120** arm **134** or **136** translates to a hover position directly over the task board test area. A stereo pair of images is taken by the calibrated and synchronized OTCM **138** cameras, and these images are then downlinked, and the OTCM offset from the calibration fixture is calculated. A command is then sent to correct the arm position for the offset. Once camera calibration is complete, the DR **120** is commanded to move by a predetermined amount, and the ORPE process is repeated to ensure ORPE functionality. Other tests that optionally may be done at this time include a force moment accommodation test (to compensate for forces and moments placed on the DR **120** when transporting tools and instruments during a task), an OTCM torquer test (to verify the running torque profile of the OTCM torque drive), and an OTCM umbilical connector checkout (to power payloads in its grasp via an umbilical connector) The preferred RS **106** motion might be categorized into two distinct types: constrained movement and free-space movement. Constrained motion is defined as any task that occurs in close proximity to other structures, including the EM **104**, DM **102** and HST **50**. Free-space motion is movement that takes place away from a structure, such as the movement of the RS **106** from one worksite location to another, or the movement of the DR **120** to a grapple fixture hover position. Preferably, the delineation between constrained and free-space motion is based on the maximum braking distances of the GA **108** and DR**120**.

[0205] Free-space motion is preferably done using supervised autonomy (described in more detail below). In this embodiment, GA **108** translations between the EM **104** and the HST **50** preferably are considered free-space motions. Other examples might include visual surveys and coarse positioning. In one embodiment, visual surveys will be required the first time the DR **120** visits a new site or when the DR **120** returns to the worksite after a significant absence. These return visual surveys are intended to be a quick visual check of the area with the purpose of verifying that there has been no change to the worksite. The visual surveys in general may be accomplished using any of the robot cameras, depending on the size of the area to be surveyed and lighting conditions.

[0206] In another embodiment, coarse positioning is described as a series of maneuvers to position the RS **108** for a task. The goal is to position one DR **120** end effecter approximately 30 cm from the intended interface, such as a micro-fixture, while the other DR **120** end effecter is positioned to obtain the necessary orthogonal camera views. FIG. **24** illustrates typical arm positioning after completion of coarse positioning. Preferably, this pose, at a distance of about 30 cm, is called a "high hover" position.

[0207] Constrained motion, according to one embodiment, is done using a combination of supervised autonomy and teleoperation, depending on the task interface (described hereafter). Fine positioning, contact operations and Object Recognition/Pose Estimation (ORPE) are all examples of constrained motion. Once the arms are sited using coarse positioning, ORPE can be used to account for any misalignment that may exist between the end effecter and the micro-fixture before contact is attempted. Preferably, arm motion is halted until this alignment is computed.

19

[0208] As one skilled in the art will realize, the fluidity of operations in manual mode is dependent on the latency of the system, which can be defined as the time from when the command to move is issued from the remote operator via a hand controller until the operator receives verification of the motion via video. The RV **100** on orbit and remote segments preferably are designed to minimize this latency and also to minimize variations in latency. According to one embodiment, this transmission latency is about two seconds.

[0209] Supervised autonomy as it applies to the RS **106**, is defined as the process of allowing the RS **106** to execute a sequence of instructions without intervention from the remote operator. Preferably, these instructions are packaged in a script that is generated remotely, and is uplinked to the RS **106** for execution upon ground command giving authority to proceed. Alternately, RS **106** may execute a series of operations based on AI logic that may be preprogrammed into RS **106** prior to launch or uplinks or updated once RS **106** in orbit. The remote operator maintains the ability to abort a script or AI initiated operation at any time.

[0210] In one embodiment, two remote operators work in tandem as an operator/co-operator team to "teleoperate" (manually control from afar) the RS **106**. Preferably, during tasks using supervised autonomy, both operators will monitor script/AI execution and resulting RS **106** motion. During teleoperation, or manual operation, the RS **106** primary operator preferably controls the GA **108** and both DR **106** arms **134** and **136** in sequence as required for a servicing task. The other operator preferably supports the primary RS **106** controller by navigating through the servicing procedures, helping to coordinate camera views, inspecting the worksite during a task, and so forth. One of skill in the art will recognize that the above division of labor between two operators and that a different division of tasks, completion of all tasks by one operator, or the use of more than two operators are all contemplated by the present invention and fall within its scope. Tele-operation is explained in greater detail hereafter.

[0211] It is preferred that supervised autonomy will be used for free-space motions. It is also preferably used for constrained motions when the target interface is robot-friendly, that is, when it is equipped with a fixture and a target designed for robot operations. Examples of robot-friendly operation include removing/returning tools from/to caddies, handling RV **100** hardware, and interfacing with HST **50** when tool design allows for self alignment onto the HST **50** interface without the use of robot-friendly targets, such as clamping a tool onto an HST handrail. A preferred decision tree for determining which tasks are not robot-friendly, and therefore done by teleoperation, is provided in FIG. **25**.

[0212] Supervised autonomy, according to one embodiment, relies on the ability to correlate RS **106** motion with an environment model at the remote station. This is done through the use of Object Recognition/Pose Estimation (ORPE), which is described as the process of detecting errors in and correcting the remote model upon which scripted commands are based. Preferably, after the RS **106** reaches the high hover position over a target area (about 30 cm), three sets of stereo images are taken with the cameras. These images are then downlinked to the remote station, preferably uncompressed (10 Mb for each set). Once the images are at the remote station, a team of image analysts studies the current position and orientation with respect to the target, and compares this with the expected model in the remote system software. This visual comparison shows any misalignment between the arm's coordinate frame and the target fixture coordinate frame.

[0213] According to one embodiment, if a misalignment is detected, a pose estimate is applied to the target coordinate frame via a transformation matrix. The new pose estimation for the robot is transmitted to the virtual environment software, which updates the target coordinate frame within the model. This updated model is then placed on the server at the remote station and a notification is sent to all remote workstations that a model correction has been made. Personnel at each workstation must acknowledge the change. Then a correction script is generated based on the new model. Before the script can be uplinked, it must be validated against the new model version number. Any attempt to validate a script with an old model will be rejected by the remote system software, thus allowing for an extra check of the model. Once the script is validated, it is loaded to the spacecraft and executed. FIGS. **26A**, **26B** and **26C** illustrate the alignment before and after the correction is applied. One of skill in the art will recognize that it also is possible to perform that above model correction using processing on board RS **106**. In one embodiment, the environmental model is stored on the RS **106** and the correlation of RS **106** motion with that model may be automatically initiated by an on board processor based on a command from the remote station, a preloaded script, or AI logic resident in the on board processor.

[0214] The arm then preferably moves to a new hover position in alignment with the target and the task continues. In accordance with this embodiment, if the position and/or orientation errors detected by ORPE are unexpectedly large, a script simulation, or rehearsal, may be required at the remote station prior to uplink. If the errors are determined on board RS **106**, the on board processor can run a simulated rehearsal or notify the ground operator of the need to perform a script simulation at the remote station.

[0215] One preferred ORPE process can take anywhere from 10 to 15 minutes, depending on image quality and the amount of correction needed. One skilled in the art will understand that lighting is important for ORPE to function properly. Thus, the preferred lighting system used to illuminate the worksites is optimized to provide sharp contrasts that create the ideal images for used by ORPE software.

[0216] As indicated earlier, a preferred RS **106** can also be operated via manual control, also called teleoperation. An operator at a remote location monitors the environment via video downlink and moves the RS **106** preferably using joystick control. Deflection of the hand controllers directly results in RS **106** movement.

[0217] This mode of operational control can be used as an alternative to supervised autonomy for a given task and is the preferred primary method for positioning the DR **106** when the interface being engaged is not designed for robot use, as, for example, in the case of installation of handling tools on the science instruments for removal from HST **50**. In one embodiment, two hand controllers located on the remote control station are used to move the arms via rate commands, meaning that the amount of controller deflection equates to how fast the arm moves. Moreover, these commands can be scalable so the same amount of deflection of the controllers can generate large motion if the arms are far from structure, or small motion if the task being carried out requires very fine positioning. During teleoperations, the operator preferably relies primarily on streaming video from a variety of cameras, including the arm's cameras, to detect misalignments and position the DR **106** or a tool in the correct location.

[0218] Therefore, teleoperator commands are preferably verified visually. Whenever possible or practical the arm **134** and **136** cameras will offer an orthogonal view of the interface to be grasped, while cameras located on the DR **106** body provide situational awareness views of the worksite. Preferably, camera switching will be done via a voice-loop request from the teleoperators at the remote station to camera operators at a separate vision system workstation. In a preferred embodiment, the switch between scripted and manual modes can be carried out quickly and easily by commanding a mode change to the RS **106** avionics and configuring the remote station for commanding via the hand controllers.

[0219] One skilled in the art will appreciate that the servicing tasks are preferably choreographed such that they can be carried out using only one DR **106** arm **134** or **136**, thereby allowing the other arm to serve as a stabilization point at a worksite (using appropriate stabilization interfaces). One embodiment makes use of this feature for servicing tasks where the dynamics of the system cause 1) inadequate positioning resolution with respect to task alignment requirements, 2) excessive overshoot during positioning or stored energy release with respect to access envelopes, 3) excessive settling time with respect to allocated task durations, or 4) excessive system deflection when force is applied with respect to task alignment requirements. The use of stabilization in this embodiment may decrease task completion times in some cases.

[0220] For each servicing task, a number of tools may be required to interface with HST **50**, or other satellite serviced, to overcome the fact that the satellite may not be equipped with robot-friendly interfaces. For example, in one embodiment, tools are used to open HST's aft shroud and radial bay doors, de-mate and mate connectors, and drive instrument latches. These tools preferably are stowed on the EM **104** in stowage compartments, although it will be recognized that tools could also be stowed on the DM **102**. Tools needed for each servicing task are preferably grouped together and placed onto a caddy prior to launch. For example, the tools needed to open the aft shroud doors are all located on one caddy, and the tools needed to carry out the servicing tasks on instruments are in another caddy. One preferred tool caddy includes a plate upon which the tools are attached with release mechanisms and targets that allow for easy removal and replacement of tools by the DR **120**. These caddies save time because the RS **106** does not need to travel back and forth to the EM **104** to retrieve tools. Instead, as part of the setup for a servicing task, the RS **106** removes the entire caddy from its stowage location on the EM **104**, transports the caddy to HST **50**, and mounts it onto the worksite preferably using a Foot Restraint (FR) socket. Tools can be used multiple times during servicing and hence each tool can be easily located by the DR **120** cameras

through the use of visual targets and released from the caddy or replaced by incorporating micro-fixtures into their design.

[0221] In one preferred embodiment, certain servicing activities can continue through a loss of communications (command and telemetry) between the remote station and the RV **100**. For example, during a TDRS Zone of Exclusion (ZOE), where no TDRS satellite is in sight, operations can be planned accordingly. Thus, approaching a ZOE, a scripted command can be sent with the resulting task continuing through the ZOE. Alternately, AI logic on board RV **100** or any of its components can continue to initiate tasks autonomously through the ZOE. Preferably, the AI logic can be preprogrammed with a plurality of safety criteria that must be met before initiating particular autonomous tasks. In one embodiment, one set of safety criteria can be established to govern autonomous action when communications are available, i.e. supervised autonomy, and a second, preferably more stringent, set of safety criteria may be established for autonomous actions when communications are not available, i.e. unsupervised autonomy.

[0222] In the event of a temporary loss of signal (LOS), teleoperated arm movements will stop immediately with a loss of commanding. Supervised autonomous movements on the other hand have the capability to be scripted to either continue through the LOS, as with a ZOE, or stop immediately, depending on the task. Scripted activities are preferably evaluated on a case by case basis to determine the level of risk associated with the completion of the activities while there are no remote communications. In either scenario, the robot reports to the remote station upon retrieval of signal.

[0223] In one preferred embodiment, after the servicing is concluded and before the EM **104** separates from the DM **102**, the serviced satellite may be boosted to a higher orbit if its orbit has deteriorated significantly. Reboost, in this case, would preferably be performed using the EM **104** propulsion system. In another embodiment, the satellite being serviced may be refueled by the EM **104** prior to separation to further extend the satellite's useful life.

[0224] The EM **104** ejection and disposal phase begins, according to one embodiment, when control authority is handed over from the DM **102** to the EM **104** and ends when controlled disposal repositioning of the EM **104** is complete. Alternately, the EM **104** may be separated from DM **102** and either (1) directed to a second satellite requiring de-orbiting/servicing; or (2) placed in a parking orbit to await instructions to proceed to a second satellite, optionally waiting serving as an on orbit repair facility to enable rapid return to service upon unexpected failure of a satellite or key component thereon.

[0225] FIG. **27** summarizes one embodiment of the EM **104** ejection and disposal phase. One embodiment of the sequence is as follows:

[0226] 1. EM **104** ejection from the RV **100**: After the RV **100** is slewed to the proper attitude, release pyrotechnics are fired to liberate the clamp band between the DM **102** and EM **104**. Preferably, springs create a relative separation velocity between the EM **104** and the DM **102**/HST **50** stack sufficient to ensure that there is no re-contact during the time required for initial EM **104** attitude determination and stabilization. One embodiment releases the EM **104** directed along the negative orbit velocity vector. Post-ejection, the EM **104** nulls its own tip-off rates while the HST **50** nulls the tip-off rates of the DM **102**/HST **50** stack. The EM **104** then performs two zenith-directed burns of the thrusters followed by a negative orbit velocity vector burn. Other separation mechanisms and methods known to those of skill in the art may be used without departing from the scope of the present invention. If EM **104** is to be placed in a parking orbit or transit directly to a second satellite in need of repair, EM **104** may be boosted into that parking orbit or an intercept trajectory to the second satellite following separation from the DM **102**/HST **50** stack.

[0227] 2. EM **104** mass properties measurement: When the EM **104** is safely in a non-interfering orbit with respect to HST **50**, the EM **104** preferably will perform a series of RCS thruster firings in order to determine its mass, center of mass, and moments of inertia, and update the appropriate table. Remote station control may verify proper operation. If EM **104** is to be immediately de-orbited, steps 3 and 4 below may be executed. If EM **104** is to be placed in a parking orbit for later servicing mission(s) for one or more additional satellites, steps 3 and 4 may be performed at the conclusion the last servicing rendezvous for EM **104**.

[0228] 3. De-orbit burn #1: At the appropriate point in the orbit to place perigee (accounting for perturbations) for the final disposal burn, the EM **104** will fire its four 100-pound thrusters for sufficient time to produce a predetermined delta V, dropping perigee to 250 km. This perigee is high enough to avoid attitude control issues associated with center-of-mass/center-of-pressure offsets. It is also high enough to allow the EM **104** to remain in orbit long enough to recover from any anomalous condition.

[0229] 4. De-orbit burn #2: At least 3 orbits later (after sufficient time to confirm a nominal burn #1), the EM **104** will fire its four 100-pound thrusters for sufficient time to result in perigee below 50 km. There will be two consecutive orbits during which burn #2 can be executed, with additional pairs of opportunities each day.

[0230] The entire sequence described above is preferably autonomous, with the remote operator continuously monitoring performance and providing go-aheads before burns #1 and #2. Any anomalies detected on board preferably result in an abort of the sequence, except during de-orbit burn #2, where a point of no return is reached. The remote operator can abort the sequence at any time prior to de-orbit burn #2 via a command or EM **104** can be set automatically to abort the sequence if an anomaly is detected.

[0231] Preferably, after the EM **104** is clear of the HST **50**/DM **102** stack, the DM **102** solar arrays **142** are deployed. FIG. **28** graphically depicts this process. The preferred science operations phase begins at the completion of EM **104** ejection and terminates when science observations and any end-of-life testing is complete. According one embodiment, after the EM **104** has been jettisoned the HST **50** is commanded from the remote station to reconfigure for science operations. This includes establishing attitude control, deploying the HGA booms **56**, opening the aperture door **58**, and so forth. One of skill in the art will recognize that, following servicing, the satellite will undergo a plural-

ity of processes to resume its normal post-service operations, which may include establishing or restoring attitude control, communications links, C&DH, thermal control, and payload operations on the satellite. The particular sequence of post servicing operations will vary depending on the configuration and payload of the satellite as well as its condition when servicing was commenced.

[0232] In another embodiment, the HST science operations will resume with the initiation of the Servicing Mission Verification Program (SMOV). The SMOV for the preferred servicing mission has been established to verify the functions of the HST **50** replacement instruments. It also includes the re-commissioning of the existing science instruments, spacecraft subsystems, and the overall observatory for science operations. FIG. **29** summarizes the science operations phase.

[0233] Due to the extended timeframe of the method of one embodiment, the on-orbit activities of the SMOV program can be grouped for execution in two phases, thereby mitigating some of the HST observing time lost due to a lengthy servicing mission. Preferably, activities in SMOV Phase A are those that can be carried out while the EM **104** is still attached to the HST **50**. Activities executed during Phase A will complement the individual hardware elements performance verification (FT of battery and gyro augmentations, and instruments). These may include, but not be limited to, engineering activation of old and new science instruments, monitoring their contamination and thermal properties, and characterizing their baseline performance. Wherever possible, science calibrations (internal and external) are performed. Also, if at all possible, science programs can be carried out during servicing, subject to the constraints imposed by the servicing mission and pending the commissioning of prerequisite capabilities. All activities performed during Phase A will not be sensitive to and will not interfere with the temporary spacecraft configuration and the established servicing mission timeline.

[0234] SMOV Phase B preferably comprises those commissioning activities that can be carried out only after completion of the servicing mission and the release of the EM **104**, with the spacecraft in final on-orbit configuration. Thus, in one embodiment, commissioning of all other science instruments and spacecraft subsystems not performed during Phase A will be accomplished in Phase B. This may include spacecraft power, pointing, thermal, and guidance, as well as existing and replacement scientific instrument characterization and calibration. Hence, science observations preferably ramp up to their normal levels as SMOV Phase B activities ramp down to completion. The HST **50**/DM **102** disposal phase preferably begins at the completion of science operations and terminates with the completion of the controlled disposal. FIG. **30** summarizes this phase.

[0235] Preferably the DM **102** slews the combined vehicle to the preferred attitude for the initial reentry burn. According to this embodiment, a small retrograde burn (engineering burn) to check out the system is initiated followed by two retrograde apogee burns. Then the final burn adjusts the perigee to 50 km and sets up the preferred controlled reentry into the Pacific Ocean.

[0236] While the invention herein revealed and described is set forth in what, at present, is considered to be the best mode contemplated for making and carrying out the invention and the preferred embodiments of this invention, it will be understood that the foregoing is given by way of illustration, rather than by way of limitation. Accordingly, any and all boundaries and restrictions imputed to the scope of this invention must be defined by the spirit and intent of the following claims.

1. A robotic system for servicing free-flying spacecraft, comprising:

a multi-axis manipulating grappling arm, the grappling arm including an end effector on one end, and

at least one dexterous arm having a first and second end, the first end including an interface for servicing the spacecraft,

wherein the robot system is autonomously controlled by commands that are subject to manual override by an operator in telecommunication with the robotic system.

2. A robotic system for servicing free-flying spacecraft, according to the limitations of claim 1, wherein the end effector of the grappling arm aids in capturing the spacecraft to be serviced.

3. A robotic system for servicing free-flying spacecraft, according to the limitations of claim 1, wherein the end effector of the grappling arm connects to the second end of the dexterous arm.

4. A robotic system for servicing free-flying spacecraft, according to the limitations of claim 1, wherein the interface for servicing the spacecraft includes tools.

5. A robotic system for servicing free-flying spacecraft, according to the limitations of claim 1, wherein the interface for servicing the spacecraft includes a vision system for providing visual monitoring capabilities to the operator.

* * * * *

US00D628609S

(12) **United States Design Patent**   (10) Patent No.:   **US D628,609 S**
Linn et al.   (45) Date of Patent: ** **Dec. 7, 2010**

(54) **ROBOT**

(75) Inventors: **Douglas Martin Linn**, White Lake, MI (US); **Chris A. Ihrke**, Hartland, MI (US); **Robert O. Ambrose**, Houston, TX (US); **Joshua S Mehling**, League City, TX (US); **Myron A Diftler**, Houston, TX (US); **Adam H Parsons**, Tulsa, OK (US); **Nicolaus A Radford**, League City, TX (US); **Lyndon Bridgwater**, Houston, TX (US); **Heather Bibby**, Houston, TX (US)

(73) Assignees: **GM Global Technology Operations, Inc.**, Detroit, MI (US); **NASA Lyndon B. Johnson Space Center**, Houston, TX (US); **Oceaneering Space Systems**, Houston, TX (US)

(**) Term: **14 Years**

(21) Appl. No.: **29/359,105**

(22) Filed: **Apr. 6, 2010**

(51) LOC (9) Cl. **15-99**
(52) U.S. Cl. **D15/199**
(58) Field of Classification Search D15/199; D21/166, 171, 177, 578, 593, 594, 621, 634; 180/8.6; 318/568.12, 568.2; 364/424.02
See application file for complete search history.

(56) **References Cited**

U.S. PATENT DOCUMENTS

3,728,815	A	*	4/1973	Tomiyama 446/291
4,095,367	A	*	6/1978	Ogawa 446/73
D251,627	S	*	4/1979	McQuarrie et al. D21/578
D288,581	S	*	3/1987	Man D21/578
5,334,073	A	*	8/1994	Tilbor et al. 446/308
D410,476	S	*	6/1999	Gomi et al. D15/199
D460,503	S	*	7/2002	Koshiishi et al. D21/578
6,430,475	B2	*	8/2002	Okamoto et al. 700/245
6,604,021	B2	*	8/2003	Imai et al. 700/245
D579,035	S	*	10/2006	Kim et al. D15/199
D541,353	S	*	4/2007	Takahashi D21/578
D550,735	S	*	9/2007	Takahashi D15/199
D561,212	S	*	2/2008	Mitchell D15/199
D572,739	S	*	7/2008	Jennings et al. D15/199
D574,404	S	*	8/2008	Maisonnier et al. D15/199
D578,170	S	*	10/2008	Chiang et al. D21/578
2005/0184697	A1	*	8/2005	Iribe et al. 318/568.12

* cited by examiner

Primary Examiner—Patricia Palasik
(74) *Attorney, Agent, or Firm*—Reising Ethington P.C.

(57) **CLAIM**

The ornamental design for a robot, as shown and described.

DESCRIPTION

FIG. **1** is a front view of a robot showing the new design;

FIG. **2** is a left perspective view thereof;

FIG. **3** is a side view thereof;

FIG. **4** is a rear view thereof;

FIG. **5** is a right front perspective view looking down on the robot; and,

FIG. **6** is a left rear perspective view looking down on the robot.

The broken lines in the drawings depict unclaimed environmental subject matter.

1 Claim, 6 Drawing Sheets

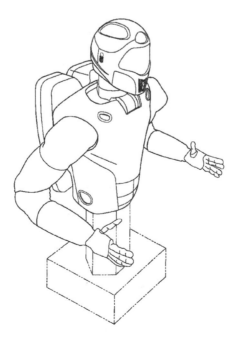

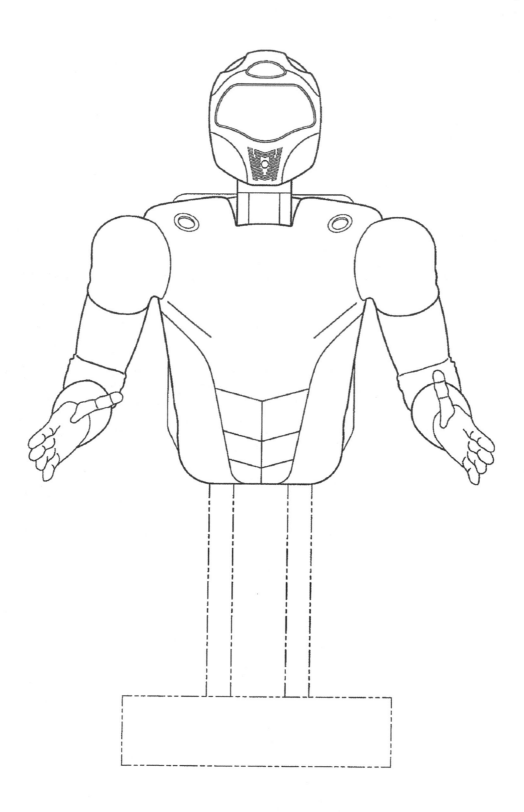

Fig-1

114

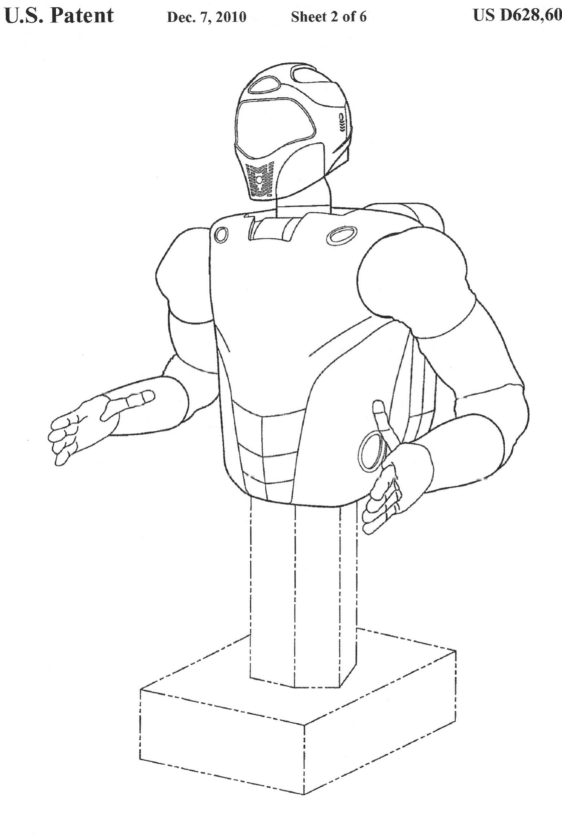

Fig-2

115

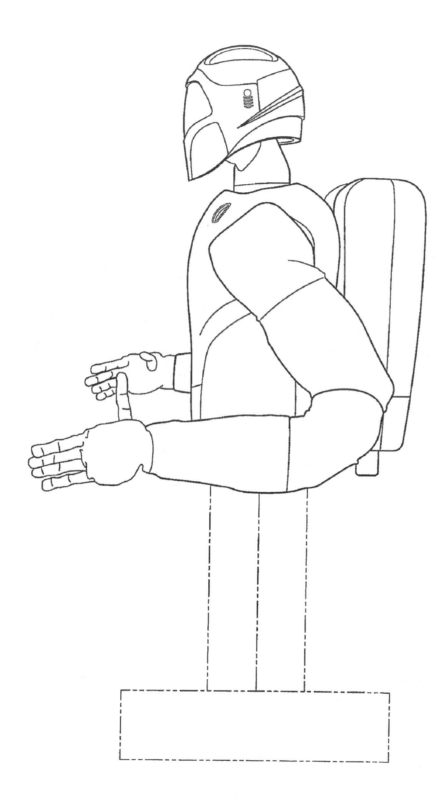

Fig-3

116

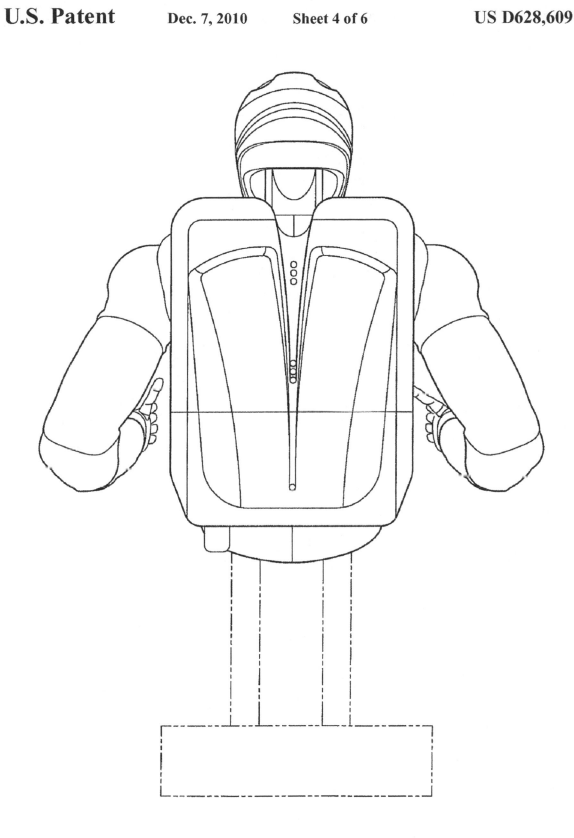

Fig-4

117

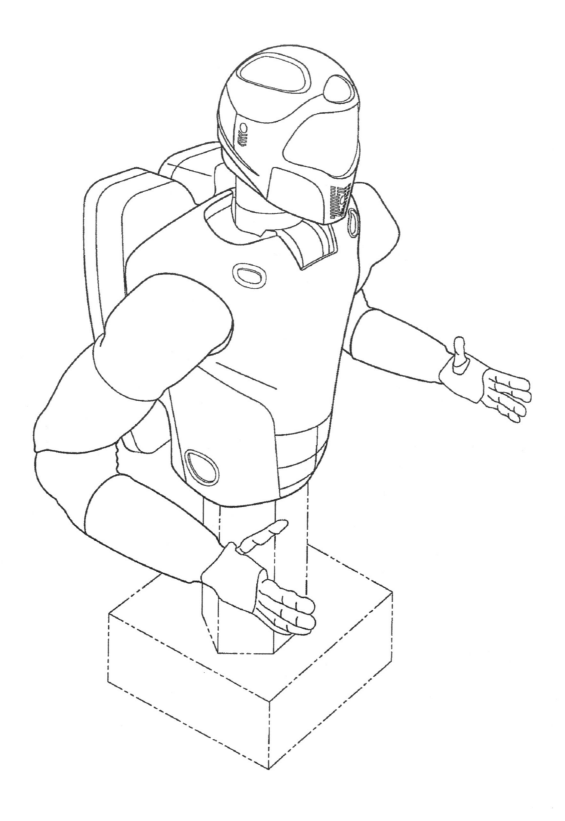

Fig-5

118

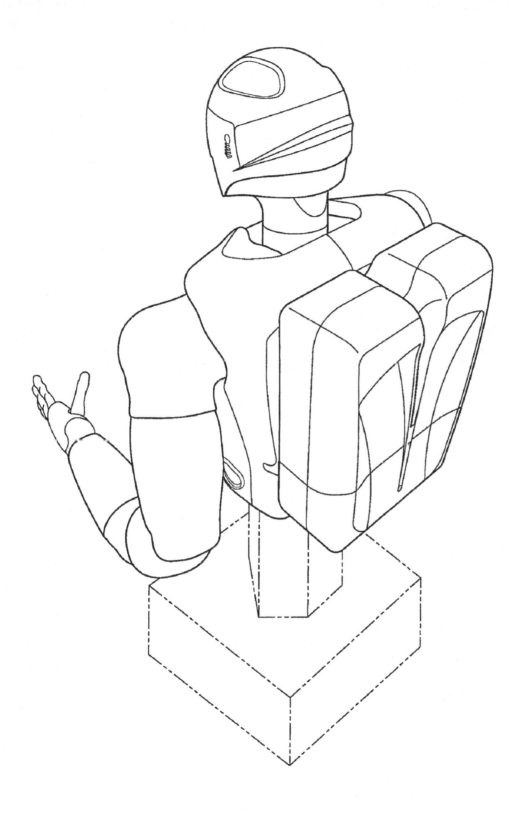

Fig-6

119

US008494782B1

(12) **United States Patent**
Stolc et al.

(10) Patent No.: **US 8,494,782 B1**
(45) Date of Patent: **Jul. 23, 2013**

(54) **RAPID POLYMER SEQUENCER**

(75) Inventors: **Viktor Stolc**, Milpitas, CA (US);
Matthew W Brock, San Francisco, CA (US)

(73) Assignee: **The United States of America as Represented by the Administrator of the National Aeronautics & Space Administration (NASA)**, Washington, DC (US)

(*) Notice: Subject to any disclaimer, the term of this patent is extended or adjusted under 35 U.S.C. 154(b) by 0 days.

(21) Appl. No.: **13/092,048**

(22) Filed: **Apr. 21, 2011**

Related U.S. Application Data

(62) Division of application No. 10/885,537, filed on Jun. 24, 2004, now Pat. No. 7,949,472.

(51) **Int. Cl.**
G01N 33/48 (2006.01)
G06F 15/00 (2006.01)

(52) **U.S. Cl.**
USPC **702/19**; 712/220

(58) **Field of Classification Search**
None
See application file for complete search history.

(56) **References Cited**

U.S. PATENT DOCUMENTS

6,740,518 B1	5/2004	Duong et al.
7,258,838 B2	8/2007	Li et al.
2002/0094526 A1	7/2002	Bayley et al.

OTHER PUBLICATIONS

Akeson, et al., Microsecond Time-Scale Discrimination Among Polycytidylic Acid, Polyadenylic Acid, and Polyuridylic Acid as Homopolymers or as Segments Within Single RNA Molecules, Biophysical Journal, Dec. 1999, 3227-3233, 77, Biophysical Society.
Blodgett, Films Built by Depositing Successive Monomolecular Layers on a Solid Surface, Journal of American Chemical Society, 1935, 1007-1022, 57.
Chechik, et al., Reactions and Reactivity in Self-Assembled Monolayers, Advanced Materials, 2000, 1161-1171, 12-16, WILEY-VCH.

Kasianowicz, et al., Characterization of individual polynucleotide molecules using a membrane channel, Proc. Natl. Acad. Sci., Nov. 26, 1996, 13770-13773, 93.
Lahann, et al., A Reversibly Switching Surface, Science, 2003, 371-374, 299.
Langmuir, The Constitution and fundamental Properties of Solids and Liquids. II. Liquids, J. Amer. Chem. Soc., 1917, 1848-1906, 39.
Li, et al., Ion-beam sculpting at nanometre length scales, Letters to Nature, 2001, 166-169, 412, Macmillan Magazines Ltd.
Marziali, et al., New DNA Sequencing Methods, Annu. Rev. Biomed. Eng., Aug. 2001, 195-223, 3, Annual Reviews.
Sagiv, Organized Monolayers by Adsorption. 1. Formation and Structure Oleophobic Mixed Monolayers on Solid Surfaces, J. Amer. Chem. Soc., Jan. 1980, 92-98, 102, American Chemical Society.
Stein, et al., Ion-Beam Sculpting Time Scales, Physical Review Letters, Dec. 20, 2002, 276106-1-276106-4, 89-27, The American Physical Society.
Non-final Rejection, mailed Jan. 28, 2008, in parent case, U.S. Appl. No. 10/885,537, filed Jun. 24, 2004, issued May 24, 2011 as patent No. 7,949,472.
Response to Non-final Rejection, mailed Jan. 28, 2008, in parent case, U.S. Appl No. 10/885,537, filed Jun. 24, 2004, issued May 24, 2011 as patent No. 7,949,472, Response filed Mar. 19, 2008.
Final Rejection, mailed Jul. 28, 2008, in parent case, U.S. Appl. No. 10/885,537, filed Jun. 24, 2004, issued May 24, 2011 as patent No. 7,949,472.
Response to Final Rejection, mailed Jul. 28, 2008, in parent case, U.S. Appl. No. 10/885,537, filed Jun. 24, 2004, issued May 24, 2011 as patent No. 7,949,472, Response filed Jan. 26, 2009.

Primary Examiner — Eric S Dejong
(74) *Attorney, Agent, or Firm* — John F. Schipper; Robert M. Padilla

(57) **ABSTRACT**

Method and system for rapid and accurate determination of each of a sequence of unknown polymer components, such as nucleic acid components. A self-assembling monolayer of a selected substance is optionally provided on an interior surface of a pipette tip, and the interior surface is immersed in a selected liquid. A selected electrical field is impressed in a longitudinal direction, or in a transverse direction, in the tip region, a polymer sequence is passed through the tip region, and a change in an electrical current signal is measured as each polymer component passes through the tip region. Each of the measured changes in electrical current signals is compared with a database of reference electrical change signals, with each reference signal corresponding to an identified polymer component, to identify the unknown polymer component with a reference polymer component. The nanopore preferably has a pore inner diameter of no more than about 40 nm and is prepared by heating and pulling a very small section of a glass tubing.

18 Claims, 9 Drawing Sheets

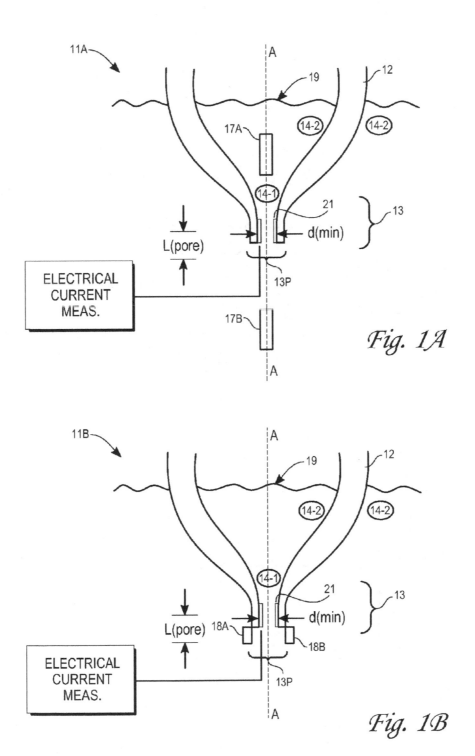

Fig. 1A

Fig. 1B

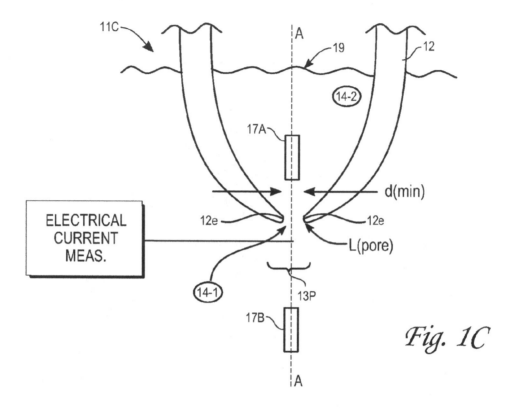

Fig. 1C

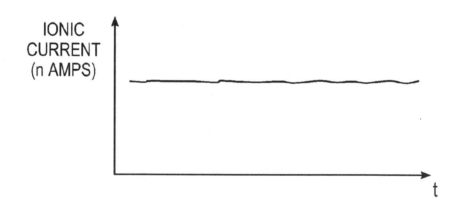

Fig. 2A (Polymer Absent)

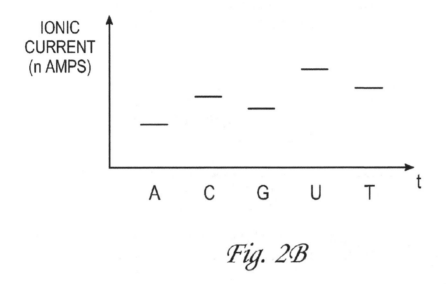

Fig. 2B

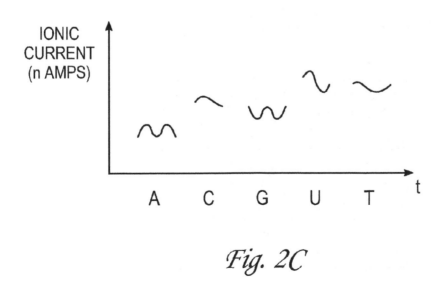

Fig. 2C

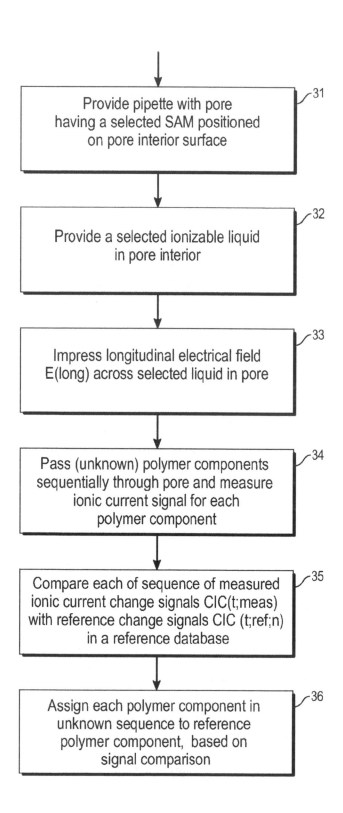

Fig. 3

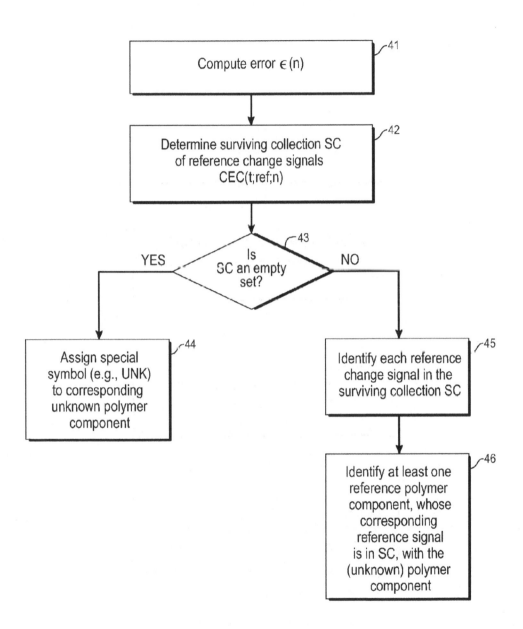

Fig. 4

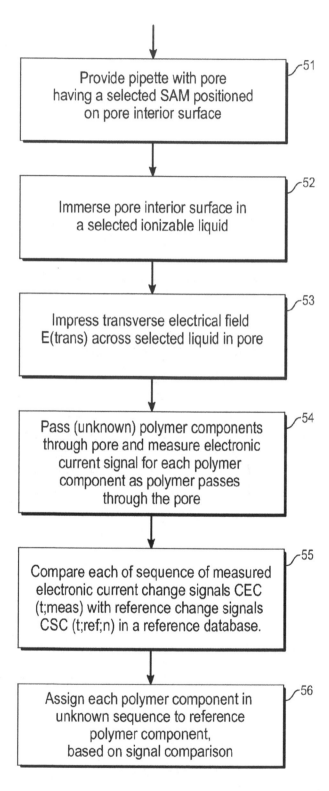

Provide pipette with pore
having a selected SAM positioned
on pore interior surface ⌐51

Immerse pore interior surface in
a selected ionizable liquid ⌐52

Impress transverse electrical field
E(trans) across selected liquid in pore ⌐53

Pass (unknown) polymer components
through pore and measure electronic
current signal for each polymer
component as polymer passes
through the pore ⌐54

Compare each of sequence of measured
electronic current change signals CEC
(t;meas) with reference change signals
CSC (t;ref;n) in a reference database. ⌐55

Assign each polymer component in
unknown sequence to reference
polymer component,
based on signal comparison ⌐56

Fig. 5

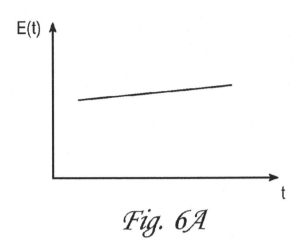

Fig. 6A

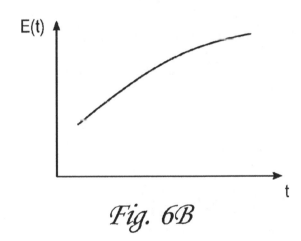

Fig. 6B

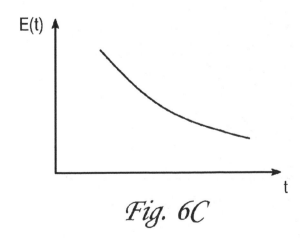

Fig. 6C

127

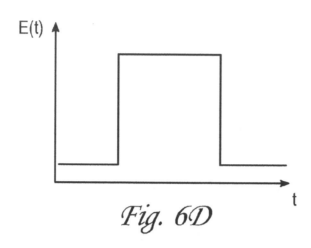

Fig. 6D

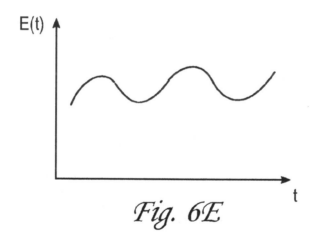

Fig. 6E

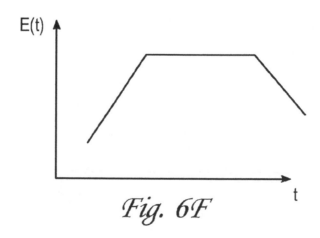

Fig. 6F

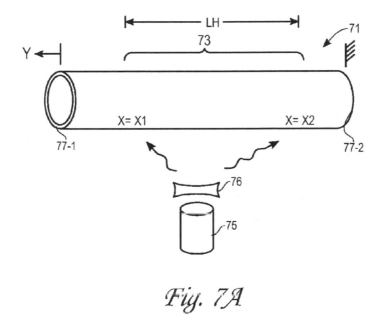

Fig. 7A

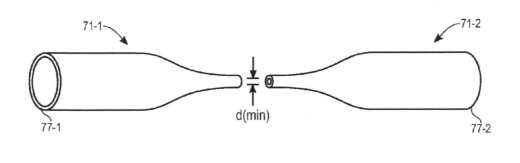

Fig. 7B

1

RAPID POLYMER SEQUENCER

ORIGIN OF THE INVENTION

The invention described herein was made, in part, by an employee of the United States Government and may be manufactured and used by or for the Government for governmental purposes without the payment of any royalties thereon or therefor.

TECHNICAL FIELD

The present invention is a method and system for rapidly and accurately determining an ordered sequence of molecular units, such as bases in a nucleic acid, such as DNA or RNA, and for fabricating a nanopore system to facilitate the sequencing.

BACKGROUND OF THE INVENTION

Nanofabrication techniques offer the possibility to create solid state pores or apertures with diameters and lengths similar to diameters and lengths of single nucleotides or proteins. Solid state nanopores permit use of non-physiological conditions for structural manipulation of biopolymers, such as non-neutral pH levels, high temperatures and/or high voltage differences. Use of a solid state substrate will allow a more straightforward manipulation of surface chemistry in the pore, which may be critical to fine-tune the rate of nucleic acid translocation or the degree of ionic current reduction associated with passage of a polymer, such as a poly-nucleotide through a nanopore.

Kasianowicz et al, in "Characterization of individual polynucleotide molecules through a membrane channel," Proc. Nat. Acad. Sci. vol. 93 (1996) 195-223, have used a pore of diameter about 1.5 nanometers (nm) in the bacterial α-hemolysin ion channel protein, and have applied an electrical field to drive a negatively charged polynucleotide through the pore from one side to the other, which transiently reduces ionic conductance through the pore. Akeson et al, in "Microsecond Time Scale Discrimination Among Polycytidylic Acis in Homopolymers or as Segments Within Single RNA Molecules," Biophys. Jour. Vol. 77 (1999) 3227-3233, have shown that polynucleotides of different lengths can be discriminated by time duration of translocation as the nucleotide sequence passes through a pore. Translocation of different nucleotide homopolymers reduces ionic conductance of α-hemolysin by characteristic amounts, which suggests that the individual nucleotides in a heteropolymer could be identified, if passed through a nanopore of appropriate dimensions and composition. However, α-hemolysin has a pore length as long as a sequence of about 20 nucleotides so that discrimination between individual nucleotides using α-hemolysin is not possible.

What is needed is a system that provides rapid and accurate identification of ordered components of a nucleic acid, protein or similar polymer, at rates up to and above one component per μsec. Preferably, the approach should adequately discriminate between the different ordered components present in the polymer and provide accurate ordering, with an acceptable error rate that is controllable by varying the rate at which the polymer components pass through and is read by the system.

SUMMARY OF THE INVENTION

These needs are met by the invention, which provides a system and associated method that relies upon a pore at a

2

pipette tip, having a pore diameter as small as 1-40 nm, preferably containing a selected alkali halide, ammonium compound (e.g., NH_4, $N(CH_3)_4$, or a suitable ionic organic compound or ionic inorganic compound (e.g., $CaSO_4$, $Mg_m(PO_4)_n$). In one embodiment, a voltage difference is impressed, in a longitudinal direction or in a transverse direction, across an ionic liquid within the pore, and a varying ionic current through the pore, or a varying electron current across the pore (referred to collectively as an "electrical current") is measured in response to passage of each of an ordered sequence of polymer components, such as nucleotides in a nucleic acid or proteins, through the pore.

In one embodiment, the method includes steps of:

providing a pipette having a longitudinal axis and having a tapered region having a pore with a selected pore diameter in a range of 1-40 nanometers (nm);

providing a selected liquid in contact with an interior surface of the pore;

impressing a selected voltage difference across the selected liquid within the pipette pore substantially parallel to the pipette longitudinal axis direction, and providing an ionic current value induced in the selected liquid; and

passing an unknown polymer molecule, having a sequence of polymer components, through the pore, and determining a change in the ionic current signal induced by passage of each of the polymer components through the pore. In another embodiment, the voltage difference is impressed transversely, across the pore, and a transverse electronic current, induced in response to passage of each of the polymer components through the pore, is measured.

In another embodiment, a method for producing the pore includes steps of:

heating a hollow cylinder of a selected pipette material, having first and second cylinder ends, having a longitudinal axis and having a selected initial inner diameter, with a selected heating source for at least one of first and second longitudinal locations for at least one of first and second selected time intervals;

translating one of the first and second cylinder ends relative to the other of the first and second cylinder ends during a selected third time interval that partly or wholly overlaps at least one of the first time interval and the second time interval; and

allowing the hollow cylinder to separate into at least first and second pipettes and at least one of the first and second pipettes has a pore with a pore diameter in a range 1-40 nanometers (nm).

BRIEF DESCRIPTION OF THE DRAWINGS

FIGS. 1A, 1B and 1C illustrate apparati for practicing the invention.

FIGS. 2A, 2B and 2C graphical views of typical sequences of ionic or electron current values measured with no polymer component present (2A), and in response to passage of a polymer component through a pore (2B, 2C).

FIGS. 3, 4 and 5 are flow charts illustrating procedures for practicing the invention according to two embodiments.

FIGS. 6A-6F graphically illustrate time variations that can be applied to an impressed voltage difference used in the invention.

FIGS. 7A and 7B illustrate formation of a pipette tip for use in the invention.

DESCRIPTION OF BEST MODES OF THE INVENTION

FIG. 1A illustrates one embodiment of apparatus for measurement of longitudinal ionic current in practicing the invention. The system **11** includes a glass pipette **12**, having a longitudinal axis AA and having a tapered tip region **13**, with a pore **13p** having a selected pore minimum inner diameter d(min) in a preferred range of 1-40 nm, or larger if necessary. A length of the interior surface of the tip region **13** is provided with a selected first liquid **14-1** including an ionizable molecule including an alkali halide (NaCl, KCl, NaBr, KBr, $MgCl_2$, $CaCl_2$, MgClBr, etc.), ammonium compound (e.g., NH_4, $N(CH_3)_4$, or a suitable ionic organic compound or ionic inorganic compound (e.g., $CaSO_4$, $Mg_m(PO_4)_n$). A portion of the pipette adjacent to the pore is immersed in a selected second liquid **14-2**, which may be, but need not be, the same as the first liquid **14-1**. The pore **13p** has a pore length L(pore) in a selected length range. A voltage difference ΔV, having a value in a range 10-2000 milliVolts, is impressed substantially in the longitudinal axis direction across the liquid in the pore, and an ionic current value IC through the pore is measured by an electrical current measurement module **15** The voltage difference may, for example, be provided by a first electrode **17A**, positioned within the first liquid **14-1** in the interior surface of the pore **13p**, and a second electrode **17B**, positioned within a "bath" **19** of the second liquid **14-2** surrounding the pore. One or both of the electrodes, **17A** and **17B**, may include Ag/AgCl or another substance known to provide reversible current and to have low offset voltage in ionic solutions.

FIG. 1B, illustrating an embodiment for measuring transverse electronic current, is similar to FIG. 1A, except that spaced apart electrodes, **18A** and **18B**, replacing the electrodes **17A** and **17B**, are arranged on or adjacent to a perimeter of the pore **13** and an electronic current flows from **18A** to **18B** in response to imposition of a voltage difference ΔV between these electrodes.

FIG. 1C illustrates a different configuration of the pore **13p**, according to the invention. In FIG. 1C, different portions of an end **12e** of the tip substantially face each other and define an effective pore length L(pore) that is approximately equal to a thickness of the pipette **12** at an end of the pipette. This configuration is preferred where the pore width d(min) is to be made as small as possible (e.g., less than or equal to 1.5 nm).

In one approach, an interior surface of the pore **13p** is left uncoated in practicing the invention. Preferably, the interior surface of the pore **13p** is coated or wetted or otherwise provided with a self-assembling monolayer ("SAM") **21** of a selected material that will manifest hydrogen bonding, van der Waals interaction and/or similar reversible, transient interactions with a class of polymers of interest. The SAM substance provided on an interior surface of the pore **13p** may be octadecyltrichlorosilane ($C_{18}H_{37}SiCl_3$ or "OTS"), as discussed by Sagiv in "Organized Monolayers by Absorption. 1. Formation and Structure of Oleophobic Mixed Monolayers on Solid Surfaces," J. Amer. Chem. Soc. vol. 102 (1980) pp. 92-98, or may be another suitable substance that will interact with a polymer components passing through the pore **13p** and allow measurement of a modulated ionic current signal or electron current signal that is characteristic of a particular polymer component. Other SAM substances that may be used include alkylsiloxane monolayers, alkylsilanes, trimethoxysilanes, mono-, di- and tri-chlorosilanes, octadecylsilanes, organochlorosilanes, aminosilanes, perfluorodecyltrichlorosilanes and aminopropylethoxysilanes.

From another perspective, a stable SAM can be formed using sulfur-containing absorbates on gold, chlorosilanes or alkoxysilanes on glass, and fatty acids on a metal oxide surface.

As used herein "SAM" includes an array of substantially identical molecules (e.g., containing a silane component) covalently attached to a glass surface and oriented substantially perpendicular to the surface, which interact, without permanent bonding, with a selected group of one or more solution molecules that pass near the SAM array. A SAM may be used to provide transient interactions with a polymer ubit passing through a nanopore and/or may be used to tailor the effective longitudinal and/or transverse dimensions (diameter, etc.) of a nanopore.

Formation of self-assembling monolayers on a gas or liquid interface were first reported by Langmuir in J. Am. Chem. Soc., vol. 39 (1917) 1848, and were first shown to be formable on a solid surface by Blodgett, J. Am. Chem. Soc., vol. 57 (1935) 1007. Spontaneous formation of a SAM on a solid substrate was first demonstrated by Bigelow, Pickett and Zisman, J. Colloid Interface Sci., vol. 1 (1946) 513 Chechik, Crooks and Stirling, in "Reactions and Reactivity in Self-Assembled Monolayers," Advanced Materials, 2000, 1161-1171, define a SAM as a monomolecular film of surfactant, formed spontaneously on a substrate upon exposure to a surfactant solution and provide a general review of use of SAMs. A SAM may be disordered or close packed, depending on the degree of wetting of the substrate surface. As noted by Chechik et al, ibid, a SAM is ideally suited as a scaffold to graft a polymer onto solid surfaces, because of the high density of functional groups, relatively small number of defects, and a well defined structure. A molecule that is part of a SAM may be terminated by various functional groups, such as OH and amines.

A second example of an SAM is (16-Mercapto)hexadecanoic acid (MHA) on a gold substrate, as studied and reported by J. Lahann et al in Science, vol. 239 (2003) pp 371-374 MHA includes hydrophobic chains capped by hydrophilic carboxylate end groups. Cleavage of the carboxylate end groups provides a low density SAM of hydrophobic chains. Application of a small electrical potential or voltage difference (e.g., −1054 mV≦V≦+654 mV to the negatively charged carboxylate groups provides an attractive force that causes a conformation change in the hydrophobic chains, whereby an all-trans conformation becomes partly trans and partly gauche conformation, with substantial qualitative and quantitative changes in associated sum-frequency generation (SFG) spectroscopic variations associated with the different conformations. The conformational changes are reversible so that removal of the applied electrical potential causes a return to the relatively featureless SFG spectroscopic variations associated with the original hydrophobic chain conformations (all trans). Viewed from another perspective, change in hydrophobic chain conformations associated with a specific change, such as a variation in translocation associated with passage of different polymer units through a nanopore in which a very thin layer of MHA on gold is provided, would cause a measurable change in electrical current or change in electrical potential (tens to hundreds of millivolts) associated with passage of each (different) polymer unit.

In the absence of passage of a polymer component through the pore, a steady ionic current through the pore (or electronic current across the pore) will develop in response to impressing a small voltage difference in a longitudinal (or transverse) direction, as shown graphically in FIG. 2A.

An ordered sequence of polymer components, such as a nucleic acid (e.g., DNA or RNA) is passed through the pore **13p**, allowing development of a sequence of changing ionic current values, as illustrated in FIGS. 2B and/or 2C. In FIG. 2B, passage of each polymer component through the pore **13p** is assumed to produce an approximately square wave signal, having an approximately constant characteristic amplitude for a small time interval that corresponds to the time required for that polymer component to pass through the tip. In FIG. 2C, passage of each polymer unit through the pore 13p is assumed, more realistically, to produce a signal having a characteristic, time varying signal shape, a characteristic average amplitude and a characteristic shape parameter, for a small time interval that corresponds to the time required for that polymer component to pass through the tip.

Where one or more polymer components passes through the pore, translocation will cause the steady ionic current shown in FIG. 2A to change with time in response to passage of the polymer component through the pore and the accompanying translocation. If, for example, the polymer sequence is a nucleic acid, such as DNA (alternatively, RNA), each nucleotide will contain one of the four bases adenine (A), cytosine (C), guanine (G) and thymine (T) (alternatively, adenine, cytosine, guanine and uracil (U) for RNA). Ideally, each of the four bases (for DNA or for RNA) will produce a distinguishable change in ionic current signal as that nucleotide passes through the pipette tip, as suggested in FIG. 2B or FIG. 2C.

Under the influence of an applied voltage difference, negatively charged nucleotides or other polymer units are driven through the pore, and a polynucleotide strand can thus be threaded from one side of a lipid biolayer to the other. A steady electrical current that is present in the pore in the absence of a polymer unit is partly occluded during translocation. In principle, polymer units of different lengths can be distinguished from each other by translocation duration, and several homopolymers of different composition can be distinguished based on characteristic levels of electrical current reduction.

FIG. 3 is a flow chart of a procedure for practicing the invention. In step 31 of FIG. 3, a pipette, having a longitudinal axis and having a tapered tip with an associated pore having a selected pore minimum inner diameter d in a preferred range (e.g., d=1-40 nm) is provided, and a selected self-assembling monolayer (SAM) is optionally provided on some portion of the pore surface. In step 32, a selected first liquid containing ions is provided in the interior surface of the pore, preferably containing an alkali halide, ammonium compounds (e.g., NH_4, $N(CH_3)_4$, or a suitable ionic organic compound or ionic inorganic compound (e.g., $CaSO_4$, $Mg_m(PO_4)_n$). More generally, the selected first liquid may be any solution that provides a concentration p of ions at least equal to a threshold value ρ(ion;thr), for example, ρ(ion;thr)$\geq 10^x$ cm^{-3}. The liquid may include the polynucleotide or other polymer that is to be identified. In step 33, a voltage difference having a value in a range ΔV=10-2000 milliVolts is impressed on the liquid in the pore, in a direction substantially parallel to the pipette longitudinal axis. If the polymer has a net electrical charge, the polarity of the voltage difference is chosen to induce the polymer to pass through (or across) the pore. In step 34, ordered components in a polymer (unknown) are sequentially passed through the pore, and each of a sequence of changes in ionic current signals is measured, resulting in a sequence of measured values such as the sequences shown in FIG. 2B or FIG. 2C.

In step 35 (optional), the sequence of changes in measured ionic current signals CIC(t;meas) is compared, one-by-one or in consecutive groups, with reference change signals CIC(t;ref;n), numbered n=1, . . . , N (N≧2) in a reference signal database. Each reference change signal corresponds to a reference polymer component. In step 36 (optional), each polymer component (e.g., a nucleotide containing a particular base) in the unknown sequence is assigned to the reference

polymer component having a reference ionic current change signal that is most similar, in some quantitative sense, to the measured (changes in) ionic current change signal. Optionally, steps 35 and 36 are performed off-line

The signal comparison step 35 is optionally implemented as follows. The ionic current change signal CIC(t;meas) for the unknown polymer sequence is measured at a sequence of time values t_m, producing a sequence of measured ionic current change values $\{CIC(t_m;meas)\}_m$. (m=1, . . . , M; M≧2) This sequence of measured ionic current change values is compared with a reference sequence (n) of ionic current change signal values $\{CIC(t_m+\tau(n);ref;n)\}_m$, where τ(n) is a selected time shift that may vary with the reference number n being considered, by computing an error value

$$\epsilon(n) = \left\{ \sum_{m=1}^{M} w_m |CIC(t_m;\text{meas}) - CIC(t_m+\tau(n);\text{ref};n)|^p \right\}^{1/p}, \quad (1)$$

where $\{w_m\}_m$ is a selected sequence of non-negative weight values (at least one positive) and p is a selected positive number (e.g., p=1, 1.6 or 2). Reference ionic current change signals $CIC(t_m+\tau;\text{ref};n)$ for which the error satisfies $\epsilon(n) > \epsilon$(thr), where ϵ(thr) is a selected positive threshold value, are discarded and not considered further for this measured ionic current change value sequence $\{CIC(t_m;\text{meas})\}_m$. When at least one error value satisfies $\epsilon(n) \leq \epsilon$(thr), the "surviving collection"

$$SC = \{CIC(t_m+\tau(n);\text{ref};n) | \epsilon(n) \leq \epsilon(\text{thr})\} \quad (2)$$

of all reference signals with error values that satisfy the inequality $\epsilon(n) \leq \epsilon$(thr), are considered, and the reference ionic current change signal $CIC(t_m+\tau(n);\text{ref};n)$ that provides the smallest error $\epsilon(n)$ is assigned to the unknown polymer unit. When the surviving collection SC is an empty set, because no error value satisfies $\epsilon(n) \leq \epsilon$(thr), the system assigns a selected symbol, such as UNK, to this polymer unit.

The comparison procedure can be summarized in a flow chart in FIG. 4. In step 41, the error $\epsilon(n)$, defined as in Eq. (1) or in another suitable manner, for each reference change signal $CIC(t_m+\tau(n);\text{ref};n)$ in the database is computed. In step 42, the surviving collection SC of reference signals is determined. In step 43, the system determines if SC is an empty set. If the answer to the query in step 43 is "yes," the system assigns a special symbol (e.g., UNK) to the corresponding measured ionic current value in step 44, indicating that no reference change signal $IC(t_m+\tau(n);\text{ref};n)$ is sufficiently similar to the measured ionic current change signal. If the answer to the query in step 43 is "no" (SC is non-empty), the system identifies, in step 45, each reference change signal $CIC(t_m+\tau(n);\text{ref};n=n')$ for which the corresponding error satisfies

$$\epsilon(n') = \min_{1 \leq n \leq N} \epsilon(n). \quad (3)$$

In step 46, the system identifies at least one reference polymer component, for which the corresponding reference change signal $CIC(t_m+\tau(n');\text{ref};n')$ is in the surviving collection SC, with the unknown polymer component whose signal was measured.

FIG. 5 is a flow chart of an alternate procedure for practicing the invention, using a transverse voltage difference. In step 51 of FIG. 5, a pipette, having a longitudinal axis and having a tapered tip with an associated pore having a selected pore minimum inner diameter d in a preferred range (e.g., d=1-40 nm) is provided, where a selected self-assembling monolayer is optionally provided on an interior surface of the pore. In step 52, the pore interior is provided with a selected first liquid, preferably containing an alkali halide, ammonium

7

8

compounds (e.g., NH_4, $N(CH_3)_4$, or a suitable ionic organic compound or ionic inorganic compound (e.g., $CaSO_4$, Mg_m $(PO_4)_n$), so that the first liquid is present within the pore. More generally, the selected liquid may be any solution that provides at least a concentration ρ of electrons at least equal to a threshold value $\rho(\text{ion};\text{thr})$, for example, $\rho(\text{ion};\text{thr}) \geqq 10^x \, \text{cm}^{-3}$. In step **53**, a voltage difference having a value in a range $\Delta V = 10\text{-}2000$ milliVolts, or more if desired, is impressed on the first liquid in the pore, in a direction substantially transverse to the pipette longitudinal axis. In step **54**, a polymer sequence (unknown) is sequentially passed through the pore, and each of a sequence of electron current change signals is measured, resulting in a sequence of measured values such as the sequences shown in FIG. 2B or FIG. 2C. The electron signals resulting from imposition of the transverse voltage difference are likely to be different from the corresponding ionic current signals resulting from imposition of a longitudinal voltage difference.

In step **55** (optional), the sequence of measured electron current change signals $\text{CEC}(t_m;\text{meas})$ is compared, one-by-one or in consecutive groups, with reference change signals $\text{CEC}(t_m+\tau(n);\text{ref};n)$, numbered $n=1, \ldots, N'$ ($N' \geqq 2$) in a reference signal database. In step **56** (optional), each polymer unit (e.g., a nucleotide containing a particular base) in the unknown sequence is assigned to the reference polymer component having a reference electron current value that is most similar to the measured electron current signal. Step **55** may, for example, be implemented by analogy with implementation of step **35** in FIG. **3**, with electronic change signals, $\text{CEC}(t_m;\text{meas})$ and $\text{CEC}(t_m+\tau(n);\text{ref};n)$ replacing the corresponding ionic current change signals in Eqs. (1) and (2).

The voltage difference amplitude $\Delta V(t)$, impressed longitudinally or transversely across the selected liquid, may be substantially uniform in time, as illustrated in FIG. 6A, may be substantially monotonically increasing in time (FIG. 6B), may be substantially monotonically decreasing in time (FIG. 6C), may be substantially a step function in time (FIG. 6D), may vary substantially sinusoidally in time (FIG. 6E), may vary substantially trapezoidally in time (FIG. 6F), with temporal length segments $\tau 1$, $\tau 2$ and $\tau 3$, or may have another suitable time varying shape. The trapezoidal variation shown in FIG. **6F** includes a triangular variation, in which the middle segment has length $\tau 2 = 0$.

A tip region of a pipette (quartz glass, aluminosilicate glass, borosilicate glass or other suitable glass) having an appropriate minimum inner diameter may be formed using the following procedure, illustrated in FIGS. 7A and 7B. A selected middle region **73**, having a preferred length LH in a range 0.1-2 cm or more, of a pipette **71** with a hollow core is heated or otherwise receives substantial thermal energy, using a laser, infrared source or a heated metal filament **75** and (optional) associated focusing system **76**, at one or more locations, $x=x1$, $x=x2$, etc., for one, two or more time intervals, of length $\Delta t1$, $\Delta t2$, etc. The time intervals may partly or wholly overlap or may be isolated from each other. As the heating or irradiation continues, one or both of first and second ends, **77-1** and **77-2**, of the pipette is pulled with a selected force F, optionally $10^1\text{-}10^7$ dynes or more, or at a selected displacement rate, v of a few mm/sec, so that the first and second ends are displaced relative to each other. The pipette **71** separates into two pipette segments, **71-1** and **71-2**, in the (last) heating cycle, and at least one of the two resulting pipette segments has a hollow core (a pore) with a pore minimum inner diameter d(min). Tip parameters (thickness, nanopore diameter, nanopore length, etc.) can be partly controlled by appropriate choice of one or more of the parameters heating rate, LH, Δt(irr), F and/or v.

Suitable applications of the invention, using ionic current or electronic current, include the following: (1) counting of genomic or non-genomic fragments, by identification of a first end and/or a second end of each fragment that passes through a nanopore; (2) identification of locations of single strand segments and double strand segments in a "mixed" DNA sequence passing through a nanopore; (3) discrimination between single strands and double strands of DNA passing through a nanopore; and (4) identification of individual nucleotides in single strand DNA passing through a nanopore; (5) identification of corresponding base pairs (e.g., cytosine-guanine, adenine-thymine and adenine-uracil) in a double strand DNA or RNA passing through a nanopore, and (6) estimation of polymer component length by correlation with length of time interval for translocation.

What is claimed is:

1. A method of fabricating a nanopore, the method comprising:

heating a hollow cylinder of a pipette material, comprising primarily at least one of quartz glass, aluminosilicate glass and borosilicate glass, by a process comprising use of at least one of a laser, an infrared light source and a heated metal for heating one or more locations on the cylinder for a first time interval, the hollow cylinder having first and second cylinder ends, having a longitudinal axis and having a non-zero initial inner diameter; and

applying a machine controlled translation force to translate at least one of the first and second cylinder ends relative to the other of the first and second cylinder ends by a change in end-to-end separation distance no greater than about 2 cm during a second time interval that partly or wholly overlaps the first time interval, in order to encourage the hollow cylinder to separate into at least first and second pipettes, each with a corresponding nanopore, with at least one pore diameter in a range of 1-40 nanometers (nm) and with at least one pore length no greater than about 2 cm.

2. The method of **1**, further comprising choosing said heating source from a group of heating sources consisting of a laser, an infrared light source, and a heated metal.

3. The method of claim **1**, further comprising:

providing a selected liquid in contact with an interior surface of said pore;

impressing a non-zero voltage difference across the selected liquid within said pore approximately parallel to a longitudinal axis direction of said cylinder, and determining at least one of an electrical current value and an ionic current value induced in the selected liquid; and

passing a polymer molecule, having a sequence of polymer components, through said pore in a first direction, determined with reference to the longitudinal axis direction, and determining at least one of an electrical current signal and an ionic current signal induced by passage of each of the polymer components through said pore.

4. The method of claim **3**, further comprising selecting material for said pipette from a group of materials including quartz glass, aluminosilicate glass and borosilicate glass.

5. The method of claim **3**, further comprising passing said polymer sequence through said pore at an average rate in a range of 1-1000 polymer components per msec.

6. The method of claim **3**, further comprising choosing said polymer sequence to be a nucleic acid sequence including the bases adenine, cytosine and guanine and at least one of the bases thymine and uracil.

9

7. The method of claim 3, further comprising selecting said voltage difference from a group of time-dependent differences including a difference that (i) is approximately uniform in time; (ii) increases monotonically with time; (iii) decreases monotonically with time; (iv) is a step function in time; (v) varies sinusoidally with time; and (vi) varies trapezoidally with time.

8. The method of claim 3, further comprising choosing said selected liquid to include at least one of an alkali halide, an ammonium compound, an ionic organic compound and an ionic inorganic compound.

9. The method of claim 1, further comprising providing a self-assembling monolayer of a selected substance on a selected portion of said interior surface of said pore.

10. The method of claim 9, further comprising choosing said self assembling monolayer to include at least one of: (i) octadecyltrichlorosilane on glass and (ii) (16-Mercapto) hexadecanoic acid on a gold substrate.

11. The method of claim 1, further comprising:

providing a selected liquid in contact with an interior surface of said pore;

impressing a non-zero voltage difference across the selected liquid within said pore transverse to a longitudinal axis direction of said cylinder, and determining an ionic current value induced in the selected liquid; and

passing a polymer molecule, having a sequence of polymer components, through said pore in a first direction, determined with reference to the longitudinal axis direction, and determining an ionic current signal induced by passage of each of the polymer components through said pore.

10

12. The method of claim 11, further comprising passing said polymer sequence through said pore at an average rate in a range of 1-1000 polymer components per msec.

13. The method of claim 11, further comprising choosing said polymer sequence to be a nucleic acid sequence including the bases adenine, cytosine and guanine and at least one of the bases thymine and uracil.

14. The method of claim 11, further comprising selecting said voltage difference from a group of time-dependent differences including a difference that (i) is substantially uniform in time; (ii) increases monotonically with time; (iii) decreases monotonically with time; (iv) is a step function in time; (v) varies sinusoidally with time; and (vi) varies trapezoidally with time.

15. The method of claim 11, further comprising choosing said selected liquid to include at least one of an alkali halide, an ammonium compound, an ionic organic compound and an ionic inorganic compound.

16. The method of claim 1, further comprising providing a self-assembling monolayer of a selected substance on a portion of said interior surface of said pore.

17. The method of claim 16, further comprising choosing said self assembling monolayer to include at least one of: (i) octadecyltrichlorosilane on glass and (ii) (16-Mercapto) hexadecanoic acid on a gold substrate.

18. The method of claim 1, further comprising applying said machine controlled translation force in a range of between 10 dynes and 10 million dynes in a direction corresponding to said longitudinal axis.

* * * * *

US007305935B1

(12) **United States Patent** (10) **Patent No.:** **US 7,305,935 B1**

Foster (45) **Date of Patent:** **Dec. 11, 2007**

(54) **SLOTTED ANTENNA WAVEGUIDE PLASMA SOURCE**

(75) Inventor: **John Foster**, Strongsville, OH (US)

(73) Assignee: **The United States of America as represented by the Administration of NASA**, Washington, DC (US)

(*) Notice: Subject to any disclaimer, the term of this patent is extended or adjusted under 35 U.S.C. 154(b) by 0 days.

(21) Appl. No.: **10/925,499**

(22) Filed: **Aug. 25, 2004**

(51) **Int. Cl.**
C23C 16/00 (2006.01)
C23F 1/00 (2006.01)
H01L 21/306 (2006.01)

(52) **U.S. Cl.** .... **118/723 MA**; 118/723 MW; 156/345.41; 156/345.42

(58) **Field of Classification Search** .... 118/723 MW, 118/723 MA, 723 MR; 156/345.36, 345.41, 156/345.42, 345.46, 345.49
See application file for complete search history.

(56) **References Cited**

U.S. PATENT DOCUMENTS

3,604,012	A	*	9/1971	Lindley	343/768
5,466,295	A	*	11/1995	Getty	118/723 MA
5,579,019	A	*	11/1996	Uematsu et al.	343/771
5,783,102	A	*	7/1998	Keller	216/68
5,891,252	A		4/1999	Yokogawa et al.	
6,033,481	A		3/2000	Yokogawa et al.	
6,190,496	B1		2/2001	DeOrnellas et al.	
6,196,155	B1	*	3/2001	Setoyama et al.	156/345.42
6,294,862	B1	*	9/2001	Brailove et al.	313/363.1

6,350,347	B1	2/2002	Ishii et al.	
6,376,796	B2	4/2002	Sato et al.	
6,380,684	B1	4/2002	Li et al.	
6,390,019	B1	5/2002	Grimbergen et al.	
6,504,159	B1	1/2003	Keller	
6,551,445	B1	4/2003	Yokogawa et al.	
6,632,324	B2	10/2003	Chan	
2001/0008171	A1	7/2001	Fukuda et al.	
2003/0062129	A1 *	4/2003	Ni	156/345.42
2003/0150562	A1	8/2003	Quon	
2004/0090290	A1 *	5/2004	Teshirogi et al.	333/237

OTHER PUBLICATIONS

Foster "Discharge Characterization of 40 cm-Microwave ECR Ion Source and Neutralizer" NASA Gleen Research Center, Cleveland, OH, no date available.

* cited by examiner

Primary Examiner—Parviz Hassanzadeh
Assistant Examiner—Rakesh K. Dhingra
(74) *Attorney, Agent, or Firm*—Howard M Cohn

(57) **ABSTRACT**

A high density plasma generated by microwave injection using a windowless electrodeless rectangular slotted antenna waveguide plasma source has been demonstrated. Plasma probe measurements indicate that the source could be applicable for low power ion thruster applications, ion implantation, and related applications. This slotted antenna plasma source invention operates on the principle of electron cyclotron resonance (ECR). It employs no window and it is completely electrodeless and therefore its operation lifetime is long, being limited only by either the microwave generator itself or charged particle extraction grids if used. The high density plasma source can also be used to extract an electron beam that can be used as a plasma cathode neutralizer for ion source beam neutralization applications.

5 Claims, 5 Drawing Sheets

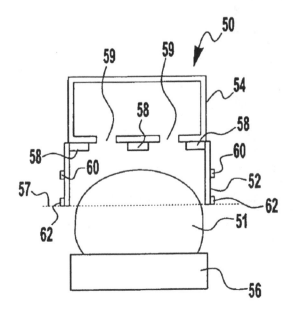

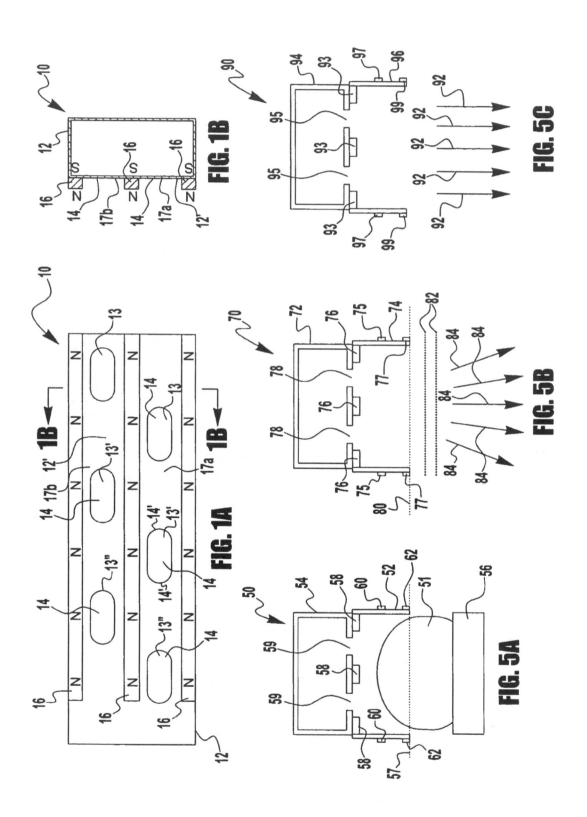

FIG. 1B

FIG. 5C

FIG. 1A

FIG. 5B

FIG. 5A

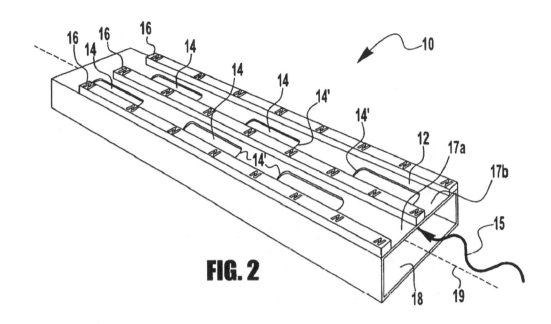

FIG. 2

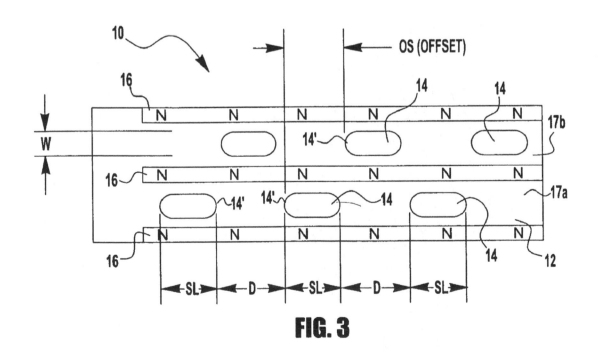

FIG. 3

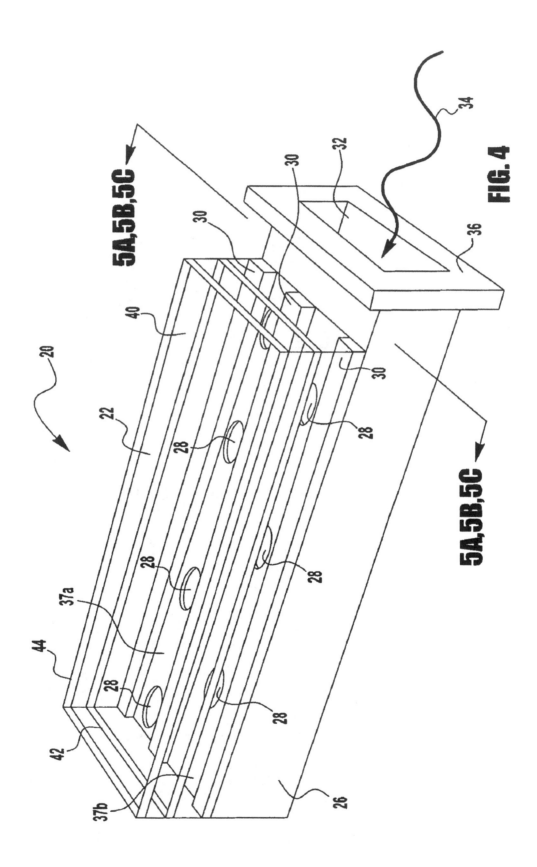

FIG. 4

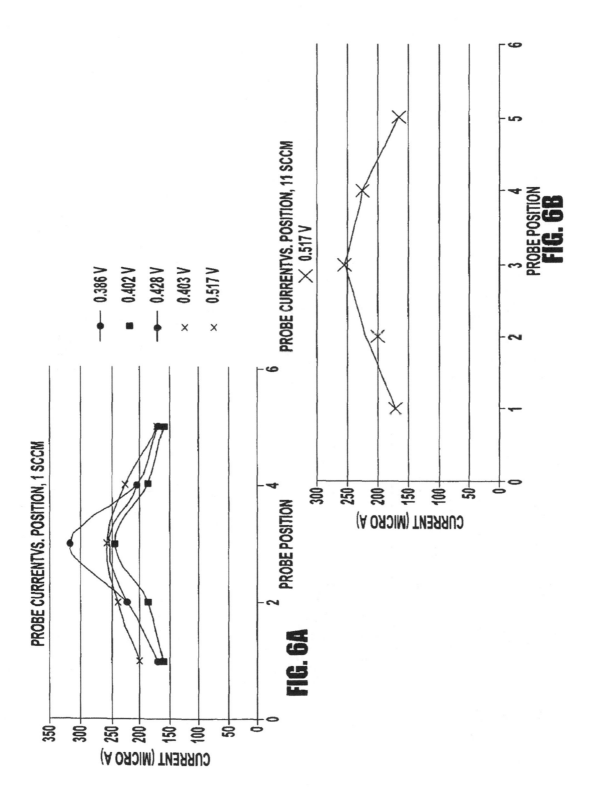

FIG. 6A

FIG. 6B

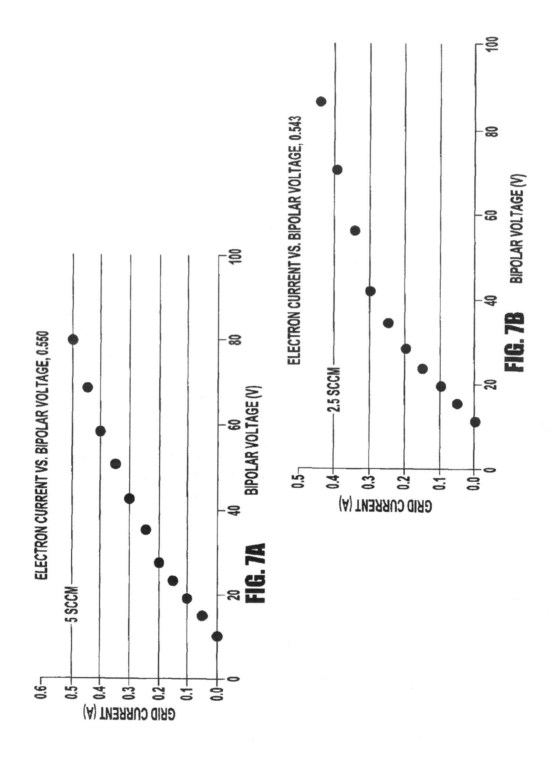

ELECTRON CURRENT VS. BIPOLAR VOLTAGE, 0.550
5 SCCM
GRID CURRENT (A)
0.0
0.1
0.2
0.3
0.4
0.5
0.6
0
20
40
60
80
100
BIPOLAR VOLTAGE (V)
FIG. 7A

ELECTRON CURRENT VS. BIPOLAR VOLTAGE, 0.543
2.5 SCCM
GRID CURRENT (A)
0.0
0.1
0.2
0.3
0.4
0.5
0
20
40
60
80
100
BIPOLAR VOLTAGE (V)
FIG. 7B

1

SLOTTED ANTENNA WAVEGUIDE PLASMA SOURCE

STATEMENT REGARDING FEDERALLY SPONSORED RESEARCH OR DEVELOPMENT

The invention described herein was made by an employee of the United States Government and may be manufactured and used by or for the Government for Government purposes without the payment of any royalties thereon or therefore.

FIELD OF THE INVENTION

The present invention relates to a plasma producing microwave antennas used for producing plasmas for use in ion thrusters, ion etching of surfaces, the embedding of ions within surfaces, production of electrons, and the like.

BACKGROUND OF THE INVENTION

Plasmas consist of gaseous complexes in which atoms or molecules are dissociated into free electrons, ions, free radicals, and neutral particles; stars, for instance, consist predominantly of plasmas. On earth, plasma occurs naturally in lightning bolts, flames, and similar phenomena, or may be manufactured by heating a gas to high temperatures, or by applying a strong electric field to a gas. Plasmas are called the "fourth state of matter" because their physical properties make them physically distinct from solids, liquids, and gases.

Ions, as well as electrons, from various kinds of plasma generators can be used in such industrial processes as etching, ashing (as with photoresist material or surfaces being chemically machined), deposition of materials such as oxides or nitrides, oxidation, sputtering, polymerization, ion implantation within surfaces and in high-specific-impulse thrusters for use on satellites and other space vehicles.

Drawbacks of existing direct current (DC) ion sources include erosion, short service life of plasma generators, and plasma non-uniformity. Erosion derives from the impacting of high-speed ions on the surfaces of the machines that produce plasmas. For example, DC ion sources eject erosion products into the discharge plasma as a consequence of the fact that the discharge cathode is constantly being bombarded by the ions of the plasma in which it is immersed. This is an undesirable attribute from the standpoint of materials processing, as contamination of the work product can result. DC ion sources (and DC electron sources) have limited lifetimes due to being constantly subjected to erosion, and the cathodes that drive such plasma sources typically, over time, lose their ability to emit electrons so that eventually the cathodes fail. Typically, DC ion sources (ion thrusters in particular) utilize a single on axis discharge cathode. This arrangement gives rise to peaked, non-uniform plasma density profiles at the exit plane. Such non-uniform profiles give rise to non-uniform wear of the ion extraction grids—thereby leading to failure by structural degradation or by electron backstreaming.

Disk shaped multi-slotted antenna designs have been used in the past to circumvent issues described above. These sources require, however, an insulating window for operation, i.e., for impedance matching and shielding. The insulating window, typically boron nitride makes such devices impractical for ion sources or ion thruster applications because the insulating window will acquire a coating over time due to wear of the extraction grids. The coating will

2

ultimately prevent microwaves form penetrating the source and thus plasma production will cease.

Prior art U.S. patents include U.S. Pat. No. 6,376,796 issued to Sato, et al entitled "Plasma processing system"; U.S. Pat. No. 6,190,496 issued to DeOrnellas, et al entitled "Plasma etch reactor and method for emerging films"; U.S. Pat. No. 6,033,481 issued to Yokogawa et al entitled "Plasma processing"; and U.S. Pat. No. 5,891,252 issued to Yokogawa et al entitled "Plasma processing apparatus."

Sato, et al., U.S. Pat. No. 6,376,796 relates to a plasma processing system utilizing an antenna supplying high power generating high density plasma for performing processing on the surface of a substrate. A slotted antenna supplies high frequency power. Sato has a disk-shaped conductor that performs impedance matching. A magnetic circuit using permanent magnets is provided close to the electromagnetic wave emitter.

DeOrnellas U.S. Pat. No. 6,190,496 claims a plasma etch reactor with a reactor chamber, two electrodes and power sources connected to the electrodes generate power at two different frequencies. A third electrode generates power at a low frequency. Magnetic confinement is utilized with the reactor chamber. The reactor is useful in etching the new class of films used in chip designs. The magnets can be permanent or electromagnets and are designed to concentrate the plasma which can reduce erosion to the electrodes and also protect the process chamber parts.

Yokogawa U.S. Pat. No. 6,033,481 discusses generation of uniform plasma over a large range for use in etching processing. High density plasma is generated in a vacuum vessel housing an electron cyclotron resonance device. An electromagnetic wave is radiated from a planar conductive plate arranged opposite to the surface of the sample being processed inside the vacuum vessel. The same patent also claims an electromagnetic wave radiation antenna consisting of strip-lines provided on an earth electrode opposite the processed sample.

Yokogawa U.S. Pat. No. 5,891,252 is similar to U.S. Pat. No. 6,033,481 and is cited because it too discusses antennas with a plasma source. The earlier patent provides a plasma processing apparatus which does not require large power consumption. It also discusses supplying an electromagnetic wave from a power source to a conductive plate in a planar shape and radiating the electromagnetic wave for forming plasma from the conductive plate.

The above-cited references do not disclose the particular combination of innovative features of present invention described hereinbelow. In Sato, et al., the design of the plasma generation antenna is the main part of the invention.

ASPECTS OF THE INVENTION

It is an aspect of the present invention to provide methods and apparatus as defined in one or more of the appended claims and, as such, having the capability of accomplishing one or more of the following subsidiary aspects.

In accordance with the foregoing, one aspect of the present electrodeless slotted antenna rectangular waveguide plasma source invention is to provide a plasma source that produces a distributed, uniform plasma density profile such as to make the plasma applicable for plasma processing applications.

Another aspect is to provide a plasma source that can be operated with permanent magnets only.

Another aspect of the present invention is to provide a plasma source that is capable of operating at low flow rates and low background pressures.

3

Another aspect of the present invention is to provide a plasma source that can be used as either an electron or an ion source.

Another aspect of the present invention is to provide a plasma source in which the plasma current densities produced at the exit plane of the device are large so as to yield high etch rates or material deposition rates.

Yet another aspect of the present invention is to provide a plasma source that does not require a microwave window.

And a final aspect of the present invention is to provide a microwave antenna approach that is straightforward to scale up to larger areas and higher powers.

SUMMARY OF THE INVENTION

The present invention is a slotted antenna waveguide plasma source that uses microwaves to drive electron cyclotron resonance (ECR) so as to create a plasma. The slotted antenna waveguide source is comprised of a waveguide having a primary axis; parallel mounted, spaced-apart bar magnets disposed along one outer wall of the waveguide; a series of matched radiating slot pairs machined in one wall of the waveguide between the externally mounted, parallel, spaced-apart, magnets; and a discharge chamber equipped with a first plasma containment ring of magnets disposed around a central perimeter of the discharge chamber and a second plasma containment/secondary ECR production ring of magnets disposed around a far perimeter of the discharge chamber. The parallel mounted, spaced-apart magnets are permanent magnets, and their magnetic poles are oriented in the same direction. All magnets are permanent magnets. The parallel, spaced-apart magnets comprise three magnets. The slots comprising the series of matched radiating slot pairs are arranged in two mutually parallel linear rows of uniformly spaced slots, each row being parallel to the primary axis or the waveguide. Each slot of each slot pair is offset from its mate in a direction parallel to the major axis of the waveguide. The uniformly spaced slots are spaced according to wavelength of microwaves being used. And each of the slots comprising the series of matched radiating slot pairs has rounded ends.

The present invention is a slotted antenna waveguide plasma source that uses microwaves to drive electron cyclotron resonance (ECR) so as to create a plasma. The slotted antenna waveguide source is comprised of a waveguide having a primary axis; parallel, spaced-apart bar magnets disposed along one outer wall of the waveguide; a single row of radiating slots machined in one wall of the waveguide between the externally mounted, parallel, spaced-apart, magnets; and a discharge chamber equipped with a first plasma containment ring of magnets disposed around a central perimeter of the discharge chamber and a second plasma containment/secondary ECR production ring of magnets disposed around a far perimeter of the discharge chamber.

The present invention is a method for producing a plasma by means of electron cyclotron resonance (ECR), the method being characterized by the steps of acquiring a microwave waveguide, determining its primary axis of the microwave waveguide and then modifying the microwave waveguide by machining a series of matched radiating slot pairs in one wall of the waveguide at regular intervals in a direction parallel to the primary axis of the waveguide; mounting parallel, spaced-apart magnets on one external wall of the waveguide in parallel alignment with the waveguide's primary axis; and mating to the waveguide a discharge chamber having an open side away from the

waveguide, and then distributing a first plasma containment ring of magnets around a central perimeter of the discharge chamber, and distributing a second plasma containment/ secondary ECR production ring of magnets around a far perimeter of the discharge chamber followed by situating the mated waveguide and discharge chamber inside of an evacuated enclosure, supplying a material to be ionized into a plasma into the enclosure and finally radiating microwaves into an opening at one end of the waveguide. The waveguide's physical dimensions and characteristics are matched with microwave wavelength to be used. The poles of the parallel, spaced apart magnets are oriented in the same direction, and all the magnets are permanent magnets. Each slot within each matched radiating slot pair is offset from one another in a direction parallel to the major axis of the waveguide. The slots are all machined so as to have rounded ends.

BRIEF DESCRIPTIONS OF THE FIGURES

The structure, operation, and advantages of the present invention will become apparent upon consideration of the description hereinbelow taken in conjunction with the accompanying FIGURES. The figures are intended to be illustrative, not limiting. Certain elements in some of the FIGURES may be omitted, or illustrated not-to-scale, for illustrative clarity. The cross-sectional views may be in the form of "slices", or "near-sighted" cross-sectional views, omitting certain background lines which would otherwise be visible in a "true" cross-sectional view, for illustrative clarity.

Although the invention is generally described in the context of these preferred embodiments, it should be understood that the FIGURES are not intended to limit the spirit and scope of the invention to these particular embodiments.

Certain elements in selected ones of the FIGURES may be illustrated not-to-scale, for illustrative clarity. The cross-sectional views, if any, presented herein may be in the form of "slices", or "near-sighted" cross-sectional views, omitting certain background lines which would otherwise be visible in a true cross-sectional view, for illustrative clarity.

Elements of the FIGURES can be numbered such that similar (including identical) elements may be referred to with similar numbers in a single FIGURE. For example, each of a plurality of elements collectively referred to as **199** may be referred to individually as **199a**, **199b**, **199c**, etc. Or, related but modified elements may have the same number but are distinguished by primes. For example, **109**, **109'**, and **109"** are three different elements which are similar or related in some way, but have significant modifications, e.g., a tire **109** having a static imbalance versus a different tire **109'** of the same design, but having a couple imbalance. Such relationships, if any, between similar elements in the same or different figures will become apparent throughout the specification, including, if applicable, in the claims and abstract.

The structure, operation, and advantages of the present preferred embodiment of the invention will become further apparent upon consideration of the following description taken in conjunction with the accompanying FIGURES, wherein:

FIG. 1A is an orthogonal schematic top view of the present electrodeless slotted waveguide plasma source invention showing the slotted waveguide and magnets;

FIG. 1B is an orthogonal schematic end view of the present electrodeless slotted waveguide plasma source invention showing the slotted waveguide and magnets;

5

6

FIG. **2** is an oblique schematic view of the present electrodeless slotted waveguide plasma source invention, showing the slotted waveguide, magnets and the inlet for microwave power;

FIG. **3** is an orthogonal schematic view top view of the present slotted waveguide plasma source invention, showing the characteristic dimensions and spacing of the slots;

FIG. **4** is an oblique schematic view of the present slotted waveguide plasma source invention, showing the slotted waveguide, magnets, inlet for microwave power, and a plasma containment/secondary ECR production ring;

FIG. **5A** is a schematic end-view of the electrodeless slotted waveguide plasma source invention showing the arrangement of the major components for plasma processing of materials;

FIG. **5B** is a schematic end-view of the electrodeless slotted waveguide plasma source invention showing the arrangement of the major components for use of the invention in the production of ions for use in an ion thruster application;

FIG. **5C** is a schematic end-view of the slotted waveguide plasma source invention showing the arrangement of the major components when the invention is used as an electron source;

FIGS. **6A** and **6B** are graphs of ion current density profiles; and

FIGS. **7A** and **7B** illustrate grid voltage as a function of extractable electron current at different flow rates when the invention is used as an electron source.

DEFINITIONS

Substrate refers to a material or workpiece that is to be etched by exposure to a plasma.

Contactor refers to a virtual "grounding rod" which serves to control charge buildup by generating a conductive plasma bridge so that excess charge can be discharged to the ambient potential.

DETAILED DESCRIPTION OF PREFERRED EMBODIMENT

Electrodeless electron cyclotron resonance (ECR) is the means employed in this slotted antenna waveguide plasma source invention. ECR is a commercially used technology primarily in the fields of high energy research and, at lower power, semiconductor wafer processing equipment for etching and material deposition.

This present invention has two factors that make it superior to any commercial ECR systems on the market.

It is electrodeless, and permanent magnets are used to generate the plasma as opposed to present-day commercial systems that use electromagnets and electrodes that are consumable. In wafer processing the electrode slowly erodes and results in some level of contamination on the wafer surface. Contaminated wafer areas are waste, thereby reducing processing throughput, efficiency, and yield. The technology eliminates the electrode and the subsequent contamination resulting in improved processing.

The configuration of the magnets above the slotted grid allows maintenance of a relatively constant power/slot ratio. Long bar-like spaced-apart parallel magnets above the slots create a series of channels. When a higher power design is required, slots are added to the grid in the channels and the input power can be increased. A full scale prototype has been operated with performance verified.

The purpose of this slotted antenna source invention is to electrodelessly generate uniform discharge plasma at reduced input powers and gas flow rates. This slotted antenna plasma source invention provides a source of ions as well as electrons in a completely electrodeless manner using ECR. It features a series of matched radiating slot pairs that are distributed at regular intervals along the length of the waveguide portion of this plasma source. This arrangement allows the plasma production to take place in a distributed fashion thereby giving rise to a uniform plasma profile. A uniform plasma profile is necessary for ion (electron) extraction optics uniformity. The slotted antenna design makes the approach scalable to much high powers. All that is required is the adding of additional matched radiating slot pairs along the length of the discharge chamber. In order for the power/slot ratio to remain constant, input microwave power must increase accordingly. Another key attribute of the slotted antenna approach described here is that it is designed so that an insulating window is not necessary. This allows the slotted antenna source to be used for ion beam and electron beam applications. The source is designed so that ECR takes place above each slot and the magnetic field at each slot provides a strong gradient to prevent plasmas backflow. The windowless nature of this invention gives it a distinct advantage over other slotted plasma source geometries which can only be used in non ion beam, non-deposition type plasma applications.

This invention produces high current densities and uniform discharge plasma. Additionally, it does not require cumbersome, energy-hungry electromagnets. The source has operated at 2.45 GHz but can be designed to operate at virtually any microwave frequency (915 MHZ to 6 GHz is a typical practical range of operation). Also, it does not require a microwave window which would otherwise be a contamination source. For ion beam applications this window could also be coated thereby preventing microwaves from coupling into the source and producing a discharge plasma.

The present electrodeless slotted antenna plasma source invention provides a uniform plasma density profile. Being an electrodeless plasma source, it has a long service life. It operates on the principle of electron cyclotron resonance (ECR). It does not require an insulating window, allowing it to be used for ion beam and electron beam applications. Thus this slotted antenna plasma source invention produces high current densities and uniform discharge plasma. This electrodeless slotted antenna plasma source invention can operate at virtually any microwave frequency, a typical range being 915 MHz to 6 Ghz. It has the potential to be used for ion thruster applications on spacecraft, including satellites, or as a source for plasmas appropriate for use in materials processing. Moreover it does not require electromagnets, as it operates with permanent magnets.

The primary advantage of this invention is the use of a slotted waveguide and a rectangular discharge that permits direct scalability to larger areas and higher power generators. As a source of ions or electrons, it can be scaled up simply by adding slots to the waveguide antenna. It is somewhat analogous to the slotted antennas used in microwave communication technologies.

Referring now to FIGS. **1A**, **1B** and **2**, the basic structure of the present invention becomes evident. FIG. **1A** is an orthogonal view of the top side (i.e., the long slotted side) of the present invention **10** comprised of the waveguide body **12**, slots **14**, and parallel, spaced-apart bar magnets **16** mounted along the external surface of one outer wall **12'** of the waveguide **12**. FIG. **1B** shows the slotted waveguide

7

8

invention **10** in cross-sectional view A-A' as that view is indicated in FIG. 1A. FIG. **2** is an oblique view of the waveguide invention **10**, showing the waveguide **12**, the slots **14**, and the permanent magnets **16**. The slots **14** comprise a series of matched radiating slot pairs (designated as **13**, **13'**, and **13"**, these numbers designating mated pairs of slots) machined in one wall **12'** of the waveguide **12**. The slots **14** and the slot pairs **13,13'** and **13"** can also be regarded as being arranged in two mutually parallel linear rows of uniformly spaced slots located within channels **17a**, **17b** lying between the parallel mounted, spaced-apart bar magnets **16**, each row being parallel to the primary axis of the waveguide.

Referring now specifically to FIG. **2**, there is shown the waveguide **12** having a primary axis **19** and with the slots **14** comprising a series matched radiating slot pairs disposed in two rows within channels **17a** and **17b**, and three bar magnets **16** disposed such as to separate and bracket each row or line of slots. The primary axis **19** is the long, or main, axis of the waveguide. Microwaves **15** are fed into the waveguide **12** at the open end **18** of the waveguide. The three magnets **16** are arranged such that their magnet poles are oriented in the same direction, shown with north pole face oriented upward in FIG. **2**. This is a preferred configuration, all polarities of the magnets **16** being the same, either N or S. However, the antenna has also been operated with alternating lines of magnets as well.

Three permanent magnets **16** is the maximum number envisioned. In this case the slots **14** are bounded by lines of magnets **16** on either side. This configuration has been validated. It is possible to use only two magnet row **16** as well. This too has been validated, especially at the higher frequencies where the spacing between slots **14** is too small to place a magnet of adequate field strength between slots. Additionally, it has been found that this configuration tends to reduce the magnetic field between slots **14** thereby allowing case of diffusion of plasma from the slotted antenna region into the plasma volume. Again, this approach has found best utility at the higher frequencies where the required field strengths are large and can thus reduce diffusion of plasma from the ECR zone.

The purpose of the lines of permanent magnets **16** is to establish the necessary magnetic field in the region above the slot (i.e., outside of the waveguide **12**) to ensure ECR. The magnets **16** also generate a field profile that prevents the backflow of plasma in the slot **14**. In this respect, at least two and no more than three magnet rows are used.

It is possible to utilize a single row of slots **14**, in which case only two permanent bar magnets **16** would be needed or required. The main requirement is that the slots **14** radiate in phase. In this regard, at most only two rows **17a,17b** of alternating slots **14** can be utilized.

It is worth noting that the slots may not necessarily be uniformly spaced perpendicular to the waveguide centerline, but they must be uniformly spaced along the axis.

During operation of this slotted antenna invention, plasma forms in the region of the desired electron cyclotron resonance (ECR) takes place on magnetic contours of sufficient magnetic field strength that satisfies the conditions for ECR. I.e., plasma production takes place at locations (plasma production sites) that are volumes of space disposed just outside of the waveguide **12** around the edges and centered on the middle of each slot **14**. During normal operation, the separate plasma productions sites associated with each slot **14** coalesce to become a single lines of plasma production that fill the channels **17a** and **17b**. That is to say, the series of matched radiating slot pairs are located below the plasma

production regions or sites which are more or less ellipsoidal until they coalesce or merge into single long strips of plasma filling, respectively, the channels **17a**, **17b**.

The slots **14** are not rectangular, rather each of the slots **14** comprising the series of matched radiating slot pairs (shown as **13**, **13'** and **13"** in FIG. 1A) has rounded ends, i.e., the short sides **14'** (FIG. 1A) of each rectangular slot is rounded. The dimensions of the slots are to be understood by referring to FIG. **3**. The length SL of each slot **14** is ½ the wavelength of the microwaves entering the end **18** of the waveguide **12**. The distance D between the slots **14** is ½ the waveguide wavelength. The distance D between the uniformly spaced slots **14** within each row or channel **17a,17b** can be longer than D so as long as the radiation field is in phase. That is, the slots **14** are spaced according to the wavelength of the microwaves to be used. The width W of the slot is chosen to be sufficiently narrow such that the aperture radiates like an idealized slot but not so narrow that the electric field causes electrical breakdown (arcing).

Note in FIGS. 1A, **2**, and **3** that the two lines of slots **14** filling the channels **17a** and **17b** between the magnets **16** are offset from one another by an amount shown as OS in FIG. **3**. That is, each slot of each slot pair is offset by an amount OS from its mate in a direction parallel to the major axis of the waveguide. The optimal offset OS of the slots sets in the respective channels **17a** and **17b** is determined either computationally or empirically. The offset OS works to intersect or interrupt the current in the wall of the waveguide **12**. In general, the displacement depends on the number of slots. If there is a large number of slot pairs, and uniform power distribution per slot is desired, then the slot displacements will not be uniform. Also, the invention does not have to have 3 slot pairs as shown in the FIGURES. More slots can be added in scaling up the power. In addition to the slot pairs, there must be one drainage slot which "empties" the remaining power.

Waveguide sizes are standardized such that the waveguide's characteristics are matched with the wavelength of microwave radiation to be used. The waveguide **12** used with this invention is WR 159 for 5.85 GHz operation, or WR 340 for 2.45 GHz operation. For each size, there is a specific frequency range over which the waveguide will operate.

FIG. **4** is an oblique view of the slotted antenna plasma source invention **20** with a discharge chamber **22** mated to the slotted waveguide **26** which has slots **28** disposed between spaced apart magnets **30**. ECR takes place near the plane **40** defining the top of (as shown in the view of FIG. **4**; the plane of the "top" is marked as a dashed line **57** in the inverted view of FIG. **5A**) the channels **37a,37b**. Microwaves **34** enter the waveguide **26** through the opening **32** in the waveguide mounting flange **36** which connects to a microwave source (not shown). The rectangular discharge chamber **22** is open at its top **40** and has disposed around its central perimeter (defined as the region of the discharge chamber about midway between the slotted wall of the waveguide **26** and the top plane **40** of the discharge chamber) a first plasma containment ring of permanent magnets **42**. The discharge chamber **22** also has a second plasma containment/secondary ECR production ring of magnets **44** disposed around its far perimeter (which lies in the plane **40** and is the portion of the discharge chamber most distal from the slotted wall of the waveguide **26**). (The plane of the top [i.e., **40** in FIG. **4**] is visible as a dashed line **57** in inverted, end-on, schematic view of FIG. **5A**.) The circumferentially disposed plasma containment ring of magnets **42** reduces diffusion losses and enhances the utilization of the hot electrons produced near the ECR zones defined by the channels **37a**, **37b** that are more or less in the region between the magnets **30**. ECR can also take place at these rings, providing additional ionization at the periphery.

FIGS. **5A**, **5B** and **5C** are end-on, inverted, sectional views (direction of view as indicated in FIG. **4**) of the waveguide plasma source shown as **20** of FIG. **4**.

FIG. **5A** is a schematic view of the present slotted antenna plasma source invention **50** as it would be used in the plasma processing of a material or substrate **56**. FIG. **5A** shows waveguide **54** mated with discharge chamber **52** disposed above a material or substrate **56** disposed near the plane **57** of the outlet of the discharge chamber. A volume of plasma **51** is shown abutting (and acting upon) a substrate **56**. That is to say, FIG. **5A** shows the approximate location of a substrate **56** relative to the waveguide **54** and the discharge chamber **52** when the present invention is used in the plasma processing of materials. FIG. **5A** also shows the spaced-apart parallel magnets **58**, slots **59**, a first plasma containment ring of magnets **60** and a second plasma containment/secondary ECR production ring of magnets **62**.

FIG. **5B** is a view of the slotted antenna plasma source invention **70** as it would appear (schematically) when used as an ion source intended for use as a thruster or ion milling/ion implantation. FIG. **5B** shows the waveguide **72**, discharge chamber **74**, spaced-apart parallel magnets **76**, slots **78**, a first plasma containment ring of magnets **75** and a second plasma containment/secondary ECR production ring of magnets **77**. The plane of the "top" or outlet **80** of the discharge chamber **74** is denoted by a dashed line, beyond which (i.e., outside of the discharge chamber) are disposed electrically charged grids **82** of the sort typically used to accelerate ions from the plasma source **70** in the direction indicated by arrows **84**.

FIG. **5C** is a view of the slotted antenna plasma source invention **90** as it would appear (schematically) when used to produce an electron beam **92**. FIG. **5C** shows waveguide **94**, discharge chamber **96**, spaced-apart parallel magnets **93**, slots **95**, first plasma containment ring of magnets **97** and a second plasma containment/secondary ECR production ring of magnets **99**. Electrons emerge from the discharge chamber **96** in the direction indicated by the arrows **92**. The electrons, having much less mass than the corresponding ions of the plasma, emerge from the discharge chamber **96** at much higher speeds than do the heavier ions.

When the present invention is used in the applications described above in relation to the FIGS. **5A**, **5B** and **5C**, mated waveguide and discharge chamber assembly is disposed such that the microwaves from the waveguide radiate into an evacuated enclosure into which a material to be ionized by radiating microwaves into a plasma is injected.

Window

A window, made of a dielectric material through which microwaves are emitted prior to producing plasmas, is used in some microwave plasma sources. No window is needed, used, or required in the present invention. And example of the use of such a dielectric window is taught in U.S. Pat. No. 6,376,796, to Sato, et al., who describe a disk-shaped multi-slotted antenna design.

In general, the function of the dielectric window is to aide in impedance matching of the microwaves from the waveguide to the vacuum. Additionally, the dielectric window can serve as a physical barrier to backflowing plasma which could potentially give rise to breakdowns and arcing that would disrupt microwave flow. In the present slotted antenna plasma source invention, the magnetic circuit in the

near the waveguide slots allows for gas breakdown and well-matched plasma production downstream of the slots. The well-matched plasma produced as a consequence of the optimized magnetic circuit eliminates the need for dielectrics to aid in impedance matching. Additionally, the magnetic field profile at each slot prevents plasma from backflowing into the slots and causing breakdowns there. Additionally, the magnetic field at and inside the slots is not sufficient to produce ECR so no plasma production can take place in the waveguide. Finally, the use of multiple slots reduces the electric field at each slot and thereby minimizes slot arcing which could be caused by the presence of the plasma. This is how the dielectric window was eliminated.

The invention of Sato, et al., utilizes a dielectric window that is described in the second paragraph, column 7, of the patent. The window covers the antenna disk comprising a hypothetical plane from which the microwaves emerge from the dielectric disk (**20**). In contrast, and as noted supra, the slotted antenna source according to the present invention does not utilize a microwave window of any kind. The microwave excitation emerges from the slots in the waveguide itself. No dielectric is required for microwave transport or matching. It should be pointed out that the device in Sato's invention is subject to coatings which could extinguish the discharge if they are conductive. That is to say, the present waveguide plasma source invention is designed so that no microwave dielectric window is not needed, and since there is no window, the issue of window coatings is thereby eliminated. Window coatings can prevent microwave flow (if the coating is metallic) or effect matching (if the coating is dielectric). The present windowless slotted antenna design can be used to generate plasma for materials processing applications where there are condensable dielectric or metal vapors present, because there is no dielectric window to coat over or otherwise fail. The dense plasma generated by this approach can be used for ion or electron extraction. In this respect it can serve as either an ion or an electron source.

Performance

FIGS. **6A** and **6B** show graphs of ion current density profiles as a function of position down the length of the rectangular plasma source at low and high flow rates between 48 and 74 W of microwave power. FIGS. **7A** and **7B** illustrate grid voltage as a function of extractable electron current at different flow rates when the slotted antenna plasma source invention is used as an electron source.

General Comments

This invention as applications in the semiconductor manufacturing sector as well as the broader area of plasma processing. Because of the unique ease of scaling to larger areas, work piece size is not a factor. The large uniform plasma produced by the above described source makes ideal for the processing of silicon wafers, implanting ions in various materials or controlling the chemistry of a deposition plasma. The scalable rectangular discharge shape is easily adaptable to commercial processes in semiconductor manufacturing and larger scale ion deposition processes that are currently limited to comparatively small work pieces. Erosion products are virtually eliminated as the plasma production is a purely electrodeless process. Manufacturers of semiconductor products either develop or utilize plasma sources for silicon wafer processing, implantation, or deposition processing.

This plasma source invention could also be used for long life ion thruster applications on commercial satellites. Additionally, satellite manufacturers may be interested in the

11

source for satellite charge control. The slotted antenna source could also serve as a plasma contactor for such applications. Also, since no windows are used or required, the device can operate in environments of condensable metal vapors.

Although the invention has been shown and described with respect to a certain preferred embodiment or embodiments, certain equivalent alterations and modifications will occur to others skilled in the art upon the reading and understanding of this specification and the annexed drawings. In particular regard to the various functions performed by the above described components (assemblies, devices, circuits, etc.) the terms (including a reference to a "means") used to describe such components are intended to correspond, unless otherwise indicated, to any component which performs the specified function of the described component (i.e., that is functionally equivalent), even though not structurally equivalent to the disclosed structure which performs the function in the herein illustrated exemplary embodiments of the invention. In addition, while a particular feature of the invention may have been disclosed with respect to only one of several embodiments, such feature may be combined with one or more features of the other embodiments as may be desired and advantageous for any given or particular application.

What is claimed is:

1. A windowless slotted antenna waveguide plasma source that uses microwaves to drive electron cyclotron resonance (ECR) so as to create a plasma, the windowless slotted antenna waveguide source being comprised of:

a slotted waveguide having a longitudinal primary axis and an open end adapted to receive the microwaves;

first, second and third parallel, spaced-apart permanent bar magnets each having a longitudinal axis mounted on an external surface of one wall of the slotted waveguide and the longitudinal axis of each of the bar magnets being parallel to the longitudinal primary axis to create first and second channels;

at least three matched radiating slot pairs in the one wall of the waveguide disposed with one slot of each of the at least three matched slot pairs disposed in the first channel between the first and second externally mounted, parallel, spaced-apart permanent bar magnets

12

and the other slot of each of the at least three matched slot pairs disposed in the second channel between the second and third externally mounted, parallel, spaced-apart permanent bar magnets whereby ECR takes place above each slot of the at least three matched slot pairs outside of the antenna waveguide and the magnetic field at each slot provides a strong gradient to prevent plasma backflow through each slot into the wave guide; and

a windowless discharge chamber open to the waveguide and equipped with:

a first plasma containment ring of permanent magnets disposed around a central perimeter of the discharge chamber; and

a second plasma containment/secondary ECR production ring of permanent magnets disposed around a far perimeter from the antenna of the windowless discharge chamber.

2. The windowless slotted antenna waveguide plasma source of claim **1** wherein the slots in each of the first and second channels are uniformly spaced from each other.

3. The windowless slotted antenna waveguide plasma source of claim **1** wherein the slots comprising each matched radiating slot pair are disposed such that one slot of each slot pair in the first channel is offset from the other slot of each slot pair in the second channel in a direction parallel to the primary axis of the waveguide.

4. The windowless slotted antenna waveguide plasma source of claim **1** wherein the magnetic poles of the first, second and third parallel, spaced-apart permanent bar magnets are oriented in the same direction whereby the same pole of each of the first, second and third, parallel, spaced-apart permanent bar magnets is disposed against the one wall of the waveguide and the opposite pole of each of the first, second and third, parallel, spaced-apart permanent bar magnets is oriented in the same direction upward from the waveguide.

5. The slotted antenna waveguide plasma source of claim **1** wherein the slots in each of the first and second channels are spaced apart according to wavelength of microwaves being used.

* * * * *

146

US007493869B1

(12) **United States Patent** (10) Patent No.: **US 7,493,869 B1**
Foster et al. (45) **Date of Patent:** **Feb. 24, 2009**

(54) **VERY LARGE AREA/VOLUME MICROWAVE ECR PLASMA AND ION SOURCE**

(75) Inventors: **John E. Foster**, Strongsville, OH (US); **Michael J. Patterson**, Brunswick, OH (US)

(73) Assignee: **The United States of America as represented by the Administration of NASA**, Washington, DC (US)

(*) Notice: Subject to any disclaimer, the term of this patent is extended or adjusted under 35 U.S.C. 154(b) by 587 days.

(21) Appl. No.: **11/311,183**

(22) Filed: **Dec. 16, 2005**

(51) **Int. Cl.**
 C23C 16/00 (2006.01)
(52) **U.S. Cl.** .... 118/723 AN; 118/723 MA; 156/345.41; 156/345.42
(58) **Field of Classification Search** ...., 118/723 MW, 118/723 MA, 723 MR, 723 AN; 156/345.41, 156/345.42; 315/111.21
See application file for complete search history.

(56) **References Cited**

U.S. PATENT DOCUMENTS

5,203,960 A	4/1993	Dandl	....	156/643
5,324,362 A	6/1994	Schneider et al.	.....	118/723 MP
5,370,765 A	12/1994	Dandl	....	156/643
5,707,452 A	1/1998	Dandl	....	118/723 MW

6,153,977 A	11/2000	Taira et al.	....	315/111.41
6,322,662 B1	11/2001	Ishii et al.	....	456/345
6,376,028 B1	4/2002	Laurent et al.	....	427/571
6,830,652 B1 *	12/2004	Ohmi et al.	....	156/345.41
7,404,991 B2 *	7/2008	Ohmi et al.	....	427/569
2002/0121344 A1	9/2002	Noguchi	....	156/345.48
2003/0173030 A1	9/2003	Ishii et al.	....	156/345.48
2003/0183170 A1	10/2003	Kato et al.	....	118/723 MW
2004/0045674 A1	3/2004	Ishii et al.	....	156/345.48

FOREIGN PATENT DOCUMENTS

JP	06151092 A	5/1994
JP	06158298 A	6/1994
WO	WO 91/12353	8/1991

* cited by examiner

Primary Examiner—David Hung Vu
(74) *Attorney, Agent, or Firm*—Howard M. Cohn

(57) **ABSTRACT**

The present invention is an apparatus and method for producing very large area and large volume plasmas. The invention utilizes electron cylcotron resonances in conjunction with permanent magnets to produce dense, uniform plasmas for long life ion thruster applications or for plasma processing applications such as etching, deposition, ion milling and ion implantation. The large area source is at least five times larger than the 12-inch wafers being processed to date. Its rectangular shape makes it easier to accommodate to materials processing than sources that are circular in shape, The source itself represents the largest ECR ion source built to date. It is electrodeless and does not utilize electromagnets to generate the ECR magnetic circuit, nor does it make use of windows.

20 Claims, 4 Drawing Sheets

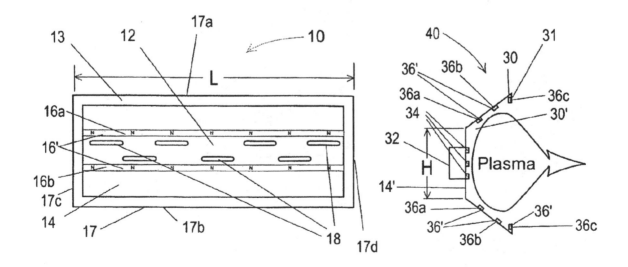

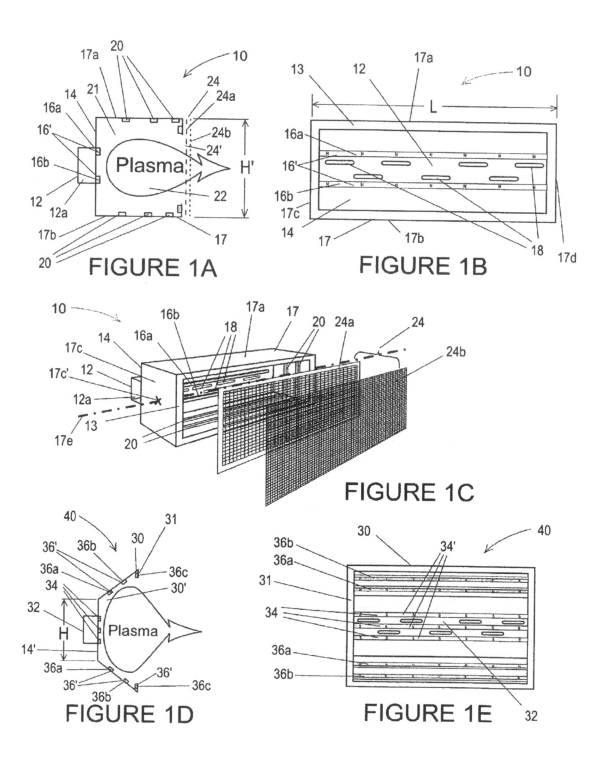

FIGURE 1A

FIGURE 1B

FIGURE 1C

FIGURE 1D

FIGURE 1E

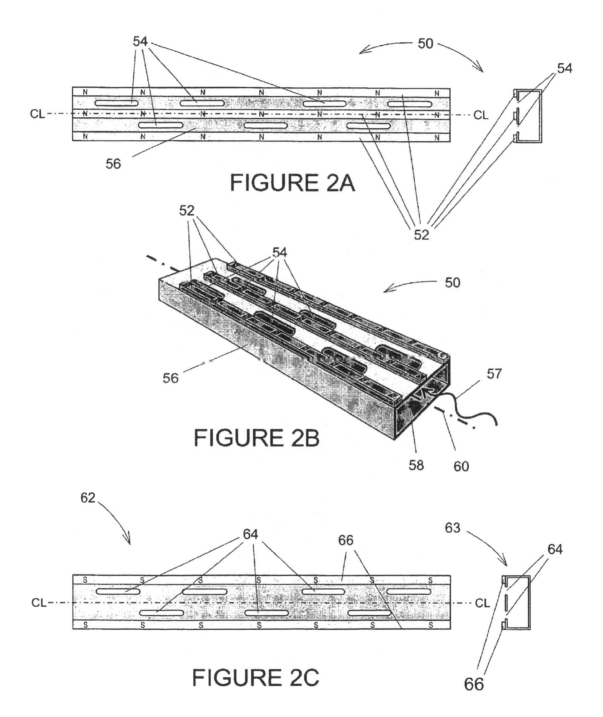

FIGURE 2A

FIGURE 2B

FIGURE 2C

149

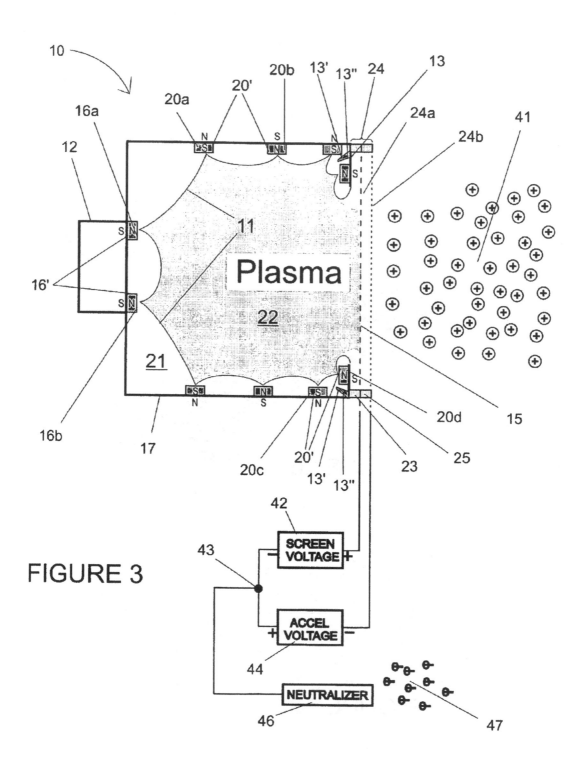

FIGURE 3

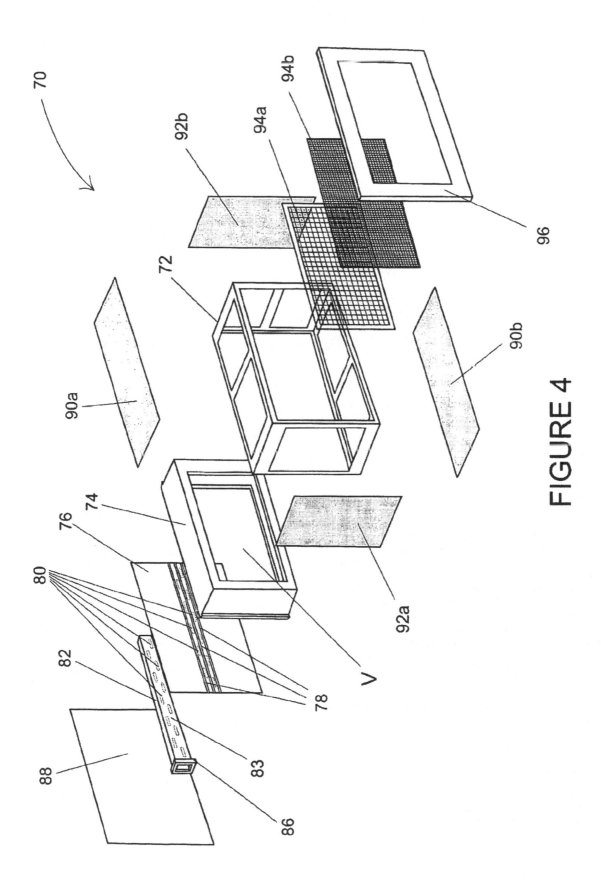

FIGURE 4

1

VERY LARGE AREA/VOLUME MICROWAVE ECR PLASMA AND ION SOURCE

STATEMENT REGARDING FEDERALLY SPONSORED RESEARCH OR DEVELOPMENT

The invention described herein was made by an employee of the United States Government and may be manufactured and used by or for the Government for Government purposes without the payment of any royalties thereon or therefore.

RELATED APPLICATIONS

U.S. application Ser. No. 10/894,225 entitled LARGE AREA PLASMA SOURCE filed Jul. 19, 2004 by J. Foster.

U.S. application Ser. No. 10/925,499 SLOTTED ANTENNA WAVEGUIDE PLASMA SOURCE filed Aug. 25, 2004 by J. Foster.

TECHNICAL FIELD OF THE INVENTION

The present invention relates to large area and large volume plasma sources and to microwave antennas used for producing plasmas for use in ion thrusters, ion etching of surfaces, the embedding of ions within surfaces, production of electrons, and the like.

BACKGROUND

Plasmas consist of gaseous complexes in which atoms or molecules are dissociated into free electrons, ions, free radicals, and neutral particles. Stars, for instance, consist predominantly of plasmas. On earth, plasmas occur naturally in lightning bolts, flames, and similar high-energy phenomena, or may be manufactured by heating a gas to high temperatures, or by applying a strong electric field to a gas. Plasmas are called the "fourth state of matter" because their physical properties make them physically distinct from solids, liquids, and gases.

Ions, as well as electrons, from various kinds of plasma generators can be used in such industrial processes as etching, ashing (as with photoresist material or surfaces being chemically machined), deposition of materials such as oxides or nitrides, oxidation, sputtering, polymerization, ion implantation within surfaces and also in high-specific-impulse thrusters for use on satellites and other space vehicles.

Drawbacks of existing direct current (DC) ion sources include erosion, short service life of plasma generators, and plasma non-uniformity. Erosion derives from the impacting of high-speed ions on the surfaces of the machines that produce plasmas. For example, DC ion sources eject erosion products into the discharge plasma as a consequence of the fact that the discharge cathode is constantly being bombarded by the ions of the plasma in which it is immersed. This is an undesirable attribute from the standpoint of materials processing, as contamination of the work product can result. DC ion sources (and DC electron sources) have limited lifetimes due to being constantly subjected to erosion, and the cathodes that drive such plasma sources typically, over time, lose their ability to emit electrons so that eventually the cathodes fail. Typically, DC ion sources (ion thrusters in particular) utilize a single on-axis discharge cathode, which gives rise to peaked, non-uniform plasma density profiles at the exit plane. Such non-uniform profiles cause non-uniform wear of the ion extraction grids—thereby leading to failure by structural degradation or by electron backstreaming.

2

Disk shaped multi-slotted antenna designs have been used in the past to circumvent the aforesaid issues. These sources require, however, an insulating window for operation, i.e., for impedance matching and shielding. The insulating window, typically boron nitride makes such devices impractical for ion sources or ion thruster applications because the insulating window acquires over time a coating due to wear of the extraction grids. Said coating will ultimately prevent microwaves form penetrating the source and thus plasma production will cease.

The production of large-area plasmas that are also large in volume and provide dense plasmas is much sought after in the area of electric propulsion and plasma processing. Achieving these plasma characteristics is generally difficult from the standpoint of issues such as recombination, collisional losses and diffusion, all of which reduce discharge efficiency and uniformity of the discharged reaction mass. Moreover, the design of plasma generators that are intended for use in electric propulsion and plasma processing applications tends toward the production of plasma discharges having minimal internal erosion of the source. From an electric propulsion thruster standpoint, this design goal provides extended operation lifetime. For plasma processing, it reduces the amount of contamination of the materials being processed.

It is also important that plasma discharges take place at reduced pressures. Hollow cathode based sources in a multipole configuration can be implemented to generate reasonably large discharge plasmas. However, such discharges tend to be of poor uniformity and to introduce erosion products due to cathode degradation (as it is exposed to the discharge plasma and bombarded by high-energy discharge ions). In this respect, conventional hollow cathode based discharge sources are not a solution to long life and low erosion plasma sources.

The prior art evidenced in patent literature shows various microwave, permanent magnet, ECR plasma sources, but they suffer from limitations that the present invention overcomes.

U.S. Patent Application 2004/0045674 A1 to Ishii, et al., "Radial Antenna and Plasma Device Using It," describes a general microwave discharge, not an electron cyclotron resonance discharge (ECR). In this system, the microwave discharge is fundamentally limited in maximum plasma density, efficiency, and pressure. It is not an efficient ion source at the kinds of low pressures that are desirable for directional etching and sputter deposition applications in microelectronics. The invention of Ishii, et al., also uses a dielectric window, which can be problematic for both ion thruster uses and many deposition microelectronics reactors where metal vapor is present in the plasma. Metal ions and atoms can condense on the window, forming a layer that eventually prevents any microwave power from entering the system. Additionally, the device of Ishii, et al., utilizes a coaxial line connection to the slotted antenna, which limits the amount of power, plasma density and thus the maximum dimension to which the source can be built, thus limiting the ability to scale it up without recourse to a complete system redesign to scale up to a larger size.

U.S. Patent Application 2003/0183170 A1, to Kato, et al., "Plasma Processing Apparatus," also describes a microwave system that lacks the potential of ECR. The comments above, in relation to US 2004/0045674 A1 apply to this source as well.

U.S. Patent Application 2003/0173030, to Ishii, et al., "Plasma Processing Apparatus," describes essentially the same device addressed in relation to US 2004/0045674 A1. In this case however, Ishii, et al., focus on plasma processing application of the device. In this regard, its size is limited and can be scaled up only with difficulty.

U.S. Patent Application 2002/0121344 A1, to Noguchi, "Plasma Generating Device and Plasma Processing Apparatus Comprising Such a Device," utilizes the same physics described in the patents described above. Power is fed to it by means of a coaxial line.

Japanese Patent 06151092 A, to Kyoichi, "Microwave Plasma Treatment Device," also describes a microwave discharge device that is similar to the ones taught in the foregoing patents. It does not describe a high density low pressure ECR source.

Japanese Patent 06158298 A, to Mutsumi, et al., "Plasma Treating Device," does not describe microwave plasma of any sort. It describes a RF glow discharge for plasma processing applications. Such devices operated at pressures ~1 Torr and plasma densities are low and not particularly suited for etching or Sputter deposition. Sputter contamination is an issue for such a source.

WO 91/12353, "Device for Treating Substrates in a Gas-Based Plasma Produced by Microwaves," describes a specialized microwave plasma source intended for the processing of optical coatings. It suffers from limitations described above in comments 1-4.

U.S. Pat. No. 5,324,362, to Schneider, et al., "Apparatus for Treating Substrates in a Microwave-Generated Gas-Supported Plasma," apparently refers to a US patent WO 91/12353. This technology suffers from limitations described above in comments 1-4. As a sputtering source it could introduce contaminants in a deposition or etching plasma. It also presents a lifetime issue as the antenna would be subject to sputtering. The source also utilizes a microwave window, which has disadvantages described herein.

U.S. Pat. No. 6,376,028, to Laurent, et al. "Device and Method for Treating the Inside Surface of a Plastic Container with a Narrow Opening in a Plasma Enhanced Process," does not describe a plasma source but rather a device and process that requires a plasma (preferably microwave generated). It is not applicable to the present invention.

U.S. Pat. No. 6,153,977, to Taira, et al., "ECR Type Plasma Generating Apparatus," refers to an ECR source that utilizes a helical antenna that presumably launches a directed microwave beam toward and ECR zone established by two permanent magnets in opposition. It is inherently a small diameter device, and the ECR zone must be established between two closely spaced magnets. The device is not scalable to larger dimensions of the sort useful for large area plasma processing, high current, or long life ion thruster applications. Moreover, it is limited with respect to plasma density, which means that a workpiece to be processed must rely on the diffusion of the magnetized plasma, which is in general a slow process and can result in non-uniformities. And because it has an internal antenna it will be subject to sputter erosion limitations on service life, while also generating contaminants. The outer ceramic shield would be subject to the formation of metal coatings over time, which could affect the microwave coupling and thus the overall operation. Also because the device is coaxially fed, it is inherently limited to reduced microwave power.

U.S. Pat. No. 5,707,452, to Dandl, "Coaxial Microwave Applicator for an Electron Cyclotron Resonance Plasma Source," describes a permanent magnet ECR source that utilizes internal coaxially fed antennas immersed in ECR zones to produce plasma. This use of the coax fed antennas circumvents issues of a similar device patented by Dandl: U.S. Pat. No. 5,203,960 and U.S. Pat. No. 5,370,765 which utilize internal antennas that are subject to erosion and therefore become likely plasma contamination sources. Additionally, as each internal antenna is coaxially fed, which makes them power limited.

U.S. Pat. No. 5,203,960, to Dandl, "Method of Operation of Electron Cyclotron Resonance Plasma Source," and U.S. Pat. No. 5,370,765, also to Dandl, "Electron Cyclotron Resonance Plasma Source and Method of Operation," cannot be utilized efficiently at lower, more commercially assessable frequencies such as 2.45 GHZ. Patent '960 has cylindrical geometry which means that scaling to larger volumes requires a complete redesign of the magnetic circuit.

U.S. Pat. No. 6,322,662, to Ishii, et al. "Plasma Treatment System," utilizes a coax fed slotted antenna which inherently limits power and complicates implementation, as the coax feed would necessarily be water cooled at modest powers. It also uses a ceramic microwave window which would be subject to coating and so preclude its application to etching and deposition plasmas where metal vapors could be deposited on the ceramic. Additionally, the slotted antenna geometry of this invention is complicated and its overall layout does not lend well to scaling up in power. The antenna geometry is sophisticated, thereby imposing or requiring significant fabrication effort. Additionally, this invention is not an ECR source, but rather utilizes microwave energy to directly sustain the discharge via pair production. In this regard, it has to operate at a high background pressures that limit its uses. In general, the devices described in the Dandl patents, by virtue of the plasma production approach, will likely not scale with increasing diameter. The ECR zones are not couple via the ring cusp magnetic circuit, which allows for very large area/volume plasma production with straightforward scaling.

SUMMARY OF THE INVENTION

The present invention is a large electrodeless and windowless plasma source comprising a plasma chamber defining an enclosed and elongated prismatic volume and comprising a rectangular top wall having an inner planar surface, a rectangular bottom wall having an inner planar surface, two parallel quadrangular end walls having inner planar surfaces having centroids that define a length axis, a planar rectangular back portion having a height dimension and a planar rectangular exit plane having a height dimension and a perimeter. A slotted waveguide microwave antenna having a main axis and a plurality of matched slot pairs on one face feeds microwave energy into the plasma chamber, which contains a magnetic circuit comprising a first magnetic circuit portion and a second magnetic circuit portion. A means for injecting gases into the plasma chamber is provided. The prismatic plasma chamber can be a rectangular volume defined by the planar inner surfaces of the rectangular top wall and the rectangular bottom wall which are parallel to one another, the two parallel quadrangular end walls having inner planar surfaces, and the a planar rectangular back portion and the planar rectangular exit plane which are parallel to one another. The main axis of the slotted waveguide microwave antenna and the length axis of the plasma chamber that is defined by centroids of the two parallel quadrangular end walls are parallel and spaced apart. The first magnetic circuit portion is comprised of at least two linear magnets mounted external to the slotted waveguide microwave antenna and parallel to the main axis of the slotted waveguide and oriented into the plasma chamber, and the at least two linear magnets are permanent magnets having magnetic poles that are oriented in the same direction. The second magnetic circuit portion is comprised of a plurality of spaced apart linear magnets having magnetic poles and disposed about the inner top and bottom walls and the end walls of the

5

prismatic volume of the plasma chamber so that each spaced apart linear magnet forms a planar rectangular magnet loop that is parallel to the planar rectangular exit plane, and the magnetic poles of adjacent spaced apart planar rectangular magnetic loops are oppositely oriented with respect to each other. The overall magnetic circuit is comprised of a plurality of spaced apart linear magnets and magnet loops having polarities that alternate. The slotted waveguide microwave antenna is mounted to the back portion of the plasma chamber and the plurality of matched slot pairs on one face of the antenna are oriented into the prismatic volume of the plasma chamber. Gas injection means is disposed about the perimeter of the exit plane. Ion optics means can be disposed across the exit plane so as to focus the exiting plasma beam of ions. The enclosed prismatic volume can, as an alternative to the rectangular volume described above, be trapezoidal in cross-sectional shape when viewed along the length axis defined by the centroids of the two parallel quadrangular end walls, said trapezoidal cross-sectional shape being further defined by the height dimension of the planar rectangular back portion being less than the height dimension of the planar rectangular exit plane, while the two parallel quadrangular end walls are trapezoidal in shape. Ion optics can be used as well with the trapezoidal shaped plasma chamber.

The present invention is a method of creating a large electrodeless and windowless plasma source, the method being characterized by the steps of assembling a plasma chamber enclosed within an elongated prismatic volume whose shape is defined by a rectangular top wall having an inner planar surface, a rectangular inner bottom wall having an inner planar surface, two parallel quadrangular end walls having inner planar surfaces and centroids that define a length axis of the plasma chamber, a planar rectangular back portion, and a planar rectangular exit plane, and the further steps of affixing to the planar rectangular back portion a slotted waveguide microwave antenna having a main axis, at least two linear permanent magnets oriented parallel to said main axis and having magnetic poles, and a plurality of matched slot pairs oriented into the prismatic volume of the plasma chamber, disposing within the prismatic volume of the plasma chamber a plurality of mutually adjacent, non-coplanar permanent magnet loops having magnetic poles, one loop of which is closest to the slotted waveguide microwave antenna and providing one or more inlets for a gas to be ionized. The method is further characterized by alignment of the main axis of the slotted waveguide microwave antenna parallel to the length axis defined by the centroids of the quadrangular end walls and includes the further step of orienting the magnetic poles of each mutually adjacent non-colinear permanent magnet loop in a direction opposite those of adjacent loops whose magnetic poles must be oriented such that each of the at least two linear permanent magnets affixed to the slotted waveguide microwave antenna are oriented in a single direction that is opposite that of the magnetic pole of the permanent magnet loop that is closest to the at least two linear permanent magnets. The method can also include the further step of installing ion optics means across the planar rectangular exit plane.

BRIEF DESCRIPTION OF THE FIGURES

The structure, operation, and advantages of the present invention will become apparent upon consideration of the description herein below taken in conjunction with the accompanying FIGURES. The FIGURES are intended to be illustrative, not limiting. Certain elements in some of the FIGURES may be omitted, or illustrated not-to-scale, for

6

illustrative clarity. The cross-sectional views may be in the form of "slices," or "near-sighted" cross-sectional views, omitting certain background lines which would otherwise be visible in a "true" cross-sectional view, for illustrative clarity.

Although the invention is generally described in the context of these preferred embodiments, it should be understood that the FIGURES are not intended to limit the spirit and scope of the invention to these particular embodiments.

Certain elements in selected ones of the FIGURES may be illustrated not-to-scale, for illustrative clarity. The cross-sectional views, if any, presented herein may be in the form of "slices", or "near-sighted" cross-sectional views, omitting certain background lines which would otherwise be visible in a true cross-sectional view, for illustrative clarity.

Elements of the FIGURES can be numbered such that similar (including identical) elements may be referred to with similar numbers in a single FIGURE. For example, each of a plurality of elements collectively referred to as **199** may be referred to individually as **199a**, **199b**, **199c**, etc. Or, related but modified elements may have the same number but are distinguished by primes. For example, **109**, **109'**, and **109"** are three different elements which are similar or related in some way, but have significant modifications, e.g., a tire **109** having a static imbalance versus a different tire **109'** of the same design, but having a couple imbalance. Such relationships, if any, between similar elements in the same or different figures will become apparent throughout the specification, including, if applicable, in the claims and abstract.

The structure, operation, and advantages of the present preferred embodiment of the invention will become further apparent upon consideration of the following description taken in conjunction with the accompanying FIGURES, wherein:

FIG. **1A** is an orthogonal schematic cut-away end view of one embodiment of the invention;

FIG. **1B** is an orthogonal schematic front view of the embodiment of FIG. **1A**;

FIG. **1C** is an oblique schematic view of the embodiment of FIG. **1A**;

FIG. **1D** is an orthogonal schematic cut-away end view of a second embodiment of the invention;

FIG. **1E** is an orthogonal schematic front view of the embodiment of FIG. **1D**;

FIG. **2A** is an orthogonal front view of a three-magnet slotted waveguide antenna and plasma source;

FIG. **2B** is an oblique view of the waveguide antenna of FIG. **2A**;

FIG. **2C** is an orthogonal front view of a two-magnet slotted waveguide antenna and plasma source;

FIG. **3** is an end-on schematic view of one embodiment of the invention, showing the magnetic circuit and the operation of the ion optics; and

FIG. **4** is an oblique exploded view of an existing embodiment of the present invention.

DETAILED DESCRIPTION OF THE PREFERRED EMBODIMENTS

The present invention is a large area and large volume microwave electron cyclotron resonance (ECR) plasma and ion source that can be used as either a high density, large area plasma source and/or as an ion source. It is electrodeless and windowless. Its applications include materials processing operations such as ion milling and ion implantation and ion propulsion for space vehicles. An analysis of the performance of the present invention, entitled, "High Power ECR Ion Thruster Discharge Characterization," was presented by the inventor at the International Electric Propulsion Conference on Nov. 2, 2005, and is incorporated herein in its entirety by reference hereto.

FIG. 1A is an orthogonal, cut-away, schematic end-view of one embodiment 10 of a large area, large volume, plasma and ion source 10 according to the present invention. FIG. 1B is an orthogonal schematic front view of this embodiment of the ion source 10, and FIG. 1C is an oblique view of the ion source 10.

The large area, large volume, plasma and ion source 10 comprises a slotted waveguide antenna 12 that is attached to the back wall 14 of the plasma and ion source 10. The slotted waveguide microwave antenna 12 is rectangular in cross section and extends along the long dimension L (FIG. 1B) on the back wall 14 of the plasma and ion source 10. The waveguide 12 is shown with two spaced apart permanent magnets 16a, 16b that are oriented along the length L of the waveguide, as shown in the orthogonal front view FIG. 1B wherein are shown the microwave radiating slots 18 whereat plasma formation takes place due to the interaction of gas atoms with microwaves. The spaced apart permanent magnets 16a,16b are the elements of a first magnetic circuit portion 16' of a total magnetic circuit 11 (FIG. 3). As described below, this first magnetic circuit 16' might include a third magnet between the two shown, 16a,16b, according to the frequency of the microwaves being used. Also as described below, plasma formation also takes place in the vicinity of a secondary magnet circuit portion 20' (FIG. 3) that is comprised of magnet rings 20 (FIG. 1A) due to electron cyclotron resonance discharge (ECR). (FIG. 3 shows the complete magnetic circuit 11, with its primary portion 16' and secondary portion 20' comprising at least the magnetic rings 20a,20b,20c,20d.) The waveguide magnets 16a,16b, comprising a first magnetic circuit portion 16', together with the secondary magnet circuit 20' (FIG. 3), form a magnetic circuit portion 11 (FIG. 3) that is described in more detail below. The magnetic circuit 11 of the invention is comprised of the first magnetic circuit portion 16', consisting of at least two linear magnets 16a,16b and the second magnetic circuit portion 20' (FIG. 3) that is contained within the plasma chamber, as described below.

The plasma chamber 21 has a prismatic volume defined by, or enclosed by, an elongated prismatic housing 17, the boundaries of which are a rectangular top wall 17a that has an inner planar surface and a rectangular bottom wall 17b that also has an inner planar surface, plus two parallel quadrangular end walls 17c,17d (FIG. 1B) having planar surfaces with centroids 17c',17d' that define a length axis 17e for the plasma chamber 21, and a planar rectangular back portion 14 having a height dimension H (shown in reference to back portion 14' in FIG. 1D) and a planar rectangular exit plane 24' having a height dimension H' and a perimeter 13. Injection of gas to be ionized is done by gas injection means 13' (FIG. 3) consisting of injection ports 13" (FIG. 3) disposed around the perimeter 13 of the plasma chamber 21 in the vicinity of the exit plane 24'. More specifically, and referring to FIG. 3, gas is injected roughly in the region between secondary magnet loops 20c and 20d. The present plasma source invention 10 can operate on virtually any common gas, including air, xenon, and CO_2, all of which have been demonstrated.

Referring to FIGS. 1A, 1B, the waveguide magnets 16a, 16b are oriented such that their north poles (N) are oriented outward from the back 14 of the housing 17. South poles (S) could as well be so oriented. In either case, north or south, the pole orientations of the waveguide magnets 16a,16b are the same so as to create magnetic field lines that are, at least in the proximity of the radiating slots 18, more or less normal to the

plane of the radiating slots. The poles of the secondary magnet rings 20 (20a,20b,20c,20d in FIG. 3) alternate in ways described below.

FIG. 1C is an oblique schematic view of the ion source invention 10, showing the slotted antenna rectangular waveguide 12 attached to the back 14 of housing 17. The waveguide magnets 16a,16b are shown, as are the radiating slots 18. Also shown in FIG. 1C is the ion optics means 24 which comprises two component electrical screen or grids 24a,24b, which are shown displaced forward of the main body 17 of the source 10. When the ion source invention 10 is used as a high-specific-impulse thruster, the grids 24a,24b of the ion optics 24 would be attached to and sealed against the front perimeter flange 13. The ion optics 24 would also be used when the ion/plasma source 10 is used in certain, but not all, materials processing operations such as ion milling and ion implantation.

FIGS. 1D and 1E show two orthogonal schematic views of a second embodiment 40 of the present plasma source invention wherein the housing 30 opens outward from the slotted waveguide 32 and encloses a plasma chamber 30' that is a prismatic volume. The waveguide 32 is shown in FIGS. 1D and 1E with three spaced-apart waveguide magnets 34. This different number of magnets is related to the microwave frequency, which is 5.85 GHz, versus 2.45 GHz used with the two-magnet set up shown in FIGS. 1A,1B and 1C. Either frequency, 5.85 GHz or 2.45 GHz, can be used in either of the embodiments 10 and 40 shown in FIGS. 1A through 1E, though with adjustments in the number of waveguide magnets 16a,16b and 34 according to the microwave frequency being used. In FIG. 1E, the three waveguide magnets 34 are shown as having their south poles facing outward.

Three spaced apart planar rectangular magnetic loops or rings 36a,36b,36c are shown disposed around the inner portion of the housing 30. The magnet planar loops 36a,36b,36c, of which only the upper and lower longitudinal portions are shown in FIG. 1E, have end segments (out of view in the FIGURE) which complete rectangular shaped circuits about the interior of the volume defined by the housing 30. The magnet planar loops 36a,36b,36c, and the corresponding magnet loops 20 in the rectangular plasma chamber embodiment portrayed in FIGS. 1A,1B and 1C, are the components of the secondary magnetic circuit portion 36' of this embodiment 40. Note in FIG. 1E that the orientation of the magnetic poles of the magnet ring 36a, which is closest to the slotted waveguide microwave antenna, is opposite that of the waveguide magnets 34 that comprise the primary magnetic circuit portion 34' of this embodiment 40.

Likewise, magnet ring 36b, which also extends around the rectangular interior of the housing 30, has its poles oriented opposite to that of the preceding ring 36a. Additionally, the third magnet ring 36c is disposed behind the forward flange 31 and has its north poles oriented so as to face into the volume defined by the housing 30. The magnetic circuit loops are made of lots of little magnets that are mounted in a linear way around the prismatic plasma chamber volume 21. No ion optics are shown with the embodiment 40 of FIGS. 1D and 1E.

FIGS. 2A,2B and 2C show views of two embodiments of the slotted waveguide portion of the present ion and plasma source invention. FIG. 2A shows a slotted waveguide 50 in orthogonal longitudinal front view and in cross sectional end view. Three spaced apart permanent magnets 52 are separated by slots 54 in the body 56 of the waveguide 50. The slots 54 are matched pairs, as discussed in detail in an earlier patent application Ser. No. 10/925,499 entitled, "Slotted Antenna Waveguide Plasma Source", to the present inventor which is

9

10

incorporated in its entirety herein. A matched pair consists of alternating slots displaced by one half of a wavelength, or equivalent multiple, from slot center to center. The slots **56** alternate about the centerline CL (denoted in FIG. 2A) of the mid-plane of the waveguide **50** and, when mounted upon the back surface **14** of the invention the matched slot pairs are oriented into the prismatic volume of the plasma chamber **21**. The main difference between the slotted antenna geometry of the present invention and the one described in the "Slotted Antenna Waveguide Plasma Source" disclosure is the absence of a center line magnet when the present plasma source invention operates with the higher frequency microwaves (5.85 GHz), as shown in FIG. 2C. That is to say, at the 2.45 GHz operating frequency, the center line magnet **54'** (located between slots **56**) was used, but at 5.85 GHz, the center magnet was eliminated to improve performance. At the higher frequency, center-row magnets interfere with microwave launching, giving rise to significant reflection. The north poles (N) of the magnets **52** are shown oriented normal to the waveguide body **56**. FIG. 2B is an oblique view of the slotted waveguide **50**. Microwaves **57** enter one end **58** of the waveguide **50**, along the waveguide main axis **60**. A complete description of the slotted waveguide antenna portion of the present invention is given in the aforementioned disclosure, "Slotted Antenna Waveguide Plasma Source." Note, with respect to FIGS. 1A,1B,1C and 2B that the waveguide main axis **60** is parallel to and spaced apart from the length axis **17***e*.

FIG. 2C shows a slotted waveguide **62** in orthogonal longitudinal front view and also in cross sectional end view **63**, with slots **64** and two spaced apart permanent magnets **66**. That use of two instead of three magnets **66** reflects the intended microwave frequency of 5.85 GHz. South poles (S) of the permanent magnets **66** are shown facing outward, though the opposite orientation, with the north poles (N) facing outward is equally possible.

In general, waveguide sizes are standardized such that the waveguide's characteristics are matched with the wavelength of the microwave radiation to be used. For each waveguide size, there is a specific frequency range over which the waveguide will operate best. Also, in relation to the slotted waveguide portions of the present plasma source invention, the magnetic circuit near the waveguide slots, which is also called herein the first magnetic circuit portion, allows for gas breakdown and well-matched plasma production on the outside of waveguide in the vicinity of the slots **64**. The plasma that is produced as a consequence of the optimized magnetic circuit that eliminates the need for dielectric windows to aid in impedance matching. Additionally, the magnetic field profile at each slot prevents plasma from backflowing into the slots and causing breakdowns there, and the magnetic field at and inside the slots is not sufficient to produce ECR so no plasma production can take place inside of the waveguide. Finally, the use of multiple slots reduces the electric field at each slot and thereby minimizes slot arcing that could be caused by the presence of the plasma, which thereby eliminates the need for a dielectric window. Plasma ions that are created near the radiating slots **54** (FIGS. 2A,2B), or **64** (FIG. 2C), emerge into the larger contained volume **21** (i.e., the plasma chamber of FIG. 1A) to create a plasma volume **22** that, in the illustration of FIG. 1A, progresses to the right in the FIGURE, through the system of plasma optics **24** comprising the two grids **24***a* and **24***b*.

The planar secondary magnet loops **20** in FIGS. 1A and **36***a*,**36***b*,**36***c* in FIGS. 1D,1E serve to direct the plasma in the directions indicated. The spacing of the planar magnet loops with respect to one another and in relation to the linear magnetic **16***a*,**16***b* disposed upon the waveguide **12**. The planar

secondary magnetic loops are aligned such that the magnet sides run parallel with the long dimension of the slots so as to ensure a strong magnetic field in the region of the slots. Permanent magnets used in this work had surface field strengths between 2.8 kG and 3 kG, which is sufficiently strong to achieve ECR all the way up to microwave frequencies of 6 GHz. At higher frequencies, stronger magnets would have to used.

FIG. 3 shows in cross-sectional end view the plasma source **10** (of FIGS. 1A,1B and 1C) and its magnetic circuit **11** which arises due to the orientation of the poles (N and S) of the magnet rings **20***a*,**20***b*,**20***c* and **20***d*, which are disposed around the rectangular interior perimeter of the rectangular housing **17** and together comprise the secondary magnetic circuit elements **20'** of the magnetic circuit **11**. The orientation of the poles of the magnet rings alternates, as illustrated with Ns and Ss. The magnetic circuit **11** is created by the field lines of the magnet rings. The process of electron cyclotron resonance takes place in the vicinities of the magnet rings **20***a*,**20***b*,**20***c*,**20***d* as electrons that have been excited by the microwaves spiral into and out of the densest portions of the magnetic field lines close to the magnet rings. The fast moving electrons induce further ionization of atoms of the feed gas when electrons collide with them, the result being the formation of a plasma within the contained volume or plasma chamber **21**.

Across the exit plane **15** of the plasma chamber **21** is disposed the screen grid **24***a* portion of the ion optics **24**. The grid **24***a* is mounted upon a suitable first insulating ring **23** attached between the periphery of the screen grid **24***a* and the exit flange **13**. Axially outward of the screen grid **24***a*, an accelerator grid **24***b* is mounted, for example on a suitable second insulating ring **25** attached between the periphery of the screen grid **24***a* and the periphery of the accelerator grid **24***b*. As is conventional in the art, the screen grid **24***a* is electrically connected to a positive terminal of a screen voltage power supply **42**, for extracting electrons from plasma **22** in the plasma chamber **21**. Furthermore, the accelerator grid **24***b* is electrically connected to a negative terminal of an accelerator voltage power supply **44**, for accelerating positive ions from the plasma **22** (that has been partially depleted of electrons) outward in an positive ion stream **41**. A negative terminal of the screen voltage power supply **42** is tied to a positive terminal of the accelerator voltage power supply **44** through a common junction point **43**.

To prevent a positive space charge from forming as an ion cloud that could obstruct or impede the ion stream **41**, a neutralizer **46** is employed to generate a stream of electrons **47** that will recombine with the ions in the ion stream **41**, thereby neutralizing the cloud back to an uncharged inert gas. A terminal of the neutralizer **46** is connected to the common junction point **43**, thereby establishing an effective ground reference for the system, and also in effect bleeding off the electrons extracted by the screen grid **24***a*. For long service life (e.g., 10 years continuous operation) with a minimum amount of erosion, the screen grid **24***a* and the accelerator grid **24***b* are composed of pyrolytic graphite. Furthermore, it should be noted that a uniform dense ECR plasma as provided by the inventive plasma source **10** minimizes grid erosion by reducing peaks in the ion current density profile at the ion extraction plane (exit plane **15**). A uniform plasma density profile at the exit plane **15** also prevents such things as crossover or over-focusing induced erosion.

Referring again to the magnetic circuit **11** that is defined by magnetic field lines that run between the magnet rings **20***a*, **20***b*,**20***c*,**20***d* (that are disposed in a rectangle shaped annulus around the rectangular inner perimeter of the housing **17**) comprising the secondary magnetic circuit **20'**, and the magnets **16a,16b** comprising the primary magnetic circuit **16'**, the orientation of the poles of the first secondary or intermediate magnet ring **20a** is such that a one of its first (S) and second (N) magnetic poles is against the outer housing **17** and the one magnetic pole's opposed magnetic pole is facing into the plasma chamber **21**. The annular exit flange **13**, which is composed of a ferromagnetic material, and that is attached to and extends into the exit edge of the plasma chamber **21** at the exit plane **15**, has attached inside it a rectangle shaped annular magnet ring **20d** such that one of its first (N) and second (S) magnetic poles is against the exit flange **13** and the one magnetic pole's opposed magnetic pole is facing into the plasma chamber **21**. Thereby, the magnetic circuit **11** derives from the magnet rings **20a,20b,20c** and **20d** and also the magnets **16a,16b**, all of which are composed of permanent magnet material such that inward facing magnetic poles (N, S) alternate polarity with respect to adjacent magnet rings while proceeding along the wall rectangular portion of the housing **17**. The waveguide magnets **16a,16b**, comprising the primary magnetic circuit portions **16'**, are accordingly oriented, as shown in FIG. **3**.

Referring once again to the FIGS. 1A through 1C, the slotted antenna rectangular waveguide **12** injects microwaves in to a rectangular discharge chamber **21** contained within the housing **17**. Because the waveguide antenna **12** extends the length L of the back **14** of the discharge chamber **21**, it allows for distributed plasma production. Unlike single hollow cathode DC devices, the distributed plasma **22** that is produced gives rise to distributed ionization thereby improving discharge uniformity. Coupled to the slotted antenna **12** is the aforementioned magnetic circuit structure consisting of the waveguide magnets **16a,16b** and the secondary magnets **20** which are arranged so as to generate contours on which ECR plasma production takes place. The secondary magnets **20a, 20b,20c,20d**, in conjunction with the magnets **16a,16b**, create the magnetically connected magnetic circuit **11** that 1) confines the produced discharge plasma and 2) circulates the hot electrons produced in the ECR zones.

The embodiments **10** and **30** in FIGS. 1D and 1E respectively have been demonstrated using two different microwave frequencies: 2.45 Ghz and 5.85 GHz. While waveguides designed to handle 2.45 GHz are commercially readily available, 5.85 MHz can be used for those applications requiring very high plasma densities even though power supplies at 5.85 Ghz are more expensive than at 2.45 GHz.

FIG. **4** is an oblique exploded view the structural components of an actual embodiment of the plasma source **70** according to the present invention. When assembled, the plasma source **70** is contained with a main support frame **72** that holds the support structure **74** for the secondary magnets or magnet rings (not shown), along with the back plate **76** has attached to it the spaced-apart waveguide magnets **78** that straddle the radiating slots **80**. The waveguide **82**, as shown in the exploded view, has an open face **83**. When the waveguide **82** is mounted against the back plate **76**, the waveguide becomes complete with its waveguide magnets **78** and radiating slots **80** whereat the plasma forms and emerges into the volume V of the support structure **74** that holds the secondary magnets. Bracket **86** enables the waveguide **82** to be connected to a microwave source (not shown). When the plasma source **70** is assembled, it has a back cover **88** and top and bottom covers **90a,90b** and side covers **92a,92b**. The ion optics grids **94a,94b** are held in place against the frame **72** and the housing **74** by the forward frame **96**.

General Comments

Novel features of this invention include:

1. Completely electrodeless (erosion issues eliminated);

2. Plasma source does not require a microwave window;

3. Very large area, large volume plasmas are possible by simply extended the length of the slotted antenna and housing of secondary magnetic circuit;

4. Scalable to very high powers (minimal modifications to magnetic circuit required to make device larger) (also waveguide approach allows for operation up to 10 to 100 kW of input power); more specifically, the characteristic length dimension, parallel to the main axis of the slotted antenna waveguide, can be increased without limit;

5. Utilizes permanent magnets for ECR and plasma confinement;

6. Adaptable to operate over a range of frequencies (2.45, 5.85 GHz already demonstrated); in fact, compared to large circular plasma sources, the present rectangular unit has a broader frequency range.

7. Plasma in interior of device is not magnetized making it desirable for ion beam applications (ions are magnetized); the invention has been operated as a high energy ion source: beam power 13 kW;

8. Different types of gases can be used (reactive or non-reactive);

9. Metal vapors plasmas can also be processed in the discharge chamber since there is no microwave window at the source;

10. Source can operated at very low background pressures 10^{-5} to 10^{-4} Torr;

11. The rectangular shape lends itself to industrial applications;

12. Prototype source represents the largest, most powerful ECR source ever built;

13. The device operates at multiple frequencies, requiring only change in size waveguide of slotted antenna;

14. Device operates with permanent magnets. Large volume minimizes heat load to magnets so that device can operate over a wide power range without overheating magnets;

15. Device though large volume is self starting;

16. Device though large volume is also capable of operating over a wide range of flow rates;

17. Device operates on different gases including but not limited to air, xenon, and CO_2;

18. Emission spectra of device discharge plasma revealed only singly charge ions and no neutrals. The lack of multiple charged species in plasma suggests that erosion due to multiply charge species is minimal;

19. The large volume source is tunable over a wide power range with very low reflected powers (<10%). The discharge though high power and large volume is stable and does not mode hop;

20. The plasma is uniform in both the lateral and transverse dimensions;

21. Plasma potentials in the discharge are low, approximately 15 Volts or less, thus minimizing erosion issues; and

21. The source is scalable to larger sizes by simply extending the slotted antenna.

The large area plasma source described in this disclosure is electrodeless. It utilizes microwave electron cyclotron resonance (ECR) to generate the discharge. A slotted antenna has been implemented with a novel magnetic circuit geometry to produce a large area plasma. The source is also designed to be windowless. Both the implementation of the slotted antenna and the primary magnetic circuit allow for both large-area and large-volume plasmas to be produced. Such plasmas have been generated using this approach. For example, a source with an effective beam area of measuring 40×90 cm (and 40 cm deep) has already been tested and validated. It is scalable in power, size and plasma density. The present invention has demonstrated high plasma density operation at both 2.45 GHz and 5.85 GHz. Additionally, it has been demonstrated with the use of a permanent magnetic circuit instead of with the kinds of bulky and energy intensive electromagnets that are typically used in conventional ECR sources. The plasma source according to the present invention represents a means to generating large-area plasmas. Uniformity of the plasma can be tailored by adjusting slot and magnet locations.

The plasma source according to the present invention can be scaled upwards in its length dimension, i.e., in the direction parallel to the axis of the slotted waveguide antenna. It can be used to process multiple work pieces such as silicon wafers, with its rectangular shape being better-suited to industrial work areas than would be circular plasma sources of comparable characteristic linear dimension. The large size and high plasma density offered by the device gives it the capacity to process many items at once, which can dramatically improve productivity of companies that produce microchips from silicon wafers, i.e., many wafers can be processed at once. The same holds true for fabs that do depositions, implantations, or etchings. This plasma and ion source can be used with reactive gases used in etching industry. Large area ion implantation source for surface modifications can also benefit from this technology.

This ion source invention offers benefits over hollow cathode technology, with perhaps the most important to the commercial industry being that a very clean (few contaminants), high volume plasma can be generated.

In the realm of ion propulsion, this invention can also be adapted to producing dense, uniform plasmas for long life ion thruster applications.

Although the invention has been shown and described with respect to a certain preferred embodiment or embodiments, certain equivalent alterations and modifications will occur to others skilled in the art upon the reading and understanding of this specification and the annexed drawings. In particular regard to the various functions performed by the above described components (assemblies, devices, circuits, etc.) the terms (including a reference to a "means") used to describe such components are intended to correspond, unless otherwise indicated, to any component which performs the specified function of the described component (i.e., that is functionally equivalent), even though not structurally equivalent to the disclosed structure which performs the function in the herein illustrated exemplary embodiments of the invention. In addition, while a particular feature of the invention may have been disclosed with respect to only one of several embodiments, such feature may be combined with one or more features of the other embodiments as may be desired and advantageous for any given or particular application.

14

The invention claimed is:

1. A large electrodeless and windowless plasma source comprising:
   a plasma chamber defining an enclosed, elongated prismatic volume and comprising:
      a rectangular top wall having an inner planar surface;
      a rectangular bottom wall having an inner planar surface;
      two parallel quadrangular end walls having inner planar surfaces having centroids that define a length axis;
      a planar rectangular back portion having a height dimension; and
      a planar rectangular exit plane having a height dimension and a perimeter;
   a slotted waveguide microwave antenna having a main axis and a plurality of matched slot pairs on one face; and
   a magnetic circuit comprising:
      a first magnetic circuit portion; and
      a second magnetic circuit portion; and
   a gas injection means.

2. The large electrodeless and windowless plasma source of claim 1 wherein the enclosed prismatic volume is a rectangular volume defined by:
   the planar inner surfaces of the rectangular top wall and the rectangular bottom wall which are parallel to one another;
   the two parallel quadrangular end walls having inner planar surfaces; and
   the planar rectangular back portion and the planar rectangular exit plane which are parallel to one another.

3. The large electrodeless and windowless plasma source of claim 1 wherein the main axis of the slotted waveguide microwave antenna and the length axis of the plasma chamber that is defined by centroids of the two parallel quadrangular end walls are parallel and spaced apart.

4. The large electrodeless and windowless plasma source of claim 1 wherein the first magnetic circuit portion is comprised of at least two linear magnets mounted external to the slotted waveguide microwave antenna and parallel to the main axis of the slotted waveguide and oriented into the plasma chamber.

5. The large electrodeless and windowless plasma source of claim 4 wherein the at least two linear magnets are permanent magnets having magnetic poles.

6. The large electrodeless and windowless plasma source of claim 5 wherein:
   magnetic poles of the at least two linear magnets are oriented in the same direction.

7. The large electrodeless and windowless plasma source of claim 1 wherein:
   the second magnetic circuit portion is comprised of a plurality of spaced apart linear magnets having magnetic poles and disposed about the inner top and bottom walls and the end walls of the prismatic volume of the plasma chamber so that each spaced apart linear magnet forms a planar rectangular magnet loop that is parallel to the planar rectangular exit plane.

8. The large electrodeless and windowless plasma source of claim 7 wherein:
   the magnetic poles of adjacent spaced apart planar rectangular magnetic loops are oppositely oriented with respect to each other.

9. The large electrodeless and windowless plasma source of claim 1 wherein:
   the magnetic circuit is comprised of a plurality of spaced apart linear magnets and magnet loops having polarities that alternate.

15

10. The large electrodeless and windowless plasma source of claim **1** wherein:

the slotted waveguide microwave antenna is mounted to the back portion of the plasma chamber and the plurality of matched slot pairs on one face are oriented into the prismatic volume of the plasma chamber.

11. The large electrodeless and windowless plasma source of claim **1** wherein the gas injection means is disposed about the perimeter of the exit plane.

12. The large electrodeless and windowless plasma source of claim **1** wherein the exit plane of the plasma chamber has ion optics means disposed across it.

13. The large electrodeless and windowless plasma source of claim **1** wherein the enclosed prismatic volume has a trapezoidal cross-sectional shape when viewed along the length axis defined by the centroids of the two parallel quadrangular end walls, said trapezoidal cross-sectional shape being further defined by the height dimension of the planar rectangular back portion being less than the height dimension of the planar rectangular exit plane.

14. The large electrodeless and windowless plasma source of claim **1** wherein the two parallel quadrangular end walls are trapezoidal in shape.

15. The large electrodeless and windowless plasma source of claim **1** wherein the planar rectangular exit plane of the plasma chamber has ion optics means disposed across it.

16. The method of creating a large electrodeless and windowless plasma source, the method being characterized by the steps of:

assembling a plasma chamber enclosed within an elongated prismatic volume whose shape is defined by a rectangular top wall having an inner planar surface, a rectangular inner bottom wall having an inner planar surface, two parallel quadrangular end walls having inner planar surfaces and centroids that define a length axis of the plasma chamber, a planar rectangular back portion, and a planar rectangular exit plane;

affixing to the planar rectangular back portion a slotted waveguide microwave antenna having a main axis, at

16

least two linear permanent magnets oriented parallel to said main axis and having magnetic poles, and a plurality of matched slot pairs oriented into the prismatic volume of the plasma chamber;

disposing within the prismatic volume of the plasma chamber a plurality of mutually adjacent, non-coplanar permanent magnet loops having magnetic poles, one loop of which is closest to the slotted waveguide microwave antenna; and

providing one or more inlets for a gas to be ionized.

17. The method of claim **16** wherein the method of affixing of a slotted waveguide microwave antenna to the rectangular back portion defining the prismatic volume of the plasma chamber includes the further step of aligning the main axis of the slotted waveguide microwave antenna parallel to the length axis defined by the centroids of the quadrangular end walls.

18. The method of claim **16** wherein the method of disposing within the prismatic volume of the plasma chamber a plurality of mutually adjacent non-coplanar permanent magnet loops, one of which is closest to the at least two linear permanent magnets of the slotted waveguide microwave antenna includes the further step of orienting the magnetic poles of each mutually adjacent non-colinear permanent magnet loop in a direction opposite those of adjacent loops.

19. The method of claim **18** wherein the method of orienting the magnetic poles of each mutually adjacent permanent magnet loop in a direction opposite those of adjacent loops includes the further step of orienting the magnetic poles of each of the at least two linear permanent magnets affixed to the slotted waveguide microwave antenna in a single direction that is opposite that of the magnetic pole of the permanent magnet loop that is closest to the at least two linear permanent magnets.

20. The method of claim **16** where in the method of creating a large electrodeless and windowless plasma source includes the further step of installing ion optics means across the planar rectangular exit plane.

* * * * *

US008680749B2

(12) United States Patent
Xu et al.

(10) **Patent No.:** **US 8,680,749 B2**

(45) **Date of Patent:** **Mar. 25, 2014**

(54) **PIEZOELECTRIC MULTILAYER-STACKED HYBRID ACTUATION/TRANSDUCTION SYSTEM**

(75) Inventors: **Tian-Bing Xu**, Hampton, VA (US); **Xiaoning Jiang**, State College, PA (US); **Ji Su**, Yorktown, VA (US)

(73) Assignees: **National Institute of Aerospace Associates**, Hampton, VA (US); **The United States of America as represented by the Administration of NASA**, Washington, DC (US)

(*) Notice: Subject to any disclaimer, the term of this patent is extended or adjusted under 35 U.S.C. 154(b) by 165 days.

(21) Appl. No.: **12/584,290**

(22) Filed: **Sep. 3, 2009**

(65) **Prior Publication Data**

US 2010/0096949 A1 Apr. 22, 2010

Related U.S. Application Data

(60) Provisional application No. 61/093,767, filed on Sep. 3, 2008.

(51) **Int. Cl.**
H01L 41/113 (2006.01)
(52) **U.S. Cl.**
USPC **310/339**; 310/328
(58) **Field of Classification Search**
USPC 310/328, 337, 339
See application file for complete search history.

(56) **References Cited**

U.S. PATENT DOCUMENTS

4,999,819 A 3/1991 Newnham et al.

5,276,657 A	1/1994	Newnham et al.	
5,632,841 A	5/1997	Hellbaum et al.	
5,639,850 A	6/1997	Bryant	
6,066,911 A *	5/2000	Lindemann et al.	..... 310/323.02
6,071,088 A *	6/2000	Bishop et al.	.... 417/322
6,614,143 B2 *	9/2003	Zhang et al.	.... 310/317
7,394,181 B2	7/2008	Su et al.	
7,446,459 B2	11/2008	Xu et al.	
2006/0197405 A1 *	9/2006	Su et al.	.... 310/311
2008/0074000 A1 *	3/2008	Bennett et al.	.... 310/328
2008/0238260 A1 *	10/2008	Xu et al.	.... 310/339

FOREIGN PATENT DOCUMENTS

JP 62-228111 A * 10/1987 .... G01C 19/56

* cited by examiner

Primary Examiner — Thomas Dougherty

(74) *Attorney, Agent, or Firm* — Kimberly A. Chasteen; Robin W. Edwards

(57) **ABSTRACT**

A novel full piezoelectric multilayer stacked hybrid actuation/transduction system. The system demonstrates significantly-enhanced electromechanical performance by utilizing the cooperative contributions of the electromechanical responses of multilayer stacked negative and positive strain components. Both experimental and theoretical studies indicate that for this system, the displacement is over three times that of a same-sized conventional flextensional actuator/transducer. The system consists of at least 2 layers which include electromechanically active components. The layers are arranged such that when electric power is applied, one layer contracts in a transverse direction while the second layer expands in a transverse direction which is perpendicular to the transverse direction of the first layer. An alternate embodiment includes a third layer. In this embodiment, the outer two layers contract in parallel transverse directions while the middle layer expands in a transverse direction which is perpendicular to the transverse direction of the outer layers.

18 Claims, 16 Drawing Sheets

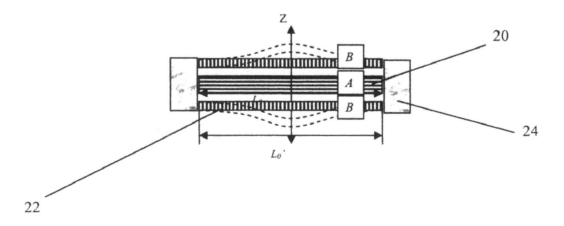

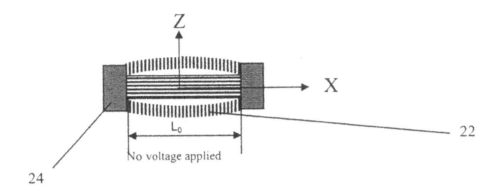

No voltage applied

FIG. 1A

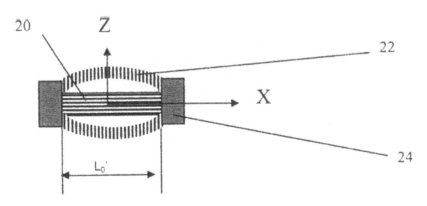

Voltage applied to all active elements

FIG. 1B

FIG. 2A

FIG. 2B

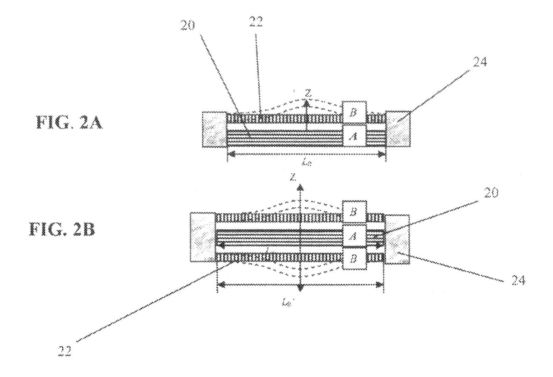

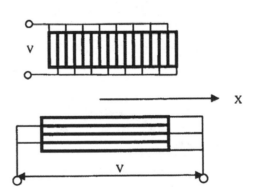

FIG 3A

FIG 3b

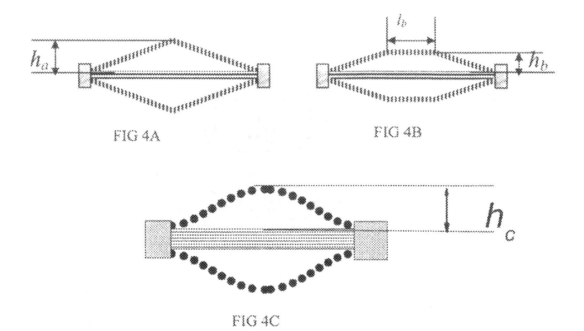

FIG 4A   FIG 4B

FIG 4C

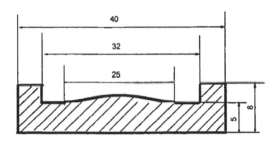

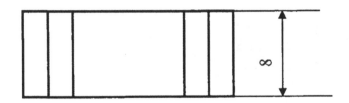

FIG. 5

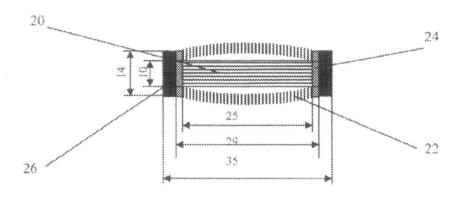

FIG 6A

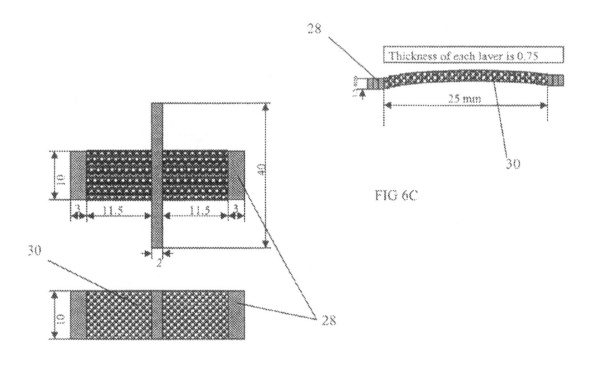

Thickness of each layer is 0.75

FIG 6C

Unit mm

FIG 6B

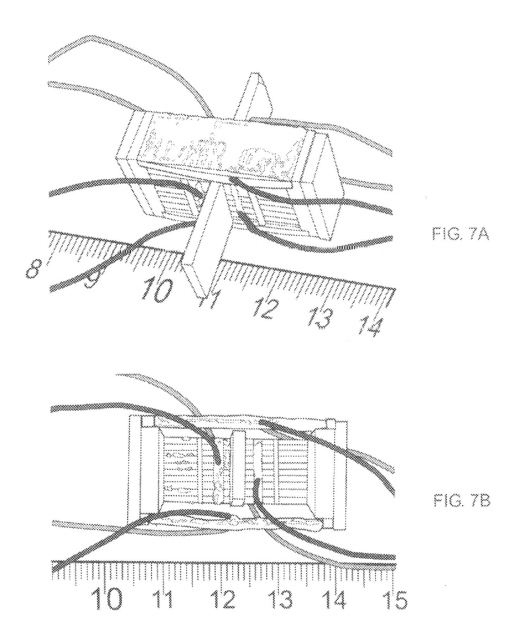

FIG. 7A

FIG. 7B

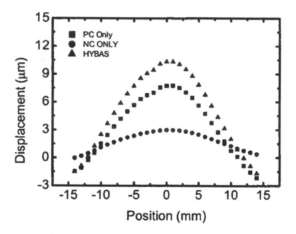

FIG. 8

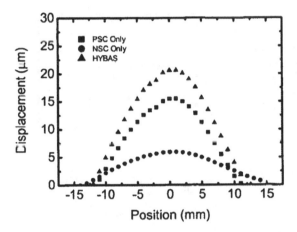

FIG. 9

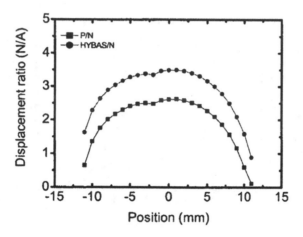

FIG. 10

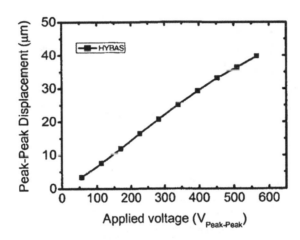

FIG. 11

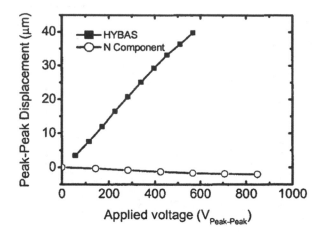

FIG. 12

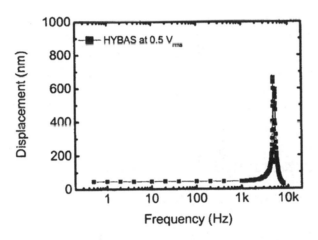

FIG. 13

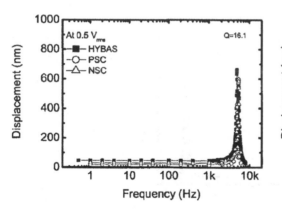

FIG. 14A   FIG. 14B

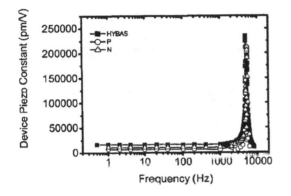

FIG 15A

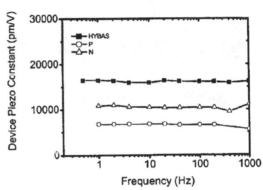

FIG 15B

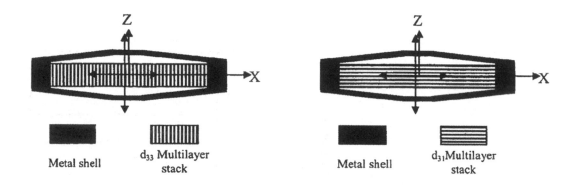

FIG 16A

FIG 16B

1

PIEZOELECTRIC MULTILAYER-STACKED HYBRID ACTUATION/TRANSDUCTION SYSTEM

CROSS REFERENCE TO RELATED APPLICATION

The present application claims priority from U.S. Provisional Application Ser. No. 61/093,767, filed Sep. 3, 2008.

STATEMENT REGARDING FEDERALLY SPONSORED RESEARCH OR DEVELOPMENT

The U.S. Government has a paid-up license in this invention and the right in limited circumstances to require the patent owner to license others on reasonable terms as provided for by the terms of Cooperative Agreement No. NCC-1-02043 awarded by the National Aeronautics and Space Administration.

BACKGROUND OF THE INVENTION

1. Field of the Invention

The present invention relates to high performance electromechanical actuators, and, more particularly to a piezoelectric actuation/transduction system.

2. Description of Related Art

Many civilian and military applications require high performance electromechanical actuators. These include active vibration control, dynamic flow control in aerospace, underwater navigation and surveillance, and microphones, etc. High displacement and electromechanical output power are two main demands for actuators needed in many applications. In the past few decades, a great deal of effort has been devoted to two research fields: 1) the development of electromechanically active materials offering the desired properties and 2) the development of electromechanical devices which utilize the materials in an efficient manner. Since metal-ceramic composite actuators were invented (the so called Moonies), many device configurations have been exploited for amplified displacement and enhanced efficiency.

Recently, a hybrid actuation system (HYBAS) was developed to utilize the characteristics of the electromechanical performance of these two types of electroactive materials in a cooperative and effective way. This system is described in issued U.S. Pat. No. 7,394,181, July 2008 "Hybrid Electromechanical Actuator and Actuation System," incorporated herein by reference. The system showed significantly-enhanced electromechanical performance compared to the performance of devices made of each constituent material individually. A theoretical model for the HYBAS was also developed, considering the elastic and electromechanical properties of the materials utilized in the system and the device configuration. A comparison was made with experimental data which showed that the model predicts the response of the HYBAS with good accuracy. More recently, new synthetic jet actuator concepts were invented copending patent application Ser. Nos. 60/842,458, 60/842,459, and 60/842,686), piezoelectric hybrid energy harvesting transducer (HYBERT) (issued U.S. Pat. No. 7,446,459, November 2008), incorporated herein by reference, and piezoelectric triple hybrid actuation system (TriHYBAS) based on the understanding of the electromechanical properties of piezoelectric materials and their applications.

In order to enhance the mechanical energy output to obtain high displacement, large mechanical load capability (high blocking force) with low applied voltage for a HYBAS, a full

piezoelectric multilayer stacked hybrid actuation/transduction system (Stacked-HYBATS) was desired.

A novel full piezoelectric multilayer stacked hybrid actuation/transduction system has been developed. The system demonstrates significantly-enhanced electromechanical performance by utilizing the cooperative contributions of the electromechanical responses of multilayer stacked negative and positive strain components. Both experimental and theoretical studies indicate that, for this system, the displacement is over three times that of a same-sized conventional flextensional actuator/transducer. The coupled resonance mode between positive and negative strain components of the system is much stronger than the resonance of a single element actuation only when the effective lengths of the two kinds of elements match. Compared with a prior hybrid actuation system, the multilayer system is designed to provide high mechanical load capability, low voltage driving, and a high effective piezoelectric constant. The present system provides extremely high effective piezoelectric constants both at resonance and off-resonance frequencies. The effective piezoelectric constant can be altered by varying the size of each component: the degree of the pre-curvature of the positive strain components, the thickness of each layer in the multilayer stacks, and the piezoelectric constant of the material used. Since all the elements are piezoelectric components, the system can serve as projector and receiver for underwater detection. The performance of the system can be enhanced by improving the piezoelectric properties. With the present system, future actuator/transducer designs and piezoelectric material applications will reach a new level. The experimental results indicate that the stacked hybrid actuation/transduction system can provide displacement over three times larger than a same-sized conventional flextensional actuator/transducer with compatible mechanical load capability. Moreover, the coupled resonance between positive strain and negative strain components of a stacked hybrid actuation/transduction system is much stronger than the resonance peak of a single element actuation when the effective lengths of the two kinds of elements match each other.

An object of the present invention is to provide a piezoelectric multilayer stacked hybrid actuation/transduction system.

An object of the present invention is to provide a piezoelectric multilayer stacked hybrid actuation/transduction system which provides increased displacement over similar sized flextensional actuator/transducers with the same level of mechanical load capability.

Another object of the present invention is to provide a piezoelectric multilayer stacked hybrid actuation/transduction system which includes positive and negative strain components.

Yet another object of the present invention is to provide a piezoelectric multilayer stacked hybrid actuation/transduction system which provides an extremely high effective piezoelectric constant at resonance frequency and off-resonance frequencies.

Finally, it is an object of the present invention to accomplish the foregoing objectives in a simple and cost effective manner.

SUMMARY OF THE INVENTION

The present invention addresses these needs by providing an electromechanical actuator which includes at least two electromechanical elements. Both electromechanical elements include an electromechanically active component which contracts in a lengthwise direction when electric power is applied thereto; however, the electromechanical elements are disposed in relation to one another such that said lengthwise directions thereof are parallel to one another, and they are mechanically coupled to one another at least at two opposing edges thereof An electric power source is coupled to the electromechanically active components for simultaneously applying electric power thereto. The electromechanically active components include at least one layer of an electroactive polymer, preferably a piezoelectric polymer or an electrostrictive polymer. Alternatively, the electromechanically active components include at least one layer of an electroactive ceramic. In a particularly preferred embodiment, the actuator further includes a third electromechanical element which includes an electromechanically active component that expands in a lengthwise direction when electric power is applied thereto. The third electromechanical element is disposed in relation to the first electromechanical element such that said lengthwise direction thereof is parallel to the lengthwise direction of the first electromechanical element, and is mechanically coupled to said first and second electromechanical elements at least at two opposing edges thereof In this embodiment, the first electromechanical element is sandwiched between said second and third electromechanical elements. The electric power source is coupled to all three electromechanically active components for the simultaneously application of electric power to each of the electromechanically active components. As with the first two electromechanically active components, the third electromechanically active component includes at least one layer of an electroactive polymer, preferably a piezoelectric polymer or an electrostrictive polymer. Alternatively, the electromechanically active component includes at least one layer of an electroactive ceramic.

BRIEF DESCRIPTION OF THE DRAWINGS

A more complete description of the subject matter of the present invention and the advantages thereof, can be achieved by the reference to the following detailed description by which reference is made to the accompanying drawings in which:

FIG. 1A shows a diagram of a full piezoelectric multilayer stacked hybrid actuation/transduction system according to the preferred embodiment of the present invention when no voltage is applied to all the active elements;

FIG. 1B shows a diagram of a full piezoelectric multilayer stacked hybrid actuation/transduction system according to the preferred embodiment of the present invention when a voltage is applied to all the active elements;

FIG. 2A shows a diagram of a single-sided full piezoelectric multilayer stacked hybrid actuation/transduction system according to the preferred embodiment of the present invention;

FIG. 2B shows a diagram of a double-sided full piezoelectric multilayer stacked hybrid actuation/transduction system according to the preferred embodiment of the present invention;

FIG. 3A shows a diagram of piezoelectric inorganic (ceramic or single crystal) positive strain (in X direction) multilayer stack according to the preferred embodiment of the present invention;

FIG. 3B shows a diagram of piezoelectric inorganic (ceramic or single crystal) negative strain (in X direction) multilayer stack according to the preferred embodiment of the present invention;

FIG. 4A shows a diagram of a configuration of a full piezoelectric multilayer stacked hybrid actuation/transduc-

tion system wherein the two positive strain components are a triangular shape under uniform loads;

FIG. 4B shows a diagram of a configuration of a full piezoelectric multilayer stacked hybrid actuation/transduction system wherein the two positive strain components are conventional flextensional actuator metal shell shape under uniform loads;

FIG. 4C shows a diagram of a configuration of a full piezoelectric multilayer stacked hybrid actuation/transduction system wherein the two positive strain components are deformations under uniform loads;

FIG. 5 shows an exemplary mode for multilayer stack processing according to the preferred embodiment of the present invention for positive strain components;

FIG. 6A shows a diagram of an exemplary piezoelectric ceramic hybrid actuation system;

FIG. 6B shows a diagram of the multilayer stack based negative strain component of a piezoelectric ceramic hybrid actuation system;

FIG. 6C shows a diagram of the multilayer stack based positive strain component of a piezoelectric ceramic hybrid actuation system;

FIG. 7A shows a top view of a full piezoelectric multilayer stacked hybrid actuation/transduction system according to the preferred embodiment of the present invention;

FIG. 7B shows a side view of a full piezoelectric multilayer stacked hybrid actuation/transduction system according to the preferred embodiment of the present invention;

FIG. 8 shows a graph of the displacement profiles of a full ceramic multilayer single-sided stacked hybrid actuation/transduction system according to the preferred embodiment of the present invention at different working modes at 150 V DC bias and 1 Hz 100 V_{rms} AC;

FIG. 9 shows a graph of the displacement profiles of a full ceramic multilayer double-sided stacked hybrid actuation/transduction system according to the preferred embodiment of the present invention at different working mode at 150 V DC bias and 1 Hz 100 V_{rms} AC

FIG. 10 shows a graph of the displacement ratio of positive strain component of stacked hybrid actuation/transduction system over the negative strain component in a double-sided stacked hybrid actuation/transduction system at 150 V DC bias and 1 Hz 100 V_{rms} AC signal;

FIG. 11 shows a graph of the displacement as a function of applied voltage for stacked hybrid actuation/transduction system, (note 1 $V_{rms}=2\times2^{0.5}$ $_{Vpeak-peak}$);

FIG. 12 shows a graph of a comparison of displacements as a function of applied voltage for the stacked hybrid actuation/transduction system and the negative component in the direction of its length, (note 1 $V_{rms}=2\times2^{0.5}$ $_{Vpeak-peak}$);

FIG. 13 shows a graph of the displacement as a function of frequency for the stacked hybrid actuation/transduction system at 0.5 V_{mrs};

FIG. 14A shows a graph, in log plot, of the displacement as a function of frequency for the stacked hybrid actuation/transduction system, positive strain elements active only, and negative strain element active only at 0.5 V_{mrs};

FIG. 14B shows a graph, in linear plot, of the displacement as a function of frequency for the stacked hybrid actuation/transduction system, positive strain elements active only, and negative strain element active only at 0.5 V_{mrs};

FIG. 15A shows a graph of effective piezoelectric constant as a function of frequency for the stacked hybrid actuation/transduction system, and positive strain elements and negative strain element active only at 0.5 V_{mrs} for full range of frequency plot;

5

6

FIG. **15**B shows a graph of effective piezoelectric constant as a function of frequency for the stacked hybrid actuation/transduction system, and positive strain elements and negative strain element active only at 0.5 V$_{mrs}$ before resonance frequency plot;

FIG. **16**A shows a diagram of multilayer stack-based flextensional actuator, inorganic d$_{33}$ mode; and

FIG. **16**B shows a diagram of multilayer stack-based flextensional actuator, inorganic d$_{31}$ mode.

ELEMENT LIST

20 negative strain component
22 positive strain component
24 ceramic
26 steel
28 passive ceramic
30 piezoelectric ceramic

DETAILED DESCRIPTION OF THE PREFERRED EMBODIMENT

The following detailed description is of the best presently contemplated mode of carrying out the invention. This description is not to be taken in a limiting sense, but is made merely for the purpose of illustrating general principles of embodiments of the invention. For example, the actuation system can be designed in various shapes, including but not limited to rectangular, circular, square, and oval.

An example of a full piezoelectric multilayer stacked hybrid actuation/transduction system is schematically shown in FIG. **1**. The negative-strain component **20** contracts and the positive-strain component **22** expands, each along its lengthwise direction, when an electric field is applied on the device as shown in FIG. **1**B. The interaction between the two elements enhances motion along the Z axis for a stacked hybrid actuation/transduction system. The difference between the stacked hybrid actuation/transduction system and the HYBAS is that all the elements can be made from one kind of material. The multilayer stacked positive and negative strain components enable the stacked hybrid actuation/transduction system to provide high mechanical load capability, low voltage driving, and high effective piezoelectric constant in one device. A stacked hybrid actuation/transduction system can be a single-sided stacked hybrid actuation/transduction system, such as the one shown in FIG. **2**A, or a double-sided stacked hybrid actuation/transduction system, such as the one shown in FIG. **2**B, which behaves similarly to a conventional flextensional actuator. In order to dominate the dynamic length of the stacked hybrid actuation/transduction system by the negative strain component, the area of the cross section for the negative strain component will be much larger than the total cross-sectional areas of the two positive strain components.

In general, the transverse strain is negative and longitudinal strain positive in inorganic materials, such as ceramics/single crystals. Different piezoelectric multilayer stack configurations can cause a piezoelectric ceramic/single crystal multilayer stack exhibit negative strain or positive strain, as shown in FIG. **3**, at a certain direction without increasing the applied voltage. The stacked hybrid actuation/transduction system utilizes the properties of different strain directions in each single element to enhance the performance of a designed transducer/actuator system for underwater transductions, mechanical motion controls, and other military and civilian applications such as optical scanners for warfare, position controls for intelligent facilities, and flow dynamic controls.

The positive strain components can be made from any type of inorganic piezoelectric ceramic materials, such as lead zirconate titanate (PZT), lead magnesium niobate-lead titanate ceramic (1-x)PbMg1/3Nb2/3O3-xPbTiO(3) (PMN-xPT), lead zinc niobate-lead magnesium niobate-lead titanate ceramics [PbZn1/3Nb2/3O3-PbMg1/3Nb2/3O3-PbTiO3 (PZN-PMN-PT)], lead lanthanum zirconate titanate (PLZT); and piezoelectric single crystal materials, such as, lead magnesium niobate-lead titanate (PMN-PT) single crystal, lead zinc niobate-lead titanate (PZN-PT)single crystal, and barium titanate (BaTiO$_3$) single crystal can be used for piezoelectric positive strain component. In order to achieve positive strain in the length direction of the multilayer stack, the stack must be configured as shown in FIG. **3**a. However, for organic piezoelectric materials, such as piezoelectric poly (vinylidene fluoride) (PVDF) polymer, and piezoelectric poly (vinylidene fluoride-trifluoroethylene) (PVDF-TrFE) copolymers the multilayer configuration will be different. It has to be configured as shown in FIG. **3**b to achieve positive strain in the length direction of the multilayer stack.

The negative strain component is preferably made as follows. The art of the invention is to optimize performance using the configuration of the piezoelectric positive and negative strain components. The negative strain component can be made utilizing the same piezoelectric materials as described for the positive strain component above. The difference lies in the configuration of the multilayer components in opposite style. For inorganic piezoelectric material (ceramics/single crystals) multilayer, it must be configured as shown in FIG. **3**b to achieve the negative strain along its length. However, for organic piezoelectric polymer multilayer, it must be configured as shown in FIG. **3**a to obtain negative strain along its length.

In order to control the deformation direction of the positive strain components in a stacked hybrid actuation/transduction system, we needed to analyze the three different pre-curvature positive components as shown in FIG. **4**. These three are typical positive strain components styles in this invention.

The dimensions of the major components are listed in Table 1. For this particular example, assume the active length of the stacked hybrid actuation/transduction system is 25 mm long and the integrated lengths of the positive strain components are 25.25 mm (1% longer than the negative strain components).

If a piezoelectric ceramic is selected, the typical maximum strain for positive strain component is 0.2%, and the negative strain component is 0.1%. The displacement for various situations for each stacked hybrid actuation/transduction system is listed in Table 2.

TABLE 1

The dimensions of the major components of stacked hybrid actuation/transduction system	
Component	Dimension
Effective length of stacked hybrid actuation/transduction system	25 mm
Negative strain components	25 mm
Integrated lengths of positive component	25.25 mm
l$_b$	6 mm
h$_a$	1.77125 mm
h$_b$	1.6014 mm
h$_c$	1.60625 mm

179

7

TABLE 2

	Displacement for various situations for each stacked hybrid actuation/transduction system		
HYBAS	Positive component actuation only (μm)	Negative component actuation only (μm)	HYBAS actuation (μm)
A-Type (FIG. 4a)	340.25	172	498
B-Type (FIG. 4b)	286.5	144.75	417.5
C-Type (FIG. 4c)	309.25	156.25	465

The displacement data indicate that the stacked hybrid actuation/transduction system with triangular shape positive components (A-Type, FIG. 4a) has maximum displacements, the stacked hybrid actuation/transduction system with conventional flextensional shape positive component (B-Type, FIG. 4B) has minimum displacements, and the stacked hybrid actuation/transduction system with the curvature of deformations under uniform loads (C-Type, FIG. 4C) has mid-level displacements. However, stacked hybrid actuation/transduction system A-Type (FIG. 4A) and B-Type (FIG. 4B) will have stress accumulations at a certain area, and the stacked hybrid actuation/transduction system C-Type (FIG. 4C) has uniform stress distribution. Overall, stacked hybrid actuation/transduction system C-Type (FIG. 4C) is one of the best choices for pre-curvature positive strain components for most applications. However, A-type and B-type stacked hybrid actuation/transduction system also have some advantages for some specific applications. For the first experimental validation for the stacked hybrid actuation/transduction system, the C-type configuration was selected in this invention.

Piezoelectric ceramic is selected as an example of an electroactive material which is acceptable for the stacked hybrid actuation/transduction system. The modeled displacements for a 25 mm long stacked hybrid actuation/transduction system with different degrees of curvature are listed in Table 3. When the pre-curvature is increased, the displacement of the stacked hybrid actuation/transduction system will decrease. Considering the process of a stacked hybrid actuation/transduction system and the stress release in the multilayer stack and other applications, the optimized integrated length of pre-curved positive strain component is at the range of 100.1% to 100.25% of the length of the stacked hybrid actuation/transduction system.

TABLE 3

The modeled displacements for a 25 mm long stacked hybrid actuation/transduction system with different degrees of curvature		
Integrated length of pre-curved positive strain components in a 25 mm long stacked hybrid actuation/transduction system	h_c (μm)	Displacement of stacked hybrid actuation/transduction system (μm)
25.25 mm (1%)	1606.25	465
25.125 mm (0.5%)	1133.75	476.25
25.075 mm (0.25%)	801.25	775
22.025 mm (0.1%)	507.5	1005

According to the theoretical modeling, the mode for the multilayer processing is designed as shown in FIG. 5.

Equation for the curvature ("0" position at the center)

$$z = \frac{1}{18600}\left(\left(\frac{L_0}{2}\right)^2 - (x)^2\right)^2$$

Where z: displacement, L_0: length of curvature, and x is the location along x axis

A diagram of the designed stacked hybrid actuation/transduction system is shown in FIG. 6. In order to control the length of the stacked hybrid actuation/transduction system by the negative strain component, the overall dimension of the cross-section of the negative strain component is more than three times higher than the overall dimension of the positive strain components, and the positive strain component is pre-curved.

In order to fabricate a pre-curved positive strain component, a pair of male and female modes are designed and shown in FIG. 5.

Piezoelectric ceramic stacks were used for the first concept study. Piezoelectric single crystal stacks are preferably used for the future real applications of high performance stacked hybrid actuation/transduction system to increase the displacement of a stacked hybrid actuation/transduction system.

A picture of the fabricated stacked hybrid actuation/transduction system according to the present invention is shown in FIG. 7.

The parameters of the full piezoelectric ceramic stacked hybrid actuation/transduction system are listed in table 4.

TABLE 4

The parameters of the full piezoelectric ceramic stacked hybrid actuation/transduction system									
		Parameters							
		Length (mm)			Thickness (mm)			Width (mm)	
Materials		Total	Single layer	Effective	total	Single layer	Total	Effective	
Negative strain piezoelectric ceramic multilayer stack	Designed	25.0		23.0	10	1.0	10.0	10.0	
	Fabricated	25.0		23.0	10	1.0			
Positive strain piezoelectric composites (each side)	Designed	31.0	0.625	25.0	1.0	1.0	10.0	10.0	
	Fabricated	31.0	0.65	27.5	1.0	1.0	10.0	10.0	

The measured displacement profiles of the full ceramic single-sided stacked hybrid actuation/transduction system at different working modes at 150 V DC bias and 1 Hz 100 V_{rms} AC are shown in FIG. 8. The experimental results indicate that the displacement of stacked hybrid actuation/transduction system is greater than that of a single element actuation. When a voltage is applied to the positive strain component (for the cases of positive strain element active only or the positive and negative component active simultaneously), the displacement goes down to under zero at the two ends of the stacked hybrid actuation/transduction system, i.e., the displacement direction is opposite with the applied electric field. This may be due to negative strain of the positive strain components perpendicular to their lengthwise directions. When a positive voltage is applied to the positive strain component, the piezoelectric component will shrink perpendicularly to the electric field direction.

The measured displacement profiles of the double-sided stacked hybrid actuation/transduction system at different working modes at 150 V DC bias and 1 Hz 100 V_{rms} AC are shown in FIG. 9. The experimental results indicate that the displacement of the stacked hybrid actuation/transduction system is always better than a single element actuation only. For the situation that the negative strain component active only is equivalent to a same sized flextensional actuator/transducer. Compared to a conventional flextensional actuator (only a negative strain component is active) the performance of a full ceramic multilayer double-sided stacked hybrid actuation/transduction system is much better than a conventional flextensional actuator.

The displacement for the positive strain components active only or the stacked hybrid actuation/transduction system (Positive strain component+Negative strain component) active over the displacement of the negative strain component active only is shown in FIG. 10. The positive strain components produced displacement 2.6 times that of the negative strain active only at the center of the stacked hybrid actuation/transduction system. This is due to the following reasons:

(a) The thickness ratio of each layer of the negative strain component over each layer of the positive strain component is 1.6. The electric field of the positive strain component is 1.6 time higher than the electric field of the negative strain component when the same voltage is applied to each element of the stacked hybrid actuation/transduction system.

(b) The piezoelectric constant of the positive strain component is two times of the negative strain component.

(c) The effective length of the positive strain component is 1.08 times that of the negative strain component. Therefore, the deformation of the positive strain component is larger than the deformation of the negative strain component when the same voltage is applied to the two kinds of components. The stacked hybrid actuation/transduction system produces displacement which is 3.5 times that of the negative strain component active only at the center of the stacked hybrid actuation/transduction system.

The displacement as a function of applied voltage for the stacked hybrid actuation/transduction system is shown in FIG. 11. The displacement increases generally constantly with the applied voltage. This indicates that the displacement of the stacked hybrid actuation/transduction system increases linearly with the applied electric field increase.

The comparison of the peak-to-peak displacements as a function of applied peak-to-peak voltage for the stacked hybrid actuation/transduction system and the negative component along its length is presented in FIG. 12. The results indicate that the ratio of the displacement for a stacked hybrid actuation/transduction system at the center over its negative

component in the length direction is −25 times. The ratio can be varied by alternating the degree of the pre-curvature of the positive strain components of the stacked hybrid actuation/transduction system, and the thickness of the layers in the multilayer stacks. It is possible to make the ratio over 100 times by a proper design.

The displacement as a function of frequency for the stacked hybrid actuation/transduction system at 0.5 V_{mrs} is shown in FIG. 13. A strong resonance peak is observed at the frequency of 4830 Hz. The mechanical Q value for the resonance peak is 16.1. The displacement at the resonance peak is 15 times of the displacement at off resonance peak.

A comparison of the displacement as a function of frequency for the stacked hybrid actuation/transduction system, and positive strain component and negative strain component actuation only at 0.5 V_{mrs} is shown in FIG. 14. In FIG. 14A all the elements have strong resonance peaks at several kHz. The displacements at below 1 kHz remain constant. In FIG. 14B, the details of the resonance peaks are observed for the stacked hybrid actuation/transduction system at 0.5 V_{mrs} and each element. One significant resonance peaks at 4850 Hz, for the positive strain element. However, two significant resonance peaks at 4850 Hz and 5300 Hz are observed for the negative strain component active only and the stacked hybrid actuation/transduction system. The ratio of the two resonance frequencies is 1.093. FIG. 7 shows that that the piezoelectric effective length of the positive strain components in the stacked hybrid actuation/transduction system is 27.5 mm instead of the designed 25 mm. The dark color portions are the active piezoelectric components and the brown portions are the passive components in FIG. 7. As shown in FIG. 7, the size difference in length for the positive strain components and the negative strain component is clear, particularly in FIG. 7b. The ratio of the length of the positive strain component over the length of the negative strain component is 1.1. The resonance peak of the negative strain component at 5300 Hz is the nature frequency of the negative component. However, the resonance peak at 4850 Hz is due to the mechanical coupling from the positive strain component. There are also two peaks at 4850 Hz and 5300 Hz for the stacked hybrid actuation/transduction system. This is also due to the size mismatch for the two kinds of components. For the resonance peak at 4850 Hz, the resonance peak shown for the stacked hybrid actuation/transduction system is much stronger than for each element actuation only. If the lengths of the positive and negative strain components match each other, the two resonance peaks will be moved together and the resonance peak will be enhanced. This indicates that the stacked hybrid actuation/transduction system can be a good candidate for underwater detection transducers.

The inventive concept described herein can be used as a transducer. In this embodiment, a first electromechanical element includes a first electromechanically active component that contracts in a lengthwise direction when electric power is applied thereto while a second electromechanical element includes a second electromechanically active component that expands in a lengthwise direction when electric power is applied thereto. These electromechanical elements are disposed in relation to one another such that said lengthwise directions thereof are parallel to one another, and are mechanically coupled to one another at least at two opposing edges thereof. As described above, both of the electromechanically active components are manufactured from the same piezoelectric material. A mechanical deflection means is coupled to at least one of said first and second electromechanically active components such that deflection causes an electrical charge to be produced.

11

The transducer may further include a third electromechanical element which includes an electromechanically active component that expands in a lengthwise direction when electric power is applied thereto. In this embodiment, the third electromechanical element is disposed in relation to the first electromechanical element such that said lengthwise direction thereof is parallel to the lengthwise direction of the first electromechanical element, and is mechanically coupled to the first and second electromechanical elements at least at two opposing edges thereof wherein the first electromechanical element is sandwiched between the second and third electromechanical elements. The mechanical deflection means may be coupled to at least one of said first, second and third electromechanically active components.

Effective piezoelectric constant is a very important parameter for measuring the sensitivity of a transduction device. The effective piezoelectric constant as a function of frequency for the stacked hybrid actuation/transduction system, and positive strain component and negative strain component actuation only at 0.5 V is shown in FIG. **15**. The effective piezoelectric constant for the stacked hybrid actuation/transduction system is 16,500 pC/N at off-resonance frequencies, and 235,720 pC/N at the resonance frequency. The effective piezoelectric constant at resonance frequency will be over 300,000 pC/N if the length of the two kinds of elements matching in the stacked hybrid actuation/transduction system. The effective piezoelectric constant will be about 1,000,000 pC/N if the piezoelectric ceramic (d33=750 pC/N, d31=−360 pC/N) elements are replaced with piezoelectric PMN-PT single crystal (d33=2000 pC/N, d31=−1000 pC/N). If the thickness of each layer in the multilayer stack decreases by another 5 times, the effective piezoelectric constant will increase another 5 times. In addition, the effective piezoelectric constant can be improved by reducing the degree of the pre-curvature of the positive strain components in the stacked hybrid actuation/transduction system.

The main purpose of this example is to demonstrate the device concept and the processing possibility for the stacked hybrid actuation/transduction system. For this example, the pre-curved multilayer positive component was made from a ceramic sheet having a thickness of 0.625 mm, the multilayer negative component was made from a ceramic sheet having a thickness of 1 mm and the piezoelectric constants are d_{33}=750 pC/N and d_{31}=−360 pC/N. The center displacement at 150 V DC bias and 1 Hz 100 V_{rms} AC for the double-sided stacked hybrid actuation/transduction system is over 20 μm. If we made the multilayer positive and negative strain components with the thickness of 0.1 mm PMN-PT single crystal sheet (d_{33}=2000 pC/N, and d_{31}=−1000 pC/N), the same size double-sided stacked hybrid actuation/transduction system at 150 V DC bias and 100 AC single (equivalent electric field is 14.14 kV/cm, still smaller than the E_c=20 kV/cm for piezoelectric single crystal) will produce 400 μm displacement. If the effective length of the double-sided stacked hybrid actuation/transduction system is 60 mm, it will produce over 1 mm displacement. This indicates that the multilayer double-sided stacked hybrid actuation/transduction system technology is available to produce displacement at the range of 1 mm to 2 mm. In addition, the mechanical load capability of the stacked hybrid actuation/transduction system may be easily controlled by alternating the thickness of the multilayer components.

Today's highest performance flextensional actuators are multilayer piezoelectric materials stack based flextensional actuators. They are either working on d_{31} mode or d_{33} mode as shown in FIG. **16**. If the thicknesses of each layer in the stacks are the same and the size of each layer is the same, the displacement of the d_{33} mode is two times that of the d_{31} mode. Comparing the stacked hybrid actuation/transduction system with multilayer piezoelectric materials stack based flextensional actuators, the displacement of a stacked hybrid actuation/transduction system will be 3 times the displacement of the same sized d_{31} mode multilayer piezoelectric materials stack based flextensional actuator, and 1.5 times the displacement of the same sized d_{33} mode multilayer piezoelectric materials stack based flextensional actuators.

In summary, a stacked hybrid actuation/transduction system was invented and successfully fabricated. The stacked hybrid actuation/transduction system demonstrates significantly enhanced electromechanical performance by utilizing the advantages of cooperative contributions of the electromechanical responses of multilayer stacked negative and positive strain components. The experimental studies indicate that for a stacked hybrid actuation/transduction system, the displacement is over three times that of a conventional flextensional actuator/transducer of the same size. The coupled resonance between positive and negative strain components of a stacked hybrid actuation/transduction system is much stronger than the resonance of a single element actuation only when the effective lengths of the two kinds of elements match each other. Since all the elements are piezoelectric components, the stacked hybrid actuation/transduction system can serve as projector and receiver for underwater detection. Compared with our previously invented hybrid actuation system (HYBAS), the multilayer stacked hybrid actuation/transduction system can be designed to provide high mechanical load capability, low voltage driving, and a high effective piezoelectric constant. The stacked hybrid actuation/transduction system can provide extremely high effective piezoelectric constant both at resonance frequency and off resonance frequencies. The effective piezoelectric constant can be altered by varying the size of each component, the degree of the pre-curvature of the positive strain components, the thickness of each layer in the multilayer stacks, and the piezoelectric constant of the material used. A high resolution of transducer can be obtained with the stacked hybrid actuation/transduction system structure. The flextensional actuator/transducer could be replaced by a stacked hybrid actuation/transduction system with higher performance. The performance of a stacked hybrid actuation/transduction system can always be enhanced by improving the piezoelectric properties. With the new stacked hybrid actuation/transduction system device concepts, the future actuator designs and piezoelectric material applications will reach a new level.

Obviously, many modifications may be made without departing from the basic spirit of the present invention. Accordingly, it will be appreciated by those skilled in the art that within the scope of the appended claims, the inventions may be practiced other than has been specifically described herein. Many improvements, modifications, and additions will be apparent to the skilled artisan without departing from the spirit and scope of the present invention as described herein and defined in the following claims.

What is claimed is:

1. An electromechanical actuator, comprising:

a first electromechanical element including a first electromechanically active component that contracts in a lengthwise direction when electric power is applied thereto;

a second electromechanical element including a second electromechanically active component that expands in a lengthwise direction when electric power is applied thereto, said first and second electromechanical elements being

(i) disposed in relation to one another such that said lengthwise directions thereof are parallel to one another, and

(ii) mechanically coupled to one another at least at two opposing edges thereof wherein the first and second electromechanically active components are manufactured from the same electromechanically active material; and

an electric power source coupled to said first and second electromechanically active components for simultaneously applying electric power thereto.

2. The actuator as set forth in claim **1** wherein said first electromechanically active component and said second electromechanically active component comprise at least one layer of an electroactive polymer.

3. The actuator as set forth in claim **2** wherein said electroactive polymer is selected from the group consisting of piezoelectric polymers and electrostrictive polymers.

4. The actuator as set forth in claim **1** wherein said first electromechanically active component and said second electromechanically active component comprise at least one layer of an electroactive ceramic.

5. The actuator as set forth in claim **1** further comprising a third electromechanical element including a third electromechanically active component that expands in a lengthwise direction when electric power is applied thereto, said third electromechanical element being (i) disposed in relation to said first electromechanical element such that said lengthwise direction thereof is parallel to said lengthwise direction of said first electromechanical element, and (ii) mechanically coupled to said first and second electromechanical elements at least at two opposing edges thereof wherein said first electromechanical element is sandwiched between said second and third electromechanical elements, said electric power source further coupled to said third electromechanically active component for simultaneously applying electric power to said first, second and third electromechanically active components.

6. The actuator as set forth in claim **5** wherein said third electromechanically active component comprises at least one layer of an electroactive polymer.

7. The actuator as set forth in claim **6** wherein said electroactive polymer is selected from the group consisting of piezoelectric polymers and electrostrictive polymers.

8. The actuator as set forth in claim **5** wherein said third electromechanically active component comprises at least one layer of an electroactive ceramic.

9. The actuator as set forth in claim **1** wherein said first electromechanically active component and said second electromechanically active component comprise at least one layer of an electroactive ceramic selected from the group consisting of single crystal ceramics and polycrystal ceramics.

10. An electromechanical transducer, comprising:

a first electromechanical element including a first electromechanically active component that contracts in a lengthwise direction when electric power is applied thereto;

a second electromechanical element including a second electromechanically active component that expands in a lengthwise direction when electric power is applied thereto, said first and second electromechanical elements being

(i) disposed in relation to one another such that said lengthwise directions thereof are parallel to one another, and

(ii) mechanically coupled to one another at least at two opposing edges thereof wherein the first and second

electromechanically active components are manufactured from a piezoelectric material, each component being manufactured from the same piezoelectric material; and

a mechanical deflection means to deflect at least one of said first and second electromechanically active components such that an electrical charge is produced.

11. The transducer as set forth in claim **10** wherein said first electromechanically active component and said second electromechanically active component comprise at least one layer of a piezoelectric material.

12. The transducer as set forth in claim **11** wherein said piezoelectric material is selected from the group consisting of piezoelectric polymers and piezoelectric ceramics.

13. The transducer as set forth in claim **10** further comprising a third electromechanical element including a third electromechanically active component that expands in a lengthwise direction when electric power is applied thereto, said third electromechanical element being (i) disposed in relation to said first electromechanical element such that said lengthwise direction thereof is parallel to said lengthwise direction of said first electromechanical element, and (ii) mechanically coupled to said first and second electromechanical elements at least at two opposing edges thereof wherein said first electromechanical element is sandwiched between said second and third electromechanical elements, said mechanical deflection means further deflecting at least one of said first, second and third electromechanically active components.

14. The transducer as set forth in claim **13** wherein said third electromechanically active component comprises at least one layer of a piezoelectric material.

15. The transducer as set forth in claim **14** wherein said piezoelectric material is selected from the group consisting of piezoelectric polymers and piezoelectric ceramics.

16. The transducer as set forth in claim **10** wherein said first electromechanically active component and said second electromechanically active component comprise at least one layer of an electroactive ceramic selected from the group consisting of single crystal ceramics and polycrystal ceramics.

17. An electromechanical actuator, comprising:

a first electromechanical element including a first electromechanically active component that contracts in a lengthwise direction when electric power is applied thereto;

a second electromechanical element including a second electromechanically active component that expands in a lengthwise direction when electric power is applied thereto, said first and second electromechanical elements being

(i) disposed in relation to one another such that said lengthwise directions thereof are parallel to one another, and

(ii) mechanically coupled to one another at least at two opposing edges thereof wherein the first and second electromechanically active components are manufactured from the same electromechanically active material;

wherein the first electromechanically active component is configured for negative strain along its lengthwise direction, wherein the second electromechanically active component is configured for positive strain along its lengthwise direction, and wherein an electric power source is coupled to said first and second electromechanically active components for simultaneously applying electric power thereto.

18. The actuator as set forth in claim **17** further comprising a third electromechanical element including a third electro-

15
16

mechanically active component that expands in a lengthwise direction when electric power is applied thereto, said third electromechanical element being (i) disposed in relation to said first electromechanical element such that said lengthwise direction thereof is parallel to said lengthwise direction of said first electromechanical element, (ii) mechanically coupled to said first and second electromechanical elements at least at two opposing edges thereof wherein said first electromechanical element is sandwiched between said second and third electromechanical elements, wherein the third electromechanically active component is configured for positive strain along its lengthwise direction, said electric power source further coupled to said third electromechanically active component for simultaneously applying electric power to said first, second and third electromechanically active components.

* * * * *

US008412469B1

(12) **United States Patent**

Bebout et al.

(10) Patent No.: **US 8,412,469 B1**

(45) Date of Patent: **Apr. 2, 2013**

(54) **ENVIRONMENTAL MONITORING OF MICROBE METABOLIC TRANSFORMATION**

(75) Inventors: **Brad Bebout**, Santa Cruz, CA (US); **Erich Fleming**, Redwood City, CA (US); **Matthew Piccini**, Belmont, CA (US); **Christopher Beasley**, Sunnyvale, CA (US); **Leslie Bebout**, Santa Cruz, CA (US)

(73) Assignee: **The United States of America as Represented by the Administrator of the National Aeronautics & Space Administration (NASA)**, Washington, DC (US)

(*) Notice: Subject to any disclaimer, the term of this patent is extended or adjusted under 35 U.S.C. 154(b) by 317 days.

(21) Appl. No.: **12/698,996**

(22) Filed: **Feb. 2, 2010**

(51) **Int. Cl.**
G01B 3/00 (2006.01)

(52) **U.S. Cl.** **702/33**

(58) **Field of Classification Search** 702/33
See application file for complete search history.

(56) **References Cited**

U.S. PATENT DOCUMENTS

2010/0005857 A1* 1/2010 Zhang et al. 73/29.02

OTHER PUBLICATIONS

McCormick, et al., *Algae* as indicators of environmental change, Journal of Applied Phycology, 1994, 509-526, 6, Kluwer Academic Publishers, Belgium.

Campanella, et al., an Algal Biosensor for the Monitoring of Water Toxicity in Estuarine Environments, Wat. Res., Nov. 14, 2000, 69-76, 35-1, Elsevier Science Ltd, Great Britain.

Levert, et al., Modeling the growth curve for *Spirulina* (*Arthrospira*) maxima, a versatile microalga for producing uniformly labelled compounds with stable isotopes, Journal of Applied Phycology, 2001, 359-367, 13, Kluwer Academic Publishers, Netherlands.

Benson, et al., The development of mechanistic model to investigate the impacts of the light dynamics on algal productivity in a Hydrau-

lically Integrated Serial Turbidostat Algal Reactor (HISTAR), ScienceDirect, Agricultural Engineering, 2007, 198-211, 36, Elsevier.

Fetscher, et al., Incorporating Bioassessment Using Freshwater *Algae* into California's Surface Water Ambient Monitoring Program (SWAMP), Technical Report prepared for California State Water Resources Control Board, May 16, 2008.

Torres, et al., Biochemical biomarkers in *algae* and marine pollution: A review, Ecotoxicology and Environmental Safety, Jul. 2, 2008, 1-15, 71, Elsevier.

Water Monitoring, Monitoring Standard for Freshwater Blue-Green *Algae*, Aquatic Ecosystem Method AEMF008, Oct. 2008, Queensland Government Natural Resources and Water.

Coad, et al., A Telemetric Monitoring System for Estuarine Algal Bloom Management, 2009, Proceeds of the 18th NSW Coastal Conference 2009.

Omar, Perspectives on the Use of *Algae* as Biological Indicators for Monitoring and Protecting Aquatic Environments, with Special Reference to Malaysian Freshwater Ecosystems, Tropical Life Sciences Research, 2010, 51-67, 21-2.

* cited by examiner

Primary Examiner — Jerry Lin

(74) *Attorney, Agent, or Firm* — John F. Schipper; Robert M. Padilla; Christopher J. Menke

(57) **ABSTRACT**

Mobile system and method for monitoring environmental parameters involved in growth or metabolic transformation of algae in a liquid. Each of one or more mobile apparati, suspended or partly or wholly submerged in the liquid, includes at least first and second environmental sensors that sense and transmit distinct first and second environmental, growth or transformation parameter values, such as liquid temperature, temperature of gas adjacent to and above the exposed surface, liquid pH, liquid salinity, liquid turbidity, O_2 dissolved in the liquid, CO_2 contained in the liquid, oxidization and reduction potential of the liquid, nutrient concentrations in the liquid, nitrate concentration in the liquid, ammonium concentration in the liquid, bicarbonate concentration in the liquid, phosphate concentration in the liquid, light intensity at the liquid surface, electrical conductivity of the liquid, and a parameter α(alga) associated with growth stage of the alga, using PAM fluorometry or other suitable parameter measurements.

31 Claims, 5 Drawing Sheets

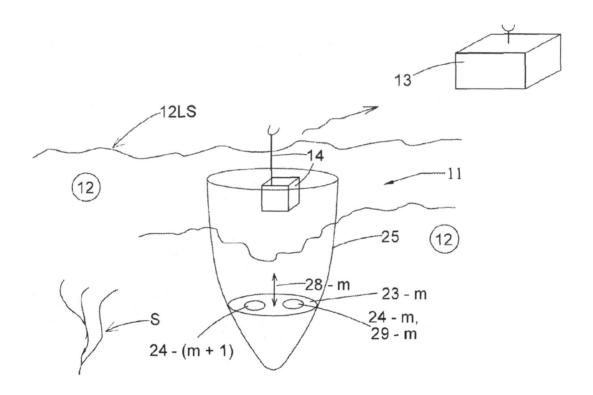

FIG. 1

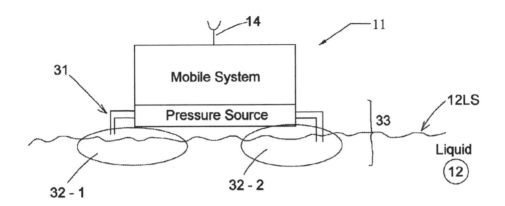

FIG. 3

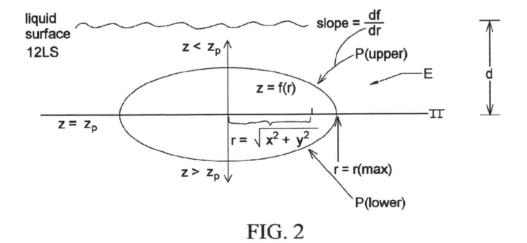

FIG. 2

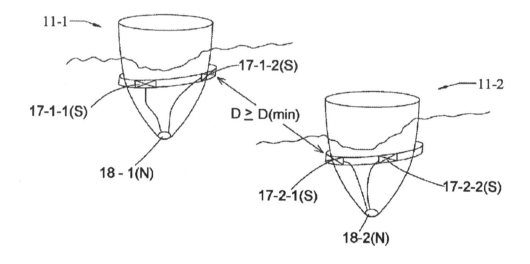

FIG. 4

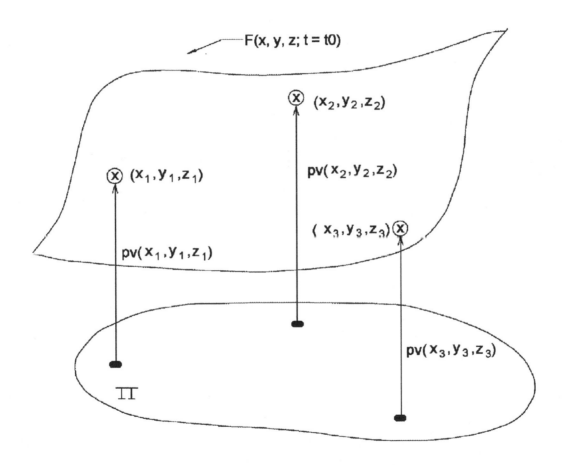

$F(x, y, z; t = t0)$

(x_2, y_2, z_2)

(x_1, y_1, z_1)

$pv(x_2, y_2, z_2)$

(x_3, y_3, z_3)

$pv(x_1, y_1, z_1)$

$pv(x_3, y_3, z_3)$

Π

FIG. 5

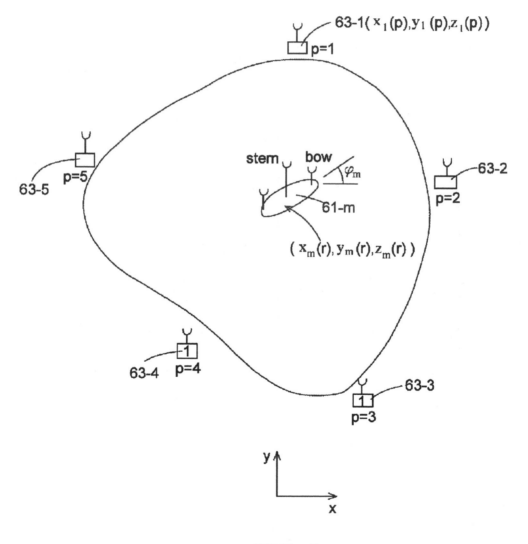

FIG. 6

190

1

ENVIRONMENTAL MONITORING OF MICROBE METABOLIC TRANSFORMATION

ORIGIN OF THE INVENTION

The invention described herein was made in the performance of work under a NASA contract and by an employee of the United States Government and is subject to the provisions of Section 305 of the National Aeronautics and Space Act of 1958, as amended, Public Law 85-568 (72 Stat. 435, 42 U.S.C. §2457), and may be manufactured and used by or for the Government for governmental purposes without the payment of any royalties thereon or therefore.

FIELD OF THE INVENTION

This invention relates to monitoring of a plurality of environmental and growth parameters associated with growth of algae and other members of the archaea, bacteria and/or eukarya domains (collectively referred to herein as "alga" or "algae" for convenient reference).

BACKGROUND OF THE INVENTION

Growth or environmental control or other controlled metabolic transformation of archaea, bacteria and/or eukarya domains in a liquid environment is challenging, in part because the ambient liquid allows transport of nutrients and other substances between the microbes, whether of the same species or of different species. Monitoring of the individual microbes for one, two or several changes in environmental, growth and/or metabolic transformation parameters is often required, if optimal control is desired.

Monitoring and control of a large number of environmental and growth parameters is often required in order to respond to predictable and unpredictable events that occur during growth, transformation and harvesting of algae. These activities should permit distinction between parameter values at different locations and different times in the growth and metabolic transformation processes, should permit optional prescription of vehicle trajectories, should provide for collection and prompt analysis of the measurements, and should permit use of multiple vehicles.

SUMMARY OF THE INVENTION

These needs are met by the invention, which provides a method of monitoring selected environmental and/or growth parameters for growth of algae and other archaea, bacteria and/or eukarya immersed in a liquid environment. The method includes the following processes: (1) one or more distinct organisms is provided in a liquid; (2) a mobile system that floats on and/or is submergible in the liquid is provided, the mobile mechanism comprising at least first and second environmental sensors that sense distinct first and second environmental parameter values, $pv(t;1)$ and $pv(t;2)$, respectively, that are drawn from liquid temperature, temperature of gas adjacent to and above the exposed liquid surface, liquid pH, liquid salinity, liquid turbidity, O_2 dissolved in the liquid, CO_2 contained in the liquid, oxidation/reduction potential of the liquid, nitrate concentration in the liquid, ammonium concentration in the liquid, bicarbonate concentration in the liquid, phosphate concentration in the liquid, other nutrient concentrations in the liquid, light intensity at the liquid surface and below the surface, electrical conductivity of the liquid, and a parameter $\eta(alga)$ associated with growth stage of the alga; (3) the first value $pv(t;1)$ is sensed at spaced apart

2

first and third sensing times, $t=t1$ and $t=t3$; (4) the second value $pv(t;2)$ is sensed at a second sensing time, $t=t2$, that is intermediate between the first and third sensing times; and (5) the sensed values, $pv(t1;1)$ and $pv(t3;1)$, sensed at the first and third sensing times, and the value $pv(t2;2)$, sensed at the second sensing time, are transmitted to a receiver that is spaced apart from the mobile system. Pulse amplitude modulation (PAM) fluorometry or another suitable mechanism is applied for some of these measurements.

Where a plurality of mobile systems are provided, the sensed values of a selected parameter at different locations are optionally combined with each other and a function, dependent upon location and time and representing a field of values of this parameter within or adjacent to the growth medium, is constructed for one or more sampling times and optionally displayed for a user. Optionally, this field of values is analyzed to estimate relevant environmental and/or growth parameter values and trends, to compare at least one such value with a range of acceptable values for such parameter, and to determine whether any change(s) should be introduced for such parameter.

Optionally, the mobile system is allowed to move with prevailing liquid currents in the liquid, and measurements of one or more parameter values are sampled and transmitted at each of a sequence of spaced apart times and locations, together with an estimate of the sampling location coordinates, angular orientations and corresponding sampling times. Alternatively, the mobile system is provided with a location sensing and/or angular orientation sensing mechanism and with a locomotion mechanism that is configured (i) to move the mobile system along a selected trajectory in the liquid and/or (ii) to alter or correct the mobile system present location to a selected corrected location and/or (iii) to alter or correct the mobile system present angular orientation to a selected corrected orientation.

Optionally, a time rate of change of at least one parameter value $pv(t;1)$ is estimated, based on an elapsed time difference, $\Delta t=t2-t1$, and this elapsed time difference is adjusted subsequently according to how quickly or slowly the parameter value $pv(t;1)$ is changing with time.

Optionally, the mobile system is provided with a submersion mechanism that permits the mobile system, or a portion of the system containing at least one of the sensors, to be submerged by a selected, continuously or discretely variable depth within the liquid.

Optionally, the mobile system has a structure with at least one aperture, through which at least one sensor performs measurements of an associated environmental parameter. Optionally, measurements of two or more parameters are performed through this aperture. Optionally, at least one sample of liquid, algae or other relevant substance can be captured through this or another aperture and preserved for subsequent analysis.

On-board, or subsequent, analyses can be implemented using procedures such as PAM fluorometry of the samples to determine photosynthetic efficiency or other parameters.

Optionally, where N mobile systems are provided (N>2), a mutual repulsion system is provided for each mobile system so that any two such mobile systems that come within a selected distance of each other will repel each other, in order to prevent "bunching" or congregation of two or more such mobile systems within a small region.

The invention described in the preceding can be applied to environmental, growth and/or metabolic transformation monitoring of algae, in a liquid environment.

BRIEF DESCRIPTION OF THE DRAWINGS

FIG. 1 illustrates use of the invention, with one mobile system, in a liquid environment.

3

FIGS. **2** and **3** illustrate an embodiment of a submersion and flotation mechanism used in the invention.

FIG. **4** illustrates a mutual repulsion system for two or more mobile systems.

FIG. **5** illustrates construction of a field of values determined according to the invention.

FIG. **6** illustrates estimation of location/angular orientation coordinates.

DESCRIPTION OF BEST MODES OF THE INVENTION

FIG. **1** illustrates an environment where the invention can be used. A mobile system **11** floats or is submerged in a liquid **12** having a liquid surface **12LS** (exposed or defined by a container surface, such as a pipe) and is intended to monitor two or more environmental, growth and/or metabolic transformation parameters (e.g., population size, population composition or metabolic activity) of the liquid or of a substance S suspended or otherwise contained in the liquid. The substance S may be one or more alga or another member of the archaea, bacteria or eukarya domains that is to be grown or otherwise transformed over a time interval. Two or more environmental and/or growth and/or metabolic transformation parameters of the substance S are to be monitored by the mobile system, as a function of time and/or as a function of location in or adjacent to the liquid **12**. These monitored parameters may include, but are not limited to, liquid temperature, temperature of gas adjacent to and above the liquid surface, liquid temperature at a selected depth below the surface, liquid pH, liquid salinity, liquid turbidity, O_2 dissolved in the liquid, CO_2 contained in the liquid, oxidization/reduction potential of the liquid, concentration of ammonia, nitrate, phosphate, carbonate or other nutrient(s) or inorganic substances in the liquid, light intensity where light enters the liquid, light intensity at one or more selected depths within the liquid, electrical conductivity of the liquid, and one or more parameters α(alga) associated with growth stage of the alga. The mobile system **11** may float on or be partially or fully submerged in the liquid or may be located within and/or move within a pipe or other container for the liquid, or the mobile system may float on or be submerged relative to an exposed liquid surface.

A first parameter value pv(t;**1**) is measured at two or more spaced apart times, t=t**1** and t=t**2** (>t**1**), and a second parameter value pv(t;**2**) is measured at one or more third times, t=t**3**, with t**1**≦t**3**<t**2**, and the measured values are transmitted to a measured signal receiver **13** that is spaced apart from the mobile system **11**, using a measured signal transmitter **14** located on the mobile system. Where M (≧2) environmental parameters are monitored, times of transmission of the M parameters may be interspersed with each other, optionally in a round robin format, so that a measured signal representing each parameter value is received at one or more spaced apart times. Optionally, one or more of the measurements may use fluorometry or a similar mechanism.

Each mobile system **11** is floatable on and/or submergible in the liquid **12** or may be located within and/or move within a pipe or other closed environment containing the liquid. The mobile system **11** optionally includes a submersion mechanism **31**, indicated in more detail in FIG. **3**, that permits a selected portion of (or all of) the mobile system to be submerged relative to a liquid surface **12LS** to a selected, continuously variable or discretely variable depth within the liquid **12**. A submergible portion of the mobile system **11** optionally includes one or more parameter value sensors **23**-*m* (FIG. **1**; m=1, 2, . . . , M; M≧2) that each sense one or

more relevant environmental, growth and/or metabolic transformation parameters of the liquid **12** and/or of the substance S in the liquid. The measured sensor values pv(t;m) (m=1, 2, . . . , M) are transmitted by the transmitter **14** to the receiver **13** for analysis and/or storage. Optionally, each sensor **23**-*m* is located in or adjacent to one or more apertures **24**-*m* in a containment structure **25** of the mobile system **11**, through which the sensor measurement can be performed. Optionally, two or more sensors are located in or associated with measurement through a common aperture.

Optionally, each mobile system **11** has a location mechanism **61** (FIG. **6**) that senses the present location coordinates (x,y,z), angular orientation (θ;φ) (optional), and present time t of a designated component of the mobile system and presents this information to the transmitter **14** for transmission to the receiver **13**. Optionally, a supplementary location mechanism is provided to measure or estimate a depth d(m) of the sensor **23**-*m* below the liquid surface **12LS**, for transmission to the data receiver **13**.

A submersion mechanism **28**-*m*, which may be but need not be the same as the mobile system submersion mechanism **31**, is optionally provided for separate depth control of the sensor **23**-*m*. The submersion mechanism **28**-*m* allows the mobile system **11** to vary the depth of the associated sensor **23**-*m* to facilitate sensor readings at arbitrarily selected depths d(m) within the liquid **12**.

One implementation of a submersion mechanism **31** provides K inflatable bags, **32**-*k* (k=1, 2, . . . , K; K>2) or other gas enclosures at spaced apart locations on the mobile system **11**, or on the sensor **23**-*m*, The mass of the mobile system **11**, with or without one or more selected masses attached, is assumed to be chosen so that, when each of the enclosures **32**-*k* includes a selected amount of gas (e.g., air) and has an associated baseline volume V0(*k*), the mobile system and submersion mechanism **31** floats on the liquid surface **12LS** of the liquid, in accord with Archimedes principle. When a selected amount of gas is released from a one, two or more of the enclosures (e.g., **32-1** and **32-2**), the enclosure gas volumes are reduced to V1(**1**)<V0(**1**) and V1(**2**)<V0(**2**). As a result of this volume reduction, the mobile system **11** and/or one or more sensors **23**-*m* are (further) submerged to a controllable depth d1 below the liquid surface **12LS** of the liquid, where the depth d1 depends upon the volume differences, V0(**1**)-V1(**1**) and V0(**2**)-V1(**2**).

When the mobile system **11** and/or a sensor **23**-*m* are to be brought closer to the liquid surface **12LS** so that the depth d of submersion is reduced to d2<d1, gas from a re-pressurization mechanism **33** is (re)admitted into one or more of the enclosures **32**-*k* (not necessarily the enclosures, **32-1** and **32-2**, that were originally partly deflated), with corresponding increases in the enclosure volumes, and the mobile system **11** and/or the sensor **23**-*m* rise to a new selected depth d2 (<d1). Appendix A contains an analysis of the dependencies of submersion depth d on enclosure volume differences.

Optionally, one or more of the sensors **23**-*m* is located adjacent to, or within, an optically or electromagnetically transparent aperture **29**-*m*, through which the sensor **23**-*m* can measure or otherwise sense the environmental parameter(s) pv(t;m) associated with this sensor. Each parameter value measured or sensed by the sensor **23**-*m* is presented to the transmitter **14**, for possible transmission to the data receiver **13**, together with a time t(meas) at which the parameter was measured or otherwise sensed. Optionally, the measured or sensed parameter value and associated measurement time pv(tmeas;m);t(meas;m)) are transmitted to the data receiver **13** only if (1) a measurement time difference satisfies

5

$$t2(\text{meas});m-t1(\text{meas};m) \geqq \text{a threshold time difference}$$
$$\Delta t(thr;m), \tag{1}$$

which may depend upon m and/or (2) a parameter value difference satisfies

$$|pv(t2;m)-pv(t1;m)| \geqq \text{a threshold pv difference } pv(thr; m), \tag{2}$$

which may also depend upon m.

Preferably, the parameter value and time value signals pv(t-meas;m),t(neas;m)) are transmitted using a low power, low data rate protocol, such as Zigbee, whose protocols are partly specified by I.E.E.E. 802.15.4 standard. Zigbee uses radio frequency signals and allows relatively long battery life and secure networking. Zigbee operates in the industrial, scientific and medical (ISM) radio bands, circa 868 MHz in Europe, circa 915 MHz in the U.S. and Australia, and circa 2.4 GHz in most jurisdictions throughout the world. Zigbee can be activated in 15 msec or less so that an transmission of a isolated signal, such as pv(t(meas);m), can be preceded by transmission activation and followed by transmission de-activation, if desired, with resulting low latency and low average power consumption. Typical Zigbee applications include commercial building monitoring and control, home awareness and security, home entertainment and control, industrial plant management and control, and mobile services, such as health care/monitoring and tele-assistance.

A Zigbee communication system requires a Zigbee coordinator, one or more Zigbee routers (optional here) for forwarding data to other devices, and a Zigbee (non-forwarding) end device. The network can form a single cluster for a single mobile system 11, or a mesh of clusters (useful for a plurality of mobile systems 11). Beacon-enabled networks and non-beacon-enabled networks (number of beacons ≦15) are supported. In a non-beacon-enabled network, a non-slotted code division multiple access/collision avoidance (CDMA/CA) channel access mechanism is used. A beacon-enabled network provides wakeup/transmit/sleep time intervals that are, in one version, multiples of 15.36 msec for transmission rates of 250 kbits/sec, to multiples of 24 msec for 40 kbits/sec, to multiples of 48 msec for 20 kbits/sec. The I.E.E.E. 802.15.4 standard specifies the physical layer and the media access control layer. Message acknowledgments, when used, do not rely upon CDMA/CA.

Zigbee routers, if any are used, are typically continuously active so that a robust power supply is required. The receiver (typically located on-shore and non-portable) can be configured to receive continuously, with the aid of a large(r) battery or power supply. The individual mobile systems can transmit in a slotted format, with each of M mobile systems typically being allotted a slot of length $\Delta t(\text{mob}) \approx 200$ msec in a round robin cycle of length several sec. Not all environmental parameter values pv(t';m) need be transmitted within each time slot. Optionally, only the parameter values pv(t;m) that have changed significantly since the preceding slot for the given mobile system will be transmitted within the present time slot, as indicated in Eq. (2).

Optionally, the housing for the mobile system also includes one or more sampling apertures 30-q (q=1, . . . , Q; Q≧1) that facilitate physical capture of one or more samples of the underwater environment (e.g., a sample of the liquid, of an alga, or of surface material in which the alga is grown). The sample, after capture, is deposited in and stored in a sample repository within the mobile system, for subsequent analysis.

Where two or more mobile systems, denoted **11-1** and **11-2** here (FIG. **4**) are present, one concern is keeping the mobile systems spaced apart from each other by a distance D that is at least a minimum distance D(min) For small but positive

6

values of D(min), for example, D(min)=1-5 cm, each mobile system is provided with at least three, preferably at least five, mutual repulsion mechanisms, **17**-*j*-*k* (j=1, 2; k=1, 2, 3) mounted on each such system that provide mutual repulsion, mobile system to mobile system. One implementation of the mutual repulsion mechanisms **17**-*j*-*k* provides three or more magnetic poles, all south poles or all north poles so that any two poles, one on mobile system **11-1** and one on mobile system **11-2**, will repel each other. The three south poles **17-1**-*k* on the mobile system **11-1** (and, similarly, the three south poles **17-2**-*k* on the mobile system **11-2**) are preferably connected to a single north pole **18**-*j* of an opposite magnetic sign, which is optionally located in a region elsewhere within the mobile system, as illustrated in FIG. **4**. Choice of the magnetic strength of the pole **18**-*j* will strongly influence s distance of closest approach of two mutually repulsive magnets (both south poles or both north poles), one located on each of the two mobile systems. By spacing P south poles on a perimeter at approximately uniform angle differences (e.g., at $\Delta\phi \approx 360°/P$ for P such poles), the mutual repulsion of like poles will be approximately equally effective, for approach of a first mobile system to a second mobile system from any direction.

Estimation of location coordinates, angular orientation coordinates and corresponding sampling times $(x,y,z;\theta;\phi;t)$ can be implemented using GPS signals, for a relatively large body LB of liquid, or may be implemented using three or more pseudolite signal generators, located at spaced apart positions adjacent to the boundary LB, as discussed in detail in Appendix B.

Appendix A. Mechanism For Control of Submersion Depth.

Consider first and second bags or other enclosures **32-1** and **32-2** (FIG. **3**) that is inflatable with a selected gas, preferably having a very low density relative to the density of the liquid **12**. The enclosures, **32-1** and **32-2**, are attached to a mobile system **11** and are attached to a controllable, pressurized source **33** of the selected gas, which can be introduced into one or both of enclosures or can be withdrawn from one or both of enclosures.

FIG. **2** illustrates a cross section of a bag or other enclosure E, which is assumed to be symmetric about a horizontal plane Π (referenced as a coordinate value, $z=-z_P$) and is assumed to be (approximately) rotationally symmetric about a z-axis (x=y=0). A cross section of the lower and upper sections of the enclosure shown in FIG. **2** are assumed to be defined as

$$z=-z_P \pm f(r), \tag{A-1}$$

$$r=\sqrt{(x^2+y^2)}, \tag{A-2}$$

where r is a radius measured in the horizontal plane Π. The function f(r) is assumed to be continuously differentiable so that the derivative or slope df/dr is defined and continuous for $0 \leqq r \leqq r(\text{max})$ (edge of the enclosure in the plane Π). Note that the corresponding slopes {df/dr} (upper) and {df/dr} (lower) on the upper section ($z>-z_P$) and on the lower section ($z<-z_P$) of the enclosure are related by

$$\{df/dr\}(\text{upper})=-\{df/dr\}(\text{lower}). \tag{A-3}$$

The total liquid force on the enclosure, assumed to be directed normal to the enclosure surface at each point, is given by

$$F(z_P)=\rho 0 g \int_0^{r(max)} \{\{[z_P-f(r)](df/dr)(\text{upper})+[z_P+f(r)]$$
$$(df/dr)(\text{lower})\} 2\pi r \, dr/\{1+(df/dr)^2\}^{1/2},=$$
$$\rho 0 g \int_0^{r(max)} \{2z_P\}(df/dr)(\text{upper}) 2\pi r \, dr, \tag{A-4}$$

$$\sin \psi=(df/dr)/\{1+(df/dr)^2\}^{1/2}. \tag{A-5}$$

7

8

where it is assumed that the horizontal plane Π is located at a depth $\Delta z = z_P$ below the surface of the liquid **12**, and that the mass or pressure equivalent of this liquid (per unit depth below the liquid surface) is ρ0 (e.g., 62.4 lbs. per cubic foot for water as the liquid **12**), A corresponding volume of the enclosure interior is

$$V = \int_0^{r(max)} 2f(r) 2\pi r \, dr. \qquad (A\text{-}6)$$

The total liquid force F is directed upward, toward negative values of the coordinate z. Note that, for any smooth shape f(r) of the enclosure cross section, the total liquid force F on the enclosure is proportional to the depth parameter z_P and is usually directed upward. Equation of the force F and the mobile system weight w(mobile) will provide an equilibrium depth z_P at which the (submerged) enclosure plus weight will settle. As the amount of the selected gas introduced into the enclosure E increases, the shape function f(r) changes, the volume within the enclosure increases, and the equilibrium value of the depth parameter z_P decreases so that the mobile system **11** rises in the liquid; and conversely. The net energy required to cause the depth parameter z_P to decrease by a controllable amount so that the mobile system **11** rises in the liquid is substantially equal to the energy required to introduce the additional gas into the enclosure interior, which is relatively small. Optionally, when the depth parameter z_P is to be increased so that the mobile system sinks by a controllable amount, a portion of the selected gas in the enclosure interior can be bled off and allowed to pass into the ambient medium, with little or no additional energy expenditure.

Assuming that the mass of an attached mobile system, including ballast masses, if desired, is m(total), the enclosure(s) E will rise in the supporting liquid to an enclosure depth $\Delta z = z_p$ for which

$$F(z_P) = m(\text{total}) {}^* g. \qquad (A\text{-}7)$$

This relation may be corrected, if desired, for the supplemental buoyancy for the mobile system **11** that is provided by the supporting liquid.

Appendix B. Estimation of Location Coordinates and Angular Orientation

Coordinates and Sampling Times.

Consider a mobile system **61**-m (m=1, . . . , M;M≧1) that is floating on or submerged in a liquid **62**, having a boundary ∂B, as illustrated in FIG. **6**. Three or more spaced apart pseudolites, **63**-k (k=1, . . . , K; K≧5) are located at selected distances from the boundary ∂B, or optionally within the liquid, each pseudolite **63**-k has known and fixed coordinates (x_k, y_k, z_k), and any three of the pseudolites are non-collinear. A signal receiver **62** is located at a selected position, relative to or on the mobile system **61**-m. The mobile system **61**-m has a timing mechanism that is coordinated with a timing mechanism on each of the pseudolites **63**-k. At each of a specified sequence of spaced apart times, $\{t = t_{k,m}\}_m$, the pseudolite **63**-k transmits a short location/timing signal $S_{L/T}(t_{k,m})$, preferably including a coded portion that identifies the pseudolite source and specifying the time this signal is transmitted. The signal $S_{L/T}(t_{k,m})$ is received by a receiver antenna on the mobile system **61**-m, which computes a time difference

$$\Delta t_{k,m} = t_{a,k,m} - t_{k,m}. \qquad (B\text{-}1)$$

between a time, $t = t_{ta,k,m}$, this signal is received by the receiver antenna (m) and the signal transmission time for the pseudolite (k). A separation distance,

$$d_{k,m}(t) = c \Delta t_{k,m} \qquad (B\text{-}2)$$

$$= \{(x_m(r)) - x_k(p))^2 + (y_m(r)) - y_k(p))^2 +$$

$$(z_m(r)) - z_k(p))^2\}^{1/2},$$

between the receiver antenna, having location coordinates $(x_m(r), y_m(r)), z_m(r))$, and the pseudolite, having location coordinates $(x_k(p), y_k(p)), z_k(p))$, is then estimated, where c is the propagation velocity of an electromagnetic signal in the ambient environment (the "speed of light").

Each pseudolite will have fixed location coordinates that do not vary with time, and preferably any temporal variation between the timers for each pair of pseudolites is immediately corrected, through p-to-p communication. However, an individual receiver associated with a mobile system (m) will have varying location coordinates, and the on-board timer for this mobile system may have a time shift, $\Delta t = \tau(t;m)$ that varies with time and varies with the particular mobile system (m) being examined. This time shift (positive, zero or negative; unknown initially) is explicitly incorporated in the equations for distance as follows:

$$\{(x_m(r)) - x_k(p))^2 + (y_m(r)) - y_k(p))^2 + (z_m(r)) - z_k(p))^2\}^{1/2} = c\{\Delta t(k.m) + \tau(t;m)\}(k=1, \ldots, K; m \text{ fixed}), \qquad (B\text{-}3(k,m))$$

where $\Delta t(k,m)$ is a time difference measured at the pseudolite number k or measured at the mobile system number m. Equations (B-3(k,m)) for k=2, 3, 4, etc. (m fixed) are squared and subtracted from Eq. (3-B(k=1 μm) as follows.

$$\{(x_m(r)) - x_k(p))^2 + (y_m(r)) - y_k(p))^2 + (z_m(r)) - z_k(p))^2\} -$$

$$\{(x_m(r)) - x_1(p))^2 + (y_m(r)) - y_1(p))^2 + (z_m(r)) - z_1(p))^2\} =$$

$$2\{x_m(r)(x_1(p) - x_k(p)) + y_m(r)(y_1(p) - y_k(p)) + z_m(r)(z_1(p) - z_k(p))\} +$$

$$x_k(p)^2 - x_1(p)^2 + y_k(p)^2 - y_1(p)^2 + z_k(p)^2 - z_1(p)^2 +=$$

$$c^2\{\Delta t(k.m) + \tau(t; m)\}^2 - c^2\{\Delta t(1.m) + \tau(t; m)\}^2 +=$$

$$c^2\{2\tau(t; m)(\Delta t(k, m) - \Delta t(1, m)) + \Delta t(k, m)^2 - \Delta t(1, m)^2\}(B\text{-}4(k, m))$$

The unknowns here are the location coordinates, $x_m(r)$, $y_m(r)$ and $z_m(r)$, and the time shift t(t;m) for the mobile system **61**-m; all other quantities are known. Equations (B-4(k,m)) can be re-expressed in matrix form as

$$M \cdot X = H, \qquad (B\text{-}5)$$

$$M = \begin{bmatrix} x_1(p) - x_k(p) & (y_1(p) - y_k(p)) & z_1(p) - z_k(p) & \Delta t(k, m) - \\ & & & \Delta t(1, m \\ x_1(p) - x_k(p) & (y_1(p) - y_k(p)) & z_1(p) - z_k(p) & \Delta t(k, m) - \\ & & & \Delta t(1, m) \\ x_1(p) - x_k(p) & (y_1(p) - y_k(p)) & z_1(p) - z_k(p) & \Delta t(k, m) - \\ & & & \Delta t(1, m) \\ x_1(p) - x_k(p) & (y_1(p) - y_k(p)) & z_1(p) - z_k(p) & \Delta t(k, m) - \\ & & & \Delta t(1, m) \end{bmatrix} \qquad (B\text{-}6)$$

-continued

$$X^{tr} = [\, x_m(r)\, y_m(r) \quad z_m(r) \quad \tau(r; m)\,],\tag{B-7}$$

$$2H^{tr} = [x_1(p)^2 - x_k(p)^2 + y_1(p)^2 -$$
$$y_k(+z_1(p)^2 - z_k(p)^2 + c^2(\Delta t(k, m)^2 - \Delta t(l, m)^2),\, x_1(p)^2 -$$
$$x_k(p)^2 + y_1(p)^2 - y_k(+z_1(p)^2 - z_k(p)^2 +$$
$$c^2(\Delta t(k, m)^2 - \Delta t(l, m)^2),\, x_1(p)^2 - x_k(p)^2 + y_1(p)^2 -$$
$$y_k(+z_1(p)^2 - z_k(p)^2 + c^2(\Delta t(k, m)^2 - \Delta t(l, m)^2),$$
$$x_1(p)^2 - x_1(p)^2 + y_1(p)^2 -$$
$$y_k(+z_1(p)^2 - z_k(p)^2 + c^2(\Delta t(k, m)^2 - \Delta t(l, m)^2)]$$

The matrix M has an inverse M^{-1} (rank 4), in part because no three of the location coordinate triples $(x_i(p),y_i(p),z_i(p))$ (i=1, 2, 3, 4, 5) for the pseudolites are collinear. The matrix solution X of Eq. (B-5) becomes

$$X = M^{-1}H.\tag{B-9}$$

The time shift $\tau(t;m)$ for mobile system 61-m may, but need not, vary with time t.

The location coordinates $(x_m(t;r),y_m(t;r),z_m(t;r))$ estimated for mobile system 61-m will vary with time t as the mobile system moves on or within the liquid 62. Two consecutive sampling times, t_n and t_{n+1}, for the mobile system 61-m may be determined by identifying a time difference, $t_{n+1}-t_n$, for which a separation distance first satisfies

$$\{(x_m(t_{n+1};r)-x_m(t_n;r))^2 + (y_m(t_{n+1};r)-y_m(t_n;r))^2 + (z_m(t_{n+1};r)-z_m(t_n;r))^2\}^{1/2} \ge d(thr),\tag{B-10}$$

where d(thr) is a selected threshold separation distance, which is chosen according to an estimated difference in one or more environmental parameters that may occur with the separation distance d(thr). This sampling frequency may vary from one environmental parameter to another.

Angular orientation coordinates (ϕ,θ)=(azimuthal angle, polar angle) for the mobile system, relative to a horizontal plane may be estimated by obtaining the location coordinates,

$(x_m(r;\text{bow}),y_m(r;\text{bow}),z_m(r;\text{bow}))$ and

$(x_m(r;\text{stem}),y_m(r;\text{stem}),z_m(r;\text{stern}))$

for spaced apart, first and second locations on the bow and on the stern, respectively, of the mobile system 61-m. These location coordinates may be estimated, applying the considerations involved in Eqs. (B-1) through (B-9) to measurements made at a second data receiver located on the bow and at a third data receiver located on the stern of the mobile system 61-m. The angles ϕ_m and θ_m for mobile system no. m are then estimated from the relations

$$\tan\phi_m = \{y_m(r;\text{bow}) - y_m(r;\text{stern})\} / \{x_m(r;\text{bow}) - x_m(r;\text{stern})\},\tag{B-11}$$

$$\tan\theta_m = \{z_m(r;\text{bow}) - z_m(r;\text{stern})\} / \{x_m(r;\text{bow}) - x_m(r;\text{stern}))^2 + (y_m(r;\text{bow}) - y_m(r;\text{stern}))^2\}^{1/2},\tag{B-12}$$

Normally, the polar angle θ_m will be close to 0, because the mobile system will be approximately horizontal in the liquid 62.

Appendix C. Construction of a Surface From a Field of Values.

Consider a field of measured values $pv(x_k,y_k,z_k,t_k;m)$ (k=1, ..., K) of a selected environmental parameter (m fixed), where the values have been measured at times $(t_k \approx t0$, a time value independent of k) that are reasonably close to each other. This is preferably done using two or more mobile systems, which may be individually stationary or may move relative to each other. If the integer K is not too large (pref-

erably, K≦20, and more preferably K≦10), a three-dimensional field or surface of values that precisely matches the values $pv(x_k,y_k,z_k,t_k;m)$ for the coordinates $(x=x_k,y=y_k,z=z_k)$ is constructed, as illustrated in FIG. 5. This field of values is defined by

$$F(x, y, z;\, t \approx t0) \sum_{k=1}^{K} pv(x_k, y_k, z_k, t_k; m) \prod_{j=1, j\ne k}^{K} \{(x -$$
$$x_j)(y - y_j)(z - zj) / (x_k - x_j)(y_j - y_k)(zj - z_k)\},\tag{C-1}$$

$$F(x_k, y_k, z_k,;\, t \approx t0) = pv(x_k, y_k, z_k, t_k; m),\tag{C-2}$$

where, for each value k, the finite product Π is formed for all ratios $(x-x_j)/(x_k-x_j)$ for which j≠k. The function F is a polynomial of degree K in each of the coordinates x, y and z and is representable as a surface S of height $pv(x_k,y_k,z_k,t_k;m)$ above a plane Π at the location (x_k,y_k,z_k), as illustrated in FIG. 5.

Where two or more measurement locations (x_k,y_k,z_k) have at least one of the same coordinate values, x_k or y_k or z_k, a new "rotated plane" with coordinates (x',y',z') is introduced, defined by

$$\begin{bmatrix} x \\ y \\ z \end{bmatrix} = M_2(\beta) \cdot M_3(\alpha) \begin{bmatrix} x' \\ y' \\ z' \end{bmatrix}\tag{C-3}$$

$$M_3(\alpha) = \begin{bmatrix} \cos\alpha & \sin\alpha & 0 \\ -\sin\alpha & \cos\alpha & 0 \\ 0 & 0 & 1 \end{bmatrix}\tag{C-4}$$

$$M_2(\beta) = \begin{bmatrix} \cos\beta & 0 & \sin\beta \\ 0 & 1 & 0 \\ -\sin\beta & 0 & \cos\beta \end{bmatrix}\tag{C-5}$$

The angular variables α and β are chosen so that an equivalent finite product

$$F'(x', y', z';\, t \approx t0) \sum_{k=1}^{K} pv(x'_k, y'_k, z'_k, t_k; m) \prod_{j=1, j\ne k}^{K} \{(x' -$$
$$x'_j(y' - y'_j)(z' - z'_j) / (x'_k - x'_j)(y'_j - y'_k)z_j - z'_k)\},\tag{C-6}$$

expressed in terms of the equivalent coordinates (x',y',z'), does not include any situation in which $x'_j=x'_k$ or $y'_j=y'_k$ or $z'_j=z'_k$. This can be achieved in a straightforward manner, because the total number of coordinates (x_j,y_j,z_j) is finite and equal to 3K. The coordinates (x',y',z') are then expressed in terms of the original coordinates (x,y,z) as

$$\begin{bmatrix} x' \\ y' \\ z' \end{bmatrix} = M_3(-\alpha) \cdot M_2(-\beta) \begin{bmatrix} x \\ y \\ z \end{bmatrix}\tag{C-7}$$

which is the inverse of Eq. (C-3). The resulting field of values function F"(x,y,z;t≈t0) will be a polynomial with the same maximum degree (K) in each of the coordinates but may not be expressible in the elegant form set forth in Eq. (C-1). In order to avoid high polynomial degrees, with the associated frequency variation in each of the location coordinates, it is preferable to limit the number K of sampled pv values to a relatively small integer, such as K=3-6.

It is important to control certain environmental parameters to insure that these parameters stay within a suitable range in order to avoid adversely interfering with the growth or metabolic transformation process for a particular microbe. These parameters include: liquid pH (preferred range=$3.5 \leq pH$ (liq)≤ 9.5); liquid temperature T ($0° C. \leq T(liq) \leq 40° C.$); CO_2 concentration (0-10 mmoles/liter); O_2 concentration (0-1 mmole/liter); nutrient concentration (0-1 mmole/liter); light irradiance I adjacent to a liquid surface (0-2500 photons/(meter)-2-sec).

Appendix D. Application of Fluorometry to Transformation Measurements.

In a fluorescence process, incident light having energy $E=hv=hc/\lambda$ is absorbed by an object, a portion of the light energy is transformed into one or more other processes, and the remainder, if any, is re-emitted at a higher wavelength, $\lambda'>\lambda$ or $v'<v$, representing a lower emission energy. The remainder of the incident energy may be absorbed and used for photosynthesis, for heat dissipation and/or for quantum processes such as (temporary) atomic or molecular excitation. This perspective may be expressed as an equation

$$E=hv+\text{photosynthesil} (E_{ps})+\text{heat dissipation}(E_{diss})+ \text{quantum processes}(E_{qp})+\text{fluorescence} (E_{FL}=hv') \quad \text{(D-1)}$$

For simplicity, the presence of quantum processes is ignored here.

When a leaf or other biological object is kept in the dark, with no energy supplied, the characteristic internal energy of the object will decrease toward a minimum energy value E_{min}. When this object is illuminated with incident light ($E=hv$), the reissued fluorescence signal energy E_{FL} will increase to a maximum value E_{max}, with the remainder, $E_{ps}+E_{diss}$, being generally not observable optically. The difference, $E_v, = E_{max}-E_{min}$, is referred to as the variable fluorescence and has a range of values, $E_v \approx 0.8 E_{max}$, for healthy, growing plants. For many algae, the ratio E_v/E_{max} has an optimal range, depending upon the process of interest., and the system approaches this optimal range monotonically as growth or other metabolic transformation proceeds.

When non-saturating light is received by a target (e.g., chlorophyll a), the target is elevated to an excited state in which an electron is transferred into an electron transport chain (ETC), which can be subsequently used for other purposes, such as production of ATP, reduction of NADP, and production of glucose. After electron transfer to and through an ETC has occurred, the electron acceptor becomes available again to accept another electron. When higher light intensity is delivered, the reaction centers become temporarily inactivated (closed) until electrons presently in the reaction centers are cleared out through transfer. When this saturation and temporary closure occurs, excess incident light is re-emitted as fluorescence, which can be measured and used as a diagnostic parameter to estimate the present status of the target. When a group of cells is under stress, saturation occurs more easily, and the system processes the incident light less efficiently than would occur in a group of cells not under such stress.

A fluorescence target is initially kept in the dark, to allow the ETC to become cleared of electrons and to open all acceptor channels. At this point, the system is most efficient in accepting small amounts of incident light and in processing the electrons produced in the excited states. As the system approaches saturation, efficiency decreases. System effi-

ciency changes more quickly when system stress is present and saturation occurs at reduced (time-integrated) incident light levels.

Photo-excitation of the fluorescence target is preferably implemented using pulse light, with an excitation interval having a temporal length in a range of 0.1 μsec-1 msec, in order to avoid saturating the target and to estimate the minimum value E_{min}. Delivery of a single, longer pulse, with an associated time interval length in a range 0.1-2 sec can be used to estimate a fluorescence saturation energy level.

A pulse amplitude modulation (PAM) fluorometer can deliver incident light pulses in one or several different wavelength ranges (λ) and at different light delivery rates r(λ), in order to estimate the efficiency parameter F_v/F_M (comparable to E_v/E_{max}) and an initial value E_{min}. The fluorescence efficiency will vary with the wavelength range used and with the light delivery rate. A PAM fluorometer uses three or four wavelength ranges to estimate the presence and concentrations of at least three groups of algae: (i) green algae (sensed by presence of chlorophyll b); (ii) cyanobacteria (sensed by presence of allophycocyanin), and (iii) diatom/dinoflagellate (sensed by presence of chlorophyll c, fucoxanthin and carotenoids). Other wavelength-related groups can also be used here. Stress of a group of cells in the target can be implemented through O_2 deprivation, CO_2 deprivation, nitrate (salt) excess or deficit, or other nutrient excess or deficit, among others.

PAM fluorometry allows control of at least four parameters for monitoring a present stage of micro-organism and selected environmental parameters: wavelength range, light intensity or irradiance, duration of exposure, and duty cycle (fraction of time the micro-organism is exposed to light).

What is claimed is:

1. A method of monitoring an environment for growth or transformation of algae, the method comprising:

providing at least one alga, immersed in, or adjacent to a surface of, a liquid;

providing a mobile system that floats on and is submersible in the liquid to a controllable depth, the mobile mechanism comprising at least first and second environmental sensors that sense distinct first and second environmental parameter values, pv(t;1) and pv(t;2), respectively, where at least one of the first and second environmental sensors senses at least one of liquid temperature at a selected depth within the liquid, temperature of gas adjacent to and above the liquid, liquid pH, liquid salinity, liquid turbidity, O_2 dissolved in the liquid, CO_2 concentration in the liquid, oxidization and reduction potential of the liquid, nitrate concentration in the liquid, ammonium concentration in the liquid, bicarbonate concentration in the liquid, phosphate concentration in the liquid, light intensity where light enters the liquid, electrical conductivity of the liquid, and an alga parameter that is a measure of growth stage of the alga, and another of the at least two environmental sensors senses light intensity at a selected depth in the liquid;

sensing the first environmental parameter value pv(t;1) at spaced apart first and third sensing times, t=t1 and t=t3;

sensing the second environmental parameter value pv(t;2) at a second sensing time, t=t2, that is intermediate between the first and third sensing times; and

transmitting the environmental parameter values, pv(t=t1; 1) and pv(t=t3;1), sensed at the first and third sensing times, and the environmental parameter value pv(t=t2; 2), sensed at the second sensing time, to a data receiver.

13

2. The method of claim **1**, further comprising providing a locomotion mechanism that is configured to move said mobile system along a selected trajectory in said liquid.

3. The method of claim **1**, further comprising providing a location sensing mechanism that provides at least first and second sets of location observation coordinates of said mobile system for at least first and second location observation times, respectively, and transmits the at least first and second sets of location observation coordinates and the at least first and second location observation times to said data receiver.

4. The method of claim **3**, wherein said location sensing mechanism provides said at least first and second sets of said location observation coordinates of said mobile system by a procedure comprising:

transmitting timed electromagnetic signals from at least first, second and third electromagnetic signal sources, spaced apart from each other and from said mobile system, at determinable first, second and third location signal emission times, respectively, to a location signal receiver on said mobile system; and

estimating at least first and second location coordinates (x,y) for a first mobile system location, determined with reference to the location signal receiver at a location signal receipt time, determined with reference to at least one of the first, second and third location signal emission times.

5. The method of claim **3**, wherein said location sensing mechanism provides at least one of two angular orientation coordinates, θ and ϕ, for said mobile system by a procedure comprising:

transmitting timed electromagnetic signals from at least first, second and third spaced apart electromagnetic signal sources at determinable first, second and third location signal emission times at a first and second, spaced apart location signal receivers located on said mobile system;

estimating at least first and second location coordinates (x_k,y_k) for each of first and second spaced apart locations, corresponding to k=1 and k=2, respectively, on said mobile system, determined with reference to the first location signal receiver and the second location signal receiver, respectively, at a location signal receipt time, determined with reference to at least one of the first, second and third location signal emission times; and

determining at least one of the angular orientation coordinates, θ and ϕ, for said mobile system with reference to an angular orientation of a line segment extending between first and second locations having the respective location coordinates (x_1,y_1) and (x_2,y_2).

6. The method of claim **3**, further comprising:

providing a locomotion mechanism that is configured to move said mobile system along a selected mobile system trajectory in said liquid;

representing the mobile system trajectory as a sequence of trajectory location coordinates representing at least first and second spaced apart locations, through which the mobile system trajectory passes, and corresponding first and second location observation times;

receiving the location observation coordinates at a location signal receiver and providing observation location coordinates for the at least first and second location observation times;

comparing the location observation coordinates with the mobile system trajectory location coordinates for the at least first and second locations through which the mobile system trajectory passes; and

when a distance between the location observation coordinates and the mobile system trajectory location coordinates, for at least one of the first and second locations through which the mobile system trajectory passes, is greater than a selected threshold distance, issuing a correction signal to vary at least one location observation coordinate of the mobile system relative to the mobile system trajectory.

7. The method of claim **1**, wherein said mobile system is permitted to move in said liquid according to prevailing liquid currents in said liquid.

8. The method of claim **1**, further comprising:

providing an elapsed time difference value between said first sensing time and said second sensing time for said first sensed parameter value;

providing an estimation of a time rate of change of said first sensed parameter value; and

adjusting the elapsed time difference so that this difference decreases monotonically with increase in the time rate of change of said first sensed parameter value.

9. The method of claim **8**, further comprising adjusting said elapsed time difference so that a change in said first sensed parameter value, between at least two consecutive sensing times, does not exceed a selected fraction f of an average value of said first sensed parameter value, where f lies in a range 0<f<1.

10. The method of claim **9**, further comprising selecting said fraction f in a range of 0.01 to 0.20.

11. The method of claim **1**, wherein said first sensed parameter value pv(t;**1**) and said second sensed parameter value pv(t;**2**) are transmitted with respective first and second parameter value reporting frequencies that are different from each other.

12. The method of claim **1**, wherein said first sensed parameter value pv(t;**1**) and said second sensed parameter value pv(t;**2**) are transmitted with respective first and second parameter value reporting frequencies that are the same.

13. The method of claim **1**, further comprising:

receiving at least 2K+1 first sensed parameter values in a selected time interval, where K is a selected positive integer;

forming a weighted average WA1 of the at least 2K+1 received first sensed parameter values; and

replacing each of the at least 2K+1 first sensed parameter values by the weighted average AW1.

14. The method of claim **1**, further comprising:

receiving a sequence of at least 2K+1 first sensed parameter values in a selected time interval, where K is a selected positive integer; and

selecting a first sensed parameter value that is a median of the sequence.

15. The method of claim **1**, further comprising:

receiving at least 2K+1 first sensed parameter values in a selected time interval, where K is a selected positive integer;

arranging the at least 2K+1 first sensed parameter values in a sequence that is monotonically increasing or monotonically decreasing; and

choosing a first sensed parameter value that represents at least one of a majority view choice and a plurality view choice among the sequence.

16. The method of claim **3**, further comprising providing a submersion mechanism, attached to said mobile system, that permits said mobile system to be submerged or raised to a selected and continuously variable or discretely variable depth.

15

17. The method of claim **16**, wherein said mobile system is submerged within said liquid by a procedure comprising:

providing at least first and second bags that are inflatable with a selected gas and that are attached at spaced apart locations on said mobile system, where the first and second bags contain first and second selected amounts, respectively, of first and second selected gases;

when said mobile system is to be raised to said selected depth within said liquid, increasing the selected amount of the selected gas in at least one of the first and second bags; and

when said mobile system is to be lowered to said selected depth within said liquid, decreasing the selected amount of the selected gas in at least one of the first and second bags.

18. The method of claim **1**, further comprising providing said mobile system with an external covering having at least one aperture through which an adjacent portion of said liquid is exposed to sense at least one of said first and second environmental parameters so that at least one of said environmental parameter values can be measured in said liquid.

19. The method of claim **18**, wherein at least two of said at least first and second environmental parameters is sensed through said at least one aperture.

20. The method of claim **18**, further comprising providing a signal transmitting mechanism, having a signal transmission antenna, on an upper portion of said external covering.

21. The method of claim **18**, further comprising providing said external covering with a lower portion that is shaped as a portion of a prolate spheroid that is partly or wholly submerged in said liquid.

22. The method of claim **18**, further comprising providing said external covering with a lower portion that is shaped as an M-hedral surface ($M \geq 3$) that is partly or wholly submerged in said liquid.

23. The method of claim **1**, further comprising:

comparing said sensed first environmental parameter value $pv(t1;1)$ for a selected alga, sensed at said first sensing time, with a range of acceptable values $pv1(ref)$ of said first parameter value;

when said sensed first parameter value $pv(t1;1)$ is not within the acceptable range of values $pv1(ref)$, interpreting this condition as indicating that growth of the selected alga should be discontinued.

24. The method of claim **1**, further comprising:

submerging said mobile system to a selected positive depth in said liquid, corresponding to a selected alga having selected location observation coordinates, at spaced apart location observation times, $t=t4$ and $t=t5$;

estimating said light intensity in said liquid at the selected location observation coordinates at the location observation times, $t=t4$ and $t=t5$; and

estimating an amount of growth of the selected alga for at least one of the times t4 and t5.

25. A method of monitoring an environment for growth or transformation of algae, the method comprising:

providing at least one alga immersed in, or adjacent to a surface of, a liquid;

providing N mobile systems ($N \geq 2$), numbered $n=1, \ldots, N$, where each mobile system floats and/or is submersible in the liquid to a controllable depth, and each mobile system, number n, comprises at least first and second environmental sensors that sense distinct at least first and second environmental parameter values, $pv(t;1)$ and $pv(t;2)$, respectively, in common, where at least one of the first and second environmental sensors senses at least one of liquid temperature, temperature of gas in the

16

liquid, liquid pH, liquid salinity, liquid turbidity, O_2 dissolved in the liquid, CO_2 contained in the liquid, oxidization and reduction potential of the liquid, nitrate concentration in the liquid, ammonium concentration in the liquid, bicarbonate concentration in the liquid, phosphate concentration in the liquid, light intensity where light enters the liquid, electrical conductivity of the liquid, and an alga parameter that is a measure of growth stage of the alga, and another of the at least two environmental sensors senses light intensity at a selected depth in the liquid;

sensing the first parameter value $pv(t;1;n)$ at spaced apart first and third sensing times, $t=t1$ and $t=t3$, for each of the N mobile systems to provide sensed first parameter values, $pv(t1;1;n)$ and $pv(t3;2;n)$ for the mobile system number n;

sensing the second parameter value $pv(t;2;n)$ at a second sensing time, $t=t2$, which is intermediate between the first and third sensing times, to provide a sensed second parameter value $pv(t2;2;n)$ for the mobile system number n;

transmitting the values, $pv(t1;1;n)$ and $pv(t2;2;n)$, to a data receiver that is spaced apart from at least one of the N mobile systems.

26. The method of claim **25**, further comprising:

allowing each of said N mobile systems to move with liquid currents in said liquid; and

providing a location sensing mechanism for each of said N mobile systems that senses and provides at least first and second sets of location observation coordinates $(x_n(t), y_n(t), z_n(t), (n=1, \ldots, N)$ for said mobile system number n for at least first and second spaced apart location observation times, $t=t1$ and $t=t2$, respectively, and transmits the at least first and second sets of location observation coordinates, and the at least first and second location observation times and said observed environmental parameter values $pv(t=tk;n)$ (k=1,2) to a data receiver.

27. The method of claim **26**, further comprising providing, at said location data receiver a computer that is programmed:

to receive said at least first and second sets of location observation coordinates and said at least first and second location observation times, $t=t1$ and $t=t2$; and

to estimate, for at least one of said location observation times, t1 and t2, and for at least one of said environmental parameter values $pv1(t;k;n)$ (k=1, 2; n=1, \ldots, N), a continuously variable environmental parameter field of values. $pv(x,y,z;t;k;field)$, whose value for said location observation coordinates for each of said mobile system number n (n=1 N), for at least one of said location observation times, t1 and t2, is equal to a corresponding environmental parameter value $pv1(t;k;n)$ at the corresponding location observation coordinates $(x_n(t), y_n(t), z_n(t))$ for at least one of said location observation times, t1 and t2.

28. The method of claim **27**, wherein said computer is further programmed:

to compare said environmental fields of parameter values $pv(x,y,z;t;$ field) for $t=t1$ and for $t=t2$ for at least one common set of location coordinates, $(x=x_c, y=y_c, z=z_c)$; and

to estimate a rate of change of said environmental parameter value $pv(x,y,z;t;$ field) at the common location coordinates $(x=x_c, y=y_c, z=z_c)$ in a time interval, defined by $t1 \leq t \leq t2$.

29. The method of claim **25**, further comprising providing each of at least two of said N mobile systems, numbers n=n1 and n=n2, with a mutual repulsion mechanism so that said systems n=n1 and n=n2 repel each other when a distance between the at least two systems is less than a selected threshold distance.

30. The method of claim **29**, further comprising:

providing, as said mutual repulsion mechanism for said mobile system number n=n1, a first magnetic pole mechanism having a first selected number M1 of magnetic north pole sources (M1≧2), spaced apart on an exposed surface of said mobile system number n=n1, and having a magnetic south pole source, positioned at a location on said mobile system number n=n1 that is spaced apart from each of the M1 north magnetic pole sources; and

providing, as said mutual repulsion mechanism for said mobile system number n=n2, a second magnetic pole mechanism having a second selected number M2 of magnetic north pole sources (M2≧2), spaced apart on an

exposed surface of said mobile system number n=n2, and having a magnetic south pole source, positioned at a location on said mobile system number n=n2 that is spaced apart from each of the M2 north magnetic pole sources,

whereby at least one of the M1 magnetic north pole sources on the mobile system number n=n1 and at least one of the M2 magnetic north pole sources on the mobile system number n=n2 will repel each other, when the at least one of the M1 magnetic north pole sources is within said threshold positive threshold distance of the at least one of the M2 magnetic north pole sources.

31. The method of claim **24**, further comprising using PAM fluorometry to estimate said light intensity in said liquid at said selected location observation coordinates.

* * * * *

United States Patent
(12)

Smith et al.

(10) **Patent No.:** **US 8,753,578 B1**

(45) **Date of Patent:** **Jun. 17, 2014**

(54) **APPARATUS FOR THE PRODUCTION OF BORON NITRIDE NANOTUBES**

(75) Inventors: **Michael W. Smith**, Newport News, VA (US); **Kevin Jordan**, Newport News, VA (US)

(73) Assignees: **Jefferson Science Associates, LLC**, Newport News, VA (US); **The United States of America as represented by the Administrator of NASA**, Washington, DC (US)

(*) Notice: Subject to any disclaimer, the term of this patent is extended or adjusted under 35 U.S.C. 154(b) by 710 days.

(21) Appl. No.: **12/322,591**

(22) Filed: **Feb. 4, 2009**

(51) **Int. Cl.**
B01J 19/08 (2006.01)

(52) **U.S. Cl.**
USPC **422/186**; 204/157.41; 423/290; 977/750; 977/752

(58) **Field of Classification Search**
CPC B01J 19/121; C04B 35/6229; C01B 21/0641; C30B 29/602; C30B 23/00
USPC 422/186; 204/157.41; 423/290; 977/750, 752
See application file for complete search history.

(56) **References Cited**

U.S. PATENT DOCUMENTS

5,300,203 A *	4/1994	Smalley	....	204/157.41
6,792,017 B2 *	9/2004	Halpin	....	372/35
6,855,659 B1 *	2/2005	Zhang	....	502/185
8,047,663 B2 *	11/2011	Pang et al.	....	359/614
2004/0265211 A1 *	12/2004	Dillon et al.	....	423/447.3
2005/0129607 A1 *	6/2005	Takehara et al.	....	423/445 B
2007/0110660 A1 *	5/2007	Liu et al.	....	423/447.3
2009/0004069 A1 *	1/2009	Kronholm et al.	....	422/171

OTHER PUBLICATIONS

Lee et al, "Catalytic-free synthhesis of boron nitride single-wall nanotubes with a preferred zig-zag configuration", Physical Review B. vol. 64 12405 (2001).*
Guo et al "Catalytic growth of single-walled nanotubes by laser vaporization", Chemical Physics letters, 243 (1995), p. 49-54.*
Yu et al "Synthesis of boron nitride nanotubes by means of excimer laser ablation at high temmperature", Applied Physics Letters, vol. 72, No. 16, p. 1966-1968 (1998).*
Shin et al "Pulsed lase ablatin of boron nitride", Material Research Society, vol. 397, p. 265-270, 1996.*

* cited by examiner

Primary Examiner — Xiuyu Tai

(57) **ABSTRACT**

An apparatus for the large scale production of boron nitride nanotubes comprising; a pressure chamber containing; a continuously fed boron containing target; a source of thermal energy preferably a focused laser beam; a cooled condenser; a source of pressurized nitrogen gas; and a mechanism for extracting boron nitride nanotubes that are condensed on or in the area of the cooled condenser from the pressure chamber.

9 Claims, 1 Drawing Sheet

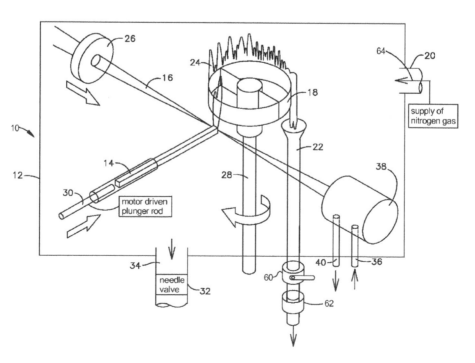

200

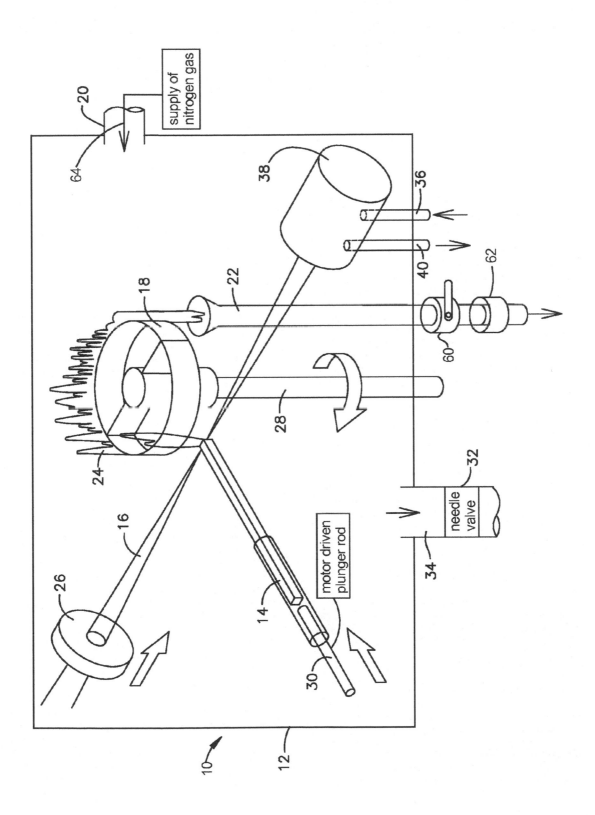

APPARATUS FOR THE PRODUCTION OF BORON NITRIDE NANOTUBES

The United States of America may have certain rights to this invention under Management and Operating Contract DE-AC05-060R23177 from the United States Department of Energy.

FIELD OF THE INVENTION

The present invention relates to the production of boron nitride nanotubes and more particularly to apparatus for the production of such structures.

BACKGROUND OF THE INVENTION

Since the announcement of the successful synthesis of high-aspect-ratio few-walled boron nitride nanotubes (FW-BNNTs) in 1995, little progress has been made in the scale-up of their synthesis. As a demonstration, in spite of the theoretical capabilities of FW-BNNTs to provide high strength-to-weight, high temperature resistance, piezo-electric actuation, and radiation shielding (via the boron content), the aerospace industry still relies on micron-sized graphite or boron fibers for structural applications. Neither FW-BNNTs nor single-wall carbon nanotubes are widely used in aerospace manufacturing, the industry generally most willing to pay a premium for high performance.

To date, high-aspect ratio FW-BNNTs have been produced in small amounts (from individual tubes to milligrams) by arc-discharge or laser heating methods. A separate class of boron nitride nanotubes has also been produced by chemical vapor deposition of nitrogen compounds (e.g. ammonia) over ball-milled precursors, but these tubes are of larger diameter and do not exhibit the continuous crystalline sp2-type bonding structure which has drawn most theoretical interest.

U.S. patent application Ser. No. 12/152,414 filed May 14, 2008 describes a process for the production of at leas centimeter-long boron nitride nanotubes. The disclosure of this application is hereby incorporated herein by reference in its entirety. In spite of this disclosure of a process for the production of boron nitride nanotubes, no apparatus has yet been described for the practical implementation of the process described in this application.

OBJECT OF THE INVENTION

It is a primary object of the present invention to provide an apparatus for the large scale production of boron nitride nanotubes using the process described in the foregoing U.S. patent application Ser. No. 12/152,414.

SUMMARY OF THE INVENTION

According to the present invention there is provided an apparatus for the large scale production of boron nitride nanotubes comprising; a pressure chamber containing; a continuously fed boron containing target; a source of thermal energy preferably a focused laser beam; a cooled condenser; a source of pressurized nitrogen gas; and a mechanism for extracting boron nitride nanotubes that are condensed on or in the area of the cooled condenser from the pressure chamber.

DESCRIPTION OF THE DRAWINGS

FIG. 1 is a schematic side view of the apparatus of the present invention.

DETAILED DESCRIPTION

Referring now to the accompanying drawing, the apparatus 10 of the present invention comprises: a pressure chamber 12 containing; a continuously fed boron nitride target 14; a source of thermal energy preferably a focused laser beam 16; a rotating cooled condenser ring 18; a supply of nitrogen gas 20; and a collection tube 22 for extracting boron nitride nanotubes from pressure chamber 12 after boron nitride vaporized by the thermal energy source forms a boron nitride plume 24 that condenses on or in the vicinity of rotating cooled condenser ring 18.

As shown in the accompanying Figure, thermal energy source 16 is preferably a laser beam introduced into pressure chamber 12 via a convex lens 26 that allows for focusing of laser beam/thermal energy source 16 within pressure chamber 12. Also as shown in the accompanying Figure, cooled condenser ring 18 is rotated continuously by virtue of its being mounted on a rotating shaft 28 such that a new surface thereof is constantly being brought into the proximity of collection tube 22.

In the preferred embodiment depicted in the accompanying Figure, boron nitride target 14 is a commercially available hot pressed hexagonal boron nitride rod 14 that is continuously fed into the field of laser beam 16 by a motor driven plunger rod 30 or similar device. According to a preferred embodiment, boron nitride target 14 is of square cross-section about 0.050" on a side and is introduced into laser beam 16 not a the focal waist of laser beam 16 but rather at a position where laser beam 16 is of approximately the same size boron nitride target rod 14. According to this preferred embodiment, target rod 14 is advanced at a rate of about 1 mm/sec into the beam 16 of a 2 kW CO_2 laser having a wavelength of about 10.6 microns and a diameter of about 12 mm.

A small flow of nitrogen gas of about 40 SCFH is maintained into pressure chamber 12 via supply of nitrogen gas 20 whose flow is regulated, for example, by a needle valve 32 in the chamber exhaust 34.

According to the preferred embodiment depicted in the accompanying Figure, laser beam 16 terminates in a copper block 38 cooled by water provided thereto by inlet and outlet 38 and 40. Copper block 38 is designed to absorb the full, continuous power of laser beam 16 without damage.

Similarly, rotating condenser 18 is water cooled by conventional means well within the skills of the skilled artisan to maintain it a temperature of about 20° C. According to the preferred embodiment depicted in the accompanying Figure, rotating condenser 18 is a hoop of about 0.025" copper attached to a water cooled rotating copper shaft 28.

In operation, as target rod 14 is converted continuously from solid to gas by the action of laser beam 16, a buoyant plume of vapors 24 rise vertically from the laser interaction zone. Plume 24 is intercepted by condenser ring 18. Where plume 24 is intercepted by condenser ring 18, boron nitride nanotubes form at a high rate. Web-like tufts of boron nitride nanotubes 4 inches in length and more, form in vertical structures which are attached at the lower end to condenser ring 18. These boron nitride nanotube structures form in fractions of a second, as recorded by videographic visualizations. As condenser 18 rotates, fresh boron nitride nanotubes grow on each newly exposed section of the advancing condenser surface.

The boron nitride nanotubes are removed from rotating condenser 18 by means of a collection tube 22 which leads to the outside of pressure chamber 12. When a ball valve 60 in

3

collection tube **22** is opened, the boron nitride nanotubes are "vacuumed" from rotating condenser ring **18** by the nitrogen gas exhausting to 1 atmosphere. Boron nitride nanotubes are collected in a wire mesh filter **62** installed in-line in collection tube **22**.

While the foregoing describes a specifically preferred embodiment of the present invention, it will be apparent that other variations of the particular parameters can be utilized. For example: for the preferred embodiment just described, the pressure was held at about 12 atmospheres, but higher pressures are anticipated to produce better results; hot-pressed boron nitride was used as the preferred target, but other targets will be suitable, given acceptable interaction with the laser. For instance, hot pressed boron powder has been produced in the literature and would make a good target, given the appropriate laser properties. Any dense version of boron or boron nitride will work; as long as the laser interacts with the target to produce a continuous stream of vapor the wavelength or other laser properties are not important. Any kW class laser should reproduce these results. Nd:YAG, or free electron lasers are 2 examples; the shape of condenser **18** can take many variations as long as it provides for free flow of the vapor plume it will work and Nb wire, W wire, Nb sheet-stock, and Cu sheetstock have all proven useful; both mechanical and suction have been shown as useful to collect boron nitride nanotubes. Since the material tends to stick to itself or to a surface, it could be wrapped around, stuck to, or sucked into any number of geometries and since boron nitride nanotubes also responds well to static charging they can be collected by this mechanism as well. Additionally, although the cooled condenser has been depicted as a cooled ring, it could equally as well comprise a cooled oscillating structure and the mechanism for collecting boron nitride nanotubes could comprise one or more collection tubes in the vicinity of the extremes of oscillation of the cooled oscillating condenser.

There has thus been described an apparatus for the practical large scale production of boron nitride nanotubes which apparatus is useful in the implementation of the methods described in U.S. patent application Ser. No. 12/152,414 filed May 14, 2008 whose disclosure has been incorporated herein in its entirety.

As the invention has been described, it will be apparent to those skilled in the art that the same may be varied in many ways without departing from the spirit and scope thereof. Any and all such modifications are intended to be included within the scope of the appended claims.

4

What is claimed is:

1. Apparatus for the large scale production of boron nitride nanotubes from a continuously fed boron containing target rod comprising:
   a pressure chamber;
   a supply of nitrogen gas into said pressure chamber; and
   a chamber exhaust;
   said pressure chamber including
   the continuously fed boron containing target rod;
      a rotating cooled condenser ring;
      a laser producing a laser beam;
      a lens for focusing said laser beam on said continuously fed boron containing target rod, said boron containing target rod is introduced into said laser beam at a position away from the focal waist of the laser beam and where said laser beam is about the same size as said boron containing target rod, said boron containing target rod being introduced into said laser beam at a position below said rotating cooled condenser ring;
      a collection tube for removing boron nitride nanotubes from said rotating condenser ring, said collection tube extending to the outside of said pressure chamber; and
      a cooled block that terminates said laser beam by absorbing the full continuous power of said laser beam.

2. The apparatus of claim **1** including a valve in said chamber exhaust for regulating said supply of nitrogen gas into said pressure chamber.

3. The apparatus of claim **1** including a motor-driven plunger rod for continuously feeding said boron containing target rod.

4. The apparatus of claim **1** wherein said cooled block is a copper block.

5. The apparatus of claim **1** wherein said lens is a convex lens.

6. The apparatus of claim **1** including a valve on said collection tube for opening and closing said collection tube.

7. The apparatus of claim **1** including an in-line wire mesh filter installed on said collection tube for collecting boron nitride nanotubes vacuumed from said rotating cooled condenser ring.

8. The apparatus of claim **2** wherein said valve in said chamber exhaust is a needle valve.

9. The apparatus of claim **1** wherein said laser is selected from the group including CO2 laser, Nd:YAG laser, and free electron laser.

* * * * *

US008217143B2

(12) United States Patent
Kim et al.

(10) Patent No.: **US 8,217,143 B2**

(45) Date of Patent: **Jul. 10, 2012**

(54) **FABRICATION OF METAL NANOSHELLS**

(75) Inventors: **Jae-Woo Kim**, Newport News, VA (US); **Sang H. Choi**, Poquoson, VA (US); **Peter T. Lillehei**, Yorktown, VA (US); **Sang-Hyon Chu**, Newport News, VA (US); **Yeonjoon Park**, Yorktown, VA (US); **Glen C. King**, Yorktown, VA (US); **James R. Elliott, Jr.**, Yorktown, VA (US)

(73) Assignees: **National Institute of Aerospace Associates**, Hampton, VA (US); **The United States of America as represented by the Administration of NASA**, Washington, DC (US)

(*) Notice: Subject to any disclaimer, the term of this patent is extended or adjusted under 35 U.S.C. 154(b) by 1224 days.

(21) Appl. No.: **11/827,567**

(22) Filed: **Jul. 12, 2007**

(65) **Prior Publication Data**

US 2008/0014621 A1   Jan. 17, 2008

Related U.S. Application Data

(60) Provisional application No. 60/830,749, filed on Jul. 13, 2006.

(51) Int. Cl.
C07K 14/00   (2006.01)

(52) U.S. Cl. **530/350**; 977/729

(58) Field of Classification Search .... None
See application file for complete search history.

(56) **References Cited**

OTHER PUBLICATIONS

Kim et al., "Cobalt oxide hollow nanoparticles derived by bio-templating", Chem. Commun. Aug. 2005 32: 4101-4103.*

* cited by examiner

Primary Examiner — Anand Desai

(74) *Attorney, Agent, or Firm* — George F. Helfrich; Kimberly A. Chasteen; Thomas K. McBride, Jr.

(57) **ABSTRACT**

Metal nanoshells are fabricated by admixing an aqueous solution of metal ions with an aqueous solution of apoferritin protein molecules, followed by admixing an aqueous solution containing an excess of an oxidizing agent for the metal ions. The apoferritin molecules serve as bio-templates for the formation of metal nanoshells, which form on and are bonded to the inside walls of the hollow cores of the individual apoferritin molecules. Control of the number of metal atoms which enter the hollow core of each individual apoferritin molecule provides a hollow metal nonparticle, or nanoshell, instead of a solid spherical metal nanoparticle.

6 Claims, 5 Drawing Sheets

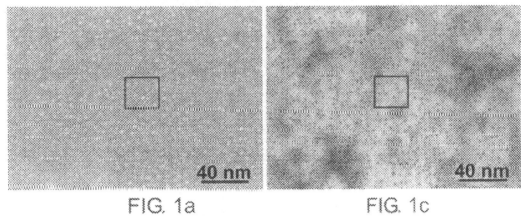

FIG. 1a   FIG. 1c

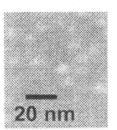

FIG. 1b

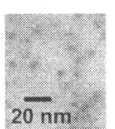

FIG. 1d

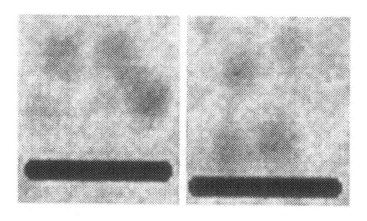

FIG. 2a

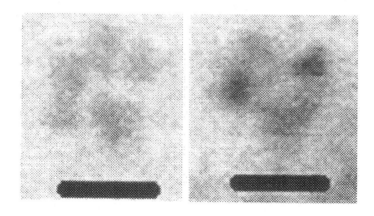

FIG. 2b

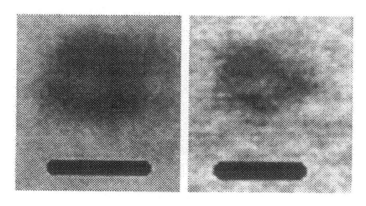

FIG. 2c

206

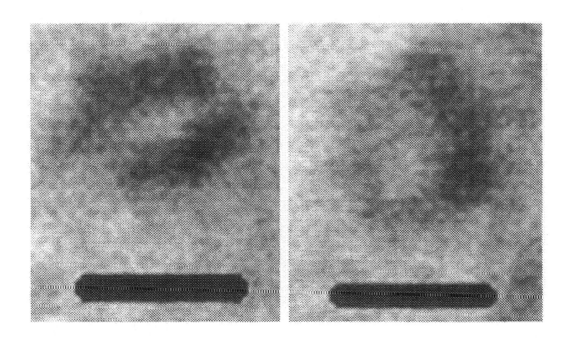

FIG. 3a

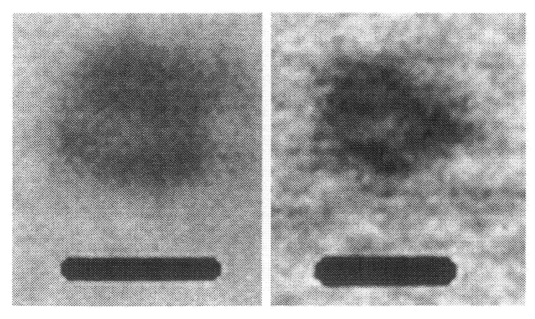

FIG. 3b

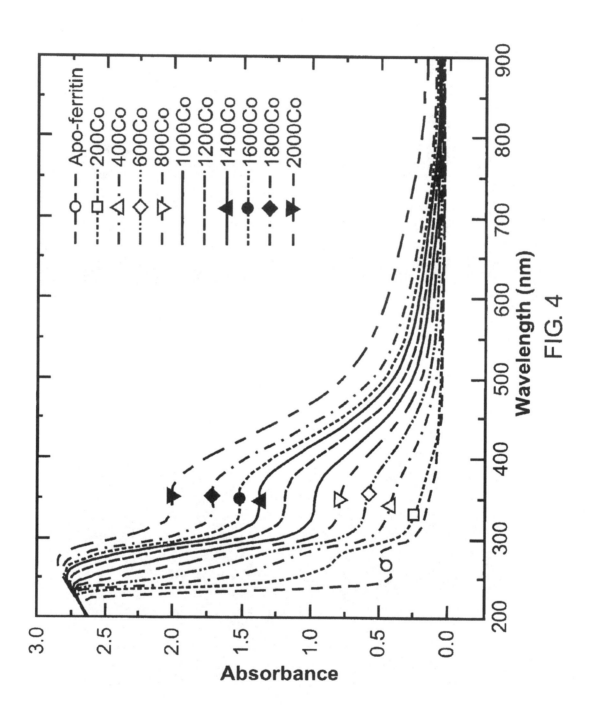

FIG. 4

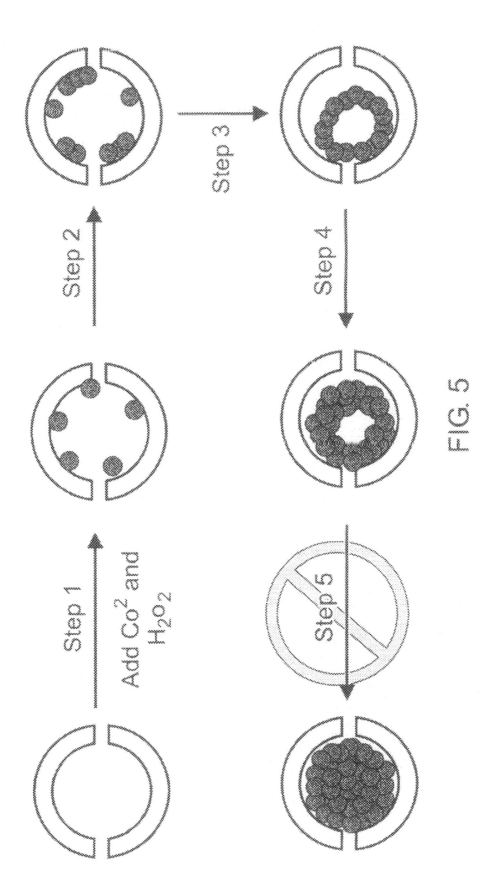

FIG. 5

1

FABRICATION OF METAL NANOSHELLS

CROSS-REFERENCE TO RELATED APPLICATION

This application claims the benefit of U.S. Provisional Application No. 60/830,749, filed on Jul. 13, 2006 for "Fabrication of Metal Nanoshells Derived By A Biotemplate."

STATEMENT REGARDING FEDERALLY SPONSORED RESEARCH OR DEVELOPMENT

The U.S. Government has a paid-up license in this invention and the right in limited circumstances to require the patent owner to license others on reasonable terms, as provided for by the terms of Contract No. NCC-1-02043 awarded by the National Aeronautics and Space Administration, and Science and Technology Corporation Contract No. L-71407D.

BACKGROUND OF THE INVENTION

1. Field of the Invention

This invention relates generally to nanoscale particles. It relates particularly to a process for fabricating hollow metal nanostructures, or metal nanoshells, employing ferritin as a bio-template.

2. Description of Related Art

A great interest currently exists in the synthesis and characterization of hollow metal nanostructures, because of their surface properties and catalytic activities, which are different from their solid counterparts. Most early work in this field involved hollow nanostructures of several hundreds of nanometers. Recently, the preparation of hollow nanostructures on the scale of tens of nanometers was demonstrated, employing a replacement reaction with a solid silver template and a nonoscale Kirkendall effect, respectively. However, such a fabrication process is very complicated, and requires the use of organic solvents. Moreover, it has been found generally difficult to form stable hollow metal nanoparticles, and even solid metal nanoparticles, because of strong magnetic interactions in magnetic particle systems.

BRIEF SUMMARY OF THE INVENTION

Accordingly, it is a primary object of the present invention to provide what is not available in the art, viz., an uncomplicated, yet highly efficacious process for the fabrication of hollow metal nanostructures, or metal nanoshells, which process does not require the employment of organic solvents or other reagents which present handling difficulties. Moreover, it is another primary object of the present invention to provide a process which produces hollow metal nanoparticles which are stable.

These primary objects and their attending benefits are achieved by providing a process for the fabrication of metal nanoshells, which process includes employing apoferritin protein molecules in aqueous solution to act as biotemplates in the formation of hollow metal nanoparticles, and to function as separators between the hollow metal nanoparticles, once they have been formed. In the present process the empty cores of the apoferritin protein molecules are reconstituted with a metal, esp. a transition metal. Controlling the number of metal atoms introduced into each apoferritin molecule results in the formation of a metal nanoshell within each

2

apoferritin protein molecule, instead of the formation of a solid metal nanoparticle therein, which would otherwise result.

Potential applications of the metal nanoshells include enhanced MRI diagnostic contrast agents, tumor hyperthermia therapies, retinal detachment therapies, and magnetic field-guided drug delivery systems and radioactive therapies.

BRIEF DESCRIPTION OF THE SEVERAL VIEWS OF THE DRAWINGS

For a more complete understanding of the present invention, including its primary objects and attending benefits, reference should be made to the DETAILED DESCRIPTION OF THE INVENTION, which is set forth below. This Detailed Description should be read together with the accompanying Drawings, wherein:

FIG. 1A and FIG. 1B are drawings prepared from field emission-scanning electron microscopy (FE-SEM) images of apoferritin protein molecules (having 1000 cobalt atoms per apoferritin protein molecule core) immobilized on a holey carbon coated copper calibration grid; the scale bars are 40 nm and 20 nm, respectively;

FIG. 1C and FIG. 1D are drawings prepared from field emission-scanning electron microscopy equipped with transmission electron microscopy (STEM) images of apoferritin protein molecules (having 1000 cobalt atoms per apoferritin protein molecule core) immobilized on a holey carbon coated copper calibration grid; the scale bars are 40 nm and 20 nm, respectively;

FIG. 2A is a drawing prepared from a STEM image of apoferritin protein molecules (having 200 cobalt atoms per apoferritin protein molecule core), immobilized on a holey carbon coated copper calibration grid; the scale bar is 8 nm;

FIG. 2B is a drawing prepared from a STEM image of apoferritin protein molecules (having 1000 cobalt atoms per apoferritin protein molecule core) immobilized on a holey carbon coated copper calibration grid; the scale bar is 5 nm;

FIG. 2C is a drawing prepared from a STEM image of apoferritin protein molecules (having 2000 cobalt atoms per apoferritin protein molecule core) immobilized on a holey carbon coated copper calibration grid; the scale bar is 5 nm;

FIG. 3A is a drawing prepared from a STEM image of apoferritin protein molecules (having 1000 cobalt atoms per apoferritin protein molecule core) immobilized on a holey carbon coated copper calibration grid; the scale bar is 5 nm;

FIG. 3B is a drawing prepared from a STEM image of apoferritin protein molecules (having 2000 cobalt atoms per apoferritin protein molecule core) immobilized on a holey carbon coated copper calibration grid; the scale bar is 5 nm;

FIG. 4 is a plot of absorbance vs. wavelength showing UV-Visible absorption spectra of apoferritin and various cobalt oxide-containing apoferritins; and

FIG. 5 is a schematic depicting the growth mechanism for incremental numbers of cobalt oxide units introduced into the hollow core of an apoferritin protein molecule.

DETAILED DESCRIPTION OF THE INVENTION

To carry out the present process for the fabrication of metallic nanoshells, a first aqueous solution is provided. This first aqueous solution is a buffered solution of molecules of an apoferritin protein. Such apoferritin protein molecules are ferritin protein molecules whose inner metallic cores have been removed, e.g., in vitro by reduction and chelation, employing the molecular channels which run through each ferritin protein molecule from its outer periphery to its inner

3

4

core. A hollow inner core is thereby presented. A preferred apoferritin protein is an apo horse spleen ferritin protein (ApoHoSF). Very beneficial results are achieved if the first aqueous solution is a 1 mg per ml ApoHoSF solution which has been adjusted to pH 8.5 in 25 mM of MOPS buffer with 50 mM NaCl.

An evenly-distributed loading of metal ions among the apoferritin protein molecules of the first aqueous solution is then provided. This is accomplished by gradually admixing a second aqueous solution, which contains the metal ions, with the first aqueous solution, which contains the apoferritin protein molecules, to form a first admixture. It is preferred if the metal ions are transition metal ions, and more preferable if the ions are of cobalt, iron, manganese, vanadium, nickel, zinc, copper, or silver. Very good results have been obtained if cobalt is employed in the present process. Especially beneficial results have been obtained if the second aqueous solution is a 50 mM solution of cobalt sulfate.

The loading or number of metal atoms per individual apoferritin protein molecule in the first admixture is determined by calculation, employing the volume of the second aqueous solution employed along with the concentration of metal ions therein, as well as the volume of the first aqueous solution employed along with the concentration of apoferritin protein therein. The optimal loading is determined empirically, as discussed below.

A third aqueous solution is then admixed with the first admixture. The third aqueous solution contains a calculated excess of oxidizing agent for the metal ions employed. Especially good results are obtained if the third aqueous solution is a 3 volume percent solution of hydrogen peroxide.

The mechanism for the formation of metallic nanoshells is considered to be as follows: Metal ions enter into the hollow core of each of the apoferritin molecules through the molecular channels therein. Chemical bonds are then formed between the metal ions and functional groups which are located on the wall of the hollow core of each apoferrition molecule during oxidation of the metal ions by the oxidizing agent. As discrete metallic nanoparticles are formed and then merged within the hollow core, a composite metallic nanoshell is formed on the wall of the hollow core where it is attached thereto, instead of a single, solid, composite metallic nanoparticle being formed within the core.

The optimal number of metal atoms per individual apoferritin protein molecule is empirically determined as that number of metal atoms which is sufficient to provide a subatantially integral, composite metallic nanoshell formed within, and attached to the wall of the hollow core, but which is insufficient to provide an integral, composite spherical metallic nanoparticle which, although formed within, and attached to the wall of the hollow core, has no empty space in the center thereof.

Very beneficial results are obtained in the practice of the present invention if the number of metal atoms per individual apoferritin protein molecule is within the range of about 1000-2000.

EXAMPLES

The following Examples are presented as being illustrative of the present invention, and are not intended to limit its scope.

ApoHoSF solution (1 mg/ml) was adjusted to a pH 8.5 in 25 mM MOPS buffer with 50 mM NaCl. $CoSO_4$ (50 mM) was used as a cobalt source and gradually added to the ApoHoSF solution, followed by the addition of an excess amount of H_2O_2 (3 vol. %). The Cobalt was added very slowly and gradually to achieve a certain loading of metal atoms evenly distributed into the ferritin. We reconstituted the ferritins having 200 Co (Co_{200}) to 2000 Co (Co_{2000}) atoms per ferritin in increments of 200 atoms.

Field emission-scanning electron microscopy (FE-SEM), and FE-SEM equipped with a scanning transmission electron microscopy (STEM, Hitachi S-5200) were used for the characterization of reconstituted Co-cored ferritins. Immobilized Co-cored ferritins on a holey carbon coated copper calibration grid were thoroughly rinsed with doubly distilled, deionized water, dried in a vacuum atmosphere, and then subjected to microscopic analysis. FE-SEM and STEM were used to obtain the whole images at the same acceleration voltage of 25 keV. FIGS. 1A, 1B, 1C and 1D show FE-SEM and STEM images of reconstituted Co-cored ferritins on a copper calibration grid. The STEM (FIGS. 1C and 1D) images show a clear view of solid cores without protein shell at a relatively low magnification. Ultraviolet-visible (UV-Vis) spectra were obtained from a Perkin-Elmer Lambda 900 light source. The ferritin protein in micro quartz cuvette was adjusted to the final concentration of 0.33 mg/ml diluted with 25 mM MOPS buffer at pH 8.5. The transmission spectra were measured from 900 nm to 200 nm at a scan speed of 150 nm/min.

FIGS. 2A, 2B and 2C are scanning transmission electron microscopy (STEM, Hitachi S-5200) images of reconstituted Co-cored ferritins on a holey carbon coated calibration grid. When the ferritin contains 200 Co atoms in the ferritin interior, cobalt oxides were formed and evenly distributed on the ferritin interior wall (FIG. 2A). The size of cobalt oxides was 2 nm. We can only see the metal cores in the ferritin through STEM imaging due to the relatively low density of the ferritin protein shell. Normally, eight hydrophilic channels along the four fold symmetric axis of the apoferritin protein shell are considered to be the pathways of metal ions into the ferritin interior. Once the metal ions enter the ferritin interior, they form chemical bonds during the oxidation process of the metal ions with the functional groups of the interior protein wall. It is very likely that the metal oxides are combined with carboxylate groups on the interior protein wall. The cobalt is thus attached to the inside wall of the hollow protein core. If there was not an interaction with the interior protein wall, a single nanoparticle would be formed within and not attached to the hollow core of an apoferritin in order to reduce surface tension. Once the seeds of metal oxides are formed, the nanoparticles inside the apoferritin grow auto-catalytically along the interior wall of the hollow core and then merge together during repetitions of Co(II) and H_2O_2 additions.

When the ferritin contains over 1000 Co atoms, the cobalt oxides form a hollow nanoparticle in the ferritin interior (FIG. 2B). STEM images show a clear circle with a hollow core through merging of the nanoparticles (FIG. 2B). The size of hollow nanoparticle was about 6 nm, which is smaller than the inner diameter of the hollow apoferritin core. FIGS. 3A and 3B show STEM images of reconstituted Co-cored ferritins with different numbers of cobalt atoms. The wall thickness and size of hollow Co_{2000} (FIG. 3B) core are somewhat larger than Co_{1000} core (FIG. 3A).

Mineralized ferritin solution with Co(II) and H_2O_2 showed a homogeneous olive-green color from the specific oxidative mineralization process at pH 8.5. The UV-Visible absorption spectra showed well-defined peaks at 280 nm (protein) and 225 nm with a shoulder at 350 nm (corresponding to cobalt oxides, especially cobalt oxyhydroxide (CoOOH)). (See FIG. 4). Addition of the Co(II) and H_2O_2 to the ApoHoSF solution results in the convolution of the protein absorption band at 280 nm with a new absorption band at 225 nm, having a shoulder at 350 nm. These two peaks related to the core material shifted to the higher wavelengths as the number of metal atoms increased within the ferritin.

The first step of metal nanoshell formation is a nucleation of small nanoparticles in the interior (hollow core) of the ferritin protein shell. Referring now to FIG. **5**, it is considered that the metal ions entered through the hydrophilic channels in the ferritin and combined with the carboxylate groups of the ferritin interior wall, thus forming discrete nanoparticles during an oxidative reaction along the ferritin interior wall (Step 1). The discrete nanoparticles continue to grow along the ferritin interior wall (Step 2). In a merging step, a hollow nanoparticle forms through the merging of discrete nanoparticles (Step 3). The size of a particular hollow nanoparticle is somewhat decreased because of the formation of metallic bonds. Finally, the hollow nanoparticle is grown with a thicker metal wall (Step 4). The nanoparticle formed has an empty core at this point. This is why one should not completely fill in the ferritin interior or hollow core with a theoretical number of Co atoms through the reconstitution procedure. Employing this growth mechanism renders hollow metal nanoparticles or metal nanoshells easily by controlling the number of metal atoms entering the interior or hollow core of the apoferritin.

We claim:

1. A process for the fabrication of metallic nanoshells, which process comprises:

(a) providing a first aqueous solution, which is a buffered solution of an apoferritin protein, wherein the apoferritin protein is selected from the group consisting of horse spleen ferritin and bacterial ferritin, each of the individual molecules of said apoferritin protein having molecular channels running therethrough from the outer periphery thereof to an inner core thereof, the channels having enabled removal of substantially all inorganic material from the inner core thereof;

(b) providing an evenly-distributed loading of metal ions, wherein the metal ions are selected from the group consisting of transition metals and noble metals, among the apoferritin protein molecules of the first solution by forming a first admixture prepared by gradually admixing a second aqueous solution containing the metal ions with the first aqueous solution, the volume of the second

aqueous solution employed, along with the concentration of metal ions in the second aqueous solution, being utilized along with the volume of the first aqueous solution employed and the concentration of apoferritin protein in the first aqueous solution, to calculate the number of metal atoms per individual apoferritin protein molecule in the first admixture, the optimum thereof being that number of metal atoms which is sufficient to provide a substantially integral, composite metallic nanoshell formed within, and attached to the wall of the hollow core, but which is insufficient to provide an integral, composite spherical metallic nanoparticle which, although formed within, and attached to the wall of the hollow core, has no empty space in the center thereof;

(c) gradually admixing a third aqueous solution with the first admixture, the third aqueous solution containing a calculated excess of oxidizing agent for the metal ions employed; whereby metal ions enter into the hollow inner core of each of the apoferritin molecules through the molecular channels therein, chemical bonds being formed between the metal ions and functional groups located on the wall of the hollow core of each of the apoferritin molecules during oxidation of the metal ions by the oxidizing agent, so that as discrete metallic nanoparticles are formed and merged within the hollow core, a composite metallic nanoshell is formed on the wall of the hollow core and attached thereto, instead of a single, solid, composite metallic nanoparticle being formed within the core.

2. The process of claim **1**, wherein the optimal number of metal atoms per individual apoferritin protein molecule is within the range of about 1000-2000.

3. The process of claim **1**, wherein the metal is a transition metal.

4. The process of claim **3**, wherein the metal is selected from the group consisting of cobalt, iron, manganese, vanadium, nickel, zinc, copper and silver.

5. The process of claim **1**, wherein the metal is cobalt.

6. The process of claim **1**, wherein the first aqueous solution is a 1 mg per ml ApoHoSF solution which has been adjusted to pH 8.5 in 25 mM MOPS buffer with 50 mM NaCl.

* * * * *

US005339821A

United States Patent [19]

Fujimoto

[11] Patent Number: 5,339,821

[45] Date of Patent: Aug. 23, 1994

[54] **HOME MEDICAL SYSTEM AND MEDICAL APPARATUS FOR USE THEREWITH**

[75] Inventor: **Jun Fujimoto**, Tokyo, Japan

[73] Assignees: **Seta Co., Ltd.; NASA Corporation Co., Ltd.**, both of Tokyo, Japan

[21] Appl. No.: **966,726**

[22] Filed: **Oct. 26, 1992**

[30] **Foreign Application Priority Data**

Feb. 13, 1992 [JP] Japan 4-059477

[51] Int. Cl.⁵ **A61N 5/04**
[52] U.S. Cl. **128/700**; 128/903; 128/904
[58] Field of Search 128/670, 671, 696, 700, 128/903, 904, 906, 908

[56] **References Cited**

U.S. PATENT DOCUMENTS

3,566,365	2/1971	Ranson et al.	128/906
3,566,370	2/1971	Worthington et al.	128/904
3,920,005	11/1975	Gombrich et al.	128/904
4,449,536	5/1984	Weaver	128/696
4,566,461	1/1986	Lubell et al.	128/700
4,722,349	2/1988	Baumberg	128/904
4,782,511	11/1988	Nemec et al.	128/904
4,803,625	2/1989	Fu et al.	128/908
4,838,275	6/1989	Lee	128/904

FOREIGN PATENT DOCUMENTS

0286456 10/1988 European Pat. Off. 128/904

Primary Examiner—William E. Kamm
Attorney, Agent, or Firm—Notaro & Michalos

[57] **ABSTRACT**

A home medical system allows any patient or healthy person to measure his or her daily condition at home and undergo a check or an inquiry diagnosis by a medical specialist or doctor. The home medical system includes equipment for measuring the electrocardiogram and other heart conditions of a user, a display for explaining the procedure and a display for displaying thereon a result of a measurement by the equipment. A communication link connects the user's equipment to a medical institution for interconnecting the medical institution to the user's system so that medical personal at the medical institution can also review the measured results obtained by the user.

9 Claims, 6 Drawing Sheets

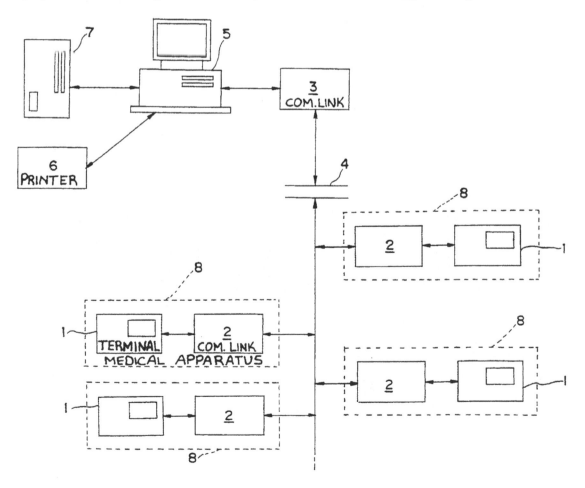

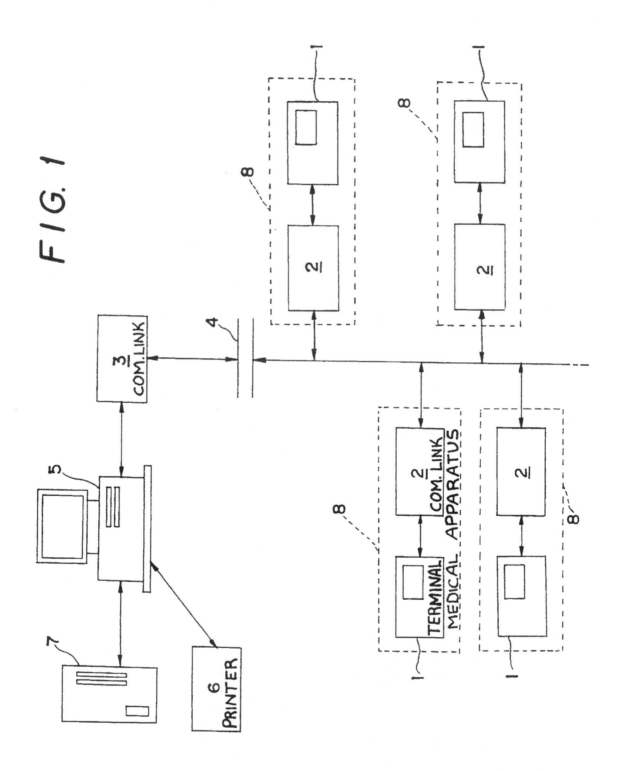

FIG. 1

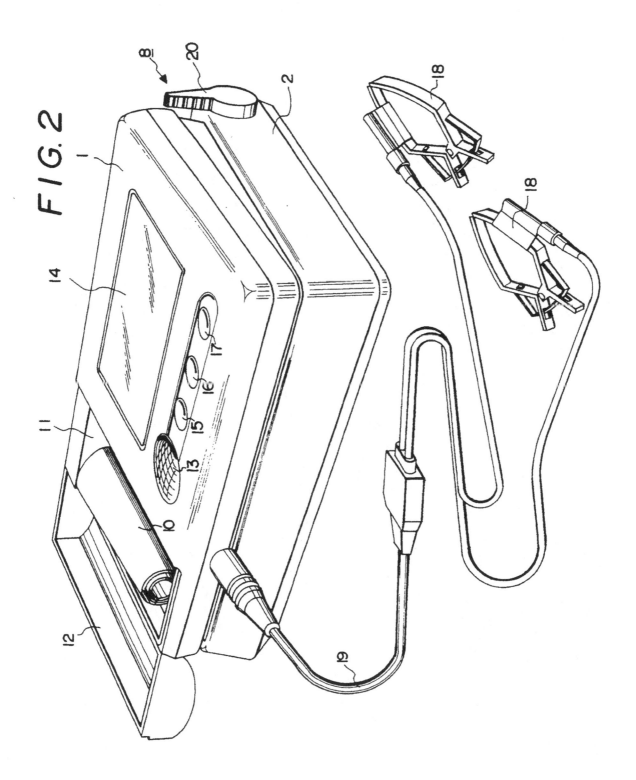

FIG. 2

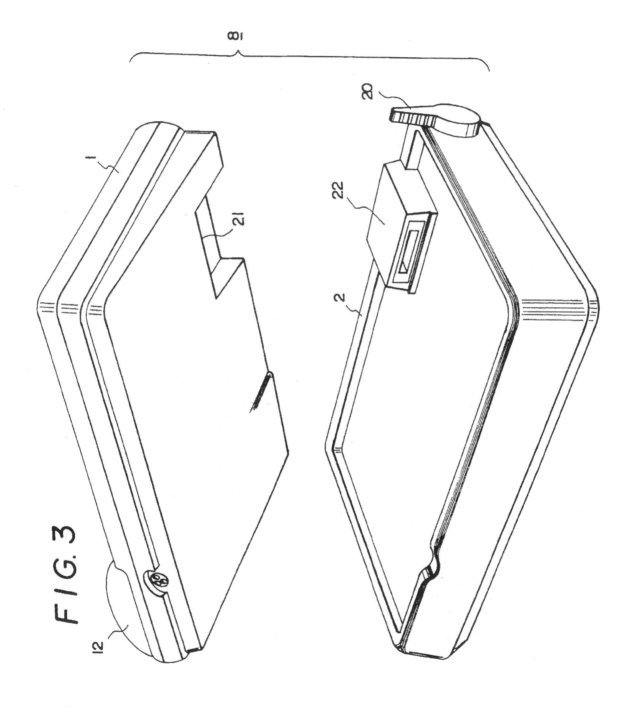

FIG. 3

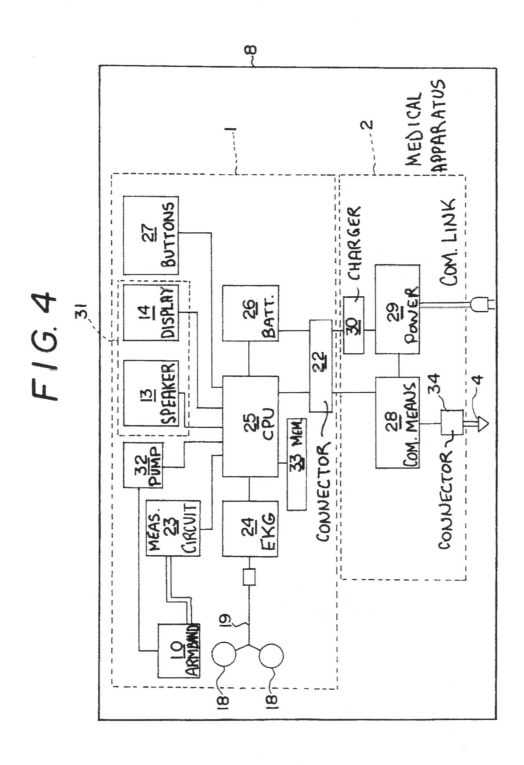

F I G. 4

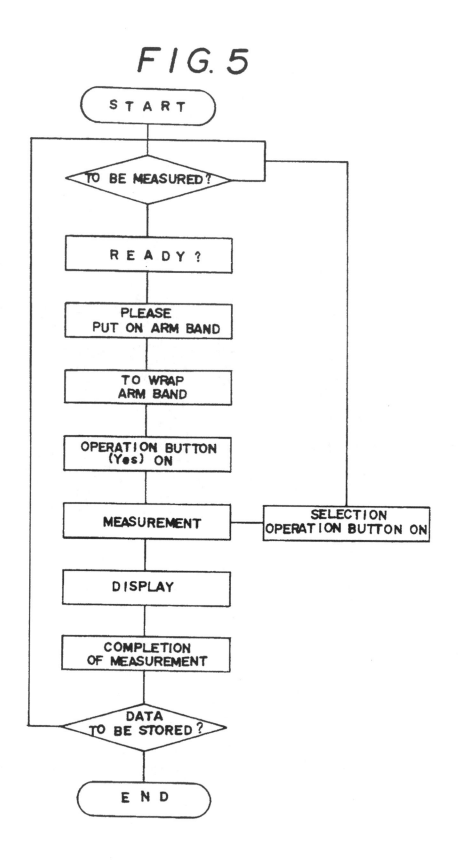

FIG. 5

FIG. 6

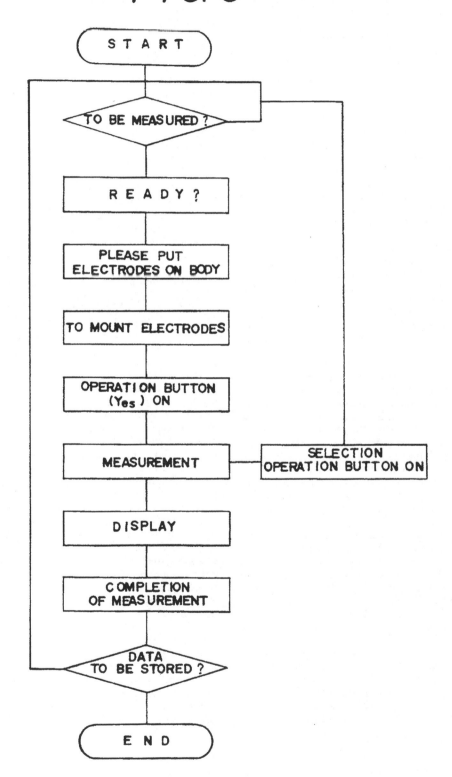

1

HOME MEDICAL SYSTEM AND MEDICAL APPARATUS FOR USE THEREWITH

BACKGROUND OF THE INVENTION

1. Field of the Invention

This invention relates to a home medical system and a medical apparatus for use therewith which are suitably applied when a common user who may be a patient having some disease effects management of the condition of the disease or health care at home.

2. Description of the Prior Art

In recent years, various home monitors have been put on the market in accordance with an increase of the necessity for the management of the condition of a disease or home care at home. However, they have not widely spread as yet due to the complexity of operation and the problem of the reliability and economy of the apparatus.

However, the variations of the blood pressure, for example, of a hypertension patient within a day and among days are very important problems. Particularly, the danger is pointed out that an excessive pressure reduction while hypertensive drugs are taken will reduce blood flow to the brain and the heart of an old hypertensive patient or a hypertension patient having a case history of cerebral infarction to cause an ischemic heart failure. Some person may, when the blood pressure is measured in front of a doctor, be strained and this can cause a rise of the blood pressure (so-called white robe hypertension) so that it is difficult to accurately grasp the original condition of the patient. Accordingly, it is very important to a hypertensive patient to observe the variation of the blood pressure in an ordinary condition at home over a long period of time.

Further, while it is recommended that a patient who has had a heart failure and has received an internal pace maker, measure his or her own pulse as a daily check in order to find out a pacing failure or a sensing failure of the internal pace maker, it is very difficult to grasp how may patients actually carry out the procedure every day. Accordingly, it is particularly useful to a pace maker embedded patient who works lively without having a particular complication that, if the patient makes use of a home medical system according to the present invention, a doctor can check an electrocardiogram monitor while the patient need not intentionally visit the hospital.

Similarly, it is an earnest desire to patients of ischemic heart diseases, patients of a heart failure, antiarrhythmic patients, patients of respiratory insufficiency, patients to whom the CAPD (continuous ambulatory peritoneal dialysis) has been performed and so forth that a patient can check the daily condition of its disease every day at home and a doctor can check the blood pressure and the electrocardiogram monitor so that the patient may live at rest every day.

On the other hand, even to healthy people having no disease, it is considered useful to early detection and early inquiry diagnosis of diseases of circulatory organs which are forecast to increase in the future that they can effect their health care easily at a low expense in order to achieve prevention and early detection of a disease.

SUMMARY OF THE INVENTION

It Is an object of the present invention to provide a home medical system and a medical apparatus for use with the home medical system by which a patient hav-

2

ing a various disease or a healthy person can measure the daily condition of the disease or the condition of health at home to undergo a check or an inquiry diagnosis by a medical specialist and which are easy to operate, high in reliability and low in expense.

The above and other objects, features and advantages of the present invention will become apparent from the following description and the appended claims, taken in conjunction with the accompanying drawings in which like parts or elements are denoted by like reference characters.

BRIEF DESCRIPTION OF THE DRAWINGS

FIG. 1 is a block diagram showing an outline of a home medical system according to the present invention:

FIG. 2 is a perspective view of a medical terminal equipment for the user side to which the present invention is applied;

FIG. 3 is a fragmentary perspective view of the medical terminal equipment shown in FIG. 2;

FIG. 4 is a block diagram of the medical terminal equipment shown in FIG. 2;

FIG. 5 is a flow chart illustrating a procedure of operation of the medical apparatus according to the present invention; and

FIG. 6 is a flow chart illustrating another procedure of operation of the medical apparatus according to the present invention.

DETAILED DESCRIPTION OF THE PREFERRED EMBODIMENT

Referring first to FIG. 1, there is shown a home medical system according to a preferred embodiment of the present invention. The home medical system shown includes a medical terminal equipment 1 for measuring the blood pressure, the pulse, the electrocardiogram and so forth, and a user side communication apparatus or link 2. A medical apparatus 8 is constituted from the medical terminal equipment 1 and the user side communication apparatus 2 and is installed at home of each user. The home medical system further includes a medical institution side communication apparatus or link 3, and a telecommunication line 4 based on, for example, a CATV (cable television) system interconnects the communication apparatus 2 and 3. It is to be noted that, though not shown, the communication apparatus and 3 may naturally be interconnected alternatively by a telephone line or by way of a radio channel. The home medical system further includes a host computer 5 with a display unit on the medical institution side, and additional equipments such as a printer apparatus 6 and an external storage apparatus 7 are provided for the host computer 5.

Referring now to FIG. 2, the medical apparatus 8 is shown in perspective view. The medical apparatus 8 shown includes the user side communication apparatus 2 and the medical terminal equipment 1 set in position on an upper face of the user side communication apparatus 2. An arm band 10 is accommodated in position at a side portion of an upper face of the medical terminal equipment 1. The arm band 10 is covered with a cover 12 which is hinged at a side portion thereof on one side of the medical terminal equipment 1. The medical terminal equipment 1 of the medical apparatus 8 includes a loudspeaker 13, a liquid crystal display apparatus 14 serving as display means, an operation button 15 for

3

entering the reply of "Yes", another operation button **16** for entering the reply of "No", and a further operation button **17** for entering a selection. A pair of measuring electrodes **18** for measuring an electrocardiogram are removaly connected to a front portion of the medical terminal equipment **1** by way of a cable **19**.

Referring now to FIG. 3, the medical terminal equipment **1** is removably mounted on the user side communication apparatus **2**, and if an operation lever **20** mounted on the user side communication apparatus **2** is tilted down and the medical terminal equipment **1** is pulled forwardly, then a connecting terminal **21** is removed from a connector **22** so that the medical terminal equipment **1** can thereafter be carried freely. It is to be noted that, in order to connect the thus removed medical terminal equipment **1** to the user side communication apparatus **2**, the connecting terminal **21** is put to the connector **22** while the operation lever **20** is in the tilted down condition, and then the operation lever **20** is tilted up, thereby completing the connection of the medical terminal equipment **1** to the user side communication apparatus **2**. Naturally, the present invention is not limited to the present embodiment with regard to the construction described just above. A battery power source is provided in the medical terminal equipment **1** as hereinafter described so that a measurement of the blood pressure and so forth and inputting of other data and so forth can be performed at a location remote from the user side communication apparatus **2**.

FIG. 4 shows in block diagram construction of the medical apparatus **8** which is constituted from the medical terminal equipment **1** and the user side communication apparatus **2**. Referring to FIG. 4, the medical apparatus **8** includes the telecommunication line **4**, the arm band **10**, the loudspeaker **13** and the liquid display unit **14** of the STU type with a backlight. The medical apparatus **8** further includes a blood and pulse measuring circuit **23**, an electrocardiogram measuring apparatus **24**, a CPU (central processing unit) **25**, a pump **32** and a memory **33**. The memory **33** is backed up by a battery for exclusive use which is different from a battery which is hereinafter described. It is to be noted that the loudspeaker **13** and the liquid crystal display apparatus **14** are controlled by the CPU **23** and also constitute explaining means **31**. The medical apparatus **8** includes a battery **26** and a plurality of operation buttons **27** which includes the operation buttons **15**, **16** and **17** described above. The elements described above are included in the medical terminal equipment **1**. Meanwhile, on the user side communication equipment **2** side, the medical apparatus **8** includes communicating means **28**, a power source circuit **29**, a battery charging circuit **30** and a connector **34**. It is to be noted that, as described above, the telecommunication line **4** may be not a line of a cable television system but a telephone line or a telecommunication line including a radio antenna or the like.

Subsequently, an outline of the home medical system according to the present invention is described. First, since the battery **26** is built in the medical terminal equipment **1**, the medical terminal equipment **1** can be used in a separate condition from the user side communication apparatus **2**, and besides, it can be utilized by a plurality of users.

If a user depresses any one of the operation buttons **15**, **16** and **17** (or alternatively a power source switch provided separately), the liquid crystal display unit **14** serving as display means is lit so that the date, the time,

4

the registered number and so forth are displayed on the liquid crystal display unit **14**. It is to be noted that, when no operation follows, the display by the liquid crystal display unit **14** is extinguished after 5 minutes or so in order to save the power of the battery power source, whereafter the liquid crystal display unit **14** enters into a waiting condition. Measurement, storage and so forth of various medical data after lighting of the liquid crystal display unit **14** are performed In such a manner, for example, as illustrated in FIGS. 5 and 6. Description of this is given below.

Measurement of the Blood Pressure and the Pulse

(1) The medical terminal equipment **1** gives to the user a question "do you want to measure the blood pressure and the pulse" by way of the screen display of the liquid crystal display apparatus **14** and sound of the loudspeaker **13**. The user enters its reply by means of either one of the operation buttons **15** and **16** for "Yes" and "No". In the case of the reply of "No", the control sequence returns to the start of the procedure without performing a measurement. On the contrary, in the case of the reply of "Yes", the control sequence advances to the next step.

(2) The medical terminal equipment **1** gives another question "are you ready ?" by way of the screen display and sound as described above.

(3) Subsequently, the medical terminal equipment **1** provides an instruction "please put on the arm band" to the user by way of the screen display and sound.

(4) The user will open the cover **12**, pick up the arm band **10** provided on the medical terminal equipment **1** and wrap it around one of the arms.

(5) After the preparation for measurement is completed, the user will depress the operation button **15** for "Yes".

(6) In response to the depression of the operation button **15**, air is automatically fed into the arm band **10** from the pump **32** and then discharged so that a measurement of the blood pressure and the pulse is started, for example, in accordance with the oscillometric method. Here, when the user wants to interrupt the measurement, the operation button **17** for "selection" will be depressed. Then, the measurement is interrupted immediately and the operation sequence returns to the step (1) described above.

(7) The result of the measurement is displayed in the following manner on the screen of the liquid crystal display unit **14**.

```
Result of Measurement
Maximum Blood Pressure = 123 mmHg
Minimum Blood Pressure = 89 mmHg
Pulse = 60/minute
```

(8) The measurement of the blood pressure and the pulse is completed with this.

(9) Subsequently, the medical terminal equipment **1** gives a question "do you want to store the data ?" by way of the screen display and sound. If the operation button **16** for "No" is depressed, then the control sequence returns to the step (1) above without storing the measurement data. On the contrary, if the operation button **15** for "Yes" is depressed, then the measurement data are stored into the memory **33**, thereby completing the procedure.

221

It is to be noted that, in the measurement of the blood pressure described above, the measurement is started with the maximum pressure value of 160 mmHg, but, if it is detected that the blood pressure exceeds the range, this is announced by sound and the measurement is started with the maximum pressure value of 240 mmHg. Further, while the arm band 10 is gradually pressurized upon measurement of the blood pressure and the pulse, in order to prepare for the case wherein a pressure higher than a necessary level is applied due to the failure of the pump 32 or the like, the medical apparatus 8 has, though not shown, a hardware safety circuit as well as a software safety circuit.

Subsequently, a measurement of an electrocardiogram is effected in accordance with such a procedure as illustrated in FIG. 6.

(1) The medical terminal equipment 1 gives a question "do you want to measure an electrocardiogram ?" to the user by way of the screen display of the liquid crystal display unit 14 and sound of the loudspeaker 13. The announcement by sound is repeated at an interval of time of 5 seconds until the user enters its reply of "Yes" by means of the operation button 15. The user will enter the reply by depression of either one of the operation buttons 15 and 16 for "Yes" and "No". In the case of the reply of "No", the control sequence returns to the start of the program. On the contrary, in the case of the reply of "Yes", the control sequence advances to the next step.

(2) The medical terminal equipment 1 gives a question "are you ready ?" by way of the screen display and sound.

(3) Subsequently, the medical terminal equipment 1 gives an instruction "put the electrodes on;" to the user by way of the screen display and sound.

(4) The user will put the measuring electrodes 18, which extend from the medical terminal equipment 1, on the arms of itself.

(5) After the user is prepared for measurement, the operation button 15 for "Yes" will be depressed.

(6) A measurement of an electrocardiogram is started. When the user wants to interrupt the measurement, the operation button 17 for "selection" will be depressed. As a result, the measurement is stopped immediately, and the control sequence returns to the step (1) above.

(7) An electrocardiographic waveform of the user during the measurement is displayed on the real time basis on the screen of the liquid crystal display unit 14.

(8) The medical terminal equipment 1 automatically ends Its measurement after one minute after completion of automatic gain adjustment after starting of the measurement.

(9) The medical terminal equipment 1 gives a question "do you want to store the data ?" by way of the screen display and sound. If the operation button 16 for "No" is depressed, then the control sequence returns to the first step (1) without storing the measurement data into the memory 33. On the contrary, if the operation button 15 for "No" is depressed, then the measurement data is stored into memory 33, thereby completing the procedure.

Subsequently, diagnosis inquiry using the system according to the present invention is described.

Minimum necessary questions for diagnosis inquiry are stored in advance in the host computer 5 and the medical terminal equipment 1, and consecutive numbers are applied in advance to the questions for diagnosis inquiry. On the medical institution side, a doctor will input the consecutive number or numbers of a question or questions for diagnosis inquiry to be asked to the user to the host computer 5, and the thus inputted number or numbers are stored into the host computer 5. After the inputting is completed, the host computer 5 transmits the inputted consecutive number or numbers of the questions for diagnosis inquiry to the medical apparatus 8 on the user side by way of the medical institution side communication apparatus 3. The medical apparatus 8 thus effects diagnosis inquiry of the received diagnosis inquiry question number or numbers to the user and transmits the result of the inquiry back to the host computer 5 by way of the user side communication apparatus 2. Since the diagnosis inquiry question number or numbers received by the medical apparatus 8 are stored in the memory 33 of the medical apparatus 8, the transmission from the host computer 5 must be performed only once. When it is desired to change the questions for diagnosis inquiry to the user, only the diagnosis inquiry question number or numbers stored in the host computer 5 should be changed. The host computer 5 transmits the thus changed diagnosis inquiry question number or numbers to the medical apparatus 8 of the user side by way of the medical institution side communication apparatus 3. Since the questions for diagnosis inquiry can be designated for each user, diagnosis inquiry effective for the disease or the condition of a particular user can be performed. The operation is performed in the following manner.

(1) The medical terminal equipment 1 gives a question "do you want to start diagnosis inquiry ?" by way of the screen display or sound.

(2) The user will enter its reply by depression of either one of the operation buttons 15 and 16 for "Yes" and In the case of the reply of "No", no diagnosis inquiry is effected. On the contrary, in the case of the reply of "Yes", diagnosis inquiry is started.

(3) The diagnosis inquiry proceeds in such a form that the user gives a reply by manual operation of either one of the operation buttons 15 and 16 for "Yes" and "No" to the question displayed on the screen of the liquid crystal display unit 14 like, for example, "Do you have a pain in the chest ?", "Yes" or "No" or "Do you feel languid ?", "Yes" or "No". When the user wants to interrupt the diagnosis inquiry, the operation button 17 for "selection" will be depressed. As a result, the diagnosis inquiry is interrupted and the procedure returns to the step (1) above.

(4) When all of the questions for diagnosis inquiry are completed, the medical terminal equipment 1 gives a question "do you wand to store the data ?" by way of the screen display and sound. If the operation button 16 for "No" is depressed, then the control sequence returns to the step (1) without storing the diagnosis inquiry data. On the contrary, if the operation button 15 for "Yes" is depressed, then the diagnosis inquiry data are stored into the memory 33, thereby completing the procedure.

Subsequently, inputting of data of the body temperature proceeds in the following manner.

(1) The medical terminal equipment 1 gives a question "do you want to record the body temperature ?" by way of the screen display of the liquid crystal display unit 14 and sound of the loudspeaker 13.

(2) The user will reply to the question by operation of the operation button 15 or 16 for "Yes" or "No". When the reply is "No", the body temperature is not recorded.

On the contrary, when the reply is "Yes", recording of the body temperature is started.

(3) The user will measure the body temperature by means of a clinical thermometer prepared by the user. Or else, the body temperature may have been measured in advance.

(4) Body temperature values from 35 to 45 degrees are displayed on the display screen, and also a cursor is displayed on the display screen. Depression of the operation button 15 or 16 for "Yes" or "No" moves the cursor in a direction in which the temperature value indicated by the cursor increases or decreases. The user will thus adjust the cursor to a body temperature value detected by the measurement by itself and depress the operation button 17 for "selection".

(5) The medical terminal equipment 1 gives a question "do you want to store the data ?" by way of the screen display and sound. If the operation button 16 for "No" is depressed, the control sequence returns to the step (1) without storing the body temperature data. On the contrary, if the operation button 15 for "Yes", then the body temperature data is stored into the memory 33, thereby completing the body temperature data inputting procedure.

An inputting procedure for data of the weight proceeds in the following manner.

(1) The medical terminal equipment 1 gives a question "do you want to record the weight ?" to the user by way of the screen display and sound.

(2) The user will reply to the question by operation of the operation button 15 or 16 for "Yes" or "No". When the reply is "No", the weight is not recorded. On the contrary, when the reply is "Yes", recording of the weight is started.

(3) The user will measure the weight by means of a weighing machine prepared by the user. Or else, the weight may have been measured in advance.

(4) The weight value of 50 Kg is displayed on the display screen of the liquid crystal display unit 14. Each depression of the operation button 15 or 16 for "Yes" or "No" increases or decreases the displayed weight value by 1 Kg. The user will thus adjust the displayed weight value to a weight value detected by the measurement by itself and depress the operation button 17 for "selection".

(5) The medical terminal equipment 1 gives a question "do you want to store the data ?" by way of the screen display and sound. If the operation button 16 for "No" is depressed, the control sequence returns to the step (1) without storing the weight value. On the contrary, if the operation button 15 for "Yes" is depressed, then the weight value is stored into the memory 33, thereby completing the weight data inputting procedure.

The medical apparatus 8 according to the present invention allows storage of data of a plurality of users into the memory 33 and also has a function of outputting, by accessing to it from the medical institution side, the stored data from the memory 33 making use of a CATV line, a telephone line or the like. When the medical apparatus 8 is to be used commonly by a plurality of users, identification information of entry numbers of the users must be inputted in advance. The inputting operation may involve displaying the identification information on the liquid crystal display unit 14 of the display means and depression of the operation button or buttons 15 or/and 16 for "Yes" and "No". The transmission of the data may be performed by accessing of the user side

to the medical institution side or may be performed by accessing of the medical institution side so that the medical institution receives data stored in the user side communication apparatus 2. The number of times of measurement and inputting of various data within a day can be selected arbitrarily in accordance with an instruction of the medical institution.

Data transmitted from the user side communication apparatus 7 are set to the medical institution side communication apparatus 3 by means of a telephone line, a CATV line or a radio channel and stored into a hard disk or an opto-magnetic disk of the host computer 5 on the medical institution side. Then, the data are displayed immediately in accordance with the necessity. The host computer 5 on the medical institution side can naturally collect and store data for several hundreds to several thousands people using the external storage apparatus 7, automatically diagnose the collected data and transmit the result of the diagnosis to the user side, and pick up those data for which a diagnosis of a doctor is considered necessary and urge a diagnosis of a doctor. In addition, the host computer 5 can print the result of the diagnosis of the doctor together with data for the last one month by means of the printer 6 so that the data thus printed out may be delivered to the user. The automatic diagnosis of the host computer 5 involves, for example, checking of the pattern of the electrocardiographic waveform for the last one month to judge whether or not it has a significant variation or some abnormality, and if some abnormal condition is detected, a warning is issued. Further, the host computer 5 can provide a display of a variation graph of the blood pressure, the pulse, the body temperature, the weight and so forth for the last one month, compare the data with national average values of the sex and the age and give a notice of the result of the automatic diagnosis like, for example, "You are overweight: how about getting thin ?" or "Your blood pressure is excessively high: take care so as not to take too much salt."

It is to be noted that, while the communication apparatus may have a different construction depending upon communicating means, since the medical terminal equipment 1 automatically discriminates the construction and performs communications, for example, suitable for a CATV line, a telephone line or the like, only the communication apparatus may be replaced. Furthermore, data compression is performed for data to be communicated so that the time for which the line is used may be minimized. For example, if data of an electrocardiogram for one minute (about 15,000 bytes) are transmitted as they are at the baud rate of 2,400 BPS, then about 50 seconds are required, but if the data are compressed to 3,000 to 1,500 bytes or so and then transmitted, then the transmission is completed in about 5 to 10 seconds or so. Since the data compression has been developed originally, even if thus compressed data are stolen, it is difficult to decompress the compressed data and the secrecy is maintained. Further, since data for which the data compression has not been performed are enciphered, there is no possibility that the secret of an individual may leak to the outside.

Further, since the medical terminal equipment 1 is constructed so that it can store and execute a program transmitted to it from the host computer 5, it can perform expansion of or modification to the functions thereof. Further, since such program data are stored in the memory 33, the transmission from the host computer 5 is necessitated only once. Instructions and/or questions for diagnosis inquiry from the host computer **5** are stored into the memory **33** and displayed on the display unit **14** or announced repetitively from the loud-speaker **13**.

Having now fully described the invention, it will be apparent to one of ordinary skill in the art that many changes and modifications can be made thereto without departing from the spirit and scope of the invention as set forth herein.

What is claimed is:

1. A medical system for measuring a user's blood pressure, pulse and electrocardiogram at home, and for communication between the user and a medical institution; the system comprising:

a home medical terminal for use by the user, the terminal including an arm band for measuring the user's blood pressure and pulse; a pair of measuring electrodes for measuring the user's electrocardiogram; explaining means for questioning a user with on-line and with preselected questions, and for presenting and explaining a measurement procedure to the user for use by the user to take measurements using said arm band and said measuring electrodes; a plurality of operation buttons operable by the user and operatively connected to the explaining means for inputting responses to the questions and for interacting with the explaining means to proceed through a measurement procedure; the home medical terminal also including display means for displaying a measurement by said arm band and a measurement by said electrodes, said display means also being operatively connected to said explaining means for displaying the questions and for presenting and explaining the measurement procedures; the home medical terminal further included a memory for storing the results of the measurements, and the answers to the questions; and a home central processing unit operatively connected to said display means, to said operation buttons, to said arm band, to said electrodes, to said explaining means and to said memory, for operating said arm band and electrodes to make the measurements, to operate said explaining means to question the user and present and explain measurement procedures to the user, and to receive signals from the operation buttons and to drive the display means and memory;

home communication means operatively connected to said home central processing unit for transmitting and receiving signals including the on-line questions for the user, responses to and from the user to those questions, and the measurements taken by the user;

institute communication means;

a communication line operatively connected between the home communication means and the institute communication means for transmitting and receiving signals therebetween;

a host computer operatively connected to the institution communication means and at the medical institution;

question means operatively connected to the host computer for initiating on-line and preselected questions for diagnosis inquiry to the host computer which are transmitted between the home and institution communication means over the commu-

nication line to the explaining means for providing questioning of the user; and

attachment means operatively connected to the host computer for storing and displaying information from the host computer, received through the home and institution communication means over the communication line, and including the results of the measurements taken by the user and stored in the memory.

2. A medical system according to claim **1**, wherein said communication line comprises a CATV line.

3. A medical system according to claim **1**, wherein said communication line comprises a radio channel.

4. A medical system according to claim **1**, including input means operably connected to said home central processing unit for use by the user to input body temperature and a weight of the user as part of the answer to the questions posed to the user by the explaining means.

5. A medical system according to claim **1**, wherein said explaining means includes a display unit and a loud-speaker.

6. A medical system according to claim **1**, wherein said communication line is a telephone line.

7. A medical apparatus, comprising:

a medical terminal equipment for a patient; and

patient side communication means;

said medical terminal equipment including an arm band for measuring a blood pressure and a pulse of the patient, a pair of measuring electrodes for measuring an electrocardiogram of the patient, explaining means for explaining a procedure and a method of a measurement by said arm band and said measuring electrodes and for displaying on-line and preselected questions to the user, operation buttons for imputing a result of the measurement and answering to a question from a medical institution, display means for displaying thereon a result of the measurement by said measuring electrodes, for displaying the data, and for displaying the questions for diagnosis inquiry from the medical institution, a memory for storing therein the result of the measurement by said arm band and said measuring electrodes, the data, the questions for diagnosis inquiry, and answers to the questions, and a central processing unit for controlling said medical terminal apparatus; and

said patient communication means including a power source circuit and a communication unit for transmitting and receiving the result of the measurement, the data, the question for diagnosis inquiry and the answers to the questions, as well as on-line questions from the medical institution, the patient communication means also operating to transmit to the medical institution a mixture of answers to the on-line and preselected questions.

8. A medical apparatus according to claim **7**, wherein said medical terminal equipment and said patient side communication means are removably coupled to each other, and said medical terminal equipment further includes a built-in battery.

9. A medical apparatus according to claim **7**, wherein said user side communication means includes data compressing means for compressing data to be transmitted.

* * * * *

US 20050151015A1

⁽¹⁹⁾ **United States**

⁽¹²⁾ **Patent Application Publication** ⁽¹⁰⁾ **Pub. No.: US 2005/0151015 A1**

Cagle et al. ⁽⁴³⁾ **Pub. Date:** **Jul. 14, 2005**

(54) **ADAPTIVE COMPOSITE SKIN TECHNOLOGY (ACTS)**

(75) Inventors: **Christopher M. Cagle,** Yorktown, VA (US); **Robin W. Schlecht,** Newport News, VA (US)

Correspondence Address:
NATIONAL AERONAUTICS AND SPACE ADMINISTR
ATION LANGLEY RESEARCH CENTER
3 LANGLEY BOULEVARD
MAIL STOP 212
HAMPTON, VA 236812199

(73) Assignee: **United States of America as represented by the Administrator of the NASA,** Washington, DC (US)

(21) Appl. No.: **10/828,528**

(22) Filed: **Apr. 9, 2004**

Related U.S. Application Data

(60) Provisional application No. 60/461,563, filed on Apr. 9, 2003.

Publication Classification

(51) Int. Cl.^{7} **B64C 1/00**
(52) U.S. Cl. **244/123**; 244/130

(57) **ABSTRACT**

A tailorable elastic skin is provided for covering shape-changing, or "morphable," structures. The skin comprises a two-dimensional "planar spring" embedded in an elastomeric material. The invention provides a smooth aerodynamic covering capable of global elongation exceeding 20% with a low input force. The design can be tailored for light-weight, lightly loaded applications, or for more heavily loaded aerodynamic or hydrodynamic conditions.

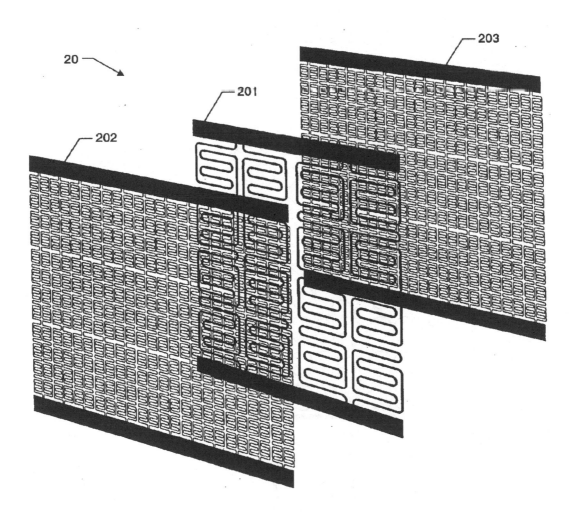

FIG. 1

FIG. 2

FIG. 3

FIG. 4

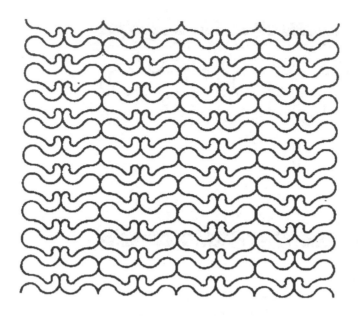

FIG. 5

FIG. 6

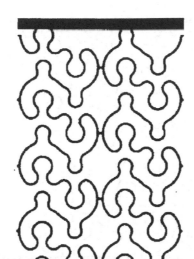

FIG. 7

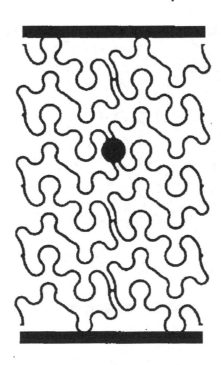

FIG. 8

FIG. 9

FIG. 10

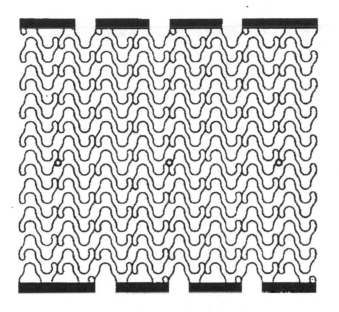

FIG. 11

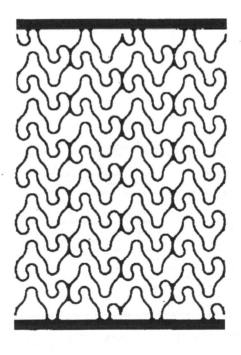

FIG. 12

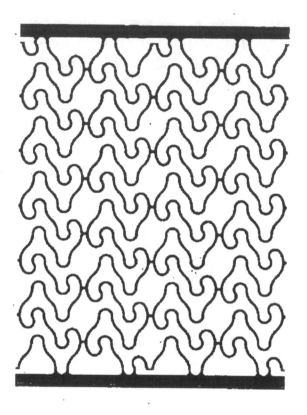

FIG. 13

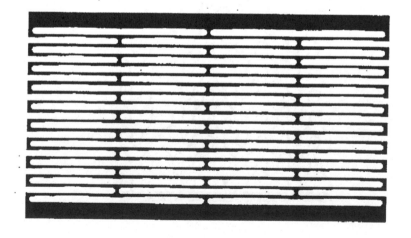

FIG. 14

FIG. 15

FIG. 16

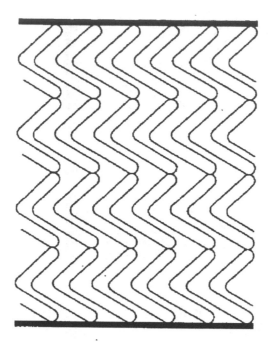

FIG. 17

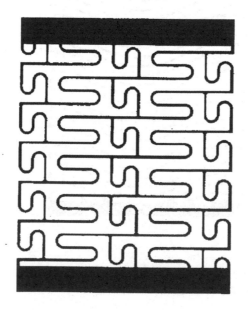

FIG. 18

FIG. 19

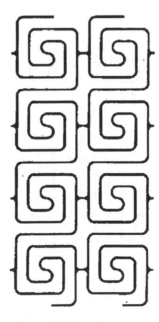

FIG. 20

FIG. 21

FIG. 22

FIG. 23

FIG. 24

FIG. 25

FIG. 26

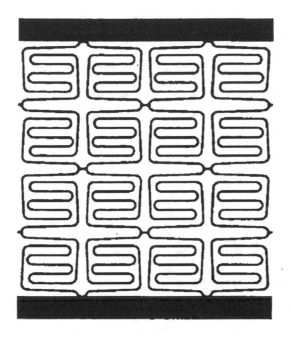

FIG. 27

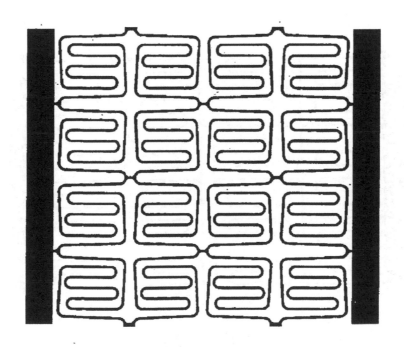

FIG. 28

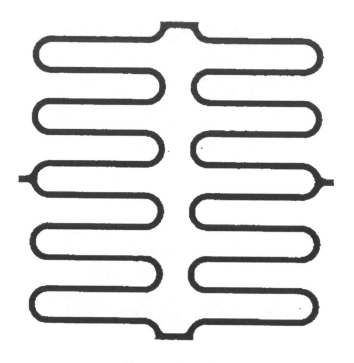

FIG. 29

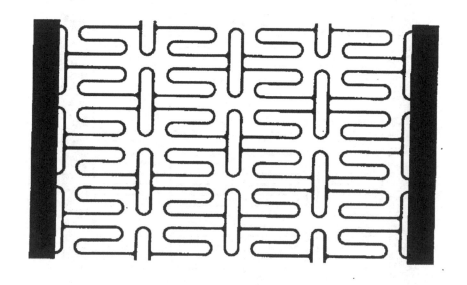

FIG. 30

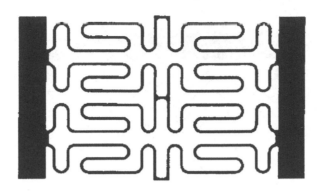

FIG. 31

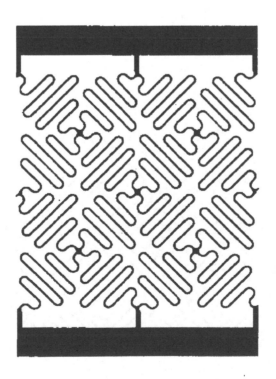

FIG. 32

FIG. 33

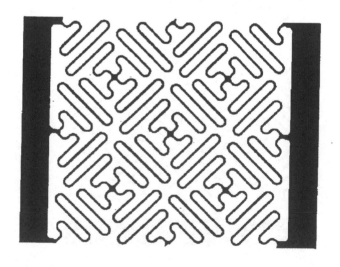

FIG. 34

FIG. 35

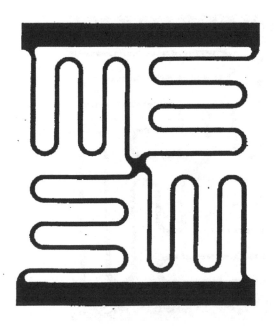

FIG. 36

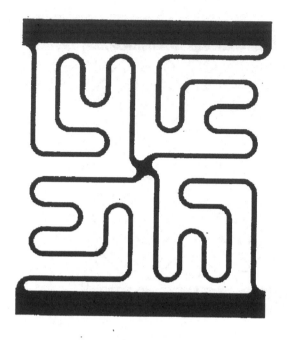

FIG. 37

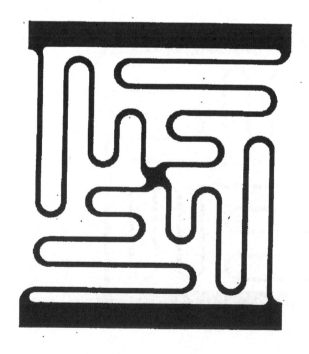

FIG. 38

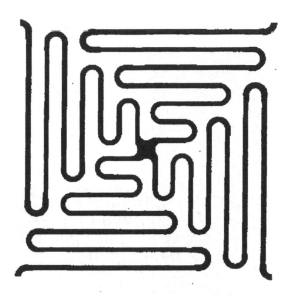

FIG. 39

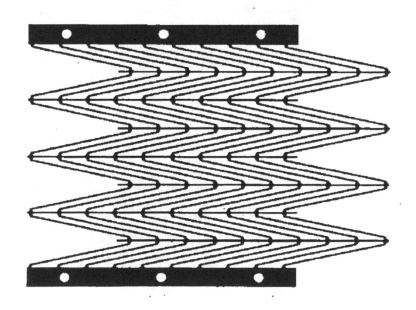

FIG. 40

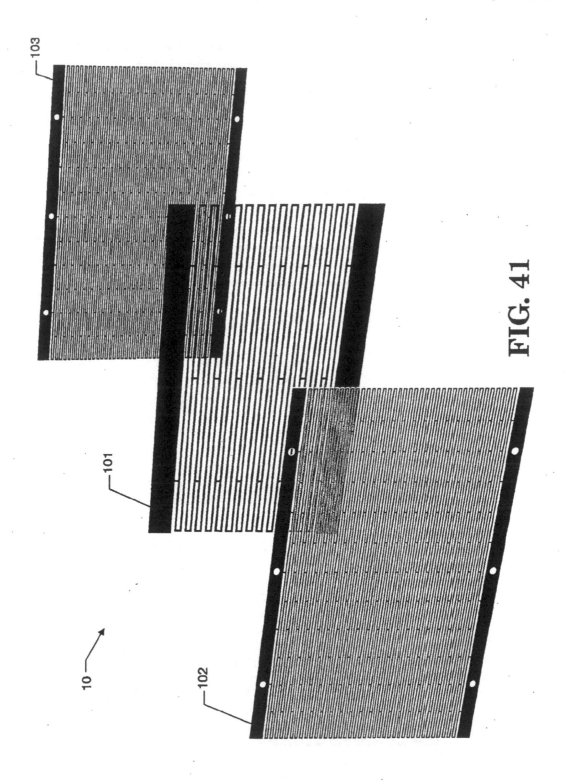

FIG. 41

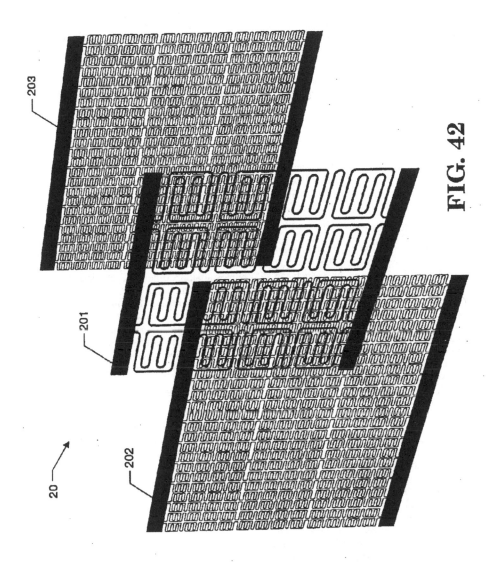

FIG. 42

ADAPTIVE COMPOSITE SKIN TECHNOLOGY (ACTS)

[0001] This application claims the benefit of U.S. Provisional Application No. 60/461,563, filed Apr. 9, 2003, and entitled "Adaptive Composite Skin Technology (ACTS)."

BACKGROUND OF THE INVENTION

[0002] 1. Field of the Invention

[0003] The subject invention relates to aerodynamic skin material, and relates more specifically to tailorable adaptive, elastic composite skins for aerodynamic or hydrodynamic applications.

[0004] 2. Description of the Related Art

[0005] Many of the proposals for aircraft that can perform large aerodynamic shape change require a flexible skin that can follow the change of some internal structure, which can be driven by conventional actuators, or possibly by "smart" actuators. These shape changes can be in the form of large bumps, conformal wing changes of platform, camber, twist, sweep, anhedral/dihedral, and integrated leading and trailing edge flaps or other devices. Presently no method exists to provide a smooth aerodynamic surface capable of large deflections while maintaining smoothness and rigidity. The only materials that come close to providing a smooth covering are latex or silicone rubber type materials, but for the required out-of-plane stiffness they require a thick section and excessive driving force.

[0006] Some prior art systems exist comprising skeletal frameworks, or structural frameworks laminated within elastomeric sheets. U.S. Pat. No. 6,588,709 by Dunne discloses a flexible skin formed by enveloping shape memory alloy rods, but does not provide the structure or capabilities offered by the present subject invention. U.S. Pat. No. 6,027,074—to Cameron discloses a reinforced elastomeric panel with rigid members and removable plate, but nothing resembling a planar spring. U.S. Pat. No. 6,337,294 to Waldrop discloses an elastic ground plane without spring qualities, and using an elastomer only for grounding purposes. Three patents to Geiger (U.S. Pat. Nos. 5,810,291, 5,931,422, and 5,958,803) disclose a variety of structurally reinforced elastomeric panels, but without planar spring structure or function. U.S. Pat. No. 4,038,040 to Nagl discloses an etched lattice grid structure which provides the capability of being formed into a geometry of compound curvature. Nagl does not, however, disclose a planar spring skeletal structure or an elastomeric component. U.S. Pat. No. 5,962,150 to Priluck similarly discloses a structural lattice configuration, but a rigid one, and one without an elastomeric component.

[0007] Generally speaking, prior art exists that discloses structurally reinforced elastomers, or lattice-like structural systems. No system exists, however, which satisfactorily provides a flexible, elastic skin, capable of significant deflection, while maintaining smoothness and rigidity, suitable for use with aerodynamic vehicles and watercraft.

BRIEF SUMMARY OF THE INVENTION

[0008] Accordingly, it is an object of the present invention to provide a flexible skin for use on aircraft and watercraft.

[0009] It is another object of the present invention to provide a flexible skin capable of large deflection while maintaining smoothness and rigidity.

[0010] It is yet another object of the present invention to provide a flexible skin that enables the real-time alteration of aircraft or watercraft external geometry.

[0011] The present invention is a tailorable, adaptive, elastic composite skin that accomplishes the objects above. These and other objects will become more readily appreciated and understood from a consideration of the following detailed description of the invention, when taken together with the accompanying drawings.

[0012] The preferred embodiment of the invention comprises at least one skeletal bi-directional spring, embedded within a flexible, preferably elastomeric, solid. The best mode of the invention varies considerably by the intended application and by the required mechanical properties of the composite skin. Although each embodiment of the present invention comprises at least one skeletal component and at least one elastomeric element, specifically selected materials, properties, and manufacturing processes may vary considerably to suit the intended use for the composite skin. The following detailed description will provide instruction on how the preferred embodiment may be modified to suit specific intended applications of the invention.

BRIEF DESCRIPTION OF THE SEVERAL VIEWS OF THE DRAWINGS

[0013] FIGS. 1-40 are two-dimensional representations of embodiments considered for the reinforcement skeleton (i.e. planar or bidirectional spring) for the present invention.

[0014] FIG. 41 is a depiction of a Computer Aided Design model of a planar spring with flexibility in one direction.

[0015] FIG. 42 is a depiction of a Computer Aided Design model of a planar spring with flexibility in two directions.

DETAILED DESCRIPTION OF THE INVENTION

[0016] The present invention is a flexible skin, which smoothly "wraps" a structural shape, with low actuation force required to stretch or warp the surface. The skin assembly consists of a relatively stiff internal skeleton, made of metallic or possibly plastic/composite material. Visual examples of internal skeleton geometry are provided in FIGS. 1-40.

[0017] One embodiment of the present invention consists of multiple layers of flexible components, including at least one internal skeleton. A first step in producing the internal skeleton is to develop the geometry of a single element of a full 2-D planar spring design that visually appears to have suitable mechanical properties, depending on the type and direction of in-plane deflection desired. Global elongation is driven by the beam bending properties of the members of the planar spring. At one extreme is a 1-dimensional spring that is very flexible in one direction and completely stiff in the orthogonal direction. Many requirements alternatively call for similar flexibility in all directions.

[0018] The selected geometry is then modeled using a Computer Aided Design (CAD) system, as illustrated in FIG. 41 and FIG. 42, and carefully shaped to have symmetry so that large planar spring prototypes can be patterned from a small section. **FIG. 41** shows components of one embodiment 10 of a composite skin, comprising a planar spring **101** designed for flexibility in one axis, and sandwiched between elastomeric sheet **102** and elastomeric sheet **103**. Similarly, **FIG. 42** shows one embodiment **20** of the present invention, having a planar spring **201** designed for flexibility in two directions, and sandwiched between elastomeric sheet **202** and elastomeric sheet **203**. A representative small section of the planar spring is computationally analyzed using a modern Finite Element Analysis program to determine flexibility and maximum stress. An iterative design process is used to optimize a shape to give the most flexibility at the least stress, without violating fabrication limitations of the material. Typical design targets for some selected embodiments of the invention are 15%-global elongation with a safety factor of 2 on yield strength. In-plane stiffness and out-of-plane bending stiffness are largely dependent on the global elongation criteria.

[0019] For a typical laminated structure having a thin surface spring coating combined with a thicker core spring structure, both elements may be independently analyzed to have similar global elongation properties. The contributions to the stiffness due to the elastomeric fill material and the joining of the independent elements are not analyzed in the initial design. This is more readily measured on sample prototype structures.

[0020] Typically 2024 or 7075 aluminum alloys, and cold-rolled stainless steel are used in the production of prototype skeletal planar springs. Preferably, but not necessarily, the skeleton material should have an ultimate tensile strength of at least 175,000 psi. The skeleton material is two-dimensionally cut to produce a planar spring, i.e. a bi-directional spring, using waterjet, laser, chemical etching, or other suitable rapid cutting process. The purpose of the produced planar spring or bi-directional spring is to provide through-plane stiffness to prevent drumming type movement normal to the surface, while allowing flexibility in the planar (bi-directional) dimension.

[0021] The skeletal spring is then embedded in a castable, elastomeric material to provide a smooth composite skin. Materials used in prototype fabrication include latex and silicone. A number of suitable materials, including an acrylic synthetic latex rubber, a water-based neoprene modified natural latex, and a single component self-curing synthetic liquid rubber are available from a manufacturer called Zeller International, of Downsville N.Y. Zeller International can be reached by telephone at (607) 363-7792, and their products can be viewed at htt://www.zeller-int.com/.

[0022] Elastomeric materials may be cast with the skeleton embedded within the casting, or the elastomer may be sprayed, dipped or brushed on. Typically, elastomers are used which have sufficient adhesive properties to allow brushing or spraying to be performed in layers without resulting in a laminated skin; i.e. the resulting elastomeric component of the skin is substantially monolithic.

[0023] In addition to this relatively simple monolithic structure, however, one embodiment of the present invention enhances the performance of the skin by layering or sandwiching the various components. Particularly for highly curved shapes such as the leading edge of a wing, the shape can be generated by laminating several sheets of thin planar

springs using the elastomer as the binder to hold the sheets together. For high performance panels with higher out-of-plane stiffness and low drive force at minimum weight, a sandwich type construction can be used with a thin, relatively stiffer material as the face (outer) spring sheet and a softer spring sheet as the core (inner) layer.

[0024] Skin stiffness is tailored by varying the material, thickness, cut shape, and local beam thickness of the internal skeleton. The internal skeleton can be designed to be less stiff in one planar direction or approximately the same stiffness in both planar directions. The former can be advantageous for 2-D hinge type applications. The latter is typically desired for more 3-D applications, such as platform changes or bump modification. Stiffness is further tailored by varying the elasticity of the elastomeric filler. Hardpoints for actuator or constraint attachments can be easily incorporated by including a threaded attachment location within the internal skeleton.

[0025] Global strain rate of the composite structure may exceed 20% in-plane, as shown in the data provided in Table 1 at the end of this written description. Table 1 provides a compilation of prototype stress and strain properties derived from finite element analysis of various embodiments of the present invention, to assist in the mechanical definition of the composite structure. "In-plane" and "planar" in the context of this description are to be understood to mean "bi-directional," or within one or two dimensions. Although the present invention may be fabricated and used in a planar configuration, it should be well understood that typical utilization of the invention would occur in three-dimensional applications, for example in aircraft wing skins or boat hulls.

[0026] Although the current embodiment of the present invention utilizes planar springs etched or cut from single monolithic sheets of metal, fabrication methods for the internal skeletal framework may include welding, brazing, bonding, or otherwise permanently joining formed strip or wire to create the desired planar spring shape. Particularly for non-metallic reinforcement, casting or injection molding methods may also be used to create the skeleton.

[0027] An additional method of construction for one embodiment of the invention utilizes a commercially made elastomeric sheet material bonded to the skeletal framework, with or without filling the core skeleton with elastomer (see again **FIGS. 41-42**). In addition, a sandwich construction method may use a stiffer, thin, elastomer-filled planar spring face sheet, bonded to a thicker core planar spring with elastomer, with or without filling the core skeleton.

[0028] Additional means of attaching the flexible skin to underlying structure include bonding to the skin assembly at node points or node lines using the elastomer as the bond agent or other compatible adhesive. Mechanical attachment points may be included in the internal skeleton as mentioned earlier, or by attaching a separate fastener hard point by means of adhesion, bonding, brazing, welding, or other suitable method. Hard points provide the attachment interface to the underlying structure by bonding, screwing, riveting, or other means.

[0029] The stiffness of the internal skeleton may be tailored to provide highly directional flexibility or nearly uniform flexibility in all directions. With proper design shaping, the relative flexibility among the different directions can be varied anywhere between these two extremes. The degree of flexibility can be varied by the methods stated above. Some commercially available elastomers can be used to vary the stiffness by varying the chemical composition within the built up structure. These can be applied in thin layers by brushing, spraying, dipping or pouring. Multiple layers can be built up in this fashion, with each additional layer permanently fusing with the previous layer. In this way the stiffness of the structure can be varied through the thickness and/or throughout the area of the skin structure.

[0030] The composite structure is designed to be loaded in a tensile manner from a natural, unconstrained state of elongation. To achieve compressive loading (negative elongation), the structure can be designed such that the skin is partially elongated to mate with the underlying structure in a neutral position (at some point between maximum compression and maximum extension). In this way the skin will be in its unconstrained position when the underlying structure is in its most compressed state. In a somewhat similar way, the elastomer may be mated with the skeletal material when the skeleton is pre-compressed. This serves to increase the allowable elongation in the skin structure by using both the compressive and tensile elastic strain of the skeletal material.

[0031] One embodiment of the present invention includes embedding electronic devices by using the planar spring sheet as a carrier for a flexible printed circuit board. This enables controls, MEMS sensors, and other instrumentation to be integral with the skin and provide a convenient means to interface to external sources. Another embodiment includes piezoelectric elements embedded within the flexible skin, or attached to the flexible skin or its skeleton. The piezoelectric elements can be used as actuators to drive the deflection of the flexible skin, or as sensors to provide measurement data in response to the skin's deflection.

[0032] This flexible skin is enabling technology for aircraft morphing applications. It provides a smooth aerodynamic covering that can flex and stretch with structural shape change. The composite skin assembly simultaneously maximizes in-plane flexibility and out-of-plane stiffness. Other applications that require large recoverable shape change can also benefit from this technology.

[0033] It is foreseen that this technology will have application in many aircraft morphing configurations. By varying the geometry, material properties, and construction methods, it may be tailored for use in wind-tunnel models, Unmanned Aerial Vehicles (UAV), and manned aircraft. It should also have application in many other transportation areas such as automotive, trucks, buses, where fuel savings can be made with improved aerodynamics. Some potential aircraft applications include aircraft wing bumps (for shock suppression), variable wing shapes, conformable control surfaces, variable nozzles, and variable engine intakes. Other applications include adaptable vehicle safety systems (e.g. impact recoverable bumpers), impact resistant skins (e.g. self healing materials), bladders, flexible/variable ducting, and conformal control surfaces for ships and submarines.

[0034] Although the invention has been described relative to a few specific embodiments, there are numerous variations and modifications that will be readily apparent to those skilled in the art, in light of the above teachings. It is therefore to be understood that, within the scope of the appended claims, the invention may be practiced other than as specifically described.

TABLE 1

material	density	modulus	yield strength	strength/modulus	modulus/density
7075 aluminum	0.1	1.5E+07	70000	6.67E-03	1.05E+08
Ti6Al4V	0.16	1.65E+07	145000	8.79E-03	1.03E+08
high strength steel	0.29	2.90E+07	140000	4.83E-03	1.00E+08

configuration	length	width	thickness	load	delta	max vm stress	effective strain	strain @ Sfy = 2	"E" psi	mat'l	
4_3	4.572	1.275	0.125	5	0.73	60,000	16.0%	9.3%	196.5	alum	
4_3	4.572	1.275	0.125	5	0.78	62,400	17.1%	9.6%	183.9	alum	
4_3	4.572	1.275	0.125	5	0.81	69,000	17.7%	9.0%	177.1	alum	
4_3	4.572	2.525	0.125	10	0.72	67,000	15.8%	8.3%	200.4	alum	
4_3	3.454	2.530	0.125	10	0.52	66,900	15.0%	7.8%	210.8	alum	
4_4	3.454	2.740	0.125	10	0.68	67,000	19.6%	10.2%	149.2	alum	
3_2	4.418	3.439	0.125	5	0.79	50,000	17.8%	12.5%	65.2	alum	
3_2	3.003	1.732	0.125	2.5	0.50	51000	16.7%	11.4%	69.4	alum	
3_3	2.953	1.827	0.125	2.5	0.55	50000	18.5%	12.9%	59.3	alum	
3_4	2.952	1.824	0.125	2.5	0.80	60000	27.0%	15.7%	40.6	alum	
3_4_a	2.952	1.820	0.125	2.5	0.80	58800	27.0%	16.7%	40.7	alum	
1	4.444	3.601	0.125	5	0.70	67000	15.6%	8.2%	71.0	alum	
1_1	4.429	3.816	0.125	5	1.00	55800	22.6%	14.2%	46.3	alum	
3_4_a	2.800	3.630	0.125	5	0.78	61000	28.0%	16.1%	39.4	alum	
3_4_b	2.800	3.500	0.125	5	0.21	41000	7.5%	6.4%	152.4	alum	
3_4_chem	0.707	0.948	0.01	0.1	0.02	25000	2.7%	7.6%	386.4	steel	
1_2	2.820	3.816	0.125	5	0.70	60000	24.8%	14.4%	42.3	alum	
1_3	2.028	2.714	0.125	2.5	0.06	13000	2.9%	7.9%	249.9	alum	
1_4	3.441	3.847	0.125	5	0.96	56800	27.8%	17.4%	37.4	alum	
1_4_chemetch_010	0.723	0.490	0.01	0.1	0.04	47000	5.9%	8.8%	344.7	steel	current
1_4_chemetch_009	0.723	0.490	0.01	0.1	0.06	57000	8.1%	9.9%	252.7		
1_4_chemetch_008	0.723	0.490	0.01	0.1	0.08	68000	11.4%	11.7%	179.3		
1_4_chemetch_007	0.723	0.490	0.01	0.1	0.12	83000	16.9%	14.2%	120.9		
1_4_ch_mod_008	0.723	0.490	0.01	0.1	0.07	56000	9.8%	12.2%	209.3		
1_4_ch_mod_007	0.723	0.490	0.01	0.1	0.11	72200	14.9%	14.2%	136.6		
1_4_ch_mod_007_2	0.723	0.490	0.01	0.1	0.11	73000	15.5%	12.2%	131.7		
1_4_ce_Ti_009	0.723	0.490	0.01	0.1	0.10	57000	13.3%	14.5%	153.7	titanium	
5_1	1.163	2.025	0.0625	2.5	0.14	34000	11.7%	12.0%	168.9	alum	
5_1_a	1.490	2.030	0.0625	2.5	0.10	25000	6.5%	9.1%	302.7	alum	
5_1_b	1.490	3.030	0.0625	2.5	0.40	41600	26.7%	22.5%	49.4	alum	
5_1_c	1.490	3.030	0.0625	2.5	0.33	35000	22.0%	22.0%	60.0	alum	
5_1_d	1.490	3.030	0.0625	2.5	0.49	51000	32.9%	22.6%	40.1	alum	
5_1_chemetch_012	0.563	0.760	0.01	0.1	0.01	13000	1.6%	8.8%	805.2	steel	
5_1_chemetch_010	0.565	0.760	0.01	0.1	0.01	21000	2.3%	7.5%	576.3	steel	
5_1_chemetch_010	0.565	0.870	0.01	0.1	0.02	22000	3.5%	11.0%	331.3	steel	
5_1_chemetch_012	0.678	1.010	0.01	0.1	0.02	17000	3.1%	12.8%	319.7	steel	
5_1_chemetch_010	0.680	0.970	0.01	0.1	0.03	23000	4.0%	12.0%	260.6	steel	final

TABLE 1-continued

Name									
5_1_steel	1.575	2.890	0.0625	1	0.07	18000	4.3%	16.8%	128.2
5_1_steel	1.585	2.885	0.0625	1	0.14	24000	8.7%	25.4%	63.7
6_1	1.700	3.025	0.0625	2.5	0.05	16000	2.8%	6.0%	478.3
6_1_b	1.860	3.020	0.0625	2.5	0.09	26600	5.1%	6.7%	260.9
6_1_b	2.025	2.125	0.0625	2.5	0.10	25600	5.1%	7.0%	259.3
11_1	1.782	2.275	0.03125	2.5	0.05	23000	2.6%	4.0%	719.2
12_1	2.813	1.775	0.0625	2.5	0.60	132100	33.4%	8.9%	105.1
13_1_025_y	2.500	2.150	0.0625	1	0.14	19400	4.8%	8.7%	187.8
13_1_025_x	2.250	2.500	0.0625	1	0.02	8000	0.7%	3.0%	1075.4
13_2_025_y	2.125	2.250	0.0625	1	0.09	11900	3.8%	11.2%	167.4
13_2_025_x	2.250	2.500	0.0625	1	0.01	5200	0.4%	2.6%	1814.1
13_2_025_y	4.000	2.000	0.0625	1	0.16	23300	7.4%	11.2%	95.6
13_2_025_x	3.000	3.000	0.0625	1	0.12	20000	5.2%	9.1%	123.1
16_1_025_x	3.750	2.000	0.0625	1	0.06	10000	1.4%	4.8%	581.8
17_1_025_x	4.500	2.500	0.0625	1	0.12	11800	3.9%	11.6%	205.1
17_1_025_y	3.750	3.000	0.0625	1	0.08	12000	2.1%	6.2%	375.0
17_2_025_x	3.000	2.500	0.0625	1	0.17	11960	3.8%	11.1%	169.4
17_2_025_y	3.000	3.000	0.0625	1	0.27	16000	7.2%	15.7%	74.3
17_3_025_x	1.438	3.000	0.0625	1	0.12	11800	3.9%	11.7%	162.7
17_3_025_y	1.500	1.313	0.0625	1	0.23	15000	7.7%	17.9%	69.6
17_3_025_x	1.500	1.500	0.0625	1	0.23	16000	7.7%	16.8%	69.6
17_3_a_1cell_x	1.500	1.500	0.0625	1	0.20	29500	13.8%	16.3%	88.5
17_3_1cell_y	1.500	1.500	0.0625	1	0.23	29000	15.5%	18.7%	69.0
17_3_1cell_x	2.750	2.750	0.0625	1	0.24	31000	15.8%	17.8%	67.5
17_3a_y	2.750	2.750	0.0625	1	0.25	31000	16.9%	19.1%	63.0
17_3a_x	1.375	1.375	0.0625	1	0.25	31000	16.4%	18.5%	65.0
17_3a_y	1.375	1.375	0.0625	1	0.19	14700	7.0%	16.6%	83.3
17_3a_x	1.250	1.250	0.0625	1	0.19	15120	6.9%	15.9%	84.7
17_3a_y	1.250	1.250	0.0625	1	0.19	29300	14.0%	16.8%	82.9
17_3a_y_opt	1.250	1.250	0.0625	1	0.18	26240	12.9%	17.3%	89.9
17_3_y_opt_125	1.250	1.250	0.0625	1	0.13	23250	10.5%	15.8%	121.6
17_3_x_opt_125	1.250	1.250	0.0625	1	0.13	22400	10.7%	16.8%	119.4
17_3_chemetch_y	0.417	0.417	0.0070	0.1	0.04	60000	10.2%	11.9%	336.1
17_3_chemetch	0.833	0.833	0.0070	0.1	0.04	29320	5.0%	21.9%	343.4
17_3_chemetch_x	0.417	0.417	0.0070	0.1	0.04	58400	10.3%	12.4%	332.2
17_3_chemetch_x_010	0.417	0.417	0.0100	0.1	0.03	42700	6.4%	10.4%	377.4
17_3_chemetch_y_010	0.417	0.417	0.0100	0.1	0.03	42950	6.1%	9.9%	395.3
18_1_cell_y	1.250	1.250	0.0625	1	0.09	24000	6.9%	10.0%	186.7
18_1_cell_x	1.250	1.250	0.0625	1	0.11	25800	8.8%	11.9%	145.5
19_1_y	1.500	3.250	0.0625	1	0.06	12400	3.8%	10.7%	129.6
19_1_x	3.250	2.250	0.0625	1	0.02	4600	0.5%	3.6%	1510.5
19_1cell_y	0.750	1.500	0.0625	1	0.03	20950	3.6%	6.0%	296.3
20_1_y	1.500	2.000	0.0625	1	0.61	46000	40.9%	31.1%	19.6
20_1_x	2.000	1.500	0.0625	1	0.02	7000	0.8%	3.8%	1422.2
21_1	2.000	2.000	0.0625	1	0.43	40870	21.6%	18.5%	37.0
21_1	2.000	2.000	0.0625	1	0.07	13600	3.4%	8.6%	238.8
21_1_a	2.000	2.000	0.0625	1	0.10	19700	5.1%	9.0%	158.4
21_1_b	2.000	2.000	0.0625	1	0.08	17600	3.9%	7.8%	205.1
21_1_a_025	2.500	2.500	0.0781	1	0.16	19000	6.3%	11.6%	81.0

(annotation "steel" appears against rows 17_3_chemetch and 17_3_chemetch_x_010)

TABLE 1-continued

21_1_1500_025	3.000	3.000	0.0625	1	0.23	18500	7.7%	14.5%	59.6
21_2	2.000	2.000	0.0625	1	0.07	13300	3.4%	8.9%	235.3
21_2_b	2.000	2.000	0.0625	1	0.07	13000	3.3%	8.8%	243.9
21_2_020	2.000	2.000	0.0625	1	0.13	19480	6.4%	11.4%	126.0
21_2_020	2.500	2.500	0.0781	1	0.20	20000	7.9%	13.9%	64.7
21_2_2_1500_025	3.000	3.000	0.0938	1	0.15	12250	4.9%	13.9%	73.1
22_1	1.000	1.000	0.0625	1	0.05	21000	5.0%	8.3%	320.0
22_1	1.250	1.250	0.0625	1	0.10	27600	7.9%	10.0%	162.1
	1.250	1.250	0.0625	1	0.12	30000	9.2%	10.7%	139.1
22_4	1.250	1.250	0.0625	1	0.14	28000	11.0%	13.8%	115.9
22_4	1.250	1.250	0.0625	1	0.21	38200	16.9%	15.5%	75.8
22_4	2.500	2.500	0.0625	1	0.20	21260	8.2%	13.4%	78.4
1_4_mfg_020	2.89	1.94		0.44	0.207	12930	7.2%	19.4%	25.3
schlecht_1_500_25	0.750	5.000	0.0625	1	0.04	13270	5.5%	14.6%	28.9
schlecht_1_375_25	0.750	3.750	0.0625	1	0.04	13230	5.5%	14.7%	38.5
schlecht_1_375_24	0.750	3.750	0.0625	1	0.05	13960	6.3%	15.7%	34.1
king_core_015end	1.034	5.000	0.0500	1	0.07	40000	6.7%	11.7%	59.9	steel
king_core_010end	1.034	5.000	0.0500	1	0.13	56000	12.2%	15.2%	32.8	steel
king_core_018end_rd	1.034	5.000	0.0500	1	0.06	35000	5.3%	10.6%	75.2	steel
king_core_018end_1_875	1.034	5.000	0.0500	1	0.08	32000	7.5%	16.5%	53.0	steel

	length	pulled	width	load	fixture	deflection	% deflection	"E" psi
0.0625	3.254	3.623	1.94	0.22	0.375	0.369	12.8%	14.16
0.0625	3.225	3.675	1.94	0.22	0.375	0.45	15.8%	11.49
0.0625	3.224	3.632	1.94	0.22	0.375	0.408	14.3%	12.67
0.0625	3.210	3.689	1.94	0.22	0.375	0.479	16.9%	10.74
0.125	3.220	3.495	1.94	0.44	0.375	0.275	9.7%	18.77
0.125	3.236	3.532	1.94	0.44	0.375	0.296	10.3%	17.54
0.125	3.252	3.577	1.94	0.44	0.375	0.325	11.3%	16.06
0.125	3.241	3.534	1.94	0.44	0.375	0.293	10.2%	17.75

The invention claimed is:

1. A flexible skin, comprising:

a bidirectional spring, encapsulated within a flexible solid.

2. A flexible skin according to claim 1, wherein the flexible solid is an elastomeric material.

3. A flexible skin according to claim 2, wherein the elastomeric material is rolled.

4. A flexible skin according to claim 2, wherein the elastomeric material is cast.

5. A flexible skin according to claim 2, wherein the elastomeric material is poured.

6. A flexible skin according to claim 2, wherein the elastomeric material is sprayed.

7. A flexible skin according to claim 2, wherein the elastomeric material is dipped.

8. A flexible skin according to claim 1, wherein the bidirectional spring has flexural properties that vary between the two axes.

9. A flexible skin according to claim 1, wherein flexible printed circuitry is carried by the bi-directional spring.

10. A flexible skin according to claim 1, further comprising:

a second bidirectional spring, encapsulated within a second flexible solid,

the second flexible solid being adhered in a layered manner to the flexible solid.

11. A flexible skin, comprising:

a bi-directional spring, skeletally attached to a flexible membrane.

12. A flexible skin according to claim 11, wherein the flexible membrane attaches to one side of the bi-directional spring.

13. A flexible skin according to claim 11, wherein the flexible membrane attaches to both sides of the bi-directional spring.

14. A method for fabricating a flexible skin, comprising the steps of:

producing a bi-directional spring, and

embedding the bi-directional spring in a flexible solid.

15. A method for fabricating a flexible skin according to claim 14, wherein the bi-directional spring is produced by chemically etching a sheet of material.

16. A method for fabricating a flexible skin according to claim 14, wherein the bidirectional spring is produced by cutting a pattern from a sheet of material, using a rapid cutting process.

17. A method for fabricating a flexible skin according to claim 16, wherein the rapid cutting process is a laser cutting process.

18. A method for fabricating a flexible skin according to claim 16, wherein the rapid cutting process is a waterjet cutting process.

19. A method for fabricating a flexible skin according to claim 14, wherein the bi-directional spring is produced from a metallic material.

20. A method for fabricating a flexible skin according to claim 14, wherein the bi-directional spring is produced from a plastic composite material.

21. A method for fabricating a flexible skin according to claim 14, wherein the bi-directional spring is embedded in the flexible solid by dipping the bi-directional spring in an uncured elastomer and then curing the elastomer.

22. A method for fabricating a flexible skin according to claim 14, wherein the bi-directional spring is embedded in the flexible solid by spraying elastomeric material over the bi-directional spring.

23. A method for fabricating a flexible skin according to claim 14, wherein the bi-directional spring is embedded in the flexible solid by pouring elastomeric material over the bi-directional spring.

24. A method for fabricating a flexible skin according to claim 14, wherein the bi-directional spring is embedded in the flexible solid by brushing elastomeric material over the bi-directional spring.

25. A method for fabricating a flexible skin, comprising the steps of:

producing a bi-directional spring, and

adhering a flexible membrane to a surface of the bi-directional spring.

26. A method for fabricating a flexible skin, comprising the steps of:

producing a bi-directional spring, and adhering a flexible membrane to each surface of the bi-directional spring.

27. A method for fabricating a flexible skin according to claim 25, further comprising the step of adhering a second flexible skin to the flexible skin.

28. A method for fabricating a flexible skin according to claim 14, further comprising the step of adhering a second flexible skin to the flexible skin.

29. A flexible skin according to claim 1, further comprising a piezoelectric element embedded within the flexible solid.

30. A flexible skin according to claim 11, further comprising a piezoelectric element bonded to a surface of the bi-directional spring.

31. A flexible skin according to claim 11, further comprising a piezoelectric element bonded to the flexible membrane.

32. A method for fabricating a flexible skin according to claim 25, further comprising the step of bonding a piezoelectric element to a surface of the bi-directional spring.

33. A method for fabricating a flexible skin according to claim 25, further comprising the step of bonding a piezoelectric element to the flexible membrane.

34. A method of fabricating a flexible skin according to claim 14, further comprising the step of embedding printed circuitry within the flexible solid.

35. A method for fabricating a flexible skin according to claim 25, further comprising the step of bonding printed circuitry to a surface of the bi-directional spring.

36. A method for fabricating a flexible skin according to claim 25, further comprising the step of bonding printed circuitry to the flexible membrane.

* * * * *

US008498756B1

(12) **United States Patent**

Sarver

(10) Patent No.: **US 8,498,756 B1**
(45) Date of Patent: **Jul. 30, 2013**

(54) **MOVABLE GROUND BASED RECOVERY SYSTEM FOR REUSEABLE SPACE FLIGHT HARDWARE**

(75) Inventor: **George L. Sarver**, Sunnyvale, CA (US)

(73) Assignee: **The United States of America as Represented by the Adminstrator of the National Aeronautics & Space Administration (NASA)**, Washington, DC (US)

(*) Notice: Subject to any disclaimer, the term of this patent is extended or adjusted under 35 U.S.C. 154(b) by 111 days.

(21) Appl. No.: **13/213,022**

(22) Filed: **Aug. 18, 2011**

(51) **Int. Cl.**
G05D 1/00	(2006.01)
G05D 3/00	(2006.01)
G06F 7/00	(2006.01)
G06F 17/00	(2006.01)

(52) **U.S. Cl.**
USPC **701/1**

(58) **Field of Classification Search**
USPC 701/1, 244/158.1, 158.9
See application file for complete search history.

(56) **References Cited**

U.S. PATENT DOCUMENTS

2,923,504	A	*	2/1960	Ortega et al. .... 244/114 R
3,093,346	A		6/1963	Faget et al.
3,132,825	A		5/1964	Postle et al.
3,310,261	A		3/1967	Rogallo et al.
3,532,179	A		10/1970	McCreary
3,702,688	A		11/1972	Faget et al.
5,064,151	A	*	11/1991	Cerimele et al. 244/172.1
5,522,470	A		6/1996	Stiegler et al.
7,392,964	B1	*	7/2008	Anderman 244/158.2
7,650,253	B2		1/2010	Weed et al.

2002/0035419	A1	*	3/2002	Lin 701/27
2007/0012820	A1		1/2007	Buehler
2007/0016371	A1	*	1/2007	Waid et al. 701/213
2010/0052948	A1		3/2010	Vian et al.
2011/0017872	A1		1/2011	Bezos et al.

FOREIGN PATENT DOCUMENTS

EP	09167658.5	A2	2/2010

OTHER PUBLICATIONS

NASA—Resusable Solid Rocket Motor and Solid Rocket Boosters, Jeane Ryba, Dec. 10, 2009.*
Johnson, Handbook of Soviet Manned Space Flight, 1980, 119-122, Univelt, Inc., San Diego, California.
Gaubatz, DC-X Results and the Next Step, Proceedings of AIAA Space Programs and Technologies Conference and Exhibit, Sep. 27-29, 1994, Huntsville, Alabama, AIAA, Washington, D.C.

* cited by examiner

Primary Examiner — Mary Cheung
Assistant Examiner — Frederick Brushaber
(74) *Attorney, Agent, or Firm* — John F. Schipper; Robert M. Padilla; Christopher J. Menke

(57) **ABSTRACT**

A reusable space flight launch system is configured to eliminate complex descent and landing systems from the space flight hardware and move them to maneuverable ground based systems. Precision landing of the reusable space flight hardware is enabled using a simple, light weight aerodynamic device on board the flight hardware such as a parachute, and one or more translating ground based vehicles such as a hovercraft that include active speed, orientation and directional control. The ground based vehicle maneuvers itself into position beneath the descending flight hardware, matching its speed and direction and captures the flight hardware. The ground based vehicle will contain propulsion, command and GN&C functionality as well as space flight hardware landing cushioning and retaining hardware. The ground based vehicle propulsion system enables longitudinal and transverse maneuverability independent of its physical heading.

19 Claims, 5 Drawing Sheets

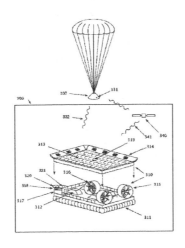

255

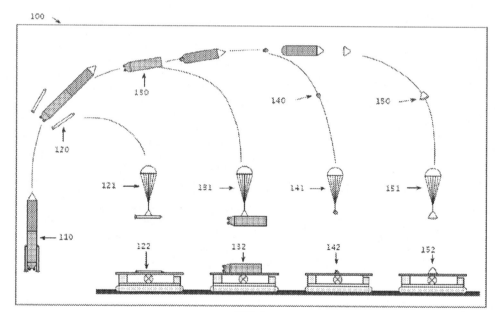

FIG. 1

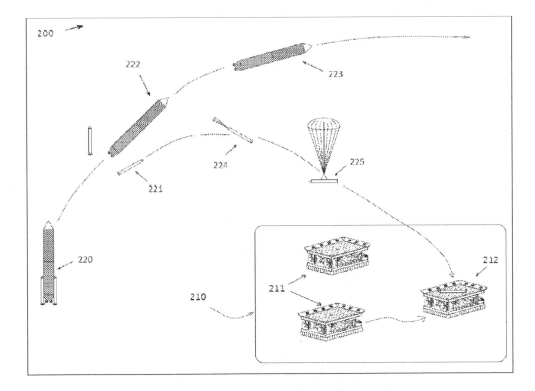

FIG.2

257

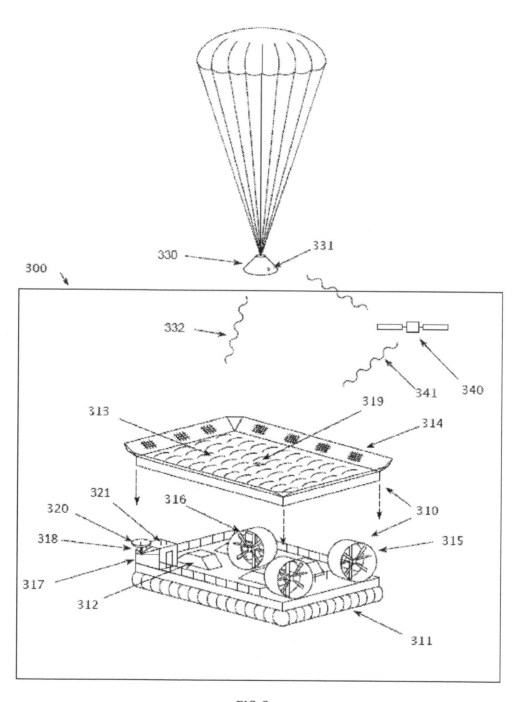

FIG. 3

258

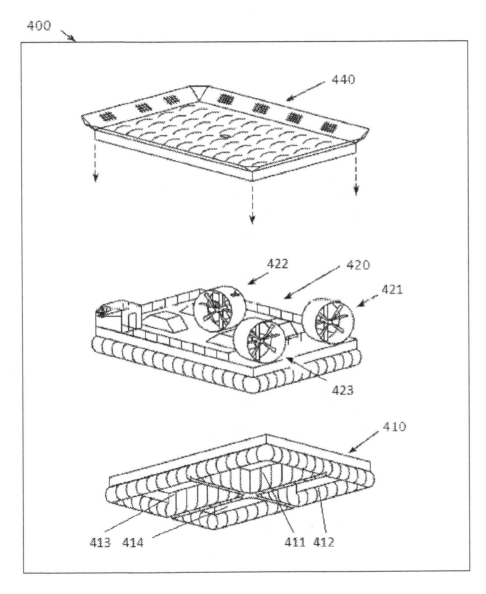

FIG. 4A

259

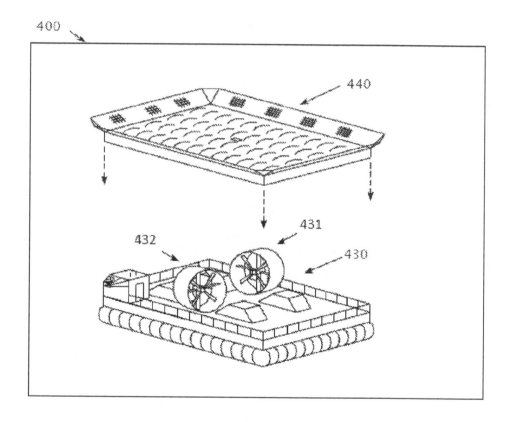

FIG. 4B

MOVABLE GROUND BASED RECOVERY SYSTEM FOR REUSEABLE SPACE FLIGHT HARDWARE

ORIGIN OF THE INVENTION

This invention was made, in part, by one or more employees of the U.S. government. The U.S. government has the right to make, use and/sell the invention described herein without payment of compensation, including but not limited to payment of royalties.

TECHNICAL FIELD OF INVENTION

An aspect of this invention relates generally to a low-cost reusable space launch system, and more particularly to a system featuring a distributed approach to configure key elements of the landing system, including guidance, navigation and control, where an actively controlled ground vehicle is used in an innovative manner to recover flight hardware such as a spacecraft or launch booster.

BACKGROUND OF INVENTION

In theory, a design incorporating a reusable spacecraft or booster can significantly reduce the cost of access to space. In order to realize these theoretical benefits, the launch vehicle must satisfy two design elements: 1) substantial elements of the launch vehicle and spacecraft must be reusable (either in full or in component) and 2) as costs scale with system size and complexity, the launch vehicle must be as small and simple as practicably possible.

Reusable suborbital or orbital flight hardware has been traditionally configured following two approaches. The first is to fit the reusable hardware with a precision landing system. The second is to fit the reusable hardware with a simple parachute and allow the hardware to fall to the surface. The Space Shuttle Orbiter is an example of the first approach to reusability. The orbiter features wings and landing gear; it glides to land on a long, but otherwise conventional runway. The Space Shuttle Solid Rocket Motors are an example of the second approach to reusability. After their fuel is expended, they fall into the ocean by parachute where they are later recovered.

Present approaches to reusable spacecraft and booster design do so at great impact to vehicle design. The inherent physics of a launch vehicle results in a system where only a few percentage points of the total gross-lift-off-weight are available for payload. (For example, the Space Shuttle has a net payload of less than 1.22% of its total gross-lift-of-weight). Any increase in fixed weight on the orbital or suborbital elements of a launch vehicle must be accounted for by a reduction in payload capability or an increase in the overall size of the system.

For a fixed size launch vehicle, with a small payload fraction, even a small percentage point increase in fixed weight among the heavier booster elements will radically reduce the launch vehicle's payload capacity.

For a conceptual launch vehicle, flying a design payload along an equivalent trajectory, these weight penalties of reusable systems will increase the gross-lift-off-weight in a multiplicative, rather than additive, fashion.

Typical reusable technologies to enable a precision landing system (lifting bodies or wings) weigh considerably more than reusable technologies that lack precision landing capability (parachutes).

2

Without precision landing capabilities, reusable spacecraft and boosters are typically retrieved at sea. A water landing, resulting in salt-water immersion of space flight hardware, is detrimental to the reusability of complex space flight hardware. After an ocean recovery, only the casings of the Space Shuttle Solid Rocket Boosters can be reused. The boosters must be otherwise re-manufactured. For example, all electronics, having been exposed to the corrosive salt-water environment, must be replaced at considerable expense.

A method to ensure precision landings of reusable space launch flight hardware (either spacecraft of boosters) that would distribute heavy elements of recovery, propulsion, guidance, navigation and control to non-flight hardware could enable a radical reduction in the size, complexity and hence cost, of hardware used to launch payloads into space.

The design of recoverable and reusable spacecraft or launch vehicle (space flight hardware) elements has been well established in practice.

In U.S. Pat. No. 3,093,346, entitled "Space Capsule," Faget illustrates a means to employ a parachute to enable the intact recovery of a returning spacecraft. A parachute is an embodiment of a concept of a lightweight, deployable membrane that provides only drag. A parachute is used to enable ballistic recovery of an object.

In U.S. Pat. No. 3,310,261, entitled "Control for Flexible Parawing," Rogallo and Sleeman illustrate the evolution of a simple parachute into a parafoil. A parafoil is an embodiment of a concept of a lightweight, deployable membrane wing that can produce lift, drag and stabilizing forces and moments. A parafoil is used to enable the gliding recovery of an object.

The McDonnell Douglas DC-X (see: "DC-X Results and the Next Step," AIAA 94-4674 demonstrated a concept for a reusable spacecraft using a retro-rocket system. The retro-rocket is used in lieu of a parachute to facilitate precision guidance, navigation and control for a soft landing. The DC-X featured space flight hardware where the engine is deployed and restarted after atmospheric reentry. The thrust from the engine is used to decelerate and orient the flight hardware vertically. With the rocket firing, the vehicle will then execute a precision vertical landing onto a specific landing site.

In U.S. Pat. No. 3,132,825, entitled "Space Atmosphere Vehicle," Postle illustrates the recovery of a spacecraft or launch vehicle element through shaping of the overall configuration into a lifting body. The lifting body is an embodiment of a concept of a rigid aeroshell with surface detailing that produces lift, drag and other stabilizing forces and moments.

In U.S. Pat. No. 3,702,688, entitled "Space Shuttle Vehicle and System," Faget teaches a more conventional approach to recovery. As found on the Space Shuttle Orbiter, this approach embodies wings and tail surfaces incorporated into the reusable flight hardware. This permits the flight hardware to glide to a landing on a conventional runway.

Examples of prior art configuration generally used to prevent a returning spacecraft lacking precision landing capabilities from destructive impact with the ground include 1) landing in water (Faget: U.S. Pat. No. 3,093,346 see above), 2) air capture using a airplane or helicopter (Mulcahy: U.S. Pat. No. 3,137,465), and 3) firing retro rockets just prior to impact (see a description of the Soyuz capsule in Handbook of Soviet Manned Space Flight, p. 119-121, ISBN 0-08803-115). In the former, the flight hardware is immersed in salt water making the design of a reusable spacecraft much more complex and heavy. In air capture, the relative size of an aircraft or helicopter to the returning flight vehicle limits its use to small capsules. This technique also is not compatible

3

with large flight vehicles due to the potential of failed capture causing the loss of the parachute and uncontrolled descent into the ground. Retro-rockets and air bags are used to cushion the landing of the flight vehicle. In these systems, the rockets or air bags add significant weight to the flight hardware and typically do not compensate for any lateral motion at landing causing significant side loads and a possibility of roll over at landing. This leads to increased structural mass of the vehicle.

Airborne recovery of spacecraft is a hazardous operation and is not suitable for manned flight vehicles. Air capture of a returning spacecraft can cause the loss of the parachute system in a failed capture event; the spacecraft would then fall to ground at a high velocity.

A ground based recovery system that occurs at zero altitude can be man rated.

Examples of prior art configurations involving a sea based recovery platform coupled with a retro-rocket technology precision vertical landing flight hardware includes US Patent Application 2011/0017872, "Sea landing of space launch vehicles and associated systems and methods." Here, Bezos describes a spacecraft recovery system comprising a ship fitted with a landing surface that is pre-positioned in the general reentry region. The reusable flight hardware elements, after re-entry, reorient themselves tail first, and perform a powered, vertical landing upon the ship mounted platform.

U.S. Pat. No. 2,923,504 ("Safety Landing Platform for Aircraft," Ortega and Wallace) teaches that a system comprising an energy absorbing landing platform attached to a moving ground based vehicle may be used to simplify the landing gear design of an airplane. While this patent describes a vehicle that is in motion at the time of capture, the wheeled has only limited steering capability.

Hovercraft are air cushion vehicles, employing the principle of aerodynamic levitation of a structure above a surface. McCreary in U.S. Pat. No. 3,532,179, entitled "Aerodynamic Lifting Device and Method of Lifting," where the air cushion is formed by means of a flexible, pneumatically stabilized diaphragm underlying the vehicle, teaches the design principles of a modern hovercraft.

All of the above references are hereby incorporated by reference.

SUMMARY OF INVENTION

An aspect of the invention is a method for capturing reusable space flight hardware that passes through an atmosphere in an approach to a terrestrial surface with a general landing region identified on the terrestrial surface in which the space flight hardware will land. One or more ground based vehicles that are movable and maneuverable are pre-positioned in the general landing region. The space flight hardware has an atmospheric deceleration system that when activated allows the space flight hardware to descend in reaction to aerodynamic and gravitational forces acting upon the space flight hardware and the deceleration system. The absolute and relative positions of the space flight hardware and the ground based vehicle are measured and the trajectory of the space flight hardware is estimated as it descends. The ground based vehicle is maneuvered using the measured absolute and relative positions and the estimated trajectory to capture the space flight hardware. In one embodiment, the components of a recovery guidance, navigation and control are located on the ground based vehicle system rather than on the space flight hardware.

4

Another aspect of the invention is drawn to a hovercraft used to capture and recover space flight hardware that passes through an atmosphere in an approach to a terrestrial surface. The hovercraft includes a surface effect levitation system comprising one or more flexible skirts and a pressurization mechanism and a landing platform to mechanically capture the space flight hardware. The hovercraft propulsion system is capable of maneuvering the hovercraft in forward/aft translation, left/right translation and directional rotation (compass heading) independently of each other. Additionally, guidance, navigation and control (GN&C) hardware located on the hovercraft that directs motion of the hovercraft to maneuver itself beneath the descending space flight hardware, substantially matching the space flight hardware speed and direction when the landing platform captures the space flight hardware.

BRIEF DESCRIPTION OF DRAWINGS

FIG. 1 is a schematic diagram illustrating the overall mission profile of a reusable space launch system where reusable booster and spacecraft elements are recovered using a translating ground based recovery system.

FIG. 2 is a schematic diagram illustrating the terminal mission profile of a reusable space launch system where reusable booster and spacecraft elements are recovered using a translating ground based recovery system.

FIG. 3 is a schematic diagram illustrating the ground based recovery system including flight hardware recovery, propulsion, steering, command and GN&C elements.

FIG. 4a is a schematic diagram of one embodiment of illustrating the ground based recovery system including flight hardware recovery, propulsion and surface effect skirts.

FIG. 4b is a schematic diagram of an alternative embodiment illustrating the ground based recovery system including flight hardware recovery, propulsion and surface effect skirts.

DETAILED DESCRIPTION

FIG. 1 shows a reusable space launch vehicle system 100 where significant elements of the launch vehicle 110 and spacecraft 150 are reusable. The reusable launch vehicle may comprise a fully reusable solid rocket booster 120, a fully reusable liquid rocket booster 130, or a partially reusable liquid rocket booster featuring a jettisonable engine pod 140.

In order to reduce the complexity of each reusable space flight hardware element, their respective recovery system will omit elements of guidance, navigation and control (GN&C) capability used for precision landing. Because any increase in the empty weight of a rocket launch system materially diminishes from its payload capability, a simple, lightweight landing parachute system to a heavier aerodynamic (wings) or propulsion (retro-rocket) based approach. Every electromechanical component required for active recovery guidance, navigation and control (GN&C) requires power. Electronics, batteries and actuators displace volume that could otherwise be used for fuel. Consequently, a design that relocates components typically found on board the space flight article to a ground based vehicle leaving only a passive parachute, will have a multiplicative effect in decreasing the complexity and weight of the booster or spacecraft. The word "ground" as generally referred to herein is intended to include both land and sea. A hovercraft, while typically operated at sea, could perform its recovery mission on land given a wide expanse of smooth, flat terrain.

Capture and recovery of these flight hardware elements will be affected by one or more translating ground based recovery vehicles **122**, **132**, **142** and **152**. These vehicles will allow the reusable flight hardware to have a dry recovery at sea; no portion of the flight hardware will ever become immersed in seawater. The protection of the flight hardware from the corrosive effects of submersion enhances reusability of all components. In addition, this means of cushioned landing is safer for any returning astronauts on board a spacecraft.

For example, a reusable solid rocket booster **120** will be fitted with a deployable parachute or parafoil **121**, suitable to decelerate it to a sufficiently low vertical velocity to affect recovery using the ground based landing system **122** without mechanical damage.

For example, a reusable liquid rocket booster **130** will be designed to return to the earth's surface without damage. The booster **130** also will be fitted with deployable parachute or parafoil **131**, suitable to decelerate it to a sufficiently low vertical velocity to affect recovery using the ground based landing system **132** without mechanical damage.

For example, reusable components (such as an engine pod) from an upper stage liquid rocket booster **140** may be jettisoned from the upper stage. These components will be designed to return to the earth's surface without damage. The engine pod **140** also will be fitted with deployable parachute or parafoil **141**, suitable to decelerate it to a sufficiently low vertical velocity to affect recovery using the ground based landing system **142** without mechanical damage.

For example, a reusable or recoverable spacecraft **150** will be designed to reenter the earth's atmosphere without damage. The spacecraft **150** also will be fitted with deployable parachute or parafoil **151**, suitable to decelerate it to a sufficiently low vertical velocity to affect recovery using the landing system **152** without mechanical damage.

For each booster or spacecraft element to be recovered, the system will employ one or more translating ground based recovery systems. For example, 1) the reusable solid rocket booster **120** will be associated with a ground recovery system **122**, 2) the reusable liquid solid rocket booster **130** will be associated with a ground recovery system **132**, 3) the reusable upper stage components **140** will be associated with a ground recovery system **142**, and 4) the reusable spacecraft **150** will be associated with a ground recovery system **152**. These systems **122**, **132**, **142** and **152** may be comprised of similar or different embodiments of this invention.

An embodiment of the present invention features a translating ground based recovery system **122**, **132**, **142** and **152**, which may comprise one or more hovercraft, or other surface vehicle, having active speed and direction control capability capable of rapid longitudinal and transverse motion upon either land or water.

Current hovercraft have been configured to have their principal propulsion system oriented to provide thrust along a dominant axis. Thrust vectoring is typically used to alter vehicle heading, rather than provide direct side force control. Thus conventional hovercraft design practice results in a vehicle that is "steered" to control position and heading in a manner consistent with a ship. However, the hovercraft principle is amenable to fitment of propulsion devices where axial and transverse thrust is directly controlled independently of the heading. With such a propulsion configuration, the hovercraft could be commanded to "crab" in translation independent of the compass heading of its structure. The propulsion system required to enable this capability will be described later.

Production hovercraft have been built in a wide variety of sizes and configurations. Commercially produced hovercraft have been engineered to operate at a maximum continuous speed of over 80 knots. Hovercraft with this speed capability

have been constructed at sizes exceeding 500 tons and 150 feet in overall length. A larger hovercraft may be desirable for capture of the largest or most critical flight hardware elements. A smaller hovercraft, of a size equivalent to the production LCAC (built by Textron for the US Navy) may prove desirable. The LCAC (180 tons overall, 150,000 pound payload, and 87 foot overall length) integrates its operations with US Navy operated amphibious well deck ships.

Current production hovercraft have been engineered to operate successfully under conditions up to Sea State 4. This sea state implies the vehicle will operate in the presence of significant waves as high as 6 feet, with the occasional 9 foot wave. Current production hovercraft have been sized for relatively short range operations, with advertised ranges of 300 to 400 nautical Miles.

The ground based recovery system **122**, **132**, **142** and **152**, comprises a heterogeneous redistribution of systems design elements. The heavy, complex and propulsive elements are allocated to the ground based hardware leaving only lightest weight and simplest elements on the flight hardware. This fractionated approach to systems design reduces the weight and complexity of the flight hardware. For equivalent payload capability, the reduction in weight and complexity of the booster or spacecraft combined with its multiplicative effect upon vehicle sizing will result in a smaller, lighter and less complex space launch system.

FIG. **2** shows a recovery scenario in **200**. Operationally, one or more ground based recovery systems **211** would be pre-positioned into the general landing area prior to launch or reentry **210**. While only one ground based vehicle would affect the actual capture of the flight hardware, in the event of high winds or speed limiting surface conditions, multiple ground based systems can be employed to recover systems that have a large landing error ellipse. Under unfavorable conditions, it is foreseeable that a single recovery system might be unable to capture the target.

The reusable launch vehicle **220** will be launched. Upon burnout, the elements to recover will be jettisoned **221** from the remainder of the launch vehicle **222**. The upper stage elements **223** will continue in flight.

The reusable flight hardware will approach the surface in reaction to aerodynamic and gravitational forces acting upon it.

During re-entry, the flight hardware would follow an essentially ballistic trajectory.

The reusable flight hardware would activate the deceleration system at an appropriate time during descent, deploying the aerodynamic device **224**. The parachute, parafoil or other aerodynamic device when fully deployed will decelerate the booster or spacecraft to a low vertical speed.

After this time, the trajectory of the flight hardware becomes dominated by aerodynamic forces where atmospheric winds interact with the aerodynamic deceleration device.

The parachute or parafoil system associated with the flight hardware will be configured to orient the flight hardware in manner best suited to reduce landing loads. Because landing design loads typically influence the weight of the flight hardware, this attribute of the ground based recovery system will directly save structural weight on the flight hardware. The parachute might hold the solid rocket booster or other cylindrical flight hardware element in a near horizontal orientation **225**.

The deceleration device need not provide any active steering or energy management capability. In one embodiment, only a passive parachute is needed; all other descent and landing systems have been transferred to ground based hardware. In another embodiment, a mixed system is envisioned where the majority of the descent and landing hardware is ground based, but the flight hardware retains limited steering or energy management systems. A system utilizing a parafoil would be an example of a system where the deceleration device has limited steering capability.

Lacking an active flight control system suitable for precision approach and landing, the flight hardware would descend to approach the surface where its trajectory will be influenced by external unsteady aerodynamic forces from atmospheric winds and turbulence.

Elements on-board the ground based recovery system **211** will measure the absolute and relative positions of the flight hardware and the ground vehicle. In one embodiment, position and velocity measurements can be made by the flight vehicle and transmitted to the ground vehicle. The GN&C system to estimate the trajectory of the flight hardware as it descends towards the ground. The GN&C system will then provide position automated guidance to the ground based vehicle based upon the estimated trajectory.

The ground based vehicle **210**, using its propulsion and steering capability will position itself so that it is beneath and matching the ground speed and direction of the descending flight hardware as closely as possible at the moment of capture **212**. This will minimize the relative velocities between the ground vehicle and the flight hardware ensuring the "softest" possible landing. The lateral relative velocities will be low, reducing the structural loads on the flight vehicle. Because landing design loads typically influence the weight of the space flight hardware, this attribute of the ground based recovery system can directly lead to lighter weight flight hardware.

The ground based vehicle will mechanically capture the descending spacecraft or booster using a passive or active capture mechanism.

As shown in FIG. 3, a ground based recovery system **300**, embodied as a hovercraft **310**, may be comprised of surface effect vehicle elements **311** and **312**, flight hardware recovery elements **313** and **314**, propulsion and steering elements **315** and **316**, a command element **317** and a guidance, navigation and control (GN&C) element **318**. These elements will be discussed in order.

To facilitate recovery, the ground vehicle should be highly maneuverable. Orientation and translational heading must be decoupled. Therefore, forwards/aft translation, left/right translation and rotation of hovercraft to different compass headings must be independently controllable. The recovery hovercraft **310** is an embodiment of a ground vehicle with high speed that can maneuver in translation and heading separately from rotation. The hovercraft will be controlled in physical heading and well as translational heading to orient its landing platform to match the principal longitudinal axis of the descending space flight hardware. This will align the center of mass of the flight hardware with the center of the landing platform. This procedure minimizes the chance that the space flight hardware overhangs the landing platform, and reduces any tendency for the hovercraft to roll or pitch due to the impact loading.

The recovery hovercraft **310** is embodied as comprising basic surface effect vehicle elements providing pressurization of one or more air cushions using a flexible pneumatically stabilized diaphragm **311**, pressurized by one or more hover fans **312**.

The ground based vehicle will mechanically capture the descending spacecraft or booster. The flight hardware recovery elements may comprise of a landing cushion **313** and recovery netting **314**. In an embodiment, the landing cushion

313 would utilize pneumatic mechanisms to absorb energy. However, other forms of cushioning or netting may be used to absorb energy during capture. The side recovery netting will prevent the flight hardware from falling overboard after capture. A passive system may comprise energy absorbing surfaces and retaining netting. An active system may comprise elements such as controllable pneumatic air bags. Pneumatic air bags, netting and cabling will secure the flight hardware after landing.

The cushioned landing platform will reduce landing loads on the recovered booster or spacecraft **330**. The capture mechanism can prevent the flight hardware from rolling over or skidding at landing.

The primary propulsion elements **315** and **316**, may be embodied by a system comprising of one or more vectored thrust propulsors and/or discrete orthogonally configured propulsors. This design permits the hovercraft ground vehicle to operate at high speeds (above 70 knots) and allows it to maneuver in two orthogonal transverse directions without the need to "steer" in rotation. Conventional practice fits the vectored thrust propulsors at one end that permits the hovercraft to move forwards and aft and to steer in direction. However, conventional practice does not permit yawing moments to be decoupled from longitudinal and transverse forces. With multiple propulsors, the hovercraft is capable of maneuvering in forward/aft translation, left/right translation and yaw independent of each other. Such a propulsion configuration will also permit the hovercraft to be conventionally "steered" to a specific heading.

The command element **317** may comprise of fully automatic, electronic system or may include a human operator as an on-board or remote pilot. The command element will coordinate the overall operation of the hovercraft. It will coordinate and direct the operation of the hovercraft when it is not being used to effect capture of flight hardware. During the hardware capture process, the command element will coordinate any active recovery cushioning **313** or netting **314** functionality as well as propulsion **315** and **316** and GN&C elements **318**.

The GN&C system **318** may comprise elements that will determine the absolute and relative positions of the descending flight hardware and the ground based recovery system. The GN&C system may be comprised of elements that: 1) estimate the present and future location of the ground based recovery system, 2) estimate the present and future location of the descending flight hardware, 3) compute speed and direction necessary to ensure that the ground based recovery system is beneath the flight hardware with minimal relative motion at the moment of capture.

The GN&C system **318** will infer real-time descent trajectories of the flight hardware resulting from atmospheric winds. The GN&C system will be comprised of a number of distinct elements, with relatively few, if any, elements placed on-board the flight hardware.

In an embodiment, GN&C elements include those that optically **319** estimate the location and trajectory of the descending flight hardware **330**. Electro-optical trackers and seekers use ambient visible light to locate the flight hardware.

GN&C elements may also comprise a RADAR system **320** to estimate the location and trajectory of the descending flight hardware **330**. RADAR uses actively generated radio frequency signals to locate the flight hardware.

GN&C elements may also comprise a global positioning system (GPS) receiver **321** on board the ground based recovery system to infer positions from global positioning system satellites **340** that broadcast signals **341**.

GN&C elements may also comprise a global positioning system (GPS) receiver **331** and active transponder **332** on the flight hardware to estimate its location and transmit that information to the ground based recovery system **300**.

Knowledge of the absolute and relative positions of the descending flight hardware and the ground based recovery system will allow the GN&C system to infer the basic trajectory as well as the effects of atmospheric winds upon the present and future location of the descending flight hardware. This information can be utilized by the command guidance algorithm in the GN&C system in order to affect capture of the flight hardware.

The recovery hovercraft **310** is sized to be large enough to capture the returning flight hardware. As noted, production hovercraft, such as the LCAC have been sized to accommodate payloads as heavy as 150,000 pounds. In comparison, the first stage of a Titan IIIb launch vehicle is 70 feet long, but weighs only 10,500 pounds empty. Similarly, the planned weight of the Orion space capsule is 19,650 pounds. Therefore, a useful hovercraft ground recovery system may be derived from existing production hardware.

Typical reentry flight hardware is fitted with a parachute sized to provide a ballistic coefficient high enough to reduce the terminal vertical velocity of the flight hardware to a speed of approximately 25 feet per second (or 15 knots). Reentry navigation is sufficiently accurate to provide an error ellipse approximately 3.25 nautical miles long by 2.75 nautical miles wide at the time of main parachute opening. With the main parachute opening at altitudes of approximately 10,000 feet above sea level, the flight hardware will have approximately 400 seconds of descent under the main parachute before touchdown.

Apollo spacecraft recovery wind speeds ranged from calm to 18 knots and the wave height ranged from calm to 6 ft. These conditions approximate those experienced in conditions from sea states 0 through sea state 4. Winds aloft may be stronger yet, with sustained winds of 19 knots and gusts.

In order to affect capture, the hovercraft would be prepositioned in the center of the predicted error ellipse. As the spacecraft maneuvers to enter the atmosphere and while it is entering, it sends its position and velocity information to the hovercraft that updates the landing error ellipse prediction using the telemetry and latest weather, winds, etc. The hovercraft continually maneuvers to the center of the landing error ellipse as the prediction is updated.

Once the parachutes open, the hovercraft moves to intercept the descending space flight hardware. The hovercraft must be able to traverse the distance from its starting point to the spacecraft and then track the motion of the flight hardware as it descends, remaining directly underneath the spacecraft until the spacecraft lands on the hovercraft platform. A typical guided spacecraft would be expected to land within about 3 nautical miles of the predicted landing location. Typical parachute opening altitudes and decent speeds result in about 5 minutes from parachute opening to landing. In this foreseeable scenario, where the parachute opens near the edge of the error ellipse, and prevailing winds blow the flight hardware further off course, the hovercraft would need to attain a mean speed of approximately 45 knots to traverse the 4 nautical miles in order to place itself beneath the flight hardware one minute prior to landing. This sort of mean speed is entirely realistic; current hovercraft have demonstrated peak speeds in excess of 80 knots.

Operationally, two or more hovercraft would be employed in a mission critical scenario in order to provide coverage of vehicles with significantly larger landing error ellipses.

In a reasonable scenario, during the final 60 seconds, the hovercraft would continue to maneuver itself to position itself directly beneath the descending flight hardware. In order to attain precision positioning of the hovercraft to affect capture, it must have a propulsion system to enable the required agility. It is desired that the hovercraft can maneuver in two orthogonal transverse directions at speeds of the same order of magnitude as the expected steady and transient winds (roughly 20 knots).

For example, if the winds are prevailing to the east at 20 knots, the descending flight hardware will be blown eastward at that speed. The hovercraft would need to head east at 20 knots. If there were unsteady gusts blowing alternatively to the north and south, the hovercraft would need to track this transient motion in order to affect capture. Ideally, to obtain this positional authority would not require the vehicle to "steer" in rotation in order to affect translation. Thus, the hovercraft could align itself in heading to capture flight hardware such as slender booster rockets without affecting its positional accuracy. This enables the hovercraft to match the mean and instantaneous surface speed and direction of the descending flight hardware.

As shown in FIG. 4A, the hovercraft **400** will have an air cushion surface effect levitation system that will comprise of one or more chambers provided by flexible, pneumatically stabilized diaphragms **410**. In an embodiment, the hovercraft air cushion is subdivided into four chambers, **411**, **412**, **413** and **414**. These chambers will be configured to provide roll and pitch stability commensurate with both the expected speed of the hovercraft and the expected impact loading resulting from flight hardware capture. The four chambers will provide additional stability at capture.

The hovercraft propulsion system will be sized to provide the necessary speed, agility and maneuverability for the hovercraft **400** to place itself beneath the descending flight hardware at the time of capture. The overall thrust and its frequency response to modulation will be chosen commensurate with the need of the hovercraft guidance, navigation and control system.

Using a GN&C system comprising elements such as optical **319**, RADAR **320** and GPS **321** sub-elements, differential position measurements between the hovercraft and the flight hardware can be determined to the order of a few inches. The feedback control system would modulate the thrust of the various propulsion units in order to ensure minimum relative lateral and transverse motion with respect to the descending flight hardware at the time of capture.

In an embodiment, shown in FIG. 4A, the hovercraft propulsion system **420** will be comprised of three or more propulsion unit fans fixed relative to the hovercraft structure mounted in a manner to permit the hovercraft to maneuver in two orthogonal transverse directions without a need to "steer" in rotation. In one embodiment, the orientation of propulsion units **421**, **422** and **423** are essentially orthogonal to one another. Propulsors **421** and **423** provide longitudinal forces, propulsor **422** provides transverse forces. Differential longitudinal forces between propulsors **421** and **423** will provide yawing moments. Modulation of thrust among the various propulsors will provide acceleration to move the hovercraft in any compass direction independently of the compass heading of its front. Modulation of thrust among the various propulsors will rotate the hovercraft so that it may "steer" in rotation in a more conventional manner. Thrust modulation may be attained either by varying the speed or the pitch of fan blades within the propulsor. A constant speed fan with variable pitch blades will offer more rapid thrust modulation than a variable speed fan.

In another embodiment, shown in FIG. 4B, the hovercraft propulsion system **430** will be comprised of one or more vectored thrust propulsion unit fans **431** and **432** mounted in a manner to permit the hovercraft to maneuver in two orthogonal transverse directions with or without a need to "steer" in rotation. Propulsor **431** and **432** can independently vector and modulate thrust. These forces will provide acceleration to move the hovercraft in any compass direction independently of the compass heading of its front. Vectoring and modulation of thrust among the various propulsors will rotate the hovercraft so that it may "steer" in rotation in a more conventional manner. Thrust modulation may be attained either by varying the speed or the pitch of fan blades within the propulsor. Vectoring may be arraigned either by rotating the entire fan assembly, or by fitting air deflectors, ducts or rudders to each fan assembly. A constant speed fan with variable pitch blades will offer more rapid thrust modulation than a variable speed fan. Movable air deflector "rudders" will offer faster response times than a rotating fan assembly.

The landing platform **440**, shown in both FIGS. 4A and 4B, will capture the flight hardware without damage or exposure to seawater. The platform **440** may be comprised of one or more embodiments of the invention. In one form of an embodiment, the platform **440** is an inflatable pneumatic surface. In an alternative embodiment, the landing platform **440** is a flexible solid surface. In a third embodiment, the landing platform **440** is a flexible open surface such as a net. Other embodiments may include elements of each type into an overall system.

In one embodiment of the invention, once the space flight hardware has been recovered and secured to the landing platform **440**, the hardware and platform may be removed from the hovercraft as a unit, potentially facilitating safe transfer of the hardware to other locations.

The hovercraft **400** must be sized to contain a usable amount of fuel. If the hovercraft is sized to operate from shore-based points, it must have sufficient fuel to travel from its base to the general recovery region and back. In the event that the hovercraft is sized to be compatible with existing amphibious well deck ships, as operated by the US Navy, it may be sized for shorter unrefueled range and operate far from any port. In this scenario, once the hovercraft recovers the flight hardware, it is cocooned inside the amphibious well of the mothership. The recovered flight hardware would be fully protected from the elements.

What is claimed is:

1. A method for capturing reusable space flight hardware that passes through an atmosphere in an approach to a terrestrial surface, the method comprising:
   estimating a trajectory of the space flight hardware as the hardware descends;
   identifying a target landing region on the terrestrial surface that the estimated trajectory will intersect as the hardware approaches the terrestrial surface;
   providing at least one ground based vehicle that is movable and maneuverable and that comprises a hovercraft having a landing platform on which the hardware is to be captured;
   pre-positioning the at least one ground based vehicle in the target landing region so that the estimated trajectory intersects at least a portion of the landing platform;
   providing an atmospheric deceleration system on the space flight hardware;
   activating the deceleration system on the space flight hardware as the hardware approaches the terrestrial surface;

   allowing the space flight hardware to descend in reaction to aerodynamic and gravitational forces acting upon the space flight hardware and the deceleration system;
   measuring relative positions of the space flight hardware and at least one of the landing platform and the ground based vehicle; and
   maneuvering the ground based vehicle using measured relative positions and the estimated trajectory to capture the space flight hardware as the hardware descends to the terrestrial surface.

2. The method of claim **1**, wherein said deceleration system comprises a simple parachute.

3. The method of claim **1**, wherein said deceleration system comprises a variable ballistic coefficient parachute or parafoil that has limited steering and energy management capability.

4. The method of claim **1**, wherein maneuvering said ground based vehicle comprises moving said ground based vehicle in at least two independent directions, drawn from forward direction, rearward direction, leftward direction, rightward direction and rotation about a selected axis that intersects said terrestrial surface.

5. The method of claim **1**, further comprising providing a recovery guidance, navigation and control (GN&C) system on said at least one ground based vehicle.

6. The method of claim **5**, wherein said GN&C system incorporates measurement of absolute and relative position and velocity information of the space flight hardware and ground based vehicle into its command guidance algorithm.

7. The method of claim **5**, wherein said GN&C system enables position guidance information to control the ground based vehicle based upon the estimated trajectory of the space flight hardware.

8. The method of claim **1**, wherein maneuvering said ground based vehicle comprises substantially matching the descending flight hardware ground position, ground speed, and ground heading at capture of said space flight hardware.

9. The method of claim **8**, wherein said landing platform is oriented to match said descending space flight hardware principal longitudinal axis, aligning the space flight hardware center of mass with the center of the landing platform.

10. The method of claim **1**, wherein said space flight hardware is a booster.

11. The method of claim **1**, wherein said space flight hardware is a spacecraft.

12. The method of claim **1**, wherein said space flight hardware is an engine or equipment pod.

13. A hardware capture system used to capture and recover space flight hardware that passes through an atmosphere in an approach to a terrestrial surface, the system comprising:
   a surface effect levitation system comprising one or more flexible skirts and a pressurization mechanism;
   a landing platform, comprising an energy absorbing open surface that comprises netting, to mechanically receive and capture the space flight hardware;
   a hovercraft propulsion system capable of maneuvering a hovercraft in forward/aft translation, left/right translation and directional rotation (compass heading) independently of each other;
   guidance, navigation and control (GN&C) hardware located on the hovercraft that directs motion of the hovercraft to maneuver itself beneath the descending space flight hardware, to approximately match the space flight hardware speed and direction when the space flight hardware approaches the landing platform.

14. The system of claim **13**, wherein said landing platform is comprised of an energy absorbing open surface.

15. The system of claim **14**, wherein said energy absorbing open surface comprises netting.

16. The system of claim **13**, wherein said propulsion system comprises at least two propulsion units fixed relative to said hovercraft and configured to propel said hovercraft in forward, rearward, leftward and rightward translation, independent of rotation.

17. The system of claim **13**, wherein said propulsion system includes at least two vectored thrust propulsion units configured to propel said hovercraft in forward, rearward, leftward and rightward translation, independent of rotation.

18. The system of claim **13**, wherein said hovercraft includes an air cushion, the air cushion being subdivided into four or more chambers that are configured to provide roll and pitch stability.

19. A method for capturing reusable space flight hardware that passes through an atmosphere in an approach to a terrestrial surface, the method comprising:

estimating a trajectory of the space flight hardware as the hardware descends;

identifying a target landing region on the terrestrial surface that the estimated trajectory will intersect as the hardware approaches the terrestrial surface;

providing at least one ground based vehicle that is movable and maneuverable and that provides a dry landing platform for the space flight hardware at an ocean landing site;

pre-positioning the at least one ground based vehicle in the target landing region so that the estimated trajectory intersects at least a portion of the landing platform;

providing an atmospheric deceleration system on the space flight hardware;

activating the deceleration system on the space flight hardware as the hardware approaches the terrestrial surface;

allowing the space flight hardware to descend in reaction to aerodynamic and gravitational forces acting upon the space flight hardware and the deceleration system;

measuring relative positions of the space flight hardware and at least one of the landing platform and the ground based vehicle;

maneuvering the ground based vehicle using the measured relative positions and the estimated trajectory to capture the space flight hardware as the hardware descends to the terrestrial surface.

*   *   *   *   *

US 20030191411A1

(19) **United States**

(12) **Patent Application Publication** (10) Pub. No.: US 2003/0191411 A1
Yost et al. (43) Pub. Date: Oct. 9, 2003

(54) **NON-INVASIVE METHOD OF DETERMINING ABSOLUTE INTRACRANIAL PRESSURE**

(75) Inventors: **William T. Yost**, Newport News, VA (US); **John H. Cantrell JR.**, Williamsburg, VA (US); **Alan R. Hargens**, San Diego, CA (US)

Correspondence Address:
NATIONAL AERONAUTICS AND SPACE ADMINISTR
ATION LANGLEY RESEARCH CENTER
3 LANGLEY BOULEVARD
MAIL STOP 212
HAMPTON, VA 236812199

(73) Assignee: **National Aeronautics and Space Administration as represented by the Administrator (NASA)**, Washington, DC (US)

(21) Appl. No.: **10/263,286**

(22) Filed: **Sep. 25, 2002**

Related U.S. Application Data

(60) Provisional application No. 60/371,601, filed on Apr. 8, 2002.

Publication Classification

(51) Int. Cl.[7] A61B 5/02
(52) U.S. Cl. 600/561

(57) **ABSTRACT**

A method is presented for determining absolute intracranial pressure (ICP) in a patient. Skull expansion is monitored while changes in ICP are induced. The patient's blood pressure is measured when skull expansion is approximately zero. The measured blood pressure is indicative of a reference ICP value. Subsequently, the method causes a known change in ICP and measures the change in skull expansion associated therewith. The absolute ICP is a function of the reference ICP value, the known change in ICP and its associated change in skull expansion, and a measured change in skull expansion.

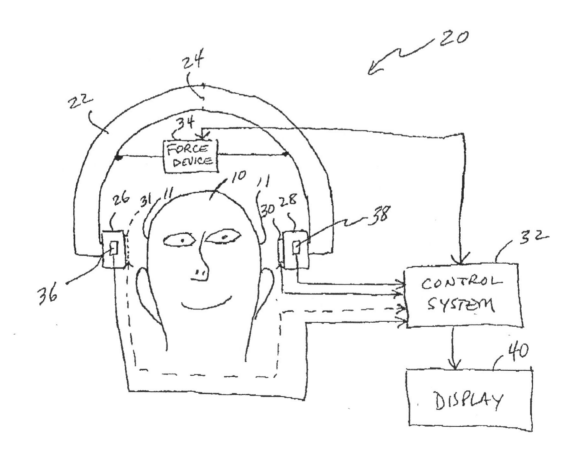

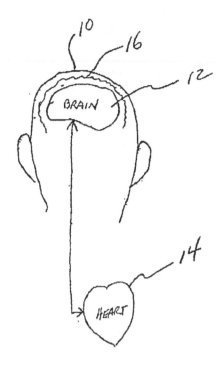

FIG. 1

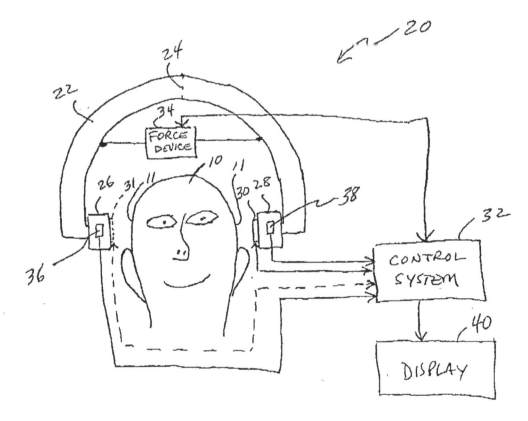

FIG. 2

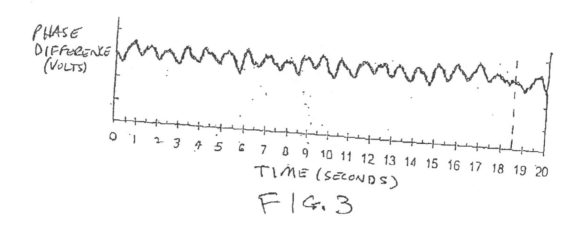

FIG. 3

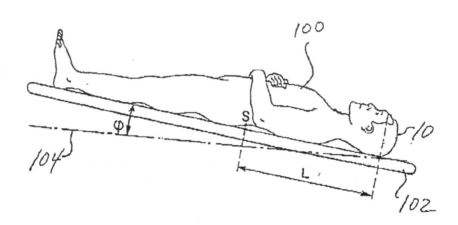

FIG. 4

270

NON-INVASIVE METHOD OF DETERMINING ABSOLUTE INTRACRANIAL PRESSURE

CLAIM OF BENEFIT OF PROVISIONAL APPLICATION

[0001] Pursuant to 35 U.S.C. Section 119, the benefit of priority from provisional application 60/371,601, with a filing date of Apr. 8, 2002, is claimed for this non-provisional application.

ORIGIN OF THE INVENTION

[0002] The invention described herein was made by employees of the United States Government and may be manufactured and used by or for the Government for governmental purposes without the payment of any royalties thereon or therefor.

CROSS REFERENCE TO RELATED APPLICATIONS

[0003] This patent application is co-pending with one related patent application entitled "NON-INVASIVE METHOD OF DETERMINING DIASTOLIC INTRACRANIAL PRESSURE" (NASA Case No. LAR 16440-1), by the same inventors as this patent application.

BACKGROUND OF THE INVENTION

[0004] 1. Field of the Invention

[0005] This invention relates to determination of intracranial pressure. More specifically, the invention is a non-invasive method for determining the absolute intracranial pressure in a patient.

[0006] 2. Description of the Related Art

[0007] The human brain and the spinal cord are immersed in a fluid called the cerebrospinal fluid (CSF) which is continuously generated and reabsorbed by the body. The CSF is contained in a membrane covering the inside of the skull and the spinal cord which terminates in a sack located at the sacrum. The brain and the membrane containing the CSF also contain blood vessels, which are in direct communication with the CSF and add to the total volume of the cerebrospinal system. The blood volume in these blood vessels varies rhythmically with the heartbeat thereby causing corresponding oscillations in the intracranial pressure (ICP). An accurate regulating process in the brain normally controls generation and reabsorption of CSF as well as the blood volume in the brain to maintain a constant ICP average value of about 40 mmHg. However, ICP changes when the regulating process is disturbed by, for example, tumors in the brain or trauma to the brain. Unfortunately, as little as 10 mmHg increase above average value in the ICP can cause insidious damage to the brain.

[0008] Given the above, monitoring ICP is of significant diagnostic and post-operative importance for patients with cranial injuries, pathologies or other conditions that may affect the pressure of the subarachnoidal fluid around the brain, and for patients who have undergone brain surgery. ICP has traditionally been measured and monitored by means of a pressure sensor inserted through the skull into the brain. Usually a hole is drilled in the skull and a catheter with a pressure sensor is inserted into the brain fluid. This known procedure, while simple and accurate is not suitable for long-term monitoring because an open wound must be maintained in the skull. Antibiotics are only partially effective in treating cranial infections so the pressure sensor typically can only be left in place for two weeks or less.

[0009] Long-term monitoring of ICP is currently achieved by implanting a pressure sensor and transmitter into the brain. The ICP is thereafter monitored by means of a receiver located outside the skull. However, this solution is not preferred because it includes the risks associated with implanting anything in the brain, and because of the problems of providing power to an implanted transmitter.

[0010] A variety of non-invasive systems and/or methods of measuring relative changes in ICP have been described in each of U.S. patent application Ser. Nos. 09/459,384, 09/493,044, 10/094,023, and 10/121,932. However, none of these provide for the measurement or determination of an absolute ICP. U.S. Pat. No. 5,617,873 discloses a method and system for monitoring absolute ICP, but requires the use of two known changes in the volume of CSF while recording corresponding changes in ICP by means of a calibrated measurement device.

SUMMARY OF THE INVENTION

[0011] Accordingly, it is an object of the present invention to provide a method of determining absolute ICP in a non-invasive fashion.

[0012] Another object of the present invention is to provide a method of determining absolute ICP that minimizes the number of procedures used.

[0013] Other objects and advantages of the present invention will become more obvious hereinafter in the specification and drawings.

[0014] In accordance with the present invention, a method is presented for determining absolute intracranial pressure (ICP) in a patient. In at least one embodiment, skull expansion of the patient is monitored as a function of time while changes in ICP in the patient are induced. Blood pressure of the patient is then measured at a time when skull expansion is approximately zero. The measured blood pressure at this time is indicative of a reference ICP value. A known change in ICP in the patient is caused after the time of zero skull expansion. A change in skull expansion associated with this known change in ICP is then measured. The absolute ICP is a function of the reference ICP value, the known change in ICP and the change in skull expansion associated with the known change in ICP.

BRIEF DESCRIPTION OF THE DRAWINGS

[0015] FIG. 1 is a schematic view of the skull and brain of a patient with the brain being coupled to the patient's heart;

[0016] FIG. 2 is a schematic view of a system that can be used to measure/monitor skull expansion in a patient for use by a method of the present invention;

[0017] FIG. 3 is a graph of a patient's skull expansion versus time as measured by, for example, the system in FIG. 2; and

[0018] FIG. 4 is a side view of a patient lying in a supine position on a tiltable bed for mechanical manipulation of the patient as a means to induce/cause changes in intracranial pressure (ICP) in the patient.

DETAILED DESCRIPTION OF THE INVENTION

[0019] Referring now to the drawings, and more particularly to **FIG. 1,** a patient's skull **10** is illustrated with his brain referenced by numeral **12**. As is well known, brain **12** is a venous structure that is coupled to the patient's heart **14** and, therefore, undergoes systolic-diastolic changes in blood pressure. The blood pressure in the venous bed of the brain is known as venous bed pressure and will be referenced herein as P_{VB}. Surrounding brain **12** is the patient's cerebrospinal fluid (CSF) **16**, the pressure of which is known as intracranial pressure or ICP as it will be referenced herein.

[0020] Skull **10** tends to expand and contract with changes in ICP. However, the compliance (i.e., the ability of skull **10** to expand with increasing ICP) of skull **10** is not sufficient to accommodate the pressure regulation needed for proper circulation of blood within brain **12** and the patient's CSF system (not shown). Accordingly, pressure within skull **10** is controlled by compliance of the brain's venous bed in association with the addition/removal of CSF **16**. The determination and/or continuous monitoring of the absolute ICP of CSF **16** is important in determining whether or not a patient has a problem interfering with the body's natural ability to control ICP.

[0021] In terms of skull expansion, the present invention takes note of the fact that the venous bed pressure P_{VB} will be equal to ICP when skull **10** is neither expanding nor contracting for a skull expansion of "zero." As is known in the art, venous bed pressure P_{VB} can be determined from a standard arterial blood pressure measurement thereby making ICP easily determined at a time of zero skull expansion. Once ICP at zero skull expansion (or ICP_{REF} as it will be referred to hereinafter) is determined, the present invention goes on to determine absolute ICP by measuring skull expansion changes brought about by associated known changes in ICP.

[0022] Before describing the details of a method of the present invention, it is to be understood that skull expansion measurements, the inducement of changes in ICP, and/or the measurement of changes in ICP, can be carried out in a variety of ways without departing from the scope of the present invention. For example, skull expansion can be measured/monitored by means of sophisticated micrometers (not shown) or by other non-invasive means such as the mechanical-acoustic system that will be described herein. The intentionally induced changes in ICP can be brought about by mechanical manipulation of the patient (e.g., pressure applied to the skull, through the use of a tilt bed, immersion of the patient in a negative pressure chamber, etc.) or by chemical manipulation of the patient (e.g., giving the patient drugs to: alter blood gas concentration, decrease production of CSF, increase the uptake rate of CSF, etc.). Measurement of changes in ICP can be measured/determined by a variety of acoustic systems (e.g., pulse-echo, pitch-catch, etc.) such as the constant frequency pulsed phase-locked-loop ultrasonic measuring system described in U.S. Pat. No. 5,214,955, which patent is incorporated herein by reference as if set forth in its entirety.

[0023] By way of a non-limiting example, **FIG. 2** illustrates a system **20** that monitors skull expansion of a patient in order to determine when there is zero skull expansion. System **20** includes an adjustable headband **22** hinged at its central portion as indicated by dashed line **24**. Pressure pads **26** and **28** are positioned at either end of headband **22** such that, when headband **22** is fitted over a patient's skull **10**, pressure pads **26** and **28** are positioned at approximately diametrically opposed positions about skull **10**. Each of pressure pads **26** and **28** can define a conforming pad (e.g., a gel-filled pad) to assure uniform contact with skin **11** adjacent skull **10**.

[0024] Mounted to pressure pad **28** is a transducer **30** capable of transmitting and receiving acoustic signals for use in a pulse-echo measurement approach. Signals are provided to transducer **30** by a control system **32** and acoustic echoes received by transducer **30** are provided to control system **32**. In the pulse-echo approach, pressure pad **26** can be constructed as an anechoic chamber to reduce reflections from the skin-air interface adjacent the side of the skull subjected to the acoustic signals. Separate transmission and reception transducers could also be used for either pulse-echo or pitch-catch measurement approaches. For example, in terms of a pitch-catch measurement approach, transducer **30** could be a dedicated transmitter and a transducer **31** (shown in phantom) could be a dedicated receiver mounted on pad **26**.

[0025] A force device **34** is coupled to headband **22** on either side of hinge **24**. Force device **34** is any controllable device capable drawing headband **22** together about hinge **24** such that an increasing pressure is applied to skull **10** via each of pads **26** and **28**. Examples of force device **34** can include, but are not limited to, solenoids, screw drives, hydraulic drives, gear drives, etc., where system response is linear. That is, force device **34** should preferably be "linear" in its expansion and contraction characteristics as it follows skull expansion. Such linearity is manifested by a force device having a constant (i.e., linear) and known stiffness (or modulus).

[0026] Control of force device **34** is maintained by control system **32** which can be entirely automatic or can include means for accepting manual inputs. To monitor the amount of pressure applied to skull **10**, pressure sensors **36** and **38** can be provided at each of pressure pads **26** and **28**, respectively. The pressure readings can be used by control system **32** as a feedback control for force device **34**. Pressure outputs can also be displayed on a display **40**.

[0027] To monitor skull expansion using the pulse-echo approach, headband **22** is placed on skull **10** such that pads **26** and **28** are in contact with the patient's skin **11** adjacent skull **10**. With respect to pad **28**, note that transducer **30**, as well as portions of pad **28** to the sides of transducer **30**, will contact skin **11**. This insures good coupling of acoustic signals transmitted into skull **10** from transducer **30** as well as good coupling of acoustic signal reflections from skull **10** to transducer **30**.

[0028] Prior to monitoring skull expansion using system **20**, it may be desirable to establish and apply a differential pressure bias to skull **10** at each of the transmission, reception and, if applicable, reflection locations about skull **10** in order to reduce or eliminate the effects associated with pulsatile blood perfusion, i.e., the small amount of systolic-diastolic blood located between the patient's skin **11** and skull **10**. The amount of differential pressure required to reduce or eliminate the influence of pulsatile blood perfusion can be determined by monitoring skull expansion as a function of applied differential pressures. Initially, the slope of a plot of these two parameters will be fairly steep. However, the slope will level off to a constant once the effects of pulsatile blood perfusion are reduced/eliminated. Note that this step is not required if acoustic signals can be coupled directly to/from the skull **10** as opposed to indirectly through the patient's skin **11**.

[0029] In general, system **20** monitors skull expansion during a period of time that changes in ICP are induced in the patient. At the time when skull expansion is zero (or approximately so), the patient's venous bed pressure (or P_{VB}) will be equal to the patient's ICP. In accordance with the teachings of U.S. Pat. No. 5,214,955, system **20** measures phase difference between the acoustic signal transmitted into skull **10** and the acoustic signal measured at a detection location. As mentioned above, the detection location can be: i) the same as the transmission location when a single transmission/reception transducer **30** is used, ii) adjacent the transmission location if a dedicated reception transducer is mounted adjacent transducer **30**, or iii) at another location that is spaced apart form the transmission location, e.g., at a location diametrically-opposed to the transmission location as would be the case if dedicated reception transducer **31** were used. Thus, in terms of system **20**, zero (or approximately zero) skull expansion is indicated when the phase difference between the transmission and reception locations is approximately zero. For example, as illustrated in **FIG. 3**, when phase difference is measured by system **20** in terms of an output voltage, (approximately) zero skull expansion (i.e., (approximately) zero slope) occurs at approximately 18.5 seconds. Note that in tests of the present invention, the phase difference waveform depicted in **FIG. 3** correlated well with an absolute ICP measurement that used an invasive probe.

[0030] During the time that skull expansion is being monitored, the patient can be "manipulated" to bring about changes in ICP. Such manipulations can be mechanical or chemical in nature. Mechanical manipulations can include the use of additional pressure being applied by force device **34** of system **20**, the use of a tilt bed while system **20** maintains a differential pressure bias, the immersion of the patient in a negative pressure chamber, etc. Chemical manipulations include drug intervention techniques for increasing/decreasing ICP.

[0031] At the time of zero skull expansion, venous bed pressure P_{VB} of the patient's brain can be determined from a standard arterial blood pressure measurement. The value of P_{VB} at this time is essentially equal to ICP which, as mentioned above, will be used as a reference value ICP_{REF}. From this point in time, known changes in ICP are brought about while corresponding changes in skull expansion are monitored. The causing of known changes in ICP can be brought about by the tilt bed/angle method, which has been described in U.S. Pat. No. 5,617,873, which patent is incorporated herein by reference. Briefly, as shown in **FIG. 4, a** patient **100** lies supine on a tiltable bed **102**. Note that while a system, for example system **20**, would remain coupled to patient **100**, it has been omitted from **FIG. 4** for clarity of illustration. With bed **102** tilted by an angle φ with the legs of patient **100** higher than skull **10**, a change (increase in this case) in ICP (or ΔICP) can be given as

$$\Delta ICP = \rho g L \sin\phi \qquad (1)$$

[0032] where ρ is the mass density of spinal fluid, g is the earth's gravitational constant, L is the distance from the center of the patient's sacrum (the location of which is indicated at S) to the center of skull **10**, and φ is the amount of tilt angle of bed **102** relative to a (horizontal) datum **104** used when determining ICP_{REF}. The present invention is not limited to a measurement of L that originates at the patient's sacrum. For example, L could be measured with respect to another reference point such as the point at which pressure in the spinal column does not change with tilt angle. Thus, for any given patient with a known/measurable distance L, ΔICP can be calculated using equation (1).

[0033] Changes in skull expansion measured by system **20** are essentially defined by changes in path length that the acoustic signal travels between its transmission and reception locations. That is, between any two measurement points in time, the path length "l" that the acoustic signal travels gets longer in the case of positive skull expansion or shorter in the case of negative skull expansion (i.e., skull contraction). Path length l could be defined by one or more paths across skull **10** depending on the number of such lengths traversed by the acoustic signal between its transmission and reception locations. Thus, the change in path length between any two points in time is "Δl."

[0034] The change in path length, Δl, for the change in ICP, ΔICP, can be measured by system **20**. The two values can be used to determine the skull expansion calibration factor, K, by,

$$K = \Delta ICP/\Delta l \qquad (2)$$

[0035] For any measured path length change, Δl_M, where,

$$\Delta l_M = l_M - l_{REF}, \qquad (3)$$

[0036] The absolute ICP or ICP_{ABS} is given as

$$ICP_{ABS} = ICP_{REF} + K(\Delta l_M) \qquad (4)$$

[0037] The advantages of the present invention are numerous. Absolute ICP is determined through the use of easily taken measurements. The process is non-invasive in nature and can, therefore, be used for both one-time and longer term monitoring scenarios. Thus, the present invention will find great utility in both critical and non-critical ICP-related pathologies as well as other medical applications requiring knowledge of absolute ICP.

[0038] Although the invention has been described relative to a specific embodiment thereof, there are numerous variations and modifications that will be readily apparent to those skilled in the art in light of the above teachings. For example, rather than using the tilt bed approach to causing known changes in ICP, system **20** could be used to apply incremental increases in headband pressure to bring about changes in skull dimensions. The changes in skull dimensions can then be used to infer changes in ICP resulting from skull expansion/contraction. It is therefore to be understood that, within the scope of the appended claims, the invention may be practiced other than as specifically described.

What is claimed as new and desired to be secured by Letters Patent of the United States is:

1. A method of determining absolute intracranial pressure (ICP) in a patient, comprising the steps of:

monitoring skull expansion of the patient as a function of time;

inducing changes in ICP in the patient;

measuring blood pressure of the patient at a time when said skull expansion is approximately zero during said step of inducing wherein said blood pressure at said time is indicative of a reference ICP value;

causing a known change in ICP in the patient after said time;

measuring a change in said skull expansion of the patient associated with said known change in ICP; and

determining a skull expansion calibration factor, wherein the absolute ICP is a function of said reference ICP value, said measured change in skull expansion and said skull expansion calibration factor.

2. A method according to claim 1 wherein each of said steps of monitoring said skull expansion and measuring said change in said skull expansion comprises the steps of:

coupling an acoustic signal to a first location on the patient's skin adjacent the skull of the patient;

detecting said acoustic signal at a second location on the patient's skin adjacent the skull of the patient; and

measuring a phase difference between said acoustic signal so-coupled at said first location and said acoustic signal so-detected at said second location, wherein said phase difference is indicative of said skull expansion.

3. A method according to claim 2 further comprising the step of applying pressure to the patient's skin at each of said first location and said second location prior to said steps of coupling and detecting, wherein pulsatile blood perfusion at said first location and said second location is reduced.

4. A method according to claim 2 wherein said first location and said second location are approximately dia-metrically-opposed to one another on either side of the skull of the patient.

5. A method according to claim 2 wherein said first location and said second location are approximately the same location.

6. A method according to claim 1 wherein said step of inducing comprises the step of manipulating the patient in a mechanical fashion.

7. A method according to claim 1 wherein said step of inducing comprises the step of manipulating the patient in a chemical fashion.

8. A method according to claim 1 wherein said step of causing comprises the step of manipulating the patient in a mechancal fashion.

9. A method according to claim 1 wherein said step of causing comprises the step of manipulating the patient in a chemical fashion.

10. A method of determining absolute ICP in a patient, comprising the steps of:

monitoring skull expansion of the patient as a function of time, wherein said skull expansion is defined in terms of a length l of a path traversing at least a portion of the skull of the patient;

inducing changes in ICP in the patient;

measuring blood pressure of the patient at a time when said skull expansion is approximately zero during said step of inducing wherein said blood pressure at said time is indicative of a venous bed pressure of the

patient, and wherein said venous bed pressure at said time is equal to a reference ICP value ICP_{REF};

causing a known change ΔICP in ICP in the patient after said time;

measuring a change Δl in said path associated with said known change in ICP; and

determining a skull expansion calibration factor, wherein the absolute ICP is equal to $ICP_{REF} + K(\Delta l_M)$, wherein Δl_M is the change in l between any measurement of l, and the measurement of l when the skull expansion was approximately zero.

11. A method according to claim 10 wherein each of said steps of monitoring said skull expansion and measuring said change Δl comprises the steps of:

coupling an acoustic signal to a first location on the patient's skin adjacent the skull of the patient;

detecting said acoustic signal at a second location on the patient's skin adjacent the skull of the patient; and

measuring a phase difference between said acoustic signal so-coupled at said first location and said acoustic signal so-detected at said second location, wherein said phase difference is indicative of said change Δl.

12. A method according to claim 11 further comprising the step of applying pressure to the patient's skin at each of said first location and said second location prior to said steps of coupling and detecting, wherein pulsatile blood perfusion at said first location and said second location is reduced.

13. A method according to claim 11 wherein said first location and said second location are approximately dia-metrically-opposed to one another on either side of the skull of the patient.

14. A method according to claim 11 wherein said first location and said second location are approximately the same location.

15. A method according to claim 10 wherein said step of inducing comprises the step of manipulating the patient in a mechanical fashion.

16. A method according to claim 10 wherein said step of inducing comprises the step of manipulating the patient in a chemical fashion.

17. A method according to claim 10 wherein said step of causing comprises the step of manipulating the patient in a mechancal fashion.

18. A method according to claim 10 wherein said step of causing comprises the step of manipulating the patient in a chemical fashion.

19. A method of determining absolute ICP in a patient, comprising the steps of:

coupling an acoustic signal to a first location on the patient's skin adjacent the skull of the patient;

detecting said acoustic signal at a second location on the patient's skin adjacent the skull of the patient;

measuring a phase difference between said acoustic signal so-coupled at said first location and said acoustic signal so-detected at said second location, wherein said phase difference is indicative of skull expansion of the patient;

repeating said steps of coupling, detecting, and measuring for a period of time;

inducing changes in ICP in the patient during said period of time;

determining a time during said time period when said phase difference is approximately zero;

measuring blood pressure of the patient at said time, wherein said blood pressure at said time is indicative of a reference ICP value;

causing a known change in ICP in the patient after said time;

measuring a change in said skull expansion of the patient associated with said known change in ICP; and

determining a skull expansion calibration factor, wherein the absolute ICP is a function of said reference ICP value, said measured change in skull expansion, and said skull expansion calibration factor.

20. A method according to claim 19 further comprising the step of applying pressure to the patient's skin at each of said first location and said second location prior to said steps of coupling and detecting, wherein pulsatile blood perfusion at said first location and said second location is reduced.

21. A method according to claim 19 wherein said first location and said second location are approximately diametrically-opposed to one another on either side of the skull of the patient.

22. A method according to claim 19 wherein said first location and said second location are approximately the same location.

23. A method according to claim 19 wherein said step of inducing comprises the step of manipulating the patient in a mechanical fashion.

24. A method according to claim 19 wherein said step of inducing comprises the step of manipulating the patient in a chemical fashion.

25. A method according to claim 19 wherein said step of causing comprises the step of manipulating the patient in a mechanical fashion.

26. A method according to claim 19 wherein said step of causing comprises the step of manipulating the patient in a chemical fashion.

27. A method of determining absolute ICP in a patient, comprising steps for:

monitoring skull expansion;

inducing changes in ICP;

determining a reference ICP; and

determining a skull expansion calibration factor, wherein absolute ICP is a function of said reference ICP, said skull expansion factor, and a measured change in skull dimension.

28. A method according to claim 27, wherein said step for determining a reference ICP comprises the step of measuring blood pressure corresponding to a time when skull expansion equals approximately zero during said step for inducing.

29. A method of claim 27 wherein said step for determining a skull expansion calibration factor comprises the steps of:

causing a known change in ICP in the patient; and

measuring the change in skull expansion associated with said known change in ICP.

30. A method according to claim 29 wherein each of said steps for monitoring skull expansion and measuring said change in skull expansion comprises the steps of:

coupling an acoustic signal to a first location on the patient's skin adjacent the skull of the patient;

detecting said acoustic signal at a second location on the patient's skin adjacent the skull of the patient; and

measuring phase differences between said acoustic signal so-coupled at said first location and said acoustic signal so-detected at said second location, wherein said phase differences are indicative of said skull expansion.

31. A method according to claim 30 further comprising the step of applying pressure to the patient's skin at each of said first location and said second location prior to said steps of coupling and detecting, wherein pulsatile blood perfusion at said first location and said second location is reduced.

32. A method according to claim 30 wherein said first location and said second location are approximately diametrically-opposed to one another on either side of the skull of the patient.

33. A method according to claim 30 wherein said first location and said second location are approximately the same location.

34. A method according to claim 27 wherein said step for inducing comprises the step of manipulating the patient in a mechanical fashion.

35. A method according to claim 27 wherein said step for inducing comprises the step of manipulating the patient in a chemical fashion.

36. A method according to claim 29 wherein said step for causing comprises the step of manipulating the patient in a mechanical fashion.

37. A method according to claim 29 wherein said step for causing comprises the step of manipulating the patient in a chemical fashion.

* * * * *

US008409845B2

(12) **United States Patent**
Trent et al.

(10) **Patent No.:** **US 8,409,845 B2**
(45) **Date of Patent:** **Apr. 2, 2013**

(54) **ALGAE BIOREACTOR USING SUBMERGED ENCLOSURES WITH SEMI-PERMEABLE MEMBRANES**

(75) Inventors: **Jonathan D Trent**, La Selva Beach, CA (US); **Sherwin J Gormly**, Carson City, NV (US); **Tsegereda N Embaye**, Boulder Creek, CA (US); **Lance D Delzeit**, Santa Clara, CA (US); **Michael T Flynn**, Corte Madera, CA (US); **Travis A Liggett**, Redkey, IN (US); **Patrick W Buckwalter**, La Selva Beach, CA (US); **Robert Baertsch**, Menlo Park, CA (US)

(73) Assignee: **The United States of America as Represented by the Administrator of the National Aeronautics & Space Administration (NASA)**, Washington, DC (US)

(*) Notice: Subject to any disclaimer, the term of this patent is extended or adjusted under 35 U.S.C. 154(b) by 1044 days.

(21) Appl. No.: **12/316,557**

(22) Filed: **Dec. 5, 2008**

(65) **Prior Publication Data**

US 2010/0216203 A1 Aug. 26, 2010

(51) **Int. Cl.**
C12N 1/12 (2006.01)
C12M 3/06 (2006.01)
A01G 13/00 (2006.01)

(52) **U.S. Cl.** **435/257.1**; 435/292.1; 435/297.1; 47/1.4

(58) **Field of Classification Search** 435/257.1, 435/292.1; 47/1.4
See application file for complete search history.

(56) **References Cited**

U.S. PATENT DOCUMENTS

3,955,317	A	*	5/1976	Gudin 435/420
4,043,903	A	*	8/1977	Dor 47/1.4
4,868,123	A		9/1989	Berson et al.
4,888,912	A		12/1989	Murray
6,509,188	B1		1/2003	Trosch et al.
7,980,024	B2	*	7/2011	Berzin et al. 47/1.4
2006/0148071	A1	*	7/2006	Bauer et al. 435/290.1
2008/0009055	A1		1/2008	Lewnard
2008/0153080	A1		6/2008	Woods et al.

(Continued)

FOREIGN PATENT DOCUMENTS

WO	WO 2008134010 A2	11/2008
WO	WO 2009/152175 A1	12/2009

OTHER PUBLICATIONS

Carvalho,et al., Microalgal Reactors: A Review of Enclosed System Designs and Performances, Biotechnol. Prog., Nov. 15, 2006, 1490-1506, 22, American Chemical Society and American Institute of Chemical Engineers.

(Continued)

Primary Examiner — William H Beisner

(74) *Attorney, Agent, or Firm* — John F. Schipper; Robert M. Padilla; Christopher J. Menke

(57) **ABSTRACT**

Methods for producing hydrocarbons, including oil, by processing algae and/or other micro-organisms in an aquatic environment. Flexible bags (e.g., plastic) with CO_2/O_2 exchange membranes, suspended at a controllable depth in a first liquid (e.g., seawater), receive a second liquid (e.g., liquid effluent from a "dead zone") containing seeds for algae growth. The algae are cultivated and harvested in the bags, after most of the second liquid is removed by forward osmosis through liquid exchange membranes. The algae are removed and processed, and the bags are cleaned and reused.

39 Claims, 7 Drawing Sheets

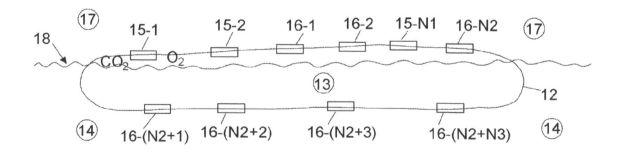

U.S. PATENT DOCUMENTS

2008/0160591	A1	7/2008	Willson et al.
2008/0178739	A1	7/2008	Lewnard et al.
2008/0181999	A1	7/2008	Yang
2009/0011492	A1	1/2009	Berzin
2009/0130706	A1	5/2009	Berzin et al.
2009/0305389	A1	12/2009	Willson et al.
2010/0028976	A1	2/2010	Hu et al.

OTHER PUBLICATIONS

Cheng, et al., Carbon Dioxide Removal From Air by Microalgae Cultured in a Membrane-Photobiorector, Separation Purification Technology, 2006, 324-329, 50, Elsevier B. V.

Fan, et al., Optimization of Carbon Dioxide Fixation by *Chlorella vulgaris*, Cultivated in a Membrane-Photobiorector, Chem. Eng. Technol., 2007, 1094-1099, 30-8, Wiley-VCH Verlag GmbH & Co. KGaA, Weinheim.

Lee, et al., Supplying CO2 to Photosynthetic Algal Cultures by Diffusion through Gas-Permeable Membranes, Applied Microbiology Biotechnology, 1989, 298-301, 31, Springer-Verlag.

Lee, Microalgal Mass Culture Systems and Methods: Their Limitation and Potential, Journal of Applied Phycology, 2001, 307-315, 13, Kluwer Academic Publishers, the Netherlands.

Xu, et al., A Simple and Low-Cost Airlift Photobioreactor for Microalgal Mass Culture, Biotechnology Letters, 2002, 1767-1771, 24, Kluwer Acedemic Publishers, the Netherlands.

* cited by examiner

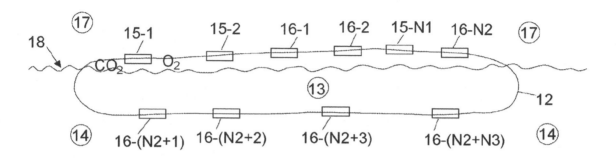

FIG. 1

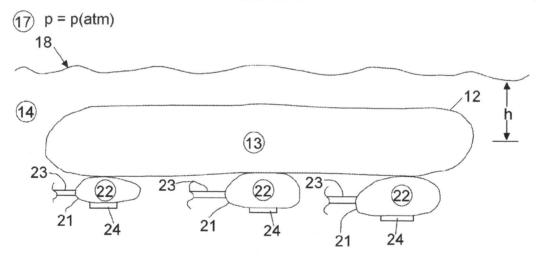

FIG. 2

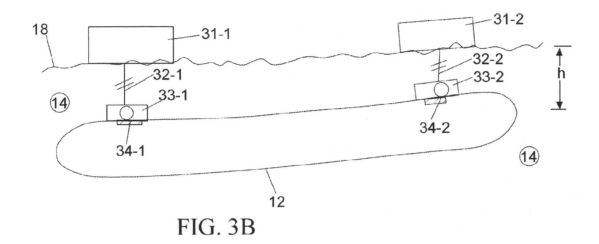

FIG. 3B

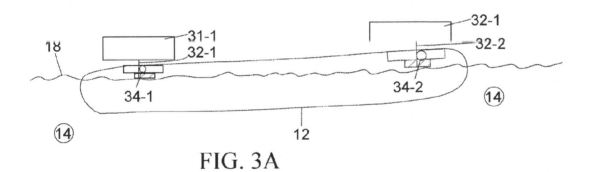

FIG. 3A

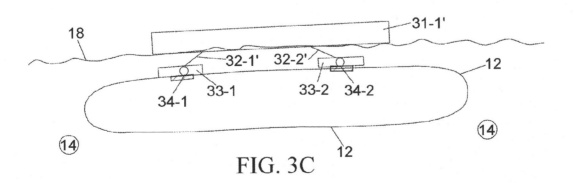

FIG. 3C

279

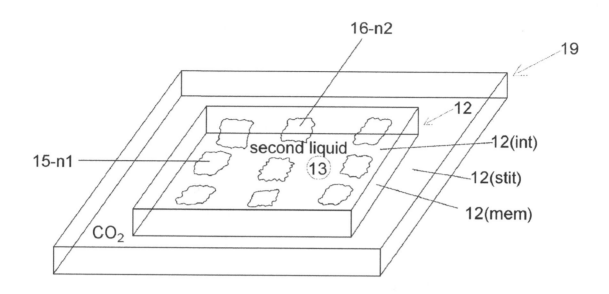

FIG. 4A

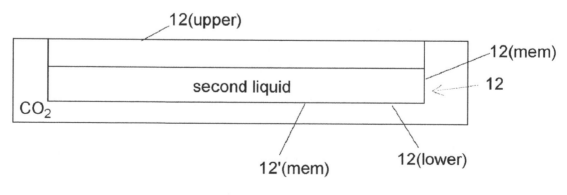

FIG. 4B

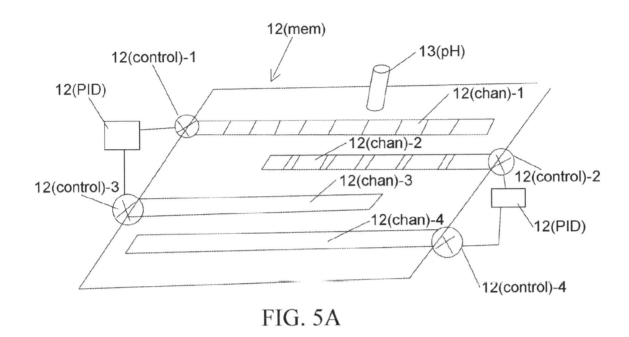

FIG. 5A

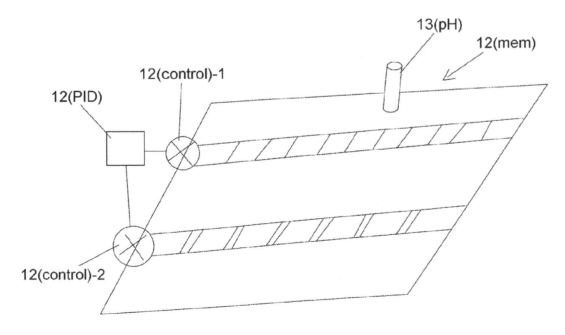

FIG. 5B

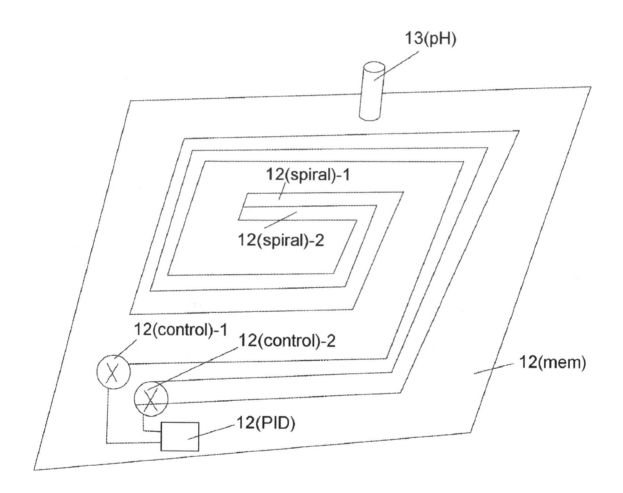

FIG. 5C

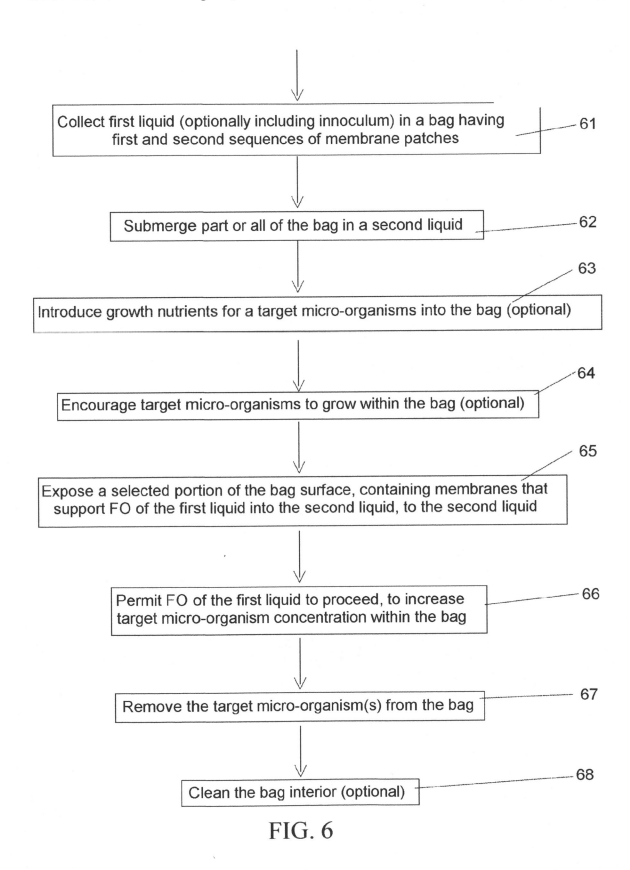

FIG. 6

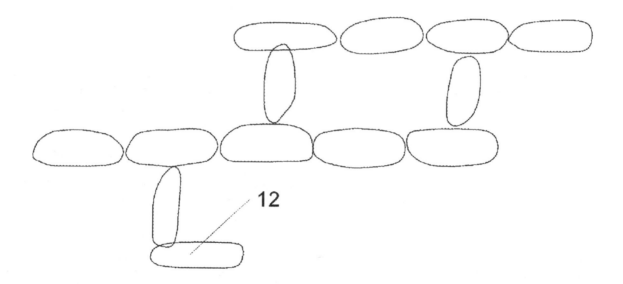

FIG. 7

1

ALGAE BIOREACTOR USING SUBMERGED ENCLOSURES WITH SEMI-PERMEABLE MEMBRANES

ORIGIN OF THE INVENTION

This invention was made, in part, by one or more employees of the U.S. government. The U.S. government has the right to make, use and/or sell the invention described herein without payment of compensation, including but not limited to payment of royalties.

FIELD OF THE INVENTION

This invention relates to using flexible enclosures with inflatable, semi-permeable regions in aquatic environments to grow algae and/or other micro-organisms that can be used in the production of oil and other products.

BACKGROUND OF THE INVENTION

Various species of algae are known to produce valuable products ranging from food to fertilizer to biofuels. The large-scale commercial production of these algae however, particularly for commodity products like biofuels, has been limited by the unfavorable economics of the current cultivation and harvesting methods. The two dominant cultivation methods are (1) open raceways and (2) closed bioreactors and two of the dominant harvesting methods are (1) centrifugation and (2) tangential-flow filtration. These cultivation approaches have problems with high associated operating costs, high land costs, uncontrolled evaporation, contamination and/or limited flexibility.

What is needed is a relatively low cost, low maintenance approach for cultivation of the algae and separation of the algae and/or other micro-organisms from other substances. Preferably, the approach should have little or no evaporation or contamination problems and should allow flexibility in throughput, algae choice and other parameters that affect the resulting product(s).

SUMMARY OF THE INVENTION

These needs are met by the invention, which provides a system for cultivating microorganisms, such as algae, some of which are products in themselves and others produce useful byproducts, including oil, food additives, fertilizers, nutriceuticals, and pharmaceuticals. This new cultivating system is an enclosure consisting of plastic or similar bags with patches of inflatable, semi-permeable membranes incorporated into their surfaces. These bags are used in aquatic environments where the water provides infrastructural support through flotation and temperature regulation, the water motion provides mixing within the bag from currents and wave action, and in some locations (e.g., "dead zones") the water chemistry in the surrounding water provides the required nutrients for growing algae or other microorganisms. In addition, by cultivating freshwater organisms in bags deployed in a marine or brackish environment, the surrounding salt water provides a means of dewatering the contents of the bag using patches of membranes that permit forward osmosis (FO).

The bags can be made of a variety of plastics or other impermeable materials and may vary in size and shape. For cultivating algae, the bags will have a transparent upper surface to allow light penetration and may have a reflective lower surface to increase light availability in the bags, provided this

does not adversely impact the native populations of algae and/or other micro-organisms in the surrounding environment. The diameter of the individual bag can range from meters to kilometers, but for algae and/or other micro-organisms, the bag thickness is limited to a value, usually no more than about 10 cm, that allows adequate light penetration through water. The bags are made of light-weight, flexible, durable plastic (e.g., polyurethane) or similar material that will be shaped by its flotation on the surface of the water and in some cases by structural components. The shape and flexibility of bags allows the external water currents and waves to mix the bag contents, and the shape and thermal properties of the bag material allows the temperature inside the bag to be regulated by the heat capacity of the surrounding water.

While the size and shape of the bag (other than its depth for growth of algae and/or other micro-organisms) are not critical to the bioreactor's function, the semi-permeable membranes and the offshore location of the bioreactor are critical. The bags have patches of different kinds of semi-permeable membranes on their surfaces, which include gas-permeable, water-permeable, and/or nutrient-permeable membranes. The different membranes function by influencing the dissolved gases, the nutrients, and the concentration of nutrients, salts, and algae and/or other micro-organisms in the bags. Not all the different kinds of membranes are needed, depending on the conditions.

Under most conditions, patches of gas-permeable membranes on the upper surface of the bag, which may be exposed to air, are needed. These membranes allow oxygen and other gasses to pass out of the bag and carbon dioxide to pass into the bag. In some embodiments, pressurized carbon dioxide, available externally or stored in a bladder within the bag, in addition to atmospheric carbon dioxide, will pass through the gas-permeable membranes into the bag.

The liquid-permeable membrane (forward osmosis [FO] membrane) is used to remove liquid from the bag, thereby concentrating the remaining contents of the bag. Liquid, but not algae or other selected micro-organisms, diffuses through the FO membrane into the surrounding liquid, provided there is a chemical gradient between the liquid inside the bag and the liquid outside the bag. Methods of establishing this gradient include: (i) provision of freshwater inside the bag and marine water outside, (ii) provision of marine water inside and brine outside, amd (iii) provision of another substantial concentration differential between the liquids inside and outside the bag. As liquid leaves the bag, chemicals and algae and/or other micro-organisms inside the bag are concentrated within the bag. The concentrated chemicals in the bag may be used to artificially stress the algae and/or other micro-organisms to encourage their production of oil or to induce them to produce other products. Artificial stressors include presence of excess salt and nutrient starvation. The removal of liquid from the bag also concentrates the algae and/or other micro-organisms, which facilitates their harvesting and processing. Under most conditions, after harvesting the bag can be used again.

In one embodiment, the patches of FO membrane are located on the upper surface of the bag so the patches are mostly exposed to air or another ambient atmosphere and do not significantly remove liquid from the bag. In this configuration, osmosis-based liquid removal is initiated by submerging the bags. In another embodiment, the FO membrane is located on the lower surface of the bag, and osmosis proceeds slowly during the entire culturing period. For convenient reference herein, the liquids inside and outside the bag will be collectively referred to as "water."

3

The nutrient-permeable membranes can be used under conditions in which the nutrients in the surrounding water are higher than in the bag, but are not needed when the bag is filled with high-nutrient water and the nutrient concentration in the surrounding water is low. In environments with high concentrations of nutrients (e.g., "dead zones"), patches of nutrient-permeable membrane are incorporated into the lower surface of the bag to take up nutrients from the surrounding water. Nutrient-permeable membranes, such as nitrate membranes, create an equilibrium between the inside and outside of the bag, but the uptake of nutrients by the algae and/or other micro-organisms (innoculum) inside the bag creates a net flux of nutrients into the bag.

In some embodiments, the bags are filled with nutrient-rich freshwater (non-marine/low salt), for example, from a river mouth or a sewage outfall. The bag is allowed to fill at one end with liquid effluent and either the native population of algae is allowed to grow or the bag is inoculated with an alga or consortium of algae and/or other micro-organisms. Specific strains of algae and/or other micro-organisms can be encouraged to grow by the size of the innoculum and/or by influencing the conditions inside the bag (e.g., light levels, nutrients, pH, salinity, temperature, trace elements).

These culturing and dewatering methods address many of the technical challenges of the existing cultivation and harvesting methods for algae and/or other micro-organisms that impact their cost-effective implementation. A key feature of the new system is that it consists of flexible bags or enclosures that are deployed in aquatic environments. Because the new system is made of light-weight material, such as plastic, and is deployed offshore, this system not only avoids the problems of land costs and competition with other land uses, but the surrounding water provides infrastructure, cooling water, mixing from wave action, and local nutrient supplies. The design of the system avoids problems associated with water use, evaporation, and contamination by "weed" species. When deployed in the contaminated or eutrophied coastal areas known as "dead zones," the system will help to remediate these zones by removing contaminating nutrients. The system will also remove carbon dioxide from the atmosphere and may help to mitigate the contribution carbon dioxide is making to global warming. The energy-intensive de-watering step for conventional algae: harvesting is achieved by the new system, using forward osmosis membranes and requiring little or no external input of energy.

This invention solves many of the current problems associated with cultivating algae in open pond raceways or closed bioreactors on land. These problems include competing land-uses and environmental impact, water requirements, evaporation control, contamination control, temperature regulation, provision of energy for mixing and harvesting, and invasion by "weed" species. The invention also contributes to the remediation of dead zones by removing polluting nutrients and reduces global warming by sequestering carbon dioxide from the atmosphere.

This new system can also be used for cultivating aquatic organisms, including algae and/or other micro-organisms, provided there is a chemical gradient between the growth conditions inside the enclosure and the surrounding environment. The system can also be used for dewatering.

BRIEF DESCRIPTION OF THE DRAWINGS

FIG. 1 is a sectional side view of an embodiment of the invention.

4

FIGS. 2 and 3A/3B/3C illustrate submersion of the bag in FIG. 1 to a continuously controllable depth using two approaches.

FIGS. 4A/4B illustrate apparatus for controllable CO_2/O_2 exchange between the bag interior and an external region.

FIGS. 5A/5B/5C illustrate alternative channel arrangements for membranes for CO_2/O_2 exchange.

FIG. 6 is a flow chart of a procedure for practicing the invention.

FIG. 7 schematically illustrates a connected structure for bag transport.

DESCRIPTION OF THE INVENTION

The invention uses an enclosure, such as a plastic bag, as a bioreactor with patches of semi-permeable membranes used for exchanges between the inside and the outside of the bioreactor, in an aquatic environment. For cultivation of algae and/or other micro-organisms, the bag allows light to enter through the upper surface and may have a light-reflective surface on the lower surface to increase the light available for algae cultivation. The bag is filled with a nutrient-rich liquid effluent, which promotes the growth of extant or introduced algae and/or other micro-organisms. The bioreactor is used offshore in an aquatic or marine environment, which provides support, cooling, mixing, dewatering, and in some cases nutrients. The bag-bioreactor is not intended to be used on land, although it can be used in artificial aquatic environments, such as a brine pond, a waste-water basin or a reservoir.

The patches of semi-permeable membranes on the bag allow the bag contents to beneficially interact with the surroundings. For example, a gas exchange membrane removes excess O_2 from the bag interior and allows CO_2 to enter, which aids algae growth. FIG. 1 is a sectional side view of an embodiment 11 of the system. A bag 12, containing a liquid effluent (second liquid) 13 and one or more selected algae and/or other micro-organism(s), is partly submerged in a first liquid 14 of a type different from the second liquid. An upper surface of the bag includes a first sequence 15-$n1$ ($n1=1$, 2, ..., N1; N1$\geqq$1) of permeable membrane patches that permit exchange of CO_2 outside the bag 12 with O_2 inside the bag. The upper surface of the bag 12 optionally includes a second sequence, 16-$n2$ ($n2=1$, ..., N2; N2$\geqq$0) of liquid-permeable membrane patches that permit transport of the second liquid 13 from within the bag 12 into the first liquid 14 by forward osmosis (FO). A lower surface of the bag 12 also includes further members, 16-(N2+1), 16-(N2+2), ..., 16-(N2+N3) (N3$\geqq$1), of the second sequence of membrane patches that permit transport of the second liquid 13 from within the bag 12 into the first liquid 14. The upper surface of the bag 12 is preferably surrounded by a gas atmosphere 17, such as air, at an ambient pressure, such as 1 atm. The bag is defined by upper and lower bag surfaces, attached to each other to form a closable container, where the upper and lower surfaces are substantially parallel to the surface of the first liquid 14.

The patches of FO membrane 16-$n2$ remove water to concentrate nutrients, to promote growth of algae and/or other micro-organisms, to concentrate salts or added reagents that induce algal oil production, and to concentrate-algae and/or other micro-organisms to assist in their harvesting and processing. By placing the patches of FO membrane 16-$n2$ on the upper surface of the bag, dewatering can be regulated by controlling the average depth h of the bag below the surface (FIG. 2). When the FO membrane 16-$n2$ is at the surface and mostly exposed to air, little dewatering occurs. When the FO membranes are submerged, the membranes actively dewater

5

6

the interior of the bag **12**. In this first embodiment, the bag **12** is submerged by an average depth h below the surface **18** of the water **14**, as illustrated in FIG. **2**, to activate the FO process and/or to protect the bag from inclement weather, such as a storm at sea.

In an incubation position, the upper surface of the bag **12** floats adjacent to the water surface **18**; and in a second (inverted) position the upper surface and the lower surface positions are exchanged with each other so that the upper surface of the bag is submerged to a selected average depth h (e.g., h=2-20 cm), and all surfaces of the bag are exposed to the surrounding liquid **14** in this second position. Gas exchange ceases and FO (now activated) depletes the bag interior of most of its water **13** and concentrates the algae and/or other micro-organisms grown in the bag interior. In the first approach, the bag **12** is submerged by a ballast arrangement or a tethering arrangement, illustrated in FIGS. **2** and **3A/3B**.

The rate of dewatering depends on the properties of the membrane **16**-$n2$ and the difference in composition between the water inside and outside the bag as indicated by

$$J(\text{eff})=A\{\Delta\pi-\Delta p\}, \tag{1}$$

where A is the hydraulic permeability of the membrane by liquid effluent, $\Delta\pi$ is a difference in osmotic pressures (inside versus outside), and Δp is a difference in hydrostatic pressure (inside versus outside).

Where hydrostatic pressures are approximately the same, inside and outside the bag **12**, $\Delta\pi$ is approximately 400 pounds/in^2 across the membrane **16**-$n2$ so that the liquid portion of the effluent, not including salts, microorganisms and/or other particles, will diffuse into the surrounding marine water. Where the bag **12** has a depth, measured perpendicular to the water's surface, of no more than about 20 cm, the associated hydraulic pressure difference (water pressure outside the bag minus water pressure inside the bag) is less than 40 pounds/in^2 so that the osmotic pressure term M dominates until the bag interior is nearly drained of its liquid effluent. When the bag **12** is nearly fully drained, the bag interior will contain the algae and/or other micro-organisms and other chemicals produced therein, plus a small amount of liquid effluent **13**. Before the flux J(eff) changes sign, indicating that some water **14** may flow into the bag **12**, it is preferable to terminate the liquid transport, for example, by returning the bag to the surface.

The micro-organisms in the bags will grow over a time interval of 1-10 days or longer. During or at the end of this incubation period, oil-producing algae may be subjected to stresses, such as nitrogen starvation or increased salts to promote oil production in association with algal growth. Some algal species have been found to produce over 40 percent oil, as a fraction of micro-organism dry weight.

When cultures are ready for dewatering, the bag is submerged so that the area primarily exposed to the ambient atmosphere during cultivation is under water. This activates the FO process, which will proceed until the contents of the bag are sufficiently concentrated to facilitate their transport for further processing. Where algae and/or other micro-organisms are present in the bag interior, when the FO has removed sufficient amounts of water to make a thick slurry within the bag interior, the algae and/or other micro-organisms will be pumped out of the bags into a transporting container such as a barge. In the transporting container, the dewatering process can continue to further concentrate the algae and/or other micro-organisms, using FO into sea water or brine (concentrated seawater produced by solar evaporation). After the algae and/or other micro-organisms have been removed from the bag, the bag is available for refilling with

nutrient-rich freshwater to re-initiate the growth cycle. The algae and/or other micro-organisms left in the bag after harvesting become the innoculum for the next growth cycle.

To improve the period of use of the bags and clean the semi-permeable membranes, the bag interiors can be periodically rinsed with water. The freshwater algae that will be released into the aquatic environment by this process will not be able to live in seawater or brine.

Another feature of submerging the bags is the enhanced ability of the system to withstand foul weather or harsh sea conditions. For example, when a storm is present or developing locally, submerging the bag **12** to a depth greater than about one half of the wavelength (crest-to-crest distance) of waves, or to depths >20 meters, should allow the bags to withstand severe wind and wave conditions on the surface.

Depth control for a bag is provided, in one embodiment by a fluid-based ballast system that allows the bag to be submerged in a liquid, assumed to be homogeneous, to any reasonable average depth h. One begins with a ballast bag **21**, illustrated in FIG. **2**, filled with a fluid having an interior pressure p0 and a corresponding volume V0 at atmospheric pressure p(atm). The ballast bag **21** is partly or wholly filled with a fluid **22** at initial pressure p0, using a ballast control mechanism **23**, and Boyle's law

$$pV=\text{constant} \tag{2}$$

applies to the bag contents, in the absence of temperature variations. Modest size masses **24** are attached at K spaced apart locations (K≧2) to an underside of the bag exterior or ballast bag exterior, where the individual mass sizes are chosen so that, with the ballast bag interior pressure at p=p0, the bag **12** floats on the surface of the (first) liquid **14**. With the bag **12** submerged to an average depth h (≧0) below the liquid surface **18**, the pressure on the exterior surface of the bag becomes

$$p=p(\text{atm})+p1\cdot h, \tag{3}$$

where p1 is a numerical constant that is characteristic of the liquid **22**. At an average depth h for the bag, Boyle's law becomes

$$pV=(p(\text{atm})+p1\cdot h)V=p(\text{atm})V0, \tag{4}$$

which can be re-expressed as

$$h=(p(\text{atm})/p1)\{(V0/V)-1\}, \tag{5}$$

which expresses the average depth h of the bag in terms of the volume V of the bag interior. As fluid is withdrawn from the bag interior (V<V0), the bag average depth h increases continuously and controllably as the bag is submerged below the liquid surface. The average depth h of submersion is preferably limited to values such that the difference, $\Delta\pi-\Delta p$ in Eq. (1) is positive.

The appropriate value for initial bag volume V0, where the bag floats on the (first) liquid surface **18**, is determined by taking into account the density and mass of one or more weights attached to the bag. The total mass of the composite bag (bag plus interior fluid plus bag weights) is

$$m_c=m_{bag}+\rho_{fluid}V+m_{weight}, \tag{6}$$

where ρ_{fluid} is the fluid density. The mass of the first liquid displaced by the partly inflated bag is

$$m_{Liquid}=\rho_{Liquid}V+m_{weight}(\rho_{Liquid}/\rho_{weight}), \tag{7}$$

Setting m_c and m_{Liquid} equal to each other results in

$$V0=\{m_{bag}+m_{weight}\{1-(\rho_{Liquid}/\rho_{weight})\}\}/(\rho_{Liquid}/\rho_{fluid}). \tag{8}$$

7

The average depth h of bag submersion may also be controllable by providing hollow, inflatable ribs in the bar surface. When the ribs are partly or wholly inflated with a fluid (e.g., air), the ribs (1) will tend to stiffen and to provide some structure for the bag surface and (2) will act as a flotation device to reduce the bag's tendency to submerge in the surrounding first liquid. The density of the fluid in the bag ribs should be substantially less than the density of the surrounding liquid for the bag.

FIGS. 3A and 3B schematically illustrate a second approach for alternatively floating and submerging the bag 12 to a controllable average depth h, relative to a surface 18 of the surrounding water 14. Two or more float modules, 31-1 and 31-2, are connected by respective tethers, 32-1 and 32-2, to floats (optional), and tether roll-up mechanisms, 33-1 and 33-2, respectively, and weights (optional), 34-1 and 34-2, respectively, which are attached at spaced apart locations to the bag 12. In a first position, shown in FIG. 3A, the bag 12 is adjacent to the surface 18 of the water, with the tethers, 32-1 and 32-2, being rolled up or reeled in to the floats, 31-1 and 31-2. In a second position, shown in FIG. 3B, the tethers, 32-1 and 32-2, are rolled out or reeled out a controlled distance d so that the bag 12 is now submerged by an average depth h below the surface 18 of the water 14. FIG. 3C illustrates how two or more tethers, 32-1' and 32-2', can be attached to a single float module 31-1'.

As an alternative to submersion of the bag to a controlled depth, the bag may be "flipped" or inverted so that the bag upper surface (not submerged) and the lower surface (submerged) are interchanged. This maneuver will expose the new lower surface of the bag to the surrounding first liquid; and if this new lower surface has membranes that support FO, the second liquid in the bag interior will be preferentially transported across the membrane(s) in to the surrounding liquid, which will increase the concentration of algae and/or other micro-organisms in the bag interior.

A controlled amount of CO_2 is introduced into the bag interior to encourage growth of algae and/or other microorganisms. If the CO_2 forms "bubbles" with average diameters greater than a threshold value, most of the bubbles may rise to an upper surface of the second liquid in the bag and be lost, without contributing to algae growth. One approach for increasing the percentage of CO_2 that actually contributes to algae growth is to decrease the average diameter of the CO_2 bubbles so that a higher percentage of these bubbles will be absorbed into the second liquid in the bag interior, using a fine mesh screen or a membrane having pores no larger than a selected diameter.

FIG. 4A illustrates one apparatus for delivering CO_2 to the interior 12(int) of the bag. The bag 12 is a rectangular parallelepiped or curvilinear body containing the second liquid 13 and having a sequence of membrane patches, 15-$n1$ and/or 16-$n2$, on an upper surface and/or on a lower surface of the bag. The bag 12 is surrounded by a gas exchange bag 19, and an interstitial space 12(stit) between the bag 12 and the gas exchange bag 19 is filled with CO_2 at a selected pressure $p(CO_2)$, at a partial pressure in a range 1-150 psi. One or more surfaces of the bag 12 contains a membrane 12(mem) that is permeable to CO_2 contained in the interstitial space 12(stit), and is, therefore, also permeable to O_2 that is produced and accumulates in the bag interior 12(int). Preferably, the CO_2 pressure in the interstitial space 12(stit) is greater than the CO_2 pressure in the bag interior 12(int) so that the net CO_2 flow is into the bag interior. Preferably, the O_2 pressure in the bag interior 12(int) is greater than the O_2 pressure in the interstitial space 12(stit) so that the net O_2 flow is into the interstitial space. The gas exchange bag walls are not perme-

able to CO_2 or to O_2. Proceeding in this manner, a net transfer of CO_2 into bag interior occurs and a net transfer of O_2 into the interstitial space occurs. The O_2 in the interstitial space 12(stit) can be partly or wholly removed by methods known in the art so that an appreciable amount of O_2 does not accumulate in the interstitial space.

An alternative apparatus, shown in side view in FIG. 4B, provides a lower region 19(lower) and/or an upper region 19(upper) that also contains CO_2 at the selected pressure $p(CO_2)$. The lower region 19(lower) and/or the upper region 19(upper) is optionally separated from the bag interior 12(int) by a membrane 12(mem) that is permeable to CO_2 (and to O_2).

FIGS. 5A/5B/5C illustrate a suitable arrangement of gaspermeable membranes 12(mem) that can be provided on an upper surface, a bottom surface and/or a side surface of the bag 12, to facilitate exchange of CO_2 and of O_2 between regions outside the bag and inside the bag. In FIG. 5A, the membranes 12(mem) extend as M linear or curvilinear channels or fingers 12(chan)-m ($m=1, \ldots, M$; $M \geq 1$) from a first surface toward a second surface of the bag 12. In FIG. 5B, the membranes 12(mem) extend as channels or fingers (12 (chan)-m from a first surface to a second surface of the bag 12. One or more of the channels contains a CO_2 control valve mechanism 12(control)-m that either shuts off flow of CO_2 into the associated finger or permits flow of CO_2 at a selected pressure $p(CO_2)$ into the associated channel. The control mechanisms 12(control)-m are individually controlled by one or more PID controllers 12(PID) that determine which valves 12(control)-m are open and which valves are closed.

FIG. 5C illustrates a spiral arrangement of channels in which each of M adjacent spiral channels 12(spiral)-m ($m=1, \ldots, M$; $M \geq 1$; here, $M=2$) has a membrane along one surface that interfaces with the bag interior, to permit CO_2 exchange with the bag interior. In each of the embodiments in FIGS. 5A, 5B and 5C, a pH meter 13(pH) is preferably provided to monitor the pH in the bag interior (not shown here) for purposes of growth of the algae and/or other μorgs.

The algae may include one or more of *botryococcus braunii, chlorella vulgaris* or another lipid-producing algae that is useful for producing hydrocarbons or other desired products. *Botryococcus braunii* (Bb) is a pyramid-shaped, freshwater green algae, with colonies held together by a lipid biofilm matrix. The species is best known for its ability to produce large amounts of hydrocarbons, especially oils in the form of triterpenes, which are typically 30-40 percent of the dry weight of the triterpenes. Bb is believed to grow best at a temperature $T \approx 23° C.$, with a light intensity of 60 Watts/cm^2, with a light period of about 12 hours per day, at a salinity level of 0.15 M NaCl. The oils produced are usually unbranched isoprenoid triterpenes having a chemical composition C_nH_{2n-10}, ($n=23-37$), with $n=30-37$ accounting for as much as about 70 percent of the total triterpenes. The oils produced through hydro-cracking include octane (gasoline), kerosene, diesel, aviation fuel, residual oil, alkanes, alkenes, alkynes, alcohols, ethers, aldehydes, ketones, esters, amines, amides, benzene ring-based hydrocarbons and cyclic hydrocarbons.

Bb performs moderately well as a lipid-based feedstock for fuel production, with a doubling time for growth of 48-72 hours, depending on the growth environment. Some experimental results indicate that, where supplemental CO_2 (1-2 percent) is provided, the concentrations of palmitic acid and oleic acid produced are increased by factors of 2-3, relative to the corresponding concentrations produced in air; hydrocarbon content was found to be above 20 percent where 2 percent supplemental CO_2 was provided. Other experimental results indicate that growth of Bb in water with salinity levels of

9

0.034 M and 0.085 M NaCl, produces approximately two-fold increases in concentrations of palmitic acid and oleic acid in the Bb grown.

Chlorella vulgaris (Cv) is a spherical-shaped, single-celled green algae and contains green photosynthetic pigments, chlorophyll-a and chlorophyll-b, with associated photosynthetic efficiency as high as about 8 percent. When dried, the plant is about 45 percent protein, 20 percent fat, 20 percent carbohydrate, 5 percent fiber and 10 percent minerals and vitamins. The genus, *chlorella* can grow in direct sunlight, with a solar energy conversion efficiency of about 20 percent, in the presence of high levels of nitrates and phosphates. Cv is more often associated historically with food and food additive feedstocks than with feedstocks for oil production. However, Cv can also serve as a feedstock for algal oil, for trans-esterification into bio-diesel. Cell wall rupture is an essential step in extracting lipids and reusing the cell walls for fermentation into ethanol, subsequently used in the trans-esterification process. Bio-diesel and ethanol, produced from trans-esterification of Cv, provide 3.20 and 1.34 energy-equivalent units, relative to the 1.0 energy-equivalent unit solar energy input. The estimated energy gain for bio-diesel produced from Cv is about 4:1. One concern is the choice of enzymes to optimize production (increase the production rate) of bio-diesel fuel. Another concern is removal of products of the process that are not algal oil.

Thus far, the discussion of this invention has focused on growth of algae and/or other micro-organisms within the bag interior, for provision of oil for diesel, aircraft and automotive vehicles and for provision of other useful products for nutritional needs and other chemical applications. This invention can also used to encourage growth of other macro-organisms within the bag interior, such as shrimp, prawns, crayfish and/or crabs.

FIG. 6 is a flow chart illustrating a method for practicing the invention. In step **61**, effluent or eutrophied second liquid is collected in a bag. The liquid effluent may include a modest concentration of target micro-organisms, such as algae, bacteria, etc., that provide an innoculum or "seed" for one or more desired species to be grown within the bag. In step **62**, a selected surface, or all of the surface, of the bag is submerged in a first liquid, which has a differential concentration of at least one chemical substance relative to the second liquid.

In step **63** (optional), CO_2, NH_3 and/or other growth nutrients for a target micro-organism are introduced into the bag interior. In step **64** (optional), the target micro-organisms are permitted, or encouraged, to grow within the bag. In step **65**, a selected portion of the bag surface, containing membranes that support FO of the second liquid into the first liquid, is exposed to the first liquid. In step **66**, FO of the second liquid into the first liquid, across the FO membranes, is permitted to proceed so that at least a portion of the second liquid is removed from the bag interior, thereby increasing a relative concentration of the target micro-organism within the bag contents. In step **67**, the target micro-organism(s), now at increased concentration, and remainder of the second liquid are removed from the bag interior. In step **68** (optional), the bag interior is cleaned and made ready for a new cycle.

The contents of the bag interior may include lipid-based substances that can be further processed to provide oil for diesel, aircraft, automotive vehicles and other uses, using processes that are well known in the art. Alternatively or additionally, non-marine water (originally the second liquid) that is transported through the second sequence of FO membrane patches 16-*n*2 (FIG. 1) can be used to locally modify or remediate the high-nutrient-load water (first liquid) that surrounds the bag. Where a sufficient number of bags is provided

10

in a given "dead zone," this dead zone can be partly or fully converted to a reduced-nutrient zone that again supports aquatic life.

Two or more bags **12** can be attached to each other to form a "connected structure," illustrated in FIG. **7**, for immobilizing the bags or for transport of the bags in the water. In a connected structure, resembling a linear or branched carbon (backbone) chain, each bag is attached to at least one other bag, and a first bag in the structure can be reached from a second bag in the structure by a path that stays within the structure.

What is claimed is:

1. A method for producing at least one micro-organism ("μorg"), the method comprising:
   providing a closeable enclosure, having an enclosure interior and being defined by first and second opposed enclosure surfaces that are joined together;
   partially or fully immersing the enclosure in a first type liquid;
   partially filling the enclosure with the at least one μorg and a second type liquid;
   closing the enclosure with the second type liquid and the at least one μorg contained in the enclosure interior, where at least one of the enclosure first and second surfaces comprises one or more semi-permeable first membranes that are permeable to the second type liquid and are substantially impermeable to the at least one μorg;
   allowing at least a portion of the second type liquid within the enclosure interior to pass through the one or more first membranes into the first type liquid by forward osmosis, to thereby remove at least a portion of the second type liquid in the enclosure interior;
   providing at least one of the enclosure first surface and the enclosure second surface with at least one CO_2 transport membrane having a CO_2 transport rate across the transport membrane that can be changed; and
   increasing or decreasing the rate of CO_2 transport across the transport membrane into said enclosure, in order to bring a present CO_2 concentration value, $C(CO_2)$, into closer agreement with a selected CO_2 concentration value, $C(CO_2; ref)$.

2. The method of claim **1**, further comprising removing said at least one μorg from said enclosure interior when said at least one μorg has reached at least a selected μorg growth stage.

3. The method of claim **1**, further comprising:
   providing said at least one or more semi-permeable first membranes on said enclosure first surface; and
   submerging said enclosure first surface in order to promote transport of said second type liquid through said one or more first membranes into said first type liquid.

4. The method of claim **1**, further comprising choosing said first type liquid/second type liquid to have a non-zero gradient of a selected chemical across at least one of said one or more first membranes.

5. The method of claim **4**, further comprising choosing a combination of said first type liquid/second type liquid to be at least one of marine water/non-marine water, brine/marine water, and brine/non-marine water.

6. The method of claim **4**, further comprising choosing said second type liquid to comprise effluent water.

7. The method of claim **1**, further comprising initially positioning said enclosure so that a portion of said enclosure second surface is initially submerged in said first type liquid to influence passage of said second type liquid through at least one of said one or more of said first membranes.

11

8. The method of claim **1**, further comprising providing de-eutrophication of a portion of said first type liquid adjacent to said enclosure first surface by passage of said portion of said second type liquid through said one or more first membranes into said first type liquid.

9. The method of claim **1**, further comprising increasing salinity of said second type liquid within said enclosure.

10. The method of claim **1**, further comprising selecting at least one of said one or more first membranes from a group of semi-permeable membranes that contain small pores and are hydrophobic.

11. The method of claim **1**, further comprising choosing said one or more first membranes to have a thickness in a range 1-20 mils.

12. The method of claim **1**, further comprising choosing said at least one μorg to be an alga that produces at least one lipid.

13. The method of claim **12**, further comprising choosing said at least one lipid-producing alga to include at least one animal feed compound.

14. The method of claim **12**, further comprising choosing said at least one lipid-producing alga to include at least one fertilizer component.

15. The method of claim **12**, wherein said at least one lipid-producing compound produces a compound drawn from a group of hydrocarbons consisting of fuel oil, diesel fuel, aviation fuel, gasoline, kerosene, alkanes, alkenes, alkynes, alcohols, ethers, aldehydes, ketones, esters, amines, amides, benzene ring-based hydrocarbons and cyclic hydrocarbons.

16. The method of claim **1**, further comprising removing a portion of said second type liquid and said at least one μorg from said enclosure interior at first and second selected times that are spaced apart from each other.

17. The method of claim **16**, further comprising choosing a difference between said second selected time and said first selected time to be no greater than about ten days.

18. The method of claim **1**, further comprising removing, from said enclosure, and processing said at least one μorg, to produce at least one lipid with a lipid weight of at least 20 percent dry weight of said at least one μorg, and to serve as an inocculum for subsequent growth of said μorg.

19. The method of claim **1**, further comprising submerging said enclosure in said first type liquid to a continuously variable or discretely variable, selected depth h so that said enclosure is substantially completely submerged below a surface of said first type liquid.

20. The method of claim **19**, wherein said process of submerging said enclosure in said body of said first type liquid to said selected depth h comprises:

providing at least two inflatable submersion enclosures, attached to said enclosure to be submerged, with each submersion enclosure having a selected weight attached thereto and being partly filled with a selected fluid that has a lower density than said first type liquid and a lower density than said second type liquid, where the sum of the weights attached to a submersion enclosure is selected so that (i) when all of the selected fluid is withdrawn from all the submersion enclosures, the enclosure to be submerged will sink toward a bottom of said first type liquid and (ii) when sufficient fluid is admitted into the plurality of submersion enclosures, the enclosure to be submerged will float on said surface of said first type liquid,

whereby said depth of said enclosure is continuously or discretely varied by withdrawing the selected fluid from, or adding the selected fluid to, at least one submersion enclosure.

21. The method of claim **19**, wherein said process of submerging said enclosure to be submerged in said body of said first type liquid to said selected depth h comprises:

providing one or more float modules that are capable of floating on or near said liquid surface;

providing one or more tethers, each tether having a first end attached to at least one float module and having a second end attached to or associated with said enclosure;

providing a tether roll-up/reel-out mechanism, located adjacent to the first end or adjacent to the second end of each of the one or more tethers, that decreases a length d of the associated tether or increases the length d of the associated tether, upon receipt of a roll-up command signal or a reel-out command signal, respectively; and

providing a roll-up/reel-out command control mechanism, connected to each of the at least two tether roll-up/reel-out mechanisms, to provide a roll-up command signal or, alternatively, a reel-out command signal to the tether roll-up/reel-out mechanism,

whereby said depth h of said enclosure is continuously varied or discretely varied by varying the length d of the associated tether.

22. The method of claim **19**, further comprising controllably submerging said enclosure first surface to a depth in a range of 0-20 meters below said first type liquid surface.

23. The method of claim **19**, further comprising providing at least one of said enclosure first surface and said enclosure second surface with at least one hollow core rib that can be inflated by introduction of a selected fluid into the at least one hollow core rib.

24. The method of claim **1**, further comprising:

providing N enclosures (N≧2), produced according to claim **3**; and

attaching each of the N enclosures to at least one of the other N–1 enclosures so that the N enclosures form a connected structure that can be moved in said body of first type liquid from a first location to a second location that is spaced apart from the first location.

25. The method of claim **1**, further comprising:

partially or fully immersing said enclosure in said first type liquid; and

allowing heat capacity of said first type liquid to subsequently maintain a temperature of said second type liquid approximately equal to a temperature of said first type liquid.

26. The method of claim **1**, further comprising allowing wave action in said first type liquid to thereby promote mixing of contents of said second type liquid within said enclosure.

27. The method of claim **1**, further comprising providing said second type liquid within said enclosure with an average depth having a range within said enclosure of 5-20 cm.

28. The method of claim **1**, further comprising allowing light that is incident on said enclosure, to illuminate said at least one μorg and to promote growth of said at least one μorg within said enclosure.

29. The method of claim **28**, further comprising providing said enclosure second surface with an enclosure interior surface that receives and reflects substantially all light incident thereon within a selected wavelength range.

30. The method of claim **1**, further comprising providing said enclosure first surface with an enclosure substance that receives incident light and transmits the incident light into

said second type liquid only if at least one wavelength of the incident light is within a selected wavelength range.

31. The method of claim 1, wherein said at least one CO_2 transport membrane includes a plurality of mesh screen apertures that provide gas bubbles containing CO_2 gas having gas bubble diameters less than a selected threshold diameter, within said enclosure interior, to thereby promote absorption of said CO_2 gas bubbles within said second type liquid.

32. The method of claim 1, further comprising:
providing at least one second membrane that permits transport of O_2 from said enclosure interior to an exterior of said enclosure.

33. The method of claim 1, further comprising:
providing a controller that controls said present CO_2 concentration value $C(CO_2)$ within said second type liquid relative to said selected CO_2 concentration value, $C(CO_2; ref)$.

34. A method for producing at least one micro-organism ("µorg"), the method comprising:
providing a first type liquid;
providing a sealable enclosure, having an enclosure interior and being defined by first and second enclosure surfaces;
partially filling the enclosure interior with a second type liquid, and providing at least one selected micro-organism ("µorg") in the enclosure interior;
closing the enclosure;
positioning the enclosure in the first type liquid;
providing at least one of the first and second enclosure surfaces with one or more semi-permeable first membranes that are permeable to at least one of CO_2 gas and NH_3 gas and are substantially impermeable to the at least one selected µorg,
providing an exterior source of at least one of CO_2 gas and NH_3 gas in contact with the one or more first membranes;
providing a controller that senses a pH value, pH(sens), within the second type liquid, compares the value pH(sens) with a reference value, pH(ref), for the pH value within the second type liquid, and introduces at least one of the CO_2 gas and the NH_3 gas into the second type liquid in order to bring pH(sens) into closer agreement with pH(ref);
providing a semi-permeable second membrane, positioned on at least one of the first and second enclosure surfaces, that is permeable to the second liquid and is not permeable to the at least one µorg; and
allowing at least a portion of the second type liquid within the enclosure interior to pass through the second membrane, positioned on at least one of the first and second enclosure surfaces, into the first type liquid by forward osmosis, to thereby remove at least part of the second type liquid from the enclosure interior.

35. The method of claim 34, further comprising choosing said pH reference value in a range $3.5 \leq pH(ref) \leq 9.5$.

36. A method for producing at least one micro-organism ("µorg"), the method comprising:
providing a sealable enclosure, having an enclosure interior and being defined by first and second opposed enclosure surfaces that are joined together;
partially or fully immersing the enclosure in a first type liquid;
partially filling the enclosure with the at least one µorg and a second type liquid;
closing the enclosure with the second type liquid and the at least one µorg contained in the enclosure interior, where at least one of the enclosure first and second surfaces

comprises one or more semi-permeable first membranes that are permeable to the second type liquid and are substantially impermeable to the at least one µorg;
allowing at least a portion of the second type liquid within the enclosure interior to pass through the one or more first membranes into the first type liquid by forward osmosis, to thereby remove at least a portion of the second type liquid in the enclosure interior;
providing the one or more first membranes on the enclosure first surface; and
positioning at least one of the one or more first membranes above a surface of the first type liquid in order to reduce or suppress transport of said second liquid through the first membrane into said first type liquid.

37. A method for producing at least one micro-organism ("µorg"), the method comprising:
providing a sealable enclosure, having an enclosure interior and being defined by first and second opposed enclosure surfaces that are joined together;
partially or fully immersing the enclosure in a first type liquid;
partially filling the enclosure with the at least one µorg and a second type liquid;
closing the enclosure with the second type liquid and the at least one µorg contained in the enclosure interior, where at least one of the enclosure first and second surfaces comprises one or more semi-permeable first membranes that are permeable to the second type liquid and are substantially impermeable to the at least one µorg;
allowing at least a portion of the second type liquid within the enclosure interior to pass through the one or more first membranes into the first type liquid by forward osmosis, to thereby remove at least a portion of the second type liquid in the enclosure interior; and
providing one or more second membranes on at least one of the first enclosure surface and the second enclosure surface, which are permeable to at least one selected nutrient for the at least one µorg.

38. A method for producing at least one micro-organism ("µorg"), the method comprising:
providing a sealable enclosure, having an enclosure interior and being defined by first and second opposed enclosure surfaces that are joined together;
partially or fully immersing the enclosure in a first type liquid;
partially filling the enclosure with the at least one µorg and a second type liquid;
closing the enclosure with the second type liquid and the at least one µorg contained in the enclosure interior, where at least one of the enclosure first and second surfaces comprises one or more semi-permeable first membranes that are permeable to the second type liquid and are substantially impermeable to the at least one µorg;
allowing at least a portion of the second type liquid within the enclosure interior to pass through the one or more first membranes into the first type liquid by forward osmosis, to thereby remove at least a portion of the second type liquid in the enclosure interior; and
adding a selected chemical to the second type liquid to promote production of at least one of CO_2 and NH_3 within the enclosure.

39. A method for producing at least one micro-organism ("µorg"), the method comprising:
providing a sealable enclosure, having an enclosure interior and being defined by first and second opposed enclosure surfaces that are joined together;

15

partially or fully immersing the enclosure in a first type liquid;

partially filling the enclosure with the at least one μorg and a second type liquid;

closing the enclosure with the second type liquid and the at least one μorg contained in the enclosure interior, where at least one of the enclosure first and second surfaces comprises one or more semi-permeable first membranes that are permeable to the second type liquid and are substantially impermeable to the at least one μorg;

allowing at least a portion of the second type liquid within the enclosure interior to pass through the one or more

16

first membranes into the first type liquid by forward osmosis, to thereby remove at least a portion of the second type liquid in the enclosure interior; and

applying a process of inverting positions of said enclosure first surface and said enclosure second surface, relative to a surface of said first liquid, to reduce or terminate forward osmosis that has begun across the one or more first membranes.

* * * * *

(12) United States Patent
Zell

(10) **Patent No.:** **US 7,662,459 B1**

(45) **Date of Patent:** **Feb. 16, 2010**

(54) **VERSATILE HONEYCOMB MATRIX HEAT SHIELD**

(75) Inventor: **Peter T. Zell**, Moss Beach, CA (US)

(73) Assignee: **The United States of America as represented by the Administrator of the National Aeronautics and Space Administration (NASA)**, Washington, DC (US)

(*) Notice: Subject to any disclaimer, the term of this patent is extended or adjusted under 35 U.S.C. 154(b) by 0 days.

(21) Appl. No.: **12/175,379**

(22) Filed: **Jul. 17, 2008**

(51) **Int. Cl.**
B64C 1/06 (2006.01)
B32B 3/12 (2006.01)

(52) **U.S. Cl.** **428/116**; 244/123.5; 244/123.6; 428/117

(58) **Field of Classification Search** .... 428/116, 428/117, 118, 119; 244/171.7, 171.8, 99.1, 244/121, 119, 123.13, 123.12, 123.4, 123.5, 244/133, 117 A, 52/81.1, 81.2, 81.4, 202, 52/576, 578, 784.14, 784.15, 787.11, 793.11
See application file for complete search history.

Primary Examiner—Timothy M Speer
Assistant Examiner—Gordon R Baldwin
(74) *Attorney, Agent, or Firm*—John F. Schipper; Robert M. Padilla

(57) **ABSTRACT**

A thermal protection system for atmospheric entry of a vehicle, the system including a honeycomb structure with selected cross sectional shapes that receives and holds thermally cured thermal protection (TP) blocks that have corresponding cross sectional shapes. Material composition for TP blocks in different locations can be varied to account for different atmospheric heating characteristics at the different locations. TP block side walls may be attached to all, or to less than all, the corresponding honeycomb structure side walls.

16 Claims, 2 Drawing Sheets

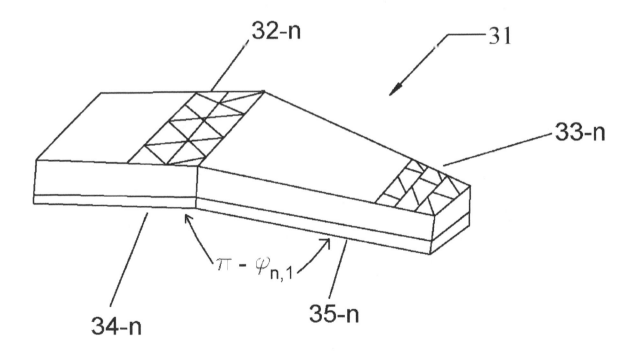

293

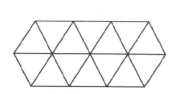

FIG. 1A

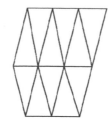

FIG. 1B

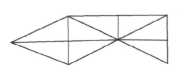

FIG. 1C

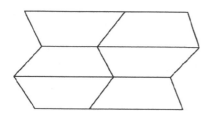

FIG. 1F

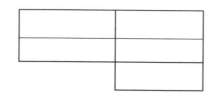

FIG. 1E

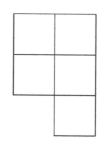

FIG. 1D

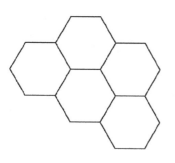

FIG. 1G

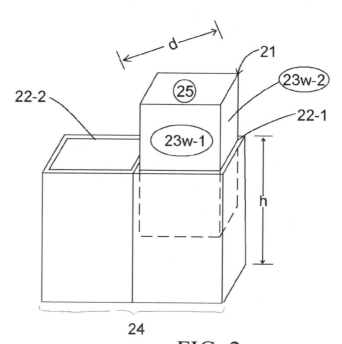

FIG. 2

294

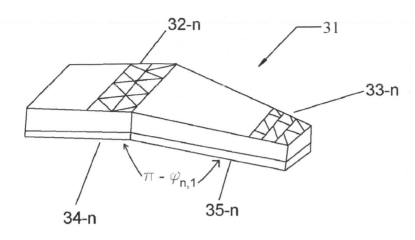

FIG. 3

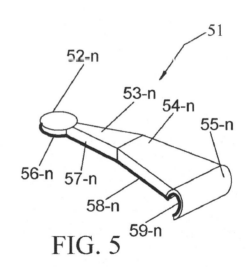

FIG. 5

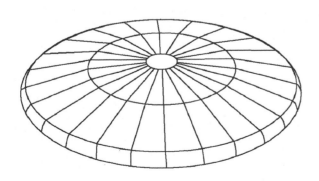

FIG. 4

1

VERSATILE HONEYCOMB MATRIX HEAT SHIELD

ORIGIN OF THE INVENTION

This invention was made, in part, by one or more employees of the U.S. government and may be made, used and/or sold by the U.S. government without payment of royalties or other compensation thereon.

FIELD OF THE INVENTION

This invention relates to thermal protection systems for vehicles entering or re-entering an atmosphere.

BACKGROUND OF THE INVENTION

When an entrant vehicle enters or re-enters an atmosphere adjacent to a surface of a planet or satellite body, the atmospheric density at the entrant vehicle surface abruptly increases from substantially zero (≈ 1 particle/cm^3) to a value at least millions of times as large in a very short time interval, of the order of a few seconds for a vehicle that enters or re-enters at velocities of the order of 10,000-30,000 kilometers per hour. This transition causes an abrupt and sustained increase in heating at and adjacent to surfaces exposed to the atmosphere, and the associated surface temperatures can exceed 3000° F. for an extended period.

What is needed is a heat shield for an entrant vehicle that can withstand the anticipated surface temperatures and that can be adapted to correspond to different entrant configurations of the vehicle (entrant velocity, entrant angle, atmosphere density distribution, etc.)

SUMMARY OF THE INVENTION

These needs are met by the invention, which provides a honeycomb matrix heat shield with honeycomb components that can be varied according to the anticipated heat dissipation needs of the entrant vehicle. The heat shield includes a honeycomb structure having thermal protection (TP) blocks inserted within each honeycomb aperture, where each TP block is thermally cured before insertion and is adhered to all, or optionally to less than all, of the adjacent walls of the honeycomb structure. The honeycomb structure and inserted TP blocks are positioned on an assembly of planar segments, as substrates, that surround one or more entrant vehicle surfaces that will be initially exposed to entrant heating. The TP blocks may have cross sectional shapes drawn from a variety of configurations, and the material compositions of the blocks may be varied across the surface to account for different anticipated heating distributions.

BRIEF DESCRIPTION OF THE DRAWINGS

FIGS. 1A-1G illustrate some of the cross sectional shapes of the TP blocks that can be used with the invention.

FIG. 2 illustrates insertion of a TP block into a honeycomb matrix aperture.

FIGS. 3 and 5 illustrate positioning of different honeycomb matrices on heat shield wedge segments according to the invention.

FIG. 4 illustrates assembling of a plurality of heat shield segments from FIG. 3 to protect an end surface of an entrant vehicle from atmospheric heating.

2

DESCRIPTION OF BEST MODE OF THE INVENTION

FIGS. 1A-1G illustrate some of the cross sectional shapes of thermal protection (TP) blocks that can be used as inserts in a honeycomb (HC) structure according to the invention. These cross sectional shapes include equilateral triangles (FIG. 1A), isoceles triangles (1B), right triangles (1C), squares (1D), rectangles (1E), symmetrical trapezoids (1F), regular hexagons (1G), and many other suitable shapes.

FIG. 2 illustrates insertion of a TP block 21, having a diameter d=2.5-10 cm, or larger if desired, and a depth h=2-12 cm, or larger if desired, into an aperture 22-1 defined by part of a HC structure 24. An adjacent aperture 22-2 does not yet have a TP block inserted therein. The TP block 21 is thermally cured before insertion into the HC structure, by exposing the TP block to heating temperatures up to about 400° F. for time intervals of length 30-180 min.

In a preferred embodiment, two or more (but less than all) contiguous side walls, 23w-1 and 23w-2, of the TP block 21 have thicknesses of the order of 0.04-0.08 cm are provided with a suitable adhesive that allows these TP side walls to adhere to corresponding walls of an aperture 22-1 of the HC structure. In a preferred embodiment, all side walls of a TP block 21 are provided with adhesive.

By providing adhesive on at least two contiguous side walls, but less than all of the sidewalls, of the TP block 21, the TP block can be allowed to thermally expand in the presence of atmospheric heating, partly independently of the thermal expansion of the confining HC structure. Where the HC structure pattern is triangular (e.g., FIGS. 1A, 1B and 1C), adhesive is optionally provided for one side wall or for two contiguous side walls of the corresponding triangular cross section TP block, to allow for thermal expansion of the TP block relative to the HC structure. Where the HC structure is an M-gon (M=4, 5, 6, etc.), m=2, 3, . . . , M−1 contiguous side walls of the corresponding M-gon TP block are optionally provided with adhesive, to allow for thermal expansion of the TP block relative to the HC structure. Alternatively, all walls of the TP block are provided with adhesive.

Each TP block 21 includes a selected TP material, such as PICA, SLA, carbon ablator and similar thermal protection materials, where an individual block may have an approximately uniform material composition. One composition of PICA (phenolic impregnated carbon ablator) is disclosed in U.S. Pat. No. 6,955,853, which is incorporated by reference herein. A composition of SLA (super lightweight ablator, a carbon char or silica char) is disclosed in U.S. Pat. No. 4,031,059, which is incorporated by reference herein. A combination of PICA and SLA thermal protection materials has been used in at least one space vehicle application, the Space Probe vehicle developed by Lockheed Martin and used for the Stardust mission that flew through the coma (tail) of the Wild 2 Comet in 2004.

However, two or more TP blocks may have different compositions, depending upon their respective locations in the HC structure, to take account of different anticipated heating environments for different contiguous TP blocks in the HC structure. Through a process of varying the composition of TP blocks in different locations on a heat shield, the weight of the heat shield may be reduced or optimized for a given anticipated heating distribution associated with a specified entrant environment. A first end 25 of each of the TP blocks in FIG. 2 is directly exposed to the atmosphere and will experience the greatest amount of heating. In some instances, a portion of the TP block (preferably, no more than 10-30 percent by volume) will ablate or otherwise chemically dissociate and

3

disappear during (re)entry. Preferably, a second end (not shown in FIG. **2**) of a TP block can be provided with adhesive to attach the TP block to an underlying substrate (**34**-*n* and **35**-*n* in FIG. **3**).

The HC structure provides a structural lattice for insertion of the TP blocks in the lattice and has a material composition, such as carbon phenolic or another suitable material, that is chosen to be compatible with the TP block material. For example, the HC structure material is preferably mechanically and/or thermally stronger than, but should ablate at approximately the same rate as, the TP block material, when exposed to the same entrant thermal environment. Optionally, the HC structure and substrate are bonded or otherwise attached to a space vehicle, and the HC structure can be tested in place, before the TP blocks are inserted.

FIG. **3** illustrates positioning of two adjacent HC structures, **32**-*n* and **33**-*n*, on respective substrates, **34**-*n* and **35**-*n* (*n*=1, . . . , N; N≧3), as part of an embodiment of the heat shield invention **31**. The substrate pairs, **34**-*n* and **35**-*n*, are preferably planar, oriented at a non-zero angle $\phi_{n,1}$ relative to each other, and N substrate pairs are assembled as part of a faceted substrate, to provide a heat shield in this embodiment, as illustrated in FIG. **4**. Each of the HC structures, **32**-*n* and **33**-*n*, in FIG. **3** may have an independently chosen pattern or HC aperture shape, such as one of the patterns shown in FIGS. **1A**–**1G**, and a TP block having an appropriate cross sectional shape is inserted into an HC aperture, as illustrated in FIG. **2**. At least three such HC structures and corresponding substrates are present in one embodiment of the invention.

FIG. **5** illustrates use of four adjacent HC structures, **52**-*n*, **53**-*n*, **54**-*n* and **55**-*n*, positioned on four corresponding substrates, **56**-*n*, **57**-*n*, **58**-*n* and **59**-*n*, respectively. The HC structure **55**-*n* and substrate **59**-*n* form a shoulder that wraps around a portion of the entrant vehicle surface.

What is claimed is:

1. A thermal protection system for atmospheric entry of a vehicle, the system comprising:

a first assembly of first honeycomb components, each first honeycomb component having a first honeycomb component material composition, having at least three first honeycomb component walls, each first honeycomb component wall having substantially the same first honeycomb component diameter and having substantially the same first honeycomb component cross sectional shape, the first honeycomb components being connected together to form a first honeycomb matrix, where each first honeycomb component in the first honeycomb matrix receives and holds a first honeycomb thermal protection block having at least three first honeycomb thermal protection block side walls, where the first honeycomb thermal protection block is a selected first thermal protection block material, where the first assembly is located on and connected to a first substrate, and where at least first and second first honeycomb thermal protection block side walls are attached to first and second first honeycomb component walls, respectively;

a second assembly of second honeycomb components, each second honeycomb component having a second honeycomb component material composition, having at least three second honeycomb component walls, each second honeycomb component wall having substantially the same second honeycomb component diameter and having substantially the same second honeycomb component cross sectional shape, the second honeycomb components being connected together to form a second honeycomb matrix, where each second honeycomb component in the second honeycomb matrix

4

receives and holds a second honeycomb thermal protection block having at least three second honeycomb thermal protection block side walls of a second honeycomb component, where the second honeycomb thermal protection block is a selected second thermal protection block material, where the second assembly is located on and connected to a second substrate, where at least first and second honeycomb thermal protection block side walls are attached to first and second honeycomb component walls, respectively, and where the first and second substrates are substantially planar and are oriented at a non-zero angle relative to each other;

where at least one of the first honeycomb thermal protection blocks is thermally cured before insertion of the at least one of the first honeycomb thermal protection blocks into the first assembly of the first honeycomb components, and where at least one of the second honeycomb thermal protection blocks is thermally cured before insertion of the at least one of the second honeycomb thermal protection blocks into the second assembly of the second honeycomb components;

where each of the first honeycomb thermal protection blocks has a first honeycomb thermal protection block first end that is exposed to an atmosphere having re-entry temperatures and has a first honeycomb thermal protection block second end that is attached to the first substrate, and at least one of the first honeycomb thermal protection blocks is thermally cured before insertion of the at least one first honeycomb thermal protection block into the first assembly of the first honeycomb components; and

where each of the second honeycomb thermal protection blocks has a second honeycomb thermal protection block first end that is exposed to the atmosphere having re-entry temperatures and has a second honeycomb thermal protection block second end that is attached to the second substrate.

2. The system of claim **1**, wherein at least one of said second honeycomb thermal protection blocks in said second substrate is thermally cured before insertion of the at least one second honeycomb thermal protection block into said second assembly of said second honeycomb components.

3. The system of claim **1**, wherein said first honeycomb material includes silicon phenolic.

4. The system of claim **1**, wherein said second honeycomb material includes silicon phenolic.

5. The system of claim **1**, wherein said first thermal protection block material includes at least one of a group of thermal protection materials consisting of PICA, SLA and carbon ablator.

6. The system of claim **1**, wherein said second thermal protection block material includes at least one of a group of thermal protection materials consisting of PICA, SLA and carbon ablator.

7. The system of claim **1**, wherein said selected first thermal protection block material and said selected second thermal protection block material are substantially the same material.

8. The system of claim **1**, wherein said first honeycomb shape for said first honeycomb components is drawn from the group consisting of regular triangles, isosceles triangles, right triangles, symmetric trapezoids, rectangles, squares and regular hexagons.

9. The system of claim **1**, wherein said second honeycomb shape for said second honeycomb components is drawn from

5

6

the group consisting of regular triangles, isosceles triangles, right triangles, symmetric trapezoids, rectangles, squares and regular hexagons.

10. The system of claim **1**, wherein at least one of said first honeycomb component thermal protection block side walls is not attached by an adhesive to any of said first honeycomb component walls.

11. The system of claim **10**, wherein at least one of said second honeycomb component thermal protection block side walls is not attached by an adhesive to any of said second honeycomb component walls.

12. The system of claim **1**, wherein each of said first honeycomb component thermal protection block side walls is attached by an adhesive to at least one of said first honeycomb component walls.

13. The system of claim **12**, wherein each of said second honeycomb component thermal protection block side walls is attached by an adhesive to at least one of said second honeycomb component walls.

14. The system of claim **1**, wherein said cross sectional shape of said first honeycomb components differs from said cross sectional shape of said second honeycomb components.

15. The system of claim **1**, wherein said diameter of said first honeycomb components differs from said diameter of said second honeycomb components.

16. The system of claim **1**, wherein said first honeycomb component material differs from said second honeycomb component material.

* * * * *

US007767305B1

(12) **United States Patent**

Stewart et al.

(10) **Patent No.:** **US 7,767,305 B1**

(45) **Date of Patent:** **Aug. 3, 2010**

(54) **HIGH EFFICIENCY TANTALUM-BASED CERAMIC COMPOSITE STRUCTURES**

(75) Inventors: **David A. Stewart**, Santa Cruz, CA (US); **Daniel B. Leiser**, San Jose, CA (US); **Robert R. DiFiore**, Fremont, CA (US); **Victor W. Katvala**, San Jose, CA (US)

(73) Assignee: **The United States of America as represented by the Administrator of the National Aeronautics and Space Administration (NASA)**, Washington, DC (US)

(*) Notice: Subject to any disclaimer, the term of this patent is extended or adjusted under 35 U.S.C. 154(b) by 0 days.

(21) Appl. No.: **10/758,611**

(22) Filed: **Jan. 14, 2004**

(51) **Int. Cl.**
B32B 7/02 (2006.01)
B32B 27/32 (2006.01)
B32B 17/06 (2006.01)
B32B 9/00 (2006.01)

(52) **U.S. Cl.** **428/428**; 428/408; 428/426; 428/446; 428/704

(58) **Field of Classification Search** 428/426, 428/428, 432, 446, 688, 689, 212, 220, 408, 428/704; 501/11, 21, 94
See application file for complete search history.

(56) **References Cited**

U.S. PATENT DOCUMENTS

2,992,959 A		7/1961	Schrewlius
4,039,997 A		8/1977	Huang et al.
4,093,771 A	*	6/1978	Goldstein et al. 428/312.6
4,308,309 A		12/1981	Leiser et al.
4,381,333 A		4/1983	Beggs et al.
5,079,082 A		1/1992	Leiser et al.
5,296,288 A		3/1994	Kourtides et al.
5,308,806 A		5/1994	Maloney et al.

5,429,997 A		7/1995	Hebsur
5,677,060 A		10/1997	Terentieva et al.
5,880,439 A		3/1999	Deevi et al.
5,945,166 A		8/1999	Singh et al.
6,225,248 B1		5/2001	Leiser et al.
6,444,271 B2	*	9/2002	Wittenauer et al. 427/376.2
6,749,942 B1	*	6/2004	Wittenauer et al. 428/446
6,955,853 B1		10/2005	Tran et al.
2001/0051218 A1	*	12/2001	Wittenauer et al. 427/376.2

OTHER PUBLICATIONS

Internet website http://www.azom.com.*
Internet website http://www.micrometals.com/tantalum_silicide.htm.*

(Continued)

Primary Examiner—Timothy M Speer
Assistant Examiner—Jonathan C Langman
(74) *Attorney, Agent, or Firm*—John F. Schipper; Robert M. Padilla

(57) **ABSTRACT**

Tantalum-based ceramics are suitable for use in thermal protection systems. These composite structures have high efficiency surfaces (low catalytic efficiency and high emittance), thereby reducing heat flux to a spacecraft during planetary re-entry. These ceramics contain tantalum disilicide, molybdenum disilicide and borosilicate glass. The components are milled, along with a processing aid, then applied to a surface of a porous substrate, such as a fibrous silica or carbon substrate. Following application, the coating is then sintered on the substrate. The composite structure is substantially impervious to hot gas penetration and capable of surviving high heat fluxes at temperatures approaching 3000° F. and above.

6 Claims, 9 Drawing Sheets

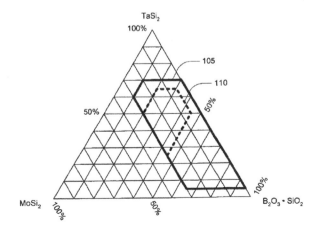

299

OTHER PUBLICATIONS

Office Action, dated Dec. 4, 2007, from a continuation-in-part, U.S. Appl. No. 10/956,516, filed Sep. 28, 2004.

Office Action, dated Aug. 19, 2008, from a continuation-in-part, U.S. Appl. No. 10/956,516, filed Sep. 28, 2004.

Nextel 312 Woven Fabrics, Foundry Service & Supplies, Inc., 1-3.

First Office Action (mailed Apr. 6, 2009) in a CIP Application, U.S. Appl. No. 11/416,508, NASA, filed Apr. 14, 2006, 25 pages.

Response to Nonfinal Action, mailed Dec. 4, 2007, Response filed May 5, 2008, in a CIP Application, U.S. Appl. No. 10/956,516, NASA, filed Sep. 28, 2004.

Response to Nonfinal Action, mailed Apr. 6, 2009, Response filed Oct. 6, 2009, in a CIP Application, U.S. Appl. No. 11/416,508, NASA, filed Apr. 14, 2006.

Final Rejection, mailed Nov. 6, 2009, in a CIP Application, U.S. Appl. No. 11/416,508, NASA, filed Apr. 14, 2006.

* cited by examiner

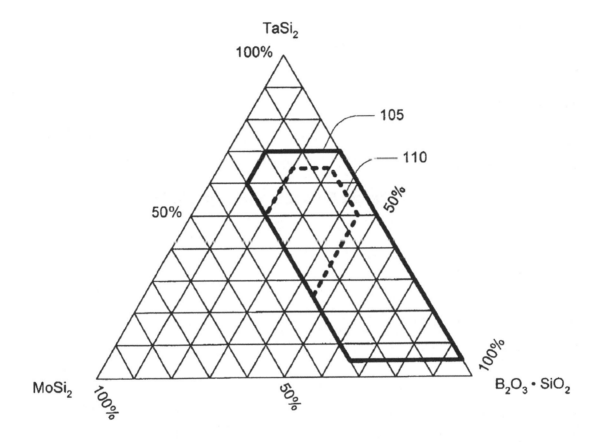

Fig. 1

301

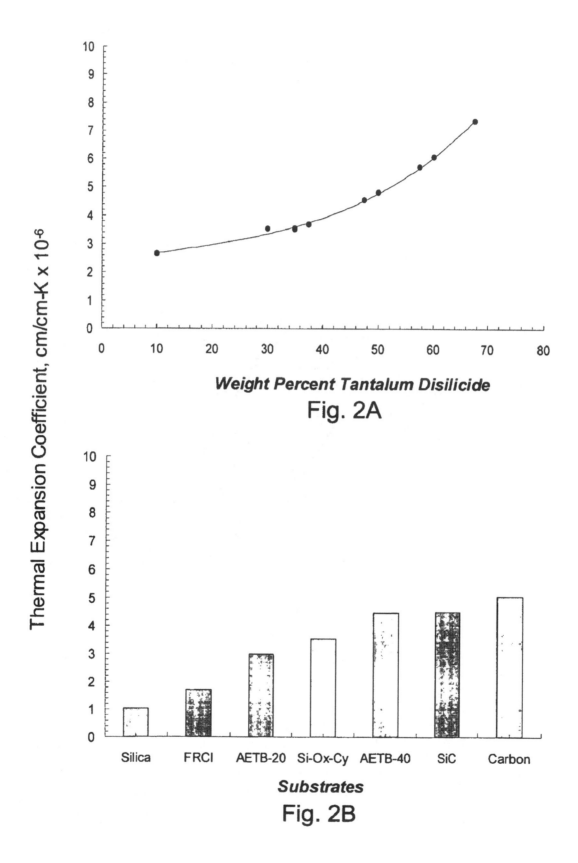

Weight Percent Tantalum Disilicide

Fig. 2A

Substrates

Fig. 2B

302

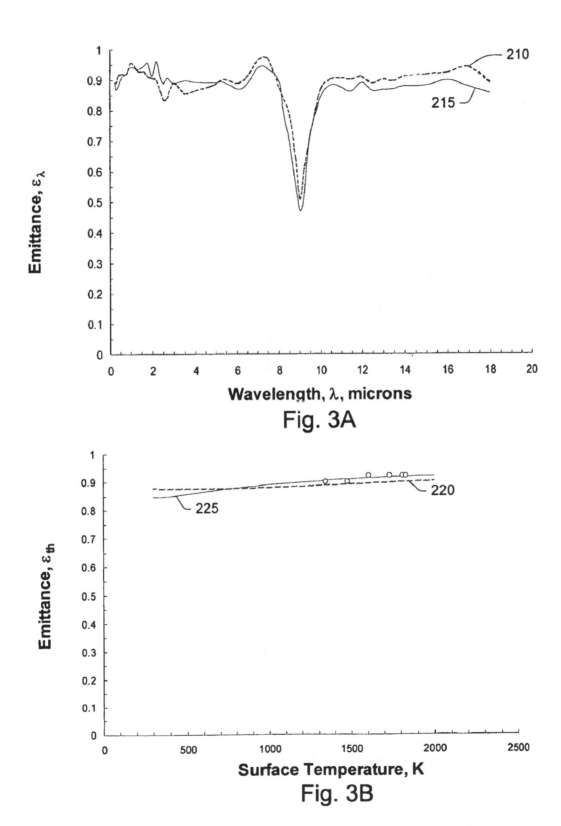

Fig. 3A

Fig. 3B

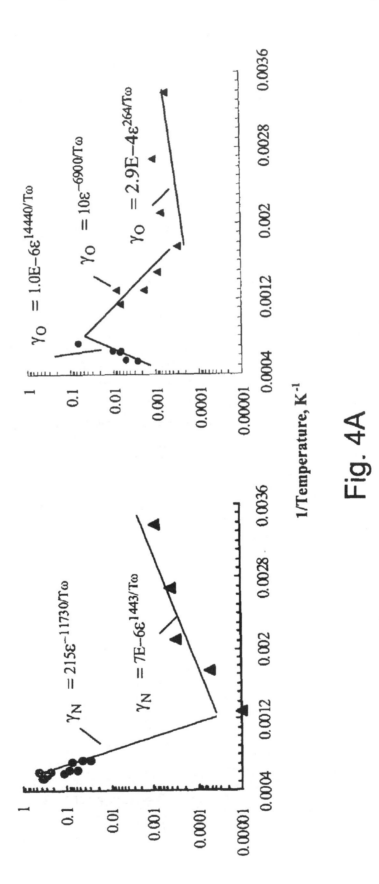

$\gamma_O = 1.0E{-}6\varepsilon^{14440/T\omega}$

$\gamma_O = 10\varepsilon^{-6900/T\omega}$

$\gamma_O = 2.9E{-}4\varepsilon^{264/T\omega}$

$\gamma_N = 215\varepsilon^{-11730/T\omega}$

$\gamma_N = 7E{-}6\varepsilon^{1443/T\omega}$

1/Temperature, K^{-1}

Fig. 4A

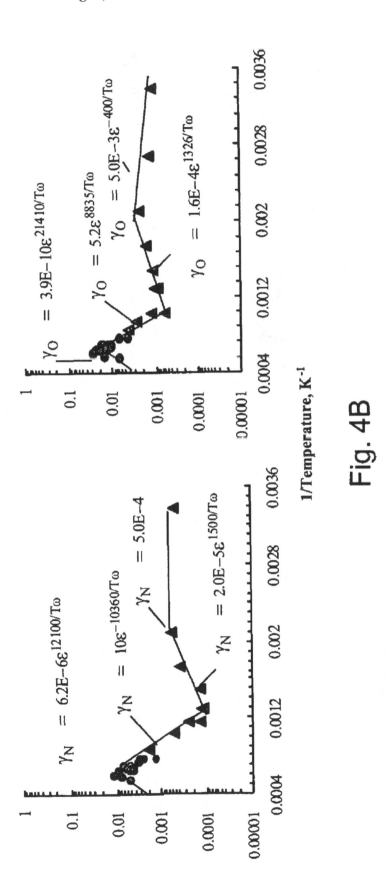

$$\gamma_O = 3.9E-10\varepsilon^{21410/T\omega}$$

$$\gamma_O = 5.2\varepsilon^{8835/T\omega}$$

$$\gamma_O = 5.0E-3\varepsilon^{-400/T\omega}$$

$$\gamma_O = 1.6E-4\varepsilon^{1326/T\omega}$$

$$\gamma_N = 6.2E-6\varepsilon^{12100/T\omega}$$

$$\gamma_N = 10\varepsilon^{-10360/T\omega}$$

$$\gamma_N = 5.0E-4$$

$$\gamma_N = 2.0E-5\varepsilon^{1500/T\omega}$$

1/Temperature, K⁻¹

Fig. 4B

305

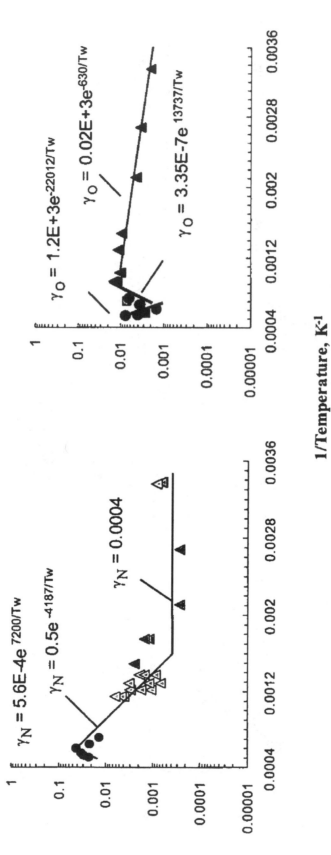

Fig. 4C

$\gamma_O = 1.2E+3e^{-22012/Tw}$

$\gamma_O = 0.02E+3e^{-630/Tw}$

$\gamma_O = 3.35E-7e^{13737/Tw}$

$\gamma_N = 5.6E-4e^{7200/Tw}$

$\gamma_N = 0.5e^{-4187/Tw}$

$\gamma_N = 0.0004$

1/Temperature, K^{-1}

306

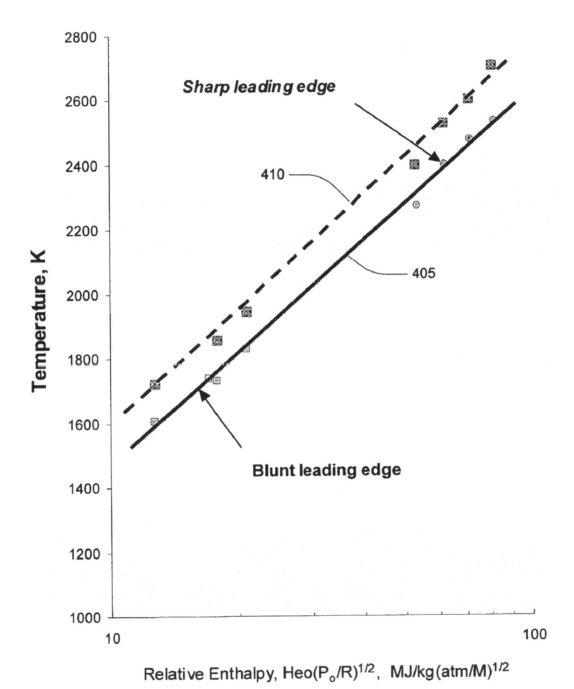

Fig. 5

307

500

510

505

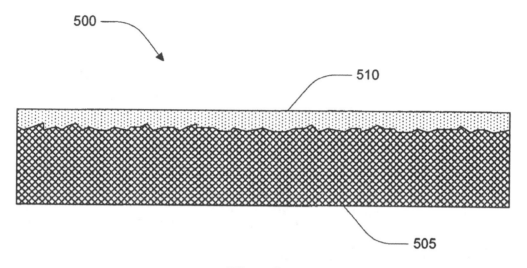

Fig. 6A

500

507

510

505

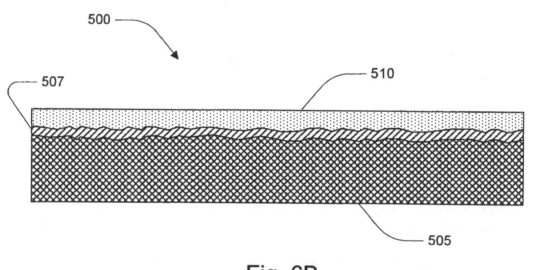

Fig. 6B

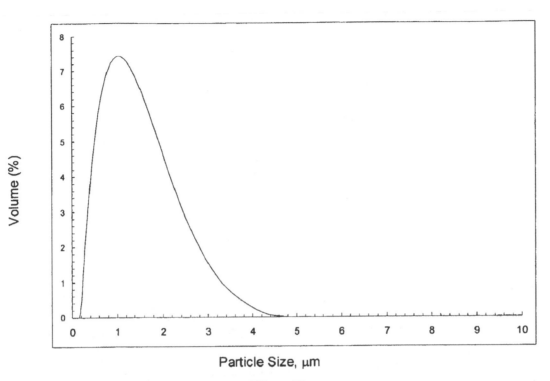

Particle Size, μm

Fig. 7

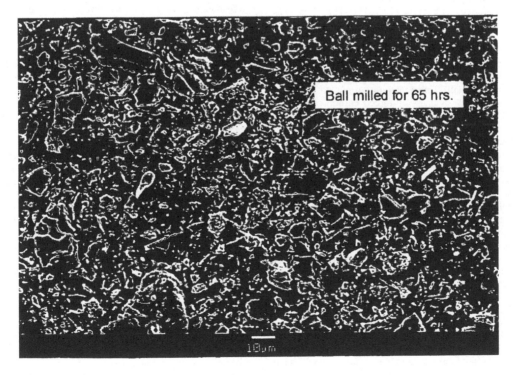

Ball milled for 65 hrs.

Fig. 8

1

HIGH EFFICIENCY TANTALUM-BASED CERAMIC COMPOSITE STRUCTURES

ORIGIN OF INVENTION

The invention described herein was made by employees of the United States Government and may be manufactured and used by or for the Government for governmental purposes without payment of any royalties thereon or therefore.

TECHNICAL FIELD OF THE INVENTION

The present invention relates generally to thermal protection systems and in particular to composite structures containing tantalum-based ceramics.

BACKGROUND OF THE INVENTION

Previous composite insulating structures intended for use in such applications as on orbital reentry vehicles, such as the Space Shuttle Orbiter, have consisted of a coating in combination with a low density insulation substrate. A borosilicate glass, Reaction Cured Glass (RCG), was chosen as the coating for the silica type of Reusable Surface Insulation (RSI) previously selected as the heat shield for the Orbiter, as disclosed in U.S. Pat. No. 4,093,771 issued Jun. 6, 1978 to Goldstein et al. This coating was prepared by blending an emittance agent, silicon tetraboride, with a specially prepared borosilicate glass powder, composed of approximately 94% by weight silica and 6% by weight boron oxide, and an ethanol carrier in a ball mill. The resulting slurry was optimized to limit penetration of the slurry into the low density insulation and limit sagging during the subsequent sintering operation. After drying, the coating was sintered (fused) to a "theoretical" density of 2.2 g/cc at 1220° C. (2225° F.). The "as fired" RCG coating weighs 0.07 g/sq cm (0.15 lbs/sq ft) and is approximately 0.3 mm (0.013 in) thick and has been applied to advanced insulation systems.

Current passive systems being proposed for use as leading edge thermal protection systems on future vehicles include hot structure, heat sink, and transpiration cooled technologies. Hot structures such as reinforced carbon-carbon are being used on the Orbiter, e.g., on the wing leading edge and nose cap, and silicon carbide systems have been proposed for other reentry vehicles such as the X-33 and X-38, etc.

The systems used on the Orbiter for the wing leading edge and nose cap typically operate at temperatures below 2700° F. (1480° C.) during Earth entry. This system, if breached, has resulted in the loss of the vehicle during Earth entry. Also, these systems are heavier, orders-of-magnitude more expensive, and require much longer lead times for delivery than a system made using rigid fibrous insulation. Other lighter weight, less expensive alternatives including coated fibrous insulation systems (such as RCG on LI-900, a low-density fibrous silica glass structure) are susceptible to excessive surface recession and/or impact damage during launch and/or landing.

The impact resistance of the fibrous insulation systems was substantially improved by the development of the Toughened Uni-Piece Fibrous Insulation (TUFI) as disclosed in U.S. Pat. No. 5,079,082 issued Jan. 7, 1992 to Leiser et al. This material represented the first family of lightweight inexpensive graded thermal protection materials. The emittance agent was molybdenum disilicide. It included a borosilicate glass matrix and a processing aid (silicon hexaboride) that permitted sintering at 2225° F. (1220° C.). TUFI is used in selected areas on the Orbiter where the temperatures of operation are

2

much lower than its capability of 2600° F. (1425° C.). The use of TUFI-like systems as a leading edge requires still higher temperature capability.

The specific disadvantages of the prior art depend upon the type of leading edge chosen. For a structural type leading edge, the major disadvantages are weight; the complexity of designing a hot structure that must perform under load and expand from room temperature to high temperature while maintaining structural integrity and while remaining attached to the vehicle; and the cost and time required to produce appropriate parts. For an insulating leading edge the disadvantage has been the relatively limited temperature capability of materials that has made it, under most circumstances, an impracticable choice due to the unacceptable limitations it imposes on the resultant atmospheric entry vehicles.

For the reasons stated above, and for other reasons stated below that will become apparent to those skilled in the art upon reading and understanding the present specification, there is a need in the art for alternative insulating structures.

SUMMARY

The various embodiments include high-efficiency tantalum-based ceramics. These low catalytic efficiency and high emittance ceramic materials were developed in order to increase the capability of a TUFI-like thermal protection system, with its high impact resistance, to temperatures above 3000° F. (1650° C.). These ceramics have been applied to both blunt and sharp wedge shaped configurations as well as the conventional shaped tile used on current high-speed atmospheric entry vehicles.

The tantalum-based ceramics contain tantalum disilicide, borosilicate glass and, optionally, molybdenum disilicide. The components are milled, along with a processing aid to facilitate sintering, then applied to a surface of a porous substrate, such as a fibrous or open pore foamed silica, carbon, aluminosilicate, silicon carbide or silicon oxycarbide substrate, as well as other substrates of silicon/carbon compositions. Following application, the coating is then sintered on the substrate. The composite structure is substantially impervious to hot gas penetration and capable of surviving high heat fluxes (temperatures approaching 3000° F. (1650° C.) and above).

For one embodiment, the invention provides a composite insulating structure. The structure includes a substrate and a coating adjoined to the substrate. The coating includes tantalum disilicide and borosilicate glass. For a further embodiment, the coating further includes molybdenum disilicide. For a still further embodiment, the coating further includes a processing aid, such as silicon hexaboride. For one embodiment, the coating impregnates the surface of the substrate. For a further embodiment, the coating impregnates the surface of the substrate to a depth of approximately 0.1 inches.

For another embodiment, the invention provides a composite insulating structure. The structure includes a porous substrate. The structure further includes a sub-layer applied to the porous substrate. The sub-layer includes molybdenum disilicide, silicon hexaboride and borosilicate glass. The sub-layer impregnates a surface of the substrate forming a functionally gradient layer transitioning from a material that is substantially the composition of the substrate to a material that is substantially the composition of the sub-layer. Density and properties gradually vary across this transition layer as a function of depth from the surface of the substrate. The structure further includes one or more second layers applied to the

3

4

sub-layer. These second layers include tantalum disilicide, molybdenum disilicide, silicon hexaboride and borosilicate glass.

For yet another embodiment, the invention provides a composite insulating structure. The structure includes a porous substrate. The structure further includes a coating applied to the substrate. The coating includes tantalum disilicide, silicon hexaboride and borosilicate glass. For one embodiment, the coating impregnates a surface of the substrate.

The invention further includes composite insulating structures of varying scope.

BRIEF DESCRIPTION OF THE DRAWINGS

FIG. 1 is composition diagram of formulations in accordance with various embodiments of the invention.

FIGS. 2A-2B are graphs of coefficients of thermal expansion typical for embodiments of the invention.

FIGS. 3A-3B are graphs of hemispherical emittance of a ceramic composite in accordance with an embodiment of the invention.

FIGS. 4A-4C are graphs comparing atom recombination coefficients for prior art materials (4A-4B) to ceramic composites in accordance with an embodiment of the invention (4C).

FIG. 5 is a graph of surface temperature versus relative enthalpy comparing a fully catalytic surface to a ceramic composite in accordance with an embodiment of the invention.

FIGS. 6A-6B are cross-sectional views of composite insulating structures in accordance with embodiments of the invention.

FIG. 7 is a graph of a particle size distribution of components for a ceramic composite in accordance with an embodiment of the invention.

FIG. 8 is a photomicrograph showing the particulate nature of a ceramic composite in accordance with an embodiment of the invention after arc-jet exposure.

DETAILED DESCRIPTION OF THE INVENTION

In the following detailed description of the preferred embodiments, reference is made to the accompanying drawings that form a part hereof, and in which is shown by way of illustration specific preferred embodiments in which the inventions may be practiced. These embodiments are described in sufficient detail to enable those skilled in the art to practice the invention, and it is to be understood that other embodiments may be utilized and that logical, mechanical and chemical changes may be made without departing from the spirit and scope of the present invention. The following detailed description is, therefore, not to be taken in a limiting sense, and the scope of the present invention is defined only by the appended claims and equivalents thereof.

The various embodiments include insulating composites capable of surviving high heating rates and large thermal gradients in the aeroconvective heating environment that entry vehicles are exposed to characteristically. For one embodiment, the composites are formed of a ceramic coating overlying a substrate. For a further embodiment, the ceramic coating impregnates a surface of the substrate to form a functionally gradient composite structure. Such ceramic coatings can be applied to blunt and sharp wedge shaped configurations as well as the conventional shaped tile used on current high-speed atmospheric entry vehicles. Tailored formulations

of this new family of tantalum silicide based materials make them compatible with a wide variety of different lightweight fibrous systems.

The ceramics of the various embodiments are formed from four primary parts. The first is tantalum disilicide ($TaSi_2$), which can act as either the emittance agent or the matrix itself depending upon the composition. The second is molybdenum disilicide ($MOSi_2$), which acts as a secondary emittance agent or as an oxygen getter within the finished composite. The third is a borosilicate glass ($B_2O_3.SiO_2$), which acts as a source for boron and an alternative matrix depending upon the composition. The fourth is silicon hexaboride (SiB_6), which acts as a processing aid. It is a minor constituent and generally ranges from about 1% to about 5% by weight of the total composition. As used herein, all composition percentages will be by weight unless otherwise noted.

FIG. 1 shows a composition diagram excluding the silicon hexaboride processing aid and illustrates the wide range of formulations that have been demonstrated for the fabrication of outer layers of ceramic coatings of the various embodiments for use in aerospace applications. The boxed area 105 approximates the range of formulations demonstrated to be suitable for such aerospace applications having borosilicate glass compositions of approximately 10% to 95%, tantalum disilicide compositions of approximately 5% to 70%, and molybdenum disilicide compositions of approximately 0% to 30%. More preferably, the composition, excluding processing aids, includes approximately 20% to 45% borosilicate glass, 10% to 65% tantalum disilicide and 5% to 30% molybdenum disilicide. Underlying or sub-layers containing approximately 20% to 60% molybdenum disilicide, approximately 40% to 80% borosilicate glass and approximately 1% to 5% of a processing aid, e.g., silicon hexaboride, may be used to aid in the integration of outer or surface layers of ceramic coatings to the substrate. The sub-layers may impregnate a portion of the substrate to create a functionally gradient composite structure. The sub-layer preferably closely matches the coefficient of thermal expansion of the substrate while subsequent layers may be used to increase the density and CTE of the coating.

Formulations, with matching CTE have been integrated into oxide-based Alumina Enhanced Thermal Barrier (AETB) tiles and carbon preforms of various compositions and density. The formulations of the various embodiments were either painted or sprayed onto the selected preform before being sintered at either 2225° F. (1220° C.) for 90 minutes or 2400° F. (1315° C.) for 10 minutes in a furnace at atmospheric pressure. The high temperature fast sintering process along with the process for applying the treatment itself minimizes the oxidation of the tantalum disilicide acting as the major constituent within the majority of the ceramics produced. The molybdenum disilicide behaves like a secondary emittance agent or as an oxygen getter inhibiting the oxidation of the tantalum compounds present. The fabrication process results in a high viscosity quasi-amorphous structure that has high emittance in one instance and high emittance ceramic in the other.

Compositions of the various embodiments have been applied to both simulated wing leading edge (WLE) and sharp wedge configurations in order to study the resulting thermal protection system (TPS) performance in high-energy arc jet flow. A blunt wedge (approximately 1.5 inch radius) made using AETB-40/12 with a coating containing a 35% tantalum disilicide/20% molybdenum disilicide formulation demonstrated reuse capability of a toughened fibrous ceramic (a functionally gradient composite) surface to heat fluxes up to 70 W/cm² in arc jet flow. FIG. 3A shows that the spectral

311

5

hemispherical emittance of this formulation is relatively unchanged. Line **210** depicts the spectral hemispherical emittance prior to arc-jet exposure while line **215** depicts the spectral hemispherical emittance after arc jet exposure. FIG. 3B demonstrates that the total hemispherical emittance remains high, approximately 0.9 or above, after arc jet exposure to surface temperatures above 2800° F. (1540° C.) for 50 minutes. Line **220** depicts the total hemispherical emittance prior to arc jet exposure while line **225** depicts the total hemispherical emittance after arc-jet exposure.

In addition, an embodiment of the invention having 65% tantalum disilicide/15% molybdenum disilicide was successfully applied to a sharp leading edge configurations (wedge with approximately 0.06 inch radius). These test articles were made using silicon oxycarbide and carbon preforms. These test articles were tested for short exposures (1.0 minute) to heat fluxes in excess of 300 W/cm^2.

Another important characteristic of the ceramic composites of the various embodiments is illustrated with reference to FIGS. 4A-4C. FIGS. 4A-4C are graphs of atom recombination coefficients for oxygen and nitrogen. The coefficients have a direct effect on the heat transfer rate to a re-entry vehicle's TPS during high-energy hypersonic flight. The lower the value the less the heat transfer rate (lower surface temperature) to the surface of the TPS due to reduced chemical heating (atom recombination). FIG. 4A represents the recombination coefficients for an RCG surface. FIG. 4B represents the recombination coefficients for a TUFI surface. FIG. 4C represents the recombination coefficients for a ceramic composite in accordance with an embodiment of the invention. As can be seen, the values of the recombination coefficients for nitrogen (γ_N) and oxygen (γ_O) for ceramics in accordance with the invention are very comparable with those for an RCG system making the material extremely advantageous. The low recombination coefficient is also indicative of an amorphous or quasi-amorphous surface structure, similar to RCG. X-ray diffraction analyses of a 35% tantalum disilicide 20% molybdenum disilicide formulation indicated that the surface actually became more amorphous after arc jet exposure.

Use of ceramic compositions in accordance with the invention into a heat shield for a spacecraft (using either a fibrous and/or foamed substrate) can facilitate a reduction of the surface temperature during Earth entry of several hundred degrees below the values calculated assuming a fully catalytic wall. This is best illustrated in FIG. **5**, which compares the measured surface temperature taken from a cone made using a ceramic composite in accordance with an embodiment of the invention, i.e., solid line **405**, with predicted values for a similar cone assuming a fully catalytic wall, i.e., dashed line **410**.

FIGS. **6A-6B** are a cross-sectional views of composite insulating structures **500** in accordance with embodiments of the invention. While the structures **500** are depicted to have substantially planar surfaces, other forms are also suitable, such as rounds, blunt wedges, sharp wedges or more complex geometries. The structures **500** include a substrate **505** and a ceramic coating **510** overlying and adjoined to the substrate **505**. In forming the coating **510**, it is preferred that the particle size of the components be reduced to allow impregnation of a surface or outer portion of the substrate **505** during application of the coating material, thereby forming a transition layer **507** containing substrate **505** and ceramic coating **510** as shown in the embodiment of FIG. 6B. Each component of the coating **510**, i.e., the MoSi$_2$, TaSi$_2$ and borosilicate glass, as well as processing aids that do not materially affect the basic and novel characteristics of the ceramic coatings described

6

herein, may be ball-milled separately or together in ethanol at 20-30% solids by weight for a suitable time to reduce particle size.

For one embodiment, the desired particle size is less than about 5 _m. For a further embodiment, the desired particle size distribution has a maximum of less than about 5 _m and a mode of approximately 1 _m. After milling, the resultant slurries are combined, if necessary, to achieve a homogeneous dispersion. The dispersion may then be sprayed, painted or otherwise applied to a surface of the substrate **505**. One or more applications may be performed to achieve a desired thickness. Alternatively, or in addition, individual applications may have the same composition, or the composition may be altered for one or more layers. For example, initial layers applied to the substrate **505** to form the transition layer **507** through impregnation may have a first composition while subsequent layers applied to the substrate **505** to form the outer surface of coating **510** overlying the substrate **505** may have a second composition.

For one embodiment, the amount of ceramic material used for coating **510** is adjusted to provide from approximately 0.07 to approximately 0.21 g/cm^2 of coating **510**. For a further embodiment, the amount of ceramic material used for coating **510** is adjusted to provide approximately 0.14 g/cm^2 of coating **510**. Suitable examples of the substrate **505** include silica, fibrous refractory composite insulation (FRCI), and AETB. Further examples include fibrous and/or foamed silicon carbide and silicon oxycarbide.

After application of the coating **510**, the structure **500** can be dried overnight at room temperature or for about two to about five hours at temperatures up to about 70° C. After drying, the coating **510** is sintered at approximately 2225° F. (1220° C.) for 90 minutes or 2400° F. (1315° C.) for 10 minutes in a furnace at atmospheric pressure. The structure **500** is normally inserted into the furnace at temperature and cooled by rapid removal from the furnace. The final coating **510** appears flat black and is pervious to water penetration. For one embodiment, the composition of the coating **510** is adjusted such that its coefficient of thermal expansion after sintering substantially matches the coefficient of thermal expansion of the underlying substrate **505**.

The following non-limiting examples describe the invention further and represent various example embodiments in which the invention may be practiced.

Example 1

For one embodiment, a composite insulating structure substantially impervious to hot gas penetration was prepared by mixing 35% tantalum disilicide with 20% molybdenum disilicide, 2.5% silicon hexaboride and 52.5% borosilicate glass. The borosilicate glass may contain from about 1% to about 10% boron oxide, but is preferably approximately 94.25% silicon dioxide and 5.75% boron oxide. All of the components were ball milled for 65 hours in an alcohol medium at 70% solids. FIG. **6** is a graph of the approximate particle size distribution measured after one such milling. After milling, the components were diluted to 25% solids prior to spraying on a substrate, e.g., AETB-40/12, with a sub-layer applied. The sub-layer was composed of 55% molybdenum disilicide, 2.5% silicon hexaboride and 42.5% borosilicate glass. All of the components of the sub-layer were ball milled for 65 hours in an alcohol medium at 70% solids and diluted to 25% solids prior to application. The sub-layer comprised 40% by weight of the total surface treatment. It was fired at 2225° F. (1220° C.) for 90 minutes and successfully tested at about 3000° F. (1650° C.) in a high-energy hypersonic arc jet flow.

7

Example 2

For another embodiment, a composite insulating structure substantially impervious to hot gas penetration was prepared by mixing 15% molybdenum disilicide with 60% tantalum disilicide, 2.5% silicon hexaboride and 22.5% borosilicate glass. All of the components were ball milled for 65 hours in an alcohol medium at 70% solids prior to spraying on a carbon preform with a sub-layer applied. The sub-layer was composed of 20% molybdenum disilicide, 2.5% silicon hexaboride and 77.5% borosilicate glass. All of the components of the sub-layer were ball milled for 65 hours in an alcohol medium at 70% solids and diluted to 25% solids prior to application. The sub-layer comprised 40% by weight of the total surface treatment. The structure was fired at 2400° F. (1315° C.) for 10 minutes and successfully tested at above 3800° F. (2095° C.) for one minute in a high-energy arc jet flow. FIG. 7 is a photomicrograph showing the particulate nature of the insulating structure after arc jet exposure.

Example 3

For yet another embodiment, a composite insulating structure substantially impervious to hot gas penetration was prepared by mixing 50% tantalum disilicide, 5% silicon hexaboride and 45% borosilicate glass. All of the components were ball milled for 65 hours in an alcohol medium at 70% solids prior to spraying on an AETB-40/12 substrate without a sub-layer applied. It was fired at 2225° F. (1220° C.) for 90 minutes and successfully tested at about 2900° F. (1595° C.) with observable foaming.

Example 4

For still another embodiment, a composite insulating structure substantially impervious to hot gas penetration was prepared by mixing 10% molybdenum disilicide with 45% tantalum disilicide, 2.5% silicon hexaboride and 42.5% borosilicate glass. All of the components were ball milled for 65 hours in an alcohol medium at 70% solids prior to spraying on an AETB-40/12 substrate with a sub-layer applied. The sub-layer was composed of 55% molybdenum disilicide and 2.5% by weight silicon hexaboride and 42.5% borosilicate glass. All of the components of the sub-layer were ball milled for 65 hours in an alcohol medium at 70% solids and diluted to 25% solids prior to application. The sub-layer comprised 40% by weight of the total surface treatment. The composite insulating structure was fired at 2400° F. (1315° C.) for 10 minutes and successfully tested in an arc jet stream at about 2830° F. (1555° C.) for 6 minutes.

Example 5

For another embodiment, a composite insulating structure substantially impervious to hot gas penetration was prepared by mixing 15% molybdenum disilicide with 40% tantalum disilicide, 2.5% silicon hexaboride and 42.5% borosilicate glass. All of the components were ball milled for 65 hours in an alcohol medium at 70% solids and diluted to 25% solids prior to spraying on an AETB-40/12 substrate with a sub-layer applied. The sub-layer was composed of 55% molybdenum disilicide, 2.5% silicon hexaboride and 42.5% borosilicate glass. All of the components of the sub-layer were ball milled for 65 hours in an alcohol medium at 70% solids and diluted to 25% solids prior to application. The sub-layer comprised 40% by weight of the total surface treatment. The

8

composite insulating structure was fired at 2400° F. (1315° C.) for 10 minutes and successfully tested at about 2870° F. (1575° C.) for 5 minutes.

Example 6

For a further embodiment, a composite insulating structure substantially impervious to hot gas penetration was prepared by mixing 20% molybdenum disilicide with 50% tantalum disilicide, 2.5% silicon hexaboride and 27.5% borosilicate glass. All of the components were ball milled for 65 hours in an alcohol medium at 70% solids and diluted to 25% solids prior to spraying on a wedge-shaped carbon preform with a sub-layer applied. The sub-layer was composed of 20% molybdenum disilicide, 2.5% silicon hexaboride and 77.5% borosilicate glass. All of the components of the sub-layer were ball milled for 65 hours in an alcohol medium at 70% solids and diluted to 25% solids prior to application. The sub-layer comprised 40% by weight of the total surface treatment. The composite insulating wedge-shaped structure was fired at 2400° F. (1315° C.) for 10 minutes and successfully tested at around 3800° F. (2095° C.) for one minute in an arc-jet hypersonic stream.

Example 7

For yet a further embodiment, a composite insulating structure substantially impervious to hot gas penetration was prepared by mixing 30% molybdenum disilicide with 10% tantalum disilicide, 2.5% silicon hexaboride and 57.5% borosilicate glass. All the components were ball milled for 65 hours in an alcohol medium at 70% solids and diluted to 25% solids prior to spraying on an AETB-40/12 substrate (using 3 micron diameter Nextel fibers) without a sub-layer applied. The composite insulating structure was fired at 2225° F. (1220° C.) for 90 minutes and successfully tested at 2950° F. (1620° C.) for 10 minutes. Although suitable for use in aerospace applications, this composite exhibited higher catalytic efficiency (200° F./110° C. higher surface temperature) than other formulations during exposure to hypersonic arc jet flow.

Example 8

For another embodiment, a functionally gradient composite insulating structure substantially impervious to hot gas penetration was prepared by mixing 20% molybdenum disilicide with 50% tantalum disilicide, 2.5% silicon hexaboride and 27.5% borosilicate glass. All the components were ball milled for 65 hours in an alcohol medium at 70% solids and diluted to 25% solids prior to spraying on a silicon oxycarbide preform with a sub-layer applied. The sub-layer was composed of 55% molybdenum disilicide, 2.5% silicon hexaboride and 42.5% borosilicate glass. All of the components of the sub-layer were ball milled for 65 hours in an alcohol medium at 70% solids and diluted to 25% solids prior to application. The sub-layer comprised 40% by weight of the total surface treatment. The composite insulating structure was fired at 2400° F. (1315° C.) for 10 minutes and successfully tested at 2900° F. (1600° C.) for 20 minutes.

Example 9

For another embodiment, a functionally gradient composite insulating structure substantially impervious to hot gas penetration was prepared by mixing 25% molybdenum disilicide with 50% tantalum disilicide, 2.5% silicon hexaboride and 22.5% borosilicate glass. All the components were ball

9   10

milled for 65 hours in an alcohol medium at 70% solids and diluted to 25% solids prior to spraying on an open pore foamed silicon carbide preform with a sub-layer applied. The sub-layer was composed of 55% molybdenum disilicide, 2.5% silicon hexaboride and 42.5% borosilicate glass. All of the components of the sub-layer were ball milled for 65 hours in an alcohol medium at 70% solids and diluted to 25% solids prior to application. The sub-layer comprised 40% by weight of the total surface treatment. The composite insulating structure was fired at 2400° F. (1315° C.) for 10 minutes and successfully tested at 3000° F. (1650° C.) in hypersonic arc jet flow for 2 minutes.

CONCLUSION

The various embodiments include high-efficiency tantalum-based ceramics. These ceramic materials were developed in order to increase the capability of a TUFI-like thermal protection system, with its high impact resistance, to temperatures above 3000° F. (1650° C.). These ceramics have been applied to various aerodynamic configurations, such as wedge, wing leading segment and conventional tile shapes used on current high-speed atmospheric entry vehicles.

In addition, this family of tantalum-based ceramics exhibits low catalytic efficiency to atom recombination during exposure to high-energy dissociated hypersonic flow. Its surface catalytic efficiency is below that of standard TUFI and is equivalent to or lower than the reaction cured glass (RCG) presently used on the Orbiter.

These high-emittance ceramic formulations extend the performance envelope of fibrous insulations to surface temperatures above 3000° F. (1650° C.) for an extended period of time in an aeroconvective heating environment. For example, after five 10-minute exposures at a stagnation point heat flux of 70 W/cm^2, a 35% TaSi$_2$/20% MoSi$_2$ formulation applied to AETB-40/12 resulted in a surface recession of less than 0.05 inch. With standard surface treatments or coatings, damage to the AETB substrate occurred at these temperatures.

These unique structures have been successfully tested in arc jet flow after they were applied to both light-weight fibrous and foamed aluminosilicate and carbonaceous substructures. Thermal protection systems made using these high-emittance ceramic formulations result in leading edge components for space vehicles that are light weight, low cost, and perform at high-efficiency during hypersonic Earth atmospheric entry. The various embodiments facilitate composite insulating structures 10 to 50 times lighter than the current hot structures being used on the Orbiter and proposed for other reentry vehicles such as X-33, X-38, etc. In addition, the various embodiments facilitate composite insulating structures that are cheaper to fabricate and maintain, and easier to design, than corresponding existing structures providing similar thermal protection.

Aside from their applicability for use with atmospheric reentry vehicles, thermal protection systems in accordance with the invention are adapted for use with standard aircraft, turbine engines, race cars, automobiles and other applications that require thermal protection surfaces that are resistant to erosion and/or impact damage. The various embodiments further may find use as heating elements for furnaces requiring higher temperature capability than the standard molybdenum disilicide type heating elements.

Although specific embodiments have been illustrated and described herein, it will be appreciated by those of ordinary skill in the art that any arrangement that is calculated to achieve the same purpose may be substituted for the specific embodiment shown. This application is intended to cover any adaptations or variations of the present invention. Therefore, it is manifestly intended that this invention be limited only by the claims and the equivalents thereof.

What is claimed is:

1. A composite structure, comprising:
   a porous substrate, having a lower surface and an upper surface and comprising a selected substrate material and having a substrate coefficient of thermal expansion;
   a first layer integrated with an exposed surface of the substrate, wherein the first layer material comprises between 20 percent and 60 percent molybdenum disilicide, between 40 percent and 80 percent borosilicate glass and a processing aid, with the first layer being positioned adjacent to and between the substrate upper surface and a second layer having a material composition different from the first layer;
   wherein the second layer material comprises between 5 percent and 70 percent tantalum disilicide, between 5 percent and 30 percent molybdenum disilicide, and between 10 percent and 95 percent borosilicate glass;
   wherein a composition of the first layer is chosen so that a coefficient of thermal expansion of the first layer is approximately the same as the coefficient of thermal expansion of the substrate; and
   wherein the combined first and second layers provide a protective layer when exposed to temperatures around 3000° F.

2. The composite structure of claim 1, wherein said processing aid comprises silicon hexaboride.

3. The composite structure of claim 1, wherein said first layer material impregnates said substrate to a depth of approximately 0.1 inches.

4. The composite structure of claim 1, wherein said substrate material is selected from the group consisting of a fibrous and open pore silica, silicon carbide, aluminosilicate, silicon oxycarbide and carbon substrates.

5. The composite structure of claim 1, wherein at least one component of said second layer has a particle size less than about 5 μm.

6. The composite structure of claim 1, wherein at least one component of said second layer has a particle size distribution having a maximum of approximately 5 μm and a mode of approximately 1 μm.

* * * * *

US008409491B1

(12) **United States Patent**
Stackpoole et al.

(10) **Patent No.:** **US 8,409,491 B1**
(45) **Date of Patent:** **Apr. 2, 2013**

(54) **IN-SITU FORMATION OF REINFORCEMENT PHASES IN ULTRA HIGH TEMPERATURE CERAMIC COMPOSITES**

(75) Inventors: **Margaret M Stackpoole**, Santa Clara, CA (US); **Matthew J Gasch**, Sacramento, CA (US); **Michael W Olson**, Sunnyvale, CA (US); **Ian W. Hamby**, Seattle, WA (US); **Sylvia M Johnson**, Piedmont, CA (US)

(73) Assignee: **The United States of America as Represented by the Administrator of the National Aeronautics & Space Administration (NASA)**, Washington, DC (US)

(*) Notice: Subject to any disclaimer, the term of this patent is extended or adjusted under 35 U.S.C. 154(b) by 0 days.

(21) Appl. No.: **13/215,206**

(22) Filed: **Aug. 22, 2011**

Related U.S. Application Data

(62) Division of application No. 11/864,471, filed on Sep. 28, 2007, now abandoned.

(51) **Int. Cl.**

B28B 1/00	(2006.01)
B28B 3/00	(2006.01)
B28B 5/00	(2006.01)
C04B 33/32	(2006.01)
C04B 35/00	(2006.01)
B32B 9/00	(2006.01)
B32B 19/00	(2006.01)

(52) **U.S. Cl.** **264/624**; 264/625; 264/626; 428/698; 428/699; 501/95.2; 501/96.2

(58) **Field of Classification Search** 501/95.1, 501/95.2, 96.1, 96.2, 96.3; 428/447, 698, 428/699, 702, 704; 264/624–627, 642, 31
See application file for complete search history.

(56) **References Cited**

U.S. PATENT DOCUMENTS

4,885,265 A		12/1989	Hillig et al.
5,081,077 A	*	1/1992	Tani et al. 501/96.3
5,356,842 A	*	10/1994	Yamakawa et al. 501/87
6,146,559 A	*	11/2000	Zank 264/29.6
6,265,337 B1		7/2001	Kukino et al.
6,287,714 B1		9/2001	Xiao et al.
6,347,446 B1		2/2002	Luthra et al.
6,350,713 B1		2/2002	Petrak
6,403,210 B1		6/2002	Stuivinga et al.
6,641,918 B1		11/2003	Sherman et al.
6,838,162 B1		1/2005	Gruber et al.
6,847,699 B2		1/2005	Rigali et al.
6,899,777 B2		5/2005	Vaidanathan et al.
6,913,827 B2		7/2005	George et al.
6,995,103 B2		2/2006	Aghajanian
7,238,219 B2		7/2007	Xiao et al.
2002/0165332 A1	*	11/2002	Pope et al. 528/25

OTHER PUBLICATIONS

Office Action-nonfinal rejection, mailed May 3, 2010, in parent case, U.S. Appl. No. 11/864,471, filed Sep. 28, 2007.

(Continued)

Primary Examiner — Kaj K Olsen
Assistant Examiner — Noah Wiese
(74) *Attorney, Agent, or Firm* — John F. Schipper; Robert M. Padilla; Christopher J. Menke

(57) **ABSTRACT**

A tough ultra-high temperature ceramic (UHTC) composite comprises grains of UHTC matrix material, such as HfB_2, ZrB_2 or other metal boride, carbide, nitride, etc., surrounded by a uniform distribution of acicular high aspect ratio reinforcement ceramic rods or whiskers, such as of SiC, is formed from uniformly mixing a powder of the UHTC material and a pre-ceramic polymer selected to form the desired reinforcement species, then thermally consolidating the mixture by hot pressing. The acicular reinforcement rods may make up from 5 to 30 vol % of the resulting microstructure.

14 Claims, 5 Drawing Sheets

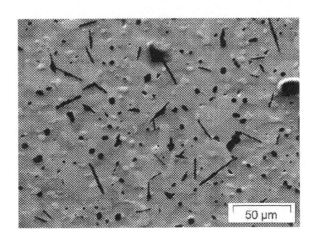

50 µm

315

OTHER PUBLICATIONS

Response to Office Action-nonfinal rejection, mailed May 3, 2010, in parent case, U.S. Appl. No. 11/864,471, filed Sep. 28, 2007. Response filed Oct. 12, 2010.

Office Action-final rejection, mailed Dec. 27, 2010, in parent case, U.S. Appl. No. 11/864,471, filed Sep. 28, 2007.

S.R. Levine et al., "Characterization of an Ultra-High Temperature Ceramic Composite", NASA/TM-2004-213085, May 2004, 28 pages.

* cited by examiner

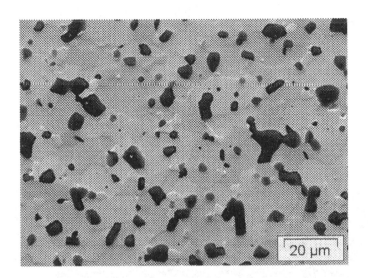

Fig. 1 (Prior Art)

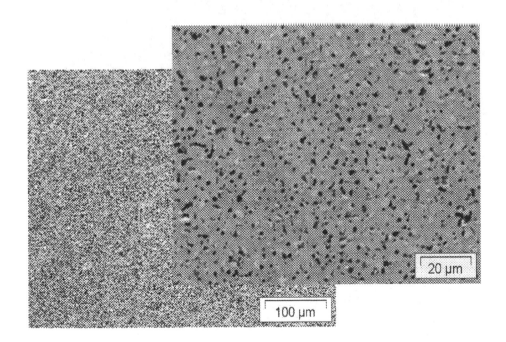

Fig. 2

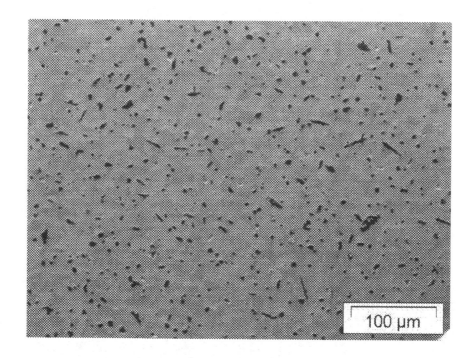

Fig. 3

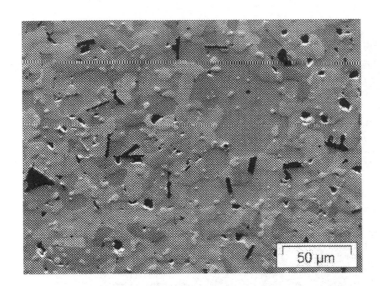

Fig. 4

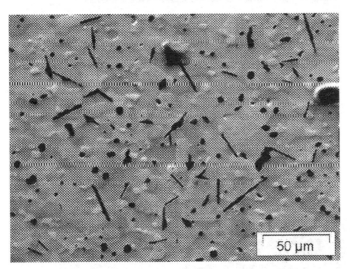

Fig. 5

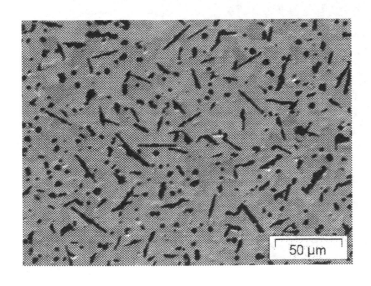

Fig. 6

319

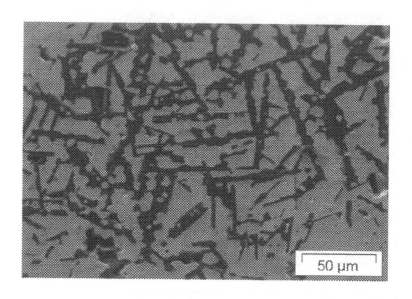

Fig. 7

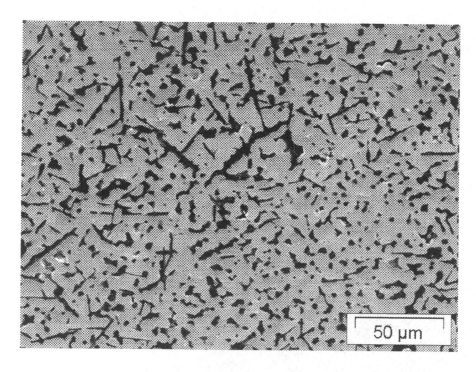

Fig. 8

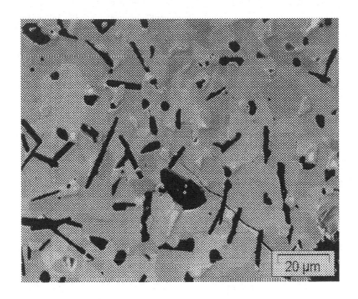

Fig. 9

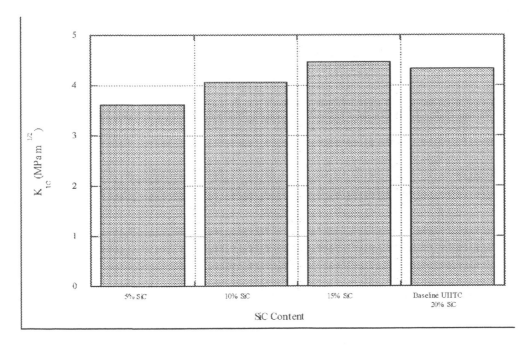

Fig. 10

1

IN-SITU FORMATION OF REINFORCEMENT PHASES IN ULTRA HIGH TEMPERATURE CERAMIC COMPOSITES

STATEMENT REGARDING FEDERALLY SPONSORED RESEARCH OR DEVELOPMENT

The invention described herein was made in the performance of work under NASA contract nos. NNA 04BC25C and NNA 05CS57A and is subject to Public Law 96-517 (35 U.S.C. 200 et seq.). The contractor has not elected to retain title to the invention.

TECHNICAL FIELD

The invention generally relates to ceramic compositions and processes of obtaining a ceramic product, especially ultra-high temperature ceramics. The invention more particularly relates to consolidated ceramic composites comprising a microstructure of a ceramic matrix incorporating a reinforcing ceramic phase, with emphasis on processes of obtaining uniform distribution of the reinforcing phase and controlling the growth of these phases.

BACKGROUND ART

The potential of various materials for use on reusable space transport vehicles with sharp leading edges is being investigated. The sharp leading edges (e.g., at the nose and wing edges) of these vehicles will experience significantly higher heating (to greater than 2000° C.) during hypersonic flight compared to the heating (~1650° C.) at the relatively blunt leading edges of the current space shuttle orbiters. This requires the development of new materials that are capable of reliably withstanding these high temperatures, including resisting oxidation and maintaining high mechanical strength at such temperatures, as well as withstanding the stresses from large spatial temperature differentials or sudden changes in temperature (improved thermal shock properties). A high thermal conductivity is also preferable, since it allows the heat energy to conduct through the material away from the hottest zones and to be re-radiated through cooler surfaces.

Ultra high temperature ceramics (UHTC), which are composed primarily of metal borides, carbides and nitrides, oxides or silicides, and especially of refractory metal diborides, are candidate materials for the sharp leading edges on hypersonic re-entry vehicles. UHTCs are a family of ceramic materials with very high melting temperatures and reasonable oxidation resistance in re-entry environments. Ground based arc-jet testing has demonstrated their potential for applications at temperatures approaching 2200° C.

However, there is concern regarding the mechanical properties and reusability of UHTC materials, in particular their low thermal shock resistance and low fracture toughness (resistance to crack propagation). Monolithic UHTCs are of concern because of their low fracture toughness and brittle behavior, leading to the possibility of sudden catastrophic failure of the material in the extreme re-entry environment. Future generation materials for use on space transport vehicles require substantial improvements in material properties, leading to increased reliability and safety. It is yet to be determined if UHTCs can be made to possess the properties necessary to reliably withstand the extreme environments experienced at the leading edges during re-entry without undergoing some recession, oxidation or thermal shock.

UHTC composites are being investigated as a possible approach to overcome the mechanical deficiencies of mono-

2

lithic UHTCs. Mechanisms responsible for enhanced toughness in ceramic composites include crack deflection, crack bridging and microcracking. It is also known that high aspect ratio microstructures can lead to enhanced performance. The mechanical performance of ceramics in general would benefit from a high aspect ratio reinforcement phase. Previous work in other ceramic systems has shown that these mechanisms can result in a fracture toughness of 10 to 30 MPa√m, compared to typical values of only 2 to 6 MPa√m in monolithic materials.

A small grain size, high aspect ratio, uniform distribution and random orientation of the reinforcing microstructures are very important for attaining the best performance from a ceramic composite. Mixing the reinforcement phase in powder form with the matrix phase (also in powder form) prior to thermal consolidation sacrifices each of these desired characteristics to some extent, as the resulting microstructure of the consolidated material has larger and rounder grains than desirable, sufficiently uniform mixing is difficult to achieve.

Early efforts with hot pressed HfB_2: 20 vol % SiC focused mainly on improving homogeneity in the resulting microstructure and on characterizing its baseline properties. The SiC reinforcement material was found to promote refinement of the microstructure in comparison with monolithic HfB_2 material, but also to decrease the thermal conductivity. Additionally, more SiC was not necessarily better from an oxidation standpoint.

U.S. Pat. No. 6,146,559 to Zank describes preparing titanium diboride ceramics by mixing titanium diboride powder with a pre-ceramic organosilicon polymer, then molding and sintering under pressure to achieve high density in these systems.

In NASA Technical Memo NASA/TM-2004-213085, S. Levine et al., "Characterization of an Ultra-High Temperature Ceramic Composite" (NASA Glenn Research Center, Cleveland Ohio, May 2004), a UHTC composite plate was produced from eleven plies of carbon fabric alternately coated with a SiC/AHPCS (allylhydrido-polycarbosilane) slurry and a HfB_2/AHPCS slurry. The coated cloth was pressed in a mold to 12 MPa, cured under inert gas to 400° C., then fired to 850° C. under inert gas to pyrolyse the AHPCS.

Kuntz et al., "Properties and Microstructure of Alumina-Niobium Nanocomposites Made by Novel Processing Methods", Ultrafine Grained Materials II, TMS 2002, pp. 225-234, indicates that the addition of refractory metals, such as niobium, to ceramic structures made by spark plasma sintering can more than double fracture toughness to greater than 6 MPa√m with only marginal decrease in hardness.

U.S. Pat. No. 6,287,714 to Xiao et al., a WC/Co cermet system has a BN grain growth inhibitor incorporated by spray drying a poly-urea-boron precursor onto the WC powder prior to densification. The resulting nanostructure material has increased toughness to 15-30 MPa√m with the grain growth inhibitor added.

An effective way to incorporate the microstructures into the ceramic composite is needed if optimum fracture toughness is to be attained.

SUMMARY DISCLOSURE

We obtain a uniform distribution of high-aspect-ratio reinforcement microstructures in UHTC materials by means of in-situ growth during thermal consolidation processing. In particular, to obtain the in-situ grown reinforcement phases, one component of the ceramic composite system is added as a pre-ceramic polymer. During powder preparation, the pre-ceramic polymer phase is uniformly distributed throughout the powder phases and coats the powder grains uniformly. Additional ceramic or refractory metal phases may also be uniformly incorporated. A traditional thermal consolidation step (such as hot pressing or spark plasma sintering) is employed, and no extra steps are necessary to obtain the reinforcement growth. Optimized hot pressing parameters are needed to achieve sufficient high aspect ratio phase growth. Optimized hot pressing parameters will differ for each material system evaluated

The reinforcement species forms as acicular rods or needle-like whiskers or filaments having a high aspect ratio, as well as uniform distribution and random orientation throughout the ceramic matrix. The ceramic composite comprises a consolidated mass of grains of UHTC material (e.g. HfB_2 or ZrB_2) surrounded by a uniform distribution of acicular reinforcement ceramic rods having an aspect ratio of at least 10:1.

The reinforcement phase imparts increased mechanical properties that lead to improved thermal shock resistance, while the UHTC matrix provides a high temperature material with reasonable oxidation properties in re-entry conditions. Initial characterization of these systems has demonstrated that crack deflection along the matrix-reinforcement interface is observed, yielding a system of improved fracture toughness over the baseline system, leading to improved mechanical performance. Initial indentation experiments on the resulting material have shown that cracks deflect at the reinforcements and grow along the reinforcement-matrix interface, indicating a system of enhanced fracture toughness compared to monolithic UHTC material. The reinforced composites should therefore reduce the risk of catastrophic failure over current UHTC systems. These high aspect ratio reinforced composites yield improved material properties, including fracture toughness and thermal shock resistance, thus offering better alternatives in microstructure to the current UHTC systems proposed for sharp leading edge applications.

BRIEF DESCRIPTION OF THE DRAWINGS

FIGS. 1-8 are magnified images of UHTC materials containing SiC. FIG. 1 represents a prior art HfB_2: SiC microstructure formed from powdered HfB_2 and powdered SiC. FIGS. 2 and 3 represent experimental results of processing a HfB_2—SiC composition with pre-ceramic polymer, but not in accord with the present invention. FIGS. 4-8 show UHTC microstructures in accord with the present invention. FIGS. 4-7 represent experimental results of processing a HfB_2—SiC composition with varying SiC volume fraction (FIG. 4: vol % SiC is 5%, FIG. 5: vol % SiC is 10%, FIG. 6: vol % SiC is 15%, FIG. 7: vol % SiC is 30%.) FIG. 8 represents experimental results of processing a ZrB_2—SiC composition.

FIG. 9 is a magnified image of a UHTC material of the present invention as in FIG. 6 after fracture toughness testing.

FIG. 10 is a bar chart showing data resulting from fracture toughness testing of UHTC materials of the present invention as in FIGS. 4-6 and a comparison baseline UHTC material of the prior art as in FIG. 1.

DETAILED DESCRIPTION

The preparation of the enhanced UHTC composite system begins with a powder assembly of grains of one or more selected inorganic metal compounds (MC). The desired ceramic matrix is composed essentially of metal borides, carbides, nitrides, oxides, silicides, borocarbides, boronitrides, carbonitrides, or oxynitrides, especially of the group IV to VI refractory metals, having melting temperatures of at least 2000° C. Exemplary materials include HfB_2, ZrB_2, TaB_2, TiB_2, TaC, HfC, NbC, TiC, ZrC, HfN, Ta_2N, and ZrN. Choice of material will depend on the intended application. For thermal protection systems on space transport vehicles, the material should have both good oxidation resistance and an extremely high melting point (e.g, near 3000° C. or higher). Hafnium and zirconium diborides are preferred candidates for use on space transport vehicles. The ceramic starting powders are milled to the desired starting size.

A second compound, a pre-ceramic polymer, is added that will form a small volume fraction (5 to 30 vol %) of the high-aspect-ratio reinforcement phase in the ceramic composite. The volume fraction should be selected to optimize one or more thermal or mechanical properties of the resultant composite material, such as its thermal conductivity, fracture toughness, thermal shock or hardness. The particular pre-ceramic polymer is selected according to the desired reinforcement species. For example, any of several available organosilicon polymers, including a polycarbosilane, polysiloxane, polysilazane, polyborosiloxane, or polyborosilazane compounds may be used to grow SiC or Si_3N_4, possibly in combination with B_4C or BN, in the ceramic matrix.

The pre-ceramic polymer compound is uniformly mixed with the refractory ceramic powder in order to coat the grains. Good mixing disperses the polymer evenly throughout the mass, resulting in a homogeneous microstructure and the desired mechanical properties in the final ceramic composite. If the pre-ceramic polymer is not mixed sufficiently to uniformly distribute the polymer throughout the refractory ceramic powder, then regions deficient in the polymer will lead to larger grains of the ceramic matrix (undesirable). If desired, a fine powder of the selected reinforcement species could also be added along with the pre-ceramic polymer in order to act as seed crystals for acicular reinforcement growth, but uniform distribution of that powder will be important to the uniformity of the grown reinforcement material.

One preferred method of ensuring uniform mixing of the pre-ceramic polymer with the ceramic powder is to create a slurry containing the ceramic powder, the pre-ceramic polymer and a compatible solvent. The slurry is fed through a nozzle that produces uniform droplets of the suspension that are captured in liquid nitrogen. The droplets are then freeze dried to remove the solvent, leaving a uniform mixture of the powder coated with the pre-ceramic polymer.

The mixture is packed in graphite dies and thermally processed using the same basic consolidation steps (such as hot pressing) that are employed in traditional UHTC processing. The heating and cooling can be controlled according to a desired schedule. In hot pressing, a more rapid heating and cooling schedule results in a finer grain structure, compared to a slower schedule. For optimum acicular reinforcement growth, a slower heating and cooling rate is preferred.

Typical pressures during hot pressing are in a range of 10 to 40 MPa (or 100 to 400 kgf/cm^2), depending on the desired volume reduction and void content of the resulting sintered body. The mixture is treated at 1800 to 2150° C. for 30 to 90 minutes, and then the ceramic is allowed to cool. Hot pressing temperatures will depend upon the particular ceramic system being consolidated. For example, systems processed with HfB_2 have a minimum processing temperature of 2050° C. with a minimum dwell time of 30 minutes. Systems processed with ZrB_2 have a minimum processing temperature of 1950° C. with a minimum dwell time of 30 minutes. In this manner, the heated pre-ceramic polymer undergoes an in situ chemical reaction that grows the desired reinforcement material around the matrix grains.

5

Where the temperature is decreased relatively slowly (e.g., over a 180 minute interval), the resulting material is an assembly of MC domains with acicular crystal rods (long, narrow, often pointed) of the reinforcement species, having an aspect ratio of the order of from 10:1 to 30:1 with randomly distributed directions. Where the temperature is decreased relatively quickly (e.g., by quenching), the resulting material is an assembly of fine grain MC domains and reinforcement grains having aspect ratios estimated as no greater than about 2:1.

The length of the acicular crystal rods or whiskers (20 to 30 μm) does not vary appreciably with volume fraction. The amount of reinforcing material does affect the number and thickness of the acicular rods. A higher volume fraction promotes higher diameter rods, with, for example, a 10 vol % of SiC yielding rod diameters on the order of 2 μm and a 15 vol % of SiC yielding rod diameters on the order of 5 μm. 20 vol % (or greater) results in a 3D network of rods that are at least partly connected to each other so as to trap the MC grains within the network of reinforcing rods. The microstructure of a composite with 20 vol % of SiC exhibits a majority of the SiC material coalesced as larger grains, but the high aspect ratio of the SiC is preserved and some finer acicular SiC grains are still evident.

Hot pressed test samples with 5, 10, 15 and 20 vol % SiC in HfB$_2$ indicate full density is achieved in samples with SiC vol % greater than 5%. It was also observed that increasing the SiC vol % results in increased toughness and for a comparable vol % of SiC the high aspect ratio UHTC has a higher toughness than the baseline UHTC system indicating that the reinforcements are enhancing toughness. Inspection of the 15 vol % sample after subject to toughness testing shows evidence of crack deflection along the acicular SiC—HfB$_2$ interfaces, as well as possible crack bridging between SiC grains, to account for the increased toughness. Preliminary work on a ZrB$_2$: 15 vol % SiC composite system likewise obtains a high aspect ratio SiC phase. The reduction in needed SiC to maintain toughness, obtained from the acicular growth, promises to enhance the composite's oxidation resistance, as arc jet testing of SiC-containing composites lead to SiC depletion near the surface if the vol % SiC is above the percolation threshold.

EXAMPLES

FIG. **1** shows a baseline hot pressed UHTC microstructure of HfB$_2$: 20 vol % SiC formed from powdered HfB$_2$ and SiC. It can be seen that this known UHTC system does not have high aspect ratio SiC reinforcements.

FIG. **2** shows a spark plasma sintered (SPS) UHTC microstructure of HfB$_2$: 10 vol % SiC formed from a mixture of powdered HfB$_2$ and a pre-ceramic polymer. The SPS process pulses electric current through a graphite die containing the ceramic mixture, thus generating heat internally at a very fast rate. It can be seen in FIG. **2** that this SPS processing results in a very refined microstructure, but no evidence of acicular reinforcing grains.

FIG. **3** shows hot pressed microstructure of HfB$_2$: 10 vol % SiC formed from a mixture of powdered HfB$_2$ and a pre-ceramic polymer, but at a dwell time of less than the minimum 30 minutes. It can be seen that short hot pressing times result in few acicular grains.

FIGS. **4-7** show hot pressed microstructures of HfB$_2$: SiC formed from a mixture of powdered HfB$_2$ and a pre-ceramic polymer, with the pre-ceramic polymer added in amounts that respectively yield 5, 10, 15 and 20 vol % of SiC in the HfB$_2$ matrix. In accord with the invention, the thermal processing in these samples was performed with longer dwell times of

6

one hour. Many acicular rods can be seen, with the number of acicular rods increasing with the volume of SiC. It is also seen that one can adjust the volume percentage of SiC in the UHTC without losing the high aspect ratio architecture. The aforementioned dimensional characteristics of the high aspect ratio reinforcing rods are evident in FIGS. **4-7**. An interconnected network of SiC is observed beginning at 20 vol %, as seen in FIG. **7**. The majority of SiC rods have coalesced to form larger grains, but some finer acicular rods are also evident.

FIG. **8** shows a hot pressed microstructure of ZrB$_2$: 15 vol % SiC formed from a mixture of powdered ZrB$_2$ and a pre-ceramic polymer in accord with the present invention. The same acicular SiC rods as in the HfB$_2$ systems are observed here as well.

FIG. **9** shows the HfB$_2$: 15 vol % SiC microstructure of FIG. **6** after having undergoing fracture toughness testing using an indentation approach. A crack is seen in the lower right portion of the image extending from a corner of the indent. The image evidences crack growth along the HfB$_2$—SiC interface with possible SiC grain bridging. The data (FIG. **10**) show that a 15% volume fraction of high aspect ratio SiC has toughness comparable to the baseline particulate composite of 20% SiC.

What is claimed is:

1. A method of forming a ceramic composite, the method comprising:

mixing a pre-ceramic polymer and a solvent into a powder of an ultra-high-temperature ceramic (UHTC) material, and allowing the pre-ceramic polymer to coat grains of the UHTC material approximately uniformly, wherein the process of mixing comprises:

(i) creating a slurry comprising the powder of the UHTC material, the pre-ceramic polymer and the solvent;

(ii) producing droplets of the slurry; and

(ii) removing or separating at least a portion of the solvent from the slurry,

wherein said UHTC material is a boron-containing material, comprising at least one of HfB$_2$ and ZrB$_2$ and having a melting temperature of at least 2000° C.;

thermally consolidating the mixture at a consolidation temperature of at least about 2000° C. for a thermal consolidation time interval in a range of about 30-180 minutes and at an applied pressure of at least 10 MPa; and

allowing acicular reinforcement rods or fibers or whiskers to grow from the UHTC grains during thermal consolidation.

2. A method of forming a ceramic composite, the method comprising:

mixing a pre-ceramic polymer and a solvent into a powder of an ultra-high-temperature ceramic (UHTC) material, and allowing the pre-ceramic polymer to coat grains of the UHTC material approximately uniformly, wherein the process of mixing comprises:

(i) creating a slurry comprising the powder of the UHTC material, the pre-ceramic polymer and the solvent;

(ii) producing droplets of the slurry; and

(ii) removing or separating at least a portion of the solvent from the slurry;

thermally consolidating the mixture at a consolidation temperature of at least about 1800° C. for a thermal consolidation time interval in a range of about 30-180 minutes and at an applied pressure of at least 10 MPa; and

allowing acicular reinforcement rods or fibers or whiskers to grow from the UHTC grains during thermal consoli-

US 8,409,491 B1

7

dation, wherein at least one of the acicular reinforcement rods or fibers or whiskers has an aspect ratio of at least 10:1.

3. The method as in claim 1, wherein said pre-ceramic polymer is selected one or more of a polycarbosilane, polysiloxane, polysilazane, polyborosiloxane, or polyborosilazane compound.

4. The method as in claim 1, wherein said acicular reinforcement ceramic rods or fibers or whiskers comprise one or more of SiC, Si_3N_4, B_4C or BN.

5. The method as in claim 1, wherein said grown acicular reinforcement ceramic rods or fibers or whiskers have a volume fraction of not more than about 20 volume percent in said thermally consolidated mixture.

6. The method as in claim 1, wherein said thermal consolidation process comprises hot pressing.

7. The method as in claim 1, further comprising uniformly distributing an additional refractory ceramic phase into said powder of UHTC material to form a new mixture, before thermally consolidating the new mixture.

8. The method of claim 1, further comprising producing said droplets of said slurry by passing said slurry through a nozzle.

9. The method of claim 1, further comprising thermally consolidating said mixture at a temperature of no more than about 2150° C.

8

10. The method of claim 1, further comprising consolidating said mixture at an applied pressure of no more than about 40 MPa.

11. The method of claim 1, further comprising thermally consolidating said mixture for said consolidation time interval in a range of about 30-90 minutes.

12. The method of claim 1, further comprising thermally consolidating said mixture for said consolidation time interval of about 180 minutes and allowing said consolidated mixture to form as an assembly of fine grain domains, with at least one of said reinforcement rods or fibers or whiskers having an aspect ratio of no more than about 2:1.

13. The method of claim 1, further comprising:
choosing said UHTC material to comprise HfB_2; and
thermally consolidating said mixture at a temperature of at least about 2050° C. for a time interval of at least about 30 minutes.

14. The method of claim 1, further comprising:
choosing said UHTC material to comprise ZrB_2; and
thermally consolidating said mixture at a temperature of at least about 1950° C. for a time interval of at least about 30 minutes.

* * * * *

US007968054B1

(12) **United States Patent**
Li

(10) **Patent No.:** **US 7,968,054 B1**
(45) **Date of Patent:** **Jun. 28, 2011**

(54) **NANOSTRUCTURE SENSING AND TRANSMISSION OF GAS DATA**

(75) Inventor: **Jing Li**, San Jose, CA (US)

(73) Assignee: **The United States of America as represented by the Administrator of the National Aeronautics and Space Administration (NASA)**, Washington, DC (US)

(*) Notice: Subject to any disclaimer, the term of this patent is extended or adjusted under 35 U.S.C. 154(b) by 941 days.

(21) Appl. No.: **11/715,785**

(22) Filed: **Mar. 7, 2007**

(51) **Int. Cl.**
  G01N 7/00 (2006.01)
  G01N 33/48 (2006.01)
  G01N 27/00 (2006.01)
  G01N 31/00 (2006.01)
  G01N 19/00 (2006.01)

(52) **U.S. Cl.** **422/83**; 422/68.1; 422/98; 702/22; 702/23; 702/27; 702/30; 977/953; 977/957; 977/742; 977/842

(58) **Field of Classification Search** 702/27; 700/266
See application file for complete search history.

(56) **References Cited**

U.S. PATENT DOCUMENTS

6,289,328 B2 *	9/2001	Shaffer	....	706/20
6,433,702 B1	8/2002	Favreau		
7,312,095 B1 *	12/2007	Gabriel et al.	....	438/49
7,318,908 B1 *	1/2008	Dai	....	422/68.1
7,477,993 B2 *	1/2009	Sunshine et al.	....	702/22
7,623,972 B1 *	11/2009	Li et al.	....	702/27

2003/0175161 A1 *	9/2003	Gabriel et al.	....	422/90
2005/0233325 A1 *	10/2005	Kureshy et al.	....	435/6
2007/0202012 A1 *	8/2007	Steichen et al.	....	422/98

OTHER PUBLICATIONS

Janata, Electrochemical Sensors, Principles of Chemical Sensors, 1989, 81-239, Plenum Press, New York.
Kong, et al., Nanotube Molecular Wires as Chemical Sensors, Science, Jan. 28, 2000, 622-625, 287, AAAS.
Li, Chemical and Physical Sensors, Carbon Nanotubes: Science and Applications, 2004, 213-233, Editor: M. Meyyappan, CRC Press, Boca Raton, FL.
Li, et al., Carbon Nanotube Sensors for Gas and Organic Vapor Detection, NanoLetters, 2003, 929-933, 3-7, American Chemical Society.
Liao, et al., Telemetric Electrochemical Sensor, Biosensors Bioelectronics, 2004, 482-490, 20, Elsevier B.V.
DWL-AB650, a commercial product, D-Link Systems Inc., http://www.dlinkshop.com/.
MICAz, a commercial product, Crossbow Technology Inc., http://www.xbow.com/.
Nanotechnology Innovation for Chemical, Biological, Radiological, and Explosive (CBRE) Detection and Protection, Workshop Report, Nanoscale . . . , Nov. 2002, http://www.nano.gov.

* cited by examiner

Primary Examiner — In Suk Bullock
Assistant Examiner — Jennifer Wecker
(74) *Attorney, Agent, or Firm* — John F. Schipper; Robert M. Padilla

(57) **ABSTRACT**

A system for receiving, analyzing and communicating results of sensing chemical and/or physical parameter values, using wireless transmission of the data. Presence or absence of one or more of a group of selected chemicals in a gas or vapor is determined, using suitably functionalized carbon nanostructures that are exposed to the gas. One or more physical parameter values, such as temperature, vapor pressure, relative humidity and distance from a reference location, are also sensed for the gas, using nanostructures and/or microstructures. All parameter values are transmitted wirelessly to a data processing site or to a control site, using an interleaving pattern for data received from different sensor groups, using I.E.E.E. 802.11 or 802.15 protocol, for example. Methods for estimating chemical concentration are discussed.

10 Claims, 13 Drawing Sheets

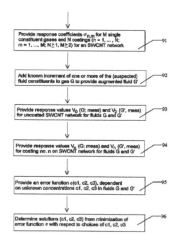

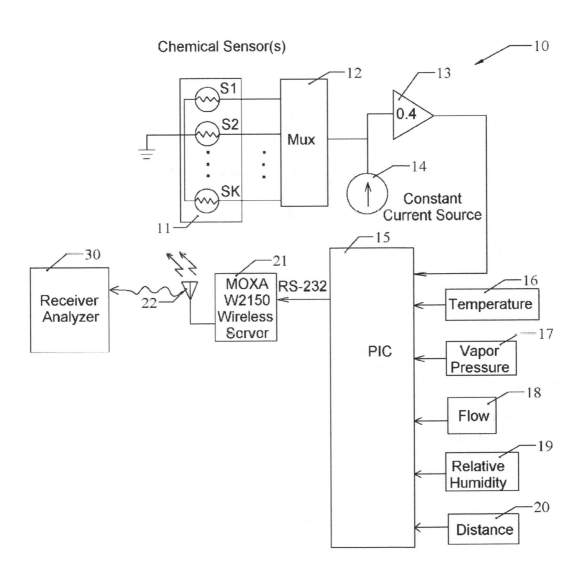

FIG. 1

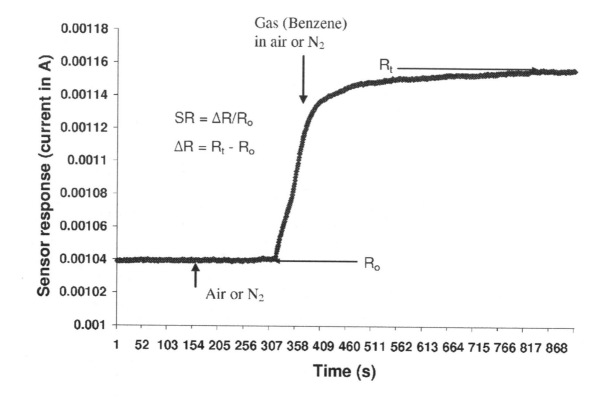

FIG. 2A

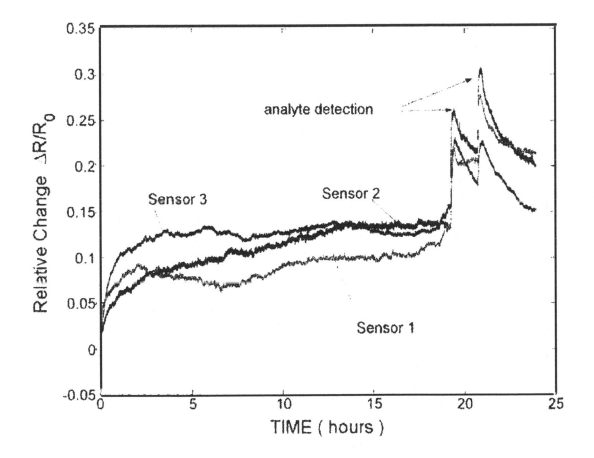

FIG. 2B

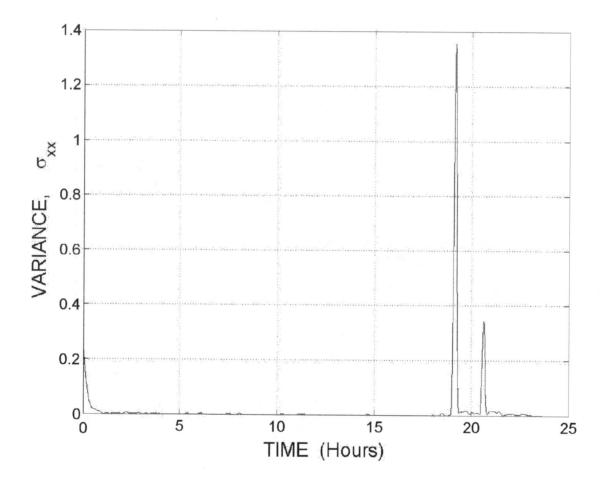

FIG. 3

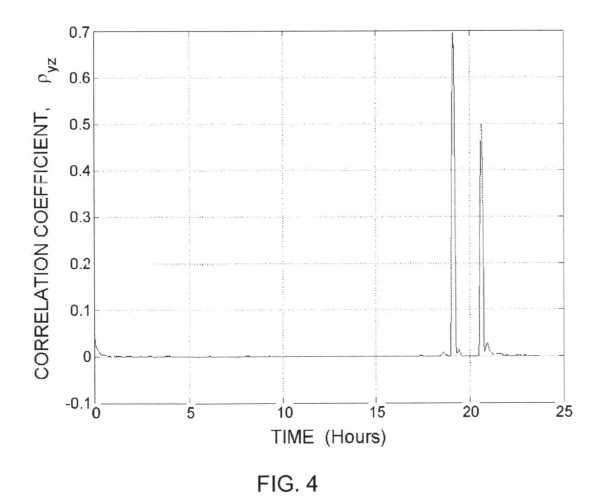

FIG. 4

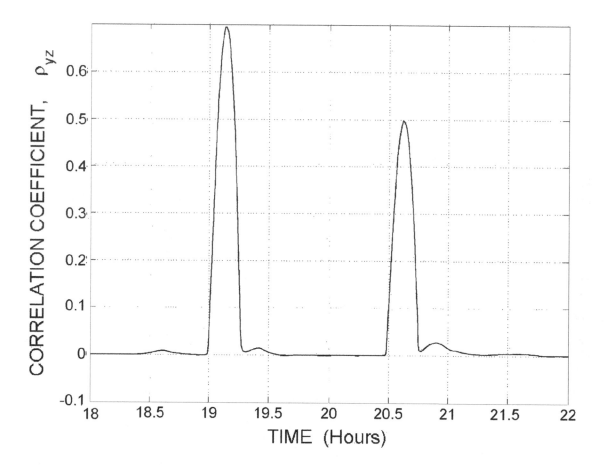

FIG. 5

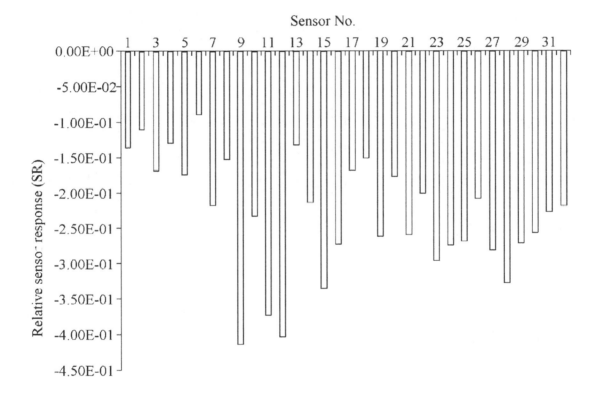

FIG. 6

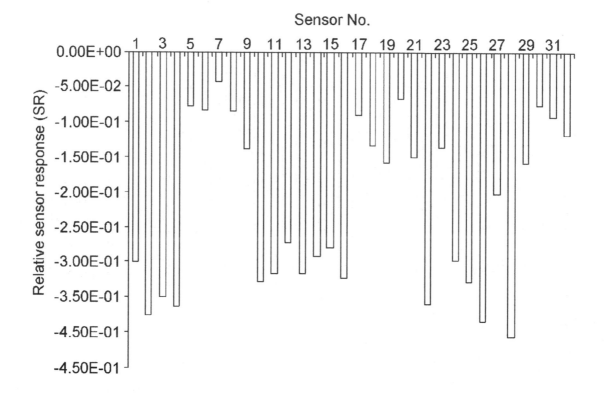

FIG. 7

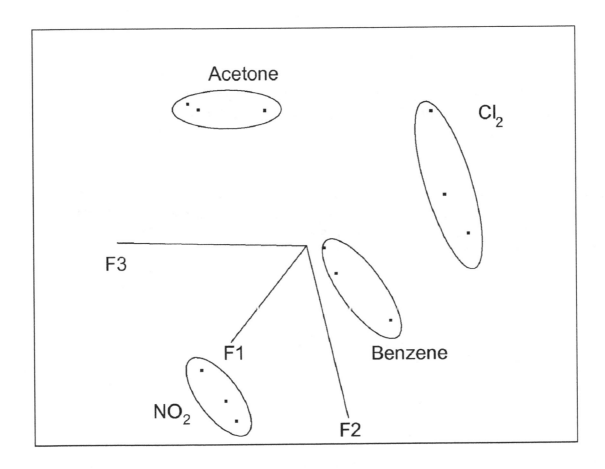

FIG. 8

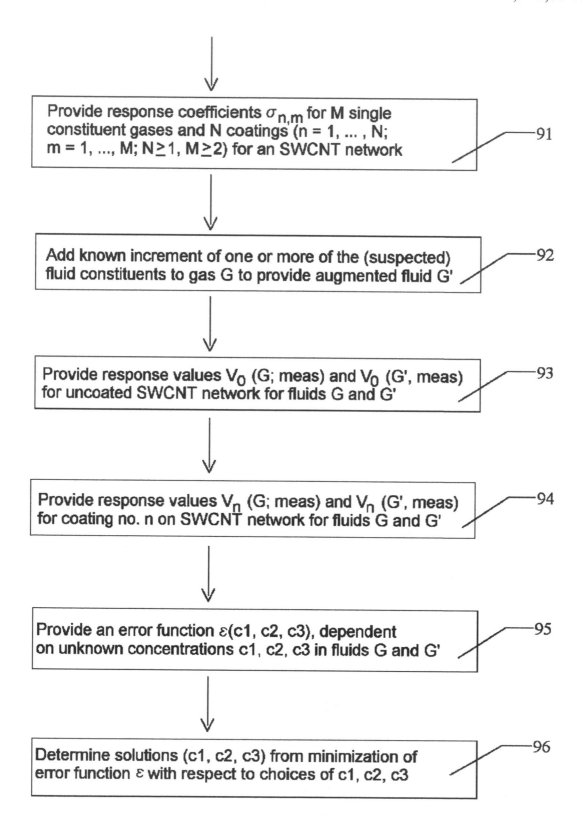

FIG. 9

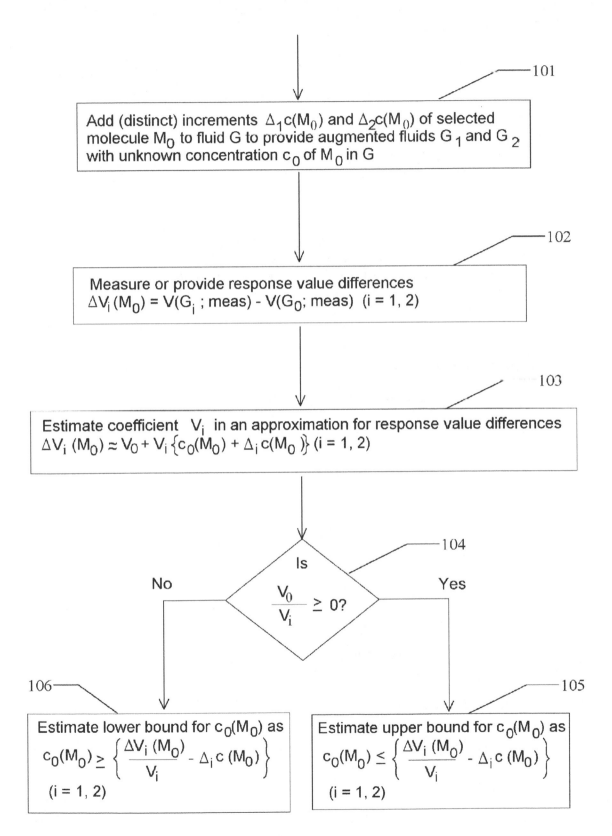

FIG. 10

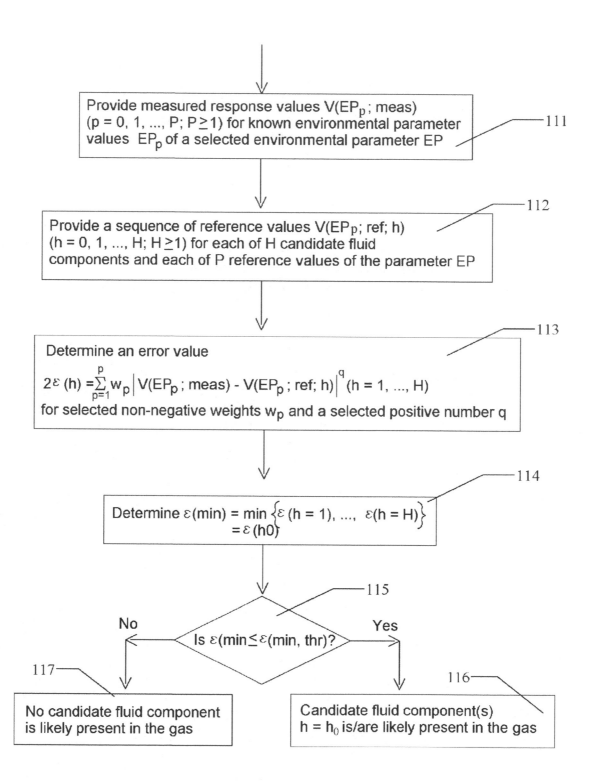

Provide measured response values $V(EP_p; meas)$ $(p = 0, 1, ..., P; P \geq 1)$ for known environmental parameter values EP_p of a selected environmental parameter EP — 111

Provide a sequence of reference values $V(EP_p; ref; h)$ $(h = 0, 1, ..., H; H \geq 1)$ for each of H candidate fluid components and each of P reference values of the parameter EP — 112

Determine an error value

$$2\varepsilon(h) = \sum_{p=1}^{p} w_p \left| V(EP_p; meas) - V(EP_p; ref; h) \right|^q \quad (h = 1, ..., H)$$

for selected non-negative weights w_p and a selected positive number q — 113

Determine $\varepsilon(min) = min\left\{\varepsilon(h = 1), ..., \varepsilon(h = H)\right\}$
$= \varepsilon(h0)$ — 114

Is $\varepsilon(min \leq \varepsilon(min, thr)$? — 115

No

Yes

No candidate fluid component is likely present in the gas — 117

Candidate fluid component(s) $h = h_0$ is/are likely present in the gas — 116

FIG. 11

338

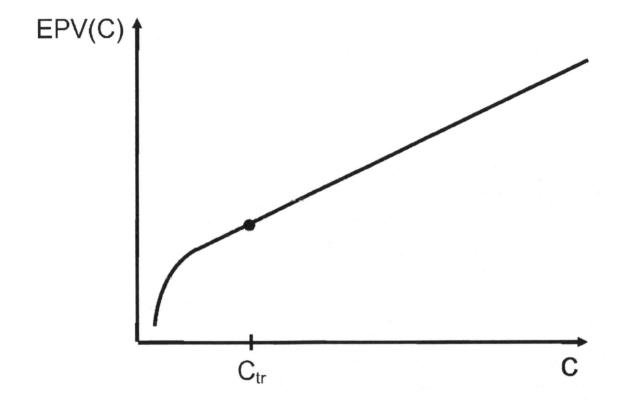

FIG. 12

1

NANOSTRUCTURE SENSING AND TRANSMISSION OF GAS DATA

ORIGIN OF THE INVENTION

Work related to this invention was performed under a joint research agreement between the National Aeronautics and Space administration and the University of California.

FIELD OF THE INVENTION

This invention relates to wireless transmission of data provided by nanostructure-based chemical and physical sensors.

BACKGROUND OF THE INVENTION

Chemical sensors have been developed for decades to detect various concentration levels of gases and vapors for deployment in a wide range of applications in industry, space mission, environment monitoring, medical, military, and others. The detection usually centers on change in a particular property or status of the sensing material (such as thermal, electrical, optical, mechanical, etc) upon exposure to the species of interest. The sensing material may be any of several elements from the periodic table, plus inorganic, semiconducting and organic compounds, in bulk or thin film form. One of the most investigated classes of chemical sensors in the past is the high-temperature metal oxide sensors due to these sensors' high sensitivity at low ppm to ppb concentration levels, with tin oxide thin films as an example. Polymer sensors have been studied in recent years because they can be operated at room temperature with low power consumption and are easily fabricated. Although commercial sensors based on these materials are available, continued research is in progress with sensing technologies using new sensing materials and new transducer platforms. New sensing technologies, such as nanotechnology-based sensors, are being developed to overcome the large power consumption and poor selectivity of metal oxides sensors, and to improve the poor sensitivity and narrow detection spectrum of polymer sensors.

Typical figures of merit expected from a chemical sensor include sensitivity (even down to a few molecules, selectivity, low power consumption, rapid response time and rapid sensor recovery time. Sensors based on the emerging nanotechnology may provide improved performance on all of the above aspects compared to current micro and macro sensors. Nanomaterials exhibit small size, light weight, very high surface-to-volume ratio, and increased chemical reactivity compared to bulk materials; all these properties are ideal for developing extremely sensitive detectors. The potential of nanomaterials for detection and for protection and remediation has been outlined in a recent report by the National Science and Technology Council ("Nanotechnology Innovation for Chemical, Biological, Radiological and Explosive Detection and Protection," November 2002).

One promising nanomaterial is the carbon nanotube ("CNT"), which exhibits extraordinary mechanical, electrical and optical properties. These interesting properties have prompted wide range investigations for applications in nanoelectronics, high strength composites, field emitting devices, catalysts, etc. A single-walled carbon nanotube ("SWCNT") has all the atoms on the surface and therefore would be exposed maximally to the environment, allowing a change in its properties sensitively. The first demonstration of an SWCNT-based sensor was for a chemical field effect transistor ("CHEMFET"), where a single semiconducting SWCNT

2

is used as the channel material and the conductivity was shown to change upon exposure to NO_2 and NH_3 (J. Kong et al, "Nanotube Molecular Wires as Chemical Sensors," Science, vol. 287, pp 622-625, January 2000). The potential for using CNTs in chemical sensors was noted in the Kong et al article. However, it still is a challenge to make practical sensors, due to difficulty in fabrication complexity, low sensor yield and poor reproducibility.

A different configuration of carbon nanotube-based chemical sensors with much easier fabrication process was introduced by J. Li et al in "Chemical and Physical Sensors, Carbon Nanotubes: Science and Applications", M. Meyyappan, ed., CRC Press, Boca Raton, Fla., 2004. First, an interdigitated electrode ("IDE") configuration is fabricated using conventional photolithographic methods with a nominal finger width of 10 μm and gap size of 8 μm. The electrode fingers are made of thermally evaporated Ti and Au (20 nm and 40 nm thickness, respectively) on a layer of SiO_2, thermally grown on top of a silicon wafer. Second, a thin layer of carbon nanotubes forming a network is laid on the fingers using a solution casting process. The conductivity of the CNT network changes upon exposure of the fingers to different gases or vapors. Such a process is significantly simpler and produces consistent sensors based on statistical properties of the CNT network with high yield (~100 percent). The IDE configuration facilitates effective electric contact between SWCNTs and the electrodes over large areas, while providing good accessibility for analytes in the form of gas/vapor adsorption or contaminants adsorption/extraction in/from liquid to all SWCNTs including semiconducting tubes.

Although carbon nanotube-based chemical sensors using the IDE configuration have been prototyped in laboratories, use of an IDE configuration for wireless sensing has not been reported in published research. Use of an IDE configuration requires frequent transmission of data measured at each of a large number of IDE fingers. A straightforward approach may consume substantial power and may require use of a relatively large footprint for the sensor system. This may be inconsistent with automated use of a remote system in a confined space.

What is needed is a wireless transmission system that (1) has a small footprint and whose size is compatible with a nanosensor system, which may have a diameter as small as 5-15 cm, (2) consumes relatively little power (e.g., about 50 μWatt-60 mWatt, or smaller with voltage regulation not activated), (3) is reliable, with a mean time to failure exceeding 8 hours (representative battery life) and (4) permits frequent data transmission from each of a large number of data sources.

SUMMARY OF THE INVENTION

These needs are met by the invention, which provides a system with one or more sensors for selected chemicals (all using nanostructure sensors with small physical sizes), one or more sensors for physical parameters, a multiplexer to receive and interleave the measured data stream values from the sensors according to a selected interleaving pattern, and a wireless transmission module to transmit the measured values to a receiver and data analyzer.

The overall sensor system consists of a chemical sensor module, a microcontroller-based data acquisition module, a multiplexer and constant current source module, and a wireless communication module. The chemical sensor module is based on use of an interdigitated electrode ("IDE") configuration. A layer of single-walled carbon nanotubes ("SWCNTs") is laid on the IDE fingers. Chemical sensing is based on detection of changes in the conductivity of the

SWCNT network. In one embodiment, the system has 32 channels of chemical sensing elements. It is self-contained and portable, and wirelessly transmits measurement data to a PC, using an I.E.E.E. 802.11a, 802.11b or 802.15 wireless LAN protocol. The footprint of the invention has a diameter as small as a few cm.

BRIEF DESCRIPTION OF THE DRAWINGS

FIG. 1 schematically illustrates a sensor array and a wireless transmitter according to an embodiment of the invention.

FIGS. 2A and 2B graphically illustrate sensor responses for identical exposures.

FIG. 3 shows the variance of measurement data from the sensor in FIGS. 2A and 2B, computed with a moving window of 1000 samples of the data.

FIGS. 4 and 5 illustrate correlation of two sensors within a moving window.

FIGS. 6 and 7 graphically illustrate relative chemical sensor response for exposure to NO_2 and for Cl_2, respectively.

FIG. 8 graphically illustrates separation of the gases NO_2, Cl_2, benzene and acetone according to principal component analysis.

FIGS. 9, 10 and 11 are flow charts of algorithm procedures for estimating concentrations of initially unknown constituents according to the invention.

FIG. 12 graphically illustrates transition from linear to logarithmic dependence upon a variable, such as concentration.

DESCRIPTION OF BEST MODE OF THE INVENTION

FIG. 1 schematically illustrates components of a system 10, constructed according to the invention, including a chemical and/or physical nanosensor module 11, whose output signals are received by a multiplexer ("MUX") 12. An output signal of the MUX 12 is augmented by a constant current source 13 and is passed through a buffer amplifier 14 (optional) and is received and processed by a microcontroller 15 (e.g., a PIC16F688, available from Microchip Technologies). In one embodiment, wherein an array of carbon nanostructures is applied to environmental sensing, the microcontroller 15 also receives a signal from at least one of a temperature microsensor 16, a vapor pressure microsensor 17, a flow microsensor (direction, velocity) 18, a relative humidity microsensor 19 and an acoustic or electromagnetic distance sensor 20. The microcontroller output signals (e.g., in RS-232 format) are received by a wireless communication module 21, which includes a wireless server 22 (e.g., a MOXA W2150), which transmits these signals, using 802.11b protocol, through an antenna 23 to a local area network (LAN). The transmitted signals are received by a receiver (not shown) that is spaced apart from the transmission system 11, for display and/or further signal processing.

Each of the individual sensors, such as 16, 17, 18 and 19, has its own data reporting cycle, and it is assumed herein that these reporting cycles are numerically compatible. In a first approach, each of the reporting cycles has the same length Δt, and the four sensors report to a multiplexer in a consecutive interleave pattern as $t_{m,n} = \{16, 17, 18, 19, 16, 17, 18, 19, 16, 17, \ldots\}$ (n=1, 2, 3, 4; m=1, 2, ...) In a second version, at least one of the sensors (16) has a reporting cycle length that is N times as long as the other cycle lengths (e.g., N=3), and the four sensors report in a second interleave pattern as $t_{m,n} = \{16, 17, 18, 19, 17, 18, 19, 17, 18, 19, 16, 17, 18, 19, 17, 18, \ldots\}$. In a third version, the reporting cycle lengths are rational,

non-integer, multiples of each other so that the reporting pattern appears random, for example, where $\Delta t(16) = (\frac{7}{4})\Delta t(17) = (\frac{3}{5})\Delta t(18) = (\frac{7}{4})\Delta t(19)$, a consistent third interleave pattern is: $t_{m,n} = \{16, 18, 16, 17, 18, 18, 19, 16, 18, 18, 16, 17, 18, 19, \ldots\}$. For any interleave pattern $\{t_{m,n}\}_{m,n}$ for data reporting, the multiplexer transmits the received data in another time sequence $\{t'_{m,n}\}_{m,n}$, where $t'_{m,n}$ is determined with reference to $t_{m,n}$ (e.g., $t'_{m,n} = t_{m,n} + \Delta t$, where Δt is a substantially constant time delay value).

In one embodiment, the chemical sensor module contains 32 sensing elements, arranged in an IDE configuration, having pure SWCNTs, having polymer coated SWCNTs, and/or having metal nanoclusters or doped SWCNTs. At the center of the data acquisition system is a microcontroller (PIC16F688) from Microchip Technologies Inc. that samples each sensor element through a set of four Texas Instruments CD4051 multiplexers. Each MUX 12 reads signals from a group of eight chemical sensing elements. The LM234 constant current source from National Semiconductor is used to provide a constant current (100 μAmp) to each sensing element. Four of these devices are used to excite each group of eight chemical sensing elements. Conductivity or resistance is measured by supplying a constant current and measuring the corresponding voltage difference across the sensor. Also included in the data system is an AD22100K temperature sensor from Analog Devices. The microcontroller reads all 32 chemical sensor and temperature values and generates a serial data output that can be connected directly (1) to a wireless serial device server, for wireless data transmission, or (2) to an RS-232 serial data output for a PC, for data logging. In this design, a W2150 serial server from Moxa Technologies, Inc. is used to wirelessly transmit data to a laptop or to a desktop PC, using an I.E.E.E. 802.11b wireless LAN protocol.

An alternative server is a Crossbow MICAz, using an I.E.E.E. 802.15.4 protocol at 2.4 GHz, can also be used for wireless transmission. This system has a data transport rate of 250 kbits/sec, and each node can also serve as a router. This allows a subset of one or more nodes to serve as a collection point for collecting data that were measured elsewhere and routing the data to a data processing module and/or to a control site that can respond to any problem encountered in the data measurements or data processing. This system uses direct sequence spread spectrum radio transmission, which is useful where two or more data collection nodes are transmitting substantially simultaneously to a data processing module and/or to a control site. Transmission range is up to 100 M outdoors and up to 30 M indoors. Device dimensions are 58×32×7 mm (diameter ≈68 mm). Analog inputs as well as digital inputs are accepted by the MICAz system.

Another alternative server is an Air-Pro D-Link dual band wireless LAN, operating at 5 GHz and 2.4 GHz, using 801.11a/b protocol with 64/128 and 152-bit, shared key data encryption for authentication and enhanced data security. Each node can also provide data collection and forwarding to a data processing module and/or to a control site. Data transport rates are 1, 2, 5.5, 11 Mbits/sec (802.11b) and 6, 9, 12, 18, 24, 36, 48 and 54 Mbits/sec (802.11a). Transmission range is up to 400 M outdoors and up to 100 M indoors. Device dimensions are 118×54×13 mm (diameter ≈133 mm).

FIG. 1 schematically illustrates components of the system 10, which includes a chemical nanosensor module 11, whose sensor output signals are received by the MUX 12. The output signal from the MUX 12 is augmented by a constant current source 13, and this signal is passed through a buffer amplifier 14 (optional) and received by a microcontroller 15 (e.g., a PIC16F688, available from Microchip Technologies). The microcontroller 15 also receives a physical sensor signal from

5

at least one of a temperature microsensor **16**, a vapor pressure microsensor **17**, a flow microsensor (direction, velocity) **18**, a relative humidity microsensor **19** and an acoustic or electromagnetic distance sensor **20**. The microcontroller output signals (presented, e.g., in RS-232 format) are received by a wireless server **21** (e.g., a MOXA W2150), which transmits these signals, using an I.E.E.E. 802.11b protocol, through an antenna **22** and are received by a receiver and analyzer **30**, spaced apart from the transmission system **10**, for display and/or further signal processing.

Sensor Response

FIG. **2A** shows typical sensor responses with the calculation. FIG. **2B** shows the sensor responses from three identical sensors that were observed over a period of 25 hours from three sensing elements. The graph illustrates change of sensor resistance changes in response to the introduction of an analyte, in this case ammonia, at approximately t=19 hours and t=20.5 hours. Data from the sensors were collected at one sample per second. For this experiment, a cotton swab soaked in ammonia hydroxide solution was placed approximately 2 cm above the sensor surface, but the concentration of the analyte was not quantified. The sensor resistance for sensors x, y, and z increases approximately 10 percent from the sensor resistance measured just prior to the time(s) of detection of the analyte. Statistical properties of the measurement data were investigated to extract the information that presents the detection of analytes. Such information can be drawn from measurement data of a single sensor or from multiple sensors.

FIG. **3** shows the variance of the measurement data from sensor "x" computed over a moving window of 1000 samples of the data. This window represents 16.7 minutes of measurement data. Small variance indicates small changes in measured data values over this period of time. A large variance indicates possible presence of analytes. In FIG. **3**, this variance is substantially larger at two instants of time (t=19 and 20.5 hours) when the analyte is introduced.

In addition to computing variance of individual sensor data values, statistical correlation of two sensors can be computed to confirm the presence of analytes. FIG. **4** shows the correlation coefficient for two sensors y and z, computed over the same moving window. FIG. **4** indicates, from an agreement between two sensors, that both sensors were exposed to the presence of analytes. An enlarged view of FIG. **4** around the two times of analyte introduction is shown in FIG. **5**. Similar results were also observed for sensor pairs (x,y) and (x,z). FIGS. **6** and **7** graphically illustrate relative sensor response for exposure of the chemical sensor array to NO_2 gas and to Cl_2 gas, respectively. The functionalized sensor-to-sensor response differences can be used to determine or estimate the gas that is present.

Chemical Discrimination

The nanomaterials used in this array were individually studied for different gases and can be classified as: 1) pristine single walled carbon nanotubes, 2) carbon nanotubes coated with different polymers (here, chlorosulfonated polyethylene and hydroxypropyl cellulose), and 3) carbon nanotubes loaded with Pd nanoparticles and monolayer protected clusters of gold nanoparticles.

When exposed to a vapor-phase analyte, each sensing element in the array responds uniquely. A reproducible combination of resistances, or "smellprint", for each vapor/gas is manifest. The sensor response is measured as a bulk relative resistance change (alternatively, current change or voltage change): $\Delta R/R_0$, as in FIG. **3A**. To calculate the relative sensor response (SR), the initial sensor resistance R_0 (or current/voltage), and the resistance R (or current/voltage) during the exposure are measured, and a normalized change,

6

$$SR = \frac{R_t - R_o}{R_o} \tag{1}$$

is computed.

By comparing the results of several gases, it is possible to determine which sensors will respond in which manner (i.e. large or small amplitude, positive or negative). Looking at the histogram of sensor responses from 32 sensors to different gases/vapors, patterns for each gas/vapor can be established for discrimination between tested gases/vapors. When the sensor responses of an unknown subject gas are compared with the smellprints of several known substances, the unknown subject gas can be identified by matching its pattern to, or minimizing a pattern difference relative to, one of the known substances in the library.

However, the sensor responses often vary with concentration of the gas, temperature, and other external factors. To account for this, the data gathered by the sensors is normalized so that the relative responses can be compared, in order to make the sensor information more accurate. In normalization, the length of all data vectors becomes the same by making the sum of the squares of vector components equal to a constant so that the vectors become fixed length vectors. The data were normalized using:

$$\sum_{k=1}^{NV} x_{ik}^2 = c_i. \tag{2}$$

Here, k designates the sensor, i identifies the gas, and NV is the total number of sensors (32 in one embodiment). Theoretically, c_i can be any positive number, such as 1.

In addition to analyzing the relative responses, the data are autoscaled to unit variance and zero mean, by mean-centering followed by dividing by the standard deviation:

$$x'_{ik} = \frac{x_{ik} - \bar{x}_k}{s_k} \tag{3}$$

where x'_{ik} is the autoscaled response, x_{ik} is the relative sensor response, $\bar{x}_k$ is the mean value of normalized response for that specific sensor, and s_k is the standard deviation:

$$s_k = \left[\frac{1}{NP-1} \sum_{i=1}^{NP} (x_{ik} - \bar{x}_k)^2 \right]^{1/2} \tag{4}$$

where NP is the number of independent responses. Autoscaling removes any inadvertent weighting that arises due to use of arbitrary physical units. In the absence of any information that would preclude its use, use of autoscaling is preferable for most applications.

The processed data set contains the sensor responses from all 32 channels. Pattern recognition algorithms are very powerful tools to deal with a large set of data. For example, principal component analysis (PCA) was applied to the data set that was collected from this carbon nanotube based sensor array. The PCA is to express the main information in the variables $X=\{x_k|k=1, 2 \ldots K)\}$ using a smaller number of variables

$$\hat{T}=\{\hat{t}_1, \hat{t}_2 \ldots \hat{t}_A\} \, (A<K), \tag{5}$$

referred to as principal components of the variable X. In this instance, the X is a matrix of 32 sensor responses to these gases and vapors from the sensor array. Here, three principal components are labeled as F1, F2, and F3 that correspond to $\hat{t}_1, \hat{t}_2,$ and $\hat{t}_3$ in Eq. (5). FIG. **8** illustrates separation of the gases NO_2, Cl_2, benzene and acetone in terms of these three principal components.

These gases and vapors are completely separated in principal component space, which indicates that this sensor array provides a high discrimination power to these gases and vapors. Because these gases were tested by this sensor array at different concentration levels in the range of 5-45 ppm, this sensor array can be used (uniquely) for high sensitive gas and vapor detection and discrimination. This sensor array discriminates the gases and vapors by their chemical nature rather than their concentrations. Also, the array responses can discriminate between gases that have some similarity in their chemical nature.

Further analysis is often required to reliably estimate concentration of one or more target chemicals c0. After exposure of a nanostructure to a gas, a measured electrical parameter value EPV (e.g., impedance, conductivity, capacitance, inductance, etc.) changes with time in a predictable manner, if a selected chemical precursor is present, and will approach an asymptotic value promptly after exposure to the target chemical. The measured EPVs are compared with one or more sequences of reference EPVs for one or more known target precursor molecules, and a most probable concentration value is estimated for each of one, two or more target molecules. An error value is computed, based on differences for the measured and reference EPVs using the most probable concentration values. Where the error value is less than an error value threshold, the system concludes that the target molecule is likely. Presence of one, two or more target molecules in the gas can be sensed from a single set of measurements.

For relatively large concentrations, it is assumed that the measured EPV for a given target molecule will vary linearly with the concentration C,

$$EPV(C)=a+b \cdot C, \tag{6}$$

where the parameters a and b are characteristic of the particular target molecule for which the measurements are made. Where $EPV(C_{1,1})$ and $EPV(C_{1,2})$ are values for a pure substance measured at the different concentration values $C_{1,1}$ and $C_{1,2}$, respectively, the parameter values a and b can be estimated by

$$a=\{EPV(C_{1,1})C_{1,2}-EPV(C_{1,2})C_{1,1}\}/\{C_{1,2}-C_{1,1}\}, \tag{7-1}$$

$$b=(EPV(C_{1,1})-EPV(C_{1,2})\}/\{C_{1,2}-C_{1,1}\}, \tag{7-2}$$

for each target molecule. For smaller concentrations ($\approx$1-50 ppm), it may be preferable to use a logarithmic approximation,

$$EPV(C)=a'+b' \cdot \log_e C, \tag{8}$$

where a' and b' are selected parameters. The parameter values a' and b' can be determined in a manner similar to that of Eqs. (7-1) and (13-2), by replacing the variables $C_{1,1}$ and $C_{1,2}$ by $\log_e\{C_{1,1}\}$ and $\log_e\{C_{1,2}\}$, respectively. FIG. **12** graphically illustrates the two concentration regimes for EPV(C), corresponding to Eqs. (6) and (8), which join together at a concentration transition value C_{tr} for which

$$a'+b' \cdot \log_e C_{tr}=a+b \cdot C_{tr}. \tag{9}$$

Given an array of N sub-arrays of CNS sensors and a set of K target molecules (k=1, . . . , K;K$\geqq$2), the EPV data for the sensors can be pre-processed in order to identify more clearly

which CNS sensor sub-arrays are more sensitive to presence of a particular target molecule. In a first embodiment, the array is exposed to a selected target molecule, such as H_2O_2, at a selected sequence $\{C_q\}_q$ (q=1, . . . , Q with Q=N) known (not necessarily distinct) concentration values (e.g., 500 ppm, 14,000 ppm, 65 ppm, 1200 ppm, 10 ppm, etc.), and a reference measurement value EPV(n;q;k;ref) (n=1, 2, . . . , N) is recorded for each sensor sub-array n, each concentration C_q of a reference gas containing a selected target molecule (k). Measurements for one or more concentration values for the selected target molecule gas can be repeated, if desired, to obtain an N×N square matrix of values. With q fixed, an N×N matrix $\{EPV(n;q;k;ref)/EPV(n;k;norm)\}$=E(n;q;k;ref) is formed, where, EPV(n;k;norm) is a normalization factor for the selected target molecule gas no. k and the sub-array no. n, which may be chosen as

$$EPV(n; k; norm) = \left\{\sum_{q=1}^{N} u_q EPV(n; q; k; ref)^{\rho}\right\}^{1/\rho}, \tag{10}$$

where $\{u_q\}_q$ is a selected set of non-negative weight numbers whose sum is a selected positive number (e.g., 1 or N) and p is a selected positive number. The normalization factor E(n;k;norm) may be a single EPV (e.g., u_{q1}=1 and u_q=0 for q≠q1), or may be a weighted sum of two or more EPVs. This normalization (optional) is intended to compensate for the concentration dependence of the particular target molecule.

For each sub-array n (fixed), the mean and standard deviation for each of K reference gases, numbered k=1, . . . , K (K$\geqq$2) are computed, as

$$\mu(n; k) = \sum_{q=1}^{N} E(n; q; k; ref)/N, \tag{11A}$$

$$\mu(n) = \sum_{k=1}^{K} \mu(n; k)/K, \tag{11B}$$

$$\sigma(n; k) = \left\{\sum_{q=1}^{N} \{E(n; q; k; ref) - \mu(n; k)\}^2/N\right\}^{1/2}, \tag{12A}$$

$$\sigma(n) = \sum_{q=1}^{N} \sigma(n; k)/K. \tag{12B}$$

One now forms K autoscaled N×N matrices, defined by

$$S(n;q;k)=\{E(n;q;k;ref)-\mu(n)\}/\sigma(n), \tag{13-k}$$

and analyzes K eigenvalue equations

$$S(n;q;k) \, V(k;\lambda(k))=\lambda(k) \, V(k;\lambda(k)), \tag{14-k}$$

where k (=1, . . . , K) is fixed and V(k;λ(k)) is a normalized N×1 vector that will usually depend upon the reference gas (k). If, as is likely, the N eigenvalues λ(k) for a fixed reference gas k are distinct, the corresponding eigenvectors V(k;λ,(k)) are mutually orthogonal (non-degeneracy). In the unusual event (degeneracy) that two or more of the N eigenvalues λ(k)are equal, different non-zero linear combinations of the corresponding eigenvectors V(k;λ(k)) can be constructed that are orthogonal to each other, within a sub-space spanned by the reduced set of eigenvectors corresponding to the identical eigenvalues.

9

Each matrix equation (14-k) has a sequence of N (eigenvalue;eigenvector) pairs, $\{(\lambda_n(k);V_n(k;\lambda_q(k))\}_n$, for a fixed reference gas k, and it is assumed here that the eigenvalues are arranged so that

$$|\lambda_1(k)| \geq |\lambda_2(k)| \geq \ldots \geq |\lambda_N(k)| \qquad (15\text{-}k)$$

and so that the highest magnitude eigenvalue in each set satisfies

$$|\lambda_1(k1)| \geq |\lambda_1(k2)| \geq \ldots |\lambda_1(kN)|, \qquad (16)$$

where $\{k1, k2, \ldots, kN\}$ includes each of the integers $\{1, 2, \ldots, N\}$ precisely once. The eigenvector $V(k1;\lambda_1(k1))$ is identified as a first basis vector $V'(1)$:

$$V'(k1;\lambda_1(k1))=V(k1;\lambda_1(k1)) \qquad (17\text{-}1)$$

A second modified vector

$$V'(k2;\lambda_1(k2))=V(k2;\lambda_1(k2))-\{V(k2;\lambda_1(k2)), V'(k1;\lambda_1(k1))\}V'(k1;\lambda_1(k1)) \qquad 17\text{-}2$$

is computed, where $\{V(k2;\lambda_2(k2)), V'(1)\}$ is the scalar product (also referred to as the inner product) of the vectors $V(k2;\lambda_2(k2))$ and $V'(k1)$. More generally, a pth modified vector

$$V'(kp;\lambda_1(kp)) = \qquad (17\text{-}p)$$

$$V(kp;\lambda_1(kp)) - \sum_{r=1}^{p-1} \{V(kp;\lambda_1(kp)), V'(kr;\lambda_1(kr))\}V'(kr;\lambda_1(kr))$$

is computed for $p=2, \ldots, K$. The set of vectors $\{V'(kr;\lambda_1(kr))\}_k(r=1, \ldots, K)$ is mutually orthogonal, in the sense that the scalar products satisfy

$$\{V'(kr;\lambda_1(kr)), V'(ks;\lambda_1(ks))\} = \delta_{r,s}. \qquad (18)$$

$$> 0(r = s)$$

$$= 0(r \neq s).$$

Each of the set of vectors $\{V'(kr;\lambda_1(kr))\}_r(r=1, \ldots, K)$ is maximally independent of each of the other vectors in the set, in the sense of mutual orthonormality (Eq. (18)). Each vector $V'(kr;\lambda_1(kr))$ will have relatively large (primary) contributions from some of the sensor sub-arrays and will have smaller (secondary) contributions from the remainder of the N sub-arrays. The vectors $V'(kr;\lambda_1(kr))$ identify a maximally independent set of linear combinations of EPV responses from the N sub-arrays that can be used to distinguish presence of one reference gas (target molecule kr) from presence of another reference gas (target molecule ks). For example, if the set of reference gases are H_2O_2, H_2O and CH_3OH, N=3 and three matrix eigenvalue equations are to be solved in Eqs. (9-k) (k=1, 2, 3). More generally, presence or absence of any of K target molecules (K$\geq$2) may be estimated.

The linear combinations LC(kp) of EPV measurements for the different sensor sub-arrays correspond to modified principal components for the particular reference gases chosen. Choice of another set of another set of reference gases will result in a different set of modified principal components, although change of one or more concentration values within a reference gas may have little or no effect on the modified principal components.

The preceding analysis concerning EPV measurements and estimates of concentration can be done wholly at the data processing site, partly at each of the data processing site and

at the chemical sensor module site, or wholly at the chemical sensor module site. The system provides an integrated chemical sensor system based on use of SWCNTs as sensing elements, including some preliminary testing results. The associated data transmission system is wireless, small, portable, and readily deployable in the field.

A nanostructure, or assembly of such structures, can be grown, for example, by a procedure discussed in connection with FIG. 1 in "Controlled Patterning And Growth Of Single Wall And Multi-wall Carbon Nanotubes," issued to Delzeit and Meyyappan in U.S. Pat. No. 6,858,197, incorporated by reference herein.

What is claimed is:

1. A system for receiving, analyzing and communicating results of sensing chemical and/or physical parameter values, the system comprising:

N sensors numbered n=1, . . . , N (N$\geq$2), of parameters, where each sensor senses an electrical parameter value $EPV(t_{m,n};n)$ of a selected chemical or a physical parameter at a selected sequence of times $\{t=t_{m,n}\}_m(m=1, 2, \ldots)$, where at least one sensor senses a data set that includes at least one of a local temperature, a local vapor pressure, a local relative humidity, at least one of an acoustic signal and an electromagnetic signal for estimating a distance between the sensor and a reference surface, and presence of a selected chemical in a test gas, and where each sensor comprises a nanostructure (NS), having a sensing element having a diameter no greater than about 20 nm;

wherein at least one NS is loaded with a selected sensitizing substance drawn from a group of sensitizing substances comprising Au particles, located between first and second ends of the at least one NS, and the first and second ends are connected to first and second terminals, respectively, of at least one of a voltage source and a current source, and to an electrical parameter value measurement mechanism that measures a change in at least one of electrical current, voltage difference, electrical resistance, electrical conductance and capacitance between the first and second ends of the at least one NS;

a multiplexer, having at least N input terminals and at least one output terminal, that receives at least one of a sensed value $EPV(t_{m,n};n)$ and a sensed value change $\Delta EPV(t_{m,n};n)$ from sensor no. n, at a sequence of times, $\{t=t'_{m,n}\}$, where the time $t'_{m,n}$ is determined with reference to a corresponding time $t_{m,n}$, and where each of a first sequence of times $\{t_{m,n1}\}_m$ is interleaved with a second sequence of times $\{t_{m,n2}\}_m$ for at least two integers, n1 and n2, satisfying $1 \leq n1 < n2 \leq N$;

a wireless transmission module, connected to the multiplexer output terminal, to receive and transmit at least one of the sensed value $EPV(t_{m,n};n)$ and the sensed value change $\Delta EPV(t_{m,n};n)$, received from the multiplexer, for at least one sensor no. n; and

a computer that is programmed to receive, from the wireless transmission module, and to compare at least one of the second value $EPV(t_{m,n};n)$ and the measured sensed value change $\Delta EPV(t_{m,n})$ in an electrical parameter value with a corresponding reference value and to estimate and indicate, based upon the comparison, presence or absence of at least one chemical in a group of K target chemicals, numbered k=1, . . . , K (K$\geq$1),

where the N sensors, the multiplexer and the wireless transmission module are contained in a volume having a diameter no greater than about 14 cm.

2. The system of claim 1, wherein said multiplexer is located adjacent to at least one of said sensors.

11

3. The system of claim **1**, wherein:

at least one of said sensors is exposed to said test gas to be interrogated for presence or absence of one or more of said K target chemicals in said test gas (k=1, . . . ,K; K≧1);

measurement values EPV(n;test) are provided of a selected electrical parameter for said test gas for each said of sensor no. n=1, . . . , N (N≧2), for each of said K target chemicals and for each of a selected sequence of concentrations Ck (k=1, . . . , K; K≦N) of the target molecule no. k; and

wherein said computer is further programmed:

to provide at least N+1 functional relationships

$$EPV(G_{ref}; meas; n) = a_{0,n} + \sum_{k=1}^{K} a_{k,n} Ck(ref),$$

$$EPV(G_{ref}; meas; n; C = 0) = a_{0,n},$$

relating a reference gas configuration, $G_{ref} = G(\{Ck(ref)\})$, in which target chemical no. k, is present in a reference gas with a known, non-negative concentration value Ck(ref) (k=1, . . . , K), to a test measurement value EPV(G_{ref};meas;n) of the reference gas that is sensed by said sensor no. n, where $a_{0,n}$ and $a_{k,n}$ are known calibration coefficients that are independent of concentration values present, and $a_{0,n}$ is an EPV value that would be measured by said sensor no. n in a test gas when all of the concentration values Ck are 0;

to receive or provide a sequence of test measurement values, V_n(G;meas) and V_0(G;meas), on said test gas in a gas configuration G=G(\{Ck\}), where at least one of the concentration values Ck of a target chemical is unknown;

to provide a numerical-valued error function $\epsilon(\{Ck\})$ associated with the test measurement values V_n(G;meas), where the error function is defined by

$$2\varepsilon(\{Ck\}) = \sum_{n=1}^{N} w_n \left| EPV(G; meas; n) - EPV(G; meas; 0) - \sum_{k=1}^{K} a_{n,k} Ck \right|^p$$

where w_n are selected non-negative weight coefficients and p is a selected positive number;

to provide at least K equations relating the calibration coefficients $a_{0,k}$ and $a_{n,k}$ for k=1, . . . , K, by partially differentiating the error function $\epsilon(\{Ck\})$ with respect to each of the concentration values Ck, and setting each of the partially differentiated expressions of $\epsilon(\{Ck\})$ equal to 0; and

to obtain solutions Ck for the at least K equations, for k=1, . . . , K, and to interpret these solutions as optimal solutions for the concentration values Ck.

4. The method of claim **3**, wherein said computer is further programmed to choose said positive number p to be p=2P, where P is a positive integer.

12

5. The system of claim **3**, wherein said computer is further programmed:

to receive a test measurement value for each of said N sensors for a new test gas, where said concentration value of at least one of said K target molecules in the new test gas is not yet known;

to provide said error function $\epsilon(\{Ck\})$, where said calibration coefficients, $a_{0,k}$ and $a_{n,k}$, are determined as in claim **3** and said concentration values Ck (k=1, . . . , K) are treated as initially unknown;

to minimize said error function $\epsilon(\{Ck\})$ with respect to a choice of value of at least one selected concentration value C(k=k1) (1≦k1≦K); and

to interpret the at least one selected concentration value C(k=k1) as a most likely value of said concentration value for said target molecule no. k1 in said new test gas.

6. The system of claim **5**, wherein said computer is further programmed:

to minimize said error function $\epsilon(\{Ck\})$ with respect to a choice of value of each of said selected concentration values Ck (1≦k≦K) for said new gas;

to compute a value of said error function $\epsilon(\{Ck\})=\epsilon(min)$ using said selected concentration values for said new gas; and

when the value $\epsilon(min)$ is no greater than a selected error function threshold, $\epsilon(thr)$, interpreting satisfaction of this condition as indicating that target gases are the primary components of said new gas.

7. The system of claim **1**, wherein a frequency of transmission of a first reporting cycle for said first sequence changes monotonically relative to a frequency of transmission of a second reporting cycle for said second sequence in response to change of a length of said first reporting cycle relative to a length of said second reporting cycle.

8. The system of claim **7**, wherein said computer is further programmed:

to minimize said error function $\epsilon(\{Ck\})$ with respect to a choice of value of each of said selected concentration values Ck (1≦k≦K) for said new gas;

to compute a value of said error function $\epsilon(\{Ck\})=\epsilon(min)$ using said selected concentration values for said new gas; and

when the value $\epsilon(min)$ is greater than a selected error function threshold, $\epsilon(thr)$, interpreting satisfaction of this condition as indicating that at least one gas that is not one of said target gases is also a primary component of said new gas.

9. The system of claim **1**, wherein said frequency of transmission of said first reporting cycle decreases monotonically, relative to said frequency of transmission of said second reporting cycle, as said length of said first reporting cycle increases relative to said length of said second reporting cycle.

10. The system of claim **1**, wherein said sensors, said multiplexer and said wireless transmission module together consume no more than about 60 mWatt electrical power in operation.

* * * * *

US007410714B1

(12) **United States Patent**   (10) **Patent No.:**   **US 7,410,714 B1**

Burke   (45) **Date of Patent:**   **Aug. 12, 2008**

(54) **UNITIZED REGENERATIVE FUEL CELL SYSTEM**

(75) Inventor: **Kenneth A. Burke**, Chardon, OH (US)

(73) Assignee: **The United States of America as represented by the Administration of NASA**, Washington, DC (US)

(*) Notice: Subject to any disclaimer, the term of this patent is extended or adjusted under 35 U.S.C. 154(b) by 401 days.

(21) Appl. No.: **10/891,599**

(22) Filed: **Jul. 15, 2004**

(51) **Int. Cl.**
    H01M 8/18   (2006.01)

(52) **U.S. Cl.** **429/26**; 429/21; 429/22; 429/24; 429/25

(58) **Field of Classification Search** .... None
See application file for complete search history.

(56)   **References Cited**

U.S. PATENT DOCUMENTS

3,975,913 A	8/1976	Erickson
3,981,745 A	9/1976	Stedman
4,087,976 A	5/1978	Morrow, Jr. et al.
4,120,787 A	10/1978	Yargeu
4,128,701 A	12/1978	Miricle
4,248,941 A	2/1981	Louis et al.
4,311,771 A	1/1982	Walther
4,344,849 A	8/1982	Grasso et al.
4,344,850 A	8/1982	Grasso
4,410,606 A	10/1983	Loutfy et al.
4,482,614 A	11/1984	Zito, Jr.
4,490,445 A	12/1984	Hsu
4,513,066 A	4/1985	Simon
4,520,081 A	5/1985	Hohne et al.
4,530,886 A	7/1985	Sederquist

4,818,637 A	4/1989	Molter et al.	
4,839,247 A	6/1989	Levy et al.	
4,906,817 A	* 3/1990	Kurz	392/442
4,990,412 A	2/1991	Hersey	
5,034,287 A	7/1991	Kunz	
5,064,732 A	* 11/1991	Meyer	429/13
5,133,928 A	* 7/1992	Oldfield	420/105
5,277,994 A	1/1994	Sprouse	
5,306,577 A	4/1994	Sprouse	
5,312,699 A	5/1994	Yanagi et al.	
5,316,643 A	* 5/1994	Ahn et al.	204/265
5,338,622 A	8/1994	Hsu et al.	
5,346,778 A	9/1994	Ewan et al.	
5,346,779 A	9/1994	Nakazawa	
5,376,470 A	12/1994	Sprouse	
5,401,589 A	3/1995	Palmer	
5,407,756 A	4/1995	Sprouse	

(Continued)

Primary Examiner—Jonathan Crepeau
Assistant Examiner—Tony Chuo
(74) *Attorney, Agent, or Firm*—Howard M. Cohn

(57)   **ABSTRACT**

A Unitized Regenerative Fuel Cell system uses heat pipes to convey waste heat from the fuel cell stack to the reactant storage tanks. The storage tanks act as heat sinks/sources and as passive radiators of the waste heat from the fuel cell stack. During charge up, i.e., the electrolytic process, gases are conveyed to the reactant storage tanks by way of tubes that include dryers. Reactant gases moving through the dryers give up energy to the cold tanks, causing water vapor in with the gases to condense and freeze on the internal surfaces of the dryer. During operation in its fuel cell mode, the heat pipes convey waste heat from the fuel cell stack to the respective reactant storage tanks, thereby heating them such that the reactant gases, as they pass though the respective dryers on their way to the fuel cell stacks retrieve the water previously removed.

7 Claims, 3 Drawing Sheets

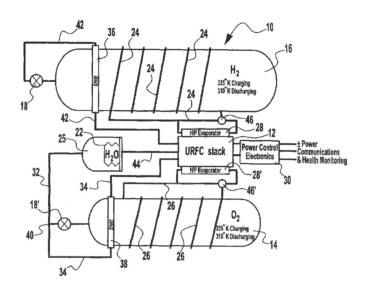

346

U.S. PATENT DOCUMENTS

5,506,066	A	4/1996	Sprouse
5,510,202	A	4/1996	McCoy
5,540,831	A	7/1996	Klein
5,678,410	A	10/1997	Fujita
5,753,383	A	5/1998	Cargnelli et al.
5,885,727	A	3/1999	Kawatsu
5,962,155	A *	10/1999	Kuranaka et al. 429/20
6,042,964	A	3/2000	Sharma et al.
6,083,636	A	7/2000	Hsu
6,399,231	B1	6/2002	Donahue et al.
6,410,180	B1	6/2002	Cisar et al.
6,447,945	B1	9/2002	Strecker et al.
6,458,477	B1	10/2002	Hsu
6,576,362	B2	6/2003	Hanton
6,579,638	B2	6/2003	Brassard
6,821,663	B2 *	11/2004	McElroy et al. 429/17
2002/0006537	A1	1/2002	Kobayashi et al.
2002/0017463	A1	2/2002	Merida-Donis
2002/0022165	A1	2/2002	Brassard
2002/0025467	A1	2/2002	Staats, III
2003/0008192	A1	1/2003	Freund et al.
2003/0011721	A1	1/2003	Wattelet et al.
2003/0031906	A1 *	2/2003	Cargnelli et al. 429/26
2003/0059664	A1	3/2003	Menjak et al.
2003/0068544	A1	4/2003	Cisar et al.
2003/0091880	A1	5/2003	Joos et al.
2003/0134172	A1	7/2003	Grande et al.
2003/0148152	A1	8/2003	Morrisey
2004/0062961	A1 *	4/2004	Sato et al. 429/19
2004/0247960	A1 *	12/2004	Sato et al. 429/20

* cited by examiner

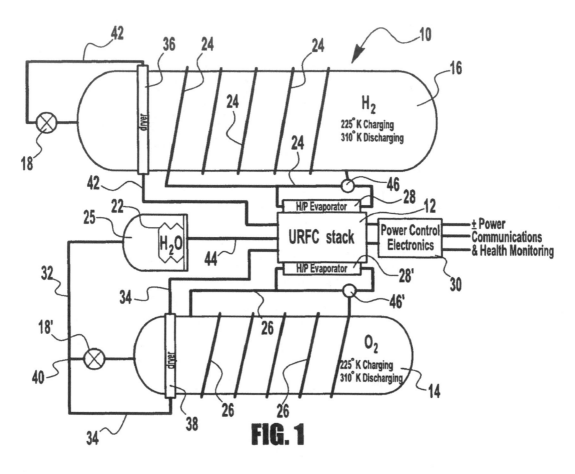

FIG. 1

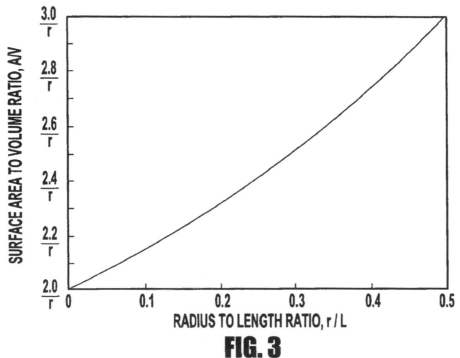

FIG. 3

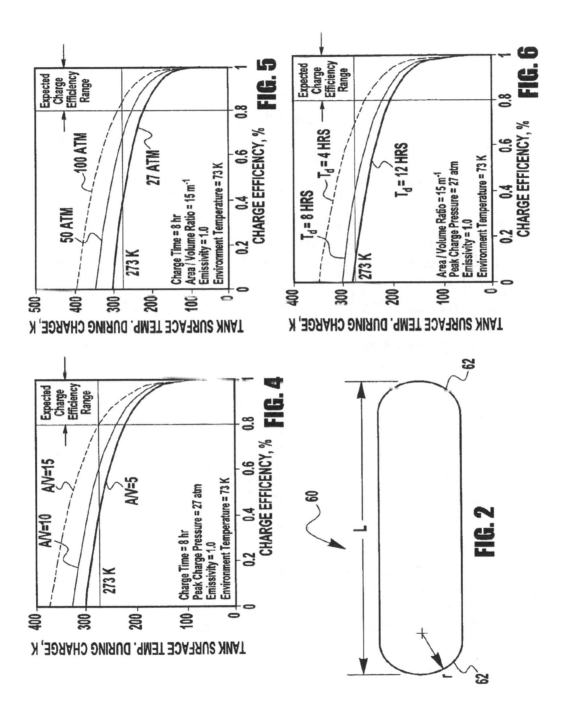

FIG. 5

FIG. 6

FIG. 4

FIG. 2

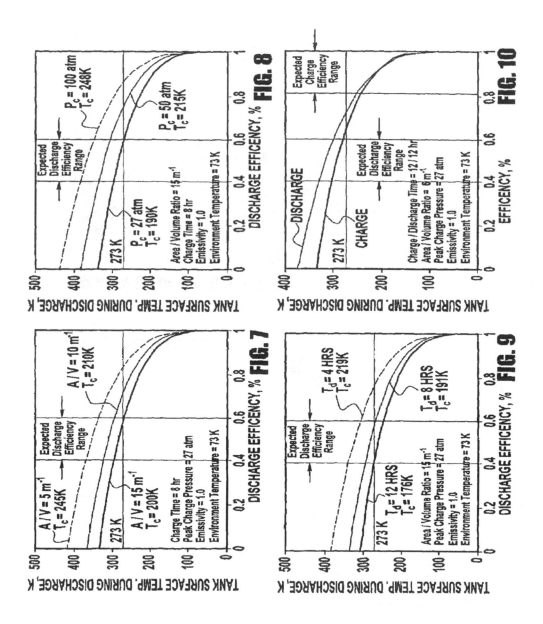

350

US 7,410,714 B1

1

UNITIZED REGENERATIVE FUEL CELL
SYSTEM

STATEMENT REGARDING FEDERALLY SPONSORED RESEARCH OR DEVELOPMENT

The invention described herein was made by an employee of the United States Government and may be manufactured and used by or for the Government for Government purposes without the payment of any royalties thereon or therefore.

TECHNICAL FIELD

The present invention relates to fuel cells, and in particular to regenerative, Proton Exchange Membrane fuel cells and to the management of waste heat associated with the use thereof in the charging and in the discharging modes of operation.

BACKGROUND OF THE INVENTION

Unitized Regenerative Fuel Cells (URFCs) are being developed by several fuel cell manufacturers. The applications for this technology are the same as for Regenerative Fuel Cell (RFC) systems. Specific NASA applications include high altitude airships, lunar or Mars-based outposts, and other secondary battery applications where the discharge period is 1 to 2 hours long or longer.

The URFCs developed to date are all based on the Proton Exchange Membrane (PEM) technology. The key advantage of the URFC over other RFC systems is that the URFC does both the process of electrolysis of water as well as the process of recombining of the hydrogen and oxygen gas byproducts to produce electricity. Because of this advantage, a one cell stack of a URFC system replaces the one electrolysis cell stack and one fuel cell stack of the prior art RFC systems. This reduction in fuel cell stacks saves a substantial amount of weight since the cell stacks are the major components of a RFC system. Besides saving the weight of one cell stack, the plumbing, wiring and ancillary equipment for one cell stack is also eliminated.

The operation of the URFC system is also simpler. A RFC requires that when the fuel cell stack is active, the electrolysis cell stack must be kept warm to avoid freezing water lines and transient warm-up periods. Likewise, as the electrolysis cell stack is active, the fuel cell stack must be kept warm to avoid freezing water lines, excessive condensation, and transient warm-up periods. Maintaining cell stacks in standby conditions complicates the overall system design, resulting in greater mass, volume, and parasitic power.

Early efforts to develop a regenerative cell resulted in cells with poor performance or cells not easily reversed in their operation. Dedicated fuel cells or electrolysis cells often have the reactants circulated through the cell stack. Usually the circulating reactants function to remove the byproducts of the fuel cell reaction (product water during fuel cell operation, and product gases during electrolysis cell operation). Sometimes the reactants are also circulated for cooling of the cell stack during its operation. For a URFC to act without circulation pumps requires that the reactants not be circulated through the cell stack, but instead, be "dead-ended" into the cell stack.

As an energy storage system, the URFC system "charges" and "discharges" like a rechargeable battery. While charging, the URFC operates the electrolysis process, which splits water into hydrogen and oxygen. While discharging, the URFC operates the fuel cell process, which combines hydrogen and oxygen and produces electricity.

2

The gases produced during electrolysis are expelled from the cell stack by the production of still more gas inside the cell stack. The continued production of gases by the cell stack pushes the gases into the reactant storage tanks, gradually "pumping" the gases to higher and higher pressure where they are stored. In addition to the oxygen and hydrogen, a certain level of water vapor also accompanies these gases when they are expelled from the cell stack.

During the URFC fuel cell process, as gases are consumed inside the cell stack, more gas is delivered to the cell stack by the pressurized reactant storage tanks.

The management of reactants inside the URFC cell stack is highly influenced by both the materials and the construction inside the cell stack. Besides the development of the reversible electrodes, proper and reliable reactant management inside the cell stack is most important to achieving acceptable URFC performance. Achieving this level of reactant management inside the cell stack during both electrolysis and fuel cell operation, and the transitions between these different processes, is currently the single biggest hurdle yet to be accomplished.

In the past, a number of reversible or regenerative fuel cells designs were known.

For example, U.S. Pat. No. 3,975,913 to Erickson discloses a closed-cycle gas generator in which one chemical, such as water, is reacted with a metal, such as molten aluminum, to produce hydrogen gas which, along with O_2 from a separate storage tank, is conveyed to a fuel cell. Waste heat from the gas generator drives a closed-cycle heat engine.

U.S. Pat. No. 4,490,445 to Hsu discloses a reversible "solid oxide electrochemical energy converter" having a counterflow heat exchanger that disposes of waste heat by directing it to heating the incoming fuel gases.

U.S. Pat. No. 5,338,622 to Hsu, et al discloses a fuel cell system that specifically addresses the issue of waste heat management by means of a counterflow heat exchanger assembly.

U.S. Pat. No. 5,401,589 to Palmer, et al discloses a fuel cell with a reformer, wherein the reformer receives waste heat from the fuel cell. Waste heat is also conveyed to a space heating system and also to a 'bottoming cycle' engine and, if at too low a temperature, is discharged to the atmosphere.

U.S. Pat. No. 5,506,066 ('066) to Sprouse discloses an 'ultra passive,' variable pressure RFC having a single H_2 storage tank "that encloses a plurality of smaller gaseous O_2 storage tubes." No pumping elements are used. A heating/cooling coil inside the H_2 tank prevents icing or overheating. The source or sink of the heat for said coil is not specified.

U.S. Pat. No. 5,510,202 ('202) to McCoy discloses a variable pressure fuel cell. McCoy uses prior art images similar to those of in the '066 patent, suggesting a possible similarity of the '202 patent's waste heat management system to that of the '066 patent.

U.S. Pat. No. 5,678,410 to Fujita et al discloses a fuel cell system for use with cars. For example. "The combined system preferably includes a heat storage tank disposed in a conduit of a heating medium . . . ." A heat transfer medium, "such as water," is used to convey heat to various heat exchangers including one that moves heat to or from a metal-hydride storage tank.

U.S. Pat. No. 5,885,727 to Kawatsu discloses a fuel cell arrangement in which waste heat is conveyed, by way of apparently integral cooling water tubes, to reaction tanks 30 and 50 wherein, respectively, oxygen and hydrogen are generated for use in the fuel cell.

In addition to the above US patents, a PCT patent US 2003/001721 A1 to Wattelet et al discloses a mobile and

351

3

compact fuel cell system having "an integrated heat exchanger unit" that combines the fuel cell cooling system and a cathode exhaust gas condenser, both being cooled, in parallel, by a shared cooling air stream. A cooling tube (callout number **38**) appears integrated with the fuel cell.

ASPECTS OF THE INVENTION

It is an aspect of the present invention to provide methods and apparatus as defined in one or more of the appended claims and, as such, having the capability of accomplishing one or more of the following subsidiary aspects.

In accordance with the foregoing, one aspect of the present unitized regenerative fuel cell (URFC) invention is to minimize system components to "bare essentials," eliminating ancillary equipment that would add unnecessary mass, volume, and parasitic power usage.

Another aspect of the present invention is to provide a reversible or regenerative electric-energy storage system that operated in a way that is equivalent to that of a rechargeable battery in which the active fuel cell portions and the electrolysis portions are one and the same and in which pumps are not used or needed to circulate coolant and otherwise manage waste heat.

Another aspect of the present invention is to minimize the system weight, volume, and parasitic power of the URFC.

Yet another aspect of the present invention is to use a heat pipe method of heat transfer for the removal of waste heat from the active proton exchange membrane portion of the fuel cell.

And a still further aspect of the present invention is to provide a way to remove water that is carried in the fuel gases generated during the electrolysis or charging mode of operation.

SUMMARY OF THE INVENTION

The present invention is a unitized regenerative fuel cell (URFC) system comprising reactant storage tanks, a water storage reservoir, a fuel cell stack, fuel cell pressure control devices, reactant gas feed lines, and power input/outputs and controls. The reactant gas storage tanks are sized and shaped to act as heat sinks and/as waste heat radiators to the ambient environment. Heat pipes convey waste heat from the fuel cell stack to the reactant gas storage tanks. Portions of the heat pipes thermally communicate with the respective reactant gas storage tanks. The reactant gas storage tanks are cylindrical and have hemispherical ends. A reactant gas dryer is disposed within each of the respective reactant gas feed lines communicating between the respective reactant gas storage tanks and the fuel cell stack. Each of the dryers is in thermal contact with the respective reactant gas storage tank. Each dryer is able to operate reversibly, returning water to the reactant gases as said reactant gases flow toward the fuel cell stack. An expandable bellows type water storage reservoir is contained within a pressure dome. Said bellows type water storage reservoir opens to a maximum volume when no internal or external forces act upon it. A reactant gas pressure line communicates between one of the reactant gas feed lines and the expandable water storage reservoir. The expandable water storage reservoir is spring-loaded in such a way as to cause its volume to increase to a maximum when no other force acts upon the storage tank.

4

BRIEF DESCRIPTION OF THE DRAWINGS

Reference will be made in detail to preferred embodiments of the invention, examples of which are illustrated in the accompanying drawing figures. The figures are intended to be illustrative, not limiting. Although the invention is generally described in the context of these preferred embodiments, it should be understood that it is not intended to limit the spirit and scope of the invention to these particular embodiments.

Certain elements in selected ones of the drawings may be illustrated not-to-scale, for illustrative clarity. The cross-sectional views, if any, presented herein may be in the form of "slices", or "near-sighted" cross-sectional views, omitting certain background lines which would otherwise be visible in a true cross-sectional view, for illustrative clarity.

The structure, operation, and advantages of the present preferred embodiment of the invention will become further apparent upon consideration of the following description taken in conjunction with the accompanying drawings, wherein:

FIG. **1** is a schematic diagram of the Unitized Regenerative Fuel Cell (URFC) system according to the present invention;

FIG. **2** is a graphic definition of the dimensional parameters of a schematized cylindrical tank having hemispherical ends according to the present invention;

FIG. **3** is a graph showing the relationship of surface area of a cylindrical tank with hemispherical ends as a function of the ratio of tank length and the radius of the hemispherical ends according to the present invention;

FIG. **4** is a graph showing the temperature of the cylindrical tank surface as a function of electrical charging efficiency, for various surface area to volume ratios for the tanks according to the present invention;

FIG. **5** is a graph showing the temperature of the cylindrical tank surface as a function of electrical charging efficiency, for various tank pressures when the ratio of surface area to tank volume is held constant according to the present invention;

FIG. **6** is a graph showing the temperature of the cylindrical tank surface as a function of electrical charging efficiency, for electrical charging times according to the present invention;

FIG. **7** is a graph showing the temperature of the cylindrical tank surface as a function of electrical discharging efficiency, for various surface area to volume ratios for the tanks according to the present invention;

FIG. **8** is a graph showing the temperature of the cylindrical tank surface as a function of electrical discharging efficiency, for various tank pressures when the ratio of surface area to tank volume is held constant according to the present invention;

FIG. **9** is a graph showing the temperature of the cylindrical tank surface as a function of electrical discharging efficiency, for electrical discharging times according to the present invention; and

FIG. **10** is a graph showing the temperature of the cylindrical tank surface during charging and discharging as a function of overall efficiency of the URFC according to the present invention.

DEFINITIONS

Reactant gases refers to such reactants as oxygen and hydrogen which can be combined in a fuel cell to produce water and electric power. The term 'reactants' is sometimes used herein to mean the same thing as 'reactant gases' or 'reactants.'

5

URFC stands for Unitized Regenerative Fuel Cell.

URFC stack refers to the operative part of the present invention, namely the reversible fuel cell stack that uses proton exchange membrane technology or its equivalent in a way that can be used to create electric power from reactants such as hydrogen and oxygen, or it can be used to produce reactants such as hydrogen and oxygen when electric power is used to drive the process so as to dissociate a material such as water. The terms 'fuel cell stack,' 'FC stack,' or 'cell stack,' are used hereinbelow to mean the same thing as 'URFC stack.'

DETAILED DESCRIPTION OF THE PREFERRED EMBODIMENT

The Unitized Regenerative Fuel Cell (URFC) system 10 of FIG. 1 "charges" and "discharges" like a rechargeable battery. While charging, the URFC system 10 operates the electrolysis process, which splits water into hydrogen and oxygen. While discharging, the URFC system 10 operates the fuel cell process, which combines hydrogen and oxygen and produces electricity. Most generally, the URFC system 10 according to the present invention comprises reactant gas storage tanks, a water storage reservoir, a fuel cell stack, fuel cell pressure control devices, reactant gas feed lines communicating between the fuel cell stack and the reactant gas storage tanks, and power input/outputs and controls.

Generally speaking, a URFC system operates either to electrolyze a substance such as water into its chemical constituents or as a fuel cell in which the chemical constituents are chemically combined and electricity is produced.

When the URFC stack is used as an electrolytic cell, so as to store chemical energy in the form of stored reactants produced from an electrical energy input, the reactant gases produced during electrolysis are expelled from the fuel cell stack by the production of still more gases from the cell stack. The continued production of gases by the cell stack pushes the gases into the reactant gas storage tanks, gradually "pumping" the gases to higher and higher pressures within the tanks where they are stored. In addition, to the reactant gases such as oxygen and hydrogen, a certain amount of water vapor also accompanies these reactant gases as they are expelled from the cell stack and pushed toward their respective storage tanks.

When operated as a fuel cell (producing electric power from chemical reactants), reactant gases flow into the fuel cell stack where they chemically react with each other so as to produce electric power. In the specific instance wherein the reactants are oxygen (O_2) and hydrogen (H_2), the resultant water (H_2O) that forms inside of the URFC stack is removed by either the capillary action of wicking material that is in close proximity to the active electrode sites, or the water is driven out of the cell stack by pressure differentials inside the stack. That is to say that the water is pushed out of the cell by a pressure difference between the water pressure inside the cell stack and the water pressure inside an external water storage reservoir.

The management of reactants inside the URFC cell stack is influenced by both the materials and the designs of the components inside the cell stack. In addition to the development of the reversible electrodes, proper and reliable reactant management inside the cell stack is most important in achieving acceptable URFC performance. The present invention is directed toward ways to manage the reactants inside the cell stack during both electrolysis and fuel cell operation, and also during transitions between these different processes.

6

URFC System

Referring now to FIG. 1, there is shown in schematic format an entire URFC system 10, according to the present invention. The system 10 consists of the URFC stack 12, a reactant gas storage tank system 14,16, bi-directional reactant pressure controls 18, 18' between the URFC stack and the reactant gas storage tanks, a bellows type expandable water storage reservoir 22 disposed within a pressure dome 25, a first heat pipe 24 communicating heat between the URFC stack and one reactant storage tank 16, a second heat pipe 26 communicating heat between the URFC stack and a second reactant storage tank 14, a thermal control system 28, 28', and a power/system control interface 30. The bellows type water storage reservoir is made of metal and is prestressed to open to a maximum volume when no internal or external forces act upon it. There is also shown in FIG. 1 a pipe 32 communicating between the pressure dome 25 and the reactant input pipe 34. Gas dryers 36,38 are in thermal communication with the reactant storage tanks 16,14, respectively. The operation of the gas dryers 36,38 is described herein. Waste heat from the URFC stack 12 is conveyed by the heat pipes 24,26 to the reactant storage tanks 16,14, respectively, by way of the heat pipe evaporators 28,28' respectively, which are in thermal contact with URFC stack. That is, portions of each heat pipe 24,26 thermally communicate with the respective reactant gas storage tanks 16,14.

The environmental settings within which this invention is intended to operate are anticipated to be cold. In other words, the applications for this URFC system 10 according to the present invention are envisioned to be those of outer space, high atmospheric altitudes, or the surfaces of the moon or Mars and like places wherein typical ambient temperature would be about –40° C. However, it is within the terms of the present invention for the to operate in other settings having less harsh environmental characteristics.

In summary, the present invention is a Unitized Regenerative Fuel Cell (URFC) system 10 that uses heat pipes to convey waste heat from the fuel cell stack 12 to the reactant storage tanks, 14,16. The storage tanks 14,16 are sized and shaped to act as heat sinks and radiators of waste heat from the fuel cell stack 12 to the ambient environment. During charge up, i.e., the electrolytic process, gases are conveyed to the reactant storage tanks 14,16 by way of tubes 34,42 that include dryer portions 36,38 that are integral with the respective surfaces of the storage tanks to which the gases are being conveyed. In other words, each reactant gas dryer is disposed within each of the respective reactant gas feed lines communicating between the respective reactant gas storage tanks and the fuel cell stack. Reactant gases moving through the dryers to their respective storage tanks give up energy to the cold tanks, causing water vapor mixed with the gases to condense out and freeze on the internal dryer surfaces. During operation in its fuel cell mode, the heat pipes 24,26 convey waste heat from the fuel cell stack to the respective reactant gas storage tanks, thereby heating them such that the reactant gases, as they pass though the respective dryers on their way to the fuel cell stacks retrieve the water previously removed. The dryers are able to operate reversibly, returning water to the reactant gases as said reactant gases flow toward the fuel cell stack. An expandable water storage reservoir is also used. It is disposed within a pressure dome that communicates with a reactant gas pressure line associated with a reactant gas feed line to one of the reactant gas storage tanks. The pressure dome is thus pressurized by reactant gas pressure communicated to it by said feed line to the said one of the reactant gas storage tanks.

7

Discussed below are the details of operation of an exemplary URFC system **10** according to the present invention that uses oxygen and hydrogen as the reactant gases and chemical energy storage media. Specifically discussed below in detail are the operation of the present invention during its two respective modes of (1) charging, during which water is electrolyzed into oxygen and hydrogen, and (2) discharge when the fuel cell operates to cause the chemical combination of the reactant gases, hydrogen and oxygen, so as to produce electrical power.

Electrolysis—O_2

During the electrolysis process oxygen is produced inside the URFC stack **12**. A mixture of oxygen and water vapor that is in equilibrium with the temperature and pressure of the URFC stack exits the URFC stack by means of the tube/pipe **34** which leads to the gas dryer **38** and thence to junction point **40** where the line bifurcates, one portion leading to the oxygen storage tank **14** by way of the bi-directional pressure control **18'**, and the other portion communicating with the pressure dome **25** that contains the expandable water storage reservoir **22**. As is noted below, the expandable water storage reservoir **22** has two counteracting forces acting on it: (1) pressure from the oxygen line **34**, which pushes inward on it, tending to shrink the volume of the tank **22** and (2) it is spring-loaded in such a way as to cause its volume to increase.

The oxygen regenerative gas dryer **38** communicates with the oxygen gas pipe **34**. The oxygen regenerative dryer is in close thermal contact with the surface of the oxygen tank **14**. As the oxygen water vapor mixture flows through the dryer **38**, heat from the gas mixture is transferred to the surface of the oxygen tank. The loss of energy from the oxygen mixture causes the water vapor in the mixture to condense and/or freeze on the inside wall of the oxygen regenerative dryer **38**. Water that is thus separated from the gaseous oxygen remains inside the dryer tubing **34** while the dried oxygen eventually is conveyed to the tank **14** by way of the bi-directional pressure control **18'**. The oxygen pipe **34** bifurcates at junction **40**, allowing a portion of the oxygen to move into (and later, during fuel cell operation, out of) the pressure dome **25** that surrounds the water storage reservoir **22**. The bi-directional pressure control **18'** acts as a back-pressure regulator that controls the oxygen pressure inside the URFC stack **12** and the water tank pressure dome **25** and allows this pressure to gradually increase all the while keeping this pressure within user-defined limits with respect to the hydrogen pressure inside the URFC stack. The dried oxygen that passes through the bi-directional pressure control **18'** enters the oxygen storage tank **14** where it accumulates until needed during the discharge (or fuel cell) cycle of operation described below. This process continues until either the electrical input charging energy is stopped, the oxygen tank reaches it's maximum pressure, or the water tank reaches its minimum level.

Electrolysis—H_2

During the electrolysis process hydrogen is also produced inside the URFC stack **12**. A mixture of hydrogen and water vapor that is in equilibrium with the temperature and pressure of the URFC stack exits the URFC stack by way of the pipe **42** and into a hydrogen regenerative dryer portion **36**, which is in close thermal contact with the surface of the hydrogen tank **16**. As the hydrogen water vapor mixture flows through the dryer **36**, heat from the gas mixture is transferred to the surface of the hydrogen tank. The loss of energy from the hydrogen mixture causes the water vapor in the mixture to condense and/or freeze on the inside wall of the hydrogen regenerative dryer. As with the water in the oxygen pipe, described hereinabove, water that is separated from the gas

8

phase remains inside the dryer tubing **36** while the dried hydrogen eventually makes its way to the bi-directional hydrogen pressure control **18** and then to the storage tank **16**. The bi-directional pressure control **18** acts as a backpressure regulator that controls the hydrogen pressure inside the URFC stack **12** and allows this pressure to gradually increase all the while keeping this pressure within user-defined limits with respect to the oxygen pressure inside the URFC stack. Dried hydrogen that passes through the bi-directional pressure control **18** enters the hydrogen storage where it gradually accumulates until needed during the discharge cycle of operation. This process continues until either the charging energy is stopped, the hydrogen tank reaches its maximum pressure, or the water tank reaches its minimum level.

Electrolysis—H_2O

During the electrolysis, or charging, process, the URFC **12** electrolyzes water. As the water is consumed, the URFC draws in water from the external water storage reservoir **22** by a siphon-like action through the pipe **44**. The water storage reservoir **22** consists of a bellows inside the aforementioned pressure dome **25**. The bellows has a spring-like action that, left unrestrained, would cause the bellows to expand to nearly the entire volume of the pressure dome. The water is stored inside the bellows. Outside the bellows **22**, but inside the pressure dome **25**, pressurized oxygen is present. This arrangement allows the water volume inside the bellows **22** to expand or contract as needed (during either electrolytic or fuel cell operation) all the while keeping the water pressure slightly less than the oxygen pressure that exists outside the bellows **22**. It is important to maintain the water pressure slightly below the oxygen pressure, because this pressure difference keeps liquid water separated from the oxygen and hydrogen gas inside the URFC stack **12**. The expandable bellows type water storage reservoir is contained within the pressure dome **25**. The gas pressure line **32** communicates between the reactant gas feed lines **34** and the dome **25** that contains the expandable water storage reservoir **22**.

Electrolysis—Thermal Control System

One of the key features of the URFC system **10** according to the present invention is the heat pipe thermal control system. During electrolysis, the waste heat produced by the URFC stack **12** is transferred to the system of heat pipes **24,26**. Bypass valves **46,46'** in the respective heat pipes **24,26** allow fluid within the heat pipes to bypass the heat radiating surfaces of oxygen and hydrogen storage tanks **14,16**, respectively, when URFC stack **12** is not at optimum operating temperature. When the URFC stack is at its proper operating temperature, the fluid in the respective heat pipes flows through portions of the heat pipes that are wrapped around the oxygen and hydrogen storage tanks, **14,16**. The portions of the heat pipes that are wrapped around the respective gas storage tanks are in close thermal contact with the surfaces of the tanks so that, as heat pipe fluid flows through the tubing wrapped around the tanks, heat is transferred from the heat pipe system to the surface of the gas storage tanks. The tank walls act in a way that is equivalent to cooling fins on the heat pipes, spreading the waste heat across the surfaces of both the oxygen and hydrogen storage tanks, which thence radiate the waste heat to the cold ambient environment. Because the amount of waste heat produced during electrolysis is small per unit area over which that heat is spread, the tank surface temperature of both the oxygen and hydrogen storage tanks, **14,16**, drops below 0° C.

Electrolysis—Power and Control

The power control system **30** of the URFC system **10** matches the voltage of the electrical power source (not shown) to the required voltage needed by the URFC stack **12** for electrolysis. A computer control manages the pressure controls as well as the health monitoring and communications.

Fuel Cell Operation—O₂

When the present URFC system **10** is operated in the fuel cell mode (i.e., generating electric power from the chemical combining of the reactant gases), oxygen is consumed inside the URFC stack **12**. As oxygen is consumed, oxygen pressure inside the URFC stack **12** and inside the water tank pressure dome **25** is reduced from the pressure levels that existed during the previous electrolysis operation described hereinabove. Oxygen pressure inside the URFC stack **12** falls until the pressure is at the steady-state fuel cell operating pressure (about 50 psi). Once at this pressure, oxygen flows from the oxygen storage tank **14** as needed to maintain the steady-state fuel cell operating pressure. The oxygen flows from the water tank **22** inside the pressure dome **25** and from the oxygen storage tank **14** through the oxygen regenerative dryer **38** on its way to the URFC stack **12**. As the oxygen flows through the regenerative dryer **38**, it absorbs heat and water vapor from the inside surface of said dryer. The dryer tube **38** is in turn warmed by the surface of the tank **14** which is dissipating the substantially higher amount of waste heat generated during the fuel cell operation. Due to the lower pressure and relatively high temperature, the oxygen gas, as it flows from the tank **14** to the URFC stack **12**, eventually evaporates all of the water previously trapped on the wall of the dryer tube **38** during the electrolysis process. In doing so, the dryer tube is "regenerated" and thereby made ready for the next electrolysis phase of operation. During the fuel cell operation the bi-directional oxygen pressure control **18'** acts as a forward, or pressure reducing, regulator that controls the oxygen pressure inside the URFC stack **12** and water tank pressure dome **25** and allows these pressures to gradually decrease to the steady-state fuel cell operating pressure. The bi-directional pressure regulator **18'** does this while keeping the oxygen pressure in the URFC stack within prescribed limits with respect to the hydrogen pressure inside the URFC stack. The fuel cell mode of operation continues as long as electrical energy is withdrawn from the URFC system or until the oxygen storage tank falls below its minimum pressure or the water storage reservoir **22** reaches its maximum filled state.

Fuel Cell Operation—H₂

During the fuel cell mode of operation, hydrogen is consumed inside the URFC stack **12**. As hydrogen is consumed the hydrogen pressure inside the URFC stack is reduced from the pressure achieved during the previous electrolysis operation. Hydrogen pressure within the URFC stack decreases until the pressure is at the steady state fuel cell operating pressure (about 50 psi). Once at this pressure, hydrogen flows from the hydrogen storage tank **16** to maintain the steady-state operating pressure of the fuel cell stack **12**. Hydrogen flows from the hydrogen storage tank **16** through the hydrogen regenerative dryer **36** on its way to the URFC stack. As the hydrogen flows through the regenerative dryer **36**, it absorbs heat and water vapor from the inside surface of said dryer tube. The dryer tube is in turn warmed by the surface of the tank **16**, which is dissipating the substantially higher amount of waste heat generated during the fuel cell operation. Due to the lower pressure and warm temperature inside the dryer **36**, the hydrogen gas, as it flows back to the URFC stack **12**, eventually evaporates all of the water previously trapped on the wall of the dryer tube during the electrolysis process. In doing so, the dryer tube is "regenerated" and ready for the next electrolysis phase. During the fuel cell operation, bi-

directional pressure control **18** acts as a forward (pressure reducing), regulator that controls the hydrogen pressure inside the URFC stack **12** and allows this pressure to gradually decrease to the steady state fuel cell operating pressure. The bi-directional pressure regulator **18** does this while keeping the URFC stack hydrogen pressure within prescribed limits with respect to the oxygen pressure inside the URFC stack. The fuel cell operation continues as long as electrical energy is withdrawn from the URFC system or until the hydrogen storage tank falls below its minimum pressure or the water storage reservoir reaches its maximum filled state.

The water formed inside of the URFC during fuel cell operation (i.e., electricity production) is removed by the capillary action of wicking material that is in close proximity to the active electrode sites inside the cell stack. The water is pushed out of the cell by a pressure difference between the water pressure inside the cell stack and the water pressure inside an external water storage reservoir.

Fuel Cell Operation—H₂O

During fuel cell operation the URFC stack **12** (FIG. 1) produces water. As the water is produced, the water cavities inside the URFC system **10** draw in the water from the electrode surfaces. The water is eventually drawn into the water storage reservoir **22** by a siphon-like action. The spring-like action of the water storage reservoir bellows ensures that the pressure of the water storage cavities within the URFC stack are always lower in pressure than the oxygen cavities within the URFC stack regardless of how full the water storage reservoir **22** is. This pressure difference within the URFC stack maintains the gas/liquid separation within the URFC stack, and prevents cell flooding during fuel cell operation.

Fuel Cell Operation—Thermal Control System

During the fuel cell mode operation of the reversible fuel cell system **10**, the waste heat produced by the URFC cell stack **12** is transferred to the system heat pipes **24,26**. Bypass valves **46,46'** in the heat pipe system allow the heat pipe fluid to bypass the heat radiating surfaces of oxygen and hydrogen storage tanks (**14,16** respectively) when the URFC stack **12** is not at its optimum operating temperature. When the URFC stack is at its desired operating temperature, the heat pipe fluid flows through heat pipes **26,24** that are wrapped around the oxygen and hydrogen storage tanks **14,16**. The heat pipes are in close thermal contact with the gas storage tank surface so that as the heat pipe fluid flows through the tubing wrapped around the tanks, heat is transferred from the heat pipe system to the surface of the gas storage tanks. The tank walls, acting as a heat fins, spread this waste heat across the entire tank surface of both the oxygen and hydrogen storage tanks. The tank surfaces radiate this waste heat to the cold ambient environment. Because the amount of waste heat produced during fuel cell operation is large per unit area over which that heat is spread, the tank surface temperature of both the oxygen and hydrogen storage tanks goes to well above freezing temperatures.

Fuel Cell Operation—Power and Control

The power control system **30** of the URFC system **10** matches the required voltage of the electrical loads being supplied by the URFC system. A computer system control provides the software control of the pressure controls as well as the health monitoring and communications.

Storage Tank/Radiator Analysis

As described hereinabove, the amount of heat per unit of radiator area is smaller during the electrolysis charge phase of the URFC system operation than during the fuel cell discharge phase of operation. The effect of this is to produce

11

freezing storage tank surface temperatures during the charge phase and above freezing temperatures during the discharge phase. (FIG. 1 shows hypothetical near steady state temperatures of the tanks 14,16 during electrolysis ['charging'] and fuel cell operation ['discharging']. Those hypothetical or exemplary temperatures are, during charging 225° K. and 310° K. during discharging. This is so for both tanks.)

The following analysis characterizes the waste heat management process in terms of the parameters that influence it.

The Stefan-Boltzmann Law states that,

$$Q/A=e\sigma(T^4-T_E^4) \tag{1}$$

where

Q=Heat radiation rate, watts
A=Heat radiation area, m^2
e=Emissivity, %
$\sigma=5.6703\times10^{-8}$ watt-m^2-K^{-4}
T=Temperature of radiating body, K
T_E=Temperature of surrounding environment, K

Using equation (1) to describe the heat radiation during URFC system charging,

$$Q_C/A_T=e\sigma(T_C^4-T_E^4) \tag{2}$$

where

Q_C=Heat radiation rate during charging, watt
A_T=Total tank surface area, m^2
T_C=Tank surface temperature during charging, K

Similarly, the heat radiation during URFC system discharging can be expressed as,

$$Q_D/A_T=e\sigma(T_D^4-T_E^4) \tag{3}$$

where

Q_D=Heat radiation rate during disharging, watt
T_D=Tank surface temperature during discharging, K

The heat radiation rate during charging and during discharging can be expressed as,

$$Q_C=(1-\eta_C)\xi_C \tag{4}$$

$$Q_D=(1-\eta_D)\xi_D \tag{5}$$

where

η_C=Energy efficiency during charging, watt/watt
η_D=Energy efficiency during discharging, watt/watt
ξ_C=Theoretical power required during charging, watt
ξ_D=Theoretical discharge power produced, watt

Based on the higher heating value of hydrogen of 4405 watt-hr per kg of water produced, the average theoretical power during charging and discharging is:

$$\xi_C=4405M_Wt_C^{-1} \tag{6}$$

$$\xi_D=4405M_Wt_D^{-1} \tag{7}$$

where

M_W=Mass of water used or produced, kg
t_C=Charging time, hours
t_D=Discharging time, hours

The heat dissipation area is the combined surface area of the oxygen and hydrogen storage tanks.

$$A_T=A_O+A_H \tag{8}$$

where

A_O=Oxygen tank surface area, m^2
A_H=Hydrogen tank surface area, m^2

12

Substituting Equations (4), (6), and (8) into Equation (2) to get an expression for the storage tank surface temperature during the charging phase,

$$[(1-\eta_C)4405M_Wt_C^{-1}/(A_O+A_H)]=e\sigma(T_C^4-T_E^4) \tag{9}$$

Likewise substituting Equation (5), (7), and (8) into Equation (3) to get an expression for the storage tank surface temperature during the discharging phase,

$$[(1-\eta_D)4405M_Wt_D^{-1}/(A_O+A_H)]=e\sigma(T_D^4-T_E^4) \tag{10}$$

The surface area of each gas storage tank can be expressed as the ratio of surface area to volume multiplied by the volume,

$$A_O=(A_OV_O^{-1})V_O \tag{11}$$

$$A_H=(A_HV_H^{-1})V_H \tag{12}$$

Where

V_O=Oxygen tank volume, m^3
V_H=Hydrogen tank volume, m^3

Referring to FIG. 2, there is shown in schematic side view a cylindrical tank 60 which corresponds to the shapes of the reactant storage tanks 14,16 in FIG. 1. This idealized cylindrical tank 60 has hemispherical ends 62, each having a radius r. The overall length of the tank 60 is shown as L. Thus each reactant gas storage tanks is cylindrical and has hemispherical ends. The ratio of the storage tank surface area to volume, A/V, can be expressed as,

$$A/V=2/[r-(2/3)(r^2/L)] \tag{13}$$

where

A=Tank surface area, m^2
V=Tank volume, m^3
r=Tank radius, m
L=Tank length, m

FIG. 3 shows a graphical plotting of Equation (13) showing the relationship of the ratio of the tank surface area to its volume, A/V, as a function of the ratio of the radius, r, and the length, L. As the tank gets more and more spherical (i.e., as r/L ¥→1/2) the ratio A/V approaches a value of 3/r. As the tank gets less and less spherical (i.e., as r/L→O) the ratio A/V ratio approaches a value of 2/r.

Substituting Equation (11) and (12), into equations (9) and (10), and assuming that the oxygen and hydrogen tanks have identical A/V ratios, the heat radiation expression during the charge and discharge phase can be expressed as,

$$(1-\eta_C)4405M_Wt_C^{-1}/[(A/V)(V_O+V_H)]=e\sigma(T_C^4-T_E^4) \tag{14}$$

Likewise substituting Equation (5), (7), and (8) into Equation (3) to get an expression for the storage tank surface temperature during the discharging phase,

$$(1-\eta_D)4405M_Wt_D^{-1}/[(A/V)(V_O+V_H)]=e\sigma(T_D^4-T_E^4) \tag{15}$$

The volume of the oxygen and hydrogen storage tanks can be expressed as,

$$V_O=n_ORT_O/P_O \tag{16}$$

$$V_H=n_HRT_H/P_H \tag{17}$$

where

n_O=Moles of oxygen, gmoles
n_H=Moles of hydrogen, gmoles
T_O=Temperature of oxygen, K
T_H=Temperature of hydrogen, K
P_O=Pressure of oxygen, atm
P_H=Pressure of hydrogen, atm
R=8.2×10^{-5}, atm-m^3-gmole-K^{-1}

13

The volumes of the gas storage tanks don't change during operation of the URFC according to the present invention, and are sized to accommodate the mass of each gas volume stored at the peak level of charge. Under these conditions, it is assumed that the peak charge pressure is approximately the same for both oxygen and hydrogen. It is also assumed that, at peak charge, the oxygen gas temperature is approximately the same as the hydrogen gas temperature for this sizing calculation, and that these temperatures are also equal to the surface temperature of the gas storage tanks during charging of the URFC. Using these assumptions, Equations (14) and (15) can be rewritten as,

$$(1 - \eta_C)4405M_w t_C^{-1}/[(A/V)RT_C P_C^{-1}(n_O + n_H)] = e\sigma(T_C^4 - T_E^4) \quad (18)$$

$$(1 - \eta_D)4405M_w t_D^{-1}/[(A/V)RT_C P_C^{-1}(n_O + n_H)] = e\sigma(T_D^4 - T_E^4) \quad (19)$$

where

P_C=Peak charge pressure, atm

It should be noted that the denominators on the left-hand side of equations (18) and (19) are constants and equal to each other (the combined surface area of the tanks does not change from charge to discharge once the tanks have been sized).

The moles of oxygen and hydrogen can be expressed as,

$$n_O + n_H = 1.5n_W \quad (20)$$

where

n_W=mass of water used or produced, gmoles

The moles of water can be expressed as,

$$n_W = M_W/0.018 \quad (21)$$

Substituting Equations (20) and (21) into Equations (18) and (19) yields,

$$(1 - \eta_C)4405M_w t_C^{-1}/[(A/V)RT_C P_C^{-1}(1.5M_W/0.018)] = \\ e\sigma(T_C^4 - T_E^4) \quad (22)$$

$$(1 - \eta_D)4405M_w t_D^{-1}/[(A/V)RT_C P_C^{-1}(1.5M_W/0.018)] = \\ e\sigma(T_D^4 - T_E^4) \quad (23)$$

Simplifying Equations (22) and (23)

$$(1 - \eta_C)(4405t_C^{-1})(0.012)/[(A/V)RT_C P_C^{-1}] = e\sigma(T_C^4 - T_E^4) \quad (24)$$

$$(1 - \eta_D)(4405M_w t_D^{-1})(0.012)/[(A/V)RT_C P_C^{-1}] = e\sigma(T_D^4 - T_E^4) \quad (25)$$

Referring now to FIG. 4, the surface temperature, T_C, of a cylindrical reactant storage tank is graphed as a function of charging efficiency for three different various A/V ratios, is shown according to Equation (24). Peak charging pressures in the tanks, and the charging times, are held constant. FIG. 5, like FIG. 4, is a graphical representation of T_C from Equation (24), for three peak charging pressures, with A/V and charging time being held constant. FIG. 6 is also a graphical representation of T_C from Equation (24) as a function of charge efficiency for three different charging times, with A/V and peak charging pressure being held constant.

In each of the FIGS. 4,5 and 6, the expected range of charging energy efficiency is highlighted on the right sides. The freezing point of water is also indicated. The three FIG-

URES show that within the expected charge energy efficiency range and the range of tank's A/V ratio, discharge time, and peak charge pressure, the surface temperature of the storage tanks during charging generally stay below freezing.

Equation (25) is also shown graphically in FIGS. 7,8 and 9, with the tank surface temperature, T_D, during discharge, being shown as a function of discharge energy efficiency. In FIG. 7, peak discharging pressure and the discharging time are held constant for three different A/V ratios. FIG. 8 also shows T_D as a function of discharging efficiency, with discharge time, t_D, and peak charge pressure, P_C, being held constant for three different tank ratios, A/V. In FIG. 9, the A/V ratio and the peak charge pressure are constant, for three different discharge times, t_D, according to Equation (25). In each of the FIGS. 7,8 and 9, the expected range of discharge phase energy efficiency is highlighted, and the freezing point of water is indicated. The FIGS. 7,8, and 9 show that within the expected discharge energy efficiency range and the range of tank A/V ratio, discharge time, and peak charge pressure, the surface temperature of the gas storage tanks during discharging stays above freezing.

FIG. 10 is a graphical representation of the preceding graphical representations, showing tank surface temperature for both a charge and discharge as a function of charge and discharge efficiency. FIG. 10 shows that for a system with a 12/12 hour charge/discharge where the peak charge pressure is 27 atmosphere (400 psia), during charging the surface temperature of the tanks is well below the freezing temperature, whereas during the discharge phase the tank surface temperature is well above freezing.

PRIOR ART CONSIDERATIONS

Except for the partially pressurized water storage reservoir of the present URFC invention, the other features of the URFC that are deemed patentable all relate to the management of waste heat from the two modes of operation of the FC as a fuel cell or as an electrolysis cell. More specifically, the present invention incorporates a spring loaded water storage reservoir that is externally pressurized by gas from one of the reactant tanks, and waste heat from the fuel cell stack is conveyed by heat pipes to the reactant storage tanks, from which the waste heat is radiated to the local environment.

In reference to the specific prior art teachings cited in the Background section above, U.S. Pat. No. 3,975,913 to Erickson describes a closed-cycle gas generator in which waste heat is used to drive closed cycle heat engine, rather than being conducted to gas storage tanks. No provision is made for storing water in, or retrieving it from an expendable, spring load storage tanks.

U.S. Pat. No. 4,490,445 ('445) to Hsu discloses a reversible 'solid oxide electrochemical energy converter' having a counter-flow heat exchanger that disposes of waste heat by directing it to heating the incoming fuel gases. However, the counter-flow heat exchanger of '445 is distinct from the present invention wherein heat that is delivered to the "dryer" (36,38 in FIG. 1) portion of the present invention receives its heat from the surface of the reactant storage tanks.

U.S. Pat. No. 5,338,622 to Hsu, et al discloses a fuel cell system that addresses specifically the issue of waste heat management, but, as in '445 to Hsu above, the heat transfer means is that of a counter-flow heat exchanger assembly.

U.S. Pat. No. 5,401,589 to Palmer, et al discloses a fuel cell with a reformer, wherein the reformer receives waste heat from the fuel cell. The use of a heat pipe is mentioned, but then dismissed because "heat pipes are not preferred due to the risk of leakage."

U.S. Pat. No. 5,506,066 to Sprouse discloses an 'ultra passive,' variable pressure RFC having a single H_2 storage tank "that encloses a plurality of smaller gaseous O_2 storage tubes." No "pumping elements" are used. A heating/cooling coil inside the H_2 tank prevents icing or overheating, said heating/cooling coil (**400** in FIG. **5**) has an unspecified source or sink for heat.

U.S. Pat. No. 5,510,202 to McCoy discloses a variable pressure fuel cell. McCoy uses prior art images similar to those of Sprouse in '066, suggesting that this patent's waste heat management system might be similar to that of Sprouse '066. However, the single reference to a "heating/cooling coil," in relation to a metal hydride storage tanks, does not specify a heat source or sink.

U.S. Pat. No. 5,678,410 to Fujita et al discloses a fuel cell system for use with cars. From Abstract: "The combined system preferably includes a heat storage tank disposed in a conduit of a heating medium . . . " A heat transfer medium "such as water" is used to convey heat to various heat exchangers including one that moves heat to or from a metal-hydride storage tank. Whereas waste heat from the fuel cell portion of this invention is discarded into metal hydride storage tanks during the discharge phase of operation of the system, the coolant is driven by two pumps **81** and **82** (FIG. **1**) and the coolant flow is managed by a plurality of solenoid valves. This is not the passive system of the sort described in the present disclosure, and no heat pipe system is mentioned.

U.S. Pat. No. 5,885,727 to Kawatsu discloses a fuel cell arrangement in which waste heat is conveyed, by way of apparently integral cooling water tubes, to reaction tanks **30** and **50** wherein, respectively, oxygen and hydrogen are generated for use in the fuel cell. While waste heat is conveyed, by water in tubes, to reaction tanks, the coolant is water and it is actively pumped. In one embodiment, a heat pump links separate, isolated cooling loops for the fuel cell stack and at least one reactant source (FIG. **9**), while a second embodiment (FIG. **11**) includes an external radiation.

US 2003/001721 A1 to Wattelet et al discloses a mobile and compact fuel cell system having "an integrated heat exchanger unit" that combines the fuel cell cooling system and a cathode exhaust gas condenser, both being cooled, in parallel, by a shared cooling air stream. A cooling tube **38** appears integrated with the fuel cell. No heat pipes are used, though, and any storage tanks involved are not used as heat sinks.

Although the invention has been shown and described with respect to a certain preferred embodiment or embodiments, certain equivalent alterations and modifications will occur to others skilled in the art upon the reading and understanding of this specification and the annexed drawings. In particular regard to the various functions performed by the above described components (assemblies, devices, circuits, etc.) the terms (including a reference to a "means") used to describe such components are intended to correspond, unless otherwise indicated, to any component which performs the specified function of the described component (i.e., that is functionally equivalent), even though not structurally equivalent to the disclosed structure which performs the function in the herein illustrated exemplary embodiments of the invention. In addition, while a particular feature of the invention may have been disclosed with respect to only one of several embodiments, such feature may be combined with one or more features of the other embodiments as may be desired and advantageous for any given or particular application.

What is claimed is:

1. A unitized regenerative fuel cell (URFC) system that operates either in a fuel cell mode while discharging or in an

electrolytic cell mode when charging comprising first and second reactant gas storage tanks, a water storage reservoir, and a fuel cell stack, comprising:

first and second reactant gas feed lines communicating between the fuel cell stack and the first and second reactant gas storage tanks for conveying reactant gases from the fuel cell stack to the first and second reactant gas storage tanks and for returning reactant gases from the first and second reactant gas storage tanks to the fuel cell stack:

the first and second reactant gas storage tanks acting as heat sinks and radiators of waste heat to an ambient environment below 0° C. so that during the electrolytic cell mode the surface temperature of the first and second reactant gas storage tanks is below 0° C. and during the fuel cell mode the tank surface temperature of the first and second reactant gas storage tanks is above freezing temperature;

first and second heat pipes thermally communicating with said fuel cell stack and first and second reactant gas storage tanks, respectively for conveying waste heat from the fuel cell stack to the surface of the first and second reactant gas storage tanks;

first and second reactant gas dryers in thermal communication with the first and second reactant gas storage tanks, respectively, and disposed within the first and second reactant gas feed lines, respectively, each of the first and second reactant gas dryers is integral with a surface of the first and second reactant gas storage tanks, respectively; whereby reactant gases conveyed from the fuel cell stack to the first and second reactant gas storage tanks during the electrolytic cell mode give up energy to storage tanks so that water vapor mixed with the reactant gases condenses out and freezes on internal gas dryer surfaces and during the fuel cell mode reactant gases passing from the first and second reactant gas storage tanks through the first and second reactant gas dryers on their way to the fuel cell stack are heated by the first and second reactant gas storage tanks from heat generated by the fuel cell stack whereby water on the internal gas dryer surfaces melts and returns to the reactant gases flowing to the fuel cell stack;

an expandable water storage reservoir formed as a bellows contained within a pressure dome, said water storage reservoir having water stored inside the bellows and being connected to the fuel cell stack for allowing the water volume inside the bellows to expand or contract depending upon the operation of the fuel cell stack; and

a gas pressure line communicating between the first reactant gas feed lines and the pressure dome that contains the expandable water storage reservoir for directing pressurized gas from the first reactant gas storage tank into the pressure dome and outside of the bellows so that the water pressure in the bellows is less than the gas pressure outside of the bellows.

2. The URFC system of claim **1** in which the first and second reactant gas storage tanks are cylindrical and have hemispherical ends.

3. The URFC system of claim **1** in which the first and second reactant gas dryers operate reversibly, and enable gas flow of first and second reactant gases between the first and second reactant gas storage tanks, respectively, and the fuel cell stack and between the fuel cell stack and the first and second reactant gas storage tanks.

4. The URFC system of claim **1** in which the expandable water storage reservoir is spring-loaded in such a way as to cause its volume to increase.

17

5. A unitized regenerative fuel cell (URFC) system that operates either in a fuel cell mode while discharging and in an electrolytic cell mode when charging comprising:

first and second reactant gas storage tanks acting as heat sinks and radiators of waste heat from the fuel cell stack to an ambient environment of below 0° C.,

a fuel cell stack,

first and second reactant gas feed lines communicating between the fuel cell stack and the first and second reactant gas storage tanks for conveying reactant gases from the fuel cell stack to the first and second reactant gas storage tanks and for returning reactant gases from the first and second reactant gas storage tanks to the fuel cell stack,

first and second heat pipes thermally communicating with said fuel cell stack and in thermal contact with the first and second reactant gas storage tanks, respectively for conveying waste heat from the fuel cell stack to the surface of the first and second reactant gas storage tanks so that during the electrolytic cell mode the surface temperature of the first and second reactant gas storage tanks is below 0° C. and during the fuel cell mode the tank surface temperature of the first and second reactant gas storage tanks is above freezing temperature; and

first and second reactant gas dryers means disposed within the first and second reactant gas feed lines, respectively, and in thermal communication with and integral with a surface of the first and second reactant gas storage tanks, respectively, for causing reactant gases conveyed from

18

the fuel cell stack to the first and second reactant gas storage tanks during the electrolytic cell mode to give up energy to storage tanks whereby water vapor mixed with the reactant gases condenses out and freeze as water on internal gas dryer surfaces and for causing reactant gases passing through the first and second reactant gas dryers on their way to the fuel cell stack during the fuel cell mode from the first and second reactant gas storage tanks to be heated by the heat generated by the fuel cell stack whereby water on the internal gas dryer surfaces melts and returns to the reactant gases flowing.

6. The URFC system of claim **5** including:

an expandable water storage reservoir formed as a bellows contained within a pressure dome, said water storage reservoir having water stored inside the bellows and being connected to the fuel cell stack for allowing the water volume inside the bellows to expand or contract depending upon the operation of the fuel cell stack; and

a gas pressure line communicating between the first reactant gas feed lines and the pressure dome that contains the expandable water storage reservoir for directing pressurized gas from the first reactant gas storage tank into the pressure dome and outside of the bellows so that the water pressure in the bellows is less than the gas pressure outside of the bellows.

7. The URFC system of claim **6** in which the expandable water storage reservoir is spring-loaded in such a way as to cause its volume to increase.

* * * * *

US008200486B1

(12) **United States Patent**
Jorgensen et al.

(10) **Patent No.:** **US 8,200,486 B1**
(45) **Date of Patent:** **Jun. 12, 2012**

(54) **SUB-AUDIBLE SPEECH RECOGNITION BASED UPON ELECTROMYOGRAPHIC SIGNALS**

(75) Inventors: **Charles C. Jorgensen**, Palo Alto, CA (US); **Diana D. Lee**, Palo Alto, CA (US); **Shane T. Agabon**, Millbrae, CA (US)

(73) Assignee: **The United States of America as represented by the Administrator of the National Aeronautics & Space Administration (NASA)**, Washington, DC (US)

(*) Notice: Subject to any disclaimer, the term of this patent is extended or adjusted under 35 U.S.C. 154(b) by 832 days.

(21) Appl. No.: **10/457,696**

(22) Filed: **Jun. 5, 2003**
(Under 37 CFR 1.47)

(51) **Int. Cl.**
G10L 15/00 (2006.01)
G10L 15/16 (2006.01)
G10L 15/20 (2006.01)
G10L 17/00 (2006.01)

(52) **U.S. Cl.** **704/233**; 704/231; 704/232; 704/236; 704/246

(58) **Field of Classification Search** 704/231–233, 704/236, 246
See application file for complete search history.

(56) **References Cited**

U.S. PATENT DOCUMENTS

3,383,466	A	*	5/1968	Fry et al. 704/235
5,027,408	A	*	6/1991	Kroeker et al. 704/254
5,729,694	A	*	3/1998	Holzrichter et al. 705/17
5,794,190	A	*	8/1998	Linggard et al. 704/232
6,151,571	A		11/2000	Pertrushin
6,182,039	B1		1/2001	Rigazio et al.
6,208,963	B1	*	3/2001	Martinez et al. 704/232
6,366,908	B1		4/2002	Chong et al.
6,720,984	B1	*	4/2004	Jorgensen et al. 715/863
7,062,093	B2	*	6/2006	Steger 382/216
2003/0163306	A1	*	8/2003	Manabe et al. 704/220
2003/0171921	A1	*	9/2003	Manabe et al. 704/232
2004/0044517	A1		3/2004	Palmquist
2006/0129394	A1		6/2006	Becker et al.

OTHER PUBLICATIONS

Hecht-Nielsen, "Theory of the Backpropagation Neural Network", International Joint Conference on Neural Networks, Jun. 1989.*
Basmajian, et al., Muscles Alive Their Functions Revealed by Electromyography, 1985, 429-469, Williams & Wilkins, Baltimore, MD, London, England, and Sydney, Australia.
Chan, et al., Hidden Markov Model Classification of Myoelectric Signal . . . , Proceedings of 23rd Annual EMBS International Conference, Oct. 25-28, 2001, IEEE, Istanbul, Turkey.
Chan, et al., Hidden Markov Model Classification of Myoelectric Signals in Speech, IEEE Engineering in Medicine and Biology, 2002, 143-146, IEEE.

(Continued)

Primary Examiner — Eric Yen
(74) *Attorney, Agent, or Firm* — John F. Schipper; Robert M. Padilla

(57) **ABSTRACT**

Method and system for processing and identifying a sub-audible signal formed by a source of sub-audible sounds. Sequences of samples of sub-audible sound patterns ("SASPs") for known words/phrases in a selected database are received for overlapping time intervals, and Signal Processing Transforms ("SPTs") are formed for each sample, as part of a matrix of entry values. The matrix is decomposed into contiguous, non-overlapping two-dimensional cells of entries, and neural net analysis is applied to estimate reference sets of weight coefficients that provide sums with optimal matches to reference sets of values. The reference sets of weight coefficients are used to determine a correspondence between a new (unknown) word/phrase and a word/phrase in the database.

18 Claims, 7 Drawing Sheets

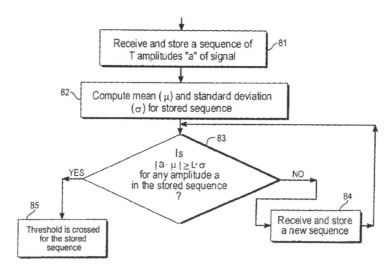

OTHER PUBLICATIONS

Chan, et al., A Multi-Expert Speech Recognition System Using Acoustic . . . , Proceedings of the Second Joint EMBS/BMES Conference, Oct. 23-26, 2002, 72-73, IEEE, Houston, Texas.

Englehart, et al., Classification of the Myoelectric Sign . . . , Medical Engineering and Physics on Intelligent Data Analysis in Electromyography and Electroneurography, 1999.

Hudgins, et al., A New Strategy for Multifunction Myoelectric Control, IEE Transaction on Biomedical Engineering, 1993, 82-94, 40-1, IEEE.

Jorgensen, et al., Sub Auditory Speech Recognition Based on EMG Signals, Proceedings of the International Joint Conference on Neural Networks, 2003, 3128-3133, 4, IEEE.

Kingsbury, et al., Wavelet Transforms in Ima . . . , Proceedings of the 1st Euroopean Conference on Signal Analysis & Predictions, Jun. 24-27, 1997, 23-34, Prague, Zcech Republic.

Manabe, et al., Unvoiced Speech REcognition Using EMG—Mime Speech Recognition -, New Horizons, 2003, 794-795, Ft. Lauderdale, Florida.

Misiti, et al., Wavelets: A New Tool for Signal Analysis, Wavelet Toolbox for Use with MATLAB, User's Guide Version 1, 1996, The Math Works, Inc.

Morse, et al., Research Summary of a Scheme to Ascertain the Availability ofSpeech Info . . . , Comput. Biol. Med., 1986, 399-410, 16-6, Pergamon Journals Ltd., Great Britain.

Morse, et al., Use of Myoelectric Signals to . . . , Proceedings of IEEE Engineering in Medicine & Biology Society 11th Annual International Conference, 1989, 1793-1794, IEEE.

Morse, et al., Time Domain Analysis of . . . , Proceedings of Annual International Conference of IEEE Engineering in Medicine and Biology Society, 1990, 1318-1319, 12-3, IEEE.

Morse, et al., Speech Recognition Using M . . . , Proceedings of Annual International Conference of IEEE Engineering in Medicine & Biology Society, 1991, 1877-1878, 13-4, IEEE.

Morse, Preliminary Design and Implementation of a Scheme to Recognize Speech from Myoelec . . . , A Dissertation Presented to the Graduate School of Clemson Universtity, 1985.

Partridge, et al., Speech Through Myoelectric Signal Recognition SMyLES, Proceedings 28th Annual Southeast Regional Conference, Apr. 18-20, 1990, 288-295, ACM, Greenville, SC.

Press, et al., Nonlinear Models, Numerical Recipes in C,The Art of Scientific Computing, Second Edition, 1992, 681-689, Cambridge University Press.

Sugie, et al., A Speech Prosthesis Employing a Speech Synthesizer—Vowel Discrimination from . . . , IEEE Transactions on Biomedical Engineering, 1985, 485-490, BME-32-7, IEEE.

Trejo, et al., Multimodal Neuroelectric Interface Development, IEEE Transactions on Neural Systems and Rehabilitation Engineering, 2003, 199-204, 11-2, IEEE.

Wheeler, et al., Gestures as Input: Neuroelectric Joysticks and Keyboards, Pervasive Computing, 2003, 56-61, IEEE CS and IEEE ComSoc.

Graciarena, et al., Combining Standard and Throat Microphones for Robust Speech Recognition, IEEE Signal Processing Letters, Mar. 2003, 72-74, 10-3, IEEE.

Junqua, et al., the Lombard Effect: A Reflex to Better Communicate With Others in Noise, IEEE International Conference on Acoustics, Speech, and Signal Processing, Mar. 15-19, 1999, 2083-2086, 4, IEEE.

NG, et al., Denoising of Human Speech Using Combined Acoustic and EM Sensorsignal Processing, IEEE International Conference on Acoustics, Speech, and Signal Processing, Jun. 5-9, 2000, 229-232, 1, IEEE.

Nonfinal Rejection in related case, U.S. Appl. No. 11/169,265, mailed Jun. 19, 2008.

Response to Nonfinal Rejection in related case, U.S. Appl. No. 11/169,265, mailed Jun. 19, 2008. Response filed Dec. 16, 2008.

* cited by examiner

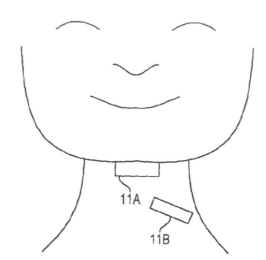

Fig. 1

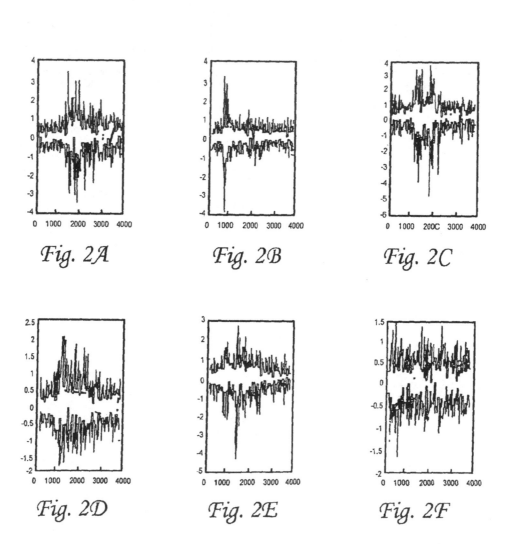

Fig. 2A   *Fig. 2B*   *Fig. 2C*

Fig. 2D   *Fig. 2E*   *Fig. 2F*

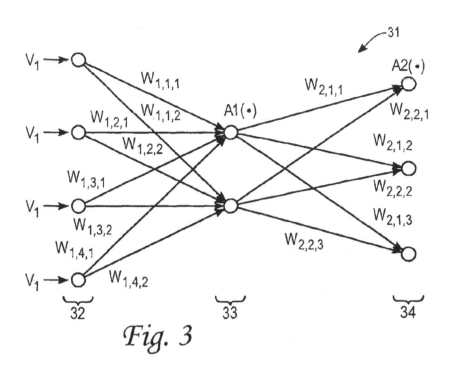

Fig. 3

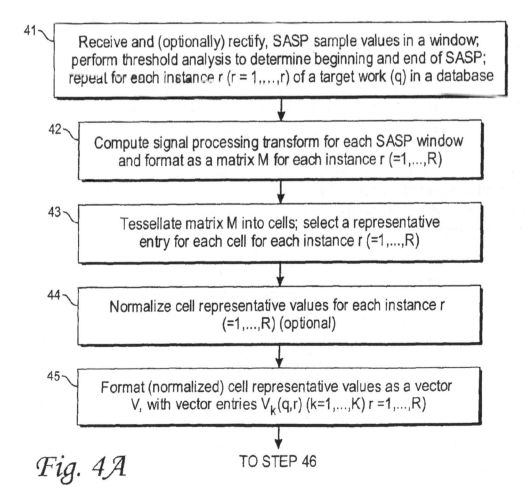

41 — Receive and (optionally) rectify, SASP sample values in a window; perform threshold analysis to determine beginning and end of SASP; repeat for each instance r (r = 1,...,r) of a target work (q) in a database

42 — Compute signal processing transform for each SASP window and format as a matrix M for each instance r (=1,...,R)

43 — Tessellate matrix M into cells; select a representative entry for each cell for each instance r (=1,...,R)

44 — Normalize cell representative values for each instance r (=1,...,R) (optional)

45 — Format (normalized) cell representative values as a vector V, with vector entries $V_k(q,r)$ (k=1,...,K) r =1,...,R)

TO STEP 46

Fig. 4A

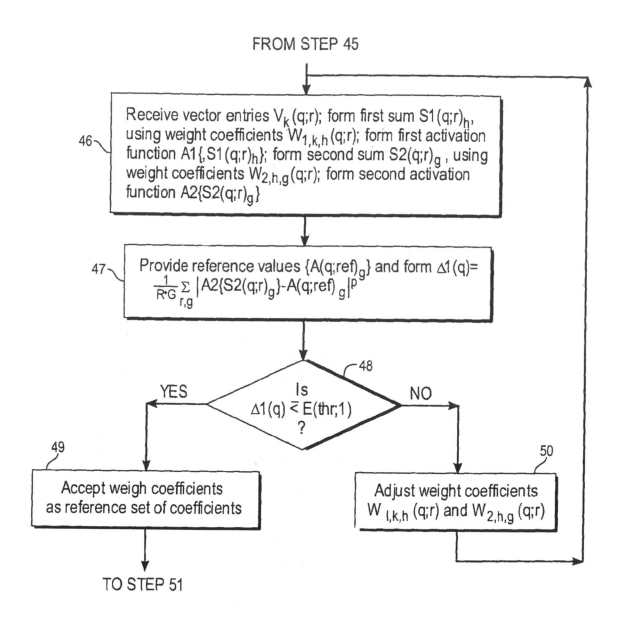

FROM STEP 45

46 — Receive vector entries $V_k(q;r)$; form first sum $S1(q;r)_h$, using weight coefficients $W_{1,k,h}(q;r)$; form first activation function $A1\{,S1(q;r)_h\}$; form second sum $S2(q;r)_g$, using weight coefficients $W_{2,h,g}(q;r)$; form second activation function $A2\{S2(q;r)_g\}$

47 — Provide reference values $\{A(q;ref)_g\}$ and form $\Delta1(q)= \frac{1}{R \cdot G} \sum_{r,g} |A2\{S2(q;r)_g\}-A(q;ref)_g|^p$

48

Is $\Delta1(q) \lessgtr E(thr;1)$?

YES   NO

49 — Accept weigh coefficients as reference set of coefficients

50 — Adjust weight coefficients $W_{1,k,h}(q;r)$ and $W_{2,h,g}(q;r)$

TO STEP 51

Fig. 4B

364

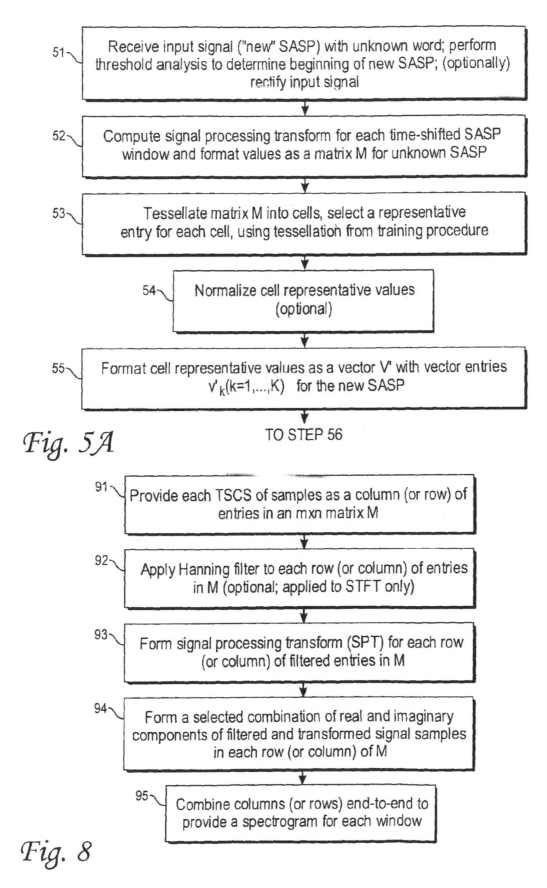

51 — Receive input signal ("new" SASP) with unknown word; perform threshold analysis to determine beginning of new SASP; (optionally) rectify input signal

52 — Compute signal processing transform for each time-shifted SASP window and format values as a matrix M for unknown SASP

53 — Tessellate matrix M into cells, select a representative entry for each cell, using tessellation from training procedure

54 — Normalize cell representative values (optional)

55 — Format cell representative values as a vector V' with vector entries $v'_k(k=1,...,K)$ for the new SASP

TO STEP 56

Fig. 5A

91 — Provide each TSCS of samples as a column (or row) of entries in an $m \times n$ matrix M

92 — Apply Hanning filter to each row (or column) of entries in M (optional; applied to STFT only)

93 — Form signal processing transform (SPT) for each row (or column) of filtered entries in M

94 — Form a selected combination of real and imaginary components of filtered and transformed signal samples in each row (or column) of M

95 — Combine columns (or rows) end-to-end to provide a spectrogram for each window

Fig. 8

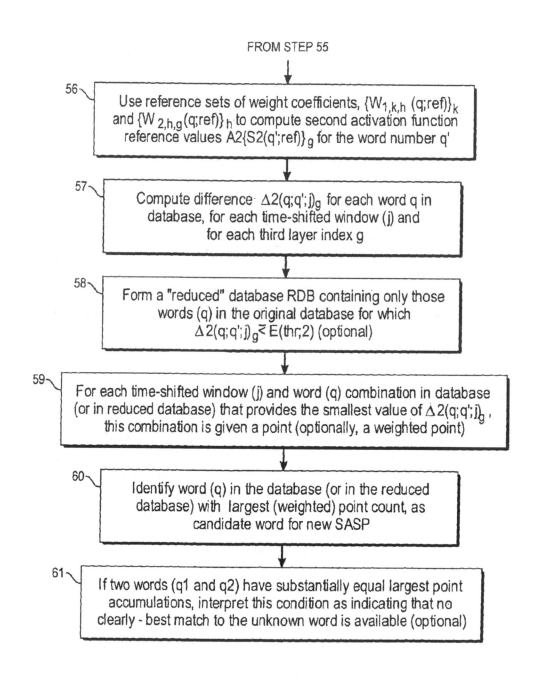

FROM STEP 55

56 — Use reference sets of weight coefficients, $\{W_{1,k,h}(q;ref)\}_k$ and $\{W_{2,h,g}(q;ref)\}_h$ to compute second activation function reference values $A2\{S2(q';ref)\}_g$ for the word number q'

57 — Compute difference $\Delta2(q;q';j)_g$ for each word q in database, for each time-shifted window (j) and for each third layer index g

58 — Form a "reduced" database RDB containing only those words (q) in the original database for which $\Delta2(q;q';j)_g \lesseqgtr E(thr;2)$ (optional)

59 — For each time-shifted window (j) and word (q) combination in database (or in reduced database) that provides the smallest value of $\Delta2(q;q';j)_g$, this combination is given a point (optionally, a weighted point)

60 — Identify word (q) in the database (or in the reduced database) with largest (weighted) point count, as candidate word for new SASP

61 — If two words (q1 and q2) have substantially equal largest point accumulations, interpret this condition as indicating that no clearly - best match to the unknown word is available (optional)

Fig. 5B

366

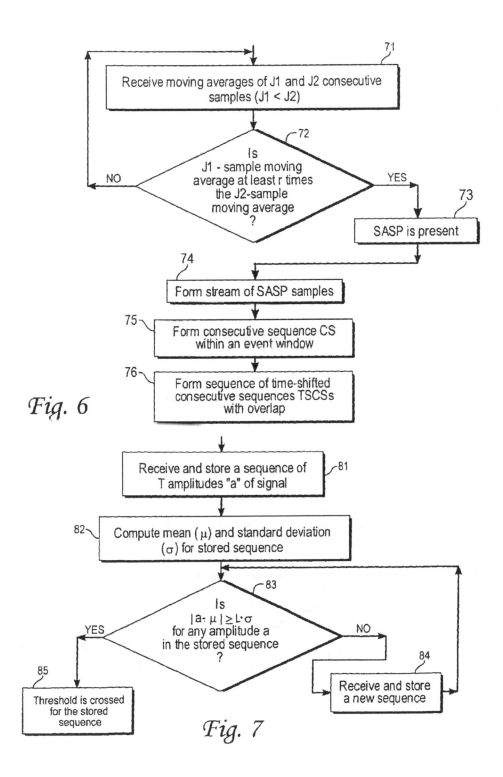

Fig. 6

Fig. 7

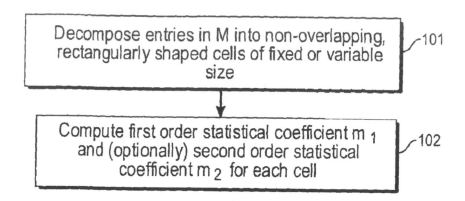

Fig. 9

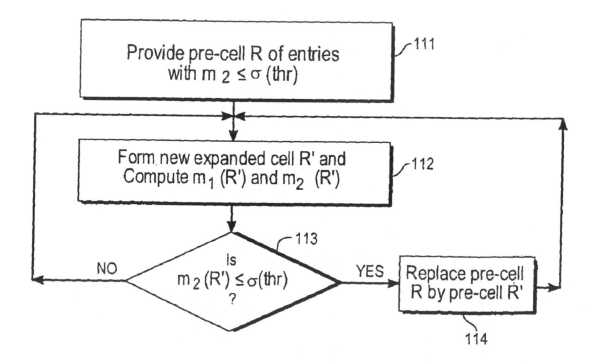

Fig. 10

1

SUB-AUDIBLE SPEECH RECOGNITION BASED UPON ELECTROMYOGRAPHIC SIGNALS

FIELD OF THE INVENTION

This invention relates to analysis of electromyographic signals produced in a human body

BACKGROUND OF THE INVENTION

Communications between two or more humans, or between a human and a machine, is traditionally dominated by visual and verbal information and alphanumeric input. Efforts to automate human-to-human or human-to-machine communication, such as commercial speech recognition have emphasized the audible aspects. A totally auditory communication strategy places a number of constraints on the communication channels, including sensitivity to ambient noise, a requirement for proper formation and enunciation of words, and use of a shared language. The physical limitations of sound production and recognition also become problematic in unusual environments, such as those involving hazardous materials (HAZMATs), extra vehicular activity (EVA) space tasks, underwater operations and chemical/biological warfare (CBW). Conventional auditory expression may be undesirable for private communication needed in many situations encountered daily, such as discrete or confidential telephone calls, offline or sotto voce comments during a teleconference call, certain military operations, and some human-to-machine commands and queries. Communication alternatives that are both private and not dependent upon production of audible signals are valuable.

One proposed method for studying alternative means of communication is direct understanding of brain signals, which bypasses speech and its analysis altogether. J. R. Wolpaw et al, "Brain-computer interface technology: a review of the first international meeting," I.E.E.E. Trans. on Rehabilitation Engineering, vol. 8 (2000) 164-171, recently published a review of the state of electroencephalograph (EEG) analysis. Several practical difficulties are encountered for near term application of pure EEG approaches, due to use in EEG of aggregated surface measured brain potential. Additionally, one confronts the nonlinear complexity and idiosyncratic nature of the signals. An alternative, invasive EEG measurement and analysis, is not considered practical for widespread use, except for extreme medical conditions.

What is needed is a sub-audible communication system that provides one or more tiers, in addition to conventional audible communication, to exchange or transfer information compactly, reliably and reasonably accurately. Preferably, the amount of computation required should be modest and not be out of proportion to the information obtained through the signal processing.

SUMMARY OF THE INVENTION

These needs are met by the invention, which provides a system for receipt and analysis of sub-audible signals to estimate and provide a characterization of speech that is sotto voce or is not fully formed for purposes of normal speech recognition. This system relies on surface measurement of muscle signals (i.e., electromyographic or EMG signals) to discriminate or disambiguate speech signals produced with relatively little acoustic input. In one alternative, EMG signals are measured on the side of a subject's throat, near the larynx, and under the chin near the tongue, to pick up and

analyze surface signals generated by a tongue (so-called electropalatogram or throat EPG signals). This approach relies on the fact that audible speech muscle control signals must be highly repeatable, in order to be understood by others. These audible and sub-audible signals are intercepted and analyzed before sound is generated using these signals. The processed signals are fed into a neural network pattern classifier, and near-silent or sub-audible speech that occurs when a person "talks to himself or to herself" is processed. In this alternative, the tongue and throat muscles still respond, at a lowered intensity level, as if a word or phrase (referred to collectively herein as a "word") is to be made audible, with little or no external movement cues present. Where sufficiently precise sensing, optimal feature selection and good signal processing are available, it is possible to analyze these weak signals to perform, or direct performance of, useful tasks without conventional vocalization, thus mimicking an idealized thought-based approach.

In a training phase, the beginning and end of a sub-audible speech pattern ("SASP") is first determined for each of R spoken instances of a word in a database including Q words in a window of temporal length 1-4 sec (preferably about 2 sec), are provided and processed. A Signal Processing Transform (SPT) operation (characterized in the text) is performed on each data sample. The resulting transforms, evaluated at a selected sequence of transform parameter values, become entries in a matrix M, where a first matrix axis may represent different scale factors and a second matrix axis may represent a time associated with a window. The matrix M is tessellated into groups of cells (e.g., of rectangular shape), and each cell is represented by a feature for that cell. The cell features are rearranged as a vector, having K entries $v_k(q;r)$. For each word (q) in the database and for each spoken instance (r) of a (known) word, a sum $S1(q;r)_h$ is formed of cell representative number k multiplied by a first set of weight coefficients $w_{1,k,h}(q,r)$ and summed over k=1, . . . , K, and a first activation function (or functions) $A1\{S1(q;r)_h\}$ of the first sum $S1$. The first activation value is multiplied by a second set of weight coefficients $w_{2,h,g}(q;r)$ and summed over h=1, . . . , H to form a second sum $S2(q;r)_g$, and a second activation function (or functions) $A2\{S2(q;r)_g\}$ is computed. The weight coefficients $w_{1,k,h}(q;r)$ and $w_{2,h,g}(q;r)$ are adjusted, using a neural net learning procedure, to provide at least one reference activation function value $A(q;ref)_g$ for which a difference, $\Delta1(q;r)_g=|A(q;ref)_g-A2\{S2(q;r)_g\}|$, is no greater than a first error threshold $\epsilon(thr;1)$. for all spoken instances, r=1, . . . , R and all value of the weight index g, with corresponding sets of weight coefficients $\{w_{1,k,h}(q;ref)\}$ and $\{w_{2,h,g}(q;ref)\}$. This completes the training phase of the invention.

An SASP including an unknown word is provided and sampled in a sequence of windows, as in the training phase. Signal Processing Transforms are computed for the sample values in each of these windows, a matrix M' is formed and tessellated into cells, and a representative value for each cell is optionally normalized, as before. The representative cell values are formatted as a vector, with entries v_k. Using the already-determined weights $w_k(q;ref)$ for each word (q), a sum $S'(q;ref)$ of the vector entries v_k, multiplied by the corresponding weights $v_k(q;ref)$ is formed, an activation function value $A\{S'(q;ref)\}$ is computed, and differences $\Delta2(q)_g=|A(q;ref)_g-A2\{S2(q;r;j)_g\}|$ are computed and compared with a second error threshold $\epsilon(thr;2)$. If at least one word (q=q0) can be found for which $\Delta2(q0)\leq\epsilon(thr;2)$, at least one word (q=q0) with minimum value $\Delta2(q0)$ is interpreted as corresponding to the unknown word.

The first phase of the technique is a learning procedure, whereby the system learns to distinguish between different known words in a database and provides reference sets of neural net weight coefficients for this purpose. In a second, word recognition phase, the weight coefficients are applied to one or more unknown words to determine if an unknown word is sufficiently similar to a word in the database. This technique provides several advantages, including minimization of word variations through use of a shared language and shared sound production, a potential to connect the sub-audible signal recognition to a flexible, highly developed speech recognition architecture non-invasive sensing, reasonably robust response to physiological variations, and privacy.

BRIEF DESCRIPTION OF THE DRAWINGS

FIG. **1** illustrates placement of signal recording electrodes in an initial experiment on sub-audible speech analysis.

FIGS. **2A-2F** are graphical views of sub-audible signals corresponding to the generic words "stop", "go", "left", "right", "alpha" and "omega."

FIG. **3** illustrates a simplified neural network classifier, with one hidden layer, that may be applied in practicing the invention.

FIGS. **4** and **5** are high level flow charts of procedures for practicing a training procedure and a word recognition procedure according to the invention.

FIGS. **6-10** are flow charts of intermediate procedures associated with the steps in the FIG. **4** or FIG. **5** flow chart.

DESCRIPTION OF BEST MODES AND THE INVENTION

In some initial tests, sub-audible pronunciation of six English words ("stop", "go", "left", "right", "alpha" and "omega") and ten numerals ("1", "2", "3", "4", "5", "6", "7", "8", "9" and "0") were recorded for each of three subjects, ages 55, 35 and 24, to provide a control set of words for a small graphic model that might be used to provide commands on a Mars Rover system, for example. The words "alpha" and "omega" may be used to enter a command to move faster or slower, or up or down, or forward or backward, as appropriate under the circumstances. EMG data were collected for each subject, using two pairs of self-adhesive AG/AG-C1 electrodes, located near the left and right anterior external area of the throat, about 0.25 cm back from the chin cleft and about 1.5 cm from the right and left sides of the larynx, as indicated in FIG. **1**. Initial results indicate that one pair, or more pairs if desired, of electrodes, located diagonally between the cleft of the chin and the larynx in a non-symmetrical relationship, will suffice for recognition in small word sets. Signal grounding usually relies on attachment of an additional electrode to the right or left wrist or another location on the body. When data are acquired using wet electrodes, each electrode pair is connected to a commercial Neuroscan or equivalent signal amplifier and recorder that records the EMG responses at a sampling rate of up to 20 KHz. A 60 Hz notch filter is used to reduce ambient signal interference.

One hundred or more exemplars for each word were initially recorded for each subject over a six-day interval, in morning and afternoon sessions. In a first group of experiments, the signals were sectioned offline into two-second time windows with variable window start times, and extraneous signals (coughs, swallows, body noises, etc.) were removed using SCAN 4 Neuroscan software. FIGS. **2A**, **2B**, **2C**, **2D**, **2E** and **2F** graphically illustrate representative EMG blocked signals for six windows, corresponding to the words "stop", "go", "left", "right", "alpha" and "omega", respectively. The blocked signals for these words are not wholly

reproducible and may be affected by the test subject's health and the time (of day) the particular signal is recorded and analyzed. The technique must also take into account the changing signal-noise ratio and/or changing amplitudes of the signals.

For signal feature processing, Matlab scripts were developed to provide a uniform signal processing system from recording through network training. These routines were used to receive and transform the raw signals into feature sets, to dynamically apply a threshold to the transformed signals, to compensate for changes in electrode locations, to adjust signal-noise ratios, and to implement neural network algorithms for pattern recognition and training. EMG artifacts, such as swallowing, muscle fatigue tremors and coughs, were removed during preprocessing of the windowed samples. In a real time application, artifact filters would be incorporated and applied to introduction of new words into the lexicon.

Sectioned signal data for each word were transformed into usable classifier feature vectors using preprocessing transforms, combined with a coefficient reduction technique. Several transforms were tested, including: (i) a short time interval Fourier Transform (STFT), requiring multiple overlapping windows; (ii) discrete wavelets (DWTs) and continuous wavelets (CWTs) using Daubechies 5 and 7 bases; (iii) dual tree wavelets (DTWTs) with a near_sym_a 5,7 tap filter and a Q-shift 14,14 tap filter; (iv) Hartley Transforms; (v) Linear Predictive Coding (LPC) coefficients and (vi) uniformly and nonuniformly weighted moving averages. Feature sets were created differently for each of these transform approaches, depending upon the unique signal processing approaches, with different pattern discriminations.

The most effective real time SPTs were the windowed STFTs and the DTWT coefficient matrices, each of which was post-processed to provide associated feature vectors. One suitable procedure is the following. Transform coefficient vectors are generated for each word, using, for example, the STFT or the DWT applied to the magnitude (absolute value) of the raw signal amplitude. Where unipolar, rather than bipolar, electrodes are used, positive and negative sign signals are distinguishable, and STFTs and DWTs could be applied to the raw signal amplitudes without automatic formation of an absolute value. Vectors were post processed using a Matlab routine to create a matrix of spectral coefficients. This matrix is tessellated into a set of sub-matrices or cells, depending upon the spectral information complexity. Tessellation sizes were determined in part by average signal energy in a given region of the spectral matrix. Uses of equal and unequal segmentation sizes were considered. A representative value was calculated for each candidate sub-matrix, to reduce the number of features or variables presented to the pattern recognition algorithm and to represent average coefficient energy.

A simple mean or average signal energy within a cell was used as a cell representative or "feature." Other first order statistical values, such as medians, modes and maximum sub-matrix values, can be used but appear to provide no substantial improvement over use of a simple mean of signal energy. The result of this approach is a fixed length feature vector for each sub-audible word tested. Dual tree wavelets are attractive here, as opposed to standard discrete wavelets, to minimize the normal wavelet sensitivity to phase shifts. Continuous wavelets (CWTs) are not presently practical for real time computations. The Hartley Transform, which provides additional information on signal behavior along a non-real line in the transform plane, was also explored, as was use of moving averages of various lengths.

5

Feature vectors for each instance of a word are used to train a neural network (NN) word recognition engine. Accuracy of recognition is evaluated using about 20 percent of the untrained word exemplars and signals from only one electrode pair, which is randomly drawn from the collection of electrode pairs, in a data recording session.

Five NN paradigms were considered for signal training classification, using the entire feature set: (1) scaled conjugate gradient nets; (2) Leavenberg-Marquardt nets; (3) probabilistic neural nets (PNNs); (4) modified dynamic cell structure (DCS) nets; and (5) linear classifiers. After comparison of the results, a scaled conjugate gradient net was chosen, for the following reasons. A Leavenberg-Marquardt net reaches the lowest mean square error level but requires too much system memory when dealing with large data sets, even where reduced memory variations are used. A signal having a low mean square error (MSE) does not necessarily correspond to, or produce, an improved generalization for new signals, where high sensor noise is present. PNN nets provide reasonable classifications but require very large training sample sizes to reach stable probabilities and do not appear to be superior in ultimate pattern discrimination ability. A dynamic cell structure (DCS) net provides fast net training, which is attractive for real time adaptation, but is less compact for the anticipated applications that are memory sensitive. A scaled conjugate gradient network has fast convergence with adequate error levels for the signal-noise ratios encountered in the data; and the performance is comparable to the Leavenberg-Marquardt performance. The scaled conjugate gradient network uses a "trust" region gradient search criterion, which may contribute to the superior overall results of this approach.

In other EMG tasks, we successfully applied Hidden Markov Models (HMMs), but these appear to be most effective for non-multi-modal signal distributions, such as are associated with single discrete gestures, rather than with the temporally non-stationary, sub-audible signal patterns of concern here. An HMM approach also requires sensitive pre-training to accurately estimate transition probabilities. A hybrid HMM/neural net approach, is an alternative.

In order to quickly explore many experimental situations using different transform variations, we have operated in a simulated real time environment that has been developed and used at N.A.S.A. Ames, wherein EMG signals are recorded to file and are later used to train and test the signal recognition engines. Our initial three test subjects were not given immediate feedback about how well their sub-audible signals were recognized. However, some learning occurred as each test subject was permitted to view the subject's EMG signals.

FIG. 3 illustrates a simplified example of a neural network classifier 31 with one hidden layer, configured to analyze a vector of feature values provided according to the invention. The NN configuration 31 includes a first (input) layer 32 having four input nodes, numbered k=1, . . . , K (K=4 here), a second (hidden) layer 33 having two intermediate nodes, numbered h=1, . . . , H (H=2 here), and a third (output) layer 34 having three output nodes, numbered g=1, . . . , G (G=3 here). A practical neural net classifier may have tens or hundreds of input nodes, hidden layer(s) nodes and output nodes. The input values v_k received at the first layer of nodes are summed and a first activation function A1 is applied to produce

$$u_h = A1 \left\{ \sum_{k=1}^{K} w_{1,k,h} \cdot v_k + 1 \cdot b \right\} \ (h = 1, \dots, H), \tag{1}$$

where the quantities $w_{1,k,h}$ are weight coefficients connecting the nodes in the first layer to the nodes in the second layer and b is a bias number. The intermediate values received at the second layer are summed and a second activation function A2 is applied to produce

$$t_g = A2 \left\{ \sum_{h=1}^{H} w_{2,h,g} \cdot u_h + 1 \cdot b \right\} \ (g = 1, \dots, G), \tag{2}$$

where the quantities $w_{2,h,g}$ are weight coefficients connecting the nodes in the second layer to the nodes in the third layer. Here, A1 and A2 may be, but need not be, the same activation function, and more than one activation function can be used in a given layer. More than one hidden layer can be included, by obvious extensions of the notation. This formalism will be used in the following development of the NN analysis, in FIGS. 4 and 5.

Training Procedure.

The term "training procedure," according to one embodiment of the invention, includes the following actions: (1) receive R spoken instances, of a sub-audible EMG signal, for at least one known word; (2) detect the beginning of each SASP containing an instance, using a thresholding procedure; (3) for each SASP, create a window, having a selected length Δt(win), that includes the SASP; (4) apply a "signal processing transform" (SPT) to each instance of one of the SASPs; (5) form a matrix (which can be one-dimensional, a vector) from the SPT values for each instance of the SASP; (6) tessellate the matrix into cells, with each cell represented by a cell "feature", for each instance; (7) (re)format the cell features as entries or components of a vector; (8) (optionally) normalize the vector entries; (9) receive the vector entries for each instance of the SASP in a neural network classifier; (10) for all instances of each word, identify sets of reference weight coefficients for the vector entry values that provide a best match to a reference pattern that corresponds to the words considered; and (11) use the reference weight coefficients in a neural network analysis of an unknown word received by the system.

FIG. 4 is a high level flow chart illustrating a procedure for practicing a training procedure according to the invention. In step 41, a sequence of length Δt(win)=1-4 sec (preferably, Δt(win)≈2 sec) of sampled signal values is received, and a sample thresholding operation is performed to determine where, in the sequence, a sub-audible speech pattern (SASP) begins. SASPs representing samples of a known word at a selected rate (e.g., about 2 KHz) are identified, recorded and optionally rectified. Signal rectification replaces the signal at each sampling point by the signal magnitude (optional). R spoken instances, numbered r=1, . . . , R (R≧10), of a given word (SASP) are preferably used for training the system to recognize that SASP.

In step 42, a Signal Processing Transform operation is performed on the pattern SASP over the window length Δt(win) for each spoken instance r=1, . . . , R, and for each word, numbered q=1, . . . , Q in a database, to provide a spectrum for the received signal for each of the windowed samples. As used herein, a "Signal Processing Transform" (SPT) has a finite domain (compact support) in the time

7

8

variable, provides a transform dependent upon at least one transform parameter (e.g., window length, number of samples used in forming the transform, scale factor, frequency, etc.), allows summation or integration over this parameter, and a collection of these transforms for different values of the transform parameter is mathematically complete.

The SPT operation in step **42** may rely upon a short time interval Fourier transforms (STFTs), discrete wavelets (DWTs) and continuous wavelets (CWTs) using Daubechies 5 and 7 bases; dual tree wavelets (DTWTs) with a near_sym_a 5,7 tap filter and a Q-shift 14,14 tap filter; Hartley Transforms; Linear Predictive Coding (LPC) coefficients, and uniformly and nonuniformly weighted moving averages, or any other suitable transforms. The spectrum obtained by this operation (expressed as a function of one or more transform parameters) is a sequence of data transform samples, formatted as an m-row-by-n-column matrix M (or as a vector, with m=1 or n=1) having a first matrix axis (along a row) and a second matrix axis (along a column), with each matrix entry representing a concentration or intensity associated with a scale factor and/or window time. In a preferred embodiment, for a wavelet SPT, the n columns (e.g., n=30) represent an increasing sequence of window times for constant scale factor, and the m rows (e.g., m=129) represent a dyadic sequence of scale factors used to provide the spectrum for a given window time. Alternatively, the m rows may represent window times and the n columns may represent scale factors. A sequence of further operations is performed on the matrix, as discussed in the following,

In step **43**, the matrix entries (e.g., wavelet coefficients) are tessellated or decomposed into "cells," with each cell representing a grouping of adjacent matrix entries (e.g., a rectangular grouping of one or more sizes), where the entries in a given cell resemble each other according to one or more criteria and associated metric(s). A matrix may be divided into uniform size cells or may be divided according to statistical similarity of cell entries or according to another criterion.

As an example, consider the following 4×6 matrix

$$M = \begin{vmatrix} 1 & 2 & 3 & 4 & 5 & 6 \\ 1 & 3 & 5 & 7 & 9 & 11 \\ 2 & 6 & 12 & 20 & 15 & 8 \\ 3 & 18 & 14 & 7 & 9 & 6 \end{vmatrix} \quad (3)$$

The matrix M may be expressed as a vector or single stream of data entries. If one decomposes this matrix M into four 2×3 non-overlapping rectangular groups of entries (cells), the corresponding arithmetic means of the four cells become

$$< M >= \begin{vmatrix} 2.5 & 7 \\ 9.17 & 10.83 \end{vmatrix} \quad (4)$$

which can represent each of the four cells, and the corresponding standard deviations of the four cells become

$$< \Delta M >= \begin{vmatrix} 42.75 & 291 \\ 628, 97 & 117.36 \end{vmatrix} \quad (5)$$

Tessellation of the matrix entries into the four 2×3 non-overlapping groups of entries in this example may depend, for example, upon the relative sizes of the entries in the matrix M. More generally, each cell is represented by a "feature" associated therewith, which may be one or more associated numerical coefficient values, such as the entries in the matrix <M> shown in Eq. (4), or a maximum or minimum value from the cell entries.

In step **44**, each cell representative value or feature in the tessellated matrix is optionally normalized by dividing this value by (i) a sum of all values of the cell representatives, (ii) a sum of the magnitudes of all values of the cell representatives, (iii) the largest magnitude of the cell representative values or (iv) another selected sum. Alternatively, a normalized cell representative value is formed as a difference between the cell representative value and a mean value for that population, divided by a standard deviation value for that population. Alternatively, a normalized cell representative value is formed as a difference between the cell representative value and a maximum or minimum cell representative value for the tessellated matrix. One goal of normalization is to reduce the dynamic range of the cell representative values for each instance $r=1, \ldots, R$ and each word $q=1, \ldots, Q$.

In step **45**, the (normalized) cell representative values determined in step **34** are arranged as a vector of length K=number of cells) or other suitable entity for subsequent processing.

In step **46**, the vector entries $v_k(q;r)$ are received and processed by a neural net (NN) classifier by multiplying each vector entry $v_k(q;r)$ by a first set of weight coefficients $w_{1,k,h}(q;r)$ $(0 \leq w_{1,k,h} \leq 1; k=1, \ldots, K; h=1, \ldots, H)$ and summing these weighted values to form

$$S1(q; r)_h = \sum_k w_{1,k,h}(q; r) \cdot v_k(q; r) \ (h = 1, \ldots, H) \quad (6)$$

This process is repeated for each of the R spoken instances of the known word. Each of the weighted sums $S1(q;r)_h$ becomes an argument in a first activation function $A1\{S1(q; r)_h\}$, discussed in the following, also in step **46**. Also in step **46**, a second set of sums is formed

$$S2(q; r)_g = \sum_h w_{2,h,g}(q; r) \cdot A1\{S1(q; r)_h\}, \ (g = 1, \ldots, G) \quad (7)$$

which becomes an argument in a second activation function $A2\{S2(q;r)_g\}$.

In step **47**, the system provides a set of reference values $\{A(q;ref)_g\}_g$ for the word number q and computes a set of differences

$$\Delta 1(q) = (1/R \cdot G) \sum_{r,g} |A2\{S2(q; r)_g\} - A(q; ref)_g|^P \quad (8)$$

where p is a selected positive number. The system determines, in step **48**, if $A1(q) \leq \epsilon(thr,1)$, where $\epsilon(thr;1)$ is a selected threshold error, preferably in a range 0.01 and below.

If the answer to the query in step **48** is "yes," the system accepts this estimated reference set, in step **49**, for use in the word recognition procedure, illustrated in FIG. **5**. If the answer to the query in step **48** is "no," the first and second

US 8,200,486 B1

9

weight coefficients, $w_{1,k,h}(q;r)$ and $w_{2,h,g}(q;r)$, are adjusted to provide another set of estimated reference values $A(q;ref)_g$, in step **50**, using a neural net analysis approach, and steps **46-48** are repeated. In the neural net analysis, a gradient method is applied to a geometric space with coordinates $w_{1,k,h}(q;r)$ and $w_{2,h,g}(q;r)$, as discussed subsequently.

In the procedure illustrated in FIG. **4**, two suitable activation functions are

$$A\{S\}=\tanh(S)=\{\exp(a\cdot S)-\exp(-a\cdot S)\}/\{\exp(a\cdot S)+\exp(-a\cdot S)\}, \quad (9A)$$

$$A\{S\}=1/\{1-\exp(-a\cdot S)\}, \quad (9B)$$

having the respective ranges of $[-1,1]$ and $[0,1]$ for $-\infty<S<\infty$, where a is a selected positive number. Other monotonically increasing, finite range functions can also be used as activation functions.

For each word q, each reference value $A(q;ref)_g$ ($q=1,\ldots,$ Q) may be determined by different first reference sets of weight coefficients, $\{w_{1,k,h}(q;ref)\}_k$ and/or by different second reference sets of weight coefficients $\{w_{2,h,g}(q;ref)\}_h$, which are now fixed for the word number q. The reference values $A(q;ref)_g$ and the associated first and second reference sets of weight coefficients will henceforth be used for comparison with not-yet-identified SASP words. Optionally, the NN has F hidden layers and F+1 sets of weight coefficients ($F\geq1$).

In an alternative embodiment, in steps **46-50**, a first universal set of weight coefficients, $\{w_{1,k,h}(ref)\}_k$ and a second universal set of weight coefficients $\{w_{2,h,g}(ref)\}_h$, not dependent upon the particular word (q), replace the first and second sets of weight coefficients $\{w_{1,k,h}(q;ref)\}_k$ and $\{w_{2,h,g}(q;ref)\}_h$. In this alternative embodiment, where the database includes at least two words, the order of the instances of different (transformed) words must be randomized, and the neural network classifier seeks to identify first and second universal sets of weight coefficients, $\{w_{1,k,h}(ref)\}_k$ and $\{w_{2,h,g}(ref)\}_h$, that are accurate for all words in the database.

Word Recognition Procedure.

The word recognition procedure, according to one embodiment of the invention, includes the following actions: (1) receive a sub-audible EMG signal, representing an unknown word; (2) detect the beginning of an SASP, using a thresholding procedure; (3) create a window, having a selected length $\Delta t(win)$, that includes the SASP; (4) create a sequence of time-shifted windowed versions of the received SASP, with time shifts equal to a multiple of a time displacement value $\Delta t(displ)$; (5) apply a signal processing transform (SPT) to each of the time-shifted versions of the SASP, (6) form a matrix (which can be one-dimensional, a vector) from the SPT values for each of the time-shifted versions of the SASP; (7) tessellate the matrix into cells, with each cell represented by a cell "feature"; (8) (re)format the cell features as entries or components of a vector; (9) (optionally) normalize the vector entries; (10) receive the vector entries, for each time-shifted version of the SASP in a trained neural network classifier, and identify a word from a database that provides a best match to an activation function value corresponding to each time-shifted version of the SASP, (11) accumulate a point for each best match; and (12) identify a word, if any, with the highest point count as the best match to a word corresponding to the received SASP.

FIG. **5** is a high level flow chart of a word recognition procedure that uses the results of the training procedure shown in FIG. **4**. In step **51**, A sub-audible signal pattern (SASP) representing a sample of a "new" (unknown) word (referred to as number q') is received and optionally rectified.

10

A sequence of sample values is received at the selected rate used in FIG. **4**. A sample thresholding operation is performed to determine where, in the sequence, the sub-audible speech pattern (SASP) begins. A sequence of J time-shifted, partially overlapping windows, numbered $j=1,\ldots,J$ ($J\geq2$), is formed from the signal representing the new word, with consecutive start times displaced by multiples of a selected displacement time such as $\Delta t(displ)=0-\Delta t(win)/2$.

In step **52**, an SPT operation is performed on the new SASP over the window length $\Delta t(win)$, to provide a first spectrum for the new word for each of the windowed samples. In step **53**, the matrix entries are tessellated or decomposed into the same cells that were used for each word in step **43** of FIG. **4**. In step **64**, each cell representative value or feature in the tessellated matrix is optionally normalized. In step **55**, the cell representative values are arranged as a vector V' having vector entries v'_k ($k=1,\ldots,K$) or other suitable entity for subsequent processing. In step **56**, the first and second reference sets of weight coefficients, $\{w_{1,k,h}(q;ref)\}_k$ and $\{w_{2,h,g}(q;ref)\}_h$, (or $\{w_{1,k,h}(ref)\}_k$ and $\{w_{2,h,g}(ref)\}_h$) used to compute the activation function reference value $A2\{S2(q;ref)\}_g$ (or $A\{S(ref)\}_g$) for the word number q are used to compute an activation function $A2\{S2'(q';ref)\}_g$, as in Eq. (6).

In step **57**, the system computes differences

$$\Delta2(q,q';j)_g=|A2\{S2'(q';j;ref)\}_g-A(q,ref)_g| \quad (10)$$

for each word (q) in the database, for each time shifted window (j) and for each NN third layer index g. Optionally, in step **58**, only those words (q) in a "reduced" database RDB, for which

$$\Delta2(q;q';j)_g\leq\epsilon(thr;2)$$

is satisfied, are considered in accumulating points in step **49**, where $\epsilon(thr;2)$ is a selected second threshold error, preferably in a range 0.01 and below. Optionally $\epsilon(thr;1)=\epsilon(thr;2)$, but this is not required.

In step **59**, for each time-shifted window (numbered $j=1,\ldots,J$), each word (q) in the database (or in the reduced database RDB) that provides the smallest value $\Delta2(q;q';j)_g$, among the set of values computed in Eq. (11), is given one point or vote. In step **60**, the word (q) in the database with the largest number of points is interpreted as the unknown word (q') that was received. Optionally, the point(s) accumulated according to the minimum value of $\Delta2(q;q';j)_g$ can be weighted, for example, by multiplying the number 1 by a weight function $WF\{\Delta2(q;q';j)_g\}$ that is monotonically decreasing as the argument $\Delta2(q;q';j)_g$ increases. Two examples of suitable weighting functions are

$$WF(s)=a+b\cdot\exp[-\alpha s], \quad (12A)$$

$$WF(s)=\{c-d\cdot(s)^\beta\}^e, \quad (12B)$$

where a, b, c, α and β and the product $d\cdot e$ are non-negative numbers, not all 0. If two or more words (e.g., q1 and q2) in the database have substantially the same largest point accumulation, the system optionally interprets this condition as indicating that no clearly-best match to the unknown word (q') is available, in step **61**.

FIG. **6** sets forth in more detail a first embodiment for a thresholding operation for step **41** in FIG. **4**. In step **71**, two or more moving averages of consecutive sequences of H1 sampled values and H2 sampled values are formed (H1<H2), where, for example, H1=10 and H2=20 is a suitable choice. Initially, the sample amplitudes and both moving averages are substantially 0, except for the presence of noise. As the system encounters the beginning of a sub-audible speech pattern (SASP), the shorter H1-sample will rise before the longer

373

11

H2-sample rises, when applied to consecutive sample runs with the same starting point. In step **72**, the system determines if the moving average of the H1-samples is at least a multiple μ of the moving average of the H2-samples, where μ is a selected ratio $\geqq 1$. If the answer to the query in step **62** is "no," the system returns to step **71** and continues to receive samples and to form the two moving averages. If the answer to the query in step **72** is "yes," the system infers that an SASP is present and that an "SASP threshold" has been crossed; and the system begins to divide succeeding time intervals into epochs, in step **73**. Other methods of determining when an SASP threshold has been crossed can also be used here.

In step **74** of FIG. **6**, a set of signal samples is received, preferably as a stream of data, and the magnitude or absolute value of each SASP signal sample is formed (optional). In step **75**, a consecutive sequence CS of the signal samples is formed within an event window, preferably of length $\Delta t(win)=1-4$ sec. In step **76** the system creates a new sequence TSCS of time shifted consecutive sequences, with the beginning of each TSCS being shifted by a selected time delay amount $\Delta t(displ)$ relative to the immediately preceding TSCS. Each TSCS will be processed and classified by a neural network classifier. The number of (above-threshold, consecutive) TSCSs may be used as a parameter in the comparisons in FIG. **4**. The system then proceeds to step **42** of FIG. **4** and continues.

FIG. **7** illustrates a dynamic threshold adjustment procedure, relying in one implementation on a Bollinger band, that may be used in step **41**. In step **81**, a sequence of T amplitudes "a" of the signal are received and stored. In step **82**, a mean (μ) and standard deviation (σ) are computed for the stored sequence. In step **83**, the system determines if the magnitude of the difference $|u-\mu|$ is at least equal to $L\cdot\sigma$ for at least one amplitude u in the stored sequence, where L is a selected positive number (e.g., $L=4-10$). If the answer to the query in step **83** is "no", the system replaces the stored sequence by a new sequence (e.g., shifted by one sample value), in step **84**, and returns to step **82**; no threshold has yet been crossed in this situation. If the answer to the query in step **83** is "yes", a threshold has been crossed within the stored sequence and a position representing the beginning of the word can be identified, in step **85**.

FIG. **8** is a flow chart providing more detail on step **42** in FIG. **4**, where a Fourier transform is used for the SPT operation In step **91**, the data stream is optionally reformatted into a sequence of columns (or into rows) of signal samples, with each column (or row) corresponding to a TSCS, according to the format required for computer analysis. In step **92**, a Hanning filter is optionally applied to each STFT window. In step **93**, an SPT operation is performed for each row of (filtered) signal samples. The particular SPT used may be a conventional Fourier transform (applied to a window of finite width), a dual wave tree wavelet transform, a Daubechie transform, a Hartley transform, a moving average with uniform or nonuniform weights, or similar transforms. The particular choice will depend upon the known characteristics of the data received for analysis. Preferably, the SPT of the signal sample sequences will provide real and imaginary components that can be combined and processed as appropriate. In step **94**, the system forms a selected combination of real and imaginary components of the (filtered and transformed) signal samples in each row. In step **85**, the columns (or rows) are combined, end-to-end, to provide a spectrogram for each (time-overlapped) window.

FIG. **9** is a flow chart providing more detail on step **43** in FIG. **4**, according to a first embodiment for tessellation of the matrix M. In step **101**, the entries within the matrix M are

decomposed into non-overlapping, rectangularly-shaped cells of one or more selected sizes (e.g., 2×3 or 5×5 or 10×7) so that every entry belongs to precisely one cell. Cells adjacent to a boundary of the matrix M may have a different (residual) size. In step **102**, a first order statistical coefficient m_1 (e.g., arithmetic mean, median, mode or largest value) is computed for, and associated with, each cell, representing an average magnitude or other feature for the entries within the cell. A second order statistical coefficient m_2 (e.g., standard deviation) is optionally computed for each cell. Here, the individual values within each cell may be substantially different so that the first order coefficient m_1 associated with a given cell may not be very representative of the individual entries. However, the cells in this embodiment are of fixed size, which is useful in some of the following computations. At one extreme, each cell may be a single entry in the matrix M.

FIG. **10** is a flow chart of an alternative embodiment for tessellation of the matrix M (step **43** in FIG. **4**). In step **111**, the matrix entries are tentatively aggregated into "pre-cells," with each pre-cell initially being a single entry and having a second order statistical coefficient m_2 of 0. Consider a general pre-cell, such as a rectangular set E of entries, having a selected first order statistical coefficient m_1 (arithmetic mean or median or mode) and having a second order statistical coefficient m_2 no larger than a selected positive threshold value $\sigma(thr)$. In step **112**, an expanded pre-cell set E', having one more row or one more column than E, is formed, and statistical coefficients m (E') and m_2(E') are computed for this pre-cell E'. In step **113**, m_2(E') is compared with the threshold value $\sigma(thr)$. If the coefficient m_2(E') for the expanded set E' is no larger than the threshold value $\sigma(thr)$, the pre-cell is redefined, in step **114**, to include the expanded set E', and the system returns to step **112**. The redefined set E' is further expanded in step **115** by one row or one column to form a new set E", and the system returns to step **112**. If m_2(E') is larger than the threshold $\sigma(thr)$, the expanded set E' is rejected, the pre-cell includes the set E but not this particular expanded set E', and the system returns to step **112**. However, another expanded set can be formed from E, by adding a different row or column, and the coefficient m_2 for this new expanded set can be computed and compared with $\sigma(thr)$. At some level, the system identifies a rectangular or other shape set $\hat{E}$ of maximum size whose coefficient $m_2(\hat{E})$ is no larger than the threshold value $\sigma(thr)$, and this maximum size set becomes a cell. This process is repeated until every entry in a cell is "similar" to every other entry in that cell, as measured by the threshold value $\sigma(thr)$. The number of matrix entries has been reduced to a smaller number of cells. The cells may be rectangular but do not necessarily have the same size. In this approach, the entries in a cell are represented by the coefficient m_1 for that cell, but the cell size is determined by the adjacent entries for which $m_2(E)\leqq\sigma(thr)$.so that the entries may be more "similar" to each other.

One practical approach for neural network training is back-propagation of errors, together with conjugate gradient analysis to identify global minima. This approach is discussed, for example, by T. Masters in *Practical Neural Network Recipes in C++*, Morgan Kaufman Publ., 1993, pp. 102-111.

With reference to step **50** in FIG. **4** in the preceding, a conjugate gradient algorithm with trust region (to limit the extension in any direction in coordinate space) is applied to the error term sum, $\epsilon(q)$ with q fixed, to determine an extremum point (minimum) for the received cell representatives.

13

For example, the basic Fletcher-Reeves algorithm can be utilized, wherein a direction of steepest descent

$$p_0 = -g_0 \qquad (13)$$

for the surface or function is first identified; a line search is performed to estimate the optimal distance to be moved along the current search direction (p_k)

$$x_{k+1} = x_k + \alpha_k p_k; \qquad (14)$$

and a conjugate direction

$$p_k = g_k + \beta_k p_{k-1}, \qquad (15)$$

is determined for the new search direction. For the Fletcher-Reeves update, the parameter β_k is chosen according to

$$\beta_k = g_k \cdot g_k / \{g_{k-1} \cdot g_{k-1}\}. \qquad (16)$$

For the Polak-Ribiere update, the parameter β_k is chosen according to

$$\beta_k = \Delta g_{k-1} \cdot g_k / \{g_{k-1} \cdot g_{k-1}\}, \qquad (17)$$

where $\Delta g_{k-1} = g_{k-1} - g_{k-2}$ is the preceding change in the direction of steepest descent. In any conjugate gradient approach, it is preferable to periodically reset the search direction to the steepest descent gradient. In a particular approach developed by Powell and Beale, resetting occurs when little orthogonality remains between the present gradient and the preceding gradient; the corresponding test is whether the inequality

$$|g_{k-1} \cdot g_k| \geq 0.2 |g_k|^2. \qquad (18)$$

is satisfied. Other variations on the corresponding algorithms can also be used here.

What is claimed is:

1. A method for training and using a system to identify a sub-audible signal formed by a source of sub-audible sounds, the method comprising providing a computer that is programmed to execute, and does execute, the following actions::

(1) receiving R signal sequences, numbered r=1, . . . , R (R≧2), with each sequence comprising an instance of a sub-audible speech pattern ("SASP"), uttered by a user, and each SASP including at least one word drawn from a selected database of Q words, numbered q=1, . . . , Q with Q≧2;

(2) estimating where each of the R SASPs begins and ends in the sequences;

for each of the signal sequences, numbered r=1, . . . , R:

(3) providing signal values of a received signal, number r, within a temporal window having a selected window width $\Delta t(win)$; and

(4) transforming each of the R SASPs, using a Signal Processing Transform ("SPT") operation to obtain an SPT value that is expressed in terms of at least first and second transform parameters comprising at least a signal frequency and a signal energy associated with the SASP;

(5) providing a first matrix M with first matrix entries equal to the SPT values for the R SASPs, ordered according to the at least first and second transform parameters along a first matrix axis and along a second matrix axis, respectively, of the matrix M;

(6) tessellating the matrix M into a sequence of exhaustive and mutually exclusive cells of matrix entries, referred to as M-cells, with each M-cell containing a collection of contiguous matrix entries, where each M-cell is characterized according to at least one selected M-cell criterion;

(7) providing, for each M-cell, an M-cell representative value, depending upon at least one of the first matrix entries within the M cell;

(8) formatting the M-cell representative values as a vector V with vector entry values $v_k(q;r)$, numbered k=1, . . . , K (K≧2);

(9) analyzing the vector entry values $v_k(q;r)$ using a neural net classifier, having a neural net architecture, and a sequence of estimated weight coefficient values associated with at least one of the neural net classifier layers, where the neural net classifier provides a sequence of output values dependent upon the weight coefficient values and upon the vector entry values $v_k(q; r)$;

(10) receiving the vector entries $v_k(q;r)$ and forming a first sum

$$S1(q;r)_h = \Sigma_k W_{1,k,h}(q;r) \cdot v_k(q;r),$$

where $\{w_{1,k,h}(q;r)\} \cdot$ is a first selected set of adjustable weight coefficients that are estimated by a neural net procedure;

(11) forming a first activation function $A1\{S1(q;r)_h\}$, that is monotonically increasing as the value $S1(q;r)_h$ increases;

(12) forming a second sum

$$S2(q;r)_g = \Sigma_h w_{2,h,g}(q;r) \cdot A1\{S1(q;r)_h\} \ (g=1, . . . , G; G≧1),$$

where $w_{2,h,g}(q;r) \cdot$ is a second selected set of adjustable weight coefficients that are estimated by the neural net procedure;

(13) forming a second activation function $A2\{S2(q;r)_g\}$ that depends upon the second sum $S2(q;r)$, that is monotonically increasing as the value $S2(q;r)$ increases;

(14) providing a set of reference output values $\{A(q; ref)_g\}$ as an approximation for the sum $A2\{S2(q,r)_g\}$ for the R instances of the SASP;

(15) forming a difference $\Delta 1(q) = (1/R \cdot G) \ \Sigma_{r,g} |A2 \{S2(q;r)_g\} - A](q; ref)_g|^{p1}$, where p1 is a selected positive exponent;

(16) comparing the difference $\Delta 1(q)$ with a selected threshold value $\epsilon(thr;1)$;

(17) when $\Delta 1(q)[[>]]$ is greater than $\epsilon(thr;1)$, adjusting at least one of the weight coefficients $w_{1,k,h}(q;r)$ and the weight coefficients $w_{2,h,g}(q;r)$, returning to step (10), and repeating the procedures of steps (10)-(16); and

(18) when $\Delta 1(q)$ is no greater than $\epsilon(thr;1)$, interpreting this condition as indicating that at least one of an optimum first set of weight coefficients $\{w_{1,k,h}(q;r;opt)\}$ and an optimum second set of weight coefficients $\{w_{2,h,g}(q;r; opt)\}$ has been obtained, and using the at least one of the first set and second set of optimum weight coefficients to receive and process a new SASP signal and to estimate whether the received new SASP signal corresponds to a reference word or reference phrase in the selected database.

2. The method of claim 1, wherein said computer is further programmed to execute, and does execute, said step (18) by a procedure comprising the following actions:

(19) receiving a new sub-audible speech pattern SASP signal uttered by said user containing an instance of at least one unknown word, referred to as a "new" word, indexed with an index q' that may be in said database of Q;

(20) estimating where the new word begins and ends in the new SASP

(21) providing signal values for the new SASP within each of said temporal windows, numbered j=1, . . . , J with J≧2, that are shifted in time relative to each other by selected multiples of a selected displacement time $\Delta t(displ)$;

15

(22) for the signal values within each of the time-shifted windows, numbered j=1, ... , J:

(23) transforming each of the signal values of the new SASP, using said Signal Processing Transform (SPT) operation to obtain new SASP SPT values with said at least first and second transform SPT values;

(24) providing a second matrix M' with second matrix entries equal to the new SASP SPT values, ordered according to said at least first and second transform parameters along a first and second matrix axes, respectively, of the second matrix M';

(25) tessellating the second matrix M' into a sequence of exhaustive and mutually exclusive M'-cells that correspond to said M-cells for said tessellated matrix M, where each M'-cell is characterized according to at least one selected M'-cell criterion;

(26) providing, for each M'-cell in the second matrix M', a M'-cell representative value depending upon at least one of the second matrix entries within the M'-cell;

(27) formatting the M'-cell representative values as a vector V' with vector entry values where $v'_k(q';r)$ refers to new word or phrase index (k=1, ... , K);

(28) applying said neural net classifier and said reference set of said optimum first set and said optimum second set of weight coefficients to compute said neural net classifier output values for each of the time-shifted sequences of the new SASP;

(29) receiving the vector entries $v'_k(q;r)$ and forming a first sum

$$S1'(q';q'';r)_h = \Sigma_k w'_{1,k,h}(q'';r;opt) \cdot v'_k(q';r),$$

where weight coefficients $w'_{1,k,h}(q'';r;opt)$ are said optimized first weight values coefficients found for a candidate word or phrase (q'') in the database;

(30) forming a first new word activation function $A1'\{S1'(q';q'';r)_h\}$ that depends upon the first sum $S1'(q';q'';r)_h$;

(31) forming a second sum

$$S2'(q';q'';r)_g = \Sigma_h w'_{2,h,g}(q'';ropt) \cdot A1'\{S1'(q';q'';r)_h\}$$
$$(g=1,....G; G\geqq1),$$

where weight coefficients $w'_{2,h,g}(q'';r) \cdot$ are said optimized second weight coefficients found for a candidate word or phrase (q'') in the database;

(32) forming a second new word activation function $A2'\{S2'(q';q'';)_g\}$ that depends upon the second sum $S2'(q';q'';r)_h$;

(33) providing a set of reference output values $\{A'(q'';ref)_g\}$ associated with each candidate word or phrase (q'') in the database;

(34) forming a comparison difference

$$\Delta1'(q'';q')=(1/R \cdot G)\Sigma_{r,g}|A2'\{S2'(q';q'';r)_g\} - A'(q'';ref)_g|^{p2},$$

where p2 is a selected positive exponent;

(35) comparing the difference $\Delta1(q'';q')$ with a selected threshold value $\epsilon(thr;2)$;

(36) when the difference $\Delta1(q'';q')$ is greater than $\epsilon(thr;2)$, returning to step (28) and repeating the procedures of steps (28)-(35) with another candidate word or phrase (q'') in the database; and

(37) when $\Delta1(q'';q')$ is no greater than $\epsilon(thr;2)$, interpreting this condition as indicating that the present candidate word or phrase (q'') is the "new" word (q'), and indicating that the present candidate word or phrase q'' is likely to be the "new" word q'.

3. The method of claim **2**, wherein said computer is further programmed to execute, and does execute, the following actions:

replacing at least one of said matrix cell features by a normalized feature for each of said cells corresponding to said matrix M.

4. The method of claim **2**, wherein said computer is further programmed to execute, and does execute, the following actions:

when at least two distinct words, number q1 and q2, in said database satisfy $\Delta1'(q';q''=q1)\approx\Delta1'(q';q''=q2)$, and $\Delta1'(q';q1)$ and $\Delta1'(q';q2)$ are substantially less than $\Delta1'(q'q'')$ for any word $q''\neq q1$ and $q''\neq q2$ in said database, and interpreting this condition as indicating that said new word included in said new SASP cannot be unambiguously identified.

5. The method of claim **2**, wherein said computer is further programmed to execute, and does execute, the following actions:

choosing said weighting for said weighted points from the group of weighting consisting of (i) substantially uniform weighting and (ii) a weighting that decreases monotonically as said magnitude of said comparison difference increases.

6. The method of claim **2**, wherein said computer is further programmed to execute, and does execute, the following actions:

determining said reference set of said weight coefficients to be independent of said word number q in said database.

7. The method of claim **2**, wherein said computer is further programmed to execute, and does execute, the following actions:

determining said reference set of said weight coefficients so that at least one reference setnof said weight coefficients so that at least one reference set weight coefficient for a first selected word number q1 in said database differs from a corresponding reference set weight coefficient for a second selected word number q2 in said database.

8. The method of claim **2**, wherein said computer is further programmed to execute, and does execute, the following actions:

selecting said window width $\Delta t(win)$ in a range 1-4 sec.

9. The method of claim **2**, wherein said computer is further programmed to execute, and does execute, the following actions:

selecting each of said matrix cells to be rectangularity shaped.

10. The method of claim **9**, wherein said computer is further programmed to execute, and does execute, the following actions:

selecting at least two of said matrix cells to have different sizes.

11. The method of claim **2**, wherein said computer is further programmed to execute, and does execute, the following actions:

choosing said SPT operations from the group of SPT operations consisting of (i) a windowed short time interval Fourier Transform (STFT); (ii) discrete wavelets (DWTs) and continuous wavelets (CWTs) using Daubechies 5 and 7 bases; (iii) dual tree wavelets (DTWTs) with a near sym_a 5,7 tap filter and a Q-shift 14,14 tap filter; (iv) Hartley Transform; (v) Linear Predictive Coding (LPC) coefficients; (vi) a moving average of a selected number of said sample values with uniform weighting; and (vii) a moving average of a selected number of said sample values with non-uniform weighting.

17

12. The method of claim **2**, wherein said computer is further programmed to execute, and does execute, the following actions:

selecting said database to include at least one of the words "stop", "go", "left", "right", "alpha", "omega", "one", "two", "three", "four", "five", "six", "seven", "eight", "nine" and "ten".

13. The method of claim **2**, wherein said computer is further programmed to execute, and does execrute, the following actions:

selecting said error threshold number to lie in a range $e(thr;1) \leqq 0.01$.

14. The method of claim **2**, wherein said computer is further programmed to execute, and does execute, the following actions:

applying a backpropagation of error method in said neural net classifier analysis of said features of said cells of said matrix M.

15. A method for training and using a system to identify a sub-audible signal formed by a source of sub-audible sounds, the method comprising providing a computer that is programmed to execute, and does execute, the following actions:

(1) receiving R signal sequences, numbered r=1, . . . , R(R$\geqq$2), with each sequence comprising an instance of a specified sub-audible speech pattern ("SASP"), uttered by the user, and each SASP including at least one word drawn from a selected database of Q words, numbered q=1, . . . , Q (Q$\geqq$2);

(2) estimating where each SASP begins and ends for each of the signal sequences;

(3) providing signal values of the received signal, number r, within a temporal window having a selected window width $\Delta t(win)$;

(4) transforming each of the R SASPs, using an Signal Processing Transform ("SPT") operation to obtain an SPT value that is expressed in terms of at least one transform parameter having a sequence of parameter values, including a signal frequency an a signal energy associated with the SASP;

(5) providing a first matrix M with first matrix entries equal to the SPT values for the R SASPs, ordered according to each of the at least first and second transform parameters along a first matrix axis and along a second matrix axis, respectively of the matrix M;

(6) tessellating the matrix M into a sequence of exhaustive and mutually exclusive, cells of the matrix entries, referred to as M-cells, with each M-cell containing a collection of contiguous matrix entries, where each M-cell is characterized according to at least one selected M-cell criterion;

(7) providing, for each M-cell, an M-cell representative value depending upon at least one of the first matrix entries within the M-cell;

(8) formatting the cell representative values as a vector V with vector entry values $v_k(q;r)$ numbered k=1, . . . , K (K$\geqq$2);

(9) analyzing the vector entry values $v_k(q;r)$ using a neural net classifier, having a neural net architecture with at least one neural net hidden layer, and a sequence of estimated weight coefficient values $w_k(q,r)$ associated with that at least one neural net hidden layer, where the neural net classifier provides a sequence of neural net output values A(q,r), equal to a sum over the index k of each of the vector entry values $v_k(q,r)$ multiplied by a corresponding weight coefficient value $w_k(q,r)$;

18

(10) providing a set of neural net reference output values {A(q; ref)} .as an approximation for the sum A(q,r) for the R instances of the SASP (r=1, . . . , R);

(11) forming a difference $\Delta(q) = \Sigma_r |A(q;r)\} \ A(q;ref)|^p$, where p is a selected positive exponent

(12) comparing the difference $\Delta(q)$ with a first threshold value $\epsilon(thr;1)$;

(13) when $\Delta(q)$ is greater than a first positive threshold value $\epsilon(thr;1)$, adjusting at least one of the weight coefficients $w_k(q;r)$, returning to step (9), and repeating the procedures of steps (9)-(12); and

(14) when $\Delta(q)$ is no greater than $\epsilon(thr;1)$, interpreting this condition as indicating that at least one of an optimum set of weight coefficients $\{w_k(q;r;opt)\}$ has been obtained, and using the set of optimum weight coefficients to receive and process a new SASP signal and to estimate whether the received new SASP signal corresponds to a reference word or reference phrase in the selected database.

16. The method of claim **15** wherein said computer is further programmed to execute, and does execute, the following actions:

choosing said SPT operations from a group of SPT operations consisting of (i) a windowed short time interval Fourier Transform (STFT); (ii) discrete wavelets (DWTs) and continuous wavelets (CWTs) using Daubechies 5 and 7 bases; (iii) dual tree wavelets (DTWTs) with a near sym_a 5,7 tap filter and a Q-shift 14,14 tap filter; (iv) Hartley Transform; (v) Linear Predictive Coding (LPC) coefficients;

(vi) a moving average of a selected number of said sample values with uniform weighting; and (vii) a moving average of a selected number of said sample values with non-uniform weighting.

17. The method of claim **15**, wherein said computer is further programmed to execute, and does execute, the following actions:

selecting at least first and second of said matrix cells to have a cell dimension, measured along a corresponding matrix axis of said matrix M, that is different for the first cell and for the second cell.

18. The method of claim **15**, wherein said computer is further programmed to execute, and does execute, the following actions:

(15) receiving a new sub-audible speech pattern SASP1 uttered by said user, comprising an instance of at least one unknown word, referred to as a "new" word, identified with an index q1, that may be but is not necessarily drawn from said database of Q words;

(16) estimating where the new word begins and ends in the new SASP1;

(17) providing signal values of the received SASP1 within each of said temporal windows;

(18) transforming each of the signal values of the new SASP1, using said Signal Processing Transform (SPT) operation to obtain new SASP1 SPT values, where each SASP1 SPT value is expressed in terms of said at least first and second transform parameters, including a signal frequency and a signal energy associated with the SASP1;

(19) providing a second matrix M1 with second matrix entries equal to SPT values for the SASP1, ordered according to each of said at least first and second transform parameters along first and second matrix axes of the second matrix M1;

(20) tessellating the matrix M1 into a sequence of exhaustive and mutually exclusive M1-cells that correspond to

said sequence of said M-cells for said matrix M where each M1-cell is characterized according to said or more cell criteria for said M-cells;

(21) providing, for each M1-cell, an M1-cell representative value depending upon at least one of the second matrix entry values within the M1-cell;

(22) formatting the M1-cell representative values as a vector V1 with vector entries $v1_k(q1)$, numbered k=1, . . . , K (K$\geq$2), where q1 refers to said index associated with said new word;

(23) analyzing the vector entry values $v1_k(q1)$ using said neural net classifier, having said neural net architecture with said at least one neural net hidden layer, and a sequence $w_k(q1,opt)$ of said optimum weight coefficients $w_k(q1,r1;opt)$, associated with said at least one neural net hidden layer, and averaged over said R instances (r1=1, . . . , R) of said SASP uttered by said user in claim **15**,

(24) providing a neural net output value A1(q1), equal to a sum over the index k of each of the vector entry values $v1_k(q1)$ multiplied by the corresponding averaged optimum weight coefficient value $w_k(q1,opt)$;

20

(25) providing a set of neural net reference output values {A1(q'; ref)} as an approximation for the sum A1(q1) for the R1 instances of the SASP1, where q' is one of said indices corresponding to said database of Q words;

(26) forming a comparison difference $\Delta1(q1,q')=|A1(q1)\} —A(q'; ref)|^p$, where said quantities A1(q';ref) and p are determined as in claim **15**;

(27) comparing the difference $\Delta1(q1,q')$ with said first threshold value $\epsilon(thr;1)$.

(28) when $\Delta1(q1,q')$ is greater than said first threshold value $\epsilon(thr;1)$, interpreting this condition as indicating that said sub-audible speech pattern SASP1 received is not a sub-audible speech pattern from said database with the corresponding number q1=q'; and

(29) when $\Delta1(q1,q')$ is no greater than $\epsilon(thr;1)$, interpreting this condition as indicating that said sub-audible speech pattern SASP1 received is likely to be a sub-audible speech pattern from said database, indexed by q', with the corresponding index q1.

*   *   *   *   *

United States Patent [19]

Dellacorte

[11] **Patent Number:** 6,007,068

[45] **Date of Patent:** Dec. 28, 1999

[54] **DYNAMIC FACE SEAL ARRANGEMENT**

[75] Inventor: **Christopher Dellacorte**, Medina, Ohio

[73] Assignee: **US Government as represented by the Administrator of NASA Headquarters**, Washington, D.C.

[21] Appl. No.: **08/753,346**

[22] Filed: **Nov. 25, 1996**

[51] Int. Cl.[6] **F16J 15/34**

[52] U.S. Cl. .... **277/82**; 277/81 R; 277/85; 277/96.2

[58] Field of Search .... 277/81 R, 82, 277/85, 88, 91, 96.2

[56] **References Cited**

U.S. PATENT DOCUMENTS

1,964,063	6/1934	Kagi	277/88
1,983,855	12/1934	Jenkins	277/88
1,998,790	9/1935	Potter	277/88
2,595,926	5/1952	Chambers, Jr.	277/91
2,708,124	5/1955	Robb	277/82
3,356,378	12/1967	Tracy	277/88
3,554,559	1/1971	Dahlheimer .	
3,751,046	8/1973	Goluber et al.	277/88
4,094,514	6/1978	Johnson .	
4,103,904	8/1978	Tankus .	
4,323,255	4/1982	Wiese .	
4,502,694	3/1985	Uhrner .	
4,591,167	5/1986	Vossieck et al. .	
4,648,605	3/1987	Marsi .	
4,728,448	3/1988	Sliney	252/12.2
4,836,560	6/1989	Haberberger .	
4,872,517	10/1989	Shaw et al. .	
5,188,377	2/1993	Drumm .	

Primary Examiner—Daniel G. DePumpo
Attorney, Agent, or Firm—Kent N. Stone; Susan Reinecke

[57] **ABSTRACT**

A radial face seal arrangement is disclosed comprising a stationary seal ring that is spring loaded against a seal seat affixed to a rotating shaft. The radial face seal arrangement further comprises an arrangement that not only allows for preloading of the stationary seal ring relative to the seal seat, but also provides for dampening yielding a dynamic sealing response for the radial face seal arrangement. The overall seal system, especially regarding the selection of the material for the stationary seal ring, is designed to operate over a wide temperature range from below ambient up to 900° C.

24 Claims, 2 Drawing Sheets

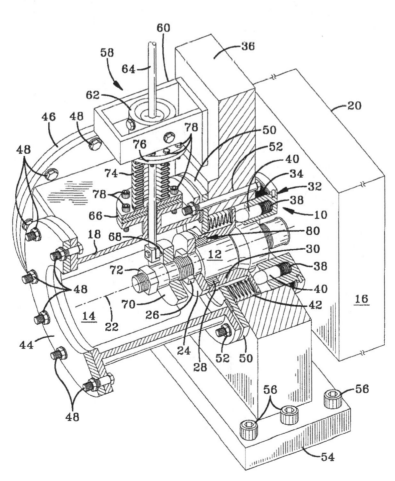

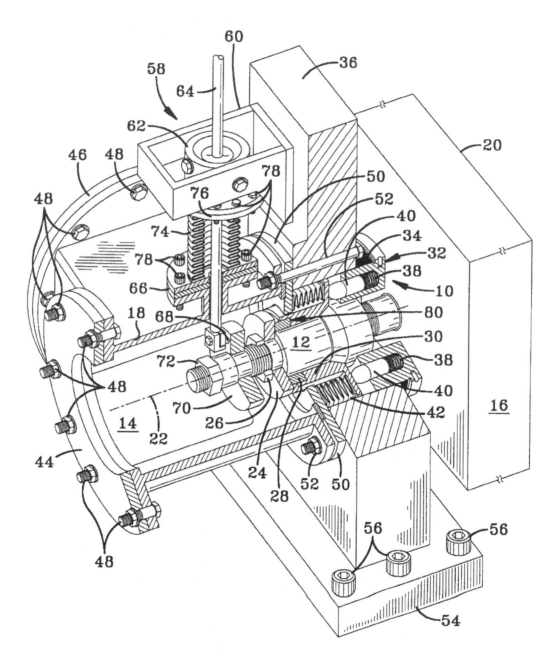

FIG—1

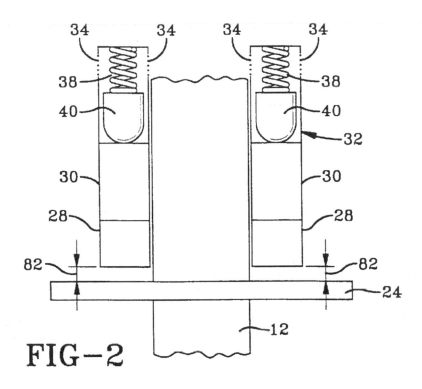

FIG-2

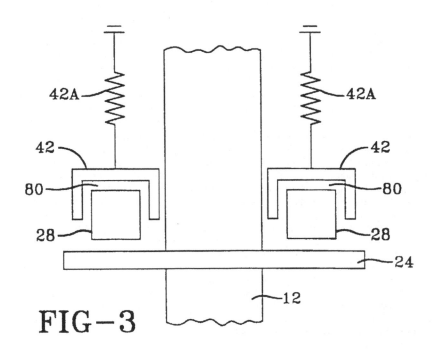

FIG-3

1

DYNAMIC FACE SEAL ARRANGEMENT

ORIGIN OF THE INVENTION

The invention described herein was made by an employee of the U.S. Government and may be manufactured and used by or for the Government for governmental purposes without the payment of any royalties thereon or therefor.

TECHNICAL FIELD

This invention relates to face seals and arrangements thereof for providing a fluid seal around a rotating shaft operating in inert, oxidizing, or reducing environments, such as argon, air, and hydrogen. The invention is particularly directed to a radial face seal arrangement located between high pressure and low pressure regions for sealing thereof over a wide range of temperatures. The invention is specifically concerned with such face seal arrangements that operate between about 25° C. to about 900° C. and seal a region where the rotating shaft passes through a housing.

Face-type fluid seals generally comprise a non-rotating, stationary or stator seal and a rotor ring serving as a seal seat and having means so as to rotate with a shaft. The seal seat has a face opposing that of the stator seal. The opposing faces extend radially outward from the periphery of the shaft and provide a seal typically between low pressure and high pressure regions each containing a fluid. Radial face seals and arrangements thereof operate with extremely small gaps between the stator seal and the opposing face of the rotating seal seat.

Prior art radial face seals and arrangements thereof have removable carbon face seals which are utilized for inert or reducing gas sealing applications. When operated in an oxidative environment to prevent carbon degradation, the seals are commonly removed and sealing is provided by clearance or labyrinth type seals. It is desired that face seals and their related arrangements be provided without the need to remove the seal to compensate for a changing environment.

Other types of face seals and arrangements thereof, such as non-contact labyrinth seals, are known in the art; however, such seals generally exhibit high leakage rates and have inadequate tolerances for thermal gradients and thermal expansions which commonly accompany high temperature applications thereof. It is desired that face seals and arrangements be provided that withstand high temperatures while having low, or even no leakage.

Hermetic face seals and arrangements thereof utilized for ferrofluid applications are also known. However, these seals encounter problems caused by high temperature applications and by being exposed to high magnetic fluxes.

The disadvantages of prior art devices may be generally summarized as including limited temperature capability, inability to tolerate high thermal growth, i.e., expansion of related elements, inability to withstand wide ranges of atmospheres, e.g., inert, oxidizing or argon, the inability to operate in regions of high magnetic fluxes, the inability to compensate for wear and, finally, the inability to compensate for seal dynamics. It is desired that face seals and their related arrangements be provided that do not suffer from these prior art disadvantages and drawbacks.

It is, therefore, an object of the present invention to provide a sealing arrangement successfully operable over a wide temperature range from about 25° C. to about 900° C.

Another object of the invention is to provide for a sealing arrangement having a wide variety of applications covering gases, such as inert, oxidizing or argon.

2

Still another object of the invention is to provide a seal arrangement that automatically compensates for thermal growth and wear while also providing for damping so as to compensate for seal dynamics.

Still further, it is another object of the invention to provide a seal arrangement having manual control means that compensates for thermal growth and wear while providing for damping so as to adjust for seal dynamics.

BACKGROUND ART

U.S. Pat. No. 3,554,559 to Dahlheimer describes a face seal arrangement for use on a rotating shaft which utilizes a sealing bellows in combination with a spring biasing arrangement. The seal has a stationary component which includes an annular seal seat. A rotating portion includes a spring bias seal washer and a bellows which mates with the stationary seat.

U.S. Pat. No. 4,094,514 to Johnson is directed to a sealing mechanism for use on a rotating shaft. The sealing device is comprised of a ferrous metal alloy material that is selected to provide high strength, wear resistance, and corrosion resistance.

U.S. Pat. No. 4,103,904 to Tankus discloses an elastic bellows used in a seal to provide a positive drive or inherent bias applied against a sealing member.

U.S. Pat. No. 4,323,255 to Wiese discloses a rotating shaft seal which uses springs to urge a seal ring into a central ring.

U.S. Pat. No. 4,502,694 to Uhrner describes a rotating shaft seal which provides primary and secondary sealing by utilizing a spring bias seal to form a primary seal that is forced into engagement with a bellows acting as a secondary seal.

DISCLOSURE OF THE INVENTION

This invention comprises a stationary sealing ring, a seal seat, a spring bias mechanism, and a bellows arrangement. The stationary seal ring serves as a primary seal and is spring biased against the seal seat. The bias spring mechanism is provided with preload characteristics that are adjustable using a threaded collar. The bellows is preferably constructed of a superalloy and is used as a secondary seal to trap leakage from the primary seal formed by the stationary seal ring in cooperation with the seal seat. An important feature of the invention is the use of a self-lubricating material for the stationary seal ring.

BRIEF DESCRIPTION OF THE DRAWINGS

The foregoing, as well as the other objects, features, and advantages of this invention, will become more apparent from the following detailed description when taken in conjunction with the appended figures in which:

FIG. 1 illustrates an axial section view of a radial face seal arrangement constructed in accordance with the present invention.

FIG. 2 is a schematic that illustrates the interrelationship of the primary elements of the radial face seal arrangement of FIG. 1.

FIG. 3 is a schematic that illustrates the interrelationship of the primary (stationary seal ring-seal seat) and secondary (bellows) seals of the radial face seal arrangement of FIG. 1.

DETAILED DESCRIPTION OF THE PREFERRED EMBODIMENTS

With reference to the drawings, wherein the same reference numbers indicate the same elements throughout, there is shown in FIG. **1** a radial face seal arrangement **10** for sealing a region where a rotating shaft, such as **12**, passes through a housing. More particularly, FIG. **1** is shown partially in section to illustrate the radial face seal arrangement **10** which is located between high pressure **14** and low pressure **16** regions respectively contained within chambers **18** and **20**. The shaft **12** rotates about its axis **22** that passes through both chambers **18** and **20**, each of which contains a fluid that provides an oxidizing, inert or reducing environment, e.g., air, argon or hydrogen, and that experiences a temperature spectrum of not less than 25° C. and not more than 900° C.

The radial face seal arrangement **10** comprises a seat seal **24** mounted, via a nut fastener **26**, onto the shaft **12** for rotation therewith. The radial face seal arrangement **10** further comprises a stationary seal ring **28** preferably positioned at one end of a seal ring carrier **30** but may be merged with the carrier to form a one-piece device. The radial face seal arrangement **10** further comprises a collar **32** having threads **34** that mate with complementary threads of a support member **36**. The collar **32** may be manually adjusted so that the devices that it carries, that is, springs **38** and mating push pins **40**, may be moved inward and outward relative to the stationary seal ring **28**. This manual adjustment allows for preloading of the stationary seal ring **28** with respect to the seat seal **24** in a manner as to be more fully described with reference to FIG. **2**.

The preload adjusting collar **32** of FIG. **1** carries springs **38** that preferably cooperates with mating push pins **40** lodged in chambers that are preferably filled with a lubricating grease. A solid lubricant could be used in place of the lubricating grease to facilitate coulomb damping. There are preferably eight (8) springs **38**, eight (8) mating push pins **40**, and eight (8) greased chambers all in correspondence with each other, and all equally spaced apart from each other circumferentially about the preload adjusting collar **32**. The radial face seal arrangement **10** preferably further comprises a bellow **42**.

The high pressure chamber **18** has end cap members **44** and **46** that are separately clamped together by means of fasteners **48** as shown in FIG. **1**. Further, the high pressure chamber **18** has end cap members **50** that are clamped together and attached to the support member **36**, via fastener **52**. The support member **36** is fixed to a plate member **54** via fasteners **56**.

The embodiment of FIG. **1**, illustrates an evaluation configuration **58** which does not form part of the present invention, but rather is included to further describe the possible techniques that may be used to evaluate the practice of the present invention. More particularly, the evaluation configuration **58** is provided for measuring the wear that is anticipated that the stationary seal ring **28** may be encountering. The evaluation configuration **58** has a housing **60** that is affixed to the support member **36** by appropriate means such as spot welding and includes a two (2) axis gimbal **62** which provides the proper orientation for a load/friction force rod **64**. The load/friction force rod **64** passes through a circular bracing arrangement **66** and carries a wear-pin specimen **68** on one of its ends that is in contact with a wear-disk specimen **70** which, in turn, is connected to the shaft **12** by means of a threaded nut fastener **72**.

The evaluation configuration **58** further comprises a shock absorbing member **74** that joins together the circular bracing arrangement **66** and a platform member **76** located at the bottom (as viewed in FIG. **1**) of the housing **60**, wherein all connections for the circular arrangement **66** and the platform

76 are provided by fasteners **78**. As previously mentioned, the evaluation configuration **58** is not considered part of the present invention and, thus, is not to be further described herein. However, the face seal arrangement **10** is of importance to the present invention and includes the primary elements **24**, **28**, **30**, **32**, **38** and **40**.

The seal seat **24** is preferably comprised of a high temperature alloy, sometimes referred to as a superalloy, that may be a nickel-based superalloy, commercially known as Inconel.

The stationary seal ring **28** is comprised of a self-lubricating, friction and wear reducing material comprising about 60–80 by weight metal-bonded chromium carbide, 10–20 by weight soft noble metal, and 10–20 by weight metal fluoride mixture. More particularly, the stationary seal ring **28** preferably comprises a material of about 70 percent by weight metal-bonded chromium carbide, about 15 percent by weight silver, and about 15 percent by weight metal fluoride. The material comprising the stationary seal ring **28** may be that described in U.S. Pat. No. 4,728,448 ('448) of H. E. Sliney, which is herein incorporated by reference. As more fully described in the '448 patent, the composite material forming the stationary seal ring **28** is a self-lubricating and very wear-resistant for use over a wide temperature spectrum from cryogenic temperatures of about 25° C. to about 900° C. in a chemically reactive environment. The stationary seal ring **28** has a face and rear portion, with the face thereof positioned in the direction of the high pressure chamber **14** so as to come into contact with the rear portion of the seat seal **24**. The stationary seal ring has its rear portion in the direction of the low pressure chamber **16**. If desired, the directions of orientation of the face and rear portions of the stationary seal ring **28** may be reversed.

The seal ring carrier **30** is preferably of a high temperature alloy such as Inconel and has one of its ends shaped so as to extend over the rear portion of stationary seal ring **28** in a manner as generally indicated by reference number **80** shown in FIG. **1**. The seal ring carrier **30** has an extending portion on its other end that comes into contact with both the mating push pins **40** and the bellows **42**. The seal ring carrier **30** is connected by appropriate means, such as by spot welding, to the bellows **42**.

The springs **38** have one of their ends fixed in position against the adjustable collar as shown in FIG. **1**, whereas the other end of each of the springs **38** provides an urging force preferably against the corresponding mating push pins **40** which, in turn, urge against the seal ring carrier **30**. The springs **38** are preferably coil springs and formed of a superalloy material, such as that of Inconel. If desired, although not preferred, the springs **38** may be selected to directly contact the seal ring carrier **30** so as to eliminate the need of the mating push pins **40** which are also preferably of a superalloy material, such as Inconel.

The bellows **42** is connected, by appropriate means such as spot welding, between the end cap **50** and the seal ring carrier **30**. The bellows **42** is preferably comprised of a superalloy material, such as Inconel, and operates in a known manner, such as that more fully described in the previously mentioned U.S. Pat. Nos. 3,554,559 and 4,502, 694, both of which are herein incorporated by reference. As will be further described, the bellows **42** is axially arranged along the seal ring carrier **30** so that one of its ends is connected and located in proximity with the rear portion of the stationary seal ring **28** and its other end is connected so that the bellows **42** encloses a defined region and confines any fluid within the boundaries of that defined region.

5

In general, the radial face seal arrangement **10** provides a dynamic seal and keeps fluid on the face of stationary seal ring **28**, that is, the side of the stationary seal ring **28** facing the high pressure chamber **14**, from penetrating the housing or chamber at the region where the rotating shaft **12** passes through the housing, that is, the low pressure chamber **16**. The stationary seal ring **28** is spring loaded against the seal seat **24** which is affixed to rotating shaft **12**. The extent of the spring **38** preloading is adjustable using the threaded collar **32** as is to be more fully described with reference to FIG. **2**. The bellows **42** prevents secondary leakage, that is, fluid leakage at the rear portion of the stationary seal ring **28**. The preload springs **38** act upon the mating push pins **40** sliding in grease so as to provide dynamic seal dampening response. The operation of the radial face seal arrangement **10** may be further described with reference to FIG. **2**.

FIG. **2** is a schematic illustrating the interrelationship between the primary elements **24**, **28**, **30**, **32**, and **38**, and preferably element **40**, of the radial face seal arrangement **10**. As seen in FIG. **2**, the adjustable collar **32** carries the springs **38** and the mating push pins **40**. The collar **32**, by means of its threads **34**, may be moved so as to adjust a gap **82** located between the seal seat **24** that rotates with the axial shaft member **12** and the stationary seal ring **28**. The adjustable collar **32**, in cooperation with the springs **38** and the mating pins **40** as well as with the preferred seal ring carrier **30**, provides means for urging the stationary seal ring **28** into engagement with the metal seal seat **24**. The adjustment of the collar **32** is commonly referred to as a preloading condition in which the threaded collar **32** is used for changing the position of the springs **38** and preferably push pins **40** relative to the stationary seal ring **28** which, in turn, changes the preloading of the stationary seal ring **28** with respect to the seal seat **24**, that is, the adjustment establishes the gap **82**.

In operation, the adjustable collar **32** is positioned to establish a preload condition, wherein the mating push pins **40** apply urging force against the seal ring carrier **30** which, in turn, provides an urging force against the stationary seal ring **28** so as to adjust the gap **82** to any desired distance. The dynamic response of the arrangement shown in FIG. **2**, is provided by the mating push pins **40** moving in their lubricating grease filled chamber so that any sudden movement of the stationary seal ring **28** relative to the seal seat **24** is absorbed or dampened by the mating push pins **40** sliding in the lubricating grease within their respective chambers.

As previously described, the composition of the stationary seal ring **28** allows the stationary seal ring **28** to successfully operate in a temperature spectrum from about 25° to 900° C. and this capability, in combination with the adjustable collar **32**, springs **38** and preferably the mating pins **40**, allows the radial face seal arrangement **10** to also operate successfully in the temperature spectrum of at least from 25° C. to 900° C.

It should now be appreciated that the practice of the present invention provides for a radial face seal arrangement **10** having the stationary seal ring **28** that allows it to operate in various fluid environments and provides the capability of successfully withstanding temperatures from 25° C. to about 900° C. The radial face seal arrangement **10** having its components illustrated in FIG. **2** provides for a primary seal. The radial face seal arrangement **10** also has a secondary sealing arrangement that may be further described with reference to FIG. **3**.

FIG. **3** is a schematic illustrating the interrelationship between the bellows **42** and the stationary seal ring **28**. The

6

bellows **42** has an inherent bias and is arranged to surround the general region **80** (see FIG. **1**) of the stationary seal ring **28**. The bellows **42** because of its accordion-like construction, its material and its spot welded connections at each end provides a flex characteristic to expand and compensate for high temperatures that may be experienced by bellows **42**, while at the same time confine the fluid that may pass by the rear portion of the stationary seal ring **28**. The flex characteristic is generally indicated with reference nomenclature **42A**.

In operation, the bellows **42**, having the characteristic **42A**, serves as the means for inhibiting any fluid leakage outward from the primary seal formed by the stationary seal ring in contact with the rotating seat seal **24**. The inhibition is referred to as a secondary seal and captures and confines the fluid passing by the rear portion of the stationary seal ring **28**.

It should now be appreciated that the practice of the present invention provides for both primary and secondary sealing arrangements that operate in various fluids both of high and low pressures along with temperatures that may range from 25° C. to about 900° C.

While the invention has been described with reference to certain preferred embodiments thereof, those skilled in the art will appreciate the various modifications, changes, omissions and substitutions that may be made without departing from the spirit of the invention. It is intended, therefore, that the invention be limited only by the scope of the appended claims.

What I claim is:

1. In a radial face seal arrangement between high pressure and low pressure regions of fluid located along a rotating axial member having a metal seal seat mounted on said axial member for rotation therewith, the improvement comprising:

a stationary seal ring for sealably engaging said metal seal seat, said stationary seal ring having a face for engaging said seal seat and a rear portion and comprising a self-lubricating, friction and wear reducing material comprising about 60–80 percent by weight metal-bonded chromium carbide, 10–20 percent by weight soft noble metal, and 10–20 percent by weight metal fluoride mixture,

means for urging said stationary seal ring into engagement with said metal seal seat,

means for inhibiting a secondary leakage at said rear portion of said stationary seal ring, and

means for damping axial motion between said stationary seal ring and against said seal seat.

2. The radial face seal arrangement according to claim **1**, wherein said stationary seal comprises a material comprising about 70 percent by weight metal-bonded chromium carbide, about 15 percent by weight silver, and about 15 percent by weight metal fluoride mixture.

3. The radial face seal arrangement according to claim **1**, wherein said means for urging includes:

a spring for urging the stationary seal ring toward the seal seat thereby preloading the engagement of said stationary seal ring with said seal seat, and

an adjustable threaded collar for changing the position of said spring relative to said stationary seal ring which, in turn, changes the preloading of said stationary seal ring with respect to said seal seat.

4. The radial face seal arrangement according to claim **3** further comprising a mating push pin interposed between said spring and said stationary seal ring.

5. The radial face seal arrangement according to claim **4**, wherein a plurality of springs operates in conjunction with a corresponding plurality of mating push pins.

6. The radial face seal arrangement according to claim **5**, wherein said springs and said mating push pins are each comprised of a superalloy.

7. The radial face seal arrangement according to claim **6**, wherein said plurality of mating push pins are housed in a corresponding plurality of chambers.

8. The radial face seal arrangement according to claim **7**, wherein said chambers are each filled with a lubricating grease.

9. The radial face seal arrangement according to claim **1**, wherein said means for inhibiting comprises a bellows having one end connected and located in proximity with said rear portion of said stationary seal ring and its other end connected so that said bellows encloses a defined region.

10. The radial face seal arrangement according to claim **9**, wherein said bellows is comprised of a superalloy.

11. A radial face seal arrangement for sealing a region where a rotating shaft passes through a housing, said sealing arrangement comprising:

(a) a seal seat mounted on said shaft for rotation therewith;

(b) a stationary seal ring for sealably engaging said seal seat, said stationary seal ring having a face for engaging said seal seat and a rear portion and comprising a material of about 60–80 percent by weight metal-bonded chromium carbide, 10–20 percent by weight soft noble metal, and 10–20 percent by weight metal fluoride mixture;

(c) means for urging said stationary seal ring into engagement with said metal seal seat; and

(d) means for damping axial motion of said stationary seal ring relative to said seal seat.

12. The radial seal arrangement according to claim **11** further comprising means for inhibiting a secondary leakage at said rear portion of said stationary seal ring.

13. The radial face seal arrangement according to claim **12**, wherein said stationary seal ring is carried by a seal ring carrier.

14. The radial face seal arrangement according to claim **11**, wherein said stationary seal comprises a material comprising about 70 percent by weight metal-bonded chromium carbide, about 15 percent by weight silver, and about 15 percent by weight metal fluoride mixture.

15. The radial face seal arrangement according to claim **13**, wherein said means for urging includes:

a spring for urging the seal ring carrier that carries said stationary seal ring toward said seal seat; and

an adjustable threaded collar for changing the position of said spring relative to said stationary seal ring.

16. The radial face seal arrangement according to claim **15** further comprising a mating push pin interposed between said spring and said stationary seal ring.

17. The radial face seal arrangement according to claim **16**, wherein a plurality of springs operates in conjunction with a corresponding plurality of mating push pins.

18. The radial face seal arrangement according to claim **17**, wherein said springs and said mating push pins are each comprised of a superalloy.

19. The radial face seal arrangement according to claim **18**, wherein said plurality of mating push pins are housed in a corresponding plurality of chambers.

20. The radial face seal arrangement according to claim **19**, wherein said chambers are each filled with a lubricant.

21. The radial face seal arrangement according to claim **20**, wherein said lubricant is in the form of a grease.

22. The radial face seal arrangement according to claim **20**, wherein said lubricant is a solid.

23. The radial face seal arrangement according to claim **13**, wherein said means for inhibiting comprises a bellows having one end connected and located in proximity with said rear portion of said stationary seal ring and its other end connected to said seal ring carrier.

24. The radial face seal arrangement according to claim **23**, wherein said bellows is comprised of a superalloy.

* * * * *

(12) **United States Patent**

Meyyappan

(10) **Patent No.:** **US 8,333,810 B1**

(45) **Date of Patent:** **Dec. 18, 2012**

(54) **CARBON NANOTUBE TOWER-BASED SUPERCAPACITOR**

(75) Inventor: **Meyya Meyyappan**, San Jose, CA (US)

(73) Assignee: **The United States of America as Represented by the Administrator of the National Aeronautics & Space Administration (NASA)**, Washington, DC (US)

(*) Notice: Subject to any disclaimer, the term of this patent is extended or adjusted under 35 U.S.C. 154(b) by 481 days.

(21) Appl. No.: **12/398,854**

(22) Filed: **Mar. 5, 2009**

(51) **Int. Cl.**
H01G 9/00 (2006.01)
(52) **U.S. Cl.** **29/25.03**
(58) **Field of Classification Search** 29/25.03
See application file for complete search history.

(56) **References Cited**

U.S. PATENT DOCUMENTS

6,454,816 B1	9/2002	Lee et al.
6,682,677 B2	1/2004	Lobovsky et al.
6,764,628 B2	7/2004	Lobovsky et al.
7,056,455 B2	6/2006	Matyjaszewski et al.
7,061,749 B2	6/2006	Liu et al.
7,199,997 B1	4/2007	Lipka et al.
7,211,350 B2	5/2007	Amatucci
7,247,290 B2	7/2007	Lobovsky et al.
7,435,476 B2	10/2008	Viswanathan et al.
7,466,539 B2	12/2008	Dementiev et al.
2006/0233692 A1	10/2006	Scaringe et al.
2008/0010796 A1*	1/2008	Pan et al. 29/25.03

OTHER PUBLICATIONS

Wang, et al., Nucleation and growth of well-aligned, uniform-sized carbon nanotubes by microwave plasma chemical vapor depositon, Applied Physics Letters, Jun. 18, 2001, 4028-430, 78-25, American Institute of Physics.

Park, et al., Synthesis of carbon nanotubes on metallic substrates by a sequential combination of PECVD and thermal CVD, Carbon, 2003, 1025-1029, 41, 2002 Elsevier Science Ltd.

Hiraoka, et al., Synthesis of Single- and Double-Walled Carbon Nanotube Forests on Conducting Metal Foils, Journal of American Chemical Society, Sep. 22, 2006, 13338-13339, 128, 2006 American Chemical Society.

Masarapu, et al., Direct Growth of Aligned Multiwalled Carbon Nanotubes on Treated Stainless Steel Substrates, Langmuir, Jul. 17, 2007, 9046-9049, 23, 2007 American Chemical Society.

* cited by examiner

Primary Examiner — Seahvosh Nikmanesh

(74) *Attorney, Agent, or Firm* — John F. Schipper; Robert M. Padilla

(57) **ABSTRACT**

A supercapacitor system, including (i) first and second, spaced apart planar collectors, (ii) first and second arrays of multi-wall carbon nanotube (MWCNT) towers or single wall carbon nanotube (SWCNT) towers, serving as electrodes, that extend between the first and second collectors where the nanotube towers are grown directly on the collector surfaces without deposition of a catalyst and without deposition of a binder material on the collector surfaces, and (iii) a porous separator module having a transverse area that is substantially the same as the transverse area of at least one electrode, where (iv) at least one nanotube tower is functionalized to permit or encourage the tower to behave as a hydrophilic structure, with increased surface wettability.

8 Claims, 1 Drawing Sheet

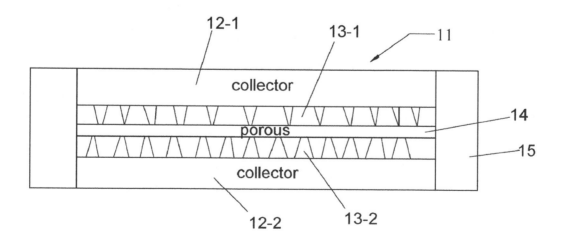

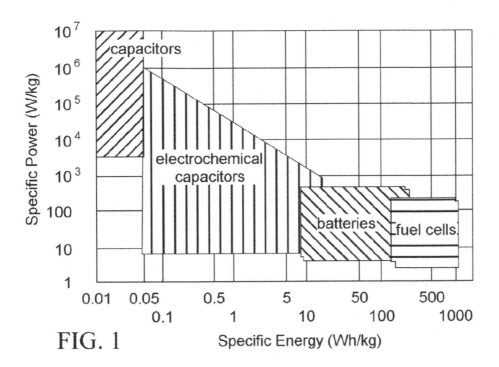

FIG. 1

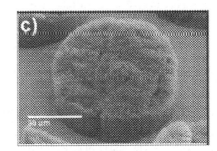

FIG. 2

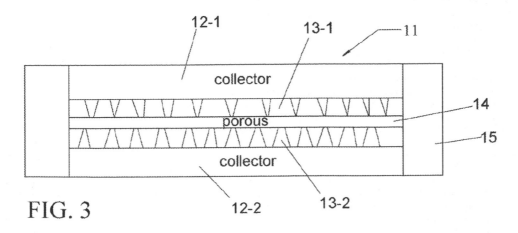

FIG. 3

1

CARBON NANOTUBE TOWER-BASED SUPERCAPACITOR

ORIGIN OF THE INVENTION

This invention was made, in part, by an employee of the U.S. government. The U.S. government has the right to make, use and/or sell the invention described herein without payment of compensation, including but not limited to payment of royalties.

FIELD OF THE INVENTION

This invention relates to energy storage, using electrochemical capacitor devices.

BACKGROUND OF THE INVENTION

Supercapacitors (sometimes referred to as ultra-capacitors) have received much attention recently in the technical literature, in industry and in the venture capital community, as a potential energy storage medium. This technology promises to provide a high power density (in units of kW/kg) and long cycle life (0.5-1.0 million cycles) while providing reasonable energy density (kWh/kg units). A number of companies, such as Maxwell (San Diego, USA), and Panasonic, Asahi Glass, Matsushita, NEC, and Nippon Chemicals and others, have been actively engaged in commercialization as well as advanced development. Although the technology has been around for thirty years, only recently commercial acceptance has arrived due to acceptable reliability and performance, at least for some applications such as memory backup and niche markets such as standby power mode in copying machines.

For many other commercial applications including hybrid/electric vehicles and military applications, development has a long way to go in terms of balance between power and energy densities, reliability, size, mass, safety and above all, price. Innovations in the electrode materials, electrolytes, other components, cell construction and almost everything else on cell design are on the table for further improvement. The focus in recent years has been on exploitation of nanostructured materials and principles of nanotechnology to improve the supercapacitor performance. The result so far has been promising and the performance has been steadily climbing. Nanostructured materials offer a high surface area and useable porosity for a given volume and mass, both of which are highly desirable for supercapacitor operation, which is the focus of this project.

Specifically, multiwalled carbon nanotubes (MWCNTs) have been grown in towers directly on metal alloys like nichrome, kanthal and stainless steel to reduce interface resistance; the nanotube towers will be treated quickly to improve surface wettability by the electrolyte; and if the design warrants, a psuedocapacitance component will be added by coating the MWCNT or SWCNT tower with an electrically conducting polymer (ECP). To understand all this, some background information is appropriate.

FIG. 1 (A. G. Pandolfo and A. E. Hollenkamp, Jour. Of Power Sources, vol. 157 (2006) p 11) graphically compares the specific power (Watts/Kg) versus specific energy available (Watt-hr/Kg) for four classes of energy storage devices: capacitors, electrochemical capacitors, batteries and fuel cells. High specific power and high specific energy available appear to vary inversely with each other so that one cannot have both in a single device.

Supercapacitors attempt to combine the best of capacitors and batteries to create an alternative form of energy storage

2

device. Conventional capacitors provide a very high specific power exceeding 100 KWatts/Kg and long cycle life. The long life is due to the fact there are no chemical reactions and associated decays. However, the energy density of a commercial capacitor is small, only tens of mWatt-hr/Kg. At the other extreme, batteries provide high energy density, about 100 Watt-hr/Kg, but battery power density is about 100 Watts/Kg. An additional issue with batteries is the anticipated cycle life, limited by the chemical interconversions and concomitant phase changes. The supercapacitor, which is a hybrid between a battery and a capacitor, is not new as the first patent to SOHIO was granted in 1966 and NEC first marketed it for memory backup applications 20 years ago.

Two types of supercapacitors are available, based on how energy is stored within each device: electrochemical double layer capacitors (EDLCs) and redox capacitors. A redox capacitor, also known as a pseudocapacitor, relies on electron transfer reactions (Faraday redox) that occurs during the charge/discharge cycle of the cell and is thus not an electrostatic. Most common redox capacitors rely on oxides, such as ruthenium oxide and manganese oxide, as well as electrically conducting polymers (ECPs), such as polyaniline and polypyrrole. A chemical reaction-based operation in pseudocapacitors more nearly resembles a battery than a capacitor in its operation. In the EDLC, a pair of symmetric electrodes, usually carbon, separated by a porous medium is soaked in an electrolyte. When the electrodes are biased, ions move towards the opposite polar electrodes and charge separation is confined to a very thin region near the electrode called a double layer. In this sense, each electrode-electrolyte interface is a capacitor and, therefore, the device shown in FIG. 2 consists of two capacitors in series, with a circular pattern of high density MWCNTs. The cell capacitance is then given by

$$1/C = 1/C1 + 1/C2, \tag{1}$$

where C1 and C2 are capacitance values of two adjacent electrodes, each given by

$$C = \in A/d \tag{2}$$

where $\in$ is a dielectric constant for the material, A is the surface area of the carbon electrode and d is the double-layer thickness. When the electrodes are symmetric, the total capacitance is half that of a single electrode. If one electrode is far smaller than the other, the total capacitance is approximately the smaller of the two capacitance values. The energy, E and the power, P of the supercapacitor are given by:

$$E = CV^2/2, \tag{3}$$

$$P = V^2/4R, \tag{4}$$

where C is capacitance, V is cell voltage, and R is the equivalent series resistance (ESR).

A capacitance value is primarily determined by the surface area and pore volume. Many carbon materials, such as activated carbon and carbon aerogel, have very large surface areas ($\approx 2000 \, m^2/gm$). However, carbon materials often suffer from a significant fraction of unusable nanopores, which are pores with diameters 2 nm or less; mesopore diameters are 2-50 nm and macropore diameters are greater than 50 nm. The nanopores contribute heavily to the measured surface area but may not contribute to increasing the capacitance. Ion transport through such small pores may be restricted. Mesopores are the most ideal for supercapacitor operation. Therefore, a simple metric of large surface area from adsorption isotherm measurements alone is not adequate to evaluate various carbon forms for capacitance enhancement; pore size distribution must also be considered.

3

A capacitor operating voltage is determined, in part, by the choice of the electrolyte, because electrolyte stability is severely compromised above certain voltages. Aqueous electrolytes, such as acids, have an operating voltage of only 1.0-1.5 Volts but are inexpensive and exhibit high ionic conductivity. Numerous nonaqueous electrolytes, such as polycarbonate and acetonitrile, allow higher operating voltages, for example 2.5 Volts. However, their electrical resistivity is at least one order of magnitude higher than the aqueous electrolytes. According to Eq. (4), a high value for R is detrimental for obtaining high power. R consists of several contributions:

$$R = R_c + R_{em} + R_{int} + R_{elec} + R_{ion} + R_{sep} \qquad (5)$$

where R_c is collector metal resistance, electrode material (carbon) resistance, R_{em}; is resistance of the interface between the carbon and the current collector metal, R_{int} is electrolyte resistance, R_{ele}, is resistance due to ion transport through the pores, R_{ion}, and R_{sep}. is separator resistance.

What is needed is a capacitor device that allows adequate transport between capacitor electrodes but suppresses electrical shorting between electrodes, that has a relatively low interface resistance between each electrode and any substance that physically separates the electrodes, and that has reduced capacitance, where the separator includes apparatus that can be made hydrophilic.

SUMMARY OF THE INVENTION

These needs are met by the invention, which provides a system, including (i) first and second, spaced apart planar collectors, (ii) first and second arrays of multi-wall carbon nanotube (MWCNT) towers, serving as electrodes, that extend between the first and second collectors, where the MWCNT towers are grown directly on the collector surfaces without deposition of a catalyst or a binder material on the collector surfaces, and (iii) a separator module having a transverse area that is substantially the same as the transverse area of either electrode, where (iv) at least one MWCNT tower is functionalized to permit or encourage the MWCNT tower to behave as a hydrophilic structure, with improved surface wettability.

BRIEF DESCRIPTION OF THE DRAWINGS

FIG. 1 graphically compares the specific power (Watts/Kgm) versus specific energy available (Watt-hr/Kgm) for four classes of energy storage devices.

FIG. 2 is an SEM image of a patterned MWCNT array grown on a metal array surface.

FIG. 3 schematically illustrates an embodiment of the invention.

DESCRIPTION OF PREFERRED EMBODIMENTS OF THE INVENTION

FIG. 3 illustrates an embodiment of a supercapacitor 11 constructed according to the invention. Substantially planar, first and second collectors, 12-1 and 12-2, are spaced apart and facing each other. First and second arrays, 13-1 and 13-2 of carbon nanotube towers, of multi-wall carbon nanotubes (MWCNTs) and/or single wall carbon nanotubes (SWCNTs), serve as electrodes and are positioned contiguous to the respective first and second collectors, 12-1 and 12-2, and between the collectors. The CNT electrodes have electrode areas, A1 and A2, and are spaced apart a selected distance d. A porous separator module 14 of thickness d is positioned between the first and second electrodes, 13-1 and

4

13-2, with a separator transverse area A(sep) that is substantially equal each of the electrode transverse areas, A1 and A2. The separator module 14 is surrounded on its sides by a gasket 15. An electrolyte is preferably soaked into or occupies unoccupied space within the electrodes, 13-1 and 13-2.

The range of pore sizes for the separator module 14 is chosen (i) to facilitate charged particle transport between the electrodes, 13-1 and 13-2, and (ii) to suppress electrical shorting between the electrodes. The porous separator module 14 may be of conventional design and materials, such as celgard, polypropylene membrane, glass fiber, cellulose fiber and similar materials. Optionally, a spacer 16 surrounds the gasket 14 and holds the first and second collectors, 12-1 and 12-2 apart.

The CNTs that comprise the electrodes, 13-1 and 13-2, are grown directly on the collectors, 12-1 and 12-2 without depositing a catalyst, such as Fe or Ni or Co, to enhance this growth, and without using a binding material. The collector material is preferably nichrome, kanthal, stainless steel or a similar material containing at most trace amounts of iron, nickel or cobalt. In the absence of a catalyst deposited on the collectors, the interface resistance R(int) between an MWCNT and a contiguous collector surface is reduced substantially, and catalyst impurities are no longer present.

A variety of carbon materials have been used in the past to construct super-capacitors. This innovation uses carbon nanotubes (CNTs), single-wall carbon nanotubes (SWCNTs) and, preferably, multiwalled nanotubes (MWCNTs). These MWCNTs have been found to be superior in many ways: their conductivity is very high relative to other forms of carbon, thus providing a relatively small value of R_{em} in Eq. (5). MWCNTs also have a highly porous structure characterized by sizeable fraction of mesopores (diameters ≥ 50 nm), have good useable surface area, and are stable and chemically inert.

One of the biggest problems to date with use of CNTs in supercapacitors is presence of a high interfacial resistance, R_{int} in Eq. (4), which can dominate all other components. Typically, MWCNTs and SWCNTs are mixed with a binder and applied as a paste onto the collector metal. This procedure adds a problem: the binder material adds to the weight but adds nothing to the capacitance value. Applying a paste to the collector does not allow thickness control, and it is difficult to obtain thickness values less than 0.3-0.5 mm. The associated interface resistance R_{int}, with a paste applied, is high. There is evidence that direct growth on the collector can help to reduce the interface resistance. The innovation disclosed and claimed here does not involve deposition of a catalyst, such as Ni, Fe or Co layers, which would also add to the resistance problem.

The growth of MWCNT and/or SWCNT towers will be done directly on polished, ultra-smooth alloy substrates containing Fe and/or Ni, such as nichrome, kanthal and stainless steel. The growth process for generating an MWCNT pillar or tower array requires heating the collector metal substrate in an inert Ar gas atmosphere to 750° C. After thermal equilibration, 1000 sccm of 8/20 ethylene/Hs gas flow results in the growth of CNT towers. The height of the structures may be controlled with time of reaction.

CNTs are normally hydrophobic, and when using (liquid) electrolytes, surface wettability becomes an issue. CNTs can be made hydrophilic in several ways. Surface functionalization, such as treatment with fluorine, chlorine or ammonia, is known to improve surface wettability. Eliminating oxygen groups is equally important because these groups add resistance to charged particle transport. The invention uses a plasma discharge to quickly treat (within a few minutes) the

5

CNT surfaces with NH_3 or F_2 to improve wettability. This is relatively fast, relatively inexpensive, scalable, and eliminates use of expensive chemicals and hazardous waste disposal issues associated with conventional wet chemical methods used for functionalization.

CNTs are hydrophobic materials and therefore wetting could be an issue when using aqueous electrolytes and even other electrolytes. Any surface treatment that increases the contact angle would be helpful as long as the approach is quick, inexpensive and does not introduce other unwanted problems.

Previously, functionalized SWCNT bundles have been used with H_2, NH_3 and F_2 (or CF_4) respectively. In all these cases, complete surface coverage was found to occur within about two minutes, as evidenced by the unchanging intensity of the observed peak (such as the C—H bond). This type of plasma, commonly used in semiconductor industry, is amenable to automation where the electrode from the CVD chamber can be passed onto the plasma chamber next.

Another issue can arise, when CNTs, acting as a nonpolar material, tend to aggregate or segregate easily in a polar solvent. This is an issue for consideration if loose bundles of nanotubes with binder are used. The use of MWCNT tower electrode may not face this as a serious problem. In any case, CNT surface functionalization with fluorine or ammonia is known to avoid this problem.

In one embodiment, the electrode is treated first for a few minutes under an argon plasma to drive out surface oxygen. This is followed by NH_3 or F_2 plasma to increase the contact angle/wettability and surface area of the MWCNT tower.

Surface oxygen increases the resistance of CNTs and they can also contribute to leakage currents. Typically high temperature treatment in an inert environment is used to eliminate the surface oxygen.

One can add a pseudo-capacitance component by modifying an array of CNTs, either by loading with oxide particles or by coating with electrically conductive polymers (ECPs). Here, the Faraday behavior of this addition is known to become attenuated with the passage of time, where this approach is combined with use of activated carbons. A trade-off between capacitance performance and capacitance endurance requires optimization. MWCNTs provide unique opportunities for coating with an ECP, such as polypyrrole, and for retaining the coating in the pores over a long period.

The capacitor charging time is primarily contributed by RC charging and ionic mass transport. The device capacitance value C is determined from Eqs. (1) and (2), and the equivalent series resistance is given by Eq. (5). It is assumed that an electrode area L×W (which is the geometrical area and different from the total surface area of the porous electrode), separation distance of a between the electrodes and equal area or symmetric electrodes.

For highly useable power density, the RC time constant must be reduced as much as possible, the specific capacitance must be increased, and the ionic transport time must be reduced. These requirements indicate a need to make the electrode thinner Currently carbon cloth electrodes and similar preparations make electrode thicknesses in a range of 0.3-0.5 μm. Chemical vapor deposition (CVD) can grow towers as small as 5 μm tall and as tall as 1000 μm, for a range of tower thicknesses. Thin MWCNT or SWCNT towers allow a reduction of R_{em} in Eq. (5) directly. Faster mass transport through thin(ner) electrodes also reduces R_{ion} in Eq. (5).

Typically, collectors are metal sheets with small resistance. Reduction of interface resistance R_{int} is achieved here through direct growth of MWCNT or SWCNT towers on a collector. Bulk produced materials also require clean up of

6

amorphous carbon and catalytic impurities, which together can account for 30 percent or more of total weight. Purified material is much more expensive; and a temptation exists to use unpurified material due to its lower cost. The impurities present may interfere with device performance and add to the cell weight without contributing to the performance. By contrast, the direct growth eliminates most of these problems; conventional growth using catalysts is not desirable.

Another critical aspect of the electrode is its surface area, because the double-layer capacitance increases with area as in Eq. (2). Unlike a conventional capacitor where the area is the geometrical area of the collector plate, the area in the supercapacitor design disclosed here uses the porous areas of the carbon electrode; this increases the area beyond what the geometry would normally allow. However, care is needed in measuring and interpreting surface area, which is typically done using N_2-adsorption isotherm measurements or the so-called BET adsorption isotherm. Although N_2 can pass through the smallest of the pores as a gas, passage of ions through the pores is not as easy because the ions are larger. The micropores, having diameters less than 2 nm, contribute heavily to the measured area but these apertures are useless for ion transport. Most of the activated carbons with impressive surface areas suffer from this problem of too many micropores. Macropores, with diameters greater than 50 nm, do not contribute much to the measured area and simply serve to connect to the collector edges and separator module in the extremities.

Ideally, a substantial fraction, at least 30 percent, of the total area would be associated with the mesapores (2-50 nm) MWCNTs with their central cavities meet this need. Further, the growth density in the MWCNT towers can be controlled with optimum mesapore distances between nanotubes as well. This approach appears to provide an optimum combination of R_{int}, surface area, and pore accessibility. Because bulk materials are not used, cost issues associated with purification, binder addition and adhesive addition are eliminated. Direct growth and assembly line operation reduce the cost concerns associated with typical electrode construction.

The choice of electrolyte determines the value of R_{elec} in Eq. (5), which will affect the power density. Beyond that, the operating voltage is primarily determined by the stability of the electrolyte during operation. Common aqueous electrolytes include 38 percent sulfuric acid or potassium hydroxide, for example. These electrolytes are characterized by low resistance (0.2-0.5 Ohms/cm²) or 1-2 Ohm-cm resistivity. This reduces R_{elec} in Eq. (5). Aqueous electrolytes allow rapid charging and discharging, which is necessary for high power applications. Electrolyte stability, however, requires an operating voltage that does not exceed 1 Volt. From Eq. (3), this limits the energy density.

There are several organic electrolytes such as propylene carbonate, and acetonitrile and its compounds, which have much higher decomposition threshold up to 3 Volts; this will yield a factor of 9 higher energy density than with aqueous electrolytes according to Eq. (3). However, the organic electrolytes exhibit a higher resistance of 1-2 Ohms/cm², equivalent to 20-60 Ohm-cm resistivity, which substantially affects the power. Some organic electrolytes, such as acetonitrile, are toxic and can release cyanide when burning.

The electrolyte choice cannot be made independently but must be consistent with electrode design. Typically, organic electrolyte ions are larger and thus require larger pores for efficient transport. The MWCNT tower electrode used here are believed to easily accommodate transport of such large ions and also possibly help to achieve a level of 3.0 Volt operation.

7

Another attractive electrolyte class is room temperature ionic liquids (RTILs), which are a much better alternative to organic electrolytes. RTILs have no solvent, are composed of only ions, and thus provide an even higher potential window (up to 5 Volts) than do organic electrolytes. The intrinsic resistance of an RTIL is also lower, and the flammability, toxicity and volatility characteristics are less troublesome

Use of a porous separator prevents shorting of the electrodes while providing access to transport. Equation (5) demands a thin (but stable) separator made of a low resistance material. Available choices include polymers, such as celgard, polypropylene membrane, glass fiber, cellulose fiber and similar materials.

What is claimed is:

1. A method for producing a supercapacitor, the method comprising:

    providing first and second substantially planar collectors, having respective first and second collector surfaces facing each other and spaced apart a selected distance apart

    growing spaced apart first and second arrays of single wall carbon nanotube (SWCNT) towers or multi-wall carbon nanotube (MWCNT) towers directly on the first and second collector surfaces, with no catalyst substance and no binder material deposited on the collector surfaces, the towers having heights in a range of about 10-1000 μm;

    positioning a porous separator module, having a substantial portion of its pores with diameters in a range 2-50 nm, between and contiguous to the first array and the second array of towers, the separator module having a thickness no greater than a height of a nanotube tower and having a separator module transverse area A(sep)

8

that is substantially equal to a transverse area A(el) of at least one of the first and second collector surfaces;

    functionalizing at least one MWCNT tower or SWCNT tower to increase surface wettability of the at least one tower.

2. The method of claim 1, further comprising functionalizing said at least one tower by addition to a tower surface of molecules of at least one of F and NH_3, to thereby eliminate or reduce a number of oxygen groups attached to said nanotube towers.

3. The method of claim 1, further comprising functionalizing said at least one MWCNT by a process comprising exposing said at least one MWCNT to a low temperature plasma discharge in presence of at least one of F and NH_3.

4. The method of claim 1, further comprising including in at least one of said first and second collector surfaces an electrically conductive material drawn from a group consisting of nichrome, kanthal and stainless steel.

5. The method of claim 1, further comprising choosing said separator module to include at least one of celgard, polypropylene membrane, glass fiber and cellulose fiber.

6. The method of claim 1, further comprising providing an electrolyte for said supercapacitor that replaces a common aqueous, organic molecule by at least one room temperature ionic liquid.

7. The method of claim 1, further comprising coating at least one of said nanotube towers with an electrically conducting polymer.

8. The method of claim 7, further comprising choosing said electrically conducting polymer to comprise polypyrrole.

* * * * *

US008679300B2

(12) **United States Patent**
Smith et al.

(10) **Patent No.:** **US 8,679,300 B2**
(45) **Date of Patent:** **Mar. 25, 2014**

(54) **INTEGRATED RIG FOR THE PRODUCTION OF BORON NITRIDE NANOTUBES VIA THE PRESSURIZED VAPOR-CONDENSER METHOD**

(75) Inventors: **Michael W. Smith**, Newport News, VA (US); **Kevin C. Jordan**, Newport News, VA (US)

(73) Assignees: **Jefferson Science Associates, LLC**, Newport News, VA (US); **The United States of America as represented by the Administrator of Nasa**, Washington, DC (US)

(*) Notice: Subject to any disclaimer, the term of this patent is extended or adjusted under 35 U.S.C. 154(b) by 8 days.

(21) Appl. No.: **13/200,315**

(22) Filed: **Sep. 22, 2011**

(65) **Prior Publication Data**

US 2012/0175242 A1 Jul. 12, 2012

Related U.S. Application Data

(63) Continuation-in-part of application No. 12/387,703, filed on May 6, 2009, which is a continuation-in-part of application No. 12/322,591, filed on Feb. 4, 2009.

(60) Provisional application No. 61/460,993, filed on Jan. 11, 2011.

(51) **Int. Cl.**
B01J 19/12 (2006.01)
C04B 14/32 (2006.01)
B01J 19/08 (2006.01)

(52) **U.S. Cl.**
USPC **204/157.41**; 204/157.45; 204/157.46; 422/186

(58) **Field of Classification Search**
USPC 204/157.45, 157.41, 157.46; 422/186; 977/896
See application file for complete search history.

(56) **References Cited**

U.S. PATENT DOCUMENTS

6,680,041 B1 *	1/2004	Kumar et al.	.... 75/330
7,184,614 B2 *	2/2007	Slatkine	.... 385/5
7,575,784 B1 *	8/2009	Bi et al.	.... 427/567
7,663,077 B1 *	2/2010	Smith et al.	.... 977/844
7,767,270 B1	8/2010	Khare et al.	
2002/0148560 A1	10/2002	Carr	
2002/0175278 A1 *	11/2002	Whitehouse	.... 250/281
2003/0203205 A1 *	10/2003	Bi et al.	.... 428/402
2006/0096393 A1 *	5/2006	Pesiri	.... 73/863.21
2007/0295702 A1 *	12/2007	Tenegal et al.	.... 219/121.84
2008/0199389 A1	8/2008	Chiu et al.	
2008/0225464 A1 *	9/2008	Lashmore	.... 423/447.2
2009/0044705 A1 *	2/2009	Takayanagi et al.	.... 96/381

(Continued)

OTHER PUBLICATIONS

"Synthesis of nanoparticles by a laser-vaporization-controlled condensation technique," Samy S. El-Shall, Shoutian Li, Proc. SPIE. 3123, Materials Research in Low Gravity 98 (Jul. 7, 1997) doi: 10.1117/12.277711.*

(Continued)

Primary Examiner — Keith Hendricks
Assistant Examiner — Colleen M Raphael

(57) **ABSTRACT**

An integrated production apparatus for production of boron nitride nanotubes via the pressure vapor-condenser method. The apparatus comprises: a pressurized reaction chamber containing a continuously fed boron containing target having a boron target tip, a source of pressurized nitrogen and a moving belt condenser apparatus; a hutch chamber proximate the pressurized reaction chamber containing a target feed system and a laser beam and optics.

18 Claims, 3 Drawing Sheets

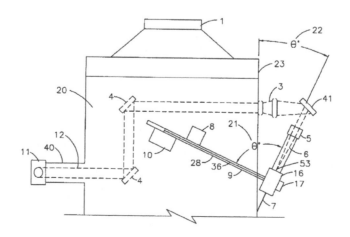

(56) **References Cited**

U.S. PATENT DOCUMENTS

2009/0117021 A1	5/2009	Smith et al.
2010/0192535 A1	8/2010	Smith et al.
2010/0219383 A1	9/2010	Eklund

OTHER PUBLICATIONS

Smith, M.W. et al., Very Long single-and Few-walled Boron nitride Nanotubes Via the Pressurized Vapor/condenser Method; Nanotechnology 20 (2009) 505604.

Ma, Renzhi et al., Synthesis and Properties of B-C-N And BN Nanostructure, Phil. Tran.:Math., Phys. and Eng. Sciences, vol. 362, No. 1823, (Oct. 15, 2004), pp. 2161-2186.

Goldberg, Dmitri et al., Nanotubes in Boron Nitride Laser Heated at High Pressure, Appl. Phys. Lett. 69 (14), Sep. 30, 1996, 2045-2047.

Goldberg, Dmitri et al., Boron Nitride Nanotubes, Adv. Mater., 2007, 19, 2413-2434.

Zhi, Chunyi et al., Effective Precursor for High Yield Synthesis of Pure BN Nanotubes, Solid State Communications 135 (2005) 67-70.

Bansal, Narottam et al., Boron Nitride Nanotubes-Reinforced Glass Composites, NASA/TM 2005-213874, Aug. 2005.

* cited by examiner

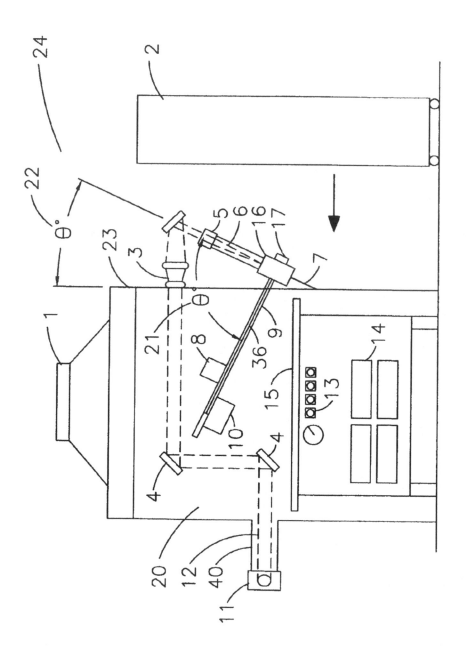

FIG. 1

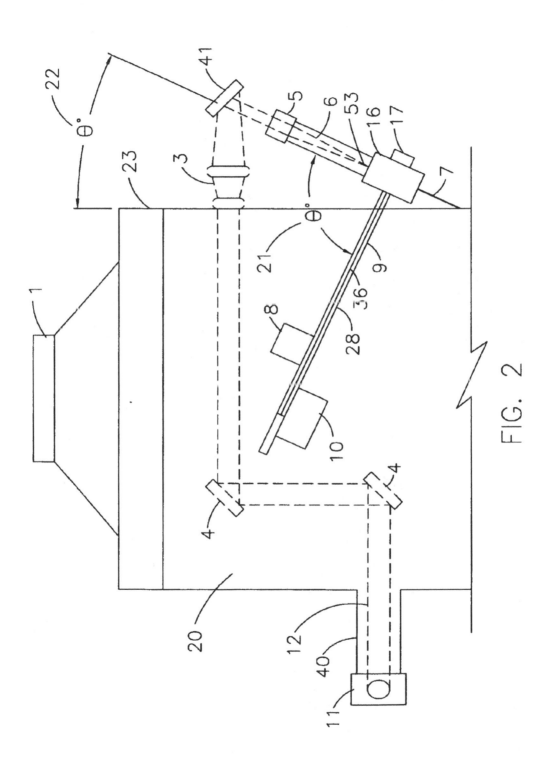

FIG. 2

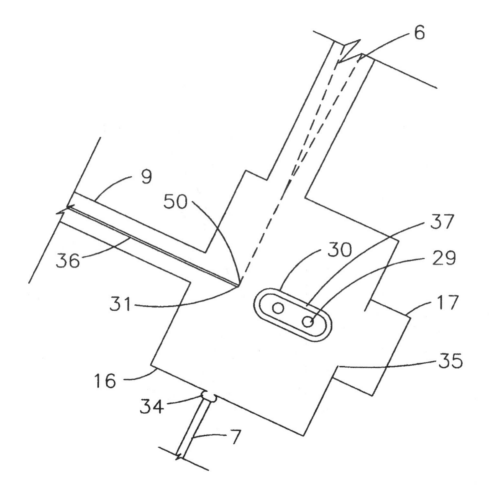

FIG. 3

1

INTEGRATED RIG FOR THE PRODUCTION OF BORON NITRIDE NANOTUBES VIA THE PRESSURIZED VAPOR-CONDENSER METHOD

This application claims the benefit of U.S. Provisional Application No. 61/460,993 filed on Jan. 11, 2011 for an Integrated Rig For The Production of BNNTs Via The PVC Method and is a Continuation-In-Part of U.S. patent application Ser. No. 12/387,703, filed on May 6, 2009 and entitled "Boron Nitride Nanotube Fibrils and Yarns", which is a Continuation-In-Part of U.S. patent application Ser. No. 12/322,591, filed on Feb. 4, 2009 and entitled "Apparatus for the Production of Boron Nitride Nanotubes".

The United States government may have certain rights to this invention under the National Aeronautics and Space Administration and/or Management and Operating Contract No. DE-AC05-060R23177 from the Department of Energy.

FIELD OF THE INVENTION

The invention relates generally to an apparatus for the production of nanostructures in particular to the formation of long strand boron nitride nanotube fibers or filaments.

BACKGROUND

Since the announcement of the successful synthesis of high-aspect-ratio-few-walled boron nitride nanotubes (FW-BNNTs) in 1995, little progress had been made until very recently in the scale-up of their synthesis. In spite of the theoretical capabilities of FW-BNNTs to provide high strength-to weight, high temperature resistance, piezo actuation, and radiation shielding (via the boron content), the aerospace industry has had to rely on micron-sized graphite or boron fibers for structural applications. Further, despite their very desirable properties, neither FW-BNNTs nor single wall carbon nanotubes are used widely in aerospace manufacturing, as the industry is generally unwilling to pay the premium price for these high performance materials.

Prior to recent inventions of the present inventors, high-aspect ratio FW-BNNTs had only been produced in small amounts by arc-discharge or laser heating methods. Further, these small amounts of FW-BNNTs were in the form of films not strands or fibers several centimeters in length. A separate class of boron nitride nanotubes known in the prior has been produced by chemical vapor deposition of nitrogen compounds (e.g. ammonia) over ball-milled precursors, but these tubes are of large diameter, do not exhibit the continuous crystalline sp2-type bonding structure which has drawn most theoretical interest, and are not strands or fibers.

The Inventors' recent work in the field of boron nitride nanotubes is described in four US patent applications. Inventors' U.S. patent application Ser. No. 12/152,414 filed May 14, 2008 and incorporated herein by reference in its entirety describes a process for the production of at least centimeter-long boron nitride nanotube strands or fibers. Inventors' U.S. patent application Ser. No. 12/322,591 filed Feb. 4, 2009 and incorporated herein by reference in its entirety describes an apparatus for production of boron nitride nanotubes and a method of continuous removal of the formed boron nitride nanotubes from the synthesis chamber. Inventors' U.S. patent application Ser. No. 12/387,703 filed May 6, 2009 and incorporated herein by reference in its entirety describes a method for production of fibrils and yarns. Inventor's U.S. patent application Ser. No. 13/199,101 filed Aug. 19, 2011 and incorporated herein by reference in its entirety for a feedstock

delivery device describes the delivery of material to a reaction chamber or process-controlled zone.

As high-aspect ratio boron nitride nanostructures with high crystallinity bonding structure are be highly desirable, improved methods and equipment for their production is likewise highly desirable.

SUMMARY OF INVENTION

The invention provides an integrated production apparatus for production of boron nitride nanotubes via the pressure vapor-condenser method. The apparatus comprises: a pressurized reaction chamber containing a continuously fed boron containing target having a boron target tip, a source of pressurized nitrogen and a moving belt condenser apparatus; a hutch chamber proximate the pressurized reaction chamber containing a target feed system wherein the target feed system provides a continuously fed boron containing target to the pressurized reaction chamber, a nitrogen control system in communication with the pressurized nitrogen; a laser beam and optics wherein the optics direct the laser beam though a laser beam tube, the hutch and into the pressurized reaction chamber; and a sliding safety shield positionable to surround at least a portion of the pressurized chamber.

The invention also provides a method of making boron nitride nanotubes having a high-aspect ratio and a high crystallinity bonding structure.

BRIEF DESCRIPTION OF THE DRAWINGS

FIG. 1 is a schematic representation of an integrated rig apparatus for the production of boron nitride nanotubes.

FIG. 2 is an expanded view of the hutch chamber and pressure chamber of an integrated rig apparatus for the production of boron nitride nanotubes.

FIG. 3 is an expanded cross sectional view of the pressure chamber region of an integrated rig apparatus for the production of boron nitride nanotubes.

DETAILED DESCRIPTION OF THE INVENTION

The generation of very long single- and few-walled boron nitride nanotubes (BNNT) has been demonstrated via a pressurized vapor/condenser method. (See Inventors' U.S. patent application Ser. No. 12/152,414 incorporated herein by reference in its entirety.) In the pressurized vapor/condenser method few walled boron nitride nanotubes of high-aspect ratio and highly crystallinity fibers grow continuously by surface nucleation from seemingly arbitrary asperities at a high linear rate (centimeters per sec) in the line of flow of vaporized boron mixed with nitrogen under elevated pressures.

The inventors describe herein their invention of an integrated apparatus for the production of boron nitride nanotubes having a high-aspect ratio and a high crystallinity bonding structure. Boron nitride nanotubes and nanotube fibers are formed via a process in which hot boron vapor flows into nitrogen held in a pressurized synthesis chamber at an elevated pressure. The hot boron vapor flows through nitrogen towards a filament nucleation site. The filament nucleation site has a surface and the boron nitride nanotubes attach to the surface and boron nitride nanotube filaments propagate away there from in the direction of flow of the stream of boron vapor. Unlike in prior art in which films are typically formed over a surface, only a small portion of the boron nitride nanotube material actually attaches to the surface of the

3

4

nucleation site, most of the material attaches to other boron nitride nanotubes to build filaments a centimeter or more in length.

As used herein a "boron nitride nanotube filament" means a fiber or strand. Typically, the boron nitride nanotube filaments are at least a centimeter long. When it is being formed the boron nitride nanotubes may appear as "streamers" to the naked eye because they extend outward and follow the flow of the hot boron vapor in the synthesis chamber and have sufficient length to have a flapping motion similar to a kite tail in the wind. In some embodiments, particularly in one in which the filament nucleation site is moved during the synthesis process, the streamers may intertwine to give a material that has a web like appearance.

As used herein the term "boron nitride" should be taken to include nanotubes comprising boron and nitrogen and accordingly includes nanotubes of the general formula $B_xC_yN_z$, for example.

As used herein a "filament nucleation site" is a structure which provides an attachment point for forming boron nitride nanotube filaments. The filament nucleation site is in the flow path of the hot boron vapor, but it should have a form and/or position that only minimally impacts the flow of the hot boron vapor.

Referring to FIG. 1 which is a schematic drawing of one embodiment of the integrated production apparatus for production of boron nitride nanotubes via the pressure vapor-condenser method. The apparatus comprises a pressurized reaction chamber 16, a hutch chamber 20 proximate the pressurized reaction chamber 16, a laser beam 12, and a sliding safety shield 2. The hutch chamber 20 further comprises a target feed system 9, an optical bench 15, gas pressure and flow controls 13 and electronic controls 14. The target feed system 9 provides for supporting and continuously feeding a boron target 36 into the pressurized reaction chamber 16. The gas pressure and flow controls 13 comprise a needle valve, pressure gauge and a regulator and are used for admitting nitrogen into the system and regulating the flow of nitrogen to maintain pressure in the pressurized reaction chamber 16. Flow rate is monitored by a chamber exhaust meter (not shown). The electronic controls 14 provide for control of the target feed system 9, control of the boron target 36 position and feed rate and laser beam 12 manipulation. During operation of the apparatus the operator may adjust the flow rate, pressure, laser power, laser focus, feed rate of the boron target 36, and position of the boron target 36 by adjusting one or more appropriate gas pressure and flow control 13 and/or one or more appropriate electronic control 14. The electronic controls 14 also provide for the control and adjustment of the rate of motion and position of the moving belt condenser (not shown in FIG. 1) in the pressurized chamber 16.

The entire integrated production apparatus is preferably enclosed in a metal and/or fire resistant box beneath an exhaust hood 1. For safety purposes, it is preferable to exhaust the system though a HEPA filter system. The metal and/or fire resistant box may have movable doors to provide access to the integrated production apparatus. The sliding safety shield 2 is movable. For operation the sliding safety shield 2 is positionable to surround at least a portion of the pressurized chamber 16 (i.e. is moved to cover the pressurized reaction chamber 16 portion of the apparatus). In a preferred embodiment the sliding safety shield 2 is lined with bullet proof (9 mm round) fiber board.

Referring to FIG. 2, which is an enlarged schematic view of a portion of the integrated production apparatus, the target feed system 9 provides for supporting and continuously feeding a boron target 36 into the pressurized reaction chamber

16. The target feed system 9 is described in detail in Inventor's U.S. patent application Ser. No. 13/199,101 filed Aug. 19, 2011 and incorporated herein by reference in its entirety. The target feed system 9 comprises a target support 28 that supports the boron target 36 and mechanisms and controls for positioning the boron target 36 and continuously feeding the boron target 36 into the pressurized reaction chamber 16. A vertical/horizontal adjuster 10 controls the target feed system's 9 pitch and yaw. The boron target 36 is advanced into the pressurized reaction chamber 16 by a motor-driven chain drive 8. The rate of feed of the boron target 36 into the pressurized reaction chamber 16 can be adjusted and controlled in real time.

A laser (not shown) is used to produce the laser beam 12. Exemplary lasers suitable for use include, but are not limited to, gas lasers such as CO_2 lasers, free electron lasers, fiber lasers, and solid state lasers. The laser beam 12 is introduced into the integrated production apparatus via a pico-motor adjustable mirror 11 through beam tube 40. A plurality of transparent turning mirrors 4 direct the laser beam 12 through the hutch chamber 20 and through beam shaping optics 3. Upon passing though the beam shaping optics 3 a laser beam end portion turning mirror 41 directs the laser beam 12 toward the pressurized reaction chamber 16. That portion of the laser beam 12 beyond the laser beam end portion turning mirror 41 is referred to herein as the laser beam end portion 6. The laser beam end portion 6 is aligned to impact the boron target 36 tip at an impact angle 21 approximately normal to the boron target 36 tip (i.e. the impact angle 21 is approximately 90°). In a preferred embodiment the beam path 53 of the laser beam end portion 6 is aligned to form an alignment angle 22 between the first chamber wall 23 of the hutch chamber 20 and the beam path 53 of the laser beam end portion 6 that is about 23°±5°. In a preferred embodiment a ZnSe input window 5 admits the laser beam 12 into the pressurized reaction chamber 16.

FIG. 3 is an enlarged schematic view of one embodiment of the pressurized reaction chamber 16 region of the integrated production apparatus of the invention. The boron target 36 is continuously moved into the pressurized reaction chamber 16 by the target feed system 9. The target feed system 9 is adjusted in position and/or rate of feed so that the target tip 31 intercepts the laser beam terminus 50 at an angle approximately normal to the target tip 31. The laser power delivered to the target tip 31 should be sufficient to vaporize the boron target tip 31 as the boron target 36 is continuously moved into the pressurized reaction chamber 16.

The pressurized reaction chamber 16 is pressurize by admitting nitrogen via nitrogen supply line 7 and valve 34 into the pressurized reaction chamber 16. In one representative embodiment, the nitrogen gas is maintained at a pressure of about 150 to about 200 psi. The introduction of nitrogen is controlled by a nitrogen control system.

Hot boron vapor is formed as the laser beam 12 vaporizes the boron target tip 31 of the boron target 36 and the boron vapor mixes with the nitrogen gas which dissociates to atomic nitrogen under the conditions present in the pressurized reaction chamber 16. The mixture of vaporized boron and nitrogen travels toward the continuous belt condenser 29. The continuous belt condenser 29 is has a moving belt 37 with a belt surface 30. In a preferred embodiment, both the position of the continuous belt condenser 29 and the rate of movement of the belt 37 are adjustable. The belt surface 30 acts as a filament nucleation site.

Boron nitride nanotubes attach to the belt surface 30 and boron nitride nanotube filaments propagate away there from in the direction of flow of the stream of boron vapor. Only a very small portion of the boron nitride nanotube material actually attaches to the surface of the nucleation site (i.e. belt surface **30**.) Most of the material attaches to other boron nitride nanotubes to build filaments a often a centimeter or more in length. During the production process the belt **37** is moved to bring a fresh portion of the belt surface **30** in proximity to the target tip **31**. While the nanotube fibers are preferentially formed on the portion of the belt **31** proximate the target tip **31**, the portion of the belt **37** nearest to the target tip **31** at a given time should be sufficiently spaced away from the target tip **31** to allow for mixing of the vaporized boron with the nitrogen and to avoid damage to the belt **37** by the laser beam end portion **6**.

Port **35** covered during operation by flange **17**, provides access to the pressurized reaction chamber **16** to remove boron nitride nanotube product at the end of a production run. Optionally, the flange **17** may be equipped with chamber view ports (not shown) for visually monitoring the reaction via video monitoring.

The invention also provides a method of producing boron nitride nanotubes utilizing the apparatus described herein. In one embodiment, the boron nitride nanotubes are produced in the pressurized reaction chamber in the presence of nitrogen gas maintained at a pressure of about 150 to about 200 psi and hot boron vapor produced by vaporizing the boron target with a laser.

The boron-containing target is continuously introduced into the pressurized reaction chamber by the target feed system. The tip of the target is positioned so that it is impacted by the laser beam terminus at an angle substantially normal to the target tip. The laser beam is produced at a laser power of between about 1000 and about 2500 W. Boron target introduction and positioning is maintained and regulated by a motor driven target feed chain and a pitch and yaw target position adjuster.

The hot boron vapor contacts the nitrogen gas atomizing a portion of the nitrogen gas. The mixture of the hot boron vapor and nitrogen gas moves towards the moving belt condenser which is positioned proximate but spaced apart from the tip of the boron target. The surface of the moving belt condenser acts as a nucleation site. The boron nitride nanotubes attach to the surface of the moving belt condenser and boron nitride nanotube filaments propagate away there from in the direction of flow of the stream of boron vapor. The belt on the moving belt condenser is moved during the process to provide additional surface for collection of more nanotube filaments. This permits continuous collection of boron nitride nanotubes over a production run which can last for substantial period of time.

During a production run, the operator can control and adjust the flow rate of nitrogen gas, pressure, laser power, laser focus, feed rate of the target, position of the target and position and speed of the condenser loop via the feedback and control systems of the apparatus. Optionally, the operator may monitor the nanotube formation visually via a video monitoring system on the pressurized reaction chamber port. Preferably during operation, a positionable safety shield is positioned to cover the pressurized reaction chamber.

At the completion of a production run, boron nitride nanotubes can be removed manually via the pressurized reaction chamber port.

In one exemplary embodiment using a CO_2 laser, boron nitride nanotubes were produced at a rate of about 25 mg per hour. The nanotubes thus produced have a high-aspect ratio and a high crystallinity bonding structure. In one embodiment least 30% of the collected boron nitride nanotubes were boron nitride nanotube filaments at least 1 cm in length. In another

embodiments least 50% of the collected boron nitride nanotubes were boron nitride nanotube filaments at least 1 cm in length and in another embodiment least 60% of the collected boron nitride nanotubes were boron nitride nanotube filaments at least 1 cm in length.

The boron-containing target may be compressed boron powder, compressed boron nitride powder, and mixtures thereof, for example. Typically a temperature of at least about 3200 to 4000° C. is needed to create the hot boron vapor.

Further, the inventors believe, without wishing to be bound to the theory, that no chemical catalyst and/or catalytic surface is needed to initiate the formation of the boron nitride nanotube fibers. The boron nitride nanotube fibers appear to form spontaneously and continuously by propagation outward (root growth) from the initial point of attachment on any suitable surface when hot boron vapor, vaporized carbon and nitrogen are present. This renders the Inventors' process fundamentally less complicated than carbon nanotube production in which a gas-borne cloud or coated surface of catalytic particles must be produced and kept active during the growth process. Accordingly, unlike for carbon nanotubes, the Inventors' production of boron nitride nanotube fibers is readily amendable to continuous production of material. Further the Inventors' process yields fibers which are at least a centimeter in length and typically centimeters in length which are highly desirable for commercial applications.

What is at present considered the preferred embodiment and alternative embodiments of the present invention has been shown and described herein. It will be obvious to those skilled in the art that various changes and modifications may be made therein without departing from the scope of the invention as defined by the appended claims.

What is claimed is:

1. An integrated production apparatus for production of boron nitride nanotubes via the pressure vapor-condenser method, the apparatus comprising:
   a. a pressurized reaction chamber containing a continuously fed boron containing target having a boron target tip, a source of pressurized nitrogen and a moving belt condenser apparatus;
   b. a hutch chamber proximate the pressurized reaction chamber containing a target feed system wherein the target feed system provides the continuously fed boron containing target to the pressurized reaction chamber, and a nitrogen control system in communication in communication with the source of pressurized nitrogen;
   c. a beam tube extending through said hutch chamber;
   d. an end portion turning mirror external to said hutch chamber; and
   e. a laser beam and optics wherein the optics direct the laser beam through said beam tube and to said end portion turning mirror, said end portion turning minor aligning said laser beam to impact said boron target in said pressurized reaction chamber.

2. The integrated production apparatus of claim **1** wherein the laser beam has a laser beam end portion and the laser beam end portion has a laser beam terminus and the laser beam terminus is aligned to impact the boron target tip at an angle approximately normal to the boron target tip.

3. The integrated production apparatus of claim **2** wherein the hutch chamber has a first chamber wall proximate the pressurized chamber and the laser beam end portion has a beam path wherein the angle formed between the first chamber wall and the beam path of the laser beam end portion is about 23°±5°.

4. The integrated production apparatus of claim 2, wherein said end portion turning minor directs said laser beam end portion and said laser beam terminus into the pressurized reaction chamber.

5. The integrated production apparatus of claim 1, wherein said integrated production apparatus is equipped with an exhaust.

6. The integrated production apparatus of claim 5, wherein the exhaust is equipped with a HEPA filter and a flow meter.

7. The integrated production apparatus of claim 1, wherein the nitrogen source is a pressurized line and the nitrogen control system comprise a needle valve, pressurized gauge and a regulator.

8. The integrated production apparatus of claim 1, wherein a plurality of transparent turning minors direct the laser beam though the hutch chamber.

9. The integrated production apparatus of claim 1, wherein the target feed system comprises a target support, a motor driven target feed and a target position adjuster.

10. The integrated production apparatus of claim 1, wherein the moving belt condenser apparatus comprises a moving belt having an adjustable rate of movement and a belt surface.

11. The integrated production apparatus of claim 10, wherein the position of the moving belt condenser is adjustable.

12. The integrated production apparatus of claim 11, wherein the moving belt condenser is placed proximate and spaced apart from the target tip and the position of the belt surface is adjustable with respect to the position of the target tip.

13. The integrated production apparatus of claim 1 further comprising a safety shield positionable to surround at least a portion of the pressurized reaction chamber.

14. A method of producing boron nitride nanotubes, the method comprising:

  a. providing an integrated production apparatus, the apparatus comprising: a pressurized reaction chamber containing a continuously fed boron containing target hav-

ing a boron target tip, a source of pressurized nitrogen and a moving belt condenser apparatus including a belt surface; a hutch chamber proximate the pressurized reaction chamber containing a target feed system wherein the target feed system provides the continuously fed boron containing target to the pressurized reaction chamber, a nitrogen control system in communication with the pressurized nitrogen, a beam tube extending through said hutch chamber, an end portion turning minor external to said hutch chamber, a laser beam and optics wherein the optics direct the laser beam through said beam tube and to said end portion turning mirror, said end portion turning mirror aligning said laser beam to impact said boron target in said pressurized reaction chamber; and a safety shield positionable to surround at least a portion of the pressurized chamber;

  b. providing nitrogen gas to the pressurized reaction chamber to maintain a pressure of about 150 to 200 psi in the pressurized reaction chamber;

  c. providing a laser beam and maintaining a laser power of about 1000 to about 2500 W;

  d. directing the laser beam to the tip of the boron target; and

  e. collecting boron nitride nanotubes on the belt surface of the moving belt condenser apparatus.

15. The method of claim 14, further comprising positioning the safety shield to cover the pressurized reaction chamber.

16. The method of claim 14, further comprising moving the belt surface to change the position of the belt surface with respect to the target tip.

17. The method of claim 14, wherein the laser beam is produced by a CO_2 laser.

18. The method of claim 14, wherein at least 30% of the collected boron nitride nanotubes are boron nitride nanotube filaments at least 1 cm in length.

* * * * *

US008673120B2

(12) **United States Patent**   (10) **Patent No.:**   **US 8,673,120 B2**

Whitney et al.   (45) **Date of Patent:**   **Mar. 18, 2014**

(54) **EFFICIENT BORON NITRIDE NANOTUBE FORMATION VIA COMBINED LASER-GAS FLOW LEVITATION**

(75) Inventors: **R. Roy Whitney**, Newport News, VA (US); **Kevin Jordan**, Newport News, VA (US); **Michael W. Smith**, Newport News, VA (US)

(73) Assignees: **Jefferson Science Associates, LLC**, Newport News, VA (US); **The United States of America, as Represented by the Administrator of NASA**, Washington, DC (US)

(*) Notice: Subject to any disclaimer, the term of this patent is extended or adjusted under 35 U.S.C. 154(b) by 155 days.

(21) Appl. No.: **13/200,316**

(22) Filed: **Sep. 22, 2011**

(65) **Prior Publication Data**

US 2012/0168299 A1   Jul. 5, 2012

Related U.S. Application Data

(60) Provisional application No. 61/460,534, filed on Jan. 4, 2011.

(51) **Int. Cl.**
B01J 19/12   (2006.01)

(52) **U.S. Cl.**
USPC **204/157.41**; 204/157.45; 204/157.47; 204/157.46

(58) **Field of Classification Search**
USPC 204/157.45, 157.46, 157.41, 157.47
See application file for complete search history.

(56) **References Cited**

U.S. PATENT DOCUMENTS

3,562,530	A	*	2/1971	Consoli et al. 250/251
3,580,731	A		5/1971	Milewski et al.
3,808,550	A	*	4/1974	Ashkin 372/97
5,814,152	A		9/1998	Thaler
6,331,477	B1	*	12/2001	Vekris et al. 257/E21.14
6,484,539	B1		11/2002	Nordine et al.
6,967,011	B1	*	11/2005	Saboungi et al. 423/249
7,291,317	B1		11/2007	Saboungi et al.
8,028,541	B2	*	10/2011	Yono et al. 423/297
8,206,674	B2	*	6/2012	Smith et al. 204/157.4
2004/0063113	A1		4/2004	Agnes et al.
2004/0179808	A1		9/2004	Renn
2008/0224100	A1		9/2008	Smalley et al.
2009/0117021	A1		5/2009	Smith et al.
2010/0192535	A1		8/2010	Smith et al.

FOREIGN PATENT DOCUMENTS

JP   2001270707   10/2001

OTHER PUBLICATIONS

Glorieux et al, "Electronic conduction in liquid boron," Europhys. Lett., 56 (1) pp. 81-85 (2001).*

Millot et al, "High-temperature properties of liquid boron from contactless techniques," Intl. J. Thermophys., vol. 23, No. 5, Sep. 2002, pp. 1185-1195.*

(Continued)

Primary Examiner — Keith Hendricks
Assistant Examiner — Colleen M Raphael

(57) **ABSTRACT**

A process for producing boron nitride nanotubes and/or boron-carbon-nitrogen nanotubes of the general formula $B_xC_yN_z$. The process utilizes a combination of laser light and nitrogen gas flow to support a boron ball target during heating of the boron ball target and production of a boron vapor plume which reacts with nitrogen or nitrogen and carbon to produce boron nitride nanotubes and/or boron-carbon-nitrogen nanotubes of the general formula $B_xC_yN_z$.

20 Claims, 2 Drawing Sheets

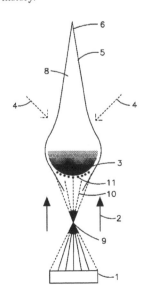

(56) **References Cited**

OTHER PUBLICATIONS

Kim et al, "Double-walled boron nitride nanotubes grown by floating catalyst chemical vapor deposition," Nano Letters 2008, vol. 8, No. 10, pp. 3298-3302 (with supporting information).*

Okada et al, "Viscosity of liquid boron," Phys. Rev. B 81, 140201(R) (2010).*

Yu et al,"Synthesis of boron nitride nanotubes by means of excimer laser ablation at high temperature," Appl. Phys. Lett., vol. 72, No. 16, Apr. 20, 1998, pp. 1966-1968.*

Arenal, "Root-growth mechanism for single-walled boron nitride nanotubes in laser vaporization technique," JACS Articles 2007, vol. 129, pp. 16183-16189.*

Smith, M.W. et al., Very Long single- and Few-walled Boron nitride Nanotubes via the Pressurized Vapor/condenser Method; Nanotechnology 20 (2009) 505604.

Ma, Renzhi et al., Synthesis and Properties of B—C—N and BN Nanostructure, Phil. Tran.:Math., Phys. and Eng. Sciences, vol. 362, No. 1823, (Oct. 15, 2004), pp. 2161-2186.

Goldberg, Dmitri et al., Nanotubes in Boron Nitride Laser Heated at High Pressure, Appl. Phys. Lett. 69 (14), Sep. 30, 1996, 2045-2047.

Goldberg, Dmitri et al., Boron Nitride Nanotubes, Adv. Mater., 2007, 19, 2413-2434.

Zhi, Chunyi et al., Effective Precursor for High Yield Synthesis of Pure BN Nanotubes, Solid State Communications 135 (2005) 67-70.

Bansal, Narottam et al., Boron Nitride Nanotubes—Reinforced Glass Composites, NASA/TM 2005-213874, Aug. 2005.

* cited by examiner

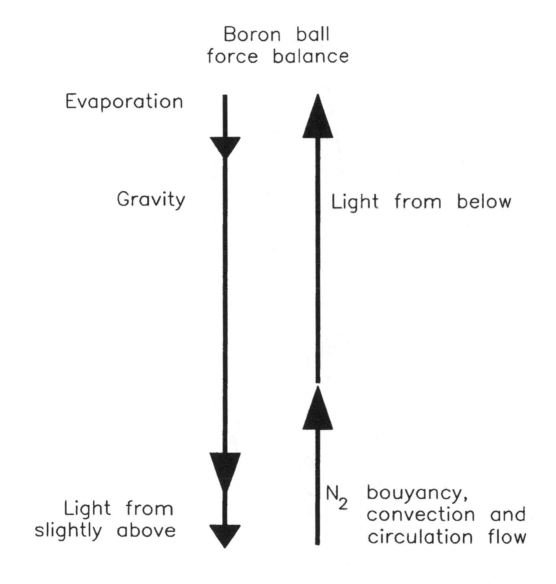

FIG. 1

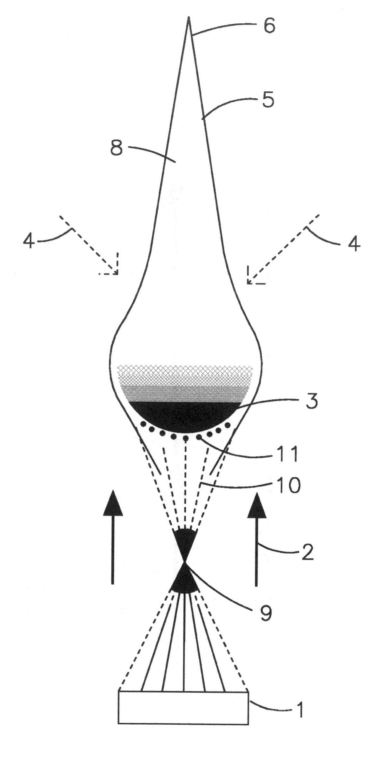

FIG. 2

1

EFFICIENT BORON NITRIDE NANOTUBE FORMATION VIA COMBINED LASER-GAS FLOW LEVITATION

This application claims the benefit of U.S. Provisional Application No. 61/460,534 filed on Jan. 4, 2011 for Efficient Boron Nitride Nanotube (BNNT) & BxCyNz Formation Via Combined Laser-Gas Flow Levitation incorporated herein by reference in its entirety.

The United States government may have certain rights to this invention under The National Aeronautics and Space Administration and/or Management and Operating Contract No. DE-AC05-06OR23177 from the Department of Energy.

FIELD OF THE INVENTION

The invention relates generally to the production of nanotubes and in particular to the formation of long-strand boron nitride and boron carbon and nitrogen ($B_xC_yN_z$) nanotubes.

BACKGROUND

Since the announcement of the successful synthesis of high-aspect-ratio-few-walled boron nitride nanotubes (FW-BNNTs) in 1995, little progress had been made until very recently in the scale-up of their synthesis. In spite of the theoretical capabilities of FW-BNNTs to provide high strength-to weight, high temperature resistance, piezo actuation, and radiation shielding (via the boron content), the aerospace industry has had to rely on micron-sized graphite or boron materials for structural applications. Further, despite their very desirable properties, neither FW-BNNTs nor single wall carbon nanotubes are used widely in aerospace manufacturing and similar industries, as industries are generally unwilling to pay the premium price for these high performance materials.

Prior to recent inventions of the present inventors, high-aspect ratio FW-BNNTs had only been produced in small amounts (from individual tubes to milligrams) by arc-discharge or laser heating methods. Further, these small amounts of FW-BNNTs were in the form of films not strands or fibers several centimeters in length. A separate class of boron nitride nanotubes know in the prior has been produced by chemical vapor deposition of nitrogen compounds (e.g. ammonia) over ball-milled precursors, but these tubes are of large diameter, and do not exhibit the continuous crystalline sp2-type bonding structure which has drawn most theoretical interest.

The Inventors' recent work in the field of boron nitride nanotubes is described in three U.S. patent application Ser. No. 12/152,414 filed May 14, 2008, U.S. patent application Ser. No. 12/322,591 filed Feb. 4, 2009 and U.S. patent application Ser. No. 12/387,703 filed May 6, 2009 incorporated herein by reference in their entirety and Inventor's article "Very Long Single- and Few-walled Boron Nitride Nanotubes Via the Pressurized Vapor/condenser Method" by Smith, Jordan, Park, Kim Lillehei, Crooks and Harrison; Nanotechnology 20 (2009) 505604. Inventors' U.S. patent application Ser. No. 12/152,414, describes the generation of very long single- and few-walled boron nitride nanotubes (BNNT) via a pressurized vapor/condenser method. In the pressurized vapor/condenser method few walled boron nitride nanotubes fibers grow continuously by surface nucleation from seemingly arbitrary asperities at a high linear rate (many cm per sec) in the line of flow of vaporized boron produced from a solid boron containing target mixed with nitrogen under elevated pressures.

2

Boron nitride nanotubes have electrical insulating properties in contrast to carbon nanotubes which are electrical conductors. This means that boron nanotubes with insulating properties have very different potential applications than carbon nanotubes which conduct. Accordingly, nanotubes, which combine boron nitride with carbon, are of considerable interest because of their potential as semiconductors.

While the pressurized vapor/condenser method has significant advantages over the prior art the energy efficiency of the pressurized vapor/condenser method is relatively low due to a large loss of heat to the solid boron support that is used both to supply and support the boron target being vaporized by the heat source (laser) driving the process.

Hence a method for producing boron nitride nanomaterials in a more energy efficient manner is highly desirable.

SUMMARY OF INVENTION

The invention provides process for producing boron nitride nanotubes. The process comprising the steps of (a) providing a boron ball target, a first laser beam having an adjustable power level and a gas flow comprising nitrogen; (b) positioning the boron ball target in a reaction position above the first laser beam and in the gas flow, the reaction position comprising a vertical reaction position and a horizontal reaction position; (c) adjusting the power level of the first laser beam to provide sufficient force from the first laser beam to the boron ball target to balance the force of gravity and the force of a light from above the boron ball target acting downward on the boron ball target and maintain the boron ball target in the vertical reaction position; (d) heating the boron ball target with the first laser beam wherein the heating evaporates a portion of the boron ball target and forms a boron vapor plume; (e) adjusting the power level of the first laser beam to maintain the heated boron ball target balanced in the vertical reaction position as the boron vapor plume moves upward from the boron ball target; (f) providing at least one second laser beam positioned above and to the side of the boron ball target, wherein the at least one second laser beam exerts a second laser beam force to maintain the heated boron ball target balanced in the horizontal reaction position; and (g) forming a plurality of boron nitride nanotubes as the upward moving boron vapor plume contacts the nitrogen in the gas flow.

The invention also provides a process for producing boron-carbon-nitrogen nanotubes of the general formula $B_xC_yN_z$. The process comprising the steps of (a) providing a boron ball target, a first laser beam having an adjustable power level, a gas flow comprising nitrogen, and a carbon source; (b) positioning the boron ball target in a reaction position above the first laser beam and in the gas flow, the reaction position comprising a vertical reaction position and a horizontal reaction position; (c) adjusting the power level of the first laser beam to provide sufficient force from the first laser beam to the boron ball target to balance the force of gravity and the force of a light from above the boron ball target acting downward on the boron ball target and maintain the boron ball target in the vertical reaction position; (d) heating the boron ball target with the first laser beam wherein the heating evaporates a portion of the boron ball target and forms a boron vapor plume and vaporizes the carbon source to form carbon atoms; (e) adjusting the power level of the first laser beam to maintain the heated boron ball target balanced in the vertical reaction position as the boron vapor plume moves upward from the boron ball target; (f) providing at least one second laser beam positioned above and to the side of the boron ball target, wherein the at least one second laser beam exerts a second

3

laser beam force to maintain the heated boron ball target balanced in the horizontal reaction position; and (g) forming a plurality of boron-carbon-nitrogen nanotubes of the general formula $B_xC_yN_z$ as the upward moving boron vapor plume contacts the nitrogen in the gas flow and carbon atoms.

DESCRIPTION OF THE DRAWINGS

FIG. 1 is a schematic representation of the forces acting on the boron ball target in the in combined laser-gas flow levitation process.

FIG. 2 is a schematic representation of the formation of boron containing nanotubes in the combined laser-gas flow levitation process.

DETAILED DESCRIPTION OF THE INVENTION

The process described herein utilizes a combination of laser light and nitrogen gas flow to support a boron ball target during heating of the boron ball target and production of a boron vapor plume.

Boron nitride nanotubes are formed when hot boron vapor (about 4000° C.) from a boron ball target combines with atomic nitrogen near the correct 1:1 stoichiometric ratio. If a source of carbon is present with the hot boron and atomic nitrogen, boron-carbon-nitrogen nanotubes of the general formula $B_xC_yN_z$ are formed. The carbon may be supplied as a carbon rich gas such as methane or acetylene that is mixed with the nitrogen gas that is supplied to the reaction system or alternatively may be solid carbon such as carbon fibers, carbon powder or graphite included in a solid boron target which is vaporized as the boron is vaporized. Lasers including, but not limited to a free electron laser(s), a fiber laser(s), a solid state laser(s), or a gas laser(s) including standard commercial CO_2 laser(s) may supply the energy for the process of the invention, for example. The laser(s) should be sufficiently powerful to produce a laser beam(s) that maintain the hot boron ball target in the reaction position and heat the boron ball target to produce boron vapor. The light from the laser beam both directly heats the boron and indirectly heats nitrogen gas flowing past the boron ball to disassociate the nitrogen gas into atomic nitrogen.

Referring to FIG. 1 which is a schematic representation of the forces acting on the boron ball target in the combined laser-gas flow levitation process. As the diagram shows the boron ball target experiences upward forces from nitrogen gas buoyancy, convection and circulation flow and the laser light from below; and downward forces due to evaporation of boron vapor from the boron ball target, gravity and light from above and slightly to the side of the boron ball target.

FIG. 2 is a schematic representation of the formation of boron containing nanotubes in the combined laser-gas flow levitation process. As FIG. 2 shows a boron ball target 3 which has a somewhat spherical or teardrop shape and a ball underside 11 is placed in a nitrogen gas flow 2 introduced below the boron ball target 3 and creating a circulation flow upward toward the boron ball target 3. First laser beam 10 from the laser 1 impinges the boron ball target 3 from below on the ball underside 11. The first laser beam 10 is focused though optics to give optical focal point 9 positioned between the laser 1 and the boron ball target 3 which facilitates keeping the boron ball target 3 in the correct location as boron evaporates from the boron ball target 3. As the first laser beam 10 impinges the boron ball target, the boron ball target heats to the melting point and evaporates, boron vapor plume 8 thus formed rises upward from the boron ball target 3 and contacts the nitrogen gas flow 2 creating a nanotube formation inter-

4

face 5 in which boron nitride nanotubes are formed. If carbon is introduced into the system as a carbon rich gas mixed with the nitrogen gas flow 2 and/or as a component of the boron ball target boron-carbon-nitrogen nanotubes of the general formula $B_xC_yN_z$ may be formed in the nanotube formation interface 5. The nanotubes thus formed are carried upward by the boron vapor plume 8 and/or nitrogen gas flow 2 and are collected at the terminus 6 of the boron vapor plume 8.

An at least one second laser beam 4 is positioned to impinge from above and slightly to the side onto the upper portion of the boron ball target 3 and/or forming boron vapor plume 8 to facilitate balancing the sideways or horizontal force acting on the boron ball target 3 and maintaining the boron ball target 3 in a balanced substantially constant position. FIG. 2 shows two second laser beams which is representative of a typical system. The at least one second laser beam may be produced by beam splitting a beam from a second laser, produced by a plurality of lasers or produced by splitting the beam of the laser 1 to give a plurality of beams. If beam splitting is employed, it is preferable the each of the plurality of the resulting beams be independently controllable. As the boron ball target 3 is heated from ambient temperature to about 4000° C. the evaporation begins and then continues as the boron ball target 3 evaporates, the power of the first laser beam 10 below and the nitrogen gas flow 2 are adjusted to stabilize the position of the boron ball target. In one embodiment evaporation of the boron ball target 3 continues until the boron ball target 3 is entirely evaporated.

As shown in FIG. 2, one laser is used to produce the first laser beam that impinges on the bottom of the boron ball target, however, as one skilled in the art will appreciate, in some embodiments the use of a plurality of lasers to produce the first laser beam that impinges on the bottom of the boron ball may be desirable. Similarly, the at least one second laser beam that impinges onto the upper portion of the boron ball target from above and slightly to the side may be produced by a plurality of lasers or alternatively the beam of a single laser may be split into a plurality of beams and directed through optics to produce light that impinges at more than one position on the upper portion of the boron ball target and/or boron vapor plume. Alternatively, laser beam from a single laser may be split to provide multiple laser beams that can be used for one or more of the first laser beam and the at least one second laser beam. If beam splitting is employed it is preferable to that each of the resulting beams is independently controllable.

The boron ball target should be maintained in a nearly constant position (i.e. a reaction position) throughout the process. The reaction position comprises a vertical reaction position and a horizontal reaction position. The reaction position is maintained by balancing the four main forces on the boron ball target. The four main forces in effect on the ball are gravity, light pressure, gas flow including buoyancy, and evaporation.

Gravity.

The boron ball target is forced down due to the force of gravity. As the boron ball evaporates (vaporizes to form the boron vapor plume), the force of gravity is lessened. The force of gravity is: $F_g=mg$ where m is the mass of the ball and g is the acceleration due to gravity (i.e. 9.8 m/s²).

Light Pressure.

Light carries momentum (i.e., p=E/c, or in terms of power of the light, P, force is $F_l=P/c$ where F_l is the force of light, and c is the speed of light). When light is absorbed, the impacted object absorbs the momentum. If light is perfectly reflected, the momentum is twice as much. The net force of the light along the vertical is also dependent on the direction of the light. For the geometry shown in FIG. 2, the light coming from below has most of its force directed upward to the boron ball target and light coming from above and slightly to the side of the boron ball target has most of its force substantially directed towards the sides of the boron ball target and/or boron vapor plume such that the net sideways or horizontal force on the boron ball target is balanced so that the net sideways or horizontal force on the boron ball target is zero. As the boron ball target is very hot during the process there is a small downward net force from the radiated light coming from the top of the boron ball target being slightly more radiated than the radiated light from the bottom of the boron ball target.

Gas Flow.

There are two sources of gas flow. These sources are: (1) a fan or pump system that moves the nitrogen gas or combinations of nitrogen gas and carbon bearing gas in the desired direction and (2) the hot boron ball target and boron vapor plume heating the surrounding gas flow thereby creating a convective flow. The sum of the two sources is maintained such that gas going around the boron ball target remains non-turbulent, i.e. laminar flow conditions. This speed is dependent on the size of the ball, the gas temperature near the ball and the gas pressure. The range of applicable gas pressure is from about atmospheric of about 15 psi to around 20,000 psi, the pressure where the boron ball would become buoyant and simply float up and away with pressures of about 100 to about 2,000 psi preferred in some embodiments. The vertical flow force, F_f from the gas flow is dependent on the diameter of the boron ball, buoyancy effects, the speed of the gas flow, the gas pressure and the temperature.

Evaporation.

When the ball approaches its vaporization temperature, i.e. about 4000° C, it begins to produce boron vapor (i.e. a boron vapor plume). The cooler part of the boron ball target will be near the bottom of the boron ball target due to the additional heat being provided by the laser(s) producing light from above and slightly to the side and the tendency of the hotter material which is lighter to rise to the top. The preferential release of boron as boron vapor on the top of the boron ball target will create a net evaporative force, F_e, downwards on the ball though there will be some upwards evaporative force from boron evaporating on the bottom side of the ball.

The process for producing boron nitride nanotubes and/or boron-carbon-nitrogen nanotubes of the general formula $B_xC_yN_z$) comprises the steps of:

1. A room temperature boron ball target is placed into a reaction position. Suitable methods for placing the boron ball target into position include, but are not limited to, using a boron target ball that has slight whiskers attached that are used to mechanically place and hold the ball in position until heating is initiated, or alternatively propelling the boron ball target upward such that the top of its near parabolic arc (slightly modified by drag) is at the desired position.

2. Once the boron ball target is in position, a laser is activated to produce a laser beam of a sufficient force to add the additional force (in addition to buoyancy and the gas flow forces) needed to balance the downward force due to gravity and light from above and to side of the boron ball target on the boron ball target

3. The boron ball target heats and as it heats it acquires additional upwards force due to convection heating of the gas flow. There are several sources of feedback to stabilize the position of the boron ball target in the reaction position. First, the first laser beam is focused at a point below the boron ball target such that some of the light near the periphery of the boron ball target impinges at an angle such that the vertical

force on the boron ball target increases as the boron ball target moves downwards closer to the focal point. Secondly, feedback from the location of the boron ball target is monitored and the power of the first laser beam and the rate of flow of the gas are adjusted based on this feedback to keep the forces on the ball vertically balanced. Thirdly, the horizontal position of the boron ball target is also monitored and the strength of the at least one second laser beam's horizontal components of force is adjusted to keep the ball directly above the focal point of the first laser beam coming from below. The horizontal forces are due to a combination of the force of the at least one second laser beam and the differential evaporation rates in the horizontal directions. Any combination or all of the effects may be employed to provide feedback for maintaining the boron ball target in a substantially stable reaction position.

4. When the boron ball target reaches the vaporization temperature of boron, the power levels of the laser(s) are adjusted in real-time to stabilize both the vaporization rate and the position of the boron ball target.

5. As the boron ball target continues to vaporize the laser(s) are further adjusted in real-time to stabilize both the vaporization and position of the boron ball target by balancing the forces of gravity, impinging light, gas flow and evaporation acting on the boron ball target (i.e. the sum of the forces gravity, impinging light, gas flow and evaporation acting on the boron ball target should be about zero.)

6. The vaporized boron formed rises upward from the boron ball target as a plume of boron vapor and contacts the nitrogen gas flow creating a nanotube formation interface in which nanotubes are formed. The nanotubes thus formed are carried upward by the boron vapor plume and/or nitrogen gas flow and are collected at the terminus of the boron vapor plume.

In a preferred embodiment the steps of the process described above are performed sequentially in the order set forth above. The process can continue until the boron ball target becomes so small that it is carried away in the gas flow. The process may be repeated by obtaining a new boron ball target.

The process for the production of boron-carbon-nitrogen and nanotubes of the general formula $B_xC_yN_z$ formation comprises essentially the same steps as for the production of few-walled boron nitride nanotubes. The specific compositional empirical formula of the $B_xC_yN_z$ nanotubes is determined by the relative amounts of boron, carbon and nitrogen used. For boron nitride nanotubes a boron-containing target of compressed boron powder, compressed boron nitride powder, and mixtures thereof, for example is suitable and no carbon is used in either the target or the gas flow. For nanotubes of the general formula $B_xC_yN_z$, carbon is introduced into the reaction. The carbon may be a solid component of the target, a carbon rich gas, mixture of carbon rich gases or a combination thereof. When a carbon rich gas is used, the proportion used is readily controlled by regulating the fractional pressure of the carbon rich gas in the nitrogen carbon rich gas mixture. Solid forms of carbon suitable for inclusion in the boron ball target are carbon fibers, carbon powder (carbon black) and mixtures thereof. Suitable carbon rich gases include, but are not limited to, hydrocarbons such as methane, ethane, ethylene, acetylene, substituted acetylenes, propane, propene, aromatic hydrocarbons such as benzene, toluene, xylene, aniline, and polyaromatic hydrocarbons, and combinations thereof.

Optionally, multiple types of carbon rich gases can be introduced simultaneously into the reaction or alternatively a

7

combination of one or more carbon rich gases and solid carbon included in the boron ball target may be used a carbon source.

The boron target is thermally excited sufficiently to form atomic boron vapor. In targets containing carbon as well as boron, both the boron and carbon are vaporized. The inventors believe, without wishing to be bound to the theory, that the when a laser heats a boron (or a boron and carbon) target to form a boron (or boron and carbon) vapor plume in the presence of nitrogen, the nitrogen is disassociated in to atomic nitrogen and the boron nitride and/or $B_xC_yN_z$ nanotubes form at the interface between the boron (or boron and carbon) vapor and the atomic nitrogen. In the case in which solid carbon is intermixed with the boron in the target, the carbon vaporizes near the same temperature as boron and both mix in the formation. In the case in which a carbon rich gas (or gases) is used as the carbon source or a portion of the carbon source, the carbon rich gas dissociates into atomic carbon and atomic hydrogen intermixed with the atomic nitrogen. The atomic carbon joins with the atomic nitrogen and boron to form the $B_xC_yN_z$ nanotubes.

Further, the inventors believe, without wishing to be bound to the theory, that no chemical catalyst and/or catalytic surface is needed to initiate the formation of boron nitride and/or $B_xC_yN_z$ nanotubes. The boron nitride nanotubes appear to form spontaneously when hot boron vapor, and nitrogen are present and or $B_xC_yN_z$ nanotubes appear to form spontaneously when hot boron vapor, vaporized carbon and nitrogen are present. This renders the Inventors' process fundamentally less complicated than carbon nanotube production in which a gas-borne cloud or coated surface of catalytic particles must be produced and kept active during the growth process. Accordingly, unlike for carbon nanotubes, the Inventors' production of boron nitride and/or $B_xC_yN_z$ nanotubes is readily amendable to continuous production of material.

The inventors believe without wishing to be bound to the theory that their process is a factor of 100 to 1000 more efficient in energy and materials usage than existing methods as well as being a method for rapid production of quantities of nanotube material as compared to known methods.

Example 1

The following example is provided for illustrative purposes. For an example using a 1.5 mm diameter boron ball target, the downward force of gravity is about 3.5×10^{-5} N. If an 8 kW laser is used to produce the light that impinges on the under side of the boron ball target the available upward force of the light is about 2.5×10^{-5} N assuming that the force due to the reflection term roughly cancels the angular effect.

To balance the force in this example, the upward force needed for the gas buoyancy and flow and heating convection terms approaches 1.0×10^{-5} N. The buoyancy component of the gas flow would be roughly equal to this at 5,000 psi so the pressure is kept below this level. For operational reasons (including safety) relying more on flow rather than buoyancy indicates that pressures of about 100 to about 2,000 psi can be used with suitable flow. As the laser power and hence force of the laser beam impinging on the bottom of the boron ball target can be rapidly changed, it is preferable in some embodiments to keep the gas low rate constant and vary the laser power to stabilize or maintain the reaction position of the boron ball target as boron evaporates from the boron ball target.

What is at present considered the preferred embodiment and alternative embodiments of the present invention has been shown and described herein. It will be obvious to those

8

skilled in the art that various changes and modifications may be made therein without departing from the scope of the invention as defined by the appended claims.

What is claimed is:

1. A process for producing boron nitride nanotubes, the process comprising the steps:
   a. providing a boron ball target, a first laser beam having an adjustable power level and a gas flow comprising nitrogen;
   b. positioning the boron ball target in a reaction position above the first laser beam and in the gas flow, the reaction position comprising a vertical reaction position and a horizontal reaction position;
   c. adjusting the power level of the first laser beam to provide sufficient force from the first laser beam to the boron ball target to balance the force of gravity and the force of a light from above the boron ball target acting downward on the boron ball target and maintain the boron ball target in the vertical reaction position;
   d. heating the boron ball target with the first laser beam wherein the heating evaporates a portion of the boron ball target and forms a boron vapor plume;
   e. adjusting the power level of the first laser beam to maintain the heated boron ball target balanced in the reaction position as the boron vapor plume moves upward from the boron ball target;
   f. providing at least one second laser beam positioned above and to the side of the boron ball target, wherein the at least one second laser beam exerts a second laser beam force on the boron ball target to maintain the boron ball target in the horizontal reaction position; and
   g. forming a plurality of boron nitride nanotubes as the upward moving boron vapor plume contacts the nitrogen in the gas flow.

2. The process of claim 1, wherein the steps are performed in sequence.

3. The process of claim 1, wherein the boron ball target has attached whiskers which are positioned mechanically to position the boron ball target above the first laser beam.

4. The process of claim 1, wherein the boron ball target is positioned above the first laser beam by propelling the boron ball upward in a near parabolic arc of motion with a top wherein the top of the near parabolic arc of motion is at the reaction position.

5. The process of claim 1, wherein the heated boron ball target is acted upon by the forces of gravity, light, gas flow including buoyancy and evaporation and the forces are balanced such that the net force acting on the heated boron ball target is zero.

6. The process of claim 1, further comprising collecting the boron nitride nanotubes.

7. The process of claim 1, wherein the first laser beam is provided by a first laser and the at least one second laser beam is provided by at least one second laser.

8. The process of claim 1, wherein the first laser beam and the at least one second laser beam are provided by a single laser and wherein the single laser produces a single laser beam and wherein a first portion of the single laser beam forms the first laser beam and a second portion of the single laser beam forms the at least one second laser beam.

9. The process of claim 1, where in the gas flow is at a pressure of about 15 to about 20,000 psi.

10. The process of claim 1 wherein the gas flow is at a pressure greater than 5,000 psi.

11. The process of claim 1 wherein the gas pressure of said nitrogen is greater than 5,000 psi.

12. A process for producing boron-carbon-nitrogen nano-tubes of the general formula BxCvNz the process comprising the steps;

    a. providing a boron ball target, a first laser beam having an adjustable power level, a gas flow comprising nitrogen, and a carbon source;

    b. positioning the boron ball target in a reaction position above the first laser beam and in the gas flow, the reaction position comprising a vertical reaction position and a horizontal reaction position;

    c. adjusting the power level of the first laser beam to provide sufficient force from the first laser beam to the boron ball target to balance the force of gravity and the force of a light from above the boron ball target acting downward on the boron ball target and maintain the boron ball target in the reaction position;

    d. heating the boron ball target with the first laser beam wherein the heating evaporates a portion of the boron ball target and forms a boron vapor plume and vaporizes the carbon source to form carbon atoms;

    e. adjusting the power level of the first laser beam to maintain the heated boron ball target balanced in the reaction position as the boron vapor plume moves upward from the boron ball target;

    f. providing at least one second laser beam positioned above and to the side of the boron ball target, wherein the at least one second laser beam exerts a second laser beam force on the boron ball target to maintain the boron ball target in the horizontal reaction position; and

    g. forming a plurality of boron-carbon-nitrogen nanotubes of the general formula BxCvNz as the upward moving boron vapor plume contacts the nitrogen in the gas flow and carbon atoms.

10

13. The process of claim 12, wherein the steps are performed in sequence.

14. The process of claim 12, wherein the boron ball target has attached whiskers which are positioned mechanically to position the boron ball target above the first laser beam.

15. The process of claim 12, wherein the boron ball target is positioned above the first laser beam by propelling the boron ball upward in a near parabolic arc of motion with a top wherein the top of the near parabolic arc of motion is at the reaction position.

16. The process of claim 12, wherein the heated boron ball target is acted upon by the forces of gravity, light, gas flow and evaporation and the forces are balanced such that the net force acting on the heated boron ball target is zero.

17. The process of claim 12, further comprising collecting the boron-carbon-nitrogen nanotubes of the general formula BxCyNz.

18. The process of claim 12, wherein the first laser beam is provided by a first laser and the at least one second laser beam is provided by at least one second laser.

19. The process of claim 12, wherein the first laser beam and the at least one second laser beam are provided by a single laser and wherein the single laser produces a single laser beam and wherein a first portion of the single laser beam forms the first laser beam and a second portion of the single laser beam forms the at least one second laser beam.

20. The process of claim 12, wherein the boron ball target comprises boron and a carbon source.

*   *   *   *   *

US008733706B1

(12) **United States Patent**
Fernandez et al.

(10) Patent No.: **US 8,733,706 B1**
(45) **Date of Patent:** **May 27, 2014**

(54) **TRANSFORMABLE AND RECONFIGURABLE ENTRY, DESCENT AND LANDING SYSTEMS AND METHODS**

(75) Inventors: **Ian M. Fernandez**, Boulder Creek, CA (US); **Ethiraj Venkatapathy**, Los Altos, CA (US); **Kenneth R. Hamm**, Tracy, CA (US)

(73) Assignee: **The United States of America as Represented by the Administrator of the National Aeronautics & Space Administration (NASA)**, Washington, DC (US)

(*) Notice: Subject to any disclaimer, the term of this patent is extended or adjusted under 35 U.S.C. 154(b) by 203 days.

(21) Appl. No.: **13/472,283**

(22) Filed: **May 15, 2012**

(51) **Int. Cl.**
B64C 1/10 (2006.01)

(52) **U.S. Cl.**
USPC **244/158.7**; 244/159.1; 244/139

(58) **Field of Classification Search**
USPC .... 244/158.7, 159.1, 139, 172.6, 110 D, 244/138 A
See application file for complete search history.

(56) **References Cited**

U.S. PATENT DOCUMENTS

4,832,288 A	*	5/1989	Kendall et al.	244/159.2
4,896,847 A	*	1/1990	Gertsch	244/159.1
5,108,047 A	*	4/1992	Puech	244/113
5,201,832 A	*	4/1993	Porter et al.	244/158.7
6,550,720 B2	*	4/2003	Fleeter et al.	244/158.7
7,837,154 B2	*	11/2010	Trabandt et al.	244/159.1

OTHER PUBLICATIONS

Drake, Bret G., editor, "Human Exploration of Mars Design Reference Architecture 5.0," NASA-SP-2009-566, Jul. 2009.
Dwyer-Cianciolo, A. M. et al., "Entry, Descent and Landing Systems Analysis Study: Phase 1 Report," NASA/TM-2010-216720, Jul. 2010.
Goetz, A. C., and Jensen, D. L., "Deployable Heatshields for Future Multistage Missiles," Journal of Spacecraft and Rockets, vol. 17, No. 1, pp. 53-57, 1980.
Venkatapathy, E. et al., "Adaptive Deployable Entry and Placement Technology (ADEPT):A Feasibility Study for Human Missions to Mars," AIAA-2011-2608, 21st AIAA Aerodynamic Decelerator Systems Technology Conference and Seminar, Dublin, Ireland, May 23-26, 2011.
Beck, R, White, S, Arnold, J, Fan, W, Stackpoole, M, Agrawal, P, and Coughlin, S, "Overview of Initial Development of Flexible Ablators for Hypersonic Inflatable Aerodynamic Decelerators," AIAA Paper presented at the 21st AIAA Aerodynamic Decelerators Conference and Seminar, Dublin, Ireland, May 2011.
Edquist, K. T. et al., "Aerothermodynamic Design of the Mars Science Laboratory Heatshield," AIAA 2009-4075, 41st AIAA Thermophysics Conference, San Antonio, TX, Jun. 2009.

(Continued)

Primary Examiner — Christopher P Ellis
(74) *Attorney, Agent, or Firm* — Christopher J. Menke; Robert M. Padilla

(57) **ABSTRACT**

A deployable aerodynamic decelerator structure includes a ring member disposed along a central axis of the aerodynamic decelerator, a plurality of jointed rib members extending radially from the ring member and a flexible layer attached to the plurality of rib members. A deployment device is operable to reconfigure the flexible layer from a stowed configuration to a deployed configuration by movement of the rib members and a control device is operable to redirect a lift vector of the decelerator structure by changing an orientation of the flexible layer.

20 Claims, 10 Drawing Sheets

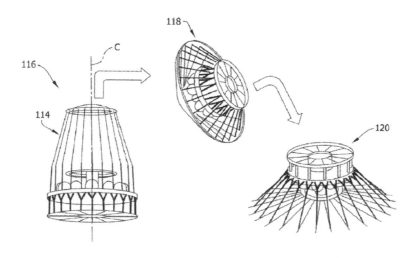

(56)   **References Cited**

OTHER PUBLICATIONS

McGuire M. K. et al., "TPS Selection and Sizing Tool Implemented in and Advanced Engineering Environment," AIAA-2004-342, 42nd AIAA Aerospace Sciences Meeting and Exhibit, Reno NV, Jan. 2004.

Milos, F.S. and Chen, Y-K, "Two-Dimensional Ablation, Thermal Response, and Sizing Program for Pyrolyzing Ablators," AIAA Paper 2008-1223, AIAA Aerospace Sciences Meeting and Exhibition, Jan. 2008.

* cited by examiner

FIG. 1

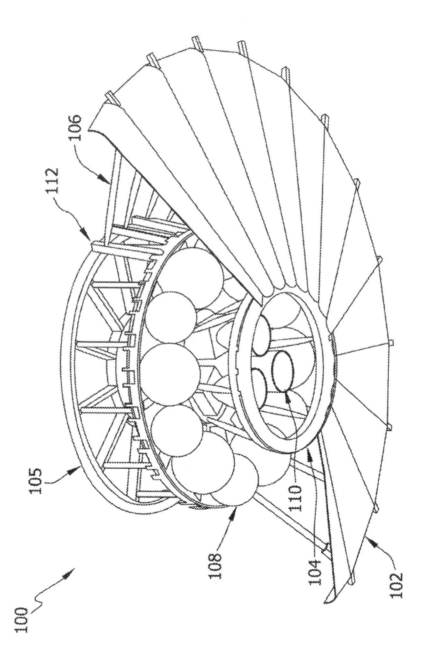

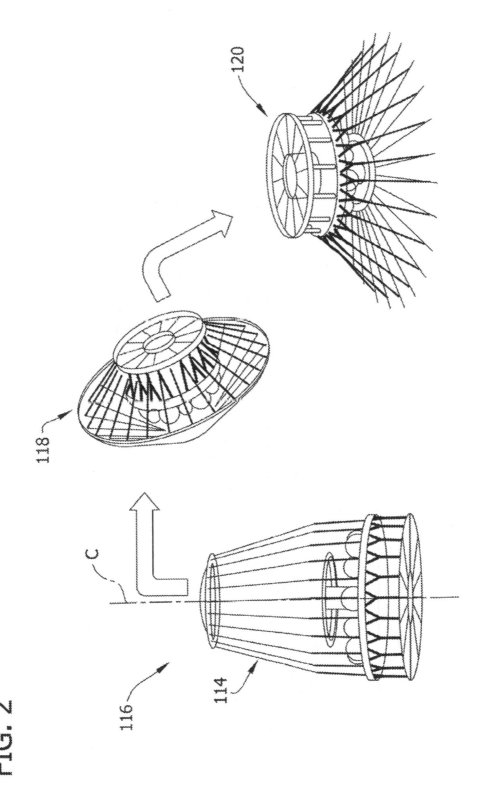

FIG. 2

FIG. 3

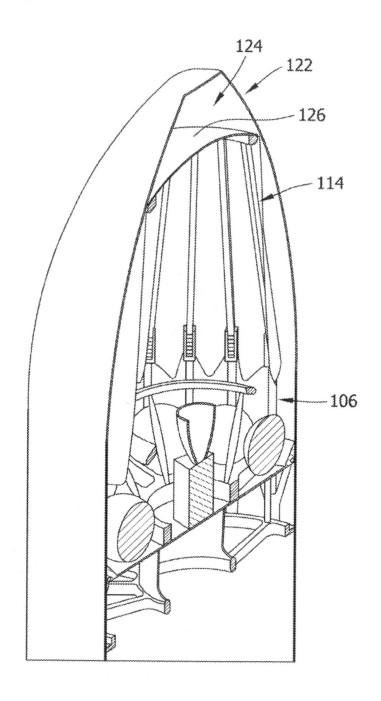

FIG. 4

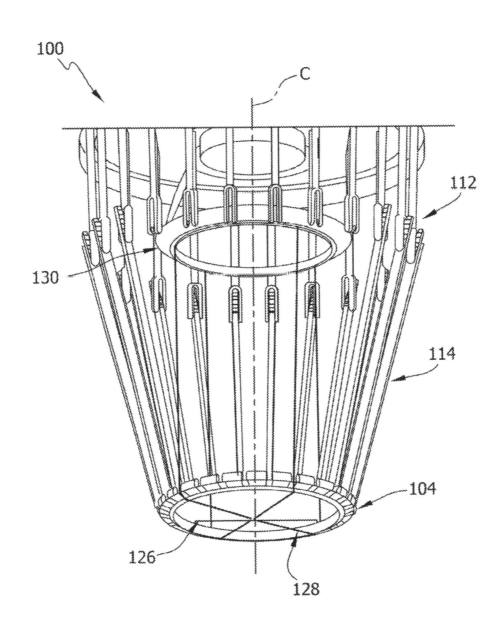

FIG. 5

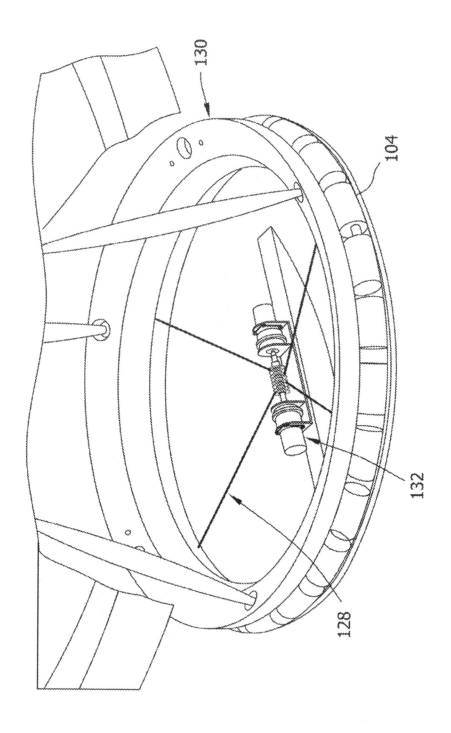

FIG. 6

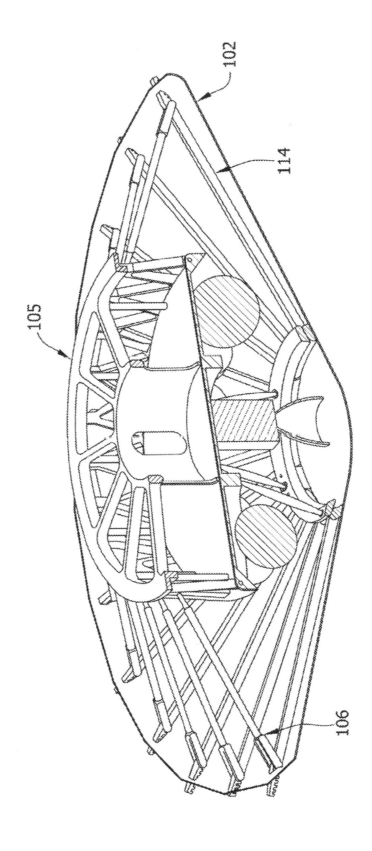

FIG. 7

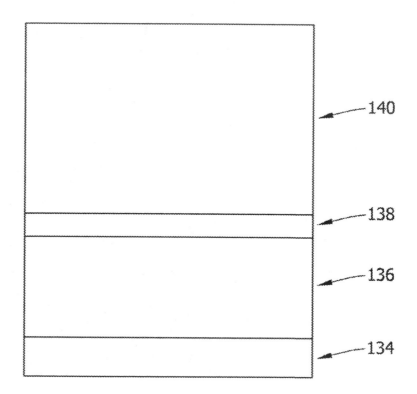

102

140

138

136

134

FIG. 8

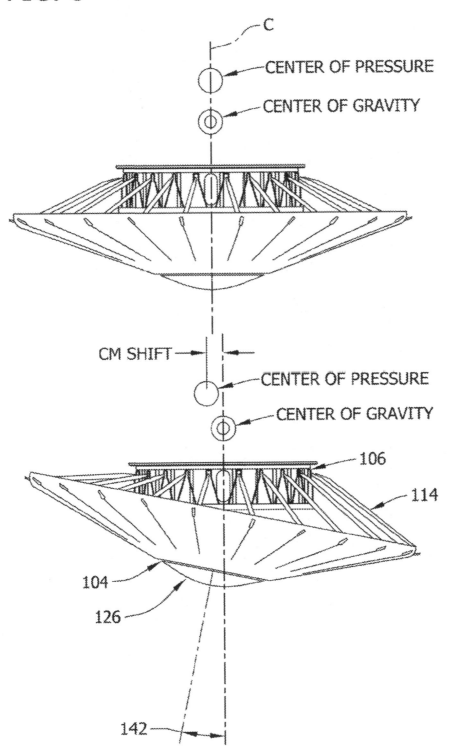

419

FIG. 9

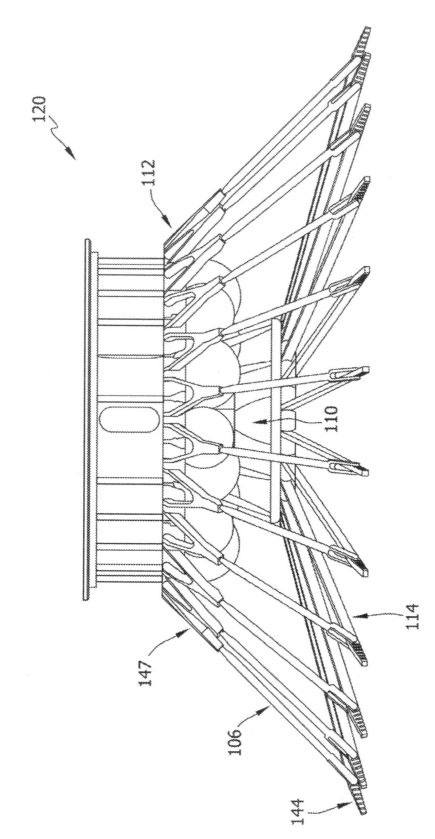

120

112

110

147

106

114

144

FIG. 10

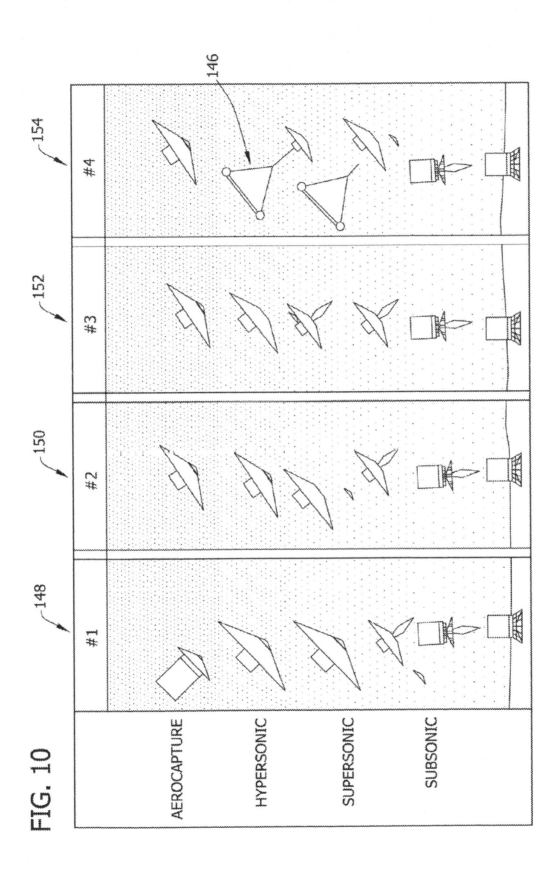

1

TRANSFORMABLE AND RECONFIGURABLE ENTRY, DESCENT AND LANDING SYSTEMS AND METHODS

ORIGIN OF INVENTION

The invention described herein was made by employees of the United States Government and may be manufactured and used by or for the Government of the United States of America for governmental purposes without the payment of any royalties thereon or therefor.

TECHNICAL FIELD OF THE INVENTION

The present disclosure relates generally to aerodynamic decelerators. More particularly, the present disclosure relates to transformable and reconfigurable, aerodynamic decelerator systems.

BACKGROUND OF THE INVENTION

Conventionally, entry, descent and landing (EDL) technology utilizes a rigid aeroshell structure for both aerodynamic braking and thermal protection of a payload. Typically, the rigid aeroshell structure has a size that is constrained by the launch vehicle carrying the rigid aeroshell structure (i.e., the size is constrained to a size that fits within the launch vehicle). Due to such size limitations of the rigid aeroshell structure, the mass of the payload for which the rigid aeroshell structure is designed is also limited. The limitations of size and the resulting mass that can be packaged within the rigid aeroshell structure often results in a severe entry condition.

Increasingly, large missions and campaigns to near and far solar system destinations, such as inner and outer planets and moons, as well as human and sample return to Earth, are planned. Such large missions and campaigns require large payloads and heatshield structures capable of safely and effectively landing the payload at these destinations.

The effectiveness of the rigid aeroshell structure for aerodynamic braking and thermal protection is dependent upon, among other factors, the size of the structure and the density of the atmosphere in which the rigid aeroshell structure is utilized. For a planet such as Mars, the atmosphere is not dense enough to allow typical rigid aeroshell structures to be effective for payloads over approximately two metric tons (mT). However, the Martian atmosphere is dense enough to cause significant heating from aerodynamic friction during descent.

Further, typical EDL technologies utilize a reaction control system (RCS) using propulsive thrust for directional control of the payload during descent. However, conventional propulsive thrust technologies may be inefficient and inadequate for large payloads.

BRIEF DESCRIPTION OF THE INVENTION

In one aspect a deployable aerodynamic decelerator structure includes a ring member disposed along a central axis of the aerodynamic decelerator, a plurality of jointed rib members extending radially from the ring member and a flexible layer attached to the plurality of rib members. A deployment device is operable to reconfigure the flexible layer from a stowed configuration to a deployed configuration by movement of the rib members, and a control device is operable to redirect a lift vector of the decelerator structure by changing an orientation of the flexible layer.

2

In another aspect, an entry, and decent system includes a ring member disposed along a central axis of the system, a plurality of rib members hinged and connected to the ring member, and a flexible layer attached to the plurality of rib members. A deployment device is operable to reconfigure the flexible layer and the plurality of rib members by movement of the rib members to control and redirect the lift vector of the decelerator structure during entry and descent maneuvers.

In another aspect, an entry, decent and landing system includes a ring member disposed along a central axis of the system, a plurality of rib members hingedly connected to the ring member, and a flexible layer attached to the plurality of rib members. A deployment device is operable to reconfigure the flexible layer from a deployed configuration to a landing configuration by moving the ring member along the central axis and a payload adaptor member is configured to connect the system to a payload.

In yet another aspect, a method of landing a payload includes providing a payload and attaching the payload to a deployable aerodynamic decelerator structure. The structure includes a ring member disposed along a central axis of the aerodynamic decelerator, a plurality of jointed rib members extending radially from the ring member, a flexible layer attached to the plurality of rib members, a deployment device operable to reconfigure the flexible layer from a stowed configuration to a deployed configuration, and a control device operable to redirect a lift vector of the decelerator structure. The deployment device is operated to reconfigure the flexible layer into the deployed configuration to attenuate the impact energy experienced by the payload. The control device is operated to redirect the lift vector of the decelerator structure and the deployment device is operated to reconfigure the flexible layer into a landing configuration.

BRIEF DESCRIPTION OF THE DRAWINGS

FIG. 1 is perspective view of an aerodynamic decelerator system according to the present disclosure.

FIG. 2 shows the aerodynamic decelerator system of FIG. 1 in each of three exemplary configurations.

FIG. 3 shows the aerodynamic decelerator system of FIG. 1 in a first configuration and stowed within a launch vehicle.

FIG. 4 shows the aerodynamic decelerator system of FIG. 1 including cables for deployment.

FIG. 5 shows a close-up view of the aerodynamic decelerator of FIG. 4 including a cable deployment mechanism.

FIG. 6 shows a perspective view of the aerodynamic decelerator of FIG. 1 in an exemplary deployed configuration.

FIG. 7 shows a cross section of a flexible layer according to the present disclosure.

FIG. 8 shows the aerodynamic decelerator system of FIG. 1 in exemplary zero lift and lift producing configurations.

FIG. 9 shows the aerodynamic decelerator system of FIG. 1 in an exemplary landing configuration.

FIG. 10 shows a plurality of exemplary aerodynamic decelerators during multiple phases of entry, decent and landing.

DETAILED DESCRIPTION OF THE INVENTION

The transformable and reconfigurable aerodynamic decelerator systems of the present disclosure are stowable within an air vehicle or launch vehicle. For example, the aerodynamic decelerators are deployable into a large aerosurface for aerocapture and atmospheric entry and descent. The aerodynamic decelerator systems are, in one embodiment, reconfigurable for efficient control during flight and include thermal protection materials. The aerodynamic decelerator systems, in another embodiment, are transformable into a final landing configuration. The aerodynamic decelerator systems described herein may also be referred to as Adaptive DEployable Placement Technology (ADEPT).

Shown generally in FIG. 1 is an exemplary embodiment of an aerodynamic decelerator 100 according to the present disclosure. The aerodynamic decelerator includes a flexible layer 102, ring member 104, payload adaptor member 105, a plurality of links 106, a plurality of fuel storage containers 108, a retro propulsion device 110, and a deployment device 112.

In one embodiment, flexible layer 102 spans between a plurality of rib members, such as spokes 114 (shown in FIG. 2). In another embodiment, flexible layer 102 is connected to spokes 114 via an integral continuous member (not shown) that is woven into flexible layer 102. In one embodiment, each continuous tang extends substantially along the entire length of the each respective spoke.

Shown generally in FIG. 2 are three exemplary configurations of aerodynamic decelerator 100 according to the present disclosure. The three configurations include: stowed configuration 116, deployed configuration 118 and landing configuration 120. In one embodiment, stowed configuration 116 is a configuration allowing aerodynamic decelerator structure 100 to fit inside a shroud 122 of a launch vehicle, for example as shown in FIG. 3. In stowed configuration 116, aerodynamic decelerator 100 is configured to fit within a volumetric envelope 124 of shroud 122. A ratio of the diameter of the stowed configuration to the deployed configuration may be referred to as a packaging efficiency. In embodiments, the packaging efficiency may be between about 2 to 5 (i.e., in a linear dimensional ratio). For example, for an exemplary Mars mission, the packaging efficiency is between about 2.3 to 4.4 (i.e., the stowed configuration diameter is 10 m whereas the deployed configuration diameter is between about 23 m to 44 m). For an exemplary mission to Venus, the packaging efficiency is about 4.0.

In one embodiment, flexible layer 102 is attached to ring member 104 and deployment device 112 in a manner that allows the flexible layer to fold around links 106 and spokes 114, for example straight radial folds (e.g., similar to an umbrella) and the like. In stowed configuration 116, links 106 and spokes 114 extend longitudinally outward with respect to a central axis C of aerodynamic decelerator 100, as shown in an exemplary manner in FIG. 3. In one embodiment, stowed configuration 116 allows for a minimum bend radius of flexible layer 102 to be approximately 40-60 mm, more particularly approximately 51 mm. In other embodiments, the minimum bend radius is any radius that allows the aerodynamic decelerator to function as described herein. In another embodiment, rigging (not shown) is utilized to constrain flexible layer 102 against launch loads.

Aerodynamic decelerator 100 is configured to extend into one or more deployed configurations. For example, after leaving Earth orbit (e.g., outside of Earth's atmosphere) and before entry into a planetary or moon atmosphere when there is little to no aerodynamic loading, aerodynamic decelerator structure 100 is reconfigured to deployed configuration 118. Generally, such deployment occurs after shroud 122 is ejected or otherwise removed. In some embodiments, aerodynamic decelerator 100 is deployed in one or more partial deployment stages. Shown generally in FIG. 4 is an exemplary embodiment of deployment device 112. In some embodiments, deployment device 112 includes one or more electrical and mechanical components configured to deploy flexible layer 102 to deployed configuration 118.

In one embodiment, a nose 126 is removably attached to ring member 104 by an adhesive, mechanical attachment such as clasps or the like. In another embodiment, nose 126 and/or flexible layer 102 is made of a heat shielding material, such as a flexible thermally protective shield. In some embodiments, the thermally protective shield material is Silicone Impregnated Reusable Carbon Ablator (SIRCA) material or Phenolic Impregnated Carbon Ablator (PICA) material or the like. In other embodiments, the thermally protective shield material is made of any suitable ablative material. Ring member 104 is hingedly connected to spokes 114 around central axis C of aerodynamic decelerator 100. Deployment of aerodynamic decelerator 100 to deployed configuration is accomplished, in one embodiment, by use of cables 128. In one embodiment, cables 128 are made of Dyneema® fiber ropes, however cables 128 may be made of any material that allows aerodynamic decelerator 100 to function as described herein. Cables 128 are affixed to ring member 104 and are configured to pull ring member 104 longitudinally along central axis C with respect to a control device 130. As ring member 104 is pulled along the longitudinal axis, spokes 114 extend radially outwardly from the hinged connection to expand flexible layer 102 into deployed configuration 118. Extending spokes radially outwardly, unfolds and/or stretches flexible layer, as shown for example in FIG. 6 into deployed configuration 118. In one embodiment, as shown in FIG. 5, cables 128 are spooled/pulled using a winding device 132 (e.g., a winch), which may be mounted in a central region of nose 126. Each of cables 128 may be individually wound on a separate pulley to individually control a length of each of cables 128. In one embodiment, winding device 132 is connected to a controller which allows an operator to control the extent of deployment. In one embodiment, winding device 132 includes dual motors and/or gearboxes for redundancy. In another embodiment, actuators (not shown), such as hydraulic, pneumatic or electromechanical actuators, are utilized to push/pull ring member 104 longitudinally along central axis C. In deployed configuration 118, aerodynamic decelerator structure has an increased drag coefficient as compared to stowed configuration 116 and is thus is configured for atmospheric aerocapture.

In one embodiment, to substantially prevent excessive local heating due to sudden acceleration of the air or other gases flowing around the shoulder from the high pressure to low pressure regions, a shoulder radius is formed at or near the end of deployment using a mechanism (not shown) that bends edges of the flexible layer inwardly (i.e., in a hoop direction). When in deployed configuration 118, flexible layer 102 extends between spokes 114 and/or links 106 (as shown in FIG. 6), which allows for the flexible layer to transfer an aerodynamic load to payload adaptor 105. In deployed configuration 118, flexible layer 102 also functions as a thermal shield to other components of aerodynamic decelerator 100. In some embodiments, flexible layer 102 forms a sphere-cone shape in deployed configuration 118, such as a 70° sphere cone shape.

In one embodiment, at least some of flexible layer 102 is made of a thermally protective material to provide the thermal shielding capability. Flexible layer 102 is configured to be strong enough to withstand the aerodynamic loads of decelerating the structure in an atmosphere and also flexible enough to fold into the stowed configuration. In one embodiment, flexible layer 102 is made of a woven carbon fiber cloth as a base material. In another embodiment, flexible layer 102 is gas impermeable and covered with a flexible thermally protective material that is boned or stitched to the woven carbon fiber cloth. Shown in FIG. 7, is a cross section of an

5

exemplary embodiment of flexible layer **102**. As shown in FIG. **7**, flexible layer **102** may itself contain one or more sub-layers in a stacked configuration. In one embodiment the sublayers may include one or more of a carbon fiber layer **134**, an insulative layer **136**, a carbon cloth layer **138** and an ablative layer **140**. In embodiments, ablative layer **140** is made of an ablative material like SIRCA or PICA. In another embodiment, at least a portion of flexible layer **102** is made of a material capable of radiating heat from front and back surfaces of flexible layer **102**.

Spokes **114** and links **106** are configured to transmit aerodynamic loads from flexible layer **102** to payload adaptor **104**. In some embodiments, spokes **114** and links **106** are made of the same or different materials, such as insulated carbon fiber composites, non-insulated carbon-carbon composites, an insulated titanium matrix or the like. In one embodiment, spokes **114** and links **106** have a rectangular cross section up to approximately 152 mm×457 mm, but may be formed in any shape and size to allow the aerodynamic decelerator to function as described herein.

In embodiments, aerodynamic decelerator includes between 16 and 32 spokes, for example, 16, 24 or 32 spokes. In one embodiment, under an applied aerodynamic loading (e.g., during aerocapture), flexible layer **102** deflects inwardly producing a scalloped shape between spokes **114**. In one embodiment, to reduce scalloping, flexible layer **102** has a thickness of approximately 0.30 mm to 0.35 mm, more particularly 0.33 mm.

To control aerodynamic decelerator **100** during descent, control device **130** controls the center of gravity and center of pressure, as shown for example in FIG. **8** by moving the payload (not shown) and or the ring member **104**. In one embodiment, control device **130** is configured to move or rotate the payload relative to aerodynamic decelerator **100** by using one or more actuators to push or pull the payload with respect to aerodynamic decelerator **100**. For example, the payload may be pushed/pulled by the actuators such that the center of mass of the payload is offset from central axis C of aerodynamic decelerator **100**. In another embodiment, control device **130** is configured to gimbal one or more of nose **126** and flexible layer **102** to shift the center of mass and/or center of pressure of aerodynamic decelerator **100**. In one embodiment, the gimbaling is implemented by adjusting tension on cables **128** such that ring member **104** and nose **126** moves relative to central axis C, as shown in an exemplary manner in FIG. **8**. In another embodiment, one or more actuators are used to push and/or pull ring member **104** and nose **126** relative to central axis C. As ring member **104** moves, spokes **114** and links **106** pivot around hinges to allow the gimbaling action and to maintain flexible layer **102** in the deployed configuration. For example, as one side of ring member **104** is pulled longitudinally upwardly with respect to central axis C, links **106** and spokes **114** on the upwardly pulled side of ring member **104** will move inwardly and upwardly and spokes **114** and links **106** on the opposite side will extend outwardly and down to maintain flexible layer **102** in the deployed configuration. In another embodiment, as shown in FIG. **8**, spokes **114** include a telescopic member which translates along a longitudinal axis of spokes **114** to preserve the outer diameter of flexible layer **102** in the deployed configuration. Control device **130** is operable to gimbal the nose **126** in a frustum normal to a plane of the ring member **104**. In one embodiment, a maximum excursion **142** of the gimbaling is approximately between about 10 degrees to 20 degrees, for example 12.5 degrees, from center, which provides a shift of the center of mass +/−0.7 meters in a first direction and 1.2 meters in a second direction. In other

6

embodiments, the maximum excursion is any excursion that allows the aerodynamic decelerator to function as described herein. Control mechanism **130** is thus operable to redirect a lift vector of aerodynamic decelerator **100** to control the direction of travel of aerodynamic decelerator **100**.

In one embodiment, aerodynamic decelerator **100** is reconfigurable for landing into landing configuration **120**, as shown for example in FIG. **9**. In one embodiment, to facilitate reconfiguration to landing configuration **120**, nose **126** (not shown in FIG. **9**) is ejected to expose retro-propulsion device **110**. In some embodiments, cables **128** are cut using cable cutters (not shown) to facilitate ejection of nose **126**. Deployment device **112** is operated to invert spokes **114** over a center of aerodynamic decelerator **100**, which places spokes **114** in a position to act as landing legs. To facilitate reconfiguration into landing configuration **120**, spokes **114** and/or links **106** are configured to translate inward toward a central axis C to preserve the outer diameter of flexible layer **102**. In another embodiment, flexible layer **102** is flexible to an extent necessary to allow spokes **114** to invert to landing configuration **120**. In one embodiment, spokes **114** include landing feet **144**. In one embodiment, landing feet **144** are formed with a surface having increased traction, such as a series of grooves or notches formed therein. In yet another embodiment, feet **144** include a repositionable hinge connecting links **106** to spokes **114**.

In the inverted position, flexible layer **102** (not shown in FIG. **9**) acts as a protective layer to protect the payload from surface debris during landing. In another embodiment, during firing of retro-propulsion device **110**, flexible layer **102** is configured to interact with the exhaust plume creating a cushioning due to ground effects before touchdown. In another embodiment, a trailing ballute **146** (FIG. **10**), or parachute, is used for supplementary aerocapture during landing in conjunction with, or instead of retro-propulsion device **110**. In another embodiment, links **106** are mounted by shock absorbers **147**, which provide shock attenuation during landing. After touchdown/landing of aerodynamic decelerator **100**, winding device **132** (shown in FIG. **5**) is operable to wind cables **128** to level the payload. In another embodiment, actuators are utilized to level the payload.

Shown generally in FIG. **10**, are four exemplary embodiments of aerodynamic decelerator **100** during a baseline mission. The baseline mission involves an aerocapture phase, a hypersonic entry phase, a supersonic entry phase, a subsonic entry phase and a landing phase. In mission profile **148**, during a first phase of aerocapture, flexible material is deployed to a first outer diameter, for example 23 meters. Prior to a second phase of entry, flexible material is deployed to a second outer diameter, for example 44 meters. As such, the ratio of payload to total landing mass of the system is within a range of from about 0.55 to 0.65. For example, in one embodiment, the payload mass is 40.0 mT and the total landed mass is 67.2 mT.

In another embodiment, as shown at numeral **150**, aerodynamic decelerator is deployed to a single outer diameter, for example 35 m, for both the aerocapture and entry phases of mission profile **150**. As such, the ratio of payload to total landing mass of the system is within a range of from about 0.45 to 0.55. For example, in one embodiment, the payload mass is 40.0 mT and the total landed mass is 78.8 mT.

In mission profile **152**, aerodynamic decelerator is deployed to a single outer diameter, for example 23 m, during aerocapture and entry, and the retro-propulsion device is activated during the supersonic phase of mission profile **152** to provide further deceleration. As such, the ratio of payload to total landing mass of the system is within a range of from about 0.5 to 0.6. For example, in one embodiment, the payload mass is 40.0 mT and the total landed mass is 65.3 mT.

In yet another embodiment, shown in mission profile **154**, flexible material **102** is deployed to a single outer diameter during the aerocapture and entry phases and trailing ballute **146** is deployed during a transition from the hypersonic phase to the supersonic phase to provide further deceleration of the payload. As such, the ratio of payload to total landing mass of the system is within a range of from about 0.5 to 0.6. For example, in one embodiment, the payload mass is 40.0 mT and the total landed mass is 64.5 mT.

In some embodiments, the above described systems and methods are electronically or computer controlled. The embodiments described herein are not limited to any particular system controller or processor for performing the processing and tasks described herein. The term controller or processor, as used herein, is intended to denote any machine capable of performing the functions, calculations, or computations, necessary to perform the tasks described herein. The terms controller and processor also are intended to denote any machine that is at least capable of accepting a structured input and of processing the input in accordance with prescribed rules to produce an output. The phrase "configured to" as used herein means that the component, controller, or processor is equipped with a combination of hardware and/or software for performing the tasks of embodiments of the invention, as will be understood by those skilled in the art. The term controller/processor, as used herein, refers to central processing units, microprocessors, microcontrollers, reduced instruction set circuits (RISC), application specific integrated circuits (ASIC), logic circuits, and any other circuit or processor capable of executing the functions described herein.

The embodiments described herein may embrace one or more computer readable media, including non-transitory computer readable storage media, wherein each medium may be configured to include or includes thereon data or computer executable instructions for manipulating data. The computer executable instructions include data structures, objects, programs, routines, or other program modules that may be accessed by a processing system, such as one associated with a general-purpose computer capable of performing various different functions or one associated with a special-purpose computer capable of performing a limited number of functions. Aspects of the disclosure transform a general-purpose computer into a special-purpose computing device when configured to execute the instructions described herein. Computer executable instructions cause the processing system to perform a particular function or group of functions and are examples of program code means for implementing steps for methods disclosed herein. Furthermore, a particular sequence of the executable instructions provides an example of corresponding acts that may be used to implement such steps. Examples of computer readable media include random-access memory ("RAM"), read-only memory ("ROM"), programmable read-only memory ("PROM"), erasable programmable read-only memory ("EPROM"), electrically erasable programmable read-only memory ("EEPROM"), compact disk read-only memory ("CD-ROM"), or any other device or component that is capable of providing data or executable instructions that may be accessed by a processing system.

A computer or computing device such as described herein has one or more processors or processing units, system memory, and some form of computer readable media. By way

of example and not limitation, computer readable media comprise computer storage media and communication media. Computer storage media include volatile and nonvolatile, removable and non-removable media implemented in any method or technology for storage of information such as computer readable instructions, data structures, program modules or other data. Communication media typically embody computer readable instructions, data structures, program modules, or other data in a modulated data signal such as a carrier wave or other transport mechanism and include any information delivery media. Combinations of any of the above are also included within the scope of computer readable media.

This written description uses examples to disclose the invention, including the best mode, and also to enable any person skilled in the art to practice the invention, including making and using any devices or systems and performing any incorporated methods. The patentable scope of the invention is defined by the claims, and may include other examples that occur to those skilled in the art. Such other examples are intended to be within the scope of the claims if they have structural elements that do not differ from the literal language of the claims, or if they include equivalent structural elements with insubstantial differences from the literal languages of the claims.

What is claimed is:

1. A deployable aerodynamic decelerator structure, comprising:
 a ring member disposed along a central axis of the aerodynamic decelerator;
 a plurality of jointed rib members extending radially from the ring member;
 a flexible layer attached to the plurality of rib members;
 a deployment device operable to reconfigure the flexible layer from a stowed configuration to a deployed configuration by movement of the rib members; and
 a control device operable to redirect a lift vector of the decelerator structure by changing an orientation of the flexible layer.

2. The decelerator structure according to claim **1**, further comprising:
 an ejectable heat shield.

3. The decelerator structure according to claim **1**, further comprising a retro-propulsion device, said retro-propulsion device being exposed upon deployment of the heat shield.

4. The decelerator structure according to claim **1**, wherein the control device is configured to gimbal the ring member with respect to the central axis.

5. The decelerator structure according to claim **1**, the deployment device operable to reconfigure the flexible layer to a landing configuration by reconfiguring the rib members into an inverted position with respect to the stowed configuration.

6. The decelerator structure according to claim **1**, the deployment device comprising a payload adaptor member configured to be connected to a payload.

7. The decelerator structure according to claim **1**, wherein the flexible layer has a stowed configuration diameter and a deployed configuration diameter, the deployed configuration diameter is larger than the stowed configuration diameter.

8. The decelerator structure according to claim **7**, wherein the plurality of jointed rib members comprises a plurality of links hingedly attached to the rib members, the deployment device operable to move the links to change the diameter of the flexible layer.

9

9. An entry, decent and landing system, comprising:
a payload adaptor member configured to connect to a payload;
a ring member disposed along a central axis of the system;
a plurality of rib members hingedly connected to the ring member on one end and connected to the payload adaptor member on another end thereof;
a flexible layer attached to the plurality of rib members; and
a deployment device operable to reconfigure the flexible layer from a deployed configuration to a landing configuration by moving the ring member along the central axis.

10. The system according to claim **9**, further comprising a control device operable to redirect a lift vector of the decelerator structure, wherein the control device is operable to shift the center of mass of the payload with respect to the central axis.

11. The system according to claim **9**, further comprising a retro-propulsion device.

12. The system according to claim **9**, further comprising a plurality of links configured to transmit aerodynamic forces acting on the flexible layer to the payload adaptor member.

13. The system according to claim **12**, wherein the deployment device is operable to place the rib members into a landing configuration wherein an end portion of the rib members is configured to support the payload.

14. The system according to claim **9**, wherein the flexible layer is at least partially made of a heat shielding material.

15. The system according to claim **9**, further comprising a retro-propulsion device and a nose cone, the retro-propulsion device being disposed intermediate the payload and the nose cone.

16. The system according to claim **9**, wherein the flexible layer comprises a carbon fabric.

10

17. A method of landing a payload, comprising:
providing a payload;
attaching the payload to a deployable aerodynamic decelerator structure, comprising:
a ring member disposed along a central axis of the aerodynamic decelerator;
a plurality of jointed rib members extending radially from the ring member;
a flexible layer attached to the plurality of rib members;
a deployment device operable to reconfigure the flexible layer from a stowed configuration to a deployed configuration; and
a control device operable to redirect a lift vector of the decelerator structure;
operating the deployment device to reconfigure the flexible layer into the deployed configuration to reduce a velocity of the payload; and
operating the control device to redirect the lift vector of the decelerator structure; and
operating the deployment device to reconfigure the flexible layer into a landing configuration.

18. The method according to claim **17**, further comprising operating a retro-propulsion device to further reduce the velocity of the decelerator structure.

19. The method according to claim **17**, further comprising operating the deployment device to reconfigure the flexible layer into a landing configuration wherein the plurality of rib members are inverted with respect to a position of the rib members in the deployed configuration.

20. The method according to claim **17**, wherein operating the control device comprises sending an electronic signal to a gimbaling device to move the ring member with respect to the payload.

* * * * *

US008529825B2

(12) **United States Patent**
Chu et al.

(10) Patent No.: **US 8,529,825 B2**
(45) **Date of Patent:** **Sep. 10, 2013**

(54) **FABRICATION OF NANOVOID-IMBEDDED BISMUTH TELLURIDE WITH LOW DIMENSIONAL SYSTEM**

(75) Inventors: **Sang-Hyon Chu**, Newport News, VA (US); **Sang H. Choi**, Poquoson, VA (US); **Jae-Woo Kim**, Newport News, VA (US); **Yeonjoon Park**, Yorktown, VA (US); **James R. Elliott**, Vesuvius, VA (US); **Glen C. King**, Yorktown, VA (US); **Diane M. Stoakley**, Ashland, VA (US)

(73) Assignees: **National Institute of Aerospace Associates**, Hampton, VA (US); **The United States of America as represented by the Administration of NASA**, Washington, DC (US)

(*) Notice: Subject to any disclaimer, the term of this patent is extended or adjusted under 35 U.S.C. 154(b) by 185 days.

(21) Appl. No.: **12/928,128**

(22) Filed: **Dec. 3, 2010**

(65) **Prior Publication Data**

US 2011/0117690 A1 May 19, 2011

Related U.S. Application Data

(62) Division of application No. 11/831,233, filed on Jul. 31, 2007, now Pat. No. 8,020,805.

(60) Provisional application No. 60/834,547, filed on Jul. 31, 2006.

(51) **Int. Cl.**
B28B 1/00 (2006.01)

(52) **U.S. Cl.**
USPC **264/620**; 264/614

(58) **Field of Classification Search**
USPC 264/614, 620
See application file for complete search history.

(56) **References Cited**

U.S. PATENT DOCUMENTS

4,491,679 A	*	1/1985	Moore	136/203
4,686,320 A	*	8/1987	Novak et al.	136/239
5,487,952 A	*	1/1996	Yoo et al.	428/552
6,849,361 B2	*	2/2005	Fukuda et al.	429/235
8,083,986 B2	*	12/2011	Choi et al.	264/620
2003/0032709 A1	*	2/2003	Toshima et al.	524/439
2007/0240749 A1	*	10/2007	Ohtaki	136/200
2009/0004086 A1	*	1/2009	Kuhling et al.	423/276
2009/0185942 A1	*	7/2009	Choi et al.	419/30

FOREIGN PATENT DOCUMENTS

WO WO 2007/077065 * 7/2007

* cited by examiner

Primary Examiner — Joseph S Del Sole
Assistant Examiner — Russell Kemmerle, III
(74) *Attorney, Agent, or Firm* — Kimberly A. Chasteen

(57) **ABSTRACT**

A new fabrication method for nanovoids-imbedded bismuth telluride (Bi—Te) material with low dimensional (quantum-dots, quantum-wires, or quantum-wells) structure was conceived during the development of advanced thermoelectric (TE) materials. Bismuth telluride is currently the best-known candidate material for solid-state TE cooling devices because it possesses the highest TE figure of merit at room temperature. The innovative process described here allows nanometer-scale voids to be incorporated in Bi—Te material. The final nanovoid structure such as void size, size distribution, void location, etc. can be also controlled under various process conditions.

23 Claims, 22 Drawing Sheets

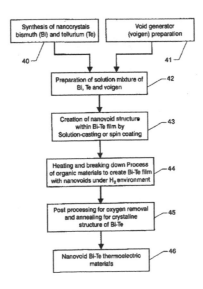

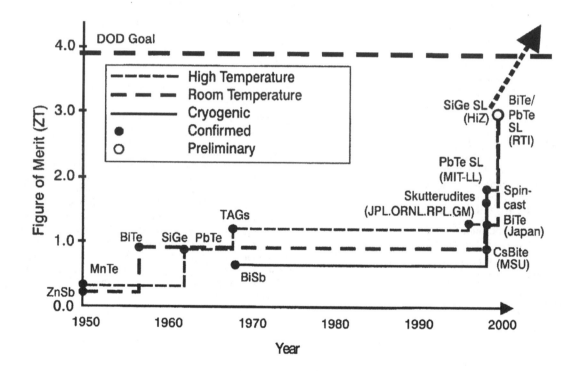

FIG.1

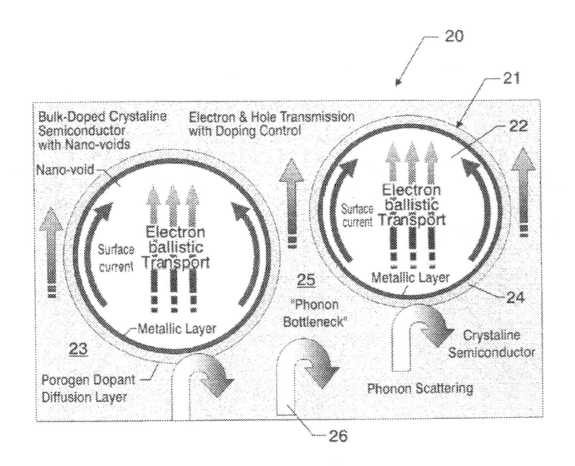

FIG.2

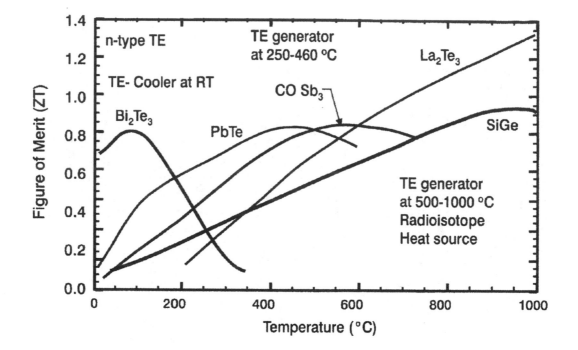

FIG.3

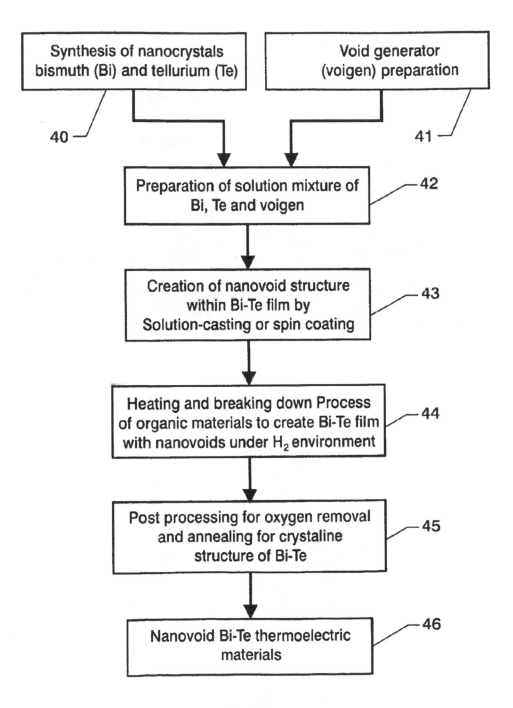

FIG.4

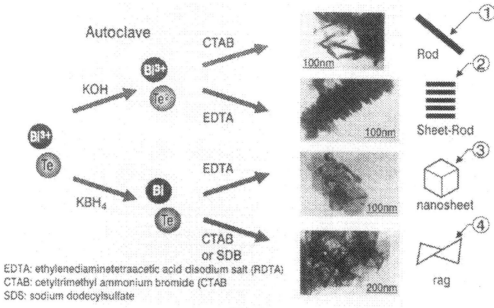

Autoclave

EDTA: ethylenediaminetetraacetic acid disodium salt (RDTA)
CTAB: cetyltrimethyl ammonium bromide (CTAB
SDS: sodium dodecylsulfate

FIG.5

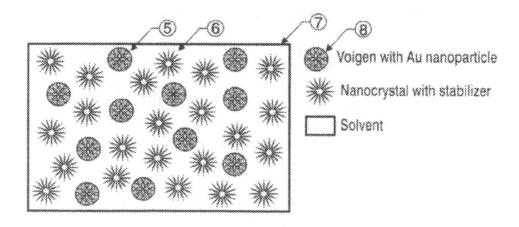

Voigen with Au nanoparticle

Nanocrystal with stabilizer

Solvent

FIG.6

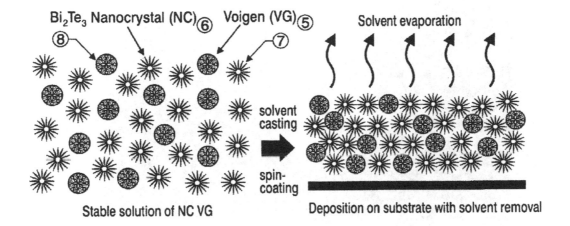

Bi$_2$Te$_3$ Nanocrystal (NC) ⑥   Voigen (VG) ⑤

⑧   ⑦

Solvent evaporation

solvent casting

spin-coating

Stable solution of NC VG

Deposition on substrate with solvent removal

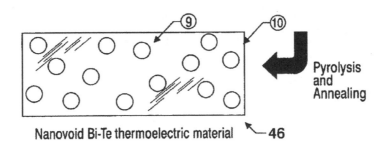

⑨   ⑩

Pyrolysis and Annealing

Nanovoid Bi-Te thermoelectric material   46

FIG. 7

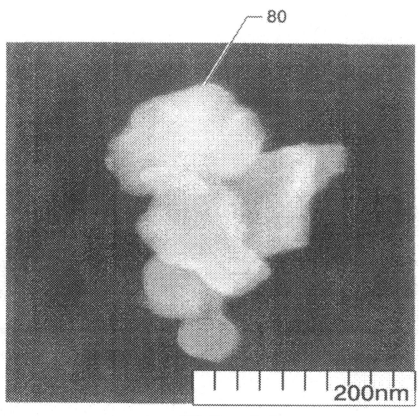

FIG. 8A

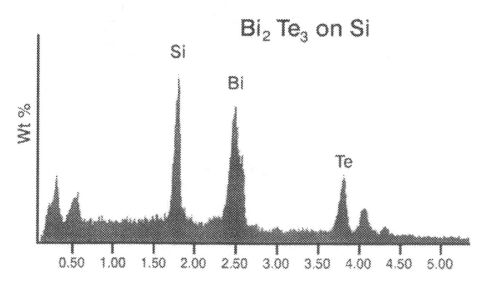

FIG. 8B

434

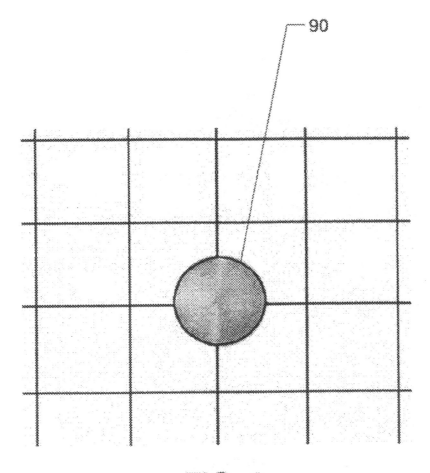

FIG. 9

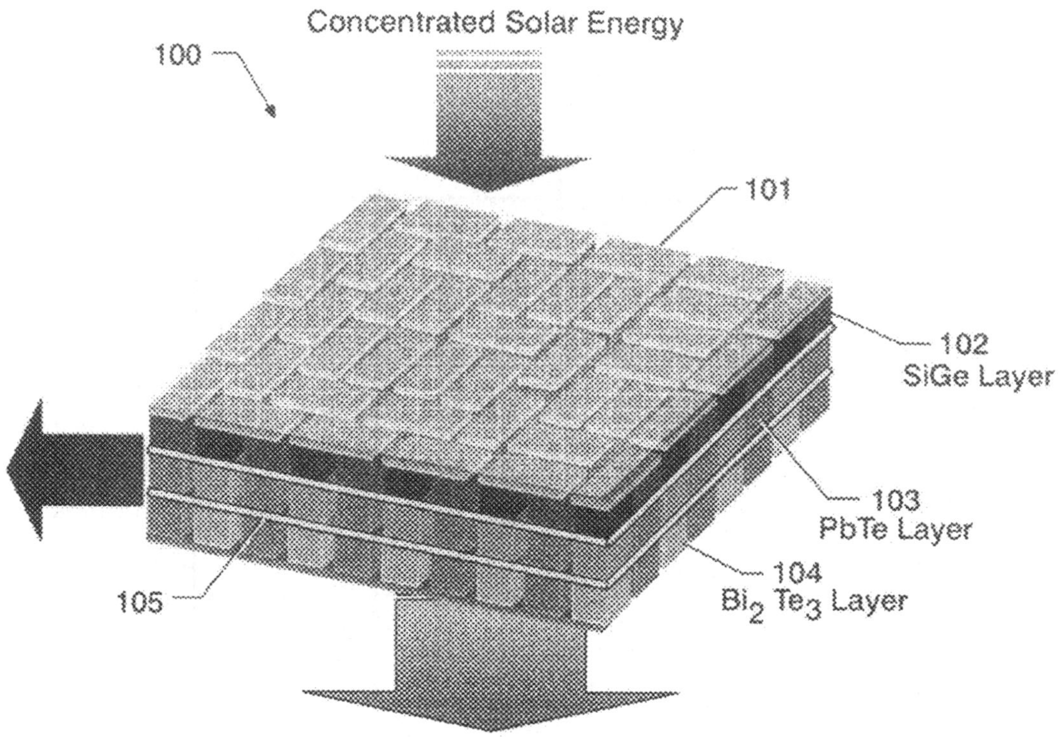

Fig. 10

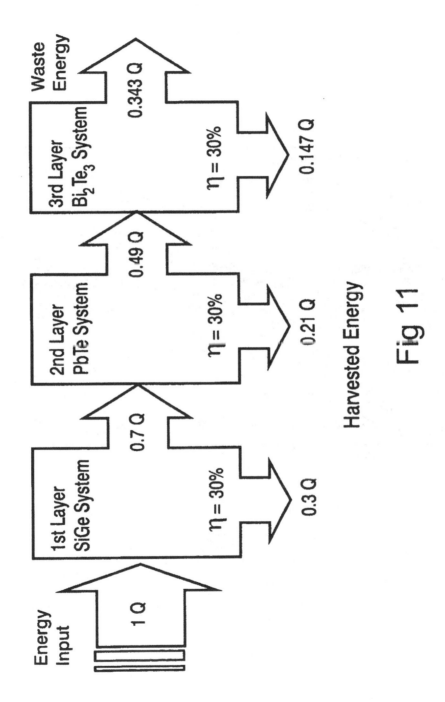

Fig 11

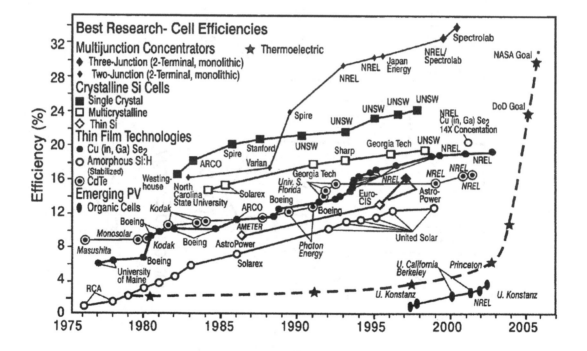

Fig. 12

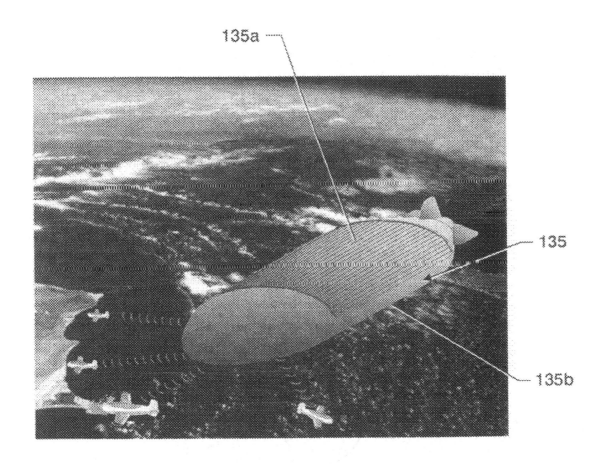

Fig 13A

439

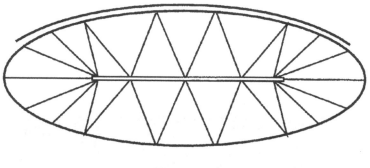

Fig 13B

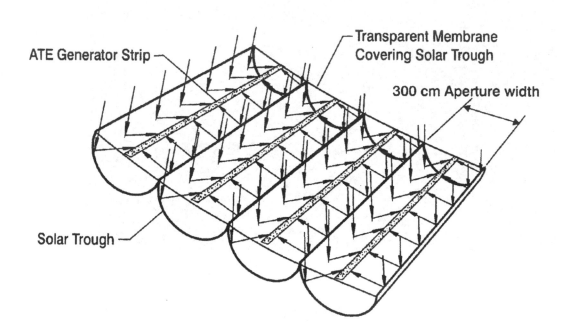

ATE Generator Strip

Transparent Membrane
Covering Solar Trough

300 cm Aperture width

Solar Trough

Fig 13C

440

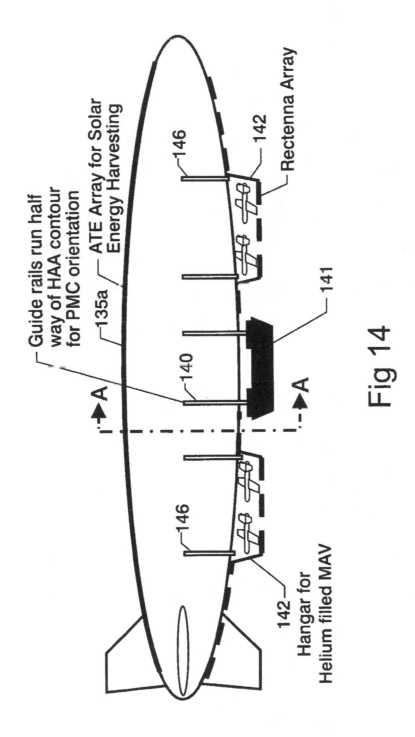

Fig 14

441

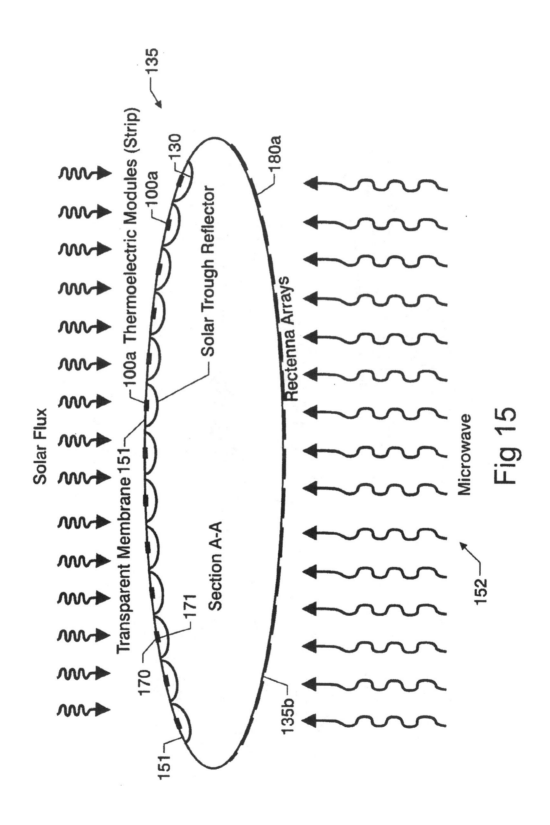

Fig 15

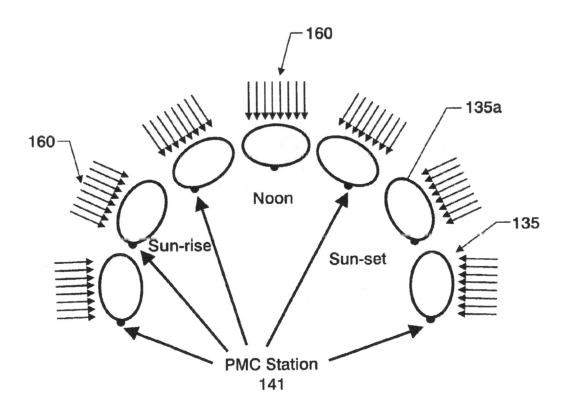

Fig 16

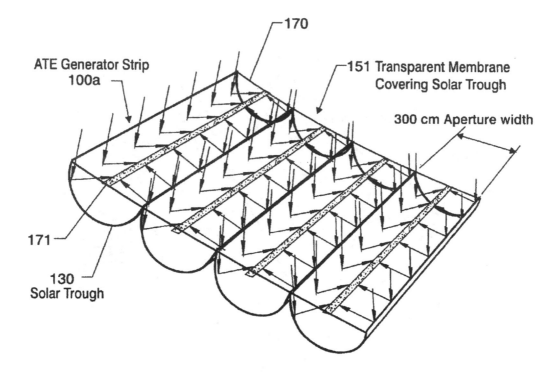

ATE Generator Strip
100a

170

151 Transparent Membrane
Covering Solar Trough

300 cm Aperture width

171

130
Solar Trough

Fig. 17

444

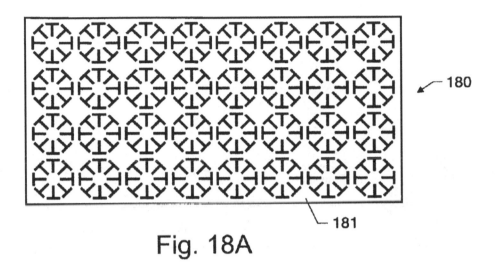

180

181

Fig. 18A

Circuit of Thin-Film Rectenna Dipole Element

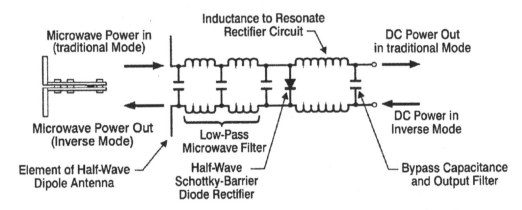

Microwave Power in
(traditional Mode)

Inductance to Resonate
Rectifier Circuit

DC Power Out
in traditional Mode

Microwave Power Out
(Inverse Mode)

Low-Pass
Microwave Filter

DC Power in
Inverse Mode

Element of Half-Wave
Dipole Antenna

Half-Wave
Schottky-Barrier
Diode Rectifier

Bypass Capacitance
and Output Filter

Fig. 18B

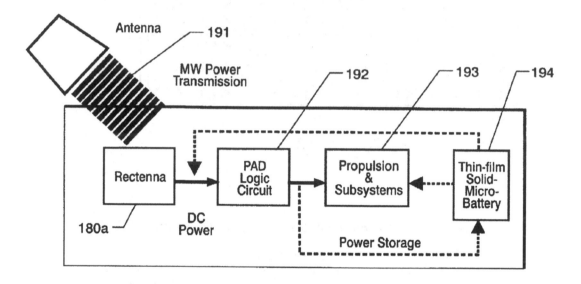

Fig. 19

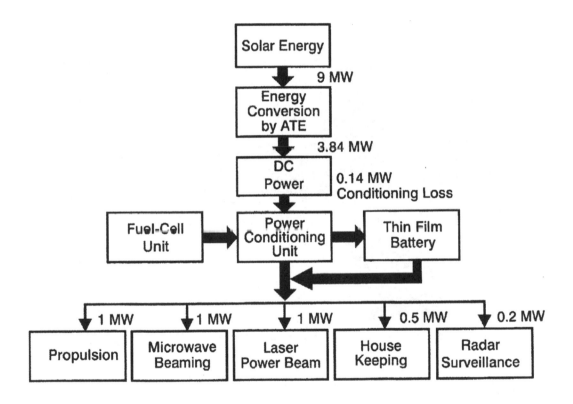

Fig. 20

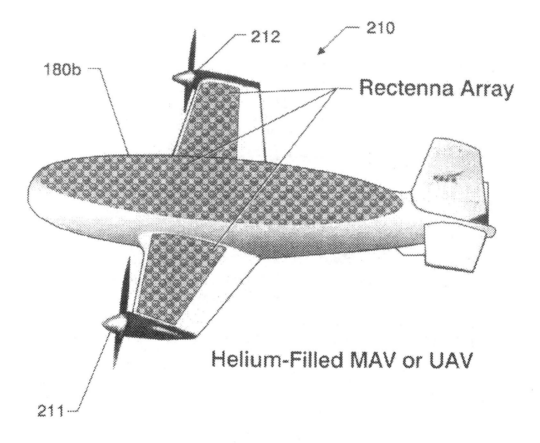

Fig. 21

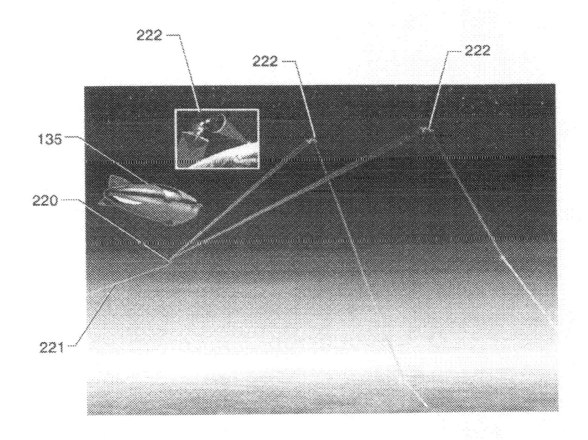

Fig. 22

1

FABRICATION OF NANOVOID-IMBEDDED BISMUTH TELLURIDE WITH LOW DIMENSIONAL SYSTEM

CROSS-REFERENCE TO RELATED APPLICATIONS

This application is a Divisional application of prior pending U.S. patent application Ser. No. 11/831,233 filed Jul. 31, 2007 now U.S. Pat. No. 8,020,805 and published Mar. 19, 2009 as U.S. 2009/0072078, which claims the benefit of U.S. provisional application 60/834,547, with a filing date of Jul. 31, 2006. The entire disclosure of the prior application is hereby incorporated by reference herein in its entirety. This invention was made in part by employees of the United States Government and may be manufactured and used by or for the Government of the United States of America for governmental purposes without the payment of any royalties thereon or therefor.

STATEMENT REGARDING FEDERALLY SPONSORED RESEARCH OR DEVELOPMENT

The U.S. Government has a paid-up license in this invention and the right in limited circumstances to require the patent owner to license others on reasonable terms, as provided for by the terms of Contract No. NCC-1-02043 awarded by the National Aeronautics and Space Administration, and Science and Technology Corporation Contract Nos. L-71200D and L-71407D.

BACKGROUND OF THE INVENTION

1. Field of the Invention

This invention generally relates to a fabrication method for a thermoelectric material. More specifically, the invention relates to a fabrication method for a nanovoid-imbedded bismuth telluride with a high figure of merit.

2. Description of the Related Art

To date, void-incorporated thermoelectric (TE) materials have been studied in only a few compound systems, such as bismuth, silicon, Si—Ge solid solutions, Al-doped SiC, strontium oxide and strontium carbonate. Si—Ge samples prepared by Pulverized and Intermixed Elements Sintering (PIES) method exhibited 30% increase in TE performance with 15-20% void fraction. Based on recent experimental research, theoretical calculations also indicated that it is possible to increase the ZT of certain materials by a factor of several times their bulk values by preparing them in 1D or 2D nanostructures. Bi—Te materials, especially with low-dimensional system, have been fabricated through solvo-thermal method (1D or 2D nanocrystals), metal-organic chemical vapor deposition (MOCVD) (2D superlattice structure), electrodeposition in porous alumina substrates (1D nanowire), and reverse micelle method (0-D quantum dots).

Typical void sizes in most of prior-art studies were in the micrometer range and no appreciable reduction in thermal conductivity was realized. Lower thermal conductivity contributes to the thermoelectric performance and in the prior-art studies, no noticeable phonon disruption was observed. Aside from theoretical predictions, there are no TE materials, based on Bi—Te, that have demonstrated such an enhancement in ZT values due to low-dimensional crystalline system. The previous studies also showed most of voids in Bi—Te film existed in an interconnected form which causes poor electron

2

mobility, resulting in lower electrical conductivity and hence, lower thermoelectric performance.

SUMMARY OF THE INVENTION

Accordingly, it is an object of the present invention to provide a fabrication method for a thermoelectric material.

Another object of the present invention is to provide a fabrication method for a thermoelectric material having a high figure of merit.

Another object of the present invention is to provide a fabrication method for a thermoelectric material having increased electrical conductivity.

Another object of the present invention is to provide a fabrication method for a thermoelectric material having reduced thermal conductivity.

Another object of the present invention is to provide a fabrication method for nanovoid-imbedded bismuth telluride with low dimensional system.

Another object of the present invention is to provide a fabrication method for nanovoid-imbedded bismuth telluride with a high figure of merit.

Other objects and advantages of the present invention will become more obvious hereinafter in the specification and drawings.

In accordance with the present invention, a method for forming high figure of merit thermoelectric materials is disclosed. The method includes providing nanocrystals of bismuth and tellurium and preparing a void generator material including a plurality of nanoparticles each having a metallic outer coating. The void generator material is preferably an organic material and more preferably a ferritin protein. A solution mixture of the bismuth nanocrystals, tellurium nanocrystals and the void generator material is prepared and deposited onto a substrate, preferably silicon. The deposition method may be spin-coating, dipping, or solvent casting or any other appropriate method. The deposited solution mixture is heated in an oxygen environment to create a plurality of nanovoid structures from the nanoparticles to provide a nanovoid incorporated bismuth-tellurium film. In the preferred method, the deposited solution mixture is heated to no more than 400° C. for approximately one hour in an oxygen environment which is 99.999% pure oxygen. Following the heating, the film is treated to remove any oxygen components remaining from heating the mixture in the oxygen environment and to cause the formation of a crystalline structure in the film. Such treatment is preferably accomplished by hydrogen calcination and hydrogen plasma quenching.

BRIEF DESCRIPTION OF THE DRAWINGS

For a more complete understanding of the present invention, including other objects and advantages, reference should be made to the Detailed Description of the Invention set forth below. This Detailed Description should be read together with the accompanying drawings, wherein:

FIG. 1 is a graph depicting the History of Thermoelectric Figure of Merit (ZT);

FIG. 2 is an illustration of a morphological design of an advanced thermoelectric material to enhance the ZT by increasing electrical conductivity while concurrently reducing thermal conductivity by populating nanovoids into the material, which material can be utilized in at least one embodiment of the present invention;

FIG. 3 is a graph of the figure of merit of several TE materials which could be utilized in at least one embodiment of the present invention;

3

4

FIG. 4 is a flow chart of the fabrication of a nanovoid bismuth telluride (Bi—Te) thermoelectric material that could be utilized in at least one embodiment of the present invention;

FIG. 5 is a diagram depicting a portion of the fabrication process of the Bi—Te thermoelectric material referenced in FIG. 4, i.e., the formation of low-dimensional bismuth telluride nanocrystals using solvo-thermal process;

FIG. 6 is a diagram depicting a portion of the fabrication process of the Bi—Te thermoelectric material referenced in FIG. 4, i.e., a three-phase mixture of Be—Te NCs, voigens, and cosolvent;

FIG. 7 is diagram depicting a portion of the fabrication process of the Bi—Te thermoelectric material referenced in FIG. 4, i.e., fabrication of nanovoid Bi—Te material by deposition and pyrolysis process that creates nanovoid structure in thermoelectric material;

FIG. 8A is an image of two-dimension nanosheets fabricated using bismuth telluride crystals which can be utilized in at least one embodiment of the present invention;

FIG. 8B is a graph of element analysis data by EDAX of same the nanosheets shown in FIG. 8A;

FIG. 9 is an image of a bismuth telluride disk fabricated by a cold press method, which can be utilized in at least one embodiment of the present invention;

FIG. 10 is a perspective view of one possible embodiment of the Advanced Thermoelectric (ATE) energy conversion system of the present invention;

FIG. 11 is a flow chart depicting the cascaded efficiency of a 3-layer ATE system in a tandem mode in accordance with at least one embodiment of the present invention;

FIG. 12 is a graph depicting the efficiencies of state-of-the art solar, and thermoelectric cells;

FIG. 13A is a perspective view of a flattened airship with ellipsoidal cross-section to maximize the reception of solar flux in accordance with at least one embodiment of the present invention;

FIG. 13B depicts the ellipsoidal cross section of the airship shown in FIG. 13A;

FIG. 13C is an expanded view of the solar troughs disposed on the top surface of the airship shown in FIG. 13A, utilizing the ATE conversion system;

FIG. 14 is a side-view drawing of another embodiment of an HAA of the present invention;

FIG. 15 is the cross-sectional view of the HAA along the plane indicated by dashed line A-A in FIG. 14;

FIG. 16 are front views of an HAA, depicting a method of operation of the HAA, in accordance with at least one embodiment of the present invention;

FIG. 17 is a drawing of the troughs shown in FIG. 13C, depicting ATE power modules utilized with linear parabolic troughs to collect solar flux, in accordance with at least one embodiment of the present invention;

FIG. 18A is a drawing of a flexible thin-film rectenna array that, in at least one embodiment of the present invention, can be attached under the bottom surface of an HAA to receive and convert microwave power into DC Power;

FIG. 18B illustrates an example of a circuit that could be utilized in the rectennas depicted in FIG. 18A;

FIG. 19 is a logic diagram of potential microwave power use by an HAA equipped with a rectenna array, such as the array depicted in FIG. 18;

FIG. 20 is flow chart depicting a possible power distribution scenario of an HAA for various application devices that might be onboard;

FIG. 21 is a perspective view of a novel unmanned or manned aerial (UAV or MAV) configured for electric propulsion power to be wirelessly transmitted; and

FIG. 22 is an image depicting an HAA utilizing a sophisticated relay system of laser power.

DETAILED DESCRIPTION OF THE INVENTION

The present invention comprises incorporation of controllable nanovoid structures into bismuth telluride (Bi—Te) thermoelectric materials using Bi—Te nanocrystal process, in order to achieve high figure of merit for TE devices. One advantageous embodiment of the present inventive system, or device, is based on advanced thermoelectric (ATE) materials which can be developed for a targeted figure of merit (FoM) goal, advantageously, greater than 5. This inventive power technology enables many application specific scenarios which might not have been possible with prior technology.

As shown in FIG. 1, the FoMs of most TE materials developed to date are still below 2. A FoM of 1 is equivalent to a thermal to electrical energy conversion efficiency greater than 6%. To achieve advanced TE (ATE) materials 20 with a high FoM, nanovoids 21 can be incorporated, as shown in FIG. 2, into the TE materials 23 to increase the electrical conductivity (EC) while reducing the thermal conductivity (TC). The nanovoids 21 are essentially nano spherical shells 24 having internal voids 22. In one embodiment, spherical shells 24 of approximately 10 nm to approximately 20 nm in outer diameter can be made from a metallic component such as gold or cobalt using a bio-template, as discussed in more detail below. The void 22 inner diameter can range from approximately 10 nm to approximately 12 nm. The void diameter needs to be small enough to avoid a reduction in electrical conductivity and a change in morphology of the bulk material to poly-crystalline.

Typically, within a crystalline structure of a material, the heat transfer mechanism is mainly dictated by phonon transmission (>70%) rather than by energetic electrons (<30%) for temperatures below 900 K. Accordingly, a method to manipulate the phonon transmission within a crystalline medium offers a capability to control the thermal conductivity. The metallic nanovoids 21 populated inside bulk matrix TE materials 23 create large phonon scattering cross-sections that effectively block the transfer of thermal energy through them. The TE material 23 in an unoccupied area 25 that is sandwiched between nanovoids 21 will become a phonon 26 bottleneck since the narrowly sandwiched bulk material is under a high tension induced from the spherical formation of the TE material boundary around the nanovoids, as shown in FIG. 2. The phonon bottleneck is essentially the combination of unoccupied area 25 and the nanovoids 21. The individual phonon 26 merely indicates that the phonon 26 cannot propagate easily through the unoccupied area 25. The structure of the TE material boundary surface around the spherical nanovoids 21 may be framed of a high energy bonding group that develops high tension over the surface. The material structure with high tension would be less subjected to an oscillatory mode transmission than material structures in normal tension. Therefore, both the high tension and the narrow passage 25 between nanovoids are resistive to phonon transmission and accordingly regarded as a phonon bottleneck. Ultimately, the imbedded nanovoids 21 create the phonon scattering cross-sections and bottlenecks throughout the matrix material as shown in FIG. 2.

The selection basis of TE materials for the present invention can be according to the temperature at which the performance of the particular TE material is best-suited. For

5

example, in at least one advantageous embodiment of the present invention, the materials selected can be silicon-germanium (SiGe) and bismuth telluride (Bi_2Te_3), along with lead telluride (PbTe). Currently pending U.S. patent application Ser. No. 11/242,415, entitled "Silicon Germanium Semiconductive Alloy and Method of Fabricating Same, by Park, et al., filed on Sep. 27, 2005, and hereby incorporated by reference as if set forth in its entirety herein, discloses additional detail relative to a lattice-matched silicon germanium semiconductive alloy and its fabrication that is suitable for use in at least one layer of the present invention. Materials desirable for use would also include nanovoid-imbedded forms of Si Ge, PbTe, and Bi_2Te_3.

Nanovoid-imbedded Bi—Te would be suitable for use in one or more different layers. Bismuth Telleride is currently used in solid-state TE cooling devices due to its high figure of merit at room temperature, as shown in FIG. 3, but its applications are still limited by poor TE properties. To improve TE performance, nanometer-scale voids can be incorporated into Bi—Te material, with the void size, size distribution, void location, etc. controlled under various process conditions. The nanovoids reduce thermal conductivity by disrupting phonons without sacrificing electron transport, thereby allowing for the reduction of thermal conductivity while increasing electrical conductivity. The nanovoid incorporation is controlled by thermodynamic miscibility and kinetic mobility of two phases, TE precursor and voigen. Metal nanoparticles such as but not limited to gold, cobalt, platinum, manganese, and iron, anchored on the voigen material surface eventually form a metal layer or lining through an annealing process. The spherical void by metal lining becomes a passage of mobile electrons and aids the electrons to move through the nanovoid structure.

There are several methods for imbedding nanovoids into a matrix material. For example, in the solvo-thermal method which can be used for Bi_2Te_3, the nanocrystals of bismuth telluride are created and then mixed with nanovoids before solvent casting. Through solvent casting on a substrate after mixing, a cake of bismuth telluride is made. This cake goes through calcination and hydrogen plasma etching processes to remove unwanted impurity elements. Finally, the sponge form of bismuth telluride is sintered to become a matrix of single crystal deposition.

To date, the void-incorporated TE materials have been studied in several compound systems, such as bismuth, silicon, Si—Ge solid solutions, Al-doped SiC, strontium oxide and strontium carbonate. Si—Ge samples prepared by Pulverized and Intermixed Elements Sintering (PIES) method exhibited 30% increase in TE performance with 15-20% void fraction. Theoretical calculations also indicate that it is possible to increase the ZT of certain materials by a factor of several times their bulk values by preparing them in 1D or 2D nanostructures. Bi—Te materials, especially with low-dimensional system, have been fabricated through solvo-thermal method (1D or 2D nanocrystals), metal-organic chemical vapor deposition (MOCVD) (2D superlattice structure), electrodeposition in porous alumina substrates (1D nanowire), and reverse micelle method (0-D quantum dots).

Nanovoids are incorporated, in a controllable manner, into bismuth telluride (Bi—Te) thermoelectric materials using a Bi—Te nanocrystal process, in order to achieve a high figure of merit. The fabrication process is shown in FIG. 4. An important element in developing high figure of merit TE materials is to fabricate void generators ("voigens") and to populate voigens into the bulk TE materials. The population distribution of voigens into bulk TE materials determines the reduction level of thermal conductivity by setting up phonon

6

bottlenecks between voigens where phonon scattering takes place. As such, the population density will depend on the desired thermal conductivity.

First, precursor materials are prepared for syntheses of Bi—Te nanocrystals 40. Various Bi—Te nanocrystals can be prepared by employing the solvo-thermal process. Nanocrystals of various sizes and shapes can be made by changing synthesis conditions, as illustrated in FIG. 5. Possible geometries of nanocrystals include nanorod, nanosheet, nanosheet-rod, nanorag, etc.

Another important part of material preparation is to synthesize voigen materials 41. Voigen materials are designed to meet several important roles for high figure of merit TE materials: (1) phonon scattering centers, (2) reduced thermal conductivity, and (3) enhanced electrical conductivity. Creation of nanovoids with size and shape uniformity is also an important issue that will determine void fraction within bulk TE materials. To enhance electrical conductivity, voigen materials (e.g., ferritin protein), which are in a nano-scale, generally approximately 8 nm inner diameter and 12 nm outer diameter are coated with a metal lining, such as but not limited to gold, cobalt, platinum, manganese, and iron. While the voigen material is not limited to ferritin protein and may be other bio-templates, the ferritin protein is generally desirable due to its ability to form the spherical shape with void. The metal nanoparticles anchored on the voigen material surface eventually form a metal layer or lining through an annealing process. The annealing process comprises hydrogen calcination and hydrogen plasma quenching. The metal lining is approximately several atomic layer thick and generally no more than approximately 3 to 4 nanometers. Nanometer-scaled voigen molecules can be dispersed in a cosolvent system with Bi—Te nanocrystals 42, as illustrated in FIG. 6. The nanoscale phase separation between the precursor and voigen is induced by their thermodynamic miscibility, and determines the final nanovoid structure. The diameter of voigen materials is designed to be less than approximately 20 nm after coated with the metal nanoparticles. The metal nanoparticles will remain as a metal lining that forms a spherical void after a pyrolysis process. The metal lining that forms the spherical void forms the passage for electrons which provides for high electrical conductivity. In conjunction with the reduced thermal conductivity attributed to the phonon scattering of nanovoids, the enhancement of electrical conductivity is desirable for high figure of merit TE performance. Overall TE performance can be possibly deteriorated by the aggregation of metallic spherical voids without spreading within the bulk material. Accordingly, the distribution of nanovoids throughout the TE material is important.

The mixture of the three-phase system (bismuth, tellurium, and voigens) is deposited on a substrate using solution-based thin-film coating methods. Known substrates, such as silicon, are suitable. Suitable coating methods include spin-coating, dipping, solvent casting, etc. 43. After coating or casting, the films are placed in a vacuum chamber and heated under the environment of ultra pure hydrogen (approximately 99.999%) 44. A temperature of less than approximately 400° C. is generally desirable. The heating time is dependent on the thickness of the film, but generally approximately one hour. Voigen material which is organic, such as ferritin protein, and other organic components from the solution used are thermally decomposed and removed during pyrolysis process 44 until nanovoid-incorporated Bi—Te film 46 is obtained, as illustrated in FIG. 7. Hydrogen calcination and hydrogen plasma quenching 45 are then used, which first remove oxygen components that are the residue of organic breakdown with hydrogen plasma and second make crystalline structure in Bi—Te films through the annealing process, respectively.

A solvothermal pre-process to make the Bi_2Te_3 nanoparticles successfully produced black powder of bismuth telluride crystal with low dimension. FIG. **8**A shows two-dimensional nanosheets **80** fabricated using potassium hydroxide (KOH) and ethylenediamine tetraacetic acid (EDTA), following the synthesis process described in FIG. **5**. The nanosheets varied in size, all thicker than approximately 30 nm, and Energy dispersive X-ray spectroscopy (EDAX) analysis using FE-SEM (Field Emission Scanning Electron Microscopy) confirmed the existence of Bi_2Te_3 by element energy analysis, as shown in FIG. **8**B. The thickness of the nanosheet is dependent on the repetition of the coating process.

Disk-type samples were prepared using a cold press method at room temperature. FIG. **9** shows the bismuth telluride disk **90** fabricated with its nanocrystal powder. The nanoscale, nanovoid structure causes phonon scattering without disturbing electron mobility, thus increasing the figure of merit from low-dimensional nanocrystal Bi—Te materials.

The same or similar skills and/or techniques used to fabricate the nanovoid-imbedded Bi_2Te_3 ATE material described above can be readily extended to the fabrication of other nanovoid-embedded TE materials, such as cobalt antimonide ($CoSb_3$) and lead telluride (PbTe), for optimal thermoelectric performance at temperature ranges different from Bi_2Te_3 and SiGe. FIG. **3** shows several TE materials along with their associated best-suitable temperature ranges.

The present inventive energy conversion system is not limited to the above-noted layer materials. Other TE materials, and nanovoid embedded TE materials would also be suitable, and would be chosen based on the specific applications and temperature ranges. In general, suitable materials will have a high Seebeck coefficient, a high electrical conductivity and a low thermal conductivity.

In accordance with the present invention, these ATE materials can be utilized in the manufacturing of ATE energy conversion devices and systems, as illustrated in FIG. **10**. To make a p-n junction for TE energy conversion, the TE matrix materials developed can undergo conventional doping processes to create N-type and P-type materials (i.e., semiconductors).

As understood in the art, "doping" refers to the process of intentionally introducing impurities into an intrinsic semiconductor in order to change its electrical properties. A P-type semiconductor is obtained by carrying out a process of doping wherein a certain type of atoms are added to the semiconductor in order to increase the number of free positive charge carriers. When the doping agent (acceptor material) is added, it accepts weakly-bound outer electrons from the semiconductor's atoms, and creates holes (i.e., atoms that have lost an electron). The purpose of P-type doping is to create an abundance of such holes. When these holes move away from its associated negative-charged dopant ion, one proton in the atom at the hole's original location is now "exposed" and no longer cancelled by an electron, resulting in a hole behaving as a quantity of positive charge. When a sufficiently large number of acceptor atoms are added, the holes greatly outnumber the thermally-excited electrons. Thus, the holes are the majority carriers in P-type materials, and the electrons are the minority carriers. In contrast, an N-type material is obtained by adding a doping agent known as a donor material, which donates weakly bound outer electrons to the semiconductor atoms. For example, an impurity of a valence-five element can be added to a valence-four semiconductor in order to increase the number of free mobile or carrier electrons in the material. These unbound electrons are only

weakly bound to the atoms and can be easily excited into the conduction band, without the formation of a "hole," thus the number of electrons is an N-type material far exceeds the number of holes, and therefore the negatively charged electrons are the majority carriers and the holes are the minority carriers.

Non-limiting examples of doping material that could be used in the instant invention are boron and phosphor, which doping could be done in a known manner, such as by ion implantation or diffusion. In general, an array of pairs of p-n junction materials, or elements, is utilized to increase the thermal exposure area. As shown in FIG. **10**, a TE module **100** can consist of three layers of p-n-junction arrays **102**, **103**, **104** in a tandem mode that operate most efficiently at high, medium, and low temperatures, correspondingly in a tandem mode, providing a cascaded conversion efficiency. In at least one advantageous embodiment, these TE layers **102**, **103**, **104** comprise advanced TE materials, making a cascaded efficiency greater than about 60 percent obtainable, as indicated in FIG. **11**. While the shown embodiment consists of three layers, it should be understood that depending upon the desired application, the number of layers can be varied accordingly. Additionally, these layers can be assembled in the manner known in the art, for example, a metallized ceramic **105** could potentially be layered between them.

Such a tandem arrangement allows efficient energy harvesting from a heat source, thus allowing the present inventive energy conversion system to be effectively utilized in High Altitude Airship (HAA) applications where solar energy is considered as an energy source. In order to address the power-related requirements for lighter-than-air vehicles, including airships and hybrid fixed-wing configurations, the integration of the ATE devices can take on many different forms, dependent on configuration needs and mission requirements. As explained above, in general, an array of a pair of p-n junction materials is necessary to increase the thermal exposure area, and the ATE energy conversion device **100** may consist of multiple layers of p-n-junction arrays, as shown in FIG. **10**. The first, or top, layer **102** is built from the array of thermoelectric material segments **101** that operate optimally at the higher temperatures, such as SiGe. The subsequent layers, or stages, are driven by the propagating thermal energy of the preceding layer. The selection of the appropriate thermoelectric material for each of these subsequent layers is chosen dependent on the optimal thermoelectric figure of merit, ZT, for the respective operating temperature ranges. Referring again to the general example as shown in FIG. **10**, the second and third layers **103**, **104** of this 3-layer thermoelectric power system **100** are respectively built from PbTe and Bi_2Te_3 in a regenerative cycle mode of operation. Further, in at least one embodiment of the invention, it is desirable to utilize ATE materials such as nanovoid embedded Bi_2Te_3 and PbTe, and lattice-matched SeGi as the three layers. The invention, however, is not limited to these materials and may use only one or more layers of ATE materials.

In operation, the incident solar flux first heats up the initial layer **102** which is built with an optimized high temperature thermoelectric material. The unused thermal energy from the first layer is subsequently utilized by the second layer **103** which is built with an optimized mid-temperature thermoelectric material, such as PbTe. Repeating this process again, the third layer **104**, such as Bi_2Te_3, uses the unused energy from the second layer to maximize the conversion of the energy that is otherwise underutilized. With this repeated process, the number of different thermoelectric material layers needed, also depends on the overall temperature range available and desired. With the available thermal energy from the solar flux, the ATE can harness more energy than photovoltaic cells that use quantized electrons of the photons from the solar flux. The integration of advanced TE materials can provide significant levels of electrical energy because of this cascaded efficiency of multiple-layer TE modules **100** that are much higher than the efficiency of a single layer and the broad use of the solar thermal energy. The layered structure of the advanced TE materials is specifically engineered to provide maximum efficiency for the corresponding range of operational temperatures. A representative three layer system of advanced TE materials, as shown in FIG. **10**, generally operates at high, medium, and low temperatures, correspondingly in a tandem mode. The cascaded efficiency of such an arrangement is estimated to be greater than 60% as indicated in FIG. **11**. With multiple advanced thermoelectric material stages, a highly effective and efficient energy harvesting system may then be optimized for representative operational requirements such as maximum power, minimum weight, minimum size, etc.

As mentioned above, these ATE materials can be chosen to fit specific applications depending upon the overall temperature range available and desired. This same procedure can be used to construct specialized TE energy conversion devices in accordance with the present invention, for many different applications, including a variety of different heat sources. That is to say, by understanding each application prior to fabricating the inventive TE energy conversion device, the appropriate ATE materials can be chosen and layered (e.g. depending upon the original thermal load and a calculation of how much heat must be removed from this load by each layer, to achieve the desired performance objectives for each layer and overall).

Additionally, as would be known to one with ordinary skill in the art, the thickness of each layer can also be varied (for example, by increasing the number of sub-layers of the ATE material) until a desired temperature reduction is achieved prior to the thermal energy passing into the next layer, so that, optimally, when the energy is passed to the next layer it is at a temperature that will permit peak, or close to peak, thermal energy conversion performance by the receiving layer. Typically, a layer thickness might range from less than 1 mm to several millimeters, or more, in thickness, depending upon the material and application.

In this inventive fashion the overall efficiency of the system increases beyond that achieved by known methods (for example, where only one known TE material is used). Additionally, the ATE devices of the present invention become more effective than solar cells because the performance of solar cells is monolithically tied to band-gap energy structure, so that they only couple with certain spectral lines. Also, the higher the efficiency of the solar cells, the higher the cost and complexity of fabrication. For comparison purposes, FIG. **12** shows the layout of predicted figure of merits as a goal to achieve, which is added onto an existing diagram of solar cell efficiencies. As compared to solar cell technology in efficiency, the ATE system is competitive. However, considering the available energy from solar flux, the ATE system, using thermal energy, can harness more energy than photovoltaic cells that use the quantized electrons by photons from solar flux.

While solar energy conversion is discussed in detail herein, and specifically in reference to HAAs, it should be reiterated that the instant power conversion invention is not so limited in scope, rather the instant ATE energy conversion system can be used to harvest heat from a wide variety of sources (e.g., power plants, radioisotopes, automotive cooling systems, etc.) for many different energy generation and/or cooling

applications. Additionally, the completion of the fabrication of the final circuitry and fabrication of an operable thermoelectric conversion system using the inventive system disclosed herein, would be understood by someone with ordinary skill in the art as these techniques are well-known in the art.

There are several potential candidate energy harvesting technologies for HAAs, such as solar cells, fuel cells, Sterling engines, and TE generators. Due to the above-mentioned restrictions, ATE devices are extremely attractive because of the cascaded efficiency of the multi-layer TE modules of the present invention, that are much higher efficiency than the efficiency of a single layer and the broad use of solar thermal energy. As explained above, the layered structure of the ATE materials is specifically engineered to provide maximum efficiency for the corresponding range of operational temperatures. The present invention essentially functions like regenerative cycles in tandem. Such a highly effective energy harvesting feature of this tandem system based on multiple layers of advanced TE materials can be the basis of an HAA power budget plan.

In accordance with the present invention, to maximize the reception of solar thermal energy, an ellipsoid cross-sectioned high altitude airship (HAA) **135** has been designed, as shown in FIG. **13A**. In at least one embodiment, such an HAA can be 150 meters long, 60 meters wide, and 24 meters high. In size, this HAA is about 2.5 times larger than a Goodyear® blimp, which is 60 meters long. With this dimension of HAA **135**, the perpendicularly incident solar power amounts to about 9 MW. However, the daytime exposure varies with sun location. As shown in FIG. **16** (a cross-sectional view), if it is necessary, the HAA **135** can be reoriented to receive the maximum solar energy by keeping the top surface **135a** of the HAA **135** always substantially perpendicular to the solar angle **160**. In at least one embodiment, a vectored electric propulsion system can be used for this purpose.

When the top surface **135a** of HAA **135** follows the sun, the power management and control (PMC) station **141** installed under the belly of HAA **135** is designed to move on a guide rail **140** (shown in FIG. **14**), to reposition itself, always dangling at, or near, the bottom, or lowest point, of HAA **135** for every collector orientation. FIG. **16** shows the repositioned PMC **141** at the nadir point of HAA **135** along with the sun position **160**. In such a manner, the energy harvested from sun-rise to sun-set becomes effectively maximized, regardless of exposure variation over the course of the day. Using 20% efficient photovoltaic (PV) cells, the maximum converted power would be less than 2 MW. With the inventive advanced TE system of the same efficiency, the converted power would be greater than 4 MW because the cascaded efficiency of three layers is calculated to be approximately 49%. Considering a three-layered structure of the advanced TE materials having a FOM **5**, the cascaded efficiency amounts to be close to 66% (see FIG. **11**). If the amount of losses (35%) due to geometrical orientation (23%), reflection (7%), absorption (3%), and transmittance (2%) is considered for the estimation of cascaded efficiency, the total harvestable unit becomes 0.427 under the condition of 0.65Ω input instead of 1Ω used in FIG. **11**. Accordingly, the obtainable power amounts to be 3.84 MW which is substantial to accommodate several roles of the HAA. FIG. **13A** depicts some of the scenarios that might be feasible, such as feeding power to off-shore or isolated locations, for example, in lieu of having to build expensive power stations. The HAA can also become a mothership to wirelessly feed power to deployed unmanned vehicles.

11

Referring to FIGS. **13**, **15** and **17**, in one embodiment of the present invention, the ATE power module **100** (FIG. **10**) can be used in conjunction with linear parabolic troughs **130**. These troughs **130** can have a 300 cm aperture width to collect solar power, as shown in FIG. **17**. In at least one application, the back-surface **170** of ATE strips **100a** is reflective to reduce solar energy absorption and faces outside directly to the cold environment of high altitude to drop the surface temperature by convective cooling. The temperature at 70,000 feet or above in the atmosphere is extremely cold and hovers below −73° C. Accordingly, to maximize the performance of the ATE system, the solar trough concentrators are used to focus solar flux to the surface **171** of the 1st layer that faces the reflector trough **130** while the back side **170** of the 3rd layer faces the cold atmosphere to increase the temperature gradient. In at least one embodiment, the material of the reflector trough **130** can be, for example, enhanced aluminum coated thin-film membrane which is sufficiently hardened to maintain its parabolic shape. Each reflector **130** can be covered by a transparent membrane **151** that allows sun light to impinge into the parabolic trough **130**. The strip of ATE power module **100a** is located on a focal line of the parabolic trough **130** and connected to the transparent thin film window material **151**, for example, both edges of the strip **100a** can be connected to the transparent material **151**. An additional advantage of this type of ATE energy conversion system is that the structural formation of such solar trough **130** will enhance the strength of large sized HAA.

The nighttime power requirements of HAAs may not be alleviated because the HAA's nighttime operation frequently has the same importance as their daytime operation. Therefore, the power for nighttime operation typically must be the same level as that of the daytime usage. Based on the daytime figure for required power, three components of power infrastructure are actively involved to supply necessary power. That is to say, for nighttime, the power required can be augmented from the onboard fuel cells, battery and a rectenna array **180a** that is attached at the bottom surface **135b** of HAA **135** (see FIGS. **14** and **15**, where the rectenna array is indicated by a dashed line). These combined systems provide at least a megawatt level of power for the intermittent operation.

Hydrogen fuel-cells with the capacity of several hundreds kilo-watt level are onboard for the nighttime power generation. The water which is an end product of fuel-cell process is collected and dissociated into hydrogen and oxygen through electrolysis process using the power harvested during daytime. The hydrogen and oxygen is collected and fed back to fuel cells later at nighttime.

The power stored in the thin-film battery during daytime can be drained out for nighttime use. The battery storage capacity (~600 Coulomb/gram) is proportional to its own weight increase. Therefore, the battery is not regarded as the major power provider for night time use. It can be used for emergency purposes.

The arrays of thin-film rectennas **180**, as shown in FIG. **18A**, can be readily fabricated on a flexible film **181** which can be used within the structural envelope of the HAA. In at least one embodiment, the arrays **180/180a** are patched under the bottom surface **135b** of HAA **135** (see FIG. **15**, which depicts a cross-sectional view of the HAA shown in FIG. **14**), to receive and convert microwave power **152** into DC Power, as illustrated schematically in FIG. **18B**. The conversion efficiency of rectennas is unusually high (~85%), but the collection efficiency is poor because of the dispersive nature of microwave. The bottom surface area of HAA **135** is wide and nearly flat to enable the HAA **135** to collect most of dispersed microwave energy. At the 21 km (~70,000 ft) altitude, the area

required to collect the W-band (90~100 GHz) microwave is approximately 48 meters in diameter. This number is calculated by the Gaubau relationship, which is defined by the following formula:

$$\tau = \frac{\sqrt{A_r \cdot A_t}}{\lambda Z}$$

wherein: A_r is the area of receiving antenna; A_t is the area of transmitting antenna; Z is the distance between the transmitting and receiving antennas; λ is the wavelength of microwave; and τ is the parameter determined for 100% reception which, in the case for microwaves, is 3.

In at least one embodiment of the present invention, the bottom surface **135b** of HAA **135** can be 150 meters long and 60 meters wide. Accordingly, the microwave power at the W-band can be delivered to the array of rectennas **180a** at the bottom surface **135b** of HAA **135** almost all without loss. FIG. **19** shows a logic diagram of microwave power use. The power **191** received by rectenna arrays **180a** is allocated and distributed by the power allocation and distribution (PAD) logic circuit **192** to specific nodal points where the power is mostly needed, such as propulsion unit or subsystems **193**. Otherwise, the excessive power can be stored in an array of thin-film solid-state batteries **194** for later use. Thus, a large amount of microwave power can be delivered to the HAA **135** from a ground or a ship-board microwave power beaming station. Even for a remotely dispatched HAA **135**, wireless airborne electro-refueling by airplanes is possible. Multiple microwave stations combined can aim their beams onto a rectenna equipped HAA **135** to feed the power required for the operation at night.

The power harvested by the inventive ATE generator can be utilized for the power transmission to UAVs, for onboard systems operation, and for internal power requirements such as propulsion and control. FIG. **13A** illustrates a graphical scenario of operational mode of an HAA **135**. If more power is required, of course, in at least one embodiment, it is solved by the enlargement of HAA **135**, and the utilized ATE system **100a** with troughs **130**. The total power harvested (3.84 MW) can be distributed for propulsion for stationary positioning and maneuvering, power storage, microwave beaming for MAV or UAV operations, laser power beaming to ground locations, such as for illumination or telecommunication purposes, and house-keeping activities. Such applications require a continuous power source that will run for several hours in a sequential or a pulse mode anytime throughout the day and the night. FIG. **20** shows the power flow diagram based on the power estimation that is to be harvested by the ATE array placed on top of the HAA. The power allocated for the operations of those onboard devices is estimated to give a glimpse at one possible power picture.

The power harvested by the inventive ATE generator can also be utilized for propulsion for position correction and maneuver. The wind at an altitude of 21 km (70,000 feet) or above is substantially lower than typical seasonal jet-streams that exist within the northern hemisphere. Nevertheless, the large cross-section of the HAA is vulnerable to drifting along with wind. Continuous positioning and maneuvering operation of the HAA against the wind is necessary and crucial for the stationary operation and maximum solar exposure over solar angle variation. Otherwise, the HAA will drift away to an undesirable location where the use of onboard devices may be impossible. The propulsion for position correction and maneuvering is also required during the night time.

13

Another potential embodiment of the inventive HAA configuration includes a base for UAV or MAV airships. A novel lightweight, high performance, long endurance UAV configuration, as shown in FIG. 21, has been developed that combines a polymer structure with an electrical power generating system to produce new missions and capabilities for air vehicles. As presently envisioned, this class of UAV satisfies aeronautical missions for high altitude, characterized by long endurance, electric propulsion, propellantless, and emissionless. The configuration utilizes a polyimide structural material for creating the primary wing and fuselage elements of the vehicle. The polymer structure functions to carry normal, bending, and pressure loads as experienced from sea-level to cruising altitudes. The polymer structure incorporates arrays of rectennas **180***b* to form a wireless power generation system. The rectenna system **180***b* has been demonstrated at microwave wavelengths (X-Band) to provide 275 volts from 18 milli-Watts of incident energy. The rectenna system **180***b* can be designed for other and higher frequencies depending on configuration requirements, atmospheric transmissibility, etc. The resulting electrical energy can be used as power for electrical motors for propulsion of the UAV's alone, in combination with electrical storage systems, or in combination with other hydrocarbon engines, including hybrid modes of operation.

As conceived, the UAV is air-launched from and returned to the HAA base. The HAA base for UAVs is built under the HAA, as shown in FIGS. 14 and 15. The UAVs may also be launched or retrieved by hand, machine, towing, or dropped from other aircraft and/or helicopters. By nature of the structural material and concept of utilization, the UAV does not require landing gear or skids. As such, the structural design requirements for takeoff, landing, and taxiing are reduced or eliminated and thereby relax the overall structural design loads and requirements.

To sustain a long duration operation, the helium or helium/hydrogen mixture filled fat-body airframe of UAVs is considered to reduce the power requirement for propulsion by both reducing the body weight and increasing the lift force by buoyancy. The fat-body framed UAV mode **210** to be propelled by electric motors is shown in FIG. 21. Two electric motor driven propellers **211**, **212** are located at both the wing-tips and control the flight direction by changing rotational speed. The power for these planes is obtained from microwave through rectenna arrays **180***b* that are integrated on the skin of the airframe. The range of maneuver is determined by the envelope of microwave beaming column and the guided direction of beam. As long as any MAVs or UAVs are within the beam column, the power is continuously fed into them.

Suppose that a UAV has a 10 m² rectenna arrays that are integrated into the skin of fuselage and both wings as shown FIG. 21. If 1 MW of microwave power as described in the block diagram of FIG. 20 is transmitted at w-band, the power flux density of microwave at the ground level will be approximately 60 mW/cm². The power received by a UAV which is a 20 km away to the ground level and has a 10 m² rectenna arrays will amount to be 6 kW within the power beam column of 50 meters in diameter. Using the same logic shown in FIG. 19, the power is allocated to the propulsion system and other functional systems, such as probes. Suppose that the maneuver of the UAV requires 4 kW of the received power. The rest can be used for sensors and probes for other operations. However, the power receiving area of MAVs or UAVs is limited due to their own limited sizes. Therefore, they require an extra lifting force to stay aloft. The helium-filled MAV or UAV **210** as shown in FIG. 21 will gain an extra lifting force.

14

The UAV size of 5 m³ helium filled will gain the buoyancy force of 51 N which will reduce the weight by approximately 5 kg.

Another scenario for HAA use is for laser power transmission technologies for space applications which were developed in late 1970 through the 1980's using the directly solar pumped iodine laser and also a high power diode laser array. The efficiencies of continuous wave (CW) lasers are, in general, poor, especially for the short wavelength lasers. If we consider a laser with 10% efficiency, the actual laser power to be conveyed through the beam becomes 100 kW level. With a pulse forming network, the laser power output would be much higher to a few tera-watts (TW) level by pulse compression. The reflectors **220** that are installed on a HAA can also be used to relay the laser beam power **221** to selected locations through the relay satellite **222** as shown in FIG. **22**. However, if the HAA has sufficient power available from utilization of the ATE conversion device of the present invention, the relay station would not be necessary. Additionally, energy harvested by the ATE device **100/100***a* can also be used for internal power requirements of the HAA. The internal power requirement is determined from the power consumption by the PMC station movement over the guide rail, communication equipment, and system monitoring devices. Additionally, onboard radar systems can also be operated with this energy. The onboard radar operation can be used for monitoring any flying objects or ground or sea level activities of interest.

The new concept HAA, as described above, has an elliptical cross-section perpendicular to the thrust axis to expand the solar exposure area, unlike the conventional airships with a circular cross-section. FIG. 13B shows the elliptical cross section of an embodiment of the airship. Accordingly, the overall shape of the new concept airship is flattened as illustrated in FIGS. 13A and 15. Although the elliptical cross-section **131** of the airship **135** may be structurally less sturdy or slightly heavier than the circular cross-section, the benefits of the elliptical shape are greater in consideration of the lift force and the stability of flight that might compensate the shortcomings of elliptical cross-section. If the structural reinforcement of the elliptical cross section should be required to maintain the same strength level of a circular cross sectioned, the weight increase due to the elliptical cross section of airship would be less than 20%. The near flat-top surface **135***a* of the airship **135** offers a wide area to accommodate a energy harvesting device from sun light, such as solar cells or the advanced thermoelectric generators of the present invention. As shown in FIG. **14**, the HAA can have guide rail systems **140/146** to locate the PMC station **141** and the UAV hangers **142** to the nadir position of HAA **135**. The purpose of rotational capability along the guide rail **140** is to maximize the incidence of solar flux by setting the top surface of HAA **135** always perpendicular to sun light **160**. Whenever the PMC station **141** moves on the guide rail **140**, the HAA rotates the PMC station **141** and sets the PMC station **141** at the lowest level as shown in FIGS. **14** and **16** since the PMC station **141** is typically the heaviest unit of the HAA. Movement of PMC **141** on guide rail **140** can be accomplished through conventional means (e.g. computer controlled and electric motor driven). Similarly, in at least one embodiment, guide rails **146** can be provided, to move the UAV hangars **142** in the same manner as the PMC station **141**.

Although the invention has been described relative to specific embodiments thereof, there are numerous variations and modifications that will be readily apparent to those skilled in the art in light of the above teachings. It is therefore to be understood that, with in the scope of the appended claims, the invention may be practiced other than as specifically described herein.

What is claimed is:

1. A method for forming high figure of merit thermoelectric materials, comprising:

providing nanocrystals of bismuth and tellurium;

preparing a void generator material including a plurality of nanoparticles each having a metallic outer coating, wherein the void generator material is ferritin protein;

preparing a solution mixture of the bismuth nanocrystals, tellurium nanocrystals and the void generator material;

depositing the solution mixture onto a substrate;

heating the deposited solution mixture in an oxygen environment to create a plurality of nanovoid structures from the nanoparticles resulting in a nanovoid incorporated bismuth-tellurium film;

following the heating, treating the film to remove any oxygen components remaining from heating the mixture in the oxygen environment; and

causing the formation of a crystalline structure in the film.

2. The method of claim 1, wherein the metallic outer coating of the nanoparticles is selected from the group consisting of gold, cobalt, platinum, manganese, and iron.

3. The method of claim 1, wherein the metallic outer coating of the nanoparticles is in the range of 3 to 4 nm thick.

4. The method of claim 1, wherein the nanoparticles are generally spherical in shape.

5. The method of claim 1, wherein the nanoparticles have an inner diameter of 8 nm and an outer diameter of 12 nm.

6. The method of claim 1, wherein the substrate is silicon.

7. The method of claim 1, wherein the solution mixture is deposited on the substrate by a method selected from the group consisting of spin-coating, dipping, and solvent casting.

8. The method of claim 1, wherein the oxygen environment is 99.999% pure oxygen.

9. The method of claim 1 wherein the deposited solution mixture is heated to no more than 400° C.

10. The method of claim 1 wherein the deposited solution mixture is heated for approximately 1 hour.

11. The method of claim 1, wherein the film is treated to remove any oxygen components remaining from heating the mixture in the oxygen environment and formation of a crystalline structure in the film are accomplished by performing hydrogen calcination and hydrogen plasma quenching.

12. A method for forming high figure of merit thermoelectric materials, comprising:

providing nanocrystals of bismuth and tellurium,

preparing a void generator material including a plurality of nanoparticles each having a metallic outer coating;

preparing a solution mixture of the bismuth nanocrystals, tellurium nanocrystals and the void generator material;

depositing the solution mixture onto a substrate;

heating the deposited solution mixture in an oxygen environment to create a plurality of nanovoid structures from the nanoparticles resulting in a nanovoid incorporated bismuth-tellurium film;

following the heating, treating the film to remove any oxygen components remaining from heating the mixture in the oxygen environment; and

causing the formation of a crystalline structure in the film, wherein the film treatment and formation of a crystalline structure in the film are accomplished by performing hydrogen calcination and hydrogen plasma quenching.

13. The method of claim 12, wherein the void generator material is an organic material.

14. The method of claim 12, wherein the void generator material is ferritin protein.

15. The method of claim 12, wherein the metallic outer coating of the nanoparticles is selected from the group consisting of gold, cobalt, platinum, manganese, and iron.

16. The method of claim 12, wherein the metallic outer coating of the nanoparticles is in the range of 3 to 4 nm thick.

17. The method of claim 12, wherein the nanoparticles are generally spherical in shape.

18. The method of claim 12, wherein the nanoparticles have an inner diameter of 8 nm and an outer diameter of 12 nm.

19. The method of claim 12, wherein the substrate is silicon.

20. The method of claim 12, wherein the solution mixture is deposited on the substrate by a method selected from the group consisting of spin-coating, dipping, and solvent casting.

21. The method of claim 12, wherein the oxygen environment is 99.999% pure oxygen.

22. The method of claim 12 wherein the deposited solution mixture is heated to no more than 400° C.

23. The method of claim 12 wherein the deposited solution mixture is heated for approximately 1 hour.

* * * * *

US 20060256975A1

(19) United States
(12) Patent Application Publication
Brooks et al.

(10) Pub. No.: US 2006/0256975 A1

(43) Pub. Date: Nov. 16, 2006

(54) DECONVOLUTION METHODS AND SYSTEMS FOR THE MAPPING OF ACOUSTIC SOURCES FROM PHASED MICROPHONE ARRAYS

(75) Inventors: **Thomas F. Brooks**, Seaford, VA (US); **William M. Humphreys JR.**, Newport News, VA (US)

Correspondence Address:
NATIONAL AERONAUTICS AND SPACE ADMINISTRATION
LANGLEY RESEARCH CENTER
MAIL STOP 141
HAMPTON, VA 23681-2199 (US)

(73) Assignee: **United States of America as represented by the Administrator of the NASA**, Washington, DC

(21) Appl. No.: **11/126,518**

(22) Filed: **May 10, 2005**

Publication Classification

(51) Int. Cl.
H04R 3/00 (2006.01)

(52) U.S. Cl. 381/92

(57) **ABSTRACT**

A method and system for mapping acoustic sources determined from a phased microphone array. A plurality of microphones are arranged in an optimized grid pattern including a plurality of grid locations thereof. A linear configuration of N equations and N unknowns can be formed by accounting for a reciprocal influence of one or more beamforming characteristics thereof at varying grid locations among the plurality of grid locations. A full-rank equation derived from the linear configuration of N equations and N unknowns can then be iteratively determined. A full-rank can be attained by the solution requirement of the positivity constraint equivalent to the physical assumption of statically independent noise sources at each N location. An optimized noise source distribution is then generated over an identified aeroacoustic source region associated with the phased microphone array in order to compile an output presentation thereof, thereby removing the beamforming characteristics from the resulting output presentation.

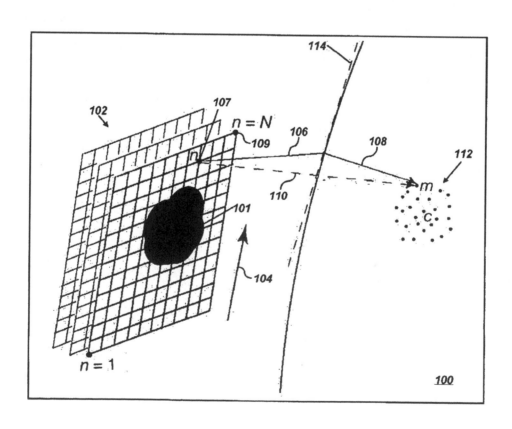

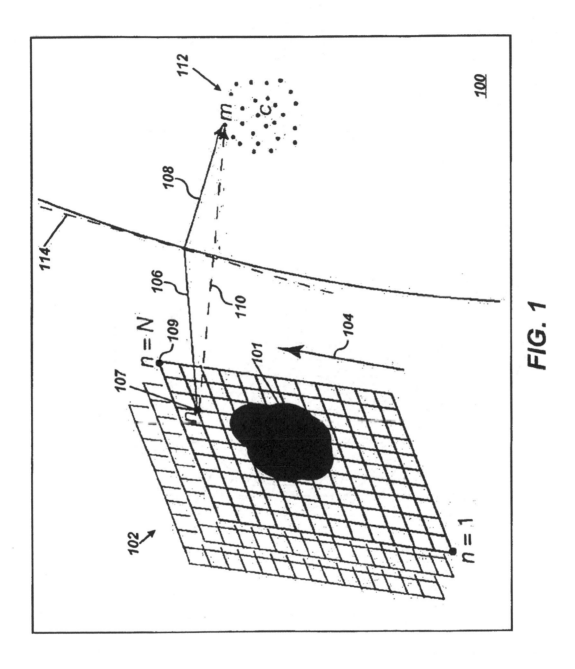

FIG. 1

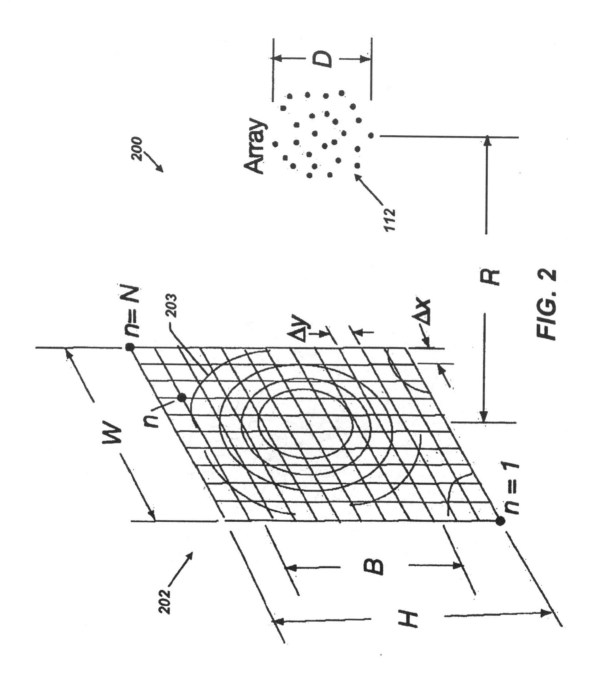

FIG. 2

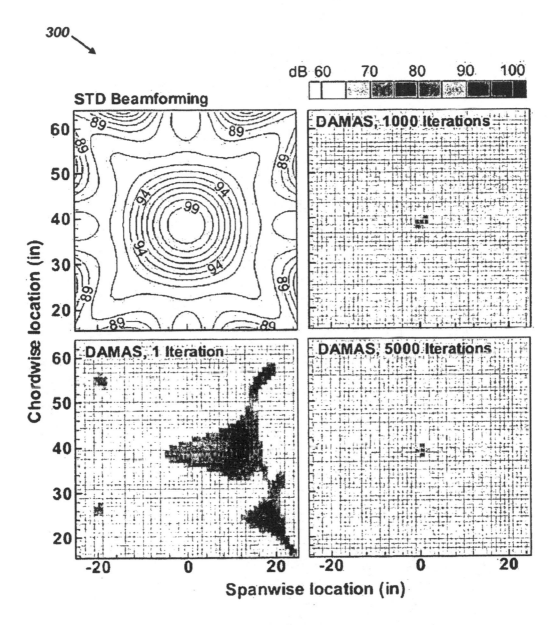

FIG. 3

461

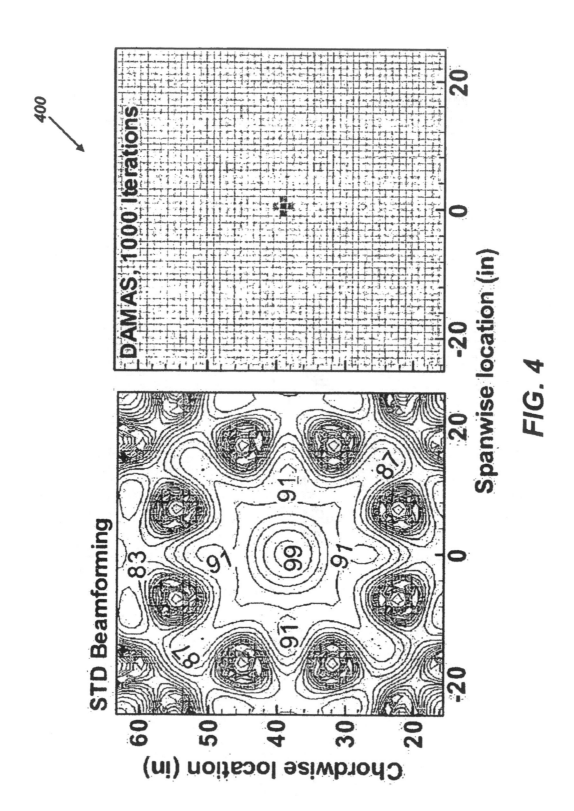

FIG. 4

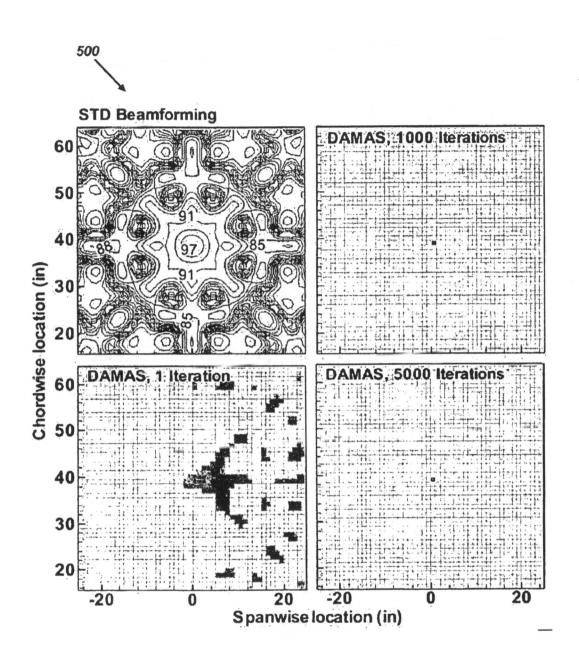

FIG. 5

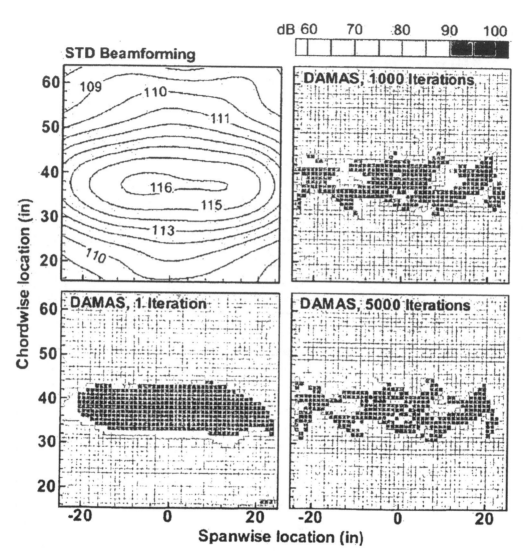

FIG. 6

464

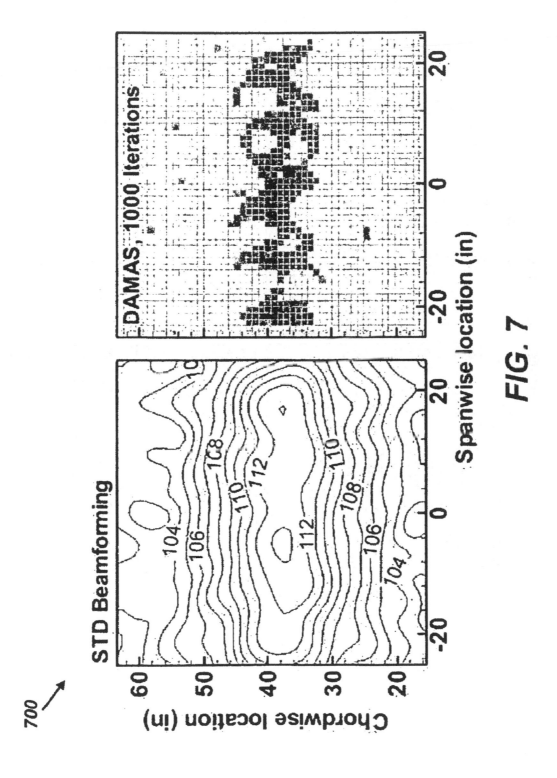

FIG. 7

800

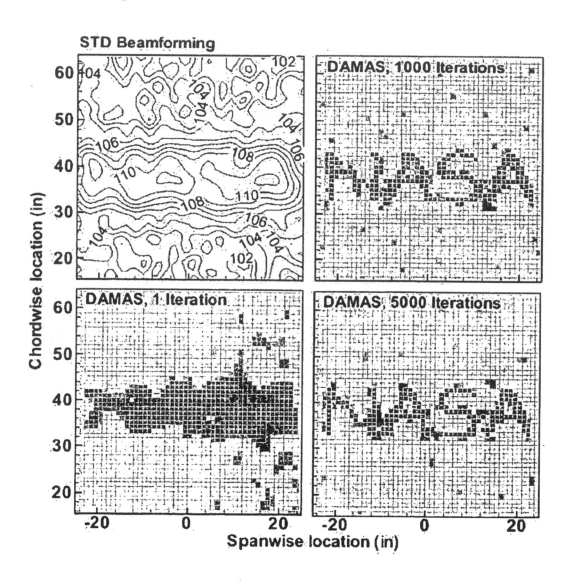

FIG. 8

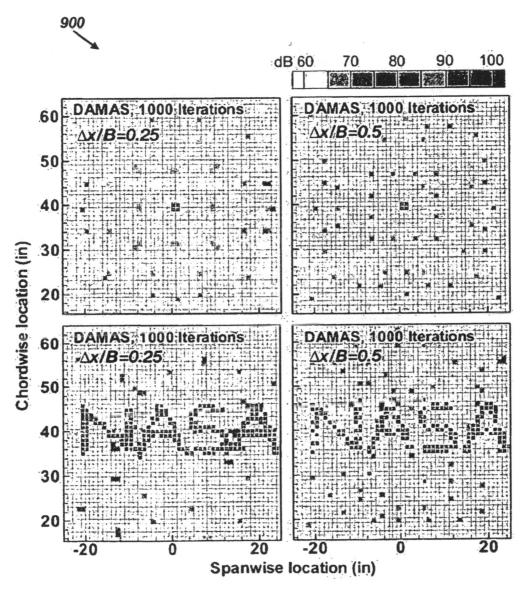

FIG. 9

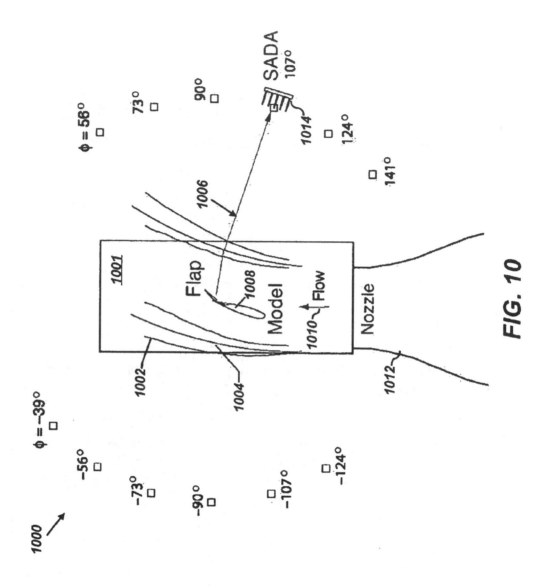

FIG. 10

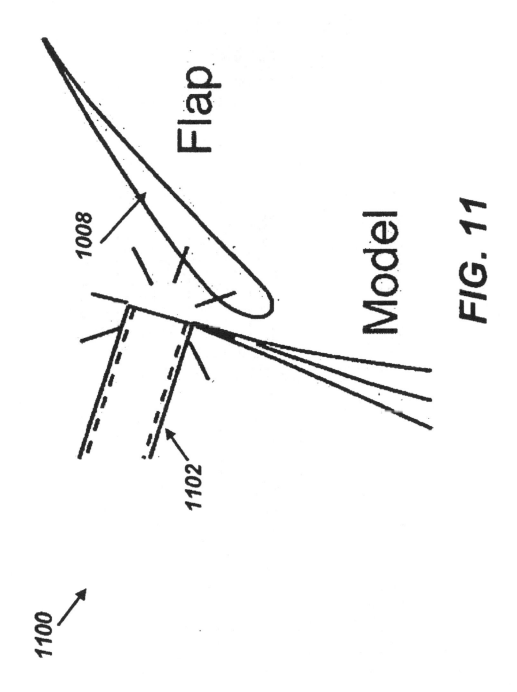

Flap

Model

1008

1102

1100

FIG. 11

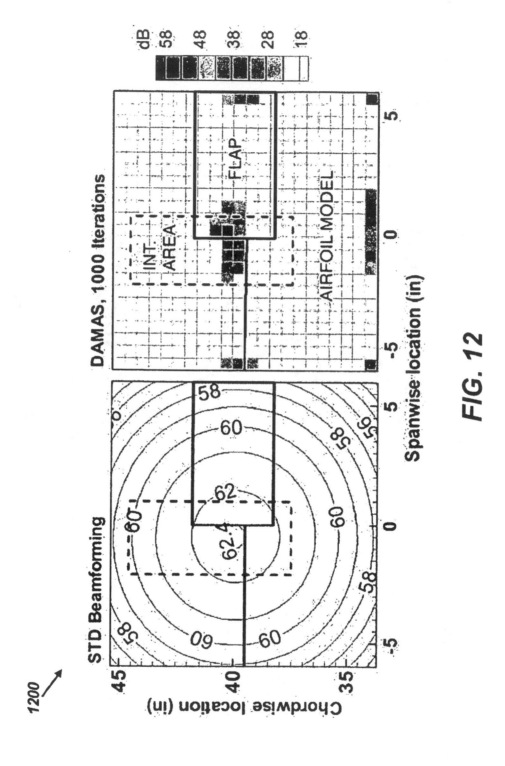

FIG. 12

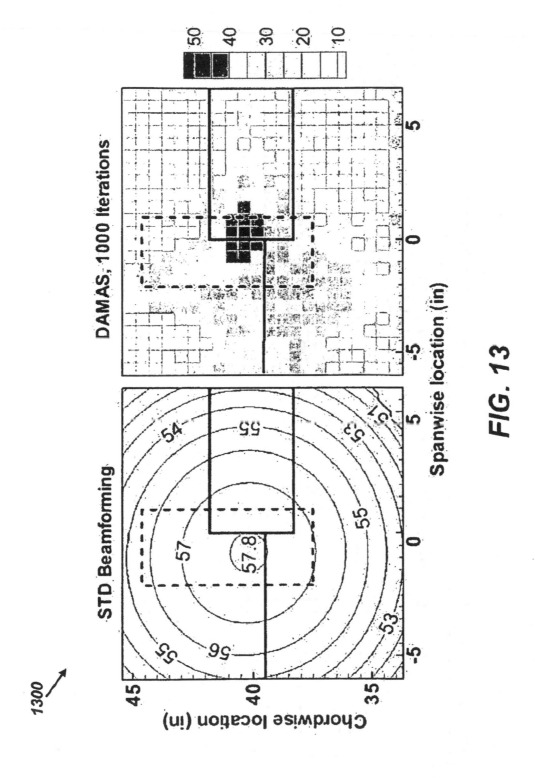

FIG. 13

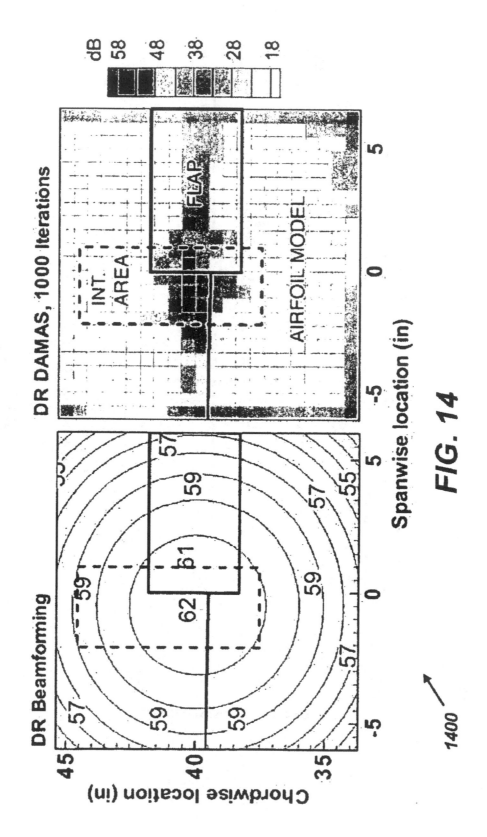

FIG. 14

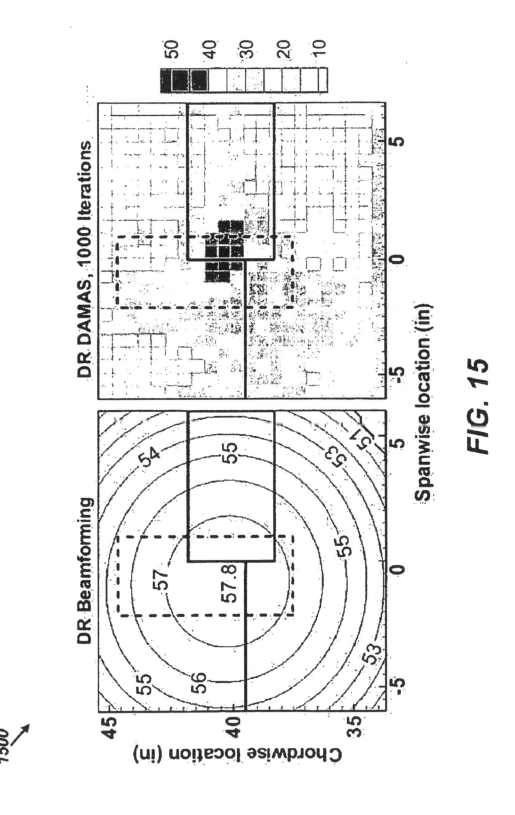

FIG. 15

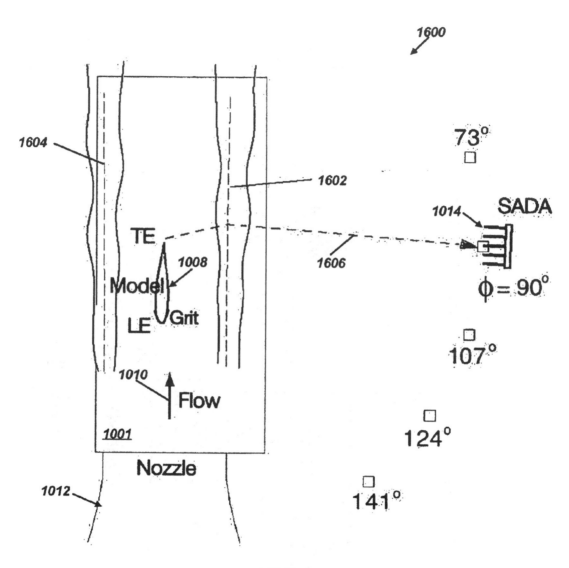

FIG. 16

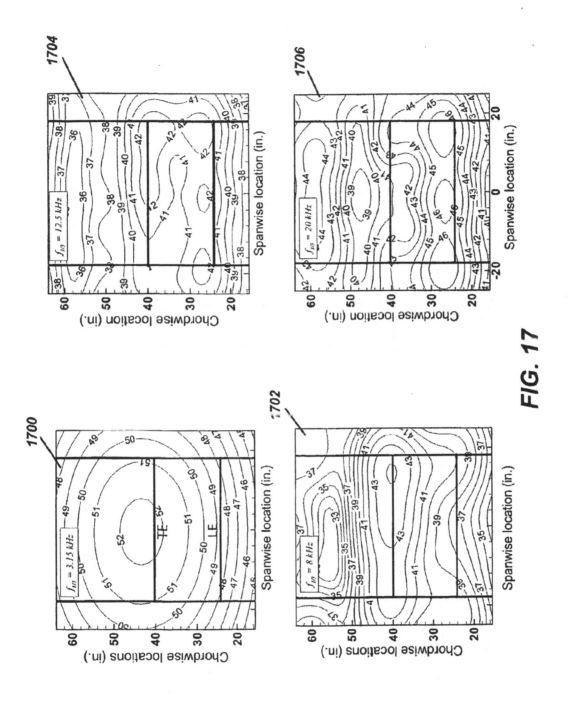

FIG. 17

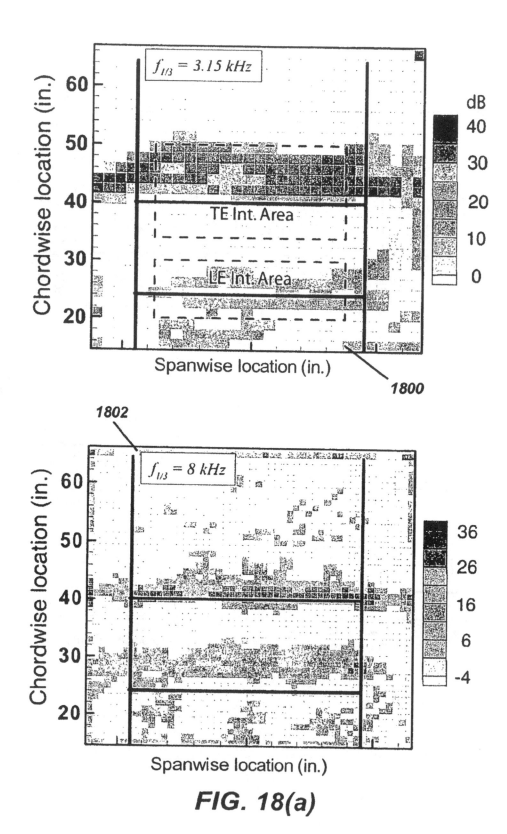

FIG. 18(a)

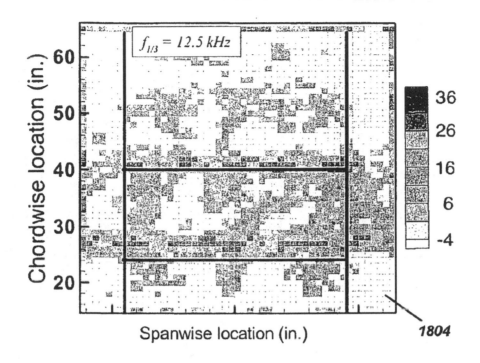

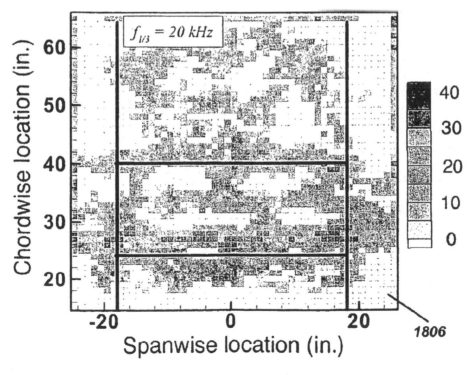

FIG. 18(b)

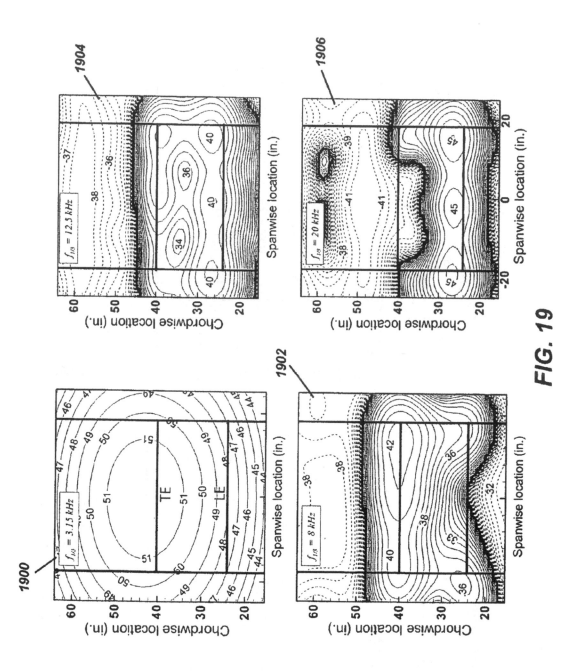

FIG. 19

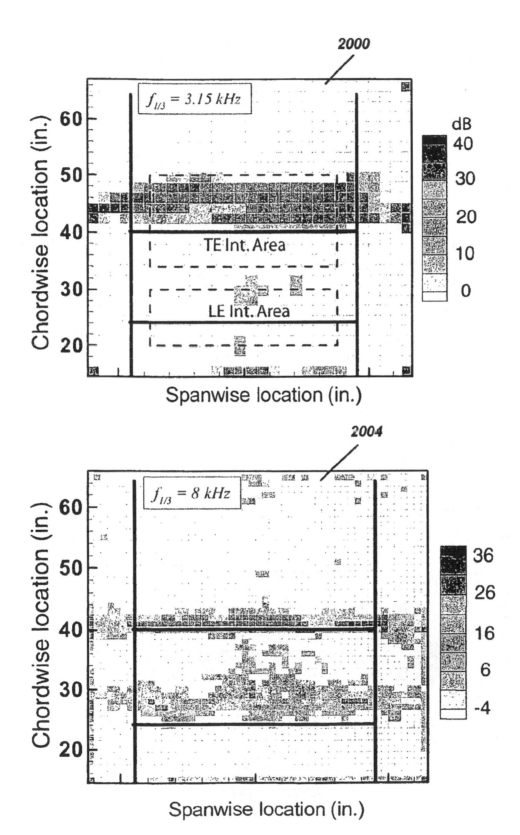

FIG. 20(a)

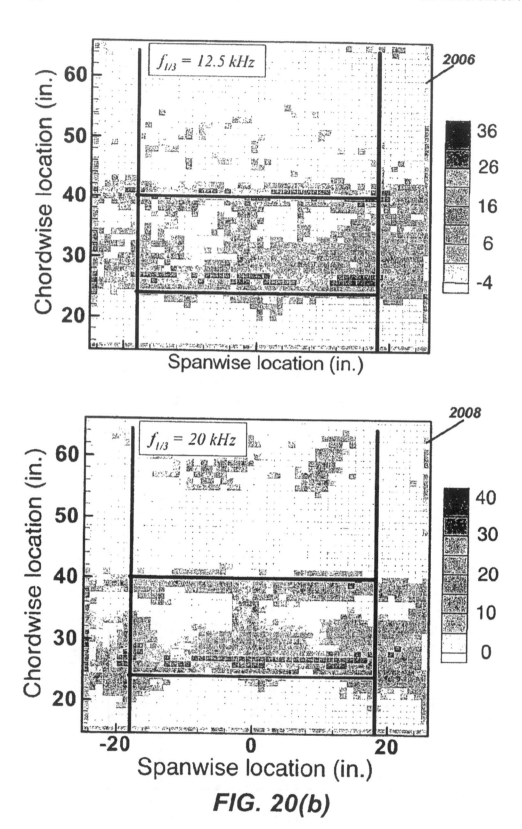

FIG. 20(b)

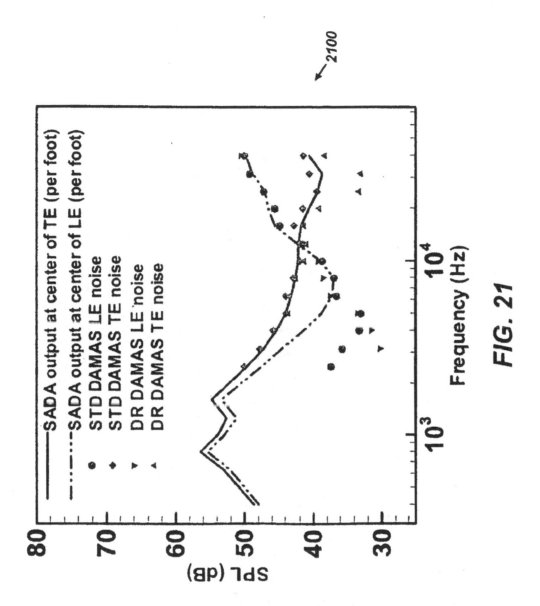

FIG. 21

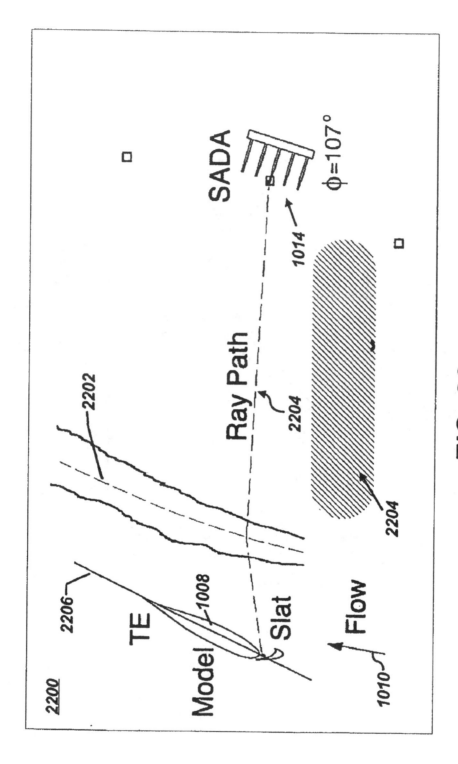

FIG. 22

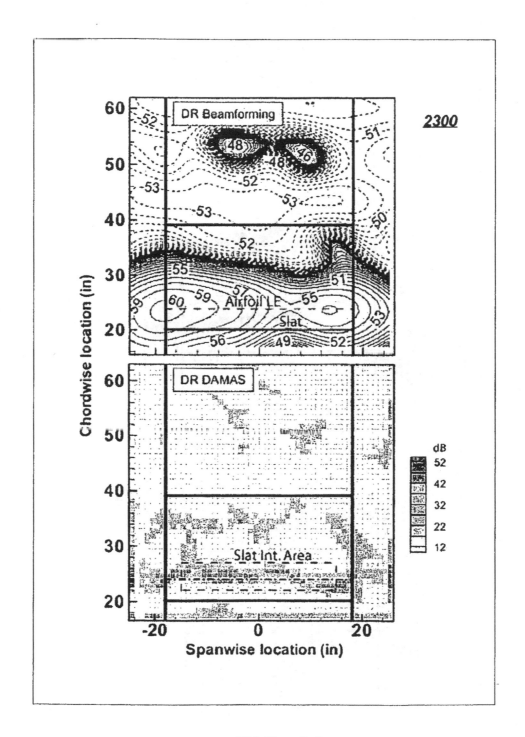

FIG. 23

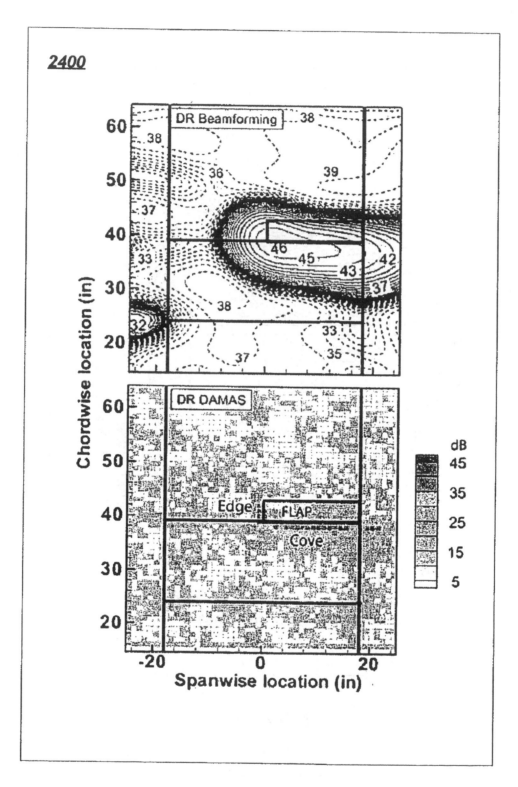

FIG. 24

DECONVOLUTION METHODS AND SYSTEMS FOR THE MAPPING OF ACOUSTIC SOURCES FROM PHASED MICROPHONE ARRAYS

TECHNICAL FIELD

[0001] Embodiments are generally related to phased microphone arrays. Embodiments are also related to devices and components utilized in wind tunnel and aeroacoustic testing. Embodiments additionally relate to aeroacoustic tools utilized for airframe noise calculations. Embodiments also relate to any vehicle or equipment, either stationary or in motion, where noise location and intensity are desired to be determined.

BACKGROUND OF THE INVENTION

[0002] Wind tunnel tests can be conducted utilizing phased microphone arrays. A phased microphone array is typically configured as a group of microphones arranged in an optimized pattern. The signals from each microphone can be sampled and then processed in the frequency domain. The relative phase differences seen at each microphone determines where noise sources are located. The amplification capability of the array allows detection of noise sources well below the background noise level. This makes microphone arrays particularly useful for wind tunnel evaluations of airframe noise since, in most cases, the noise produced by wings, flaps, struts and landing gear models will be lower than that of the wind tunnel environment.

[0003] The use of phased arrays of microphones in the study of aeroacoustic sources has increased significantly in recent years, particularly since the mid 1990's. The popularity of phased arrays is due in large part to the apparent clarity of array-processed results, which can reveal noise source distributions associated with, for example, wind tunnel models and full-scale aircraft. Properly utilized, such arrays are powerful tools that can extract noise source radiation information in circumstances where other measurement techniques may fail. Presentations of array measurements of aeroacoustic noise sources, however, can lend themselves to a great deal of uncertainty during interpretation. Proper interpretation requires knowledge of the principles of phased arrays and processing methodology. Even then, because of the complexity, misinterpretations of actual source distributions (and subsequent misdirection of engineering efforts) are highly likely.

[0004] Prior to the mid 1980's, processing of array microphone signals as a result of aeroacoustic studies involved time delay shifting of signals and summing in order to strengthen contributions from, and thus "focus" on, chosen locations over surfaces or positions in the flow field. Over the years, with great advances in computers, this basic "delay and sum" processing approach has been replaced by "classical beamforming" approaches involving spectral processing to form cross spectral matrices (CSM) and phase shifting using increasingly large array element numbers. Such advances have greatly increased productivity and processing flexibility, but have not changed at all the interpretation complexity of the processed array results.

[0005] Some aeroacoustic testing has involved the goal of forming a quantitative definition of different airframe noise sources spectra and directivity. Such a goal has been achieved with arrays in a rather straight-forward manner for the localized intense source of flap edge noise. For precise source localization, however, Coherent Output Power (COP) methods can be utilized by incorporating unsteady surface pressure measurements along with the array. Quantitative measurements for distributed sources of slat noise have been achieved utilizing an array and specially tailored weighting functions that matched array beampatterns with knowledge of the line source type distribution for slat noise. Similar measurements for distributed trailing edge noise and leading edge noise (e.g., due in this case to grit boundary layer tripping) have been performed along with special COP methodologies involving microphone groups.

[0006] A number of efforts have been made at analyzing and developing more effective array processing methodologies in order to more readily extract source information. Several efforts include those that better account for array resolution, ray path coherence loss, and source distribution coherence and for test rig reflections. In a simulation study of methods for improving array output, particularly for suppressing side lobe contamination, several beamforming techniques have been examined, including a cross spectral matrix (CSM) element weighting approach, a robust adaptive beamforming, and a CLEAN algorithm. The CLEAN algorithm is a deconvolution technique that was first implemented in the context of radio astronomy.

[0007] The CSM weighting approach reduces side lobes compared to classical beamforming with some overall improvement in main beam pattern resolution. The results for the adaptive beam former, used with a specific constant added to the CSM matrix diagonal to avoid instability problems, have been encouraging. The CLEAN algorithm has been found to possess the best overall performance for the simulated beamforming exercise. The CLEAN algorithm has also been examined in association with a related algorithm referred to as RELAX, utilizing experimental array calibration data for a no-flow condition.

[0008] The result of such studies involves a mixed success in separating out sources. In other studies, using the same data, two robust adaptive beamforming methods have been examined and found to be capable of providing sharp beam widths and low side lobes. It should be mentioned that the above methods, although perhaps offering promise, have not produced quantitatively accurate source amplitudes and distributions for real test cases. In the CLEAN methodology in particular, questions have been raised with regard to the practicality of the algorithm for arrays in reflective wind tunnel environments.

[0009] A method that has shown promise with wind tunnel aeroacoustic data is the Spectral Estimation Method (SEM). SEM requires that the measured CSM of the array be compared to a simulated CSM constructed by defining distributions of compact patches of sources (i.e., or source areas) over a chosen aeroacoustic region of interest. The difference between the two CSM's can be minimized utilizing a Conjugate Gradient Method. The application of positivity constraints on the source solutions had been found to be difficult. The resultant source distributions for the airframe noise cases examined are regarded as being feasible and realistic, although not unique.

[0010] As a consequence of the drawbacks associated with the foregoing methods and approaches, an effort has been made to develop a complete deconvolution approach for the mapping of acoustic sources to demystify two-dimensional and three-dimensional array results, to reduce misinterpretation, and to more accurately quantify position and strength of aeroacoustic sources. Traditional presentations of array results involve mapping (e.g., contour plotting) of array output over spatial regions. These maps do not truly represent noise source distributions, but ones that are convolved with the array response functions, which depend on array geometry, size (i.e., with respect to source position and distributions), and frequency.

[0011] The deconvolution methodology described in greater detail herein therefore can employ these processed results (e.g., array output at grid points) over the survey regions and the associated array beamforming characteristics (i.e., relating the reciprocal influence of the different grid point locations) over the same regions where the array's outputs are measured. A linear system of "N" (i.e., number of grid points in region) equations and "N" unknowns is created. These equations are solved in a straight-forward iteration approach. The end result of this effort is a unique robust deconvolution approach designed to determine the "true" noise source distribution over an aeroacoustic source region to replace the "classical beam formed" distributions. Example applications include ideal point and line noise source cases, as well as conformation with well documented experimental airframe noise studies of wing trailing and leading edge noise, slat noise, and flap edge/flap cove noise.

BRIEF SUMMARY

[0012] The following summary is provided to facilitate an understanding of some of the innovative features unique to the embodiments disclosed and is not intended to be a full description. A full appreciation of the various aspects of the embodiments can be gained by taking the entire specification, claims, drawings, and abstract as a whole.

[0013] It is, therefore, one aspect of the present invention to provide for a method and system for mapping acoustic sources determined from microphone arrays.

[0014] It is another aspect of the present invention to provide for a "Deconvolution Approach for the Mapping of Acoustic Sources" (DAMAS) determined from phased microphone arrays.

[0015] It is yet a further aspect of the present invention to provide for improved devices and components utilized in wind tunnel and aeroacoustic testing.

[0016] It is also an aspect of the present invention to provide for aeroacoustic tools utilized for airframe noise calculations.

[0017] The aforementioned aspects and other objectives and advantages can now be achieved as described herein. A method and system for mapping acoustic sources determined from a phased microphone array, comprising a plurality of microphones arranged in an optimized grid pattern including a plurality of grid locations thereof. A linear configuration of N equations and N unknowns can be formed by accounting for a reciprocal influence of one or more beamforming characteristics thereof at varying grid locations among the plurality of grid locations. One or more full-rank equations among the linear configuration of N equations and N unknowns can then be iteratively determined. The full-rank can be attained by the solution require-

ment of the positivity constraint equivalent to the physical assumption of statically independent noise sources at each N location. An optimized noise source distribution is then generated over an identified aeroacoustic source region associated with the phased microphone array in order to compile an output presentation thereof, in response to iteratively determining at least one full-rank equation among the linear configuration of N equations and N unknowns, thereby removing the beamforming characteristics from the resulting output presentation.

BRIEF DESCRIPTION OF THE DRAWINGS

[0018] The accompanying figures, in which like reference numerals refer to identical or functionally-similar elements throughout the separate views and which are incorporated in and form a part of the specification, further illustrate the embodiments and, together with the detailed description, serve to explain the embodiments disclosed herein.

[0019] FIG. 1 illustrates an open jet configuration system wherein an array of microphones is indicated as out of flow and a scanning plane thereof positioned over an aeroacoustic source region, in accordance with one embodiment;

[0020] FIG. 2 illustrates a system including key geometric parameters of an array of microphones and a source scanning plane, in accordance with an embodiment;

[0021] FIG. 3 illustrates a graphical representation of array output based on standard processing methodologies, wherein frequency is equal to 10 kHz and $\Delta x/B$ is generally equivalent to 0.083 in accordance with one embodiment;

[0022] FIG. 4 illustrates a graphical representation of array output based on standard processing methodologies, wherein frequency is equal to 20 kHz and $\Delta x/B$ is generally equivalent to 0.167 in accordance with one embodiment;

[0023] FIG. 5 illustrates a graphical representation of array output based on standard processing methodologies, wherein frequency is equal to 30 kHz and $\Delta x/B$ is generally equivalent to 0.25 in accordance with one embodiment;

[0024] FIG. 6 illustrates a graphical representation of array output based on standard processing methodologies, wherein frequency is equal to 10 kHz and $\Delta x/B$ is generally equivalent to 0.083 in accordance with an alternative embodiment;

[0025] FIG. 7 illustrates a graphical representation of array output based on standard processing methodologies, wherein frequency is equal to 20 kHz and $\Delta x/B$ is generally equivalent to 0.167 in accordance with an alternative embodiment;

[0026] FIG. 8 illustrates a graphical representation of array output based on standard processing methodologies, wherein frequency is equal to 30 kHz and $\Delta x/B$ is generally equivalent to 0.25 in accordance with an alternative embodiment;

[0027] FIG. 9 illustrates a graphical representation of spatial aliasing with point source and image shifted between grid points in accordance with an alternative embodiment;

[0028] FIG. 10 illustrates a configuration of a noise flap from a flap edge to an SADA, in accordance with an alternative embodiment;

[0029] **FIG. 11** illustrates an open end of a calibrator source positioned next to the flap edge depicted in **FIG. 10**, in accordance with an alternative embodiment;

[0030] **FIG. 12** illustrates a graphical representation of calibrator source test data wherein M=0 with an integrated level of 62.8 dB and a DAMAS of 62.9 dB, in accordance with an alternative embodiment;

[0031] **FIG. 13** illustrates a graphical representation of calibrator source test data wherein M=0.17, with an integrated level of 58.1 dB and a DAMAS of 57.3 dB, in accordance with an alternative embodiment;

[0032] **FIG. 14** illustrates a graphical representation of a calibrator source test, wherein M=0 with an integrated level of 62.2 dB and a DAMAS of 61.6 dB, in accordance with an alternative embodiment;

[0033] **FIG. 15** illustrates a graphical representation of a calibrator source test, wherein M=0.17 with an integrated level of 57.9 dB and a DAMAS of 56.9, in accordance with an alternative embodiment;

[0034] **FIG. 16** illustrates a configuration of a test set-up for TE and LE noise testing, in accordance with an alternative embodiment;

[0035] **FIG. 17** and FIGS. **18**(a)-**18**(b) illustrate SADA response contours for shaded STD processing for TE and LE noise testing, in accordance with an alternative embodiment;

[0036] **FIG. 19** illustrates DAMAS results corresponding to **FIGS. 17-18**, in accordance with an alternative embodiment;

[0037] **FIG. 20**(a) and **FIG. 20**(b) illustrate SADA response contours for shaded DR processing with respect to TE and LE noise tests, in accordance with an alternative embodiment;

[0038] **FIG. 21** illustrates a graphical representation of a comparison of one-third octave spectra from TE and LE noise measurements and reprocessing by DAMAS, in accordance with an alternative embodiment;

[0039] **FIG. 22** illustrates shows an airfoil/slat in a deflected open jet, with a SADA positioned at ϕ=107°;

[0040] **FIG. 23** illustrates the array output and corresponding DAMAS result for $f_{1/3}$=20 kHz using shaded DR processing over a scanning plane through an airfoil; and

[0041] **FIG. 24** illustrates beamforming contours and DAMAS results for shaded DR processing over a scanning plane placed through an airfoil chord-line.

DETAILED DESCRIPTION

[0042] The particular values and configurations discussed in these non-limiting examples can be varied and are cited merely to illustrate at least one embodiment and are not intended to limit the scope thereof. Additionally, acronyms, symbols and subscripts utilized herein are summarized below.

Symbols and Acronyms

[0043] a_m shear layer refraction amplitude correction for e_m

[0044] $\hat{A}$ DAMAS matrix with $A_{nn'}$ components

[0045] $A_{nn'}$ reciprocal influence of beamforming characteristics between grid points

[0046] B array "beamwidth" of 3 dB down from beam peak maximum

[0047] c_0 speed of sound without mean flow

[0048] CSM cross spectral matrix

[0049] D nominal diameter of array

[0050] DR diagonal removal of $\hat{G}$ in array processing

[0051] $\hat{e}$ steering vector for array to focus location

[0052] e_m component of $\hat{e}$ for microphone m

[0053] f frequency

[0054] Δf frequency bandwidth resolution of spectra

[0055] FFT Fast Fourier Transform

[0056] ϕ array elevation angle

[0057] $G_{mm'}$ cross-spectrum between p_m and $p_{m'}$

[0058] $\hat{G}$ matrix (CSM) of cross-spectrum elements $G_{mm'}$

[0059] H height of chosen scanning plane

[0060] i iteration number

[0061] k counting number of CSM averages, also acoustic wave number

[0062] l representative dimension of source geometry detail

[0063] LADA Large Aperture Directional Array

[0064] LE leading edge

[0065] m microphone identity number in array

[0066] m' same as m, but independently varied

[0067] m_0 total number of microphones in array

[0068] n grid point number on scanning plane(s)

[0069] M wind tunnel test Mach number

[0070] N total number of grid points over scanning plane(s)

[0071] p_m pressure time records from microphone m

[0072] P_m Fourier Transform of p_m

[0073] QFF Quiet Flow Facility

[0074] Q_n idealized P_m for modeled source at n for quiescent acoustic medium

[0075] r_c distance r_m for m being the center c microphone

[0076] r_m retarded coordinate distance to m, $\tau_m c_0$

[0077] R nominal distance of array from scanning plane

[0078] SADA Small Aperture Directional Array

[0079] STD standard or classical array processing

[0080] T complex transpose (superscript)

[0081] TE trailing edge

[0082] τ_m propagation time from grid point to microphone m

[0083] w_m frequency dependent shading (or weighting) for m

[0084] $\hat{W}$ shading matrix of w_m terms

[0085] W width of scanning plane

[0086] Δx widthwise spacing of grid points

[0087] $\hat{X}$ matrix of X_n terms

[0088] X_n "noise source" at grid point n with levels defined at array, Q_n*Q_n

[0089] Δy heightwise spacing of grid points

[0090] $Y(\hat{e})$ output power response of the array at focus location

[0091] $\hat{Y}$ matrix of Y_n terms

[0092] Y_n $Y(\hat{e})$, when focused at grid point n

Subscripts

[0093] bkg background

[0094] diag diagonal

[0095] m:n term associated with m, as it relates to grid position n

[0096] mod modeled

[0097] The first step in a DAMAS formulation or analysis is to beamform over the source region, using what have become traditional methods. Post processing of simultaneously acquired data from the microphones of an array begins with computation of the cross-spectral matrix for each test case data set. The computation of each element of the matrix is performed using Fast Fourier Transforms (FFT) of the original data ensemble. The transform pairs $P_m(f,T)$ and $P_m'(f,T)$ are formed from pressure time records $p_m(t)$ and $p_{m'}(t)$, defined at discrete sampling times that are Δt apart, of data block lengths T from microphones m and m', respectively. The cross-spectrum matrix element can be provided as indicated in equation (1) below:

$$G_{mm'}(f) = \frac{2}{Kw_s T}\sum_{k=1}^{K}[P_{mk}^*(f,T)P_{m'k}(f,T)] \qquad (1)$$

[0098] This one-sided cross-spectrum can be averaged over K block averages. The total record length is $T_{tot}=KT$. The term w_s represents a data-window (e.g., such as Hamming) weighting constant. $G_{mm'}(f)$ can be seen as a complex spectrum with values at discrete frequencies f, which are Δf apart. The bandwidth is $\Delta f=1/T$ (Hz). The full matrix is, with m_0 being the total number of microphones in the array,

$$\hat{G} = \begin{vmatrix} G_{11} & G_{12} & \cdots & G_{1m_0} \\ \vdots & G_{22} & & \vdots \\ \vdots & & \ddots & \vdots \\ G_{m_01} & & & G_{m_0 m_0} \end{vmatrix} \qquad (2)$$

[0099] Note that the lower triangular elements are complex conjugates of the upper triangular elements. The cross-spectral matrix can be employed in conventional beamforming approaches to electronically "steer" to chosen noise source locations about an aeroacoustic test model.

[0100] FIG. 1 illustrates an open jet configuration system 100 wherein a phased microphone array 112 is indicated as out of flow and a scanning plane thereof positioned over an aeroacoustic source region, in accordance with one embodiment.

[0101] FIG. 1 generally depicts a particular test setup of a distribution of microphones of a phased array 112 located outside the flow field containing an aeroacoustic model. A scanning plane 102 of grid points can be defined over a noise source region 101. A tangent array crossing 114 is depicted in FIG. 1 between array 112 and the scanning plane 102. Air flow can be indicated by arrow 104 in FIG. 1. (A scanning plane may, for example, be placed through the chordline of an airfoil section when studying trailing edge and/or leading edge noise.) The beamforming approach involves steering vectors associated with each microphone with respect to a selected steering location. The steering location can be designated as grid point n, which is illustrated as point 107 in FIG. 1. At point 109, the value n is equal to the value N. The ray path indicating flow is generally represented by lines 106, 108 in FIG. 1, while the ray path for no flow indicated by line 110. The steering vector can be generally provided by equation (3) below:

$$\hat{e} = col[e_1 e_2 \ldots e_{m_0}] \qquad (3)$$

where the component for each microphone m is

$$e_m = a_m \frac{r_m}{r_c}\exp\{j2\pi f\tau_m\} \qquad (4)$$

[0102] The vector components serve to phase shift each microphone signal to allow constructive summing of contributions from the chosen locations. τ_m is the time required to propagate from grid point n to microphone m. The phase can be designated as indicated in equation (5) below:

$$2\pi f\tau_m = (\vec{k}\cdot\vec{x}_m)+2\pi f\Delta t_{m,shear} \qquad (5)$$

[0103] The term $\vec{k}$ is the acoustic wave vector, $\vec{x}_m$ is the distance vector from the steering location to the microphone m. The steering vector components contain terms that account for the mean amplitude and phase changes due to convected and refracted sound transmission through the shear layer to each microphone. The corrections can be calculated through the use of Snell's law in Amiet's method, and adapted to a curved three-dimensional mean shear layer surface defined in the shear layer. Note that the variable a_m represents the refraction amplitude correction.

[0104] The value $\Delta t_{m,shear}$ represents the additional time (compared to a direct ray path with no flow) it takes an acoustic ray to travel to microphone m from the steering location n, due to the convection by the open jet flow and refraction by the shear layer. As indicted by equation (4), the ratio (r_m/r_C) can be included to normalize the distance related amplitude to that of the distance r_C from the source location to the array center microphone at c. Both r_m and r_C are in terms of "retarded" coordinates. With this, $r_m=\tau_m c_0$, where c_0 equals the speed of sound without mean flow.

[0105] For classical or standard array beamforming, the output power spectrum (or response) of the array can be obtained utilizing equation (6) below:

$$Y(\hat{e}) = \frac{\hat{e}^T \hat{G} \hat{e}}{m_0^2} \qquad (6)$$

where the superscript T denotes a complex transpose of the steering vector. Here the term $Y(\hat{e})$ can be a mean-pressure-squared per frequency bandwidth quantity. The division by the number of array microphones squared serves to reference levels to that of an equivalent single microphone measurement. Note that the cross-spectral matrix (CSM) $\hat{G}$ often has a corresponding background cross-spectral matrix $\hat{G}_{bkg}$ (i.e., obtained for a similar test condition except that the model is removed) subtracted from it to improve fidelity.

[0106] Shading algorithms can be used over distributions of array microphones to modify the output beampattern. The shaded steered response can be provided as indicated by equation (7) below:

$$Y(\hat{e}) = \frac{\hat{e}^T \hat{W} \hat{G} \hat{W}^T \hat{e}}{\left(\sum\limits_{m=1}^{m_0} w_m\right)^2} \qquad (7)$$

where w_m represents the frequency dependent shading (or weighting) for each microphone m. The variable $\hat{W}$ represents a row matrix containing the w_m terms. When all w_m terms can be set to one and W becomes an identity matrix, all microphones are fully active in the beamforming to render the formulation of equation (6). Note that in some implementations, a special shading can be used to maintain constant beamwidth over a range of frequencies by shading out ($w_m=0$) inner microphone groups at low frequencies and by shading outer groups at high frequencies.

[0107] A modified form of equation (6) can be used to improve the dynamic range of the array results in poor signal-to-noise test applications. The primary intent is to remove the microphone self noise contamination (i.e., particularly caused by turbulence interacting with the microphones). Such an action can be accomplished by removing (i.e., zeroing out) the diagonal terms of $\hat{G}$ and accounting for this change in the number of terms of $\hat{G}$ in the denominator. The output of Diagonal Removal (DR) processing can be provided equation (8) below:

$$Y(\hat{e}) = \frac{\hat{e}^T \hat{G}_{diag=0} \hat{e}}{m_0^2 - m_0} \qquad (8)$$

[0108] This modifies the beamform patterns compared to equation (6). The diagonal can be viewed as expendable in the sense that it duplicates information contained in the cross terms of $\hat{G}$. However, great care must be taken in physical interpretation of resulting array response maps, for example, negative "pressure-squared" values are to be expected over low-level noise source regions. The corresponding shaded version of equation (8) can be provided as indicated by equation (9) below:

$$Y(\hat{e}) = \frac{\hat{e}^T \hat{W} \hat{G}_{diag=0} \hat{W}^T \hat{e}}{\left(\sum\limits_{m=1}^{m_0} w_m\right)^2 - \left(\sum\limits_{m=1}^{m_0} w_m\right)} \qquad (9)$$

[0109] The common practice for studying aeroacoustic source of noise with arrays are to determine the array response, using either equations (6), (7), (8), or (9), over a range (grid) of steering locations about the source region. For particular frequencies, contours of the response levels are plotted over planes where sources are know to lie, or over volume regions in some cases. To extract quantitative contributions to the noise field from particular source locations, a number of methods are used. Integration methods can be utilized as well as special methods tailored to fit particular noise distributions, depending upon design considerations. Still the methods can be difficult to apply and care must be taken in interpretation. This is because the processing of equations (6)-(9) produces "source" maps which are as much a reflection of the array beamforming pattern characteristics as is the source distribution being measured.

[0110] The purpose here is to pose the array problem such that the desired quantities, the source strength distributions, are extracted cleanly from the beamforming array characteristics. First, the pressure transform P_m of microphone m of equation (1) is related to a modeled source located at position n in the source field as indicated by equation (10) below:

$$P_{m:n} = Q_n e_{m:n}^{-1} \qquad (10)$$

[0111] Here Q_n represents the pressure transform that $P_{m:n}$ (or P_m) would be if flow convection and shear layer refraction did not affect transmission of the noise to microphone m, and if m were at a distance of r_c from n rather than r_m. The $e_{m:n}^{-1}$ term represents simply those components that were postulated in equation (4) to affect the signal in the actual transmission to render the value P_m. The product of pressure-transform terms of equation (1) therefore becomes as indicated in equation (11) below:

$$P_{m:n}^* P_{m':n} = (Q_n e_{m:n}^{-1})^* (Q_n e_{m':n}^{-1}) \qquad (11)$$
$$= Q_n^* Q_n (e_{m:n}^{-1})^* e_{m':n}^{-1}$$

When this equation is substituted into equation (1), one obtains the modeled microphone array cross-spectral matrix for a single source located at n

$$\hat{G}_{n_{mod}} = X_n \begin{bmatrix} (e_1^{-1})^* e_1^{-1} & (e_1^{-1})^* e_2^{-1} & \cdots & (e_1^{-1})^* e_{m_0}^{-1} \\ (e_2^{-1})^* e_1^{-1} & (e_2^{-1})^* e_2^{-1} & & \vdots \\ \vdots & & \ddots & \vdots \\ & & & (e_{m_0}^{-1})^* e_{m_0}^{-1} \end{bmatrix}_n \qquad (12)$$

where X_n is the mean square pressure per bandwidth at each microphone m normalized in level for a microphone at $r_m=r_c$. It is now assumed that there are a number N of statistically independent sources, each at different n positions. One obtains for the total modeled cross-spectral matrix

$$\hat{G}_{mod} = \sum_n \hat{G}_{n_{mod}} \tag{13}$$

Employing this in equation (6),

$$Y_{n_{mod}}(\hat{e}) = \left[\frac{\hat{e}^T \hat{G}_{mod} \hat{e}}{m_0^2} \right]_n \tag{14}$$

$$Y_{n_{mod}}(\hat{e}) = \frac{\hat{e}_n^T \sum_{n'} X_{n'} [\ ]_{n'} \hat{e}_n}{m_0^2} = \sum_{n'} \frac{\hat{e}_n^T [\ ]_{n'} \hat{e}_n}{m_0^2} X_{n'} \tag{15}$$

where the bracketed term is that of equation (12). This can be shown to equal

$$Y_{n_{mod}}(\hat{e}) = \hat{A} X_n \tag{16}$$

where the components of matrix $\hat{A}$ are

$$A_{nn'} = \frac{\hat{e}_n^T [\ ]_{n'} \hat{e}_n}{m_0^2} \tag{17}$$

By equating $Y_{n_{mod}}(\hat{e})$ with processed $Y(\hat{e})$ from measured data, we have

$$\hat{A}\hat{X} = \hat{Y} \tag{18}$$

Equation (18), for $\hat{X}$, also applies for the cases of shaded standard, DR, and shaded DR beamforming, with components $A_{nn'}$ of $\hat{A}$ becoming

$$A_{nn'} = \frac{\hat{e}^T \hat{W} [\ ]_{n'} \hat{W}^T \hat{e}}{\left(\sum_{m=1}^{m_0} w_m \right)^2}, \tag{19}$$

$$A_{nn'} = \frac{\hat{e}_n^T ([\ ]_{n'})_{diag=0} \hat{e}_n}{m_0^2 - m_0}, \tag{20}$$

and

$$A_{nn'} = \frac{\hat{e}_n^T \hat{W} ([\ ]_{n'})_{diag=0} \hat{W}^T \hat{e}_n}{\left(\sum_{m=1}^{m_0} w_m \right)^2 - \left(\sum_{m=1}^{m_0} w_m \right)^2} \tag{21}$$

respectively. For standard beamforming (shaded or not) the diagonal terms for $\hat{A}$ are equal to one. For Diagonal Removal beamforming (shaded or not), the diagonal terms for $\hat{A}$ are also equal to one, but the off-diagonal components differ and attain negative values when n and n' represent sufficiently distant points from one another, depending on frequency.

[0112] Equation (18) represents a system of linear equations relating a spatial field of point locations, with beam-formed array-output responses Y_n, to equivalent source distributions X_n at the same point locations. The same is true of equation (18) when Y_n is the result of shaded and/or DR processing of the same acoustic field. X_n is the same in both cases. (One is not restricted to these particular beamforming processing as long as $\hat{A}$ is appropriately defined.) Equation (18) with the appropriate $\hat{A}$ defines the DAMAS inverse problem. It is unique in that it or an equivalent equation must be the one utilized in order to disassociate the array itself from the sources being studied. Of course, the inverse problem must be solved in order to render $\hat{X}$. Equation (18) can therefore be thought of as constituting a DAMAS inverse formulation. Equations (22) to (24), on the other hand, which are describe in greater detail below, make solutions possible and thus function as a unique iterative method.

[0113] Equation (18) represents a system of linear equations. Matrix $\hat{A}$ is square (of size N×N) and if it were nonsingular (well-conditioned), the solution would simply be $\hat{X}=\hat{A}^{-1}\hat{Y}$. However, it has been found for the present acoustic problems of interest that only for overly restricted resolution (distance between n grid points) or noise region size (spatial expanse of the N grid points) would $\hat{A}$ be nonsingular. Using a Singular Value Decomposition (SVD) methodology for determining the condition of $\hat{A}$, it is found that for resolutions and region sizes of common interest in the noise source mapping problem in aeroacoustic testing that the rank of $\hat{A}$ can be quite low—often on the order of 0.25 and below.

[0114] Rank here can be defined as the number of linearly independent equations compared to the number of equations of equation (18), which is N=number of grid points. This means that generally very large numbers of "solutions" are possible. Equation (18) and the knowledge of the difficulty with equation rank were determined early in the present study. The SVD solution approach with and without a regularization methodology special iterative solving methods such as Conjugate Gradient methods and others did not produce satisfactory results. Good results were ultimately obtained by a very simple tailored iterative method where a physically-necessary positivity constraint (making the problem deterministic) on the X components could be applied smoothly in the iteration. This is described below.

[0115] A single linear equation component of equation (18) is

$$A_{n1}X_1 + A_{n2}X_2 + \ldots + A_{nn'}X_n + \ldots + A_{nN}X_N = Y_n \tag{22}$$

With $A_{nn}=1$, this is rearranged to give

$$X_n = Y_n - \left[\sum_{n'=1}^{n-1} A_{nn'} X_{n'} + \sum_{n'=n+1}^{N} A_{nn'} X_{n'} \right] \tag{23}$$

This equation is used in an iteration methodology to obtain the source distribution X_n for all n between 1 and N as per the following equation.

$$X_1^{(i)} = Y_1 - \left[0 + \sum_{n'=1}^{N} A_{1n'} X_{n'}^{(i-1)} \right] \tag{24}$$

$$X_1^{(i)} = Y_n - \left[\sum_{n'=1}^{n-1} A_{nn'} X_{n'}^{(i)} + \sum_{n'=n+1}^{N} A_{nn'} X_{n'}^{(i-1)} \right]$$

$$X_N^{(i)} = Y_N - \left[\sum_{n'=1}^{N-1} A_{Nn'} X_{n'}^{(i)} + 0 \right]$$

[0116] For the first iteration (i=1), the initial values X_n can be taken as zero or Y_n (the choice appears to cause little difference in convergence rates). It is seen that in the successive determination of X_n, for increasing n, the values are continuously fed into the succeeding X_n calculations. After each X_n determination, if it is negative, its value is set to zero. Each iteration (i) can be completed by like calculations, but reversed, moving from n=N back to n=1. The next iteration (i+1) starts again at n=1. Equation (24) is the DAMAS inverse problem iterative solution.

[0117] FIG. 2 illustrates a system 200 including key geometric parameters of a phased microphone array 112 and a source scanning plane 202, in accordance with an embodiment. Note that the source scanning plane 202 depicted in FIG. 2 is generally analogous to the source scanning plane 102 depicted in FIG. 1. In general, FIG. 2 provides identified important parameters in defining the solution requirements for DAMAS for a scanning plane 102. The array has a spatial extent defined by the "diameter" D. It is at a nominal distance R from a scanning plane containing N grid points, which represent beamforming focal points, as well as the n locations of all the acoustic sources X_n that influence the beamformed results Y_n. Note that in FIG. 2, circles 203 generally represent dB level contours over the grid(s) of the source scanning plane 202.

[0118] For a particular frequency, the array's beamformed output is shown projected on the plane as contour lines of constant output Y, in terms of dB. The scanning plane has a height of H and a width of W. The grid points are spaced Δx and Δy apart. Although not illustrated in FIG. 2, there are defined noise source sub-regions of size l within the scanning plane (subsets of X_n), where details are desired. This relates to source resolution requirements and is considered below. For the scanning plane, the total number of grid points,

$$N=[(W/\Delta x)+1][(H/\Delta y)+1] \tag{25}$$

[0119] The array beamwidth B is defined as the "diameter" of the 3 dB-down output of the array compared to that at the beamformed maximum response. For standard beamforming of equation (6),

$$B \approx const \times (R/fD) \tag{26}$$

For the SADA (Small Aperture Directional Array with a outer diameter of D=0.65 feet) in a traditional QFF configuration[1] with R=5 feet, the beamwidth is B≈(10^4/f) in feet for frequency f in Hertz. When using shading of equation (7), B is kept at about 1 ft. for 10 kHz ≦ f ≦ 40 kHz.

[0120] In the applications of this report, some engineering choices are made with regard to what should represent

meaningful solution requirements for DAMAS source definition calculations. Because the rank of matrix Â of equation (18) equals one when using the iterative solution equation (24), there is no definitive limitation on the spacing or number of grid points or iterations to be used. The parameter ratios Δx/B (and Δy/B) and W/B (and H/B) appear to be most important for establishing resolution and spatial extent requirements of the scanning plane.

[0121] The resolution Δx/B must be small or fine enough such that individual grid points along with other grid points represent a reasonable physical distribution of sources. However, too fine of a distribution would require substantial solution iterative times and then only give more detail than is realistically feasible, or believable, from a beampattern which is too broad. On the other hand, too coarse of a distribution would render solutions of X̂ which would reveal less detail than needed, and also which may be aliased (in analogy with FFT signal processing), with resulting false images.

[0122] The spatial extent ratio W/B (and H/B) must be large enough to allow discrimination of mutual influence between the grid points. Because the total variation of level over the distance B is only 3 dB, it appears reasonable to require that 1<W/B (and H/B). One could extend W/B (and H/B) substantially beyond one—such as to five or more. In the following simulations, resolution issues are examined for both a simple and a complicated noise source distribution. Two distributions types are considered because, as seen below with respect to l/B, source complexity affects source definition convergence. The simulations also serve as an introduction to the basic use of DAMAS.

[0123] Regarding execution efficiency of the DAMAS technique, it is noted that the per-iteration execution time of the methodology depends solely on the total number of grid points employed in the analysis and not on frequency-dependent parameters. In general, the iteration time can be expressed by time=C(2N)^{2}i, where C is a hardware-dependent constant. A representative execution time is 0.38 seconds/iteration running a 2601-point grid on a 2.8-GHz, Linux-based Pentium 4 machine using Intel Fortran to compile the code. For this study, a Beowulf cluster consisting of nine 2.8 GHz Pentium 4 machines was used to generate the figures shown subsequently. Note that in FIG. 2, the value B generally represents the diameter of three circles.

[0124] FIG. 3 illustrates a graphical representation 300 of array output based on standard processing methodologies, wherein frequency is approximately equal to 10 kHz and Δx/B is generally equivalent to 0.083 in accordance with one embodiment. FIG. 4 illustrates a graphical representation 400 of array output based on standard processing methodologies, wherein frequency is equal to 20 kHz and Δx/B is generally equivalent to 0.167 in accordance with one embodiment. Likewise, FIG. 5 illustrates a graphical representation 500 of array output based on standard processing methodologies, wherein frequency is approximately equal to 30 kHz and Δx/B is generally equivalent to 0.25 in accordance with one embodiment;

[0125] In a traditional contour type presentation, the top left frame of the graphical representation of FIG. 3 illustrates an array output based on standard processing methodology of equation (6), being plotted in terms of constant dB contours over a scanning plane. In this simulation, the SADA is placed 5 feet from the plane that is positioned through a typical model location. In terms of the aforementioned parameters, H=W=50" and $\Delta x=\Delta y=1$". The resultant number of grid points is 2601 (underlying grid points are not shown in top left frame). With a chosen frequency of 10 kHz and the beamforming of equation (6), B≈12", so H/B=W/B=4.17 and Δx/B=0.083.

[0126] A single synthetic point source is placed at a grid point in the center of the plane, at n=1301. This is done by defining X_{1301} to give 100 dB=$10LogX_{1301}$ and all other $\hat{X}$ values to zero in equation (18), and then solving for $\hat{Y}$. The values of dB=$10LogY_n$ are then contour plotted. This, as with real array test data, is the starting point for the use of DAMAS. Equation (18) is solved for $\hat{X}$ using equation (17) for $A_{nn'}$, by way of equation (24), using $X_n=Y_n$ at the start of the iteration. The bottom left frame of the graphical representation 300 depicted in FIG. 3 illustrates the values of X_n after one iteration (i=1). Rather than showing contours, the presentation is one of X_n values in terms of dB at the grid points. Each grid point is actually located at the bottom left corner of the "blocks", each of dimension $\Delta x=\Delta y=1$".

[0127] In the top right and bottom right frames of graphical representation 300 the results after the one thousandth (i=1000) and the five thousandth (i=5000) iteration, respectively, are shown. At the highest iteration value, the original input value of 100 dB has been recovered within 0.1 dB and that the surrounding grid values over the plane are down in level by about 40 dB, except for the adjoining grid points at about 15-20 dB down. At the lesser iteration numbers, although there is some spreading of the source region, the integrated (obtained by simple summing of values over the spread region) levels are very close to 100 dB. One obtains 99.06 dB for 100 iteration (not shown in FIG. 3) and 100.03 dB for 1000 iterations.

[0128] The solution dependence on reducing the beamwidth B by a factor of two (Δx/B=0.167) is demonstrated in FIG. 4 where the frequency used is 20 kHz using the same standard processing over the same grid. The contour pattern is similar, but contracted, as shown in the left frame. The DAMAS result for 1000 iterations is given in the right frame. Comparing this to the results of FIG. 3, it is seen that here a more exact solution is attained with substantially less iterations. One obtains at peak of 99.97 dB, with all adjoining grid points lower by 27 dB.

[0129] FIG. 6 illustrates a graphical representation 600 of an array output based on standard processing methodologies, wherein frequency is approximately equal to 10 kHz and Δx/B is generally equivalent to 0.083 in accordance with an alternative embodiment. Likewise, FIG. 7 illustrates a graphical representation 700 of array output based on standard processing methodologies, wherein frequency is approximately equal to 20 kHz and Δx/B is generally equivalent to 0.167 in accordance with an alternative embodiment. Additionally, FIG. 8 illustrates a graphical representation 800 of array output based on standard processing methodologies, wherein frequency is approximately equal to 30 kHz and Δx/B is generally equivalent to 0.25 in accordance with an alternative embodiment. FIG. 9 illustrates a graphical representation 900 of spatial aliasing with point source and image shifted between grid points in

accordance with an alternative embodiment. FIG. 9 demonstrates the implementation of a DAMAS methodology with 1000 iterations.

[0130] The results of a more demanding simulation are depicted in FIGS. 6-8, where particular n locations were defined with same X_n values (for 100 dB) and others zero. This gives a test of the solution procedure for a group of line source distributions. The important scanning plane parameters, including the number of solution iterations, given for FIGS. 6-8 are generally the same as above for FIGS. 2-5. In FIG. 6, for example, for Δx/B=0.083, the beamforming contour plot has an elongated appearance as one would expect to obtain for a line source. After using 5000 iterations, however, one begins to see structure other than a line source. Still, the image has not converged (i.e., although not shown, it starts to converges at higher iterations). In FIG. 7, for Δx/B=0.167, an image of very prominent character emerges at 1000 iterations (i.e., although not shown, even at only 100 iterations the image is recognizable). In FIG. 8, for Δx/B=0.25, all images are apparent. With regard to integrated power, it is found that when integrating (e.g., by summing grid point values), that the total noise from the image converges to the correct value rapidly with iterations.

[0131] Such simulations demonstrate that DAMAS successfully extracts detail noise source information from phased array beamformed outputs. It is seen that finer Δx/B resolutions require more iterations to get the same "accuracy." This becomes even more valid as the noise source region becomes more complicated. However, the number of iterations required should not be the major driving issue as the DAMAS methodology is proven to be efficient and robust. Also, it is found that all solutions, examined to date, improve with increasing iterations (i.e., using double precision computations). Caution is noted for potential error if Δx/B is made too large (e.g., Δx/B above 0.2 may be borderline) in real data cases where significant sources may be in-between chosen grid points. As previously mentioned for any such error, analogy can be made with the common data analysis subject of aliasing errors with respect to FFT sampling rates. No problems of this nature are possible in these simulations because the sources are collocated at the grid points.

[0132] Experimental applications have been implemented to demonstrate the DAMAS methodology described herein. For example, experimental data from several airframe component noise studies can be re-examined with DAMAS. In such applications, DAMAS is not used with necessarily optimum resolution and scanning plane size. However, all cases fall at or near an acceptable range of $0.05 \leq \Delta x$/B (i.e., and Δy/B)≤ 0.2. For consistency with the simulations, (except for the calibrator case) the same scanning plane and resolution sizes are used with the same resultant number of grid points. The number of iterations used for all is 1000. In contrast with the simulations, the experimental results are presented in terms of one-third octave values, for the array using several different array beamforming methodologies, in order to compare to the results of the previous studies.

[0133] FIGS. 10 and 11 respectively illustrate configurations 1000 and 1100 of a test set up for flap edge noise test and calibration. In configuration 1000 of FIG. 10, for example, the noise path from the flap edge to a SADA device 1014 is illustrated as represented by ray path 1006. A mean shear layer **1004** is depicted in **FIG. 10** in association with a shear layer **1002**. Arrow **1010** depicted in **FIG. 10** represents airflow from a nozzle **1012**. A flap model **1008** is also depicted in **FIG. 10**. The nozzle **1012** is located adjacent to and/or integrated with a side plate **1001**.

[0134] In configuration **1000** of **FIG. 11**, on the other hand, the open end of a calibrator source is depicted positioned next to the edge of flap **1008**. Note that in **FIGS. 10-11**, identical or similar parts or elements are generally indicated by identical reference numerals. Thus, **FIGS. 10-11** should be interpreted together. A sketch of the flap edge noise experimental setup is therefore depicted in configuration **1000** of **FIG. 10**, wherein an airfoil main element is located at a 16° angle-of-attack to the vertical plane. The SADA device **1014** is shown positioned out of or away from the flow represented by arrow **1010** in **FIG. 10**. For configuration **1000** depicted in **FIG. 10**, the calibration test can be performed using a noise source, comprised of an open end of a one-inch diameter tube, placed next to the flap edge, as depicted in configuration **1100** of **FIG. 11**. Note that in the configuration illustrated in **FIG. 11**, a calibration source **1102** is shown proximate to the flap **1008**.

[0135] **FIG. 12** illustrates a graphical representation **1200** of calibrator source test data wherein M=0 with an integrated level of 62.8 dB and a DAMAS of 62.9 dB, in accordance with an alternative embodiment. Similarly, **FIG. 13** illustrates a graphical representation **1300** of calibrator source test data wherein M=0.17, with an integrated level of 58.1 dB and a DAMAS of 57.3 dB, in accordance with an alternative embodiment. **FIG. 14** illustrates a graphical representation **1400** of a calibrator source test, wherein M=0 with an integrated level of 62.2 dB and a DAMAS of 61.6 dB, in accordance with an alternative embodiment. **FIG. 15** illustrates a graphical representation **1500** of a calibrator source test, wherein M=0.17 with an integrated level of 57.9 dB and a DAMAS of 56.9, in accordance with an alternative embodiment;

[0136] **FIGS. 12 and 13** respectively illustrate DAMAS results from an experimental implementation thereof. For the calibrator source operating with no tunnel flow M=0, **FIG. 12** shows SADA response contours for standard (STD) processing with shading, equation (7), over a scanning plane positioned through the airfoil chord-line. This is a one-third octave presentation for $10 \log Y$ for $f_{1/3}$=40 kHz. The result was obtained by performing and summing **546** single-frequency beamforming maps (each with frequency resolution bandwidth of Δf=17.44 Hz). Note that with this array-shading, only the inner SADA diameter of 1.95 inches is active. For this no-flow case, the convective and shear layer refraction terms are absent in the steering vector definition, equations (4) and (5).

[0137] The right frame of **FIG. 12** illustrates the result for the rendered source X distribution when DAMAS is applied, solving equation (18), and using equation (19), by way of equation (24). The scanning plane used is H=W=12". Consistent with the contour presentation, the DAMAS result is a one third octave presentation obtained by separately solving for the 546 separate bands and then summing. With B=12" and a chosen $\Delta x = \Delta y = 0.55$", one has a resolution of $\Delta x/B$=0.046 (which is close to the recommended lower limit of 0.05). The number of grid points is 441 and the number of iterations used is 1000 for each frequency.

[0138] Note that a characteristic of the DAMAS solution is the non-negligible amplitudes distributed at grid points around the border of the scanning planes in **FIG. 13**. This is a scanning plane "edge" effect that is found to occur only for experimental data, where noise in the scanning plane is influenced to some degree by sources outside (or extraneous to) the plane. DAMAS constructs noise distribution solutions on the scanning plane grid points totally based on whatever is measured by beamforming on those grid points. The edge effect was examined by expanding the scanning plane to eliminate any edge problem in the region of interest. A result almost identical to **FIG. 12** was found over regions other than at the edge. Thus the edge effect has negligible impact on these results. This subject is dealt with subsequently for other applications.

[0139] A small rectangular integration region, illustrated by dashed lines in **FIG. 12**, can be used to calculate an integrated value of 62.8 dB. Correspondingly, for the present DAMAS result, one simply adds the pressure-squared values of the grid points within the source region. One obtains a value of 62.9 dB. **FIG. 13** illustrates the SADA response contour for the tunnel flow at M=0.17. Here, the convective and shear layer refraction terms are important in the steering vector definition. The integrated value from Ref. 1 is 58.1 dB, whereas the DAMAS value is 57.3 dB. It is seen by comparing the somewhat smeared image of **FIGS. 12-13** that the affect of the tunnel flow and the resultant turbulent shear layer is to spread the apparent noise region. The DAMAS result in **FIG. 13** is of particular interest because, to the knowledge of the authors, it may be the first direct measure of spatial dispersion of noise due to turbulence scatter.

[0140] For the same test cases as **FIGS. 12-13**. **7**, **FIGS. 14-15** illustrate results when diagonal removal (DR), equation (9), is employed in the beamforming. Correspondingly, DAMAS is applied using equation (21) for $A_{nn'}$. It is seen that although the DR processing modifies the Y distributions, the X source distributions and values are calculated to be almost identical to those of **FIGS. 12-13**. DR processing has the advantage of removing the auto-spectra (and possible microphone noise contamination) from the processing, while still maintaining full rank for the solution equations.

[0141] Although it is beyond the scope of this paper to evaluate the use of DAMAS for different array designs than the SADA, a limited application using Large Aperture Directional Array (LADA) data produced good comparisons for a case corresponding to a frame of **FIG. 12**. The LADA has an outer diameter of D=2.83 feet, which is 4.35 times the size of SADA (i.e., 17.4 times the active diameter of the SADA at 40 kHz for shaded processing). For a similar calibration test to that of **FIG. 12** but for array processing without shading, the integrated LADA value is 60.3 dB, and the corresponding DAMAS summed value is 61.4 dB.

[0142] A test configuration can be implemented where an airfoil, with a 16" chord and 36" span, is positioned at a −1.2° angle-of-attack to the vertical flow is depicted in **FIG. 16**. Note that in **FIGS. 10-11** and **16**, identical or similar parts or elements are generally indicated by identical reference numerals. As indicated in **FIG. 16**, a mean shear layer **1602** and **1604** are illustrated with respect to side-plate **1001** and flap **1008**. Flow is generally indicated by arrow **1010**, while a ray path **1606** to the SADA device **1014** is also depicted.

[0143] The flap **1008** can be removed and a cove thereof filled in such a manner as to produce a span-wise uniform sharp Trailing Edge (TE) of 0.005". A grit of size #90 is generally distributed over the first 5% of the Leading Edge (LE) to ensure fully turbulent flow at the TE. The SADA position is at φ=90°. **FIG. 16** generally illustrates the array output over a scanning plane placed through the chord-line. The scanning plane of size H=W=50" extends "beyond" the side-plates that hold the 36" span airfoil. The side-plate **1001** regions as seen from the viewpoint of the array, to the left of the –18" span-wise location and to the right of the 18" location as depicted in **FIG. 17**, represent reflected source regions. In general, FIGS. **17-18**(*b*) illustrate SADA response contours **1700, 1702, 1704, 1705** and **1800, 1802, 1804** and **1806** for shaded STD processing for TE and LE noise testing, in accordance with an alternative embodiment.

[0144] The array output illustrated in **FIG. 17** is presented for four one-third octave frequencies for STD processing with shading, equation (7). As before, individual frequency results are processed and are then summed to obtain the results shown. It is seen that for the $f_{1/3}$=3.15 kHz case, that the most intense region is just aft of the airfoil TE. As frequency is increased, the intense regions appear to first concentrate near the TE, and then to shift towards the LE.

[0145] **FIG. 19** presents DAMAS results corresponding to **FIGS. 17-18**. Such results are shown as graphs **1900, 1902, 1904** and **1906**. For $f_{1/3}$=3.15 kHz, Δx=Δy=1.8" is used to obtain the chosen lower-limit resolution of Δx/B=0.047. For 8, 12.5, and 20 kHz, the chosen Δx=Δy=1" give Δx/B=0.066, 0.083, and 0.083, respectively, for shaded beamforming. The results shown appear to very successfully reveal noise source distributions, even those not apparent from **FIGS. 17-18**. The TE and LE line sources are particularly well defined. The images at and beyond ±18 inches are model-side-plate noises and/or side plate reflections. There are apparent phantom images, particularly aft of the TE and around the edges of the scanning plane. These are addressed below.

[0146] **FIG. 20** generally corresponds to **FIGS. 17 and 18**, except that DR processing is used for beamforming, equation (9), and for DAMAS, equation (21). **FIG. 20**(*a*) and **FIG. 20**(*b*) illustrates SADA response contours **2000, 2002, 2004, 2006** for shaded DR processing with respect to TE and LE noise tests, in accordance with an alternative embodiment. The contours **2000, 2002, 2004, 2006** depicted in FIGS. **20**(*a*)-**20**(*b*) demonstrate that although the beam-forming contours differ significantly, the source distributions essentially match. The exception is that the DR results appear to produce cleaner DAMAS results, with much of the phantom images removed. That is, the apparent source distributions over regions away from surfaces where no "real" sources are likely to exist are significantly diminished. Also removed with DR is an "apparent" LE noise source distribution from the result of 3.15 kHz. Considering that the present STD method results are to some degree contaminated with turbulence buffeting microphone self noise, the DR results are considered more correct.

[0147] Note that also present in FIGS. **18**(*a*)-**18**(*b*) are edge effects as are found in and discussed for **FIGS. 12-13** and **14-15**. The edge effects can be readily eliminated by expanding the scanning frame beyond the regions of strong sources, thereby reducing the edge amplitudes and thus any potential influence on the regions of interest. This has been verified but this is not shown here, as the edge effect's presence in **FIG. 18**(*a*) and **FIG. 18**(*b*) is instructive. For example, an area where the edge effect appears to negatively affect DAMAS results is the side-plate region on the left side near the LE (chord-wise location **26** in. and span-wise location –21 in.).

[0148] The strong array responses (i.e., FIGS. **17, 18**(*a*), **18**(*b*) and **20**) at that location are not correspondingly represented by the DAMAS source distributions in that region. Instead, DAMAS puts strong sources along the scanning plane edge and the LE corner to explain the array response. (Note that it is well recognized that the array response over such a corner location may well be influenced by reflected (and thus correlated) noise sources, whereas the DAMAS modeling is based on an equivalent statistically independent source distribution. The edge effect is unrelated to this modeling/reality physical difference. Such reflections undoubtedly cause strengthening or weakening and/or shifting of apparent sources, but it would not cause source concentration along the edges.) Still, even with the scanning plane edge effect, away from the edges the TE and LE noise source regions are unaffected and the following noise spectra serve to verify this.

[0149] TE noise spectra were determined from amplitudes of the array response at the center of the TE, along with a transfer function based on an assumed line source distribution. Also, corresponding spectra from the LE noise region were determined to show grit-related LE noise, which due to beam-width characteristics were contaminated by TE noise at low frequencies. **FIG. 21** illustrates a graphical representation **2100** of a comparison of one-third octave spectra from TE and LE noise measurements and reprocessing by DAMAS.

[0150] Regarding graph **2100**, it is important to note that one-third octave spectra (per foot) curves for the test conditions depicted therein generally correspond to the data illustrated in **FIGS. 17, 18, 19,** and **12**. These spectra are compared to spectra of TE noise and LE noise determined from DAMAS using both STD and DR methods. These results are determined by simply summing the pressure-squared values of each grid point within the rectangular box region surrounding the TE and LE regions shown superimposed in **FIG. 19**. The region's span-wise length is 2.5 feet. The sums are divided by 2.5 to put the spectral results on a per-foot basis.

[0151] The spectral comparisons are quite good and serve as a strong validation for the different analyses. Where low-frequency results of DAMAS are not plotted, the integration regions lacked contributions (not surprising with the very large beam-widths B). The spectra are seen to agree well with results over parts of the spectra where each source is dominant. Of course in such spectra shown from Ref. 4, as in the beamformed solutions of **FIGS. 17, 18** and **20**, the TE and LE noise region amplitudes are contaminated by the mutual influence of the other source over different parts of the spectra. The present DAMAS results exclude such interference.

[0152] The slat configuration tested in the QFF can be achieved by removing the flap, filling the flap cove (as for the TE noise test above), removing the grit boundary layer trip at the LE, tilting the airfoil main element to 26° from vertical, mounting the slat, and setting the slat angle and gap. The large 26° angle is required to obtain proper aerodynamics about the slat and LE region. **FIG. 22** illustrates a system **2200** in which an airfoil/slat is present in a deflected open jet, with the SADA positioned at φ=107°, in accordance with an alternative embodiment. Note that in **FIGS. 10 and 22**, identical or similar parts or components are generally indicated by identical reference numerals. System **2200** generally includes a scanning plane **2206** and a mean shear layer **2202**. A ray path **2204** is also indicated in **FIG. 22** as extending generally from the SADA device **1014** to the flap **1008**. Airflow is indicated by arrow **1010**, white a non flow region **2204** is also depicted generally in **FIG. 22**.

[0153] **FIG. 23** illustrates a graphical representation or graph **2300** depicting an array output and a corresponding DAMAS result for $f_{1/3}$=20 kHz using shaded DR processing over the scanning plane through an airfoil. The distributed slat noise is seen to be well identified. There are higher levels toward the left side of the slat, likely due to a model mount irregularity. The aforementioned scanning plane edge effect is seen around the edge of the DAMAS presentation, and it likely has a mild impact on the source definition details at this left side. Away from the edge, the slat noise is generally uniform. The amplitude of the slat noise is determined by summing across the span within the integration box shown. For this one-third octave band, the DAMAS level of 57.9 dB (per foot) compares with 59.1 dB, which has been used as an approximate procedure involving the array output at the slat center and a derived transfer function.

[0154] The flap edge noise test configuration is illustrated in **FIG. 12** for the SADA. The flat edge flap test condition of 29° flap angle and M=0.11 is reexamined for a one-third octave frequency band of $f_{1/3}$=20 kHz. **FIG. 24** illustrates a graphical representation **2400** of beamforming contours and DAMAS results for shaded DR processing over the scanning plane placed through the airfoil chord-line. The DAMAS results appear to successfully isolate the flap edge noise from substantial flap cove noise. By using a similar rectangular integration region, shown in **FIGS. 12-13** and **14-15**, one finds a level of 44.6 dB for the flap edge noise. This compares to 47.5 dB for a spectrum level determined for this flap edge noise case. In that spectrum, this frequency corresponds to a localized spectral hump. These present results show that the cove noise contributed to the higher level measured. DAMAS is seen to allow one to readily separate and quantify these cover and flap edge contributions, where previously this was not possible.

[0155] The DAMAS technique described herein represents a radical step in array processing capabilities. It can replace traditional presentations of array results and make the array a much more powerful measurement tool than is presently the case. The DAMAS equation $\hat{A}\hat{X}=\hat{Y}$ is a unique equation that relates a classical beamformed array result $\hat{Y}$ with the source distribution $\hat{X}$. The sources are taken as distributions of statistically independent noise radiators, as does traditional array processing/integration analysis. DAMAS does not add any additional assumption to the analysis. It merely extracts the array characteristics from the source definition presentation. The iterative solution for $\hat{X}$ is found to be robust and accurate. Numerical application examples show that the actual rate and accuracy at which solutions converge depend on chosen spatial resolution and evaluation region sizes compared to the array beam width.

Experimental archival data from a variety of prior studies are used to validate DAMAS quantitatively. The same algorithm is found to be equally adept with flap edge/cove, trailing edge, leading edge, slat, and calibration noise sources

[0156] The foregoing methodology thus is generally directed toward overcoming the current processing of acoustic array data, which is burdened with considerable uncertainty. Such a methodology can serve to demystify array results, reduce misinterpretation, and accurately quantify position and strength of acoustic sources. As indicated earlier, traditional array results represent noise sources that are convolved with array beam form response functions, which depend on array geometry, size (with respect to source position and distributions), and frequency. The Deconvolution Approach for the Mapping of Acoustic Sources (DAMAS) methodology described above therefore removes beamforming characteristics from output presentations. A unique linear system of equations accounts for reciprocal influence at different locations over the array survey region. It makes no assumption beyond the traditional processing assumption of statistically independent noise sources. The full rank equations are solved with a new robust iterative method.

[0157] DAMAS can be quantitatively validated using archival data from a variety of prior high-lift airframe component noise studies, including flap edge/cove, trailing edge, and leading edge, slat, and calibration sources. Presentations are explicit and straightforward, as the noise radiated from a region of interest is determined by simply summing the mean-squared values over that region. It is believed DAMAS can fully replace existing array processing and presentations methodology in most applications. Such a methodology appears to dramatically increase the value of arrays to the field of experimental acoustics.

[0158] It is important to note that the methodology described above with respect to **FIGS. 1-23** and equations (1) to (26), which is referred to generally by the DAMAS acronym, can be implemented in the context of a module(s). In the computer programming arts, a module (e.g., a software module) can be implemented as a collection of routines and data structures that perform particular tasks or implement a particular abstract data type. Modules generally can be composed of two parts. First, a software module may list the constants, data types, variable, routines and the like that that can be accessed by other modules or routines. Second, a software module can be configured as an implementation, which can be private (i.e., accessible perhaps only to the module), and that contains the source code that actually implements the routines or subroutines upon which the module is based.

[0159] Thus, for example, the term "module," as utilized herein generally refers to software modules or implementations thereof. The world module can also refer to instruction media residing in a computer memory, wherein such instruction media are retrievable from the computer memory and processed, for example, via a microprocessor. Such modules can be utilized separately or together to form a program product that can be implemented through signal-bearing media, including transmission media and recordable media.

[0160] It will be appreciated that variations of the above-disclosed and other features and functions, or alternatives thereof, may be desirably combined into many other different systems or applications. Also that various presently unforeseen or unanticipated alternatives, modifications, variations or improvements therein may be subsequently made by those skilled in the art which are also intended to be encompassed by the following claims.

What is claimed is:

1. A method for mapping acoustic sources determined from a phased microphone array, comprising a plurality of microphones arranged in an optimized grid pattern including a plurality of grid locations thereof, comprising:

forming a linear configuration of N equations and N unknowns by accounting for a reciprocal influence of a beamforming characteristic thereof at varying grid locations among said plurality of grid locations;

iteratively determining a full-rank equation from said linear configuration of N equations and N unknowns based on a DAMAS inverse formulation; and

generating an optimized noise source distribution over an identified aeroacoustic source region associated with said phased microphone array in order to compile an output presentation thereof, in response to iteratively determining said full-rank equation among said linear configuration of N equations and N unknowns, thereby removing said beamforming characteristic from said output presentation.

2. The method of claim 1 wherein said linear configuration further comprises a system of linear equations comprising $\hat{A}\hat{X}=\hat{Y}$, wherein said system of linear equations relates a spatial field of point locations with beamformed array-output responses thereof to equivalent source distributions at a same location.

3. The method of claim 2 wherein a variable $\hat{A}$ among said system of linear equations is utilized to disassociate an array thereof from acoustic sources of interest.

4. The method of claim 2 further comprising solving for a variable $\hat{X}$ among said system of linear equations comprising $\hat{A}\hat{X}=\hat{Y}$.

5. The method of claim 1 wherein iteratively determining said full-rank equation among said linear configuration of N equations and N unknowns, further comprises attaining said full rank equation utilizing a solution requirement of a positivity constraint that is equivalent to a physical assumption of statically independent noise sources associated with at least one N location thereof.

6. The method of claim 2 wherein said full-rank equation represents a rank thereof based on a number of linearly independent equations compared to a number of equations associated with said system of linear equations $\hat{A}\hat{X}=\hat{Y}$, wherein N represents a number of grid points thereof.

7. A system for mapping acoustic sources determined from a phased microphone array, comprising a plurality of microphones arranged in an optimized grid pattern including a plurality of grid locations thereof, comprising:

a linear configuration of N equations and N unknowns formed by accounting for a reciprocal influence of said beamforming characteristic thereof at varying grid locations among said plurality of grid locations;

a full-rank equation iteratively determined from said linear configuration of N equations and N unknowns based on a DAMAS inverse formulation; and

an optimized noise source distribution generated over an identified aeroacoustic source region associated with said phased microphone array in order to compile an output presentation thereof, in response to iteratively determining said full-rank equation among said linear configuration of N equations and N unknowns, thereby removing said beamforming characteristic from said output presentation.

8. The system of claim 7 wherein said linear configuration further comprises a system of linear equations comprising $\hat{A}\hat{X}=\hat{Y}$, wherein said system of linear equations relates a spatial field of point locations with beamformed array-output responses thereof to equivalent source distributions at a same location.

9. The system of claim 8 wherein a variable $\hat{A}$ among said system of linear equations is utilized to disassociate an array thereof from acoustic sources of interest.

10. The system of claim 8 further comprising solving for a variable $\hat{X}$ among said system of linear equations comprising $\hat{A}\hat{X}=\hat{Y}$.

11. The system of claim 7 wherein iteratively determining said full-rank equation among said linear configuration of N equations and N unknowns, further comprises attaining said full rank equation utilizing a solution requirement of a positivity constraint that is equivalent to a physical assumption of statically independent noise sources associated with at least one N location thereof.

12. The system of claim 7 wherein said full-rank equation represents a rank thereof based on a number of linearly independent equations compared to a number of equations associated with said system of linear equations $\hat{A}\hat{X}=\hat{Y}$, wherein N represents a number of grid points thereof.

13. A program product for mapping acoustic sources determined from a phased microphone array, comprising a plurality of microphones arranged in an optimized grid pattern including a plurality of grid locations thereof, said program product comprising:

Instruction media residing in a computer memory for forming a linear configuration of N equations and N unknowns by accounting for a reciprocal influence of a beamforming characteristic thereof at varying grid locations among said plurality of grid locations;

Instruction media residing in a computer for iteratively determining a full-rank equation from said linear configuration of N equations and N unknowns based on a DAMAS inverse formulation; and

Instruction media residing in a computer for generating an optimized noise source distribution over an identified aeroacoustic source region associated with said phased microphone array in order to compile an output presentation thereof, in response to iteratively determining said full-rank equation among said linear configuration of N equations and N unknowns, thereby removing said beamforming characteristic from said output presentation.

14. The program product of claim 13 wherein said linear configuration further comprises a system of linear equations comprising $\hat{A}\hat{X}=\hat{Y}$, wherein said system of linear equations relates a spatial field of point locations with beamformed array-output responses thereof to equivalent source distributions at a same location.

15. The program product of claim 14 wherein a variable A among said system of linear equations is utilized to disassociate an array thereof from acoustic sources of interest.

16. The program product of claim 14 further comprising solving for a variable $\hat{X}$ among said system of linear equations comprising $\hat{A}\hat{X}=\hat{Y}$.

17. The program product of claim 13 wherein iteratively determining said full-rank equation among said linear configuration of N equations and N unknowns, further comprises attaining said full rank equation utilizing a solution requirement of a positivity constraint that is equivalent to a physical assumption of statically independent noise sources associated with at least one N location thereof.

18. The program product of claim 13 wherein said full-rank equation represents a rank thereof based on a number of linearly independent equations compared to a number of equations associated with said system of linear equations $\hat{A}\hat{X}=\hat{Y}$, wherein N represents a number of grid points thereof.

19. The program product of claim 13 wherein each of said instruction media residing in a computer comprises signal-bearing media.

20. The program product of claim 19 wherein said signal-bearing media comprise at least one of the following types of media: transmission media or recordable media.

* * * * *

US008725470B1

(12) **United States Patent**
Brown et al.

(10) Patent No.: **US 8,725,470 B1**
(45) **Date of Patent:** **May 13, 2014**

(54) **CO-OPTIMIZATION OF BLUNT BODY SHAPES FOR MOVING VEHICLES**

(75) Inventors: **James L. Brown**, Cupertino, CA (US); **Joseph A Garcia**, Belmont, CA (US); **David J. Kinney**, Manteca, CA (US); **Jeffrey V Bowles**, Mountain View, CA (US); **Nagi N Mansour**, Hillsborough, CA (US)

(73) Assignee: **The United States of America as Represented by the Administrator of the National Aeronautics & Space Administration (NASA)**, Washington, DC (US)

(*) Notice: Subject to any disclaimer, the term of this patent is extended or adjusted under 35 U.S.C. 154(b) by 442 days.

(21) Appl. No.: **13/109,954**

(22) Filed: **May 17, 2011**

Related U.S. Application Data

(60) Provisional application No. 61/397,146, filed on May 17, 2010.

(51) **Int. Cl.**
G06F 7/60 (2006.01)
G06F 17/10 (2006.01)

(52) **U.S. Cl.**
USPC **703/2**

(58) **Field of Classification Search**
None
See application file for complete search history.

(56) **References Cited**

U.S. PATENT DOCUMENTS

7,431,242 B1   10/2008   Brown et al.

OTHER PUBLICATIONS

Barr, Superquadrics and Angle-Preserving Transformations, IEEE Computer Graphics and Applications, Jan. 1981, 11-23, 1 (1).
Barr, Rigid Physically Based Superquadrics, Graphics Gems III—Ch. 111.8, edited by D. Kirk, 1992, 137-159.
Brown, The Effect of Forebody Geometry on Turbulent Heating and Thermal Protection System Sizing for Future Mars Missions Concepts, Proceedings of the International Planetary Probe Workshop, Jun. 4, 2006.
Brown, et al., An Asymmetric Capsule Vehicle Geometry Study for CEV, 45th AIAA Aerospace Sciences Meeting and Exhibit, Jan. 8-11, 2007, Reno, Nevada, American Institute of Aeronautics and Astronautics.
Garcia, et al., Parametric Co-Optimization of Lifting Blunt Body Vehicle Concepts for Atmospheric Entry, 21st International Conference on Parallel Computational Fluid Dynamics, May 18-22, 2009, Moffett Field, California.
Wright, et al., Mars Aerocapture Systems Study, NASA TM-2006-214522, Nov. 2006.

Primary Examiner — Saif Alhija
(74) *Attorney, Agent, or Firm* — John F. Schipper; Christopher J. Menke; Robert M. Padilla

(57) **ABSTRACT**

A method and associated system for multi-disciplinary optimization of various parameters associated with a space vehicle that experiences aerocapture and atmospheric entry in a specified atmosphere. In one embodiment, simultaneous maximization of a ratio of landed payload to vehicle atmospheric entry mass, maximization of fluid flow distance before flow separation from vehicle, and minimization of heat transfer to the vehicle are performed with respect to vehicle surface geometric parameters, and aerostructure and aerothermal vehicle response for the vehicle moving along a specified trajectory. A Pareto Optimal set of superior performance parameters is identified.

30 Claims, 21 Drawing Sheets

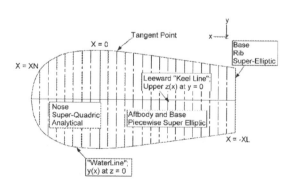

498

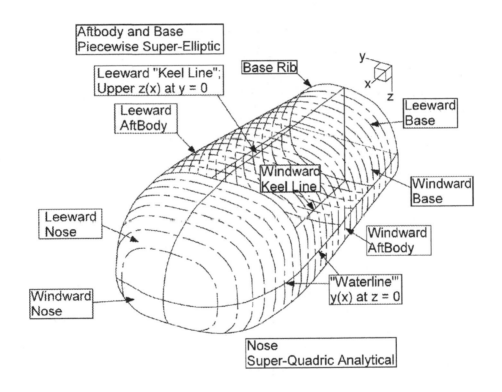

FIG. 1A

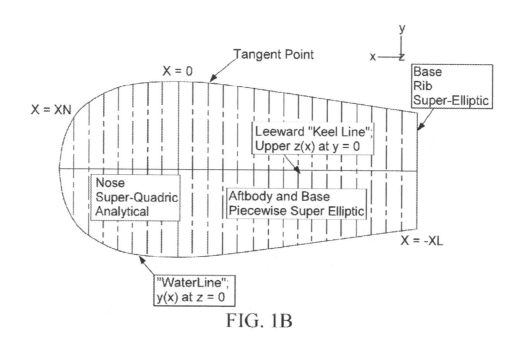

FIG. 1B

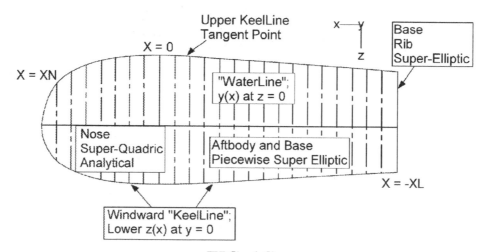

FIG. 1C

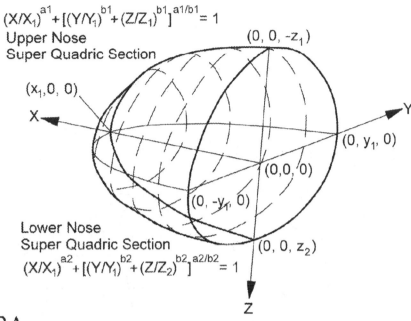

$$(X/X_1)^{a1} + [(Y/Y_1)^{b1} + (Z/Z_1)^{b1}]^{a1/b1} = 1$$

Upper Nose
Super Quadric Section

$(0, 0, -z_1)$

$(x_1, 0, 0)$

$(0, y_1, 0)$

$(0, 0, 0)$

$(0, -y_1, 0)$

Lower Nose
Super Quadric Section

$(0, 0, z_2)$

$$(X/X_1)^{a2} + [(Y/Y_1)^{b2} + (Z/Z_2)^{b2}]^{a2/b2} = 1$$

FIG. 2A

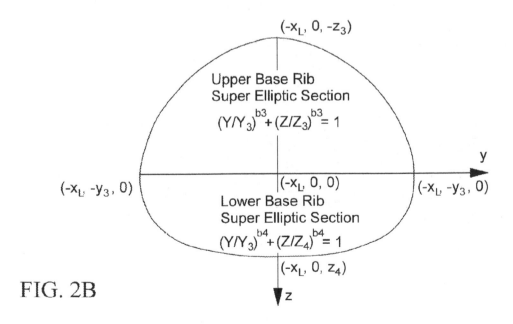

$(-x_L, 0, -z_3)$

Upper Base Rib
Super Elliptic Section

$$(Y/Y_3)^{b3} + (Z/Z_3)^{b3} = 1$$

$(-x_L, -y_3, 0)$ $(-x_L, 0, 0)$ $(-x_L, -y_3, 0)$

Lower Base Rib
Super Elliptic Section

$$(Y/Y_3)^{b4} + (Z/Z_4)^{b4} = 1$$

$(-x_L, 0, z_4)$

FIG. 2B

501

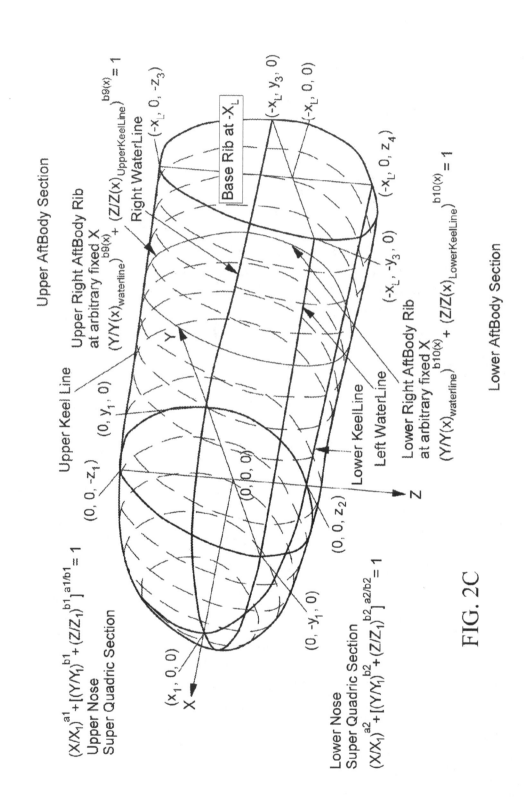

FIG. 2C

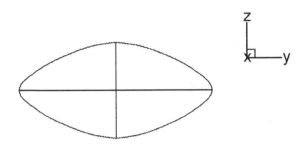

FIG. 3A

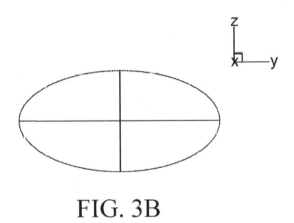

FIG. 3B

FIG. 3C

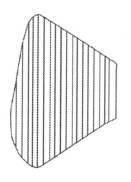

FIG. 4A

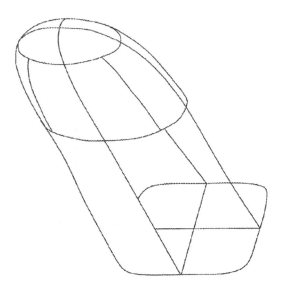

FIG. 4B

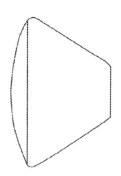

FIG. 4C

504

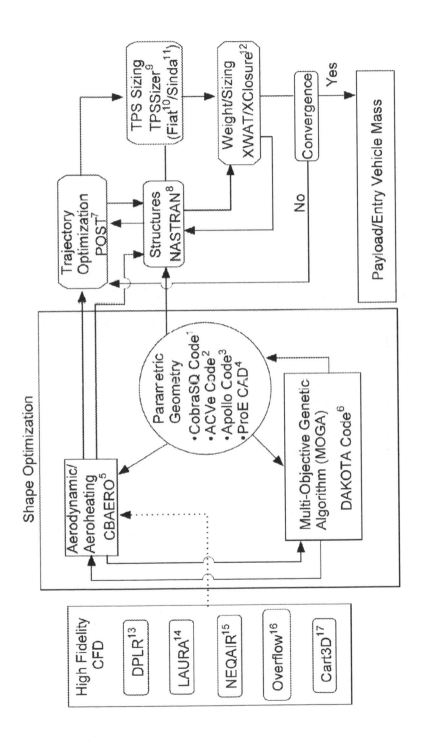

FIG. 5

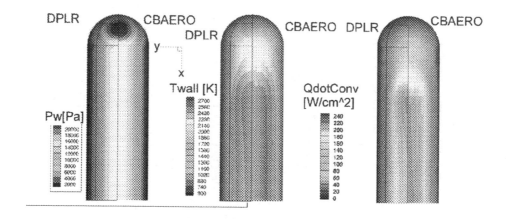

FIG. 6

506

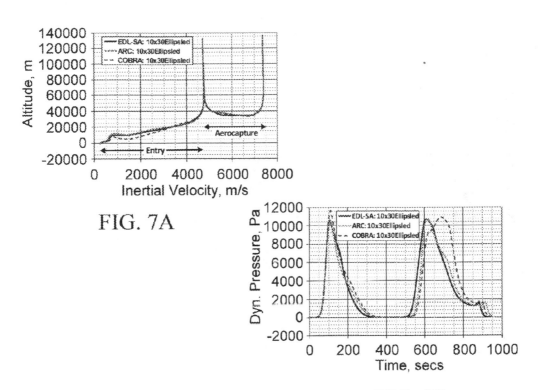

FIG. 7A

FIG. 7B

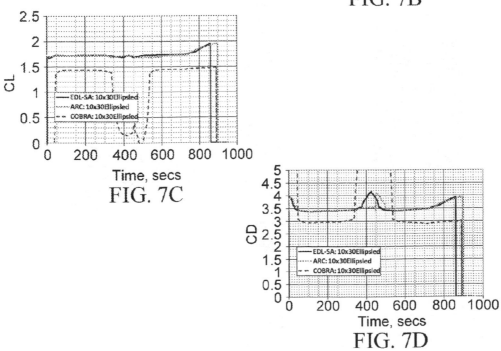

FIG. 7C

FIG. 7D

507

FIG. 8

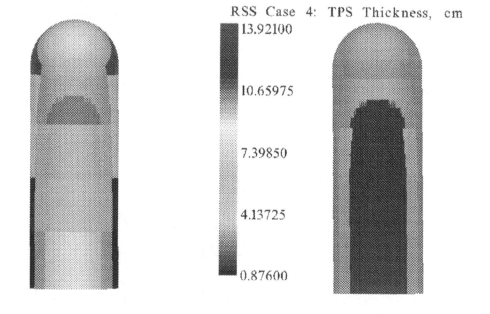

RSS Case 4: TPS Thickness, cm

13.92100

10.65975

7.39850

4.13725

0.87600

FIG. 9

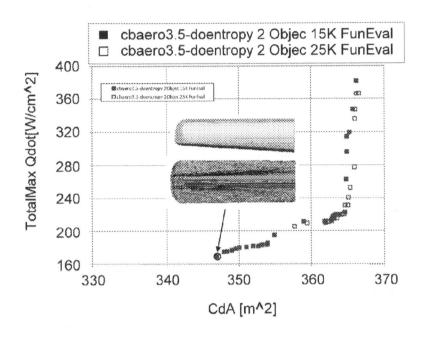

FIG. 10

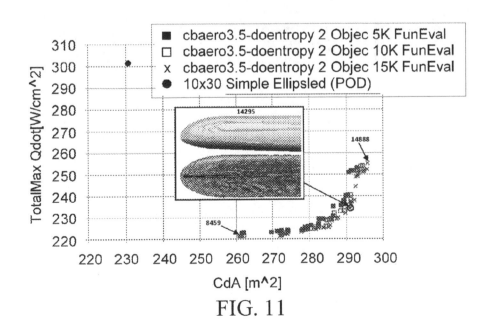

FIG. 11

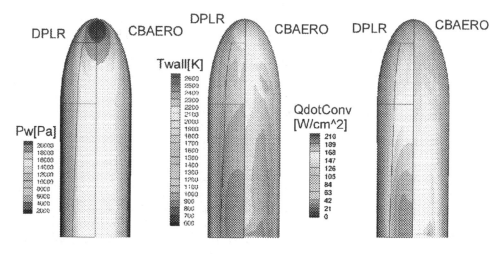

FIG. 12

510

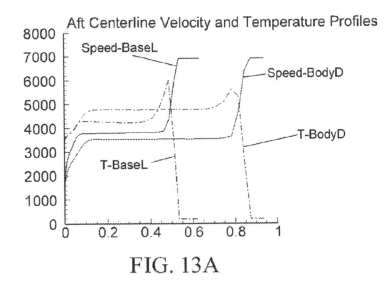

FIG. 13A

Windward Surface Normal Comparison
Out-of-Pitch-Plane Component

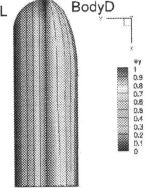

FIG. 13B

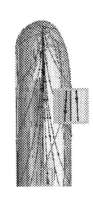

FIG. 13C

511

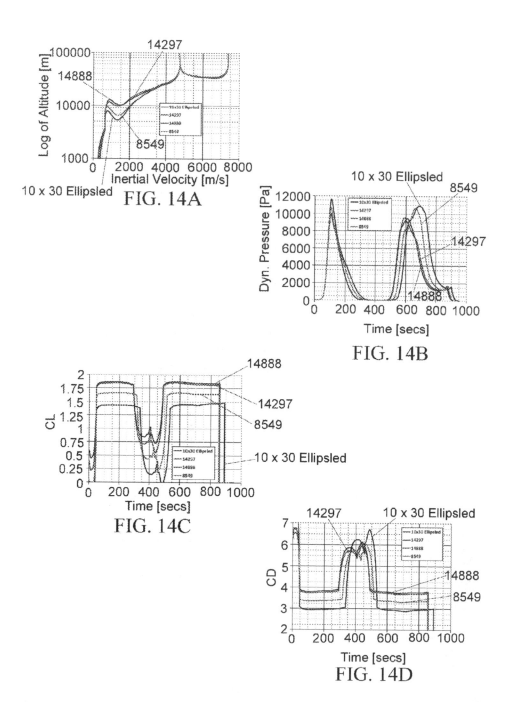

FIG. 14A

FIG. 14B

FIG. 14C

FIG. 14D

512

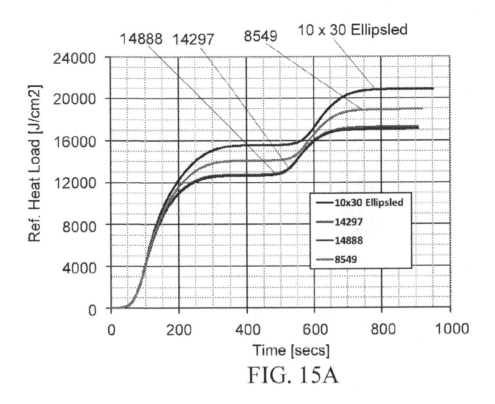

FIG. 15A

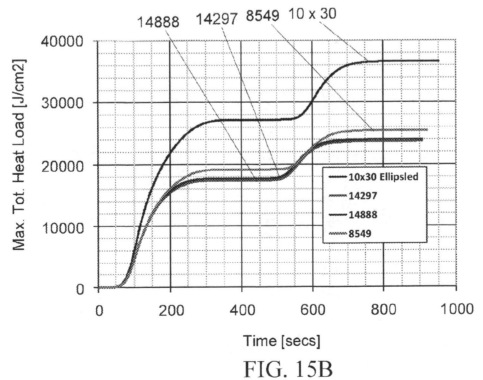

FIG. 15B

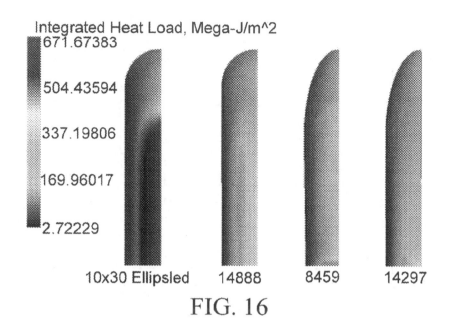

FIG. 16

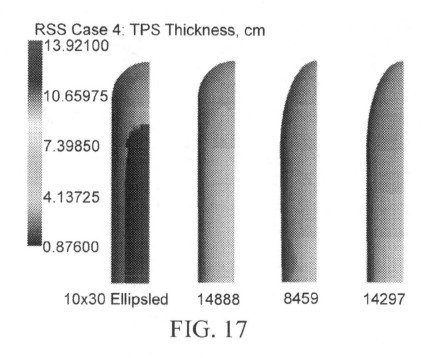

FIG. 17

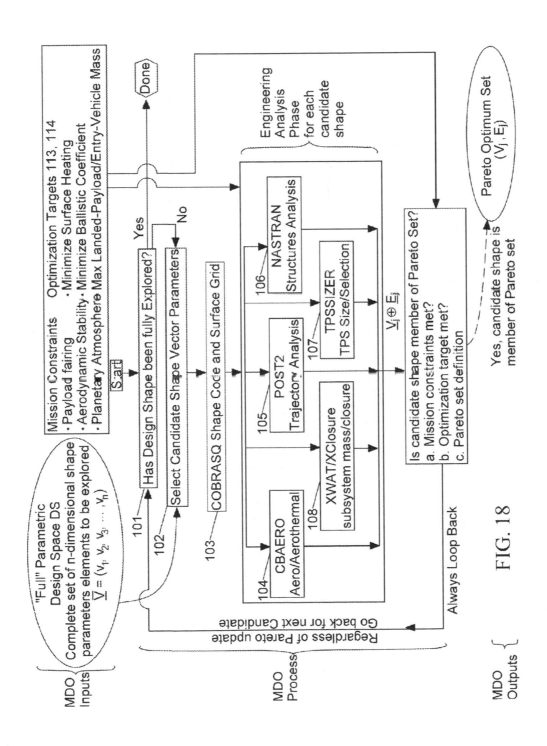

FIG. 18

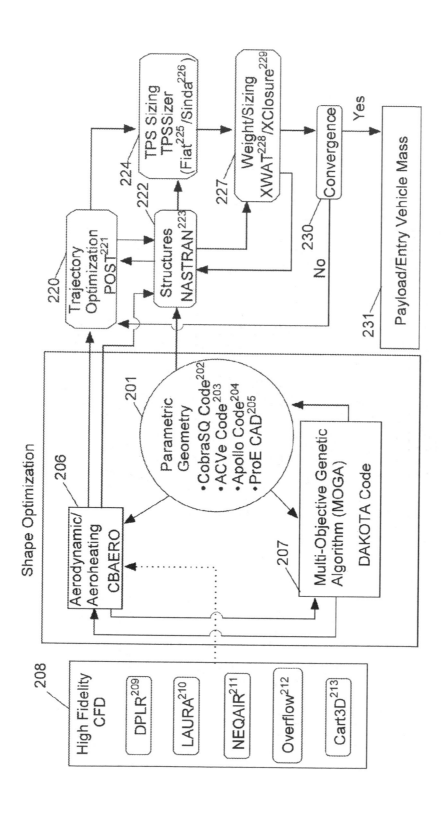

FIG. 19

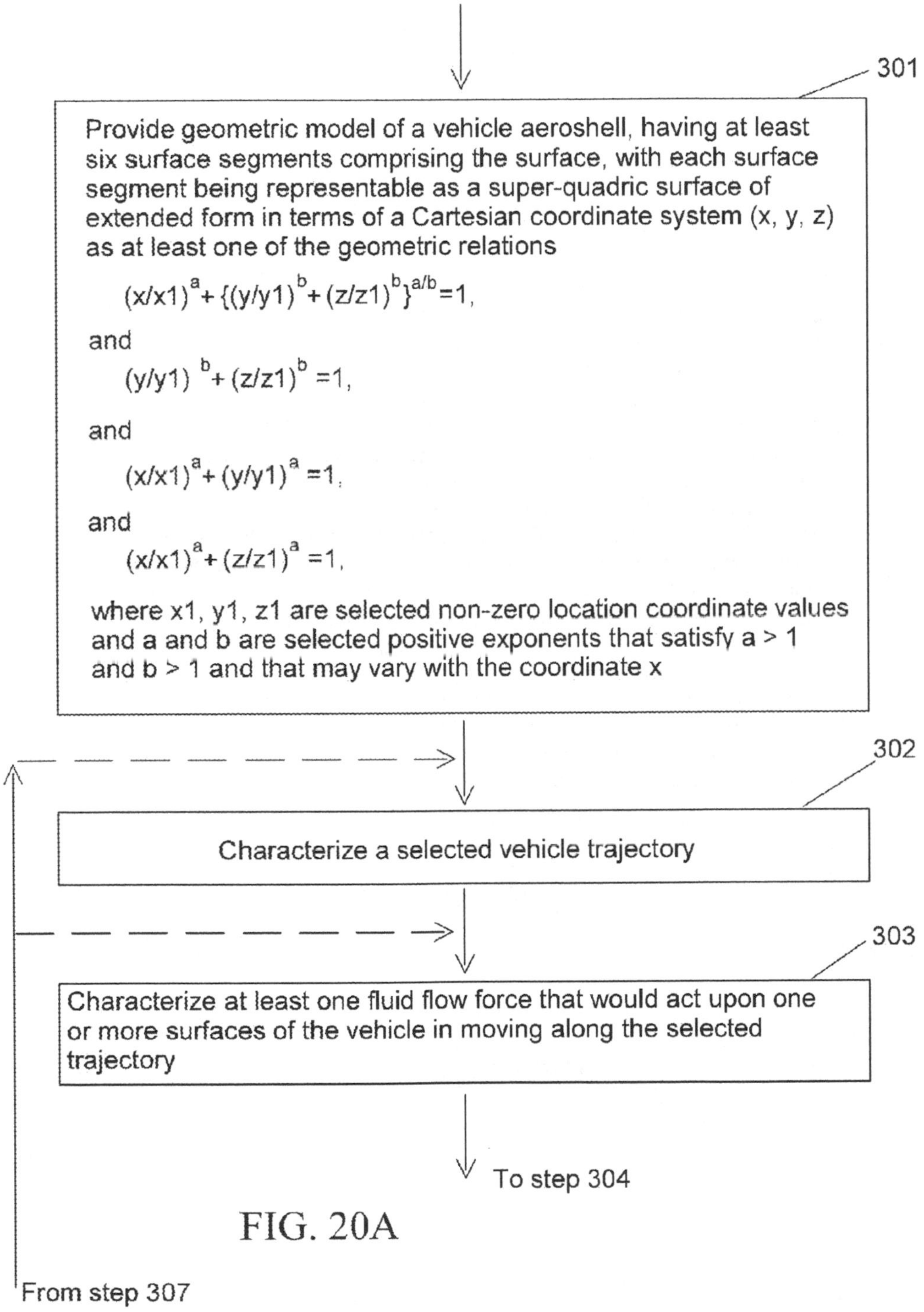

— 301

Provide geometric model of a vehicle aeroshell, having at least six surface segments comprising the surface, with each surface segment being representable as a super-quadric surface of extended form in terms of a Cartesian coordinate system (x, y, z) as at least one of the geometric relations

$$(x/x1)^a + \{(y/y1)^b + (z/z1)^b\}^{a/b} = 1,$$

and

$$(y/y1)^b + (z/z1)^b = 1,$$

and

$$(x/x1)^a + (y/y1)^a = 1,$$

and

$$(x/x1)^a + (z/z1)^a = 1,$$

where x1, y1, z1 are selected non-zero location coordinate values and a and b are selected positive exponents that satisfy a > 1 and b > 1 and that may vary with the coordinate x

— 302

Characterize a selected vehicle trajectory

— 303

Characterize at least one fluid flow force that would act upon one or more surfaces of the vehicle in moving along the selected trajectory

To step 304

FIG. 20A

From step 307

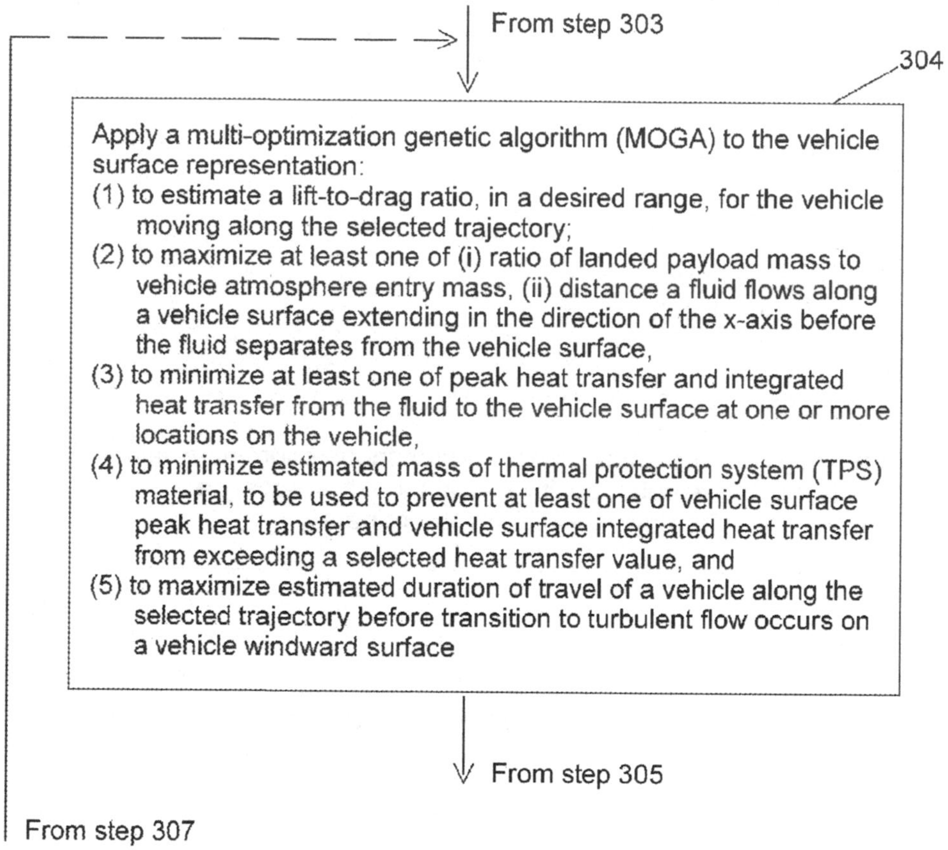

From step 303

304

Apply a multi-optimization genetic algorithm (MOGA) to the vehicle surface representation:

(1) to estimate a lift-to-drag ratio, in a desired range, for the vehicle moving along the selected trajectory;

(2) to maximize at least one of (i) ratio of landed payload mass to vehicle atmosphere entry mass, (ii) distance a fluid flows along a vehicle surface extending in the direction of the x-axis before the fluid separates from the vehicle surface,

(3) to minimize at least one of peak heat transfer and integrated heat transfer from the fluid to the vehicle surface at one or more locations on the vehicle,

(4) to minimize estimated mass of thermal protection system (TPS) material, to be used to prevent at least one of vehicle surface peak heat transfer and vehicle surface integrated heat transfer from exceeding a selected heat transfer value, and

(5) to maximize estimated duration of travel of a vehicle along the selected trajectory before transition to turbulent flow occurs on a vehicle windward surface

From step 305

From step 307

FIG. 20B

518

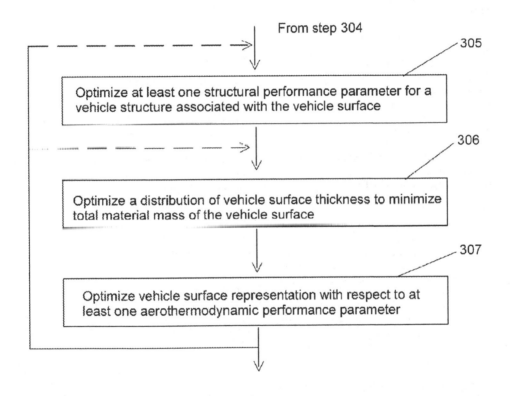

FIG. 20C

1

CO-OPTIMIZATION OF BLUNT BODY SHAPES FOR MOVING VEHICLES

PRIORITY CLAIM

This application claims the benefit of U.S. Provisional Application No. 61/397,146, filed May 17, 2010, which is hereby incorporated by reference.

ORIGIN OF THE INVENTION

The invention described herein was made by employees of the United States Government and may be manufactured and used by or for the Government of the United States of America for governmental purposes without the payment of any royalties thereon or therefor.

FIELD OF THE INVENTION

This invention relates to optimization of geometric parameters for blunt bodies for moving vehicles, such as re-entry vehicles, based upon control of heat transfer, aerothermodynamics, aerodynamics and structural responses.

BACKGROUND OF THE INVENTION

Vehicles designed for exploration of the planets, satellites and other atmospheric bodies in the Solar System favor the use of mid-L/D (Lift/Drag) lifting blunt body geometries. Such shapes can be designed to yield favorable hypersonic heat transfer and aerothermodynamic properties for low heating and hypersonic aerodynamic properties for maneuverability and stability, coupled with desirable terminal low supersonic/transonic aerodynamics, flexible trajectory design based on long down-range and cross-range performance. This includes precise control of landing site and high delivered payload mass with low packing density to better satisfy mission goals and economics. Entry trajectory selection will influence entry peak heating and integrated heat loads, which in turn will influence selection and design of the vehicle thermal protection system (TPS). Thus, a nominal trajectory must be determined for each shape considered. The vehicle will be subject to both launch and entry loading to meet structural integrity constraints that may further influence shape design. Further, such vehicles must be practical, be sized to fit on existing or realizable launch vehicles, often within existing launch payload-fairing constraints.

Past missions to planets, such as Mars and Venus, and even reentry into Earth have predominantly used a capsule configuration, either with a truncated sphere section, such as the Apollo and Soyuz configurations, or with a sphere-cone design, such as the Viking and Pathfinder series of probes. However, these vehicles are of limited lift and maneuverability and have probably reached the upper limit of their practical payload deliverability. In contrast, high-lift winged vehicles such as NASA's Shuttle Orbiter have proven to be expensive to operate and vulnerable to launch debris as a consequence of their launch configuration.

What is needed is a simultaneous optimization approach that (1) takes account of the atmosphere and environmental characteristics through which the vehicle will move, (2) uses a multi-disciplinary approach to simultaneously optimize structural, aerodynamic, aerothermodynamic, heat transfer and material responses of the vehicle, through choice of geometric parameters and materials associated with the vehicle,

2

and (3) provides a mechanism for comparison of optimal vehicle performances using different approaches.

SUMMARY OF THE INVENTION

These needs are met by the invention, which provides a parametric class of closed convex hull shapes, herein referred to as Co-Optimized Blunt Re-entry Aeroshell-Super Quadric vehicle geometry (COBRA-SQ) shapes, and a multi-disciplinary optimization (MDO) process, herein referred to as COBRA MDO, which may be used to perform a sequence of design optimization and performance confirmation processes. Initially, classes of shapes and corresponding flow characteristics are examined to identify the most appropriate classes of vehicle geometry to achieve specified key performance parameters, given the applicable constraints. Initial optimization studies of the surviving classes are performed to broadly identify the best-performing sub-classes, based on relative weights assigned to integrated and localized heat transfer rates, structural and aerothermodynamic responses, using multi-disciplinary analyses of these factors.

These responses will depend upon environmental parameters, such as the characteristics of the atmosphere traveled through, the weight distribution within the vehicle initial velocity of (re)entry, the mass of the planetary body, the initial angle of attack, and other relevant factors, and these parameters will change with the environment. The top candidates within a sub-class are analyzed further to identify parameter values for maximum performance and sensitivity of these maximum performance values to small changes in one or more environmental and/or geometric parameters.

The general shape of the COBRA-SQ defines the vehicle aeroshell shape, without any additional human effort being required. This permits automated optimization, or search for optimum aeroshell shape(s) with the desired aerodynamic and aerothermal properties. These parameters determine certain aerostability properties, such as lift and drag forces and pitch and yaw moments on the vehicle. In addition, the aeroshell shape optimization will determine the structural design required, because of the aeroloads and the thermal protection design requirements arising from the convective and radiative heating.

The following sections provide a detailed description of the parametric CobraSQ geometry family of shapes, and of construction of a generic form of the Cobra MDO design process, making use of the geometry, along with stated constraints and objectives, and describe a specific multi-disciplinary optimization (MDO) software implementation and application of these concepts and software in the design of a prototype Mars reentry vehicle of intermediate payload. FIGS. 1A, 1B and 1C illustrate sectional views of a general blunt body surface used for analysis in the invention, in perspective, top and side views, respectively.

We have developed a parametric class of mid-value Lift/Drag ratio (L/D) lifting blunt body vehicle geometries or shapes that are suitable for entry into and maneuvering within the atmospheres of those various planets and bodies which have atmospheres and which are suitable for use within a multi-objective optimization design process. The vehicle outer shape is based on piecewise C2 continuous, analytical geometric segments joined together at a limited number of seam lines with at least C1 continuity for which the geometry and analysis grids can be rapidly created from a limited set of parameters which, once defined, can be interpreted in a clear and intuitive manner.

At most eight sets of geometric parameters are used to describe the entry body shape, expressed as a super-quadric

3

(resembling an ellipsoid, but with generalization of the usual second degree exponents). The shape functions independently characterize a nose section shape (upper and lower), a base rib section shape (upper and lower), an aft-body section shape (upper and lower), a keel line shape and a water line shape, which are required to join together with at least C1 continuity at certain interfaces. Each of these five body section shapes is expressed as a super-quadric function in Cartesian coordinates (x,y,z) of the form,

$$(x/x1)^a+((y/y1)^b+(z/z1)^b)^{a/b}=1, \quad (1)$$

where x1, y1 and z1 are positive semi-axis lengths, a and b are exponents with values greater than 1, and the x-axis is oriented from back to front, as illustrated in FIGS. 2A, 2B and 2C; or for some of the surface segments (base rib, lower keel line, upper keel line and water line), only two of the three coordinates (x,y,z) are present in the corresponding shape function which may be expressed making use of a combination of linear segment and/or segments of a super-ellipse of the form,

$$(y/y1)^b+(z/z1)^b=\{1-(x/x1)^a\}^{b/a}=const \text{ at fixed } x, \quad (2A)$$

$$(x/x1)^a+(y/y1)^a=\{1-(z/z1)^a\}^{b/a}=const \text{ at fixed } z, \quad (2B)$$

$$(x/x1)^a+(z/z1)^a=\{1-(y/y1)^a\}^{b/a}=const \text{ at fixed } y \quad (2C)$$

If the exponents, a and b, are both equal to 2, the shape functions are three-dimensional ellipsoids or two-dimensional ellipses. A general re-entry body shape is thus characterized parametrically by semi-axis lengths {x1, y1, z1, y2, z2, x3, y3, z3, x4, z4, x5, z5, x6, y6,x7, x8, y7, y8}, by exponents {a1, b1, a2, b2, a3, b3, a4, b4, a5, b5, a6, b6}, and where required by shifts in x-axis coordinate origins. Some of the semi-axis lengths and exponent parameters may vary with the coordinate x.

BRIEF DESCRIPTION OF THE DRAWINGS

FIGS. 1A, 1B and 1C illustrate a COBRASQ class blunt body surface used for analysis according to the invention, in perspective, top and side views, respectively.

FIGS. 2A-2C illustrate the geometric shape parameters used to describe the different vehicle sections or views used in the invention.

FIGS. 3A-3C illustrate super-quadric surfaces in a plane with exponents a=b=1.5, a=b=2.0 and a=b=2.5.

FIG. 4 illustrates different exemplary re-entry vehicle shapes.

FIG. 5 briefly illustrates an MDO Cobra analysis process.

FIG. 6 compares aerothermal values between a DPLR Code and a CBAERO Code.

FIGS. 7A-7D graphically illustrate altitude versus velocity, and dynamic pressure, lift and drag coefficients versus time for a typical trajectory.

FIG. 8 illustrates zone assignments for a surface of a representative vehicle.

FIG. 9 illustrates TPS sizing results according to the invention.

FIGS. 10 and 11 graphically illustrate initial and final Pareto Front results according to a MOGA shape optimization.

FIG. 12 compares aerothermal values computed using a CBAERO Code and a DPLR Code.

FIGS. 13A-13C compare flow velocity and temperature versus distance from the surface (dn) and other flow variables for an optimized surface shape.

4

FIGS. 14A-14D compare trajectories for three optimized shapes with trajectories for the 10×30 Ellipsled POD.

FIGS. 15A-15B compare integrated heat load plots and TPS thicknesses for the three optimized shapes with corresponding values for the 10×30 Ellipsled POD.

FIGS. 16 and 17 compare heat loads and TPS thicknesses for different surface shapes.

FIGS. 18, 19 and 20 illustrate three procedures for practicing the invention.

DESCRIPTION OF BEST MODES OF THE INVENTION

The present invention is a blunt body hypersonic atmospheric vehicle of a shape, derived from the COBRASQ parametric geometric class described in the following, which can be used in a multi-discipline optimization design method in a manner similar as described making use of said parametric geometric class of shapes. The particular parametric form or shape of the vehicle heat shield provides a motivation for the invention and meets the need for an optimizable shape with favorable aerodynamic and heating level properties.

The COBRASQ class of geometries is intended to generate an outer shape suitable for operation as a mid-L/D ratio, hypersonic reentry blunt body vehicle and is constructed using piecewise analytical surfaces or segments joined together with at least C1 continuity at definable seam lines. An exception to the C1 continuity condition is at the base seam, which need only be C0 continuous. At launch, the COBRASQ class of geometries is normally intended for its lengthwise x-axis to be aligned vertically coincident with the vertical launch axis of the launch vehicle. On atmospheric entry, the COBRASQ class of geometries are intended to be oriented at a substantial angle of attack α with the windward side (z>0) presented to the oncoming atmosphere.

In FIGS. 2A, 2B and 2C, the geometries are illustrated along with Cartesian coordinate system (x,y,z). The x-axis is oriented along the lengthwise axis of the vehicle with the nose being in the positive x-direction and the aft-body and base being oriented towards the negative x-direction. The positive y-axis is oriented toward the right of the vehicle (facing forward), and the positive z-axis is oriented so the vehicle is pointed in what will generally be the windward direction when the vehicle is at a positive angle-of-attack (AoA).

The vehicle shape is shown in FIGS. 1A, 1B, 1C, as composed of the several surface and seam line segments:

a. Windward Forebody or Nose section (z>0, and approximately x>0),

b. Leeward Forebody or Nose section (z<0, and approximately x>0),

c. Windward Aftbody Section (z>0, and approximately x<0),

d. Leeward Aftbody Section (z<0, and approximately x<0), and

e. Base Rib Section, being the rib section or yz-plane cut of constant x at the most rearward location (x=−x_L).

The Seam lines where these segments join are:

1. Fore/Aft Seam (at approximately x=0),

2. Waterline Seam, defined at z=0, for regions with z>0 being windward sections, and z<0 being leeward sections;

3. Upper or Leeward Keel or Spine, defined as the curve or line segments at y=0 for regions with z<0; and

4. Lower or Windward Keel or Spine, defined as the curve or line segments at y=0 for z>0.

The surface segments can be described by a collection of super-quadric surfaces, with the curve seams being defined by a collection of curve segments, either linear or curvilinear.

5

Without loss of generality, in a preferred embodiment, the upper Nose section (FIG. 2A), both windward and leeward, is defined by a super-quadric of the following form:

$$(x/x1)^{a1}+\{(y/y1)^{b1}+(z/z1)^{b1}\}^{a1/b1}=1, \qquad (3)$$

where x1, y1 and z1 are specified semi-lengths and a1 and b1 are specified exponents, both greater than 1. FIGS. 3A, 3B and 3C graphically illustrate a two-dimensional representation of a super-quadric with a=b=1.5, 2.0 (ellipse) and 2.5 for comparison. In FIG. 2A, the lower Nose section is similarly defined as

$$(x/x2)^{a2}+\{(y/y2)^{b2}+(z/z2)^{b2}\}^{a2/b2}=1, \qquad (4)$$

where x2=x1, y2=y1, and a2=a1 (>1) are required for C1 continuity, and z1 and z2 are independently specified semi-lengths, and b1 and b2 are independently specified exponents, greater than 1.

The origin of the super-quadric is positioned at (x,y,z)=(0, 0,0) with the most forward point on the nose section being at (x1,0,0). Each of the upper and lower Nose sections thus defined is symmetric about the xz-plane. Where the exponents, a1, b1, a2 and b2, are all equal to 2.0, and x1=y1=z1=x2=y2=z2, a simple hemispherical nose is obtained as a geometrically degenerate case.

The upper base rib (located at x=−x_L), is a super-quadric planar surface, as shown in FIG. 2B and defined by:

$$(y/y3)^{b3}+(z/z3)^{b3}=1, \qquad (5)$$

where y3 and z3 are specified semi-axis lengths of the body surface in the yz-plane, and the specified base exponent b3 is also specified but must be >1. The lower base rib (located at x=−x_L), is a super-quadric planar surface, as shown in FIG. 2B) and is similarly defined by:

$$(y/y4)^{b4}+(z/z4)^{b4}=1. \qquad (6)$$

The origin of the base rib is located at (x,y,z)=(−x_L,0,0), and for continuity y3=y4, but z3 and z4 and b3 and b4 may be specified independently. The geometrically degenerate case of a circle is obtained with y3=z3=y4=z4 and b3=b4=2.

To define the aft-body region between the (upper/lower) Nose section and the (upper/lower) Base Rib section, both the Waterline curve segment and the (upper/lower) Keel curve segments must first be defined.

The Waterline curve segment is shown in FIG. 2C as an xy-planar cut through the vehicle shape at z=0. In the preferred embodiment, the Water line will be a continuous concatenation of at least two surface segments, defined by

$$(x/x5)^{a5}+(y/y5)^{a5}=1, \text{for } x \geq x(\text{WaterlineTangent}Pt), \text{with } z=0 \qquad (7)$$

$$y=y6(x), \text{for } x<x(\text{WaterlineTangent}Pt, \text{with } z=0, \qquad (8)$$

where the first Waterline curve segment, Eq. (7), for x>x (WaterlineTangentPt) is a super-quadric segment contribution from the Nose super-quadric, and the second Water line curve segment, Eq. (6), for x<x(WaterlineTangentPt), is a linear segment (or spline segment, if desired) that is constructed to be tangent to the Nose super-ellipse and passes through the Base Rib at (x=−xL, y3, 0). The tangent point, at x(WaterlineTangentPt), can be found analytically or by iterative numerical means. Thus, the Waterline segment can be found at any x-station as given above and will be referred hereafter by the general equation, y(x,z=0)=yWaterLine(x).

The upper and lower Keel lines are treated similarly to the Water line and are shown in FIG. 2C, which shows sectional views from a xz-planar cut through the vehicle shape at y=0,

6

each cut being composed of a continuous concatenation of at least two segments. The upper Keel line segments are defined by

$$(x/x7)^{a7}+(z/z7)^{a7}=1, \text{for } x>x(\text{UpperKeelTangent}Pt), \text{with } y=0,z>0 \qquad (9)$$

$$z=z7(x), \text{for } x<x(\text{UpperKeelTangent}Pt), \text{with } y=0,z>0 \qquad (10)$$

and the lower Keel line segments are defined by

$$(x/x8)^{a8}+(z/z8)^{a8}=1, \text{for } x>x(\text{LowerKeelTangent}Pt), \text{with } y=0,z<0 \qquad (11)$$

$$z=z8(x), \text{for } x<x(\text{LowerKeelTangent}Pt), \text{with } y=0,z<0 \qquad (12)$$

where the first curve segment for each of the upper and lower Keel lines (Eqs. (7) and (9), respectively) is a super-quadric segment contribution from the Nose super-quadric, and the second curve for each of the upper and lower Keel lines (Eqs. (8) and (10), respectively) are straight lines (or splines, if desired) that are constructed to be tangent to the super-quadric Nose segment and to pass through the Base Rib segment at (−xL,0,−z3) and (−xL,0,z4), respectively. The exponents a5, a7 and a9 will all be equal to a1, the parameters x5, x7 and x9 will all be equal to x1, and the parameter z7 and z8 will be equal to z1 and z2, respectively, as these correspond to contributions from the Nose segment(s).

The tangent point location(s), expressed as x(WaterlineTangentPt), x(UpperKeelTangentPt), and x(LowerKeelTangentPt) are found by analytical or known iterative numerical methods to enforce at least C1 continuity for the Waterline, Upper Keel line and Lower Keel line.

Thus, the (upper/lower) Keel-line segments can be found at any x-station as given above, and will be defined hereafter by the general equations

$$z(x,y=0)=z(\text{UpperKeelLine}(x)), \text{for } x1>x>-x_L, \text{and } z<0, \qquad (13)$$

$$z(x,y=0)=z(\text{LowerKeeLine}(x)), \text{for } x1>x>-x_L, \text{and } z>0. \qquad (14)$$

The Aft-body, shown in FIG. 2C, is specified for each point on the surface by the following procedure. For the Aft-body, at any given x-station, the yz-cut through the vehicle shape will be given by an upper and lower super-equadric rib defined by

$$\{(y/y(\text{Waterline}(x))^{b9(x)}+(z/z\text{UpperKeelLine}(x)\}^{b9(x)}=1, \qquad (15)$$

$$\{(y/y(\text{Waterline}(x))^{b10(x)}+(z/z\text{LowerKeelLine}(x)\}^{b10(x)}=1, \qquad (16)$$

where the exponents b9(x) or b10(x) are found by any known continuous curves (spline, cosine, or linear) segments passing from b10(x)=b1 at the greater x-value of x(WaterlineTangentPt) and x(UpperKeelTangentPt), and b9(x)=b3 at x=−x_L. Similarly, the exponent b10(x) is found by any known (spline, cosine or linear) continuous curve segments passing from b1(x)=b1 at the greater x-value of x(WaterlineTangentPt) and x(LowerKeelTangentPt), and b10(x)=b4 at x=−x_L. The vehicle is symmetric about the xz-plane at y=0.

Using the above procedure at any x-station, each rib or (x,z) curve of the Aft-body can be described entirely and without ambiguity, and such a vehicle shape is C2 continuous, except at the seam lines given above, where it is C1 continuous. In the preferred embodiment described above it appears sufficient to specify the parameters, {xL,x1-x10, y1-y10,z1-z10, a1-a10, b1-b10} to entirely determine the vehicle shape. All other parameters mentioned in the description of the preferred embodiment may be derived during execution of the procedure described above.

7

A Fortran-based COBRASQ.F program implements the preceding procedure and provides a surface grid, as either a structured Plot3D ASCII text file, or as an unstructured surface mesh file suitable for with the CBAero engineering analysis program, or as an unstructured Tecplot ASCII text file suitable for plotting, using commonly available visualization software such as either Plot3D or Tecplot.

Such a surface grid can be generated with human intervention or without human intervention by means of a Multi-discipline Design Optimization procedure by providing a limited number of intuitive parameters, such as for a shape symmetric about the yz-plane. Although the number of surface segments discussed in the preceding is 6, the vehicle surface may be defined more generally by M surface segments, with M≥1.

For this particular instance of the invention (with M=6), a minimum of 15 independent parameters define the vehicle shape from which surface grids can be automatically generated. This number of independent parameters may be large or smaller than 15, depending upon the number M of surface segments.

Such surface grids can also be used with engineering-fidelity analysis codes such as CBAERO to provide wall pressure and heating, hypersonic aerodynamic properties such as lift and drag and stability, and structural codes such as MSC NASTRAN to provide structural strength and mass estimates of such a body, or to provide a basis for generating volume grids capable of use with hi-fidelity Real-Gas Navier-Stokes fluid mechanics and chemistry codes such as DPLR.

Note that, as shown in FIGS. 3A, 3B and 3C, when the super-quadric exponents, a and b are equal to 2.0, an ellipse is formed; whereas when a and b are less than 2.0 and near 1.0, the cross-sectional shape generated approaches a rhombus; and if they are much greater than 2.0, the cross-sectional shape becomes increasingly rectangular. As a consequence, a large class of practical 3D shapes, suitable for study as possible hypersonic re-entry vehicles, can be configured by means of the above sets of geometric parameters and methods.

The general parametric shape of the present invention defines the vehicle shape without the need for intense human labor, which allows for automated optimization or search throughout a large variety of possible shapes in order to find the best aerodynamic, aerothermal properties, including stability, lift, drag, both convective and gas-phase radiation heating.

The disclosed Multi-disciplinary Design Optimization (MDO) framework takes account of the aeroshell shape, trajectory, thermal protection system, and vehicle subsystem closure, along with a Multi Objective Genetic Algorithm (MOGA) for the initial shape. This is accomplished using a combination of engineering and higher-fidelity physics-based tools along with optimization methods and engineering judgment. This process demonstrates that the proposed family of optimized medium L/D aeroshell shapes exhibits a significant improvement over the present art. Further, a trade-off between the vehicle TPS and structural mass is identified for these aeroshell shapes and their corresponding vehicle trajectories which yields an overall decrease in total vehicle mass, or a corresponding increase in delivered payload, as compared to the state of the art.

As an entry vehicle's aeroshell becomes larger, the Reynolds Number (Re) increases, causing the flow to become turbulent. Studies have shown that the legacy Viking 70-degree sphere-cone aeroshell shape, classically used for entry into Mars, exhibits high turbulent heating levels on the leeward side as well as early transition to a turbulent flow for

8

large diameters. This phenomenon has especially impacted the planned Mars Science Laboratory (MSL) aeroshell, also a 70-degree sphere-cone shape, which is predicted to experience a peak margin heating rate approaching 200 Watts/cm^2 during entry. This maximum heating occurs on the leeward side of the fore-body aeroshell, and reaches heating augmentation levels up to a factor of six higher than laminar heating levels rather than the expected turbulent heating increase by a factor of three. This high leeward side aeroshell turbulent heating has been attributed [1,2] to entropy layer swallowing effects associated with the legacy 70-degree shape at high Reynolds number, Mach number and angle of attack. The high turbulence-induced heating rates on the MSL aeroshell were a primary reason that the MSL program changed its thermal protection system (TPS) material from lighter SLA-561V to more robust PICA in 2008. The PICA material, in one embodiment, is described in U.S. Pat. Nos. 5,536,562, 5,672,389 and 6,955,853, issued to Tran et al and incorporated by reference herein.

The aeroshell shape affects several primary design areas for hypersonic entry vehicles. This includes the aerothermal environment which determines vehicle's TPS layout and design, the aerodynamics which affects deceleration and maneuverability coupled with trajectory shaping and the aerodynamic loading which affects the underlying structural subsystem. Because of this, it is crucial that alternate aeroshell designs account for these multiple disciplines in order to evaluate them in a system level view and to understand how each subsystem is affected. In order to do this and to explore the design space, an integrated Multi-disciplinary Design Optimization (MDO) technique accounting for shape, trajectory, thermal protection system (TPS), and vehicle closure was utilized in this effort. A combination of engineering and higher-fidelity physics analysis tools along with optimization methods and engineering judgment is used to accomplish a system level view and lead to a multi-discipline solution. The integrated MDO process environment allows engineers to efficiently and consistently analyze multiple design options. In addition, this integrated MDO framework allows for assessing the relative impacts of new discipline tool capabilities and identifying trade-offs between multiple objectives through the use of the Genetic Algorithm (GA) optimization Pareto front. The framework described is referred to as COBRA, an acronym for "Co-Optimization of Blunt-body Re-entry Analysis"[3].

Vehicle Geometry.

The vehicle geometry is based on one of several FORTRAN codes written specifically to provide an analytic description of the vehicle shape with a small number of geometric parameters. Shape examples are shown in FIGS. 1A-1C.

These codes that can be used to define a geometry include: 1) a low-L/D, high-ballistic coefficient symmetric/asymmetric capsule body code [4,5]; 2) a medium L/D lifting body code as described above, or 3) a low-L/D, Apollo/CEV-type truncated-sphere/torus capsule shape code. Each code can generate surface mesh descriptions in either structured Plot3d or as unstructured triangulations of the surface shape. These codes allow the use of a small set of geometric parameters to define the vehicle's outer mold line (OML) and to provide shapes with a range of aerodynamic and aerothermodynamic properties useful for optimization. The general parametric shapes of the COBRA process entirely define the vehicle shape without the need for intense human interaction. This reduction in direct interaction allows for automated optimization within a large design space to find the best combination of aerodynamic stability and aeroheating for the vehicle performance.

Aerodynamics/Aerothermodynamics.

The aerodynamic and aerothermodynamic characteristics of each particular vehicle shape are computed using either the CBAERO engineering code [6] and/or the DPLR [7] Computational Fluid Dynamic (CFD) code. CBAERO is an engineering analysis code based on independent panel methods, such as the modified Newtonian method, along with a surface streamline algorithm and an extensive set of validated engineering correlations to determine surface pressure, convective and radiative heating, shear stress, and boundary layer properties. DPLR is a high-fidelity, physics-based real-gas Navier-Stokes code used in conjunction with NEQAIR [8], a high-fidelity radiation code, to give results either in support of or in place of CBAERO data.

It is in this discipline that a hybrid approach which leverages high fidelity analyses with engineering methods using sophisticated interpolation techniques, ("anchoring"), is utilized. Traditionally, analytical tools applied in the early phases of vehicle design rely on engineering methods because of their rapid turnaround time, ease of use, and robustness. The drawbacks of engineering methods are that such methods only approximate the physics governing the process to be modeled and such methods may not accurately model the flow physics. Unlike engineering methods, high fidelity methods are based on solutions to the basic equations of physics to be modeled and yield more accurate results, if used within their limitations. However, these high fidelity methods tend to be difficult to set up and computationally expensive (typically hundreds of times more CPU-intensive than engineering methods). The anchoring approach addresses the deficiencies with the engineering and high fidelity methods by utilizing a rapid and intelligent engineering-based interpolation method. Further detail of this anchoring approach can be found in Reference [9].

Trajectory Analysis.

During optimization of the vehicle, the nominal design trajectory is dependent on the aerodynamic and aeroheating properties of the particular vehicle shape, in particular, L/D, ballistic coefficient, and peak heating. Constraints on the trajectory flight dynamics, such as gravitational loading on the vehicle, also must be imposed. To find a nominal trajectory for each vehicle under consideration, the Program to Optimize Simulated Trajectories (POST2) [10] code is used.

In this work, the trajectory used for entry and landing on a surface of a planetary body consists of two phases: (1) an initial aerocapture phase to decelerate the entry vehicle into a 1-SOL orbit about the Martian atmosphere; and (2) an entry phase down to the surface. Both trajectories are modeled with 3DOF. POST2 is wrapped inside the COBRA environment to expose input parameters necessary to simulate the aerocapture and entry trajectories. By exposing a limited set of input variables from POST2, the trajectory wrapper greatly simplifies the tedious work for the analyst and makes it suitable for integrations into the COBRA environment. However, it does not replace critical expert judgment. Results should be carefully inspected to ensure correctness. The wrapper also exposes output variables needed for downstream tools such as TPS sizing, structure, and the weight and sizing closure tools.

Structure Analysis.

In performing conceptual design on a vehicle that does not closely resemble one which has flown before, or that has undergone higher fidelity analysis, it can be difficult to develop appropriate mass predictions for the vehicle components. One component which is very sensitive to the vehicle

configuration is the structure of the aeroshell. The structure mass is determined, not only by the aeroshell configuration, but also by the aerodynamic loading, vehicle scale, and payload configuration. This presents a serious problem when performing a design space exploration or stochastic optimization where the configuration of the conceptual vehicle is allowed to vary largely. Traditionally, the options available are: (1) to apply existing Mass Estimating Relations (MERs), (2) to extrapolate from similar vehicle designs, and (3) to select a general vehicle configuration and generate a parameterized mass model to be used in the analysis. In some cases these approaches are suitable. However, there are situations when there are no MERs available for a given configuration, or the existing ones have to be extrapolated to such an extent that their associated error is either unknown or unacceptable. In many cases, larger margins are applied to the structures, making the structures infeasible as far as mass is concerned. To address these issues, in this work, a structure module has been developed to allow for direct simulation and optimization of the vehicle structure components using automated scripts. This is done by extracting the pressure load from the engineering aerodynamic tool, assigning structure elements for each aeroshell shape, and performing a structural optimization to minimize the structural subsystem mass using MSC NASTRAN [11].

Thermal Protection System Sizing.

To assess the thermal protection system (TPS), the nominal trajectory for each shape is generated and its aerodynamic and aeroheating characteristics, including the time history of the heating environments, are provided to the TPSSIZER [12] set of programs. TPSSIZER includes the FIAT [13] thermal analysis code for ablative TPS materials. The result is an optimized TPS sizing for a vehicle shape with its own nominal trajectory for the mission constraints being considered. The TPS sizing process begins by computing the maximum temperature and integrated heat load for each point on the surface of the vehicle. This is done by simulating flight by each surface geometry through the aerocapture, cool-off, and entry trajectory phases, by interpolating in Mach number, dynamic pressure, and angle-of-attack within the CBAERO aerothermal database at each trajectory time step. Appropriate design margins are applied to the heating rates based on those developed for the NASA Orion capsule [14]. The TPS material distribution is determined by the maximum heating/temperature for each body point. Approximately 10 to 20 TPS sizing points are selected for each body region based on maximum integrated heat load values. Detailed heating environments as a function of time are generated for the TPS sizing body points. For each TPS sizing point, the corresponding thermal analysis material stack-up is created, reflecting the TPS material concept and the associated aeroshell structural definition, and including sublayer material thicknesses determined by the structural analysis. At each sizing point, a transient heat transfer analysis is computed that varies the insulation thickness until the desired back wall temperature limit is satisfied. This process is repeated for all body TPS sizing points and the TPS mass is computed assuming uniform insulation thickness over each body zone.

Vehicle Mass and Sizing.

Among the constraints for optimization of a mission being considered are the particular launch vehicle, payload fairing, and delivered vehicle total mass at entry interface for the planetary body of interest. Combining the TPS sizing obtained from TPSSIZER and the propellant mass estimate for the trajectory tool POST2, the weight/sizing vehicle closure analysis code, XWAT/XClosure [15] provides an estimate of the delivered payload for the particular vehicle shape parameters selected by the MDO analysis. XWAT, the XML based Weight/Mass Analysis Tool, is an XML based C++ application to compute mass/sizing of any space vehicle concept. XWAT can be applied, not only to launch vehicles, but also EDL studies. For our study, the MER's and associated parameters for all the major subsystem elements are collected in an XML format within the LVL framework. Several of the subsystem MER's depend on the total entry mass, resulting in an implicit dependence. XWAT tries to solve a fully nonlinear mass equation system by iterating on the total entry mass until the masses of all the subsystems converge. Upon convergence, XWAT produces a mass and volume statement for the closed configuration. In this work, the payload mass is prescribed and the total entry vehicle mass is computed using the XWAT program. Optimization of either the maximum delivered payload or the minimum entry vehicle mass (where a payload is specified), becomes an objective function for the COBRA MDO environment.

Shape Optimization.

Shape optimization is performed using a Multi Objective Genetic Algorithm optimization (MOGA) package within the DAKOTA tools suite [16]. The basic idea associated with a genetic algorithm ("GA") approach is to search for a set of optimal solutions using an analogy to the theory of evolution. The problem is parameterized into a set of design variables, also referred to as "genes." Each set of design variables that fully defines one design is called a design or a chromosome. A set of chromosomes is called a population or a generation. Each design or chromosome is evaluated using a fitness function that determines survivability of that particular chromosome. In this invention, the genes are a series of geometric parameters associated with the aeroshell outer-mode-line (OML) and are optimized to meet two thermal objectives. Each evaluation is performed at a single trajectory point based on what is expected to be the maximum heat flux experienced by an entry vehicle into Mars. This maximum heat flux for the baseline 10×30 simple Ellipsled has been determined to occur during the Aerocapture trajectory phase at a Maxh number of approximately 32.0 and dynamic pressure of 0.15 bars. The GA function evaluation is performed at the flight conditions set forth in the preceding for a vehicle trim alpha design such that its aerodynamics achieves a lift-to-drag ratio of 0.5.

The two objectives are (1) to minimize the peak total heat flux on the vehicle and (2) to maximize the drag area (C_DA). Maximizing CdA leads to a minimization of ballistic coefficient. During solution advancement, each chromosome is ranked according to its fitness. The higher-ranking chromosomes are selected and continue to the next generation. The newly selected chromosomes in the next generation are manipulated using various operators (combination, crossover or mutation) to create the final set of chromosomes for the new generation. These chromosomes are evaluated for fitness and the process continues until a suitable level of convergence is obtained.

Constraints are included in the GA optimization approach, either by direct inclusion into the objective function definition as penalty constraints, or by including them into a fitness function evaluation procedure. For example, if a design violates a constraint, its fitness is set to zero, and the design does not survive to the next generation. Because GA optimization is not a gradient-based optimization technique, it does not need sensitivity derivatives. GA theoretically works well in non-smooth design spaces containing many local minimums and maximums. General GA details, including descriptions of basic genetic algorithm concepts, can be found in References [18] and [19].

Summaries of some of the computer codes (COBRASQ, CBAERO, DPLR, POST2, 3DOF, TPSSIZER, FIAT, MER, MSC NASTRAN, XWAT/XClosure, EDL-SA and ADB) used here are contained in an Appendix. Alternate MDO algorithms, as known to the practitioners of the art, can be substituted for the GA optimization algorithm.

MDO Overview.

An overview of the COBRA integrated system optimization analysis environment based on the discipline tools discussed above is illustrated in FIGS. 2A-2C and 3A-3C. The COBRA environment, as configured, allows for either a top down approach to determine the maximum landed payload mass for a given entry total entry vehicle mass, or a bottom up approach to determine the required entry vehicle mass for a given landed payload. Here, a bottom up approach is used where the landed payload required is specified, and the co-optimization process is to minimize the entry vehicle mass at atmospheric entry.

The global system optimization is achieved through a multistep process. The MOGA driver is used to find a Pareto front among the allowed range of vehicle shape parameters being considered using engineering fidelity analysis tools to explore the initial vehicle shape design space. This is followed by an integrated MDO analysis including structures, trajectory, and TPS sizing, followed by a weight and sizing analysis to perform the final vehicle closure.

COBRA Environment Calibration/Verification.

Because of the complexity of integrating the MDO analysis, it is critical that experts in different disciplines are involved in both the setup and verification of the results being generated. For our work we selected the EDL-SA rigid aeroshell Architecture 1 as described in Reference [20] as the point of departure (POD) for our baseline. Under the EDL-SA, multiple architectures are explored. The rigid aeroshell configuration was based on a vehicle with an outer model line (OML) shape including a 5-meter radius hemispherical nose with a cylindrical aft-body of diameter 10 meters and length of 25 meters yielding a total vehicle length of 30 meters, referred to in our work as the 10×30 Ellipsled. This process provides a means to allow us to perform a verification analysis and to setup and calibrate the trajectory and MERs for the chosen baseline. Each of the technical discipline analyses is performed independently on the baseline configuration and the results are compared to values reported in [20]. This process is also used to provide a point of departure (POD) for the aeroshell shape optimization and the subsequent integrated system analysis.

10×30 Ellipsled High Fidelity POD Comparison of Engineering Aero/Aerothermal.

To assess the accuracy of the CBAERO engineering tool, the aerodynamics and aerothermal heating on our POD architecture must be evaluated. To accomplish this, a comparison of the surface pressure, surface temperatures and convective heating is performed against a high fidelity DPLR simulation as shown in FIG. 4. This comparison is performed at a Mach number of 32.5, dynamic pressure of 0.114 bar, and angle-of-attack of 56.4 degrees. These qualitative comparisons illustrate that the engineering CBAERO results compare well with DPLR for this geometry.

FIG. 5 illustrates a system for practicing the invention.

10×30 Ellipsled POD Trajectories.

The trajectory is divided into energy phases using the initial and final energy states. In the COBRA environment, POST2 modulates the bank angles to achieve the final conditions while trying to satisfy a set of constraints. The aerocapture trajectory is formulated as a targeting problem. For this work, the entry trajectory is run with a reference stagnation heat load minimization option. Other options include: maximizing the landed mass, or optimizing a user defined variable through a generalized table. The aerocapture trajectory can also be constrained with specified minimum altitude, maximum g-load, and maximum heat flux. The entry trajectory is constrained with maximum g-load, maximum heat flux, maximum q-alpha, freestream dynamic pressure and cross/down range to achieve the same retro rocket initiation as is utilized in the EDL-SA effort documented in Reference [19].

Table-1 presents the trajectory initial conditions and constraints obtained from EDL-SA Architecture 1 [19] for both the aerocapture to 1-SOL orbit and the entry trajectory from the 1-SOL orbit. The Entry from 1-SOL trajectory starts at the apogee with a de-orbit DV=15.309 m/s. A cool down period is allowed after capture into 1-SOL, but to save execution time, the un-powered entry trajectory begins at the entry interface and ends at the point when the Mach number reaches 2.67. Throughout the entry trajectory, bank modulation controls is performed to minimize the reference heat load. Four constraints are implemented for the trajectory design: 1) deceleration must be less than 3 Earth G values (3 g_E), 2) q-alpha must be less than 12,000 psf-degrees (575,000 Pascal-degrees), 3) down range must exceed 1220 km, and 4) free stream dynamic pressure at Mach number M_{s1}=2.67, for aeroshell ejection, must remain below 1240 Pascal. The vehicle free falls until Mach number M_{s2}=2.72 is attained. After meeting these constraints, the vehicle continues its final descent using retro rockets until touch down at an altitude of 885 m below MOLA with a relative touchdown velocity of 2.5 m/s. The retro rocket max thrust is 1,677,200 Newton.

TABLE 1

EDL-SA 1-SOL Trajectoires		
	Aerocapture	Entry
M_{em} (kg)	110,164	109,595
Aeroshell Mass (kg)	41,222	41,222
L/D @ peak dyn. pressure	0.5	0.5
Ballistic Coef. (kg/m2)	460	460
E.I. Altitude (m)	136,097	128,772
E.I. Inertial Velocity (m/s)	7,360	4,714
Inertial F.P.A. (deg.)	−12.77	−11.005
Inertial Azimuth Angle (deg.)	89.93	0.0004
Max. G Constraint (Earth Gs)	3	3
Max. dynamic Pressure Constraint (Pa)	10,600	10,700
Retro Rocket ISP (sec)		349.2
Mach no. @ Retro Rocket		2.7

An independent trajectory analysis is first generated using the aerodynamic and atmospheric data extracted from the EDL-SA baseline trajectories, referred to as "ARC" in FIGS. 7A-7D. This is done to calibrate our trajectory simulations in COBRA, through bank modulations, and to ensure that the trajectory module can produce similar trajectories as the EDL-SA baseline. The lift and drag coefficients are constructed as functions of the vehicle specific energy. The POST2 trajectory setup is configured in the integrated COBRA environment where it receives the aerodynamic data from CBAERO. Results of the POST2 trajectories are passed to, and used by, the downstream tools. FIGS. 7A-7D compare the 10×30 Ellipsled aeroshell shape trajectory with the EDL-SA trajectory, from NASA Langley Research Center (black lines), the calibrated trajectory (green lines), and the COBRA baseline trajectory (red lines). The aerocapture and entry trajectory are concatenated into a single trajectory. The 12 hours flight time for the entry trajectory from the apogee to the entry interface is not plotted.

As shown in the plots in FIGS. 7C-7D, the integrated COBRA simulation for the 10×30 Ellipsled flies at approximately 12 percent lower drag and higher lift coefficient than that predicted by EDL-SA. However, both achieve the same lift-to-drag ratio but at different trim angles-of-attack. Hence, in order for the COBRA predicted trajectory to dissipate the same energy and permit capture into 1-SOL orbit or reach the surface, the trajectory dips lower into the atmosphere, resulting in higher free stream dynamic pressure and slightly less deceleration. It should be noted that the COBRA trajectory shows very low lift coefficients and high drag coefficients for an initial portion of a descent trajectory, where the vehicle experiences very low dynamic pressure and aerodynamic forces are negligible. These predictions are attributed to the very large viscous forces that the engineering tool predicts and which would be better evaluated with a free molecular flow computation. However, this will not affect the results of the trajectory, because the low dynamic pressure corresponds to low aero force.

10×30 Ellipsled POD Structures.

The structural module within COBRA is designed to generate a finite element (FE) model based on a user input file and a supplied surface mesh from the COBRASQ shape generation tool. The module is coded to generate a beam-stringer-skin type FE model. Using the input file, the user has control over parameters such as number and location of beam and longeron members, beam and longeron cross sections and materials, payload mass, distribution of mass over the vehicle structure, and even skin material and stackup for composite and laminate structures. The user selects from a series of analysis types including entry and/or launch analysis for a given configuration or a design optimization for either an entry load only situation or both launch and entry load cases. In an optimization run, the objective is to minimize the mass of the structure and the design variables are the dimensions of the beam member cross section and the laminate thicknesses in the stackup. The user has the option of selecting a single beam and longeron dimension to optimize (e.g., the height of an "I" beam) or any number of dimensions up to the maximum number that define a particular cross section. Further, the user has an option of dividing the vehicle into multiple zones that are optimized independently to produce a more optimized structure. On completion of the optimization run the mass of the structure is passed to XWAT, and the supplied stackup files for each zone are updated with the optimized thicknesses and passed on to the TPS sizing module allowing for a consistent structural stackup between TPSSIZER and MSC NASTRAN.

The structural optimization is performed using Solution 200 in MSC NASTRAN. This optimization was configured to yield the lowest structure mass while remaining within allowable stress and shear constraints. Most of the components in the model were constrained by their allowable stress. For this purpose, the A-Base values were used from the 1998 MIL Handbook. The only material not constrained by stress is a honeycomb material used in the laminate skin layup. For this material, the allowable shear is used to constrain the design and these properties were obtained from the Hexcel.com website.

To verify how the POD structures architecture compares to that of the EDL-SA, a comparison case was run using the information that was available about the 10×30 Ellipsled's beam locations, and the assumed materials. The EDL-SA NASTRAN FEA model was divided into six longitudinal zones. For a comparable analysis we split our FEA model into six zones and obtain a mass of 1993 kg using aluminum beams and

15

longerons and a composite laminate for the skin. Dividing the vehicle up differently may lead to a more optimal shape. By applying a ten-zone decomposition to the vehicle, as opposed to six zones (five windward zones and five leeward zones), as shown in FIG. **8**, the optimized mass is brought down to 4333 kg.

10×30 Ellipsled POD Thermal Protection Systems Sizing.

Initially MER's were developed for the Thermal Protection System mass as part of the overall entry mass calibration process discussed in the preceding. The baseline TPS concept for the Mars EDL-SA vehicle consists of a dual-layer TPS concept, made up of an outer ablative TPS layer to accommodate the high heating rates encountered during the aerocapture phase, with a lighter weight sublayer TPS material to address the more benign aerothermal environments of entry. For the current shape optimization trade study, a more conventional single layer TPS concept was selected. This resulted in a simplification of the TPS design analysis by avoiding the complication of modeling the dual layer concept without impacting the relative comparison between the varying geometric configurations (effects of modifying the aeroshell shape to infer how it will affect the TPS mass).

The TPSSIZER code is used to conduct the TPS sizing for the entry vehicle. The TPS sizing trajectory includes the initial aerocapture phase concatenated with the 1-Sol entry trajectory, with an intermediate cool down period. This cooldown allows the TPS and structure to re-radiate the aerocapture heat pulse and return to the initial pre-entry temperature distribution. Due to the magnitude of the convective and shock-layer heating incurred during aerocapture, Phenolic Impregnated Carbon Ablator (PICA) is selected for windward applications, with Shuttle derived ceramic tile (LI-900) used on the cooler leeward surfaces.

For the baseline 10×30 Ellipsled configuration, the resulting TPS material distribution includes 493.7 m^2 of LI-900 tile and 527.3 m^2 of PICA. Maximum RSS PICA thickness is 14.8 cm, with an average a real thickness of 8.16 cm. Maximum thickness for the LI-900 tile is 3.37 cm, with most of the LI-900 tile at minimum gauge thickness. The TPS windward splitline and thickness distributions are shown in FIG. **7**. Total LI-900 mass is 1170 kg, with an average areal unit mass of 2.37 kg/m^2 and total PICA mass is 12,188 kg, with an average areal unit mass of 23.11 kg/m^2. The net total TPS mass is 13358 kg with an average areal unit mass of 12.63 kg/m^2. This compares with a total TPS mass for the dual-layer concept, used by EDL-SA, of 9,217 kg at an areal unit mass of 8.96 kg/m^2. It should also be noted that the structural concept for the baseline EDL-SA Ellipsled is titanium skin-stringer with an allowable 560° K back-face temperature. By comparison, the POD Ellipsled aeroshell is composite honeycomb with an allowable maximum temperature of 450° K.

10×30 Ellipsled POD Entry Vehicle Mass Estimates.

The entry vehicle total mass was computed using Mass Estimating Relationships (MER's) developed at the major subsystem level for the 40 MT payload Ellipsled configuration, including structures, induced environments, DHCC, auxiliary systems (separation system), RCS, prime power generation and distribution, surface control actuation and RCS propellant. Fixed masses included the lander vehicle and payload. The form of the MER's was derived from Reference [20], with the leading coefficients calibrated to replicate the Mars EDL Architecture No. 1 subsystem weight statement [20]. Mass growth allowance of 15 percent was applied to all dry subsystem masses.

As an example, the aeroshell structural mass is estimated using the unit areal structural mass (UWT_Body$_{REF}$) presented in Reference [20], with correlation parameters derived

16

from the body length/body diameter trade-off study. Additional correlation parameters are applied to reflect variations in entry mass and aero-loading anticipated in the geometry trade/optimization process. The form of the aeroshell structural MER is:

$$UWT\_Body = UWT\_Body_{REF}*(L_B/L_{B\_REF})^{0.967}*(D_B/D_{B\_REF})^{-0.988}$$

$$*(m\_Entry*g_{MAX\_Lat}/(m\_Entry_{REF}*g_{MAX\_REF\_Lat}))_{0.23}$$

L_{B_REF}=30 m

D_{B_REF}=10 m

m_Entry$_{REF}$=110100 kg

$g_{MAX\_REF\_Lat}$=2.5 Earth g's)

UWT_Body$_{REF}$=5.865 kg/m^2

All of the "REF" values are taken from the reference Architecture No. 1 mass statement and associated trajectory. This form of the structural MER will return the reference unit areal mass with all the parameters set equal to the reference values. Within the shape optimization process, as the geometric parameters change, along with the associated change in the trajectories due to changes in the aerodynamic coefficients with the varied shape, the unit areal structural weight will vary to reflect the geometric and trajectory related parameter variations. This process is generally extended to the other major subsystems through the MER formulation (e.g. surface actuation mass, scaled with maximum free-stream dynamic pressure and body flap planform area).

Using the reference values for the Architecture No. 1 Ellipsled as inputs to XWAT, Table 2 compares the XWAT estimated entry mass with the values from Reference [20], as shown in the second column. The third column presents the XWAT mass estimation using the MER's for all subsystem masses. Ideally the subsystem and total masses should agree. However, differences in assumed parameters, slightly different WBS definition and the nonlinear nature of the MER's result in non-zero estimated mass differences. As an example, the maximum lateral g-load during entry is found to be 2.79 g_E's, as compared to the value of 2.5 g_E's used in Reference 19. The net result is the XWAT predicted aeroshell mass of 6129 kg, compared to 5980 kg from Reference [20]. Finally, the overall difference in estimated entry vehicle mass is approximately 1 percent.

The next step in the analysis process replaces the XWAT MER's for body structure and TPS with the integrated COBRA tools discussed above and re-closes the vehicle. The resulting subsystem masses and vehicle total entry mass are presented in column 3 of Table 2. The TPS mass has increased, reflecting the effects of not using the lighter weight dual-layer TPS system used by the EDL-SA baseline configuration. However, some of this mass increase is offset by the lower structural mass with the COBRA vehicle total entry mass being higher by 3,307 kg (3 percent) over the reference vehicle entry mass.

With the calibration of the MER's to reproduce the baseline Mars EDL-SA mass estimate, the XWAT model was integrated into the COBRA environment, with data links established to capture and transmit computed parameters and values to and from the other discipline tools within the design and analysis environment.

17

TABLE 2

Mass Comparisons of COBRA MERs with EDL-SA Predictions

Mass Element	Mars EDL-SA, kg	XWAT MER, kg	XWAT/COBRA, kg
Body Structure	6417	6695	5983
Aeroshell	5980	6129	5417
Body Flap	437	565	565
Induced Environment	16022	16063	20203
Body TPS	9217	9217	13358
Body Flap TPS	390	430	430
Acoustic Blankets	6415	6415	6415
DHCC	228	228	228
Instrumentation	—	13	13
Auxiliary Systems	1598	1598	1598
RCS	4522	4501	4517
Prime Power	—	62	63
Power Conversion/Distribution	302	322	322
Surface Actuation	442	438	454
Contingency	4430	4486	5011
Dry Mass	33962	34405	38433
RCS Propellant	5500	6304	6551
Consumables	23	23	24
Payload	68400	68400	68400
Entry Mass	110100	109133	113407

Aeroshell Shape Optimization Results.

In order for the shape optimization analysis to be performed, it is important that the objective and constraints for the shape optimization be defined to meet the intended mission requirements. For this analysis, the mission is to land 40MT on the surface of Mars using an aerocapture, followed by an entry trajectory as discussed in the preceding. One goal is to minimize the total entry vehicle mass. As discussed in the preceding, we use a multi-objective genetic algorithm (MOGA) approach to perform the shape optimization necessary to achieve the objectives. From our POD trajectory results, it has been determined that a good estimate of the peak heating trajectory point occurs at a Mach number of approximately 32.5 and a dynamic pressure of 0.15 bars. In addition a target L/D ratio of 0.5 was chosen to match the L/D used in the EDL-SA work [19]. From these values, a MOGA optimizer is run to explore the shape parameter space by utilizing the parametric COBRASQ shape code and the CBAERO engineering aerothermo-dynamics tool. This is done by specifying a set of constraints and objectives with a range of shape parameters for the MOGA optimizer to explore.

The constraints for the optimization study are: 1) determine the number of surface shape triangles which violate the AresV launch fairing envelope limits, 2) impose the conditions $\partial Cm/\partial\alpha<0$ and 3) $\partial Cm/\partial\beta<0$. The launch fairing triangle check is used to assure that the vehicle shapes do not violate the launch fairing payload dynamic envelope. The constraints $\partial Cm/\partial\alpha<0$ and $\partial Cm/\partial\beta c<0$ are aerodynamic constraints to assure that the aeroshell shapes are statically stable in the pitch plane (α) and in the yaw plane (β), respectively. The objectives are to minimize the peak total heat flux on the vehicle (Total MaxQdot) and to maximize the drag area (C_DA), which correlates directly with how quickly the vehicle will decelerate through the atmosphere before reaching the supersonic parachute deployment altitude. Here, higher C_DA is desirable.

The initial MOGA analysis results in a Pareto front set of shapes as shown in FIG. 10. Reasonable convergence is seen by the limited change in the Pareto front for 15,000 to 25,000 function evaluations. However, the shapes are found to have very boxy nose shapes, and the flow at the nose has an attachment line, not an attachment point. Utilizing engineering

18

judgment/experience we realized that these features would under-predict the heating on the nose with the engineering models and that a better range of shape design parameter for the MOGA optimizer to explore would provide more realistic heating and better predictive capability from the aerothermal engineering model.

The results of the updated MOGA shape optimization are plotted in FIG. 11. Because any point on the plot in FIG. 9 is a potential solution and the Pareto front includes the solutions that best meet the two objectives there can be multiple solutions. For our purposes the point denoted in FIG. 11 with the open black circle at $C_DA=293$ m^2 and a Total MaxQdot=203 W/cm^2 was chosen as the vehicle shape to assess further in the following sections.

Optimized Shape Comparison with High Fidelity Aero/Aerothermal.

An engineering aerothermal tool has been used to predict the aerodynamics and aeroheating within the MOGA shape optimization process. This approach allows us to evaluate a vast number of shapes and to explore sufficiently the design space. In order to verify the accuracy of the tool for these optimized shapes, we choose a point of the new Pareto front to compare with higher fidelity computations. For this purpose, we use the DPLR aerothermodynamic tools and compare at one point on the Pareto front. The comparison point, denoted in FIG. 11 with the black circle "○," will be referred to as "design14927," because it is the 14,927th design evaluated by the GA. Comparison of the surface pressure, temperatures and convective heating are shown in FIG. 12 for this shape at a Mach number of 32.5, dynamic pressure of 0.114 bar, and angle-of-attack of 56.4 degrees.

As with the earlier 10×30Ellipsled results of FIG. 6, the surface pressure comparison between DPLR and unanchored CBAERO for this "14297 shape" (FIG. 11) show excellent agreement. The unanchored CBAERO heating results appear to be about 10 percent lower than the DPLR real-gas Navier-Stokes results. The anchoring process referred to earlier would normally be performed on the downselected shapes which would provide the heat transfer corrections on the engineering CBAERO model results with a sparse set of DPLR solutions. For the purposes of this current study, the present level of agreement, in the range of anticipated heating uncertainty, is believed to be adequate.

Discussion of the Physics Behind the MOGA Shape Selection.

The advantage in hypersonic aerothermal performance of the optimized body over the baseline body can be understood through examination of FIG. 13A. Both bodies exhibit an attachment line topology along the windward centerline, and it is expected that heating will vary inversely with shock standoff (dn) of the optimized body relative to the baseline body. This greater shock standoff is associated with the larger spanwise radius of curvature. This is confirmed in FIG. 13A, which shows graphs of velocity and temperature profiles normal to the surface as obtained from the DPLR turbulent, real gas Navier-Stokes solutions. These profiles are for comparable locations just forward of the base on the aft-body windward centerline for both the baseline and the optimized body. As can be seen, the shock standoff for the optimized body is approximately 0.85 meters, compared to 0.55 meters for the baseline body. Further, the boundary layer thickness is greater for the optimized body (0.15 m) compared to the boundary layer thickness of the baseline body (0.10 m) at this aft windward centerline location. An additional factor in promoting a thick boundary layer and lower heating for the optimized body is the reduced spanwise streamline divergence associated with a larger spanwise radius of curvature.

19

FIG. **13B** provides additional insight into why the optimized body provides enhanced aerodynamic performance over the baseline body. Consider that the maximum lift of a flat plate in hypersonic flow can be found, using Newtonian methods, at approximately 55 degrees angle of attack (AoA). The surface normal of an arbitrary surface element is a unit length vector expressed as (n_x, n_y, n_z). At a given angle of attack, Newtonian methods will predict a pressure on this surface element proportional to $U*(Sin(AoA)*n_z*n_z+Cos(AoA)*n_x*n_y)$, with a contribution by the surface element to the total lift that is roughly proportional to $Sin(AoA)$ and a contribution of this surface element to the total drag roughly proportional to $Cos(AoA)$. Note that the out-of-pitch-plane component of the surface normal component, n_y, does not contribute to the generation of surface pressure, nor does it contribute to the integrated lift, nor to the integrated drag of the body. Rather, the yaw component n_y of the surface normal is ineffective in contributing to hypersonic aerodynamic performance (with the exception of yaw stability effects). FIG. **13B** contrasts the n_y component for the windward surfaces of the optimized body (Body D=14297), as compared to the baseline body (BaseL=POD), with the region about the centerline for the optimized body having a more extensive area of lower e_y surface normal. This greater extent of lower n_y surface normal about the centerline is related to the larger spanwise radius of curvature for the optimized body as described in connection with that body's lower heating. These rather

simple physical arguments help explain the greater lift, drag and lower heating for the optimized body.

As for the effect of streamlines between the two shapes, the windward aft centerline streamtube for the optimized aeroshell has reduced streamtube divergence when compared to the baseline. This is believed to be related to the spanwise radius of curvature along the attachment line (centerline) for the optimized aeroshell being greater than the curvature of the baseline body which is geometrically related to the yaw component n_y, increasing more slowly as y increases away from the centerline. These geometric and streamtube observations likely contribute to the greater shock standoff and the larger boundary layer thickness, strongest along the windward centerline, for the optimized body relative to the baseline body. COBRA Integrated System Architecture Optimization Results.

In the following sections the results for the integrated system optimization analysis performed within the COBRA environment are discussed. Three optimized aeroshell shapes from the Pareto front in FIG. **14A-14D**, including designs 8459, 14297 and 14888, are selected for an integrated system optimization. This requires performance of optimization for trajectory, structures, and TPS sizing, followed by vehicle closure. Tables 3 and 4 show system optimization results for the three optimized aeroshell architectures compared to our POD architecture.

TABLE 3

Comparison of Integrated System Analysis Optimization Part I									
GA Objectives									
AEROSHELL SHAPES	CDa m²	Max Qdot Total W/cm²	αtrim deg	Swet m²	Aerocapture Peak Q-alpha Pa-deg	Entry Peak Q-alpha Pa-deg	As-Built Structure Mass Kg	RSS TPS Mass Kg	TPS Volume m³	Total Vehicle Mass Kg
10 × 30 POD (Baseline)									
Front View Rear View Left View Bottom View	231	302	51.78	1021	601601	564194	5417	13358	51	113407
14888									
Front View Rear View Left View Bottom View	296	255	56.09	937	555650	530860	6967	8676	34	108745

heat load comparison shows how the aerodynamic effects of

TABLE 4

	Comparison of Integrated System Analysis Optimization Part II									
	GA Objectives									
AEROSHELL SHAPES	CDa m²	Max Qdot Total W/cm²	αtrim deg	Swet m²	Aerocapture Peak Q-alpha Pa-deg	Entry Peak Q-alpha Pa-deg	As-Built Structure Mass Kg	RSS TPS Mass Kg	TPS Volume m³	Total Vehicle Mass Kg
8459										
	261	221	56.90	877	605732	604257	5517	8468	33	106234
14297										
	291	234	56.77	882	567992	542518	6110	7748	30	106088

Integrated Trajectory Optimization Results.

In FIGS. **14A-14D**, trajectory comparisons between the three optimized shapes are compared to the 10×30 Ellipsled POD. Note that the dynamic pressure is reduced with the optimized aeroshell shapes and is attributed to the higher drag coefficient (FIG. **14D**) that these shapes provide which allows them to more efficiently dissipate the energy higher in the atmosphere (FIG. **14A**) as compared to the POD, and results in lower free stream dynamic pressure. leading to lower heating. In addition the optimized shapes also provide higher lift, as shown in FIG. **14C**, which also allows the body to maneuver and to achieve the same end conditions as the POD.

In FIGS. **15A-15B**, the integrated heat load plots and TPS thicknesses for the three optimized shapes are compared with the 10×30 Ellipsled POD. FIG. **15A** is a plot of the reference integrated heat load versus trajectory, based on a referenced one meter nose radius that is used in the COBRA trajectory module optimization to minimize the reference heat load. Although this is only an estimate of the actual heat load experienced by each shape, this approach provides a means by which the trajectory optimization can utilize the vehicles' lift and drag to achieve the trajectory objective. Providing a reference heat load also isolates its impact on the trajectory for configurations, apart from the local surface heating experienced by each aeroshell shape. The result of this reference

the optimized shapes, allow for lower heat load as compared to the baseline 10×30 Ellipsled. This is attributed to the aerodynamic performance of the optimized shapes, shown in FIGS. **14A-14B** which exhibit higher lift and drag and allow these aeroshell shapes to loft higher in the atmospheric while dissipating the same energy needed to reach the 1-SOL orbit or the surface of Mars. This, in turn, keeps the aeroshell at a lower dynamic pressure and helps reduce the vehicle heating. FIG. **15B** shows a more representative integrated heat load of each shape along the trajectory by tracking a nominal peak heat flux point throughout the trajectory. Note that the final integrated heat-load for each of the optimized aeroshells is lower than the integrated heat load of the baseline. This is attributed to the improved trajectories obtained by the higher performing aeroshell shapes, and to the lower heat flux around these optimized aeroshell shapes. Table 5 summarizes maximum values of key trajectory parameters that influence subsystem masses presented below.

23

TABLE 5

Comparison of maximum trajectory parameters

	10X30 POD	14888	8459	14297
Max g_E's	2.81	3.10	2.05	3.08
Max Lateral g_E's	2.74	3.07	2.93	3.01
Max qBAR, pa	11630	9907	10645	10005
Max q-α, pa-deg	602200	555644	605728	568020
Ref. Heat Load, J/cm^2	28055	17105	18944	17283
Max Heat Load, J/cm^2	36639	24010	25648	23729

Integrated Structure Optimization Results.

With the trajectory information obtained for each shape, the peak dynamic pressure loading information is extracted from the ADB (Aerothermal-Database). The pressure loading is used to perform structural optimization to evaluate the aeroshell structural mass to be used in the vehicle closure analysis. The structural stack-up is also passed to the TPS sizing tool. This provides for a consistent structural layout for the TPS sizing analysis to be performed. An unexpected result of coupling these analyses is that the increased structural weight of the optimized shapes, with their flatter windward surfaces, increases the structural thickness stack up on the windward surface, providing additional thermal mass for the TPS where the highest heat load occurs. Further details of this finding are discussed in the following TPS section.

Integrated TPSSIZER Results

At this point the optimized nominal trajectory obtained from POST is used to estimate the integrated heat load from the ADB for each aeroshell shape. FIGS. 16 and 17 show surface contour comparisons of integrated heat load and TPS thickness on the windward side for the three Pareto optimum aeroshell shapes as compared to the POD. Note that there is a significant decrease in the maximum heat load and TPS thickness distribution for each Pareto optimal aeroshell shape as compared to the 10×30 Ellipsled POD.

Integrated Vehicle Sizing

Table 5 presents a comparison of the final mass estimates for the 10×30 POD and the Pareto optimal aeroshell configurations. The structural and TPS masses have been discussed above. The reduction in acoustic blanket mass for the Pareto optimal designs depends upon the reduced wetted area. All other subsystem masses are comparable to the 10×30 POD configuration, with reduction in power generation, conversion & distribution and surface actuation systems attributable to lower trajectory g-loads and to free-stream dynamic pressure which drive the MER's for these subsystems.

Configuration design 14888 has an 11 percent reduction in dry mass compared to the 10×30 POD, while the other two Pareto front designs reduce dry mass by 18 percent. Comparing these other two designs, the 8459 design configuration trades lower structural mass for higher TPS mass, with configuration design 14927 having higher structural mass and lower TPS mass. The sum of the two masses is approximately the same for both designs. Finally, the total vehicle entry mass for the three Pareto optimal designs shows an overall reduction between 4 percent and 6 percent compared to the 10×30 POD. This translates into approximately 4,000-7,000 Kg mass savings that could be used to increase the useful landed payload mass of 40,000 kg by 10-16 percent.

TABLE 6

Comparison of mass statements

Mass Element	10X30 POD, kg	14888	8459	14297
Body Structure	5983	7532	6082	6675
Aeroshell	5417	6967	5517	6110
Body Flap	565	565	565	565
Induced Environment	20203	14996	14407	13722
Body TPS	13358	8676	8468	7748
Body Flap TPS	430	431	41	431
Acoustic Blankets	6415	5889	5509	5543
DHCC	228	228	228	228
Instrumentation	13	13	13	13
Auxiliary Systems	1598	1598	1598	1598
RCS	4517	4495	4459	4457
Prime Power	63	58	58	57
Power Conversion/Distribution	322	267	284	266
Surface Actuation	454	410	409	402
Contingency	5011	4112	4130	4112
Dry Mass	38433	34041	31675	31537
Dry Mass Fraction	.3389	.3130	.2982	.2873
RCS Propellant	6551	6282	6137	6128
Consumables	24	22	22	22
Payload	68400	68400	68400	68400
Entry Mass	113407	108745	106234	106088

Economic Impact of Mission/System Optimization.

The projected increase of 4000 to 7000 kg of useful landed payload mass from the current 40,000 kg projected, may at first be interpreted as a 12-19 percent gain. However, this gain in landed payload is for a fixed launch mass and approximately fixed mission costs. A more realistic perspective on true economic impact of these present methods on National Space policy, is that the extra potential landed payload mass represents additional value from each mission. Where each mission to Mars costs approximately $2 billion per launch (based on MSL), and as much as $20 billion for an Ares V launch [24], the additional landed payload represents an additional economic value of approximately $200 Million per launch.

An alternative interpretation is that, if the comparison is robotic precursor mission versus human exploration mission, requiring landing multiple large payloads on Mars, approximately one out of ten launches could be eliminated to achieve the same total landed payload mass to Mars. Again the total saving become large, given the substantial costs of landing payloads on Mars. This increases the economic viability of such a proposed program. Because the current approach is also applicable to Earth LEO and ISS access, the potential impact on economic viability of private commercial efforts should also be appreciable.

The references cited herein are incorporated by reference in this document.

Application of an integrated Multi-Disciplinary Optimization (MDO) system analysis procedure for a Mars heavy mass entry payload mission has been conducted and is described in this paper. The MDO system analysis procedure utilizes a multi objective genetic algorithm (MOGA) optimization of the entry vehicle's outer mode line (OML) based on a parametric family of aeroshell shapes, and incorporates the thermal protection system (TPS) sizing and structural optimization along with trajectory optimization specific to each aeroshell shape being considered. One goal is to minimize projected total vehicle entry mass for a given desired landed mass, or to maximize projected landed payload for a given launch mass.

The engineering disciplines of aerodynamics, aerothermodynamics, trajectory optimization, structural optimization,

TPS sizing, are incorporated in the MDO procedure by means of either evaluating engineering-fidelity or high-fidelity physics-based analysis codes. All other mass-driven subsystems are represented by Mass Estimating Relations (MERs) to allow for vehicle closure. The MDO system optimization approach is used with system constraints and objectives, including launch vehicle payload fairing, hypersonic aerodynamic stability, such as ballistic coefficient, lift and drag, trajectory down- and cross-range constraints, and aerothermodynamic considerations such as peak heating, and integrated heat load. Two global system objectives are: (1) to choose a shape that minimizes entry mass for a given payload, and (2) to maximize landed payload for a given vehicle entry mass. A point-of-departure (POD) architecture is used to validate and provide a reference point upon which to evaluate the improvements resulting from the MDO system procedure. For the optimized shape selected, a decrease in entry vehicle mass is achieved, which translates into a increase in landed payload of approximately 4000-7000 Kg over the 40,000 Kg useful payload mass being considered.

An additional advantage of the integrated MDO environment is in the clarification of the interaction of disparate discipline experts in mission design by providing a well-defined means by which their expert input is incorporated into the system design analysis, while providing the opportunity for consistent and fair comparison among the various design architectures and options for engineering tradeoffs. This MDO environment also provides automatic archiving of results and assumptions to be used as a basis for later review and/or re-analysis due to changes in mission constraints and/or objectives.

Finally, the projected economic benefit of the optimized architectures found by this MDO process shows that approximately one in ten launches could be eliminated based on the increased predicted landed payload mass translating into an approximate savings of $200 million per launch for a Mars heavy payload mass mission.

Appendix A. The Super-Quadric Equation and Generalizations Thereof.

The super-quadric equation is itself a generalization of a three-dimensional ellipsoid equation, (where all exponents equal 2) and may be written in Cartesian coordinates (x,y,z) in the x-specific form of the standard super-quadric equation,

$$(x/x1)^a+((y/y1)^b+(z/z1)^b)^{a/b}=1, \qquad \text{(A-1a)}$$

where x1, y1 and z1 are the positive semi-axis lengths, a and b are exponents with values greater than 1. With appropriate coordinate rotations, one can obtain either a y-specific or z-specific form of the standard super-quadric equation:

$$(y/y1)^a+((x/x1)^b+(z/z1)^b)^{a/b}=1 \qquad \text{(A-1b)}$$

$$(z/z1)^a+((y/y1)^b+(x/x1)^b)^{a/b}=1 \qquad \text{(A-1c)}$$

In these x-, y-, or z-specific standard super-quadratic equation forms, the semi-axis lengths and exponents are treated as constant.

However, to accomplish a first generalization of the x-specific form, it is possible to express the semi-axis lengths of y1 and z1, and the exponent b is a function of x:

$$(x/x1)^a+\{(y/y1(x))^{b(x)}+(z/z1(x))^{b(x)}\}^{a/b(x)}=1 \qquad \text{(A-2a)}$$

Similarly y-specific and z-specific super-quadric generalizations of the first type can be expressed as

$$(y/y1)^a+\{(x/x1(y))^{b(y)}+(z/z1(y))^{b(y)}\}^{a/b(y)}=1 \qquad \text{(A-2b)}$$

$$(z/z1)^a+\{(y/y1(z))^{b(z)}+(x/x1(z))^{b(z)}\}^{a/b(z)}=1 \qquad \text{(A-2c)}$$

26

The now variable coefficient functions, e.g. $b(x)$, $y1(x)$, etc., should be continuous and the variable exponents should also be constrained to be equal to 1 or greater.

To arrive at another or second generalization form of the super-quadric equation first consider that an yz plane cut at constant x in the range of $[-x1,x1]$ of the x-specific form of the standard super-quadric equation can be made and the resulting curve can be expressed as the x-specific form of the standard super-ellipse equation:

$$(y/y1)^a+(z/z1)^a=1, \qquad \text{(A-3a)}$$

where, as before "a" is a constant greater than 1, and y1 and z1 are constant semi-axis lengths. Likewise, the y-specific and z-specific form of the standard superellipse equation can be expressed as:

$$(x/x1)^a+(z/z1)^a=1, \qquad \text{(A-3b)}$$

$$(y/y1)^a+(x/x1)^a=1, \qquad \text{(A-3c)}$$

A second generalization of the super-quadric equation can now be expressed in x-specific, y-specific and z-specific forms

$$(y/y1(x))^{a(x)}+(z/z1(x))^{a(x)}=1, \qquad \text{(A-4a)}$$

$$(x/x1(y))^{a(y)}+(z/z1(y))^{a(y)}=1, \qquad \text{(A-4b)}$$

$$(y/y1(z))^{a(z)}+(x/x1(z))^{a(z)}=1, \qquad \text{(A-4c)}$$

where the semi-axis and exponents are no longer treated as constants but suitably constrained parameters, themselves functions of x, y or z, giving a greater range of shapes than is otherwise possible. Equations (A-4a), (A-4b), and (A-4c) may be referred to as the x-specific, y-specific and z-specific super-quadric generalizations of the second type, or collectively as either super-elliptic or super-quadric generalizations of the second type.

Note that the standard super-elliptic forms can be derived from the equations for the super-quadric generalizations of the second type, and the standard super-quadric equations forms can be derived from the equations for the super-quadric generalizations of the first type. Thus the standard forms of these equations may be considered to be included as a subset of possible equation in the set of generalized parametric super-quadric or super-elliptic equations, and we may use the known behavior of the standard super-quadric and super-elliptic equations as an intuitive guide to the behavior of the extended forms of these equations.

Appendix B. Computer Code Summaries.

COBRASQ: Given the geometric parameters describing the six sectional shapes for the vehicle, this Code applies C1 continuity at interfaces of adjacent sections to provide a "smooth" surface with no corners or discontinuities. The code generates surface mesh descriptions in either structured plot3d or as unstructured triangulations enabling the use of a small set of geometric parameters to define the vehicle's outer mold line (OML) which provides shapes with a range of aerodynamic and aerothermodynamic properties useful for optimization.

ACVe: Is a parametric geometry code for a low Lift to Drag (L/D) re-entry capsule vehicle shape with enhance performance based on an asymmetric ellipsoidal heatshield shape. Similar to the COBRASQ code, this code generates surface mesh descriptions in either structured plot3d or as unstructured triangulations enabling the use of a small set of geometric parameters to define the vehicle's outer mold line (OML)

ApolloMesher: Is a parametric geometry code based on the Apollo/CEV-type truncated-sphere/torus capsule shape. Similar to the COBRASQ code, this code generates surface mesh descriptions in either structured plot3d or as unstructured triangulations enabling the use of a small set of geometric parameters to define the vehicle's outer mold line (OML)

ProE: Pro Engineer (ProE) is a Commercial CAD tools which provides Integrated, parametric, 3D CAD/CAM/CAE solutions and has been integrated into the Cobra MDO process to provide a similar small set of parametric shape control as the above parametric geometry codes however for more complicated geometries manipulation but limited to unstructured surface geometry triangulations.

CBAERO is an engineering analysis code based on independent panel methods, such as modified Newtonian flow adjacent to a flow-defining surface, along with a surface streamline algorithm and an extensive set of validated engineering correlations to determine surface pressure, convective and radiative heating, shear stress, and boundary layer properties.

DPLR: The Data-Parallel Line Relaxation (DPLR) code is a high-fidelity, physics-based, 3-D real-gas time-dependent Navier-Stokes formulation, including heat and energy transfer. DPLR provides viscous real-gas hypersonic aerodynamics and aerothermodynamic predictions which can be used to anchor the CBAERO aerodynamic database at hypersonic down to high supersonic speeds.

NEQAIR is a high-fidelity radiation code, to give radiation effect results, either in support of or replacing CBAERO data.

LAURA: The Langley Aerothermodynamic Upwind Relaxation Algorithm (LAURA) code is a high-fidelity, physics-based, 3-D real-gas Navier-Stokes formulation, a kin to DPLR providing viscous real-gas hypersonic aerodynamics and aerothermodynamic predictions which can be used to anchor the CBAERO aerodynamic database at hypersonic down to high supersonic speeds.

OVERFLOW: The OVERset grid FLOW (OVERFLOW) solver—is a high-fidelity software package for simulating compressible 3-D perfect-gas time-dependent Navier-Stokes equations using multiple overset structured grids. OVERFLOW provides viscous aerodynamic predictions which can be used to anchor the CBAERO aerodynamic database at low supersonic down to subsonic speeds.

Cart3D: Cart3D is a mid-fidelity, 3-D perfect-gas time-dependent Euler formulation code using 3-D Cartesian grids to provide inviscid aerodynamic predictions which can be used to anchor the CBAERO aerodynamic database at low supersonic down to high transonic speeds.

POST2: a Program to Optimize Simulated Trajectories for a specified atmosphere, including L/D, ballistic coefficients, and peak heating. Constraints on the trajectory flight dynamics, such as gravitational loading on the vehicle are also imposed. This code identifies nominal trajectories for each vehicle under consideration. POST2 is wrapped inside the Cobra MDO environment (discussed in the preceding) to identify input parameters necessary to simulate the aerocapture trajectory and entry trajectory that are part of the analysis and optimization.

TPSSIZER: The Thermal Protection Sizer (TPSSIZER) code is use to predict TPS thicknesses and mass estimates at prescribed surface zone locations on the vehicle shape by computing the maximum temperature and integrated heat load for a set of selected points on the surface of the vehicle based on flying a defined set of trajectories through the aerodynamic database space and meeting specific mission constraints such as maximum TPS bond line temperatures.

FIAT: The Fully Implicit Ablation and Thermal response program (FIAT) simulates one-dimensional transient thermal energy transport in a multilayer stack of thermal protection system (TPS) materials and structure that can ablate from the top surface and decompose in-depth. FIAT is integrated into the Cobra MDO process as through TPSSIZER which calls FIAT for analyzing TPS ablative materials sizing.

SINDA: Analysis software for conduction, convection, and radiation heat transfer material response modeling utilized for analyzing non-ablating TPS materials sizing and is integrated into the Cobra MDO process through TPSSIZER.

MSC NASTRAN: Vehicle structure response code, including normal stress, shear stress, bending stress and other mechanical responses. NASTRAN is integrated into the Cobra MDO process by transferring the surface pressure loading which are extracted either from the CBAERO engineering aerodynamic database or from an anchored aerodynamic database based on the higher fidelity aero/aerodynamic tools to the structure elements assigned for each geometry to perform a structural optimization to minimize the vehicle aeroshell structural mass.

XWAT/XClosure: Provides an estimate of the delivered payload or the entry vehicle mass utilizing mass estimating relationships (MER) which are empirical vehicle mass scaling of subsystems from historical mass distributions for other missions and scaled to the particular vehicle shape parameters selected by the MDO algorithm. XWAT is an XML based C++ application that computes weight/mass of any space vehicle. XWAT can be applied to launch vehicles and to EDL studies.

DAKOTA: The Design Analysis Kit for Optimization and Terascale Applications (DAKOTA) toolkit is a flexible extensible interface between analysis codes and iterative systems analysis methods. DAKOTA contains algorithms for optimization with gradient and nongradient-based methods; uncertainty quantification with sampling, reliability, stochastic expansion, and epistemic methods; parameter estimation with nonlinear least squares methods; and sensitivity/variance analysis with design of experiments and parameter study methods. DAKOTA is integrated into the Cobra MDO process in order to utilizing its Multi-Optimization Genetic Algorithm (MOGA) to simultaneously optimize the vehicle aeroshell shape with respect to aerodynamic and aerothermodynamic objectives in order to then optimized the structural, TPS, and overall entry mass or payload mass from a multidimensional Pareto-Edgeworth optimal front of aeroshell shapes.

The Codes referred to by name in the preceding can be replaced by other equivalent codes. At the minimum, this invention requires use of a COBRASQ code for estimation of vehicle surface geometric parameters, as indicated in Eq. (1) in the preceding, a hydrodynamics code, with or without real gas effects included, an aerothermodynamics code (optionally including heat transfer effects), a structure response code and a trajectory code.

Multi-Disciplinary Computer Code Fidelity			
Discipline	Code Name	Description	Fidelity
Geometry/mesh generation	COBRASQ	Parametric surface tool	Analytic
Aero/Aerothermo	CBAERO	Engineering Aerothermo	Engrg.
Aerothermodynamics Aero/convective heat	DPLR	High fidelity CFD	High
Aerothermo/radiative Heating	NEQAIR	Predict shock radiation vehicle heating	High
Trajectory optimiz.	POST2	Traj. Optimization	Mixed
Ablative/non-ablative	TPSSIZER	1-dim heat	High

-continued

Multi-Disciplinary Computer Code Fidelity			
Discipline	Code Name	Description	Fidelity
TPS analysis		conduction/ TPS analysis	
Mass/volume estimation	XWAT	Mass/volume estimation	Engrg.

Appendix C. Discussion of Flow Charts in FIGS. **18**, **19** and **20**.

The purpose of the Cobra MDO Multi-Discipline Optimization process is to explore the full set of design space to determine if all of the specified mission constraints are met and to perform the required engineering analysis for each considered set members so as to evaluate performance optimization goals and in so doing to establish and fully populate the Pareto-optimal subset. The particular MDO algorithm chosen and details of the MDO process may be accomplished by many approaches known to practitioners of the art. A brute force approach simply evaluates each and every member of the full design space, or of a suitable dense subset, to determine if any particular member meets all constraints and evaluate performance so as to retain only those members which meet the Pareto optimum criterion. However, more efficient MDO algorithms exist and are known to practitioners of the art and are considered to be included by reference. The particular approach described herein is that of the Multi-Objective Genetic Algorithm. Further, the details of any particular flowchart can vary considerably depending on the details of the mission constraints and optimization objectives, and the flowcharts discussed in this Appendix summarize three possible approach. Variations in such a process are known to practitioners of the art and are incorporated by reference.

Design alternatives represented by members of the full design space set that are not members of the Pareto Optimum set produced by the described MDO process, are sub-optimal in some sense and need not be considered further in a design process. It is anticipated, with appropriate assignment of mission constraints and optimization goals, that the Pareto Optimum set will be much reduced in size relative to the full design space. Once found by the process described, the Pareto Optimum set consists only of those design alternatives which may be efficiently considered further in detailed engineering tradeoff studies or by other means invoking detailed human interaction, such as human values and human judgment.

A vector in design space is described by an P-tuple vector $Vj=(v1(j), v2(j), \ldots, vP(j))$, where $j=1, 2, \ldots$ is an index referring to the number of the present iteration, in parameter space, where $v1(j), v2(j) \ldots$ are the COBRASQ shape parameters described elsewhere. Upon evaluation, a candidate vector Vj is considered to be Pareto-Efficient and to be a member of the Pareto-Optimum subset, for a given mission being considered, the member meets all specified mission constraints and, further, in evaluating those performance standards being optimized, that a small variation in parameter space will not lead to a more desirable solution, where a neighboring point, $Vj+\Delta Vj$ is preferred in terms of at least one performance standard being optimized without also being less desirable in at least one other candidate performance parameter being optimized.

FIG. **18** is a general overall flow chart showing a general form of the Cobra MDO process. The inputs to the Cobra MDO process will include (1) the specified full design parameter space, (2) the mission constraints, and (3) the perfor-

mance standards being optimized. The MDO process will include (1) The MDO driver, (2) the COBRASQ shape code, or equivalent, (3) Engineering Analysis codes, such as CBAERO, MSC NASTRAN, POST2, TPSSIZER, XWAT, etc, (4) a Pareto-Optimum subset to be populated, which is the desired output. In step **101**, the system determines if the design space DS is fully explored, based on selected criteria. In step **102**, the MDO driver algorithm selects a candidate shape vector Vj and provides a corresponding set of shape parameters or components $v1, v2, \ldots, vP$ for that candidate vector for the COBRASQ shape code. In step **103**, the COBRASQ shape code generates the candidate vehicle shape as a candidate surface grid. The candidate surface grid is provided by the MDO driver for separate and interacting analyses by the associated engineering analysis codes, including CBAERO (step **104**), POST2 (step **105**), MSC NASTRAN (step **106**), TPSSIZER (step **107**), XWAT (step **108**), etc. and provides communication between these codes as required by each code, in step **109**. The outputs of these engineering analysis codes are optionally expressed as components of a composite shape/engineering vector <Vj,Ej>, in step **110**, where Ej is a vector including the candidate engineering analysis parameters.

For example, the hypersonic aerodynamic performance may be calculated by the CBAERO code for the candidate vehicle shape, which the MDO driver provides for the POST2 code for trajectory optimization. The POST2 code establishes or adopts a candidate trajectory for that candidate shape. The candidate trajectory specific corresponding to the candidate shape is delivered by the MDO driver as a second instantiation of the CBAERO code, and this instantiation evaluates aerothermodynamics and aeroheating heating of the candidate vehicle shape along its candidate trajectory. The CBAERO-POST2 aerothermodynamic-trajectory analysis is preferably optimized to keep the peak heating below a maximum specified threshold value, and to keep integrated heat load below a maximum threshold value. The results of this process are provided to the MDO driver for evaluation in the Pareto-Optimum Determination step. In parallel to the CBAERO-POST2 aerothermodynamic engineering analysis step, a CBAERO-MSC NASTRAN structures process can be conducted which will take the aerodynamic loads experienced by the candidate shape, travelling on its candidate trajectory, and evaluate for suitable structural mass distribution to keep induced stresses on the structure below some specified maximum threshold value(s). Additional analysis may be incorporated in the engineering analysis stage, and the outputs may be provided to the MDO driver. The MDO driver includes, for the candidate shape under consideration, a mission constraint stage, where the shape and engineering analysis outputs (optionally expressed as a candidate composite vector <Vj,Ej>) are evaluated and compared against defined mission constraints to determine if any constraints are violated. (step **111**)

If one or more of these mission constraints is violated, in step **111**, the MDO driver determines, in step **112**, that the candidate shape is not a member of the Pareto Optimum set and returns to the initial step to choose another candidate shape vector V(j+1). If none of the mission constraints is violated, the engineering analysis performance outputs are evaluated against the Pareto Optimization statement, in step **113**, to determine if the candidate shape meets the statement definition for Pareto Optimum membership. If the candidate shape satisfies the Pareto Optimization statement, the candidate vector <Vj,Ej> is added to the Pareto Optimization set, in step **114** If not, the candidate vector is not added to the Pareto Optimization set. Whatever is the conclusion here, the MDO driver will return to the beginning step to select another candidate shape vector V(j+1) and corresponding shape, in step **115**. The process described above is repeated, with the MDO algorithm returning each iteration to the initial step, to continue examining further candidate shape vectors from the full set of design space for possible membership in the Pareto Optimization set until the full set of design parameters is fully explored.

As a further example, FIG. **19** (same as FIG. **5**) is an overall flow chart illustrating another procedure for implementing a Multi-Objective Generic Algorithm (MOGA) for multi-dimensional optimization of various groups of parameters associated with one or more of the 17 computer codes briefly discussed in Appendix B. Only one loop (among many such loops) for one candidate shape is described, with the MDO driver needing to conduct an outer loop so as to examine the full design space. The procedure begins the Parametric Geometry code module **201**, which initially specifies approximately 30 geometric parameters (not all independent) that define the M segments of an aeroshell surface (e.g., M=6) and includes one or more of a COBRASQ code **202**, an ACVe code **203**, an Apollo code **204** and a ProE CAD code **205**. A reference or initial vehicle trajectory is preferably specified, which may be subsequently modified. The Parametric Geometry module **201** communicates with an Aerodynamic/Aeroheating module **206**, which is primarily the CBAERO code, and communicates with a multi objective genetic Algorithm (MOGA) module **207**, which is primarily the DAKOTA code. The CBAERO code relies upon a High Fidelity CFD module **208** that includes one or more of a DPLR code **209**, a LAURA code **210**, a NEQAIR code **211**, an Overflow code **212** and a CART3D code **213**.

The CBAERO code and the DAKOTA codes interact with each other throughout the following procedures. The Parametric Geometry module **201**, the Aerodynamic/Aeroheating module **206** and the MOGA module **207** provide iterative shape optimization, using the MOGA code **207**.

An output from the Aerodynamic/Aeroheating module **206** is received by a Trajectory Optimization module **220** that includes a POST2 code **221**. The Trajectory Optimization code **220** exchanges data with a Structures code **222**, including an MSC NASTRAN code **223**. The Trajectory Optimization module **220** and the Structures module **223** both exchange data with a TPSSIZER module **224**, including one or more of a Fiat code **225**, and a Sinda code **226**. The Structures module **223** and the TPSSIZER module **224** both exchange data with a Weight/Sizing module **227**, which includes one or more of an XWAT code **228** and an XClosure code **229**, and which exchanges data between the Trajectory module **210** and the Structures module **223**. An output of the Weight/Sizing module **225** is received by a Convergence Test module **230**, which determines if the various optimization codes are converging. If the answer to the convergences query is "no," the results are returned to the Trajectory Optimization module **210** and elsewhere for further processing. If the answer to the convergence query is "yes," the results are delivered to a Payload/Entry Vehicle Mass module **231**

FIG. **20** is a flow chart illustrating another alternatively described procedure for implementing a Multi-Objective Generic Algorithm (MOGA) for multi-dimensional optimization of various groups of parameters associated with one or more of the 17 computer codes briefly discussed in Appendix A. Again only one outer loop (among many such loops) is described for one candidate shape. In step **301**, a geometric model of a vehicle aeroshell surface is provided, having M surface segments (M≥1, for example, M=6) of the vehicle surface at selected locations and orientations, with at least one

surface segment being representable mathematically as a super-quadric surface of extended form in terms of a Cartesian coordinates system (x,y,z) as at least one geometric relation, drawn from

$$(x/x1)^a + \{(y/y1)^b + (z/z1)^b\}^{a/b} = 1,$$

and

$$(y/y1)^b + (z/z1)^b = 1,$$

and

$$(x/x1)^a + (y/y1)^a = 1,$$

and

$$((x/x1)^a + (z/z1)^a = 1,$$

where x1, y1 and z1 are positive semi-axis lengths, and y1 and z1 may vary with x, a and b are exponents with values greater than 1, which may vary with x, the x-axis is oriented from back to front along the vehicle surface, and x is measured along a centerline of the vehicle surfaces Each surface segment may involve all three coordinates, x, y and z, or may involve two of these three coordinates, depending upon location and orientation of the segment. Surface segment interfaces between any two adjacent segments are at least C1 continuous.

In step **302**, a selected (initial) trajectory of the vehicle through a selected fluid atmosphere is characterized. In step **303**, at least one fluid flow force that would act upon one or more surface of the vehicle in moving along the selected trajectory, is characterized.

In step **304**, a multi-optimization genetic algorithm (MOGA) is applied to the surface representation of the vehicle: (1) to estimate a lift-to-drag ratio, in a desired range, for the vehicle moving along the selected trajectory, (2) to maximize at least one of (2-i) ratio of landed payload mass to vehicle atmosphere entry mass and (2-ii) distance a fluid flows along the vehicle surface extending in the direction of the x-axis before the fluid separates from the vehicle surface; (3) to minimize at least one of peak heat transfer and integrated heat transfer from the fluid to the vehicle surface at one or more locations on the vehicle; (4) to minimize estimated mass of thermal protection system (TPS) material to be used to prevent at least one of the vehicle surface peak heat transfer and vehicle surface integrated heat transfer from exceeding a selected heat transfer limit value; and (5) to maximize estimated duration of travel of the vehicle along the selected trajectory before transition to turbulent flow occurs on a vehicle windward surface. In step **305**, a vehicle structure, associated with the vehicle surface, is optimized with respect to at least one structural performance parameter for the vehicle. In step **306**, a distribution of vehicle surface thickness is optimized to minimize total material mass of the vehicle surface. In step **307**, the vehicle surface representation is optimized with respect to at least one aerothermodynamic/aeroheating performance parameter for the vehicle. Steps **302**, **303**, **304**, **305**, **306** and/or **307** are optionally iterated upon in a multi-level optimization procedure.

One often begins with a (target) total mass of the (loaded) vehicle and an selected trajectory and iteratively optimizes the groups of parameters in steps **301-307** in order to move closer to the total target mass and to a preferred trajactory. If the computed total mass proves to be too large to reach the target mass, the target mass may be incremented in one or more mass steps Am until the (modified) target mass can be

33

reached by the iterative optimization. Likewise, if the computed total mass is already much smaller than the target mass.

REFERENCES

1 Brown, J. L. "The Effect of Forebody Geometry on Turbulent Heating and Thermal Protection System Sizing for Future Mars Missions Concepts," International Planetary Probe Workshop 4, June, 2006.

2 Wright, Henry, S., Oh, David, Y., Weshelle, Carlos H., Fisher, Jody L., Dyke, R. Eric, Edquist, Karl T., Brown, James L., Justh, Hilary L., Munk, Michelle M., "Mars Aerocapture Sytems Study," NASA TM-2006-214522, November 2006.

3 Garcia, J. A., Brown, J. L., Bowles J. V., Kinney, D. J., and Huynh L. C., "A Parametric Co-Optimization of Lifting Blunt Body Vehicle Concepts for Atmospheric Entry", 21st International Conference on Parallel Computational Fluid Dynamics, May 18-22, 2009, Moffett Field, Calif.

4 Brown, J. L., Garcia, J. A., Kinney, D. K., "An Asymmetric Capsule Vehicle Geometry Study for CEV", 45th AIAA Aerospace Sciences Meeting and Exhibit, January 2007, Nevada.

5 Brown, J. L., Garcia, J. A., Prahbu, D. K., NASA, Moffett Field, Calif. U.S. Pat. No. 7,431,242 B1 for "Re-Entry Vehicle Shape for Enhanced Performance", issued 7 Oct. 2008.

6 Kinney D., "Aero-Thermodynamics for Conceptual Design," AIAA-2004-31, 42nd AIAA Aerospace Sciences Meeting and Exhibit, Reno Nev., January 2004.

7 Wright, M. J., Candler, G., and Bose, D., "Data-Parallel Line Relaxation Method for the Navier-Stokes Equations," AIAA J., Vol. 36, No. 9, 1998, pp. 1603-1609.

8 Whiting, E. E., Park, C, Liu, Y, Arnold, J 0, and Paterson, J A, "NEQAIR96, Nonequilibrium and Equilibrium Radiative Transport and Spectra Program: User's Manual," NASA RP-1389, December 1996.

9 Kinney D., "Aerothermal Anchoring of CBAERO Using High Fidelity CFD," AIAA-2007-0608, 45th AIAA Aerospace Sciences Meeting and Exhibit, Reno Nev., January 2007.

10 G. L. Brauer, et al, "Capabilities and Applications of the program to Optimize Simulated Trajectories (POST)," NASA CR-2770, February 1977.

11 MSC. Nastran V2008.0 (Intel Windows .NET 5.2), MSC. Software Corporation, Santa Ana, Calif. URL: http://www.mscsoftware.com/Products/Default.aspx

12 McGuire M. K., Bowles J., Yang L., Kinney D., Roberts C., "TPS Selection & Sizing Tool Implemented in an Advanced Engineering Environment," AIAA-2004-342, 42nd AIAA Aerospace Sciences Meeting and Exhibit

13 Chen, Y.-K., and Milos, F. S., "Ablation and Thermal Analysis Program for Spacecraft Heatshield Analysis," J. Spacecraft and Rockets, vol. 36, No. 3, 1999, pp. 475-483.

14 CEV Thermal Protection System (TPS) Margin Management Plan ID: C-TPSA-A-DOC-7005.

15 X. Jiang, P. Gage, J. C. Vander Kam, M. Qu, "Weights Analysis of Space Launch Vehicles in an Advanced Engineering Environment", 10th AIAA/ISSMO Multidisciplinary Analysis and Optimization Conference 2004.

16 Eldred, M. S., Brown, S. L., Adams, B. M., Dunlavy, D. M., Gay, D. M., Swiler, L. P., Giunta, A. A., Hart, W. E., Watson, J.-P., Eddy, J. P., Griffin, J. D., Hough, P. D., Kolda, T. G., Martinez-Canales, M. L. and Williams, P. J., "DAKOTA, A Multilevel Parallel Object-Oriented Framework for Design Optimization, Parameter Estimation, Uncertainty Quantification, and Sensitivity Analysis: Version 4.0 Users Manual," Sandia Technical Report SAND2006-6337, October 2006. Updated September 2007 (Version 4.1) and November 2008 (Version 4.2).

17 Goldberg, D. E., "Genetic Algorithms in Search, Optimization and Machine Learning," Addison-Wesley, Reading, Mass., 59-88, 1989.

18 Davis, L., "Handbook of Genetic Algorithms," Van Nostrand Reinhold, New York, 1991.

19 "Entry, Descent and Landing Systems Analysis (EDL-SA) for High Mass Exploration and Science Mars Mission Systems", Year 1 Report Document No.: EDLSA-002rev1, 4 December, 2009 (NASA TM to be published) and communications with key EDL-SA team members.

20 Bowles, J. V., "Conceptual Studies Activities", Proceedings of the Second National Aerospace Plane Symposium, Applied Physics Laboratory, Laurel, Md. November 1986.

34

What is claimed is:

1. A method for simultaneously optimizing performance of a baseline lifting blunt body vehicle to an optimized lifting blunt body vehicle that moves through a fluid medium at speeds greater than the speed of sound through the fluid, the method comprising:

providing a computer and computer code that is programmed:

(1) to provide a geometric model of a vehicle aeroshell surface of the baseline lifting blunt body vehicle having M surface segments ($M \geq 1$) of the vehicle surface at selected locations and orientations, with at least one surface segment being representable mathematically as a super-quadric surface with an associated candidate shape vector V including N geometric parameters ($N \geq 5$) that describe the super-quadric surface in terms of a Cartesian coordinates system (x,y,z) as at least one geometric relation, drawn from

$$(x/x1)^a + \{(y/y1)^b + (z/z1)^b\}^{a/b} = 1$$

and

$$(y/y1)^b + (z/z1)^b = 1$$

and

$$(x/x1)^a + (y/y1)^a = 1$$

and

$$((x-x0)/x1)^a + (z/z1)^a = 1,$$

where x1, y1 and z1 are positive semi-axis lengths, and y1 and z1 may vary with x, a and b are exponents with values greater than 1, which may vary with x, the x-axis is oriented from back to front along the vehicle surface, and (x0,0,0) is a selected origin for the vehicle planar section on a centerline of the vehicle surface, where each section may involve all three coordinates, x, y and z, or may involve two of these three coordinates, depending upon location and orientation of the planar section, and where interfaces between any two adjacent surface segments are at least C1 continuous;

(2) to provide a candidate vehicle trajectory that the vehicle is postulated to follow through a selected fluid atmosphere;

(3) to provide a candidate vehicle structure mass distribution for the vehicle;

(4) to provide a candidate distribution of thermal protection system (TPS) mass on the vehicle;

(5) to analyze a vehicle-fluid interaction between the vehicle structure, the candidate structure mass distribu-

tion and candidate TPS mass distribution, traveling along the candidate trajectory, and the fluid atmosphere;

(6) to analyze structural responses of the vehicle, traveling along the candidate trajectory,

(7) to compute at least one vehicle performance parameter associated with a combination of the candidate shape vector V, the candidate vehicle trajectory, the candidate structure mass distribution and candidate TPS mass distribution, traveling along the candidate trajectory;

(8) to provide a Pareto Optimum set, which may initially be an empty set, of vehicle performance values representing performance of at least one preceding choice of candidate shape vector V, candidate vehicle trajectory, candidate structure mass distribution, and candidate TPS mass distribution as the vehicle moves along a corresponding preceding candidate trajectory in the fluid atmosphere, where the Pareto Optimum set includes only performance values that equal or exceed a specified Pareto threshold value;

(9) to determine if the at least one vehicle performance parameter satisfies a specified set of constraints associated with flight of the vehicle through the fluid atmosphere;

(10) where at least one of the set of constraints in not satisfied, to return to step (1) and to repeat steps (1)-(9);

(11) where all of the constraints in the set are satisfied, to compare the at least one candidate vehicle performance parameter for the candidate shape vector V, combined with a candidate engineering performance vector E including the candidate vehicle trajectory, the candidate structure mass distribution, and the candidate TPS mass distribution with a corresponding performance parameter for each of the Pareto Optimum set of performance values

(12) when the candidate vehicle performance parameter is not at least equal to the Pareto threshold value, to return to the step (1) and to repeat steps (1)-(9); and

(13) when the candidate vehicle performance parameter is at least equal to the Pareto threshold value, to add the vehicle performance parameter and the associated candidate shape vector V and the candidate engineering performance vector E to the Pareto Optimum set, and to return to step (1) at least once and to repeat steps (1)-(12) at least once,

whereby using the computer and computer code, the baseline lifting blunt body vehicle is optimized based on at least one vehicle performance parameter to thereby determine the optimized lifting blunt body vehicle.

2. The method of claim 1, further comprising choosing at least one of said at least six surface segments of said vehicle surface to be at least one of an upper Nose section and a lower Nose section, described by said geometric relation

$$(x/x1)^a\{(y/y1)^b+(z/z1)^b\}^{a/b}=1.$$

3. The method of claim 1, further comprising choosing at least one of said at least six surface segments of said vehicle surface to be mid-body Base Rib section, oriented substantially perpendicular to said x-axis and described by said geometric relation

$$(y/y1)^b+(z/z1)^b=1,$$

and at least one of said semi-length values, y1 and z1, is a specified function of said coordinate x.

4. The method of claim 1, further comprising choosing at least one of said at least six surface segments of said vehicle surface to be at least one of an upper Aft-body section and a lower Aft-body section, described by said geometric relation

$$(x/x1)^a+\{(y/y1)^b+(z/z1)^b\}^{a/b}=1,$$

and said semi-length values, y1 and z1, and the exponent b are specified functions of said coordinate x.

5. The method of claim 1, further comprising choosing at least one of said at least six surface segments of said vehicle surface to comprise at least one of a lower Keel line and an upper Keel line, oriented parallel to an xz-plane and described by said geometric relation

$$(x/x1)^a+\{(y/y1)^b+(z/z1)^b\}^{a/b}=1.$$

where at least one of y1 and z1 is a specified function of said coordinate x.

6. The method of claim 1, further comprising choosing at least one of said at least six surface segments of said vehicle surface to comprise at least one of a forward Water line and an aft Water line, oriented parallel to an xy-plane and described by said geometric relation

$$((x-x0)/x1)^a+(y/y1)^b=1$$

where at least one of x1 and y1 is a specified function of said coordinate x and said exponent b is a specified function of x, b(x).

7. The method of claim 6, further comprising choosing said exponent b(x) for said aft Water line to vary linearly with said coordinate x.

8. The method of claim 6, further comprising choosing said exponent b(x) for said aft Water line as a spline fit over a selected interval of said coordinate x.

9. The method of claim 1, further comprising choosing said desired range of said lift-to-drag ratio for said vehicle to be 0.3-0.5.

10. The method of claim 1, further comprising choosing said TPS material to be PICA.

11. A method for simultaneously optimizing performance of a baseline lifting blunt body vehicle to an optimized lifting blunt body vehicle that moves through a fluid medium at speeds greater than the speed of sound through the fluid, the method comprising:

providing a computer and computer code that is programmed:

(1) to provide a geometric model of a vehicle aeroshell surface of the baseline lifting blunt body vehicle having M surface segments (M≥1) of the vehicle surface at selected locations and orientations, with at least one surface segment being representable mathematically as a super-quadric surface with an associated candidate shape vector V including N geometric shape parameters (N≥5) that describe the super-quadric surface in terms of a Cartesian coordinates system (x,y,z) as at least one geometric relation, drawn from

$$(x/x1)^a+\{(y/y1)^b+(z/z1)^b\}^{a/b}=1$$

and

$$(y/y1)^b+(z/z1)^b=1$$

and

$$(x/x1)^a+(y/y1)^a=1$$

and

$$((x-x0)/x1)^a+(z/z1)^a=1,$$

where x1, y1 and z1 are positive semi-axis lengths, and y1 and z1 may vary with x, a and b are exponents with values greater than 1, which may vary with x, the x-axis is oriented from back to front along the vehicle surface, and (x0,0,0) is a

37

selected origin for the vehicle planar section on a centerline of the vehicle surface, where each section may involve all three coordinates, x, y and z, or may involve two of these three coordinates, depending upon location and orientation of the planar section, and where interfaces between any two adjacent surface segments are at least C1 continuous;

(2) to provide a characterization of a selected trajectory of the vehicle through a selected fluid atmosphere;

(3) to provide a characterization of aerodynamics and aero-heating in non-equilibrium air, based on computer fluid dynamics (CFD) of at least one surface segment of the vehicle as the vehicle moves along the selected trajectory;

(4) to estimate forces on the vehicle structure that arise in response to the CFD forces as the vehicle moves along the desired trajectory;

(5) to optimize the forces on the vehicle structure to achieve at least one of the following: (i) a peak force or stress on the vehicle structure is no greater than a first threshold value, and (ii) an integrated value of a force or stress on a portion of the vehicle surface is no greater than a second threshold value;

(5) to optimize mass distribution of thermal protection materials on the vehicle surface in order to achieve at least one of the following objectives: (i) peak heating at a selected location on the vehicle surface is no greater than a third threshold value and (ii) integrated heating of a selected portion of the vehicle surface is no greater than a fourth threshold value;

(6) to optimize vehicle surface mass so that total vehicle surface mass is no greater than a fifth threshold value; and

(7) to optimize choice of the geometric parameters to achieve at least one of the optimizations in steps (4) and (5),

whereby using the computer and computer code, the baseline lifting blunt body vehicle is optimized based on at least the mass distribution of thermal protection materials to thereby determine the optimized lifting blunt body vehicle.

12. The method of claim **11**, further comprising choosing at least one of said at least six surface segments of said vehicle surface to be at least one of an upper Nose section and a lower Nose section, described by said geometric relation

$$(x/x1)^a+\{(y/y1)^b+(z/z1)^b\}^{a/b}=1.$$

13. The method of claim **11**, further comprising choosing at least one of said at least six surface segments of said vehicle surface to be mid-body Base Rib section, oriented substantially perpendicular to said x-axis and described by said geometric relation

$$(y/y1)^b+(z/z1)^b=1,$$

and at least one of said semi-length values, y1 and z1, is a specified function of said coordinate x.

14. The method of claim **11**, further comprising choosing at least one of said at least six surface segments of said vehicle surface to be at least one of an upper Aft-body section and a lower Aft-body section, described by said geometric relation

$$(x/x1)^a+\{(y/y1)^b+(z/z1)^b\}^{a/b}=1,$$

and said semi-length values, y1 and z1, and the exponent b are specified functions of said coordinate x.

15. The method of claim **11**, further comprising choosing at least one of said at least six surface segments of said vehicle surface to comprise at least one of a lower Keel line and an upper Keel line, oriented parallel to an xz-plane and described by said geometric relation

38

$$(x/x1)^a+\{(y/y1)^b+(z/z1)^b\}^{a/b}=1,$$

where at least one of y1 and z1 is a specified function of said coordinate x.

16. The method of claim **11**, further comprising choosing at least one of said at least six surface segments of said vehicle surface to comprise at least one of a forward Water line and an aft Water line, oriented parallel to an xy-plane and described by said geometric relation

$$((x-x0)/x1)^a+(y/y1)^b=1$$

where at least one of x1 and y1 is a specified function of said coordinate x and said exponent b is a specified function of x, b(x).

17. The method of claim **16**, further comprising choosing said exponent b(x) for said aft Water line to vary linearly with said coordinate x.

18. The method of claim **16**, further comprising choosing said exponent b(x) for said aft Water line as a spline fit over a selected interval of said coordinate x.

19. The method of claim **11**, further comprising choosing said desired range of said lift-to-drag ratio for said vehicle to be 0.3-0.5.

20. The method of claim **1**, further comprising choosing said TPS material to be PICA.

21. A method for simultaneously optimizing performance of a baseline lifting blunt body vehicle to an optimized lifting blunt body vehicle that moves through a fluid medium at speeds greater than the speed of sound through the fluid, the method comprising:

providing a computer and computer code that is programmed:

(1) to provide a geometric model of a vehicle aeroshell surface of the baseline lifting blunt body vehicle having M surface segments (M≥1) of the vehicle surface at selected locations and orientations, with at least one surface segment being representable mathematically as a super-quadric surface with an associated candidate shape vector V including N geometric shape parameters (N≥5) that describe the super-quadric surface in terms of a Cartesian coordinates system (x,y,z) as at least one geometric relation, drawn from

$$(x/x1)^a+\{(y/y1)^b+(z/z1)^b\}^{a/b}=1$$

and

$$(y/y1)^b+(z/z1)^b=1$$

and

$$(x/x1)^a+(y/y1)^a=1$$

and

$$((x-x0)/x1)^a+(z/z1)^a=1,$$

where x1, y1 and z1 are positive semi-axis lengths, and y1 and z1 may vary with x, a and b are exponents with values greater than 1, which may vary with x, the x-axis is oriented from back to front along the vehicle surface, and (x0,0,0) is a selected origin for the vehicle planar section on a centerline of the vehicle surface, where each section may involve all three coordinates, x, y and z, or may involve two of these three coordinates, depending upon location and orientation of the planar section, and where interfaces between any two adjacent surface segments are at least C1 continuous;

(2) to provide a characterization of a selected trajectory of the vehicle through a selected fluid atmosphere;

(3) to estimate at least one fluid flow force that would act upon one or more surface of the vehicle in moving along the selected trajectory;

(4) to apply a multi-optimization genetic algorithm (MOGA) to the surface representation of the vehicle: (1) to estimate a lift-to-drag ratio, in a desired range, for the vehicle moving along the selected trajectory, (2) to maximize at least one of (2-i) ratio of landed payload mass to vehicle atmosphere entry mass and (2-ii) distance a fluid flows along the vehicle surface extending in the direction of the x-axis before the fluid separates from the vehicle surface; (3) to minimize at least one of peak heat transfer and integrated heat transfer from the fluid to the vehicle surface at one or more locations on the vehicle; (4) to minimize estimated mass of thermal protection system (TPS) material to be used to prevent at least one of the vehicle surface peak heat transfer and vehicle surface integrated heat transfer from exceeding a selected heat transfer limit value; and (5) to maximize estimated duration of travel of the vehicle along the selected trajectory before transition to turbulent flow occurs on a vehicle windward surface,

(5) to optimize a distribution of vehicle surface thickness to minimize total material mass of the vehicle surface; and,

(6) to optimize the vehicle surface representation with respect to at least one aerothermodynamic performance parameter for the vehicle; and

(7) to optimize a distribution of vehicle surface thickness to minimize total material mass of the vehicle surface,

whereby using the computer and computer code, the baseline lifting blunt body vehicle is optimized based on at least vehicle surface thickness to thereby determine the optimized lifting blunt body vehicle.

22. The method of claim 21, further comprising choosing at least one of said at least six surface segments of said vehicle surface to be at least one of an upper Nose section and a lower Nose section, described by said geometric relation

$$(x/x1)^a+\{(y/y1)^b+(z/z1)^b\}^{a/b}=1.$$

23. The method of claim 21, further comprising choosing at least one of said at least six surface segments of said vehicle surface to be mid-body Base Rib section, oriented substantially perpendicular to said x-axis and described by said geometric relation

$$(y/y1)^b+(z/z1)^b=1,$$

and at least one of said semi-length values, y1 and z1, is a specified function of said coordinate x.

24. The method of claim 21, further comprising choosing at least one of said at least six surface segments of said vehicle surface to be at least one of an upper Aft-body section and a lower Aft-body section, described by said geometric relation

$$(x/x1)^a+\{(y/y1)^b+(z/z1)^b\}^{a/b}=1,$$

and said semi-length values, y1 and z1, and the exponent b are specified functions of said coordinate x.

25. The method of claim 21, further comprising choosing at least one of said at least six surface segments of said vehicle surface to comprise at least one of a lower Keel line and an upper Keel line, oriented parallel to an xz-plane and described by said geometric relation

$$(x/x1)^a+\{(y/y1)^b+(z/z1)^b\}^{a/b}=1.$$

where at least one of y1 and z1 is a specified function of said coordinate x.

26. The method of claim 21, further comprising choosing at least one of said at least six surface segments of said vehicle surface to comprise at least one of a forward Water line and an aft Water line, oriented parallel to an xy-plane and described by said geometric relation

$$((x-x0)/x1)^a(y/y1)^b=1$$

where at least one of x1 and y1 is a specified function of said coordinate x and said exponent b is a specified function of x, b(x).

27. The method of claim 26, further comprising choosing said exponent b(x) for said aft Water line to vary linearly with said coordinate x.

28. The method of claim 26, further comprising choosing said exponent b(x) for said aft Water line as a spline fit over a selected interval of said coordinate x.

29. The method of claim 21, further comprising choosing said desired range of said lift-to-drag ratio for said vehicle to be 0.3-0.5.

30. The method of claim 21, further comprising choosing said TPS material to be PICA.

* * * * *

US008408707B1

(12) **United States Patent**
Watson et al.

(10) Patent No.: **US 8,408,707 B1**
(45) Date of Patent: **Apr. 2, 2013**

(54) **PREDICTION OF VISUAL ACUITY FROM WAVEFRONT ABERRATIONS**

(75) Inventors: **Andrew B. Watson**, Los Gatos, CA (US); **Albert J. Ahumada**, Mountain View, CA (US)

(73) Assignee: **The United States of America as Represented by the Administrator of the National Aeronautics and Space Administration (NASA)**, Washington, DC (US)

(*) Notice: Subject to any disclaimer, the term of this patent is extended or adjusted under 35 U.S.C. 154(b) by 37 days.

(21) Appl. No.: **12/428,441**

(22) Filed: **Apr. 22, 2009**

(51) Int. Cl.
A61B 3/00 (2006.01)
A61B 3/02 (2006.01)

(52) **U.S. Cl.** **351/246**; 351/239; 351/241

(58) **Field of Classification Search** 351/239, 351/241, 246
See application file for complete search history.

(56) **References Cited**

U.S. PATENT DOCUMENTS

3,905,688	A	9/1975	Decker et al.
4,239,351	A	12/1980	Williams et al.
5,121,981	A	6/1992	Waltuck et al.
5,309,185	A	5/1994	Harper et al.
6,142,631	A	11/2000	Murdoch et al.
7,470,026	B2 *	12/2008	Kaido et al. 351/223

OTHER PUBLICATIONS

Cheng, et al., Predicting subjective judgment of best focus with objective image quality metrics, Journal of Vision, Apr. 23, 2004, 310-321, 4, http://journalofvision.org/4/4/7/, 2004 ARVO.
Guirao, et al., A Method to Predict Refractive Errors from Wave Aberration Data, Optometry and Vision Science, Jan. 2003, 36-42, 80-1, 2003 American Academy of Optometry.
Marsack, et al., Metrics of optical quality derived from wave aberrations predict visual performance, Journal of Vision, Apr. 23, 2004, 322-328, 4, http://journalofvision.org/4/4/8/, ARVO 2004.
Thibos, et al., Accuracy and precision of objective refraction from wavefront abberations, Journal of Vision, Apr. 23, 2004, 329-351, 4, http://journalofvision.org/4/4/9/, 2004 ARVO.
Dalimier, et al., Use of a customized vision model to analyze the effects of higher-order ocular aberrations and neural filtering on contrast threshold performance, J. Opt. Soc. Am. A, Jul. 23, 2008, 2078-2086, 25-8.
Nestares, et al., Bayesian Model of Snellen Visual Acuity, J. Opt. Soc. Am. A, Jul. 2003, 1371-1381, 20-7, 2003 Optical Society of America.
Applegate, et al., Metrics of retinal image quality predict visual performance in eyes with 20/17 or better acuity, Optom. Vision Sci., Sep. 2006, 635-640, 83, 2006 American Academy of Optometry.

* cited by examiner

Primary Examiner — Jack Dinh
(74) *Attorney, Agent, or Firm* — John F. Schipper; Robert M. Padilla; Christopher J. Menke

(57) **ABSTRACT**

A method for generating a visual acuity metric, based on wavefront aberrations (WFAs), associated with a test subject and representing classes of imperfections, such as defocus, astigmatism, coma and spherical aberrations, of the subject's visual system. The metric allows choices of different image template, can predict acuity for different target probabilities, can incorporate different and possibly subject-specific neural transfer functions, can predict acuity for different subject templates, and incorporates a model of the optotype identification task.

6 Claims, 3 Drawing Sheets

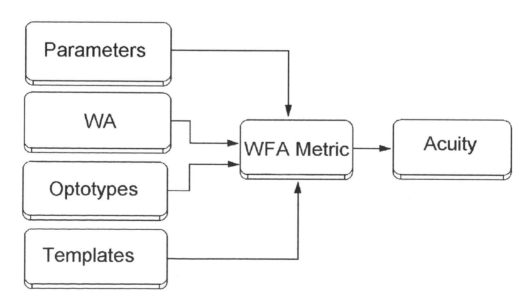

540

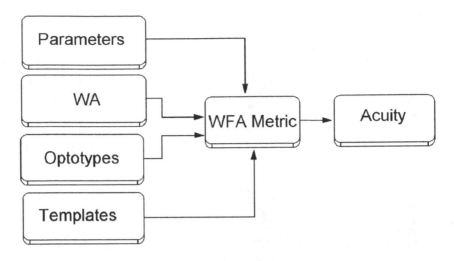

FIG. 1

CDHKNORSVZ

FIG. 2

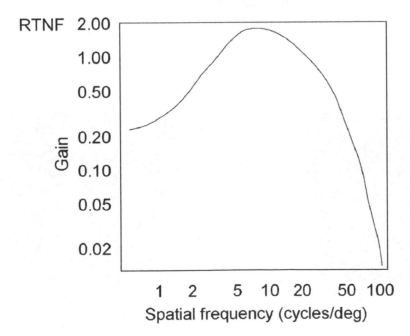

FIG. 4

541

Pupil Aperture

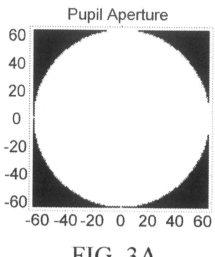

FIG. 3A

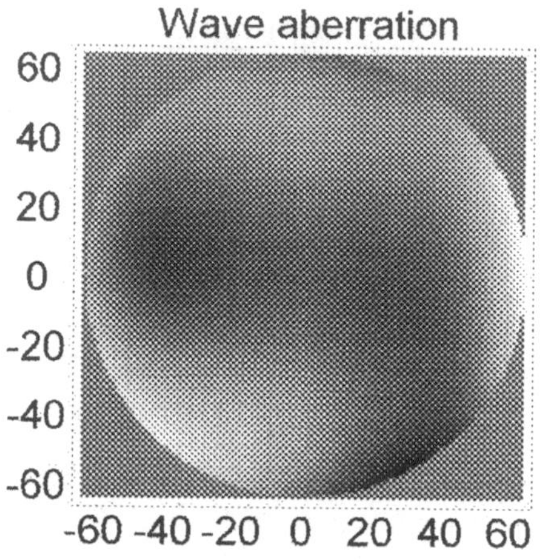

Wave aberration

FIG. 3B

Generalized pupil

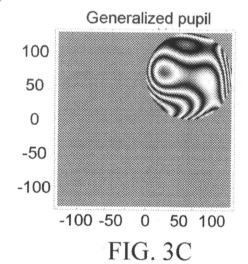

FIG. 3C

PSF

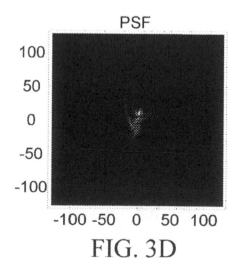

FIG. 3D

OTF

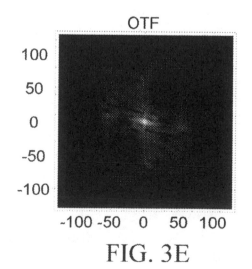

FIG. 3E

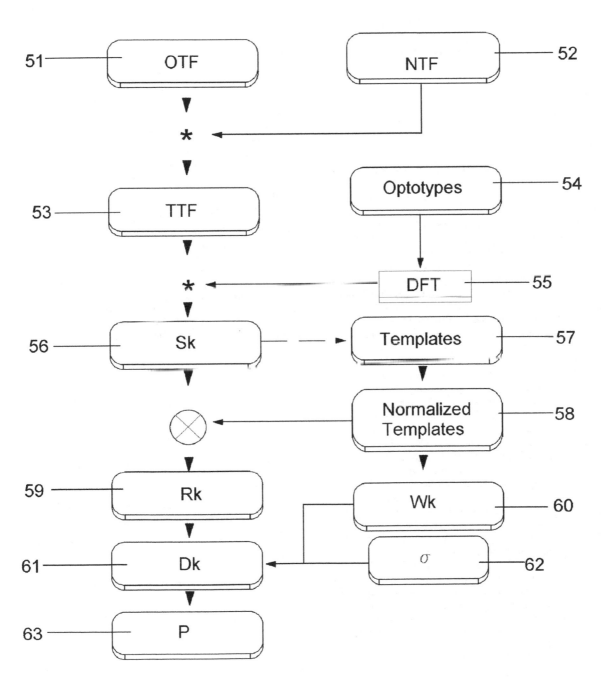

FIG. 5

543

1

PREDICTION OF VISUAL ACUITY FROM WAVEFRONT ABERRATIONS

ORIGIN OF THE INVENTION

This invention was made by one or more employees of the U.S. government. The U.S. government has the right to make, use and/or sell the invention described herein without payment of compensation, including but not limited to payment of royalties.

FIELD OF THE INVENTION

This invention relates to visual acuity of a human or other animal, based on wavefront aberrations associated with the animal's visual imaging system.

BACKGROUND OF THE INVENTION

It is now possible to routinely measure the monochromatic aberrations of the human eye. However, one cannot yet measure the visual acuity that will result from a given set of wavefront aberrations. One reason to seek a prediction of acuity from aberrations is the possibility of automated objective measurement of visual acuity, and of automated prescription of sphero-cylindrical corrections. However, it has been shown that correcting the spherical and cylindrical components of the aberrations (equivalent to minimizing the RMS error of the wavefront) does not provide best acuity. Thus these automated procedures must await a more sophisticated metric that can predict acuity from an arbitrary set of aberrations.

In the last decade there has been a revolution in measurement and treatment of visual optical defects. This revolution has included the development of aberrometers simple enough to be used in the clinic, refinement of methods of laser surgery for optical correction, and development of various optical implants, notably intra-ocular lenses (IOL). In all of these, measurement and interpretation of wavefront aberrations (WFAs) has played an important role. They are a simple and comprehensive way of describing the state of the optical system. In spite of this, there is at present no accepted, reliable way of converting WFAs to visual acuity, which is a standard measure of quality of vision. The WFA Metric allows calculation of visual acuity from wavefront aberrations.

What is needed is an approach, including one or more metrics, that allows a prediction of visual acuity, for a human or other animal, based on estimated wavefront aberrations (WFAs) measured or otherwise determined for the test subject. Preferably, the approach should allow acuity predictions for different optotypes, such as Sloan letters, Snellen e's, Landolt C's, Lea symbols, Chinese or Japanese characters and others. Preferably, the approach should permit incorporation of different, possibly subject-specific, neural transfer functions.

SUMMARY OF THE INVENTION

These needs are met by the invention, which develops and applies an optical-based and neural-based metric that allows prediction of visual acuity of the subject. For a given choice of an optotype set (e.g., Sloan letters), an optical transfer function OTF(x,y) is generated, using Zernike polynomials and the associated Zernike coefficients and a specification of a pupil aperture image PA(x,y) for two dimensional coordi-

nates (x,y) for the subject. A generalized pupil image and associated point spread function PSF(x,y) is computed, from which an OTF is computed.

A neural transfer function NTF(x,y) is specified, and a total transfer function TTF(x,y) is computed as a product of the OTF and the NTF. A proportion correct function P(k) is estimated from the neural images and a noise value, using one of three or more methods for such estimation. A probability criterion P(target) for measurement of visual acuity is specified, normally between 0.5 and 0.8. A numerical procedure returns a final index value j (final), which is converted to an estimate of acuity using a standard logMAR calculation. The output of the logMAR computation is a WFA metric that provides an estimate of visual acuity for the subject.

The metric(s) developed here is designed to predict symbol acuity from wavefront aberrations. One embodiment of the metric relies on Monte Carlo simulations of a decision process and relies on an ideal observer, limited by optics, neural filtering, and neural noise. A second metric is a deterministic calculation involving optics, symbols, and a hypothetical neural contrast sensitivity function CSF.

A WFA Metric is an algorithm for estimating the visual acuity of an individual with a particular set of visual wavefront aberrations (WFAs). The WFAs represent arbitrary imperfections in an optical system, and can include low order aberrations, such as defocus and astigmatism, as well as high order aberrations, such as coma and spherical aberration. WFAs can now be measured routinely with an instrument called an aberrometer. In modern practice, the WFAs are represented as a sum of Zernike polynomials Z(x,y), each multiplied by a Zernike coefficient. A typical measurement on the eye of a subject will consist of a list of about 16 numbers, which are the coefficients of the polynomials. The WFA Metric converts the list of numbers into an estimate of the visual acuity of the subject. If changes are planned to the WFA of the subject (through surgery or optical aids) the predicted change in visual acuity can be calculated.

BRIEF DESCRIPTION OF THE DRAWINGS

FIG. 1 illustrates an embodiment of a structure for computation of a WFA metric according to the invention.

FIG. 2 illustrates the ten Sloan letters, expressed in a sans serif font, that provide one of the optotype sets that can be used with the invention.

FIGS. 3A-3E illustrate steps in creation of the OTF.

FIG. 4 graphically illustrates a representative radial neural transfer function.

FIG. 5 is an embodiment of a procedure for evaluation of a probability correct index for one size optotype.

DESCRIPTION OF THE INVENTION

0. Notation and Terminology

In this presentation, an "image" refers to a finite discrete digital image represented by a two-dimensional array of integers or real numbers. It has a width and height measured in pixels. Where the size is specified it will be given as a list {rows,columns}. The image has a resolution measured in pixels/degree. The pixel indices of the image are x (columns) and y (rows). Images will usually be an even number of pixels wide and tall. If the image size is {2h,2h}, then the indices x and y each follow the sequence {−h, ..., 0, ..., −h−1}. This places the origin of the image at the center. An image may be written with explicit row and column arguments A(x,y), or without the coordinates as A.

3

In this presentation, a dft refers to a two-dimensional finite discrete digital array of complex numbers representing a Discrete Fourier Transform (DFT). It has a width and height measured in pixels. Where the size is specified it will be given as a list {rows,columns}. A dft has a resolution measured in pixels/cycle/degree. The pixel indices of the dft are a (columns) and v (rows). Dfts will usually be an even number of pixels wide and tall. If the dft size is {2h,2h}, then the indices u and v each follow the sequence {0, . . . , h–1, –h . . . , --1}. This places the origin of the dft at the first pixel. This is the conventional ordering of indices in the output of the Fast Fourier Transform (FFT) operator. The FFT is a particular algorithm for implementation of the DFT. In the body of this document we refer to the DFT, but this will usually be implemented by the FFT.

In this presentation, vectors will be written with one subscript A_k, and matrices will be written with two subscripts $A_{j,k}$, where the first subscript indicates the matrix row. Frequently, we will deal with vectors or matrices whose elements are images, in which case the image coordinates x.y are omitted.

We make use of the notation A:B to indicate Frobenius inner product of two matrices

$$A : B = \sum_y \sum_x A(x, y) B(x, y)$$

This is useful to describe a sum over pixels of the product of two images. The modulus or norm of an image is given by

$$\|A\| = \sqrt{A : A}$$

1. Inputs and Output

The WFA metric has four inputs. A first input is a set of wavefront aberrations, represented as a weighted sum of Zernike coefficients $z_n(x,y)$. A second input is a set of optotypes, represented in a standard graphic format, such as a font description, a set of raster images, or graphic language descriptors. One example set of optotypes is the Sloan font for the letters {C, D, H, K, N, O, R, S, V, Z}, a set often used in the measurement of acuity). A third input is a set of templates, equal in number to the number of optotypes in the set. By default, the templates are derived from the optotype set and are not a distinct input. A fourth input is a set of parameters, some of which may have default values that are permanently stored within the program. Some parameters may be changed on every calculation of the metric, while others are unlikely to be changed often. The parameters are described throughout this description.

A single output, the visual acuity, is expressed as a decimal acuity or log of decimal acuity (logMAR). An overall system structure is shown in FIG. 1.

2. Overview of the Algorithm

a. Generate the Optical Transfer Function (OTF)
b. Generate the Neural Transfer Function (NTF)
c. Generate the Total Transfer function (TTF)
d. Define the Proportion Correct function P(size)
e. Find the size for which P(size)≈P_{target}
Each of these steps is described in detail in the following.

3. Select a Set of Optotypes

The optotypes are a set of graphic symbols that the human observer is asked to identify in the course of an acuity test.

4

Examples are Sloan letters, Snellen e's, Landolt Cs, Lea symbols, Chinese or Japanese characters, or other pictograms of various sorts. Each optotype set will have a fixed number K of elements, and a defined size specification.

By way of example, the optotype set used here is the Sloan letters {C, D, H, K, N, O, R, S, V, Z}, with K=10. These letters are shown in FIG. 2. Each Sloan letter has a stroke width MAR, expressed in minutes of arc of visual angle, and each letter is 5 MAR tall by 5 MAR wide. The size specification used here is Log_{10} MAR, expressed as

$$\log MAR(mar) = \log_{10}(mar)$$

4. Determine the Usable Range of Optotype Sizes

The usable range will be limited by the resolution and size of the PSF image. As discussed below, these are determined by the pupil size, the wavelength (λ), and the pupil magnification (m). If the PSF image has a width of r, expressed in pixels, and d in degrees, the smallest stroke-width possible is one pixel, or

$$\log MAR_{min} = \log_{10}\left(\frac{60d}{r}\right)$$

The largest stroke-width will be one fifth width of the largest character, which will be one half the width of the PSF image; a margin is required to accommodate blur and to avoid wraparound so that

$$\log MAR_{max} = \log_{10}(6d)$$

It is sometimes convenient to adopt a positive integer index that corresponds to size. One example is computing logMAR in steps of 1/20. In that scheme, the minimum and maximum indices would be

$$index_{min} = \text{Ceiling}(20 \log MAR_{min})$$

$$index_{max} = \text{Floor}(20 \log MAR_{max})$$

The index l then extends from 1 to $l_{max} = index_{max} - index_{min} + 1$, and log MAR is given by

$$\log MAR = \frac{l + index_{min} - 1}{20}, \quad \text{where } l = 1, \dots , l_{max}$$

Using the default parameters, the PSF image will have a width of 256 pixels, and a width of 0.815525 deg. With these values

$$index_{min} = -14$$

$$index_{max} = 13$$

The size index l will have values between 1 and $l_{max} = 28$ for this example.

5. Generate the Optical Transfer Function (OTF)

The mathematical operations required to generate an optical transfer function (OTF) from a set of Zernike polynomials are well known. Graphs of the results at several stages are shown in FIGS. 3A-3E.

a. Create the Pupil Aperture Image PA(x,y). The image is of size {2h,2h}, where h is the half width of the pupil aperture image, expressed in pixels,

5

$$PA(x, y) = 1 \text{ if } \sqrt{x^2 + y^2} \big/ h \le 1, \quad x \text{ and } y \text{ integers } \in \{-h, \ldots 0, \ldots h-1\}$$
$$0 \text{ otherwise}$$

b. From the set of Zernike coefficients C={c_0, c_1, c_2, ..., c_N} (expressed in microns), create a discrete digital image of the Wavefront Aberration Image WA(x,y), with image size {2h,2h}. If the Zernike polynomials z_n(x,y) are identified by single index (the mode) n=0, ... N; and if the c_k are the coefficients of the individual polynomials, then

$$WA(x, y) = \sum_{n=1}^{N} c_n z_n(x, y)$$

We make use of the standard form of the Zernike polynomials as defined by Thibos, 2002, Jour. Of Optical Society of America.

c. Compute the Generalized pupil image GP(x,y)

$$GP(x, y) = PA(x, y) epx\left[\frac{i2\pi}{\lambda 10^{-3}} WA(xv,)\right]$$

where λ is the wavelength of light in nm used to illuminate the optotype set.

d. Pad the image on the left and top with zeros to create an image of size {2hm, 2hm}. The parameter m is the pupil magnification.

e. Compute the Point Spread Function PSF(x,y)

$$PSF(x,y) = |DFT[GP(x,y)]|^2$$

where DFT is the Discrete Fourier Transform operator.

f. Normalize the PSF.

$$\overline{PSF}(x, y) = \frac{PSF(x, y)}{\|PSF(x, y)\|}$$

g. Compute the Optical Transfer Function OTF(u,v)

$$OTF(u,v) = 2hm DFT[\overline{PSF}(x,y)]$$

This result is a complex image of size {2hm, 2hm}.
The height and width of the PSF image in degrees of visual angle is given by

$$d = \frac{h 360 \lambda 10^{-6}}{p\pi}$$

where p is the pupil diameter in mm. The height and width of the PSF image in pixels is given by

$$r = 2hm$$

where h is a half-width. The resolution of the PSF image in pixels/degree is

$$v = \frac{r}{d} = \frac{2\pi m p}{360 \lambda 10^{-6}}$$

6. Generate the Neural Transfer Function (NTF)

a. The Radial Neural Transfer Function RNTF(u,v) is a two-dimensional real dft given by

$$RNTF(u, v) = gain\left(\exp\left[-\left(\frac{f}{f_0}\right)^b\right] - loss\exp\left[-\left(\frac{f}{f_1}\right)^2\right]\right)$$

where gain, f_0, f_1, b, and loss are parameters. An example of this function is shown graphically in FIG. **4**.

b, The Oblique Effect Filter OEF(u,v) is a two-dimensional real dft given by

$$OEF(u, v) = OEF(f, \theta) = 1 - \left(1 - \exp\left(-\frac{f - corner}{slope}\right)\right)\sin(2\theta) \quad \text{if } f \ge corner$$
$$= 1 \text{ otherwise}$$

$$f = \sqrt{u^2 + v^2}$$

$$\theta = \arctan(u, v)$$

where corner and slope are parameters.

c. Compute the Neural Transfer Function NTF(u,v), a two-dimensional real dft given by

$$NTF(u,v) = RNTF(u,v)OEF(u,v)$$

7. Generate the Total Transfer Function (TTF)

The Total Transfer Function is given by

$$TTF(u,v) = OTF(u,v)NTF(u,v)$$

8. Define the Proportion Correct Function P(k)

The steps in evaluation of the P(k) function are as follows, and are diagrammed in FIG. **5**.

a. Given a size index 1, create K optotype images O_k(x,y). This may be done by rendering images from a graphic description, or the images may be pre-computed. Each image is of size {r,r}. See above for a definition of the optotype size index 1.

b. Create the K Neural Images S_k(x,y) by computing the DFT of the each optotype image O_k, multiplying by the TTF, and taking the inverse DFT,

$$S_k = IDFT[DFT[O_k]TTF]$$

where DFT is the DFT operation and IDFT is the Inverse DFT operation.

c. Create the K template images T_k. By default, these are identical to the Neural Images S_k.

d. Compute the normalized templates. Each template is divided by its norm, equal to the square root of the sum of the squares of all its pixels.

$$\overline{T}_k = \frac{T_k}{\|T_k\|}$$

e. Compute the matrix of normalized template cross-correlations $W_{j,k}$

$$W_{j,k} = T_j : T_k$$

f. Create an array of cross-correlations between each neural images and each template. Note that the row indexes the neural image and the column, the template.

$$R_{j,k} = S_j \cdot \overline{T}_k$$

g. At this point two or more methods are available, which we identify as methods 1 and 2.

Method 1.

i. Subtract each value from the main diagonal entry in the same row, and divide by a factor that includes the parameter σ (default value$\approx$1). There are two possible versions of a matrix D, identified by subscripts 1 and 2.

$$D_{1,j,k} = \frac{R_{j,j} - R_{j,k}}{\sigma \sqrt{1 - W_{j,k}^2}}$$

ii. The probability correct for optotype j is given by

$$P_{1,j} = \int_{-\infty}^{\infty} f(t) \prod_{k \neq j} F(t - D_{1,j,k}) \, dt$$

where f(t) and F(t) are probability density function and cumulative probability

Method 2

$$D_{2,j,k} = \frac{R_{j,j} - R_{j,k}}{\sigma \sqrt{2} \sqrt{1 - W_{j,k}}}$$

$$P_{2,j} = \prod_{k \neq j} F(D_{2,j,k})$$

The final value of P is given by

$$P = \frac{1}{K} \sum_{k=1}^{K} P_k$$

9. Find the Size for which $P \approx P_{target}$

The parameter P_{target} is the criterion probability for measurement of visual acuity. It is usually set to a value between 0.5 and 0.8. This value will depend upon the number K of optotypes and must be greater than 1/K (the probability of getting the right answer by guessing). For the Sloan letters, a default value $P_{target} = 0.55$ is used. Various efficient iterative procedures may be used to locate the value of size for which $P \approx P_{target}$. Here we describe the method of bisection, though other methods may be used.

$$l_{low} = 1$$

$$l_{high} = l_{max}$$

$$P_{low} = P(l_{low})$$

$$P_{high} = P(l_{high})$$

begin loop

8

If $l_{high} - l_{low} = 1$, exit and return $l_{final} = l_{low} + \frac{l_{high} - l_{low}}{p_{high} - p_{low}}(p_t - p_{low})$

$$l_{mid} = \text{Round}\left[\frac{l_{high} + l_{low}}{2}\right]$$

$$P_{mid} = P(l_{mid})$$

If $P_{mid} < P_{target}$,

$$l_{low} = l_{mid}$$

$$P_{low} = (l_{low})$$

otherwise

$$l_{high} = l_{mid}$$

$$P_{high} = P(l_{high})$$

Go to begin loop

The returned value of l_{final} can then be converted to an acuity in logMAR using the Equation above. This is the output of the WFA Metric.

FIG. 5 illustrates a sequence of steps of a procedure for practicing the invention. In step 51, an OTF is generated. In step 52, an NTF is generated and is multiplied by the OTF, to form a TTF (step 53). In step 54, a set of optotypes is and is subjected to a DFT process, in step 55. In step 56, the processed optotypes are used to form images S_j of the optotypes. In step 57, the images S_j are used to create a set of templates T_k, and normalized templates T_k^* are created in step 58. Cross correlations $R_{j,k}$ of the images S_j and the normalized templates T_k^* are formed, in step 59. In step 60, cross-correlations W_k of the normalized templates T_k^*. Normalized difference matrices $D_{j,k}$ are formed from the cross-correlation matrix $R_{j,k}$ are formed in step 61, using information from the cross-correlations W_k. and a statistical parameter σ, in step 62. In step 63, a probability P associated with measurement of visual acuity is computed.

10. Unique Features of the WFA Metric

The WFA metric is the only known metric to compute acuity from wavefronts that:

(i) incorporates a model of the optotype identification task

(ii) can predict acuity for different target probabilities

(iii) can predict acuity for different optotypes

(iv) allows user specification of optotypes

(v) can incorporate different and possibly subject-specific neural transfer functions

(vi) can predict acuity for different subject templates

The template matching algorithm that is fundamental to this metric may have other uses in predicting performance in identification tasks.

Parameter	Default value	Unit	Definition
K			number of optotypes
k			index of optotpye, 1, . . . , K
l	556	nm	wavelength
p	5	mm	diameter of pupil
h	64	pixels	half width of pupil image
m	2		magnification
d	derived	degrees	size of the PSF image

-continued

Parameter	Default value	Unit	Definition
r	2 m h	pixels	size of the PSF image
v	r/d	pixels/deg	resolution of PSF image
corner	13.5715	cycles/deg	oblique effect parameter
slope	3.481		oblique effect parameter
gain	3.149614		NTF parameter
loss	0.9260249		NTF parameter
f_0	35.869213		NTF parameter
f_1	5.412887		NTF parameter
b	1.064181		NTF parameter
l			optotype size index
WA		image	wavefront aberration
PSF		image	point spread function
PA		image	pupil aperture
GP		complex image	generalized pupil
TTF		dft	total transfer function
NTF		dft	neural transfer function
OTF		dft	optical transfer function
OEF		dft	oblique effect transfer function
O_k			optotype with index k
S_k			neural image of optotype
T_k			template with index k
$\bar{T}_k$			normalized template with index k
$W_{j,k}$			cross-correlation between normalized templates
$R_{j,k}$			cross-correlation between normalized templates and neural images
$D_{j,k}$			template response distribution means
P_j		probability	probability correct for optotype with index k
P		probability	probability correct for optotypes of one size
σ			noise standard deviation
P_{target}	0.55		criterion proportion correct
mar		minutes	optotype stroke size
x,y			image pixel coordinates
u,v			dft pixel coordinates
j,k			row, column indices of matrices
C_n			coefficient of Zernike polynomial n
Z_n			Zernike polynomial n

What is claimed is:

1. A method of predicting visual acuity of an imaging system, the method comprising:

providing a set of K optotypes, numbered k=1,. . . , K (K≧2) of a specified size, to be used to establish a reference set of symbols to estimate visual acuity, and providing a description or image T_k(x,y) of each optotype, dependent upon location coordinates (x,y) associated with the optptype image produced by the imaging system;

constructing a Wavefront Aberration Image WAI(x,y) that manifests selected image aberrations associated with the imaging system;

computing a generalized pupil image GPI(x,y), with non-zero values confined to within a pupil aperture associated with the imaging system, that manifests the selected image aberrations and that is dependent upon at least one wavelength λ of light with which the image is viewed;

computing a Point Spread Function PSF(x,y) that is an absolute value squared of a Discrete Fourier Transform (DFT) of the image GPI(x,y);

computing a Normalized Point Spread Function NPSF(x, y), proportional to the Point Spread Function PSF (x,y), whose norm is 1:

computing an Optical Transfer Function OTF(u,v), expressed as a function of spatial frequency indice (u,v) in a Fourier transform plane, that is a Discrete Fourier

10

Transform of the Normalized Point Spread Function NPSF (x,y), multiplied by a value h of original image size and multiplied by an image magnification index m;

generating a Radial Neural Transfer Function RNTF(u,v), where RNTF(u,v) satisfies the following conditions: (i) RNTF(u,v) is a continuous, non-negative function of a spatial frequency variable $f=[u^2+v^2]^{1/2}$; (ii) RNTF(u,v) has at least one value, f=f(max), for which NRTF(u,v) is a maximum; (iii) for 0<f<f(max), RNTF(u,v) is monotonically increasing in f; (iv) for f>f(max), and RNTF (u,v) is monotonically decreasing toward 0;

computing a Neural Transfer Function NTF(u,v) as a product of the Radial Neural Transfer Function RNTF (u,v) and an Oblique Effect Filter function OER(u,v) that compensates for viewing angle of the original optotype image;

generating a Total Transfer Function TTF(u,v), defined as a product of NTF(u,v) and the Optical Transfer Function OTF(u,v);

generating a Proportion Correct index PC(j), which presents a probability associated with a correct optotype that would be identifed by a subject having the Wavefront Aberration Image WAI(x,y) for at least one optotype(j).

2. The method of claim 1, wherein said step of constructing said Waveform Aberration Image WAI(x,y) comprises:

providing a Pupil Aperture Imaging characteristic function PA(x,y) that has a first value substantially equal to 1 within a pupil aperture of a test subject and has a second value substantially equal to 0 outside the pupil aperture of the test subject, where (x,y) are location coordinates;

providing a set of Zernike polynomials Z_n(x,y) and associated coefficients c_n, and creating a discrete digital image a Wavefront Aberration Image WAI, defined as an error sum

$$WAI(x,y)=\Sigma_n c_n Z_n(x,y);$$

where the coefficients c_n are chosen to minimize a computed error between an image provided by said imaging system and the error sum;

computing a generalized pupil image GP, defined as

$$GP(x,y)=PA(x,y)exp\{2i WAI(x,y)/(\lambda/1000)\},$$

where λ refers to a wavelength used to illuminate the optotypes; and

padding said image of each of said optotype on at least two adjacent edges of said image with zeroes to create an image of size (Δx,Δy)=(mh,mh), where h represents an original image size, measured in a selected direction, and m is a multiplier index.

3. The method of claim 1, wherein said Oblique Effect Filter OEF(u,v) is determined by a procedure comprising forming

$$OEF(u, v) = OEF1(f, \theta) = 1 - \{1 - \exp\{((corner) - f)/(slope)\}\}\sin2\theta$$

$$\text{if } f \geq (corner)$$

$$= 1 \text{ otherwise}$$

$$f=(u^2+v^2)^{1/2}$$

$$\theta=arctan(u,v),$$

where corner and slope are parameter.

11

4. The method of claim **1**, wherein said process of generating said Proportion Correct index PC(j) comprises:

computing a neural image $S_j(x,y)$ ($j=1,\ldots,K$) as an inverse DFT of a product of said Total Transfer Function TTF (u,v) multiplied by a DFT of an optotype image $O_j(x,y)$;

computing a cross-correlation matrix between each of the neural images S_j and each of said templates T_k, defined as

$$R_{j,k}=S_j(x,y):T_k(x,y);$$

computing a cross-correlation matrix of each normalized template with each normalized template, $W_{j,k}=T_j:T_k$;

computing and normalizing a difference of matrix entries, $R_{j,j}-R_{j,k}$, between each diagonal entry $R_{j,j}$ and each entry $R_{j,k}$ in a corresponding row of the matrix $\{R_{j,k}\}$, to form a normalized difference matrix $D_{j,k}$;

$$D_{j,k}=\{R_{j,j}-R_{j,k}\}/\{\sigma\{1-W_{j,k}{}^2\}^{1/2}\},$$

12

where σ is a statistical value that is provided or computed; and

estimating a probability for estimation of a correct optotype by a subject by computing a probability value that is either (i) a product of functions of the matrices D_{jk}, or (ii) an integral, with an integrand equal to a normal statistical function, multiplied by the product of the functions of the matrices D_{jk}.

5. The method of claim **1**, wherein said Radial Neural Transfer Function RNTF(u,v) is defined as

$$RNTF(u,v)=(gain)\{exp[-(f/f_0)^b-(loss)\ exp[-(f/f_1)^2]\},$$

where $f=(u^2+v^2)^{1/2}$ is a spatial frequency and (gain), (loss), b, f_0 and f_1 are selected parameter values.

6. The method of claim **1**, wherein said set of optotypes includes at least one of:

Sloan letters; Snellen E's; Landolt C's; and Lea symbols.

* * * * *

US008759057B1

(12) **United States Patent**
Cullings et al.

(10) **Patent No.:** **US 8,759,057 B1**
(45) **Date of Patent:** **Jun. 24, 2014**

(54) **METHODS FOR PURIFYING ENZYMES FOR MYCOREMEDIATION**

(71) Applicant: **The United States of America as Represented by the Administrator of the National Aeronautics & Space Administration (NASA)**, Washington, DC (US)

(72) Inventors: **Kenneth W. Cullings**, Ventura, CA (US); **Julia C. DeSimone**, San Jose, CA (US); **Chad D. Paavola**, Carmel, IN (US)

(73) Assignee: **The United States of America as Represented by the Administrator of the National Aeronautics & Space Administration (NASA)**, Washington, DC (US)

(*) Notice: Subject to any disclaimer, the term of this patent is extended or adjusted under 35 U.S.C. 154(b) by 0 days.

(21) Appl. No.: **13/854,620**

(22) Filed: **Apr. 1, 2013**

Related U.S. Application Data

(63) Continuation-in-part of application No. 13/438,793, filed on Apr. 3, 2012.

(60) Provisional application No. 61/619,906, filed on Apr. 3, 2012, provisional application No. 61/471,605, filed on Apr. 4, 2011.

(51) **Int. Cl.**
C12N 9/98	(2006.01)
C12N 9/02	(2006.01)
C12N 9/00	(2006.01)

(52) **U.S. Cl.**
CPC *C12N 9/00* (2013.01); *C12N 9/0004* (2013.01); *C12N 9/98* (2013.01)
USPC **435/183**; 435/187; 435/189

(58) **Field of Classification Search**
None
See application file for complete search history.

(56) **References Cited**

FOREIGN PATENT DOCUMENTS

EP   2078755 A1 * 7/2009 .... C12P 1/02

OTHER PUBLICATIONS

Wang, H.X. et al. 2006. Purification of a laccase from fruiting bodies of the mushroom *Pleurotus eryngii*. Applied Microbiology and Biotechnology 69:521-525.*
Cullings, et al., Effects of Artificial Defoliation of Pines on the Structure and Physiology of the Soil . . . , Applied and Environmental Microbiology, Apr. 2005, 1996-2000.
Wang, et al., Purification of a laccase from fruiting bodies of the mushroom *Pleurotus eryngii*, App Microbol Biotechnol 2006, 69:521-525.

* cited by examiner

Primary Examiner — John S Brusca
Assistant Examiner — Sharon M Papciak
(74) *Attorney, Agent, or Firm* — Christopher J. Menke; Robert M. Padilla

(57) **ABSTRACT**

A process for purifying laccase from an ectomycorrhizal fruiting body is disclosed. The process includes steps of homogenization, sonication, centrifugation, filtration, affinity chromatography, ion exchange chromatography, and gel filtration. Purified laccase can also be separated into isomers.

7 Claims, 1 Drawing Sheet

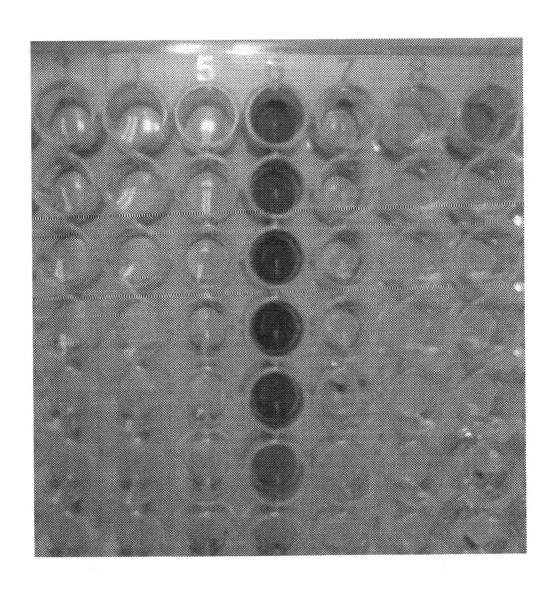

1

METHODS FOR PURIFYING ENZYMES FOR MYCOREMEDIATION

CROSS-REFERENCE TO RELATED APPLICATIONS

This application claims the benefit of U.S. Provisional Application No. 61/619,906, filed Apr. 3, 2012 and is a continuation-in-part of U.S. application Ser. No. 13/438,793, filed Apr. 3, 2012, which claims the benefit of U.S. Provisional Application No. 61/471,605, filed Apr. 4, 2011, all three of which are incorporated by reference in their entirety herein.

ORIGIN OF THE INVENTION

The invention described herein was made in part by employees of the United States Government and may be manufactured and used by or for the Government of the United States of America for governmental purposes without the payment of any royalties thereon or therefor.

BACKGROUND OF THE INVENTION

This invention relates to bioremediation of contaminants in the environment. More particularly, this invention relates to using fungi to degrade or sequester contaminants in the environment.

Bioremediation is emerging as a cost effective and efficient way to remediate environmental hazards. The work is performed naturally by microbes (bacteria and fungi) that are capable of breaking down the long- and short-chain organic backbones of solvents and fuels such as diesel. Fungi are capable of enhancing the natural process by as much as 10-fold through synergistic action with natural bacteria, and they are also capable of rapid remediation of solvents in their own right.

The fungi that perform this function are wood-rotting and ectomycorrhizal fungi. They naturally possess the enzymes necessary to break down the carbon chains found in many types of contamination. Studies of model white rot fungi (e.g., *Pleurotus ostreatus*) indicate that lignin-degrading fungi will degrade lignin and can reduce hydrocarbon contamination in soils by as much as 40% in as little as one month. Much of the work in these reductions is performed by fungal laccases.

Laccases are polyphenol oxidases that utilize a wide array of phenolic substrates that include lignin in wood and soil humic compounds, polycyclic aromatic hydrocarbons (PAH), and polychlorinated biphenyls (PCB's). PAH and PCB's are widespread soil and water contaminants of human origin that can accumulate via several sources, including diesel spills. Laccases are easily inducible, are involved in lignin beak-down, utilize a broad range of substrates, are often extracellular, and reduce toxicity of these compounds via immobilization to humic substances, thus lowering their bioavailability. Hence, laccases are considered excellent candidates for use in remediation.

In one experiment known in the art, a plot of soil contaminated with diesel was inoculated with mycelia of oyster mushrooms; traditional bioremediation techniques (i.e., inoculation with bacteria) were used on control plots. After about a month, much of the polycyclic aromatic hydrocarbons (PAH) had reportedly been reduced to non-toxic components in the mycelia-inoculated plots. It appears the natural microbial community participates with the fungi to break down contaminants, eventually into carbon dioxide and

2

water. Also known in the art, white-rot or wood-decay fungi have been found to be effective in breaking down aromatic pollutants (toxic components of petroleum), as well as chlorinated compounds (certain persistent pesticides).

H. X. Wang & T. B. Ng, Purification of a laccase from fruiting bodies of the mushroom *Pleurotus eryngii,* 69 Appl. Microbiol. Biotechnol. 521-525 (2006), describes a basic laccase purification method for the mushroom, *Pleurotus eryngii.* The disclosed method is insufficient for use in purifying laccases from fungi that contain more fleshy structures and fails to provide for separation of laccase isozymes. Therefore, an improved, broadened, and expanded method that would apply to many more types of fungi is needed.

While prior art methods of laccase purification are known and are generally suitable for their limited purposes, they possess certain inherent deficiencies that detract from their overall utility in environmental bioremediation. For example, they are not generally applicable to mushroom-forming fungi. They are generally suitable for use with some fruiting bodies, but they are not well suited for use with fleshier fungal species. As a further example, they do not provide for separation of enzyme isomers and purification of such isomers.

Bio-prospectors continue to search for new forms of mycoremediation and new methods of decontaminating the environment because prior art products and methods, though generally suitable for their limited purposes, possess certain inherent deficiencies that detract from their overall utility in environmental bioremediation.

In view of the foregoing, it will be appreciated that providing improved products and methods for environmental bioremediation would be a significant advancement in the art.

SUMMARY OF THE INVENTION

An illustrative embodiment of a process according to the present invention for purifying laccase from an ectomycorrhizal fruiting body comprises:

(A) homogenizing the fruiting body in a buffer of about pH 7 to obtain a slurry;

(B) sonicating the slurry to obtain a sonicated slurry;

(C) centrifuging the sonicated slurry at a relative centrifugal force of about 15,000 to about 20,000 and collecting a resulting first supernatant;

(D) sonicating the first supernatant to obtain a sonicated first supernatant;

(E) ultracentrifuging the sonicated first supernatant such that a resulting second supernatant separates into top and bottom supernatant layers, and collecting the bottom supernatant layer;

(F) filtering the bottom supernatant layer through a bacteria-retaining filter and collecting the filtrate;

(G) subjecting the filtrate to DEAE cellulose chromatography and eluting retained proteins with a first sodium chloride gradient;

(H) removing the sodium chloride from the eluted, retained proteins to obtain desalted proteins, subjecting the desalted proteins to ion exchange chromatography, desorbing adsorbed proteins with a second sodium chloride gradient, and collecting the first desorbed peak; and

(I) fractionating the first desorbed peak into fractions by gel filtration.

BRIEF DESCRIPTION OF THE DRAWING

FIG. **1** shows enzymatic activity of a laccase purified according to an illustrative embodiment of the present invention (column 6); a positive control is shown in column 9.

3

DETAILED DESCRIPTION OF THE INVENTION

Before the processes of the presently claimed invention are disclosed and described, it is to be understood that this invention is not limited to the particular configurations, process steps, and materials disclosed herein as such configurations, process steps, and materials may vary somewhat. It is also to be understood that the terminology employed herein is used for the purpose of describing particular embodiments only and is not intended to be limiting since the scope of the present invention will be limited only by the appended claims and equivalents thereof.

The publications and other reference materials referred to herein to describe the background of the invention and to provide additional detail regarding its practice are hereby incorporated by reference. The references discussed herein are provided solely for their disclosure prior to the filing date of the present application. Nothing herein is to be construed as an admission that the inventors are not entitled to antedate such disclosure by virtue of prior invention.

It must be noted that, as used in this specification and the appended claims, the singular forms "a," "an," and "the" include plural referents unless the context clearly dictates otherwise. Thus, for example, reference to "a laccase" includes reference to a mixture of two or more laccases, reference to "an ectomycorrhizal fruiting body" includes reference to one or more of such fruiting bodies, and reference to "the product" includes reference to a mixture of two or more of such products.

Unless defined otherwise, all technical and scientific terms used herein have the same meanings as commonly understood by one of ordinary skill in the art to which this invention belongs.

In describing and claiming the present invention, the following terminology will be used in accordance with the definitions set out below.

As used herein, "comprising," "including," "containing," "characterized by," and grammatical equivalents thereof are inclusive or open-ended terms that do not exclude additional, unrecited elements or method steps. "Comprising" is to be interpreted as including the more restrictive terms "consisting of" and "consisting essentially of."

As mentioned above, illustrative embodiments of the present invention include processes for purifying laccase from ectomycorrhizal fruiting bodies and processes for separating purified laccase into isomers. These processes will be further described in the examples that follow. The scope of the invention, however, will be limited only by the claims.

Example 1

Prior Art

H. X. Wang & T. B. Ng, Purification of a laccase from fruiting bodies of the mushroom *Pleurotus eryngii*, 69 Appl. Microbiol. Biotechnol. 521-525 (2006), describes the purification of laccase as follows:

The fruiting bodies of *Pleurotus eryngii* (2 kg) were extracted by homogenization in distilled water (2 ml/g). The homogenate was filtered through cheesecloth before centrifugation. The resulting supernatant was applied to a 5×20 cm diethylaminoethyl (DEAE) cellulose (Sigma) column in 10 mM Tris HCl buffer (ph 7.3). Following removal of unadsorbed proteins, the column was eluted with 0.8 M NaCl added to the Tris HCl buffer. The adsorbed fraction was dialyzed prior to loading on a 2.5×20 cm column of carboxymethyl (CM) cellulose

4

(Sigma) in 10 mM NH4OAc buffer (ph 5.1). After removal of unadsorbed proteins, adsorbed proteins were desorbed by addition of 1 M NaCl to the elution buffer. The unadsorbed fraction was subsequently subjected to ion exchange chromatography on a 1.5×20 cm Q-SEPHAROSE® column (Amersham Biosciences) in 10 mM NH4OAc buffer (ph 5.1). Unadsorbed proteins were eluted with the same buffer. Adsorbed proteins were desorbed with a linear 0-1 M NaCl gradient in 10 mM NH4OAc buffer (ph 5.1). The first adsorbed peak obtained was fractionated by gel filtration on a SUPER-DEX® 75 HR 10/30 column (Amersham Biosciences) by fast protein liquid chromatography (FPLC).

Example 2

Improved Laccase Purification

The method of Example 1 was carried out, with the following changes. Fruiting bodies of *Suilllus granulatus* were homogenized in 10 mM Tris-HCl buffer, pH 7.3, instead of in water. Filtration through cheesecloth was omitted, because the homogenate was too thick to pass readily through the cheesecloth filter. Instead, the slurry was sonicated, then centrifuged at 10,500 rpm (relative centrifugal force (RCF) of 18,093). The supernatant was collected, sonicated, and ultracentrifuged at 45,000 rpm. This treatment caused the supernatant to separate into two layers. The bottom supernatant layer was collected and then filtered using a 0.45 Fm syringe filter (polyethersulfone, PES). The filtrate was loaded onto a DEAE Sepharose column and eluted using an NaCl gradient. Dialysis was performed on the active fractions as described in Example 1. The CM cellulose chromatography step was omitted, but the ion exchange chromatography on Q-SEPHAROSE® and gel filtration on SUPERDEX® 75 were carried out as described in Example 1.

Example 3

Laccase purified according to the procedure of Example 2 was separated into isomers as follows. Active fractions were concentrated to <2 ml using a VivaSpin centrifugal filter (PES; 10,000 MWCO), and assayed for concentration and specific activity, then loaded onto a Phenyl Fast-Flow (low substitution) HIC (hydrophobic interaction chromatography) column. This treatment resulted in five peaks, the most active being of interest. Active fractions after HIC chromatography were concentrated to <1 ml using a VivaSpin (Vivaproducts, Inc., Littleton, Mass.) centrifugal filter (PES; 10,000 MWCO), and assayed for concentration and specific activity, resulting in separation and the obtaining of pure individual enzyme.

Example 4

Laccase purified according to the procedure of Example 2 was assayed for phenol oxidation activity in an ABTS (2,2'-azino-bis(3-ethylbenzothiazoline-6-sulfonic acid) assay according to procedures well known in the art. The sample to be assayed was placed in 100 mM sodium tartrate buffer (pH 4.3) containing ABTS. The increase in absorbance at 405 nm was recorded over 15 min.

FIG. 1 shows the results of such an assay. Laccase purified from a *Russula* species is shown in the wells in column 6. *Trametes versicolor* laccase purchased from Sigma Chemical Co. (St. Louis, Mo.) was a positive control, as shown in column 9.

These results demonstrate that laccase purified according to the present invention contains phenol oxidation activity, which is consistent with known laccase enzymes.

What is claimed is:

1. A process for purifying laccase from an ectomycorrhizal fruiting body, the process comprising:

   (A) homogenizing the fruiting body in a buffer of about pH 7 to obtain a slurry;

   (B) sonicating the slurry to obtain a sonicated slurry;

   (C) centrifuging the sonicated slurry at a relative centrifugal force of about 15,000 to about 20,000 and collecting a resulting first supernatant;

   (D) sonicating the first supernatant to obtain a sonicated first supernatant;

   (E) ultracentrifuging the sonicated first supernatant such that a resulting second supernatant separates into top and bottom supernatant layers, and collecting the bottom supernatant layer;

   (F) filtering the bottom supernatant layer through a bacteria-retaining filter and collecting the filtrate;

   (G) subjecting the filtrate to DEAE cellulose chromatography and eluting retained proteins with a first sodium chloride gradient;

   (H) removing the sodium chloride from the eluted, retained proteins to obtain desalted proteins, subjecting the desalted proteins to ion exchange chromatography, desorbing adsorbed proteins with a second sodium chloride gradient, and collecting the first desorbed peak; and

   (I) fractionating the first desorbed peak into fractions by gel filtration.

2. The process of claim 1, wherein the ultracentrifuging is at about 45,000 rpm.

3. The process of claim 1, wherein the ion exchange chromatography of step (H) is carried out on a column.

4. The process of claim 1, wherein the gel filtration of step (I) is carried out on a column by fast protein liquid chromatography.

5. The process of claim 1, further comprising assaying the fractions of step (I) for phenol oxidation activity.

6. The process of claim 5, wherein phenol oxidation activity is assayed by (2,2'-azino-bis(3-ethylbenzothiazoline-6-sulfonic acid) ("ABTS") assay.

7. The process of claim 1, further comprising separating fractions from the gel filtration step of step (I) into laccase isomers by hydrophobic interaction chromatography.

* * * * *

US006608628B1

(12) **United States Patent**

Ross et al.

(10) Patent No.: **US 6,608,628 B1**
(45) Date of Patent: **Aug. 19, 2003**

(54) **METHOD AND APPARATUS FOR VIRTUAL INTERACTIVE MEDICAL IMAGING BY MULTIPLE REMOTELY-LOCATED USERS**

(75) Inventors: **Muriel D. Ross**, Albuquerque, NM (US); **Ian Alexander Twombly**, Santa Clara, CA (US); **Steven O. Senger**, Onalaska, WI (US)

(73) Assignee: **The United States of America as represented by the Administrator of the National Aeronautics and Space Administration (NASA)**, Washington, DC (US)

(*) Notice: Subject to any disclaimer, the term of this patent is extended or adjusted under 35 U.S.C. 154(b) by 0 days.

(21) Appl. No.: **09/436,716**

(22) Filed: **Nov. 5, 1999**

Related U.S. Application Data

(60) Provisional application No. 60/107,286, filed on Nov. 6, 1998, provisional application No. 60/107,509, filed on Nov. 6, 1998, provisional application No. 60/107,284, filed on Nov. 6, 1998, and provisional application No. 60/107,390, filed on Nov. 6, 1998.

(51) Int. Cl.⁷ **G06F 9/00**; G06F 15/16; G06F 15/173; G09G 5/00

(52) U.S. Cl. **345/619**; 345/723; 345/733; 345/734; 345/751; 345/756; 709/107; 709/204; 709/231; 382/128; 382/154

(58) Field of Search 345/733, 734, 345/735, 736, 737, 740, 741, 744, 748, 750, 751, 753, 761, 619, 700, 719, 723, 732, 756; 709/223, 219, 315, 107, 201, 204, 205, 100, 200, 231, 232, 246; 703/1, 104.1

(56) **References Cited**

U.S. PATENT DOCUMENTS

5,515,491 A * 5/1996 Bates et al. 345/155

5,740,176 A * 4/1998 Gupta et al. 370/440

(List continued on next page.)

FOREIGN PATENT DOCUMENTS

EP   1058191   * 12/2000   .... G06F/11/14

OTHER PUBLICATIONS

"World Tool Kit Reference Manual," Release 8, Sense8 Corporation, 1991–1998, Chapter 1,4,7 and 22.

Ross, et al., "New Approaches To Virtual Environment Surgery," Medicine Meets Virtual Reality. J.D. Westwood, et al. (Eds), IOS Press 1999, pp. 297–301.

(List continued on next page.)

Primary Examiner—Matthew C. Bella
Assistant Examiner—Wesner Sajous
(74) *Attorney, Agent, or Firm*—Robert M. Padilla; Carla M. Wong

(57)   **ABSTRACT**

A virtual interactive imaging system allows the displaying of high-resolution, three-dimensional images of medical data to a user and allows the user to manipulate the images, including rotation of images in any of various axes. The system includes a mesh component that generates a mesh to represent a surface of an anatomical object, based on a set of data of the object, such as from a CT or MRI scan or the like. The mesh is generated so as to avoid tears, or holes, in the mesh, providing very high-quality representations of topographical features of the object, particularly at high-resolution. The system further includes a virtual surgical cutting tool that enables the user to simulate the removal of a piece or layer of a displayed object, such as a piece of skin or bone, view the interior of the object, manipulate the removed piece, and reattach the removed piece if desired. The system further includes a virtual collaborative clinic component, which allows the users of multiple, remotely-located computer systems to collaboratively and simultaneously view and manipulate the high-resolution, three-dimensional images of the object in real-time.

20 Claims, 26 Drawing Sheets

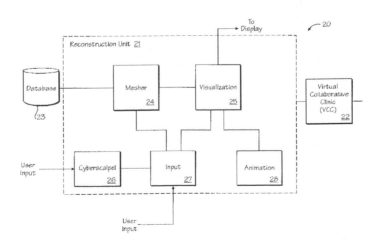

U.S. PATENT DOCUMENTS

5,742,778 A	*	4/1998	Hao 395/332
6,011,537 A	*	1/2000	Slotznick 345/619
6,148,066 A	*	11/2000	Di Santo 379/93.19
6,182,123 B1	*	1/2001	Filepp 709/217
6,192,320 B1	*	2/2001	Margrey 702/34
6,215,785 B1	*	4/2001	Batruci 370/360
6,295,513 B1	*	9/2001	Thackston 703/1
6,356,758 B1	*	3/2002	Almeida et al. 455/446
6,411,965 B2	*	6/2002	Klug 707/201
6,525,732 B1	*	2/2003	Gadh et al. 345/428

OTHER PUBLICATIONS

Montgomery, et al., "A Method for Semiautomated serial section reconstruction and visualization of Neural Tissue from TEM Images", Biomedical Image Processing and Biomedical Visualization, SPIE–The International Society for Optical Engineering, Feb. 1993, vol. 1905, pp. 114–120.

Montgomery et al., "Improvements In Semiautomated Serial–Section Reconstruction and Visualization of Neural Tissue From TEM Images," SPIE Electronic Imaging, 3D Microscopy Conf Proc., 1994, pp. 264–267.

Montgomery et al., "Non–Fiducial, Shape–Based Registration of Biological Tissue," SPIE vol. 2655, Aug. 1996, pp. 224–232.

Ross, et al., "A National Center for Biocomputation: In Search of a Patient–Specific Interactive Virtual Surgery Workbench," Medicine Meets Virtual Reality, IOS Press and Ohmsha, 1998, pp. 5323–328.

Heather Harreld, "NASA Aids In Virtual Surgery," Federal Computer Week, Nov. 2, 1998.

Andrew Wilson, "Researchers Use Visualization Tools to Render 3–D Medical Images," Vision Systems Design, Dec. 1997, pp. 30–34, 36 and 38.

Bill Curtis, "The Virtual Reality of Medicine," California Computer News, vol. XIV, Dec. 1997, pp. 38–39.

Tamara Grippi, "Robots In Surgery, SVMH Prepares for the Future," The Carmel Pine Cone, Aug. 29, 1997, pp. 10A, 14A, and 15A.

Charles F. King, "Medical Volume Visualization—The Doorway to the Future," Innovation 3, Summer 1997, pp. 40–42, 44–45.

Judy Richter, "A Cut Above Routine Surgery," The San Francisco Examiner, Apr. 6, 1997, pp. B–5–B6.

"From Tang to Robotic Surgery," Space Life Sciences Consortium Newsletter, Division of Space Life Sciences, vol. 5, No. 1, Spring 1997, pp. 1–3.

David Eggleston, "NASA Uses First Immersive Workbench for Surgery Training," Silicon Graphics World, vol. 7, No. 1 Jan. 1997.

Ferrara–Kurth, Kierith, "Researcher Creates Visualization for 3–D Bronchial Fly–Throughs", Silicon Graphics World, vol. 7, No. 1 Jan. 1997.

"Working In Virtual Worlds," Computer Graphics World, Jan. 1997.

Mike Goodkind, "Not Exactly Rocket Science," Stanford Today, Sep./Oct. 1996, pp. 31–32.

Muriel D. Ross, "Biological Neural Networks: Models For Future 'Thinking' Machines," NASA Tech Briefs, vol. 15, No. 6, Jun. 1991, pp. 10, 11 and 131.

Orla Smith, "Visible Human Project Gets Greater Exposure," Nature Medicine, vol. 2, No. 11, Nov. 1996.

"NASA Technology Assists Reconstructive Surgery," Space Technology Innovation, Sep./Oct. 1996, p. 17.

Keller et al., "Visual Cues, Practical Data Visualization," IEEE Computer Society Press, p. 155.

Thomas P. Pearsall, "Close Encounters of the Virtual Kind," Circuits and Devices, Jan. 1999, pp. 10–12.

Susan Okie, "Out of Body Medicine: Doctors Turn to Computer Simulators to Enhance Their Skills," The Washington Post, Nov. 5, 1996, p. Z12.

Grimson, et al., "Image Guided Surgery," Scientific American, Jun. 1999, pp. 63–69.

"How's That For Forward Thinking?" The Spotlight, New Media News, May 2, 1997.

"Virtual Rehearsals For Plastic Surgery," Biophotonics International, Sep./Oct. 1996, p. 33.

"Real Patients, Virtual Surgery," A Fantastic Voyage Through the Human Body, Feb. 1997.

"Surgical Simulator," Popular Mechanics, Feb. 1998, p. 26.

"Software Scalpel For Virtual Surgery," Real Time Graphics, vol. 7, No. 4, Oct./Nov. 1998.

Jane Hutchison, "Biocomputation Center Opens," Astrogram, vol. XXXIII, No. 23, Aug. 16, 1991, p. 1–2.

Scientific Computing & Automation, Jul. 1999, p. 55.

Greg Freiherr, "The Future Arrives for Medical Displays," Medical Device and Diagnostic Industry, Jan. 1997, pp. 92–97.

* cited by examiner

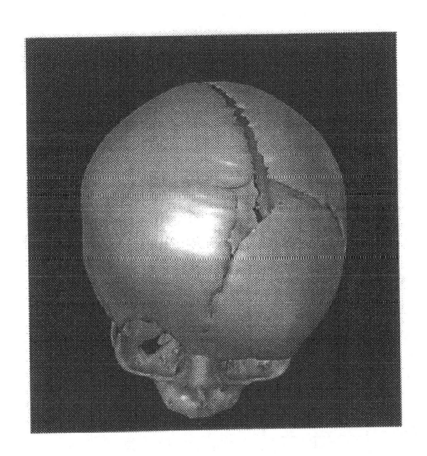

FIG. 1

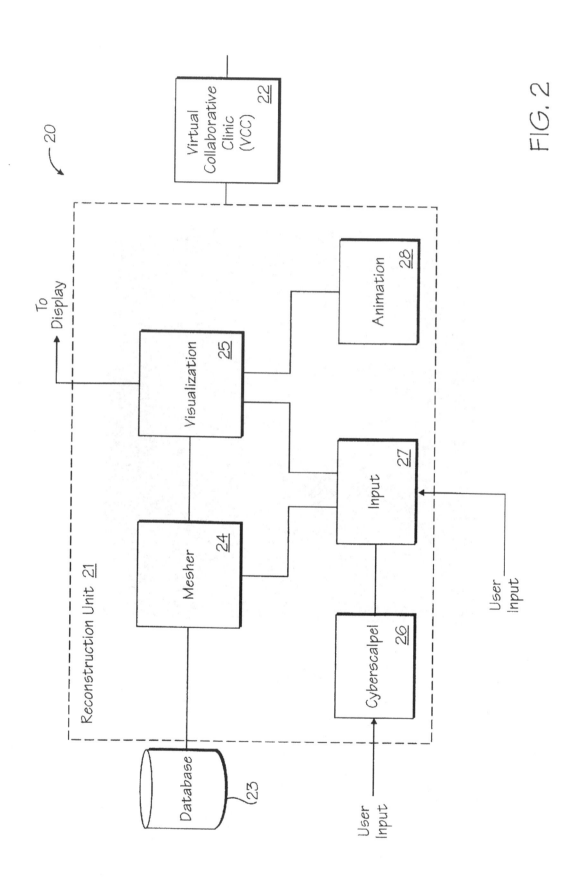

FIG. 2

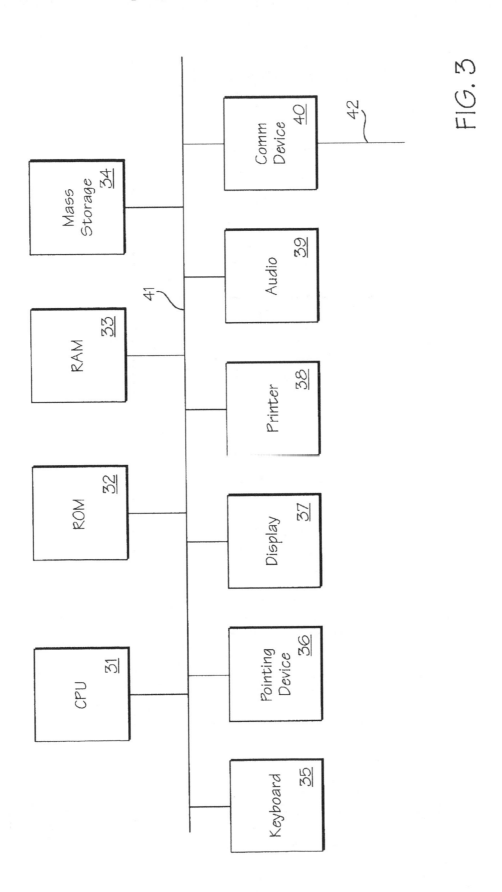

FIG. 3

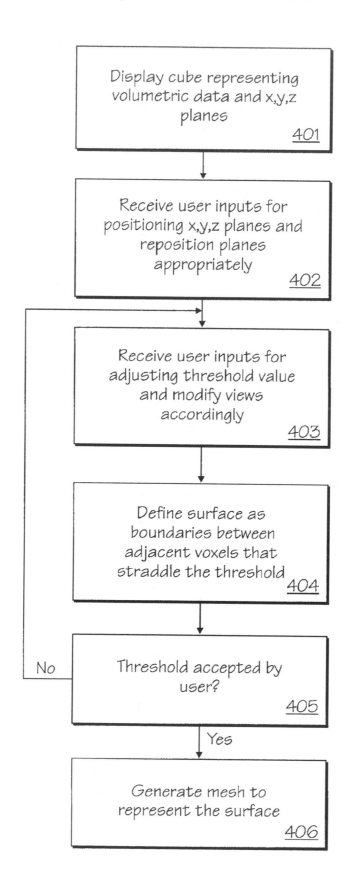

Display cube representing volumetric data and x,y,z planes
<u>401</u>

Receive user inputs for positioning x,y,z planes and reposition planes appropriately
<u>402</u>

Receive user inputs for adjusting threshold value and modify views accordingly
<u>403</u>

Define surface as boundaries between adjacent voxels that straddle the threshold
<u>404</u>

No   Threshold accepted by user?
<u>405</u>

Yes

Generate mesh to represent the surface
<u>406</u>

FIG. 4

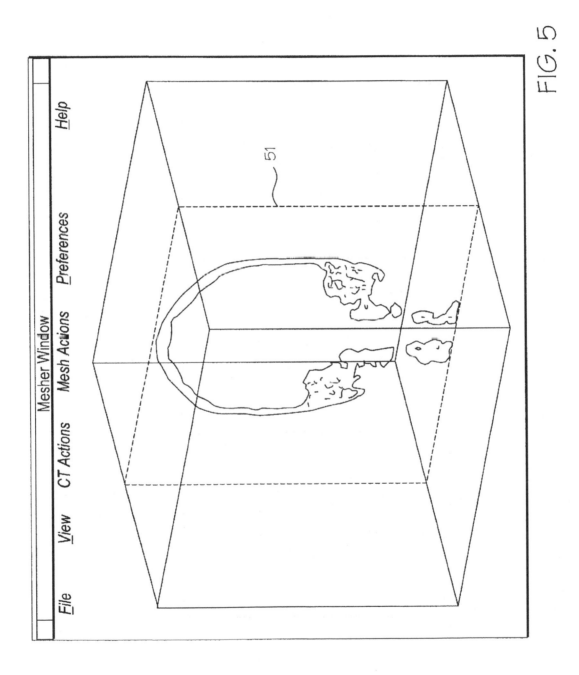

FIG. 5

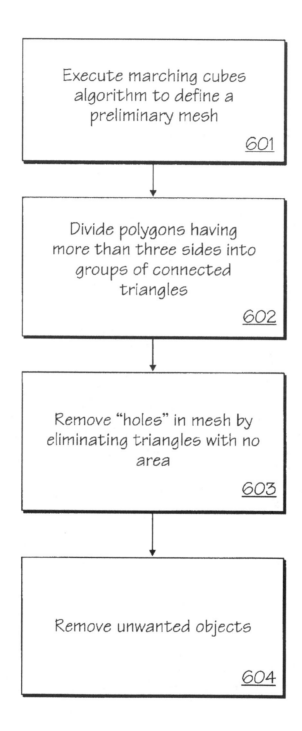

Execute marching cubes algorithm to define a preliminary mesh

<u>601</u>

Divide polygons having more than three sides into groups of connected triangles

<u>602</u>

Remove "holes" in mesh by eliminating triangles with no area

<u>603</u>

Remove unwanted objects

<u>604</u>

FIG. 6A

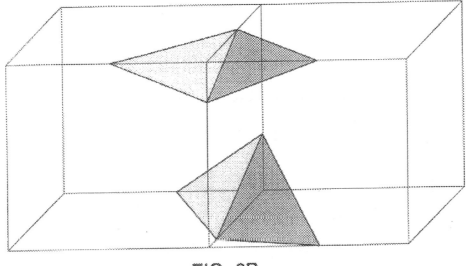

FIG. 6B

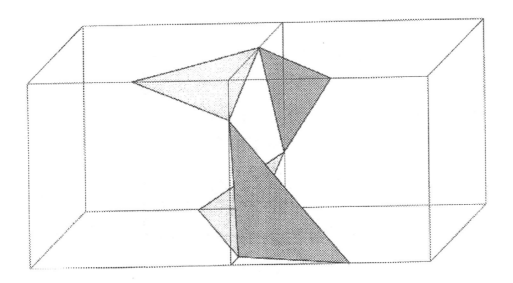

FIG. 6C

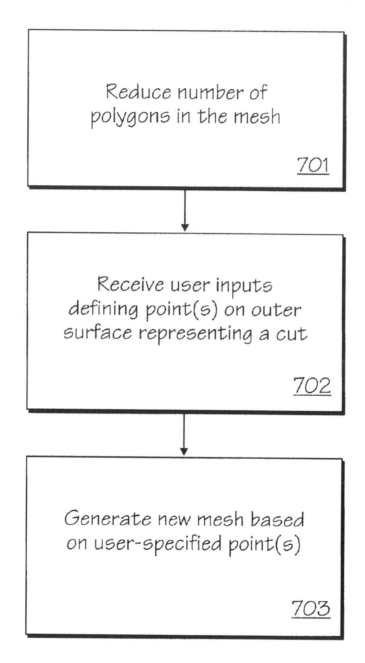

FIG. 7

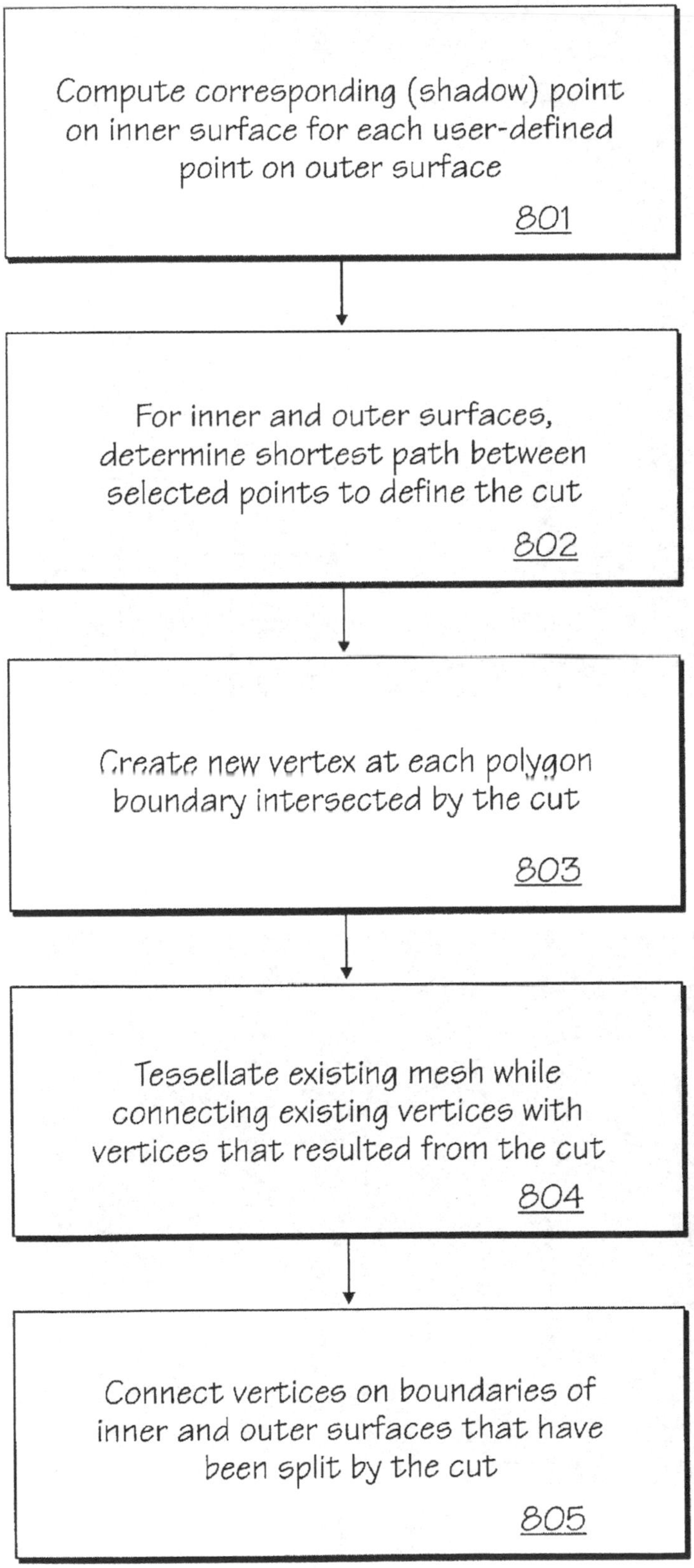

Compute corresponding (shadow) point
on inner surface for each user-defined
point on outer surface

<u>801</u>

For inner and outer surfaces,
determine shortest path between
selected points to define the cut

<u>802</u>

Create new vertex at each polygon
boundary intersected by the cut

<u>803</u>

Tessellate existing mesh while
connecting existing vertices with
vertices that resulted from the cut

<u>804</u>

Connect vertices on boundaries of
inner and outer surfaces that have
been split by the cut

<u>805</u>

FIG. 8

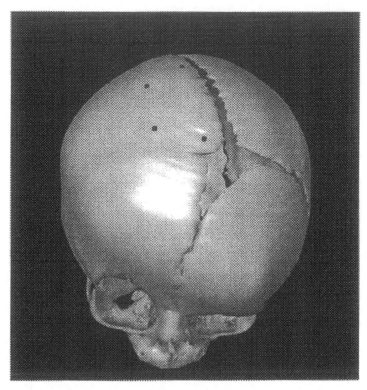

Fig. 9A

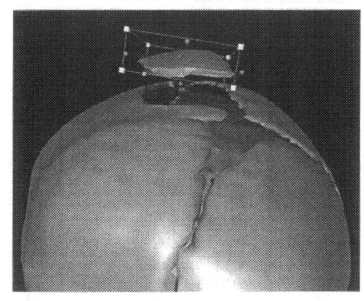

Fig. 9B

566

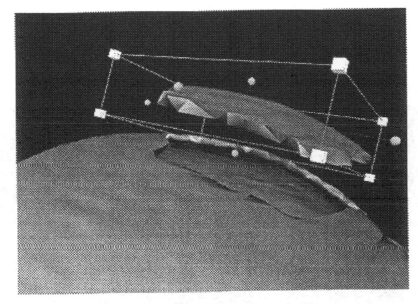

Fig. 9C

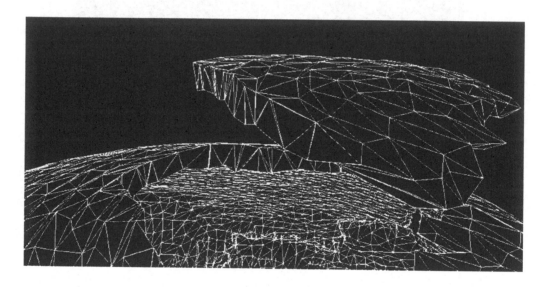

FIG. 9D

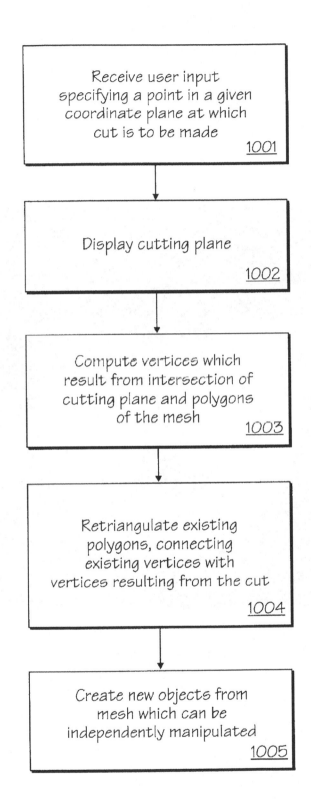

Receive user input specifying a point in a given coordinate plane at which cut is to be made 1001

Display cutting plane 1002

Compute vertices which result from intersection of cutting plane and polygons of the mesh 1003

Retriangulate existing polygons, connecting existing vertices with vertices resulting from the cut 1004

Create new objects from mesh which can be independently manipulated 1005

FIG. 10

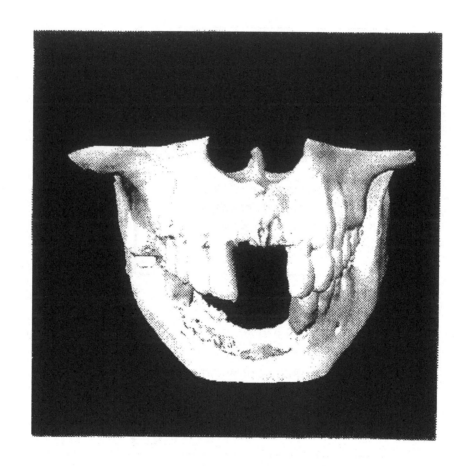

FIG. 11A

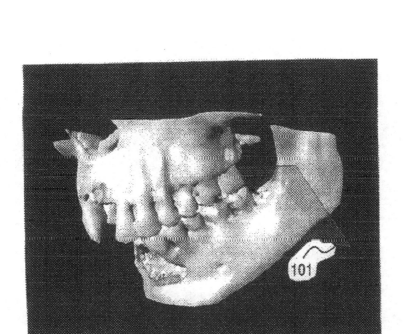

FIG. 11B

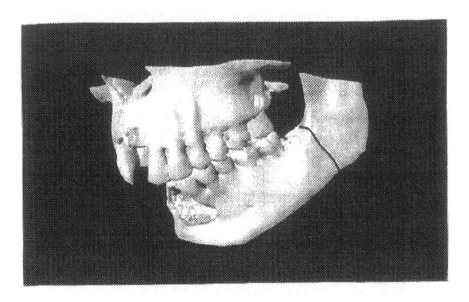

FIG. 11C

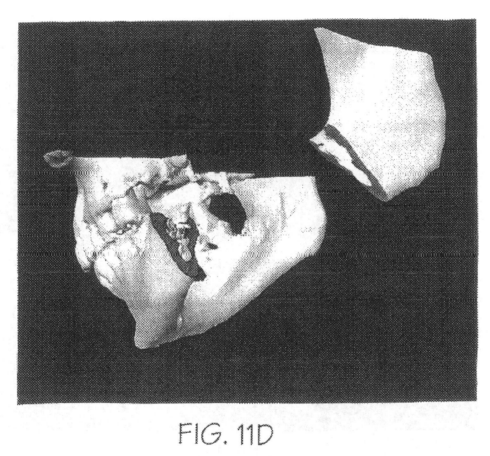

FIG. 11D

573

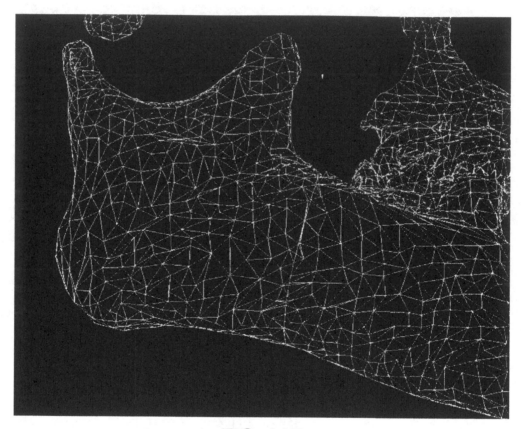

FIG. 11E

574

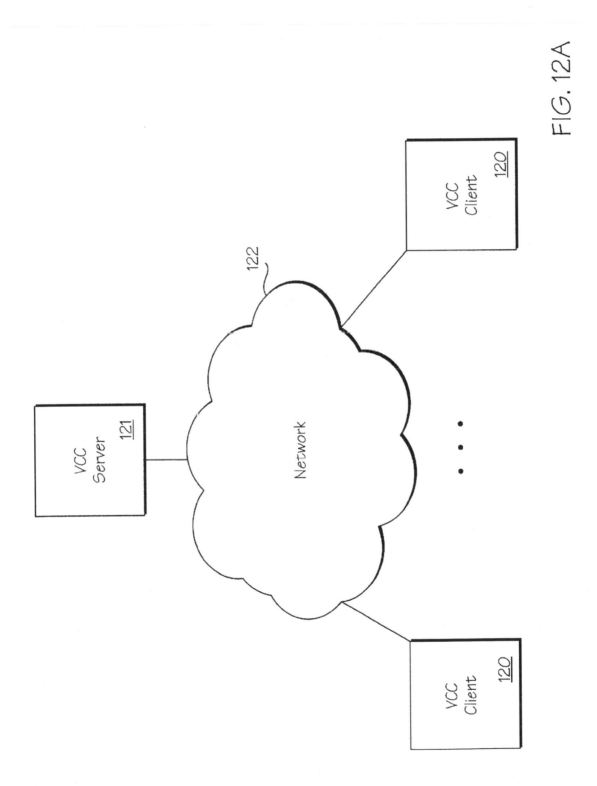

FIG. 12A

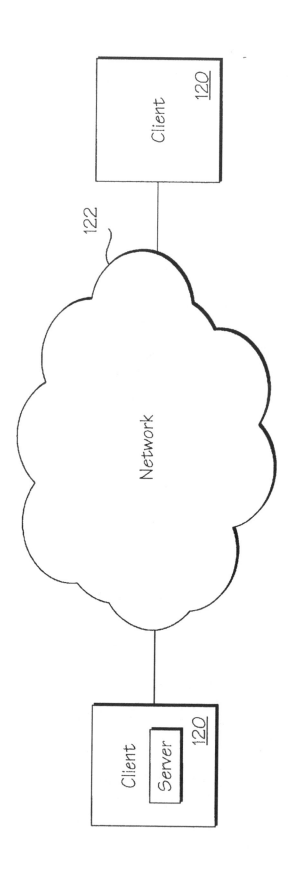

FIG. 12B

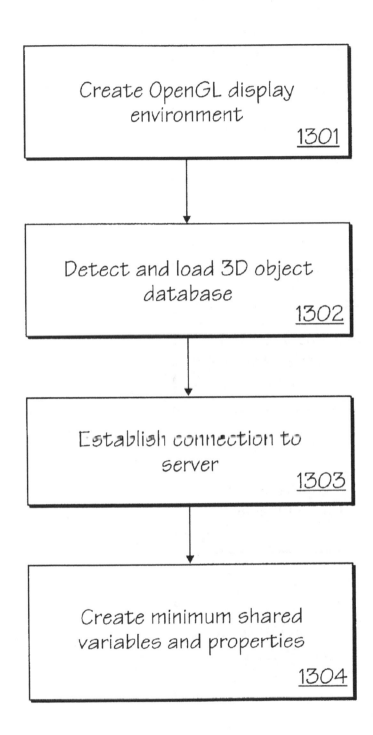

FIG. 13

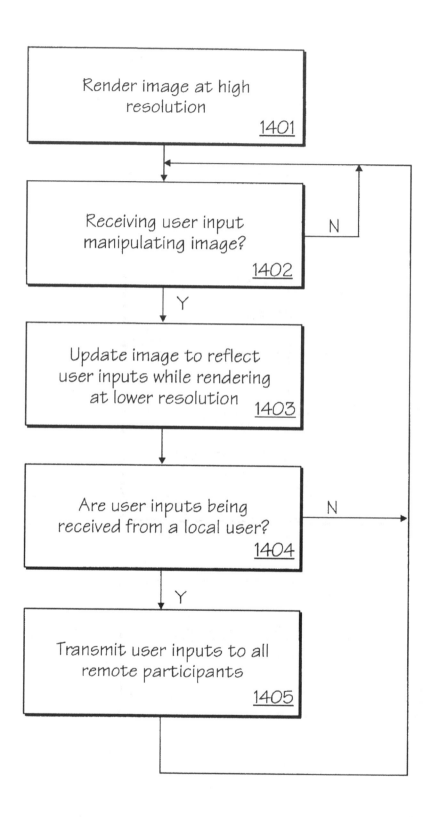

FIG. 14

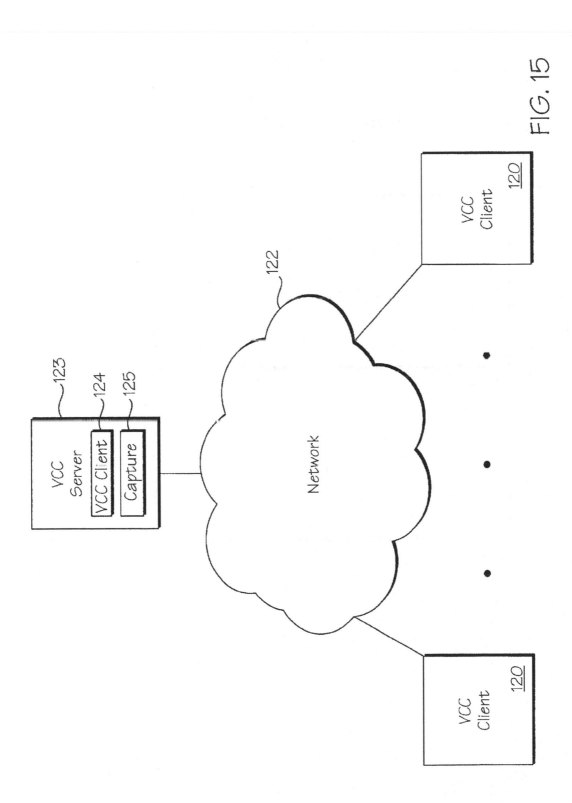

FIG.15

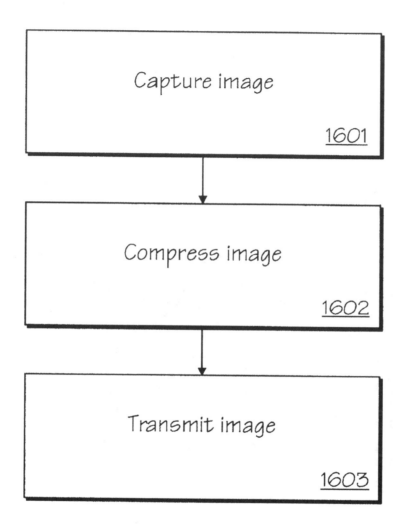

FIG. 16

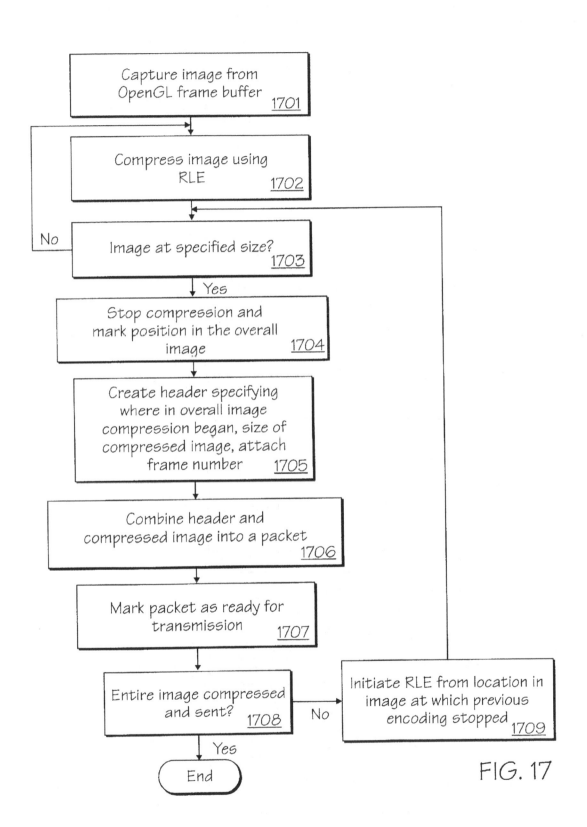

Capture image from OpenGL frame buffer   1701

Compress image using RLE   1702

Image at specified size?   1703   No

Yes

Stop compression and mark position in the overall image   1704

Create header specifying where in overall image compression began, size of compressed image, attach frame number   1705

Combine header and compressed image into a packet   1706

Mark packet as ready for transmission   1707

Entire image compressed and sent?   1708   No

Initiate RLE from location in image at which previous encoding stopped   1709

Yes

End

FIG. 17

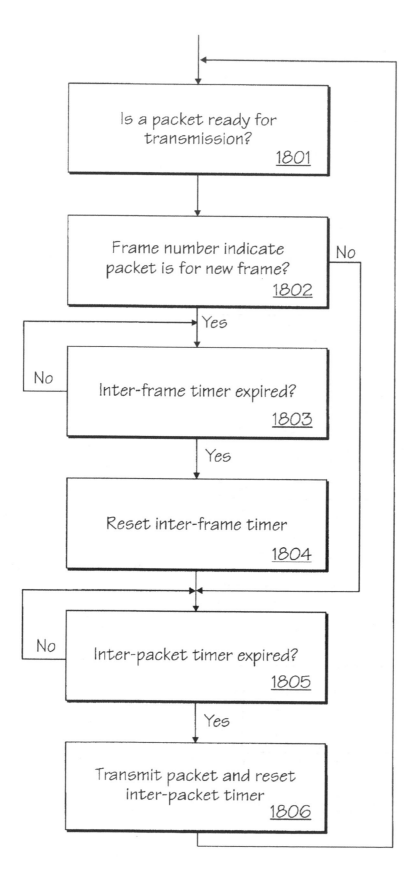

FIG. 18

1

METHOD AND APPARATUS FOR VIRTUAL INTERACTIVE MEDICAL IMAGING BY MULTIPLE REMOTELY-LOCATED USERS

This application claims the benefit of Provisional U.S. Patent Applications No. 60/107,286, filed on Nov. 6, 1998 and entitled "Reconstruction of Serial Sections (ROSS 3-D Reconstruction Program)"; Ser. No. 60/107,509, filed on Nov. 6, 1998 and entitled "Polygon Reduction in 3-Dimensional Meshes"; Ser. No. 60/107,284, filed on Nov. 6, 1998 and entitled "Mesher: Three-Dimensional Surface Generation from Volumetric Data Sets"; and Ser. No. 60/107,390, filed on Nov. 6, 1998 and entitled "Virtual Surgery Cutting Tool", each of which is incorporated herein by reference in its entirety.

ORIGIN OF THE INVENTION

The invention described herein was made in the performance of work under a NASA contract no. NCC2-1006 and is subject to Public Law 96-517 (35 U.S.C. 200 et seq.). The contractor has not elected to retain title to the invention.

FIELD OF THE INVENTION

The present invention pertains to the field of medical imaging systems and techniques. More particularly, the present invention relates to techniques for displaying and manipulating high-resolution, three-dimensional medical images.

BACKGROUND OF THE INVENTION

Various techniques have been developed for imaging internal structures and functions of the human body. Examples of such techniques include computed tomography (CT), magnetic resonance imaging (MRI), echocardigraphy, sonography, and nuclear medicine. The images are commonly generated by first acquiring three-dimensional (3D) data using a tomographic imaging system, and then "reconstructing" the images based on the data. The reconstruction process is normally performed by software executing on a computer system such as a workstation or a personal computer (PC). Advances in computer technology, including increases in the amounts of available processing power, have enabled more sophisticated ways of capturing and displaying medical image data, such as stereoscopic rendering, animation, and virtual surgery. Nonetheless, there is still a great need for improvements upon such techniques, including improvements in image quality, new ways for users to interact with such images, and greater ease of use of biomedical image display systems.

Current biomedical visualization techniques allow a user to view and manipulate a 3D image of an anatomical object, such as a skeletal structure or an organ. FIG. 1, for example, shows such an image of a skull, formed using such a technique. In that case, the data of the object acquired by the imaging system is typically reconstructed so that the surface of the object is represented as a "mesh" of interconnected polygons; the polygons, which are typically triangles, are defined by a set of interconnected vertices. One well-known technique for generating a mesh to represent the surface of an object is known as the "marching cubes" algorithm, described by W. Schroeder et al., The Visualization Toolkit, Prentice Hall PTR, Upper Saddle River, N.J., 1998, pp.159–64. A high-quality image of the surface of the object requires that the mesh represent the minute topographical details of the surface with high fidelity. The realism provided by current surface visualization techniques is limited by the

2

number of polygons used to form the mesh and the size of the polygons. To increase the accuracy with which very small features of the surface are shown, it is desirable to use a larger number of very small polygons. However, while increasing the number of polygons may provide a more realistic surface, it also tends to drastically slow down the rendering process, particularly rendering in response to user manipulation of the images. As a result of these limitations, current visualization techniques generally cannot provide the amount of surface detail that is desired by medical practitioners. In addition, current techniques tend to introduce artifacts (flaws) into the image during the reconstruction process. For example, one common problem associated with the marching cubes algorithm is that holes or tears can occur in the mesh due to inherent ambiguity in that algorithm. Hence, it is desirable to have an image visualization technique that provides more detailed surface representation with fewer artifacts and which can operate at an acceptable speed using conventional hardware.

One area of advancement in biomedical visualization techniques is virtual surgery. In virtual surgery, a user (e.g., a physician) manipulates a computer input device to define an incision or a cut in a displayed anatomical object. Special-purpose software, sometimes referred to as a virtual cutting tool, allows the user to define the cut and view internal features of the object. Current virtual cutting tools are limited in the degree of realism they can provide. As noted above, one limitation lies in the number of polygons used to represent the surface to be cut. Processing speed requirements tend to limit the number of polygons that can be practically used. In addition, current virtual cutting tools restrict the shape of the cut made by the user to the vertices of the mesh. Hence, both the surface being cut and the cut itself tend to be ragged and/or unrealistic in appearance. Further, such cutting tools often do not accurately depict tissue thicknesses. Therefore, it is desirable to have the virtual surgery cutting tool which provides more realistic visualization of incisions or cuts, without increasing processing power requirements.

Another area of interest is the ability to allow multiple users at different computer systems to collaboratively view and interact with biomedical images in real-time. For example, it is desirable to enable a number of physicians using different computer systems that are remote from each other to view an image of an anatomical object simultaneously; it is further desirable that when one user manipulates the image, the changes are instantly displayed to the other users. Such a system might be used to provide people living in remote rural areas with access to sophisticated medical knowledge, facilities, and techniques, such as are now associated mainly with urban centers. Another field where such capability would be particularly useful is in space exploration. For example, such a system might be used to allow doctors on Earth to interactively diagnose and treat astronauts in a spacecraft or on a future lunar or Martian base.

One major obstacle to accomplishing this is that images tend to require very large amounts of data. Biomedical images in particular tend to be extremely data-intensive in order to provide image quality that is adequate for diagnosis and treatment. Consequently, speedy user interaction with such images tends to require a substantial amount of processing power and sophisticated hardware at the remote stations. Allowing real-time, simultaneous interaction by multiple remote users is considerably more problematic, even with very high-speed communication links. Hence, it is desirable to have a technique for enabling multiple remote users to interact collaboratively with high-resolution medical images in real-time. It is particularly desirable that such a technique not require expensive equipment or inordinate amounts of processing power at each remote station.

SUMMARY OF THE INVENTION

The present invention includes a method and apparatus for enabling a number of geographically distributed users to collaboratively view and manipulate images of an object. A data structure including data representing the object is maintained. The data structure includes a set of variables that are shared by each of a number of remote processing systems. The data structure further includes a number of models of the object, each of which corresponds to a different image resolution. Data is then multicast to each of the remote processing systems based on the data structure, to allow the image to be displayed on each of the remote processing systems. This includes dynamically selecting from among the models of the object. Transmission of user inputs applied at each of the client systems is coordinated, to allow the image displayed on each of the client systems to be updated in real-time in response to user inputs applied at each other client system.

Other features of the present invention will be apparent from the accompanying drawings and from the detailed description which follows.

BRIEF DESCRIPTION OF THE DRAWINGS

The present invention is illustrated by way of example and not limitation in the figures of the accompanying drawings, in which like references indicate similar elements and in which:

FIG. 1 illustrates a 3-D image of a skull;

FIG. 2 illustrates a virtual interactive imaging system in accordance with the present invention;

FIG. 3 shows a block diagram of a hardware platform that may be used to implement the virtual interactive imaging system;

FIG. 4 is a flow diagram illustrating a user interactive process for configuring the virtual interactive imaging system for mesh generation;

FIG. 5 illustrates an example of a display presented to user during execution of the routine of FIG. 4;

FIG. 6A is a flow diagram illustrating a process for generating a mesh to represent the surface of an object;

FIG. 6B illustrates a portion of a mesh which is properly constructed, such that the mesh no holes;

FIG. 6C illustrates a portion of a mesh that is improperly constructed, such that the mesh has a hole;

FIG. 7 is a flow diagram illustrating an overall process associated with operation of the virtual cutting tool;

FIG. 8 illustrates a process associated with the virtual cutting tool, for use with flat bones such as the skull;

FIGS. 9A, 9B, 9C and 9D illustrate displays showing a process of removing a section from a skull using a virtual cutting tool;

FIG. 10 illustrates a process associated with the virtual cutting tool, for use with the jaw or other non-flat bones;

FIGS. 11A through 11D show a sequence of displays associated with the routine of FIG. 10;

FIG. 11E shows an example of a mesh representing a jaw bone;

FIGS. 12A and 12B show two different network configurations associated with the Virtual Collaborative Clinic (VCC);

FIG. 13 is a flow diagram showing a process for initiating the VCC environment;

FIG. 14 is a flow diagram showing a process for implementing multiresolution display for the VCC environment;

FIG. 15 shows a network configuration for an embodiment of the VCC that includes a graphics supercomputer;

FIG. 16 is a flow diagram showing the overall process implemented by the graphics supercomputer of FIG. 15;

FIG. 17 is a flow diagram illustrating a process executed by the graphics supercomputer for capturing and compressing images; and

FIG. 18 is a flow diagram showing a process executed by the graphics supercomputer for transmitting packets to VCC clients.

DETAILED DESCRIPTION

A method and apparatus are described for enabling a number of geographically distributed users to collaboratively view and manipulate high-quality, high-resolution, 3D images of anatomical objects based on tomographic data. The method and apparatus are part of a virtual interactive imaging system which, as described in greater detail below, allows the display of high-resolution, 3D images of medical data to a user and allows the user to manipulate the images. The system includes a mesh generation component that generates high resolution meshes to represent surfaces of objects, based on data from a CT or MRI scan or the like. An example of a low resolution mesh is illustrated in FIG. 11E, which shows a mesh representing part of a jaw bone. Using the techniques described herein, meshes are generated so as to avoid tears, or holes, in the mesh, providing very high-quality representations of topographical features of the object, particularly at high-resolution. The system further includes a virtual surgery cutting tool that enables the user to simulate the removal of a piece or layer of a displayed object, such as a piece of skin or bone, view the interior of the object, manipulate the removed piece, and reattach the removed piece if desired. The system further provides a virtual collaborative clinic environment, which allows the users of multiple, remotely-located computer systems to collaboratively and simultaneously view and manipulate the high-resolution, 3D images of an object in real-time. The images may be rendered in four dimensions (4D), wherein the fourth dimension is time; that is, a chronological sequence of images of an object is displayed to show changes of the object over time (i.e., an animation of the object is displayed).

FIG. 2 illustrates an embodiment of the virtual interactive imaging system 20. The imaging system 20 may be embodied as software, which may be written in C, C++, or any other suitable programming language. It should be noted, however, that the imaging system 20 may alternatively be embodied in hardware, or as a combination of hardware and software. Thus, the present invention is not restricted to any particular combination of hardware and or software. The system 20 comprises a core reconstruction unit 21, and a Virtual Collaborative Clinic (VCC) unit 22 that is operatively linked to the reconstruction unit 21. The reconstruction unit 21 accesses medical image data stored in a database 23 for purposes of generating high-resolution, stereoscopic 3-D images. The data may be CT data, MRI data, or any other type of tomographic medical data. Further, the techniques described herein can also be applied to other types of data, i.e., outside the medical field, as will become apparent from the description which follows.

The reconstruction unit 21 includes a mesher component 24, a visualization module 25, a cyberscalpel 26, an input

5

unit 27, and an animation unit 28. The mesher 24 generates meshes to represent object surfaces based on the data stored in the database 23. The visualization module 25 generates images of patient data from medical scans. The cyberscalpel 26 is a virtual cutting tool for virtual surgery which allows the user to simulate cutting of an anatomical object displayed by the visualization module 25, using a conventional user input device. The cyberscalpel 26 is operatively coupled to the input unit 27, which is operatively coupled to the mesher 24 and the visualization units 25. The visualization unit 25 is also coupled to the animation module 28. The user input module 27 receives conventional user inputs for manipulating images and performing other functions, such as may be provided from a mouse, trackball, touchpad, or other standard user input device. The animation module 28 provides the capability to animate displayed images, to show changes to the object over time (4D).

The Virtual Collaborative Clinic (VCC) unit 22 is an extension of the reconstruction unit 21 which enables multiple, remotely located users to interact with the same 3D data set. As described in detail below, the VCC unit 22 may have counterpart components that reside and execute on other, remote processing systems. The VCC unit 22 is designed to allow users at widely distributed locations to view and interact with a common set of 3D objects in a virtual environment, and to share all changes to these objects in real-time. Again, the images may be rendered in 4D in the VCC environment to show changes of the object over time.

The reconstruction unit 21 generally provides ease of use and generality in application. Realistic, 3D stereoscopic images can be produced within minutes from medical scans. High fidelity is a main feature of the software package. It allows surgeons to visualize huge datasets, as from CT scans of patients' faces and skulls, or of the lung or the heart, so that very small defects are noticeable. The visualizations are based on meshes that may use several millions of polygons to describe surfaces. The mesher 24 employs an improvement upon the marching cubes algorithm, as will be described below, which permits polygon reduction without the tearing that is common to marching cubes applications. This approach allows the number of polygons describing surfaces to be reduced drastically (by as much as 98%) without losing topographical features. Polygon reduction permits more effective use of a cyberscalpel 26, so that surgeons can plan complicated surgery ahead of time, using realistic displays.

It should be recognized that, while the embodiments described herein are directed to medical applications, many aspects of the imaging system 20 can be applied outside of the medical field. For example, using features of the imaging system 20, researchers can bisect or otherwise cut into other types of scientific reconstructions, such as geological map of a planet, to gain new insights. Polygon reduction with retention of topography also makes it possible to implement the imaging system 20 on a PC, so that stereoscopic, 3D visualizations can be manipulated in real-time on an inexpensive computer. A main benefit is to enable visualization and interaction with patient-specific data in an immersive, virtual environment, which may be PC-based. Such PC-based systems can be placed on spacecraft.

As noted above, the imaging system 20 may be embodied as software that can be implemented in a conventional PC; however, the imaging system may also be implemented on a workstation, or any other suitable platform, or it may be distributed across two or more processing systems on a network. FIG. 3 illustrates one example of a hardware platform which may be used to implement the imaging

6

system 20. Note that FIG. 3 is a high-level conceptual representation that is not intended to be limited to any one particular architecture. The illustrated hardware platform includes a central processing unit (CPU) 31, read-only memory (ROM) 32, random access memory (RAM) 33, and a mass storage device 34, each connected to a bus system 41. The bus system 41 may include one or more buses connected to each other through various bridges, controllers and/or adapters, such as are well-known in the art. For example, the bus system 41 may include a system bus that is connected through an adapter to one or more expansion buses, such as a Peripheral Component Interconnect (PCI) bus. Also coupled to the bus system 41 are a keyboard 35, a pointing device 36, a display device 37, a printer 38, and audio output subsystem 39, and a communication device 40.

The pointing device 36 may be any suitable device for enabling a user to position a cursor or pointer on the display device 37, such as a mouse, trackball, touchpad, stylus, a microphone combined with an audio input system and speech recognition software, etc. The display device 37 may be any suitable device for displaying alphanumeric, graphical and/or video data to a user, such as a cathode ray tube (CRT), a liquid crystal display (LCD), or the like, and associated controllers. Mass storage device 34 may include any suitable device for storing large volumes of data, such as a magnetic disk or tape, magneto-optical (MO) storage device, or any of various types of Digital Versatile Disk (DVD) or compact disk (CD) storage. The communication device 40 may be any device suitable for enabling the hardware platform to communicate data with another processing system over communication link 42, such as a conventional telephone modem, a cable television modem, an Integrated Services Digital Network (ISDN) adapter, a Digital Subscriber Line (XDSL) adapter, a network interface card (NIC) such as an Ethernet adapter, etc. The audio subsystem 39 may include, for example, an audio sound card and a speaker. Of course, many variations upon the illustrated architecture can be used consistently with the imaging system 20 described herein.

I. MESHER

The mesher 24 (FIG. 2) operates based on segmentation to provide surface information, and automatic registration followed by mesh generation to describe the surface(s). The mesher 24 generates surface models of 3D objects imaged in a volumetric data set. The mesher 24 is similar to existing surface generation tools, except as otherwise described herein. Although the mesher 24 is not restricted to medical datasets, a more advantageous use of this application is thought to be in the generation of surface models of anatomical objects from CT and MRI medical data and the like. Typical models include the surface of the skin and skull on patients requiring reconstructive surgery and the surface of the heart for patients undergoing bypass graft surgery. The method is tailored to the kinds of contour data provided from the source.

FIG. 4 illustrates a user-interactive process performed by the imaging system 20 in connection with mesh generation. The user interface to the mesher 24 provides an efficient means of interacting with the volumetric data to set parameters necessary for the mesh generation. A key parameter is the threshold, which determines what portion of the data will constitute the surface boundary. Accordingly, at block 401 the user is presented with a graphical window depicting the volumetric data as an outlying cube, as illustrated in FIG. 5. This cube may be manipulated by the user with a mouse (or other user input device) to an arbitrary orientation on screen.

7

Three planes corresponding to the x, y, and z planes of the data volume, an example of which is shown as plane **51**, are positioned by the user to intersect the data volume. At block **402**, the user places each plane at the desired location along its corresponding axis and displays the two-dimensional data associated with the intersection of the volume. Next, at block **403** the user adjusts the threshold value by moving a slider bar or other similar control. To view the threshold data for a desired plane, the user selects a check box for that plane. The threshold value for each plane initially may be set to a predetermined default value, so as to represent bone, for example. To facilitate the user's selection of the boundary threshold, the display in each plane shows only those pixels whose value is: 1) equal to the threshold value and to 2) have at least one adjoining pixel with a value lower than the threshold value. The purpose of this operation is to display only the outline that will constitute a surface boundary, and not display any of the internal volume of the object. Every voxel in the volumetric dataset is classified as above or below this threshold, and at block **404** the surface is interpolated to be the boundary between adjacent voxels that straddle the threshold. If the user accepts the current threshold setting at block **405**, then at block **406** the mesher **24** generates a mesh to represent the surface using the current threshold setting. Otherwise, the routine repeats from block **403**, where the user selects another threshold value.

FIG. **6A** illustrates the process for generating the mesh (block **406**) in greater detail, according to at least one embodiment. Initially, at block **601** the points that constitute the above-noted boundary are connected into a triangle-based mesh using the marching cubes algorithm. The marching cubes algorithm produces a mesh consisting of a mixture of polygon shapes. However, the mesher **24** performs additional operations to produce a more regular, triangle-based mesh from the marching cubes generalized polygon mesh. An example of such a mesh is provided in FIG. **11E**, which shows part of a mesh representing a jaw bone. The procedure includes dividing the polygons which have more than three sides into groups of connected triangles at block **602**. Hence, the mesher **24** closely approximates small changes in curvature of the object as it re-generates the mesh. The resulting more regular, triangular mesh leads to greater coherency in the surface structure and a more realistic representation of the data.

At block **603**, all triangles with no area (i.e., triangles for which two or more vertices lie on top of one another) are eliminated—this step prevents tearing (occurrence of holes) and spurious surfaces in the model during subsequent operations on the mesh. Such tears are common to 3D reconstructions that are based on the marching cubes algorithm alone. FIG. **6C** illustrates an example of a portion of a mesh that has a hole, as often results from using the marching cubes algorithm alone. Note that the triangles in the left and right cubes connect the intersections on their shared face in a different way, such that they do not share edges. The result is a single surface that contains a hole. In contrast, FIG. **6B** illustrates an example of a portion of a mesh that has no holes. Note that the triangles in the left and right cubes connect the intersections on their shared face in the same way, such that they share edges. The result is two discrete surfaces that do not contain any holes. Hence, the present technique for surface generation allows for generation of meshes that may be reduced greatly without losing surface integrity or topography. Retention of surface integrity and topographical features is important for implementation of interactive tools such as the cyberscalpel **26** (FIG. **2**), since the quality of the initial model is propagated throughout subsequent operations on the data.

8

Generation of a surface mesh tends to produce many distinct objects bounded by a surface. In general, only a few of these objects are of interest, and the others constitute artifacts produced by noise found within the volumetric data. Accordingly, as a final step in the mesh generation process, such unwanted objects are removed at block **604**.

Once the mesh is generated, the visualization module **25** takes over. The visualization module **25** has features to permit greater versatility in viewing the images. The main functionalities of the visualization module **25** include three display modes for viewing 3D models: 1) wire frame, 2) gourad shading, and 3) semi- to full-transparency of selected objects. The visualization module **25** also provides for interactive manipulation of objects with the mouse (or other user input device), such as rotation, translation, and zoom; objects can be turned off or cut into any direction by arbitrary cutting planes.

The animation module **28** provides for animations by saving key frames in sequence to create an animation file. These animations are viewable on many platforms, including the monitor screen, and can be videotaped.

One significant feature of the mesher **24** is that it was designed to use the maximum range of gray levels present in the data, rather than resampling the data to fit a standardized range. A typical standardized range of gray levels is 8 bits in length, allowing 256 distinct gray levels, whereas raw CT data is 12 bits, or 4096 distinct gray levels. Retaining the higher resolution in the volumetric data provides a smoother surface reconstruction (a finer-grain image) that leads to improved realism in visual appearance.

II. CYBERSCALPEL

The cyberscalpel **26** uses a mesh that is reduced from its original million or more polygons (as generated by the mesher **24**) to a number more practical for speedy interaction with a cutting tool. Retention of geometry during mesh reduction is essential to implementation of interactive tools, since the goal is virtual surgery that is reasonably accurate in detail. The QSlim program from Carnegie Mellon University can be used to perform mesh reduction, and is believed to yield excellent results in either Unix or NT based operating systems. Mesh reduction can alternatively be performed as a reduction in the number of vertices based on minimization of the local mesh curvature. In at least one embodiment, the mesh is reduced to 50,000 polygons, which is far in excess of that used by many who are developing tools for virtual surgery. Thus, the imaging system **20** permits use of higher fidelity 3D reconstructions than do other packages, producing a more realistic image for interaction when preparing for surgery or when learning new procedures.

Refer now to FIG. **7**, which shows an overall process associated with operation of the virtual cutting tool. Prior to initiating virtual surgery, the number of polygons in the mesh is reduced at block **701**, using techniques such as those mentioned above. At block **702**, the cyberscalpel **26** is invoked, receiving user inputs defining one or more points representing a cut on the outer surface of the displayed object. The user inputs may be entered from a conventional user input device, such as a mouse. For example, in one embodiment the operator decides where a cut should begin and how it should extend along the external surface of the object. Points are placed by the user on the surface of the object using the mouse (or other pointing device) one after another until the cut is outlined. FIG. **9A** illustrates an example of four user-defined points (dark dots) placed on the top of a skull image, using this technique. FIGS. 9A, 9B, 9C and 9D illustrate steps in the process of removing a section from a skull using the cyberscalpel 26. At block 703, the cyberscalpel 26 generates a new mesh based on the user-specified points.

Two different virtual cutting techniques are implemented by the cyberscalpel 26, as a result of differences in the geometry of bones and other tissues and organs of the body. For cutting flat bones such as those of the skull, the object is visualized as a shaded solid, as shown in FIGS. 9A, 9B and 9C. The underlying mesh is not visible. Although only the external surface is apparent to the viewer, the inner surface is also reconstructed.

FIGS. 8 illustrates a process performed by the cyberscalpel 26 for flat bones, such as the skull. At block 801, as the user defines points on the outer surface of the object (see FIG. 9A), simultaneously points on the inner surface, which shadow those on the external surface, are automatically identified. The points on the surface of the object need not be placed close together. At block 802, an algorithm determines the shortest path between the selected locations and logically defines the shape of the cut. At block 803, while following along the path from one selected location to the next, a vertex is created at the edge of each polygon that is intersected by the path between successive points. Next, at block 804 the existing mesh is tessellated (tiled with polygons) as the original vertices are connected with the new vertices, i.e., the vertices which resulted from cutting.

At block 805, vertices on the boundary created by the cut on the inner surface are connected with vertices on the boundary created by the cut on the outer surface, so that the segmented piece appears as a 3D solid when manipulated—that is, the thicknesses of the layers cut into are visible. This effect can be seen in FIGS. 9B, 9C, and 9D. FIG. 9B shows a display frame with a piece being removed from the skull based on user-defined points. FIG. 9C shows a display frame with a magnified view of the removed skull piece of FIG. 9B. FIG. 9D shows another magnified view of a removed skull section, in which the polygons of the mesh are visible, including triangles created to connect the inner and outer surfaces of the skull. This feature provides for a more realistic, 3D segment of bone to be cut from the original reconstruction and manipulated. The removed piece may be outlined by a set of "handles" by which the user can manipulate the removed piece or reattach it to the main object. Examples of such handles are shown in FIGS. 9B and 9C as the points connected by lines around the removed piece of skull.

Using this technique, in contrast with prior virtual surgery tools, points to be connected are not necessarily existing points of the mesh. In addition, in contrast with prior techniques, the vertices at the boundary of the cut are connected.

In an extension of the above technique, the user simply drags a scalpel-like instrument along the surface of the image, and new points (as well as new polygons) are established precisely along the path.

For the jaw, a variation of this technique is employed. This is because the jaw has an outer, U-shaped surface as well as other corresponding inner surfaces that are, however, more irregular. Again, polygon reduction to 50,000 polygons is performed. FIG. 10 shows a process used by the cyberscalpel 26 for cutting the jaw, according to at least one embodiment. FIGS. 11A through 11D illustrate an example of what may be displayed to the user during this process. FIG. 11A shows a frontal view of a jaw prior to the cutting

process. Referring to FIG. 10, at block 1001, a location is selected by the user about midway on the external surface of the jaw (in this example), where the cut is to be made. At block 1002, a cutting plane 101 is then displayed as intersecting the object at this user-selected location, as shown in FIG. 11B. At block 1003, an algorithm computes vertices which result from the intersection of the polygons' edges with the cutting plane. Another algorithm retriangulates the existing polygons at block 1004, connecting existing vertices with vertices created by cutting. The cut is represented by a line along the virtual jaw to assist in placement of the cuts before separation of the objects, as shown in FIG. 11C. At block 1005, an algorithm then separates the mesh into connected components, creating new objects, which can then be manipulated independently, as shown in FIG. 11D. As with the flat bone embodiment of the cyberscalpel (described above), vertices on the cut edge of the inner surface are connected with vertices on the cut edge of the outer surface, so that the removed piece appears as a 3D solid.

As many cuts can be made as are needed to capture the surgical procedure realistically. Manipulation of the plane and subsequent objects may be facilitated by the use of the Open Inventor toolkit, available from TGS of San Diego, Calif., or any other suitable software. Note that, as with the mesher 24, these techniques employed by the cyberscalpel 26 are not limited to use on the skull or the jaw, nor to anatomical objects generally.

Several extensions to the above-described techniques can also be implemented. For example, the cyberscalpel 26 may provide the capability for the user to reposition the separated components more easily in three-space, in order to properly represent the original geometric structure. This embodiment, a series of visualization workstations that are linked together via a network. The number of workstations is essentially unlimited. The system includes at least two visualization workstations (i.e., VCC clients for displaying the data) and an information server that mediates the transmission of variables between the clients. Optionally, the information server may reside within one of the visualization workstations. The VCC component 22 may implement the functionality of either the VCC client, the information server, or both.

The visualization workstations are not tied to any specific hardware, but in at least one embodiment, are based on the OpenGL graphics API of Silicon Graphics Inc. of Mountain View, Calif., which is available on a wide variety of computer platforms. Network connectivity is also independent of hardware—however, the network protocols for TCP/IP (Transport Control Protocol/Internet Protocol), UDP (User Datagram Protocol), and Multicast UDP are supported. The VCC accommodates different levels of hardware resources.

Referring to FIG. 12A, the users of two or more client computer systems 120 may collaboratively interact with a displayed 3D object via a network 122. Interaction is coordinated by the information server 121 on the network 122. As noted, the information server may reside within one of the visualization workstations, as shown in FIG. 12B. The client systems 120 may be conventional PCs, for example. The server 121 may also be a PC, although in other embodiments, the server 121 may be a workstation, or a high-end graphics supercomputer, as described further below. The clients contact the information server via an IP address across the network 122, but they are not required to be able to contact one another.

The VCC 22 described herein is particularly significant to the telemedicine arena, in which the space and humanitarian

11

12

aspects of the can be done by maintaining in memory the original geometry of the removed segment(s). The original geometry can be viewed as a semitransparent object, much like a ghost of the part, so that replacement bones can be repositioned within the ghost very easily. Computational restoration of the overlying and underlying tissues is desirable here, so that the result of the operation can be viewed in advance. In addition, the cyberscalpel 26 may be linked with other algorithms to provide structural and spatial coordinate information about the separated components. This information can be used as a template, which the user can use when harvesting bone from other sites or when fabricating implants. In the case of the jaw, replacement bones may come from the fibula. The fibula can be reconstructed with the segments of bone from a representative jaw surgery placed above it. The fibula can then be segmented, using the angles of the cuts and lengths of the segments as templates. The replacement segments can then the replaced to redefine the jaw.

III. VIRTUAL COLLABORATIVE CLINIC (VCC)

The VCC component 22 (FIG. 2) is an extension of the reconstruction unit 21 that generates a virtual environment (the "VCC environment") that enables multiple users to interact in real-time with the same stereoscopic 3D data set. One advantageous use for such a system is to examine 3D reconstructions of medical data for consultation and diagnosis by medical practitioners who are located in different parts of the world. Thus, the VCC environment is particularly suited to displaying 3D models of anatomical reconstructions used in medical diagnoses and treatment planning, and the collaborative aspects allow physicians at different geographical sites to manipulate these objects as though looking at a common display.

In brief, the VCC architecture is comprised of, in at least one applications are of enormous significance. When spacecraft are well on their way to Mars, it will be nearly impossible to send astronauts back to Earth for treatment. Development of a virtual environment, imaging and the force-feedback (haptic) devices and technologies will make it possible to send sonically scanned data back to Earth for visualization, when necessary. The method of treatment can be devised by an expert on Earth and put into a virtual environment mode. The virtual environment images can be communicated to the spacecraft (with minutes of delay, of course), where the visualizations can be replayed in virtual environment or can be used to drive a slave robotic device. An astronaut physician can thus be walked through a procedure, and can practice it in virtual environment, before working on the ill member of the team. In addition, the VCC 22 can be used to bring medical services to people in remote or poverty stricken areas. The VCC environment provides capabilities for information sharing for collaboration, as well as data manipulations at each client site, independent of other sites. In addition, the VCC environment may include graphics service from a graphics supercomputer, as described below.

The VCC provides several features to provide the remote interaction capabilities. In at least one embodiment, each computer in the collaboration contains a copy of the 3D reconstruction to be viewed, and has the graphical and computational capabilities to display such an object. Collaboration occurs by linking together the attributes of the object (i.e., location, orientation, color, etc.) on each computer so that a change to an attribute on one computer is immediately propagated to all the other participants' computers. Functionally, this system allows an individual to manipulate an object in space and show a particular aspect of the model to the other participants, as though they were all looking at a common screen. A pointer is programmed into the software, permitting a participant to point out salient structures to others as a discussion takes place.

Implementation of the VCC environment may be hindered on any one or more of the client computers 120, due to limitations in the computational and/or graphical capabilities of such client computer(s), particularly if such client computers are lower end PCs. However, the prevalence and relatively low cost of PCs (in comparison to other platforms) makes it desirable that the VCC component 26 run on PCs, so a large degree of scalability is provided. Multiresolution representations of the mesh models are used in the VCC environment to accomplish this. For example, by switching to a low resolution version of a model (for example, a model having $\frac{1}{50}$ of the triangles in the full model) during user interactions, the manipulation of an object takes on a real-time quality which allows the user to precisely position an object by hand. Upon completion of the manipulation, a high resolution version of the data is displayed, causing a slight delay but not interfering with the users actions, since the object is no longer being manipulated.

There may be situations in which the display of the high resolution data on a PC is simply not practical, because the dataset is so large that it could take minutes to render the image. Extending the idea of multiresolution display, the VCC described herein allows a graphics supercomputer to render a stationary, high resolution dataset, and to distribute the images to all of the participating client sites as their high resolution display. Using the capabilities of a high-bandwidth network such as the Next Generation Internet, a technique for real-time capture and transmission of images from the graphics supercomputer may be implemented. As described further below, this implementation uses a multicast distribution method to send the images out to all the client sites, allowing a server to provide images for potentially hundreds of client sites simultaneously. A key benefit of this component is the elimination of the need for high speed graphics systems at the client sites, allowing an institution to leverage a single high speed graphics system through their organization.

The first step in launching the VCC environment is to start the information server. This is a discrete piece of software from the VCC itself, and may be left running as a service on a machine assigned as the information server. At least one embodiment, the information server is the World2World toolkit of SENSE8 Corporation of Mill Valley, Calif. FIG. 13 illustrates the procedure for starting the VCC application.

On startup, the VCC component 22 implementing the client application performs the following procedure. At block 1301, an OpenGL display environment is created. At block 1302, the 3D object database is detected and loaded. At block 1303, a connection to the information server is established. A block 1304 the minimum shared variables and properties are created. In at least one embodiment, the minimum shared variables and properties are: 1) location and orientation of the camera (users viewpoint) in the virtual environment; 2) lighting applied to the scene; 3) name of the current object to display; and 4) name and state of any devices (i.e., the mouse or a third tracking device) connected to the workstation. If another client has already created any of these variables on the information server, the server associates the corresponding variables and properties between client sites.

The general operation of the VCC environment is as follows. Upon successful startup of the client, the user may load one of the 3D objects in the database into the viewing environment via a menu selection. Once an object has been selected, the name of the object is sent via the information server to all the other clients and triggers a load of the same object at each client site. If the object is not available in a particular client's database, a simple shape (e.g., a cube) is loaded to indicate failure to find the desired object. The failure is also signaled to the information server, which then requests that the originating client sends the object data to the clients that do not already have it.

Each object is embedded in a scenegraph, which is an organizational tree used to store all the properties of the object, such as geometric information about the object, spatial orientation, lighting conditions, colors, etc. Each scenegraph is analyzed as it is loaded, and all the variables and properties in the scenegraph (except the geometry itself) are created as shared variables and linked through the information server. Modification of any property due to scene manipulation is then automatically propagated to all the other clients, providing the collaborative aspect of the system.

Click-and-drag mouse operations or similar operations using other peripheral devices are used to perform spatial manipulation of the scene. Modifications of properties, such as color or opacity, are performed via menu operations and dialog boxes. When a user loads a new object, all of the shared variables associated with the old object scenegraph are destroyed and replaced by those in the new scenegraph.

Handling of the shared variables within the VCC is independent of the information server. Within the VCC client, a transmission queue is created that holds information that must be sent to the information server. Modification of a shared variable cause the variable and its new value to be placed in the queue, where it is held until the transmission function is executed. The transmission function gathers all the variables in the queue and sends them as a list having entries in the form (variable, value) to the information server for redistribution. Any server system that can handle data of this form may be used as the information server—examples are Microsoft's DCOM, Sun's Java Shared Data Toolkit, or the World2World toolkit from Sense8. A timer is used to trigger when the transmission function is executed—for example, transmission every 50 milliseconds may be suitable.

The display routines of the VCC are compatible with different hardware having vastly different graphics performance. The general technique is referred to as multi-resolution display. In essence, several representations (models) of each 3D object are created, each model having an order of magnitude less geometry components than the last. All of these models are stored in the scenegraph, and the VCC chooses one of them to display based on a series of pre-set criteria. One such criterion is response time to user manipulations. For example, rotations of an object by dragging the mouse should produce a smooth, animated sequence of rotations that track the users movements in real time. However, another criterion may be object detail when the object is static, provided the user does not have to wait too long for the static image to be rendered. As noted above, displaying one of the lower resolution images during scene manipulation and then displaying a higher resolution image when stopped accomplishes these goals. Providing information to the VCC about the graphics capability of the specific hardware at a client site allows the system to choose the appropriate levels of detail for these operations. Thus, different users linked in the VCC collaboration may be looking at the same object, but at different levels of detail, especially

during manipulations. Note that this is the main reason behind sharing all of the information in the scenegraph except the geometry.

FIG. 14 illustrates an embodiment of the multiresolution display process. At block 1401, the image is rendered on a client system statically at high resolution. If the user input for manipulating the image is received at block 1402, then at block 1403, the displayed image is updated to reflect the user input (i.e., rotation, translation, etc.) while being rendered at a lower resolution (based on the appropriate model in the scenegraph). If, at block 1404, the user inputs are being received from a local user, then at block 1405, shared variables representing the user inputs are transmitted to the remote participants.

Optionally, the VCC environment may include a graphics supercomputer server. The purpose of such an embodiment is to leverage the speed of a graphics supercomputer for very large (i.e. highly detailed) objects that would not be renderable on a PC desktop system. An example of such an embodiment is illustrated in FIG. 15. In this example, the network 122 is a high-bandwidth network between all clients 120 participating in the collaboration. The graphics server 123 runs a client application 124 identical to that of the VCC client systems 120, but also contains a capture process 125 designed to capture the image created by the display system and transmit it to the VCC client systems 120. Upon reception of the image from the graphics server 123, the VCC clients 120 display this image rather than generating their own through the local display system. In at least one embodiment, the graphics server 123 is an Onyx2 system with InfiniteReality2 graphics, from Silicon Graphics Inc.

The graphics server process operates in two modes: 1) continuous transmission of images, akin to streaming video, and 2) single-frame transmission in response to an event in the program. Mode "1)" is used if the VCC clients are not expected to perform any local rendering. Mode "2)"is used if the VCC clients are expected to render the low resolution images during manipulation of the object, but receive the high resolution static display from the graphics server.

The overall operation of the graphics server process is described now with reference to FIG. 16. At block 1601, the image is captured from the OpenGL frame buffer. At block 1602, the image is compressed for transmission. At block 1603, the image is transmitted to the VCC clients. More specifically, as described further below, individual portions of an overall image are compressed and transmitted sequentially.

Standard methods for capturing and sending images across a network are generally insufficient for purposes of this embodiment. The most common solutions are MPEG encoding or Apple QuickTime encoding of the video stream, which can be performed with specialized hardware to allow frame rates on the order of 30 frames per second. However, these solutions are limited to NTSC and PAL screen resolutions, which are insufficient for the very high resolutions displays needed for this application (e.g., 1024×1024 true color pixels). Software encoding using these standards is possible, but they are computationally intensive and cannot be performed in real-time on images extracted from the OpenGL frame buffer. Even in the case of single frame transmission, the software implementations of MPEG and QuickTime could take 10–100 times longer than is desired.

Consequently, the present technique employs a run length encoding (RLE) compression routine that can operate on a typical image in less than 70 msec, and provide a compression ratio in the range of 3:1 to 6:1, depending on image content. Even with a 6:1 compression, typical 3D medical images to be transmitted may be about 8 Mb ($1024 \times 1024 \times 3 \times 2$ for stereo display). A single data stream to a VCC client at 10 frames per second would require 80 Mb/sec. Multiply this bandwidth by the number of clients, and transmission can become extremely difficult. A solution is to use the multicast addressing protocol, which allows a single data stream to leave the graphics server addressed for multiple client receivers. One aspect of the multicast protocol is that the packet size (the basic unit of information transmitted across the network by the protocol) is on the order of 1.5 Kb in size; consequently, the overall image is broken into many packets for transmission. Another aspect of the multicast protocol is that transmission of each piece of information is unreliable—that is, it is impossible to guarantee that a specific packet arrives at a particular client. Because some portion of an image could be lost, and the VCC client must be able to reconstruct a partial image if information is missing, this factor is accounted for in the transmission routines implemented by the graphics server, as described below.

The RLE image encoding must retain all of the image information if it is to be decoded properly. Because information could be lost in transmission, a modified RLE method is used to selectively encode smaller portions of the image that can fit in a single packet. Rather than base the RLE encoding on a specific image size, the compression routine starts compressing data until a specified compressed file size is reached, at which point it restarts and creates a new packet. Finished packets are handed off to the transmission routines, and sent immediately to the VCC clients. Each packet also contains a header specifying where in the whole image this image fragment should be decoded, and which image frame number it belongs to in case fragments of multiple images arrive at a VCC client.

Thus, the process implemented by the graphics server is described further with reference to FIG. 17. At block **1701**, the graphics server captures the image from the OpenGL frame buffer. Next, the server compresses the image using RLE encoding at block **1702**, and checks the size of the encoded image at block **1703**. When the encoded image reaches the specified size (block **1703**), the server marks the position in the image and halts the RLE encoding at block **1704**. At block **1705**, the server creates a header specifying where in the image the RLE encoding began, exactly how large is the RLE encoded image, and attaches the image frame number generated by the graphics server for this image frame. The server combines the header and RLE encoded image into a packet at block **1706**, and marks the packet as ready for transmission at block **1707**. If the entire image has been compressed and transmitted (block **1708**), then the routine ends; otherwise the RLE compression is reinitiated at block **1709** from the location in the image at which the previous encoding was halted, and routine repeats from block **1703**.

At a VCC client, each packet received is decoded and placed in the image at the location specified by the header in the packet. When packets with a larger frame number arrive, the VCC client assumes that all packets have been sent for the current frame and transfers the image to the screen. If packets have been lost, then errors in the image will be seen at the VCC client.

Network equipment that is currently available cannot, in practice, handle the bandwidth required for the applications described above, without substantial loss of data packets. Because a reliable transmission protocol is not available, the

data flow coming out of the graphics server is regulated to minimize packet loss, at the expense of frames per second. When transmitting data at a very high data rate, too many packets may be lost, resulting in noticeable image degradation on the client systems. Accordingly, it may be desirable to maintain an average data rate that is lower than the maximum achievable rate, to reduce the number of lost packets. Creating two timers in the graphics server transmission routines, one to regulate inter-packet transmission time and the other to regulate inter-frame transmission time, can be used to accomplish this. These parameters can be modified while the system is operating, so that if network conditions change, the transmission rate can be adjusted accordingly.

The transmission process, therefore, is described further with reference to FIG. **18**. At block **1801**, the server determines if a packet is available for transmission. If the frame number of the packet indicates that the packet is for a new frame at block **1802**, then it is determined at block **1803** whether the inter-frame timer has expired. If the packet is not for a new frame, the procedure precedes directly to block **1805**, described below. If the packet is for a new frame and the inter-frame timer has not expired, the procedure loops at block **1803** until the inter-frame timer has expired. Once the inter-frame timer has expired, the timer is reset at block **1804**, and at block **1805**, it is determined whether the inter-packet timer has expired. If not, the procedure loops at block **1805** until the inter-packet timer has expired. When the inter-packet timer has expired, the packet is transmitted, and the inter-packet timer is reset at block **1806**. The procedure then repeats from block **1801**.

Note that the capture, compression, and transmission processes many run in separate threads for greater efficiency. If a single image is being sent, then the sequence of events is serial. However, in the streaming video mode, transmission of a given frame may occur concurrently with compression of the next frame and capture of a subsequent frame. Such concurrent operation allows the frame rate to be limited only by the slowest process of the three and can significantly increase the number of frames sent per second for complex images.

Thus, a method and apparatus have been described for enabling a number of geographically distributed users to collaboratively view and manipulate high-quality, high-resolution, 3D images of anatomical objects based on tomographic data. Although the present invention has been described with reference to specific exemplary embodiments, it will be evident that various modifications and changes may be made to these embodiments without departing from the broader spirit and scope of the invention as set forth in the claims. Accordingly, the specification and drawings are to be regarded in an illustrative sense rather than a restrictive sense.

What is claimed is:

1. A method of enabling users of a plurality of networked computer systems to collaboratively view and manipulate images of an object, the method comprising:

causing corresponding images of the object to be displayed on each of a plurality of computer systems at a first resolution;

receiving, at one of the computer systems, user input specifying a manipulation of the image;

transmitting information indicative of the user input to each of the other computer systems;

updating the image displayed on each of the other computer systems substantially simultaneously to depict the manipulation, including displaying the image at a second resolution lower than the first resolution while said manipulation is being depicted; and

displaying the image on each of the computer systems at the first resolution when depiction of the manipulation is complete.

2. A method as recited in claim 1, further comprising maintaining a model of the object at the first resolution and a model of the object at the second resolution, wherein said updating comprises switching from using the first model to using the second model to display the image.

3. A method as recited in claim 1, wherein the image displayed by each of the computer systems may be a three-dimensional image.

4. A method as recited in claim 1, wherein said displaying comprises displaying changes of the object over time.

5. A method of enabling a plurality of geographically distributed users to collaboratively view and manipulate images of an object, the method comprising:

maintaining a data structure including data representing the object, the data structure including a plurality of variables shared by each of a plurality of remote processing systems, the data structure further including a plurality of models of the object, each model corresponding to a different image resolution;

multicasting data to each of the remote processing systems based on the data structure to allow the image to be displayed on each of the remote processing systems, including dynamically selecting from the plurality of models; and

coordinating transmission of user inputs and values of shared variables applied at each of the client systems to allow the image displayed on each of the client systems to be updated in real-time in response to user inputs applied at each other client system.

6. A method as recited in claim 5, further comprising selecting said models of the object for said multicasting so as to cause the image to be displayed on each of the client systems at a reduced resolution during a user manipulation of the image on one of the client systems.

7. A method as recited in claim 6, wherein at least one of the client systems is configured to display changes of the object over time.

8. A method as recited in claim 5, further comprising, for each of a plurality of consecutive portions of the data representing the object:

compressing the portion until the portion reaches the specified image size; and

combining the compressed portion into a packet with information indicating a position of said portion within the image.

9. A method of enabling a plurality of geographically distributed users to collaboratively view and manipulate images of an object in real-time, the method comprising, at a server:

maintaining a data structure including data representing the object, the data structure including a plurality of variables shared by each of a plurality of remote client systems, the data structure further including a plurality of models of the object, each model corresponding to a different image resolution;

sequentially preparing a packet of each of a plurality of consecutive portions of the data representing the object for transmission to the remote client systems, based on the data structure, including selecting said models of the object according to display capabilities of the remote client systems;

multicasting each packet that is ready for transmission to each of the remote client systems to allow each of the client systems to display the image of the object based on the packets; and

coordinating transmission of user inputs applied at each of the client systems to allow the image displayed on each of the client systems to be updated in real-time in response to user inputs applied at each of the other client systems.

10. A method as recited in claim 9, wherein said maintaining comprises selecting said models of the object so as to cause the image to be displayed on each of the client systems at a reduced resolution during a user manipulation of the image at one of the client systems.

11. A method as recited in claim 9, wherein said preparing comprises:

compressing the portion until the portion reaches the specified image size;

combining the compressed portion into a packet with information indicating a position of said portion within the image; and

marking the packet as ready for transmission.

12. A method as recited in claim 9, wherein said multicasting further comprises regulating a data transmission rate to control the number of packets lost during transmission.

13. A method as recited in claim 9, wherein said coordinating comprises:

receiving values of said shared variables from each of the remote client systems, the values representing user inputs applied at each said remote client system; and

using the values to update the data structure.

14. A method of enabling a plurality of geographically distributed users to collaboratively view and manipulate images of an object in real-time, the method comprising, at a server processing system:

maintaining a data structure including data representing the object, the data structure including a plurality of properties of the object and variables shared by each of a plurality of remote client systems, the data structure further including a plurality of models of the object, each model representing an image of the object at a different resolution;

setting a specified image size;

sequentially preparing each of a plurality of consecutive portions of the data representing the object for transmission, based on the data structure, by

compressing the portion using run length encoding until the portion reaches the specified image size,

combining the compressed portion into a packet with information indicating a position of said portion within the image, and

marking the packet as ready for transmission;

sequentially multicasting each said packet that is ready for transmission to each of the remote client systems to allow each of the client systems to display an image of the object based on the packets; and

coordinating transmission of user inputs applied at each of the client systems to allow the image displayed by each of the client systems to be updated in real-time in response to user inputs applied at each other client system, said coordinating including

receiving values of said shared variables from each of the remote client systems, the values representing user inputs applied at each said remote client system, and using the values to update the data structure.

15. A method as recited in claim **14**, wherein said preparing comprises appropriately accessing said models of the object so as to cause the image to be displayed on each of the client systems at a lowered resolution during a user manipulation of the image one of the client systems.

16. A method as recited in claim **14**, wherein said transmitting comprises regulating a data transmission rate to control the number of packets lost during transmission.

17. An apparatus for enabling a plurality of geographically distributed users to collaboratively view and manipulate images of an object, the method comprising:

    means for maintaining a data structure including data representing the object, the data structure including a plurality of variables shared by each of a plurality of remote processing systems, the data structure further including a plurality of models of the object, each model corresponding to a different image resolution;

    means for multicasting data to each of the remote processing systems based on the data structure to allow the image displayed on each of the remote processing systems, including dynamically selecting from the plurality of models; and

    means for coordinating transmission of user inputs applied at each of the client systems to allow the image

displayed on each of the client systems to be updated in real-time in response to user inputs applied at each other client system.

18. An apparatus as recited in claim **11**, further comprising means for selecting said models of the object for said multicasting so as to cause the image to be displayed on each of the client systems at a reduced resolution during a user manipulation of the image on one of the client systems.

19. An apparatus as recited in claim **17**, further comprising:

    means for compressing each of a plurality of consecutive portions of the data representing the object until each said the portion reaches a specified image size; and

    means for combining each compressed portion into a packet with information indicating a position of said portion within the image.

20. An apparatus as recited in claim **17**, wherein said means for coordinating comprises:

    means for receiving values of said shared variables from each of the remote processing systems, the values representing user inputs applied at each said remote client system; and

    means for using the values to update the data structure.

* * * * *

50138085R00326

Made in the USA
Columbia, SC
02 February 2019